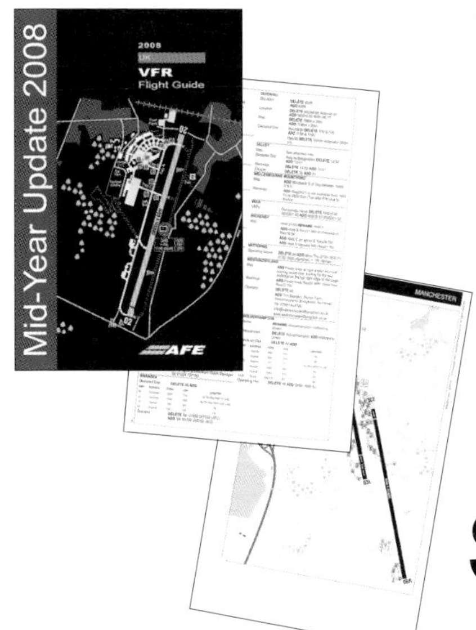

UK VFR Flight Guide

FREE Update Service

To receive your free printed and email updates, please fill in your name and address on the form below:

(Please use block capitals)

Name ____

Address ____

____

____

Postcode ____

Email ____

Return this form to:
UK VFR Flight Guide
1a, Ringway Trading Estate,
Shadowmoss Road,
Manchester M22 5LH
or register online at **www.ukvfrflightguide.co.uk**
quoting the reference number at the bottom of this page

VFR2009 0009885

2009

UK VFR
Flight Guide

In association with the Light Aircraft Association

Published by

Camber Publishing Ltd

Spiral bound ISBN 978 1 906559 038

Loose leaf ISBN 978 1 906559 052

Softback ISBN 978 1 906559 045

Distributed to the aviation trade by:

AFE Ltd (Manchester Office)
1a Ringway Trading Estate,
Shadowmoss Road,
Manchester M22 5LH

Tel: 0161 499 0023 **Fax:** 0161 499 0298

AFE Ltd (Oxford Office)
The Pilot shop
Oxford Airport
Oxford
OX5 1QX

Tel: 01865 841441 **Fax:** 01865 842495

Distributed to the book trade by:

Crécy Publishing Ltd
1a Ringway Trading Estate,
Shadowmoss Road,
Manchester M22 5LH

Tel: 0161 499 0024 **Fax:** 0161 499 0298

www.afeonline.com

2009 UK VFR Flight Guide

Editor Louise Southern

Designed by Robert Taylor
GDi studio

Contributors:

John Dale

Jeremy M Pratt

Mike Rudkin

Chris Walsh

Effective information date 25/09/08

Important

The UK VFR Flight Guide is a guide only and it is not intended to be taken as an authoritative document. In the interests of safety and good airmanship the AIP (including supplements, amendments and AIRACs), Pre-flight Information Bulletins, NOTAMS and AICs should be checked before flight as information can, and does, change frequently and often with little notice. Whilst every care has been taken in compiling this guide, relying where possible on official information sources, the publisher and editorial team will not be liable in any way for any errors or omissions whatsoever.

Regular amendments available at: **www.ukvfrflightguide.co.uk**

Note from the Editor

I cannot believe another year has passed by, and another edition of the UK VFR Flight Guide has been researched, edited and printed.

This year we have more airfields included in the UK VFR Flight than ever before.

Completely new
Abergavenny
Berrier
Charlton Park
Dunsfold
East Kirkby
Holmbeck Farm
Honington
Kirknewton
Little Rissington
Raydon Wings
Wingland

Upgraded from text to map entry
Ballykelly
Breidden
Coll
Fairford
Kimbolton
Main Hall Farm
Portmaok
Shifnall
Sollas
Strathaven
Weston on the Green

Sadly we have lost a few airfields from the guide – this does not mean the airfield is no longer in use but the owner has decided due to various reasons to remove the airfield from the guide.

Ayton Castle
Boones Farm
Donemana
Nesscliffe Camp
Sheffield City
Sennybridge
Thorne

Any airfield owners who would like to have their airfield included within the guide, please email me details of the strip and I will ensure the airfield is included in the 2010 UK VFR Flight Guide.

RNAV frequencies, bearings and distances remain part of the 2009 guide. We have only included 1 per map entry where relevant. If the distance from the beacon is greater than 30nm, we have decided to leave this information of the entry due to accuracy when flying.

New for VFR 2009 is the CD-Rom version, this has been very successful with UK AIM 2008, so it was decided to produce VFR 2009 in the same format. The disc is easy to use, but amendments to this format are not available.

During 2009 the UK VFR Flight Guide website will be launched. Please email your jollies – text and pictures to louise@afeonline.com for inclusion. Also it would be good to receive airfield reviews for airfields visited. These will be put on the website www.ukvfrflightguide.co.uk for everyone to read and comment on.

Happy and safe flying for 2009

Regards
Louise

Louise Southern
Editor
louise@afeonline.com

Contents

Flight Planning

VOLMET broadcasts ....inside front cover
Airmet 10
MetFAX 11
Automated Metar and TAF telephone service 12
Forecast Offices 13
Weathercall 14
Aeronautical meteorological codes 15-16
METFORM 215 17-18
MET chart symbols 18
ICAO UK airfield locators Decode 19
ICAO UK airfield locators Encode 20
ICAO flight plan form 21
Filing a VFR flight plan 22-23
Prevention of the Infringement of Controlled Airspace 24-25
ICAO aircraft designators 26
Customs & Excise facilities 27
Customs & Excise Regulations 28
Prevention of terrorism act 29
Police Force Contact Numbers 30
Gliding Airfields – a general guide 31
Beach Airfields – a general guide 32
Unlicensed Airfields – a general guide 33
CAA Safety Leaflet No 12 – Strip Sense 34-39
VFR minima 40
Landing & take-off distance factors 41
Temperature & pressure conversions 42
Feet/metres conversion 42
Km/nautical miles/statute miles conversion 42
Weight conversion 43
Volume conversion 43
Millibar/Inches of mercury conversion 44
Aeronautical Information Services (AIS) 45
Aviation Contact Details 45-66
Abbreviations 47-55

In-flight

Crosswind/headwind calculator 57-58
Airspace Classifications 59-64
SVFR 65
UK En-route Nav Aids 66-70
Visual Reference Points Outside Controlled Airspace 71-72
Visual Reference Points Within Controlled Airspace 73-76
Prohibited and Restricted Areas 77-78
Temporary Restricted Airspace, Red Arrows displays,
Emergency Restrictions of Flying, Royal Flights 79
Danger Areas (inc. DACS & DAAIS) 79-85
Areas of Intense Aerial Activity (AIAA) 86
Boscombe Down Advisory Radio Area 87
LARS units 88-89
MATZ units 90
Military Middle Airspace 91-92
Safetycom 93
Sunrise & sunset tables 93
County airfield listing 94-95
Airfield listing A-Z 96-98
Airfield name cross-reference 98
Key to airfield directory maps 99-101
Interception procedures ....inside back cover
Ground signals, light signals, SAR ground signals, morse code ....back cover

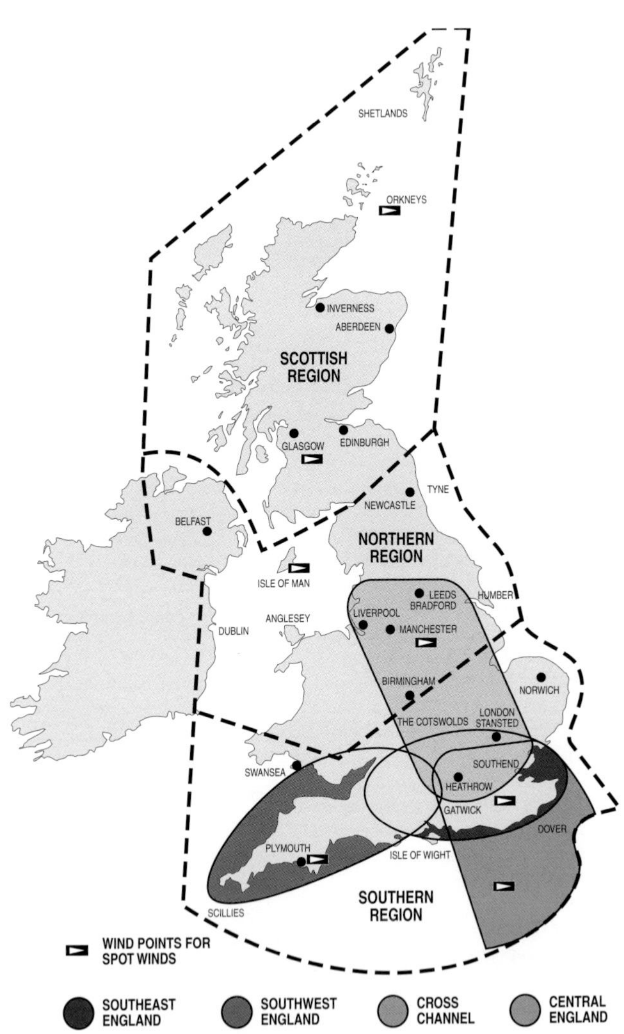

AIRMET – Fax

09060 700 510	Airmet Index Page
09060 700 507	Regional Airmet South Text
09060 700 508	Regional Airmet North Text
09060 700 509	Regional Airmet Scottish Text
09060 700 511	Airmet UK Weather Text
09060 700 512	Airmet UK Upper Winds Text
09060 700 513	Airmet UK Update and Outlook
09060 700 514	Airmet South West England Text
09060 700 515	Airmet South East England Text
09060 700 516	Airmet Central England Text
09060 700 517	Airmet Cross Channel Text

Note: 090607 calls cost 75p/minute at all times

Weather helpdesk 0871 200 3985

MetFAX Helpline:
Tel: 08700 750075
Fax: 08700 750076

Fax Number	Product Description
09060 100 400	Main Index of all Fax services
09060 700 501	Aviation Index page
09060 700 502	Surface Analysis chart
	Surface T+24 Forecast chart
09060 700 503	F215 UK Low Level Weather chart
	F214 UK Spot Wind chart
09060 700 504	Surface T+48, 72, 96 & 120 Forecast chart
	3 day planning text (S England, S Wales)
09060 700 544	Surface T+48, 72, 96 & 120 Forecast chart
	3 Day planning text (N England, N Wales)
09060 700 505	Explanatory notes for F215
09060 700 506	4 Tephigrams temp/height chart
	Satellite Images
09060 700 538	Guide to satellite images
09060 700 537	Satellite Image (Visible & Infra-Red)
09060 700 539	Satellite Image (Infra-Red)
	European
09060 700 541	RAFC European FL100-450 Sig Wx.
	F614 European med-high Spot Winds
09060 700 542	F415 European Low Level Weather
	F414 European Low Level Spot Winds
	TAF and METAR Bulletins
09060 700 520	TAF & METAR Index Page
09060 700 521	METAR 1 – S England, South Wales, Channel Islands
09060 700 522	METAR 2 – SE England, Midlands, Wales
09060 700 523	METAR 3 – North England, Scotland, Ireland
09060 700 524	METAR 4 – SE England, Channel Islands, France
09060 700 525	METAR 5 – Europe
09060 700 530	TAF – 18hr Bulletin
09060 700 531	TAF 1 – S England, South Wales, Channel Islands
09060 700 532	TAF 2 – SE England, Midlands, East Anglia. Wales
09060 700 533	TAF 3 – North England, Scotland, Ireland
09060 700 534	TAF 4 – SE England, Channel Islands, France
09060 700 535	TAF 5 – Europe
09060 700 540	TAF & METAR Decode

METAR Bulletins compiled every 30 minutes

Note: 09060 calls cost 75p/minute at all times

Automated Metar and TAF telephone service

The automated METAR and TAF service is accessed by telephoning: **09063 800 400**
This is a premium rated number.
Once connected press the star (*) key followed by the appropriate three digit code number.

Code	ICAO	Aerodrome	Hours	METAR	9hr TAF	24hr TAF
222	**PD**	Aberdeen	0500-2100	•	•	•
224	**JA**	Alderney	0700-1800	•	•	
228	**AA**	Belfast Aldergrove	H24	•	•	•
232	**AC**	Belfast City	0500-2100	•	•	
234	**PL**	Benbecula	0700-1500	•	•	
236	**KB**	Biggin Hill	0700-1900	•	•	
238	**BB**	Birmingham	H24	•	•	•
242	**NH**	Blackpool	0600-2000	•	•	
244	**DM**	Boscombe Down	H24	•		•
246	**HH**	Bournemouth	0600-2000	•	•	
252	**GD**	Bristol	H24	•	•	•
254	**VN**	Brize Norton	H24	•		•
256	**SC**	Cambridge	0600-1800	•	•	
366	**EC**	Campbeltown	0600-2400	•		•
258	**FF**	Cardiff	H24	•	•	•
262	**NC**	Carlisle	0800-1600	•	•	
266	**BE**	Coventry	H24	•	•	•
268	**TC**	Cranfield	0700-1700	•	•	
272	**DR**	Culdrose	H24	•	•	
276	**PH**	Edinburgh	H24	•	•	•
278	**TE**	Exeter	0600-2400	•	•	
282	**LF**	Farnborough	0600-1800	•		•
286	**PF**	Glasgow	H24	•	•	•
288	**BJ**	Gloucestershire	0800-1700	•	•	
292	**JB**	Guernsey	0300-2000	•	•	
296	**NJ**	Humberside	0500-2000	•	•	
298	**PE**	Inverness	0600-2000	•	•	
322	**NS**	Isle of Man	H24	•	•	
324	**JJ**	Jersey	0300-2000	•	•	
326	**QK**	Kinloss	H24	•	•	•
328	**PA**	Kirkwall	0500-1700	•	•	
334	**NM**	Leeds Bradford	H24	•	•	•
336	**XE**	Leeming	H24	•	•	
338	**QL**	Leuchars	H24	•	•	•
342	**GP**	Liverpool	H24	•	•	•
344	**LC**	London City	0600-1900	•	•	
346	**KK**	London Gatwick	H24	•	•	•
348	**LL**	London Heathrow	H24	•	•	•
352	**SS**	London Stansted	H24	•	•	•
354	**AE**	Londonderry	0500-1900	•	•	
356	**QS**	Lossiemouth	H24	•	•	•
358	**GW**	London Luton	H24	•	•	•
364	**DL**	Lyneham	H24	•	•	•
368	**CC**	Manchester	H24	•	•	•
372	**MH**	Manston	0600-2100	•	•	
374	**YM**	Marham	H24	•	•	
376	**NT**	Newcastle	H24	•	•	•
377	**WU**	Northolt	0500-2300	•	•	
378	**SH**	Norwich	0500-0100	•	•	
382	**VO**	Odiham	H24	•	•	
386	**HD**	Plymouth	0600-1800	•	•	
388	**PK**	Prestwick	H24	•	•	•
392	**DG**	St Mawgan	H24	•	•	•
394	**PM**	Scatsa	0700-1700	•	•	
396	**HE**	Scillies St Mary's	0700-1600	•	•	
398	**OS**	Shawbury	H24	•	•	
422	**KA**	Shoreham	0700-1700	•	•	
424	**HI**	Southampton	0500-1900	•	•	
426	**MC**	Southend	H24	•	•	
428	**PO**	Stornoway	0600-1500	•	•	•
432	**PB**	Sumburgh	0500-2100	•	•	
436	**NV**	Durham Tees Valley	0600-2100	•	•	
438	**PU**	Tiree	0900-1300	•	•	

Code	ICAO	Aerodrome	Hours	METAR	9hr TAF	24hr TAF
444	OV	Valley	H24	•	•	
446	XW	Waddington	H24	•		•
448	UW	Wattisham	H24	•	•	
452	PC	Wick	0600-200	•	•	
454	XT	Wittering	H24	•	•	
456	DY	Yeovilton	H24	•	•	
522	EHAM	Amsterdam		•	•	•
524	LFOB	Beauvais		•	•	
526	LFBR	Brest		•	•	•
528	EBBR	Brussels		•	•	•
532	LFRK	Caen		•	•	
536	LFRC	Cherbourg		•	•	
538	EICK	Cork		•	•	
542	LFRG	Deauville		•	•	
544	LFRD	Dinard		•	•	
546	EIDW	Dublin		•	•	•
548	LFRM	Le Mans		•	•	
552	LFAT	Le Touquet		•	•	
554	LFQQ	Lille		•	•	•
556	ELLX	Luxembourg		•	•	•
562	EBOS	Ostend		•	•	•
564	LFPG	Paris Charles De Gaulle	•	•	•	
566	LFPB	Paris Le Bourget		•	•	•
568	LFPO	Paris Orly		•	•	•
572	LFRN	Rennes		•	•	
574	LFSR	Reims		•	•	
576	EHRD	Rotterdam		•	•	•
578	EINN	Shannon		•	•	•
582	LFPN	Toussus Le Noble		•	•	

Forecast Offices

The following offices are able to provide TAFs and METARs if you are unable to obtain them from another source, and can also provide clarification of a TAF or METAR you have already received.

Belfast/Aldergrove Airport*	01849 423275
Birmingham Weather Centre	0845 3000300
Cardiff Weather Centre	02920 390492
Exeter Weather Centre	0870 900 0100
	01392 885680
Glasgow Weather Centre*	0141 221 6116
Isle of Man Airport	01624 821641
Jersey Airport	01534 492256
Jersey Airmet	01534 492256
	09006 650033
Leeds Weather Centre	01132 457687
Newcastle Weather Centre	0191 232 4245
Sella Ness	01806 242069

*These Forecast Offices can be consulted to clarify a forecast, for special forecasts and for route forecasts.

email: aviation@metoffice.com

www.metoffice.com

Weathercall is the UK's most used telephone based weather forecast.
Weathercall by telephone 6 hr town forecast updated hourly.
Weathercall by telephone 10 day forecast updated 3 time daily.
Weathercall by fax forecast updated daily at 7:00.

Weather call by phone

To use Weathercall, dial the number for your area and choose from the following list of options:
Press 1 for 10 day regional outlook forecast
Press 2 for the forecast for your town, covering the next 6 Hrs
Press 3 for a barometric pressure reading
Press 4 to leave your address to receive a Weathercall Card

Greater London	09014 722051
Kent, Surrey & Sussex	09014 722052
Dorset, Hampshire & Isle of Wight	09014 722053
Devon & Cornwall	09014 722054
Wiltshire, Gloucestershire, Avon & Somerset	09014 722055
Berkshire, Buckinghamshire & Oxfordshire	09014 722056
Bedfordshire, Hertfordshire & Essex	09014 722057
Norfolk, Suffolk & Cambridgeshire	09014 722058
Glamorgan & Monmouthshire	09014 722059
Shropshire, Herefordshire & Worcestershire	09014 722060
West Midlands, Staffordshire & Warwickshire	09014 722061
Nottinghamshire, Leicestershire, Northants & Derbyshire	09014 722062
Lincolnshire	09014 722063
Carmarthenshire, Credigion & Pembrokeshire	09014 722064
Anglesey, Gwynedd, Wrexham & Denbighshire	09014 722065
North West England	09014 722066
York, East Riding, South, West & North Yorkshire	09014 722067
Durham, Northumberland & Tyne & Wear	09014 722068
Cumbria, Lake District & Isle of Man	09014 722069
Dumfries & Galloway	09014 722070
Central Scotland & Strathclyde	09014 722071
Fife, Lothian & Borders	09014 722072
Tayside	09014 722073
Grampian & East Highlands	09014 722074
West Highlands & Islands	09014 722075
Caithness, Sutherland, Orkneys & Shetland	09014 722076
Northern Ireland	09014 722077

Weathercall by Fax

	10 day forecast 2-5 day regional forecast	5 day regional forecast
South East	09065 300128	09060 100411
South West	09065 300129	09060 100412
Wales	09065 300130	09060 100413
North West & North Wales	09065 300131	09060 100416
North East	09065 300132	09060 100417
Scotland	09065 300133	09060 100418
Northern Ireland	09065 300134	09060 100419
Midlands	09065 300135	09060 100414
National	09065 300136	09060 100410
East Anglia	09065 300137	09060 100415
Synoptic chart (today & tomorrow)	09065 300138	
Synoptic chart (following 4 days)	09065 300139	

Additional services by fax

Weather Radar Sequence	09060 100425
Surface analysis chart	09060 100444
User guide to surface charts	09060 100445
UK Plotted chart	09060 100447

Call charges (based upon calls from a BT Landline)
Weathercall by telephone (09014) 60p per minute
Weathercall 5 day forecast & fax services (09060) £1 per minute
Weathercall 10 day forecast by fax (09065) £1.50 per minute
www.metoffice.com – Aviation section

Sample METAR:

LOCATION	ISSUE DATE/TIME	OBSERVATION DATE/TIME	WIND	VISIBILITY	WEATHER	CLOUD	CLOUD	CLOUD	AIR TEMP /DEWPOINT	QNH	MILITARY WEATHER STATE CODE
EGQM	061159	061200Z	04028G39KT	3500	+RA	FEW005	SCT012	OVC020	07/05	Q0983	YLO

Sample TAF:

LOCATION	ISSUE DATE/TIME	FORECAST DATE/PERIOD	WIND	VISIBILITY	WEATHER	CLOUD	CLOUD	SUPPLEMENTARY INFORMATION
EGNT	060841Z	061019	04025G35KT	7000	RA	SCT008	BKN015	TEMPO 1019 05030G45KT 3000 BKN008

LOCATION INDICATOR
The ICAO Four Letter Code for the airfield

TIME
The first number group will be the issue time of the METAR/TAF as a six number group, the first two numbers being the date. The second six number group will be the date (first two numbers) followed by:
– METAR. The observation time in hours and minutes UTC, followed by Z (Zulu).
– TAF The period of forecast validity in UTC.

WIND
The surface wind direction is given in degrees true (three digits) rounded to the nearest 10°, followed by wind speed (two digits). Wind speed may be given in knots (KT), kilometres per hour (KMH) or metres per second (MPS).

G Wind Gust
00000 Wind Calm
VRB Variable Wind Direction
V Variation in wind direction of 60° or more

VISIBILITY
The minimum horizontal visibility is given in metres.

9999 Visibility 10km or greater
0000 Visibility less than 50 m

– METAR only. Where there is a marked difference in visibility depending on direction, more than one visibility may be reported, followed by direction in which that visibility exists e.g. S = south, NE = north east etc.

RUNWAY VISUAL RANGE – METAR Only

R RVR, followed by runway designator and the touchdown zone visibility in metres. If visibility is greater than the maximum RVR that can be assessed, or more than 1500 metres, it will be preceded by a P. M = RVR below the minimum that can be assessed.
At non-UK aerodromes the additional designator may be added after the RVR: U = Up; D = Down; N = No change. If there is a significant variability in RVR the letter V will be used in-between the minimum and maximum RVRs.

WEATHER

Weather Phenomena

Description	**Precipitation**	**Visibility Factor**	**Other**
MI Shallow	DZ Drizzle	BR Mist	PO Well developed dust/sand whirls
BC Patches			
PR Partial Covering	RA Rain	FG Fog	
DR Drifting	SN Snow	FU Smoke	SQ Squalls
BL Blowing	SG Snow Grains	VA Volcanic Ash	FC Funnel Cloud(s) (tornado or water-spout)
SH Shower(s)	IC Diamond Dust	DU Widespread Dust	SS Sandstorm
TS Thunderstorm	PE Ice-Pellets	SA Sand	DS Duststorm
FZ Super-Cooled	GR Hail	HZ Haze	
	GS Small Hail		

Intensity or Proximity Qualifier
- Light i.e. -SH
Moderate (no qualifier) i.e. SH
+Heavy i.e. +SH
VC In the vicinity (within 8 km of the airfield, but not actually at the airfield)
NSW (TAF only) = No Significant Weather

CLOUD

Cloud amount may be described as:

FEW (few)	1-2 OKTAS
SCT (Scattered)	3-4 OKTAS
BKN (Broken)	5-7 OKTAS
OVC (Overcast)	8 OKTAS
Note: 1 OKTA	1/8 cloud cover

Cloud base is given in hundreds of feet above aerodrome level (aal).f

Cloud type is not identified, except:

CB	Cumulo-nimbus
TCU	Towering Cumulus
SKC	Sky Clear
NSC	No Significant Cloud (TAF only)

If the sky is obscured the letters VV are inserted followed by the vertical visibility in hundreds of feet.

VV/// Sky obscured, vertical visibility cannot be assessed.

CAVOK

(Pronounced KAV-O-KAY) will be used to replace the visibility, RVR, weather and cloud groups if the following conditions apply:

a Visibility: 10km or more

b Cloud: no cloud below 5000ft or below highest Minimum Sector Altitude, whichever is greater and no CB at any height

c No significant weather at or near the airfield

AIR TEMPERATURE/DEWPOINT

These are given in degrees Celsius

M Minus

QNH

Rounded down to the next whole millibar and given as a four figure group in millibars/hectopascals, preceded by Q. If the value is less than 1000, the first number is 0.

SUPPLEMENTARY INFORMATION

METARs

RE Recent weather

WS Windshear

TREND. Certain major aerodromes will include a trend indicator for any forecast change in conditions during the two hours after the observation time.

BECMG Becoming, TEMPO = Temporary; may be followed by time (in hours and minutes UTC) preceded by FM (from), TL (until) or AT (at).

NOSIG No significant changes forecast during the trend period.

BECMG is an expected permanent change in conditions, expected to last less than one hour in each instance and not total more than half the forecast period.

TEMPO is a temporary fluctuation in conditions expected to last less than 1hour at a time and not occur in total during more than half the forecast period.

TAFs

Probability:

PROB 30 30% probability

PROB 40 40% probability

The abbreviations FM, TEMPO and BECMG are followed by time(s) (UTC) to the nearest hour.

AMENDMENTS

AMD is inserted after TAF and before the ICAO four letter code. AMD is used when the original TAF is withdrawn and replaced for some reason.

RETARD

(R) Used when the TAF is received late. Most often seen on METFAX.

MILITARY WEATHER STATE COLOUR CODES

– MINIMUM weather conditions

Colour	Visibility	Base of lowest cloud: 3/8 (scattered) or more
Blue	8km	2500ft AGL
White	5km	1500ft AGL
Green	3700m	700ft AGL
Yellow	1600m	300ft AGL
Amber	800m	200ft AGL
Red	Less than 800m	Below 200ft AGL or sky obscured
Black	Airfield not usable for reasons other than cloud base or visibility Black will precede actual colour code	

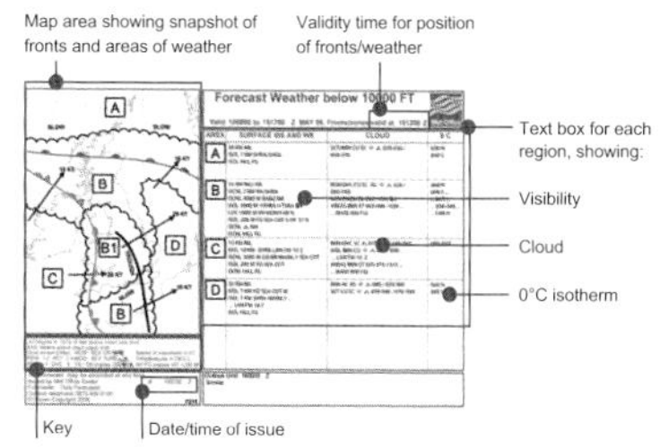

Map area

The map area will still appear on the sig Wx chart showing a snapshot of the fronts and areas of weather at a specific validity time (VT) shown at the top right of the chart.
Only sig wx areas, fronts and speed of movement will be shown on the map area. The 0 °C isotherm boxes have been moved to the text box allocated to a particular area.
The 'top' of the chart will now be 10,000 ft instead of 15,000ft.

Weather

The text boxes on the right will show the weather for each area of the map and have been designed to follow the TAF code appearing in the same order; visibility and weather followed by cloud. The METAR weather codes will also be used in this section to refer to specific forecast weather types (e.g. TS, +RA, FG etc.)

Cloud

Cloud amount will be: FEW, SCT, BKN or OVC, followed by the cloud type (e.g. ST, CU, CB, SC, AC). An additional two symbols may then appear to indicate whether MOD/SEV ICE or TURB is expected in this cloud. A key to the symbols is included in the lower left corner of the chart.
Cloud heights then appear in 100s of feet in the form 020/050 (in this case the cloud base is 2,000 ft and the top 5,000 ft AMSL). If a cloud top is expected to extend above 10,000 ft then XXX will appear. For example, BKN/OVC STSC 008/060 indicates 5 – 8 oktas of stratus and strato-cumulus base 800 ft top 6,000 ft AMSL with moderate turbulence and moderate icing expected within.

Key:

MOD ICE	Moderate icing
SEV ICE	Severe icing
MOD TURB	Moderate turbulence
SEV TURB	Severe turbulence

Mountain wave

Wherever necessary, mountain wave forecasts will appear in the 'visibility and weather' box as MTW followed by a vertical speed VSP and height(s) above mean sea level.
e.g. 'MTW MAX VSP 700 FPM AT 080'. Mountain wave maximum vertical speed 700 ft per minute at 8,000 ft with moderate/severe turbulence expected

Issue/validity times

In order to meet customer requests, the chart times have been altered slightly to cover a nine-hour period instead of just six hours. Charts will be available at similar times to those currently in place. The table below summarises the times for the new charts:

Chart	Issue time	Valid for flights between	Validity time*	Outlook to	Prognosis
UK low-level	0330	0800 and 1700	1200	0000	1800
sig weather (F215)	0930	1400 and 2300	1800	0600	0000
	1530	2000 and 0500	0000	1200	0600
	2130	0200 and 1100	0600	1800	1200
European low-level	0330	0800 and 1700	1200	n/a	n/a
sig weather (F415)	0930	1400 and 2300	1800	n/a	n/a
	1530	2000 and 0500	0000	n/a	n/a
	2130	0100 and 1100	0600	n/a	n/a

*Validity time is the time at which the position of the fronts and areas of weather are valid.
All times will remain in UTC (denoted by 'Z' or 'Zulu' on the new briefing charts).

Prognosis

The prognosis chart (forecast for six hours on) will no longer appear on the chart, but will be shown below the main F215 chart on the Met Office web site. This prognosis chart shows only the expected positions of the principal synoptic features and mean sea level isobars at the end of the period. Weather zones are not given on the prognosis chart.

UK and European spot winds charts (F214 and 414)

In response to customer requests, the Met Office has also agreed to change the chart validity times of the F214 and F414 spot winds charts in order to bring them into line with the new F215 and F415 Sig Wx charts. As a result, the spot wind charts will have improved issue times and validity times as set out in the table below:

Chart	Issue time	Valid for flights between	Validity time*	Outlook to
UK spot winds (F214)	0000	0300 and 0900	0600	n/a
	0600	0900 and 1500	1200	n/a
	1200	1500 and 2100	1800	n/a
	1800	2100 and 0300	0000	n/a
European spot winds (F414)	0000	0300 and 0900	0600	n/a
	0600	0900 and 1500	1200	n/a
	1200	1500 and 2100	1800	n/a
	1800	2100 and 0300	0000	n/a

Amendment of charts

Only the current chart will be amended, therefore a chart will be subject to amendment as soon as it has been issued.

Example for F215 and F415

If we consider three chart issues of F215/F415, the 0200 – 1100 chart issued at 2100, the 0800 – 1700 chart issued at 0300 and the 1400 – 2300 issued at 0900. If the actual weather were to change from the forecast weather at say, 1000 with un-forecast thunderstorms which are now forecast to last all day, the 0800 – 1700 chart would be amended instantly since this is the current chart. The previous chart valid 0200 – 1100 would not be amended since it is no longer current (even though it's period is unfinished). If forecasters believe that the thunderstorms will also affect the period 1400 – 2300, then this chart would also be amended.
Users are advised to use the latest chart wherever possible since this should include the most up-to-date information and amendments as necessary.

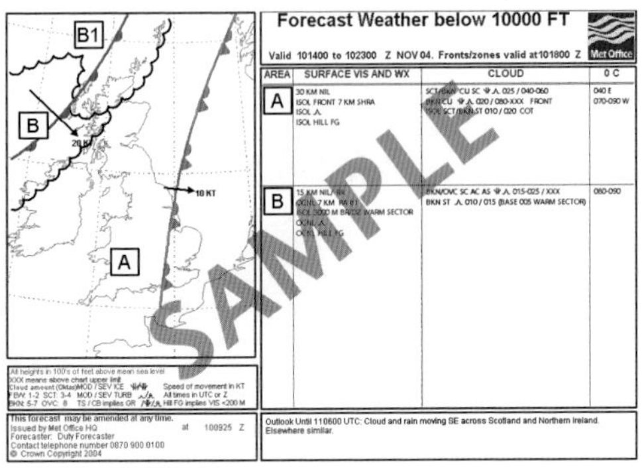

MET chart symbols

	Pressure Systems, Fronts and Convergence Zones
	Cold front at surface
	Warm front at surface
	Occluded front at surface
	Quasi-stationary front at surface
	Convergence line
	Intertropical convergence zone
L x 999	Centre of low pressure area (with indication of pressure at centre)
H ○ 1020	Centre of high pressure area (with indication of pressure at centre)
10	Speed of movement
	Direction of movement
SLW	Slow
STNR	Stationary
	Zone Boundaries
	Boudary of area of significant weasther
/// /// /// ///	Rain *
,	Drizzle *
	Snow *
	Shower *
	Hail *
	Light Icing *
=	Widespread Mist *
≡	Widespread Fog *
	Freezing Fog *
	Widespread Smoke *
	Freezing Rain
	Moderate Icing
	Severe Icing
	Freezing Precipitation
	Moderate Turbulence
	Severe Turbulence
	Severe Sand or Dust Haze
	Widespread Sandstorm or Duststorm
∞	Widespread Haze
CAT	Clear Air Turbulence
	Severe Line Squall
	Thunderstorm
	Marked Mountain Waves
	Tropical Cyclone
	* these symbols are not used at high altitude

	Temperature and Tropopause
H 400	Tropopause 'High' centre and altitude (FL 400)
340 L	Tropopause 'Low' centre and altitude (FL 340)
0°C 130	Freezing level (in thousands of feet as a Flight Level)
-62 400	Temperature and Flight Level of the tropopause
	Wind & Temperature at Altitude Charts Pressure
L	Centre of a low-pressure system
H	Centre of a high-pressure system
	Temperature
0°C	In degrees Celsius
	Wind
	Arrow shaft marks wind direction
	Each long feather equals 10 knots
	Each half feather equals 5 knots
	Each solid triangle equals 50 knots
0	Calm
FL 380	Flight level of jetstream

	Cloud Quantities
SKC	Sky Clear
FEW	Few (1 to 2 oktas)
SCT	Scattered (3 to 4 oktas)
BKN	Broken (5 to 7 oktas)
OVC	Overcast (8 oktas)
LYR	Layers
	For Cumulonimbus only:
ISOL	Isolated
OCNL	(occasional) Well Separated
FRQ	(frequent) Hardly or not at all separated
EMBD	Embedded in other cloud
	Localisation
COT	Coast
LAN	Land
LOC	Locally
MAR	At Sea (maritime)
MON	Mountains
SFC	Surface
VAL	Valleys

EGAA	Belfast Aldergrove
EGAB	Enniskillen
EGAC	Belfast City
EGAD	Newtownards
EGAE	Londonderry
EGAL	Langford Lodge
EGBB	Birmingham
EGBC	Cheltenham Racecourse
EGBD	Derby
EGBE	Coventry
EGBG	Leicester
EGBJ	Gloucestershire
EGBK	Northampton
EGBL	Long Marston
EGBM	Tatenhill
EGBN	Nottingham
EGBO	Wolverhampton Halfpenny Green
EGBP	Kemble
EGBS	Shobdon
EGBT	Turweston
EGBV	Silverstone
EGBW	Wellesbourne Mountford
EGCB	Manchester Barton
EGCC	Manchester
EGCD	Manchester Woodford
EGCE	Wrexham
EGCF	Sandtoft
EGCG	Strubby Heliport
EGCH	Holyhead
EGCJ	Sherburn-in-Elmet
EGCK	Caernarfon
EGCL	Fenland
EGCN	Doncaster Sheffield
EGOP	Southport Sands
EGCP	Thorne
EGCS	Sturgate
EGCT	Tilstock
EGCV	Sleap
EGCW	Welshpool
EGDB	Mountwise
EGDC	Chivenor
EGDD	Bicester
EGDG	St Mawgan
EGDL	Lyneham
EGDM	Boscombe Down
EGDN	Netheravon
EGDP	Portland
EGDR	Culdrose
EGDX	St Athan
EGDY	Yeovilton
EGEC	Campbeltown
EGED	Eday
EGEF	Fair Isle
EGEG	Glasgow City Heliport
EGEH	Whalsay
EGEL	Coll
EGEY	Colonsay
EGEN	North Ronaldsay
EGEO	Oban
EGEP	Papa Westray
EGER	Stronsay
EGES	Sanday
EGET	Lerwick
EGEW	Westray
EGFA	West Wales
EGFC	Cardiff Heliport
EGFE	Haverfordwest
EGFF	Cardiff
EGFH	Swansea
EGFP	Pembrey
EGGD	Bristol
EGGP	Liverpool
EGGW	London Luton
EGHA	Compton Abbas
EGHB	Maypole
EGHC	Lands End
EGHD	Plymouth
EGHE	Scilly Isles
EGHF	Lee-on-Solent
EGHG	Yeovil
EGHH	Bournemouth
EGHI	Southampton
EGHJ	Bembridge
EGHK	Penzance Heliport
EGHL	Lasham
EGHN	Sandown
EGHO	Thruxton
EGHP	Popham
EGHR	Chichester
EGHS	Henstridge
EGHT	Tresco Heliport
EGHU	Eaglescott
EGHY	Truro
EGJA	Alderney
EGJB	Guernsey
EGJJ	Jersey
EGKA	Shoreham
EGKB	Biggin Hill
EGKD	Albourne
EGKE	Challock
EGKG	Goodwood Racecourse
EGKH	Lashenden
EGKK	London Gatwick
EGKL	Deanland
EGKR	Redhill
EGLA	Bodmin
EGLB	Brooklands
EGLC	London City
EGLD	Denham
EGLF	Farnborough
EGLG	Panshanger
EGLI	Isleworth
EGLJ	Chalgrove
EGLK	Blackbushe
EGLL	London Heathrow
EGLM	White Whaltham
EGLS	Old Sarum
EGLT	Ascot Racecourse
EGLW	London heliport
EGMA	Fowlmere
EGMC	Southend
EGMD	Lydd
EGMF	Farthing Corner
EGMH	Manston
EGMJ	Little Gransden
EGML	Damyns Hall
EGNA	Hucknall
EGNB	Brough
EGNC	Carlisle
EGNE	Retford
EGNF	Netherthorpe
EGNG	Bagby
EGNH	Blackpool
EGNI	Skegness
EGNJ	Humberside
EGNL	Barrow
EGNM	Leeds Bradford
EGNO	Warton
EGNR	Hawarden
EGNS	Isle of Man
EGNT	Newcastle
EGNU	Full Sutton
EGNV	Durham Tees Valley
EGNW	Wickenby
EGNX	East Midlands
EGNY	Beverley
EGOD	Llandbedr
EGOE	Ternhill
EGOP	Pembrey
EGOS	Shawbury
EGOV	Valley
EGOW	Woodvale
EGOY	West Freugh
EGPA	Kirkwall
EGPB	Sumburgh
EGPC	Wick
EGPD	Aberdeen
EGPE	Inverness
EGPF	Glasgow
EGPG	Cumbernauld
EGPH	Edinburgh
EGPI	Islay
EGPJ	Fife
EGPK	Glasgow Prestwick
EGPL	Benbecula
EGPM	Scatsta
EGPN	Dundee
EGPO	Stornoway
EGPR	Barra
EGPS	Peterhead Heliport
EGPT	Perth
EGPU	Tiree
EGPW	Unst
EGQB	Ballykelly
EGQK	Kinloss
EGQL	Leuchars
EGQM	Boulmer
EGQS	Lossiemouth
EGSA	Shipdham
EGSB	Bedford
EGSC	Cambridge
EGSD	Great Yarmouth
EGSF	Peterborough Conington
EGSG	Stapleford
EGSH	Norwich
EGSI	Marshland
EGSJ	Seething
EGSK	Hethel
EGSL	Andrewsfield
EGSM	Beccles
EGSN	Bourn
EGSO	Crowfield
EGSP	Peterborough Sibson
EGSQ	Clacton
EGSR	Earls Colne
EGSS	London Stansted
EGST	Elmsett
EGSU	Duxford
EGSV	Old Buckenham
EGSW	Newmarket Racecourse
EGSX	North Weald
EGSY	Sheffield City
EGTA	Aylesbury
EGTB	Wycombe Air Park
EGTC	Cranfield
EGTD	Dunsfold
EGTE	Exeter
EGTF	Fairoaks
EGTG	Bristol Filton
EGTH	Shuttleworth
EGTK	Oxford
EGTO	Rochester
EGTP	Perranporth
EGTR	Elstree
EGTU	Dunkeswell
EGTW	Oaksey Park
EGUB	Benson
EGUC	Aberporth
EGUL	Lakenheath
EGUN	Mildenhall
EGUO	Colerne
EGUU	Uxbridge
EGUW	Wattisham
EGUY	Wyton
EGVA	Fairford
EGVF	Fleetlands
EGVH	Hereford
EGVN	Brize Norton
EGVO	Odiham
EGVP	Middle Wallop
EGWC	Cosford
EGWE	Henlow
EGWN	Halton
EGWU	Northolt
EGXC	Coningsby
EGXD	Dishforth
EGXE	Leeming
EGXF	Forrest Moor
EGXG	Church Fenton
EGXH	Honington
EGXJ	Cottesmore
EGXM	Benbecula
EGXP	Scampton
EGXT	Wittering
EGXU	Linton on Ouse
EGXV	Leconfield
EGXW	Waddington
EGXZ	Topcliffe
EGYB	Brampton
EGYD	Cranwell
EGYE	Barkston Heath
EGYM	Marham
EGYP	Mount Pleasant

ICAO airfield locators Encode

Aberdeen	EGPD
Aberporth	EGUC
Albourne	EGKD
Alderney	EGJA
Andrewsfield	EGSL
Ascot Racecourse	EGLT
Aylesbury	EGTA
Bagby	EGNG
Ballykelly	EGQB
Barkston Heath	EGYE
Barra	EGPR
Barrow	EGNL
Beccles	EGSM
Bedford	EGSB
Belfast Aldergrove	EGAA
Belfast City	EGAC
Bembridge	EGHJ
Benbecula	EGPL
Benson	EGUB
Beverley	EGNY
Bicester	EGDD
Biggin Hill	EGKB
Birmingham	EGBB
Blackbushe	EGLK
Blackpool	EGNH
Bodmin	EGLA
Boscombe Down	EGDM
Boulmer	EGQM
Bourn	EGSN
Bournemouth	EGHH
Brampton	EGYB
Bristol	EGGD
Bristol Filton	EGTG
Brize Norton	EGVN
Brooklands	EGLB
Brough	EGNB
Caernarfon	EGCK
Cambridge	EGSC
Campbeltown	EGEC
Cardiff Heliport	EGFC
Cardiff	EGFF
Carlisle	EGNC
Chalgrove	EGLJ
Challock	EGKE
Cheltenham Racecourse	EGBC
Chichester	EGHR
Chivenor	EGDC
Church Fenton	EGXG
Clacton	EGSQ
Colerne	EGUO
Coll	EGEL
Colonsay	EGEY
Compton Abbas	EGHA
Coningsby	EGXC
Cosford	EGWC
Cottesmore	EGXJ
Coventry	EGBE
Cranfield	EGTC
Cranwell	EGYD
Crowfield	EGSO
Culdrose	EGDR
Cumbernauld	EGPG
Damyns Hall	EGML
Deanland	EGKL
Denham	EGLD
Derby	EGBD
Dishforth	EGXD
Doncaster Sheffield	EGCN
Dundee	EGPN
Dunkeswell	EGTU
Durham Tees Valley	EGNV
Dunsfold	EGTD
Duxford	EGSU
Eaglescott	EGHU
Earls Colne	EGSR
East Midlands	EGNX
Eday	EGED
Edinburgh	EGPH
Elmsett	EGST
Elstree	EGTR
Enniskillen	EGAB
Exeter	EGTE
Fair Isle	EGEF
Fairford	EGVA
Fairoaks	EGTF
Farnborough	EGLF
Farthing Corner	EGMF
Fenland	EGCL
Fife	EGPJ
Forest Moor	EGXF
Fowlmere	EGMA
Full Sutton	EGNU
Glasgow City Heliport	EGEG
Glasgow	EGPF
Glasgow Prestwick	EGPK
Gloucestershire	EGBJ
Goodwood Racecourse	EGKG
Great Yarmouth	EGSD
Guernsey	EGJB
Halton	EGWN
Haverfordwest	EGFE
Hawarden	EGNR
Henlow	EGWE
Henstridge	EGHS
Hereford	EGVH
Hethel	EGSK
Hollyhead	EGCH
Honington	EGXH
Hucknall	EGNA
Humberside	EGNJ
Inverness	EGPE
Islay	EGPI
Isle of Man	EGNS
Isle of Wight	EGHN
Isleworth	EGLI
Jersey	EGJJ
Kemble	EGBP
Kinloss	EGQK
Kirkwall	EGPA
Lakenheath	EGUL
Lands End	EGHC
Langford Lodge	EGAL
Lasham	EGHL
Lashenden	EGKH
Leconfield	EGXV
Leeds Bradford	EGNM
Leeming	EGXE
Lee on Solent	EGHF
Leicester	EGBG
Lerwick	EGET
Leuchars	EGQL
Linton on Ouse	EGXU
Little Gransden	EGMJ
Liverpool	EGGP
Llandbedr	EGOD
London City	EGLC
London Gatwick	EGKK
London Heathrow	EGLL
London Heliport	EGLW
London Luton	EGGW
London Stansted	EGSS
Londonderry	EGAE
Long Marston	EGBL
Lossiemouth	EGQS
Lydd	EGMD
Lyneham	EGDL
Manchester Barton	EGCB
Manchester Woodford	EGCD
Manchester	EGCC
Manston	EGMH
Marham	EGYM
Marshland	EGSI
Maypole	EGHB
Middle Wallop	EGVP
Mildenhall	EGUN
Mountwise	EGDB
Mount Pleasant	EGYP
Netheravon	EGDN
Netherthorpe	EGNF
Newcastle	EGNT
Newmarket Racecourse	EGSW
Newtownards	EGAD
North Ronaldsay	EGEN
North Weald	EGSX
Northampton	EGBK
Northolt	EGWU
Norwich	EGSH
Nottingham	EGBN
Oaksey Park	EGTW
Oban	EGEO
Odiham	EGVO
Old Buckenham	EGSV
Old Sarum	EGLS
Oxford	EGTK
Panshanger	EGLG
Papa Westray	EGEP
Pembrey	EGOP
Penzance Heliport	EGHK
Perranporth	EGTP
Perth	EGPT
Peterborough Conington	EGSF
Peterborough Sibson	EGSP
Peterhead Heliport	EGPS
Plymouth	EGHD
Popham	EGHP
Portland	EGDP
Portsmouth	EGVF
Prestwick	EGPK
Redhill	EGKR
Retford	EGNE
Rochester	EGTO
Sanday	EGES
Sandtoft	EGCF
Scampton	EGXP
Scatsta	EGPM
Scilly Isles	EGHE
Seething	EGSJ
Shawbury	EGOS
Sheffield City	EGSY
Sherburn in Elmet	EGCJ
Shipdham	EGSA
Shobdon	EGBS
Shoreham	EGKA
Shuttleworth	EGTH
Silverstone	EGBV
Skegness	EGNI
Sleap	EGCV
Southampton	EGHI
Southend	EGMC
Southport Sands	EGCO
St Athan	EGDX
St Mawgan	EGDG
Stapleford	EGSG
Stornoway	EGPO
Stronsay	EGER
Strubby Heliport	EGCG
Sturgate	EGCS
Sumburgh	EGPB
Swansea	EGFH
Tatenhill	EGBM
Ternhill	EGOE
Thorne	EGCP
Thruxton	EGHO
Tilstock	EGCT
Tiree	EGPU
Topcliffe	EGXZ
Tresco Heliport	EGHT
Truro	EGHY
Turweston	EGBT
Unst	EGPW
Uxbridge	EGUU
Valley	EGOV
Waddington	EGXW
Warton	EGNO
Wattisham	EGUW
Wellesbourne Mountford	EGBW
Welshpool	EGCW
West Freugh	EGOY
Westray	EGEW
West Wales	EGFA
Whalsay	EGEH
White Whaltham	EGLM
Wick	EGPC
Wickenby	EGNW
Wittering	EGXT
Wolverhampton Halfpenny Green	EGBO
Woodvale	EGOW
Wrexham	EGCE
Wycombe Air Park	EGTB
Wyton	EGUY
Yeovil	EGHG
Yeovilton	EGDY

FLIGHT PLAN **ATS COPY**

PRIORITY ADDRESSEE(S)

<<≡ FF → <<≡

FILING TIME ORIGINATOR

→ <<≡

SPECIFIC IDENTIFICATION OF ADDRESSEE(S) AND/OR ORIGINATOR

3 MESSAGE TYPE 7 AIRCRAFT IDENTIFICATION 8 FLIGHT RULES TYPE OF FLIGHT

<<≡ (FPL – – <<≡

9 NUMBER TYPE OF AIRCRAFT WAKE TURBULENCE CAT. 10 EQUIPMENT

– / – / <<≡

13 DEPARTURE AERODROME TIME

– <<≡

15 CRUISING SPEED LEVEL ROUTE

– →

<<≡

16 DESTINATION AERODROME TOTAL EET HR.MIN ALTN AERODROME 2ND. ALTN AERODROME

– → → <<≡

18 OTHER INFORMATION

–

) <<≡

SUPPLEMENTARY INFORMATION (NOT TO BE TRANSMITTED IN FPL MESSAGES)

19 ENDURANCE EMERGENCY RADIO

HR.MIN PERSONS ON BOARD UHF VHF ELBA

–E/ → P/ → R/ U V E

SURVIVAL EQUIPMENT POLAR DESERT MARITIME JUNGLE JACKETS LIGHT FLUORES UHF VHF

→ S / P D M J → J / L F U V

DINGHIES

NUMBER CAPACITY COVER COLOUR

→ D / → → C → <<≡

AIRCRAFT COLOUR AND MARKINGS

A/

REMARKS

→ N / <<≡

PILOT-IN-COMMAND

C/) <<≡

FILED BY SPACE RESERVED FOR ADDITIONAL REQUIREMENTS

CA48/RAF F2919(Revised November 1985) Carto. D.O 8810

Use block capitals throughout, insert all clock times in 4 figures using UTC. Numbers below relate to item numbers on the flight plan form.

ITEM 7: Aircraft Identification. The aircraft's registration (when it is being used as the RT callsign, or if the aircraft in non-radio) or the flight identification, with a maximum of 7 characters.

ITEM 8: Flight Rules/Type of Flight

Flight Rules

I IFR
V VFR
Y IFR first
Z VFR first

If using Y or Z specify in ITEM 15 where flight rules will change.

Type of Flight

S Scheduled air service
N Non-scheduled air transport operation
G General aviation
M Military
X Other category

ITEM 9: Number & Type of Aircraft, **Wake Turbulence Category**.

Insert number of aircraft *only* if more than one.
Insert type of aircraft as ICAO aircraft type designator. If no such designator exists insert ZZZZ and specify at ITEM 18 preceded by TYP/.

Wake Turbulence Category

H Heavy, MTOW of 136000kg or more
M Medium MTOW 7001kg – 135999kg
L Light MTOW 7000Kg or less

ITEM 10: Equipment,

N No comm/nav equipment
S Standard comm/nav equipment (VHF RTF, ADF, VOR, ILS)
or insert one or more of the following letters as appropriate;

A Loran A
C Loran C
D DME
E DECCA
F ADF
H HF RTF
I Inertial Navigation
L ILS
M OMEGA
O VOR
P DOPPLER
R RNAV Route Equipment
T TACAN
U UHF RTF
V VHF RTF
Z Other (specify at item 18, preceded by COM/ or NAV/)

SSR Equipment; after the slash (/)

N None
A Transponder Mode A
C Transponder Mode C

ITEM 13: Departure Aerodrome and **Time**.

Insert ICAO four letter aerodrome designator. If no ICAO designator exists enter ZZZZ and specify in ITEM 18, preceded by DEP/.
Insert estimated off-block time (UTC).

ITEM 15: Cruising Speed, Level & Route.

Insert True Air Speed for cruising portion of route. Use four figures preceded by K (Kilometres) or N (Knots). For Mach number three numbers preceded by M.
Insert cruising level as Flight Level (F followed by three numbers); or Altitude (A followed by three figures showing hundreds of feet); or Standard Metric Level (S followed by tens of metres); or altitude in tens of metres (M followed by four figures) or VFR for VFR flight with no specific cruising level.
For route, designator of first ATS route (if appropriate), and each point of change of speed, level, ATS route or flight rules, followed by designator of next ATS route.
For flight outside designated ATS routes, use coded designator, or lat/long coordinates, or bearing and distance from a navigation aid. DCT (Direct) can be used to join successive points unless both points are defined as geographical co-ordinates or bearing and distance.
If the departure aerodrome is not on an ATS route, insert DCT before the first point.

ITEM 16: Destination Aerodrome, Total Elapsed Time, Alternate Aerodrome and **2nd Alternate Aerodrome**.

Insert ICAO four letter designator for destination aerodrome, if no designator exists enter ZZZZ, and specify name in ITEM 18 preceded by DEST/.
Insert Total Elapsed Time in hours/minutes.
Insert alternate aerodrome(s) as ICAO designator, or if no designator exists then ZZZZ and specify name in ITEM 18 preceded by ALTN/.

ITEM 18: Other Information.

0 if None

EET/	signficant point(s) or FIR boundary designator(s) with estimated *elapsed* time(s).
REG/	registration if different to aircraft identification in ITEM 7
OPR/	name of operator if appropriate
STS/	reason for special handling by ATC
TYP/	types of aircraft, if ZZZZ specified at item 9
COM/	comm equipment if Z specified in item 10
NAV/	nav equipment if Z specified in item 10
DEP/	Departure aerodrome name if ZZZZ inserted at item 13
DEST/	Destination aerodrome name if ZZZZ inserted at item 16
ALTN/	Alternate aerodrome name if ZZZZ inserted at item 16
RMK/	any other plain language remarks as appropriate

ITEM 19: Supplementary Information.

Endurance:
E/ – fuel endurance in a four-figure group to express hours/minutes
Persons on Board:
P/ –
Emergency Radio:
R/ Radio
Cross out U if UHF 243MHz not available.
Cross out V if VHF 121.5MHz not available.
Cross out E if emergency locater beacon – aircraft (ELBA) not available.

Survival Equipment:
S/ Survival Equipment
Cross out all indicators if survival equipment not carried
Cross out P if polar survival equipment not carried
Cross out D if desert survival equipment not carried
Cross out M if maritime survival equipment not carried
Cross out J if jungle survival equipment not carried

Jackets:
J/ Jackets
Cross out all indicators if no life-jackets are carried
Cross out L if life-jackets are not equipped with lights
Cross out F if life-jackets are not equipped with flourescein
Cross out U or V to indicate radio capability of life-jackets.

Dingies:
Number Cross out indicators D and C if no dinghies are carried, or insert number
Capacity Insert total capacity, in persons, of dinghies carried
Cover Cross out C if dinghies are not covered
Colour Insert colour of dinghies carried

Aircraft Colour and Markings:
A/ Aircraft colour and markings – insert colour of aircraft and significant markings

Remarks:
N/ Remarks – Cross out indicator N if no remarks, or indicate other survival equipment/remarks.

Pilot in Command:
C/ Pilot – Insert name of pilot in command

Filing a flight plan

A VFR flight plan must be filed at least 60 minutes before clearance to start or taxi is requested. Normally the flight plan is filed at the departure airfield who will pass it on to the relevant Parent ATSU Flight Briefing Unit. If the departure airfield will not be able to file the flight plan, it should be telephoned or faxed directly to the appropriate Parent ATSU Flight Briefing Unit:

Flight Briefing Unit Telephone Number	Fax Number
LONDON/Heathrow EGLL	
0208 745 3111	0208 745 3491
0208 745 3163	0208 745 3492
Manchester EGCC	
0161 499 5502	0161 499 5504
0161 499 5500	0161 499 5501
Scottish ACC EGPX	
01292 692679	01292 671048

The ATSU or FBU must be advised as soon as possible of any cancellations, delays that will exceed 30 minutes, or changes to flight plan details.
If the flight lands at a place other than the flightplan destination, the destination must be informed within 30 minutes of the planned ETA there.

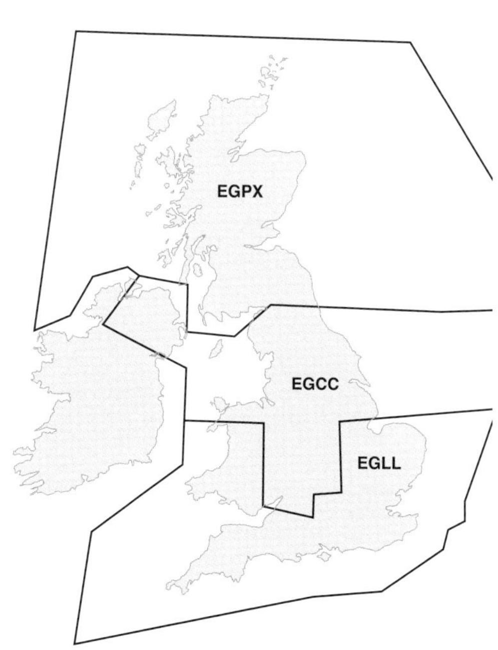

IMPORTANT NOTICE

Prevention of the Infringement of Controlled Airspace

The number of reported infringements of controlled airspace is rising

2005	412 reported infringements
2006	562 reported infringements
2007	702 reported infringements
2008	241 reported infringements (January to May)

Since 2005 NATS has asked air traffic controllers to report all controlled airspace infringements however minor, this will explain some of the increase shown that year. However the number of risk bearing infringements has increased by the same amount and these would have been previously reported.

While infringements can occur in any controlled airspace, certain hotspot areas have become apparent, some of which are listed below

Luton/Stansted Area	Red Arrows Displays (Temporary Restricted Areas)
London City Airport	Western part of London Control Zone (White Waltham Area)

Particular care should be taken while operating in these areas.

A UK based website devoted solely to Airspace Infringements is run by the General Aviation Safety Council (GASCo) on behalf of the Civil Aviation Authority. The Fly On Track Website contains lots of useful information which will aid pilots in avoiding infringements of controlled airspace; the following information is taken from the site.

The Web address for the Fly on Track Website, AIS (UK Aeronautical Information Service) and NATS (National Air Traffic Services) Website are listed below

Fly on Track	www.flyontrack.co.uk
AIS (UK Aeronautical Information Service)	www.ais.org.uk
NATS (National Air Traffic Services)	www.nats.co.uk

How NOT to Infringe – TOP TIPS FROM THE ON TRACK TEAM

1 **NOTAM Checking:**
Check NOTAMs before flying (www.ais.org.uk) and learn to use an efficient method like 'narrow route brief' features if possible. In any case, double check on any temporary airspace restrictions using the freephone 0500 354802. If using a commercial or graphical product, remember to check any that are reported as 'not-plottable' carefully.

2 **Track Through or Around CAS?**
When planning a route via controlled airspace, always have 'plan B' to avoid it too. Make a decision checkpoint on where to take this avoidance route if a clearance is not possible – it's much easier to get round a block of airspace from a few miles distant than it is to successfully divert around tight up to the boundary. Remember to plan time and fuel calculations using the longer route.

3 **Routing 'Close By' CAS:**
When routing very close to an airspace boundary but not crossing it, consider a call to that airspace ATC or a nearby formal LARS. Even when you are totally accurately on track, you may be a minor distraction for a busy controller who actually doesn't know you know exactly what you are doing. If you have to fly very close to a boundary, check for any obvious line feature that will help you stay clear. Don't be ashamed to use it, it's a way of reducing your workload.

4 **Weather:**
A pilot's workload rises rapidly in less than ideal weather and so do infringements. If the weather starts to deteriorate, consider your options early and if necessary divert or turn back, or start to use safe line features in good time. Even in good weather take note if a strong 'across track' wind is blowing towards the boundary. It doesn't take much loss of concentration whilst you admire the wonders of flying in good weather, and you can accidentally drift over a boundary.

5 **CAS Transits:**
If you wish to transit controlled airspace or a zone, think about what you need to ask in advance and call the appropriate Air Traffic Control (ATC) unit at ten nautical miles or five minutes flying time from the airspace boundary to give notice. Think about your routing and the active runway alignment. You are much more likely to get a crossing approved perpendicular to the runway than along it. Check the useful airspace guides written by local ATC for most of the 'CTR's in the UK, giving tips, photos, and preferred routings – they are all on the www.flyontrack.co.uk 'links' tab.

6 **Make Your Calls Clear and Efficient**
Thinking before you press the transmit switch. Using the correct radio phraseology helps air traffic control to help you and sounds more professional! A handy free kneeboard insert is available from the CAA or from www.flyontrack.co.uk 'tips' tab. It will help you form any request for a zone crossing by giving you a 'template' mask to slot your words into.

7 **Get a Specific Clearance**
Remember the instruction 'Standby' means just that; it is not an ATC clearance and not even a precursor to a clearance. Even if given a squawk or any sort of service (e.g. FIS), this does not mean you can enter the airspace. Only cross the boundary if the controller issues a specific crossing clearance, otherwise, consider

plan 'B' to route around or perhaps even over or under. Be aware that ATC may be busy when you call them even if you hear no-one. Just because the frequency doesn't sound busy doesn't mean that the controller isn't busy on another frequency or on landlines

8 **Can You Cope with 'Change'?**
Your planned route through controlled airspace may appear simple on your chart be prepared for a crossing clearance that does not exactly match your planned route but will allow you to transit safely. Tell the controller the moment anything is not clear, or you are unsure of exactly where you are. Even if not planning to cross any controlled airspace, don't delay in calling any ATC when uncertain of your position. Overcoming your embarrassment may prevent an infringement, which may in turn prevent an AIRPROX (or worse).

9 **Transponders**
If you have a transponder with mode C, you should use the 'altitude reporting' at all times in flight unless instructed otherwise by a ATC unit. Always use mode C, ATC will always expect you to, even if they do not tell you. Do NOT fly with the transponder only set to 'ON', train yourself to set 'ALT' automatically, as this may prevent an infringement altogether or reduce the consequences if one were to happen. ATC is there to help, so don't be afraid to talk to them OR, in certain parts of the country, you can 'advertise' that you are there to be contacted if necessary. If you don't want to enter the airspace and don't need a specific service either, if you are near any ATC unit currently trialing a 'listening in' squawk, why not tune in to their frequency without announcing yourself and use the associated squawk? You can read about this on the www.flyontrack.co.uk home page.

DON'T INFRINGE AIR DISPLAY AIRSPACE

Every year the Temporary Restricted Airspace established around certain air shows in the UK attracts infringements. For example, between 2002 and 2005 Red Arrows Temporary Restricted Airspace was infringed on 14 occasions.
At best, infringements will lead to displays – including those by the Red Arrows – being disrupted and thousands of members of the paying public being denied the chance to see solo and team aerobatic performances. Some are cancelled as a result or called off half way through – for example the 2006 Kemble display.
All such incursions have flight safety implications and could lead to accidents and loss of life.
In many cases infringements occur because pilots simply haven't briefed themselves properly before taking off. All pilots should be aware of the briefing options available to ensure that they are not one of the infringements statistics. There are several ways to obtain pre-flight briefing information:

One of the easiest ways to check on temporary restricted airspace (such as Red Arrows displays) is by calling the dedicated free phone AIS Information Line on 0500 354 802

Check NOTAMs on the AIS Website contact the NOTAM Office on 020 8745 3451 or 3450 (24 hour facility).

Alternatively, check Pre-Flight Information Bulletins (PIBs) on the AIS website. PIB Help is also available there. PIBs may also be accessed through the NATS Website, even if the AIS website is down.

Check all of the Red Arrow's display sites and certain air shows. Aeronautical Information Circulars (AICs), also on the AIS Website

Mauve AICs notify the establishment of Temporary Restricted Airspace around

Yellow AICs providing details of major displays or rallies may also be published.

A number of major events are notified by both Mauve and Yellow AICs.

Wherever and whenever you fly during the summer make sure you're properly briefed and that you don't end up as a Air Display infringement statistic.

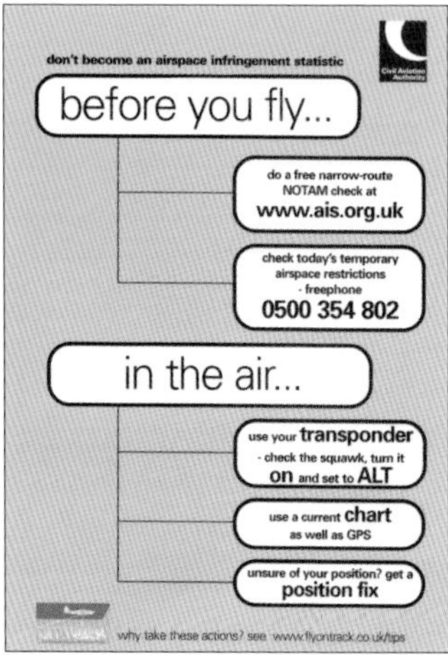

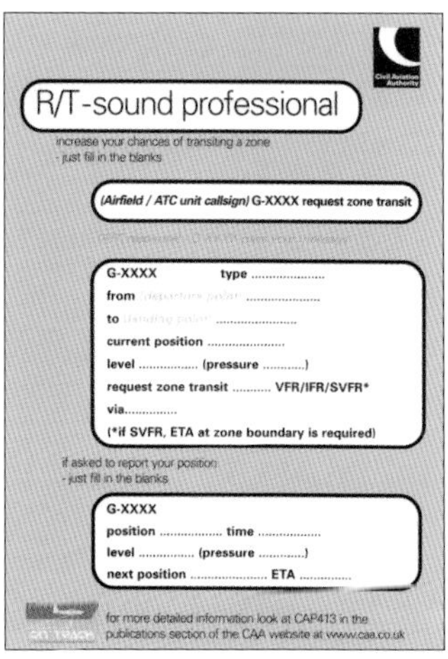

Name/Model	ICAO
2/180 Gyroplane	HG18
47G2/Bell	KH2
47G2A/Bell	KH2A
47G3B-KH4/Bell	KH4
A109/109A/II	A109
AB 47 G/G-2/2A/2A1/ 3B1/4/4A	A47G
AB 47 J/J-2A/3/3B-1	A47J
Aero145	O145
Aero Commander 685	AC85
Aero Commander 695	AC95
Aero-Jodel D-11A	AE11
Aeronca Champion	AR58
Aeronca Chief/Super Chief	AR11
Aeronca Sedan	AR15
Aero Star	TS60
Aero Star 600/700	PA60
Aircoupe A2	FO2
Aircruiser	VT11
Air Cruiser	AC72
Airtourer	VT10
ARV ARV-1	ARV1
Autogyro (Ultralight/Microlight)	GYRO
Balloons	BALL
Beagle Pup B121	BT12
Beech Bonanza 33	BE33
Beech Bonanza 35	BE35
Beech Bonanza 36	BE36
Beech Baron 55	BE55
Beech Baron 58	BE58
Beech Beech F90	BE9T
Beech Beech Jet 400	BE40
Beech Duchess 76	BE76
Beech Duke 60	BE60
Beech King Air C90, E90	BE9L
Beech King Air 100	BE10
Beech Starship, Model 2000	BEST
Beech Sundowner 23/ Musketeer 23	BE23
Beech Super King Air 200	BE20
Beech Super King Air 300	BE30
Beech Super King Air 350	B350
Beech Twin Beech 18	BE18
Bell 412	NB12
Bell B/A 206B-1	CCB4
Bell Jet Ranger/ Long Sea Ranger	B06
BN-2A/B Islander/Defender	BN2P
BN-2A Mk111 Trislander	TRIS
BO 105	NB05
BO 105A/C/D/S	MBH5
BO 105LS A-1, A-3	MDH5
BO 209, S Monsun	MB09
Brave	PA36
Buccaneer/LA-4/200EP/EPR	LA4
Buecker BUE 131 Jungmann BJ31	
CAP 10/10B	CP10
CAP 20/20L	CP20
CAP 21	CP21
CAP 230	CP23
Cessna 120	C120
Cessna 140	C140
Cessna 150	C150
Cessna 152	C152
Cessna 170	C170
Cessna 172/Skyhawk/ HawkXPII/Cutlass	C172
Cessna 172RG	C72R
Cessna 177RG	C77R
Cessna 185/Skywagon	C185
Cessna 190	C190
Cessna 195	C195
Cessna 310/T310	C310
Cessna 337	C337
Cessna Pressurised 337	P337
Cessna 340/340A	C340
Cessna 401/402/4026	C402
Cessna 411	C411
Cessna Caravan 1	C208
Cessna Cardinal 177	C177
Cessna Centurion/ Turbo Centurion 210	C210
Cessna Chancellor 414A	C414
Cessna Citation Jet 522	C525
Cessna Citation	C500
Cessna Citation II/S2	C550
Cessna Citation III/VI/VII	C650
Cessna Citation V	C560
Cessna Conquest/ Conquest II	C441
Cessna Crusader T303	C303
Cessna Golden Eagle 421	C421
Cessna Pressurised Centurion	P210
Cessna Skylane 182/RG, Turbo Skylane/RG	C182
Cessna Skymaster	C336
Cessna Stationair/Turbo Stationair/6	C206
Cessna Stationair/ Turbo Stationair 7/8	C207
Cessna Titan	C404
CFM Shadow	SHAD
CH-47	CEM47
Champion	CL60
Champion Citabria	AR7
Champion Lancer 402	CH40
Chipmunk DHC-1	DH1
Christen Eagle II	SOCH
Commander 112/114	CM11
Commander 200	M200
Commander 500	AC50
Commander 520	AC52
Commander 560	AC56
Corsair	C425
Cougar GA-7	GA7
CP 301 Emeraude	CP30
Decathlon	BL8
Diamond 1/1A	MU30
Diplomate ST 10	S10a
DO27	DO27
DR100,105,1050,1051	DR10
DR220,221	DR22
DR 250	DR250
DR 300	DR30
DR 360	DR36
DR 400	DR 40
Ecureuil AS350	S350
Ecureuil AS351	S351
Ecureuil AS355	S355
Europa	EUPA
Falco	F8L
Falcon 10	FA10
Falcon 20FJF/20C/ 20D/20E/20F	FA20
Falcon 20G/20GF, Mystere Falcon 200	FA21
Falcon 50	FA50
Falcon 900	FA90
G109/109B	G109
G115/115A	G115
Gardan GY100	GY10
Gazelle Sa341/342	GAZL
Glassair II/III	GLAS
Glider/Sailplane	GLID
Grumman Cheetah, Tiger, Traveler	AA5
Grumman Yankee AA-1B	AA1
Gulfstream I	G159
Gulfstream II/III/IV	GULF
HN-300C	BI30
Horizon GY 80	S80
HR 100	HR10
HR 200	HR20
HS125	HS25
Jet Commander	JCOM
Jet Commander 840/980/1000	AC6T
Jetstream 31/32	JSTA
Jodel D112/D120	D11
Jodel D140	D140
Kachina 2150A	MOR2
Kitfox	FOX
L-4-200 Buccaneer	LA4
LA-250	LA25
Lancair 235/320/360	LNC2
Lancair IV	LNC3
Learjet 23	LJ23
Learjet 24	LJ24
Learjet 25	LJ25
Learjet 28	LJ28
Learjet 31	LJ31
Learjet 35	LJ35
Learjet 55	LJ55
Learjet 60	LJ60
Luscombe 11	L11
Maule M-4	M4
Maule M-5	M5
Maule M-6	M6
Maule M-7	M7
Mooney 20, 21, 22, 201, 231	M20
Meta-Sokol L40	O40
MU2	MU2
P64-Oscar	OSCR
Pilatus PC-12	PC12
Piper Apache	PA23
Piper Aztec	PA27
Piper Cherokee/Archer II/ Dakota/Warrior	PA28
Piper Cherokee Arrow	P28R
Piper Cherokee 6/Lance/ Saratoga	PA32
Piper Cheyenne I/II	P31T
Piper Cheyenne III/IV	PA42
Piper Chieftain/Navajo	PA31
Piper Clipper	PA16
Piper Commanche	PA24
Piper Cub Special	PA11
Piper Cub Trainer	J2
Piper Cub Trainer 3	J3
Piper Family Cruiser	PA14
Piper Malibu	PA46
Piper Pacer	PA20
Piper Seminole	PA44
Piper Seneca	PA34
Piper Super Cruiser	PA12
Piper Super Cub	PA18
Piper Tri-Pacer/Colt	PA22
Piper Twin Commanche	PA30
Piper Vagabond	PA17
Piper Vagabond Trainer	PA15
R 1180T, 1180TD	R100
R 2160, 2160D, 2100, 2100A, 2112	R200
R 3000/3100/3120/3140	R300
Rallye	RALL
RF3	RF3
RF4	RF4
RF5	RF5
RF6	RF6
RF6B	SPF6B
RF7	SPF7
RF9	RF9
Robinson R22	R22
Robinson R44	R44
SF260	F260
SF260TP	F26T
Stagger Wing 17	BE17
Stampe	SV4
Stearman	B75
Steen Skybolt	BOLT
Super Acro Sport	ASPO
Swift	GC1
T67M Firefly 160	RF6
Tampico TB-09	TAMP
TBM 706	TBM7
Texan	T6
Tiger Moth 82A	DH82
Tobago TB-10	TOBA
Tomahawk	PA38
Trinidad TB-20/21	TRIN
Turbo Commander 690C	
Turbulent	D31
Twin Otter DHC-6	DH6
Vari-Eze	KREZ
Vari EZE/Long EZ	LGEZ
Yak 50	YK50
Yak 52	YK52
Zlin 42	Z42
Zlin 43	Z43
Z-50L	Z50

The following airports have been designated as Customs and Excise Airports by the DTLR:

Aberdeen	
Belfast Aldergrove	2
Biggin Hill	1
Birmingham	
Blackpool	1
Bournemouth	
Bristol	
Cambridge	1
Cardiff	
Coventry	1
Durham Tees Valley	
East Midlands	
Edinburgh	
Exeter	1
Glasgow	2
Humberside	1
Isle of Man	1
Leeds/Bradford	
Liverpool	
London City	1
London Gatwick	2
London Heathrow	2
London Luton	
London Stansted	
Lydd	1
Manchester	2
Manston	1
Newcastle	
Norwich	
Plymouth	2
Shoreham	1
Southampton	
Southend	
Sumburgh	1

1 Aerodromes are NOT Ports of Entry under the Immigration Act 1971
2 Aerodromes are Sanitary Airport under the International Sanitary Regulations

1 Aircrew

1.1 Arriving on Flights from other EU Countries

1.1.1 The duty/tax free allowances do not apply to intra EU crew. No declaration is required to be made. Also, there is no HMRC restriction on crew members exit route from the airport (although in practice at most larger airports their movements are constrained by security measures).

1.2 Arriving on Flights from Non-EU Countries

1.2.1 The HMRC officer at the airport of arrival will be able to advise on the arrangements in operation there for clearance of aircrew. Normally, this will involve the crew members in either:

a Making a declaration on Form C909; or

b making an oral declaration in the Red Channel or at the Red Point, if they are carrying goods in excess of the customs allowances for aircrew.

1.2.2 The terms of this paragraph apply not only to crew who have arrived on a direct flight from outside the EU, but also to crew whose aircraft has made a stopover at another EU airport.

1.3 Departing on Flights to Non-EU Destinations

1.3.1 It is not normally necessary for crews effects to be made available for HMRC inspection, except when refund of VAT is being claimed under the Retail Export Scheme. VAT leaflet 704/1/September 2004 explains the conditions under which aircrew are eligible for the Scheme, and the procedures to be followed.

2 Passengers

2.1 Arriving on Domestic Flights

2.1.1 The hold baggage of passengers who arrived in the United Kingdom from a non-EU Country and have transferred to a domestic flight will be subject to HMRC control at the destination airport, if it has not been cleared at the airport of arrival in the United Kingdom. The HMRC officer at the destination airport should be contacted for details of the arrangements.

2.2 Arriving on Flights from other EU Countries

2.2.1 Passengers on direct flights from other EU Countries are not normally required to make any declaration and at most airports proceed through a separate EU exit.

2.2.2 The only exception is for passengers who commenced their journey outside the EU and have transferred to a flight to the United Kingdom after arriving in another EU Country. After reclaiming their hold baggage, such passengers must make an oral declaration in the Red Channel or at the Red Point, if they are carrying goods in excess of Customs allowances. Passengers with nothing to declare should proceed through the Green Channel.

2.3 Arriving on Flights from Non-EU Countries

2.3.1 After disembarkation, passengers completing their journey at a United Kingdom airport reclaim any hold baggage, and if they are carrying goods in excess of Customs allowances they must make an oral declaration in the Red Channel or at the Red Point. Passengers with nothing to declare should proceed through the Green Channel. These procedures apply not only to passengers who have arrived on a direct flight from outside the EU, but also to passengers whose aircraft has made a stopover at another EU airport.

2.3.2 Passengers who are transferring to a flight to another EU Country do not reclaim their hold baggage, but must declare any goods in their cabin baggage which are in excess of customs allowances.

2.3.3 Passengers who are transferring to a flight to a non-EU Country are not required to make any declaration to HMRC.

2.3.4 The HMRC officer for the airport of arrival should be contacted for advice on the arrangements there for passengers transferring to a flight to another United Kingdom airport, as these may vary depending on local circumstances.

2.4 Departing on Flights to Non-EU Destinations

2.4.1 It is not normally necessary for passengers baggage to be made available to HMRC, except when refund of VAT is being claimed under the Retail Export Scheme. VAT leaflet 704/1/September 2004 explains the conditions under which passengers are eligible for the scheme and the procedures to be followed.

3 Further Information

3.1 Further information on the HMRC requirements for international travellers, including details of Customs allowances is in HM Customs and Excise Notice 1.

It is a requirement of the Act that the commander of any aircraft flying between Great Britain and the Republic of Ireland, Northern Ireland, the Isle of Man or the Channel Islands or Inbound to Great Britain from those places must, on exit or entry to Great Britain, land at an airport designated in the act. The same requirement exists for flights entering or leaving Northern Ireland when flying to or from Great Britain, the Republic of Ireland, the Isle of Man or the Channel Islands.

To comply with the requirements of this legislation the captains of aircraft affected by the Act **must.**

1 Obtain clearance from the examining Police officer before take-off from and after landing at an airport designated in the act.

2 Must comply with the requirements of the examining officer in respect of any examination of the captain, passengers, or crew, if carried.

Designated Airports in Gt. Britain, Northern Ireland, Isle of Man, & Channel Islands

ABERDEEN
ALDERNEY
BELFAST ALDERGROVE
BELFAST CITY
BIGGIN HILL
BIRMINGHAM
BLACKPOOL
BOURNEMOUTH
BRISTOL
CAMBRIDGE
CARDIFF
CARLISLE
COVENTRY
DURHAM TEES VALLEY
EAST MIDLANDS
EDINBURGH
EXETER
GLASGOW
GLOUCESTERSHIRE
GUERNSEY
HUMBERSIDE
ISLE OF MAN
JERSEY
LEEDS BRADFORD
LIVERPOOL
LONDON CITY
LONDON GATWICK
LONDON HEATHROW
LONDON LUTON
LONDON STANSTED
LONONDERRY
LYDD
MANCHESTER
MANSTON
NEWCASTLE
NORWICH
PLYMOUTH
PRESTWICK
SOUTHAMPTON
SOUTHEND

BRISTOL FILTON is not an airport designated under the act but the same facility will be available if application is made at least 24hrs prior to the flight. Such application should be made during normal office hours to. **Tel:** 01272 699094

Flights from Non Designated Airports

If a pilot wishes to make a direct flight from anon-designated airport he/she **must** seek prior permission from the Chief Constable in whose area then on-designated airport is located. Permission should be sought **as far in advance as possible.**

Requirements for Civil Helicopters

Pilots of civil helicopters flying into Northern Ireland are required to notify the Police Service of Northern Ireland (PSNI) control and Information centre. **Tel:** 01232 650222 Ex 22430, of the point and time for crossing the Northern Ireland coast, **this is in addition to the normal requirements of the Act.** Any amendment to the crossing point and/or time must be advised to **Belfast Aldergrove APP** who will notify the PSNI on the pilots behalf.

Avon and Somerset	**0845 456 7000**
Bedfordshire	**01234 841212**
Cambridgeshire	**0845 456 4564**
Cheshire	**0845 458 0000**
Cleveland	**01642 326326**
Cumbria	**0845 330 0247**
Derbyshire	**0845 123 3333**
Devon and Cornwall	**0845 277 7444**
Dorset	**01305 222222**
Durham	**0845 606 0365**
Dyfed-Powys	**0845 330 2000**
Essex	**01245 491491**
Gloucestershire	**0845 090 1234**
Greater Manchester	**0161 872 5050**
Gwent	**01633 838111**
Hampshire	**0845 045 4545**
Hertfordshire	**0845 330 0222**
Humberside	**0845 606 0222**
Kent	**01622 690690**
Lancashire	**0845 125 3545**
Leicestershire	**0116 222 2222**
Lincolnshire	**01522 532222**
London (Metropolitan)	**0207 230 1212**
London (City)	**0207 601 2455**
Merseyside	**0151 709 6010**
Norfolk	**0845 456 4567**
Northampton	**0845 370 0700**
Northumbria	**01661 872555**
North Wales	**0845 607 1002**
North Yorkshire	**0845 606 0247**
Nottinghamshire	**0115 9670999**
South Wales	**01656 655555**
South Yorkshire	**0114 220 2020**
Staffordshire	**0845 330 2010**
Suffolk	**01473 613500**
Surrey	**0845 125 2222**
Sussex	**0845 607 0999**
Thames Valley	**0845 850 5505**
Warwickshire	**01926 415000**
West Mercia	**0845 744 4888**
West Midlands	**0845 113 5000**
West Yorkshire	**0845 606 0606**
Wiltshire	**0845 408 7000**

Scotland

Central Scotland	**01786 456000**
Dumfries and Galloway	**0845 600 5701**
Fife	**01592 418888**
Grampian	**0845 600 5700**
Lothian and Borders	**0131 311 3131**
Northern	**01463 715555**
Strathclyde	**0141 532 2000**
Tayside	**01382 223200**

Northern Ireland

Police Service of Northern Ireland (PSNI)	**02890 650222**

Isle of Man & Channel Islands

Isle of Man	**01624 631212**
Jersey	**01534 612612**
Guernsey	**01481 725111**

(Who also have responsibility for Alderney)

As you may notice from this guide, the number of gliding airfields that will accept powered aircraft is increasing. There are a number of hazards and practices associated with such airfields which are unfamiliar to the powered pilot. The following points are designed as general guidance and pilots intending to visit a gliding airfield **are strongly advised to ensure they are properly briefed on the specific field they intend to visit.** All gliding airfields require telephone PPR so this is not another chore to remember. **There is nothing more likely to reverse the trend of gliding airfields accepting powered aircraft than demonstrations of poor airman ship or obstruction of their activities.** Having said the heavy bit, GO OUT AND ENJOY!

1 MAINTAIN A VERY GOOD LOOKOUT. Not only does steam give way to sail but remember, a glider cannot go around! Even the hottest competition model will continue to descend when committed to a landing. DO NOT OBSTRUCT THE LANDING AREA! Remember that Gliding fields are primarily for gliding, you are a guest and give preference at all times.

2 FLYING IN THE LOCAL AREA WHEN JOINING OR LEAVING THE CIRCUIT? Then there are two very relevant tips to remember. Firstly... **keep a very good lookout close to cloud base**... On thermic days this is where the Gliders will be, an unstable day with developing, or developed Cumulus will see many gliders turning beneath them, if you are descending through cloud it makes sense to do this further from your destination than you might normally do. Secondly... By the very nature of their activities glider pilots are more used to flying in close proximity to other aircraft than we powered pilots. Sometimes this can be very disconcerting! (It certainly has worried me when I've gone gliding)! But remember, as they do it a lot they are very aware of aircraft in their proximity, keep a very good lookout and may even have heard you coming! The best reaction is to assume you have not been seen and apply the Rules of the Air.

3 USE THE GLIDER COMMON FREQUENCIES. All gliding fields require PPR, when you get it make sure you know which of the common gliding frequencies are used by the local club and make circuit reports on it. You are very unlikely to get an answer but at least someone **MAY** know you are there. Remember, not all local Gliders will be listening out on radio, traffic awareness is not its primary function so **remain vigilant at all times.**

4 LOOK OUT FOR CABLES. Do not carry out overhead joins, as this is where the winch will deposit any departing gliders, sometimes up to 3000ft agl! You may see the cable drogue parachute but you will **not** see the cable. If you hit it in flight it will kill you, which would really spoil your visit! Remember also that tug aircraft will be towing cables, don't get too close and **always give them priority,** they have a job to do and this is only courteous airmanship.

5 LANDING (LOOK OUT FOR CABLES AGAIN)! After landing, roll beyond the launch point. This is because most gliders will be planning their landing to arrive at the launch point so that it is only a short push, (or tow), to regain the end of the launch queue. They'll then have plenty of room to land behind and to the right of you, (remember the Rules of the Air). It's quite obvious where the launch point is as the launch control caravan will be here and so will the launch queue of gliders. Give them a wide berth and do not land if a launch is in progress. After landing turn **left** and wait. Have a good look up final approach and on the base legs. Nothing coming? Then taxi back down the strip keeping close to the edge. If a tug or Glider should appear on final then stop and wait until it has landed. Continue to taxi back and **pass behind the launch queue. Don't taxi in front of the queue, you will be crossing the cables, the danger of this is quite obvious.** Park by the Launch control caravan but not between it and the winch as you will be obstructing the winch drivers view of the control caravan's visual signals, (a bit like an Aldis light).

6 BE AWARE OF YOUR PROPWASH. When manoeuvring or parking be very aware of your prop wash if you are using increased revs. The area around the launch point is generally very busy with people awaiting a launch, gliders being towed or manhandled, trailers, caravans, and vehicles. The possibilities for damage caused by loose stones or prop wash is self-evident.

7 DEPARTING. The same rules apply. Don't take off until the launch cable is on the ground following a launch remember the drogue chute on the cable will make this easy to accertain. Continue to be extremely vigilant until well clear of the site. At sites, which have Aerotow facilities, it is quite likely that there will be noise abatement routes or procedures. Find out if there are and follow them!

IF YOU ARE IN ANY DOUBT ABOUT LOCAL PROCEDURES THEN ASK ONE OF THE RESIDENT INSTRUCTORS. THERE WILL ALMOST CERTAINLY BE ONE NEAR THE LAUNCH CONTROL CARAVAN.

8 BAD GROUND. Many gliding fields are exactly that, a large field with useable and, sometimes, very unusable areas. Ensure you know where the area suitable for powered aircraft use is. Currock Hill is a case in point where a very large grass area has a relatively small area suitable for powered aircraft use.

Gliding fields invariably have some form of catering and facilities for an overnight stay at very reasonable cost. They are not as forbidding as they may seem to power pilots but when you do visit them show them you are a good airman. This article is by no means comprehensive and I find I learn something new at each site I visit. By showing the Gliding fraternity that we are considerate of their operations, the more likely it is that they will be willing to allow powered aircraft the use of their sites, which opens up a whole new range of airfields to visit.

Beach Airfield Operations – a general guide

There are a number of airfields within the UK VFR Flight Guide with sand/beach runways. Hazards are associated with such airfields. The following should be followed to ensure safe arrivals and departures:

1 Most beach airfields are open to the public – keep a good look out for people walking along the beach.

2 The useable portion of the beach for landing is situated below the high water mark.

3 It is recommended to carry out an inspection of the beach/Rwy prior to landing, by flying over the area a few times to establish the layout etc..

4 Pilots should exercise caution during flare and hold off as height judgement can be difficult over the featureless surface.

5 Prefered landing technique is to use power down to touchdown.

6 Ensure you have checked out the high and low tide times before departing for the beach/airfield.

7 Carry out engine run-up on a suitable area of firm sand around the high water mark.

8 If ACFT stops on the beach before commencing take off run for run up there is a danger of the wheels sinking into the sand.

Use of Unlicensed Airfields and Unlicensed Runways

Every annual edition of the UK VFR Flight Guide contains data on around 500 airfields. The majority of these are 'unlicensed' airfields – that is they may not comply with the standards of a licensed airfield, or the owner/operator may simply have decided not to go to the time and expense of having the airfield inspected to ensure that it complies with licensed airfield requirements.

Every day, hundreds if not thousands of flights operate safely to and from unlicensed airfields, but it is necessary for any pilot using an unlicensed airfield or runway to appreciate some of the essential differences between licensed and unlicensed airfields.

■ Often our only source of information for an unlicensed airfield is the airfield operator. Their information may, or may not, be as accurate or as up-to-date as that for a licensed airfield. We rarely receive 'updated' information or amendments for unlicensed airfields during the 12 month life cycle of a UK VFR Flight Guide edition and changes are rarely notified by NOTAM.

■ Runway length information in particular may be less accurate at unlicensed airfields. At one 'grass strip' airfield, the runway length can vary by up to 70 metres during a season depending on who is mowing the runway. The standard of runway markings varies, it may not be obvious where the runway starts and finishes. It is essential to contact the airfield operator for up-to-date information before using an unlicensed airfield, and it is essential to apply all the relevant performance factors and safety margins to take-off, climb and landing distance calculations.

■ Runways, facilities and even the use of the entire site may be withdrawn or changed without notice. Again, it is essential to contact the airfield operator for up-to-date information before using an unlicensed airfield.

■ Obstructions close to the airfield and runways which would not be permitted at a licensed airfield may be found at an unlicensed airfield on a permanent or temporary basis. It is essential to contact the airfield operator for up-to-date information before using an unlicensed airfield.

■ There may be obstacles such as walls or hedges right up to the runway edges, for example trees or hedges over 20ft high at the end of an unlicensed runway. These may reduce the amount of useable runway to significantly less than that depicted. Runway and taxiway surfaces, dimensions, slopes and surroundings that would not be permitted at a licensed airfield may exist at an unlicensed airfield. Uncontrolled non-aviation activities (agriculture, live stock, public rights of way etc.) may exist at unlicensed airfields. It is essential to contact the airfield operator for up-to-date information before using an unlicensed airfield.

■ We strongly recommend that pilots intending to use an unlicensed airfield have read, understood and comply with the advice in the following safety publications:

Safety Sense Leaflet 7C Aeroplane Performance

Safety Sense Leaflet 12D Strip Sense

■ We also strongly recommend that pilots intending to use an unlicensed airfield have read and understood:

CAP428 Safety Standards at Unlicensed Aerodromes

The above publications can be downloaded free at www.caa.co.uk

■ We also strongly recommend that pilots intending to use an unlicensed airfield have read, understood and comply with the advice in:

Aeronautical Information Circular (AIC) 127 (P110)/06 Performance of Light Aeroplanes – Take-Off, Climb and Landing

This AIC can be downloaded free at www.ais.org.uk

SAFETYSENSE LEAFLET 12d STRIP SENSE

1 INTRODUCTION
2 ASSESSING THE STRIP
3 OPERATIONAL CONSIDERATIONS
4 OVERNIGHT CONSIDERATIONS
5 FLYING CONSIDERATIONS
6 SETTING UP YOUR OWN STRIP
7 MAIN POINTS

1 INTRODUCTION

a. Unlicensed aerodromes and private strips are often used by pilots and private owners. They may be more convenient or cheaper than licensed aerodromes; however they do require special consideration. Approximately one third of GA Reportable Accidents in the UK occur during take off or landing at unlicensed aerodromes. The proportion of flying activity is not known.

b. This Leaflet is intended to start you thinking about the differences and particular needs of such flying, and also to give some guidelines about operating from, or establishing, your own strip. It should be read in conjunction with the relevant parts of SafetySense leaflet 6, Aerodrome Sense

2 ASSESSING THE STRIP

a. It is important to realise that the CAA criteria for the licensing of an aerodrome, e. g. clear approaches without power or other cables, no trees or obstructions close to the runway and so on, are unlikely to have been applied to the strip. Since in almost all cases **Prior Permission is Required (PPR) before landing**, your phone call should also include discussion of any difficulties, obstructions, noise sensitive areas to be avoided and the useable length of the strip.

b. Find out the arrangements for grass cutting. It is no use landing only to find the grass is so long that it prevents you taking off again. As a rule of thumb, the grass length should not be more than 30% of the diameter of the wheel.

c. Use an Ordnance Survey map to find out accurately the elevation above mean sea level of the strip –modern maps are in metres.

d. The orientation of the strip may have been laid out to fit in with the needs of agriculture. Establish the direction of the prevailing winds in the area and note the location of any windsock. Will it be affected by nearby trees or buildings? A well located windsock will give you the ground level wind speed and direction. Beware of strips near the coast; sea breezes can change rapidly from onshore to offshore, morning and evening.

e. Tell the operator of the strip what experience you have, which strips you have used recently, and what aeroplane you intend using. He has probably seen pilots with similar aeroplanes flying into and out of the strip and you can benefit from local knowledge. He does not want an accident any more than you do! Exchange telephone numbers in case of a last minute hitch. If possible visit it by road to see for yourself, but best of all carry out the advice of paras 5a, 5b and 5c.

f. The length of the strip ***must*** be accurately established. If you pace it out, remember an average pace is ***not*** one metre, but considerably less (the British army's marching pace is only 30 inches). This may decrease still further after walking several hundred metres. A proper measuring device is better; for example a rope of accurately known length.

g. The strip should be adequately drained or self-draining. Visit it after heavy rain to see whether it remains waterlogged or muddy. Rain after long dry periods may not soak away and can remain hidden by the grass.

h. The surface should be free from ruts and holes and should be properly and regularly rolled. One way of assessing the surface is to drive a car along the strip. If at about 30 mph the ride is comfortable, there should be no problems.

i. If it is a disused wartime airfield, some of the runway may be unusable, while other parts may have a surface in poor condition – including loose gravel and stones. These can be picked up by the propeller wash and can damage windscreens, tail and, of course, the propeller itself. Stone damage can be very expensive.

j. Carefully examine from the ground, air or maps the approaches to the strip and the go-around area, with particular reference to any runway slope, obstructions or hills within 5 km, windshear or turbulence from nearby woods/ buildings and other considerations.

k. Look closely at neighbouring properties; a climb out above the breeding pens or stud farm next door will soon bring an end to everyone's operation.

3 OPERATIONAL CONSIDERATIONS

a. Aeroplane performance **must** be appropriate for the proposed strip. You must be fully familiar with the contents of Safety Sense Leaflet No. 7 (Aeroplane Performance) or AIC 67/2002 (Pink 36) 'Take off, Climb and Landing Performance of Light Aeroplanes'. Remember, the figures shown in the Pilots Operating Handbook are obtained using a new aeroplane, flown by an expert pilot under near ideal conditions, i.e. the best possible results. On the strip, the grass may be different from the 'short, dry, mown grass' of the Handbook. There may be a slight uphill gradient, tall trees or cables at the far end, or a cross wind. Short wet grass should be treated with utmost caution, it can increase landing distances by 60% – it's like an icy surface! Take account of all of these most carefully and then add an additional margin for safety before deciding. (SafetySense Leaflet No. 7, Aeroplane Performance, recommends a 33% safety factor for take-off but 43% for landing.)

b. Your own abilities as a pilot need critical and honest assessment. The ability to land smoothly on a long hard runway is very different from the skills needed for this type of operation.

c. Most importantly the combination of ***YOU and YOUR*** aeroplane must be satisfactory. A weakness in either of these could show up in the accident statistics

d. The CAA poster 'AIRSTRIPS, think Hedgerow NOT Heathrow' reminds pilots of the operational considerations, and is available for free download from the CAA web site www.caa.co.uk through "safety", "general aviation" and "information".

e. Some strips are located on hills where, up to a certain wind speed, take offs are downhill and landings uphill. Re- read the above paragraphs, for although such strips are not necessarily dangerous, they should not be attempted unless you are totally confident about paragraphs a, b and c.

f. You must check that the insurance covers operation from an unlicensed aerodrome or a strip. It is important that you give Insurers fullest possible written details before the visit.

g. Find out about the local arrangements for booking in and booking out; usually a Movements Log is provided.

h. Ensure that passengers and spectators are properly briefed about where they may go, where they may stand and what they may or may not touch.

i. Leave details of route, ETA and passengers in the Movements Log **AND** with someone who will react appropriately and alert the Emergency Services if you fail to arrive/ return.

j. If you are planning to go abroad direct from the strip, then nominating a 'responsible person' is even more important.. Remember customs and immigration requirements, and those of the Terrorism Act if going to or from Northern Ireland, the Isle of Man, or the Channel Islands. Consult the UK AIP GEN 1.2.1 and SafetySense Leaflet No. 20, 'VFR Flight Plans' .

4 OVERNIGHT CONSIDERATIONS

a. If you intend to leave the aircraft overnight at a strip, it may be necessary for you to arrange your own tie- downs and wheel chocks. Ensure that control locks are in place and the aircraft is properly secured. If the wind is likely to increase, then position your aircraft so as to minimise the possibility of it moving and be prepared to reposition it if the wind direction changes. Covers should be used to keep insects and water out of the pitot tube and static vents.

b. Next morning your pre- flight inspection should be more careful than usual just in case birds or other wildlife have taken up residence; birds can build a nest overnight. Check the pitot head, static and tank vents for insects.

c. If the strip is shared with cows, horses or sheep, then an electric or other suitable fence to separate them from your aeroplane is essential. Cows are very partial to the taste of aeroplane dope and their rough tongues have been known to strip fabric from wings. Metal aeroplanes do not escape their attentions, since they make suitable back-scratchers.

d. Discuss with the strip operator the security of the aeroplane. Vandalism and fuel thefts may be a problem.

5 FLYING CONSIDERATIONS

a. Consider having a familiarisation flight to and from the strip with a pilot who knows the strip and is both current on your aeroplane and operations into grass strips.

b. In any case you must know and fly the correct speeds for your aeroplane and remember the importance of using appropriate techniques, keeping the weight off the nosewheel etc.

c. If the strip is shorter than you are used to or has difficult approaches, you should arrange for a flying instructor to appraise your flying skills and revise and improve short field, soft field, general circuit and airmanship skills. It is not the intention of this leaflet to list the skills – that is the instructor's task. Listen and learn. If an instructor is not available, at least practice your short landings on a long runway before attempting to land at a short strip.

d. Airmanship and look- out must be of the highest order; there is unlikely to be any form of ATC service to advise you of the presence of other aircraft, their position or intentions, so be especially vigilant. Low flying military aircraft may NOT avoid strips.

e. Circuit **practice** at unlicensed aerodromes could be unpopular with the neighbours and may be in breach of part of Rule 5 of the Rules of the Air if you are within 500 ft of persons, vessels, vehicles or structures. However, if you find a problem with turbulence or crosswind, surface or slope, do not hesitate to **go around in accordance with normal aviation practice**.

f. Plan your circuit using the best available QNH, for example from a nearby aerodrome. Failing that you could use the most recent 'regional pressure setting (RPS)' but be aware your altimeter will certainly over-read if you use RPS. You should already know the elevation of the strip, so add this figure to the appropriate height that you would use in a normal circuit. Thus, if the strip is 250 ft amsl, downwind will be e.g. 1250 ft QNH.

g. Get into the habit of flying a compact circuit using engine and propeller handling techniques that will minimise noise disturbance. Avoid long flat and noisy approaches, these are not conducive to good neighbourliness nor necessarily the best short landing technique. If your approach is bad, **make an early decision** to go-around. It is often useful to plan to make a go-around from your first approach (avoiding persons, vessels vehicles and structures by 500 feet).

h. Note carefully the position and height of any obstructions on the approach especially hard- to- see local power and phone cables. Make sure that you can clear them (and any crop) by an adequate margin, and provided that you maintain this clearance, always aim to touch down close to the threshold – **not halfway down the strip.**

i. Always start your take off run as close as possible to the beginning of the strip, unless there are very good reasons not to do so. Work out an acceleration check point from which you can stop if you haven't reached sufficient speed to make a safe take-off

j. Bear in mind when turning off the strip, Rule 17(7) of the Rules of the Air and other arriving aircraft.

k. When performing power checks or engine runs try to minimise any noise nuisance and ensure that the slipstream is not creating a problem. Unexpected noise etc can terrify livestock; be considerate when choosing the site for engine checks.

l. After take off, reduce power and propeller rpm when it is safe. Climb to at least 500 ft agl before turning.

m. If you are a regular strip user, decide your weather and wind limits and be clear about your Go/ No Go decision process.

6 <u>SETTING UP YOUR OWN STRIP</u>

a. If you are planning to move your aeroplane to a strip, or perhaps start your own, the points below should be considered, in addition to any others in CAP 428 'Safety Standards at Unlicensed Aerodromes'.

b. Remember that Rule 5 of the Rules of the Air includes, amongst other requirements, the prohibition of flights below 1000 feet over 'congested' areas except when aircraft are taking off or landing at a licensed or government aerodrome. It is therefore most important that climb out, approach and circuit paths at an unlicensed aerodrome are clear of 'congested' areas. Such areas are legally defined as 'in relation to a city, town, or settlement, any area which is substantially used for residential, industrial, commercial or recreational purposes'.

c. Talk to nearby aerodrome operators to ensure that you will not conflict with their activities.

d. Look again at the performance of the aeroplane and your abilities. If operating from this strip means that every take off and landing, even when the aeroplane is lightly loaded, is 'tight', change to a more suitable aeroplane or strip.

e. Remember that, unless there is 'established use', aircraft operations may be in contravention of local regulations. It may of course be possible to obtain planning permission from the outset for your strip, although this would probably involve you in a great deal of hassle. However, this is much better than having it compulsorily closed by the local council if they decide that your operations are in contravention of Planning Regulations. It is in your interests to establish this from the outset and it is furthermore a good idea to talk to all of the neighbours and the planning authority ***before*** you do anything.

f. Cutting the grass and generally maintaining the surface has been discussed earlier; however, if you are responsible for the upkeep of the strip it is important to establish who will cut the grass, roll it and how often. This needs to be a regular activity – we all know only too well how much our lawns grow in a week.

g. Beware when mowing. Instances have occurred of pilots following the mown lines instead of the strip direction.

h. Grass seed mixtures which will give reduced rolling resistance and slower growth are available. Consult a seed merchant.

i. In deciding the orientation of the strip/landing run, consider carefully the local wind effects. It may be possible to re- orientate the strip by some 10 or 20 degrees which could reduce the cross wind effect. This is particularly important for some tailwheel types where the maximum crosswind component that can be tolerated may be as little as 10 knots.

j. Remember that whilst taking off down a slope or landing up a slope is acceptable, taking off and landing across the slope is dangerous. Ensure that the orientation of the strip eliminates excessive lateral slope.

k. It is essential to mark any obstacles, potholes or bad ground at this stage and runway markers or even runway numbers will help people to line up and operate more accurately. It is also possible to have local power lines and telephone lines moved by paying the costs.

l. You must decide in advance on your fuel arrangements. If you are intending to store fuel, then you must comply with Article 101 of the Air Navigation Order and CAP 434 'Aviation Fuel at Aerodromes'. It may be possible to obtain relatively small quantities of aviation fuel by sharing the delivery with a nearby aerodrome or strip. It is normally necessary to obtain local council permission to store fuel.

m. Decide on your maintenance arrangements, your engineer may require coaxing/ persuasion to visit your strip at short notice to rectify a defect.

n. If you own or fly a wood or fabric covered aeroplane it should be hangared – ideally all aircraft should be. However, storing it in a farm barn brings its own particular problems – rodents. Mice are nimble creatures, able to climb landing gear legs and set up home in your aeroplane. We heard of a squirrel that got into the wing structure and stored its winter supply of acorns near the wing tip. Over 30 lbs of acorns were removed! A tray of rat poison encircling each wheel should be considered.

Birds also find aircraft irresistible nesting sites; a nest removed in the morning may be substantially rebuilt by late afternoon. Pre-flight checking the aeroplane becomes very important. Insects may take over your aircraft. Given a few days undisturbed progress, a wasps' nest could appear.

o. It is vital to remove all live- stock from the runway prior to take off and prior to landing. Thus, if animals have access to the strip, assistance by a friend or farmhand is essential. Animals are unpredictable.

p. Cows leave other evidence of their presence – cow pats! Not only does this look unsightly on the aeroplane, but a build up of this, and mud, add to the drag and weight of the aeroplane. Mud and animal contaminants may also be corrosive, so regular washing of the aeroplane, especially the underside, becomes a necessity. Check regularly that spats are clear of mud and grass. Temporary removal of the spats must be agreed with a CAA Regional Office.

q. The farmer and/ or his workers may need gentle reminders about the fragile nature of your aeroplane compared with farm machinery, should they need to move it. They may not know about the dangers of propellers/ helicopter rotors.

r. Consider sitting a small hut or caravan on the strip. This will give secure storage for oil, fire extinguishers, fire axe, polish, foot pump and so on. It is suggested that this should have a large letter C painted on it to make it clear that it is a reporting point for pilots and where the Movements Log is kept. A notice board inside is useful to display information such as local instructions, NOTAMs, the engineer's telephone number, accident procedures and any temporary obstructions, soft ground and grass cutting rotas. Make sure there is enough room to park visiting aircraft well clear of the landing area.

s. Get into the habit of checking the strip each day before starting flying. Any ruts, soft ground or other problems should be dealt with or publicised on the notice board so that they can be avoided on take off and landing.

7 MAIN POINTS

DO obtain permission from the owner/operator prior to visiting the strip. Talk to pilots who have used the strip before and can advise you on procedures/obstructions.
DO check that the combination of you **and** your aeroplane **can** safely cope with this strip.
DO always leave details of ETA route, destination and how many are on board in the Movements Log.
DO always nominate a 'responsible person' as described in Safety Sense Leaflet 20 'VFR Flight Plans', who knows how to raise the alarm if you fail to arrive/return.
DO follow the requirements for customs, immigration and the Terrorism Act if flying to or from overseas.
DO talk to neighbouring aerodromes or to the Flight Information Service on the radio.
DO build up a working relationship with your nearest aerodrome. You may need them for fuel, weather information and maintenance.
DO be ready for unexpected effects from trees, barns, windshear, downdraught, etc.
DO work hard at being a good neighbour and improving the Public's perception of General Aviation by minimising noise nuisance.
DO check that the strip **really** is long enough, with a 30% margin for safety.
DO check on the effect of power and other cables.
DO check whether any slope makes it a 'one way' strip.
DO obtain and display a copy of the CAA's AIRSTRIPS poster.
DO NOT 'beat up' the strip or engage in other forms of reckless, illegal and unsociable flying.
DO NOT attempt to take off or land if the grass is long, the ground is muddy or weather is marginal. There will always be a better day to fly or you can always divert into a neighbouring aerodrome.
DO NOT run- up an engine where the noise affects others or slipstream can be a nuisance.
DO NOT attempt to 'scrape' in from a bad approach.

FINALLY, ensure that safety is the first consideration. A safe flight will almost always be an enjoyable and rewarding one.

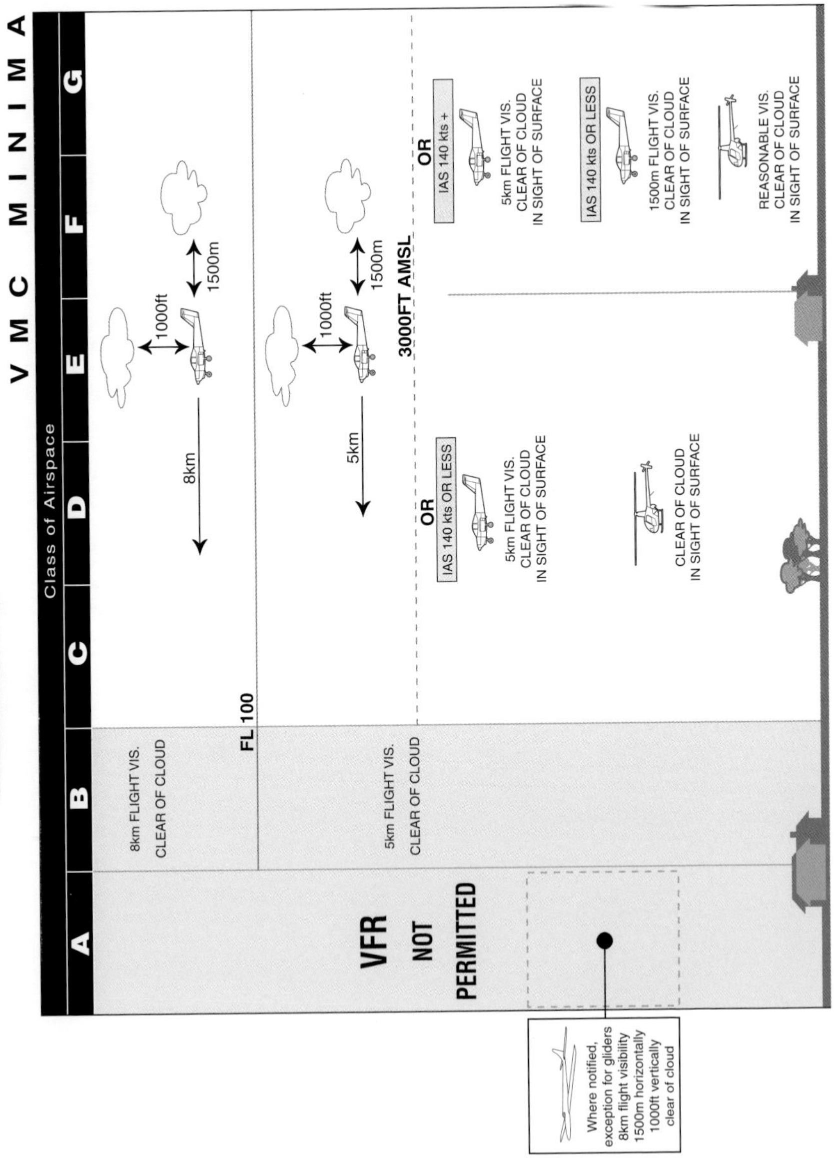

VMC MINIMA

Class of Airspace

A B C D E F G

A: VFR NOT PERMITTED

Where notified, exception for gliders 8km flight visibility 1500m horizontally 1000ft vertically clear of cloud

B (above FL 100): 8km FLIGHT VIS. CLEAR OF CLOUD

B (below FL 100): 5km FLIGHT VIS. CLEAR OF CLOUD

C–G above FL 100: 8km, 1000ft, 1500m

FL 100

C–G below FL 100, above 3000FT AMSL: 5km, 1000ft, 1500m

3000FT AMSL

C, D, E at or below 3000FT AMSL:

OR

IAS 140 kts OR LESS

5km FLIGHT VIS.
CLEAR OF CLOUD
IN SIGHT OF SURFACE

CLEAR OF CLOUD
IN SIGHT OF SURFACE

F, G at or below 3000FT AMSL:

OR

IAS 140 kts +

5km FLIGHT VIS.
CLEAR OF CLOUD
IN SIGHT OF SURFACE

IAS 140 kts OR LESS

1500m FLIGHT VIS.
CLEAR OF CLOUD
IN SIGHT OF SURFACE

REASONABLE VIS.
CLEAR OF CLOUD
IN SIGHT OF SURFACE

Take-off Distance Factors		
VARIATION	INCREASE IN TAKE-OFF DISTANCE (to 50')	FACTOR
10% increase in aircraft weight	20%	**1.2**
Increase of 1000' in runway altitude	10%	**1.1**
Increase in temperature of 10°C	10%	**1.1**
Dry Grass		
– Up to 20cm (8 in)	20%	**1.2**
Wet Grass		
– Up to 20cm (8 in)	30%	**1.3**
Wet Paved Surface	–	–
2% uphill slope	10%	**1.1**
Tailwind component of 10% of lift off speed	20%	**1.2**
Soft ground or snow *	at least 25%	**at least 1.25**
Additional safety factor	–	1.33

Landing Distance Factors		
VARIATION	INCREASE IN LANDING DISTANCE (from 50')	FACTOR
10% increase in aircraft weight	10%	**1.1**
Increase of 1000' in runway altitude	5%	**1.05**
Increase in temperature of 10°C	5%	**1.05**
Dry Grass		
– Up to 20cm (8 in)	15%	**1.15**
Wet Grass		
– Up to 20cm (8 in)	35%	**1.35**
Very short grass may increase	<60%	**<1.6**
Wet Paved Surface	15%	**1.15**
2% downhill slope	10%	**1.1**
Tailwind component of 10% of landing speed	20%	**1.2**
snow *	at least 25%	**at least 1.25**
Additional safety factor	–	1.43

The Take-off Run Available (TORA)

The TORA is the length of the runway available for the take-off ground run of the aircraft. This is usually the physical length of the runway.

The Emergency Distance (ED)

The ED is the length of the TORA plus the length of any stopway. A stopway is area at the end of the TORA prepared for an aircraft to stop on in the event of an abandoned take off. The ED is also known as the ACCELERATE – STOP DISTANCE AVAILABLE.

The Take-off Distance Available (TODA)

The TODA is the TORA plus the length of any clearway. A clearway is an area over which an aircraft may make its initial climb (to 50' in this instance). The TODA will not be more than 1.5 x TORA.

The Landing Distance Available (LDA)

The LDA is the length of the runway available for the ground run of an aircraft landing. In all cases the landing distance required should never be greater than the landing distance available.

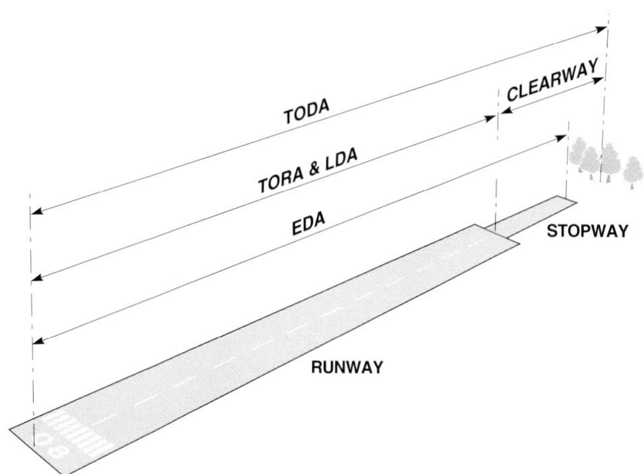

Temperature & Pressure

TEMPERATURE

°C: 50, 40, 30, 20, 10, 0, − 10, - 20, − 30, − 40, − 50, − 60

°F: 120, 110, 100, 90, 80, 70, 60, 50, 40, 30, 20, 10, 0, − 10, − 20, − 30, − 40, − 50, − 60, − 70

PRESSURE

Kg/cm^2: 7, 6, 5, 4, 3, 2, 1, 0

lbs/sq": 100, 90, 80, 70, 60, 50, 40, 30, 20, 10

Bars: 7, 6, 5, 4, 3, 2, 1, 0

Metric/Imperial Measurement

Metres	Feet
1	3.28
2	6.56
3	9.84
4	13.12
5	16.40
6	19.69
7	22.97
8	26.25
9	29.53
10	32.81
20	65.62
30	98.43
40	131.23
50	164.04
60	196.85
70	229.66
80	262.47
90	295.28
100	328.08
200	656.16
300	984.25
400	1,312.34
500	1,640.42
600	1,968.50
700	2,296.59
800	2,624.67
900	2,952.76
1000	3,280.84
2000	6,561.70
3000	9,842.50
4000	13.123.40
5000	16,404.20
6000	19,685.00
7000	22,965.90
8000	26,246.70
9000	29,527.60
10000	32,808.40

Feet	Metres
1	0.30
2	0.61
3	0.91
4	1.22
5	1.52
6	1.83
7	2.13
8	2.44
9	2.74
10	3.05
20	6.10
30	9.14
40	12.19
50	15.24
60	18.29
70	21.34
80	24.38
90	27.43
100	30.48
200	60.96
300	91.44
400	121.92
500	152.40
600	182.88
700	213.36
800	243.84
900	274.32
1000	304.80
2000	609.60
3000	914.40
4000	1,219.20
5000	1,524.00
6000	1,828.80
7000	2,133.60
8000	2,438.40
9000	2,743.20
10000	3,048.00

Km/Nautical Miles/Statute Miles

NM	Km	St
1	1.85	1.15
2	3.70	2.30
3	5.56	3.45
4	7.41	4.60
5	9.26	5.75
6	11.11	6.90
7	12.96	8.06
8	14.82	9.21
9	16.67	10.36
10	18.52	11.51
20	37.04	23.02
30	55.56	34.52
40	74.08	46.03
50	92.60	57.54
60	111.12	69.05
70	129.64	80.55
80	148.16	92.06
90	166.68	103.57
100	185.2	115.1
200	370.4	230.2
300	555.6	345.2
400	740.8	460.3
500	926.0	575.4
600	1111.2	690.5
700	1296.4	805.6
800	1481.6	920.6
900	1666.8	1035.7

Km	NM	St
1	.54	.62
2	1.08	1.24
3	1.62	1.86
4	2.16	2.49
5	2.70	3.11
6	3.24	3.73
7	3.78	4.35
8	4.32	4.97
9	4.86	5.59
10	5.40	6.21
20	10.80	12.43
30	16.20	18.64
40	21.60	24.86
50	27.00	31.07
60	32.40	37.28
70	37.80	43.50
80	43.20	49.71
90	48.60	55.92
100	54.0	62.1
200	108.0	124.3
300	162.0	186.4
400	216.0	248.6
500	270.0	310.7
600	324.0	372.8
700	378.0	435.0
800	432.0	497.1
900	486.0	559.2

Conversion Factors:

Centimetres to Inches x .3937
Inches to Centimetres x 2.54
Metres to Feet x 3.28084
Feet to Metres x 0.3048

Statute Miles to Nautical Miles x 0.868976
Statute Miles to Kilometres x 1.60934
Kilometres to Statute Miles x 0.62137
Kilometres to Nautical Miles x 0.539957
Nautical Miles to Statute Miles x 1.15078
Nautical Miles to Kilometres x 1.852

Km/Nautical Miles/Statute Miles

ST	NM	Km
1	.87	1.61
2	1.74	3.22
3	2.61	4.83
4	3.48	6.44
5	4.34	8.05
6	5.21	9.66
7	6.08	11.27
8	6.95	12.87
9	7.82	14.48
10	8.69	16.09
20	17.38	32.19
30	26.07	48.28
40	34.76	64.37
50	43.45	80.47
60	52.14	96.56
70	60.83	112.65
80	69.52	128.75
90	78.21	144.84
100	86.9	161.0
200	173.8	321.9
300	260.7	482.8
400	347.6	643.7
500	434.5	804.7
600	521.4	965.6
700	608.3	1126.5
800	695.2	1287.5
900	782.1	1448.4

Conversion Factors:

lbs to Kilograms x 0.45359

Kilograms to lbs x 2.20462

Weight lbs/Kg

lbs	Kg	Kg	lbs
1	.45	1	2.20
2	.91	2	4.41
3	1.38	3	6.61
4	1.81	4	8.82
5	2.27	5	11.02
6	2.72	6	13.23
7	3.18	7	15.43
8	3.63	8	17.64
9	4.08	9	19.84
10	4.54	10	22.05
20	9.07	20	44.09
30	13.61	30	66.14
40	18.14	40	88.18
50	22.68	50	110.23
60	27.22	60	132.28
70	31.75	70	154.32
80	36.29	80	176.37
90	40.82	90	198.42
100	45.4	100	220.5
200	90.7	200	440.9
300	136.1	300	661.4
400	181.4	400	881.8
500	226.8	500	1102.3
600	272.2	600	1322.8
700	317.5	700	1543.2
800	362.9	800	1763.7
900	408.2	900	1984.2
1000	453.6	1000	2204.6
2000	907.2	2000	4409.2
3000	1360.8	3000	6613.9
4000	1814.4	4000	8818.5
5000	2268.0	5000	11023.1
6000	2721.5	6000	13227.7
7000	3175.1	7000	15432.3
8000	3628.7	8000	17637.0
9000	4082.3	9000	19841.6
10000	4535.9	10000	22046.2

Volume (Fluid)

Litres	Imp. Gall	U.S. Gall
1	0.22	0.26
2	0.44	0.53
3	0.66	0.79
4	0.88	1.06
5	1.10	1.32
6	1.32	1.59
7	1.54	1.85
8	1.76	2.11
9	1.98	2.38
10	2.20	2.64
20	4.40	5.28
30	6.60	7.93
40	8.80	10.57
50	11.00	13.21
60	13.20	15.85
70	15.40	18.49
80	17.60	21.14
90	19.80	23.78
100	22.00	26.42
200	44.00	52.84
300	66.00	79.26
400	88.00	105.68
500	110.00	132.10
600	132.00	158.52
700	154.00	184.94
800	176.00	211.36
900	198.00	237.78
1000	220.00	264.20

U.S. Gall	Imp. Gall	Litres
1	0.83	3.79
2	1.67	7.57
3	2.50	11.36
4	3.33	15.14
5	4.16	18.93
6	5.00	22.71
7	5.83	26.50
8	6.66	30.28
9	7.49	34.07
10	8.33	37.85
20	16.65	75.71
30	24.98	113.56
40	33.31	151.41
50	41.63	189.27
60	49.96	227.12
70	58.29	264.97
80	66.61	302.82
90	74.94	340.68
100	83.27	378.54

Imp. Gall	U.S. Gall	Litres
1	1.20	4.55
2	2.40	9.09
3	3.60	13.64
4	4.80	18.18
5	6.00	22.73
6	7.21	27.28
7	8.41	31.82
8	9.61	36.37
9	10.81	40.91
10	12.01	45.46
20	24.02	90.92
30	36.03	136.38
40	48.04	181.84
50	60.05	227.30
60	72.06	272.76
70	84.07	318.22
80	96.08	363.68
90	108.09	409.14
100	120.09	454.60

Conversion Factors:

Imperial Gallons to Litres x 4.54596

Litres to Imperial Gallons x 0.219975

U.S. Gallons to Litres x 3.78541

Litres to U.S. Gallons x 0.264179

Imperial Gallons to U.S. Gallons x 1.20095

U.S. Gallons to Imperial Gallons x 0.832674

Millibars/Inches

Mbs	ins	Mbs	ins	Mbs	ins	Mbs	ins	Mbs	ins	Mbs	ins
950	28.054	970	28.644	990	29.235	1010	29.825	1030	30.416	1050	31.007
951	28.083	971	28 674	991	29.264	1011	29.855	1031	30.445		
952	28.113	972	28.703	992	29.294	1012	29.884	1032	30.475		
953	28.142	973	28.733	993	29.323	1013	29.914	1033	30.504		
954	28.172	974	28.762	994	29.353	1014	29.943	1034	30.534		
955	28.201	975	28.792	995	29.382	1015	29.973	1035	30.564		
956	28.231	975	28.821	996	29.412	1016	30.002	1036	30.593		
957	28.260	977	28.851	997	29.441	1017	30.032	1037	30.623		
958	28.290	977	28.880	998	29.471	1018	30.062	1038	30.652		
959	28.319	979	28.910	999	29.500	1019	30.091	1039	30.682		
960	28.349	980	28.939	1000	29.530	1020	30.121	1040	30.711		
961	28.378	981	28.969	1001	29.560	1021	30.150	1041	30.741		
962	28.408	982	28.998	1002	29.589	1022	30.180	1042	30.770		
963	28.437	983	29.028	1003	29.619	1023	30.209	1043	30.800		
964	28.467	984	29.058	1004	29.648	1024	30.239	1044	30.829		
965	28.496	985	29.087	1005	29.678	1025	30.268	1045	30.859		
966	28.526	986	29.117	1006	29.707	1026	30.298	1046	30.888		
967	28.556	987	29.146	1007	29.737	1027	30.327	1047	30.918		
968	28.585	988	29.176	1008	29.766	1028	30.357	1048	30.947		
969	28.615	989	29.205	1009	29.796	1029	30.386	1049	30.977		

To convert Inches into millibars multiply by 33.86
To convert millibars into Inches multiply by 0.0295

UK Aeronautical Information Service
NATS Ltd
Heathrow House
Bath Road
Hounslow
Middlesex
TW5 9AT
www.ais.org.uk

UK NOTAM Office	Tel: 0208 750 3773/3774
	Fax: 0208 750 3775
AIS Information line	Tel: 0500 354 802
AIS Publication Section	Tel: 0208 750 3777
AIS Library	Tel: 0208 750 3789

Pre-flight information bulletins can be accessed from the internet www.ais.org.uk
For information regarding Temporary Restricted Airspace
Red Arrows Displays and Emergency Restrictions of Flying
Royal Flights
Freephone telephone number is available Tel: 0500 354802

Aviation Contact Details

AOPA
Aircraft Owners & Pilots Association
Tel: 0207 834 5631
Fax: 0207 834 8623
Email: info@aopa.co.uk
Web: www.aopa.co.uk

ASG
Air Safety Group
Tel: 01483 764413
Email: secretary@airsafetygroup.org

BAEA
British Aerobatic Association
Tel: 01234 713245
Email: info@aerobatics.org.uk
Web: www.aerobatics.org.uk

BALPA
British Air Line Pilots Association
Tel: 0208 476 4000
Fax: 0208 476 4077
Email: balpa@balpa.org
Web: www.balpa.org.uk

BBAC
British Balloon & Airship Club
Tel: 0117 9531231
Email: information@bbac.org
Web: www.bbac.org

BBGA
British Business & General Aviation Association
Tel: 01844 238020
Fax: 01844 238087
Email: info@bbga.aero
Web: www.bbga.aero

BGA
British Gliding Association
Tel: 0116 253 1051
Fax: 0116 251 5939
Email: office@gliding.co.uk
Web: www.gliding.co.uk

BHAB
British Helicopter Advisory Board
Tel: 01276 856100
Fax: 01276 856126
Email: info@bhab.org
Web: www.bhab.flyer.co.uk

BHPA
British Hang Gliding & Paragliding Association
Tel: 0116 261 1322
Fax: 0116 261 1323
Email: office@bhpa.co.uk
Web: www.bhpa.co.uk

BMAA
British Microlight Aircraft Association
Tel: 01869 338888
Fax: 01869 337116
Email: general@bmaa.org
Web: www.bmaa.org

BPA
British Parachute Association
Tel: 0116 278 5271
Fax: 0116 247 7662
Email: skydive@bpa.org.uk
Web: www.bpa.org.uk

BWPA
British Women Pilots Association
Tel: 01342 892739
Email: enquires@bwpa.co.uk
Web: www.bwpa.co.uk

FFA
Flying Farmers Association
Tel: 01944 738281
Fax: 01944 738240
Email: chix@farmline.com
Web: www.ffa.org.uk

GAPAN
Guild of Air Pilots & Air Navigators
Tel: 0207 404 4032
Fax: 0207 404 4035
Email: gapan@gapan.org
Web: www.gapan.org

GASCO
General Aviation Safety Council
Tel/Fax: 01634 200203
Email: info@gasco.org.uk
Web: www.gasco.org.uk

JAA
Joint Aviation Authorities
Tel: +31 23 5679700
Fax: +31 23 5621714
Web: www.jaa.nl

LAA
Light Aircraft Association
Tel: 01280 846786
Fax: 01280 846780
Email: office@laa.uk.com
Web: www.lightaircraftassociation.co.uk

LFA
Lawyers Flying Association
Tel: 0207 796 6516
Fax: 0207 796 6783
Email: tony@stapley.co.uk
Web: www.stapley.co.uk/lfa.htm

CAA Headquarters
CAA House
45-59 Kingsway
London
WC2B 6TE
Tel: 0207 379 7311 (Switchboard)

CAA Safety Regulation Group
Aviation House
South Area London Gatwick Airport
Gatwick
Tel: 01293 567171 (Switchboard)
Web: www.caa.co.uk

NATS
4000 Parkway
Whiteley
Fareham
Hampshire
PO15 7FL
Tel: 01489 616001
Web: www.nats.co.uk

AFE Manchester
1a Ringway Trading Estate
Shadowmoss Road
Manchester
M22 5LH
Tel: 0161 499 0023
Fax: 0161 499 0298
Email: enquiries@afeonline.com
Web: www.afeonline.com

AFE Oxford
The Pilot Shop
Oxford Airport
Oxford
OX5 1QX
Tel: 01865 841441
Fax: 01865 842495
Email: oxford@afeonline.com
Web: www.afeonline.com

A

AAA	Amended Meteorological Message
AAL	Above Aerodrome Level
ABM	Abeam
ABN	Aerodrome Beacon
ABV	Above
AC	Area Control
ACARS	Aircraft Communications Addressing and Reporting System
ACAS	Airborne Collision Avoidance System
ACC	Area Control Centre or Area Control
ACCID	Notification of an Aircraft Accident
ACFT	Aircraft
ACK	Acknowledge
ACL	Altimeter Check Location
ACN	Aircraft Classification Number
ACN	Airspace Co-ordination Notification
ACP	Acceptance
ACPT	Accept or Accepted
ACT	Active or Activated or Activity
AD	Aerodrome
ADA	Advisory Area
ADDN	Addition or Additional
ADF	Automatic Direction-Finding Equipment
ADJ	Adjacent
ADR	Advisory Route
ADS B	Automatic Dependent Surveillance – Broadcast
ADS-C	Automatic Dependent Surveillance – Contract
ADSU	Automatic Dependent Surveillance Unit
ADVS	Advisory Service
ADZ	Advise
AES	Aircraft Earth Station
AEW	Airborne Early Warning
AFIL	Flight Plan Filed in the Air
AFIS	Aerodrome Flight Information Service
AFM	Yes or Afirm or Affirmative or That is Correct
AFS	Aeronautical Fixed Service
AFT	After
AFTN	Aeronautical Fixed Telecommunication Network
A/G	Air to Ground
AGA	Aerodromes, Air Routes and Ground Aids
AGL	Above Ground Level
AGN	Again
AI	Attitude Indicator
AIAA	Area of Intense Aerial Activity
AIC	Aeronautical Information Circular
AIM	ATFM Information Message
AIP	Aeronautical Information Publication
AIRAC	Aeronautical Information Regulation and Control
AIREP	Air-Report
AIREX	Air Exercise
AIS	Aeronautical Information Service
ALA	Alighting Area
ALERFA	Alert Phase
ALR	Altering
ALRS	Alerting Service
ALS	Approach Lighting System
ALT	Altitude
ALTN	Alternate or Alternating
AMA	Area Minimum Altitude
AMC	Airspace Management Cell
AMD	Amend or Amended
AMDT	Amendment
AMS	Aeronautical Mobile Service
AME	Authorised Medical Examiner
AMSL	Above Mean Sea Level
ANO	Air Navigation Order
ANS	Answer
AO	Aircraft Operators
AOC	Aerodrome Obstacle Chart
AOC	Air Operators Certificate
AOM	Aerodrome Operating Minima
AOPA	Aircraft Owners & Pilots Association
AP	Airport
APAPI	Abbreviated Precision Approach Path Indicator
APCH	Approach
APIS	Aircraft Positioning and Information System
APP	Approach Control Office or Approach Control or Approach Control Service
APR	April
APRX	Approximately
APSG	After Passing
APV	Approve or Approved or Approval
ARNG	Arrange
ARO	Air Traffic Services Reporting Office
APR	Aerodrome Reference Point
APR	Air-Report
ARQ	Automatic Error Correction
ARR	Arrival
ARS	Special Air-Report
ARST	Arresting
ASC	Ascent or Ascending to
ASDA	Accelerate Stop Distance Available
ASR	Altimeter Setting Region
ASHTAM	Special series of NOTAM notifying, by means of specific format, change in activity of a volcano, a volcano eruption and/or volcanic ash cloud that is or significance to aircraft operations
ATA	Actual Time of Arrival
ATC	Air Traffic Control
ATIS	Automatic Terminal Information Service
ATPL	Air Transport Pilot Licence (UK)
ATS	Air Traffic Services
ATSOCAS	ATS Outside Controlled Airspace
ATSU	Air Traffic Service Unit
ATTN	Attention
ATZ	Aerodrome Traffic Zone
AUG	August
AUS	Airspace Utilisation Section
AUTH	Authority
AUW	All Up Weight
AVASIS	Abbreviated Visual Approach Slope Indicator
AVBL	Available
AVG	Average
AVGAS	Aviation Gasoline
AVTUR	Aviation Turbine Fuel
AWY	Airway
AZM	Azimuth

B

B	Blue
BA	Braking Action
BAA	British Airports Authority Plc
BASE	Cloud Base
BBMF	Battle of Britain Memorial Flight
BCFG	Fog Patches
BCN	Beacon
BCST	Broadcast
BDRY	Boundary

BECMG	Becoming
BFR	Before
BKN	Broken
BL	Blowing (followed by DU = Dust, SA = Sand or SN = Snow)
BLCP	Base Level Change Point
BLDG	Building
BLO	Below Clouds
BOMB	Bombing
BOTA	Brest Oceanic Transition Area
BR	Mist
BRF	Short) Used to indicate the type of approach desired or required)
BRG	Bearing
BRKG	Breaking
B-RNAV	Basic (To be pronounced AR-NAV) Area Navigation
BS	Commercial Broadcasting Station
BTL	Between Layers
BTN	Between
C	
C	Centre (runway indentification)
C	Degrees Celcius (Centigrade)
CAA	Civil Aviation Authority
CANP	Civil Aircraft Notification Procedure
CAP	Civil Air Publication
CAS	Controlled Airspace
CAT	Category
CAT	Clear Air Turbulence
CATZ	Combined Aerodrome Traffic Zone
CAVOK	(To be pronounced 'KAV-OH-KAY') Visibility, cloud and present weather better than prescribed values or conditions
CB	(To be pronounced 'CEE-BEE') Cumulonimbus
CC	Counter Clockwise
CC	Cirrocumulus
CCA	(or CCB, CCC etc in sequence) Corrected meterological message (message type designator)
CD	Candela
CDN	Co-ordination (message type designator)
CDR	Conditional Route
CF	Change Frequency to ....
CFMU	Central Flow Management Unit (Europe)
CGL	Circuling Guidance Light(s)
CH	Channel
CHAPI	Compact Helicopter Approach Path Indicator
CHG	Modification (message type designator)
CI	Cirrus
CIDI	Common ICAO Data Interchange Network
CIT	Near or over large towns
CIV	Civil
CK	check
CL	Centre Line
CLA	Clear Type of Ice Formation
CLBR	Calibration
CLD	Cloud
CLG	Calling
CLR	Clear or Cleared to or Clearance
CLSD	Close or Closed or Closing
CM	Centimetre
CMATZ	Combined Military Aerodrome Traffic Zone
CMB	Climb to or Climbing to
CMPL	Completion or Completed or Complete
CNL	Cancel or Cancelled
CNL	Flight Plan Cancellation (message type designator)
CNS	Communications, Navigation and Surveillance
COL	Column (in tables and text)
COM	Communications
CONC	Concrete
COND	Condition
CONS	Continuous
CONST	Construction or Constructed
CONT	Continue(s) or Continued
COOR	Co-ordinate or Co-ordination
CO-ORD	Geographical Co-ordinates
COP	Change Over Point
COR	Correct or Correction or Corrected (Used to indicate corrected meteorological message; message type designator)
COT	At the Coast
COV	Cover or Covered or Covering
CPDLC	Controller to Pilot Data Link
CPL	Current Flight Plan (message type designator)
CRAM	Conditional Route Availability Message
CRZ	Cruise
CS	Cirrostratus
CTA	Control Area
CTAM	Climb to and Maintain
CTC	Contact
CTL	Control
CTN	Caution
CTOT	Calculated Take-off Time
CTR	Control Zone
CU	Cumilus
CUF	Cumuliform
CUST	Customs
CW	Continuous Wave
CWY	Clearway
D	
D..	DME Range (prefix used in graphics)
D..	Danger Area (followed by identification)
D..	Downward (tendency in RVR during previous 10 minutes)
DA	Decision Altitude
DAAIS	Danger Area Activity Information Service
DACS	Danger Area Crossing Service
DATIS	Data Link Automatic Terminal Information Service
DCD	Double Channel Duplex
DCKG	Docking
DCS	Double Channel Simplex
DCT	Direct (In relation to flight path clearances and type of approach)
DEC	December
DEG	Degrees
DEMO	Demonstration
DEP	Depart or Departure
DEP	Departure (message type designator)
DER	Departure End of the Runway
DES	Descend or Descending to
DEST	Destination
DETRESFA	Distress Phase
DEV	Deviation or Deviating
DF	Direction Finding
DFT	Department of Transport

DH	Decision Height
DIF	Diffuse
DIST	Distance
DIV	Divert or Diverting
DLA	Delay (message type designator)
DLA	Delay or Delayed
DLY	Daily
DME	Distance Measuring Equipment
DNG	Danger or Dangerous
DOC	Designated Operational Coverage
DOM	Domestic
DP	Dew Point Temperature
DPT	Depth
DR	Dead Reckoning
DR..	Low Drifting (followed by DU = Dust, SA = Sand or SN = Snow)
DRG	During
DS	Duststorm
DSB	Double Standard
DTAM	Descend to and Maintain
DTG	Date-Time Group
DTRT	Deteriorate or Deteriorating
DTW	Dual Tandem Wheels
DU	Dual
DUC	Dense Upper Cloud
DUR	Duration
DVOR	Doppler VOR
DW	Dual Wheels
DZ	Drizzle
E	
E	East or Eastern Latitude
EAT	Expected Approach Time
EB	Eastbound
ECA	Emergency Controlling Authority
ECAC	European Civil Aviation Conference
EDT	Estimated Departure Time
EET	Estimated Elapsed Time
EFC	Expected Further Clearance
EFIS	Electronic Flight Instrument System
EGNOS	Electronic Geostationary Navigation Overlay Service
EHF	Extremely High Frequency (3000 to 30000 MHz)
ELBA	Emergency Location Beacon – Aircraft
ELEV	Elevation
ELR	Extra Long Range
ELT	Emergency Locator Transmitter
EM	Emission
EMBD	Embedded in a layer (To indicate cumulonimbus embedded in layers of other clouds)
END	Stop-End (related to RVR)
ENE	East North East
ENG	Engine
ENR	En-Route
EOBT	Estimated Off-Block Time
EQPT	Equipment
ER	Here.... Or Herewith
ESE	East South East
EST	Estimate or Estimated or Estimate (message type designator)
ETA	Estimated Time of Arrival or Estimating Arrival
ETD	Estimated Time of Departure or Estimating Departure
ETFMS	Enhanced Tactical Flight Management System
ETO	Estimated Time Over Significant Point
ETOPS	Extended Twin-jet Operations
EV	Every
EXC	Except
EXER	Exercises or Exercising or To Exercise
ECP	Expect or Expected or Expecting
EXT	Extension
EXTD	Extend or Extending
F	
F	Fixed
FAC	Facilities
FAF	Final Approach Fix
FAL	Facilitation of International Air Transport
FAM	Flight Activation Monitoring
FAP	Final Approach Point
FAS	Final Approach Segment
FAT	Final Approach Track
FATO	Final Approach and Take-off Area
FAX	Facsimile Transmission
FBL	Light (Used to indicate the intensity of weather phenomena, interference or static reports, eg, FBL RA = Light Rain)
FBU	Flight Briefing Unit
FC	Funnel Cloud (tornado or water spout)
FCST	Forecast
FCT	Friction coefficient
FDOD	Flight Data Operations Division
FDPS	Flight Data Processing System
FEB	February
FG	Fog
FIC	Flight Information Centre
FIR	Flight Information Region
FIS	Flight Information Service
FISO	Flight Information Service Officer
FISA	Automated Flight Information Service
FL	Flight Level
FLAS	Flight Level Allocation System
FLD	Field
FLG	Flashing
FLR	Flares
FLT	Flight
FLTCK	Flight Check
FLUC	Fluctuating or Fluctuation or Fluctuated
FLW	Follow
FLY	Fly or Flying
FM	from
FM..	From (followed by time weather change is forecast to begin)
FMC	Flight Management Computer
FMD	Flow Management Division
FMP	Flow Management Position
FMS	Flow Management System
FMU	Flow Management Unit
FNA	Final Approach
FPL	Filed Flight Plan (message type designator)
FPM	Feet Per Minute
FPR	Flight Plan Route
FR	Fuel Remaining
FREQ	Frequency
FRI	Friday
FRNG	Firing
FRONT	Front (relating to weather)
FRQ	Frequent
FSL	Full Stop Landing
FSS	Flight Service Station
FST	First
FT	Feet
FU	Smoke
FZ	Freezing

FZDZ Freezing Drizzle
FZFG Freezing Fog
FZRA Freezing Rain
G
G Green
G/A Ground to Air
G/A/G Ground to Air and Air to Ground
GA General Aviation
GAGAN GPS & Geostationary Earth Orbit Augmented Navigation
GAT General Air traffic
GBAS Ground Based Augmentation System
GCA Ground Controlled Approach System or Ground Controlled Approach
GEN General
GEO Geographic or True
GES Ground Earth Station
GLD Glider
GLONASS Global Orbiting Navigation Satellite System
GMC Ground Movement Control
GMR Ground Movement Radar
GND Ground
GNDCK Ground Check
GNSS Global Navigation Satellite System
GP Glide Path
GPA Glide Path Angle
GPS Global Positioning System
GPWS Ground Proximity Warning System
GR Hail
GRAS Ground Based Regional Augmentation System
GRASS Grass Landing Area
GRVL Gravel
GS Ground Speed
GS Small hail and/or snow pellets
GUND Geoid Undulation
GVS Gas Venting Site
H
H24 Continuous Day and Night Service
HAPI Helicopter Approach Path Indicator
HBN Hazard Beacon
HDF High Frequency Direction-Finding Station
HDG Heading
HEL Helicopter
HEMS Helicopter Emergency Medical Service
HF High Frequency (3000 to 30000 kHz)
HGT Height or Height Above
HIAL Highlands and Islands Airports Ltd
HI High Intensity Directional Lights
HIRTA High Intensity Radio Transmission Area
HJ Sunrise to Sunset
HLDG Holding
HMR Helicopter Main Routes
HN Sunset to Sunrise
HO Service available to meet Operation requirements
Hol Holiday
HOPA Helicopter Operational Area
HOSP Hospital Aircraft
HPA Hectopascal
HR/HRS Hours
HS Service Available During Hours of Scheduled Operations
HT High Tension (power)
HTA Helicopter Training Area
HURCN Hurricane
HVDF High and Very High Frequency Direction Finding Stations (At the Same Location)
HVY Heavy
HVY Heavy (used to indicate the intensity of weather phenomena eg HVY RA = Heavy Rain)
HX No Specific Working Hours
HYR Higher
HZ Dust Haze
Hz Hertz (Cycle per Second)
I
IAC Instrument Approach Chart
IAF Initial Approach Fix
IAO In and Out of Clouds
IAP Instrument Approach Procedure
IAR Intersection of Air Routes
IAS Indicated Airspeed
IBN Identification Beacon
IC Diamond Dust (very small ice crystals in suspension)
ICE Icing
ID Identifier or Identify
IDENT Identification
IF Intermediate Approach Fix
IFF Identification Friend/Foe
IFPS Integrated Flight Planning System
IFR Instrument Flight Rules
IGA International General Aviation
ILS Instrument Landing System
IM Inner Marker
IMC Instrument Meteorological Conditions
IMG Immigration
IMPR Improve or Improving
IMT Immediate or Immediately
INA Initial Approach
INBD Inbound
INC In Cloud
INCERFA Uncertainty Phase
INFO Information
INOP Inoperative
INP If not Possible
INPR In Progress
INS Inertial Navigation System
INSTL Install or Installed or Installation
INSTR Instrument
INT Intersection
INTL International
INTRG Interrogator
INTRP Interrupt or Interruption or Interrupted
INTSF Intensify or Intensifying
INTST Intensity
IR Ice on Runway
IRS Inertial Reference System
IRVR Instrumented Runway Visual Range
IR Instrument Rating
ISA International Standard Atmosphere
ISB Independent Sideband
ISOL Isolated
J
JAN January
JMC Joint Maritime Course
JTST Jet Stream
JUL July
JUN June
K
KG Kilograms
kHz Kilohertz
KIAS Knots Indicated Airspeed

KM	Kilometres
KMH	Kilometres per Hour
KPA	Kilopascal
KT	Knots
KW	Kilowatts
L	
L	Left (Runway Identification)
L	Locator (NDB with published approach procedure, See LM, LO)
LAM	Logical Acknowledgment (message type designator)
LAN	Inland
LARS	Lower Airspace Radar Service
LAT	Latitude
LATCC (Mil)	London Air Traffic Control Centre (Mil)
LCA	Local or Locally or Location or Located
LDA	Landing Distance Available
LDG	landing
LDI	Landing Direction Indicator
LEN	Length
LF	Low Frequency
LFA	Low Flying Area
LFZ	Local Flying Zone
LGT	light or Lighting
LGTD	Lighted
LHA	Lowest Holding Altitude
LHS	Left Hand Side
LI	Low Intensity Omni-directional Lights
LIH	Light Intensity High
LIL	Light Intensity Low
LIM	Light Intensity Medium
LITAS	Low Intensity Two Colour Approach Slope Indicators at ... and ... metres from threshold bracketing approach angle of ... degrees
LLZ	Localizer
LM	Locator, Middle
LMT	Local Mean Time
LNG	Long (Used to indicate the type of approach desired or required)
LO	Locator, outer
LOC	Localizer
LONG	Longitude
LORAN	LORAN (Long Range Air Navigation System)
LRG	Long Range
LTD	Limited
LTT	Landline Teletypewritter
LV	Light and Variable (Relating to Wind)
LVE	Leave or Leaving
LVL	Level
LVP	Low Visibility Procedures
LYR	Layer or Layered
M	
M	Mach Number (Followed by figures)
M	Metres (Preceded by Figures)
MAA	Maximum Authorised Altitude
MAG	Magnetic
MAINT	Maintenance
MAP	Aeronautical maps and charts
MAPt	Missed Approach Point
MAR	At Sea
MAR	March
MAS	Manual A1 Simplex
MASA	Multifunctional Transport Satellite (MTSAT) Satellite Based Augmentation System
MATZ	Military Aerodrome Traffic Zone
MAX	Maximum
MAY	May
MB	Millibar
MCA	Minimum Crossing Altitude
MCW	Modulated Continuous Wave
MDA	Minimum Descent Altitude
MDF	Medium frequency Direction Finding Station
MDH	Minimum Descent Height
MEA	Minimum En-route Altitude
MEDA	Military Emergency Diversion Aerodrome
MEHT	Minimum Eye Height over Threshold (For VASIS and PAPI)
MET	Meteorological or Meteorology
METAR	Aviation routine weather report (In aeronautical meteorological code)
MF	Medium Frequency (300 to 3000 kHz)
MHDF	Medium and High Frequency Direction Finding Stations (At the same location)
MHVDF	Medium, High and Very High Frequency Direction Finding Stations (At the same location)
MHz	Megahertz
MID	Mid-point (related to RVR)
MIFG	Shallow Fog
MIL	Military
MIN	Minutes
MKR	Marker radio beacon
MLS	Microwave Landing System
MM	Middle Marker
MNM	Minimum
MNPS	Minimum Navigation Performance Specifications
MNPSA	Minimum Navigation Performance Specifications Airspace
MNT	Monitor or Monitoring or Monitored
MNTN	Maintain
MOA	Military Operating Area
MOC	Minimum Obstacle Clearance (required)
MOCA	Minimum Obstacle Clearance Altitude
MOD	Moderate (Used to indicate the intensity of weather phenomena, interference or static reports, eg MOD RA = Moderate Rain
MOGAS	Motor Gasoline
MON	Above Mountains
MON	Monday
MOTNE	Meteorological Operational Telecommunications Network Europe
MOV	Move or Moving or Movement
MPH	Statue Mile per Hour
MPS	Meters per Second
MRA	Minimum Reception Altitude
MRG	Medium Range
MRP	ATS/MET Reporting Point
MRSA	Military Mandatory Radar Service Area
MS	Minus
MSA	Minimum Sector Altitude
MSG	Message
MSL	Mean Sea Level
MT	Mountain
MTA	Military Training Area
MTOW	Maximum Take Off Weight
MTRA	Military Temporary Reserved Airspace
MTU	Metric Units
MTW	Mountain Waves
MTWA	Maximum Total Weight Authorised

MVDF	Medium and Very High Frequency Direction Finding Stations (At the same location)
MWO	Meterological Watch Office
MX	Mixed type of ice formation (white and clear)
N	
N	North or Northern Lattitude
N	No distinct tendency (in RVR during previous 10 minutes)
NADP	Noise Abatement Departure Procedure
NAT	North Atlantic
NAV	Navigation
NB	Northbound
NBFR	Not Before
NC	No Change
NDB	Non-Directional Radio Beacon
NDS	Non Deviating Status
NE	North East
NEB	North East Bound
NEG	No or Negative or Permission not granted or That is correct
NERS	North Atlantic European Routing System
NGT	Night
NIL	None or I have nothing to send to you
NM	Nautical Miles
NML	Normal
NNE	North North East
NNW	North North West
NOF	International NOTAM Office
NOSIG	No Significant Change (Used in trend-type landing forecast)
NOTA	Northern Oceanic Transition Area
NOTAM	A notice containing information concerning the establishment, condition or change in any aeronautical facility, service, procedure or hazard, the timely knowledge of which is essential to personnel concerned with flight operations.
NOV	November
NPA	Non Precision Approach
NRP	Noise Preferential Routeing
NR	Number
NRH	No Reply Heard
NS	Nimbostratus
NSC	No Significant Cloud
NSF	Non Standard Flights
NSW	Nil Significant Weather
NVG	Night Vision Goggles
NW	North West
NWB	North West Bound
NXT	Next
O	
OAC	Oceanic Area Control Centre
OAS	Obstacle Assessment Surface
OAT	Operational Air Traffic
OBS	Observe or Observed or Observation
OBSC	Obscure or Obscured or Obscuring
OBST	Obstacle
OCA	Obstacle Clearance Altitude
OCA	Oceanic Control Area
OCC	Occulting (light)
OCNL	Occasional or Occasionally
OCS	Obstacle Clearance Surface
OCT	October
OFZ	Obstacle Free Zone
OHD	Overhead
OLDI	On-line Data Interchange
OM	Outer Marker
OPA	Opaque, white type of ice formation
OPC	The control indicated is operational control
OPMET	Operational Meteorological (information)
OPN	Open or Opening or Opened
OPR	Operator or Operate, Operative or Operating or Operational
OPS	Operations
O/R	On Request
ORCA	Oceanic Route Clearance Authorisation System
ORD	Indication of an order
OSV	Ocean Station Vessel
OTLK	Outlook (used in SIGMET messages for volcanic ash and tropical cyclones)
OTP	On Top
OTS	Organised Track System
OUBD	Outbound
OVC	Overcast
P	
P	Prohibited area (Followed by identification)
PALS	Precision Approach Lighting System (specify category)
PANS	Procedures for Air Navigation Services
PAOAS	Parallel Approach Obstacle Assessment Surfaces
PAPA	Parallax Aircraft Parking Aid
PAPI	Precision Approach Path Indicators
PAR	Precision Approach Radar
PARL	Parallel
PAX	Passengers
PCD	Proceed or Proceeding
PCN	Pavement Classification Number
PDG	Procedure Design Gradient
PER	Performance
PERM	Permanently
PH	Public Holidays
PIB	Pre-flight Information Bulletin
PJE	Parachute Jumping Exercise
PLA	Practice Low Approach
PLN	Flight Plan
PLVL	Present Level
PN	Prior Notice Required
PNdB	Perceived Noise Decibels
PNR	Point of No Return
PO	Dust Devils
POB	Persons on Board
POSS	Possible
PPI	Plan Position Indicator
PPR	Prior Permission Required
PPSN	Present Position
PRI	Primary
PRKG	Parking
PROB	Probability
PROC	Procedure
PROV	Provisional
PS	Plus
PSG	Passing
PSN	Position
PSP	Pierced Steel Plank
PTN	Procedure Turn
PTS	Polar Track Structure
PWR	Power
Q	
QDM	Magnetic Heading (zero wind)

QDR Magnetic Bearing
QFE Atmospheric Pressure at aerodrome elevation (or runway threshold)
QFU Magnetic Orientation of Runway
QNH Altimeter sub-scale setting to obtain elevation when on the ground
QTE True Bearing
QUAD Quadrant

R

R Rate of Turn
R Red
R.. Restricted Area (followed by identification)
R.. Radial (prefix for use in graphics)
R Right (runway identification)
RA Rain
RA Resolution Advisory
RAC Rules of the Air and Air Traffic Services
RAD Radar Approach Aid
RAD Radius
AD Route Availability Document
RAF Royal Air Force
RAFC Regional Area Forecast Centre
RAFAT Royal Air Force Aerobatic Team
RAFCT Royal Air Force Combined Training
RAG Ragged
RAG Runway Arresting Gear
RAI Runway Alignment Indicator
RAS Radar Advisory Service
RASA Radar Advisory Service Area
RASC Regional AIS System Centre
RA(T) Restricted Area (Temporary)
RB Rescue Boat
RCA Reach Cruising Altitude
RCC Rescue Co-ordination Centre
RCF Radio Communications Failure (message type designator)
RCH Reach or Reaching
RCL Runway Centre Line
RCLL Runway Centre Line Light(s)
RCLR Recleared
RDH Reference Datum Height (For ILS)
RDL Radial
RDO Radio
RE Recent (Used to qualify wethaer phenomena, eg RERA – Recent Rain)
REC Receive
REDL Runway Edge Light(s)
REF reference
REG Registration
REQ Request or Requested
RERTE Re-route
RESA Runway End Safety Area
RET Rapid Exit Taxiway
RETIL Rapid Exit Taxiway Indicator Light
RFF Fire and Rescue Equipment
RG Range (lights)
RHAG Rotary Hydraulic Arrester Gear
RHS Right Hand Side
RIF Reclearance In Flight
RIS Radar Information Service
RITE Right (Direction of Turn)
RL Report Leaving
RLA Relay to
RLLC Royal Low Level Corridor
RLLS Runway Lead-in Lighting System
RLNA Requested Level Not Available
RMK Remark
RN Royal Navy
RNAV (To be pronounced 'AR-NAV' Area Navigation
RNG Radio Range
RNHF Royal Navy Historical Flight
RNP Required Navigation Performance
ROBEX Regional OPMET Bulletin Exchange (Scheme)
ROC Rate of Climb
ROD Rate of Descent
ROFOR Route Forecast (In aeronautical meteorological code)
RON Receiving Only
RPL Receptive Flight Plan
RPLC Replace or Replaced
RPS Radar Position Symbol
RQMNTS Requirements
RQP Request Flight Plan (message type designator)
RR Report Reaching
RRA (or RRB, RRC... etc in sequence) Delayed meteorological message (message type designator)
RSC Rescue Sub-Centre
RSCD Runway Surface Condition
RSP Responder beacon
RSR En-Route Surveillance Radar
RTD Delayed (used to indicate delayed meteorological message, message type designator)
RTE Route
RTF Radiotelephone
RTG Radiotelegraph
RTHL Runway threshold light(s)
RTN Return or Returned or Returning
RTOAA Rejected Take-off Area Available
RTR Radar Termination Range
RTS Return to Service
RTT Radioteletypewriter
RTZL Runway Touchdown Zone Light(s)
RUT Standard regional route transmitting frequencies
RV Rescue Vessel
RVA Radar Vectoring Area
RVP Rendezvous Point
RVR Runway Visual Range
RVSM Reduced Vertical Separation Minimum
RWY Runway

S

S South or Southern Latitude
SA Sand
SALS Simple Approach Lighting System
SAN Sanitary
SAP As soon as possible
SAR Search and Rescue
SARPS Standards and Recommended Practices (ICAO)
SARSAT Search and Rescue Satellite Aided Tracking System
SAT Saturday
SATCOM Satellite Communication
SB Southbound
SBAS Satellite Based Augmentation System
SC Stratocumulus
ScACC Scottish Area Control Centre
ScATCC Scottish Area and Terminal Control Centre
SCT Scattered
SDBY Stand by
SDF Step Down Fix

SE	South East
SEB	South East Bound
SEC	Seconds
SEC	sector
SECT	Sector
SEG	Stand Entry Guidance
SELCAL	Selective Calling System
SEP	September
SER	Service or Servcing or Served
SEV	Severe (Used eg to qualify icing and turbulence reports)
SFC	Surface
SG	Snow Grains
SGL	Signal
SH	Showers (followed by RA = Rain, SN = Snow, PL = Ice pellets, GR = Hail, GS = Small hail and/or snow pellets or combinations thereof, eg SHRASN = Showers of rain and snow)
SHF	Super High Frequency (3000 to 3000 MHz)
SI	International Systems of Units
SI	Statutory Instruments
SID	Standard Instrument Departure
SIF	Selective Identification Feature
SIGMET	Information concerning en-route weather phenomena which may affect the safety of aircraft operations
SIGWX	Significant weather
SIMUL	Simultaneous or Simultaneously
SIWL	Single Isolated Wheel Load
SKC	Sky Clear
SKED	Schedule or Scheduled
SLP	Speed Limiting Point
SLW	Slow
SMB	Side Marker Boards
SMC	Surface Movement Control
SMR	Surface Movement Radar
SN	Snow
SNOCLO	Aerodrome closed due to snow (used in METAR/SPECI)
SNOWTAM	A special series NOTAM notifying the presence or removal of hazardous conditions due to snow, ice, slush or standing water associated with snow, slush and ice on the movement area, by means of a specific format
SOC	Start of Climb
SOTA	Shannon Oceanic Transition Area
SPECI	Aviation selected special weather report (In aeronautical meteorological code)
SPECIAL	Special meteorological report (In abbreviated plain language)
SPL	Supplementary flight plan (message type designator)
SPOT	Spot wind
SQ	Squall
SR	Sunrise
SRA	Surveillance Radar Approach
SRD	Standard Route Document
SRE	Surveillance Radar Equipment of precision approach radar system
SRG	Short range
SSR	Search and Rescue Region
SRY	Secondary
SS	Sandstorm
SS	Sunset
SSB	Single Sideband
SSE	South South East
SSR	Secondary Surveillance Radar
SST	Supersonic transport
SSW	South South West
ST	Stratus
STA	Straight in Approach
STAR	Standard Instrument Arrival
STD	Stabdard
STF	Stratiform
STN	Station
STNR	Stationary
STOL	Short Take Off and Landing
STS	Status
STWL	Stopway light(s)
SUBJ	Subject to
SUN	Sunday
SUP	Supplement (AIP Supplement)
SUPPS	Regional Supplementary Procedures
SVC	Service message
SVCBL	Serviceable
SVFR	Special Visual Flight Rules
SW	South West
SWB	South West Bound
SWY	Stopway
T	
T	Temperature
TA	Traffic Advisory
TA	Transition Altitude
TACAN	Tactical Air Navigation Aid
TAF	Aerodrome Forecast
TAIL	Tail wind
TAR	Terminal Area Surveillance Radar
TAS	True Air Speed
TAX	Taxiing or Taxi
TC	Terminal Control
TC	Tropical Cyclone
TCAS	Traffic Alert and Collision Avoidance System
TCH	Threshold Crossing Height
TCU	Towering Cumulus
TDA	Temporary Danger Area
TDO	Tornado
TDZ	Touch Down Zone
TECR	Technical Reason
TEL	Telephone
TEMPO	Temporary or Temporarily
TFC	traffic
TGL	Touch and Go Landing
TGS	Taxiing Guidance System
THR	Threshold
THRU	Through
THU	Thursday
TIL	Until
TIP	Until past ... (place)
TKOF	Take-Off
TL	Till (followed by time by which weather change is forecast to end)
TLOF	Toumchdown and Lift off Area
TLP	Tactical Leadership Programme
TMA	Terminal Control Area
TNA	Turn Altitude
TNH	Turn Height
TO	To ... (place)
TOC	Top of Climb
TODA	Take off Distance Available
TODAH	Take off Distance Available, Helicopter
TOP	Cloud Top
TORA	Take of Run Available
TP	Turning Point

TR	Track
TRA	Temporary Reserved Airspace
TRANS	Transmits or Transmitter
TRL	Trnsition Level
TROP	Tropopause
TS	Thunderstorm (in aerodrome repots and forecasts TS used alone means thunder heard but no precipitation at the aerodrome)
TS...	Thunderstorm (followed by RA = Rain, SN = Snow, PL = Ice pellets, GR = Hail, GS = Small hail and/or now pellets or combinations thereof, eg, TSRASN – thunderstorm with rain and snow)
TT	Teletypewriter
TUE	Tuesday
TRUB	Turbulence
TVOR	Terminal VOR
TWR	Aerodrome control tower or aerodrome control
TWY	Taxiway
TWYL	Taiway Link
TYP	Type of Aircraft
TYPH	Typhoon
U	
U	Upward (tendency in RVR during previous 10 minutes)
UAA	Unusual Aerial Activity
UAB	Until Advised by ...
UAC	Upper Area Control Centre
UAR	Upper Air Route
UAV	Unmanned Aerial Vehicle
UDF	Ultra High Frequency Direction Finding System
UFN	Until Further Notice
UHDT	Unable Higher Due Traffic
UHF	Ultra High Frequency (300 to 3000 MHz)
UIR	Upper Flight Information Region
UIC	Upper Information Centre
UIR	Upper Flight Information Region
UK	United Kingdom
U/L	Unlicensed
ULR	Ultra Long Range
UNA	Unable
UNAP	Unable to Approve
UNL	Unlimited
UNREL	Unreliable
U/S	Unservicable
UTA	Upper Control Area
UTC	Co-ordinated Universal Time
V	
VA	Volcanic Ash
VAC	Visual Approach Chart
VAL	In Valleys
VAN	Runway Control Van
VAR	Magnetic Variation
VAR	Visual-aural radio range
VASIS	Visual Approach Slope Indicator System
VC	Vicinity of aerodrome (followed by FG = Fog, FC = Funnel cloud, SH = Showers, PO = Dust/sand whirls, BLDU = Blowing dust, BLSA = Blowing sand or BLSN = Blowing snow, eg VC FG = Vicinity Fog
VCY	Vicinity
VDF	Very High Frequency Direction Finding Station
VER	Vertical
VFR	Visual Flight Rules
VHF	Very High Frequency (3 to 300 MHz)
VLR	Very Long Range
VMC	Visual Meteorological Conditions
VM(C)	Visual Manoeuvring (Circling)
VOLMET	Meteorological information for aircraft in flight
VOR	Very High Frequency Omni-directional Radio Range
VORTAC	VOR and TACAN combination
VOT	VOR airborne equipment test facility
VRB	Variable
VRP	Visual Reference Point
VSA	By visual reference to the ground
VSP	Vertical speed
VSTOL	Very Short Take-off and Landing
VTOL	Vertical Take-off and Landing
W	
W	West or Western Longitude
W	White
WAAIS	Wide Area Augmentation System
WAC	World Aeronautical Chart – ICAO 1:1 000,000
WAFC	World Area Forecast Centre
WB	Westbound
WBAR	Wing bar lights
WDI	Wind Direction Indicator
WDSPR	Widespread
WED	Wednesday
WEF	With effect from or Effective from
WGS	World Geodetic System
WI	Within
WID	Width or Wide
WIE	With Immediate Effect or Effectively Immediately
WILCO	Will comply
WINTEM	Forecast upper wind and temperature for aviation
WIP	Work in Progress
WKN	Weaken or Weakening
WNW	West North West
WO	Without
WPT	Way-point
WRNG	Warning
WS	Windshear
WSW	West South West
WT	Weight
WTSPT	Waterspout
WWW	Worldwide web
WX	Weather
X	
X	Cross
XBAR	Crossbar (of approach lighting system)
XNG	Crossing
XS	Atmospheres
Y	
Y	Yellow
YCZ	Yellow caution zone (runway lighting)
YR	Your
Z	
Z	Co-ordinated Universal Time (in meteorological messages)

In-flight

Crosswind/Headwind calculator – use of the wind component graph

This graph can be used to find the head/tail wind component and the crosswind component, given a particular wind velocity and runway direction.

EXAMPLE:
Runway 27
Surface wind 240°/15 knots

The angle between the runway direction (270°) and wind direction(240°) is 30°. Now on the graph locate a point on the 30° line, where it crosses the 15 knot arc. From this point take a horizontal line to give the headwind component (13 knots) and a vertical line to give the crosswind component (8 knots).

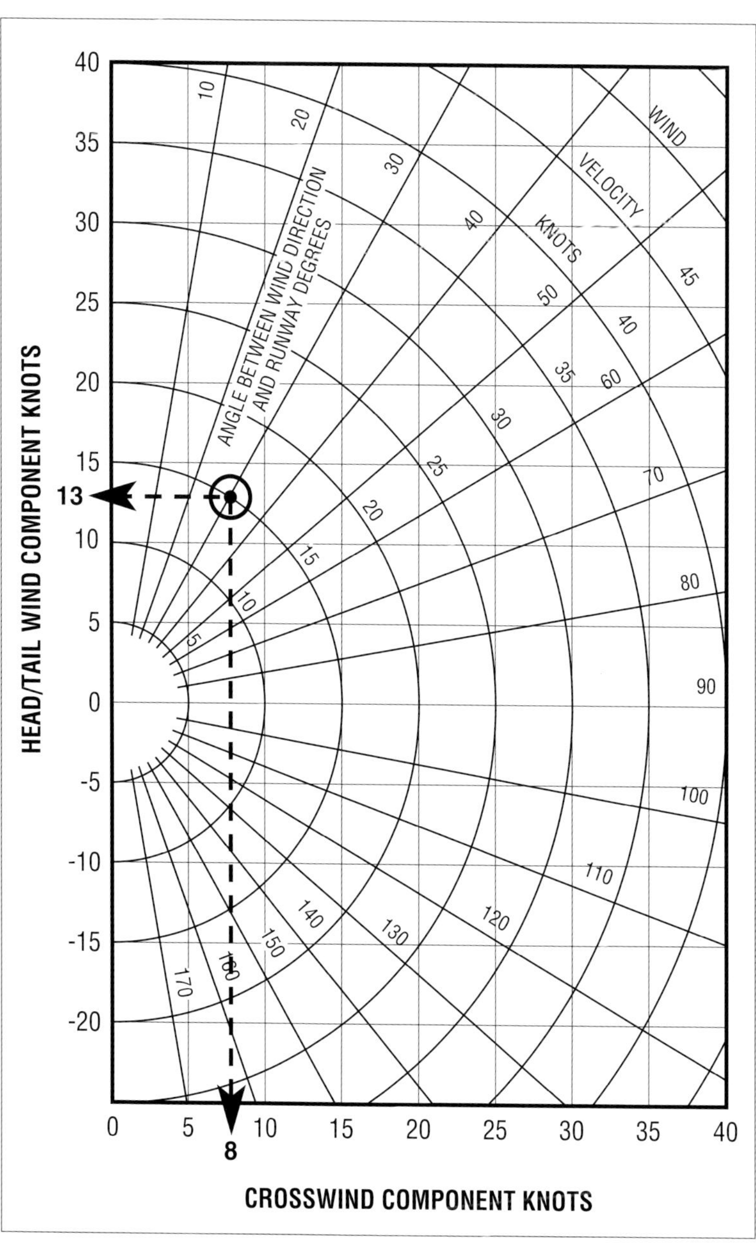

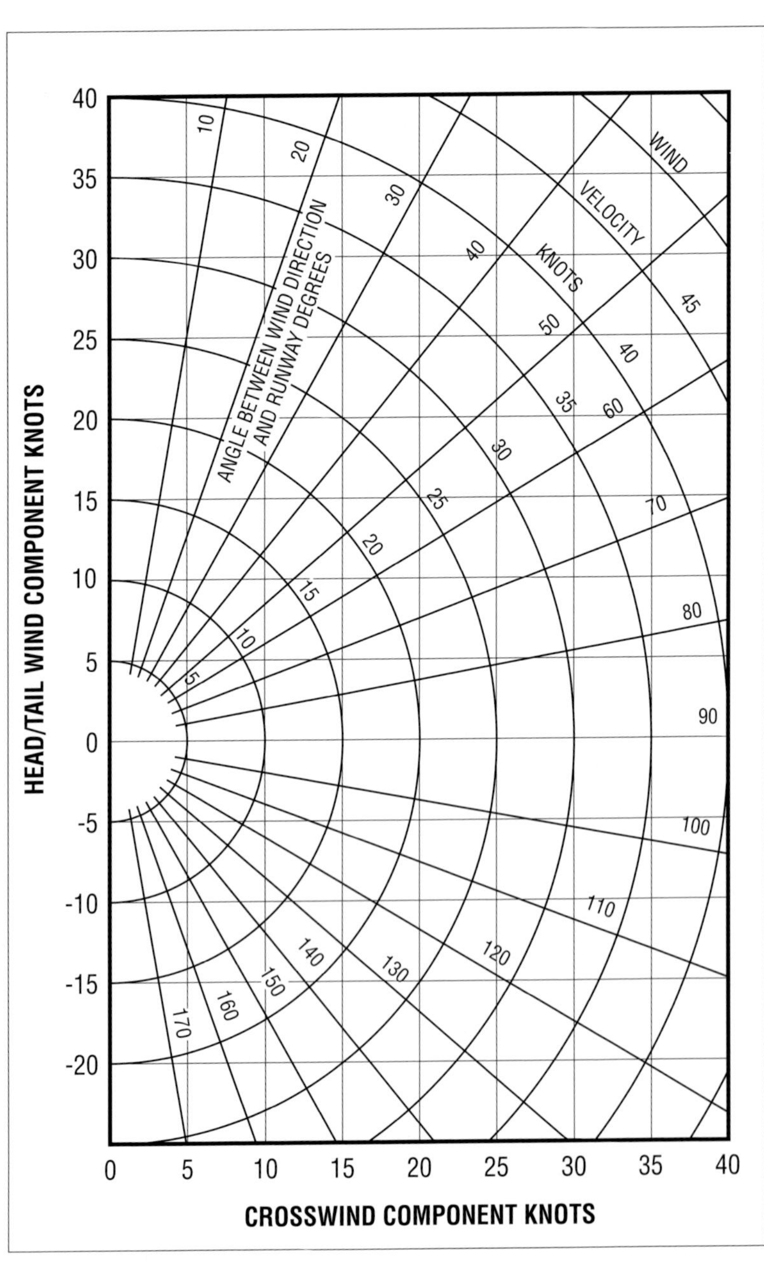
HEAD/TAIL WIND COMPONENT KNOTS
CROSSWIND COMPONENT KNOTS
ANGLE BETWEEN WIND DIRECTION AND RUNWAY DEGREES
WIND VELOCITY KNOTS
40
35
30
25
20
15
10
5
0
-5
-10
-15
-20
0
5
10
15
20
25
30
35
40
10
20
30
40
50
60
70
80
90
100
110
120
130
140
150
160
170
45

Class A Airspace

	IFR	VFR
Service	Air Traffic Control Service	VFR FLIGHT NOT PERMITTED
Separation	Separation provided between all IFR flights by ATC	
ATC Rules	Flight plan required (**See Note 1**) ATC clearance required Radio communication required ATC instructions are mandatory	
VMC Minima	Not applicable (**See Note 2**)	
Speed Limitations	As published in procedures or instructed by ATC	

Note 1: In certain circumstances, Flight Plan requirements may be satisfied by passing flight details on RTF (detailed at ENR 1.10).

Note 2: For the purposes of:

(a) Climbs and descents maintaining VMC;

(b) powered aircraft – Airways crossings (ENR 1.1.1.3, paragraph 5.1.6.1); and

(c) powered aircraft – other penetrations of Airways (ENR 1.1.1.3, paragraph 5.1.6.2).

In Class A Airspace, the VMC minima are to be:

At or above FL 100:	8km flight visibility 1500 m horizontal and 1000ft vertical distance from cloud
Below FL 100:	5km flight visibility 1500 m horizontal and 1000ft vertical distance from cloud

Class B Airspace

	IFR	VFR
Service	Air Traffic Control Service	
Separation	Separation provided between all flights by ATC	
ATC Rules	Flight plan required (See Note) ATC clearance required Radio Communications required ATC instructions are mandatory	
VMC Minima	Not applicable	**At or above FL100** 8km flight visibility Clear of cloud **Below FL100** 5km flight visibility Clear of cloud
Speed Limitations	As published in procedures or instructed by ATC	

Note: In certain circumstances, Flight Plan requirements may be satisfied by passing flight details on RTF (detailed at ENR 1.10). No UK Airspace currently designated Class B,

Class C – Controlled Airspace

	IFR	VFR
Service	Air Traffic Control Service	
Separation	Separation provided between all IFR flights	All VFR flights separated from all IFR flights by by ATC. Traffic information provided on other VFR flights to enable pilots to effect own traffic avoidance and integration
ATC Rules	Flight plan required (See Note) ATC clearance required Radio communication required ATC instructions are mandatory	
VMC Minima	Not applicable	**At or above FL100** 8km flight visibility 1500m horizontal and 1000ft vertical distance from cloud **Below FL100** 5km flight visibility 1500m horizontal and 1000ft vertical distance from cloud **or** **At or below 3000ft** **(a)** aircraft (except helicopters) 140ft IAS or less: 5km flight visibility and clear of cloud and in sight of the surface; **(b)** helicopters: clear of cloud and in sight of the surface
Speed Limitation	As published in procedures or instructed by ATC	**Below FL100** 250kt IAS **or** Lower when published in procedures or instructed by ATC

Note: In certain circumstances, Flight Plan requirements may be satisfied by passing flight details on RTF (detailed at ENR 1.10).

Class D Airspace

<table>
<tr><th></th><th>IFR</th><th>VFR</th></tr>
<tr><td>Service</td><td colspan="2">Air Traffic Control Service</td></tr>
<tr><td>Separation</td><td>Separation provided between all IFR flights by ATC
Traffic information provided on conflicting ATC VFR flights</td><td>ATC separation not provided
Traffic information provided on IFR and other VFR flights to enable pilots to effect own traffic avoidance and integration.</td></tr>
<tr><td>ATC Rules</td><td colspan="2">Flight plan required (See Note 1)
ATC clearance required
Radio communication required
ATC instructions are mandatory</td></tr>
<tr><td>VMC Minima</td><td>Not applicable</td><td>At or above FL100
8km flight visibility
1500m horizontal and 1000ft vertical distance from cloud
Below FL100
5km flight visibility
1500m horizontal and 1000ft vertical distance from cloud
or
At or below 3000ft
(a) aircraft (except helicopters)
140kt IAS or less
5km flight visibility and clear of cloud and in sight of the surface.
(b) helicopters
clear of cloud and in sight of the surface.</td></tr>
<tr><td>Speed Limitation</td><td colspan="2">Below FL100
250kt IAS
or
Lower when published in procedures or instructed by ATC</td></tr>
</table>

Note 1: In certain circumstances, Flight Plan requirements may be satisfied by passing flight details on RTF (detailed at ENR 1.10).

Class E Airspace

	IFR	VFR
Service	Air Traffic Control Service	Air Traffic Control Service to communicating flights
Separation	Separation provided between all IFR flights by ATC Traffic information provided on conflicting VFR flights	ATC separation not provided Traffic information provided on request, as far as practicable on IFR and other known VFR flights to enable pilots to effect own traffic avoidance and integration
ATC Rules	Flight plan required (See Note) ATC clearance required Radio Communications required ATC instructions are mandatory	None However pilots are encouraged to contact ATC and comply with instructions
VMC Minima	Not applicable	**At or above FL100** 8km flight visibility 1500m horizontal and 1000ft vertical distance from cloud **Below FL100** 5km flight visibility 1500m horizontal and 1000ft vertical distance from cloud **or** **At or below 3000ft** **(a)** Aircraft (except helicopters): 140kt IAS or less 5km visibility and clear of cloud and in sight of surface **(b)** helicopters: clear of cloud and in sight of surface
Speed Limitations	Below FL100 250kt IAS **or** lower when published in procedures or instructed by ATC	

Note: In certain circumstances, Flight Plan requirements may be satisfied by passing flight details on RTF (detailed at ENR 1.10).

Class F Airspace

	IFR	VFR
Service	Air Traffic Advisory Service to participating Flights	Air Traffic Services as appropriate
Separation	Separation provided between participating IFR flights by ATC	ATC separation not provided
ATC Rules	Participating flight Flight plan required (See Note) ATC clearance required Radio communication required ATC instructions are mandatory	None
VMC Minima	Not applicable	**At or above FL100** 8km flight visibility 1500m horizontal and 1000ft vertical distance from cloud **Below FL100** 5km flight visibility 1500m horizontal and 1000ft vertical distance from cloud **or** **At or below 3000ft** **(a)** aircraft (except helicopters) greater than 14kt IAS 5km flight visibility and clear of cloud and in sight of the surface **(b)** aircraft (except helicopters) 140kt IAS or less 1500m flight visibility clear of cloud and in sight of the surface **(c)** helicopters at a speed which, having regard to the visibility, is reasonable: clear of cloud and in sight of the surface
Speed Limitations	**Below FL100** 250kt IAS **or** lower when published in procedures or instructed by ATC	

Note: In certain circumstances, Flight Plan requirements may be satisfied by passing flight details on RTF (detailed at ENR 1.10).

Class G Airspace

	IFR	VFR
Service	Air Traffic Services as appropriate	
Separation	ATC separation not provided (See Note 1)	
ATC Rules	None (See Note 2)	
VMC Minima	Not applicable	**At or above FL100** 8km flight visibility 1500m horizontal and 1000ft vertical distance from cloud **Below FL100** 5km flight visibility 1500m horizontal and 1000ft vertical distance from cloud **or** **At or below 3000ft** **(a)** Aircraft (except helicopters) greater than 140kt IAS 5km flight visibility clear of cloud and in sight of the surface **(b)** Aircraft (except helicopters) 140kt IAS or less 1500m flight visibility clear of cloud and in sight of the surface **(c)** helicopters at a speed which, having regard to the visibility, is reasonable clear of cloud and in sight of the surface.
Speed Limitations	**Below FL100** 250kt IAS **or** lower when published in procedures or instructed by ATC	

Note 1: Where Air Traffic Control units provide ATS to traffic outside Controlled Airspace, separation may be provided between known flights.

Note 2: Aircraft receiving services from Air Traffic Control units are expected to comply with clearances and instructions unless the pilot advises otherwise.

Special VFR Flight: A flight made at any time in a Control Zone which is Class A airspace, or in any other control zone in Instrument Meteorological Conditions or at night, in respect of which the appropriate air traffic control unit has given permission for the flight to be made in accordance with special instructions given by that unit instead of in accordance with the Instrument Flight Rules and in the course of which the aircraft complies with any instructions given by that unit and remains clear of cloud and in sight of the surface.

1 Clearance for Special VFR flight in the UK is an authorisation by ATC for a pilot to fly within a Control Zone although he is unable to comply with IFR. In exceptional circumstances, requests for Special VFR flight may be granted for aircraft with an all-up-weight exceeding 5700kg and capable of flight under IFR. Special VFR clearance is only granted when traffic conditions permit it to take place without hindrance to the normal IFR flights, but for aircraft using certain notified lanes, routes and local flying areas see paragraph 2.2. Without prejudice to existing weather limitations on Special VFR flights at specific aerodromes (as detailed within the AD 2 Section) ATC will not issue a Special VFR clearance to any fixed-wing aircraft intending to depart from an aerodrome within a Control Zone, when the official meteorological report indicates that the visibility is 1800m or less and/or the cloud ceiling is less than 600ft.
2 Aircraft using the access lanes and local flying areas notified for Denham, White Waltham and Fairoaks in the London CTR and any temporary Special Access Lanes which may be notified from time to time will be considered as Special VFR flights and compliance with the procedures published for the relevant airspace will be accepted as compliance with ATC clearance. Separate requests should not be made nor will separate clearances be given. Separation between aircraft which are using such airspace cannot be given, and pilots are responsible for providing their own separation from other aircraft in the relevant airspace.
3 When operating on a Special VFR clearance, the pilot must comply with ATC instructions and remain at all times in flight conditions which enable him to determine his flight path and to keep clear of obstacles. Therefore, it is implicit in all Special VFR clearances that the aircraft remains clear of cloud and in sight of the surface. It may be necessary for ATC purposes to impose a height limitation on a Special VFR clearance which will require the pilot to fly either at or not above a specific level
4 A full flight plan, Form CA48/RAF2919, is not required for Special VFR flight but ATC must be given brief details of the call sign, aircraft type and pilots intentions. These details may be passed either by RTF or, at busy aerodromes, through the Flight Clearance Office. A full flight plan must be filed if the pilot wishes the destination aerodrome to be notified of the flight.
5 Requests for Special VFR clearance to enter a Control Zone, or to transit a Control Zone, may be made to the ATC authority whilst airborne. Aircraft departing from aerodromes adjacent to a Control Zone boundary and wishing to enter may obtain Special VFR clearance either prior to take-off by telephone or by RTF when airborne. In any case, all such requests must specify the ETA for the selected entry point and must be made 5-10 minutes beforehand.
6 ATC will provide standard separation between all Special VFR flights and between such flights and other aircraft under IFR. However, pilots with a Special VFR clearance should note that they cannot be given separation from aircraft flying in the lanes, routes and local flying areas detailed in paragraph 2.2; nor from aircraft flying in any temporary Special Access Lanes which may be notified from time to time.
7 A Special VFR clearance within a Control Zone does not absolve the pilot from the responsibility for avoiding an Aerodrome Traffic Zone unless prior permission to penetrate the ATZ has been obtained from the relevant ATC Unit.
8 Because Special VFR flights are made at the lower levels, it is important for pilots to realise that a Special VFR clearance does not absolve them from the need to comply with the relevant low flying restrictions of Rule 5 of the Rules of the Air Regulations 1996 (other than the 1500ft rule where the clearance permits flight below that height). In particular, it does not absolve pilots from the requirement that an aircraft, other than a helicopter, flying over congested areas must fly at such a height as would enable it to clear the area and alight without danger to persons or property on the ground in the event of an engine failure and that a helicopter, whether flying over a congested area or not, must fly at such a height as would enable it to alight without danger to persons or property on the ground in the event of an engine failure. In addition there are special rules applicable to flight by helicopters over London.

En-route nav aids

Note: DMEs associated with a specific runway normally read distance from the threshold of the runway in use.

Station	Navaid	Ident	Freq	Range	Co-ordinates
Aberdeen	Lctr	ATF	348.00	25	N5704.65 W00206.34
	NDB	AQ	336.00	15	N5708.30 W00224.28
	VOR/DME	ADN	114.30		N5718.63 W00216.03
	DME 16	I-AX	109.90		N5712.07 W00212.04
	DME 34	I-ABD	109.90		N5712.07 W00212.04
Alderney	Lctr	ALD	383.00	30	N4942.53 W00211.98
Barkway	VOR/DME	BKY	116.25		N5159.38 E00003.71
Barra	NDB	BRR	316.00	15	N5701.55 W00726.95
Barrow	NDB	WL	385.00	15	N5407.61 W00315.78
	DME	WL	109.40		N5407.59 W00315.79
Belfast Aldergrove	VOR/DME	BEL	117.20		N5439.66 W00613.79
	Lctr	OY	332.00	15	N5441.56 W00605.12
	DME 25	I-AG	109.90		N5439.63 W00612.02
	DME 17	I-FT	110.90		N5439.31 W00613.74
Belfast City	Lctr	HB	420.00	15	N5436.93 W00552.86
	DME 22	I-BFH	108.10		N5437.17 W00552.50
	DME 04	HBD	108.10		N5437.17 W00552.50
Benbecula	VOR/DME	BEN	113.95		N5728.67 W00721.92
	DME	BCL	108.10	25	N5728.51 W00722.22
	NDB	BBA	401.00	40	N5728.57 W00722.15
Benson	TACAN	BSO	110.00		N5136.88 W00105.96
Berry Head	VOR/DME	BHD	112.05		N5023.91 W00329.61
Biggin Hill	DME 21	I-BGH	109.35		N5120.22 E00002.10
	VOR/DME	BIG	115.10		N5119.85 E00002.08
Birmingham	Lctr	BHX	406.00	25	N5227.27 W00145.14
	DME 15	I-BIR	110.10		N5227.27 W00145.14
	DME 33	I-BM	110.10		N5227.27 W00145.14
Blackbushe	NDB	BLK	328.00	15	N5119.40 W00050.69
	DME	BLC	116.20		N5119.40 W00050.69
Blackpool	Lctr	BPL	420.00	15	N5346.37 W00301.67
	DME 28	I-BPL	108.15		N5346.22 W00301.71
Boscombe Down	TACAN	BDN	108.20		N5108.93 W00145.15
Bournemouth	Lctr	BIA	339.00	20	N5046.66 W00150.54
	Lczr 26	IBH	110.50		N5046.64 W00151.56
	DME 08	I-BMH	110.50		N5046.72 W00150.38
	DME 26	I-BH	110.50		N5046.72 W00150.38
Bovingdon	VOR/DME	BNN	113.75		N5143.56 W00032.98
Brecon	VOR/DME	BCN	117.45		N5143.53 W00315.78
Bristol	Lctr	BRI	414.00	40	N5122.89 W00243.05
	DME 09	I-BON	110.15		N5122.89 W00243.20
	DME 27	I-BTS	110.15		N5122.89 W00243.20
Bristol Filton	Lctr	OF	325.00	25	N5131.31 W00235.41
	DME 09	I-BRF	110.55		N5131.25 W00235.48
	DME 27	I-FB	110.55		N5131.25 W00235.48
Brize Norton	TACAN	BZN	111.90		N5144.89 W00136.21
	Lctr	BZ	386.00	20	N5144.95 W00136.10
Brookmans Park	VOR/DME	BPK	117.50		N5144.98 W00006.40
Brough	NDB	BV	372.00	15	N5343.52 W00034.89
Burnham	NDB	BUR	421.00	15	N5131.13 W00040.61
Caernarfon	NDB	CAE	320.00	15	N5306.00 W00420.40
Cambridge	Lctr	CAM	332.50	15	N5212.65 E00010.96
	DME 23	I-CMG	111.30		N5212.42 E00010.88
Campbeltown	NDB	CBL	380.00	15	N5526.14 W00541.28
Cardiff	Lctr	CDF	388.50	40	N5123.60 W00320.27
	DME 12	I-CDF	110.70		N5123.92 W00320.43
	DME 30	I-CWA	110.70		N5123.92 W00320.43
Carlisle	Lctr	CL	328.00	20	N5456.40 W00248.33
	DME	CO	110.70		N5456.40 W00248.31
Carnane	NDB	CAR	366.50	25	N5408.46 W00429.50
Chiltern	NDB	CHT	277.00	25	N5137.38 W00031.11
Clacton	VOR/DME	CLN	114.55		N5150.91 E00108.85
Compton	VOR/DME	CPT	114.35		N5129.50 W00113.18
Compton Abbas	NDB	COM	349.50	10	N5057.97 W00209.31
Coningsby	TACAN	CGY	111.10		N5305.46 W00010.14
	DME 25	CY	110.70		N5307.34 W00001.02

Station	Navaid	Ident	Freq	Range	Co-ordinates
Cottesmore	TACAN	CTM	112.30		N5244.12 W00039.04
Coventry	Lctr	CT	363.50	20	N5224.66 W00124.35
	DME 23	I-CT	109.75		N5222.23 W00128.84
	DME 05	I-CTY	109.75		N5222.23 W00128.84
Cranfield	Lctr	CIT	850.00	15	N5207.81 W00033.41
	VOR	CFD	116.50		N5204.45 W00036.64
Cranwell	NDB	CWL	423.00	25	N5301.58 W00029.34
	TACAN	CWZ	117.40		N5301.72 W00029.13
	DME 27	I-CW	108.50		N5301.90 W00028.90
Cumbernauld	NDB	CBN	374.00		N5558.53 W00358.48
	DME	CBN	117.55		N5558.53 W00358.47
Daventry	VOR/DME	DTY	116.40		N5210.81 W00106.83
Dean Cross	VOR/DME	DCS	115.20		N5443.31 W00320.43
Detling	VOR/DME	DET	117.30		N5118.23 E00035.83
Doncaster Sheffield	NDB	FNY	338.00		N5328.49 W00100.10
	DME	I-FNL	110.95		N5328.49 W00100.12
	DME 02	I-FIN	110.95		N5328.49 W00100.12
Dover	VOR/DME	DVR	114.95		N5109.75 E00121.55
Dundee	Lctr	DND	394.00	25	N5627.30 W00306.90
	DME 10	I-DDE	108.10		N5627.10 W00301.55
Durham Tees Valley	Lctr	TD	347.50	25	N5433.63 W00120.02
	DME 05	I-TSE	108.50		N5430.49 W00125.68
	DME 23	I-TD	108.50		N5430.49 W00125.68
East Midlands	Lctr	EME	353.50	20	N5249.96 W00111.67
	Lctr	EMW	393.00	10	N5249.72 W00127.27
	DME 09	I-EMW	109.35		N5249.97 W00119.67
	DME 27	I-EME	109.35		N5249.97 W00119.67
Edinburgh	Lctr	EDN	341.00	35	N5558.70 W00317.12
	Lctr	UW	368.00	25	N5554.30 W00330.15
	DME 06	I-VG	108.90		N5557.10 W00322.37
	DME 24	I-TH	108.90		N5557.10 W00322.37
Enniskillen	NDB	EKN	357.50	15	N5423.97 W00739.32
	DME	ENN	116.75		N5423.97 W00739.22
Epsom	NDB	EPM	316.00	25	N5119.16 W00022.31
Exeter	Lctr	EX	337.00	25	N5045.13 W00317.70
	DME 08	I-ET	109.90		N5044.12 W00324.86
	DME 26	I-XR	109.90		N5044.12 W00324.86
Fairford	TACAN	FFA	113.40		N5140.81 W00147.86
	DME 09	I-FFD	111.10		N5140.90 W00147.86
	DME 27	I-FFA	111.10		N5140.90 W00147.86
Fairoaks	NDB	FOS	348.00	8	N5120.82 W00033.83
	DME	FRK	109.85		N5120.82 W00033.83
Farnborough	DME 24	I-FNB	111.50		N5116.59 W00046.68
	DME 06	I-FRG	111.55		N5116.59 W00046.68
Gamston	VOR/DME	GAM	112.80		N5316.88 W00056.83
Glasgow	VOR/DME	GOW	115.40		N5552.23 W00426.74
	DME 05	I-UU	110.10		N5552.18 W00426.04
	DME 23	I-OO	110.10		N5552.18 W00426.04
	Lctr	GLW	331.00	25	N5552.19 W00426.02
Gloucestershire	Lctr	GST	331.00	25	N5153.51 W00210.07
	DME	GOS	115.55		N5153.53 W00210.08
Goodwood	VOR/DME	GWC	114.75		N5051.31 W00045.40
Great Yarmouth	Lctr	ND	417.00	10	N5238.15 E00143.62
Guernsey	VOR/DME	GUR	109.40		N4926.23 W00236.22
	NDB	GUY	361.00	30	N4926.23 W00236.03
	DME 09	I-UY	108.10		N4926.00 W00236.00
	DME 27	I-GH	108.10		N4926.00 W00236.00
Haverfordwest	NDB	HAV	328.00	10	N5149.93 W00458.10
	DME	HDW	116.75		N5149.93 W00458.18
Hawarden	Lctr	HAW	340.00	25	N5310.75 W00258.77
	DME 04	I-HWD	110.35		N5310.73 W00258.73
	DME 22	I-HDN	110.35		N5310.73 W00258.73
Henton	NDB	HEN	433.50	30	N5145.58 W00047.41
Honiley	VOR/DME	HON	113.65		N5221.40 W00139.81
Humberside	Lctr	KIM	365.00	15	N5334.43 W00021.22
	DME 21	I-HS	108.75		N5334.43 W00021.20

Station	Navaid	Ident	Freq	Range	Co-ordinates
Inverness	VOR/DME	INS	109.20		N5732.55 W00402.49
	DME 05	I-LN	108.50		N5732.51 W00402.77
	DME 23	I-DX	108.50		N5732.51 W00402.77
	NDB	IVR	328.00		N5732.72 W00402.12
Islay	NDB	LAY	395.00	20	N5540.97 W00614.96
	DME	ISY	109.95		N5540.97 W00614.96
Isle of Man	VOR/DME	IOM	112.20		N5404.01 W00445.81
	Lctr	RWY	359.00	20	N5404.86 W00437.37
	DME 26	I-RY	111.15		N5404.86 W00437.37
	DME 08	I-RH	111.15		N5404.86 W00437.37
Jersey	Lctr	JW	329.00	25	N4912.35 W00213.20
	VOR/DME	JSY	112.20		N4913.26 W00202.76
	DME 09	I-JJ	110.90		N4912.50 W00212.12
	DME 27	I-DD	110.30		N4912.57 W00211.34
Kinloss	NDB	KS	370.00	20	N5738.99 W00335.21
	TACAN	KSS	109.80		N5739.56 W00332.11
Kirkwall	Lctr	KW	395.00	40	N5857.56 W00253.96
	VOR/DME	KWL	108.60		N5857.58 W00253.63
	DME 09	I-ORK	110.10		N5857.54 W00253.96
	DME 27	I-KIR	110.10		N5857.54 W00253.96
Lakenheath	TACAN	LKH	110.20		N5224.39 E00032.88
Lambourne	VOR/DME	LAM	115.60		N5138.76 E00009.10
Lands End	VOR/DME	LND	114.20		N5008.18 W00538.21
Lashenden	DME	HLS	115.95		N5109.28 E00038.88
	NDB	LSH	340.00	15	N5109.28 E00038.88
Leeds Bradford	Lctr	LBA	402.50	25	N5351.90 W00139.17
	DME 32	I-LF	110.90		N5351.78 W00139.57
	DME 14	I-LBF	110.90		N5351.78 W00139.57
Leeming	TACAN	LEE	112.60		N5417.83 W00132.21
Leicester	NDB	LE	383.50	10	N5236.38 W00102.10
Lerwick	NDB	TL	376.00	25	N6011.30 W00114.78
Leuchars	TACAN	LUK	110.50		N5622.37 W00251.82
Lichfield	NDB	LIC	545.00	50	N5244.80 W00143.16
Linton-On-Ouse	TACAN	LOO	109.00		N5403.03 W00114.94
Liverpool	Lctr	LPL	349.50	25	N5320.38 W00243.51
	DME 09	LVR	111.75		N5319.95 W00250.95
	DME 27	I-LQ	111.75		N5319.95 W00250.95
London	VOR/DME	LON	113.60		N5129.23 W00028.00
Londonderrry	Lctr	EGT	328.50	25	N5502.73 W00709.30
	DME 26	I-EGT	108.30		N5502.51 W00709.56
London City	NDB	LCY	322.00	10	N5130.27 E00004.05
	DME 10	LST	111.15		N5130.35 E00003.32
	DME 28	LSR	111.15		N5130.35 E00003.32
London Gatwick	NDB	GE	338.00	15	N5109.86 W00004.14
	Lctr	GY	365.00	15	N5107.83 W00018.95
	DME 08R	I-GG	110.90		N5109.16 W00011.53
	DME 26L	I-WW	110.90		N5109.16 W00011.53
London Heathrow	DME 09R	I-BB	109.50		N5127.83 W00027.51
	DME 09L	I-AA	110.30		N5128.73 W00027.55
	DME 27R	I-RR	110.30		N5128.65 W00027.55
	DME 27L	I-LL	109.50		N5127.83 W00027.51
London Luton	Lctr	LUT	345.00	20	N5153.68 W00015.15
	DME 08	I-LTN	109.15		N5152.39 W00022.10
	DME 26	I-LJ	109.15		N5152.39 W00022.10
London Stanstead	NDB	SSD	429.00	20	N5153.68 E00014.70
	DME 05	I-SED	110.50		N5153.21 E00014.10
	DME 23	I-SX	110.50		N5153.21 E00014.10
Lydd	DME 21	I-LDY	108.15		N5057.24 E00056.37
	Lctr	LZD	397.00		N5057.53 E00056.35
Lyneham	NDB	LA	282.00	40	N5130.49 W00200.36
	TACAN	LYE	109.80		N5130.61 W00159.54
Machrihanish	VOR/DME	MAC	116.00		N5525.80 W00539.02
Manchester	Lctr	MCH	428.00	15	N5321.20 W00216.38
	VOR/DME	MCT	113.55		N5321.42 W00215.73
	DME 05L	I-MM	109.50		N5321.19 W00216.38
	DME 23R	I-NN	109.50		N5321.19 W00216.38
	DME 05R	I-MC	111.55		N5320.35 W00217.57

Station	Navaid	Ident	Freq	Range	Co-ordinates
Manchester Woodford	Lctr	WFD	380.00	15	N5320.26 W00209.50
	DME 25	I-WU	109.15		N5320.33 W00209.00
Manston	DME	I-MSN	111.75		N5120.48 E00120.78
	Lctr	MTN	347.00	20	N5120.27 E00120.46
Marham	TACAN	MAM	108.70		N5238.84 E00033.20
Mayfield	VOR/DME	MAY	117.90		N5101.03 E00006.96
Midhurst	VOR/DME	MID	114.00		N5103.23 W00037.50
Mildenhall	TACAN	MLD	115.90		N5221.80 E00029.30
Newcastle	VOR/DME	NEW	114.25		N5502.31 W00141.90
	Lctr	NT	352.00	40	N5503.02 W00138.56
	DME 07	I-NC	111.50		N5502.22 W00141.35
	DME 25	I-NWC	111.50		N5502.22 W00141.35
New Galloway	NDB	NGY	399.00	35	N5510.65 W00410.11
Northampton	NDB	NN	378.50	15	N5217.95 W00047.86
Northolt	DME 25	I-NHT	108.55		N5133.22 W00024.63
Norwich	Lctr	NH	371.50	20	N5240.59 E00123.08
	Lctr	NWI	342.50	20	N5240.65 E00117.49
	DME 27	I-NH	110.90		N5240.65 E00116.99
Nottingham	NDB	NOT	430.00	10	N5255.30 W00104.77
Ockham	VOR/DME	OCK	115.30		N5118.30 W00026.83
Odiham	TACAN	ODH	109.60		N5113.97 W00056.91
Ottringham	VOR/DME	OTR	113.90		N5341.90 W00006.21
Oxford	Lctr	OX	367.50	25	N5149.95 W00119.39
	DME	OX	117.70		N5149.95 W00119.37
	DME 19	I-OXF	108.35		N5150.23 W00119.31
Penzance	NDB	PH	333.00	15	N5007.70 W00531.70
Perth	VOR	PTH	110.40		N5626.55 W00322.11
Plymouth	Lctr	PY	396.50	20	N5025.46 W00406.74
	DME31	I-PLY	109.50		N5025.46 W00406.71
Pole Hill	VOR/DME	POL	112.10		N5344.63 W00206.20
Prestwick	NDB	PIK	355.00	30	N5530.37 W00434.64
	Lctr	PW	426.00	30	N5532.66 W00440.89
	DME 31	I-KK	110.30		N5530.47 W00435.65
	DME 13	I-PP	110.30		N5330.47 W00435.65
Redhill	NDB	RDL	343.00	10	N5112.97 W00008.33
Rochester	NDB	RCH	369.00	10	N5121.23 E00030.22
St Abbs	VOR/DME	SAB	112.50		N5554.45 W00212.38
St Athan	TACAN	SAT	114.80		N5124.38 W00326.09
St Mawgan	NDB	SM	356.50	20	N5026.89 W00459.70
	TACAN	SMG	112.60		N5026.07 W00501.82
Scampton	TACAN	WAD	117.10		N5309.92 W00031.62
Scatsta	Lctr	SS	315.50	25	N6027.61 W00112.92
Scilly Isles	Lctr	STM	321.00	15	N4954.85 W00617.47
Scotstownhead	NDB	SHD	383.00	80	N5733.55 W00149.03
Seaford	VOR/DME	SFD	117.00		N5045.63 E00007.31
Shawbury	VOR/DME	SWB	116.80		N5247.88 W00239.75
Sherburn-In-Elmet	NDB	SBL	323.00	10	N5347.37 W00112.50
Shipdham	NDB	SDM	348.50	10	N5237.42 E00055.50
Shobdon	NDB	SH	426.00	20	N5214.68 W00252.55
Shoreham	Lctr	SHM	332.00	10	N5050.13 W00017.73
	DME	SRH	109.95		N5050.17 W00017.60
Sleap	NDB	SLP	382.00	10	N5250.02 W00246.07
Southampton	Lctr	EAS	391.50	15	N5057.30 W00121.36
	DME 20	I-SN	110.75		N5057.31 W00121.36
Southend	Lctr	SND	362.50	20	N5134.56 E00042.01
	DME 24	I-ND	111.35		N5134.22 E00041.86
Stornoway	Lctr	SAY	431.00	40	N5812.93 W00619.74
	DME 18	STW	110.90		N5812.91 W00619.75
	DME 36	SOY	110.90		N5812.91 W00619.75
	VOR/DME	STN	115.10		N5812.41 W00610.98
Strumble	VOR/DME	STU	113.10		N5159.68 W00502.41
Sumburgh	Lctr	SBH	351.00	25	N5952.94 W00117.69
	VOR/DME	SUM	117.35		N5952.73 W00117.19
	DME 09	SUB	108.50		N5952.95 W00117.63
	DME 27	I-SG	108.50		N5952.95 W00117.63
Swansea	Lctr	SWN	320.50	15	N5136.30 W00404.31
	DME	SWZ	110.30		N5136.36 W00404.24

Station	Navaid	Ident	Freq	Range	Co-ordinates
Talla	VOR/DME	TLA	113.80		N5529.95 W00321.16
Tattenhill	NDB	TNL	327.00	10	N5248.88 W00146.00
Tiree	VOR/DME	TIR	117.70		N5629.59 W00652.53
Trent	VOR/DME	TNT	115.70		N5303.23 W00140.20
Turnberry	VOR/DME	TRN	117.50		N5518.80 W00447.03
Valley	TACAN	VYL	108.40		N5315.45 W00432.65
Waddington	TACAN	WAD	117.10		N5309.92 W00031.60
Wallasey	VOR/DME	WAL	114.10		N5323.51 W00308.06
Warton	NDB	WTN	337.00	15	N5345.10 W00251.13
	TACAN	WTN	113.20		N5344.42 W00253.57
	DME 26	I-WQ	109.90		N5344.85 W00252.27
Wattisham	TACAN	WTZ	109.30		N5207.32 E00056.43
Welshpool	NDB	WPL	323.00	10	N5237.80 W00309.23
	DME	WPL	115.95		N5237.78 W00309.23
Westcott	NDB	WCO	335.00	30	N5151.18 W00057.75
West Wales	NDB	AP	370.50	15	N5206.99 W00433.58
Whitegate	NDB	WHI	368.50	25	N5311.10 W00237.38
Wick	Lctr	WIK	344.00	30	N5826.80 W00303.78
	VOR/DME	WCK	113.60		N5827.53 W00306.02
Wittering	TACAN	WIT	117.60		N5236.47 W00029.92
Wolverhampton	Lctr	WBA	356.00	25	N5230.95 W00215.71
Halfpenny Green	DME	WOL	108.60		N5230.95 W00215.71
Woodley	NDB	WOD	352.00	25	N5127.16 W00052.73
Yeovil	Lctr	YVL	343.00	20	N5056.48 W00239.87
	DME	YVL	109.05	25	N5056.45 W00239.20
Yeovilton	TACAN	VLN	111.00		N5100.30 W00238.32

Airfield	VRP	Position
Benbecula	Lochmaddy Pier	N5735.77 W00709.40
	Monarch Isles Lighthouse	N5731.57 W00741.67
Biggin Hill	Sevenoaks	N5116.60 E00010.90
Blackpool	Fleetwood Golf Course	N5355.13 W00302.72
	Inskip Disused AD	N5349.63 W00250.05
	Kirkham	N5346.95 W00252.28
	Marshside	N5341.78 W00258.23
	Poulton Railway Station	N5350.90 W00259.42
Boscombe Down	Alderbury	N5102.90 W00143.90
Bristol Filton	M5 Bridge over River Avon	N5129.33 W00241.58
	Old Severn Bridge	N5136.67 W00238.62
	Thornbury	N5136.67 W00231.10
Carlisle	Gretna	N5459.73 W00304.05
	Halthwistle	N5458.13 W00227.73
	Penrith	N5439.87 W00245.02
	Wigton	N5449.48 W00309.67
Coventry	Bitteswell Disused AD	N5227.47 W00114.78
	Cement Works	N5216.35 W00123.07
	Draycott Water	N5219.57 W00119.58
	Nuneaton Disused AD	N5233.90 W00126.88
Cranfield	Olney Town	N5209.20 W00042.10
	Stewartby Brickworks	N5204.40 W00031.05
	Woburn Town	N5159.40 W00037.15
Dundee	Broughty Castle	N5627.75 W00252.18
Exeter	Axminster	N5046.90 W00259.90
	Crediton	N5047.43 W00339.08
	Cullompton	N5051.47 W00323.63
	Exmouth	N5037.48 W00324.13
	Topsham	N5041.38 W00328.82
Farnborough	Alton	N5109.12 W00057.97
	Bagshot	N5120.95 W00041.95
	Farnborough Railway Station	N5117.79 W00045.30
	Guilford	N5114.37 W00035.10
	Hook	N5116.77 W00057.72
Humberside	Brigg	N5333.20 W00029.20
	Castor	N5329.77 W00019.10
	Elsham Wolds	N5336.52 W00025.68
	Immingham Docks	N5337.70 W00011.60
	Laceby Crossroads	N5332.12 W00010.82
	North Tower Humber Bridge	N5342.85 W00027.03
Inverness	Dingwall	N5735.97 W00425.88
	Dores	N5722.92 W00419.92
	Invergordon	N5741.53 W00410.05
	Lochindrob	N5724.17 W00342.95
	Tomatin	N5720.02 W00359.50
Islay	Mull of Oa	N5535.50 W00620.30
	North Coast	N5556.00 W00609.90
	Port Ellen	N5538.00 W00611.40
	Rhinns Point	N5540.40 W00629.10

Airfield	VRP	Position
Kirkwall	Foot	N5901.72 W00248.38
	Lamb Holm Island	N5853.23 W00253.60
	Stromberry	N5901.82 W00256.02
Londonderry	Buncrana	N5508.00 W00727.40
	Coleraine	N5507.90 W00640.30
	Dungiven	N5455.70 W00655.50
	Moville	N5511.40 W00702.40
	New Buildings	N5457.50 W00721.50
Middle Wallop	Andover	N5112.54 W00131.65
	Grateley	N5110.24 W00136.57
	Harewood	N5110.64 W00127.64
	Stockbridge	N5106.81 W00129.22
Plymouth	Avon Estuary	N5017.00 W00353.00
	Ivy Bridge	N5023.08 W00355.10
	Saltash Roundabout	N5025.13 W00414.08
	Yelverton Roundabout	N5029.52 W00405.22
Scatsta	Brae	N6023.82 W00121.23
	Fugla	N6026.95 W00119.43
	Hillswick	N6028.55 W00129.32
	Voe	N6021.00 W00115.97
Scilly Isles	Pendeen Lighthouse	N5009.88 W00540.30
	St Martins Head	N4958.05 W00615.95
Shoreham	Brighton Marina	N5048.65 W00006.05
	Lewes Int A27/A26 Jct	N5051.87 E00001.45
	Littlehampton	N5048.77 W00032.78
	Washington Int A24/A283	N5054.57 W00024.47
Southend	Billericay	N5138.00 E00025.00
	Maldon	N5143.70 E00041.00
	Sheerness	N5126.50 E00044.90
	South Woodham Ferrers	N5139.00 E00037.00
	St Marys Marsh	N5128.50 E00036.00
Warton	Blackburn	N5344.85 W00228.78
	Formby Point	N5333.12 W00306.32
	Garstang	N5354.38 W00246.55
	M6 Jct 28/M58 Jct	N5332.07 W00241.87
	Castletown Disused AD	N5835.07 W00321.01
Wick	Duncansby Head Lighthouse	N5838.60 W00301.50
	Keiss Village	N5832.00 W00307.40
	Loch Watten	N5829.00 W00320.10
	Lybster Village	N5818.00 W00317.10
	Thrumster Masts	N5823.58 W00307.43

Airfield	VRP	Position
Aberdeen	Banchory	N5703.00 W00230.10
	Meldrum TV Mast	N5723.20 W00224.00
	Insch	N5720.57 W00236.85
	Peterhead	N5730.42 W00146.60
	Stonehaven	N5657.75 W00212.60
	Turiff	N5732.32 W00227.60
Belfast Aldergrove	Ballymena	N5451.80 W00616.40
	Cluntoe Disused AD	N5437.23 W00632.03
	Divis	N5436.45 W00600.57
	Glengormley M2 J4	N5440.83 W00558.90
	Larne	N5451.20 W00549.52
	Portadown	N5425.50 W00626.85
	Toome Disused AD	N5445.47 W00629.67
Belfast City	Comber	N5433.05 W00544.75
	Groomsport	N5440.50 W00537.08
	Saintfield	N5427.62 W00549.97
	Whitehead	N5445.17 W00542.57
Bournemouth	Hengistbury Head	N5042.72 W00144.93
	Sandbanks	N5041.00 W00156.83
	Stoney Cross Disused AD	N5054.70 W00139.42
	Tarrant Rushton Disused AD	N5051.00 W00204.70
Bristol	Barrow Tanks Reservoirs	N5124.58 W00239.77
	Bath	N5122.70 W00221.42
	Cheddar Reservoir	N5116.78 W00248.08
	Chew Valley	N5119.50 W00235.70
	Churchill	N5120.00 W00247.60
	Clevedon	N5126.35 W00251.08
	East Nailsea	N5125.80 W00244.10
	Hicks Gate Roundabout	N5125.52 W00231.00
	Portishead	N5129.70 W00246.42
	Radstock	N5117.53 W00226.92
	Weston Super Mare	N5120.70 W00258.33
Brize Norton	Bampton	N5143.50 W00132.80
	Burford	N5148.40 W00138.20
	Charlbury	N5152.30 W00128.90
	Faringdon	N5139.30 W00135.20
	Farmoor Reservoir	N5145.20 W00121.40
	Lechlade	N5141.60 W00141.40
	North Leach Roundabout	N5150.25 W00150.15
Cardiff	Cardiff Docks	N5127.40 W00309.10
	Flat Holm Lighthouse	N5122.55 W00307.13
	Lavernock Point	N5124.38 W00310.23
	M4 J36	N5131.93 W00334.40
	Minehead	N5112.35 W00328.50
	Nash Point Lighthouse	N5124.08 W00333.33
	Nash South	N5122.88 W00333.45
	St Hilary TV Mast	N5127.45 W00324.18
	Wenvoe TV Mast	N5127.57 W00316.90

Airfield	VRP	Position
Channel Islands	Alderney NDB	N4942.53 W00211.98
	Carteret Lighthouse	N4922.00 W00148.00
	Casquets Lighthouse	N4943.00 W00222.00
	Corbiere Lighthouse	N4911.00 W00215.00
	East of Iles Chausey	N4853.00 W00139.00
	Granville	N4850.00 W00139.00
	Ile de Brehat	N4851.00 W00300.00
	Minquiers	N4857.00 W00208.00
	North East Point	N49.30.42 W00230.52
	South East Corner	N4910.00 W00202.00
	St Germain	N4914.00 W00138.00
	West of Minquiers	N4857.00 W00218.00
Durham Tees Valley	A1(M)/A66(M) Jct	N5430.00 W00137.60
	Hartlepool	N5441.00 W00112.83
	Northallerton	N5420.33 W00125.92
	Redcar Racecourse	N5436.43 W00103.85
	Sedgefield Racecourse	N5438.75 W00128.10
	Stokesley	N5428.18 W00111.68
East Midlands	Bottesford	N5257.88 W00046.90
	Church Boughton	N5253.17 W00141.90
	M1 J22	N5241.73 W00117.55
	M42 J11	N5241.33 W00132.88
	Melton Mowbray	N5244.37 W00053.57
	Trowell	N5257.70 W00116.05
Edinburgh	Arthurs Seat	N5556.63 W00309.70
	Bathgate	N5554.17 W00338.42
	Cobbinshaw Reservoir	N5548.47 W00334.00
	Dalkeith	N5553.60 W00304.10
	Forth Rd Bridge North Tower	N5600.37 W00324.23
	Hillend Ski Slope	N5553.30 W00312.50
	Kelty	N5608.08 W00323.25
	Kirkcaldy Harbour	N5606.83 W00309.00
	Kirkliston	N5557.33 W00324.18
	Kirknewton	N5553.25 W00325.08
	M9 J2	N5558.90 W00330.72
	Musselburgh	N5556.83 W00302.42
	Penicuik	N5549.92 W00313.42
	Polmont	N5559.33 W00341.00
	West Linton	N5545.17 W00321.45
Glasgow	Alexandria	N5559.33 W00434.59
	Ardmore Point	N5558.29 W00441.96
	Baillieston	N5551.17 W00405.37
	Barrhead	N5548.00 W00423.50
	Bishopton	N5554.13 W00430.10
	Dumbarton	N5556.67 W00434.10
	East Kilbride	N5545.84 W00410.33
	Erskine Bridge	N5555.22 W00427.77
	Greenock	N5556.83 W00445.08

Airfield	VRP	Position
	Inverkip Power Station	N5553.90 W00453.20
	Kilmacolm	N5553.67 W00437.65
	Kilmarnock	N5536.75 W00429.90
	Kingston Bridge	N5551.37 W00416.18
Isle of Man	Laxey	N5413.75 W00424.10
	Peel	N5413.33 W00441.50
Leeds Bradford	Dewsbury	N5341.50 W00138.10
	Eccup Reservoir	N5352.27 W00132.60
	Harrogate	N5359.50 W00131.60
	Keighley	N5352.00 W00154.60
Liverpool	Aintree Racecourse	N5328.60 W00256.58
	Burtonwood	N5325.00 W00238.28
	Chester	N5311.70 W00250.68
	Kirkby	N5328.80 W00252.90
	Neston	N5317.50 W00303.60
	Oulton Park	N5310.57 W00236.80
	Seaforth	N5327.68 W00302.08
	Stretton Disused AD	N5320.77 W00231.58
London Gatwick	Billinghurst	N5100.90 W00027.00
	Dorking	N5113.62 W00020.10
London Gatwick	Guildford	N5114.37 W00035.10
	Handcross	N5103.17 W00012.13
	Haywards Heath	N5100.45 W00005.77
	Tunbridge Wells	N5108.00 E00015.90
London Luton	Hemel	N5145.37 W00024.97
	Hyde	N5150.65 W00021.96
	Pirton	N5158.30 W00019.90
London Stansted	Audley End Railway Station	N5200.25 E00012.42
	Braintree	N5152.70 E00033.23
	Chelmsford	N5144.00 E00028.40
	Diamond Hangar	N5152.67 E00014.15
	Epping	N5142.00 E00006.67
	Great Dunmow	N5152.30 E00021.75
	Haverhill	N5204.95 E00026.07
	North End Hangar 4	N5153.32 E00013.53
	Nuthampstead AD	N5159.40 E00003.72
	Puckeridge A10/A120 Jct	N5153.10 E00000.27
	Ware	N5148.70 W00001.60
Lyneham	Avebury	N5125.68 W00151.28
	Blakehill Farm	N5137.00 W00153.10
	Calne	N5126.20 W00200.30
	Chippenham	N5127.60 W00207.40
	Clyffe Pypard	N5129.40 W00153.70
	Devizes	N5120.80 W00159.30
	M4 J15	N5131.60 W00143.48
	M4 J16	N5132.70 W00151.25
	M4 J17	N5130.88 W00207.30
	Malmesbury	N5135.10 W00206.20

Airfield	VRP	Position
	Marlborough	N5125.20 W00143.70
	Melksham	N5122.50 W00208.30
	South Marston	N5135.40 W00144.10
	Wroughton	N5130.55 W00147.98
Manchester	Alderley Edge Hill	N5317.72 W00212.73
	Barton AD	N5328.27 W00223.42
	Buxton	N5315.35 W00154.77
	Congleton	N5309.90 W00210.85
	Jodrell Bank	N5314.18 W00218.55
	Rostherne	N5321.23 W00223.12
	Sale Water Park	N5326.00 W00218.17
	Stretton Disused AD	N5320.77 W00231.58
	Swinton Intercharge	N5331.40 W00221.60
	Thelwall Viaduct	N5323.43 W00230.35
Newcastle	Blaydon	N5458.10 W00141.62
	Blyth Power Station	N5508.50 W00131.50
	Bolam Lake	N5507.88 W00152.47
	Durham	N5446.43 W00134.60
	Hexham	N5458.25 W00206.17
	Morpeth Railway Station	N5509.75 W00140.97
	Ouston Disused AD	N5501.50 W00152.52
	Stagshaw Masts	N5502.00 W00201.42
	Tyne Bridges	N5458.05 W00136.42
Prestwick	Culzean Bay/Castle	N5522.17 W00446.08
	Cumnock	N5527.33 W00415.45
	Doonfoot	N5526.25 W00439.03
	Heads of Ayr	N5525.97 W00442.78
	Irvine Harbour	N5536.50 W00440.90
	Kilmarnock	N5536.75 W00429.90
	Pladda	N5525.58 W00507.07
	West Kilbride	N5541.13 W00452.08
Southampton	Bishops Waltham	N5057.28 W00112.58
	Calshot	N5049.07 W00119.75
	Romsey	N5059.45 W00129.75
	Totton	N5055.20 W00129.33
Sumburgh	Bodam	N5955.10 W00116.10
	Mousa	N6000.00 W00109.60

PROHIBITED Area (prefix P). Airspace within which the flight of ACFT is prohibited.
RESTRICTED Area (prefix R). Airspace within the flight of ACFT is restricted in accordance with certain specified condition.

All prohibited and restricted areas extend upwards from the surface, unless otherwise noted.
# indicates an area where pilots are warned that entry (even if in advertent) might make the ACFT liable to counter measures.
The phrase 'subject to appropriate permission' should be taken to mean that prior written permission must be obtained from the authority listed in the RAC section of the AIP, and the flight must be carried out subject to any conditions contained within such permission.

ALWAYS CHECK PROHIBITED/RESTRICTED AREA INFORMATION BY THE LATEST AIP & NOTAM INFORMATION, IF IN DOUBT – STAY OUT!

Identification/ Name	Upper Vertical Limit (AMSL)	Type of restriction	Remarks
R002 Devonport	2000	Restricted	Flight permitted if taking off or landing at HMS Drake Helicopter Landing Site subject to appropriate permission. Helicopters are permitted to take-off or land at a ship in the Devonport Dockyard subject to appropriate permission.
P047 Winfrith	1000	Prohibited	
R063 Dungeness	2000	Restricted	Flight permitted if taking off or landing at the helicopter area at Dungeness, subject to appropriate permission. Flight permitted if taking off or landing at London Ashford Airport (Lydd) in accordance with normal practice, remaining at least 1.5nm from Dungeness.
R095 Sark	2374	Restricted	Flight not permitted without permission from States Board of Administration, Guernsey. Sark is within UK territorial waters although within Brest FIR.
R101 Aldermaston	2400	Restricted	Flight permitted if taking off or landing at the helicopter landing area at Aldermaston, subject to appropriate permission.
R104 Burghfield	2400	Restricted	Flight permitted if taking off or landing at the helicopter landing area at Burghfield, subject to appropriate permission.
R105 Highgrove House	2000	Restricted	Applies only to helicopters and microlight ACFT.
P106 Harwell	2500	Prohibited	Flight permitted if taking off or landing at the helicopter landing area at Harwell, subject to appropriate permission.
R107 Belmarsh	2000	Restricted	Applies only to helicopters. Flight by helicopter permitted if carrying out an IFR approach from the E to London City AD. Flight permitted by any helicopter operated by or on behalf of a Police Force for any area within the UK.
R153 Hinkley Point	2000	Restricted	Flight permitted if taking off or landing at the helicopter area at Hinkley Point, subject to appropriate permission. Flight permitted by a helicopter flying within Bridgewater Bay Danger Area with permission from person in charge of the area, remaining at least 1nm from Hinkley Point.
R154 Oldbury	2000	Restricted	Flight permitted if taking off or landing at the helicopter area at Oldbury, subject to appropriate permission.
R155 Berkeley	2000	Restricted	Flight permitted if taking off or landing at the helicopter area at Berkeley, subject to appropriate permission.
R156 Bradwell	2000	Restricted	Flight permitted if taking off or landing at the helicopter area at Bradwell, subject to appropriate permission. Flight at a height >1500ft amsl whilst conducting Instrument APP procedure at Southend Airport.
R157 Hyde Park	1400	Restricted	Flight permitted by any aircraft flying in accordance with a special notification flight or any helicopter flying on route H4 with clearances issued by the appropriate ATC unit.
R158 City of London	1400	Restricted	Flight permitted by any aircraft flying in accordance with a special notification flight or any helicopter flying on route H4 with clearances issued by the appropriate ATC unit.
R159 Isle of Dogs	1400	Restricted	Flight permitted by any aircraft flying in accordance with a special notification flight or any helicopter flying on route H4 with clearances issued by the appropriate ATC unit.
R160 The Specified Area	Unlimited	Restricted	Except with PPR from CAA helicopters shall not fly over this area of Central London below such height deemed safe in the event of engine failure.
R204 Long Lartin	2200	Restricted	Applies only to helicopters other than Police Force Operations.
R212 Whitemoor	2000	Restricted	Applies only to helicopters other than Police Force Operations.
R214 Woodhill	2400	Restricted	Applies only to helicopters other than Police Force Operations.
R217 Sizewell	2000	Restricted	Flight permitted if taking off or landing at the helicopter area at Sizewell, subject to appropriate permission.
R218 Trawsfynydd	2700	Restricted	Flight permitted if taking off or landing at the helicopter area at Trawsfynydd, subject to appropriate permission.

Identification/ Name	Upper Vertical Limit (AMSL)	Type of restriction	Remarks
R311 Capenhurst	2200 Upper Vertical	Restricted	
R312 Springfields	2100	Restricted	Flight permitted at not less than 1670ft amsl for the purpose of landing at Blackpool AD. Flight permitted S of a line N5346.44 W00244.54 to N5345.13 W00250.44 for the purpose of landing or taking off at Warton AD. Flight permitted if taking off or landing at the helicopter landing area at Springfields, subject to appropriate permission.
R313 Scampton	9500	Restricted	Active Mon-Fri 0830-1700 (Winter), 0730-1600 (Summer) and as notified by NOTAM when Red Arrows are training. Pre-flight information Tel: 01522 733055 Tel: 01522 727451/727452. Waddington RAD 127.35
R315 Full Sutton	2000	Restricted	Applies only to helicopters other than Police Force Operations.
R319 Manchester	1700	Restricted	Applies only to helicopters other than Police Force Operations
R321 Wakefield	1600	Restricted	Applies only to helicopters other than Police Force Operations
R322 Wylfa	2100	Restricted	Flight permitted <2000ft agl, whilst operating in accordance with RAF Valley. Flight permitted if taking off or landing at the helicopter area at Valley, subject to the appropriate permission.
R413 Sellafield	2200	Restricted	Flight permitted if taking off or landing at the helicopter landing area at Sellafield, subject to appropriate permission.
R431 Maghaberry #	2000	Restricted	Flight permitted for the purpose of landing or taking off at Belfast Aldergrove if the ACFT is under the control of Belfast Aldergrove ATC.
R432 Frankland/Durham	2200	Restricted	Applies only to helicopters other than Police Force Operations
R444 Heysham	2000	Restricted	Flight permitted if taking off or landing at the helicopter area at Heysham, subject to appropriate permission. Microlight access to Middleton Sands obtained via BMAA office.
R445 Barrow in Furness	2000	Restricted	Flight permitted if taking off or landing at the helicopter area at Barrow in Furness, subject to appropriate permission.
R446 Hartlepool	2000	Restricted	Flight permitted if taking off or landing at the helicopter area at Hartlepool, subject to appropriate permission. Flight <1800ft amsl whilst conducting an Instrument APP to Durham Tees Valley AD.
R501 Chapelcross	2400	Restricted	Flight permitted if taking off or landing at the helicopter landing area at Chapelcross. Subject to appropriate permission.
R504 Shotts	2800	Restricted	Flight permitted by any helicopter operated by or on behalf of a Police Force for any area of the UK
R515 Hunterston	2000	Restricted	Flights permitted for purpose of landing or take off at the Helicopter area at Hunterston. Subject to appropriate permission.
R516 Torness	2100	Restricted	Flights permitted for purpose of landing or take off at the Helicopter area at Torness. Subject to appropriate permission.
R603 Rosyth	2000	Restricted	Flight permitted within Kelty Lane if APP to land at, or Dept from, Edinburgh AD
R610A The Highlands	5000	Restricted	Flight permitted outside the Hrs of the Highlands Restricted Area (HRA) and during Scottish public holidays. Areas generally active Mon-Thu 1500-2300 (Winter) 1400-2200 (Summer) When HRA is active, crossing permission may be possible from Tain Range 122.75. Entry may also be possible subject to authorisation if requested from the Military Tactical Booking Cell Tel: 0800 515544 before the proposed flight.
R610B The Highlands	5000 750	Restricted	Lower limit 750ft AMSL. See notes for R610A.
R610C The Highlands	2000	Restricted	See notes for R610A.
R610D The Highlands	2000	Restricted	See notes for R610A.
P611 Coulport/Faslane	2200	Prohibited	
R612 Arbroath	6000	Restricted	Activity info available from Leuchars Tel: 01334 838722
P813 Dounreay	2100	Prohibited	

Temporary Restricted Airspace, Red Arrows Displays, Emergency Restrictions of Flying and Royal Flights

The latest information regarding Temporary Restricted Airspace, Red Arrows displays, Emergency Restrictions of Flying and Royal flights is all available by dialling a specially provided Freephone number. The number is:

0500 354802

Danger Areas

DANGER Area (D) Airspace within which activities dangerous to the flight of ACFT may exist or take place.
DACS Danger Area Crossing Service
DAAIS Danger Area Activity Information Service

The first frequency given is the primary frequency to be contacted during the Hrs of operation. Where a second frequency is given , this should be called if contact cannot be established on the first frequency. The second frequency is sometimes a FIR controller frequency. These frequencies often very busy, or even not manned, so you cannot always rely on establishing contact and obtaining a DACS/DAAIS on such a frequency.
All danger areas extend upwards from the surface, unless otherwise noted.
= Hrs of activity are one hour earlier during the summer period.

ALWAYS CHECK DANGER AREA INFORMATION BY THE LATEST AIP, PRE-FLIGHTINFORMATION BULLETIN & NOTAM INFORMATION. AND IF IN DOUBT – STAY OUT!

*Subject to co-ordination procedures above 22000

Identification/ Name	Upper Limit (AMSL)	Hours of Activity (UTC)	Remarks
D001 Trevose Head	1000	Mon-Thu 0800-2359 Fri 0800-1800 #	DACS: St Mawgan APP 128.725 DAAIS: London Info 124.750
D003 Plymouth	Up to 55000 SFC*	Mon-Thu 0800-2359 Fri 0800-1600 # & as notified	DACS: Plymouth Mil 121.250 London Info 124.750 Pre-flight Info Tel: 01752 557550
D004 Plymouth	Up to 55000 SFC*	Mon-Thu 0800-2359 Fri 0800-1600 # & as notified	DACS: Plymouth Mil 121.250 London Info 124.750 Pre-flight Info Tel: 01752 557550
D006 Falmouth Bay	1500	Mon-Thu 0800-2359 Fri 0800-1600 # & as notified	DACS: Culdrose APP 134.050 DAAIS: London Info 124.750 Pre-flight Info Tel: 01326 552201
D006A Falmouth Bay	Up to 22000	Mon-Thu 0800-2359 Fri 0800-1600 # & as notified	DACS: Plymouth Mil 121.250 London Info 124.750 Pre-flight Info Tel: 01326 552201
D007 Fowey Inner	2000	Mon-Thu 0800-2359 Fri 0800-1600 # & as notified	DACS: Plymouth Mil 121.250 London Info 124.750 Pre-flight Info Tel: 01637 872201 Ex 2045/2046
D007A Fowey	Up to 22000	Mon-Thu 0800-2359 Fri 0800-1600 # & as notified	DACS: Plymouth Mil 121.250 London Info 124.750 Pre-flight Info Tel: 01752 557550
D007B Fowey	Up to 22000	Mon-Thu 0800-2359 Fri 0800-1600 # & as notified	As for D007A
D008 Plymouth	Up to 55000	Mon-Thu 0800-2359 Fri 0800-1600 # & as notified	As for D007A
D008A Plymouth	Up to 22000	Mon-Thu 0800-2359 Fri 0800-1600 # & as notified	As for D007A
D008B Plymouth	Up to 55000 SFC*	Mon-Thu 0800-2359 Fri 0800-1600 # & as notified	As for D007A
D009 Wembury	Up to 22000	Mon-Thu 0800-2359 Fri 0800-1600 # & as notified	As for D007A
D009A Wembury	Up to 55000	Mon-Thu 0800-2359 Fri 0800-1600 # & as notified	As for D007A
D011 Dartmoor	10000 OCNL Notification to 24100	Mon-Fri 0800-2359 # & as notified	Nil
D012 Lyme Bay	Up to 18000 OCNL Notification to 25000	Mon-Thu 0800-2359 # Fri 0800-1600 # & as notified	DACS: Plymouth Mil 124.150 or London Info 124.750 Pre-flight Info Tel: 01752 557550

Identification/ Name	Upper Limit (AMSL)	Hours of Activity (UTC)	Remarks
D013 Lyme Bay	Up to 60000	Mon-Thu 0800-2359 # Fri 0800-1600 # & as notified	As D012
D014 Portland	5000 OCNL Notification to 15000	Mon-Thu 0800-2359 Fri 0800-1600 # & as notified	DACS: Plymouth Mil 124.150 or London Info 124.750 Tel: 01752 557550
D015 Bovington	3600	When notified	DAAIS: Bournemouth TWR 125.600
D017 Portland	22000 OCNL Notification to 55000	Mon-Thu 0800-2359 # Fri 0800-1600 # & as notified	DACS: Plymouth Mil 124.15 or London Info 124.750 Pre-flight Info Tel: 01752 557550
D021Portland	Up to 15000	Mon-Thu 0800-2359 # Fri 0800-1600 # & as notified	As D017
D023 Portland	22000 OCNL Notification to 55000	Mon-Thu 0800-2359 # Fri 0800-1600 # & as notified	As D017
D026 Lulworth	15000	Mon-Thu 0800-2359 Fri 0800-1600 & as notified	DAAIS: London Info 124.750 Pre-flight Info Tel: 01752 557550
D031 Portland	As notified up to 15000	Mon-Thu 0800-2359 # Fri 0800-1600 # & as notified	DACS: Plymouth Mil 124.150 London Info 124.750 Pre-flight Info Tel: 01752 557550
D036 Portsmouth	19000 OCNL Notification to 55000	Mon-Thu 0800-1700 # Fri 0800-1400 # & as notified	DACS: Plymouth Mil 124.150 DAAIS: London Info 124.750 Pre-flight Info Tel: 01752 557751
D037 Portsmouth	55000	Mon-Fri 1000-1800 # & as notified	DAAIS: London Info 124.750 or 124.600
D038 Portsmouth	55000	Mon-Fri 0800-1800 # & as notified	As D037
D039 Portsmouth	55000	Mon-Fri 0800-1800 # & as notified	As D037
D040 Portsmouth	22000 OCNL Notification to 55000	Mon-Fri 0800-1800 # & as notified	As D037
D044 Lydd Ranges	4000	H24	DAAIS: Lydd Info 120.700 London Info 124.600
D061 Woodbury Common	1500	When notified	DAAIS: Exeter APP 128.975 when open
D064A South West MDA	FL 660 10000 ONCL Notification from ALT 5000 to FL 660	When Notified	Air combat and training exercises of ACFT engaged in high energy manoeuvres Pre flight notification Tel: RAF Boulmer 01665 572312
D064B South West MDA	FL 660 10000 ONCL Notification from AIT 5000 to FL 660	When notified	As D064A
D064C South West MDA	FL 660 10000 ONCL Notification from ALT 5000 to FL 660	When notified	As D064A
D110 Braunton Burrows	2000	When notified	DAAIS: London Info 124.750
D113A Castlemartin	15200 ONCL Notification to 40000	Mon-Fri 0830-2359 # & as notified	DAAIS: London Info 124.750

Identification/ Name	Upper Limit (AMSL)	Hours of Activity (UTC)	Remarks
D113B Castlemartin	15200 ONCL Notification up to 45000 Upper	Mon-Fri 0830-2359 # & as notified	DAAIS: London 124.750
D115A Manorbier	23000 ONCL Notification to 27000	Mon-Fri 0830-1700 # & as notified	DAAIS: London Info 124.750
D115B Manorbier	40000 OCNL Notification to 50000	Mon-Fri 0830-1700 # & as notified	DAAIS: London Info 124.750
D117 Pendine	23000 ONCL Notification to 27000	Mon-Fri 0800-1800 # & as notified No firing during public holidays	DAAIS: Pembrey Range 122.750 London Info 124.750
D118 Pembrey	23000 5000	Mon-Thu 0900-1700 # Fri 0900-1400 # & as notified SR-SS outside main activity ops Hrs	DAAIS: Pembrey Range 122.750 DAAIS: not available
D119 Bridgewater Bay	5000	When notified	DAAIS: Yeovilton APP 127.350 London Info 124.750
D121 St. Thomas Head	600	H24	DAAIS: Bristol APP 125.650 London Info 124.750
D123 Imber	Up to 50000	H24	DACS: Salisbury Ops 122.750 DAAIS: ATIS 122.75 0 Pre-flight Info Tel: 01980 674730 or Tel: 01980 674710 DAAIS: Tel: 01980 674739
D124 Lavington	As notified up to unlimited	When notified	As D123
D125 Larkhill	Up to 50000	H24	As D123
D126 Bulford	1400 OCNL Notification to 2500	H24	As D123
D127 Porton	12000 8000 OCNL Notification to 12000	0600-1800 daily 1800-0600 daily	DAAIS: Boscombe Down Zone 126.700 London Info 124.750
D128 Everleigh	1400 OCNL Notification to 50000	H24	As D123
D129 Weston-on-Green	FL120	H24	DAAIS: Brize RAD 124.275
D130 Longmoor	1800 2300	H24 Mon-Fri	Farnborough APP 125.250 London Info 124.600 Pre flight Info Tel: 0208 7453451
D131 Hankley Common	1400	When notified	DAAIS: Farnborough APP 125.250 London Info 124.600
D132 Ash Ranges	As notified up to 2500	When notified	DAAIS: Farnborough APP 125.250 London Info 124.600
D133 Pirbright	1200 OCNL Notification to 2400	0800-2359# & as notified	DAAIS: Farnborough APP 125.250 London Info 124.600
D133A Pirbright	1200	0800-2359 # & as notified	As D133
D136 Shoeburyness	10000	When notified Mon-Fri 0800-1800 #	DAAIS: Southend APP 130.775 London Info 124.600
D138 Shoeburyness	Up to 35000 OCNL Notification to 60000	Mon-Fri 0600-1800 # & when notified	As D136

Identification/ Name	Upper Limit (AMSL)	Hours of Activity (UTC)	Remarks
D138A Shoeburyness	Up to 35000 OCNL Notification to 60000	Mon-Fri 0600-1800 # & when notified	As D136
D138B Shoeburyness	5000	When notified as D138	As D136
D139 Fingringhoe	1500 OCNL Notification to 2000 Upper	H24	Nil
D141 Hythe Ranges	3200	H24	DAAIS: Lydd Info 120.700 London Info 124.600
D145 Hullavington	2000	When notified	DAAIS: Lyneham Zone 123.400
D146 Yantlet	3000	When notified 0800-1700 #	DAAIS: Southend APP 130.775
D147 Pontrilas	10000	H24	Nil
D201 Aberporth	Unlimited	Mon-Fri 0800-2300 # & as notified	DACS: Aberporth Info 119.650 Swanwick Mil 135.150
D201A Aberporth	Unlimited	Mon-Fri 0800-2300 # & as notified	As D201
D201B Aberporth	Unlimited	When notified	As D201
D201C Aberporth	Unlimited FL 55	Mon-Fri 0800-2300 # & as notified	As D201
D201D Aberporth	Unlimited FL 55	Mon-Fri 0800-2300 # & as notified	As D201
D203 Sennybridge	23000 OCNL Notification to 50000	Mon-Fri 0800-1800 #	Nil
	18000 ONCL Notification to	Mon-Fri 1800-0800 #	Nil
	50000	When notified	Nil
D206 Cardington	6000	Mon 0400 to Fri 2259 & as notified	Nil
D207 Holbeach	23000	Mon-Thu 0900-1700 Fri 0900-1200 # Sept – April inc Tue & Thur 1700-2200 # & as notified	DAAIS: London Info 124.600 DAAIS: Not available
	5000	SR-SS outside main activity Ops Hrs	Nil
D208 Stanford	2500 OCNL Notification to 7500	H24	DAAIS: Lakenheath Zone 128.900
D211 Swynnerton	As notified up to 2400	When notified	Nil
D213 Kineton	2400	When notified	DAAIS: Coventry APP 119.250 Coventry ATIS 126.050
D215 North Luffenham	2400	When notified	DAAIS: Cottesmore APP 130.200
D216 Credenhill	2300 OCNL Notification to	H24	Nil
	10000	When notified	Nil
D304 Upper Hulme	3500	When notified 0800-1800 # occassionaly up to 2100 Oct-Mar inc	DAAIS: Manchester APP 135.000
D305 Beckingham	1500	When notified	Nil
D306 Cowden	5000	SR-SS	Nil
D307 Donna Nook	20000 OCNL Notification to 23000	Mon-Thu 0900-1630 Fri 0900-1500 # Sep-Apr inc Tue & Thu 1630-2200 # & as notified	DAAIS: Donna Nook Range Control 122.750
	5000	SR-SS outside main activity Ops Hrs	DAAIS: Not available
D308 Wainfleet	23000	Mon & Wed 1400-2200 # Tue & Thurs 0900-1700 # Fri 0900-1500 # & as notified Mon-Fri only	DAAIS: Wainfleet Range Control 122.750
	5000	SR-SS outside main activity Ops Hrs	DAAIS: Not available
D314 Harpur Hill	2900	Mon-Fri 0800-1900 #	DAAIS: Manchester APP 135.000
D323A Southern MDA	As notified up to FL 660 As notified up from FL 50	When notified	Pre-flight RAF Boulmer Tel: 01665 572312 Airspace Booking Tel: 01489 612495

Identification/ Name	Upper Limit (AMSL)	Hours of Activity (UTC)	Remarks
D323B Southern MDA	As notified up to FL 660 As notified up from FL 50	When notified	As D323A
D323C Southern MDA	As notified up to FL 660 As notified up from FL 50	Mon-Fri 0800-1800 # & as notified	As D323A
D323D Southern MDA	As notified up to FL 660 As notified up from FL 250	When notified	As D323A
D323E Southern MDA	As notified up to FL 660 As notified up from FL 250	When notified	As D323A
D323F Southern MDA	As notified Up to FL 660 As notified up From FL 250	When notified	As D323A
D401 Ballykinler	3200	0800-2359 # daily	Nil
D402A Luce Bay (N)	3000 OCNL Notification to 23000	When notified	DACS/DAAIS: Range Control 130.050 Scottish Mil via Scottish Info 119.875
D402B Luce Bay (N)	3000 OCNL Notification to 23000	When notified	As D402A
D402C Luce Bay (N)	4000	Mon-Fri 0730-1530 #	As D402A
D403 Luce Bay	Up to 35000 & as notified	Mon-Thu 0900-2230 # Fri 0900-1630 #	As D402A
D403A Luce Bay	3000	Mon-Thu 0900-1800 Fri 0900-1630	As D402A
D405 Kirkcudbright	15000 OCNL Notification to 50000	Mon-Fri 0800-2359 # & when notified	Kirkcudbright Range 122.100 (0800-1630 (L)
D405A Kirkcudbright	1000	Mon-Fri 0800-2359 #	As for D405
D406 Eskmeals	Up to 50000 OCNL Notification to 80000	Sep-Mar: Mon-Fri 0800-1700 Apr-Aug: Mon-Fri 0700-1900 # & as notified	DAAIS: London Info 125.475
D406B Eskmeals	As notified up to 50000 OCNL Notification to 80000	When notified	DAAIS: London Info 125.475
D406C Eskmeals	As notified up to 50000	When notified	DACS: Eskmeals Range 122.750
D407 Warcop	10000 OCNL Notification to 13500	Mon-Sat 0730-0200 Sun 0730-1300 #	Nil
D408 Feldom	2500 OCNL Notification to 5600	Tue-Sun 0830-1630 # & as notified	DAAIS: Leeming APP 127.750 London Info 125.475
D409 Catterick	3400	When notified	DAAIS: Leeming APP 127.750 London Info 125.475
D410 Strensall	1000	When notified 0800-1800 #	Nil
D412 Staxton	10000	When notified	DAAIS: London Info 125.475 Airspace Booking Tel: 01489 612495
D442 Bellerby	3000	H24	Nil
D505 Magilligan	2000 OCNL Notification to 6500	0800-2359 # daily	Nil
D508 Ridsdale	4100	Mon-Fri 0800-1700 # & as notified	DACS: Newcastle APP 124.375 Pre-flight Info Newcastle ATC Tel: 0870 122 1448 Ex 3251

Identification/ Name	Upper Limit (AMSL)	Hours of Activity (UTC)	Remarks
D509 Campbeltown	As notified up to 55000	When notified	DAAIS: Scottish Info 119.875
D510 Spadeadam	5500 ONCL Notification to 18000	Mon-Thurs 0900-1700 # Fri 0900-1600 # & as notified	DAAIS: Newcastle APP 124.375 Carlisle TWR 123.600 DACS: Spadeadam 128.725
D510A Spadeadam	5500 ONCL Notification to 15000	Mon-Thurs 0900-1700 # Fri 0900 1600 # & as notified	As D510
D512 Otterburn	18000 OCNL Notification to 25000	H24	DAAIS: Scottish Info 119.875
D512A Otterburn	22000	When notified	As D512
D513 Druridge Bay	10000	When notified	DAAIS: Scottish Info 119.875 Tel: 01489 612495
D513A Druridge Bay	As notified up to 23000	When notified	As D513
D513B Drurudge Bay	As notified up to 23000	When notified	As D512
D601 Garelochhead	4000	0800-2359 # daily & as notified	Nil
D602 Cultybraggan	2500	When notified	Nil
D604 Barry Buddon	1500 OCNL Notification to Max ALT 9000	H24	DAAIS: Leuchars APP 126.500
D609 St. Andrews	1000 OCNL Notification to 5000	H24	DAAIS: Scottish Info 119.875
D613A Central MDA	As notified up to FL 660 As notified up from FL 100	When notified	Pre-flight RAF Boulmer Tel: 01665 572312 Airspace Booking Tel: 01489 612495
D613B Central MDA	As notified up to FL 660 As notified up from FL 100	When notified	As D613A
D613C Central MDA	As notified up to FL 660 As notified up from FL 100	When notified	As D613A
D701 Hebrides	Up to 30000	Mon-Fri 1000-1800 # & as notified.	DAAIS: Scottish Info 127.275. When D701A is activated, D701 becomes an integral part of it & is activated to the same altitude.
D701A Hebrides	As notified up to unlimited	When notified	DAAIS: Scottish Info 127.275
D701B Hebrides	As notified up to unlimited	When notified	DAAIS: Scottish Info 127.275 Above FL 55 Stationary Temporary Airspace Reservation will be iniated by RSO Hebrides via Shanwick Oceanic.
D701C Hebrides	10000 OCNL Notification to 15000	When notified	DAAIS: Scottish Info 127.275
D701D Hebrides	As notified up To unlimited	When notified	DAAIS: Scottish Info 127.275 Above FL 55 Stationary Temporary Airspace Reservation will be iniated by RSO Hebrides via Shanwick Oceanic.
D701E Hebrides	10000	When notified Mon-Fri 1630-SS Sat 1300-SS #	DAAIS: Scottish Info 127.275 Activated after normal civilian ACFT movements at Benbecula have ceased.
D702 Fort George	2100	0800-1600 # daily & as notified	DAAIS: Inverness TWR 122.600 Scottish Info 129.225

Identification/ Name	Upper Limit (AMSL)	Hours of Activity (UTC)	Remarks
D703 Tain	15000 ONCL Notification to 22000 5000	Mon-Thu 0900-2200 Fri 0900-1400 SR-SS outside main Ops Hrs	ACFT visiting Dornoch or Fearn AD during range opening Hrs Contact Tain Range 122.750 DAAIS: not available
D710 Raasay	1500	When notified Mon-Sat SR-SS	DAAIS: Scottish Info 127.275
D712A Northern MDA	As notified up to FL 660 As notified up from FL 245	When notified	Pre-flight RAF Boulmer Tel: 01665 572312 Airspace Booking Tel: 01489 612495
D712B Northern MDA	As notified up to FL 660 As notified up from FL 245	When notified	As D712A
D712C Northern MDA	As notified up to FL 660 As notified up from FL 245	When notified	As D712A
D712D Northern MDA	As notified up to FL 660 As notified up from FL 245	When notified	As D712A
D801 Cape Wrath (NW)	As notified up to 55000	When notified	DAAIS: Scottish Info 129.225
D802 Cape Wrath (SE)	As notified up to 55000	When notified	As D801
D803 Garvie Island	As notified up to 40000	When notified Mon-Fri 0800-1800 #	DAAIS: Scottish Info 129.225
D807 Moray Firth	1500	Mon-Fri 0700-2359 # & as notified	DAAIS: Lossiemouth Dept 119.350
D809 (N) Moray Firth (North)	As notified up to 55000	When notified	DAAIS: Scottish Info 129.225
D809 (C) Moray Firth (Central)	As notified up to 55000	When notified	As D809 (N)
D809 (S) Moray Firth (South)	As notified up to 55000	When notified	As D809 (N)

Culdrose

Vertical limits:	Surface to 5800ft
Activity:	Considerable helicopter & fixed-wing activity. Night operations may take place with ACFT using reduced navigation/anti-collision lights.
Active Times:	Peak activity Mon-Thur 0730-1600 Fri 0730-1530 (Summer) + 1Hr (Winter)
Contact Frequencies:	Culdrose LARS 134.050

Kinloss/Lossiemouth

Vertical limits:	Surface to FL150
Activity:	Intensive military activity
Active Times:	Peak activity Mon-Thur 0700-2259 Fri 0700-1700 (Summer) + 1Hr (Winter)
Contact Frequencies:	Lossiemouth LARS 119.350

Lincolnshire

Vertical limits:	2500ft ALT to FL180
Activity:	Considerable military flight training
Active Times:	Peak activity Mon-Fri 0600-1500 (Summer) + 1Hr (Winter)
Contact Frequencies:	Waddington LARS 127.350 Cottesmore LARS 130.200 Coningsby LARS 120.800

Oxford

Vertical limits:	Surface to 5000ft ALT
Activity:	Intensive military and civilian activity from the many aerodromes in this area, heavy jet, training, instrument etc.
Active Times:	Permanently active
Contact Frequencies:	Brize Radar LARS 124.275

Spadeadam

Vertical limits:	Surface to 4500ft
Activity:	Military activity associated with electronic warfare training range D510
Active Times:	Peak activity Mon-Thur 0800-1600 Fri 0500-1500 (Summer) + 1Hr (Winter) and as notified
Contact Frequencies:	DACS: Spadeadam APP 122.100 Hrs as above DAAIS: Newcastle LARS 124.375 H24 Carlisle APP 123.600

Shawbury

Vertical limits:	Surface to FL70
Activity:	Intensive instrument training, general handling and training by military helicopters and fixed-wing ACFT. Night operations may take place with ACFT using reduced navigation/anti-collision lights.
Active Times:	Permanently active Mon-Thu 0600-1230 Fri 0600-1600 (Summer) + Hr (Winter)
Contact Frequencies:	Shawbury LARS 120.775

Vale of York

Vertical limits:	Surface to FL190
Activity:	Considerable military flight training
Active Times:	Peak activity Mon-Thur 0600-2259 Fri 0600-1500 (Summer) + 1Hr (Winter)
Contact Frequencies:	Leeming LARS 127.750 Linton LARS 129.150

Valley

Vertical limits:	2000ft to 6000ft
Activity:	Considerable flight training
Active Times:	Peak activity Mon-Thur 0700-1700 Fri 0700-1600 (Summer) + 1Hr (Winter)
Contact Frequencies:	Valley LARS 125.225 London Flight Info 124.750

Wash

Vertical limits:	Surface to FL50
Activity:	Holding patterns associated with Danger Areas D207 & D308
Active Times:	Permanently active Mon-Fri
Contact Frequencies:	Waddington LARS 127.350 H24 Coningsby LARS 120.800 Marham LARS 124.150

Yeovilton

Vertical limits	Surface to 6000ft ALT
Activity	Intense helicopter instrument flying training. Night operations may take place with ACFT using reduced navigation/anti-collision lights.
Active Times	Mon-Thu 0730-1600 Fri 0730-1500 (Summer) + 1Hr (Winter)
Contact Frequencies	Yeovilton LARS 127.350 Plymouth Military Radar 124.150

Boscombe Down Advisory Radio Area

Vertical limits:	FL50 to FL245, but excluding controlled airspace.
Activity:	Considerable test flight activity. Such flights often have limited manoeuvrability and may not be able to comply with the rules of the air.
Hours of operation:	Mon-Thu 0830-1700 Fri 0830-1600 (Summer) Mon-Thu 0930-1830 Fri 0930-1030(Winter)
Contact Frequencies:	Boscombe Down 126.700 Boscombe LARS 126.700 Bournemouth APP 119.475 Bristol LARS 125.650 Bristol Filton LARS 122.725 Brize LARS 124.275 Cardiff LARS 126.625 Exeter LARS 128.975 Farnborough LARS 125.25 London Radar 135.180 Lyneham Zone 123.400 Middle Wallop APP 118.275 Plymouth LARS 121.25 & 124.15 Southampton APP 128.850 Yeovilton LARS 127.350

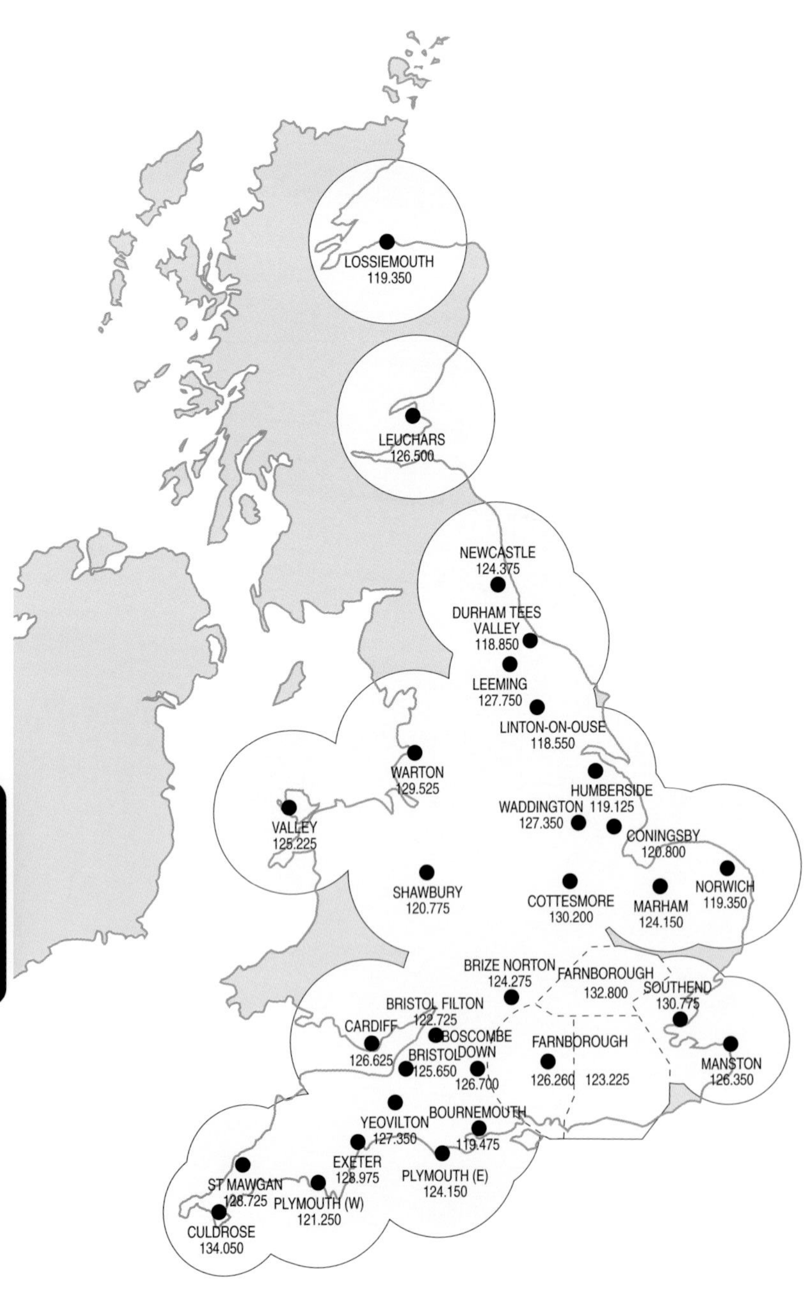
LOSSIEMOUTH
119.350
LEUCHARS
126.500
NEWCASTLE
124.375
DURHAM TEES
VALLEY
118.850
LEEMING
127.750
LINTON-ON-OUSE
118.550
WARTON
129.525
HUMBERSIDE
119.125
WADDINGTON
127.350
VALLEY
125.225
CONINGSBY
120.800
NORWICH
119.350
SHAWBURY
120.775
COTTESMORE
130.200
MARHAM
124.150
BRIZE NORTON
124.275
FARNBOROUGH
132.800
SOUTHEND
130.775
BRISTOL FILTON
122.725
CARDIFF
126.625
BOSCOMBE
DOWN
126.700
BRISTOL
125.650
FARNBOROUGH
126.260
123.225
MANSTON
126.350
YEOVILTON
127.350
BOURNEMOUTH
119.475
EXETER
128.975
PLYMOUTH (E)
124.150
ST MAWGAN
128.725
PLYMOUTH (W)
121.250
CULDROSE
134.050

Lower Airspace Radar Service (LARS) Units

Even outside the published hours, pilots should attempt to contact the LARS unit in case it is open beyond normal hours. Some LARS units (mostly military ones) may close for up to a week during holiday periods - see Pre-flight Information Bulletins.

LARS	Contact Frequency	ATC Hours
Boscombe Down	Boscombe Zone 126.700	H24 not available weekends & PH
Bournemouth	Bournemouth 119.475	0630-2130
Bristol	Bristol APP 125.650	H24
Bristol Filton	Filton APP 122.725	Mon-Fri 0700-1700 (Summer) + 1Hr (Winter) Service north of River Avon
Brize Norton	Brize 124.275	H24
Cardiff	Cardiff APP 126.625	0500-2200 (Summer) + 1Hr (Winter)
Coningsby	Coningsby 120.800	Mon-Fri 0800-1700
Cottesmore	Cottesmore 130.200	Mon-Fri 0800-1700
Culdrose	Culdrose 134.050	Mon-Thu 0830-1700 or SS Fri 0830-1400 or SS
Durham Tees Valley	Teeside APP 118.850	H24
Exeter	Exeter APP 128.975	Mon 0600-2359 Tue-Fri 0001-0100 0600-2359 Sat 0001-0100 0530-2000 Sun 0700-2359 (Summer) Mon 0001-0100 0700-2359 Tue-Fri 0001-0200 0700-2359 Sat 0001-0200 0800-1700 Sun 0830-2359 (Winter)
Farnborough West	Farnborough West 125.250	0700-1900 (Summer) + 1Hr (Winter)
Farnborough East	Farnborough East 123.225	0700-1900 (Summer) + 1Hr (Winter)
Farnborough North	Farnborough North 132.800	0700-1900 (Summer) + 1Hr (Winter)
Humberside	Humberside APP 119.125	Sun-Fri 0530-1915 Sat 0530-1900 (Summer) + 1Hr (Winter)
Leeming	Leeming 127.750	H24
Leuchars	Leuchars 126.500	H24
Linton-On-Ouse	Linton 118.550	Mon-Thu 0730-1715 Fri 0730-1700
Lossiemouth	Lossiemouth 119.350	Mon-Fri during Inverness AD Op Hrs
Manston	Manston 126.350	0800-1600
Marham	Marham 124.150	Mon-Thu 0800-2359 Fri 0800-1800
Newcastle	Newcastle APP 124.375	H24
Norwich	Norwich APP 119.350	0900-1700
Plymouth*	Plymouth MIL 121.250	Mon-Fri 0630-2230
	Plymouth MIL 124.150	Mon-Fri 0630-2230
St Mawgan	St Mawgan 128.725	Mon-Thu 0650-2359 Fri-Sun 0650-2200
Shawbury	Shawbury 120.775	Mon-Thu 0830-1730 Fri 0830-1700
Southend	Southend 130.775	0900-1800
Valley	Valley 125.225	Mon-Thu 0800-1800 Fri 0800-1700
Waddington	Waddington 127.350	H24
Warton	Warton 129.525	Mon-Thu 0630-1900 Fri 0630-1600 (Summer) + 1Hr (Winter)
Yeovilton	Yeovilton 127.350	Mon-Thu 0830-1700 Fri 0830-1400

Military Aerodrome Traffic Zone (MATZ) Units

ATZ	Contact Frequency	ATC Hours
Barkston Heath	Cranwell 119.375	Mon-Thu 0830-1730 Fri 0830-1700
Benson	Benson 120.900	H24
Boscombe Down	Boscombe Zone 126.700	H24
Church Fenton	Fenton 126.500	H24
Coningsby	Coningsby 120.800	H24
Cottesmore	Cottesmore 130.200	H24
Cranwell	Cranwell 119.375	H24
Culdrose	Culdrose 134.050	H24
Dishforth	Leeming 127.750	H24
Fairford	Brize Radar 119.000	H24
Honington	Lakenheath 128.900	H24
Kinloss	Lossiemouth 119.350	H24
Lakenheath	Lakenheath 128.900	H24
Leeming	Leeming 127.750	H24
Leuchars	Leuchars 126.500	H24
Linton-On-Ouse	Linton 118.550	Mon-Thu H24 Fri-Sun 0700-2359 Summer 1Hr earlier
Lossiemouth	Lossiemouth 119.350	H24
Marham	Marham 124.150	H24
Merryfield	Yeovilton 127.350	Mon-Fri 0700-1700 Summer 1Hr earlier
Middle Wallop	Boscombe Zone 126.700	H24
Mildenhall	Lakenheath 128.900	H24
Mona	Valley 125.225	H24
Odiham	Odiham 131.300	H24
Predannack	Culdrose 134.050	H24
St Mawgan	St Mawgan 128.725	H24
Scampton	Waddington 127.350	H24
Shawbury	Shawbury 120.775	H24
Ternhill	Shawbury 120.775	H24
Topcliffe	Leeming 127.750	H24
Valley	Valley 125.225	H24
Waddington	Waddington 127.350	H24
Warton	Warton 129.525	H24
Wattisham	Wattisham 125.800	H24
Wittering	Cottesmore 130.200	H24
Yeovilton	Yeovilton 127.350	H24

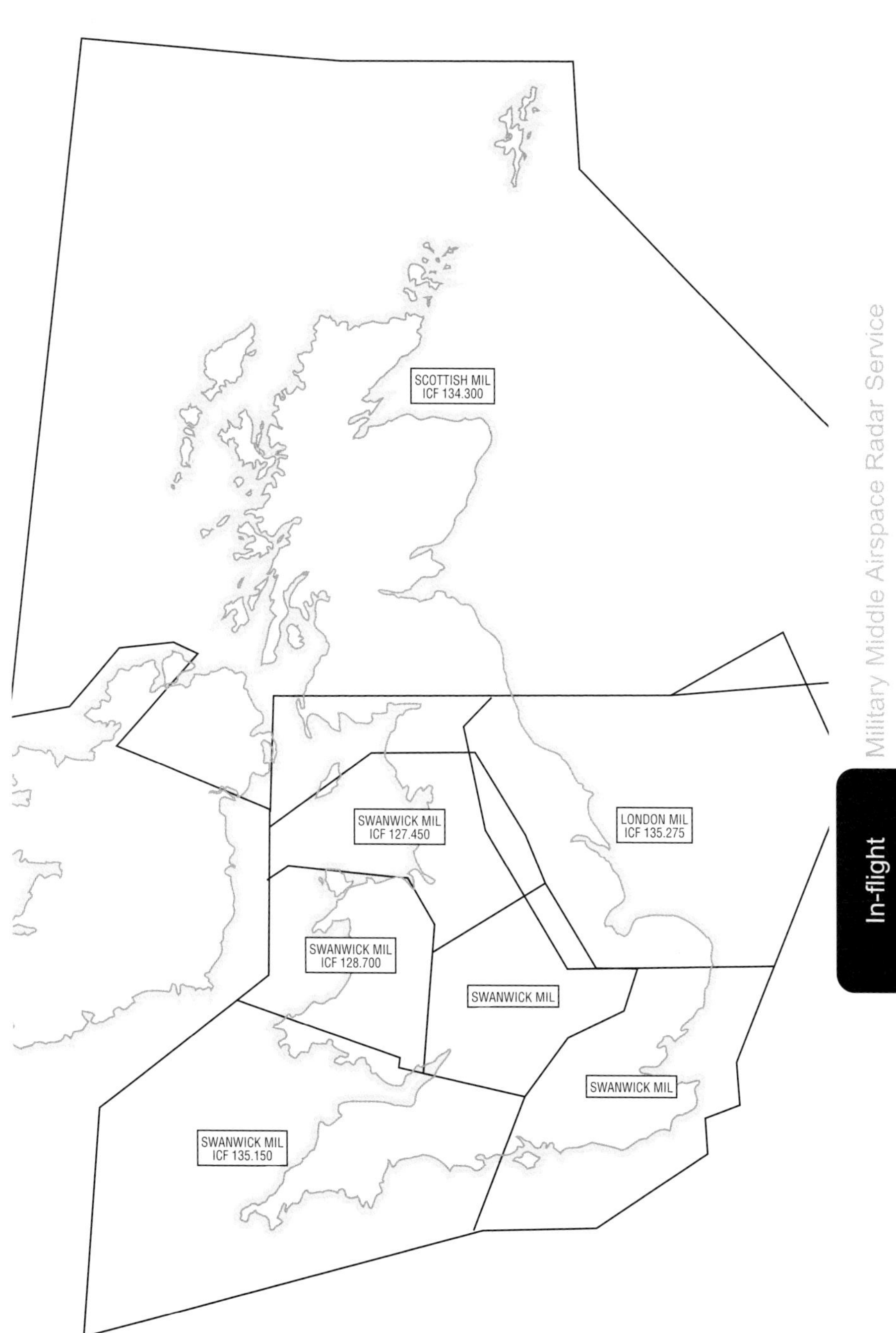
SCOTTISH MIL
ICF 134.300
SWANWICK MIL
ICF 127.450
LONDON MIL
ICF 135.275
SWANWICK MIL
ICF 128.700
SWANWICK MIL
SWANWICK MIL
SWANWICK MIL
ICF 135.150

1 Availability of Service

1.1 This service is available to all aircraft flying outside Controlled airspace in the UK FIR except for flight along advisory routes and for flight within the Sumburgh FISA. It is available from FL 100 to FL 240. This service is subject to Unit capacity.

1.2 The military Units providing this service together with their boundaries are depicted on the chart at ENR 6-1-6-4. The table below shows their hours of operation, the RTF operating frequency on which this service is normally provided and a telephone number for pre-flight contact.

Unit & Callsign	Operating Hours	Initial frequency (ICF)	Contact telephone number
London Military	H24	135.275 MHz	01895 426464
Swanwick Military	H24	135.150 MHz 128.700 MHz 127.450 MHz	01489 612417
Scottish Military	H24	134.300 MHz	01292 479800 Ex 6020 or 6002

1.3 Participating aircraft must be equipped with a serviceable transponder.

2 Type of Service

2.1 The service provided will be a Radar Advisory Service or Radar Information Service (See ENR 1.6.1.1/2).

3 Procedures

3.1 In order to comply with the requirements of the FPPS at London/Swanwick Military captains of aircraft requiring a radar service in the Upper, Middle or Lower Airspace within the London/Swanwick Military area of responsibility are to pre-notify their intended flight details to London/Swanwick Military by one of the following methods:

(a) Pre-flight Notification – Flight Plans. As the preferred method of notification flight plans (F2919/CA48) should be submitted as far in advance of ETD as possible and in any case not less than 30 minutes before service is required. The London/Swanwick Military signals address – EGWDZQZX – must be included on the flight plan. When appropriate these additions to the standard flight plan format must also be included:

(i) Item 18. The point and the time at which a radar service is required to commence;

(ii) Item 15. The point of entry into the area and the point of exit.

Note: Item 15. If a flight is planned to enter any Controlled Airspace (CAS) within the London/Swanwick Military area of responsibility and a service is required before joining or after leaving CAS, both parts of the route may be entered in Item 15 of the same flight plan. In this case both IFPS – EGZYIFPS – and London/Swanwick Military EGWDZQZX must appear as addressees.

(b) Pre-Flight Notification – Military Prenote. When it has not been possible to file a flight plan, as sub-paragraph (a), relevant details of the intended flight should be telephoned by the pilot or by his aerodrome operations or ATC to London/Swanwick Military, Main Flight Plan Reception Section, (ATOTN Telephone Ext 6710) at least 15 minutes before service is required. Flight details should be passed in this order:

(i) Callsign;

(ii) number of aircraft (if more than 1) and aircraft type(s);

(iii) position and time at which service is required to commence;

(iv) speed and flight level at commencement of service;

(v) route (including any required speed or level changes);

(vi) position of leaving the delineated area (if applicable); and

(vii) destination (ICAO Location Indicator).

(c) In-Flight Notification (Air Filing). Exceptionally, when neither form of pre-flight notification has been made the flight details listed in sub-paragraph (b) above, may be notified in flight (Air Filed) by radio to:

(i) ATCRU. Airfile with the ATCRU, currently providing a service for onward transmission by them to London/Swanwick Military at least 15 minutes in advance of service being required;

(ii) London/Swanwick Military. Request radar service by calling London Radar on the appropriate (ICF), at least 5 minutes before service is required passing the details listed in sub-paragraph (b) above.

3.2 Changes to Flight Details

(a) Pre-Flight Notification. Changes to pre-flight notifications are to be passed to LATCC (Mil) as soon as possible by:

(i) Amended flight plan if time permits (as in paragraph 3.1 (a) (ii)); otherwise

(ii) by telephone (as in paragraph 3.1 (b)).

(b) In-Flight Notification (Air Filing). By RT as soon as possible (as in paragraph 3.1 (c))

SAFETYCOM. It is a common frequency for use by aircraft operating in the vicinity of an aerodrome or landing site within the UK that does not have an assigned frequency.

SAFETYCOM Frequency – 135.475 MHz

SAFETYCOM is NOT an air traffic service. It is available to assist pilots to avoid potential collisions between arriving and departing aircraft and should be only used to broadcast the pilot's intentions.
Transmissions made on SAFETYCOM are to be made only when the aircraft is below 2000ft, above an aerodrome or location elevation or below 1000ft above circuit height (if applicable). SAFETYCOM transmissions can only be made within 10nm of the aerodrome or landing location.
The SAFETYCOM frequency must only be used to transmit information regarding the pilot's intentions, there will be NO response from the ground, except when the pilot of an aircraft on the ground needs to transmit his intentions.
The SAFETYCOM frequency must NOT be used as a 'chat' frequency at any time.
Pilots are advised to brief themselves on the format of calls using CAP413.
The use of SAFETYCOM is not mandatory.
SAFETYCOM is not recommended for use at aerodromes that have assigned frequencies for communications. Pilots remain responsible for obtaining any clearance that is necessary to enter controlled airspace.

Sunrise and sunset tables

DATE	EGAA Belfast Aldergrove **SR/SS**	EGBB Birmingham **SR/SS**	EGFF Cardiff **SR/SS**	EGPH Edinburgh **SR/SS**	EGLL London Heathrow **SR/SS**	EGCC Manchester **SR/SS**
Jan 1	0848/1609	0818/1604	0819/1616	0845/1550	0807/1602	0825/1601
Jan 15	0840/1630	0811/1623	0812/1634	0835/1612	0800/1621	0817/1621
Feb 5	0808/1711	0743/1700	0746/1710	0801/1655	0733/1657	0748/1700
Feb 19	0739/1740	0716/1727	0720/1736	0730/1726	0708/1723	0720/1727
Mar 5	0706/1808	0645/1753	0651/1800	0656/1755	0638/1747	0648/1754
Mar 19	0631/1836	0613/1818	0619/1824	0619/1824	0607/1812	0615/1820
Apr 1	0558/1901	0542/1841	0550/1846	0545/1851	0537/1833	0544/1844
Apr 15	0523/1928	0510/1905	0519/1909	0509/1919	0506/1857	0511/1909
May 6	0436/2008	0427/1941	0437/1944	0419/2002	0424/1931	0426/1947
May 20	0411/2033	0404/2003	0415/2005	0453/2028	0402/1953	0402/2020
June 3	0354/2053	0349/2021	0401/2022	0334/2050	0348/2010	0346/2029
June 17	0347/2105	0344/2033	0356/2032	0327/2102	0343/2020	0340/2040
July 1	0352/2105	0349/2033	0401/2033	0332/2102	0348/2021	0345/2040
July 15	0407/2054	0402/2023	0414/2024	0348/2050	0401/2012	0359/2030
Aug 5	0441/2019	0433/1952	0443/1955	0424/2013	0430/1943	0431/1958
Aug 19	0507/1949	0456/1925	0505/1928	0452/1941	0452/1916	0455/1929
Sept 2	0533/1915	0519/1854	0527/1858	0519/1906	0514/1846	0519/1857
Sept 16	0559/1840	0542/1821	0549/1826	0546/1829	0536/1814	0544/1823
Oct 7	0638/1747	0618/1731	0623/1739	0627/1734	0610/1726	0621/1732
Oct 21	0705/1713	0642/1700	0647/1708	0656/1659	0634/1656	0646/1700
Nov 4	0733/1643	0708/1632	0711/1642	0726/1627	0659/1629	0713/1632
Nov 18	0801/1619	0733/1610	0735/1621	0755/1601	0723/1608	0739/1609
Dec 2	0825/1603	0756/1557	0757/1608	0821/1544	0745/1555	0802/1554
Dec 16	0843/1558	0812/1553	0813/1605	0839/1539	0800/1552	0819/1550

ENGLAND

Bedfordshire
Cranfield
Dunstable Downs
Henlow
Holmbeck Farm
Little Staughton
London Luton
Long Acres Farm
Sackville Farm
Shuttleworth
Berkshire
Brimpton
Newbury Racecourse
White Waltham
Bristol
Bristol
Bristol Filton
Buckinghamshire
Aylesbury
Finmere
Halton
Thornborough Grounds
Wycombe Air Park
Cambridgeshire
Bourn
Cambridge
Chatteris
Duxford
Jubilee Farm
Kimbolton
Kingfisher Bridge
Lark Engine Farmhouse
Little Gransden
Main Hall Farm
Marshland
Mitchels Farm
Newnham
Peterborough Conington
Peterborough Sibson
Sutton Meadows
Wallis International
Wyton
Cheshire
Arclid
Ashcroft
Lymm Dam
Stretton
Cornwall
Bodmin
Culdrose
Davidstow Moor
Lands End
Lower Botrea
Perranporth
Predannack
Roserrow
St Mawgan
Truro
Woodlands
Cumbria
Barrow
Berrier
Cark
Carlisle
Glassonby
Kirkbride
Derbyshire
Camphill
Coal Aston
Derby
Devon
Belle Vue
Chivenor
Dowland
Dunkeswell
Eaglescott
Eggesford
Exeter
Farway Common
Gorrell Farm
Halwell
Lundy Island
Plymouth City
Salcolmbe
Sheepwash
Stoodleigh Barton
Dorset
Bournemouth
Bowerswain Farm
Compton Abbas
Newton Peveril
Stalbridge
Co Durham
Durham Tees Valley
Fishburn
Peterlee
East Yorkshire
Beverley
Breighton
Eddsfield
Full Sutton
Garton Field
Hollym
Melbourne
Octon
Pocklington
South Cave
East Sussex
Deanland
Old Hay
Swanborough Farm
Essex
Andrewsfield
Audley End
Clacton
Damyns Hall
Earls Colne
Fanners Farm
Gerpins Farm
Great Oakley
Laindon
London Stansted
Nayland
North Weald
Rayne Hall Farm
Southend
Stapleford
Thurrock
West Hordon
Gloucestershire
Badminton
Bowldown
Eastbach
Fairford
Glendoe
Gloucestershire
Kemble
Little Rissington
Nympsfield
Upper Harford
Greater London
London City
Greater Manchester
Manchester
Manchester Barton
Manchester Woodford
Hampshire
Bourne Park
Chilbolton
Colemore Common
Farnborough
Hook
Lasham
Middle Wallop
Odiham
Popham
Southampton
Thruxton
Herefordshire
Allensmore
Berrow
Broadmeadow
Cottered
Harwicke
Lane Farm
Ledbury
Shobdon
Woonton
Hertfordshire
Elstree
Fowlmere
Graveley
Hundson
Nuthampstead
Panshanger
Plaistows
Rush Green
Top Farm
Humberside
Humberside
Isle of Man
Andreas
Isle of Man
Isle of Wight
Bembridge
Binstead
Isle of Wight
Isle of Scilly
Scilly Isles
Kent
Challock
Clipgate
Farthing Corner
Folkestone
Laddingford
Lashenden
Lydd
Manston
Maypole
Payden Street
Pent Farm
Rochester
Stoke
Lancashire
Blackpool
Rossall Field
St Michaels
Tarn Farm
Temple Breuer
Warton
Leicestershire
Battleflat Farm
Bruntingthorpe
Cottesmore
East Midlands
Husbands Bosworth
Leicester
Measham Cottage Farm
Wharf Farm
Lincolnshire
Ashley's Field
Barkston Heath
Bucknall
Coningsby
Cranwell
Crowland
East Kirkby
Fenland
Haxey
Hougham
Manby
Louth
New York
North Coates
North Moor
Saltby
Scampton
Skegness
Strubby
Sturgate
Temple Bruer
Waddington
Wickenby
Wingland
Wittering
Merseyside
Haydock Park
Ince
Liverpool
Woodvale
Middlesex
Denham
London Heathrow
Northolt
Norfolk
Boughton North
Cromer
East Winch
Felthorpe
Great Massingham
Gunton Park
Kings Lynn
Langham
Little Snoring
Long Stratton
Ludham
Marham
Norwich
Old Buckenham
Seething
Shipdham
Tibenham Priory Farm
Tibenham
Weybourne
North Yorkshire
Bagby
Burn
Church Fenton
Dishforth
Elvington
Felixkirk
Kirkbymoorside
Leeming
Linton on Ouse
Sutton Bank
Topcliffe
Whitby
Wombleton
Yearby
York
Northamptonshire
Bakersfield
Deenethorpe
Easton Maudit
Hinton in the Hedges
Newark
Northampton
Pitsford
Rothwell

Spanhoe
Tower Farm
Turweston
Northumberland
Currock Hill
Eshott
Milfield
Newcastle
Nottinghamshire
Forwood Farm
Grassthorpe Grange
Hucknall
Lambley
Langar
Newark
Nottingham
Retford
Syerston
Oxfordshire
Benson
Bicester
Brize Norton
Chalgrove
Chiltern Park
Drayton St Leonard
Enstone
Hook Norton
Oaklands
Oxford
Shennington
Shotteswell
Weston on the Green
Rutland
Shacklewell
Shropshire
Briedden
Knockin
Nesscliffe Camp
Peplow
Rednall
Seighford
Shawbury
Sherlowe
Shifnall
Sleap
Ternhill
Tilstock
Somerset
Clutton Hill Farm
Henstridge
Merryfield
Shepton Mallet
Weston Zoyland
Yeovil
Yeovilton
South Yorkshire
Doncaster Sheffield
Finningley Village
Haxey
Netherthorpe
Sandtoft
Willow Farm
Staffordshire
Abbots Bromley
Otherton
Roddige
Sittles Farm
Tatenhill
Sufffolk
Beccles
Crowfield
Cuckoo Tye Farm
Debach
Elmsett
Honington
Ipswich Monewden
Lakenheath
Mildenhall
Nayland
Newmarket Heath
Raydon Wings
Rougham
Waits Farm
Wattisham
Surrey
Biggin Hill
Blackbushe
Dunsfold
Fairoaks
London Gatwick
Redhill
Vallance by Ways
Tyne & Wear
Currock Hill
Newcastle
Warwickshire
Alcester
Baxterley
Bidford
Bromsgrove
Green Farm
Home Farm
Little Chase Farm
Long Marston
Stoke Golding
Wellesbourne Mountford
West Midlands
Birmingham
Cosford
Coventry
Wolverhampton
West Sussex
Chichester
Chilsfold Farm
Jackrells Farm
London Gatwick
Shoreham
Truleigh Farm
West Yorkshire
Fadmoor
Garforth
Huddersfield
Leeds Bradford
Oxenhope
Sherbern in Elmet
Walton Wood
Wiltshire
Boscombe Down
Charlton Park
Clench Common
Colerne
Craysmarsh Farm
Draycott Farm
Garston Farm
Lydeway Field
Lyneham
Manor Farm
Netheravon
Oaksey Park
Old Sarum
Redlands
Sandhill Farm
Upavon
Wadswick Strip
Wing Farm
Worcestershire
Bromsgrove
Defford
Hanley William
Milson
Pound Green

WALES

Cardiff
Cardiff
Carmarthenshire
Pembrey
Denbigshire
Greenlands
Rhedyn Coch
Dyfed
Haverfordwest
Flintshire
Hawarden
Gwynedd
Caernarfon
Talybont
Gwent
Upfield Farm
Isle of Anglesey
Mona
Valley
Monmouthshire
Abergavenny
Pembrokeshire
Rosemarket
Powys
Breidden
Lane Farm
Welshpool
Rhondda Cynon Taff
Rhigos
Swansea
Swansea
West Wales
Vale of Glamorgan
St Athan
Wrexham
Chirk

SCOTLAND

Aberdeenshire
Aberdeen
Hatton
Insch
Kirknewton
Whiterashes
Angus
Aboyne
Argyll & Bute
Bute
Campbeltown
Colonsay
Coll
Gigha Island
Glenforsa
Islay
Oban
Tiree
Berwickshire
Charterhall
Nether Huntley Wood
Borders
Midlem
Dumfries & Galloway
Castle Kennedy
Wigtown
Dundee City
Dundee
Fife
Crail
Fife
Kingsmuir
Leuchars
Highland
Dornoch
Fearn
Feshiebridge
Glendoe
Inverness
Isle of Skye
Knockbain Farm
Plockton
Strathaven
Wick
Lothian
East Fortune
Edinburgh
Kirknewton
Morayshire
Kinloss
Lossiemouth
North Lanarkshire
Cumbernauld
Orkney Islands
Eday
Flotta
Kirkwall
Lamb Holm
North Ronaldsay
Papa Westray
Sanday
Stronsay
Westray
Perth & Kinross
East Lochlane Farm
Errol
Perth
Portmoak
Strathallan
Shetland Islands
Fair Isle
Fetlar
Foula
Lerwick
Out Skerries
Papa Stour
Scatsta
Sumburgh
Unst
Whalsay
South Ayrshire
Prestwick
Strathclyde
Glasgow
Western Isles
Barra
Benbecula
Sollas

CHANNEL ISLANDS

Alderney
Guernsey
Jersey

IRELAND

Northern Ireland
Ballykelly
Belfast Aldergrove
Belfast City
Bellarena
Donaghcloney
Dunnyvadden
Enniskillen
Londonderry
Movenis
Newtownards

Airfields in BLOCK CAPITALS are in the main listing with an airfield diagram. Airfields in Lower Case are in the Private Airfields text listing.

ABBOTS BROMLEY
ABERDEEN
ABERGAVENNY
Aboyne
Alcester
ALDERNEY
Allensmore
ANDREAS
ANDREWSFIELD
ARCLID
ASHCROFT
ASHLEY'S FIELD
AUDLEY END
AYLESBURY
BADMINTON
BAGBY
BAKERSFIELD
BALLYKELLY
BARKSTON HEATH
BARRA
BARROW
BATTLEFLAT FARM
BAXTERLEY
BECCLES
BELFAST ALDERGROVE
BELFAST CITY
BELLARENA
BELLE VUE
BEMBRIDGE
BENBECULA
BENSON
BERRIER
BERROW
BEVERLEY
BICESTER
BIDFORD
BIGGIN HILL
Binstead
BIRMINGHAM
BLACKBUSHE
BLACKPOOL
BODMIN
BOSCOMBE DOWN
BOUGHTON NORTH
BOURN
BOURNE PARK
BOURNEMOUTH
Bowerswaine Farm
BOWLDOWN
BREIGHTON
BRIEDDEN
BRIMPTON
BRISTOL
BRISTOL FILTON
BRIZE NORTON
Broadmeadow
Bromsgrove
BRUNTINGTHORPE
BUCKNALL
BURN
BUTE
CAERNARFON
CALAIS DUNKIRK
CAMBRIDGE
CAMPBELTOWN
Camphill
CARDIFF
CARK
CARLISLE
CASTLE KENNEDY
Caunton
CHALGROVE
Challock
CHARLTON PARK
CHARTERHALL
CHATTERIS
CHICHESTER
CHILBOLTON
CHILSFOLD FARM
CHILTERN PARK
CHIRK
CHIVENIR
CHURCH FENTON
CLACTON
CLENCH COMMON
CLIPGATE
CLUTTON HILL FARM
COAL ASTON
COLEMORE COMMON
COLERNE
COLL
COLONSAY
COMPTON ABBAS
CONINGSBY
COSFORD
COTTERED
COTTESMORE
COVENTRY
CRAIL
CRANFIELD
CRANWELL
CROMER
CROWFIELD
CROWLAND
Craysmarsh Farm
CUCKOO TYE FARM
CULDROSE
CUMBERNAULD
CURROCK HILL
DAMYNS HALL
DAVIDSTOW MOOR
DEANLAND
DEBACH
DEENTHORPE
DEFFORD
DENHAM
DERBY
DINARD
DISHFORTH
DONAGHCLONEY
DONCASTER SHEFFIELD
DORNOCH
Downland
DRAYCOTT FARM
DRAYTON ST LEONARD
DUBLIN
DUNDEE
DUNKESWELL
DUNNVADDEN
DUNSFOLD
Dunstable Downs
DURHAM TEES VALLEY
DUXFORD
EAGLESCOTT
EARLS COLNE
EAST FORTUNE
EAST KIRKBY
East Lochlane Farm
EAST MIDLANDS
East Winch
EASTBACH
EASTON MAUDIT
EDAY
EDDSFIELD
EDINBURGH
EGGESFORD
ELMSETT
ELSTREE
ELVINGTON
ENNISKILLEN
ENSTONE
Errol
ESHOTT
EXETER
FADMOOR
FAIR ISLE
FAIRFORD
Fanners Farm
FARIOAKS
FARNBOROUGH
FARTHING CORNER
FARWAY COMMON
Fearn
FELIXKIRK
FELTHORPE
FENLAND
FESHIEBRIDGE
FETLAR
FIFE
FINMERE
FINNINGLEY VILLAGE
FISHBURN
Flotta
Folkestone
Forwood Farm
FOULA
FOWLMERE
FULL SUTTON
GARFORTH
GARSTON FARM
GARTON FIELD
GERPINS FARM
GIGHA ISLAND
GLASGOW
GLASSONBY
Glendoe
GLENFORSA
GLOUCESTERSHIRE
GORREL FARM
GRASSTHORPE GRANGE
GRAVELEY
GREAT MASSINGHAM
GREAT OAKLEY
Green Farm
GREENLANDS
GUERNSEY
Gunton Park
HALTON
Halwell
HANLEY WILLIAM
HARDWICKE
Hatton
HAVERFORDWEST
HAWARDEN
HAXEY
HAYDOCK PARK
HENLOW
HENSTRIDGE
HINTON IN THE HEDGES
HOLLYM
HOLMBECK FARM

Home Farm
HONINGTON
Hook
Hook Norton
HOUGHAM
HUCKNALL
HUDDERSFIELD
HUMBERSIDE
HUNSDON
HUSBANDS BOSWORTH
INCE
INSCH
INVERNESS
IPSWICH MONEWDEN
ISLAY
ISLE OF MAN
ISLE OF SKYE
ISLE OF WIGHT
JACKRELLS FARM
JERSEY
JUBILEE FARM
KEMBLE
KIMBOLTON
Kingfisher Bridge
Kings Lynn
KINGSMUIR
KINLOSS
KIRKBRIDE
KIRKBYMOORSIDE
KIRKNEWTON
KIRKWALL
Knockbain Farm
KNOCKIN
LA ROCHELLE
LADDINGFORD
Laindon
LAKENHEATH
LAMB HOLM
LAMBLEY
LANDS END
Lane Farm
LANGAR
Langham
Lark Engine Farmhouse
LASHAM
LASHENDEN
LE TOUQUET
LEDBURY
LEEDS BRADFORD
LEEMING
LEICESTER
LERWICK
LEUCHARS
LINTON ON OUSE
Little Chase Farm
LITTLE GRANSDEN
LITTLE RISSINGTON
LITTLE SNORING
LITTLE STAUGHTON
LIVERPOOL
LONDON CITY
LONDON GATWICK
LONDON HEATHROW
LONDON LUTON
LONDON STANSTED
LONDONDERRY
LONG ACRES FARM
LONG MARSTON
LONG STRATTON
LOSSIEMOUTH
LOUTH
Lower Botrea
LUDHAM
LUNDY ISLAND
LYDD
LYDEWAY FIELD
LYMM DAM
LYNEHAM
MAIN HALL FARM
Manby
MANCHESTER
MANCHESTER BARTON
MANCHESTER WOODFORD
MANOR FARM
MANSTON
MARHAM
MARSHLAND
MAYPOLE
MEASHAM COTTAGE FARM
Melbourne
MERRYFIELD
MIDDLE WALLOP
MIDLEM
MILDENHALL
MILFIELD
MILSON
MITCHELS FARM
MONA
MOVENIS
NAYLAND
NETHERAVON
NETHERTHORPE
Nether Huntly Wood
NEW YORK
Newark
NEWBURY RACE COURSE
NEWCASTLE
NEWMARKET HEATH
NEWNHAM
NEWTON PEVERIL
NEWTOWNARDS
NORTH COATES
NORTH MOOR
NORTH RONALDSAY
NORTH WEALD
NORTHAMPTON
NORTHOLT
NORWICH
NOTTINGHAM
NUTHAMPTSTEAD
Nympsfield
OAKLANDS
OAKSEY PARK
OBAN
Octon
ODIHAM
OLD BUCKENHAM
OLD HAY
OLD SARUM
OSTEND
OTHERTON
OUT SKERRIES
OXENHOPE
OXFORD
PANSHANGER
PAPA STOUR
PAPA WESTRAY
Payden Street
PEMBREY
Pent Farm
PEPLOW
PERRANPORTH
PERTH
PETERBOROUGH CONINGTON
PETERBOROUGH SIBSON
PETERLEE
PITTSFORD
PLAISTOWS
PLOCKTON
PLYMOUTH CITY
POKLINGTON
POPHAM
PORTMOAK
POUND GREEN
PREDANNACK
PRESTWICK
RAYDON WINGS
RAYNE HALL FARM
REDHILL
REDLANDS
REDNAL
RETFORD
RHEDYN COCH
Rhigos
ROCHESTER
RODDIGE
Rosemarket
ROSERROW
ROSSALL FIELD
ROTHWELL
ROUGHAM
RUSH GREEN
ST ATHAN
ST MAWGAN
ST MICHAELS
SACKVILLE FARM
SALCOMBE
SALTBY
SANDAY
SANDHILL FARM
SANDTOFT
SCAMPTON
SCATSTA
SCILLY ISLES
SEETHING
SHAWBURY
SHEEPWASH
SHENNINGTON
SHERBURN IN ELMET
SHERLOWE
SHIFNAL
SHIPDHAM
SHOBDON
SHOREHAM
SHOTTESWELL
SHUTTLEWORTH
SITTLES FARM
SKEGNESS
SLEAP
SOLLAS
SOUTH CAVE
SOUTHAMPTON
SOUTHEND
SPANHOE
STAPLEFORD
STOKE
STOKE GOLDING
Stoodleigh Barton
STORNOWAY
STRATHALLAN
STRATHAVEN
Stretton
STRONSAY
STRUBBY
STURGATE
SUMBURGH

Sutton Bank
SUTTON MEADOWS
SWANBOROUGH FARM
SWANSEA
SYERSTON
TALYBONT
TATENHILL
TEMPLE BRUER
TERNHILL
Thornborough Grounds
THRUXTON
THURROCK
TIBENHAM
TIBENHAM PRIORY FARM
TILSTOCK
TIREE
TOP FARM
TOPCLIFFE
Tower Farm
Truleigh Farm
TRURO
TURWESTON
UNST
UPAVON
UPFIELD FARM
UPPER HARFORD
Vallance by ways Gatwick
VALLEY
WADDINGTON
Wadswick Strip
WALLIS INTERNATIONAL
WALTON WOOD
WARTON
WATTISHAM
WELLESBOURNE MOUNTFORD
WELSHPOOL
WESTON ZOYLAND
West Hordon
WEST WALES
WESTON ON THE GREEN
WESTRAY
WEYBOURNE
WHALSAY
WHARF FARM
Whitby
WHITE WALTHAM
WHITERASHES
WICK
WICKENBY
Wigtown
Willow Farm
WING FARM
WINGLAND
WITTERING
WOLVERHAMPTON
WOMBLETON
Woodlands
WOODVALE
Woonton
WYCOMBE
WYTON
Yatesbury
YEARBY
YEOVIL
YEOVILTON
YORK

For	See
Aberporth	West Wales
Aldergrove	Belfast Aldergrove
Aviemore	Feshiebridge
Baldock	Newnham
Banbury	Shotteswell
Barham	Clipgate
Barton	Manchester Barton
Bedford	Castle Mill
Bembridge	Isle of Wight
Biggleswade	Shuttleworth
Bolt Head	Salcolmbe
Booker	Wycombe Air Park
Bradford	Leeds Bradford
Braintree	Rayne Hall Farm
Broadford	Isle of Skye
Buntingford	Cottered
Castle Donington	East Midlands
Cherry Tree Farm	Monewden
Chester	Hawarden
Church Farm	Shotteswell
City of Derry	Londonderry
Cleobury Mortimer	Milson
Conington	Peterborough Conington
Croft Farm	Defford
Crosland Moor	Huddersfield
Dalcross	Inverness
Doncaster	Thorne
Dyce	Aberdeen
Edgehill	Shenington
Eglington	Londonderry
Emlyn's Field	Greenlands
Emlyn's Other Field	Rhedyn Coch
Filton	Bristol Filton
Finningley	Doncaster Sheffield
Gamston	Retford
Gatwick	London Gatwick
Glenrothes	Fife
Goodwood	Chichester
Grange over Sands	Cark
Great Yarmouth	North Deenes
Halfpenny Green	Wolverhampton Halfpenny Green
Headcorn	Lashenden
Heathrow	London Heathrow
Hurn	Bournemouth
Jericho Farm	Lambley
Kidlington	Oxford
Laurelhill	Donaghcloney
Lewes	Deanland
Lichfield	Sittles Farm
Lincoln	Wickenby
Linley Hill	Beverley
Liverpool	Liverpool John Lennon
Luton	London Luton
Machrinhanish	Campbeltown
Machrins	Colonsay
Marshland	Wisbech
Monewden	Ipswich Monewden
Moors National Park	Fadmoor
Mount Airey	South Cave
Muckleburgh	Weybourne
Mull	Glenforsa
Newquay	St Mawgan
Newton le Willows	Haydock Park
Ninescores Farm	Finingley Village
North Connel	Oban
North Reston	Louth Hall Farm
Northreeps	Cromer
Old Warden	Shuttleworth
Oswestry	Knockin
Peterhead	Longside
Pickering	Wombleton
Priory Farm	Tibenham
Riseley	Sackville Farm
Robin Hood Int	Doncaster Sheffield
Ronaldsway	Isle of Man
Royston	Nuthampstead
Rufforth	York
Rugby	Husbands Bosworth
Sandown	Isle of Wight
Sandy	Long Acres Farm
Scone	Perth
Scunthorpe	North Moor
Sibson	Peterborough Sibson
Sorbie	Kingsmuir
Spalding	Crowland
Spence	Eastbach
St Angelo	Enniskillen
St Just	Lands End
St Marys	Scilly Isles
Stansted	London Stansted
Staverton	Gloucestershire
Stewton	Louth
Stoneacre Farm	Farthing Corner
Stonefield Park	Chilbolton
Sywell	Northampton
Tarn Farm	Rossall Field
Teeside	Durham Tees Valley
Thame	Aylesbury
Thirsk	Bagby
Thorne	Doncaster
Tingwall	Lerwick
Tollerton	Nottingham
York	Elvington
Velcourt	Ledbury
Walney Island	Barrow
Wasing Lower Farm	Brimpton
Westland	Yeovil
Withybush	Haverfordwest
Woodford	Manchester Woodford
Yeatsall Farm	Abbots Bromley

Key to airfield directory maps

800m x 46m	Hard Rwy, with the Rwy length and width in metres
800m x 18m	Soft Rwy, with the Rwy length and width in metres
09	The Runway QDM (the magnetic direction of the runway in tens of degrees)
	Displaced threshold
	Hard Twy, Apron or manoeuvring area
	Grass Twy, Apron or manoeuvring area
	Dissused Rwy
	Dissused Twy, Apron or manoeuvring area
H1 H	Holding point
01 LP	Launch Point
H	Helipad
H	Helicopter holding point
T	Signal square
	Windsock
C	Control, the point for pilots to report
	Parachuting area
	Buildings or built-up area (non aviation)
	Buildings (aviation)
	Track
A47	Road
M6	Dual carriageway or Motorway
	Railway
	Disused Railway
	Overhead powerlines
	Cuttings and embankments
	Trees or bushes
	Hedge
	Footpath or Bridleway
	Fence
	Stone wall
	Ditch or dyke
	Grass boundary
	Waterway
	Coastline
	High ground
	Marsh
	Do NOT overfly
	Quarry

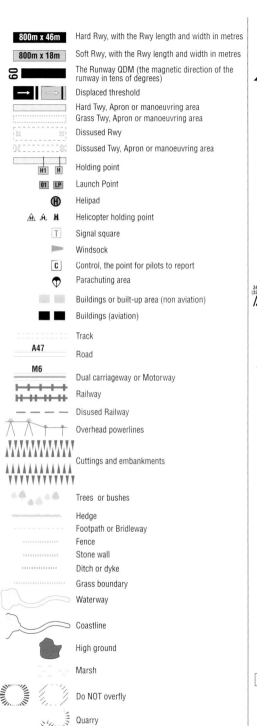

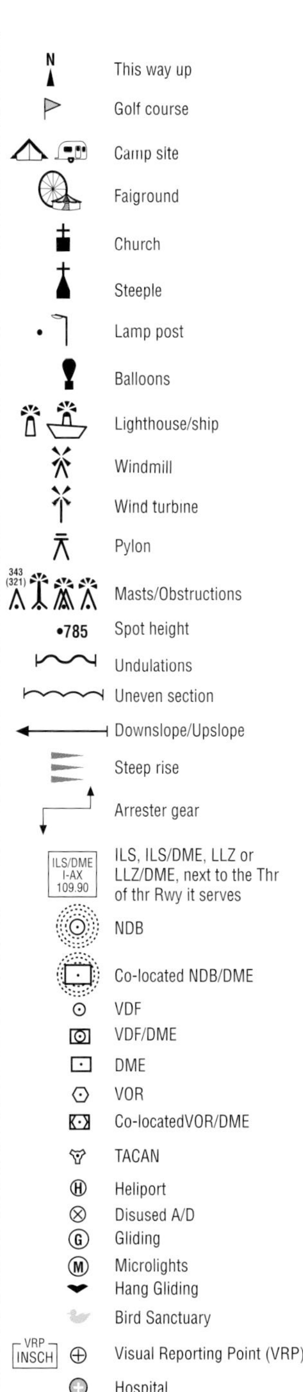

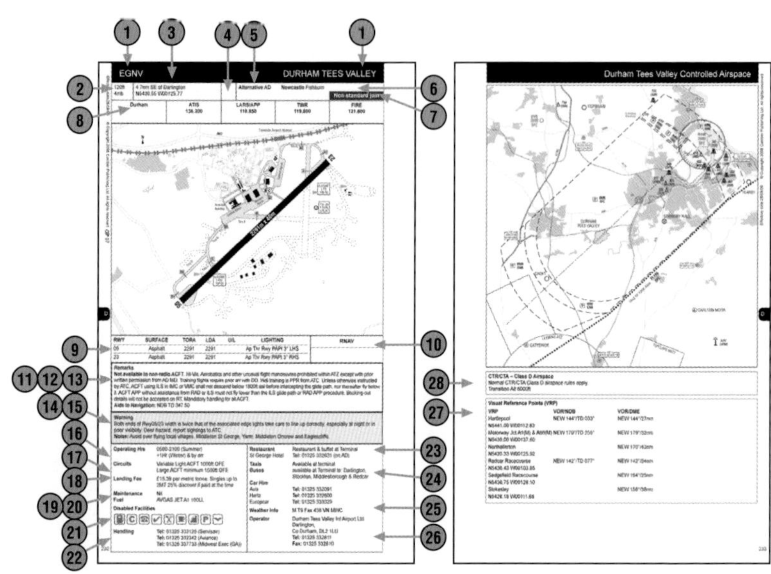

1	The airfield ICAO or NOTAM code (where applicable) and airfield name.
2	The airfield elevation in feet Above Mean Sea Level (AMSL). The figure in mbs (hPas) indicates the approximate mbs/hPas difference between QNH & QFE. The figure is based on 1 mb/hPa = 30 feet. It is only an approximate guide and should only be used to cross-check the QFE as reported by the airfield.
3	Location geographically, and by Latitude & Longitude. Lat and Long are given to 2 decimals (not seconds) of a minute.
4	PPR (Prior Permission Required). PPR should be taken to mean that a telephone call must be made before departure requesting permission to use the airfield.
5	Alternative AD. possible airfield to be used if unable to reach intended airfield. 1st alternative – IFR airfield 2nd alternative – licensed airfield within 30nm If no airfield available within this distance, the alternative listed will be a hard surface Rwy within 30nm.
6	Diversion AD – Diversion aerodrome, for use in emergency only, no PPR required and no landing fees
7	Non-standard joining procedure in operation on the airfield.
8	Radio frequencies. The name in italics is the radio callsign of the airfield. The following callsigns should be used:

Abbreviation	**Callsign**
ZONE	Zone
A Non-standard joining procedure in operation on the airfield.	
PP	Approach
RAD	Radar
TWR	Tower
GND	Ground
AFIS	Information
A/G	Radio
FIS	London/Scottish Information as applicable
FIRE	This frequency (when shown) is available only when the airport fire service is attending an incident.

9	Details of the runway directions, surface, lengths and widths (in metres) and lighting are given. TORA = Take-off Run Available LDA = Landing Distance Available.
10	RNAV location as a radial (magnetic bearing from) and range (nautical miles) from VOR/DME within 30nm radius from AD.
11	Remarks/PPR conditions. Plain language remarks regarding the use of the airfield.
12	Aids to Navigation – Radio navigation aids shown by type, ident and frequency.
13	Visual aid to location. Help for the pilot in locating/identifying the airfield
14	Warnings relevant to users of the airfield and flight in the immediate vicinity.
15	Noise. Special procedures for arr and dept airfield to help with noise abatement procedures in place at the airfield.
16	Operating hours are as notified, they may vary with little or no prior notice.
17	Circuit directions and heights, where this information is known

18 Landing fees. This information is based on supplied data. Special rates or supplements may apply at certain times, airfield pages are not amended for a change of landing fee information only.

19 Maintenance availability where known

20 Fuel availability. Please note that at many airfields fuel is not available at all times when the airfield is open.

21 Disabled Facilities

- Access to airside
- Help for refueling
- Access or help to pay landing fee and sign in/out and flight breifing where applicable
- Assistance is available with prior notice only
- Assistance is available without prior notice
- No wheelchair access available on this airfield
- Wheelchair access toilet close by
- Access to airfield café
- Access for hot drinks only
- Access to pilot shop
- Disabled parking reserved close to facilities
- Flight training for the disabled available

22 Handling agent information information if present on airfield.

23 Restaurants. Basic detail where known. Inclusion of a company name or telephone number does not imply recommendation or endorsement by the airfield operator or the publisher.

24 Taxis/Car Hire. Basic detail where known. Inclusion of a company name or telephone number does not imply recommendation or endorsement by the airfield operator or the publisher.

25 Weather Information. Weather reports & forecasts available for the airfield and where they can be obtained:

M METAR (usually only available during the normal opening hours of the airfield).
M* METAR not distributed. It will probably be necessary to contact the airfield direct for this report.
T9 9 hour TAF
T24 24 hour TAF
T TAF of other duration (mostly military airfields).
Fax METAR & TAF available via MetFAX service (see Met section of Flight Planning for full details).
123 Three figure airfield code for use with automated METAR & TAF telephone service. (see Met section of Flight Planning for full details).
A ATIS (see radio box for frequency).
VS METAR included on VOLMET South broadcast.
VN METAR included on VOLMET North broadcast.
VM METAR included on VOLMET Main broadcast.
VSc METAR included on VOLMET Scottish broadcast.
AirS Airfield is within AIRMET Southern coverage *.
AirN Airfield is within AIRMET Northern coverage *.
AirSc Airfield is within AIRMET Scottish coverage *.
AirSE Airfield is within AIRMET Southeast England coverage *.
AirCen Airfield is within AIRMET Central England coverage *
AirSW Airfield is within AIRMET Southwest England coverage *.

* Used only if TAFs are not available. Where coverage overlaps the most localised forecast is given.

Forecast office. Where no forecast office is designated, that designated to other airfields in the area is given. Forecast office telephone numbers are given in the MET section of the Flight Planning pages. For military and government airfields the stated Forecast Office may be able to provide METARs and TAFs.

MOEx Exeter Weather Centre
GWC Glasgow Weather Centre

26 The postal address, telephone and fax numbers of the airfield operator

27 Visual Reference Points (VRP's)

28 Other information, such as controlled airspace regulations, special procedures, may also be listed after the main airfield page.

ABBOTS BROMLEY

400ft 13mb	4nm N of Rugeley N5249.50 W00154.00	PPR	**Alternative AD** **East Midlands** Tatenhill

Non-Radio	APP	A/G	Safetycom
	East Mids 134.175	Tatenhill 124.075	135.475

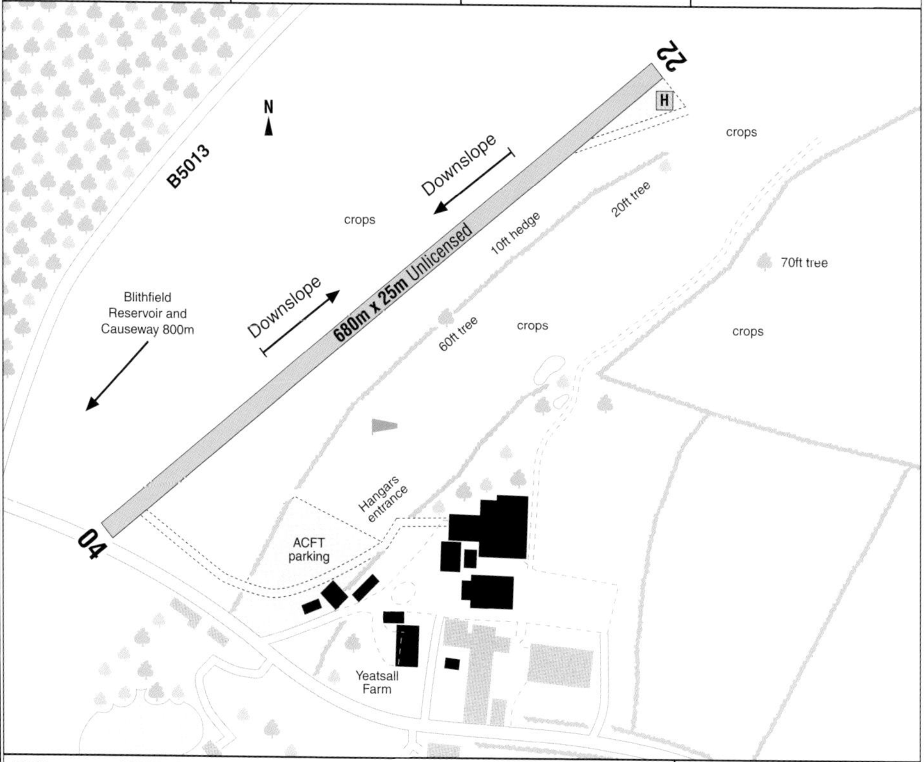

RWY	SURFACE	TORA	LDA	U/L	LIGHTING
04/22	Grass			680x25	Nil

RNAV			
TNT	115.70	215	16.1

Remarks

PPR by telephone essential. AD situated close to end of causeway carrying B5013 across Blithfield Reservoir. AD based ACFT are mainly active at weekends. AD close to Tatenhill ATZ visitors advised to call Tatenhill.

Warnings

Cross Hayes gliding site with winch launching 2nm SE of AD. Keep good lookout for Gliders. Tatenhill ATZ 4nm to E. During the week low flying military ACFT may be encountered, keep a good lookout.
Noise: Avoid over flight of Abbots Bromley village close to E of AD

Operating Hrs	SR-SS daily
Circuits	24 RH, 06 LH, 800ft QFE
Landing Fee	Nil
Maintenance	Nil
Fuel	Nil
Disabled Facilities	Nil
Accomodation	B&B available at Marsh Farm in Abbots Bromley
Marsh Farm	**Tel:** 01283 840323
Taxis	
Rugeley	**Tel:** 01889 586061
Car Hire	Nil
Weather Info	Air Cen MOEx

Operator
Mr Richard Hall
Yeatsall Farm
Abbots Bromley
Staffs
WS15 3DY
Tel: 01283 840343
Tel: 07807 886315

215ft 7mb	5nm NW of Aberdeen N5712.12 W00211.87	PPR	Alternative AD Diversion AD	Perth

Non-standard join

Aberdeen	ATIS 114.300 121.850	APP 119.050	RAD 128.300 119.050 134.100	Handling Caledonian 130.625 Flt Support 130.600 Signature 122.350 SGS 131.700 Aviance 130.075
TWR 118.100	GND 121.700	FIRE 121.600		

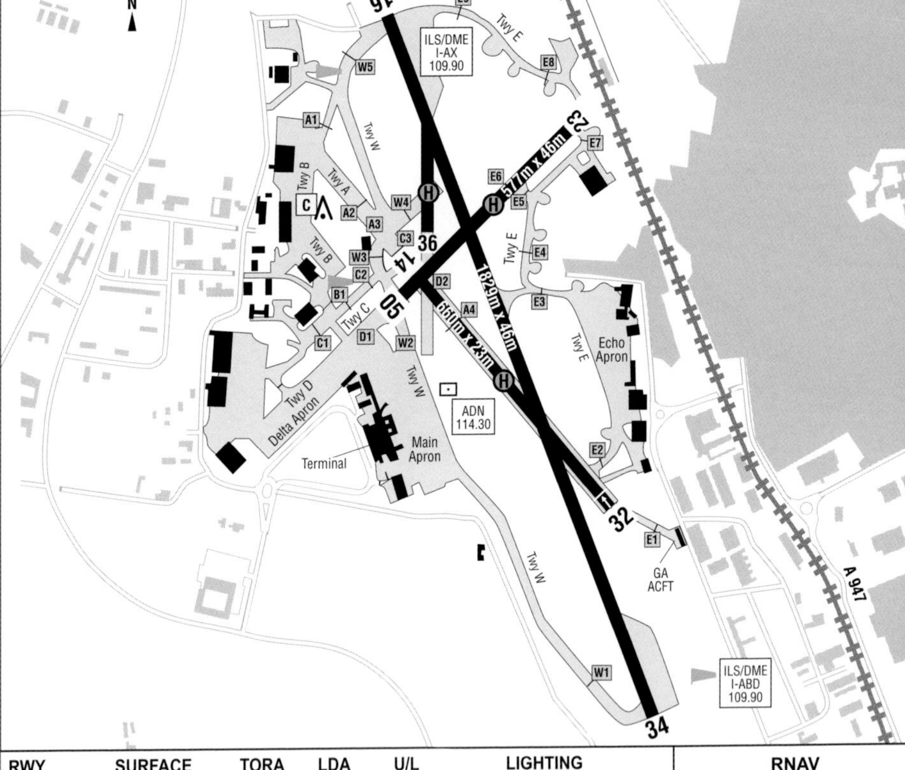

RWY	SURFACE	TORA	LDA	U/L	LIGHTING
16/34	Asphalt	1829	1829		App Thr Rwy PAPI 3° LHS
36	Asphalt	Helistrip		260x23	Nil
05/23	Asphalt	Helistrip		577x46	23-Thr Rwy CHAPI 6°
14/32	Asphalt	Helistrip		660x23	Nil

RNAV			
ADN	114.30	167	6.8

Remarks

PPR to non-radio ACFT. Helicopter operations outside published Hrs. ACFT to join final not less than 1000ft QFE. All telephone calls are recorded.

Handling: All Arr light ACFT will be directed to Signature at the Flying Club unless another handling agent has been specified.

Aids to Navigation: NDB ATF 348.00. NDB AQ 336.00

Warnings

TV masts 1290ft amsl 12.5nm NW 648ft amsl 146°/2.9nm. Intense helicopter activity adjacent to full length of E apron Light ACFT beware of large helicopter down wash/vortices. Rwy16 PAPIs should not be used until on extended centre line. Moderate/severe turbulence and windshear may be experienced on APP to all Rwys when the 1000ft wind exceeds 15kt indirection 200-320°. Model ACFT flying up to 13kg not above 400ft agl at Haremoss 1.5 NW of Portlethen.

Operating Hrs	0510-2130 (PPR 2130-0510) (Summer) +1Hr (Winter)	**Handling**	**Tel:** 01244 770222 (Caledonian) **Tel:** 01224 723357 (Flight Support) **Tel:** 01244 723636 (Signature) **Tel:** 01224 795802 (Aviance)
Landing Fee	On application		
Maintenance	By arr		
Fuel	**Tel:** 0860 310313 AVTUR JET A1		

Disabled Facilities	

Car Hire	
Avis	**Tel:** 01224 722282
Europcar	**Tel:** 01224 770770
Enterprise	**Tel:** 01224 348484
Hertz	**Tel:** 01224 722373
Budget	**Tel:** 01224 771777
Taxis	Available at terminal
Weather Info	M T9 T18 Fax 222 A Vsc GWC

Operator	Aberdeen Airport Ltd Aberdeen Airport Dyce, Aberdeenshire Scotland, AB21 7DU **Tel:** 0870 040 0006 (AD) **Tel:** 01224 723714 (NATS) **Fax:** 01224 727176 (ATC) **Fax:** 01224 725721 (AD) www.aberdeenairport.com

CTA/CTR-CLASS D AIRSPACE
Normal CTA/CTR-Class D Airspace rules apply
Transition Altitude 6000ft

Entry/Exit Lanes
To facilitate the operation of ACFT to and from Aberdeen, the following entry/exit lanes have been established. They are all 3nm wide:
1 Peterhead lane
2 Stonehaven lane
3 Inverurie lane – for ACFT taking off from Rwy16 or landing on Rwy34 follow A96 until Kintore.
Use of lanes is subject to ATC clearance. ACFT in lanes must remain clear of cloud, in sight of the surface, fly not above 2000ft QNH with a min visibility of 3 km. ACFT using the lane shall keep the centre line on the left. Pilots must maintain adequate clearance from the GND or other obstacles

Effective date:25/09/08

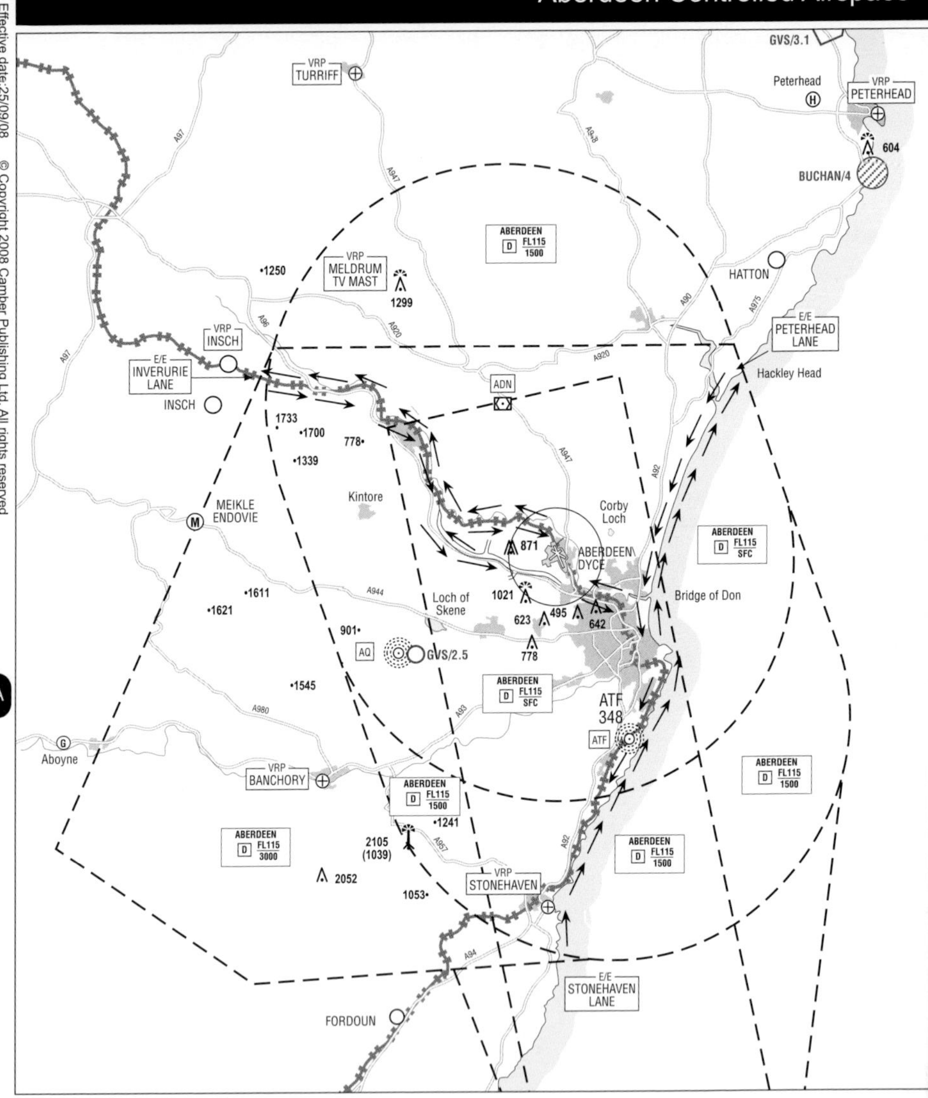

A

Visual Reference Points (VRP)

VRP	VOR/NDB	VOR/DME
Banchory N5703.00 W00230.10	ADN 210°/ATF 268°	ADN 210°/17nm
Insch N5720.57 W00236.85	ADN 284°/AQ 335°	ADN 284°/11nm
Meldrum TV Mast N5730.42 W00146.60	AND 321°/AQ 005°	AND 321°/6nm
Peterhead N5730.42 W00146.60	ADN 057°/SHD 162°	ADN 057°/20nm
Stonehaven N5657.75 W00212.60	ADN 179°/ATF 210°	ADN 179°/21nm
Turiff N5732.32 W00227.60	ADN 340°/SHD 271°	ADN 340°/15nm

220ft 7mb	2nm SE of Abergavenny N5147.64 W00259.61	PPR	Alternative AD **Gloucestershire** Shobdon

Non-Radio	LARS Cardiff 126.625	Safetycom 135.475

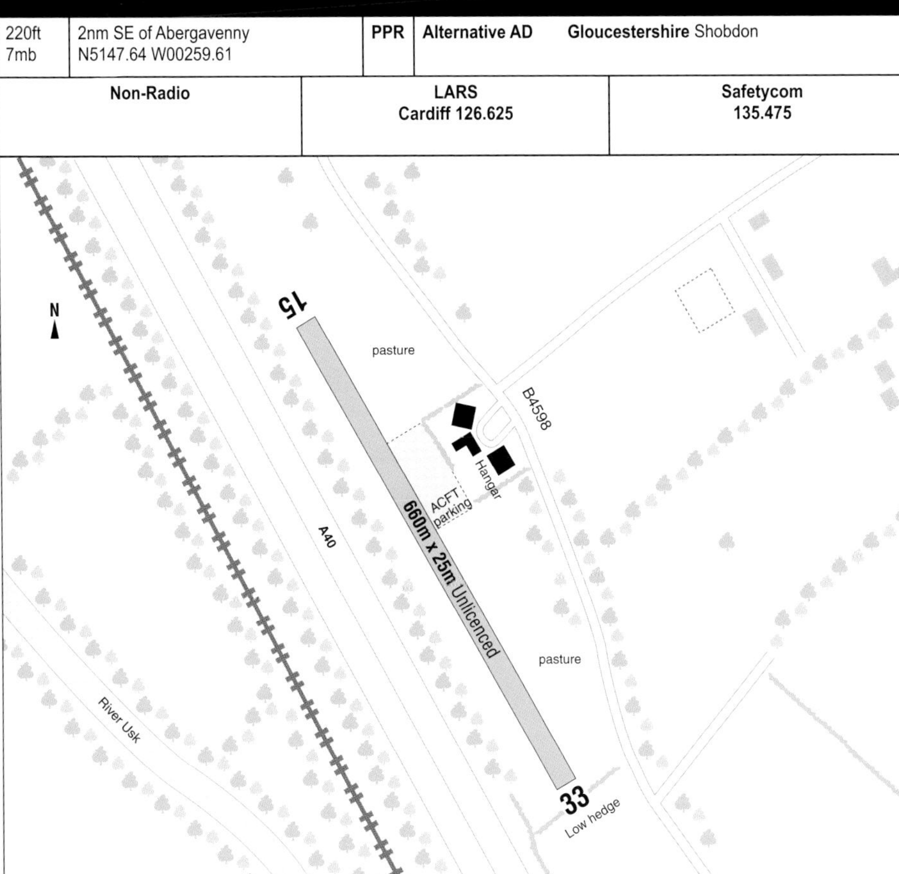

RWY	SURFACE	TORA	LDA	U/L	LIGHTING
15/33	Grass			660x25	Nil

RNAV			
BCN	117.45	070	11

Remarks
PPR by telephone essential. Home of Pioneer Aviation U.K. Visitors welcome at pilots own risk. Flat grass strip which lies alongside the A40 dual-carriageway.

Warnings
High gnd to N and W of AD up to 1955ft.

Operating Hrs	0800-2000 (L)
Circuits	LH 1000ft QFE
Landing Fee	Nil
Maintenance	Nil
Fuel	Nil
Disabled Facilities	Nil
Restaurant	Nil
Taxi	Operator can advise on local taxi operators
Car Hire	Nil
Weather Info	Air S MOEx

Operator
Frank Cavaciuti
Pioneer Aviation UK Ltd
Byre Hardwick
Abergavenny
Monmouthshire NP7 9AB
Tel: 01973 850973
keren@pioneeraviation.co.uk
www.pioneeraviation.co.uk

Effective date:25/09/08 OP C8

290ft 10mb	1nm SW of St Annes N4942.37 W00212.88		Alternative AD Diversion AD	Jersey Guernsey

Alderney	APP	TWR	GND	FIRE
	Guernsey 128.650	125.350	130.500	121.600

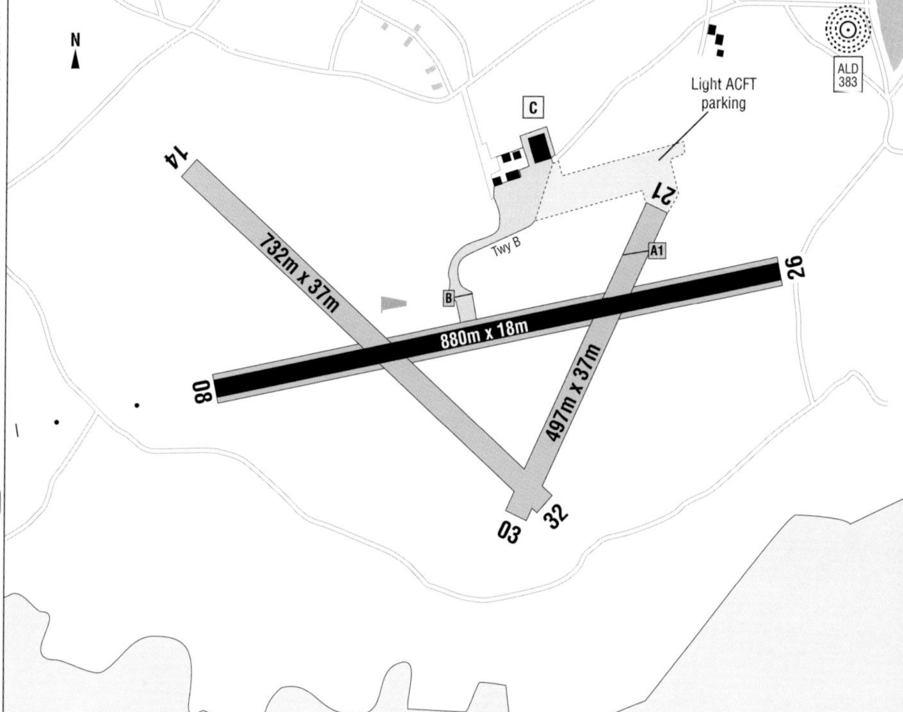

RWY	SURFACE	TORA	LDA	U/L	LIGHTING
03/21	Grass	497	497		Nil
14/32	Grass	732	732		Thr Rwy APAPI 3.5° LHS
08/26	Asphalt	880	880		App Thr Rwy APAPI 3° LHS

Rwy08/26 18m asphalt with 2.5m grass either side

RNAV			
GUR	109.40	047	22.1

Remarks

Not available to non-radio ACFT. PPR for parking on hard apron. Hi-Vis. Permit ACFT require written permission to flying from ATC (Guernsey) prior to arr. Channel Islands CTR regulations apply. ACFT must be able to maintain R/T communication with Jersey Zone, Guernsey APP & Alderney TWR. Instrument training must be booked in advance with Guernsey APP. On arrival all pilots and passengers must report to Flight Clearance to carry out Special Branch & Customs clearance. Duty free shop.

Warnings

Exercise caution because of turbulence caused by nearby cliffs. Rwy surfaces undulating. Rwy03/21 & Rwy14/32 are marked by inset concrete blocks. Low boundary fence with orange/white markers short of Rwy03 & 32 Thr. ACFT using Rwy08/26 may see a white RVR light at upwind ends when Rwy lights are on. AD boundary fence 0.9m high lies within the Rwy14/32 and Rwy03/21 Rwy strips. Animals grazing infields on final APP. Due to coastal location, birds are a hazard throughout most of the year, particularly in the migration season.
Noise: Avoid over flying St Annes below 700ft aal.

Operating Hrs Mon-Thu 0640-1730
Fri-Sun 0640-1830 (Summer)
Mon-Sat 0740-1830
Sun 0855-1830 (Winter)

Circuits 26, 32 LH, 08, 14 RH, 700ft QFE
No circuits 03/21

Landing Fee
£10.20 per 1000kgs or part there of (flights > 55nm)
£8.20 per 1000kgs or part thereof (flights < 55nm)
£6.20 per 1000kgs or part there of (local flights)
Fuel uplift or overnight stay discounts – Single £8 Twin £16
3 nights free parking

Maintenance Nil
Fuel AVGAS 100LL
0700-1730 (Daily) Sun 0900-1830 (Winter)

Disabled Facilities

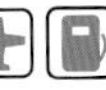      

Restaurants Light refreshments available at AD

Taxis
Alderney Taxis **Tel:** 01481 822611/822992

Cycle Hire
J B Cycle Hire **Tel:** 01481 822294/822762

Weather Info M T9 Fax 224 JER
Tel: 01481 238957 (METAR & TAF)

Operator
States of Guernsey
States of Guernsey Airport
Guernsey, Channel Islands
Tel: 01481 822851 (Alderney ATC)
Tel: 01481 237766 Ex 2130 (Guernsey APP)
Tel: 01481 237766 (Guernsey ATC)
Tel: 01481 822851 (PPR Hard apron only)
Fax: 01481 822352 (Alderney ATC)

Effective date:25/09/08

CTR Class D Airspace

Normal CTA/CTR Class D Airspace rules apply
Alderney Control Zone Radius 5nm SFC/2000ft aal

1 Unless otherwise authorised by Guernsey ATC, an ACFT shall not fly at less than 2000ft above AD elevation and within 5nm of the AD.
2 If at any time the ACFT is less than 2000ft within 5nm of the AD, then a continuous watch is to be made with Guernsey ATC
3 Carriage of SSR transponders is mandatory within the Channel Isles CTR.
4 If R/T failure occurs track 070° out of the zone from Alderney from overhead the AD at 2000ft.

Channel Island Visual Reference Points (VRP)

VRP	VOR/DME	VOR/DME	VOR/DME
Carteret Lighthouse N4922.00 W00148.00	JSY 051°/13nm	GUR 101°/32nm	
Casquets Lighthouse N4943.00 W00222.00	JSY 340°/32nm	GUR 032°/19nm	
Corbiere Lighthouse N4911.00 W00215.00	JSY 257°/8nm	GUR 141°/21nm	DIN 353°/36nm
Heauville N4934.60 W00148.06	JSY 026°/24nm	GUR 078°/33nm	
NE Point of Guernsey N4930.42 W00230.52	JSY 317°/25nm	GUR 045°/6nm	
NW corner of Jersey N4915.30 W00214.50	JSY 289°/8nm	GUR 131°/18nm	
Point de Rozel N4928.60 W00150.60	JSY 029°/18nm	GUR 088°/30nm	
St. Germain N4914.00 W00138.00	JSY 091°/16nm	GUR 111°/40nm	DIN 028°/43nm
SE Corner of Jersey N4910.00 W00202.00	JSY 176°/3nm	GUR 130°/28nm	DIN 007°/35nm
W of Cap de la Hague N4943.00 W00200.00	JSY 008°/30nm	GUR 058°/29nm	

See Channel Island transit Corridor chart – Jersey

A

XAND ANDREAS

110ft 3mb	3nm NW of Ramsey N5422.03 W00426.45	PPR	Alternative AD Ronaldsway

Andreas Base	ATIS Ronaldsway 123.875	APP Ronaldsway 120.850	A/G 130.100

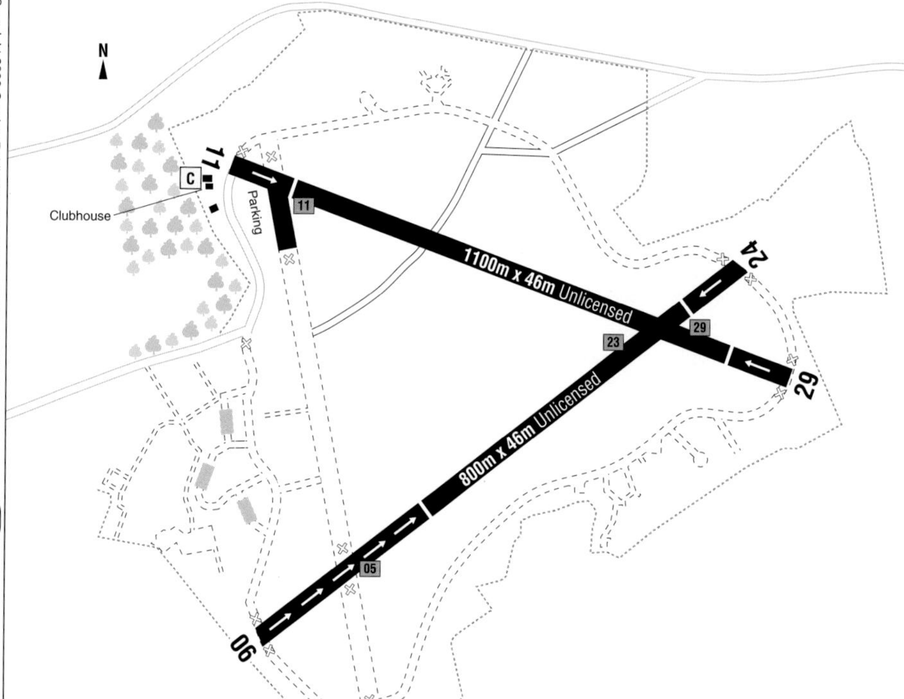

RWY	SURFACE	TORA	LDA	U/L	LIGHTING
11/29	Asphalt			1100x46	Nil
06/24	Asphalt			800x46	Nil

RNAV			
IOM	112.20	038	22.0

Remarks
PPR by telephone 24hours before visit. Visiting ACFT welcome at pilots own risk. AD uses WW2 site, marked areas are useable, Rwy surfaces may have loose stones. AD is not notified as a point of entry for I.O.M. under the prevention of Terrorism legislation, call special branch 12 hours before visit.

Warnings
Non-radio traffic occasionally operates from Andreas. Vehicle access to AD strictly controlled due to Rwy access. See website for details.
Caution: Rotor winds off hills to N of Rwy24.
Noise: Avoid over flying all local houses.

Operating Hrs	0900-1900 (Summer) 0900-1700 (Winter)
Circuits	11 & 24 LH 06 & 29 RH 1000ft QFE No overhead joins
Landing Fee	Single £15 Twin £25
Maintenance	Nil
Fuel	By arrangement
Disabled Facilities	Nil
Restaurant	Nil
Taxi	
Crenells	**Tel:** 01624 812239
Car Hire	Nil

Weather Info	Air N MOEx
Operator	Andreas Aviation Andreas Airfield Ballacorey Farm Ballacorey Road Andreas Isle of Man, IM7 4EW **Tel:** 01624 880897 **Tel:** 07624 473397 www.manxpilots.com

A

EGSL ANDREWSFIELD

286ft 10mb	4nm WNW of Braintree N5153.70 E00026.95	PPR	**Alternative AD** **Diversion AD**	**Southend** Earls Colne

Andrewsfield	LARS Farnborough North 132.800	APP Essex RAD 120.625	A/G 130.550

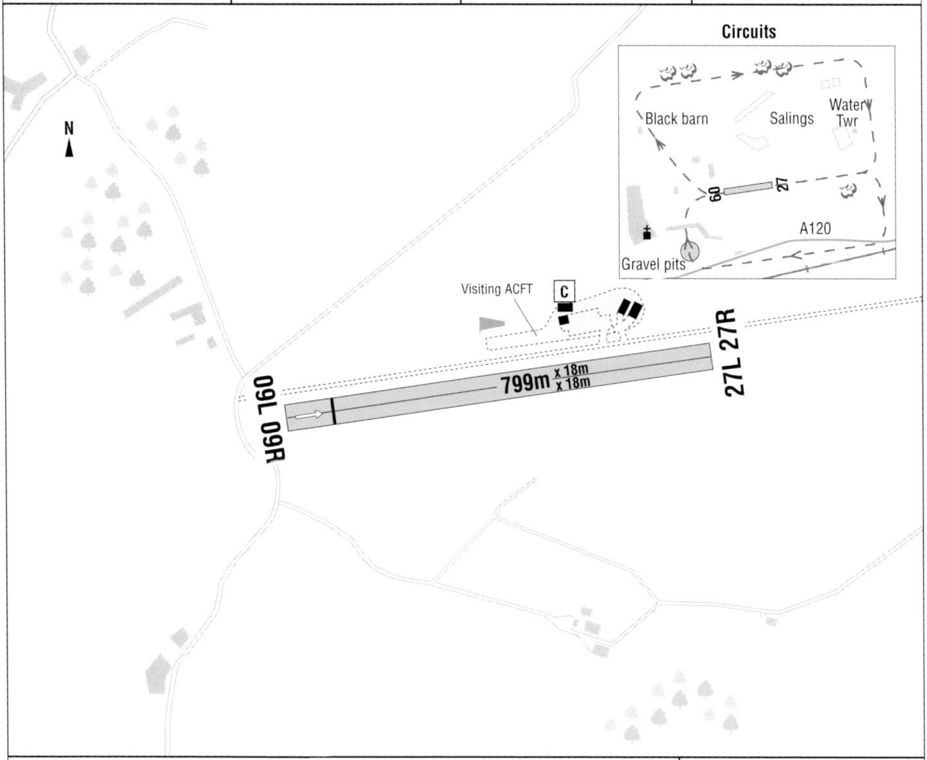

Circuits

Black barn
Salings
Water Twr
09
27
A120
Gravel pits

N
Visiting ACFT
C
09L 09R
799m x 18m x 18m
27L 27R

RWY	SURFACE	TORA	LDA	U/L	LIGHTING
09L/R	Grass	799	720		Thr Rwy
27L/R	Grass	799	799		Thr Rwy APAPI 3° LHS

Operating as two parallel Rwys

RNAV			
LAM	115.60	039	18.6

Remarks

PPR by telephone only. Not available for public transport flights. Use at night by ACFT requiring a licensed AD is confined to operations by Andrewsfield Aviation Ltd using Rwy27. Rwy09 not available for landings by night by ACFT required to use a licensed AD.

Warnings

Located on E edge of Stansted CTR and under the Stansted CTA (base 2000ft AMSL).

Operating Hrs 0700-1900 (Summer)
0830-2100 (Winter) & by arr

Circuits RH 700ft QFE

Landing Fee Single £8 Helicopters £12

Maintenance
MK Aero support **Tel:** 01371 856796

Fuel AVGAS 100LL

Disabled Facilities

Restaurants Hot & cold food available

Taxis
Style Travel **Tel:** 01371 853016

Car Hire
The Oak Garage **Tel:** 01371 820227

Weather Info Air Cen MOEx

Operator Andrewsfield Aviation Ltd
Sailing Airfield, Stebbing
Great Dunmow, Essex, CM6 3TH
Tel: 01371 856744
Fax: 01371 856500
aviation@andrewsfield.freeserve.co.uk

Effective date:25/09/08 OP 08

262ft 9mb	2nm E of Sandbach N5308.50 W00219.00	PPR	Alternative AD	**Liverpool** Manchester Barton

Non-Radio	ATIS Manchester 128.175 (Arr)	Safetycom 135.475

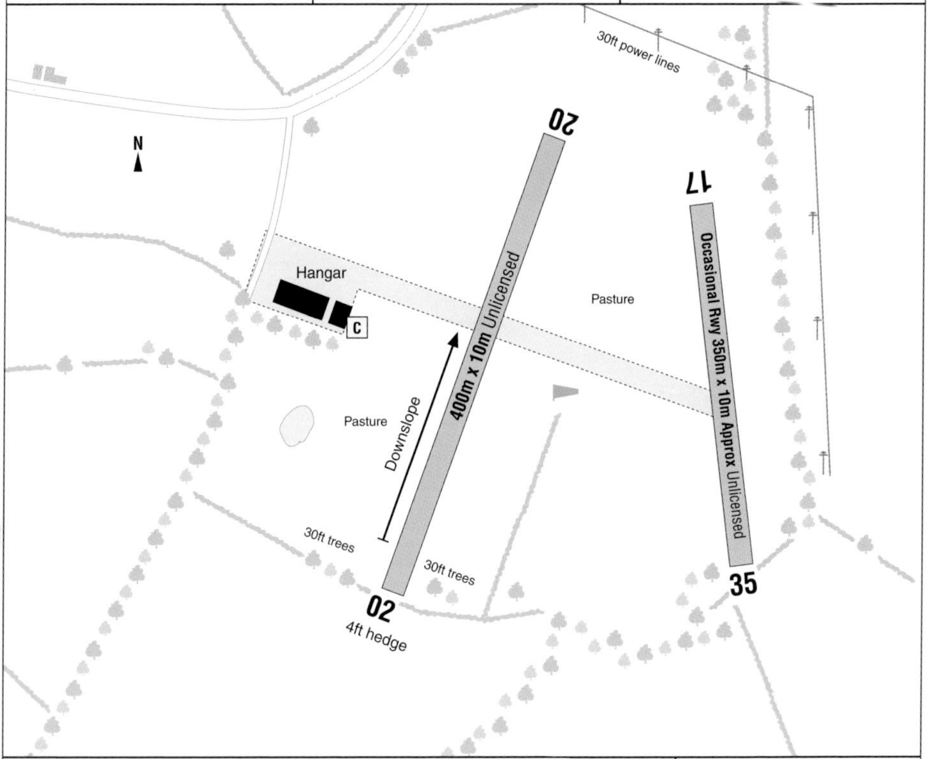

RWY	SURFACE	TORA	LDA	U/L	LIGHTING
02/20	Grass			400x10m	Nil

Rwy02/20 surface undulates
Rwy17/35 (350x10m) avail certain times due to crop rotation

RNAV			
MCT	113.55	193	13.1

Remarks
PPR by telephone essential. Visiting ACFT welcome at pilots own risk. AD used as microlight training site. Twy W of windsock can be used for landing in strong crosswinds

Warnings
Manchester CTR boundary is 2.5nm to N. 4ft hedge Rwy02 Thr. 30ft trees abeam Rwy02 Thr 30ft power lines cross final APP Rwy20 approx 175m from Thr.
Noise: See overleaf for specific noise info

Operating Hrs	SR-SS
Circuits	02 LH, 20 RH 500ft QFE
Landing Fee	£2
Maintenance	By prior arr
Fuel	By prior arr
Disbabled Facilities	Nil
Restaurants	Nil
Taxis/Car Hire	Nil
Weather Info	Air Cen MOEx

Operator
Arclid Resident Flyers
C/O John Bradbury (CFI)
Cheshire Microlight Centre
4 Adlington Drive
Sandbach
Cheshire,CW11 1DX
Tel: 01270 764713 (Home/Office)
Tel: 07831 274201 (Airfield/Mobile)
enquire@cheshiremicrolights.co.uk
www.cheshiremicrolights.co.uk

A

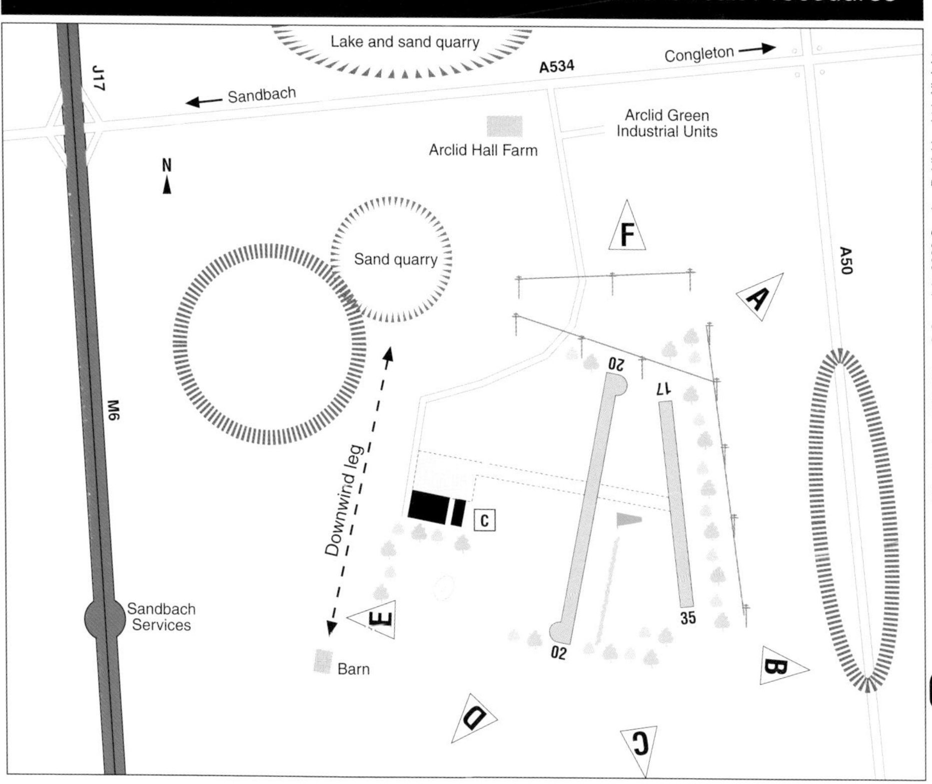

Arclid circuit procedures
Circuits should be made as tight to AD as possible to avoid the noise sensitive areas marked. Particularly those to the W.
Avoid the houses to E when possible.
Depts to follow the standard dept routes marked A-F.
When you book out, take the next SDR in turn.

Effective date:25/09/08

A

150ft 5mb	3.2nm SW of Winsford N5309.85 W00234.29	PPR	Alternative AD Diversion AD	Liverpool Hawarden Non-standard join

Ashcroft	ATIS Manchester 128.175 (Arr)	ATIS Liverpool 124.325	APP Liverpool 119.850	A/G 122.525 transmit blind

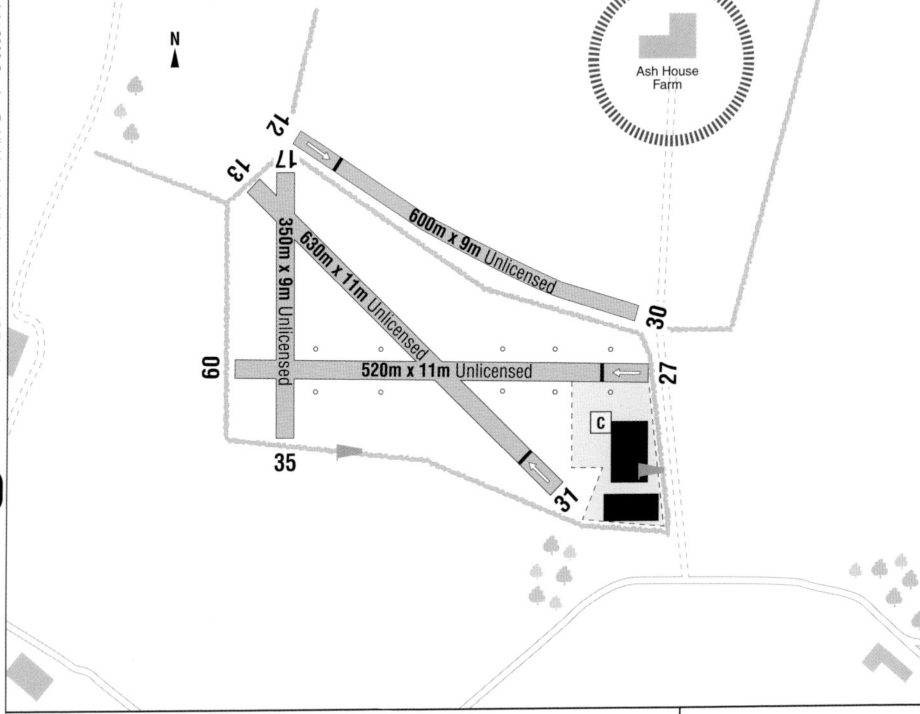

RWY	SURFACE	TORA	LDA	U/L	LIGHTING
09/27	Grass			520x11	Ltd
13/31	Grass			630x11	Nil
12/30	Grass			600x9	Nil
17/35	Grass			350x9	Nil

Displaced Thr Rwy27 50m, Displaced Thr Rwy32 50m, Displaced Thr Rwy12 100m

RNAV			
MCT	113.55	228	16.0

Remarks
Strict PPR. Pilots use the strip entirely at their own risk and discretion. There may be long grass either side of the Rwys.

Warnings
Rwy12/30 curved and slightly raised. Rwy13/31 & Rwy17/35 waterlogged after heavy rain. Raised white Rwy markers along either side of Rwy09/27. Severe downdrafts when landing on Rwy27 with SW winds >10kts. Rwy27 slopes up by 1.2%.
Noise: Essential no flying on N side of AD, avoid all local farmhouses.

Operating Hrs SR-SS
Circuits South 800ft QFE
Landing Fee Microlights £5
Parking £5 per day
ACFT < 200hp £8
ACFT > 200hp £15
Maintenance Nil
Fuel Nil
Disabled Facilities Nil
Restaurants Boot & Slipper 2nm from AD
Tel: 01270 528238

Taxis
Winsford Taxis **Tel:** 01606 550055
Tonys Taxis **Tel:** 01606 559348
Weather Info Air Cen MOEx
Operator Steve Billington
Ashcroft Farm, Darnhall
Winsford, Cheshire, CW7 4DQ
Tel: 01270 528697
ashcroftair@btinternet.com
www.ashcroftair.co.uk

8ft 0mb	4.5nm NNW of Skegness N5313.00 E00016.25	PPR	Alternative AD	**Doncaster Sheffield** Wickenby

Non Radio	LARS Waddington 127.350	LARS Coningsby 120.800	Safetycom 135.475

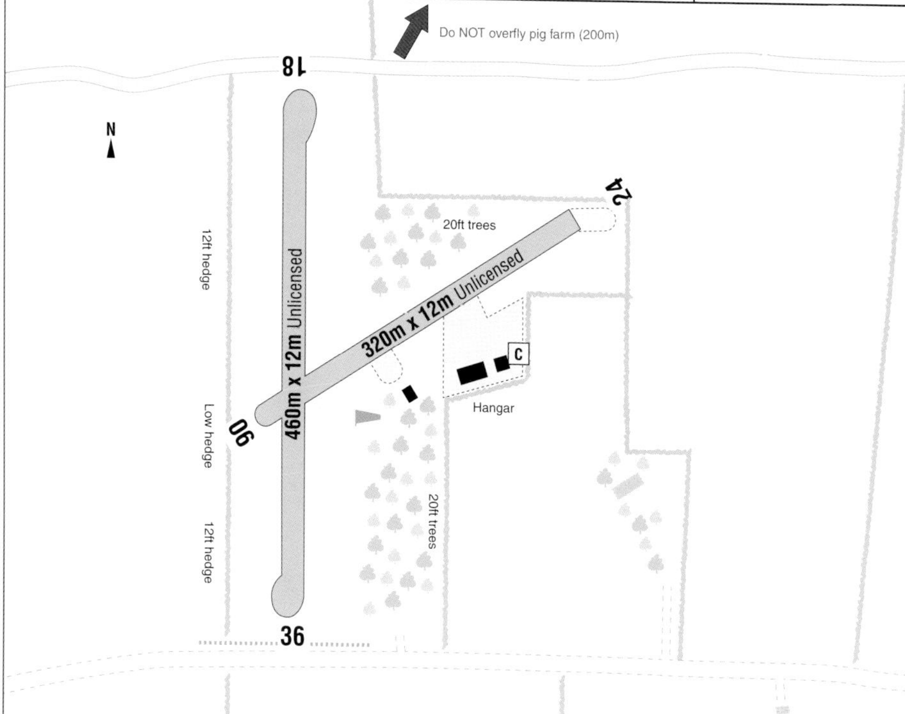

RWY	SURFACE	TORA	LDA	U/L	LIGHTING
18/36	Grass			460x12	Nil
06/24	Grass			320x12	Nil

RNAV

Remarks

PPR by telephone essential. All visitors must be met by prior arrangement AD is very isolated, no public transport is available. Rwys regularly cut and in excellent condition.

Warnings

Rwy36 has slight downslope at N end. Low hedges at Rwy06/24 Thr. Rwy36 APP is over a public road.
Caution: Vehicles on Airfield.
Noise: Avoid over flying pig farm to NNE of AD.

Operating Hrs	SR-SS
Circuits	18 & 06 RH, 24 &36 LH.
Landing Fee	Available with PPR
Maintenance	Nil
Fuel	Nil
Disabled Facilities	Nil
Restaurant	Nil
Taxi/Car Hire	Available with PPR
Weather Info	Air Cen MOEx

Operator
John Rogers
The Captain's Table
Witham Bank
Chapel Hill
Lincolnshire
LN4 4QA
Tel: 01526 343757

283ft 11mb	1nm SW of Saffron Walden N5200.52 E00013.57	PPR	**Alternative AD** **Diversion AD**	**Cambridge** Duxford

Non-radio	**APP** **Essex RAD 120.625**	**Safetycom** **135.475**

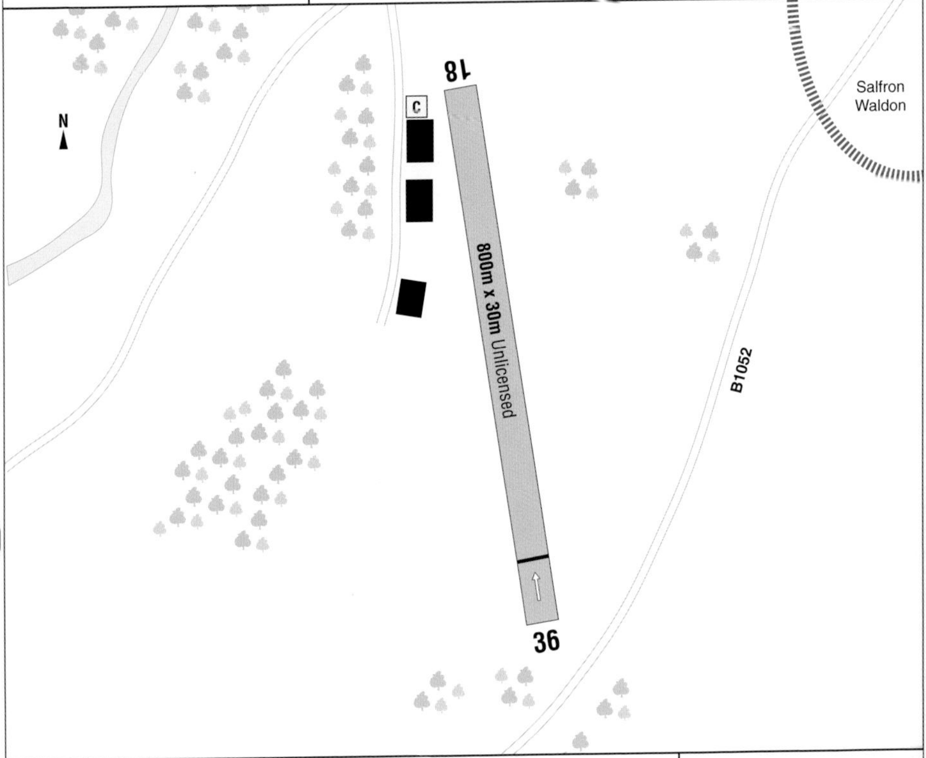

18
C
N
Salfron Waldon
800m x 30m Unlicensed
B1052
36

RWY	SURFACE	TORA	LDA	U/L	LIGHTING
18/36	Grass			800x30	Nil

Rwy18 slight upslope
Rwy36 APP tall trees reduce LDA to 700m

RNAV			
BKY	**116.25**	**083**	**6.1**

Remarks
AD situated on the edge of Stansted CTA. Inbound ACFT to contact Essex RAD. Visiting pilots must report to the control point at the green hangar to sign movements book.

Warnings
Caution is necessary on APP Rwy36 due to a line of trees across the extended centre line 50m before the AD boundary.
Noise: Avoid over flying Saffron Walden 1nm NE of AD.

Operating Hrs By arr SR-SS
Circuits 18 RH, 36 LH
Landing Fee Single £5 Twin £10 (private)
Single/Twin £10 (commercial)
Maintenance Nil
Fuel Nil
Disabled Facilities

Taxis
Adtax **Tel:** 01799 521164

Car Hire
Practical Car Hire **Tel:** 01799 541456

Weather Info Air Cen MOEx
Operator Audley End Development Co Ltd
Bruncketts Wendens Ambo
Saffron Walden
Essex
CB11 4JL
Tel: 01799 541354/541956
Fax: 01799 542134
aee@tdirect.net

A

EGTA AYLESBURY

289ft 9mb	3nm NE of Thame N5146.52 W000546.40	PPR	Alternative AD	Cranfield Wycombe

Non-standard join

Non-radio	LARS Benson 120.900	APP Luton 129.550	Safetycom 135.475

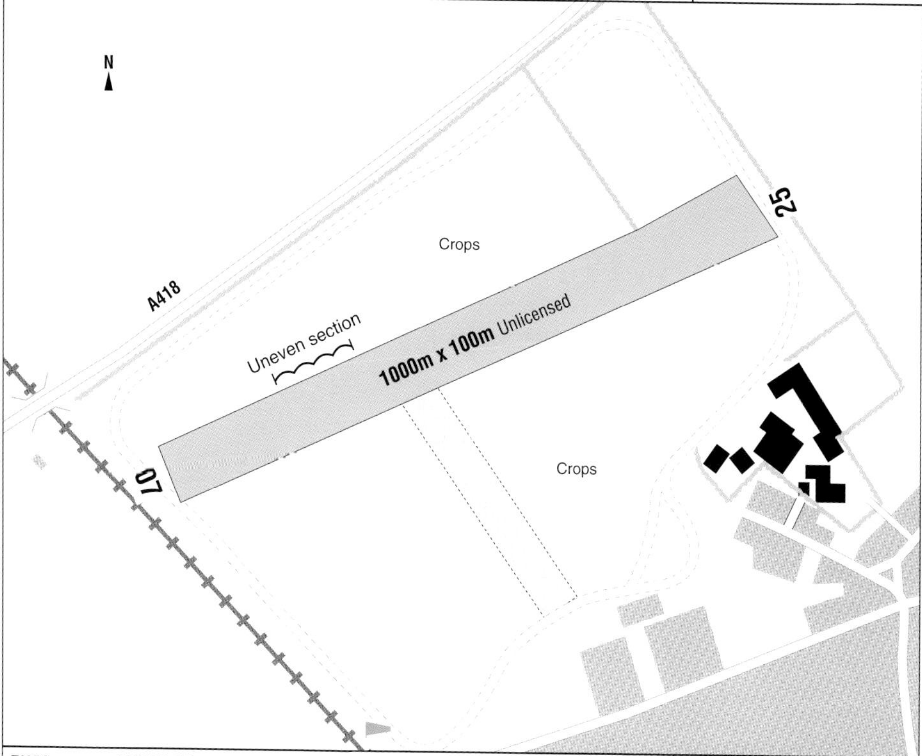

N

A418

Crops

Uneven section

1000m x 100m Unlicensed

07

25

Crops

RWY	SURFACE	TORA	LDA	U/L	LIGHTING
07/25	Grass			1000x100	Nil

RNAV			
BNN	113.75	286	13.8

Remarks

PPR by telephone essential at all times. Gliding site but light ACFT & microlights welcome at own risk. Please park adjacent to glider launch point at Thr of Rwy in use.

Warnings

No overhead joins due launch cables. AD may suffer from water logging after periods of heavy rain. The gliding club advise that although they are always happy to see powered visitors they have no facilities – not even a loo!

Noise: Avoid over flying Haddenham village 1.5nm SE of AD

Operating Hrs	Weekends only Sat-Sun (Summer) Sun only (Winter)
Circuits	All circuits on N side 1000ft QFE No overhead joins Keep good lookout for gliders
Landing Fee	Donations gratefully received
Maintenance	Nil
Fuel	Nil
Disabled Facilities	Nil
Restaurants	Nil
Taxis/Car Hire	Nil
Weather Info	Air Cen MOEx

Operator

Upward Bound Trust Gliding Club
Mr M Clark
27 Crotch Crescent
New Marston
Oxon
OX3 0JL
Tel: 01865 865165 (Day)
Tel: 01865 721090 (Evenings)
www.ubt.org.uk

495ft 17mb	3.5nm ENE of Chipping Sodbury N5132.98 W00217.92	PPR	Alternative AD	**Bristol Filton** Kemble

Badminton	APP Lyneham 123.400 Bristol Filton 122.725	A/G 123.175

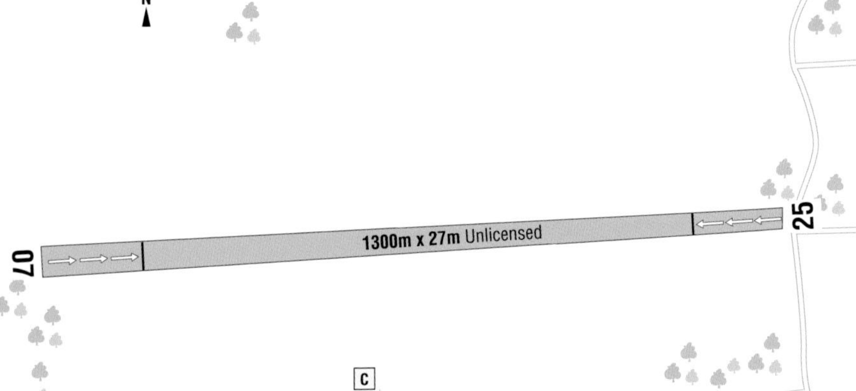

RWY	SURFACE	TORA	LDA	U/L	LIGHTING
07	Grass			1250x27	Nil
25	Grass			1250x27	Nil

Displaced Thr Rwy07 50m, Displaced Thr Rwy25 50m

RNAV

Remarks
PPR by telephone only. Rwy25 APP should be high enough to cross the public road safely.

Warnings
Care must be taken during August and March when Rwy may be fenced against stock. Horse trials in May.
Noise: Avoid over flying the villages of Badminton and Little Badminton.

Operating Hrs By arr
Circuits 07 LH, 25 RH
Landing Fee On Application
Maintenance Nil
Fuel 100LL
Disabled Facilities Nil
Restaurants Nil
Taxis/Car Hire Nil
Weather Info Air SW MOEx

Operator
Mr H Richardson
Badminton Airfield
Badminton
Glos, GL9 1DD
Tel: 01454 218888 (Hangar)
Tel: 01454 218220
Tel: 01249 721076
Fax: 01454 218159

160ft 5mb	2nm SE of Thirsk N5412.62 W00117.55	PPR	Alternative AD Diversion AD	Durham Tees Valley Wombleton

Non-standard join

Bagby	APP Topcliffe 125.000	A/G 123.250 Not always manned

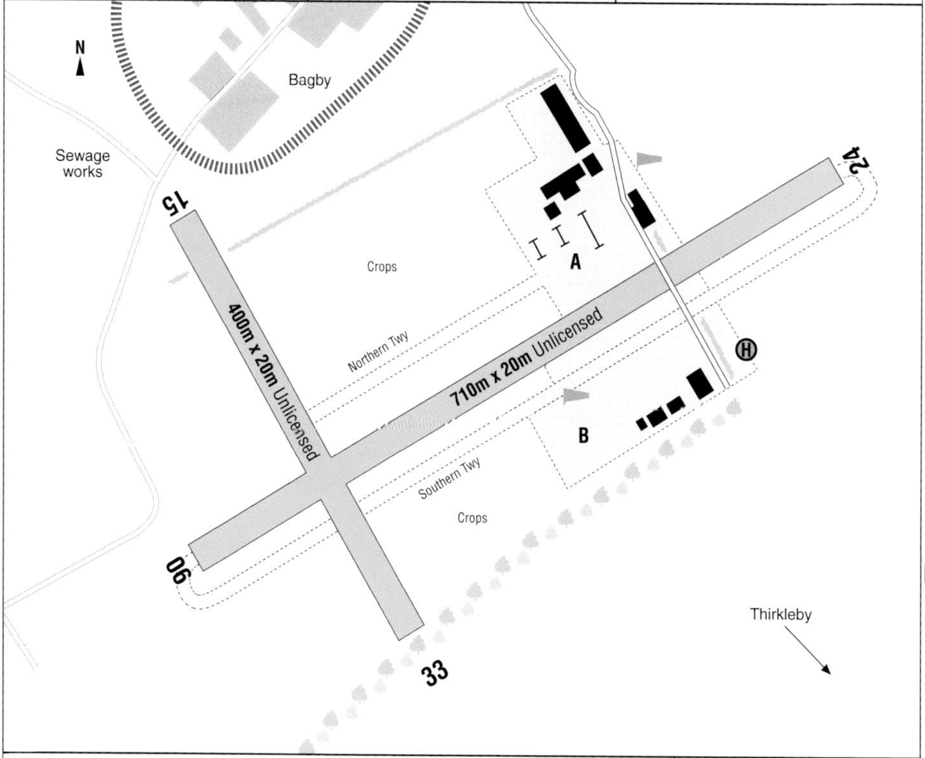

N
Bagby
Sewage works
15
24
Crops
A
Northern Twy
710m x 20m Unlicensed
400m x 20m Unlicensed
B
Southern Twy
Crops
06
33
Thirkleby

RWY	SURFACE	TORA	LDA	U/L	LIGHTING
06/24	Grass			710x20	Rwy lighting available
15/33	Grass			400x20	Nil

Rwy06 Upslope 2.5%, Rwy33 Upslope 1.5%

RNAV

Remarks
PPR essential during winter months. Light ACFT including twins are welcome. During Topcliffe Hrs of operation special dept procedures apply, details available on arrival. Microlight training takes place on AD. ACFT parking, A – short term, B – long term.

Warnings
Non radio ACFT telephone briefing recommended weekdays.
Noise: Do not over fly the villages of Bagby and Thirkleby. Compulsory routing via sewage works on Rwy15/33.

Operating Hrs Visiting ACFT 0900-1900, Home ACFT 0830-2000 (Summer) & by arr. Strictly PPR (Winter). Services available 0900-1900

Circuits To S 800ft
No overhead joins

Landing Fee All landings free with fuel uplift

Maintenance M3 G Fox Engineering
Tel: 01845 597707

Fuel AVGAS 100LL JET A1

Disabled Facilities

Accomodation Hotels In Thirsk

Restaurants Snacks/meals & club facilities at AD 0900-1700 daily

Taxis
Jeb **Tel:** 07973 443169
Chapmans **Tel:** 07960 568299

Car Hire
Moss Motors **Tel:** 01845 522042

Weather Info Air N MOEx

Operator Mr M L Scott
Bagby Airfield
Bagby, Thirsk
North Yorkshire YO7 2PH
Tel: 01845 597385
Tel: 07736 775463
info@bagby.airfield.com

340ft 11mb	2nm NE of Corby N5230.10 W00038.15	PPR	**Alternative AD**	**Cranfield** Peterborough Conington

Non-Radio	LARS Cottesmore 130.200	Safetycom 135.475

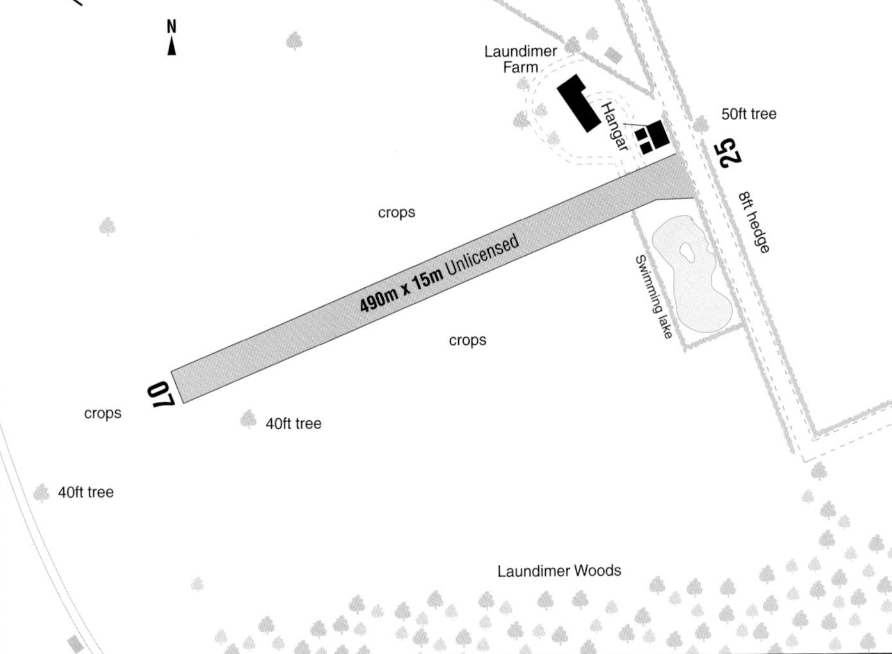

RWY	SURFACE	TORA	LDA	U/L	LIGHTING
07/25	Grass			490x15	Nil

RNAV			
DTY	116.40	046	26

Remarks
PPR by telephone. Visiting ACFT, including Microlights welcome at pilots own risk. Rwy25 boggy during Winter months. Cottesmore active Mon-Fri only.
Visual aids to location: AD located at top of hill adjacent to extensive Woods, (S of strip). Rockingham Motor Racing circuit 1.5nm to NW.

Warnings
8ft hedge at Rwy25 Thr. 50ft tree to N Rwy25 APP on very short final. 40ft tree to S Rwy07 Thr. Crops grown up to edges of strip. Deenethorpe AD 1nm NE. Lyveden Gliding site 1.5nm SE, beware of cables up to 2000ft agl. Wittering MATZ 3.5nm NNE, Harrier ACFT may be encountered mainly during weekdays, keep a good lookout.
Noise: Avoid over flying local habitation, particularly Weldon village to NW.

Operating Hrs	SR-SS daily
Circuits	25 LH, 07 RH
Landing Fee	Donations to Air Ambulance Microlights £2 ACFT £5
Maintenance	Nil
Fuel	MOGAS by arr
Disabled Facilities	Nil
Restaurants/ Accomodation	B&B available from Laundimer house

Taxis/Car Hire	Nil
Weather Info	Air Cen MOEx
Operator	Mr T D Baker Laundimer House Bears Lane, Weldon, Northants, NN17 3LH **Tel/Fax:** 01536 206770 sportscruiser@aol.co.uk (AD) Pauline@laundimerhouse.co.uk (B&B)

EGQB BALLYKELLY

18ft 0mb	5nm SW of Londonderry Airfield N5503.69 W00700.89	PPR MIL	Alternative AD Londonderry

Non-standard join

Ballykelly	APP Londonderry 123.625	APP 128.50	A/G 129.95 (Drop Zone)

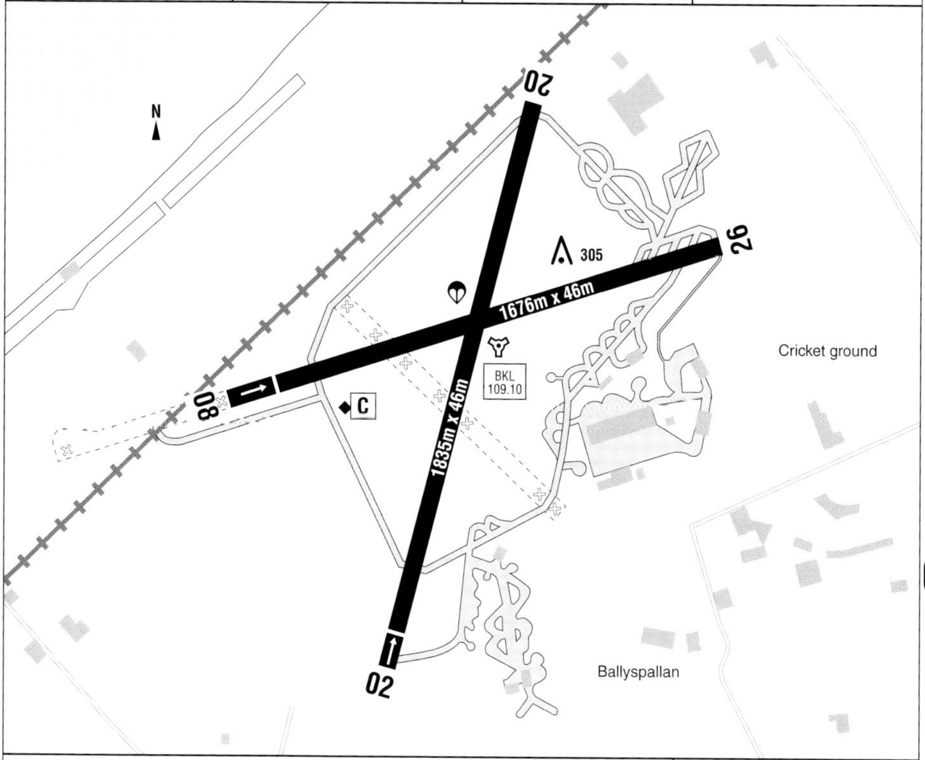

N
20
26
305
1676m x 46m
1835m x 46m
BKL 109.10
08
C
02
Cricket ground
Ballyspallan

RWY	SURAFCE	TORA	LDA	U/L	LIGHTING
02/20	Concrete	1835	1835		Nil
08/26	Concrete	1676	1676		Nil

Displaced Thr Rwy02 & Rwy08

RNAV			
BEL	117.20	319	36.2

Remarks
PPR 24 Hrs notice required.

Warnings
AD situated within R503. ACFT must not penetrate restricted area unless in contact with Londonderry APP. Pilots are warned against inadvertent entry into prohibited or restricted areas in Northern Ireland, such entry might be judged to have hostile or criminal intent and the ACFT may be liable to counter-measures. High GND to NE of AD. Railway line to W of AD boundary. 350ft mast between Rwy30 & Rwy26 Thr. Free-fall parachuting may take place at any time. Gliding at Bellarena and Benone Strand AD close by.

Operating Hrs	H24
Circuits	Nil
Landing Fee	Available with PPR
Maintenance	Nil
Fuel	Nil
Disabled Facilities	Nil
Restaurants	Nil
Taxi/Car Hire	Nil
Weather Info	Air N GWC

Operator Army
Ballykelly Airfield
Londonderry
Co Londonderry
Northern Ireland
Tel: 02827 721323

EGYE BARKSTON HEATH

367ft 12mb	5nm NE of Grantham N5257.74 W00033.70	PPR MIL	Alternative AD Diversion AD	**Cranwell** Langar

Barkston	APP Cranwell 119.375	TWR 120.425

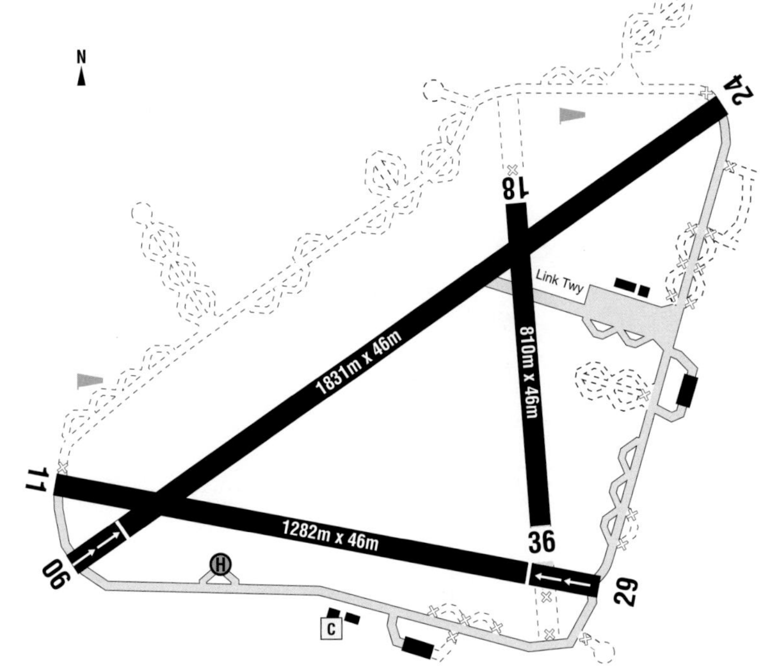

RWY	SURFACE	TORA	LDA	U/L	LIGHTING
06RH	Concrete	1831	1677		Thr Rwy PAPI 3° LH
24RH	Concrete	1831	1831		Ap Thr Rwy PAPI 3° LH
11LH	Asphalt	1282	1280		Thr Rwy PAPI 3° LH
29RH	Asphalt	1282	1125		Thr Rwy PAPI 3° LH
18/36	Asphalt	810	810		Nil

RNAV			
GAM	112.80	148	23.7

Remarks
PPR by telephone essential. AD not available for use outside published Hrs. RAF AD. Extensive military training on AD. Model ACFT club and RAF Cranwell Motor Club use AD at weekends.

Warnings
AD regularly active outside normal operational Hrs. Considerable aerobatic activity may be encountered in the ATZ and local area at any time. Due to the close proximity of neighbouring AD and over lapping RAD patterns, all ACFT on instrument APP may be subject to a RIS, FIS or procedural service.
Noise: Avoid over flying Belton, Bottesford and Ancaster villages.

Operating Hrs	Mon-Thu 0730-1630 Fri 0730-1600 (L)
Circuits	11, 18 LH, 36, 06, 24, 29, RH Piston 800ft QFE. Jet 1500ft QFE Low level 500ft QFE
Landing Fee	Available with PPR
Maintenance	Nil for visiting ACFT
Fuel	Not available to visiting ACFT
Disabled Facilities	
Restaurants	Nil
Taxis/Car Hire	Nil

Weather Info	Air Cen MOEx ATIS **Tel:** 01400 265023
Visual Reporting Points (VRP)	
Point Oscar	Roundabout on A15/A52 W of Threekingham, S of Osbournby.
Point Alpha	E of Bottesford on E edge of A1 southbound road
Operator	Defence Elementary Flying Training School RAF Barkston Heath Grantham, Lincs NG32 2DQ **Tel:** 01400 265200 (PPR) **Tel:** 01400 265201 (Ops)

EGPR BARRA

5ft 0mb	Foreshore of Traigh Mhor N5701.37 W00726.58	PPR	**Alternative AD** **Diversion AD**	**Benbecula** Tiree

Non-standard join

Barra	FIS	AFIS	APP
	Scottish 127.275	Tiree 122.700 Barra 118.075	Benbecula 119.200

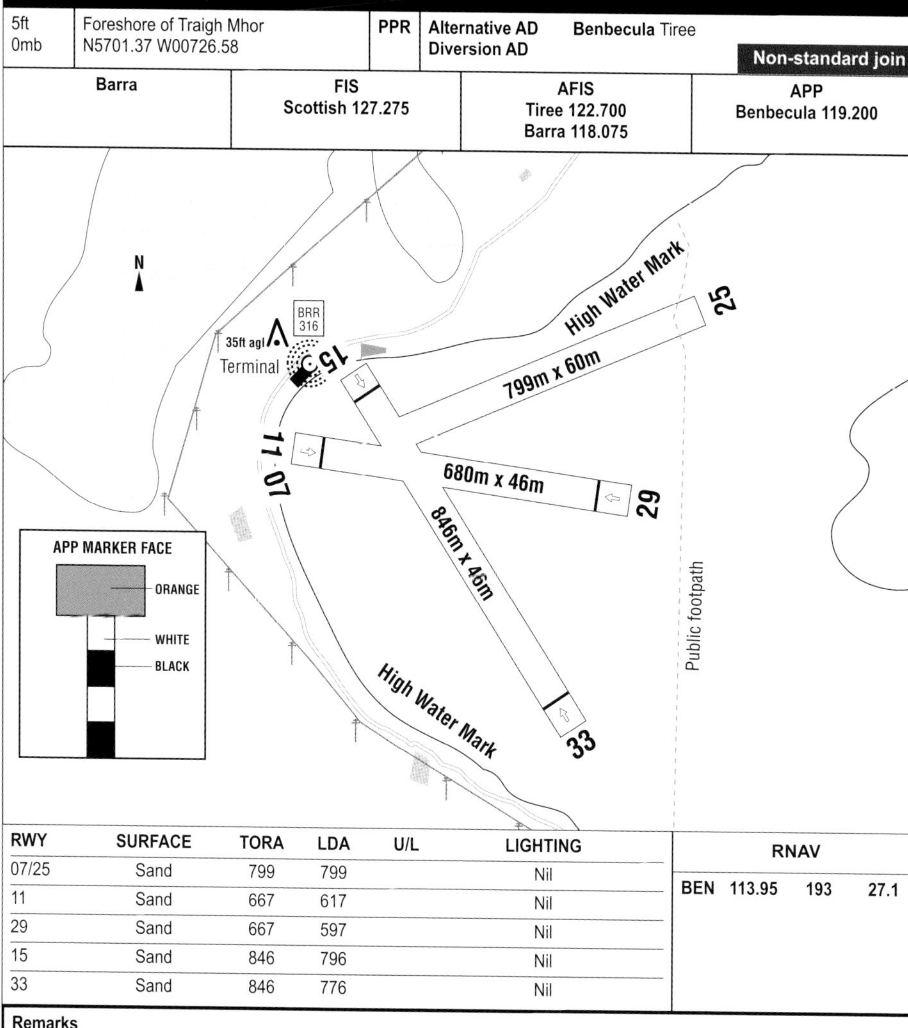

RWY	SURFACE	TORA	LDA	U/L	LIGHTING
07/25	Sand	799	799		Nil
11	Sand	667	617		Nil
29	Sand	667	597		Nil
15	Sand	846	796		Nil
33	Sand	846	776		Nil

RNAV			
BEN	113.95	193	27.1

Remarks

PPR is required to obtain information on surface conditions, in addition to other information. The obstacle clearance surfaces of Rwy07/25 are infringed at both ends. A weather minima of 3km visibility and cloud base of 1000ft aal must be strictly adhered to.

Warnings

Landing and take-off areas may be considerably ridged by hard sand and contain pools of standing water which are hazards to ACFT. The bearing strength, braking action and contamination of the beach is unknown, variable and unpredictable. Some down draughts may be experienced at the W end of Rwy07/25 in strong wind from the W through S. The E end of Rwy07/25 is generally unfit for use due to water logging & sand ridging.

Operating Hrs	Mon-Fri 0945-1215 & 1400-1630 Sat 1215-1330 Sun Closed All times subject to tidal variation
Circuits	Variable
Landing Fee	£16 up to 3000kgs Booked in advance VFR cash/cheque on the day
Maintenance	Nil
Fuel	Nil

Disabled Facilities

Restaurants
Heathbank Hotel (4 miles)
Craigard/Castlebay Hotels (12 miles)

Taxis	
J Campbell	**Tel:** 01871 810216
Car Hire	
Macmillan Self Dri.	**Tel:** 01871 890366
H MacNeil	**Tel:** 01871 810262
Bus	Drops passengers at Castlebay
Weather Info	Air Sc GWC
Operator	HIAL Barra Aerodrome Eoligarry Isle of Barra, HS9 5YD **Tel:** 01871 890212 (PPR) **Fax:** 01871 890220 www.highlands-and-islands-airports.uk.com

44ft 2mb	1.5nm NW of Barrow in Furness N5407.87 W00315.81	PPR	Alternative AD Diversion AD	Blackpool Cark

Walney	AFIS 123.200

N
17
1011m x 46m
23
1048m x 46m Unlicensed
NDB WL 385
DME I-WL 110.15
A
B
H
05
35
ILS I-WL 110.15

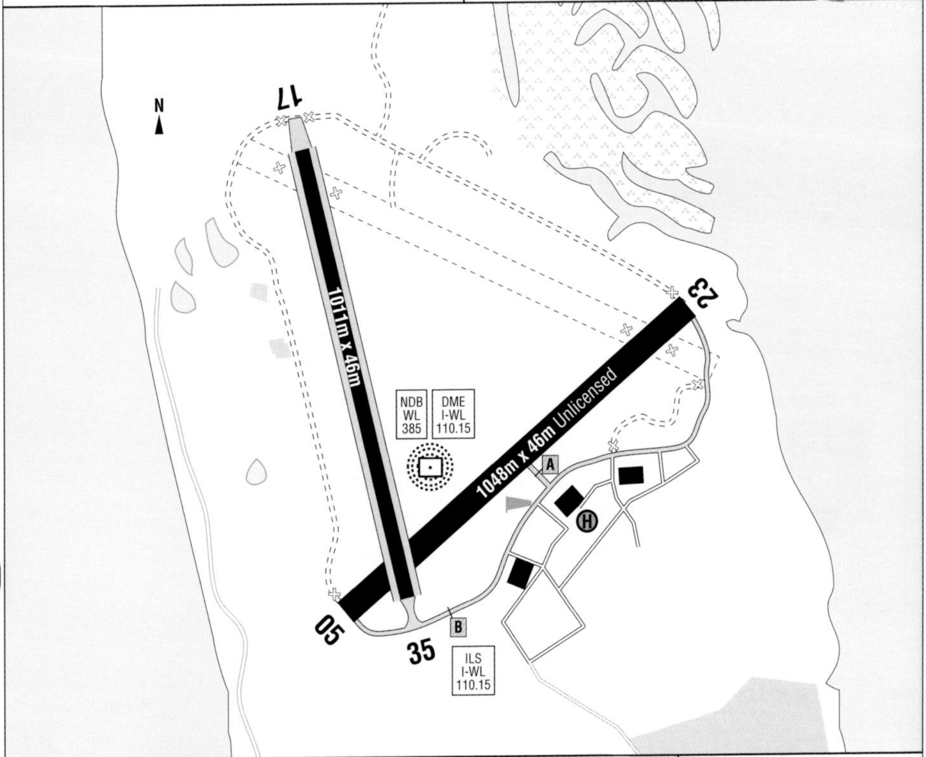

RWY	SURFACE	TORA	LDA	U/L	LIGHTING
05	Asphalt			1014x46	Thr Rwy APAPI 4° LHS
23	Asphalt			1014x46	Thr Rwy APAPI 3.5° LHS
17	Asphalt	1011	1011		Thr Rwy APAPI 4° RHS
35	Asphalt	998	998		Thr Rwy APAPI 3° LHS

RNAV

Remarks
PPR strictly by telephone. Non-radio ACFT not accepted. AD closed to all traffic except home based ACFT and gliders at weekends, PH and other notified periods. Landings absolutely prohibited when AD is closed.

Warnings
Glider launching takes place on the AD. Rwy17/35 has centre strip 23m wide, Rwy edge lights still 46m wide. Restricted area R445 2nm SE of AD

Operating Hrs	Mon Thu 0700-1530 Fri 0700-1200 (Summer) +1Hr (Winter)
Circuits	Variable
Landing Fee	£5.00 per half tonne
Maintenance	Nil
Fuel	JET A1
Disabled Facilities	

Restaurants	Ferry Hotel restaurant 20 mins walk
Taxis	
Acacia Cars	**Tel:** 01229 830055
D&S Contracts	**Tel:** 01229 822020

Car Hire	
Avis	**Tel:** 01229 829555
Hertz	**Tel:** 01229 836666
Weather Info	M* Air N MOEx
Operator	Bae Systems (Marine) Ltd Barrow/Walney Island Aerodrome Cumbria, LA14 3YJ **Tel:** 01229 470087/471407 (Flt Ops) **Fax:** 01229 470619

B

525ft 17mb	2nm S of Coalville N5241.83 W00121.02	PPR	Alternative AD	East Midlands Leicester

Non Radio	ATIS East Mids 128.225	APP East Mids 134.175	Safetycom 135.475

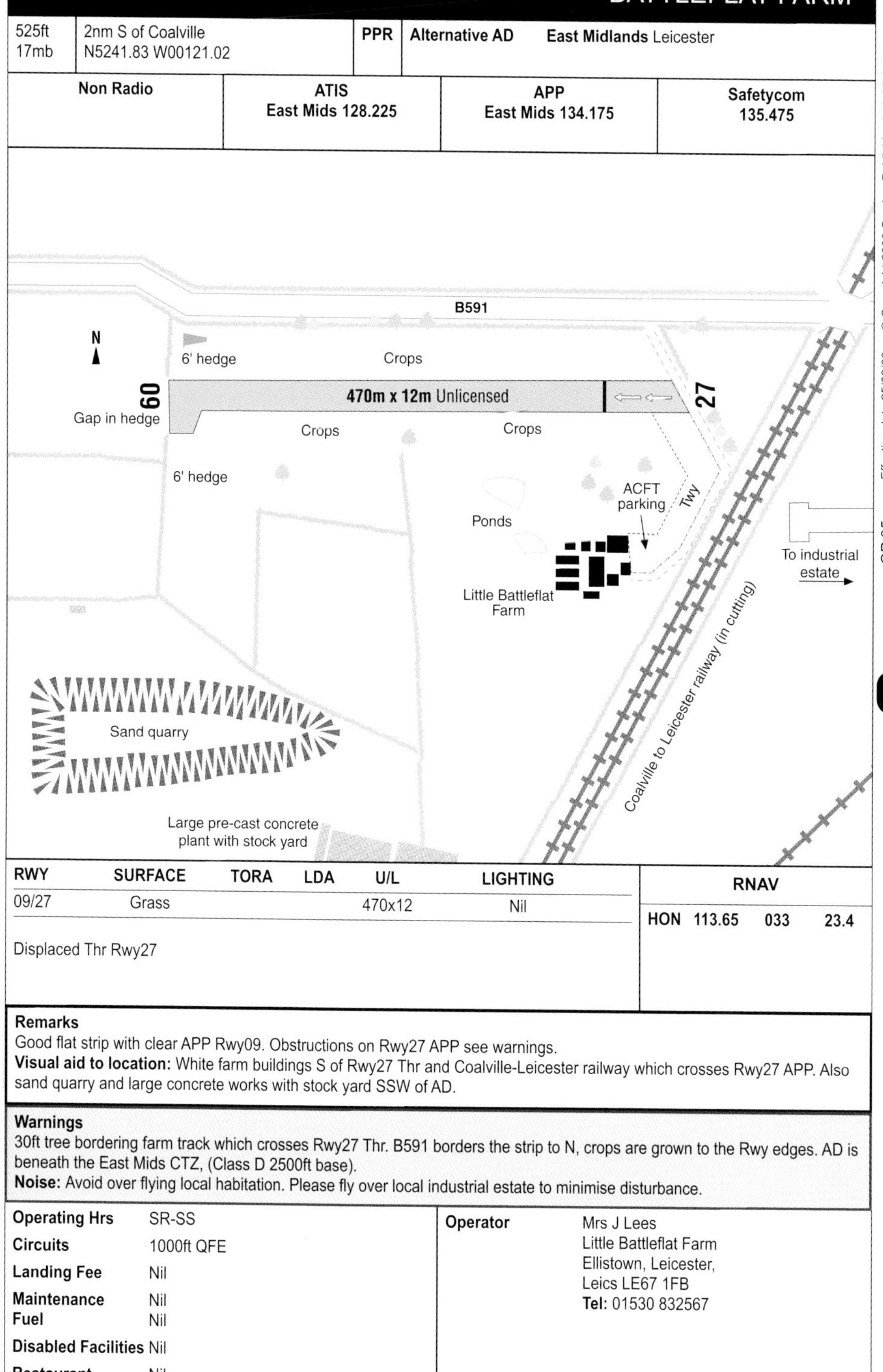

RWY	SURFACE	TORA	LDA	U/L	LIGHTING
09/27	Grass			470x12	Nil

Displaced Thr Rwy27

RNAV			
HON	113.65	033	23.4

Remarks
Good flat strip with clear APP Rwy09. Obstructions on Rwy27 APP see warnings.
Visual aid to location: White farm buildings S of Rwy27 Thr and Coalville-Leicester railway which crosses Rwy27 APP. Also sand quarry and large concrete works with stock yard SSW of AD.

Warnings
30ft tree bordering farm track which crosses Rwy27 Thr. B591 borders the strip to N, crops are grown to the Rwy edges. AD is beneath the East Mids CTZ, (Class D 2500ft base).
Noise: Avoid over flying local habitation. Please fly over local industrial estate to minimise disturbance.

Operating Hrs	SR-SS
Circuits	1000ft QFE
Landing Fee	Nil
Maintenance	Nil
Fuel	Nil
Disabled Facilities	Nil
Restaurant	Nil
Taxi/Car Hire	Nil
Weather Info	Air Cen MOEx

Operator
Mrs J Lees
Little Battleflat Farm
Ellistown, Leicester,
Leics LE67 1FB
Tel: 01530 832567

420ft 14mb	4.5nm SE of Tamworth N5234.00 W00136.60	PPR	Alternative AD	**Birmingham** Tatenhill

Baxterley	APP Brimingham 118.050	A/G 120.300 Only monitored during events

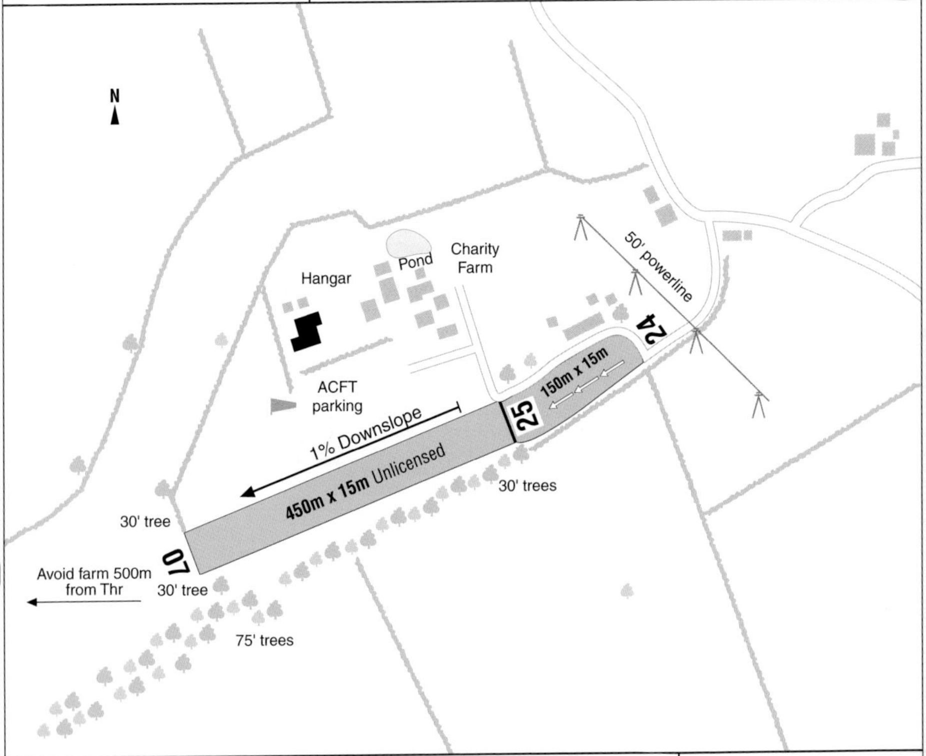

RWY	SURFACE	TORA	LDA	U/L	LIGHTING
07/25	Grass			450x15	Nil

Rwy25 150x15m dogleg 240°

RNAV			
HON	113.65	013	12.7

Remarks
PPR by telephone. Situated close to NE corner of Birmingham CTR (base 2000ft), visitors advised to contact Birmingham APP. Organised Fly-ins and events during summer months. Check aviation press for details. BAX displayed on hangar roof.

Warnings
50ft agl power lines 70m from Rwy25 Thr (measured from beginning of dogleg extension). Mature trees to S of Rwy that may cause turbulence, they decrease in size from Rwy07 Thr towards Rwy25. 1% down slope Rwy25.Occasional model ACFT activity.
Noise: Avoid over flying local habitation, particularly farm 500m out Rwy07 APP.

Operating Hrs	SR-SS
Circuits	S 1000ft QFE
Landing Fee	Nil
Maintenance	Nil
Fuel	AVGAS available by prior arr
Disabled Facilities	Nil
Restaurant	Refreshments available with 24Hrs notice
Taxi/Car Hire	Available on request
Weather Info	Air Cen MOEx

Operator
Ken Broomfield
Charity Farm
Baxterley, Warks
Tel: 01827 874572
Fax: 01827 874898
(Operates as voice info line on fly-in days)

80ft 3mb	2nm SE of Beccles N5226.12 E00137.10	PPR	**Alternative AD** **Norwich** Seething

Beccles	A/G 120.375

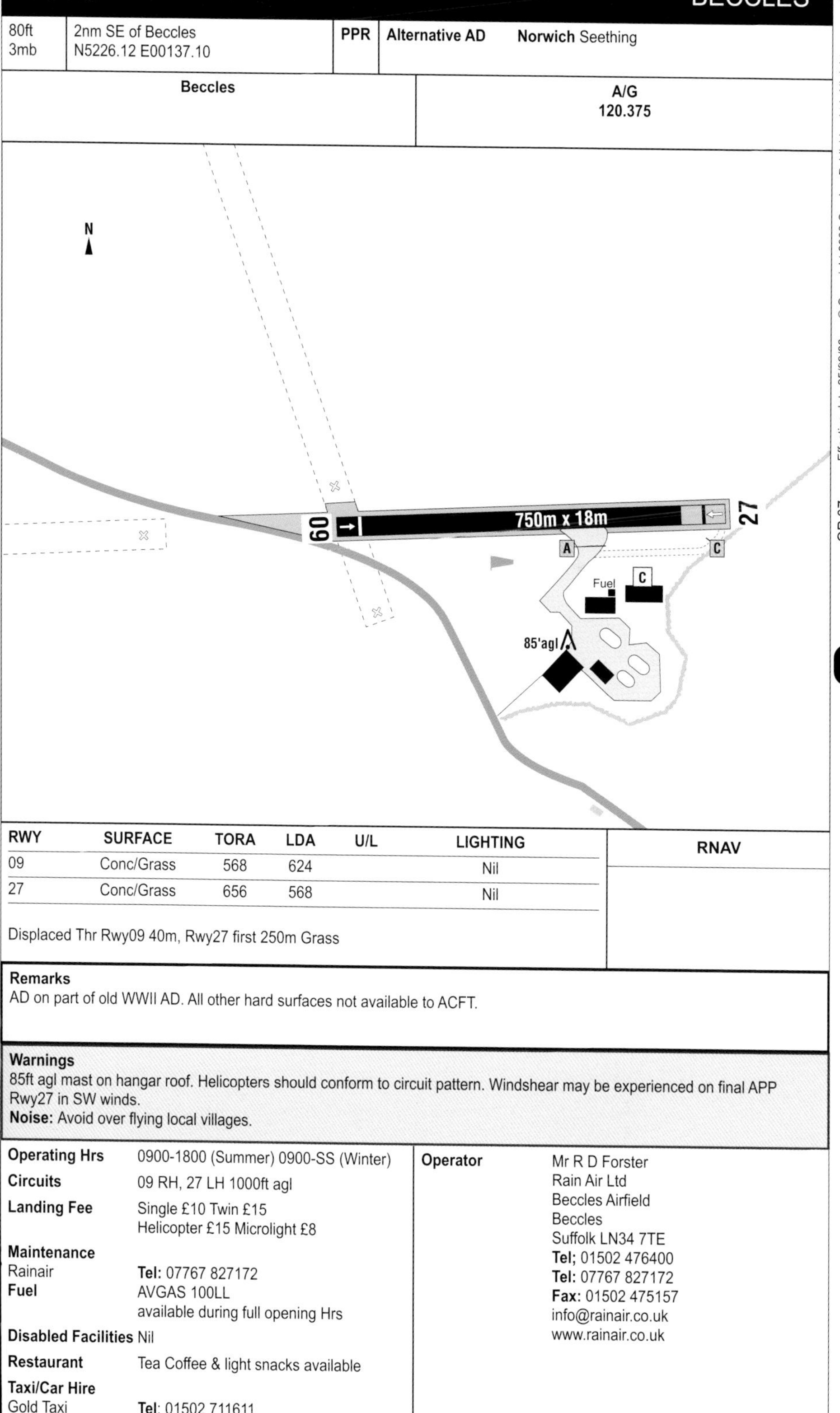

RWY	SURFACE	TORA	LDA	U/L	LIGHTING
09	Conc/Grass	568	624		Nil
27	Conc/Grass	656	568		Nil

Displaced Thr Rwy09 40m, Rwy27 first 250m Grass

RNAV

Remarks
AD on part of old WWII AD. All other hard surfaces not available to ACFT.

Warnings
85ft agl mast on hangar roof. Helicopters should conform to circuit pattern. Windshear may be experienced on final APP Rwy27 in SW winds.
Noise: Avoid over flying local villages.

Operating Hrs	0900-1800 (Summer) 0900-SS (Winter)
Circuits	09 RH, 27 LH 1000ft agl
Landing Fee	Single £10 Twin £15 Helicopter £15 Microlight £8
Maintenance Rainair	**Tel:** 07767 827172
Fuel	AVGAS 100LL available during full opening Hrs
Disabled Facilities	Nil
Restaurant	Tea Coffee & light snacks available
Taxi/Car Hire Gold Taxi	**Tel**: 01502 711611
Weather Info	Air S MOEx

Operator
Mr R D Forster
Rain Air Ltd
Beccles Airfield
Beccles
Suffolk LN34 7TE
Tel; 01502 476400
Tel: 07767 827172
Fax: 01502 475157
info@rainair.co.uk
www.rainair.co.uk

Effective date:25/09/08

EGAA BELFAST ALDERGROVE

268ft 9mb	11.5nm NW of Belfast N5439.45 W00612.95	PPR	Alternative AD	Belfast City Newtownards

Non-standard join

Aldergrove	ATIS 128.200	APP 128.500	RAD 120.900
DIR 129.000	TWR 118.300	GND 121.750	FIRE 121.600

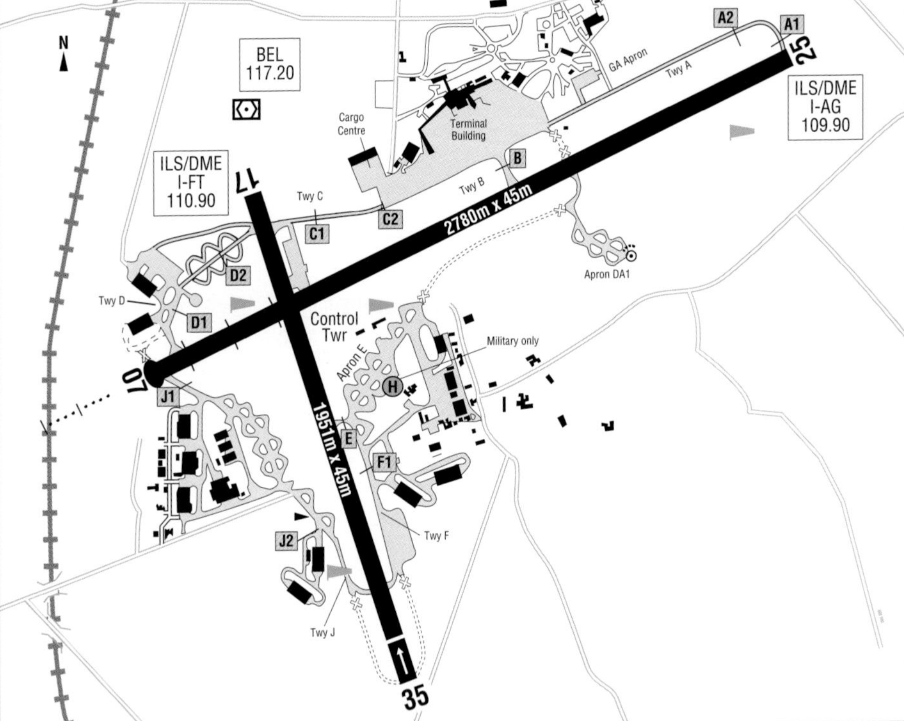

RWY	SURFACE	TORA	LDA	U/L	LIGHTING
07/25	Asphalt	2780	2780		Ap Thr Rwy PAPI 3° LHS
17	Asphalt	1791	1791		Ap Thr Rwy PAPI 3° LHS
35	Asphalt	1891	1799		Ap Thr Rwy PAPI 3° LHS

RNAV
BEL 117.20 on AD

Remarks
PPR to non-radio ACFT. Pilots must present ACFT and contents to police on Arr from and prior to Dept for international flights. Twy J U/L for civil use only. ACFT below 2000kg AUW will park, normally self-manoeuvring on the GA apron, or as directed. For training contact the AD Duty Officer. Illuminated wind direction indicators at Thr Rwy17, 25 & 35. Certain customs facilities available. Handling available from Executive Jet Centre or Woodgate Executive Air Charter.
Aids to Navigation: NDB OY 332.00

Warnings
Severe bird hazard during autumn and winter months; pilots will be advised by ATC. Helicopters frequently operate at low level S of Rwy25, but will remain at least 250m from that Rwy until further cleared by ATC. Beware of AD Langford Lodge 3nm SW of Aldergrove and ensure that you are landing at the correct AD. Langford Lodge U/L AD with crossed Rwy07/25 & Rwy03/21 situated 3nm SW of Aldergrove. Model ACFT flying takes place at Langford Lodge, not above 400ft or 200ft when Rwy07 in use. Model ACFT flying at Nutts Corner, disused AD 3nm SE of Aldergrove

Operating Hrs	H24	**Maintenance**	Woodgate Air Maintenance **Tel:** 02894 422017
Circuits	LH except Rwy25	**Fuel**	JET A1 AVGAS 100LL, 0900-1700 (L) Out of Hrs by prior arr with **Tel:** 02894 422478 (Executive Air Service)
Landing Fee	Under 2mt or flights within 185km £14.99 Parking £11.99 (per 24Hrs)		

B

Disabled Facilities	Available	**Operator**	Belfast International Airport Belfast, BT29 4AB **Tel:** 02894 484281 (ATC/Flight Planning) **Tel:** 02894 484313 (Duty Ops/Manager) **Fax:** 02894 423883 (AD)
Handling	**Tel:** 02894 422646 (Executive Jet Centre) **Tel:** 02894 422478 (Woodgate Air Charter) **Fax:** 02894 422640 (Executive Jet Centre) **Fax:** 02894 452649 (Woodgate Air Charter)		
Restaurant	Buffet & bars available at terminal		
Taxis	Available at Terminal Buses every 30 mins		
Car Hire			
Avis	**Tel:** 02894 422333		
Europcar	**Tel:** 02894 423444		
Hertz	**Tel:** 02894 422533		
Weather Info	M T9 T18 Fax 228 A VSc BEL		

TMA – Class E Airspace CTR Class D Airspace
Normal CTA/CTR Class D Airspace rules apply
Transition Alt 6000ft
1 Flight within the Belfast Aldergrove CTR shall not take place without permission of ATC, giving details of position level and track. A listening watch shall also be maintained whilst complying with any instructions from ATC.
2 Beware of AD Langford Lodge 3nm SW of Aldergrove and ensure that you are landing at the correct AD.

B

Lower limits of TMA are as shown or 700AGL whichever is higher

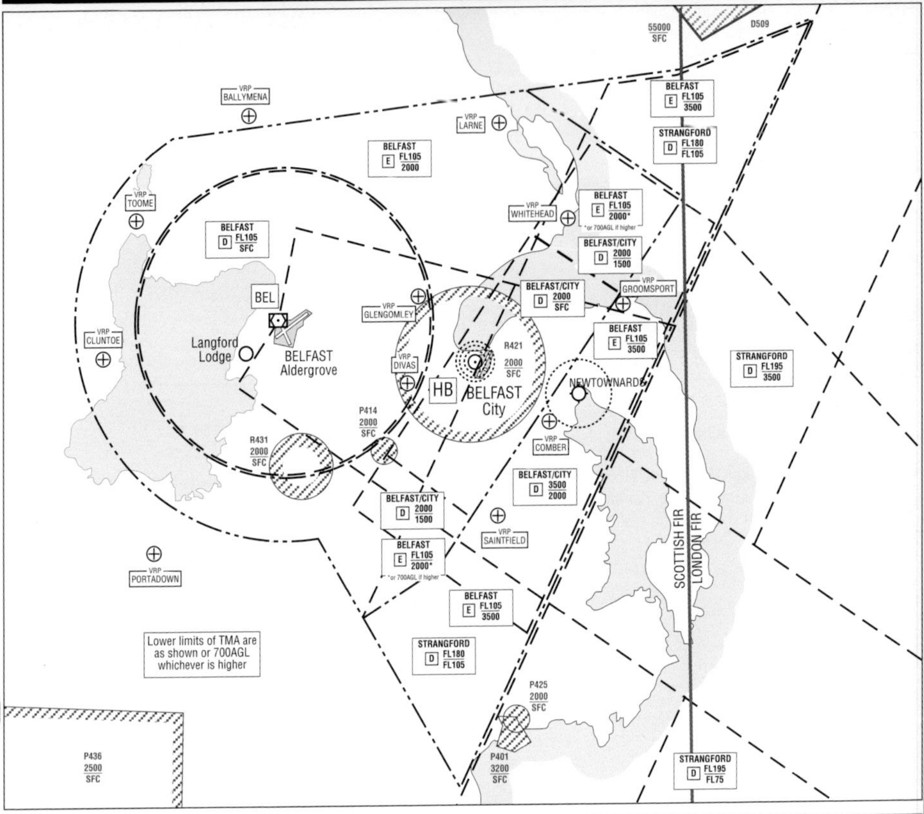

Visual Reference Points (VRP)

VRP	VOR/VOR	VOR/NDB	VOR/DME
Ballymena N5451.80 W00616.40	BEL 359°/MAC 218°	BEL 359°/HB 323°	BEL 359°/12nm
Cluntoe (Disused AD) N5437.23 W00632.03	BEL 263°/MAC 218°	MAC 218°/OY 260°	BEL 263°/11nm
Divis N5436.45 W00600.57	BEL 118°/DUB 014°	BEL 118°/HB 269°	BEL 118°/8nm
Glengormley (M2 J4) N5440.83 W00558.90	BEL 088°/TRN 232°	BEL 088°/HB 324°	BEL 088°/9nm
Larne N5451.20 W00549.52	BEL 056°/MAC 196°	MAC 197°/OY 048°	BEL 056°/18nm
Portadown N5425.50 W00626.85	BEL 214°/DUB 001°	DUB 001°/OY 224°	BEL 214°/16nm
Toome (Disused AD) N5445.47 W00629.67	BEL 308°/MAC 222°	MAC 222°/OY 291°	BEL 308°/11nm

15ft 1mb	E side of Belfast Docks N5437.08 W00552.35		**Alternative AD** **Diversion AD**	**Belfast Aldergrove** Newtownards **Non-standard join**

Belfast	**ATIS** **136.625**	**APP** **130.850**
RAD **134.800**	**TWR** **122.825**	**Handling** **129.750**

RWY	SURFACE	TORA	LDA	U/L	LIGHTING
04	Asphalt	1829	1737		Ap Thr Rwy PAPI 3° LHS
22	Asphalt	1767	1767		Ap Thr Rwy PAPI 3° LHS

RNAV			
BEL	117.20	109	12.6

Remarks
ACFT Dept under IFR and VFR must comply with published noise abatement procedures if weather conditions permit.

Warnings
Many obstacles on Rwy04 APP. Windshear on APP Rwy22 and Rwy04 Dept with wind 100°-160° >15kts.

Operating Hrs Mon-Sun 0530-2030 (Summer)
+1Hr (Winter)

Circuits 04 LH, 22 RH, 1500ft QNH

Landing Fee On Application
Ground Handling available published Hrs

Maintenance Nil

Fuel JET A1
Available published Hrs
No AVGAS

Disabled Facilities

Handling **Tel:** 02890 935027
Fax: 02890 935160

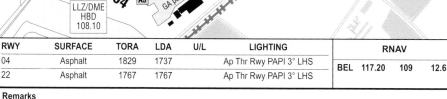

Restaurants Buffet & bar at Terminal

Taxis	Airport Taxi Rank	**Operator**	Belfast City Airport Ltd Sydenham by-Pass Belfast, BT3 9JH **Tel:** 02890 454871 (ATC) **Tel:** 02890 939093 (AD) **Tel:** 02890 935027 (GA Contact Number) **Fax:** 02890 935123 (ATC) **Fax:** 02890 939094 (Admin) **Fax:** 02890 90739582 (GA Contact Fax) airsidestandards@belfastcityairport.com www.belfastcityairport.com
Car Hire			
Avis	**Tel:** 02890 420404		
National	**Tel:** 02890 739400		
Europcar	**Tel:** 02890 450904		
Hertz	**Tel:** 02890 732451		
Weather Info	M T9 Fax 232 BEL ATIS **Tel:** 02890 935124		

CTA/CTR-Class D Airspace
Normal CTA/CTR Class D Airspace rules apply
Transition Alt 6000ft

Departure Procedures
Rwy04
ACFT <13000kg turn to 034°M on passing 500ft QNH or 0.4nm DME, climb to 1500ft QNH before commencing turn.
Rwy22
ACFT <13000kg climb straight ahead to 1500ft QNH before turning onto heading.

Visual Reference Points (VRP)

VRP	VOR/VOR	VOR/NDB	VOR/DME
Comber N5433.05 W00544.75	TRN 221°/IOM 315°	TRN 221°/HB 135°	BEL 118°/18nm
Groomsport N5440.50 W00537.08	TRN 222°/IOM 325°	IOM 325°/HB 074°	BEL 093°/21nm
Saintfield N5427.62 W00549.97	TRN 220°/IOM 307°	IOM 307°/HB 175°	BEL 137°/18nm
Whitehead N5445.17 W00542.57	TRN 228°/IOM 326°	IOM 326°/HB 042°	BEL 078°/19nm

B

BELLARENA

15ft 0mb	4nm N of Limavady (Disused AD) N5508.30 W00658.00	PPR	Alternative AD Londonderry **Non-standard join**

Bellarena Base	A/G 130.100 Used during glider ops. If no response make blind calls

RWY	SURFACE	TORA	LDA	U/L	LIGHTING
13/31	Grass			500x30	Nil
11/29	Grass			500x30	Nil

RNAV

Remarks

PPR by telephone essential. Primarily a gliding site but occasional visits by light ACFT welcome at own risk. Rwys are not marked but are the best runs on a large field of coastal turf. Although we quote Rwy widths the large run-off area make these figures academic.

Warnings

AD is surrounded to the land ward by a wire fence 4ft high. Glider launching by aerotow please keep a good lookout for tugs & gliders. High GND 1263ft amsl 1.8nm to E & SE.

Operating Hrs	0930 (L) to 30mins after SS Sat/Sun & PH 7 day Ops through Easter week & 1 week in July
Circuits	LH 1000ft QFE
Landing Fee	Nil
Maintenance	Nil
Fuel	Nil

Disabled Facilities

Restaurants/ Accommodation	There are a number of restaurants in Limavady & local hotels & B&B

Taxis	**Tel:** 02897 7750561 **Tel:** 02897 7750489
Car Hire	**Tel:** 02870 343654
Weather Info	Air N MOEx
Operator	Ulster Gliding Club Bellarena Airfield Co Londonderry Northern Ireland BT49 0LA **Tel:** 02877 750301 (Clubhouse manned at weekends) **Tel:** 07527 547829 (Control during Ops) secretary@ulsterglidingclub.org www.ulstergliingclub.org

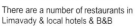

 OP 07

675ft 22mb	2.5nm NE of Torrington N5058.57 W00405.73	PPR	**Alternative AD** **Diversion AD**	**Exeter** Eaglescott

Belle Vue	**A/G** **123.575**

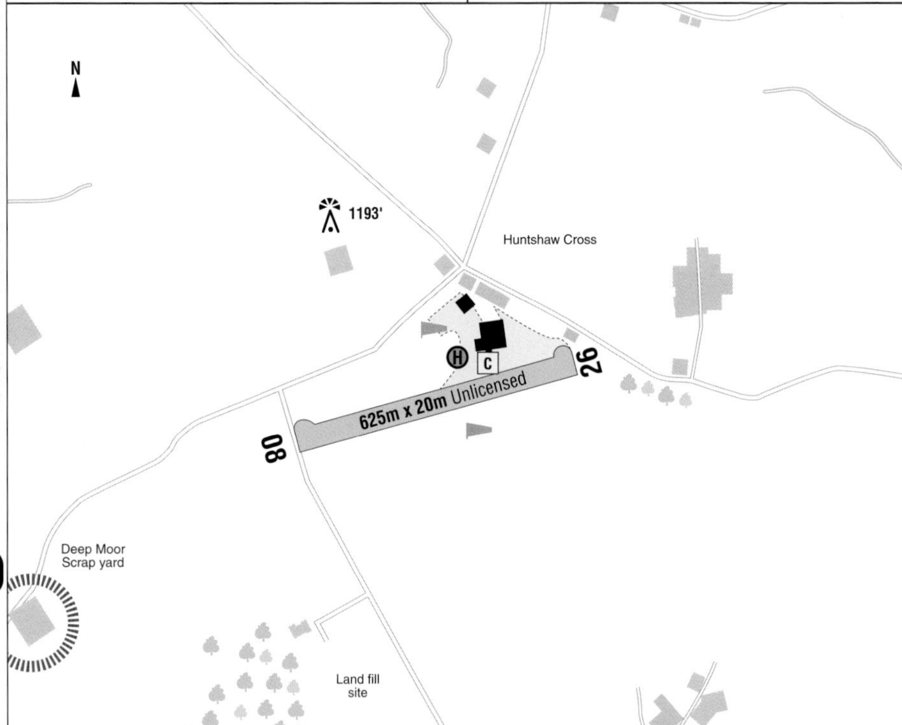

RWY	SURFACE	TORA	LDA	U/L	LIGHTING
08/26	Grass			625x20	Nil

Displaced Thr Rwy26 100m

RNAV

Remarks
PPR by telephone. Microlight activity. Visiting ACFT welcome at pilots own risk. Microlights with cruise speed above 45kts permitted. Taxi on the Rwy unless otherwise directed. Eaglescott AD, gliding parachuting, microlights and fixed wing activity 5nm SE avoid ATZ unless transit authorised. Camping and caravaning available. Model ACFT flying takes place occasionally S of AD.

Warnings
H24 operations. Radio mast with guy lines 537agl (1193ft amsl) 300m N of AD. Beware of grazing sheep. Rwy08 APP should be sufficiently high to give good clearance of public road close to Thr. Electric fences sometimes adjacent to Rwy on S side.
Noise: Avoid over flying all settlements and farms within 3nm, particularly scrap yard 0.75nm SW of Rwy08 Thr. Dept climb out on Rwy heading until 2nm to clear area.

Operating Hrs	Mon-Sat 0800-2100 or SS Sun/PH 0900-1800 landing only until 2100
Circuits	LH 1000ft QFE
Landing Fee	£5 Overnight parking £3 per night
Maintenance	Nil
Fuel	MOGAS available 1nm distance
Disabled Facilities	Nil
Restaurants	Self service refreshments at AD B&B within 1km details available from operator

Taxis/Car Hire	Details available from operator
Weather Info	Air SW MOEx
Operator	Mr D R Easterbrook Belle Vue Aerodrome Yarnscombe, Barnstaple Devon, EX313ND **Tel/Fax:** 01805 623113 **Tel:** 07971 278984 **Tel:** 01237 477248 (Tony Hodder – Wingnuts Flying Club)

B

53ft 2mb	2.3nm NE of Sandown (Isle of Wight) N5040.68 W00106.57	**Alternative AD** **Diversion AD**	**Southampton** Isle of Wight

Bembridge	A/G 123.250

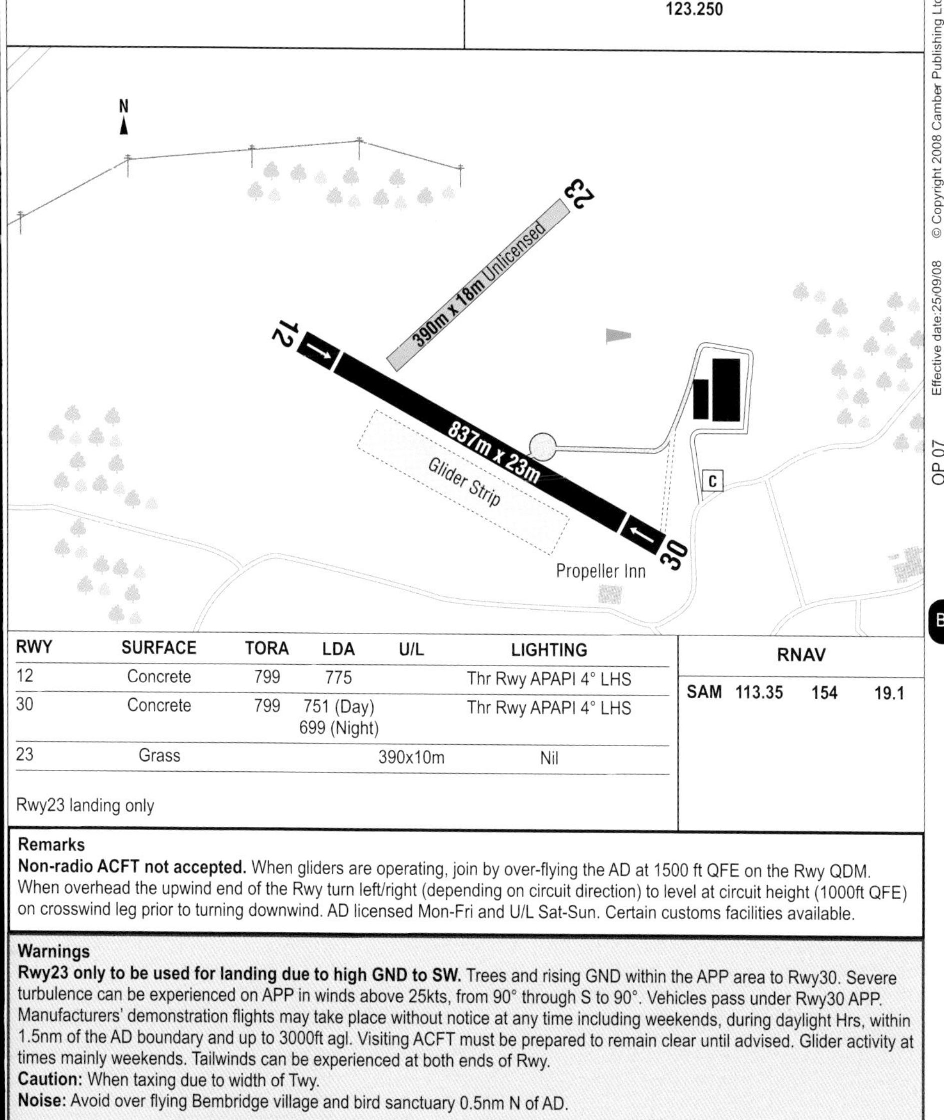

RWY	SURFACE	TORA	LDA	U/L	LIGHTING
12	Concrete	799	775		Thr Rwy APAPI 4° LHS
30	Concrete	799	751 (Day) 699 (Night)		Thr Rwy APAPI 4° LHS
23	Grass			390x10m	Nil

Rwy23 landing only

RNAV			
SAM	113.35	154	19.1

Remarks
Non-radio ACFT not accepted. When gliders are operating, join by over-flying the AD at 1500 ft QFE on the Rwy QDM. When overhead the upwind end of the Rwy turn left/right (depending on circuit direction) to level at circuit height (1000ft QFE) on crosswind leg prior to turning downwind. AD licensed Mon-Fri and U/L Sat-Sun. Certain customs facilities available.

Warnings
Rwy23 only to be used for landing due to high GND to SW. Trees and rising GND within the APP area to Rwy30. Severe turbulence can be experienced on APP in winds above 25kts, from 90° through S to 90°. Vehicles pass under Rwy30 APP. Manufacturers' demonstration flights may take place without notice at any time including weekends, during daylight Hrs, within 1.5nm of the AD boundary and up to 3000ft agl. Visiting ACFT must be prepared to remain clear until advised. Glider activity at times mainly weekends. Tailwinds can be experienced at both ends of Rwy.
Caution: When taxing due to width of Twy.
Noise: Avoid over flying Bembridge village and bird sanctuary 0.5nm N of AD.

Operating Hrs	0730-1700 (Summer) +1Hr (Winter) & by arr
Circuits	12 LH, 30 RH, 1000ft QFE Gliders will be flying opposite circuit
Landing Fee	< 750kg £5, 751-1500kg £10.75 >150001 kg £5 per 500kg Overnight parking £5 Touch & Go 50% of landing or £20 per Hr
Maintenance	Nil
Fuel	AVGAS 100LL JET A1 by prior arr during operational Hrs
Disabled Facilities	Nil

Restaurants

Bembridge Aero Club	**Tel:** 01983 87331
Crab & Lobster	**Tel:** 01983 872244

Taxis

Bembridge Harbour	**Tel:** 01983 874132

Car Hire

South Wight Rentals	**Tel:** 01983 864263
Weather Info	Air S MOEx
Operator	B-N Group Ltd The Airport, Bembridge Isle of Wight, PO35 5PR **Tel:** 01983 871538/873331 (ATC) **Tel/Fax:** 01983 871566 ats@eghj.com www.ehgj.com

19ft 1mb	W side of Isle of Benbecula N5728.87 W00721.77	PPR	**Alternative AD** **Tiree** Barra **Diversion AD**

Benbecula	ATIS	APP	TWR	AFIS	FIRE
	113.950	119.200	119.200	119.200	121.600

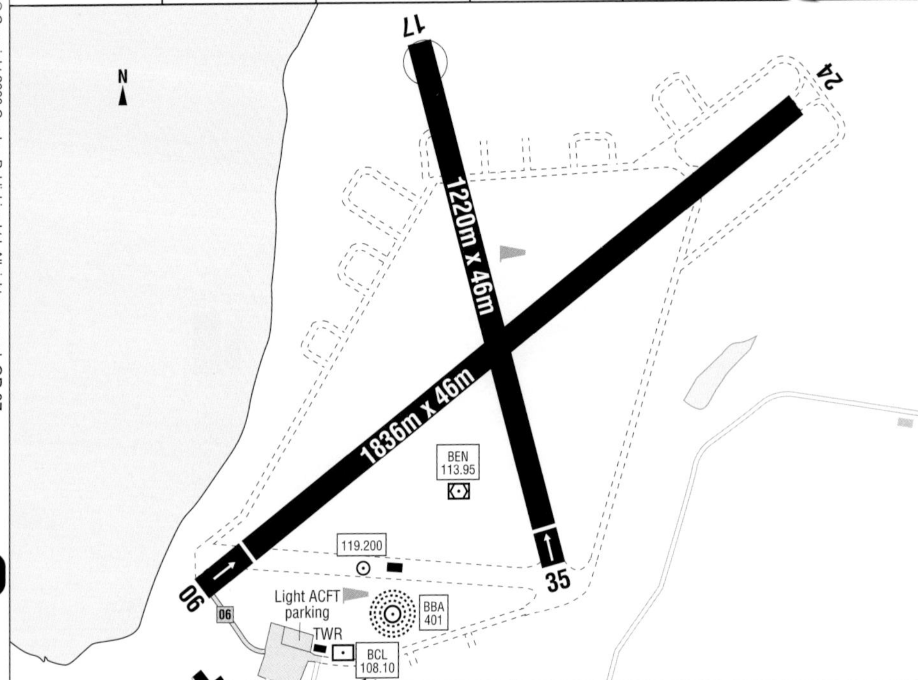

RWY	SURFACE	TORA	LDA	U/L	LIGHTING
06	Bitumen	1836	1717		Ap Thr Rwy PAPI 3°LHS
24	Bitumen	1688	1688		Ap Thr Rwy PAPI 3°LHS
17/35	Asphalt	1220	1220		Nil

Starter extension Rwy35 100m (available on request, day only)

RNAV
BEN 113.95 on AD

Remarks

PPR 3Hrs notice required. Built in tie-downs on N section of main apron. Low intensity battery edge lights available Rwy17/35 for air ambulance or SAR ACFT only. Rwy17/35 not available to ACFT >5700kg unless Rwy06/24 is not available & surface wind conditions dictate. Prefered Rwy for landing Rwy24 Dept Rwy06. AFIS may be provided outside APP/TWR Hrs of service by arr for Air Ambulance or SAR flights. Training flights are subject to prior approval from ATC.

Warnings

Twys closed except between Thr Rwy06 and apron. Rwy06 end lights visible for last 50m of landing run only. Rwy17/35 is subject to standing water. Grass areas soft and unsafe. Only marked Twy to be used. Intense military activity takes place in the vicinity. ATC will advise when Danger Area D701 A-E is active.

Operating Hrs Mon-Fri 0615-1645 Sat 0615-0930 1500-1645 Sun 1000-1130 (Summer) +1Hr (Winter)

Circuits Nil

Landing Fee £15 ACFT under 3MT VFR cash/cheque on day

Maintenance Nil

Fuel JET A1 Mon-Fri 0900-1600 (L) & by arr

Loganair Fuels **Tel:** 01870 603147/0141 842 7455 **Fax:** 01870 602714

Disabled Facilities Nil

Restaurants/Accommodation
Light refreshments available at AD Cafe/Bar
Accommodation in local Hotels

Taxi
Buchanan's **Tel:** 01870 602277
MacVicar's **Tel:** 01870 602307
Maclennan's **Tel:** 01870 602191

Car Hire
Maclennan's **Tel:** 01870 602191

Weather Info M T9 Fax 234 GWC **Tel:** 01870 604818

Visual Reference Points (VRP)
Lochmaddy Pier N5735.76 W00709.40
Monach Islands Lighthouse N5731.58 W00741.65

Operator HIAL Benbecula Aerodrome
Balvanich, Isle of Benbecula
Western Isles HS7 5LW
Tel: 01870 602051
Fax: 01870 604826
www.highlands-and-islands-airports.uk.com

B

EGUB BENSON

226ft 7mb	2nm NE of Wallingford N5136.98 W00105.75	PPR MIL	Alternative AD Diversion AD	**Oxford** Wycombe

Benson	Zone 120.900	APP 136.450	TWR 127.150	GND 121.800

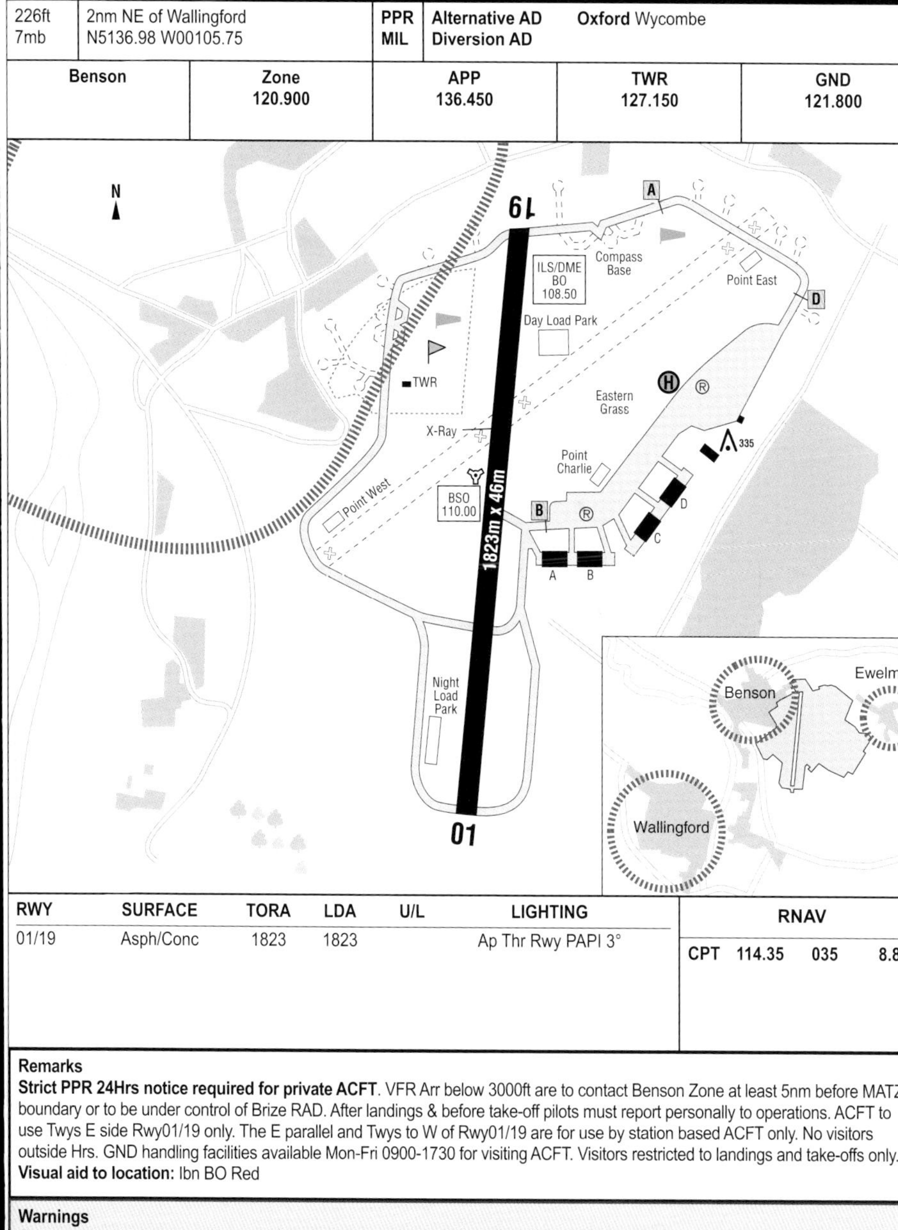

RWY	SURFACE	TORA	LDA	U/L	LIGHTING
01/19	Asph/Conc	1823	1823		Ap Thr Rwy PAPI 3°

RNAV			
CPT	114.35	035	8.8

Remarks

Strict PPR 24Hrs notice required for private ACFT. VFR Arr below 3000ft are to contact Benson Zone at least 5nm before MATZ boundary or to be under control of Brize RAD. After landings & before take-off pilots must report personally to operations. ACFT to use Twys E side Rwy01/19 only. The E parallel and Twys to W of Rwy01/19 are for use by station based ACFT only. No visitors outside Hrs. GND handling facilities available Mon-Fri 0900-1730 for visiting ACFT. Visitors restricted to landings and take-offs only.
Visual aid to location: Ibn BO Red

Warnings

Serious risk of bird strikes. Regular glider, helicopter & light ACFT activity in the MATZ. Caution on 90° bend en-route to Rwy24 from the apron, braking action poor when wet with adverse camber. High traffic density due to Oxford AIAA. Do not climb above 4000ft QNH until clear of N boundary Awy G1 S of Benson, base 4500ft. London QNH. Intensive MATZ crossing traffic. Public road crosses the undershoot of Rwy19 150m from Thr. Caution, fixed wing and rotary activity takes place outside published Hrs.
Noise: Avoid over flying the villages of Benson, Ewelme and Wallingford.

Operating Hrs	H24
Circuits	01 RH, 19 LH 1300ft QFE
Landing Fee	Charges in accordance with MOD policy Contact Station Ops for details
Maintenance	Nil
Fuel	AVGAS JET A1 100LL FSII by arr
Disabled Facilities	Nil
Restaurants	Nil
Taxis/Car Hire	Nil
Weather Info	Air SE MOEx
Operator	RAF Benson Wallingford Oxon OX10 6AA **Tel:** 01491 827017/18 **Fax**: 01491 838747 (Ops)

1020ft 3mb	6nm W of Penrith N5439.24 W00256.04	PPR	Alternative AD	Carlisle

Non-radio	APP Carlisle 123.600	Safetycom 134.475

N

07

400m x 17m Unlicensed

25

H

C

RWY	SURFACE	TORA	LDA	U/L	LIGHTING
07/25	Grass			400x17	Nil

RNAV

Remarks

PPR essential for pre-arrival briefing. Microlights, Gyroplanes and Helicopters welcome at pilots own risk. H will be marked in neighbouring field. Camping permitted. Overnight and holiday accommodation available.

Warnings

Operating Hrs	SR-SS
Circuits	Nil
Landing Fee	Nil
Maintenance	Nil
Fuel	MOGAS JET A1 during 2009
Disabled Facilities	Nil
Restaurants	Local pub near by
Taxi/Car Hire	Nil
Weather Info	Air N MOEx

Operator

Roger Savage
The Bank Barn
Croft House
Berrier
Penrith
Cumbria
Tel: 01768483859
Tel: 07836 272033
photography@rogersavage.co.uk

195ft 6mb	At Jct2 of M50 3nm SE of Ledbury N5200.22 W00221.87	PPR	**Alternative AD** **Gloucestershire** Kemble

Non-Radio	LARS	Safetycom
	Filton 122.725 **Brize 124.275**	**135.475**

N
ACFT parking
30ft powerlines
24
crops
650m x 30m Unlicensed
Downslope
crops
crops
06
crops
30ft trees
Estate access road

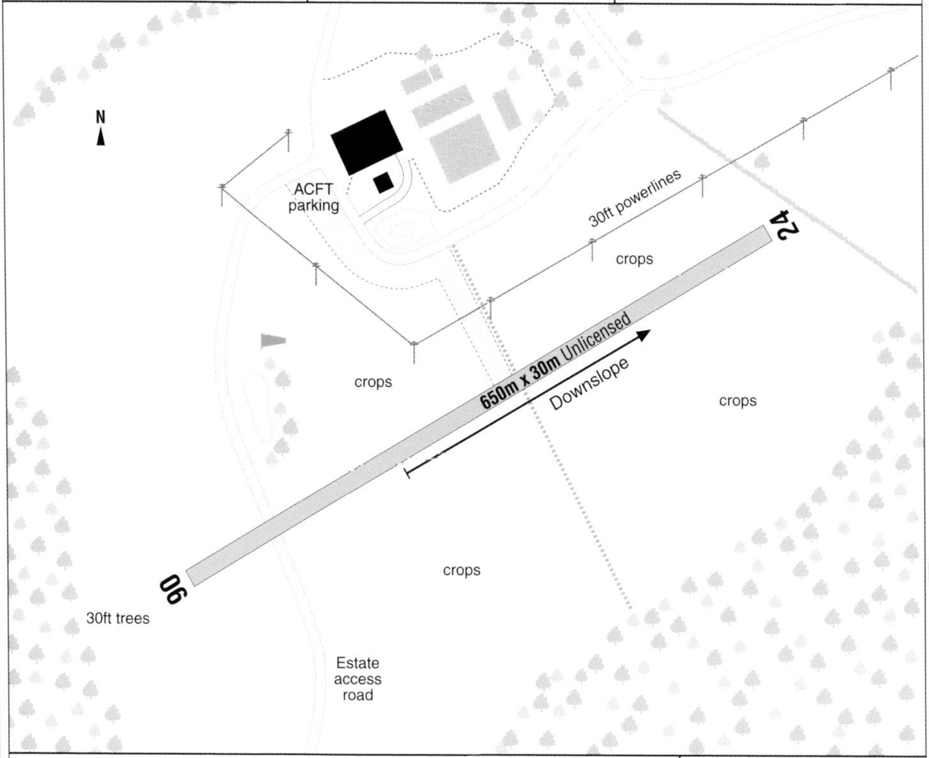

RWY	SURFACE	TORA	LDA	U/L	LIGHTING
24/06	Grass			650x30	Nil

RNAV

Remarks
PPR by telephone. Visiting ACFT welcome at pilots own risk. AD is part of a working farm. Crops may be grown up to Rwy edge.

Warnings
Rwy06 downslope particularly after Rwy midpoint. Vehicles regularly use estate access road which crosses Rwy close to Rwy06 Thr. Road surface is concrete.
Caution: Twy has a ditch on E side. Powerlines on AD diagram. Mast 0.5nm SW of AD 630ft amsl. Great Malvern HIRTA is 5nm NNE up to 4000ft amsl.
Noise: Do not over fly Bromesberrow Heath 1nm SW of AD.

Operating Hrs	SR-SS
Circuits	Variable at 1000ft QFE
Landing Fee	Advised with PPR
Maintenance	Nil
Fuel	AVGAS 100LL
Disabled Facilities	
Taxi/Car Hire	Nil
Weather Info	Air SW MOEx

Operator
Dr The Hon G Greenall
Bromesberrow Place
Ledbury
Herefordshire
HR8 1RZ
Tel: 01531 650102
Fax: 01531 650056
gilgreenall@bromesberrow.com

5ft 0mb	4nm NE of Beverley N5353.92 W00021.72	PPR	Alternative AD Diversion AD	**Humberside** Full Sutton

Beverley	A/G 123.050

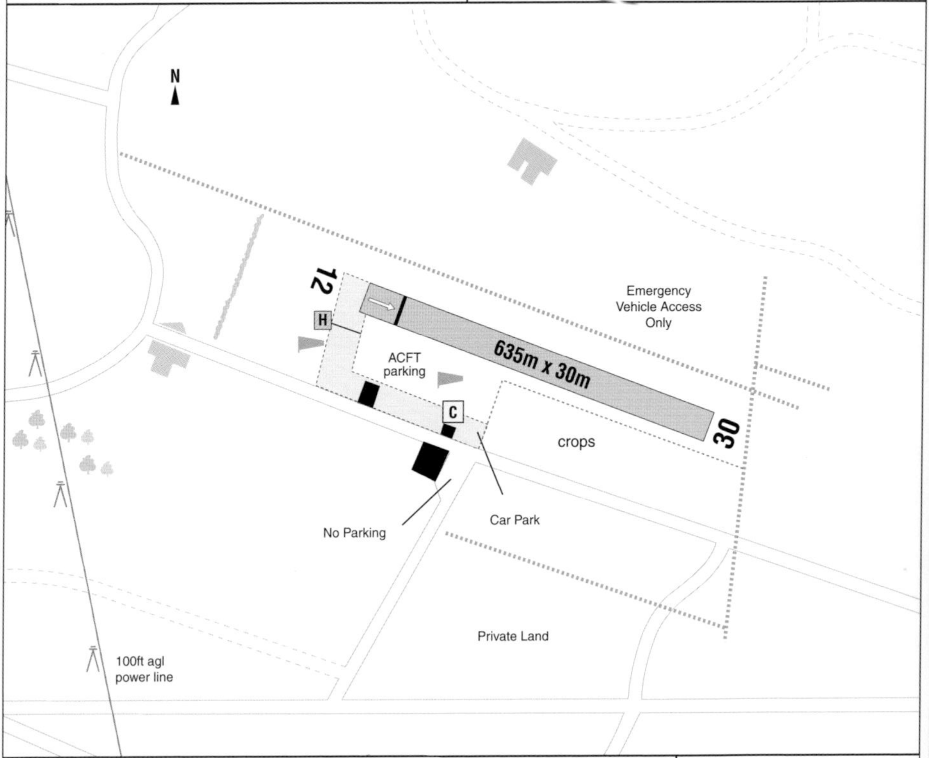

N
12
H
ACFT parking
635m x 30m
30
C
Emergency Vehicle Access Only
crops
Car Park
No Parking
Private Land
100ft agl power line

RWY	SURFACE	TORA	LDA	U/L	LIGHTING
12	Grass	635	635		Nil
30	Grass	635	635		Nil

RNAV			
OTR	113.90	327	15.1

Remarks
PPR. Non-radio ACFT not accepted. Licensed AD not available for public transport flights required to use a licensed AD. Due to the proximity of electric transmission line no right base join for Rwy12. No right turns due to possible conflict with SAR helicopter activity

Warnings
Power line 100ft aal crosses extended Rwy centre line 1200m 300° from ARP. Pilots using Rwy12 must have visual contact with the power line before starting final APP. A dyke 30m before Rwy30 Thr marked with red and white warning markings. A second dyke runs parallel to Rwy30, 23m from the right-hand edge.
Noise: Avoid over flying Leven village 1.5nm E of AD. Dept from Rwy12 turn left before reaching Leven village.

Operating Hrs 0900-1800 (Summer) 0900-SS (Winter)
Closed Monday

Circuits ACFT to join overhead at 1500 ft QFE
All circuits N. Avoid Leconfield ATZ
12 LH, 30 RH, 1000 ft QFE

Landing Fee Single £5 Twin £10 (< 2 Tonne)
Microlight £3

Maintenance Nil
Fuel AVGAS 100LL

Disabled Facilities

Restaurants Tea, coffee & sweets available in club house

Taxis
Alpha **Tel:** 01482 881461
Bradcabs **Tel:** 01482 868396

Car Hire
Andrews **Tel:** 01482 867360
Beverly Ford **Tel:** 01482 866900

Weather Info Air N MOEx

Operator Hull Aero Club
Linley Hill Airfield
Leven
East Yorkshire HU17 5LT
Tel/Fax: 01964 544994
info@hullaeroclub.co.uk

EGDD BICESTER

267ft 9mb	0.25nm NNE of Bicester N5154.91 W00108.11	PPR	**Alternative AD** **Oxford** Turweston **Non-standard join**

Bicester Radio	LARS Brize 124.275	A/G 129.975

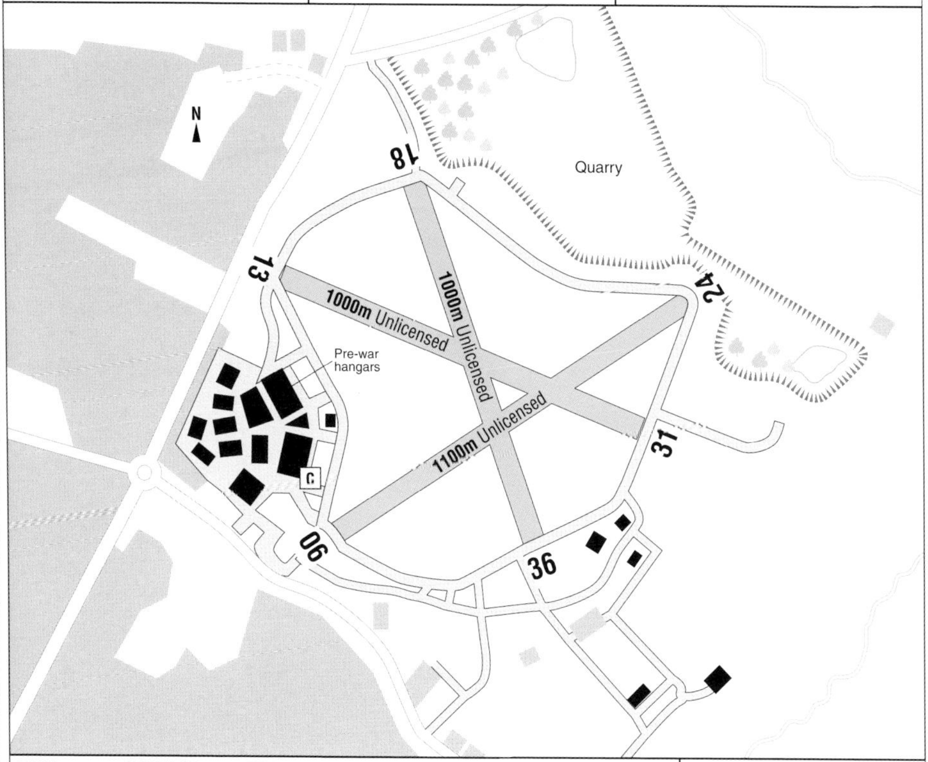

RWY	SURFACE	TORA	LDA	U/L	LIGHTING
06/24	Grass			1100	Nil
13/31	Grass			1000	Nil
18/36	Grass			1000	Nil

RNAV			
DTY	116.40	187	15.8

Remarks

PPR by telephone. Gliding takes place 7 days a week including winch launch and aerotow. AD pre-war RAF grass field. Light ACFT welcome when on gliding business. Visiting pilots keep a good lookout for Gliders at all times. AD surface within the perimeter track is short cut grass and is all landable with care. Rwys are not marked on the grass, map is an indication only. Rwy in use marked by a bus and cars at Thr. Circuit traffic is controlled with advisory instructions on A/G freq. An excellent website is available which provides local info.

Visual aid to location: 'C' type hangars in technical area in SW corner of AD.

Warnings

Gliders and powered ACFT operate on both sides of circuit. Once established in the circuit ACFT must remain on same side and land on that side of launch point. ACFT must not cross over the centre line. No overhead joins at any time due cables. D129, Weston on the Green, is close to SW of AD. Visiting pilots must ensure they do not penetrate the area.

Operating Hrs	SR-SS
Circuits	Telephone briefing essential with PPR on day of intended arrival.
Landing Fee	Nil
Maintenance	Nil
Fuel	AVGAS 100LL

Disabled Facilities

Restaurants Food & drink available weekend

Taxis/Car Hire	Nil
Weather Info	Air Cen MOEx
Operator	Windrushers Gliding Club Bicester Airfield Skimmingdish Lane Bicester Oxfordshire OX26 5HA **Tel:** 01869 252493 **Tel:** 07986 049036 fly@windrushers.org.uk www.windrushers.org.uk

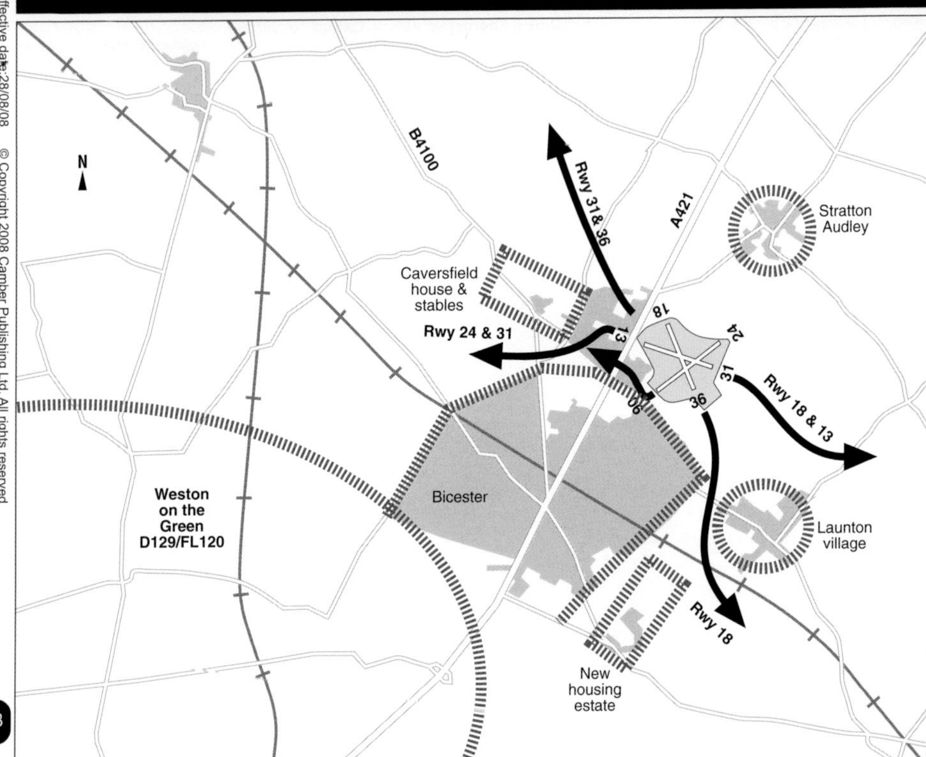

Prior to dept all non Bicester based ACFT must book out using the powered ACFT book, immediately prior to start up. A verbal dept briefing **must** be obtained from duty instructor.
All pilots must be aware of the possibility of noise complaints at ALL times. Avoid Bicester Town and all villages and farms wherever possible by following the designated routes.

Rwy24
Aim to pass left of main hangar, turn right onto 300°, keeping Bicester town on your left.

Rwy31
Turn 45° right or left after take-off to avoid Caversfield House and stables.
Low powered ACFT are advised to climb straight ahead, then turn right onto 360°.

Rwy18
Fly 130° after take off to avoid Launton village or fly 200° to pass between Launton and Bicester (following the ring road).

Rwy36 & 06
Avoid the village of Stratton Audley
Note: Engine failure options are severely limited from Rwy18, 24 and 31.

XBID BIDFORD

135ft 4mb	4nm E of Evesham N5208.03 W00150.97	PPR	**Alternative AD** **Gloucestershire** Wellesbourne Mountford **Non-standard join**

Bidford Base	**A/G** **129.975** **Glider Freq**

RWY	SURFACE	TORA	LDA	U/L	LIGHTING
06/24	Grass			800x100	Nil

RNAV			
HON	**113.65**	**211**	**15.0**

Remarks
PPR essential by telephone for daily gliding & noise briefing. Gliding site aerotow only. Powered ACFT should keep a good look out for gliders ensuring their operations are not obstructed.

Warnings
Power lines 300m from Rwy24 Thr. AD situated within Restricted area R204, applicable to helicopters only. Crops grown up to S of AD.
Noise: Avoid over flying local villages. Keep N of farmhouse Rwy06 APP.

Operating Hrs	0800-SS (L)
Circuits	S 1000ft QFE
Landing Fee	£6
Maintenance	Bidford Airfield Ltd (Gliders & powered ACFT) **Tel/Fax:** 01789 490174
Fuel	AVGAS 100LL
Disabled Facilities	Nil
Restaurants/ Accomodation	Cafe & camping on site
Taxis	**Tel:** 01789 262600
Car Hire	**Tel:** 01905 792307
Weather Info	Air Cen MOEx

Operator	Bidford Gliding Ltd Bidford Airfield Bidford-on-Avon Warks, B504PD **Tel:** 01789 772606 (AD) office@bidfordgliding.co.uk www.bidfordgliding.co.uk

599ft 20mb	12nm SSE of London N5119.85 E00001.95	Alternative AD	Southend Redhill

Biggin	LARS Farnborough East 123.225	ATIS 121.875 (dept)	APP 129.400	RAD Thames 132.700	TWR 134.800	FIRE 121.600

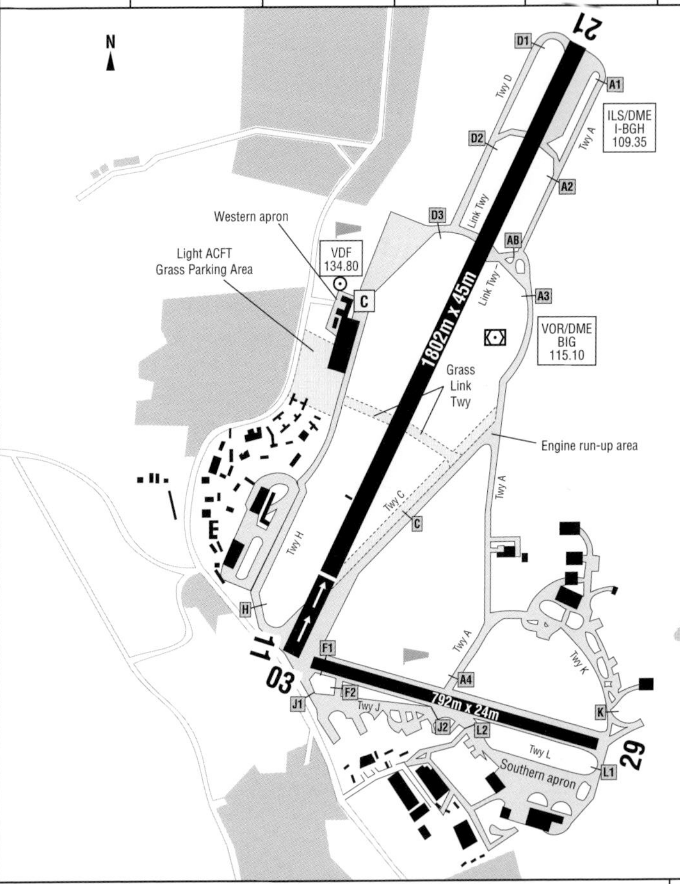

RWY	SURFACE	TORA	LDA	U/L	LIGHTING
03	Concrete	1778	1558		Thr Rwy APAPI 4° LHS
21	Concrete	1670	1670		Ap Thr Rwy PAPI 3° LHS
11/29	Asphalt	792	792		Nil

RNAV
BIG 115.10 on AD

Remarks

PPR Helicopters. AD not available to non-radio ACFT or microlights. Hi Vis. When taking off, going around or making touch and goes remain at, or below, 500ft QFE until the upwind end of the Rwy. Joining the circuit at 1000ft QFE across the upwind end of the Rwy in use. Inbound IFR flights requiring RAD service, contact Thames RAD. AD rules and conditions of use are available from the operator.

Warnings

Windshear and turbulence on short final Rwy03 with NE winds. Aerobatic manoeuvres and low fly pasts are prohibited unless participating in an organised flying display.

Caution: Reduced wing tip clearance between taxing and parked ACFT on apron adjacent to TWR. Marshalling guidance provided.

Noise: All types of ACFT and helicopters must avoid noise sensitive areas surrounding AD, helicopters must conform to normal fixed wing Dept and circuit procedures unless otherwise instructed by ATC. Routes published by AD authority.

Operating Hrs	Mon-Fri 0630-2000 Sat-Sun & PH 0800-1900 (Summer) +1Hr (Winter)
Circuits	03, 11 LH, 21, 29 RH 1000ft QFE
Landing Fee	Up to 0.8 tonnes £17.99 0.8-1.7 tonnes £21.15

Maintenance	
Shipping & Airlines Ltd	**Tel:** 01959 573404
Falcon Flying Services	**Tel:** 01959 575923
Fuel	AVGAS JET A1 100LL
Disabled Facilities	Nil
Restaurants	Restaurant/refreshments available at AD

B

Taxis	
Luxury Cars	**Tel:** 01959 578550/567
Car Hire	
Budget Rent-a-Car	**Tel:** 0208 4647736
Weather Info	M T9 Fax 236 A MOEx

Operator

Regional Airports Ltd
Biggin Hill Airport
Surrey TN16 3BN
Tel: 01959 578500 (Admin)
Tel: 01959 578525 (ATC/Ops)
Tel: 01959 578526 (Fuel)
Fax: 01959 576406 (Admin)
Fax: 01959 576404 (Ops)
enquiries@bigginhillairport.com
www.bigginhillairport.com

Effective date:25/09/08

Biggin Hill Noise Procedures

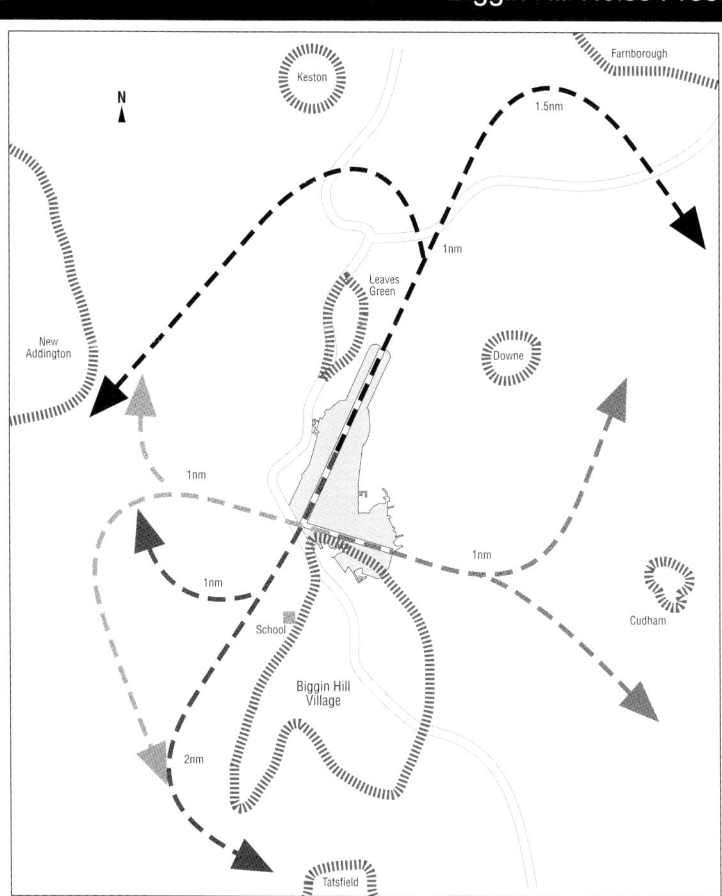

B

Visual Reference Points (VRP)

Sevenoaks	N5116.60 E00010.90

VFR Dept Routes

Transition Alt 6000ft. Light twins and singles only

Rwy21

Dept E, S or NE avoid built up areas. Keep school and silos on left. Straight ahead for 2nm then left turn. Dept to W or N straight ahead for 1nm then turn right. Keep school on left

Rwy03

Dept to E or S, NE; straight ahead for 1.5nm then right turn.

Caution; ACFT joining dead side Rwy03/21 at Alt 1600ft. Avoid Farnborough and Downe. Dept to N and W; straight ahead for 1nm then left turn. Avoid built up areas

Rwy29

Dept to S, E, straight ahead for 1nm then left turn. Keep silos on left.

Caution; ACFT joining dead side Rwy11/29 at Alt 1600ft. Dept to N, NE; straight ahead for 1nm right turn. Avoid Leaves Green. Dept to W; straight ahead for 1nm then turn on track.

Rwy11

All directions; straight ahead for 1nm then left or right on track. Avoid Cudham, Downe, Biggin Hill.

Caution; If turning W or S due to ACFT joining dead side Rwy11/29 at Alt 1600ft.

328ft 11mb	5.5nm ESE of Birmingham N5227.23 W00144.88	PPR	Alternative AD	Coventry Wellesbourne Mountford

Non-standard join

Birmingham	ATIS 136.025	APP 118.050	DEL 121.975
RAD 118.050 131.325	TWR 118.300	GND 121.800	FIRE 121.600

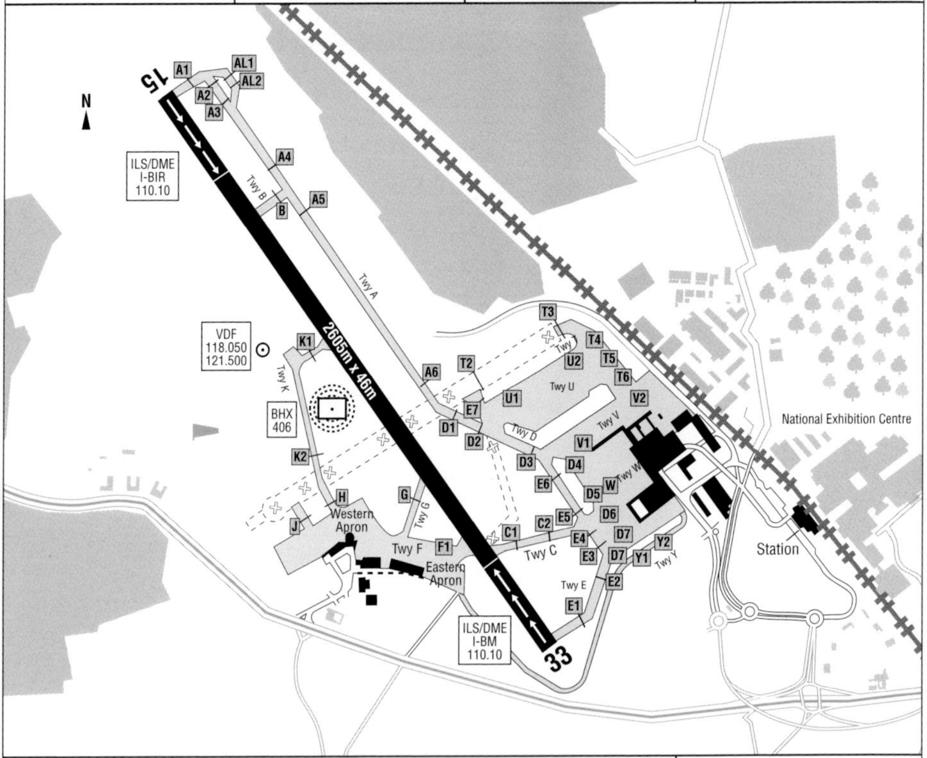

N

ILS/DME I-BIR 110.10

2605m x 46m

VDF 118.050 121.500

BHX 406

National Exhibition Centre

Western Apron

Eastern Apron

Station

ILS/DME I-BM 110.10

RWY	SURFACE	TORA	LDA	U/L	LIGHTING
15	Asphalt	2570	2280		Ap Thr Rwy PAPI 3° LHS
33	Asphalt	2595	2298		Ap Thr Rwy PAPI 3° LHS

RNAV			
HON	113.65	335	6.6

Remarks

PPR to non-radio ACFT. Hi-Vis. Use of AD for training purposes is subject to the approval of Airport Managing Director & ATC. Training ACFT must climb straight ahead to1000ft aal before turning, unless otherwise instructed by ATC. Training flights including ILS go-arounds by ACFT not based at Birmingham, likely to cause nuisance to surrounding area, are prohibited between 1800-0800 (L). ACFT must not join the final APP track to any Rwy below 1500ft aal, unless they are propeller driven ACFT whose MTWA does not exceed 5700kg in which case the minimum height is 1000ft aal. Mandatory handling for GA ACFT. Marshalling is mandatory for all ACFT parking on W apron. Twy T & U are not available at night. Use minimum power manoeuvring on Twy T & U. Use of Twy C prohibited when Rwy33 in use.

Helicopter Operations: Helicopters to land as instructed by ATC.

Visual aids to location: IBn BM Green.

Warnings

Twy D to rear of stands 44-51 restricted to ACFT with max wing span of 38.5m.

Operating Hrs	H24
Circuits	Variable circuits 1000ft QFE for light ACFT
Landing Fee	Up to 1MT £14.80 Up to 1.5MT £22.21 Up to 2MT £29.61 Up to 3MT £39.52 & parking

Maintenance	Available plus hangarage
Fuel	Arrange through handling agents AVTUR JET A1 No AVGAS

Disabled Facilities

 OP 08

B

Handling	**Tel:** 0121 782 1999 (Signature) **Tel:** 0121 767 7715 (Aviance) **Tel:** 0121 767 772 (Servisair Globeground) **Tel:** 0121 767 7518 (British Airways) **Tel**: 0121 781 0005 (Swissport) **Tel:** 0121 782 5100 (Midwest Exec Aviation) **Fax:** 0121 7821899 (Signature) **Fax:** 0121 782 7766 (Servisair Globeground) **Fax:** 0121 767 7590 (British Airways) **Fax**: 0121 781 0020 (Swissport) **Fax:** 0121 782 5101 (Midwest Exec Aviation)	**Taxis**	Available at Terminal
		Car Hire	
		Avis	**Tel:** 0121 782 6183
		Hertz	**Tel:** 0121 782 5158
		Europcar	**Tel:** 0121 782 6507
		Weather Info	M T9 T18 Fax 238 A VS MWC ATIS **Tel:** 0121 780 0910
		Operator	Birmingham International Airport Ltd Birmingham, B26 3QJ **Tel:** 08707 335511 (AD Switchboard) **Tel:** 0121 782 6227 (ATC) **Tel:** 0121 780 0907 (FBU) **Tel:** 0121 767 7139/7153 (Ops/Duty Manager) **Fax:** 0121 782 8802 (AD) **Fax:** 0121 780 0917 (ATC)
Restaurants	Restaurant, buffet & bar available at Terminal		

CTA/CTR Class D Airspace
Normal CTA/CTR Class D Airspace rules apply.
Transition Alt 4000ft
Clearance for SVFR below 1500ft QNH will not be given in the sector enclosed by the bearings 245° and 360° from AD. This is the main built-up area of Birmingham.

Ground Movement
ATC Ground Movement Control (GMC) service operates 0700-2100 (L). On the manoeuvring area, pilots will be cleared under general direction from GMC and are reminded of the importance of maintaining a careful lookout at all times. ATC instructions will normally specify the taxi route to be followed. All operators making requests for taxiing or towing clearance to GMC should state their location in the initial call. Mandatory handling is required for all visiting business and General Aviation ACFT.

Noise Abatement Procedure
All ACFT using the AD shall be operated in a manner calculated to cause the least disturbance practicable in areas surrounding the AD. Unless otherwise instructed by ATC, ACFT using the ILS in IMC or VMC shall not descend below 2000ft before intercepting the glide path nor fly below the glide path there after. An ACFT approaching without assistance from ILS or RAD must follow a descent path not lower than if following the ILS glide path.

Effective date:25/09/08

B

EGLK BLACKBUSHE

325ft 11mb	8.5nm SE by S of Reading N5119.43 W00050.85	PPR	Alternative AD Diversion AD	Farnborough Fairoaks

Non-standard join

Blackbushe	LARS Farnborough West 125.250	AFIS 122.300	A/G 122.300

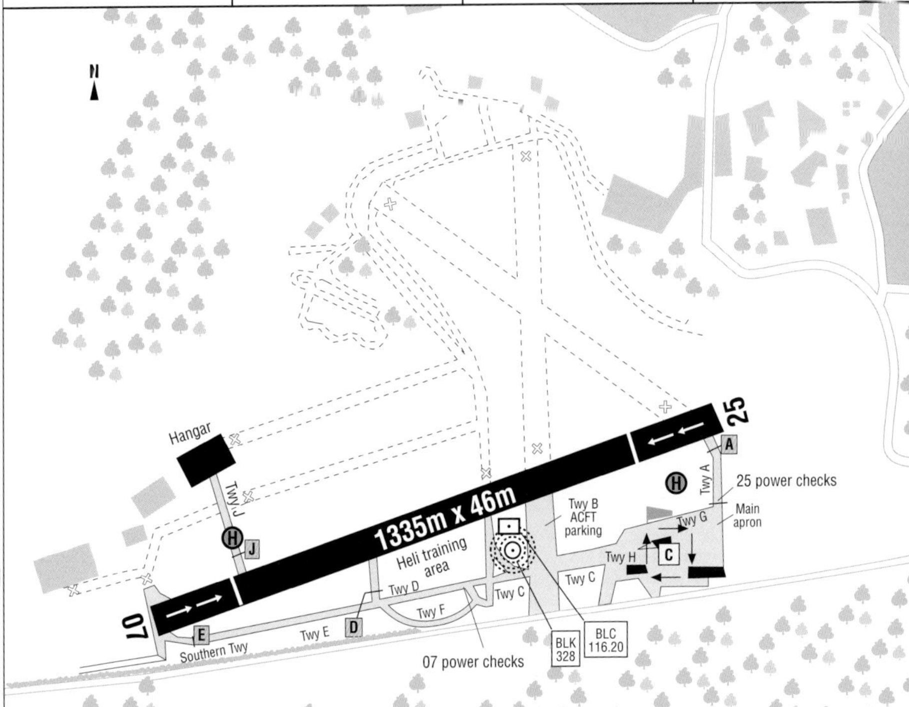

RWY	SURFACE	TORA	LDA	U/L	LIGHTING
07	Asphalt	1237	1102		Thr Rwy PAPI 3.1° LHS
25	Asphalt	1237	1059		Thr Rwy PAPI 3.1° LHS

Helipad On Twy J

RNAV			
OCK	115.30	277	15.2

Remarks
PPR by telephone. Some PHs AD is not available for ACFT required to use a licensed AD. APP Blackbushe remaining N of the M3 to avoid ACFT using Farnborough. Pilots are responsible for their passengers whilst on the airside of AD. Due to planning restrictions the following ACFT may not land at this AD: Cessna Skymaster (C336/337/L); Dornier 28D Sky Servant(D08D/L); Gates Learjet 23, 24, 25, 28, 29 (LR23, 24, 25, 28/L, 29/M); Piaggio P166 (P166/L).
Visual Aids to location: Abn White flashing.

Warnings
AD is frequently used outside the published Hrs of operation by fixed and rotary wing ACFT. Pilots operating at any time in the vicinity of the AD should therefore call Blackbushe AFIS/AG to check if the AD is active. Pilots are further cautioned that no reply does not necessarily imply no traffic in the ATZ, and a very careful lookout should be maintained. Avoidance of the ATZ if at all possible is preferable. Helicopter specific lighting aids have been installed on Twy J, these consist of illuminated Tee and CHAPI 5.0°. Fixed-wing pilots should ignore indications from this lighting. An additional AD beacon situated on the roof of a hangar (287° 0.3nm from the ARP) may be illuminated, but only outside notified AD Hrs. A section of disused Rwy01/19, to the S of Rwy07/25, is marked as ACFT parking area. The grass between Twys C & D is unsuitable for use by certain types of helicopter due to its poor grading. Pilots are cautioned to positively ascertain that the grading of this area is suitable for their operational requirements. Visual glide slope guidance signals for both Rwy07& 25 are visible to the S of the extended Rwy centre lines where normal obstacle clearance is not guaranteed. They should not be used until aligned with the Rwy. A public footpath crosses the centre of the AD from SE to NW. Fuel normally available on PH. Caution large concentrations of birds on and in the vicinity of AD.
Noise: Avoid over flying Yateley to NE and Hartley-Wintney W of AD

Operating Hrs	0700-1700 (Summer) +1Hr (Winter) & by arr	**Taxis**	
Circuits	All circuits S of AD Single engined ACFT 800ft QFE Twin engined & executive ACFT 1200ft QFE Night circuit height for all ACFT 1000ft QFE	A2B Taxis	**Tel:** 01276 64488/64499
		Car Hire	
		Avis	**Tel:** 01344 417417
		Europcar	**Tel:** 01276 451570
Landing Fee	Single from £19.50. Discount available for fuel uplift and club ACFT or LAA/AOPA members with card Single £10. Further reductions available to £7.50 at weekends	**Weather Info**	Air SE MOEx
Maintenance		**Operator**	Blackbushe Airport Ltd Blackbushe Airport Camberley, Surrey **Tel:** 01252 879449 (Admin) **Tel:** 01252 873338 (TWR) **Fax:** 01252 874444 (Admin) blackbusheairport@bca.group.com
PremiAir Aircraft Engineering	**Tel:** 01252 890089		
Fuel	AVGAS 100LL AVTUR JET A1		
Disabled Facilities			
Restaurants	Club facilities at The Bushe		

Blackbushe Circuit Diagram

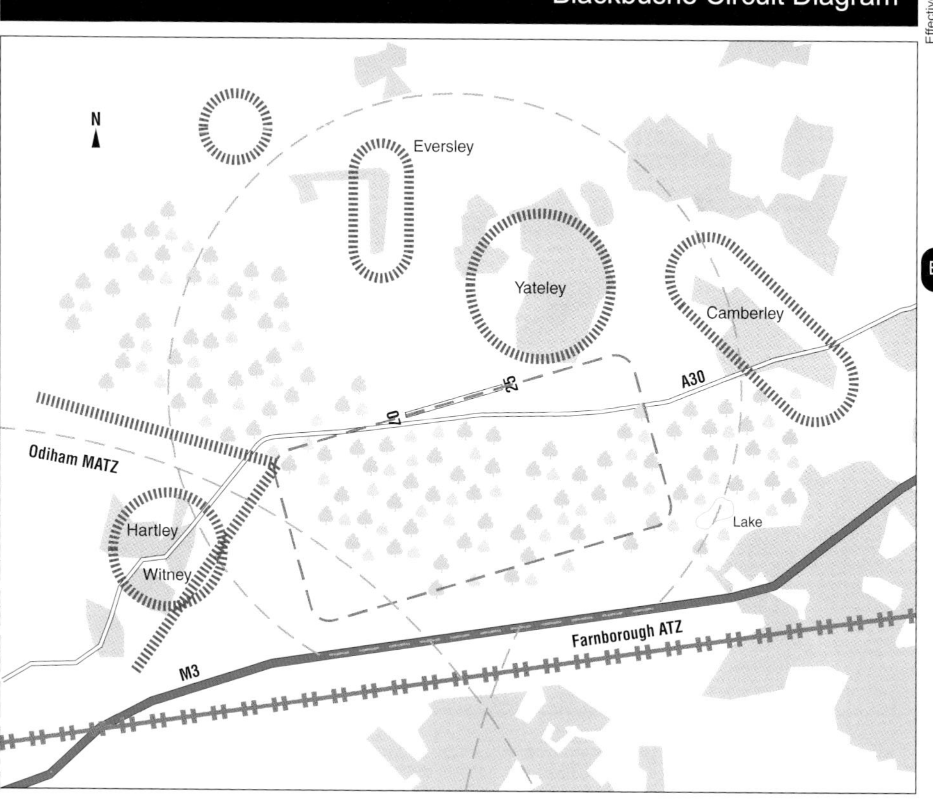

B

34ft 1mb	2.6nm SSE of Blackpool N5346.30 W00301.72	PPR	Alternative AD **Warton** Woodvale

Blackpool	ATIS 127.200	APP Warton 129.525	APP 119.950

RAD 135.950	TWR 118.400	FIRE 121.600

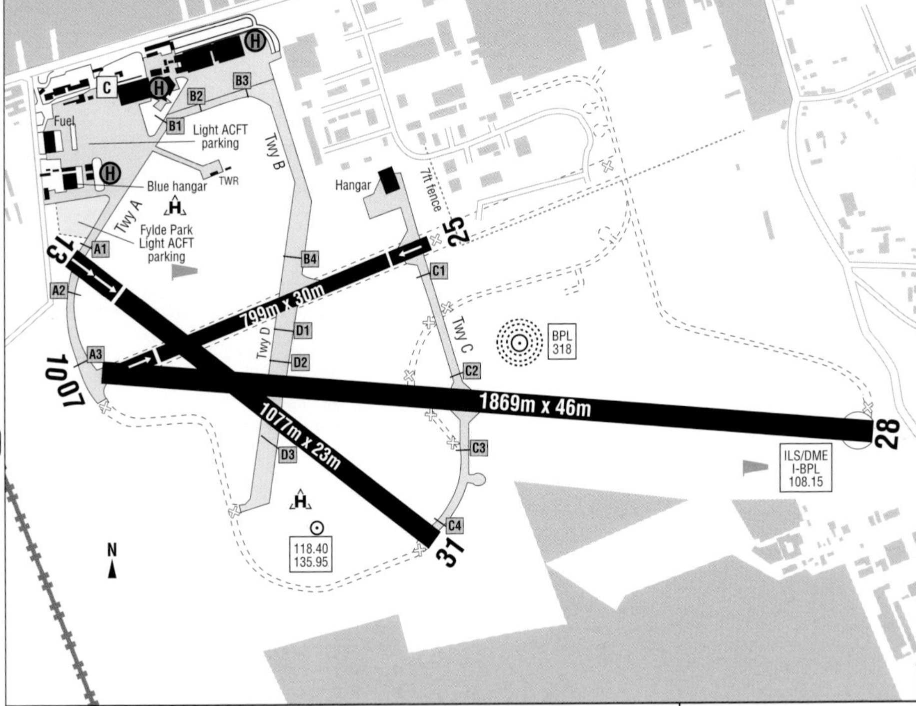

RWY	SURFACE	TORA	LDA	U/L	LIGHTING
07	Asphalt	700	610		Nil
25	Asphalt	799	700		Nil
10/28	Asphalt	1869	1869		Ap Thr Rwy PAPI 3° LHS
13	Asphalt	1077	927		Nil
31	Asphalt	927	1077		Nil

RNAV			
WAL	114.10	014	23.1

Remarks

PPR. Hi-Vis. All inbound ACFT to make initial call to APP. Landing and taxiing on grass areas by fixed-wing ACFT is prohibited. The portion of Twy which passes between the hangars and the ACFT parking area is only suitable for ACFT with wingspan of up to 19m. Grass parking known as Fylde Park is provided to N of Rwy13 under shoot. ACFT using Blackpool AD do so in accordance with Blackpool AD terms and conditions (available on application). All Depts must book out with ATC via telephone. ACFT must have at least £5m insurance.

Warnings

Operating Hrs	0600-2000 (Summer) 0700-2100 (Winter) & by arr	**Maintenance**	
		Westair	**Tel:** 01253 404925
Circuits	25, 28, 31 RH 07, 10, 13 LH	**Fuel**	AVGAS JET A1 100LL
Landing Fee	0-500kgs £7.50 501-1000kgs £15.00 1001-1500kgs £22.50	**Handling**	Blackpool Ground Handling **Tel:** 01253 472578 **Fax:** 01253 472578

B

Disabled Facilities

Restaurants	Bar/Cafe in terminal
Taxis	
Black Taxi	Freephone in terminal
Car Hire	
Hertz	**Tel:** 01253 344010
Weather Info	M T9 Fax 242 A VN MWC

Operator

Blackpool Airport Ltd
Blackpool Airport, Blackpool
Lancashire, FY4 2QY
Tel: 0871 855 6868
Fax: 01253 405009
Tel: 01253 472527 (ATC)
Fax: 01253 402004 (ATC)

Visual Reference Points (VRP)

Fleetwood Golf Course	N5355.13 W00302.72
Inskip Disused AD	N5349.63 W00250.05
Kirkham	N5346.95 W00252.28
Marshide	N5341.78 W00258.23
Poulton Railway Station	N5350.90 W00259.42

Pilots may also be requested to route via the following positions

Blackpool (Tall) TWR	338°/2.6nm
Gasometers	037°/1.8nm
St Annes Pier	185°/1.5nm

Helicopter Operations

Two helicopter APP aiming points marked with an 'H' are located 140m W of the ATC TWR (H N) and 100m from the end of Twy 02 (H S).

Arr Procedures – VFR Helicopters Arr from S will be routed abeam St Annes Pier to enter the ATZ not above 600ft QFE and route to H S prior to further clearance to requisite parking area.

Helicopters Arr from the N and E quadrants will route via the Fleetwood-Kirkham on Railway. M6 or the M55 to APP the AD via the Gasometers on the W edge of the M55, prior to crossing the ATZ not above 600ft QFE to H N.

Helicopters wishing to APP at 1500ft or above will join overhead at 1500ft QFE, descend on the dead side prior to proceeding to H N or H S.

Dept Procedures: N and E: helicopters will clear the ATZ not above 600ft QFE on track of 071°, via the Gasometers, and then route either via the M55, the Kirkham-Fleetwood railway N to Heysham, or the M6 Motorway. S and SW route seawards via abeam St Annes Pier not above 600ft QFE until clear of ATZ. Helicopter captains are warned about proximity of Warton MATZ, radio masts 700ft at Inskip, radio mast adjacent to gasometers in NE quadrant at 300ft amsl, military low level activity in Irish Sea. Captains will not overfly the ICI complex at Thornton.

VFR Flights

The following locations are established as VFR reporting points:

APP S:	Marshside
APP SE:	Warton AD
APP E:	Kirkham
APP ENE:	Inskip
APP NE:	Poulton
APP N:	Fleetwood

Pilots APP from the W should contact ATC at 5nm range. All VFR flights should leave the zone tracking to/from these locations. Arr ACFT from the S must contact Warton APP in the first instance.

B

650ft 21mb	3.5nm NE of Bodmin N5029.98 W00439.95	PPR	Alternative AD Diversion AD	St Mawgan Perranporth

Bodmin	APP St Mawgan 128.725	A/G 122.700

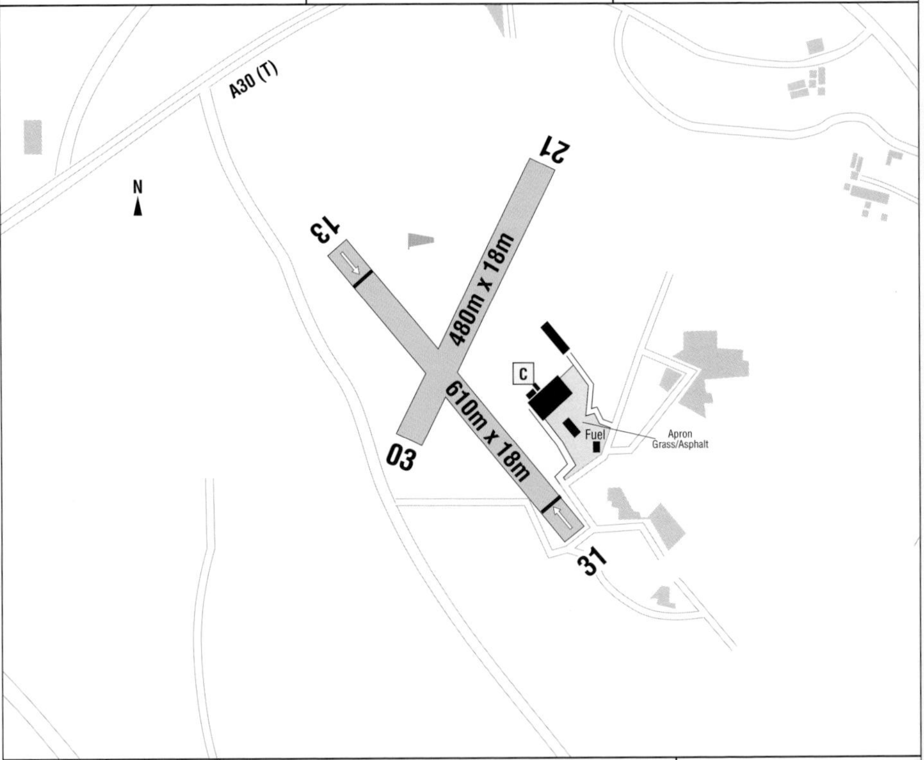

RWY	SURFACE	TORA	LDA	U/L	LIGHTING
03/21	Grass	480	480		Nil
13	Grass	598	598		Nil
31	Grass	610	540		Nil

RNAV

Remarks
PPR. AD not available for night flying. AD limited to ACFT take off weight <2490kg. AD closed 2200-0700 (L). Customs available by arr.

Warnings
Windshear may be encountered in strong winds. Due to the convex nature of the AD the Rwy stop-ends are not visible from the take-off position.
Caution: When taxiing to the apron or fuel bay. Rifle range 1.4nm to E safety height 1000ft

Operating Hrs	0830-1930 (Summer) 0830-1730 or SS (Winter) & by arr
Circuits	03, 31 LH, 21, 13 RH 800 ft QFE
Landing Fee	Single £8
Maintenance	Hangarage available
Fuel	AVGAS 100LL
Disabled Facilities	Nil
Restaurants	Restaurant open 5 days a week 1030-1500 (L) also pilot shop
Taxis	
Bodmin Taxi Serv	**Tel:** 01208 72345
Car Hire	Nil
Weather Info	Air SW MOEx

Operator
Cornwall Flying Club Ltd
Bodmin Airfield, Cardinham,
Bodmin, Cornwall, PL30 4BU
Tel: 01208 821419
Tel: 01208 821463
Fax: 01208 821711

B

EGDM BOSCOMBE DOWN

407ft 13mb	5nm NE of Salisbury N5109.13 W00144.84	PPR MIL	Alternative AD Diversion AD	**Bournemouth** Thruxton

Non-standard join

Boscombe	Zone	APP/DIR	TWR/GND	FIRE
	126.700	130.000	130.750	121.600

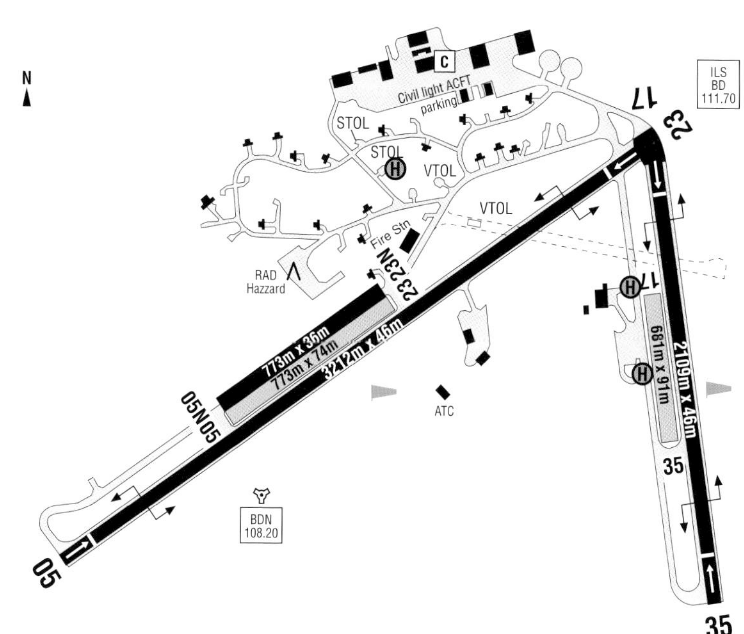

RWY	SURFACE	TORA	LDA	U/L	LIGHTING
05	Asphalt	3212	3209		Ap Thr Rwy PAPI 3°
23	Asphalt	3212	3109		Ap Thr Rwy PAPI 3°
17	Asphalt	2108	1913		Ap Thr Rwy PAPI 3°
35	Asphalt	2108	2107		Ap Thr Rwy PAPI 3°
17/35	Grass	681	681		Nil
23/05N	Asphalt	73	773		Nil
23/05	Grass	773	773		Nil

RNAV			
SAM	113.35	313	19.0

Remarks

Strict PPR from Main Flying Ops. PPR to civil ACFT is limited Mon-Thur 0900-1700 Fri 0900-1600. No training flights. Pilots operating over Salisbury Plain must, before recovery to Boscombe Down, establish RT contact for RAD Sequencing and avoidance of circuit traffic. Visiting ACFT to call at min 20nm. All procedures within 10nm and below 3000ft are flown on Boscombe QFE. After landing visiting ACFT must obtain ATC permission before vacating Rwy. Outside published Hrs VHF only ACFT inbound call Boscombe Zone 20nm from AD. If no reply contact Boscombe TWR for info on ACFT ops. No response on either freq means ATC closed. The ATZ will remain active with Bustard Flying Club ACFT.

Warnings

Intensive test flying at this AD. Beware of close proximity 'Salisbury Plain' Danger Areas D123, D124, D125, D126 – DACS Salisbury Ops and also of D127 Porton Down. After dark up to 2359 Hrs Mon-Fri MATZ may contain unlit ACFT, AD and obstruction lights may be extinguished during flying. Light ACFT & heli flying in daylight outside AD Hrs. Radiation hazard (525ft radius up to 500ft agl extends to within 500ft of Rwy05/23). Possible inadvertent actuation of electrically initiated explosive devices. RAF barriers installed for all Rwys. Arrester gears are fitted 435m from 05 Thr, 372m from 23 Thr, 273m from 17 Thr, 427m from 35 Thr. Rwy05/23 overrun cable normally up. Rwy17/35 both cables normally down. No gliding permitted. No deadside on AD below 1200ft QFE. Helicopters operate southside normally up to 500ft QFE. Light ACFT operate to parallel section of N Twy from non-standard 800ft N circuit

Noise: Avoid over flying Cholderton Rare Breeds Farm, Arundel Farm, Amesbury village and all nearby villages

MAIP 08 Effective date:25/09/08

Operating Hrs	H24	**Operator**	MOD Boscombe Down Salisbury Wiltshire SP4 0JF **Tel:** 01980 663051 (Ops) **Tel:** 01980 663246 (ATC) **Fax:** 01980 663225
Circuits	Variable		
Landing Fee	Charges in accordance with MOD policy Contact Station Ops for details		
Maintenance	Nil		
Fuel	AVGAS 100LL JET A1 with FSII		
Disabled Facilities			
Restaurants	Nil		
Taxis/Car Hire	Available by private arr		
Weather Info	M T Fax 244 MOEx ATIS **Tel**: 01980 663101		

Visual Reference Point (VRP)
Outside normal operating Hrs.
Join from W, following A303 to Stonehenge at 800ft QFE.
Report at Stonehenge

B

BOUGHTON NORTH

70ft 2mb	4nm SSW of RAF Marham N5235.52 E00030.95	**PPR**	**Alternative AD** **Norwich** Old Buckenham

Non-Radio	**APP** **Marham 124.150**	**Safetycom** **135.475**

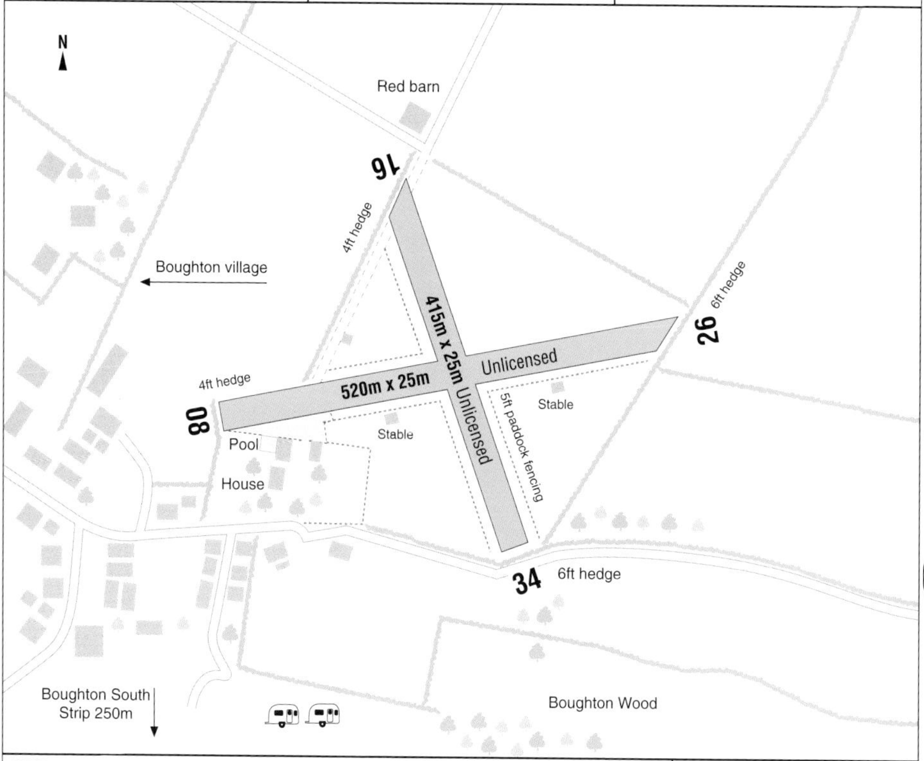

RWY	SURFACE	TORA	LDA	U/L	LIGHTING
08/26	Grass			520x25	Nil
16/34	Grass			415x25	Nil

RNAV

Remarks
PPR by telephone. Visiting pilots welcome at own risk. Free lift to Oxborough Hall for National Trust members.

Warnings
AD situated within Marham MATZ. Arr/Dept ACFT contact Marham APP. Rwys are bordered by 5ft paddock fence. There are hedges on all Thrs. Uphill slope Rwy16
Caution: There is another Boughton AD (single Rwy) to S.
Noise: Avoid over flying the village of Boughton.

Operating Hrs SR-SS + 30 mins
Circuits See remarks
Landing Fee Nil
Maintenance Nil
Fuel Nil
Disabled Facilities

Restaurants Tea & coffee available at the farmhouse

Taxis
Barry's Cars **Tel:** 01366 385888
Car Hire
Bees Motors **Tel:** 01366 384109
Fax: 01366 387109

Weather Info Air S MOEx

Operator Mr P Coulten
Oxborough Road, Boughton
Kings Lynn, Norfolk
Tel/Fax: 01366 500315 (Home)
Tel: 07771 552870
paulcoulten@btinternet.com

EGSN BOURN

216ft 7mb	7nm W of Cambridge N5212.63 W00002.55	PPR	Alternative AD Diversion AD	Cambridge Little Gransden

Bourn	A/G 124.350

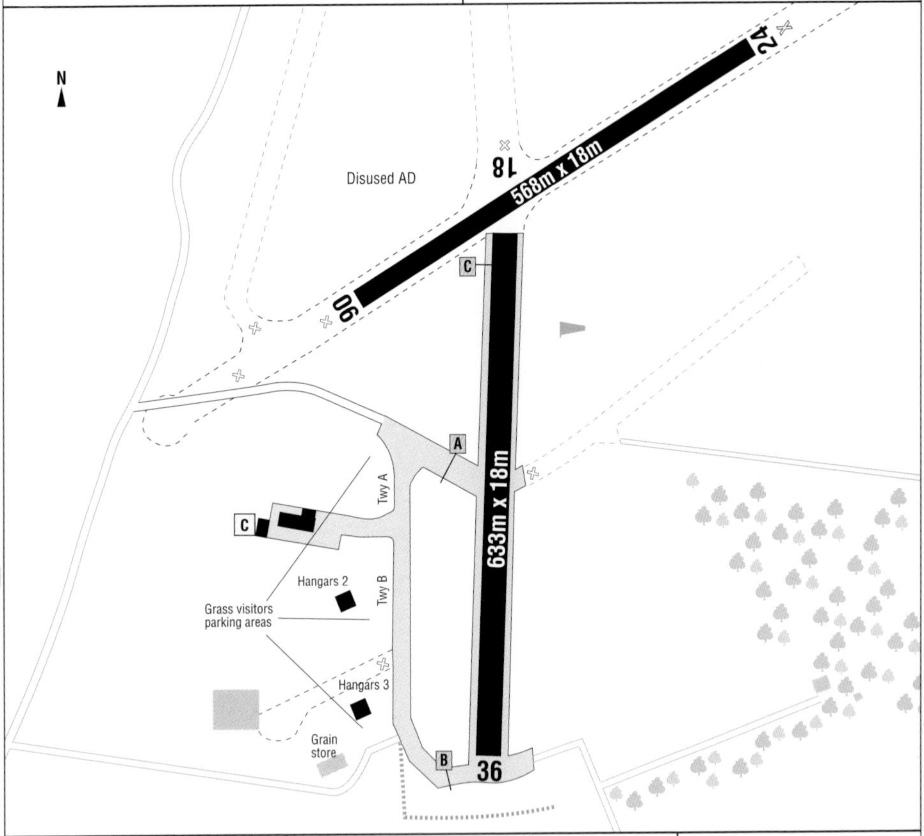

RWY	SURFACE	TORA	LDA	U/L	LIGHTING
18/36	Bitumen	633	633		Nil
06/24	Bitumen	568	568		Nil

RNAV			
BKY	116.25	346	13.8

Remarks
PPR by telephone. The licensed area is situated on WWII AD on which non-aviation activities also take place. Not available for use by public transport passenger flights required to use a licensed AD or at night. Power checks for Rwy36 to be completed at Hold A.

Warnings
There are a number of other licensed AD in the vicinity and intensive gliding with winch launching cables to 3000ft agl takes place at Gransden Lodge 3nm SW Bourn. No engine run ups at Hold B.
Noise: Avoid over flying all local villages.

Operating Hrs	0900-1700 (Summer) 0930-1700 or SS (Winter) & by arr Closed on all Bank Holiday Mondays
Circuits	36, 24 RH, 18, 06 LH 1000ft QFE
Landing Fee	Single £5 Twin £10 Microlight £1 Classic & interesting ACFT free at discretion of duty instructor
Maintenance	Nil
Fuel	Nil

Disabled Facilities

Restaurants	Tea & coffee only available at AD
Taxis/Car Hire	Arrangement on arrival
Weather Info	Air Cen MOEx
Operator	Rural Flying Corps Bourn Aerodrome Bourn, Cambs, CB23 2TQ **Tel/Fax:** 01954 719602 rfcbourn@btconnect.com www.rfcbourn.flyer.co.uk

Effective date:25/09/08 OP 08

B

550ft 18mb	3.5nm NNE of Andover N5115.96 W00127.43	PPR	Alternative AD	Southampton Thruxton

Non-Radio	LARS Boscombe 126.700	RAD Middle Wallop 123.300	Safetycom 135.475

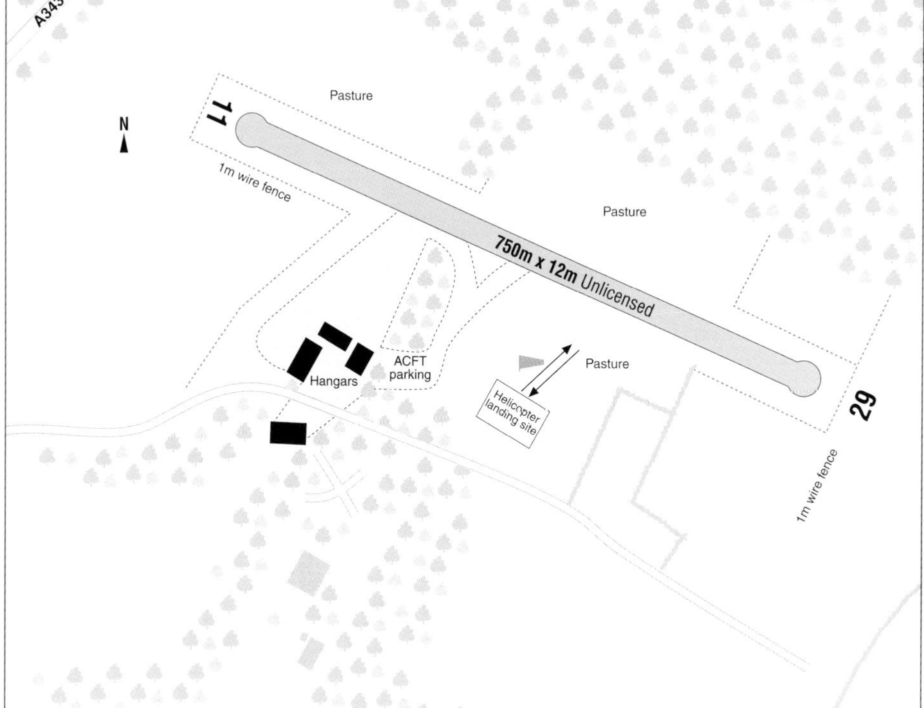

RWY	SURFACE	TORA	LDA	U/L	LIGHTING
29/11	Grass			750x12	Nil

RNAV			
CPT	114.35	217	16.2

Remarks

PPR by telephone essential. Pilots welcome at own risk. AD home to Aerofab restorations. Boscombe & Middle Wallop MATZ's are close to S/SW. Helicopters to join long finals and hover taxi from E of windsock to landing site.

Warning

Rwy11 has slight upslope. AD close to Boscombe & Middle Wallop areas of aerial activity and military aircraft, particularly helicopters may be encountered down to low level. Windshear may be encountered on Rwy11 APP when there are moderate/strong winds from E.

Noise: Avoid over flying of all local houses and villages.

Operating Hrs	SR-SS
Circuits	LH 1000ft QFE
Landing Fee	A packet of biscuits
Maintenance	M3 Aerofab Restorations (fixed wing)
Fuel	Nil
Disabled Facilities	
Restaurants	Nil
Taxis/Car Hire	Nil
Weather Info	Air SW MOEx

Operator

John King
Aerofab Restorations
Bourne Park Estates
Andover
Hants
SP11 0DG
Tel: 01264 736635
www.aerofabrestorations.co.uk

Effective date:25/09/08

OP 08

B

38ft 1mb	3.5nm NNE of Bournemouth N5046.80 W00150.55	PPR	Alternative AD Diversion AD	Southampton Compton Abbas Non-standard join

Bournemouth	ATIS	APP	RAD
	133.725	119.475	119.475 118.650

TWR	GND	FIRE
125.600	121.700	121.600

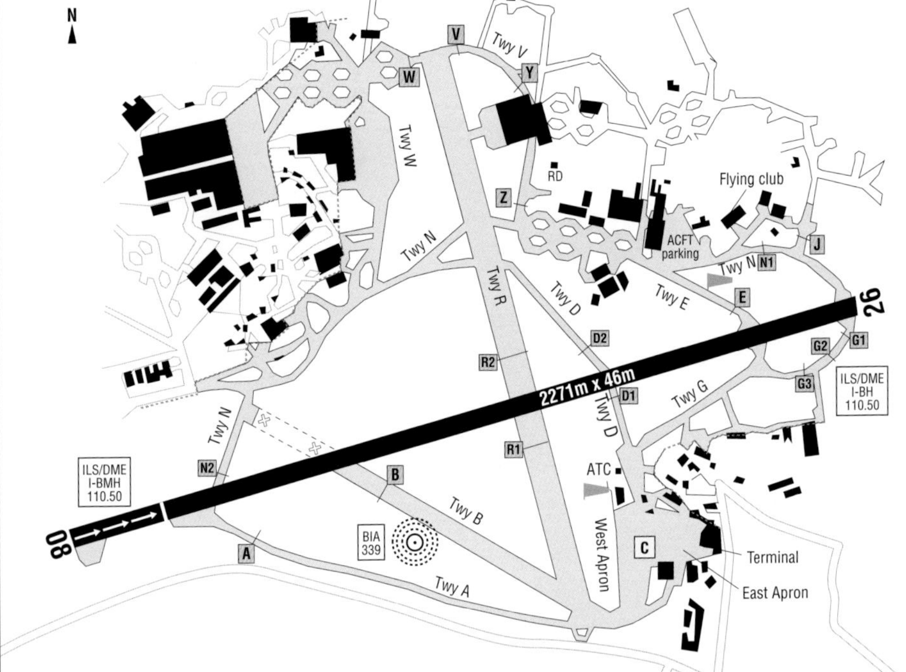

RWY	SURFACE	TORA	LDA	U/L	LIGHTING
08	Asphalt	2271	1838		Ap Thr Rwy PAPI 3° LHS
26	Asphalt	2026	1970		Ap Thr Rwy PAPI 3° RHS

RNAV			
SAM	113.35	243	21.2

Remarks

PPR for all ACFT. Hi-Vis. Escorts may accompany no more than 3 persons who do not have Hi-Vis clothing. It is prohibited to taxi any ACFT on U/L part of AD where vehicles operate on the road system. In these areas towing only approved subject to look-outs., asphalt or grass areas S of Twy G. Long or short stay ACFT to be parked at least 25m from Twy edge. Pilots to state parked position on initial contact with ATC. Booking out via RTF not permitted. Flight plans to be filed at Flight Clearance Office at Bournemouth Handling in person. Prop swinging may only be carried out as a 2-person operation, this is to include PIC and person familiar with prop swinging procedures. All ACFT MTWA 3 tonnes or greater intending to park on the E or W apron require marshaller guidance before leaving the apron taxi-lane for stand positioning. All GND running of engines must have the approval of AD Authority and be booked through ATC. All ACFT that use E or W aprons and/or the terminal facilities are required to be handled by an approved handling agent. All visiting ACFT <3 tonnes must contact Bournemouth Handling to obtain a PPR number. ACFT not complying to this will not be able to land.

Warnings

With the exception of Twy B & R all Twys are only 15m wide and so are not suitable for use by ACFT with a wheel base that exceeds 18m or a wheel span greater than 9m. Use of spur Twy that abut V and G is limited to ACFT with a wingspan not exceeding 15m or wheel base not exceeding 4.5m. The SE Twy is routed through the apron area. The entire area bounded by the S and by a single yellow painted line near the Control tower to the N is designated as apron area for air traffic control purposes. Pilots are to exercise caution in this area, and when using the NE Twy, due to movements of pedestrians and vehicles. Twy V & W & R are unlit and unsuitable for use during dark. Pilots wishing to use Twy V & W during dark should request a follow me vehicle at the earliest opportunity.

Noise: Rwy26 Dept – Climb on Rwy QDM to 0.6 DME, track 270°M to 2000ft before any other turn. **Rwy08 Dept:** – Climb on Rwy QDM to 1.0 DME, track 075°M to 4.1 DME before commencing S turn. For all other directions ACFT can commence a turn at or above 2000ft agl.

Operating Hrs	0530-2030 (Summer) 0630-2130 (Winter) & by arr	**Restaurants**	Cafeteria in terminal Flybites on NW sector of AD
Circuits	Only available to AD based ACFT ACFT less than 5700kgs 1000ft All other ACFT/jet ACFT 1500Ft After 2030 (L) all ACFT 1500ft QFE	**Taxis**	At terminal or
		Country Cabs	**Tel:** 01202 536276
		United	**Tel:** 0800 304555
		Car Hire	
Landing Fee	On application (payable at Bournemouth Handling or by invoice)	Avis	**Tel:** 01202 293218
		Hertz	**Tel:** 01202 291231
Maintenance	Available Full up to 5700kg MAUW	**Weather Info**	M T9 Fax 246 A VS MOEx METAR **Tel:** 01202 364151 TAF **Tel:** 01202 364158
Fuel	AVGAS 100LL Jet A1 Refuelling facilities available daily 0700-2130 with:		
Shell	**Tel:** 01202 575037 by prior arr only outside these times with:	**Operator**	Bournemouth Airport Plc Christchurch Dorset BH23 6SE **Tel:** 01202 364150 (ATC) **Tel:** 01202 364170 (AD Duty Manager) **Fax:** 01202 364159 (ATC) www.bournemouthairport.com
Esso	**Tel:** 01202 594000		
Disabled Facilities	Available		
Handling	**Tel:** 01202 583408 (Signature – Executive) **Tel:** 07795 243065 (Signature – Executive) **Tel:** 01202 364317 (Bournemouth Handling) **Fax:** 01202 581579 (Signature –Executive)		

B

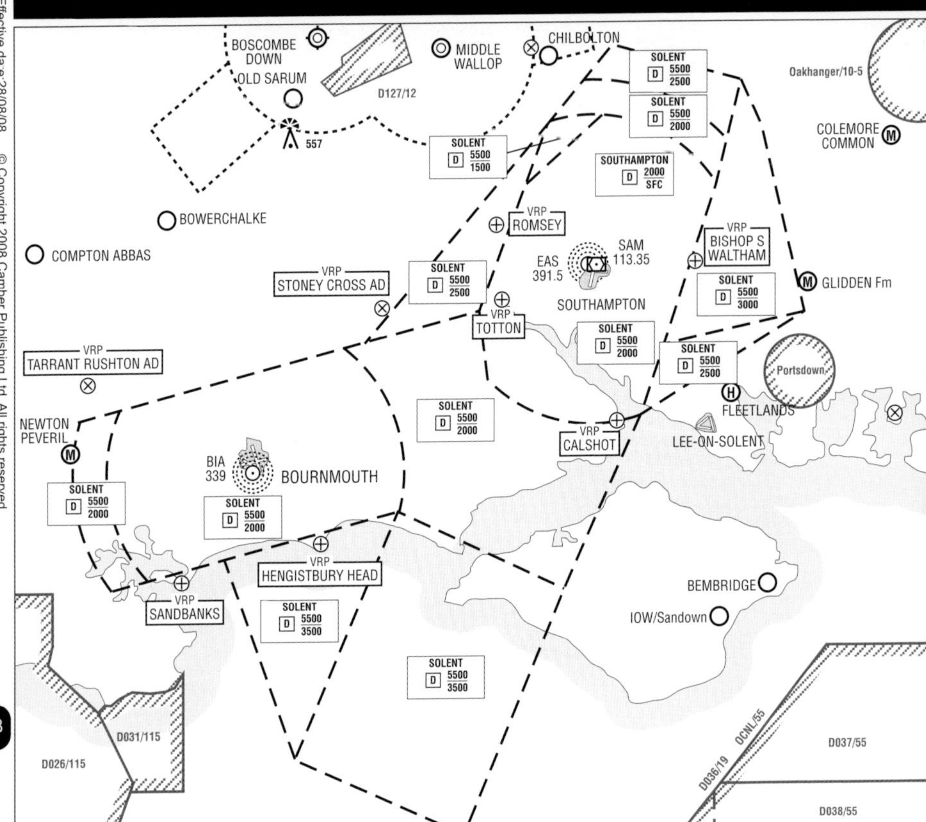

CTR–Class D Airspace

Normal CTA/CTR Class D Airspace rules apply.

Transition Alt 6000ft outside the Solent CTA notified hours Transition Alt 3000ft.

Visual Reference Points (VRP)

VRP	VOR/NDB	VOR/DME
Hengistbury Head N5042.72 W00144.93	SAM 229°/BIA 141°	SAM 229°/21nm
Sand Banks N5041.00 W00156.83	Not suitable VOR/NDB	SAM 237°/28nm
Stoney Cross (Disused AD) N5054.70 W00139.42	SAM 260°/BIA 045°	SAM 260°/12nm
Tarrant Rushton (Disused AD) N5051.00 W00204.70	SAM 260°/BIA 299°	SAM 260°/29nm

B

500ft 16mb	3.5nm WSW of Tetbury N5137.72 W00214.75	PPR	**Alternative AD** **Gloucestershire** Kemble

Non-Radio	LARS Filton 122.725	LARS Brize 124.275	Safetycom 135.475

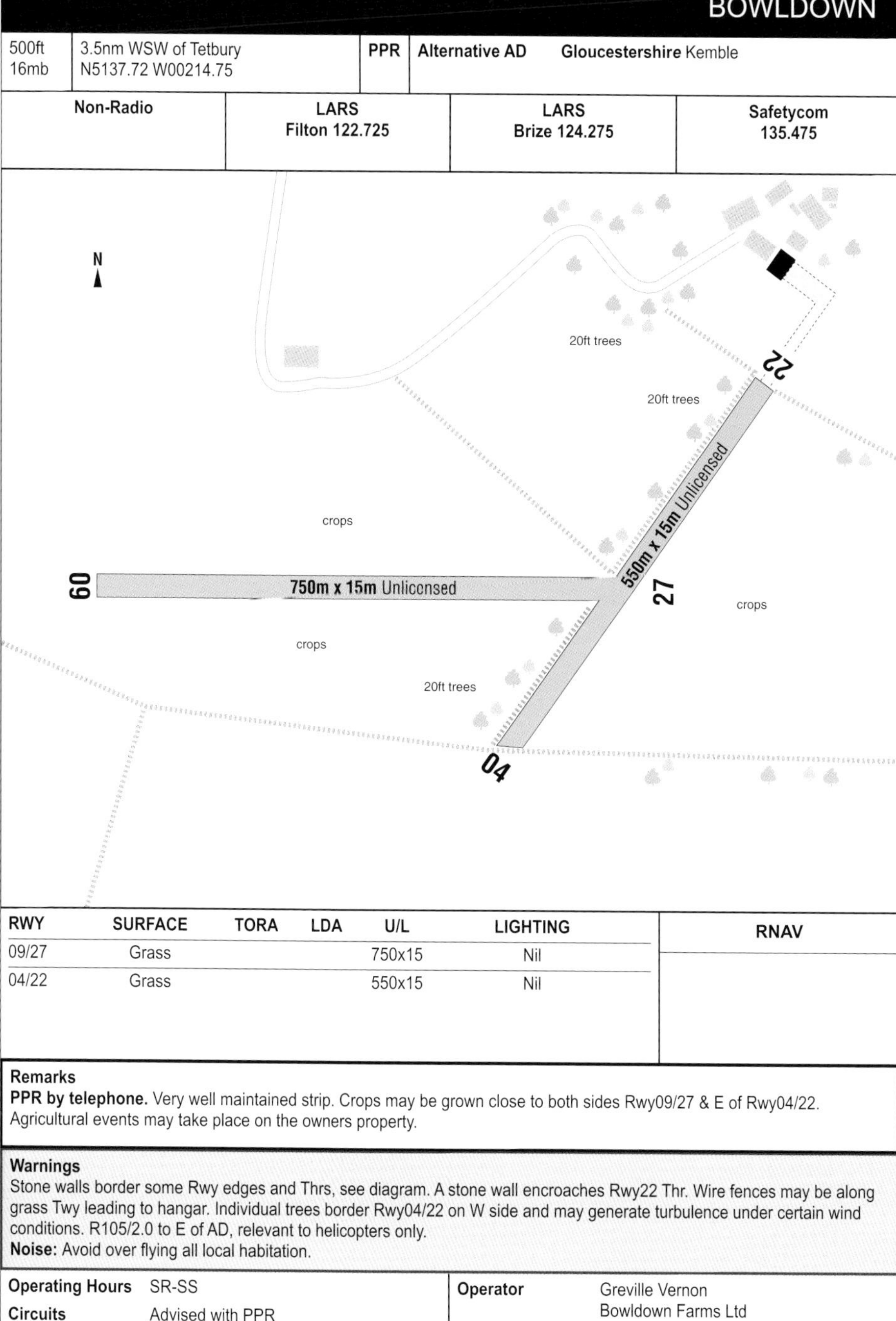

RWY	SURFACE	TORA	LDA	U/L	LIGHTING
09/27	Grass			750x15	Nil
04/22	Grass			550x15	Nil

RNAV

Remarks
PPR by telephone. Very well maintained strip. Crops may be grown close to both sides Rwy09/27 & E of Rwy04/22. Agricultural events may take place on the owners property.

Warnings
Stone walls border some Rwy edges and Thrs, see diagram. A stone wall encroaches Rwy22 Thr. Wire fences may be along grass Twy leading to hangar. Individual trees border Rwy04/22 on W side and may generate turbulence under certain wind conditions. R105/2.0 to E of AD, relevant to helicopters only.
Noise: Avoid over flying all local habitation.

Operating Hours	SR-SS
Circuits	Advised with PPR
Landing Fee	Nil
Maintenance	Nil
Fuel	Nil
Disabled Facilities	Nil
Taxi/Car Hire	Nil
Weather Info	Air SW MOEx

Operator
Greville Vernon
Bowldown Farms Ltd
Bowldown
Weston Birt
Tetbury
Gloucestershire
GL8 8UD
Tel: 01666 890224
Tel: 07764 348651
gv@bowldown.com

200ft 6mb	4nm NNE of Welshpool N5242.30 W00305.00	PPR	Alternative AD	**Hawarden** Welshpool

Non-Radio	LARS Shawbury 120.775	A/G Welshpool 128.000	Safetycom 135.475

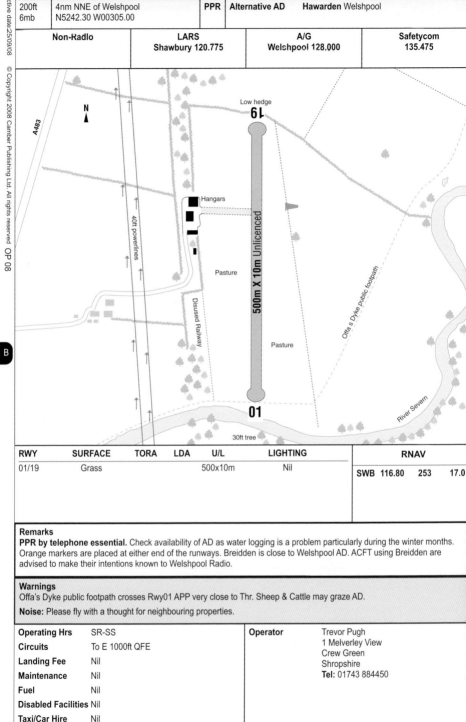

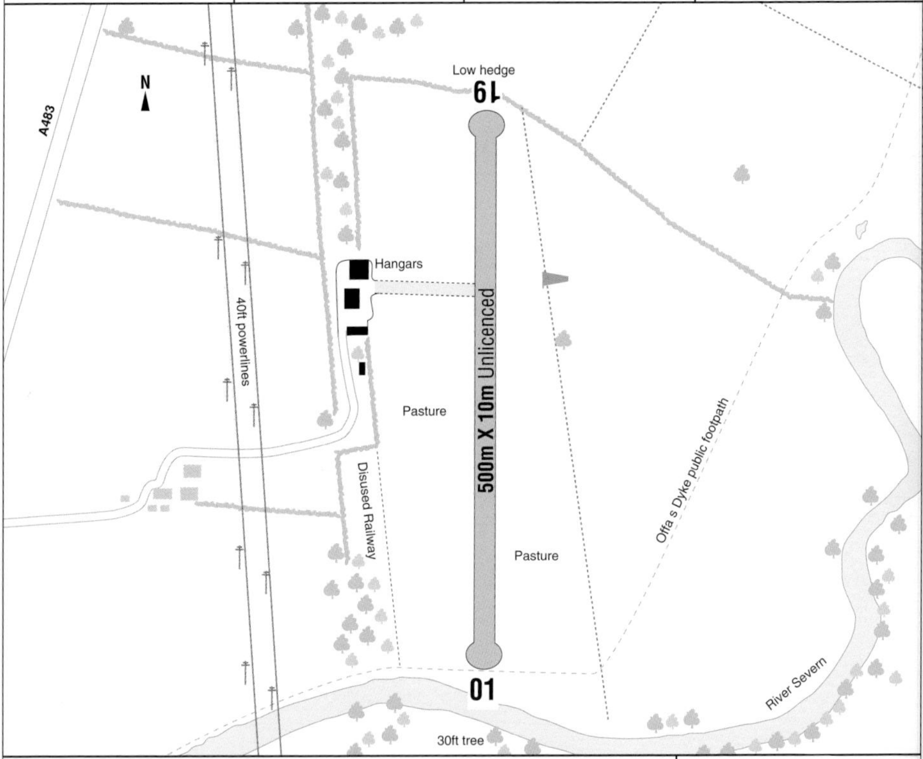

RWY	SURFACE	TORA	LDA	U/L	LIGHTING
01/19	Grass			500x10m	Nil

RNAV			
SWB	116.80	253	17.0

Remarks
PPR by telephone essential. Check availability of AD as water logging is a problem particularly during the winter months. Orange markers are placed at either end of the runways. Breidden is close to Welshpool AD. ACFT using Breidden are advised to make their intentions known to Welshpool Radio.

Warnings
Offa's Dyke public footpath crosses Rwy01 APP very close to Thr. Sheep & Cattle may graze AD.

Noise: Please fly with a thought for neighbouring properties.

Operating Hrs	SR-SS
Circuits	To E 1000ft QFE
Landing Fee	Nil
Maintenance	Nil
Fuel	Nil
Disabled Facilities	Nil
Taxi/Car Hire	Nil
Weather Info	Air N MOEx

Operator Trevor Pugh
1 Melverley View
Crew Green
Shropshire
Tel: 01743 884450

B

20ft 1mb	5nm ENE of Selby N5348.12 W00054.85	PPR	Alternative AD Diversion AD	Humberside Sherburn in Elmet

Non-standard join

Breighton	A/G 129.800

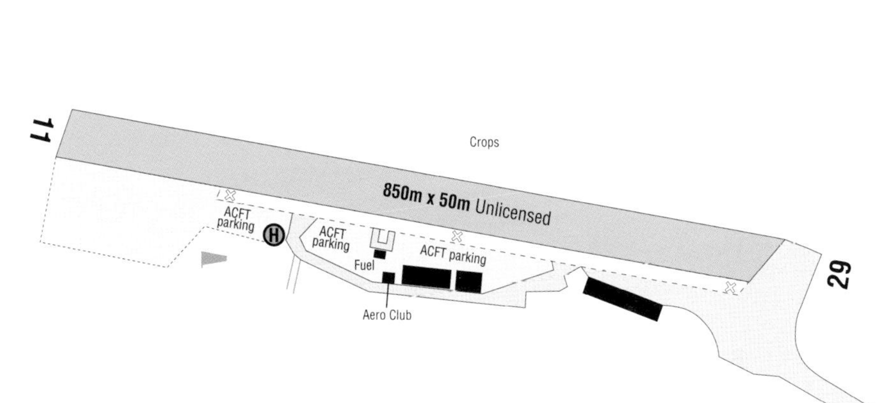

RWY	SURFACE	TORA	LDA	U/L	LIGHTING
11/29	Grass			850x50m	Nil

RNAV			
OTR	113.90	286	29.5

Remarks
PPR. Visiting ACFT, including non radio, welcome on prior permission and at pilot's own risk. Situated at SW corner of disused military AD. Home of vintage and classic ACFT. Live side join required due to frequent aerobatic activity on N side of Rwy centre line. Vintage & Classic ACFT especially welcome.

Warning
Special rules apply on display days.
Noise: Avoid over flying the villages of Breighton and Bubwith.

Operating Hrs 0900-1700 daily & by arr

Circuits 29 LH, 11 RH, 700ft QFE all circuits S
No overhead joins.

Landing Fee £5

Maintenance Real Aeroplane Co
Tel: 01757 289065

Fuel AVGAS JET A1 100LL
Limited over night hangarage available

Disabled Facilities

Taxis On request through AD
Car Hire
National **Tel:** 01904 612141

Weather Info Air N MOEx

Operator Real Aeroplane Company Ltd
The Aerodrome Breighton
Selby
East Yorkshire YO8 7DH
Tel: 01757 289065
rac-ops@tiscali.co.uk
www.realaero.com

Effective date:25/09/08 OP 08
B

210ft 7mb	5.5nm ESE of Newbury N5123.03 W00110.35	PPR	**Alternative AD** **Diversion AD**	**Farnborough** Blackbushe **Non-standard join**

Brimpton	A/G 135.125 Not always manned

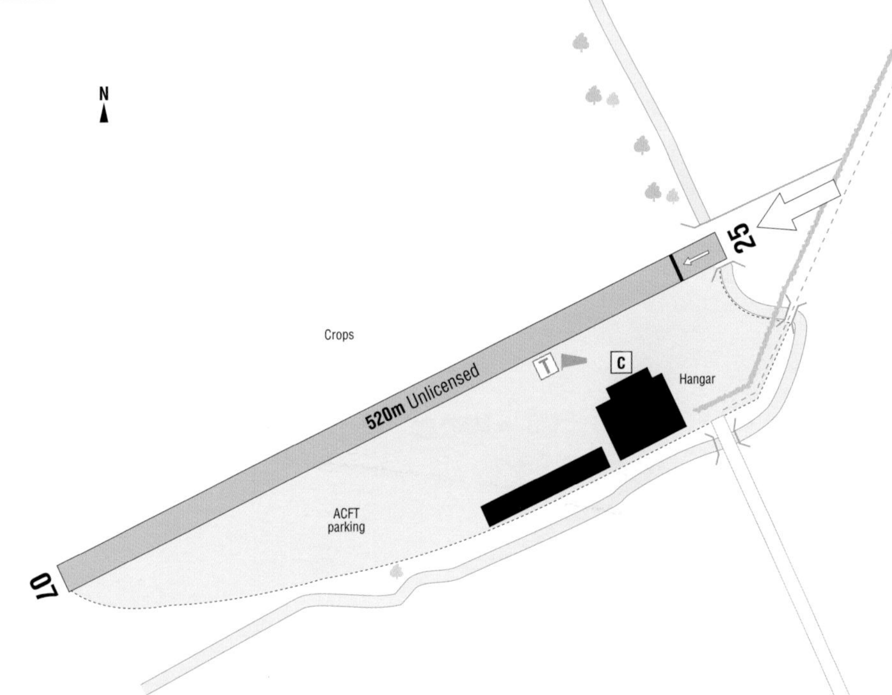

RWY	SURFACE	TORA	LDA	U/L	LIGHTING
07/25	Grass			520	Nil

Displaced Thr Rwy25 100m

RNAV			
CPT	114.35	169	6.7

Remarks
PPR strictly by telephone.

Warnings
AD situated just within NW edge of Atomic Weapons Establishment Restricted Area R101/2.4 and operates under special exemption. All APP to AD must be from N. Flying S of AD below 2400ft AGL prohibited unless landing or taking-off.
Noise: Avoid over flying the villages of Brimpton, Aldermaston, Woolhampton and local habitation.

Operating Hrs 0830-dusk (L)
Circuits 07 LH, 25 RH 800ft QFE
No overhead joins
Landing Fee Single £5 Twin £10
Maintenance Limited
Fuel Nil
Disabled Facilities

Restaurants Light snacks available in clubhouse
Taxis
JDM Taxis **Tel:** 01635 826763
CDC Taxis **Tel:** 01635 866730

Car Hire
National **Tel:** 01635 582525
Weather Info Air SW MOEx
Operator Alan House
Manor View
Hopgoods Green
Upper Bucklebury
Berkshire
RG7 6TA
Tel: 01635 866088
Tel: 07836 775557
Tel: 0118 971 3822 (Clubhouse)

EGGD BRISTOL

622ft 21mb	7nm SW of Bristol N5122.95 W00243.13	PPR	**Alternative AD** **Bristol Filton** Kemble **Diversion AD**

Non-standard join

Bristol	ATIS	APP	RAD
	126.025	125.650	136.075

TWR	GND	FIRE
133.850	121.925	121.600

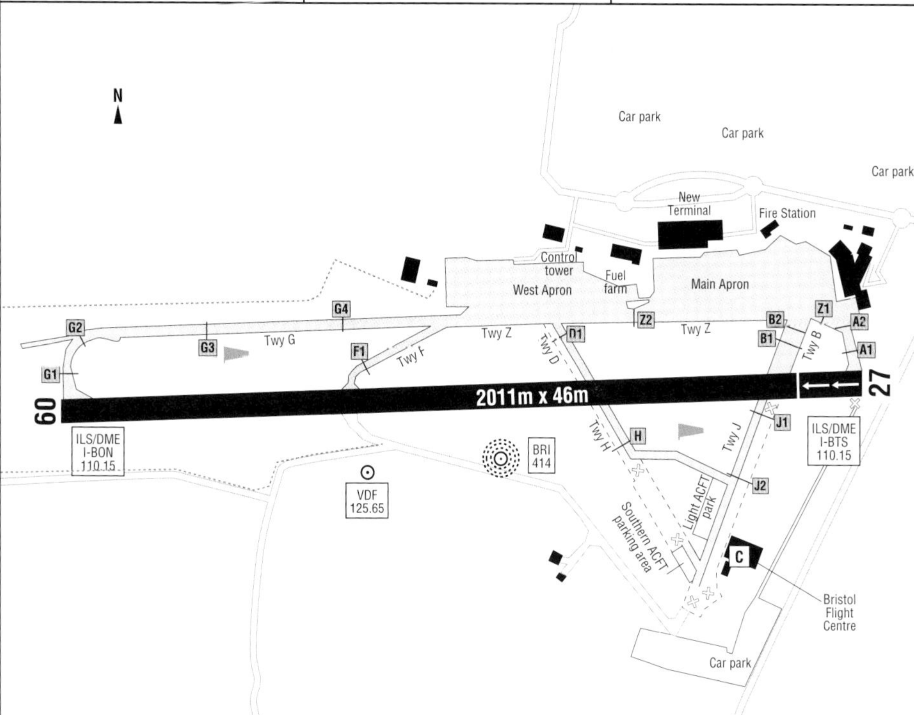

RWY	SURFACE	TORA	LDA	U/L	LIGHTING
09	Asphalt	2011	1938		Ap Thr Rwy PAPI 3° LHS
27	Asphalt	2011	1876		Ap Thr Rwy PAPI 3° LHS

RNAV			
BCN	117.45	139	28.8

Remarks

Non-radio ACFT not accepted. Hi-Vis. Training is not permitted 2200-0700 (L). See 'Booking & Training Procedures'. Propeller driven ACFT of more than 5700kg MTWA must not join final APP track to any Rwy at a height of less than 1000ft QFE. Parking & start up procedure for all ACFT on main aprons is under guidance of apron marshaller following clearance from ATC. Grass areas unsuitable for parking ACFT. Light ACFT Ops:Rwy27 – Pilots to arrange flight to minimise noise nuisance. ACFT landing Rwy27 follow descent profile not below that indicated by PAPI's. Rwy09 – Practice EFATO manoeuvres not permitted. Pilots should avoid over flying Felton Village whenever possible, when Dept Rwy09 and requiring to turn left, ACFT shall climb ahead to 1nm DME before commencing turn. GND running of engines subject to ATC approval at night. Helicopter Operation: Do not over fly noise sensitive area to N of AD boundary below 500ft QFE. Helicopters wishing to Dept/Arr via E/NE AD boundary use Rwy then turn N following A38. Helicopters Dept/Arr from W do so along line of Twy G. W Dept should not turn N until crossing AD boundary. W Arr avoid Felton Village. Helicopters avoid all noise sensitive areas & not permitted to overfly apron. Designated helicopter training area S of AD. Parallel Arr/Dept not permitted to/from Twy G except when traffic using Rwy is VFR. Due to restricted GA parking, operators of inbound GA flights must pre notify handling agents with ETA and duration of stay

Warnings

GND signals not displayed, except light signals. Hot air balloon activity in VMC & daylight Hrs from site 4.5nm NE of AD & downwind of site. Balloons may pass below CTA or if radio equipped, within the CTR/CTA. Pilots will be notified by ATC of known balloon activity which may affect their flights. Glider and hang glider activity takes place along the Mendip Hills, to the south of the AD. ATC will only be notified of such activity when gliders and hang gliders are operating within designated areas within the CTR/CTA and so pilots may not always receive warning of the activity. Bird scaring is carried out on a regular basis but birds may not always be detected on the extreme W end of the AD and on the APP and Dept tracks of all Rwys. Pilots must conform to the noise abatement techniques laid down for the type of ACFT and operate so as to cause the least disturbance practicable in areas surrounding the AD. Pilots may experience wind shear/turbulence especially if the wind is strong, SE Rwy09, W Rwy27.

Operating Hrs H24

Circuits Variable 1000ft QFE for non-jet ACFT
Rwy09 RH only but ATC may vary
Rwy27 LH. Helicopters 700ft QFE

Landing Fee On Application to BFC
Night surcharges 2300-0700 (L)

Maintenance
Bristol Flight Centre **Tel:** 01275 474501

Fuel AVGAS 0800-2000 (L)
Surcharge applies outside these Hrs
Bristol Flight Centre **Tel:** 01275 474601
AVTUR JET A1 Mon-Fri 0500-0130
Sat-Sun 0500-2300

Disabled Facilities

Handling **Tel:** 01275 472776 (Servisair)
Tel: 01275 474501 (Bristol Flight Centre)
Fax: 01275 474851 (Bristol Flight Centre)
Fax: 01275 474514 (Servisair)

Restaurants
Restaurant refreshments & club facilities available
Duty-Free Shop & 24Hr (airside) bar

Taxis
Bristol Int Cars **Tel:** 01275 474888

CarHire
Avis **Tel:** 01275 473536
Europcar **Tel:** 01275 474623
Hertz **Tel:** 01275 472807

Weather Info M T9 T18 Fax 252 A VS BCFO

Operator Bristol Airport Plc Bristol Airport
Bristol BS48 3DY
Tel: 0871 334 4444 (AD)
Tel: 0871 334 4449
Tel: 01275 473712 (ATC)
Fax: 01275 474800/474482 (ATC)
www.bristolairport.com

Booking & Training Procedures
A booking system operates for instrument training. Training periods can be booked by application to ATC. Filing of a flight plan does not constitute a booking and failure to make a booking may result in the ACFT being refused use of the facilities. Pilots are to inform ATC of booking cancellations. Circuit training by non-Bristol based ACFT is only available by prior arrangement with ATC. Booking procedures for all circuit training ACFT may be introduced by ATC during busy periods. Circuit direction for all training ACFT will be varied by ATC for air traffic and noise nuisance avoidance purposes.

Visual Reference Points (VRP)

VRP	VOR/NDB	VOR/DME
Barrow Tanks Reservoir N5124.38 W00239.77	BCN 134°/BRI 056°	BCN 134°/30nm
Bath Racecourse N5125. W00224.	BCN 123°/BRI 083°	BCN 123°/37nm
Cheddar Reservoir N5116.78 W00248.08	BCN 151°/BRI 211°	BCN 151°/32nm
Chew Valley N5119.50 W00235.70	BCN 138°/BRI 129°	BCN 138°/35nm
Churchill N5120.00 W00247.60	BCN 147°/BRI 229°	BCN 147°/29nm
Clevedon N5126.35 W00251.08	BCN 142°/LA 267°	BCN 142°/23nm
East Nailsea N5125.80 W00244.10	BCN 136°/BRI 352°	BCN 136°/27nm
Frome N5113. W00219.	BCN 133°/LA 219°	BCN 133°/27nm
Hicks Gate Roundabout N5125.52 W00231.00	BCN 127°/BRI 074°	BCN 127°/33nm
M4 J18 N5125. W00231.	BCN 115°/BRI 066°	BCN 115°/37nm
M5 Sedgemoor Services N5116. W00255.	BCN 158°/BRI 232°	BCN 158°/37nm
M5 Avon Bridge N5129. W00241.	BCN 127°/BRI 012°	BCN 127°/26nm
Old Severn Bridge (M48) N5136. W00238.	BCN 110°/BRI 015°	BCN 110/24nm
Radstock N5117.53 W00226.92	BCN 134°/LA 236°	BCN 134°/40nm
Wells Mast N5114. W00237	BCN 144°/BRI 161°	BCN 144°/38nm
Weston Aerodrome N5120. W00256.	BCN 156°/BRI 256°	BCN 156°/26nm

NB: ACFT entering the Bristol CTR/CTA via M5 Avon Bridge, Hicks Gate, Radstock or Cheddar VRP's may be required to hold at East Nailsea, Barrow Tanks Reservoirs, Churchill or Chew Valley VRPs as appropriate. The Wells Mast is referred to as the Mendip Mast at AIP ENR 5.4.1. Pilots are advised to use caution when routing via this VRP due to the nature of this lighted Air Navigation obstacle at height 1009ft agl, 2003ft amsl

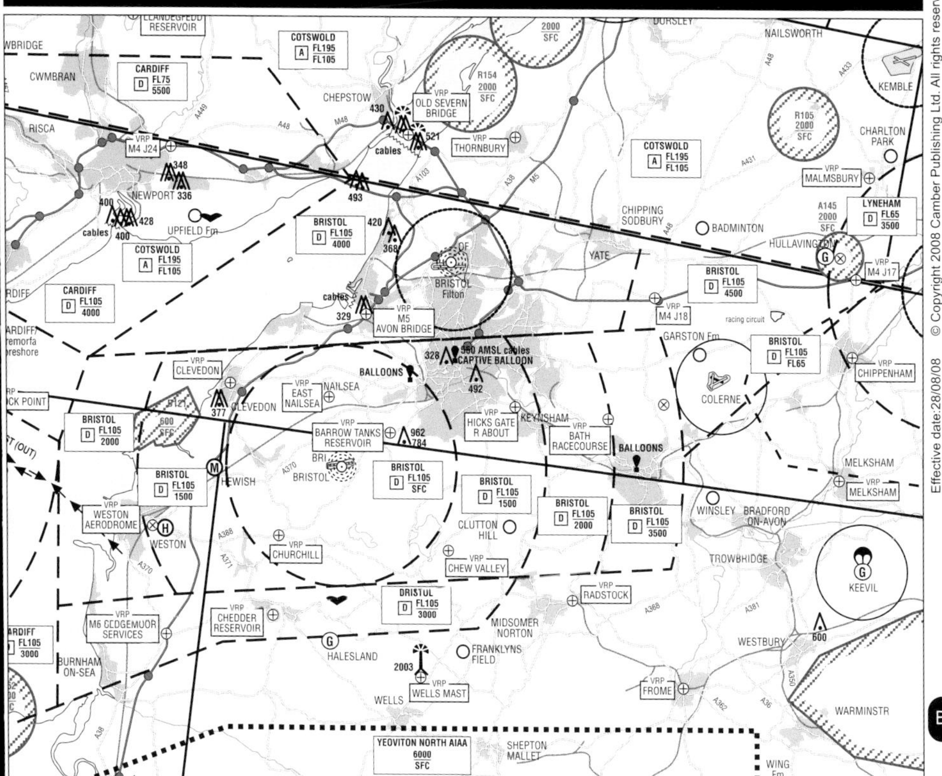

CTA/CTR-Class D Airspace

Normal CTA/CTR Class D Airspace rules apply.

Transition Alt 6000ft.

B

226ft 8mb	4nm N of Bristol N5131.17 W00235.45	PPR	Alternative AD	Bristol Kemble

Non-standard join

Bristol Filton	APP	RAD	TWR	FIRE
	122.725	122.725	132.350	121.600

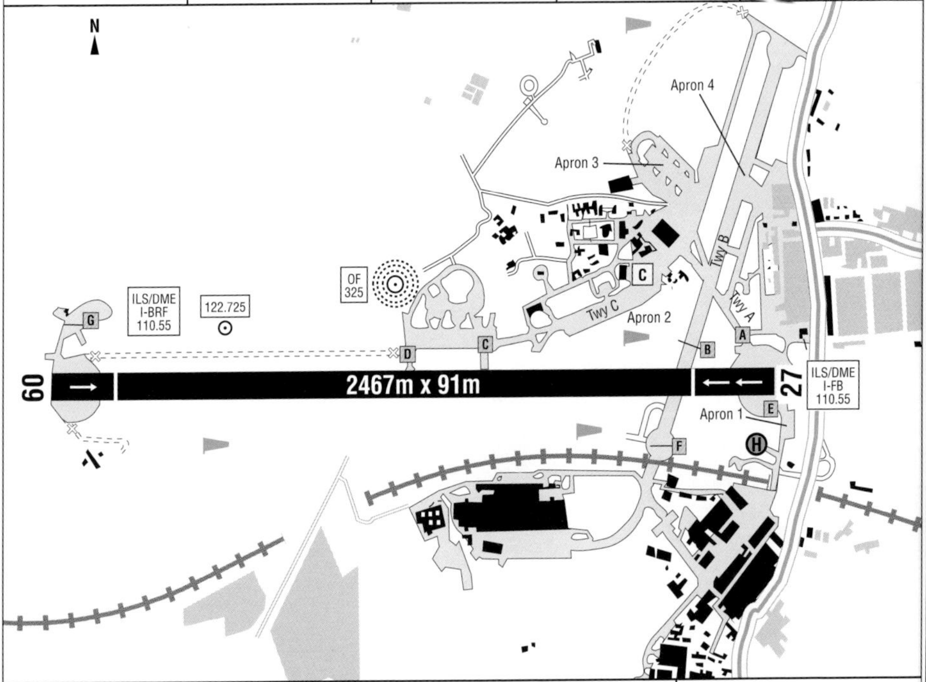

RWY	SURFACE	TORA	LDA	U/L	LIGHTING
09	Concrete	2300	2125		Ap Thr Rwy PAPI 3° LHS
27	Concrete	2300	2060		Ap Thr Rwy PAPI 3° LHS

RNAV			
BCN	117.45	120	27.8

Remarks

PPR by telephone. ACFT on APP Rwy27 are to cross A38 not below 100ft agl. Instrument training not available to ACFT without a serviceable transponder. All ACFT to contact APP not RAD at weekends. All ACFT fitted with a Ballistic Recovery System (BRS) must declare that the device is on the ACFT before arr at Filton.

Warnings

Not all Twys are available for use. Deviation from the marked manoeuvring area can be hazardous. Rwy09/27 subject to slow clearance of standing water after heavy rain. Pilots must request start clearance and have a marshaller in attendance. Pilots must ensure that at all times ACFT are operated to cause the least disturbance practicable in areas surrounding the AD.
Noise: Subject to ATC operations at the time, Dept ACFT will be offered Rwy27, Arr Rwy09 whenever possible, together with the surface wind and Rwy status. Pilots are to avoid flying over built up areas.

Operating Hrs Mon-Fri 0530-1930 Sat-Sun 0800-1600(Summer) +1Hr (Winter)

Circuits Jet/Turbo Prop ACFT, 2000ft QFE
Other ACFT variable 1500ft QFE

Landing Fee <2.5 metric tonne MTOW £25 per metric tonne or part there of, >2.5 metric tonne MTOW £19 per metric tonne or part there of

Maintenance Hangarage on request

Fuel AVGAS 100LL (subject to avail) JET A1

Disabled Facilities

Restaurants Refreshments at BAe Flight Operations

Taxis
Eurotaxis **Tel:** 01454 320101
Spirit Taxis **Tel:** 0117 3731111

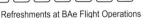

Car Hire
Hertz **Tel:** 0870 8502692
Sixt **Tel:** 0117 9793543

Weather Info M T9 Fax MOEx

Visual Reference Points (VRP)
Old Severn Bridge N5136.67 W00238.62
M5 bridge over River Avon N5129.33 W00241.58
Thornbury N5136.67 W00231.10

Operator BAe Property Services
PO Box 77
Bristol, BS99 7AR
Tel: 0117 9699094
Fax: 0117 9362474
Fax: 0117 9698428
bristolfilton.flightops@baesystems.com
www.bristolfilton.co.uk

B

EGVN BRIZE NORTON

287ft 10mb	4nm WSW of Witney N5145.00 W00135.02	PPR MIL	Alternative AD **Oxford** Kemble Diversion AD

Non-standard join

Brize	LARS	Zone	RAD	DIR
	124.275	119.000	124.275	133.750

APP	TWR	GND	OPS
127.250	123.725	121.725	130.075

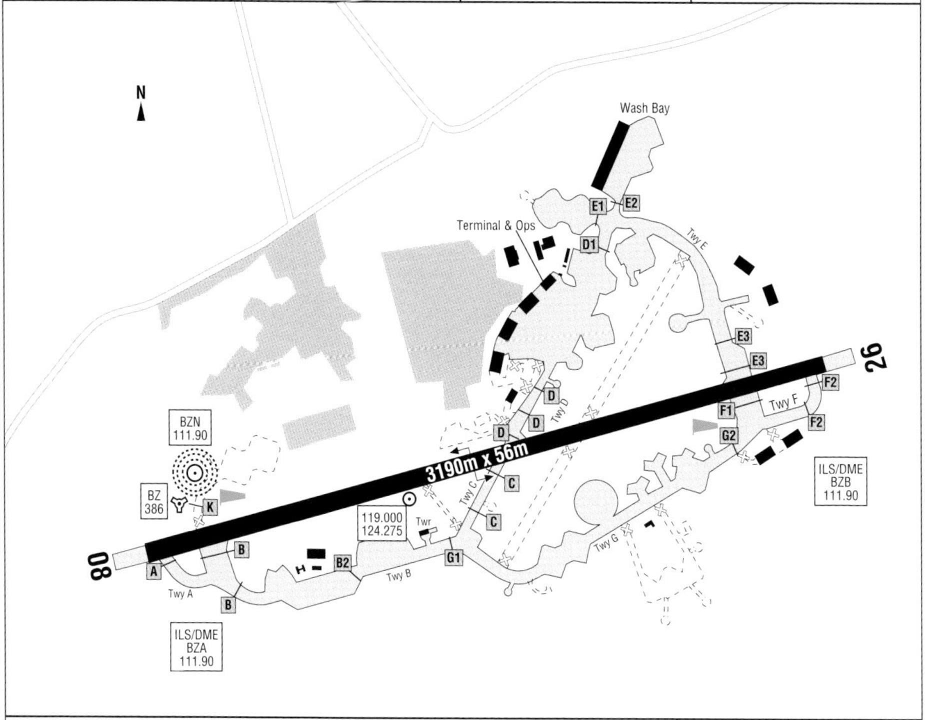

N
Wash Bay
Terminal & Ops
E1 E2 D1 Twy E E3 E3 26 F2 F1 Twy F F2 G2
D D Twy D D
3190m x 56m
C C Twy C
BZN 111.90
BZ 386 K
119.000 124.275 Twr
08 A B B2 G1 Twy B Twy G
Twy A B
ILS/DME BZA 111.90
ILS/DME BZB 111.90

RWY	SURFACE	TORA	LDA	U/L	LIGHTING
08/26	Asphalt	3050	3050		Ap Thr Rwy PAPI 3°

RNAV			
CPT	114.35	323	206

Remarks
PPR 24Hrs notice required. Located within the Brize Norton CTR. No visiting ACFT between 1700-0800 (L). No 180° turns on Rwy. Light ACFT can expect to see vehicular traffic crossing at the upwind end of the Rwy. Brize LARS available Mon-Fri 0800-2000 (L). Outside Hrs subject to controller. Brize Zone available H24. Brize Zone frequency is for Brize CTR crossing/transit.

Warnings
Free fall parachuting takes place up to FL150 SR-SS. ACFT with wing span >60m are not permitted to use Twy B.
Noise: Rwy26 Visual circuits should avoid Cotswold Wildlife Park, Shilton, Witney, Clanfield, Minster Lovell and Bampton.. Rwy08 visual circuits avoiding Witney. Light ACFT will normally be required to enter or leave the Brize Norton CTR via Burford or Faringdon VRP's. Arr ACFT are to proceed at 1000ft QFE directly from the VRP's to base leg, or as directed by ATC.

Operating Hrs H24
Circuits Light ACFT Variable 1000ft QFE
Other ACFT 1500ft
Landing Fee Charges in accordance with RAF policy
Contact Station Ops for details
Maintenance Nil
Fuel JET A1 FS11 AVGAS
Disabled Facilities

Restaurants Nil
Taxis/Car Hire Nil

Weather Info M T Fax 254 MOEx
ATIS **Tel:** 01993 848815
Operator RAF Brize Norton
Oxon OX8 3LX
Tel: 01993 842551
Tel: 01993 842551 Ex 7433 (PPR)
Tel: 01993 845886 (Brize Norton FC)

CTA/CTR-Class D Airspace
Normal CTA/CTR Class D Airspace rules apply
To assist Brize RAD in ensuring access to its airspace pilots should make an R/T call when 15nm or 5 minutes flying time from the zone boundary, whichever is the earlier.

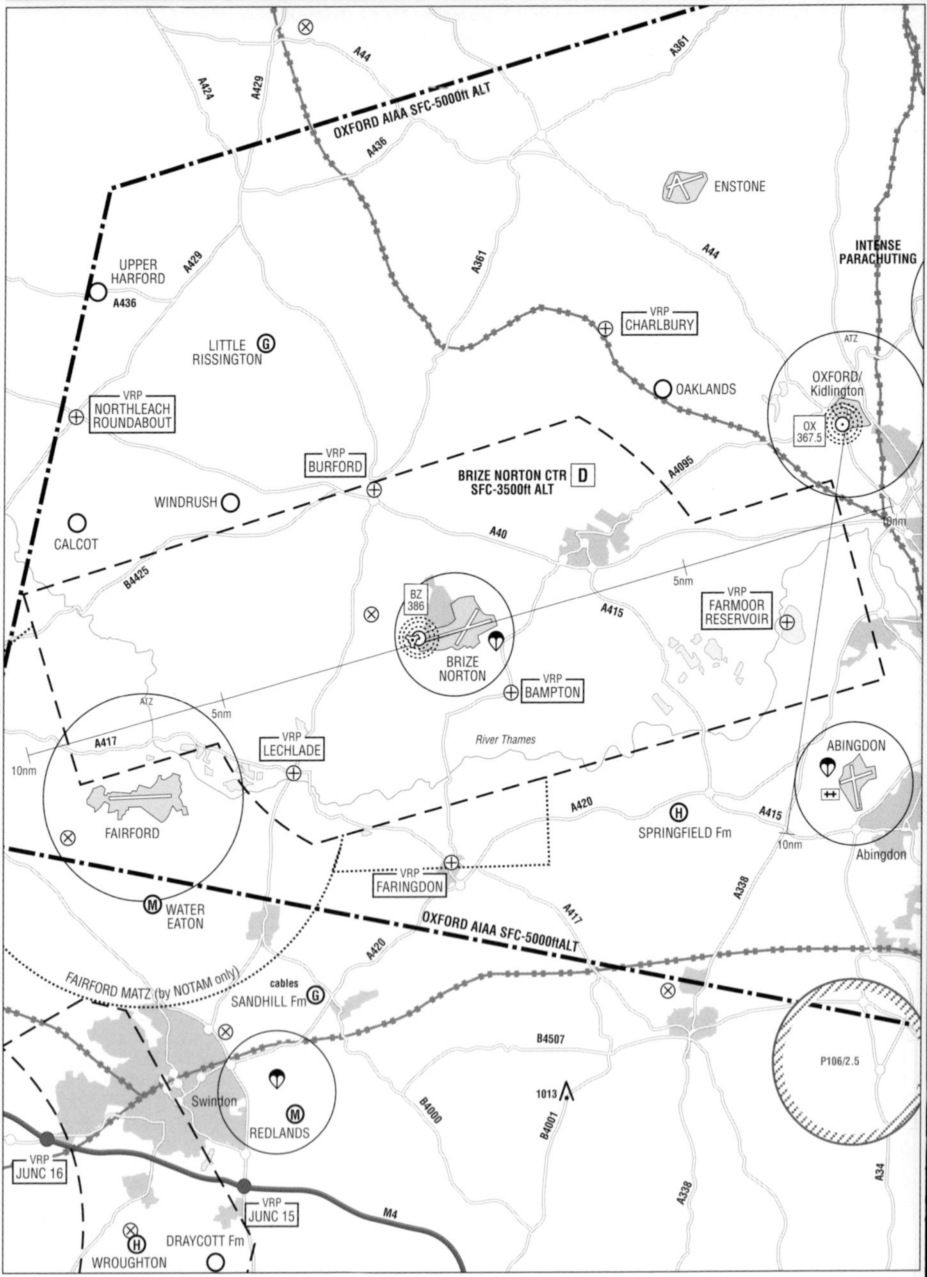

Visual Reference Points (VRP)

VRP	VOR/VOR	VOR/NDB	VOR/DME
Bampton N5143.30 W00132.48	CPT 321°/DTY 213°	CPT 321°/BZ 127°	CPT 321°/19nm
Burford N5148.24 W00132.12	CPT 323°/DTY 223°	CPT 323°/BZ 342°	CPT 323°/24nm
Charlbury N5152.18 W00128.54	CPT 339°/DTY 219°	CPT 339°/BZ 034°	CPT 339°/25nm
Faringdon N5139.18 W00135.12	CPT 308°/DTY 212°	CPT 308°/BZ 177°	CPT 308°/17nm
Farmoor Reservoir N5145.12 W00121.24	CPT 344°/DTY 202°	CPT 344°/BZ 091°	CPT 344°/17nm
Lechlade N5141.36 W00141.25	CPT 307°/DTY 219°	CPT 307°/BZ 227°	CPT 307°/21nm
Northleach Roundabout N5150.15 W00150.09	CPT 319°/DTY 235°	CPT 319°/BZ 304°	CPT 319°/31nm

467ft 16mb	6nm S of Leicester N5229.22 W00107.84	PPR	Alternative AD Diversion AD	Coventry Leicester

Bruntingthorpe	A/G 122.825 (By arr)

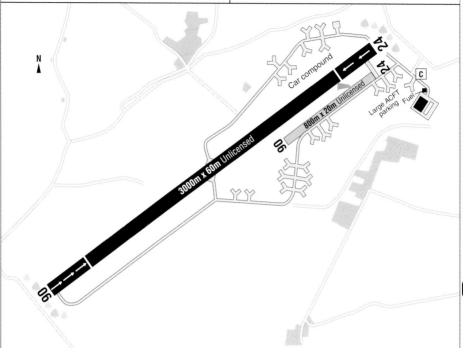

N
Car compound
3000m x 60m Unlicensed
800m x 20m Unlicensed
Large ACFT parking
Fuel
C
06
24
06
24

RWY	SURFACE	TORA	LDA	U/L	LIGHTING
06/24	Asphalt			2630x60	Nil
06/24	Grass			800x60	Nil

RNAV			
DTY	116.40	002	18.3

Remarks

PPR by telephone. AD used intensively by the motor industry for vehicle proving. Extensive long term parking/storing facilities available for large ACFT. ACFT museum unique collection of Cold War jets open Sun 1000-1600.

Warnings

Earth banks with trees up to 40' close to both Thrs. Grass Rwy has been reduced to 800m due to new track at Rwy24 Thr.
Noise: Do not over fly local villages.

Operating Hrs Available on request
Circuits Avoid over flying habitation
Landing Fee On application
Maintenance Nil
Fuel Nil
Disabled Facilities

Restaurants Pubs 10min walk in Bruntingthorpe village
Taxis/Car Hire By arrangement on arrival
Weather Info Air Cen MOEx

Operator
C Walton Ltd
Bruntingthorpe Aerodrome
Lutterworth, Leics, LE17 5QN
Tel: 01162 799300
Tel: 01162 799315 (Security)
Fax: 01162 478031
www.bruntingthorpe.com

50ft 1mb	5nm WSW of Horncastle N5311.97 W00015.17	**PPR**	**Alternative AD** **East Midlands** Wickenby

Non-Radio	**LARS** **Coningsby 120.800**	**LARS** **Waddington 127.350**	**Safetycom** **135.475**

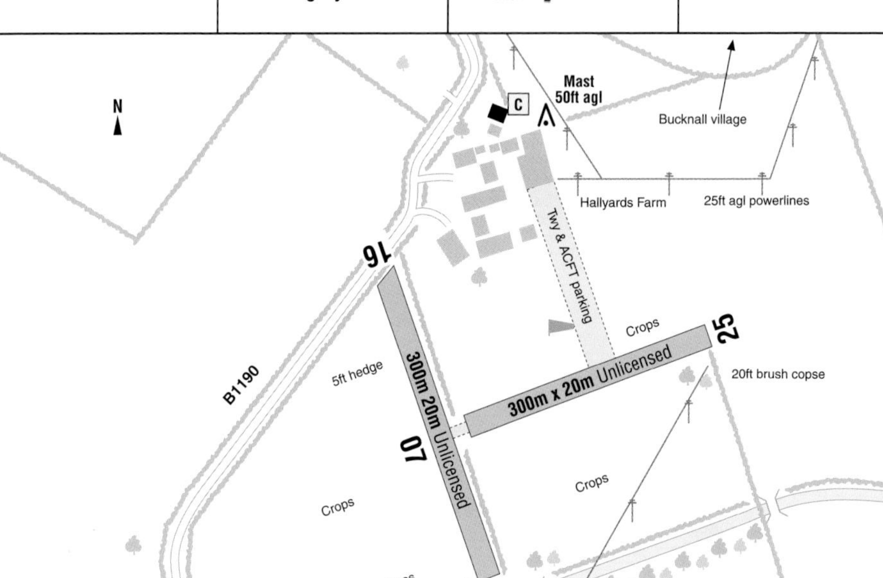

RWY	SURFACE	TORA	LDA	U/L	LIGHTING
07/25	Grass			300x20	Nil
16/34	Grass			300x20	Nil

RNAV			
GAM	112.80	108	25.1

Remarks
PPR by telephone. Suitable for Microlights or STOL ACFT. AD is bordered by drainage dyke to S and road to N. Visitors ensure they have identified current Rwys.
Visual Aid to Location: Church in Bucknall Village and Sewage Farm close NE of strip.

Warnings
Road and low hedge cross Rwy16 Thr. 30ft trees cross Rwy34 APP just short of Rwy Thr. A public bridleway crossed Rwy25 Thr. There is a low hedge, with a gap for taxiing which divides Rwy07/25 from 16/34. AD is close to N boundary of Coningsby MATZ.
Noise: Avoid over flight of Bucknall village to NE.

Operating Hrs SR-SS
Circuits 07, 25 to S, 16, 34 to W
Always away from village
Landing Fee Nil
Maintenance Nil
Fuel MOGAS available by arrangement
Disabled Facilities

Restaurants Nil
Taxis/Car Hire Nil
Weather Info Air N MOEx

Operator
Allan Todd
Hallyards Farm, Bucknall
Woodhall Spa, Lincs, LN10 5DT
Tel: 01526 388249 (Allan Todd)
Tel: 07970 496811
allan@todd.flyer.co.uk

Effective date:25/09/08 OP 05

B

XBRN BURN

20ft 0mb	2nm S of Selby N5344.73 W00104.97	PPR	**Alternative AD** **Leeds Bradford** Sherburn in Elmet **Non-standard join**

Burn Base	APP	A/G
	Fenton 126.500 Doncaster Sheffield 126.225	130.100 (Not always manned)

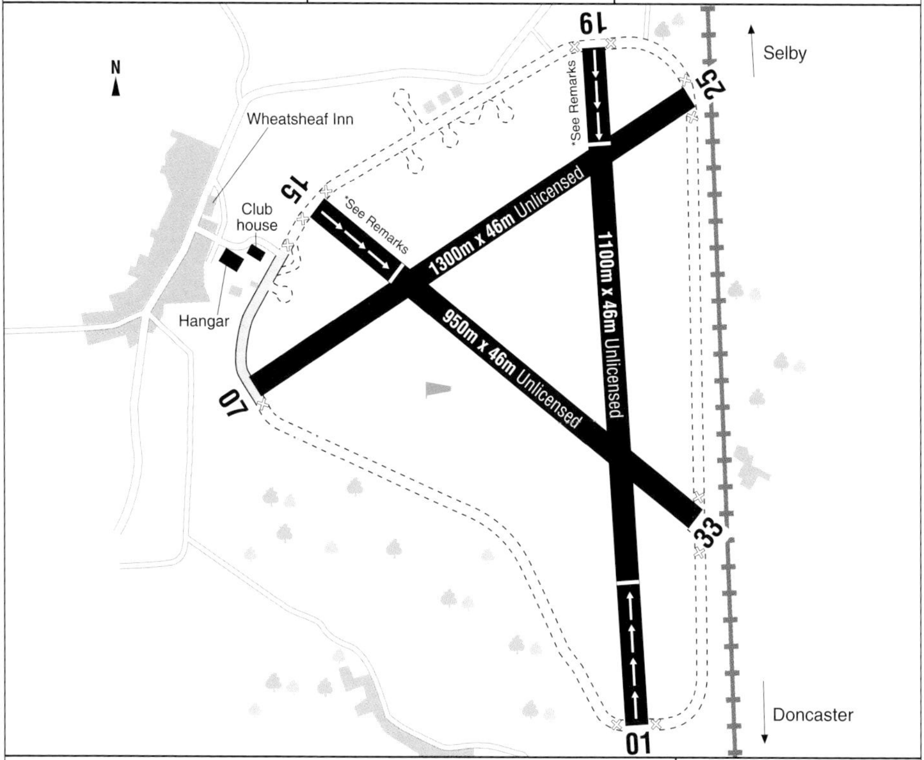

N
19
25
Selby
Wheatsheaf Inn
*See Remarks
15
Club house
*See Remarks
1300m x 46m Unlicensed
1100m x 46m Unlicensed
Hangar
950m x 46m Unlicensed
07
33
Doncaster
01

RWY	SURFACE	TORA	LDA	U/L	LIGHTING
07/25	Asphalt			1300x46	Nil
01/19	Asphalt			1100x46	Nil
15/33	Asphalt			950x46	Nil

Rwys in moderate to poor condition

RNAV			
GAM	112.80	354	28.3

Remarks
PPR by telephone. AD a gliding site, powered ACFT welcome at pilots own risk. Pilots with Silver 'C' gliding qualification are always welcome. All visiting pilots must obtain a full briefing to ensure safe integration when gliding is in progress. Rwy01/19 & Rwy15 have displaced Thr to avoid obstructions and rough portions of Asphalt; these areas must NOT be used.

Warnings
Located on edge of Doncaster Sheffield CTA. Gliding by winch launch and aerotow to 2000ft agl. DO NOT join overhead when gliding is in progress. Powered ACFT and Gliders may operate from different Rwys. When gliding club is closed all gates are locked. Access arranged with PPR gliding not in progress. Farming activity, horse riders, and walkers near Rwys. Twy are not suitable for ACFT use except between Rwy07 Thr and Clubhouse/Hangar.

Operating Hrs SR-SS

Circuits Visitors normally LH 1000ft QFE. Orbit AD at 1000ft QFE to indicate intention to land. DO NOT join overhead. Club tugs & Gliders Variable

Landing Fee £10 includes temporary membership BGA members free

Maintenance Nil

Fuel AVGAS 100LL

Disabled Facilities

Restaurants Good local Pubs

Taxis
Selby Taxis **Tel:** 01757 212285
Station Taxis **Tel:** 01757 702567
Den's Cabs **Tel:** 01757 291541

Car Hire Nil

Weather Info Air N MOEx

Operator Burn Gliding Club Ltd
Park Lane
Burn, Selby
North Yorkshire, YO8 8LW
Tel: 01757 270296 (Clubhouse)
Tel: 07712 467401 (Launch Point)
Tel: 01757 210896 (PPR/Briefing)
Tel: 01405 860144 (PPR/Briefing)

50ft 1mb	1nm SW of Kingarth N5545.00 W00503.00	PPR	Alternative AD	Glasgow Prestwick

Non-Radio	Lighting Control 130.650	Safetycom 135.475

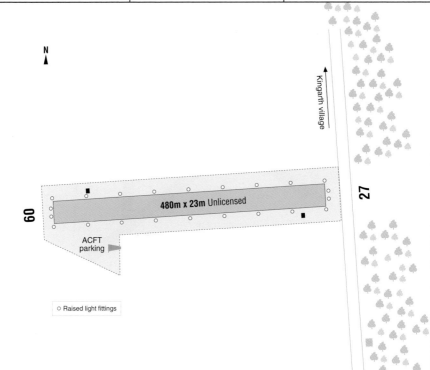

RWY	SURFACE	TORA	LDA	U/L	LIGHTING
09	Grass			500x23	Rwy Thr APAPI 4.5° LHS
27	Grass			500x23	Rwy Thr APAPI 5.0° LHS

RNAV			
GOW	115.40	257	21.6

Remarks
PPR by telephone. Available to visiting ACFT at Pilots own risk during daylight Hrs only. AD lighting not available for visitors but provided for Loganair Air Ambulance operations only.

Warnings
Rwy27 APP is through a gap cut in an extensive stand of trees. High GND to SE to 516ft amsl. Strip slopes down from Rwy27 to Rwy09 with 1 degree gradient. Caution AD light fittings raised above Rwy surface. Sector Safety Altitude for AD of 3600ft (NE sector). 2600ft (SE sector). 3900ft (SW sector) 3500ft (NW sector). **Remember- these figures are for the guidance of Air Ambulance experienced pilots. Visitors should exercise extreme caution.** There is Class E airspace, Scottish TMA with base 3000ft QNH to E of AD.

Operating Hrs SR-SS
Circuits Circuits to N
Landing Fee Nil
Maintenance Nil
Fuel Nil
Disabled Facilities

Restaurant Within walking distance of Kingarth village
Taxi/Car Hire Nil

Weather Info Air SC GWC
Operator Mr N Mellish
Mount Stuart Trust
Estate Office
Mount Stuart
Rothesay
Isle of Bute, PA20 9LR
Tel: 01700 502627
(Mon-Fri 0900-1700 (L)
Fax: 01700 505313
nick.mellish@bute-estate.com

B

14ft 0mb	3.5nm SW of Caernarfon N5306.25 W00420.42	PPR	Alternative AD Diversion AD	Liverpool Mona

Caernarfon	LARS Valley 125.225	A/G 122.250

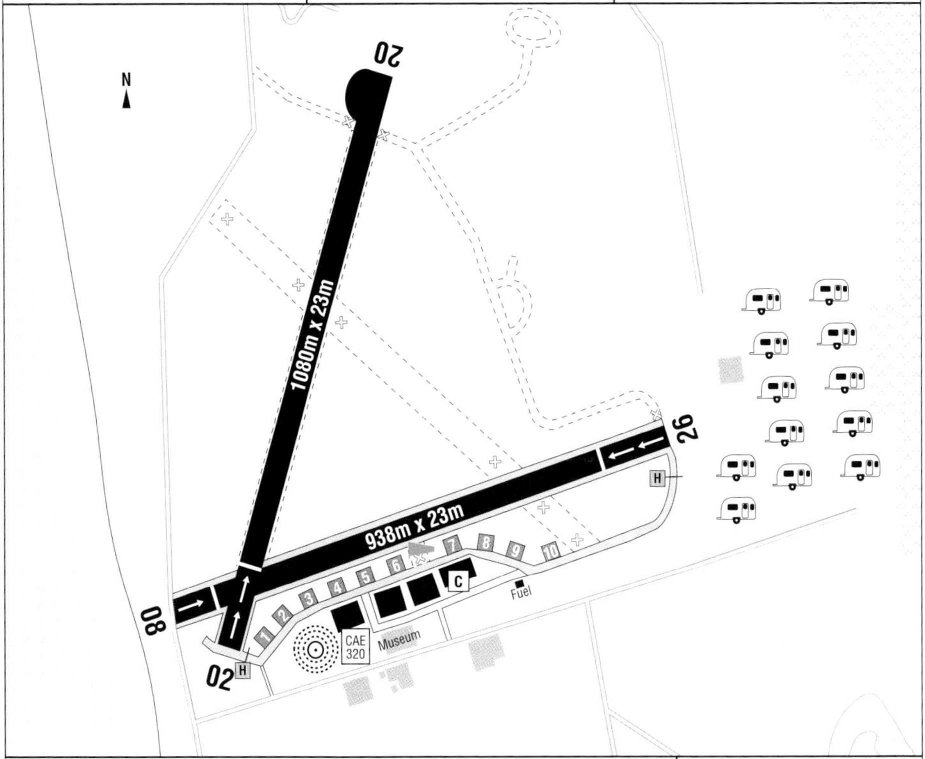

RWY	SURFACE	TORA	LDA	U/L	LIGHTING
08	Asphalt	799	880		Nil
26	Asphalt	799	759		Nil
02	Asphalt	1080	1003		Nil
20	Asphalt	1044	1044		Nil

RNAV

Remarks
PPR. Hi-Vis. Arr ACFT contact Valley. Join the circuit overhead at 1300ft QFE. No taxiing on grass surfaces. Dept ACFT, unless otherwise instructed should call Valley immediately after take-off. Certain customs facilities available. Aviation museum on AD.

Warnings
AD in vicinity of Valley CMATZ. Extensive high GND to S and E of AD. TV mast 2050ft AMSL 5nm S of AD. Transient obstacles, vehicles (16ft) on road across Rwy02 APP centre line. Microlight and gliding activity on AD.
Noise: Avoid over flight of any caravan site within ATZ (Apart from final Rwy26).

Operating Hrs 0800-1800 (Summer) 0900-1630 (Winter)

Circuits 02, 26 RH, 08, 20 LH, 800ft QFE

Landing Fee Single £15, Twin £25
Microlight £10

Maintenance Apache Aviation **Tel:** 01286 832407

Fuel AVGAS 100LL JET A1
with oils W100 & W80

Disabled Facilities

Restaurants Dakota Cafe
Tel: 01286 830800

Taxis/Car Hire AD will assist

Weather Info Air N MOEx

Operator Air Caernarfon Ltd
Dinas Dinlle
Gwynedd
LL54 5TP
Tel: 01286 830800
Fax: 01286 830280
www.air-world.co.uk

EGSC CAMBRIDGE

47ft 2mb	1.5nm E of Cambridge N5212.30 E00010.50	PPR	Alternative AD Diversion AD	Cranfield Bourn

Non-standard join

Cambridge	ATIS	APP	RAD	TWR	OPS Marshalls
	134.600	123.600	124.975	122.200	129.700

Light ACFT fuel
N
Flying clubs
CAM 332.50
Twy A
C
A
ILS/DME I-CMG 111.30
GA Grass parking
B
A2
Twy B
12 Apron
Twy C
C1
Twy C
C
1965m x 46m
B2
D1
C2
A3
B3
17 Apron
899m x 35m
D
Twy D
C3
10
D2
05
23
1
VDF 123.600
699m x 35m
28
D3
2
05

Heli hover taxi route

GA Grass parking Area

Z	1	2	3	4	5	6	7	8	9 Z
Y	1	2	3	4	5	6	7	8	9 Y
X	1	2	3	4	5	6	7	8	9 X
W	1	2	3	4	5	6	7	8	9 W

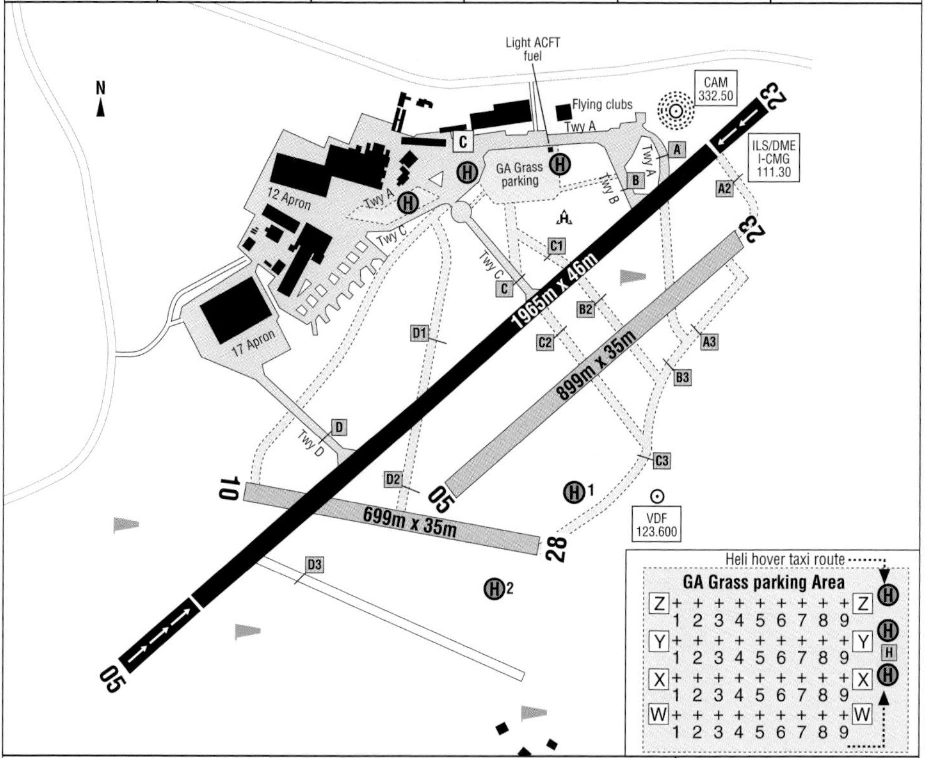

RWY	SURFACE	TORA	LDA	U/L	LIGHTING
05	Asphalt	1851	1635		Ap Thr Rwy PAPI 3° LHS
23	Asphalt	1892	1747		Ap Thr Rwy PAPI 3° LHS
05/23	Grass	899	899		Nil
10/28	Grass	699	699		Nil

RNAV			
BKY	116.25	021	13.5

Remarks

PPR for Jets and Twins only. Not available to non-radio ACFT, Microlights or gliders. Hi vis. Preferred Arr Rwy23, Dept Rwy05. ACFT APP Asphalt Rwy05/23 not below PAPI glide slope from 1000ft. Parallel Rwy ops may be in progress. Rwy05/23 grass go-arounds remain S of Rwy05/23 grass centre line. ACFT taxiing on grass to keep to Twys. Long grass is unsuitable for manoeuvring. Holding position signs and yellow Twy markings are provided between Twy A, B, C, D and the main Rwy. Holding points for grass Rwy are marked with rectangular day glo markers marked with the Rwy designator. A security charge may be levied for secure parking. Handling available. Customs available with PPR.
Helicopter Hover Taxi Route: Helicopters are to request hover to HA then onto parking as directed. Exit in reverse direction.
Visual aid to location: IBN flashing green CI.

Warnings

Turbulence and wind shear may be experienced shortly after Dept Rwy28 when there is a strong N wind.
Noise: Avoid over-flying Cambridge below 2000ft. Helicopters should APP vis Heli VRP to N E &S of AD, avoiding over flying Cambridge city and surrounding villages.

Operating Hrs	Mon-Fri 0630-1900 Sat-Sun 0700-1800 (Summer) +1Hr (Winter) & by arr
Circuits	23, 28 LH, 05, 10 RH 1500ft Twins/Jets, Fixed wing 1000ft, 700ft Helicopters (QFE)
Landing Fee	£44.50 up to 1.5MT pay on day Discounted for training ACFT.
Maintenance	Available by arr
Fuel	JET A1 AVGAS 100LL

Disabled Facilities

Handling	**Tel:** 01223 373214/3285 (Cambridge Airport Handling) enquiries@cambridgecityairport.com
Restaurants	Restaurant Mon-Fri 0730-1400 Coffee Shop Mon-Fri 0800-1630

Taxis		**Operator**	Marshall Aerospace
Panther	**Tel:** 01223 715715		Cambridge Airport
Car Hire			Newmarket Road
Hertz	**Tel:** 01223 416634		Cambridge, CB5 8RX
Avis	**Tel:** 01223 212551		**Tel:** 01223 373737 (Switchboard)
Weather Info	M T9 Fax 256 MOEx		**Tel:** 01223 293737 (ATC)
			Tel: 01223 373214 (Ops)
			Fax: 01223 37302 (ATC)
			atc.admin@marshallaerospace.com
			www.cambridgecityairport.com

Helicopter VRP

November	Reservoir/small lake 0.25nm
N5214.38 E00011.25	NE Horningsea
Echo	
N5212.47 E00014.54	Plantation S of A14
Sierra	
N5209.51 E00010.27	Golf Course

Minimum Noise Procedure

Rwy05 RTO climb ahead thru 500ft QFE before turning
Rwy05 LTO climb ahead thru 2000ft QFE before turning
Rwy23 LTO climb ahead thru 500ft QFE before turning
Rwy23 RTO climb ahead thru 2000ft QFE before turning

C

42ft 2mb	3nm WNW of Campbletown N5526.23 W00541.18	PPR	**Alternative AD** **Diversion AD**	**Prestwick**

Campbeltown	**AFIS** **125.900**

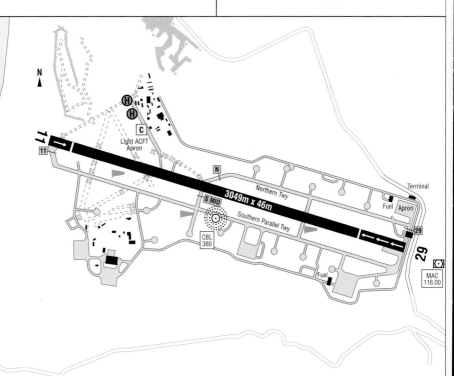

N
11
29
Light ACFT Apron
3049m x 46m
Northern Twy
Southern Parallel Twy
S MID
CBL 380
Terminal
Fuel
Apron
Fuel
MAC 116.00

RWY	SURFACE	TORA	LDA	U/L	LIGHTING
11	Conc/Asph	2869	2727		Ap Thr Rwy PAPI 3°
29	Conc/Asph	2899	2497		Ap Thr Rwy PAPI 3.5°

Rwy29 first 402m sterile for landing, Rwy11 first 322m sterile for landing

RNAV			
MAC	**116.00**	**294**	**1.3**

Remarks
Non-radio ACFT not accepted. Circling is not permitted S of AD. No GND signals.

Warnings
Serious risk of bird strikes. High GND 1159ft amsl 135°/4nm & 1465ft amsl 230°/5nm.

Operating Hrs Mon-Fri 0840-1645 (L) & by arr
Circuits 11 LH, 29 RH, 1500ft QFE
No circuits to S of AD
Landing Fee £16 up to 3MT
VFR cash\cheque\visa on day
Maintenance Nil
Fuel Nil
Disabled Facilities

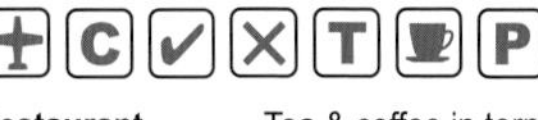

Restaurant Tea & coffee in terminal

Taxis
McKerrals **Tel:** 01586 553131
Car Hire
Campbeltown **Tel:** 01586 552772
Weather Info M T Fax 366 GWC
Operator HIAL Campbeltown
Argyll PA28 6NU
Tel: 01586 553797 (ATC)
Fax: 01586 552620
www.highlands-and-islands-airports.uk.com

EGFF CARDIFF

220ft 8mb	8.5nm SW of Cardiff N5123.80 W00320.60	PPR	Alternative AD **Bristol** Swansea

Non-standard join

Cardiff	ATIS	LARS	APP
	132.475	126.625	126.625

RAD	TWR	OPS
125.850	125.000	Signature 122.350

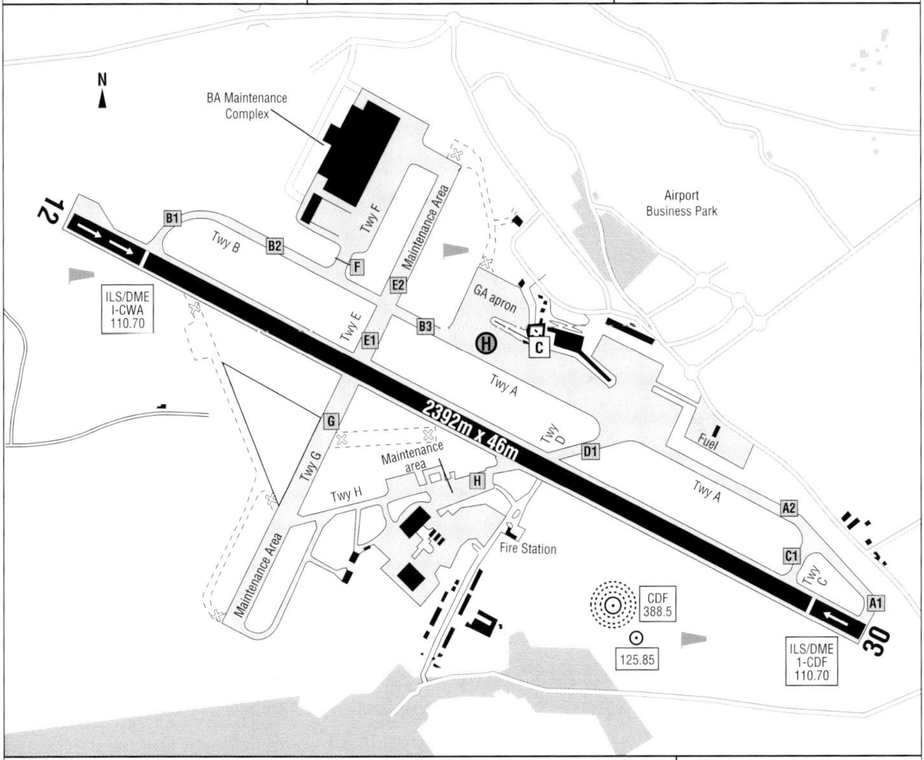

N
BA Maintenance Complex
Airport Business Park
12
30
ILS/DME I-CWA 110.70
ILS/DME 1-CDF 110.70
Twy B
Twy F
Maintenance Area
GA apron
Twy E
Twy A
2392m x 46m
Twy D
Fuel
Twy G
Maintenance area
Twy H
Fire Station
Twy C
CDF 388.5
125.85
B1 B2 B3 E1 E2 F C G H D1 A1 A2 C1

RWY	SURFACE	TORA	LDA	U/L	LIGHTING
12	Asphalt	2352	2133		Ap Thr Rwy PAPI 3° LHS
30	Asphalt	2354	2201		Ap Thr Rwy PAPI 3° LH

Displaced Thr Rwy12 227m, Displaced Thr Rwy30 183m

RNAV			
BCN	117.45	193	19.9

Remarks

PPR essential. All training in Cardiff CTR/CTA is PPR from Cardiff APP. A helicopter set-down point, marked with an 'H', is situated on Twy A to the S of stand 12. ACFT will be allowed to ground taxi or hover taxi to the H, as instructed by ATC. Flight clearance is located on the first floor of the Control TWR building. Access from airside is via the domestic pier. Asymmetric training must be approved by ATC and ACFT wishing to instrument train in Cardiff Zone must have a functioning transponder with Mode C. Landing fees can be paid at the Bureau De Change between 0800-1700 Monday to Friday, otherwise at the Information Desk in the terminal, also at Cardiff-Wales Flying Club on the S side of AD. Handling is mandatory for all ACFT other than Cardiff based flying club.

Warnings

Possible turbulence on short finals when landing on Rwy30 in strong W to S winds. Due to proximity of RAF St Athan (3nm W) overhead joining will not normally be approved. When inbound to Rwy12 or outbound from Rwy30 at Cardiff be aware of the close proximity of RAF St Athan and the St Athan Local Flying Zone to the Cardiff Arr/Dept tracks. VFR flights to/from Cardiff AD may be required to enter/leave the CTR at VRPs which avoid the St Athan Local Flying Zone.
Noise: ACFT must be operated to cause the least disturbance practicable to areas surrounding the AD. Single engine ACFT should avoid over flying the chemical complex at Barry.

Operating Hrs	H24
Circuits	30 RH, 12 LH or as instructed by ATC
Landing Fee	On application

Maintenance

LAM	**Tel:** 01446 710106
Fuel	AVGAS 100LL JET A1 JET A1 by arr with Air BP (H24) AVGAS (H24) **Tel:** 01446 710000 (H24)

Disabled Facilities

Handling Tel: 01446 712637 (Signature)

Restaurants Licensed Buffet and Cafeteria in Terminal

Taxis
Cardiff Airport Taxis **Tel:** 01446710693
Frequent buses to/from Cardiff & Barry

Car Hire
Avis **Tel:** 01446 710569
Europcar **Tel:** 01446 711924
Hertz **Tel:** 01446 711722

Weather Info M T9 T18 Fax 258 A VS MOEx
ATIS **Tel:** 01446 729319
ATIS **Tel:** Ex 3319 (Internal)

Operator Cardiff International Airport Ltd
Vale of Clamorgan, CF26 3BD
Tel: 01446 712562 (ATC)
Tel: 01446 711111 (AD Auth)
Fax: 01446 711838 (ATC)
Fax: 01446 712555 (AD Auth)

CTA/CTR – Class D Airspace
Normal CTA/CTR Class D Airspace rules apply
Transition Alt 4000ft
The attention of pilots is drawn to the close proximity of St Athan AD and Local Flying Zone. Pilots entering or leaving Cardiff CTR VFR may be required to avoid the St Athan Local Flying Zone.

VFR Flights
VFR clearance in the Cardiff CTR will be given for flights operating in VMC. Routing instructions and/or altitude restrictions may be specified in order to integrate VFR flights with other traffic. Pilots are reminded of the requirements to remain in VMC at all times and to comply with the relevant parts of the Low Flying Rules, and must advise ATC if at any time they are unable to comply with the clearance instructions issued.

VFR Routes To/From Cardiff
a In order to integrate VFR flights to/from Cardiff with the normal flow of IFR traffic, a number of standard routes are established along which ATCVFR clearances will be issued subject to the conditions specified above. These routes are defined by prominent GND features and are detailed below.
b In order to reduce RTF congestion, the standard outbound and inbound visual routes are allocated route designators. Pilots are to ensure that they are familiar with the route alignment and altitude restrictions prior to Dept/entering the CTR.

C

Standard Outbound Visual Routes

Exit point	Rwy	Max Alt	Route Designator	Route
Bridgend	12/30	1500ft	VFR St Hilary	Route N of St Hilary TV mast & leave the CTR to the N of Bridgend via J36 VRP.
Nash Point	30	1500ft	VFR Nash Point	Route E of the quarry (1nm W of Cardiff AD) & leave the CAS to the W along the coast, over water, via Nash Point.
Nash Point	12	1500ft	VFR Nash Point	Leave CAS to W along coast, over water via Nash Point
North	30/12	1500ft	VFR North	Route between St Hilary and Wenvoe TV masts and leave CAS to the N.
NE Flat Holm	12/30	1500ft	VFR South East	Route N of Barry then N of Flat Holm Island, leave CAS to E/SE of zone boundary.
N Minehead	30	1500ft	VFR South	Route E of quarry (1nm W of Cardiff AD) & leave CAS to S towards Minehead VRP
N Minehead	12	1500ft	VFR South	Route S & leave CAS to S towards Minehead VRP.

Standard Inbound Visual Routes

Entry point	Rwy	Max Alt	Route Designator	Route
Bridgend	30/12	1500ft	VFR St Hilary	Enter CAS via Bridgend, route N of St Hilary TV mast, then as directed by ATC.
North	30/12	1500ft	VFR North	Enter CAS from N between St Hilary and Wenvoe TV masts, then as directed by ATC.
Wenvoe	30/12	1500ft	VFR Wenvoe	Enter CAS via Wenvoe TV mast, then as directed by ATC.
Cardiff Docks	30/12	1500ft	VFR Cardiff Docks	Enter CAS via Cardiff Docks, then as directed by ATC.
NE of Flat	30/12	1500ft	VFR Flat Holm	Enter CAS via Weston Super Mare, route N of Flat Holm Holm Lighthouse Lighthouse towards Lavernack Point, then as directed by ATC.
N Minehead	30	1500ft	VFR South	Enter CAS form S, then as directed by ATC.
N Minehead	12	1500ft	VFR South	Enter CAS from S, remaining E of the quarry (1nm W of Cardiff AD), then as directed by ATC.
Nash Point	30	1500ft	VFR Nash Point	Enter CAS via Nash Point, route along the coast, over water, then as directed by ATC.
Nash Point	12	1500ft	VFR Nash Point	Enter CAS via Nash Point, route along coast, over water, E of quarry (1nm W of Cardiff AD), then as directed by ATC.

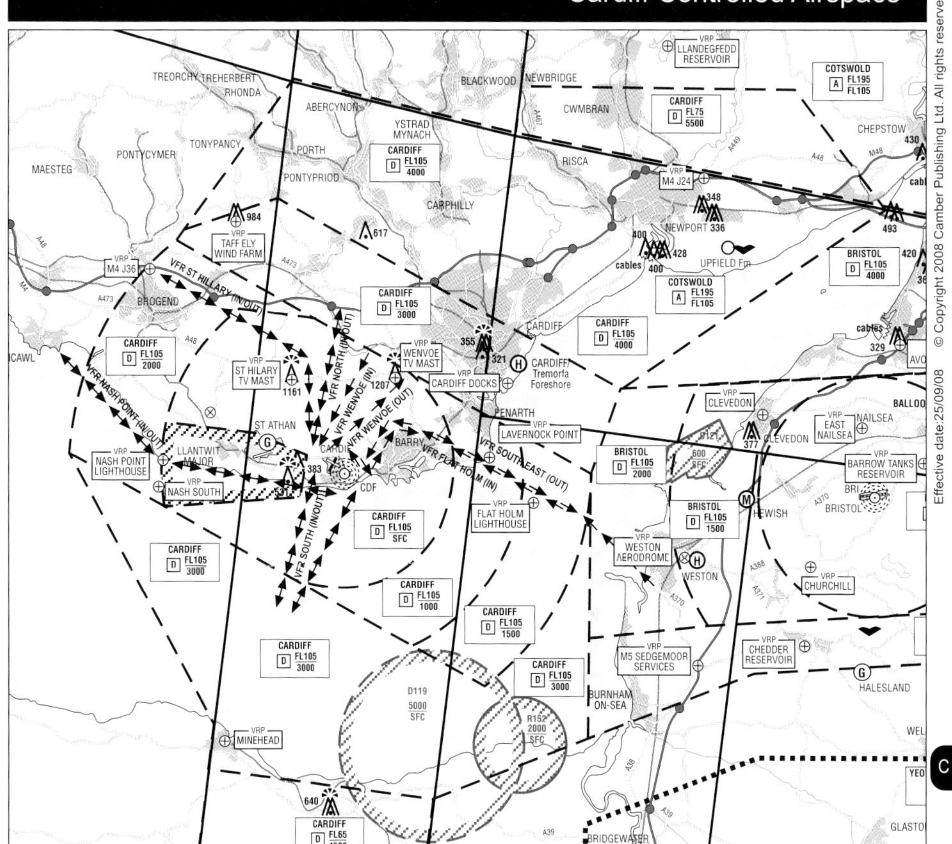

Visual Reference Points (VRP)

VRP	NDB/DME	VOR/DME
Cardiff Docks N5127.40 W00309.10	CDF 064°/*I-CWA (I-CDF) 7nm	BCN 171°/17nm
Clatworthy Reservoir N5104. W00322.	CDF 187°/*I-CWA (I-CDF) 19nm	BCN 189°/39nm
Flat Holm Lighthouse N5122.55 W00307.13	CDF 100°/*I-CWA (I-CDF) 8nm	BCN 169°/22nm
Lavernock Point N512423.38 W00310.23	CDF 086°/*I-CWA (I-CDF) 6nm	BCN 173°/20nm
Llandegfedd Reservoir N5121.00 W00258.00	CDF 041°/*I-CWA (I-CDF) 22nm	BCN 104°/11nm
M4 J24 N5136.00 W00255.00	CDF 055°/*I-CWA (I-CDF) 20nm	BCN 124°/15nm
M4 J36 N5131.93 W00334.40	CDF 317°/*I-CWA (I-CDF) 12nm	BCN 229°/16nm
Minehead N5112.35 W00328.50	CDF 207°/*I-CWA (I-CDF) 8nm	BCN 198°/32nm
Nash Point Lighthouse N5124.08 W00333.33	CDF 277°/*I-CWA (I-CDF) 7nm	BCN 213°/22nm
Nash South (on St Athan C/L 1nm S of Nash Point) N5122.88 W00333.45	CDF 269°/*I-CWA (I-CDF) 8nm	BCN 212°/23nm
Old Severn Bridge (M48) N5136.00 W00238.	CDF 067°/*I-CWA (I-CDF) 29nm	BCN 110°/24nm
St Hilary TV Mast ** N5127.45 W00324.18	CDF 330°/*I-CWA (I-CDF) 4nm	BCN 201°/17nm
Taff Ely Wind Farm N5134.00 W00328.	CDF 338°/*I-CWA (I-CDF) 117nm	BCN 223°/12nm
Wenvoe TV Mast ** N5127.60 W00316.95	CDF 031°/*I-CWA (I-CDF) 5nm	BCN 186°/16nm

Note: * DME frequency-paired with ILS gives zero range indication from the Thr of the Rwy with which it is associated
** Caution to be exercised when routing via St Hilary TV mast 1164ft amsl/745ft agl
*** Caution to be exercised when routing via Wenvoe TV mast 1212ft amsl/787ft agl

Effective date:25/09/08

17ft 0mb	7nm S of Lake Windermere N5409.87 W00257.53	PPR	**Alternative AD** **Blackpool** Barrow **Non-standard join**

Cark Drop Zone	LARS Warton 129.525	A/G 129.900

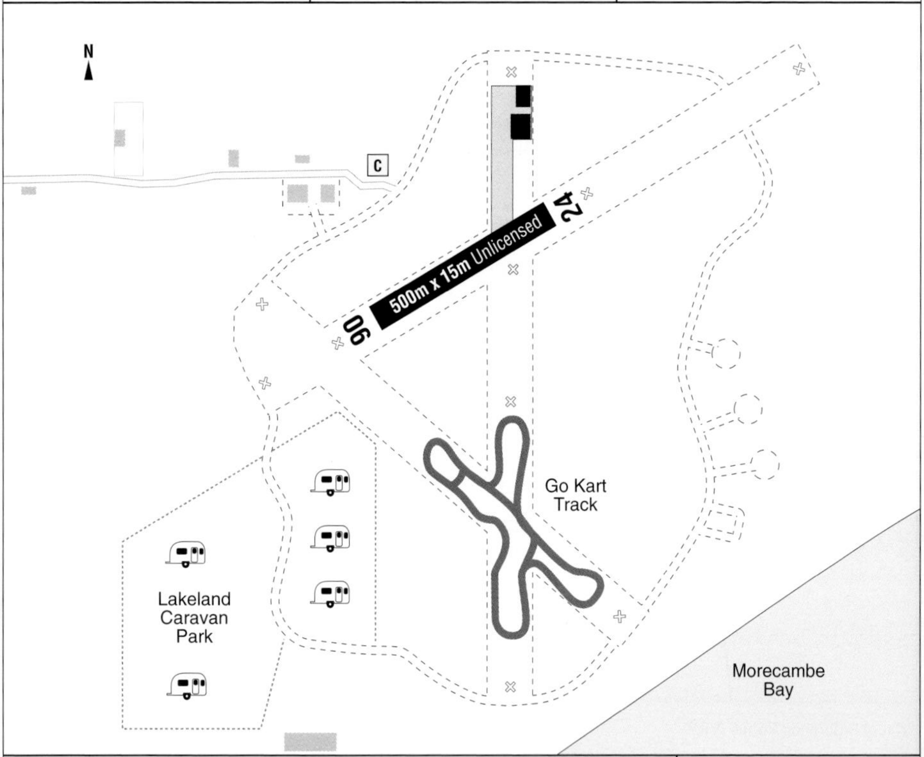

RWY	SURFACE	TORA	LDA	U/L	LIGHTING
06/24	Asphalt			400x15	Nil

Rwy06/24 200m over run, Rwy surfaces rough

RNAV

Remarks
PPR by telephone. Primarily a parachute centre but light ACFT welcome at own risk. Parachutists exit free-fall up to FL140. Parachutes open from 6000ft down. Radio usually manned only at weekends. If no reply please make blind calls.

Warnings
The 2 other Rwys are fenced off and unusable. Portions of WW II Rwy06/24 are overgrown and unusable but serviceable portion is clearly visible. Windsock at weekends only. Occasionally live stock on AD. Power lines 550m from Rwy06 Thr.
Noise: Avoid over flying local habitation.

Operating Hrs	SR-SS
Circuits	No overhead joins Circuits over the sea at 1000ft QFE
Landing Fee	Single £10, Twin £20, Microlight £10
Maintenance	Nil
Fuel	Nil
Disabled Facilities	

Restaurants	Snacks at weekends
Taxis	**Tel:** 01539 533792
Car Hire	Nil
Weather Info	Air N MOEx

Operator
North West Parachute Centre
Cark Airfield
Moore Lane
Flookburgh
Grange-over-Sands
Cumbria
Tel: 01539 558672
(PPR AD weekends)

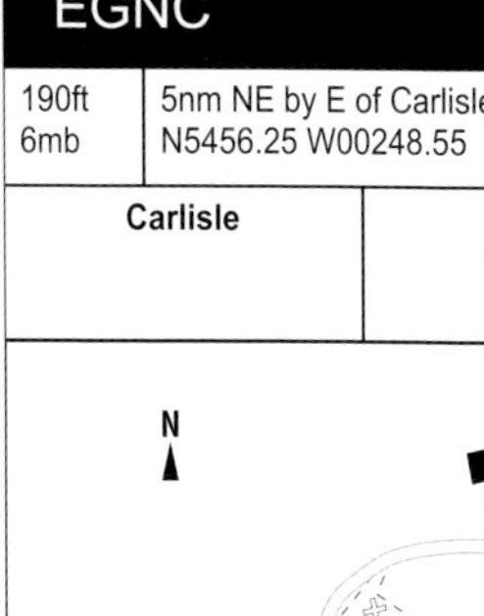

190ft 6mb	5nm NE by E of Carlisle N5456.25 W00248.55	PPR	Alternative AD	**Newcastle** Kirkbride

Carlisle	ATIS	APP	TWR	FIRE
	118.425	123.600	123.600	121.600

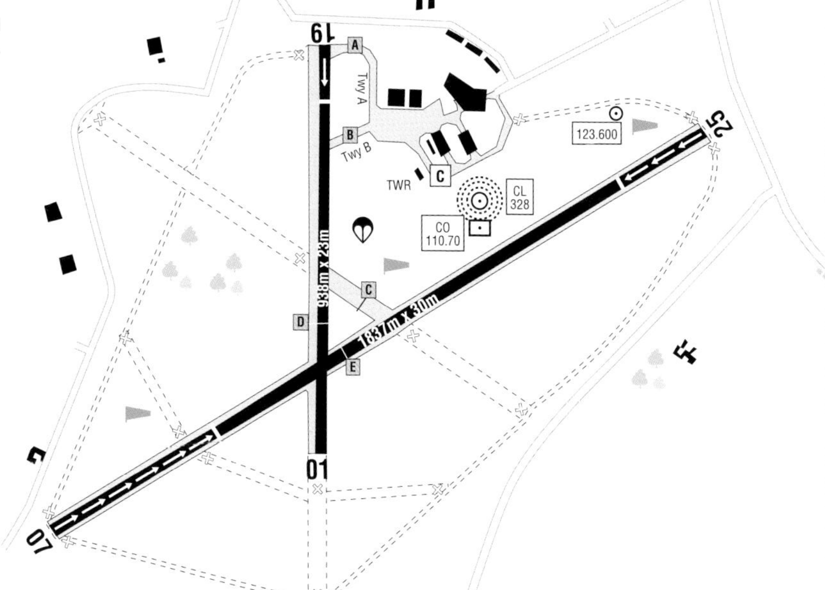

RWY	SURFACE	TORA	LDA	U/L	LIGHTING
01	Asphalt	803	803		Nil
19	Asphalt	938	809		Nil
07	Asphalt	1659	1321		Thr Rwy PAPI 3.5° LHS
25	Asphalt	1714	1469		Ap Thr Rwy PAPI 3.25° LHS

Displaced Thr Rwy25 245m, Displaced Thr Rwy19 129m, Displaced Thr Rwy07 458m

RNAV			
DCS	115.20	060	22.5

Remarks

PPR. AD is not available to non-radio ACFT. Hi-vis. All ACFT using AD must comply with the AD terms & conditions available via AD Ops. AD used out of Hrs. Certain customs facilities available. Aviation museum on AD.

Warnings

Danger Area D510 5nm NE of AD. DAAIS available from Carlisle APP. The ends of TORA/ED/LDA on Rwy07/25 are shown by red edge lights only. The red lights across the Rwys mark the end of useable pavement. Rwy07/25 lighting is at full width 46m. The only useable Twys are from the apron to the Rwy19 Thr and the disused Rwy13/31 that links Rwy01/19 with Rwy07/25. Free fall parachuting on AD. During adverse weather conditions NDB CL is subject to failure, use with caution.

Operating Hrs 0800-1730 (Summer) +1Hr (Winter) & by arr

Circuits Variable

Landing Fee On application

Maintenance Northumberland Aircraft Maintenance
Tel: 01670 731189 (M3)
Tel: 07962 167468

Fuel AVGAS 100LL AVTUR JET A1 by prior arr
Oil W80 S80 W100 S100 Multi

Disabled Facilities

Taxi
Airbus 2000 **Tel:** 01697 73735
Executive Cars **Tel:** 01228 404305

Car Hire
National **Tel:** 01228 542707
Avis **Tel:** 01228 590580
Enterprise **Tel:** 01228 599877

Weather Info M T9 Fax 262 MOEx
ATIS **Tel:** 01228 574123

Visual Reference Points (VRP)
Gretna N5459.73 W00304.05
Haltwistle N5458.13 W00227.73
Penrith N5439.87 W00245.02
Wigton N5449.48 W00309.67

Operator Stobart Air Ltd
Carlisle Airport
Carlisle, CA6 4NW
Tel: 01228 573641 (Admin/Ops)
Fax: 01228 573310
enquiries@carlisleairport.co.uk
www.carlisleairport.co.uk

70ft 2mb	2.5nm E of Stranraer N5453.52 W00456.09	PPR	Alternative AD	Prestwick Carlisle

Non-Radio	FIR Scottish 119.875	DAAIS West Freugh 130.050	Safetycom 135.475

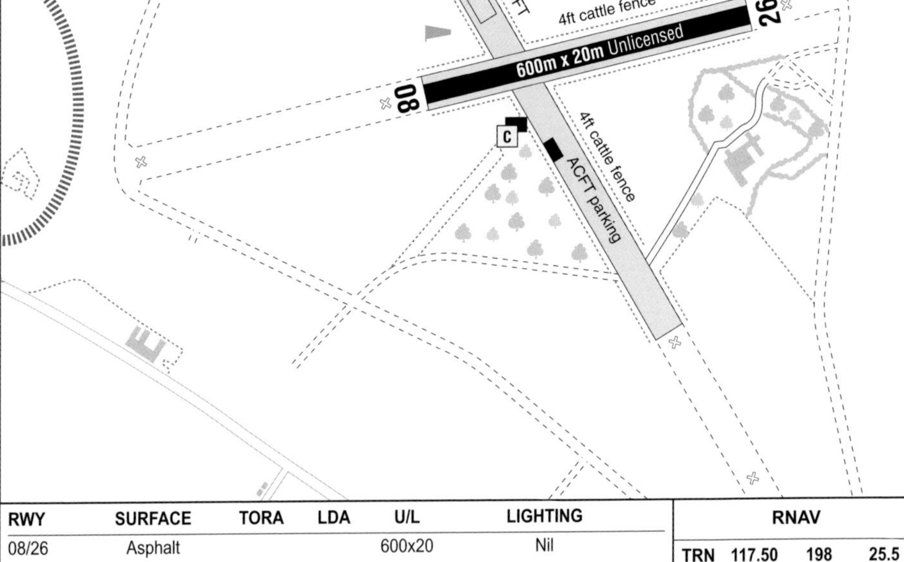

RWY	SURFACE	TORA	LDA	U/L	LIGHTING
08/26	Asphalt			600x20	Nil

RNAV			
TRN	117.50	198	25.5

Remarks
Strictly PPR due to activities on AD. Contact via website or telephone. Visiting ACFT welcome at their own risk and at pilots discretion. WW2 AD, useable areas marked with white brackets painted on Rwy. Website provides news and info on events and aerial photo.

Warnings
AD situated on the edge of D402A . Pilots to contact West Freugh Ops, and check NOTAM's to ascertain danger area activity. West Freugh is under care & maintenance, A/G is manned, provides range activity info. Military ACFT may still use West Freugh. Wind shear may be encountered due trees to N & S of Rwy. Model ACT use area N of Rwy intersection, they are forbidden from operating within 60m of Rwy08/26
Noise: Rwy26 left turn ASAP after take-off, track 240° to avoid house at W end of Rwy. Avoid over flying the village to NW of AD.

Operating Hrs SR-SS

Circuits 08 RH, 26 LH. Join over head 1200ft QFE, descend downwind leg

Landing Fee Micro/Ultralight £5, Single £10, Twin £20
All money towards developments

Maintenance Nil

Fuel Nil
See website

Disabled Facilities

Restaurants Castle Kennedy Gardens – See website
The Plantings Inn **Tel:** 01581 400633 (also B&B 400m)

Taxis
McLeans **Tel:** 01776 702222

Car Hire Nil

Weather Info Air Sc GWC

Operator Stair Estates, Estate Office
Rephad, Stranraer
Wigtownshire DG9 8BX
Tel: 01776 702024 (AD)
Tel: 07774 116424 (AD mobile)
Tel: 01776 888741 (West Freugh Ops)
Fax: 01776 706248 (AD)
enquires@castlekennedyairfield.co.uk
www.castlekennedyairfield.co.uk

C

230ft 7mb	8nm SE of Oxford N5140.53 W00104.38	PPR	Alternative AD Diversion AD	Oxford Wycombe

Non-standard join

Chalgrove	LARS Farnborough West 125.250	Zone Benson 120.900	A/G 125.400

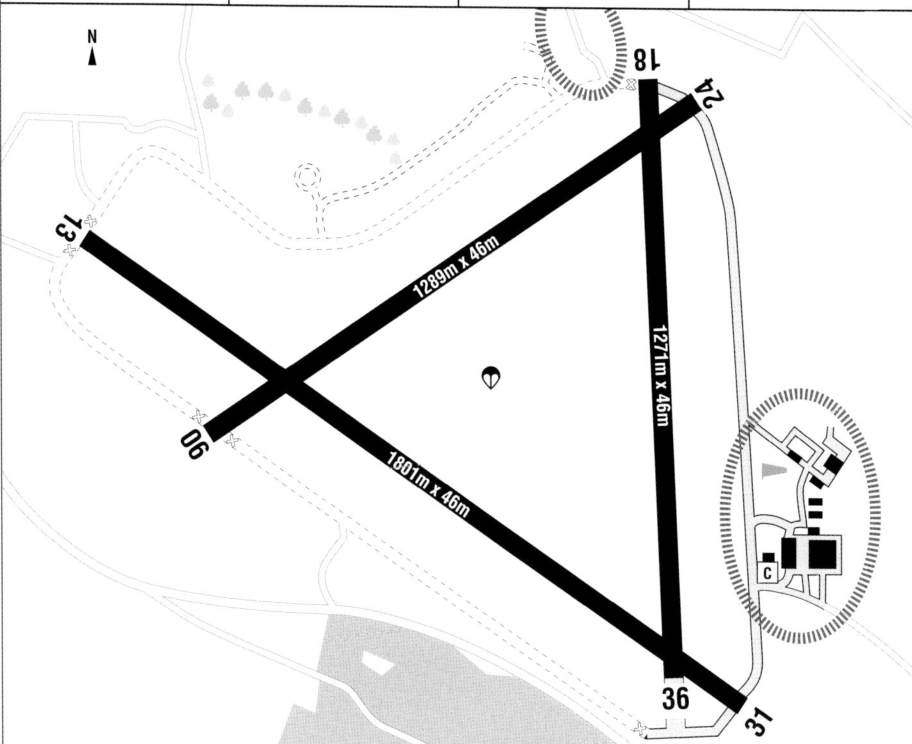

RWY	SURFACE	TORA	LDA	U/L	LIGHTING
06/24	Asphalt	1289	1289		Rwy
13/31	Asphalt	1798	1798		Thr Rwy
18	Asphalt	1270	1270		Ap Rwy
36	Asphalt	1270	1224		Rwy

Rwy18 no departures

RNAV			
CPT	114.35	028	12.0

Remarks

Strictly PPR by telephone. For ACFT visiting company only, no public transport/corporate movements will be approved. AD licensed for daytime use only, however company operations may take place at night. Visiting ACFT operations will be prohibited during testing.

Warnings

AD situated within the Benson MATZ, Arr/Dept ACFT contact Benson APP. Over flight of hangar and associated buildings prohibited below1000ft QFE. Take-off, landing, and taxiing on grass areas prohibited due to obstructions. GND level tests from a Meteor ACFT on Rwy13/31 at speeds between 60-130kts. In flight tests from a Meteor ACFT above Rwy06/24 at heights between 250-1000ft QFE at speeds up to 450kts. Ejector seat testing may take place at any time during daylight Hrs from the centre of the AD up to 600ft agl. Parachute drop tests from 5500ft QFE overhead AD from helicopters

Noise: Avoid over flying Chalgrove village

Operating Hrs	Mon-Thu 0730-1530 Fri 0730-1130 (Summer) +1Hr (Winter) AD closed at weekends & PH
Circuits	N 1000ft QFE
Landing Fee	Advised with PPR
Maintenace	Nil
Fuel	JET A1
Disabled Facilities	Nil
Restaurants	Nil
Taxis	Operator can advise
Car Hire	Nil
Weather Info	Air SE MOEx
Operator	Martin-Baker Aircraft Co Ltd Chalgrove Airfield, Chalgrove Oxford, OX44 7RJ **Tel:** 01865 892200 **Fax:** 01865 892214

Effective date:25/09/08 OP 08

366ft 12mb	6nm NW of Lyneham N5136 W00204	PPR	Alternative AD Bristol Kemble

Non-Radio	Zone Lyneham 123.400	AFIS Kemble 118.900	Safetycom 135.475

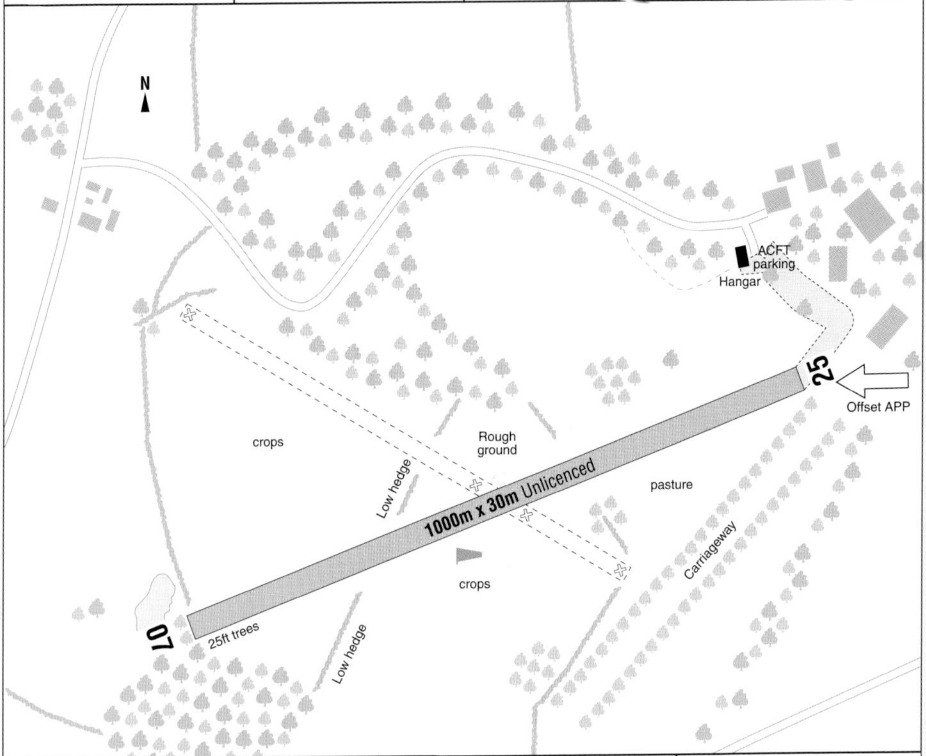

RWY	SURFACE	TORA	LDA	U/L	LIGHTING	RNAV
07/25	Grass			1000x30	Nil	

Remarks

PPR essential by telephone. Pilots welcome at their own risk. Windsock displayed.

Warnings

AD situtated on edge of Lyneham MATZ. The second,NW/SE Rwy must not be used.
Noise: Avoid over flying Charlton village and the large house on Rwy25 APP.

Operating Hrs	SR-SS
Circuits	Nil
Landing Fee	£10 for church funds
Maintenance	Nil
Fuel	Available on request
Disabled Facilities	Nil
Restaurants	Nil
Taxi/Car Hire	Nil
Weather Info	Air SW MOEx

Operator

The Earl of Suffolk and Berkshire
Charlton Park
Malmesbury
Wiltshire
SN16 9DG
Tel: 01666 823200
Tel: 07768 081188
Fax: 01666 822004
charltonpark@zoom.co.uk

XCHA — CHARTERHALL

350ft 12mb	4.5nm SSW of Duns N5542.45 W00222.64	PPR	**Alternative AD** **Edinburgh** Eshott **Diversion AD**

Non-Radio	FIS	Safetycom
	Scottish 119.875	135.475

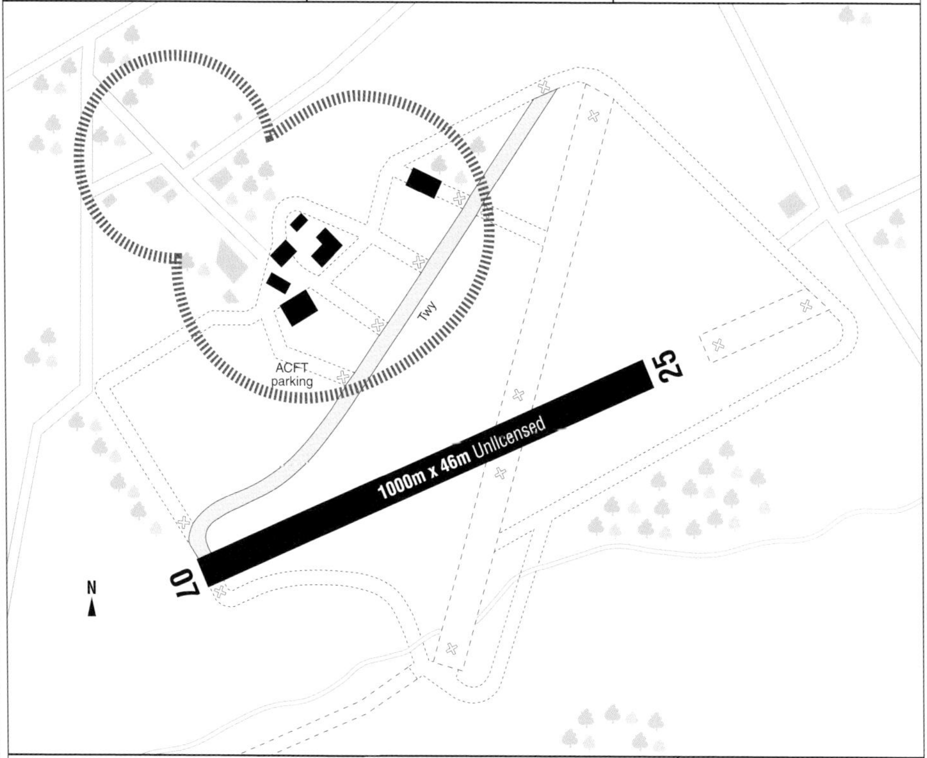

RWY	SURFACE	TORA	LDA	U/L	LIGHTING
07/25	Asphalt			1000x46	Nil

RNAV			
SAB	112.50	211	13.2

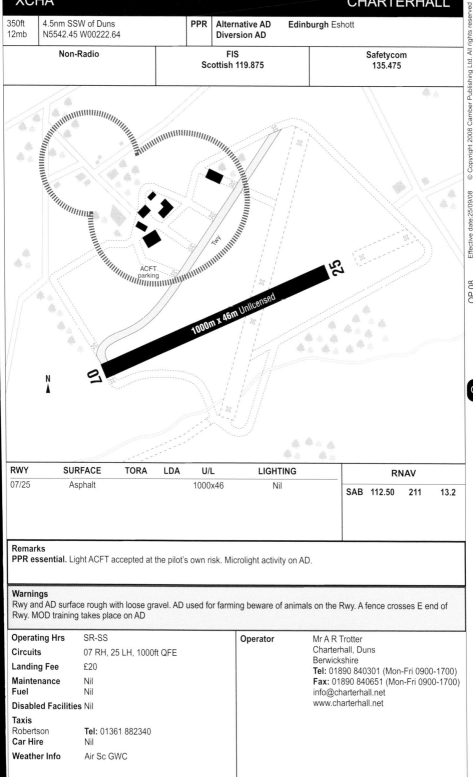

Remarks

PPR essential. Light ACFT accepted at the pilot's own risk. Microlight activity on AD.

Warnings

Rwy and AD surface rough with loose gravel. AD used for farming beware of animals on the Rwy. A fence crosses E end of Rwy. MOD training takes place on AD

Operating Hrs	SR-SS
Circuits	07 RH, 25 LH, 1000ft QFE
Landing Fee	£20
Maintenance	Nil
Fuel	Nil
Disabled Facilities	Nil
Taxis	
Robertson	**Tel:** 01361 882340
Car Hire	Nil
Weather Info	Air Sc GWC

Operator

Mr A R Trotter
Charterhall, Duns
Berwickshire
Tel: 01890 840301 (Mon-Fri 0900-1700)
Fax: 01890 840651 (Mon-Fri 0900-1700)
info@charterhall.net
www.charterhall.net

5ft 0mb	2nm N of Chatteris N5229.12 E00005.43	PPR	Alternative AD	**Cambridge** Peterborough Conington **Non-standard join**

Chatteris	A/G 129.900 Only manned during parachuting

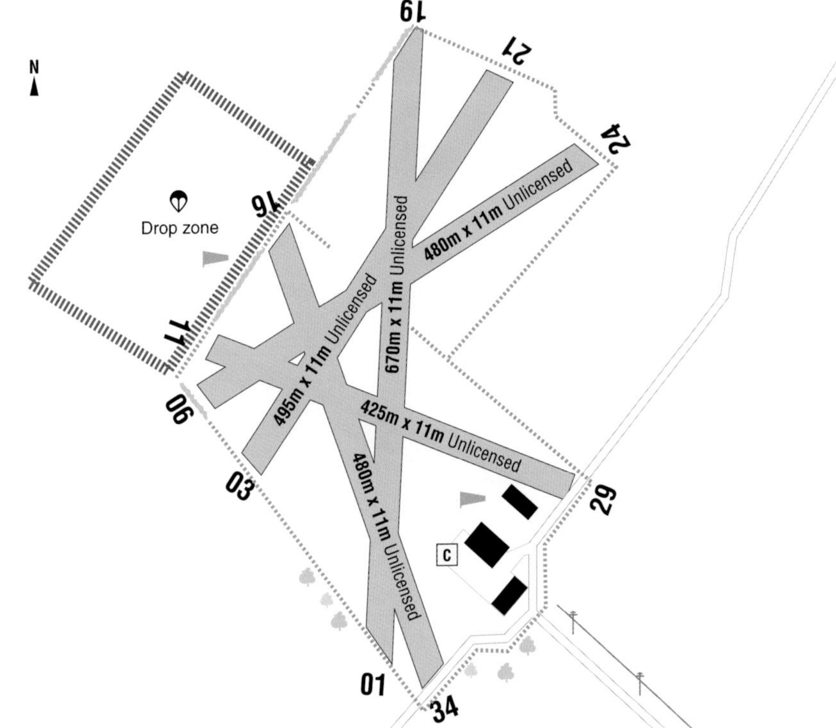

RWY	SURFACE	TORA	LDA	U/L	LIGHTING
01/19	Grass			670x11	Nil
06/24	Grass			480x11	Nil
03/21	Grass			495x11	Nil
16/34	Grass			480x11	Nil
11/29	Grass			425x11	Nil

Rwy34 & 29 microlight use only

RNAV			
BKY	116.25	005	29.7

Remarks
PPR strictly by telephone due to parachuting ops. Parachutists free-fall from FL150. Microlights also operate. No overhead joins.

Warnings
Do not over fly the drop zone at any time. Public road crosses the undershoot Rwy29, please be aware of vehicles & pedestrians. AD is in an area of intense military low flying, keep a good lookout at all times.
Noise: Avoid over flying local habitation.

Operating Hrs	SR-SS
Circuits	19, 21, 24 LH, 01, 03, 06 RH, 700ft QFE No dead side
Landing Fee	Light ACFT £5, Microlight £5 except where reciprocal arr exists
Maintenance	Nil Hangarage overnight by prior arr
Fuel	Nil
Disabled Facilities	Nil
Restaurants	Cafe at AD Mon-Sun 0900-2000 (L)

Taxis	**Tel:** 01354 658083
Car Hire	**Tel:** 01354 652361
Weather Info	Air S MOEx
Operator	Chatteris Leisure Ltd Chatteris Airfield, Stonea March, Cambs, PE15 0EA **Tel:** 01473 829982 (PPR Weekends) **Tel:** 01354 740810 (PPR AD) **Fax:** 01354 740406 chatpara@aol.com

EGHR CHICHESTER

110ft 3mb	1.5nm NNE of Chichester N5051.57 W00045.55	PPR	Alternative AD Diversion AD	Southampton Shoreham

Goodwood	LARS Farnborough West 125.250	AFIS 122.450

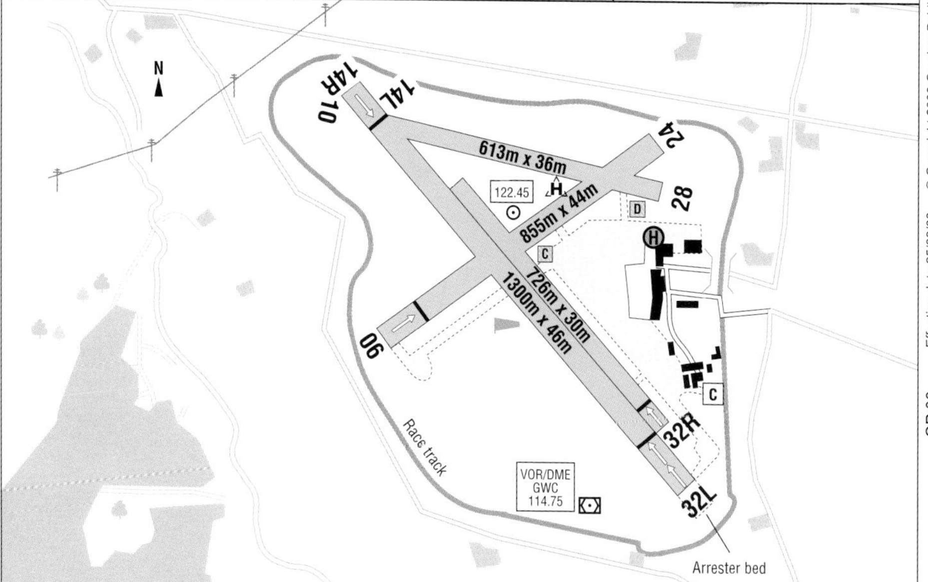

RWY	SURFACE	TORA	LDA	U/L	LIGHTING
06	Grass	855	710		Nil
24	Grass	845	845		Nil
32L	Grass	1115	1074		Thr Rwy APAPI 3° LHS
14R	Grass	1104	1073		Thr Rwy APAPI 3° LHS
14L/32R	Grass	726	726		Nil
10/28	Grass	613	613		Nil

Displaced Thr Rwy14R 67m, Displaced Thr Rwy32L 176m, Starter extension Rwy14R 67m
Starter extension Rwy14R 50m

RNAV

GWC 114.75 on AD

Remarks
All ACFT must obtain PPR before flight. Rwy14R has U/L starter extension for CEGA ACFT only. Helis must not taxi across road between fire station & TWR. Helis taxiing from parking area must taxi W of TWR. White Frangible Rwy edge markers on all Rwys.

Warning
When Rwy06/24 & 10/28 in use fixed-wing circuits, opposite direction heli circuits flown from Rwy32L Thr. Arrester bed shingle at end Rwy14R. When Relief Rwy14L/32R in use (Nov-Mar) Thr will be marked with black & white prismatic markers. Motor racing track on perimeter in constant use daylight Hrs not to be used for taxiing ACFT any time. Helis not permitted join circuit below 700ft QFE unless weather dictates lower height.
Noise: Helis avoid routing over Chichester, Westerton & Summersdale

Operating Hrs 0800-1700 (Summer)
Nov Feb & Mar 0900-1700
Dec-Jan 0900-1600 & by arr

Circuit 06, 14, 10 LH, 24, 28, 32 RH
ACFT 1200ft QFE, Heli 900ft QFE
or as directed by AFIS
Sun – no circuits after 1400(L)

Landing Fee PA28 £16.30

Maintenance Goodwood ACFT Maintenance
Tel: 01243 755064

Fuel AVGAS 100LL JET A1

Disabled Facilities

Restaurants On AD by motor circuit pits and in Goodwood Flying Club

Taxi
Dunnaways **Tel:** 01243 782403

Car Hire
Chichester Car Rental **Tel:** 01243 530133
Enterprise **Tel:** 01243 779500

Weather Info Air SE MOEx

Operator Goodwood Road Racing Co Ltd
Chichester (Goodwood) Aerodrome
Chichester
West Sussex, PO18 0PH
Tel: 01243 755061 (ATC)
Fax: 01243 755062 (ATC)
Tel: 01243 755061 (PPR)
Tel: 01243 755087 (Event Bookings & Admin)
control@goodwood.co.uk
www.goodwood.co.uk

Effective date:25/09/08
OP 08

Helicopter Circuits

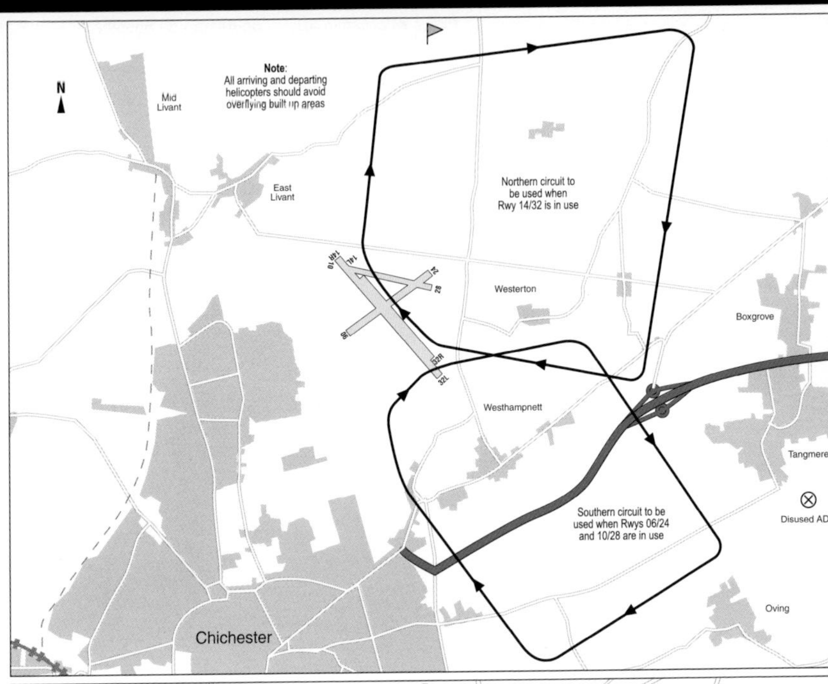

Fixed Wing Circuits

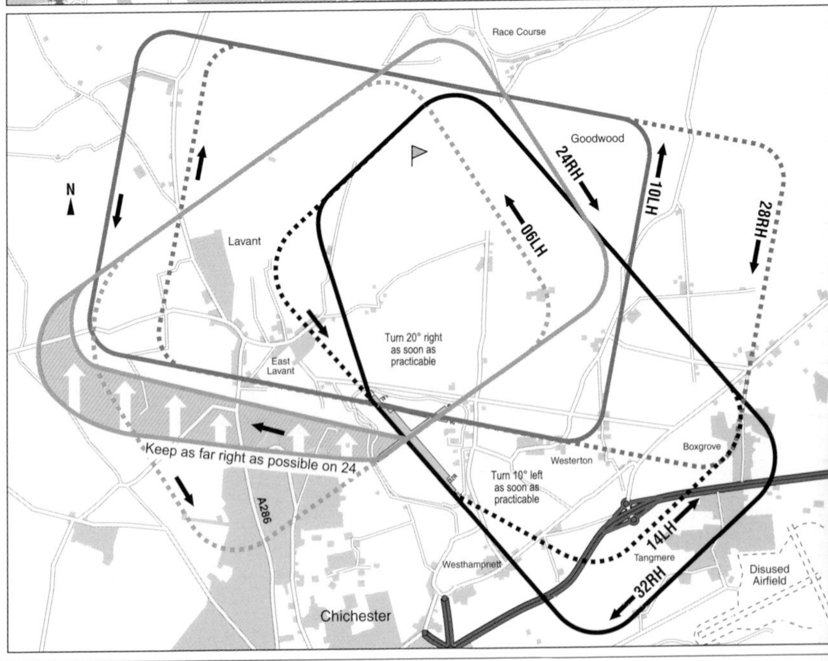

Circuit Height 1200ft QFE

Rwy06 Arr No low APP over built up areas in the undershoot

Rwy24 Dept ASAP after takeoff, turn R to avoid built up areas, maintain HDG until circuit height. No practice EFATO until W A286

Rwy14L/R Arr No low APP over East Lavant, light ACFT land beyond the intersection Rwy10/14

Rwy14L/R Dept ASAP after takeoff turn L 10° to avoid over flight of school and houses on Dept path. No practice EFATO until well clear of houses and school

Rwy32L/R Arr Follow defined circuit path turning base leg S of dual carriageway

Rwy32L/R Dept ASAP after takeoff turn R 20° to avoid East Lavant, maintain HDG until beyond village. No practice EFATO until well clear of East Lavant village

Rwy10 Arr Follow defined circuit, avoiding Lavant village on base leg

Rwy28 Dept Maintain Rwy HDG until clear of Lavant Village

292ft 10mb	5nm SSE of Andover N5108.13 W00125.28	PPR	Alternative AD **Southampton** Thruxton **Non-standard join**

Non-Radio	LARS Boscombe 126.700	TWR Middle Wallop 118.275	Safetycom 135.475

Effective date:25/09/08 OP 08

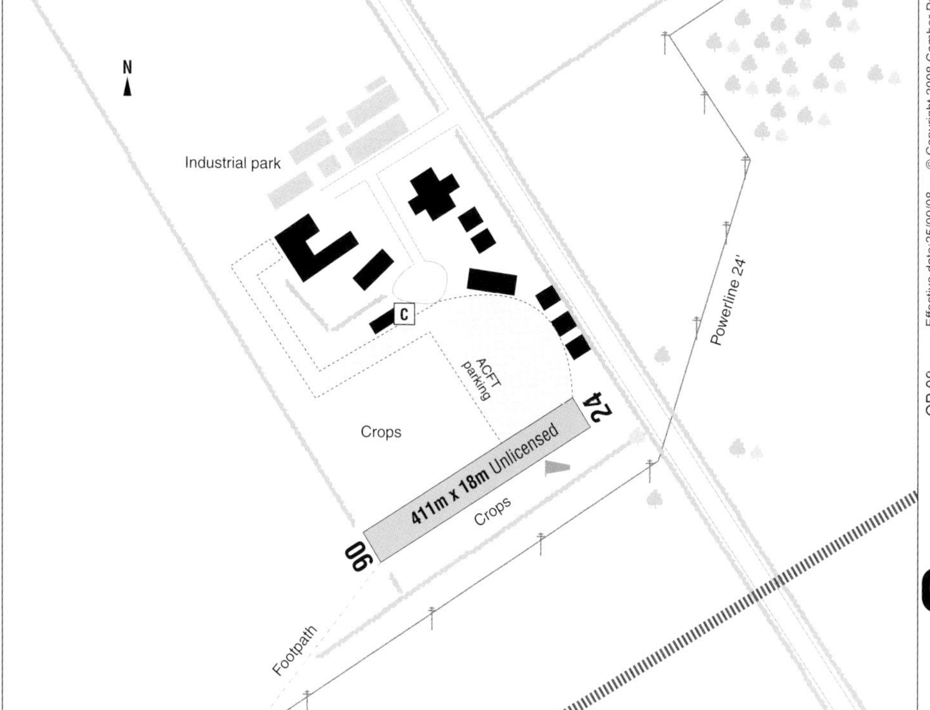

RWY	SURFACE	TORA	LDA	U/L	LIGHTING
24	Grass			411x18	Nil
06	Grass			384x18	Nil

Rwy24 2% upslope

RNAV			
SAM	113.35	351	11.3

Remarks
PPR by telephone. Microlights & light ACFT operate. Helicopters NOT permitted. AD close to boundary of Middle Wallop MATZ. In/Outbound ACFT call Boscombe APP/Zone. All flights must be logged in control caravan facing the strip & landing fees (sealed envelope) in box by flight log.

Warnings
Standard circuit join NOT available due to MATZ stub and noise sensitive areas.
Light ACFT: to fly wide circuit as if making go-around. Beware of microlights making tight circuits. Rifle range 2nm E of AD, over fly at least 500ft QFE.
Microlights: Fly across mid-point of Rwy (150°), turn late down wind without crossing A30. Beware of light ACFT on longer finals from wide circuits. Rwy24 beware of power cables and public road immediately before Thr. Army helicopters operate in surrounding area (Mon-Fri).
Noise: Do not over fly telescope site and Chilbolton village to N of AD.

Operating Hrs	0800-2100 (L) No night flying. No flying training
Circuits	24 LH, 06 RH, All circuits S 600ft QFE
Landing Fee	£3
Maintenance	M3 Hants Light Plane Services **Tel:** 01264 860056
Fuel	Nil
Disabled Facilities	Nil

Restaurants	
Les Copains D'abord	**Tel:** 01264 810738
Abbots Mitre	**Tel:** 01264 860348 (pub)
Taxis/Car Hire	Nil
Weather Info	Air SW MOEx
Operator	Stonefield Park & Chilbolton Flying Club c/o 5 Augustus Gardens Camberley Surrey GU15 1HL **Tel:** 01276 691563 (Colin Marsh PPR) www.chilboltonflyingclub.co.uk

140ft 4mb	5nm S of Dunsfold AD N5104.31 W00036.27	PPR	Alternative AD	Shoreham Goodwood

Non-Radio	LARS Farnborough West 125.250	Safetycom 135.475

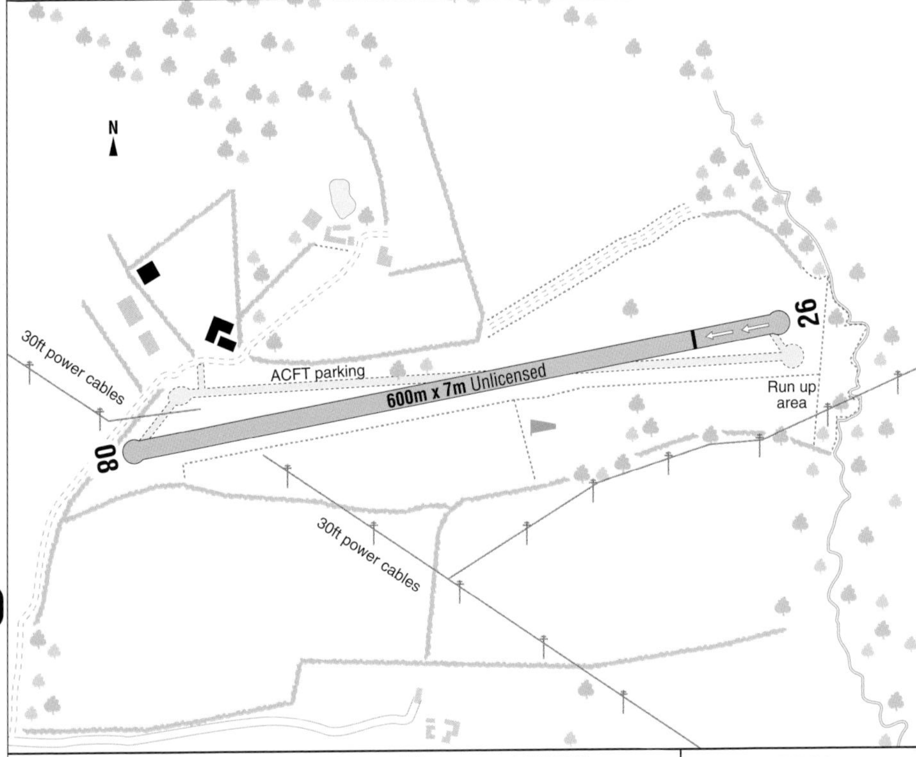

RWY	SURFACE	TORA	LDA	U/L	LIGHTING
08	Grass			470x7	Nil
26	Grass			470x7	Nil

Rwy26 2% upslope

RNAV			
MID	114.00	051	1.2

Remarks
PPR by telephone essential. Sheep may be grazing and electric wire fence established across strip. Windsock displayed.

Warnings
Domestic power cables run close to AD on SW corner. AD may be waterlogged after prolonged wet weather. Gatwick CTA close to E.
Noise: Avoid all local villages, houses and Farms. Also fields containing livestock.

Operating Hrs	SR-SS
Circuits	N over woods 1000ft QFE. Keep tight to AD
Landing Fee	Notified with PPR
Maintenance	Nil
Fuel	Nil
Disabled Facilities	Nil
Restaurants	Nil
Taxis/Car Hire	Nil
Weather Info	Air SE MOEx

Operator
Mr I Charlton
Chilsfold Farm
Northchapel
Petworth
West Sussex
GU28 9JZ
Tel: 01428 707655

C

180ft 6mb	7nm W of Henley-on-Thames N5133.36 W00106.59	PPR	Alternative AD **Oxford** Wycombe
			Non-standard join

Chiltern Park	Zone Benson 120.900	A/G 134.025

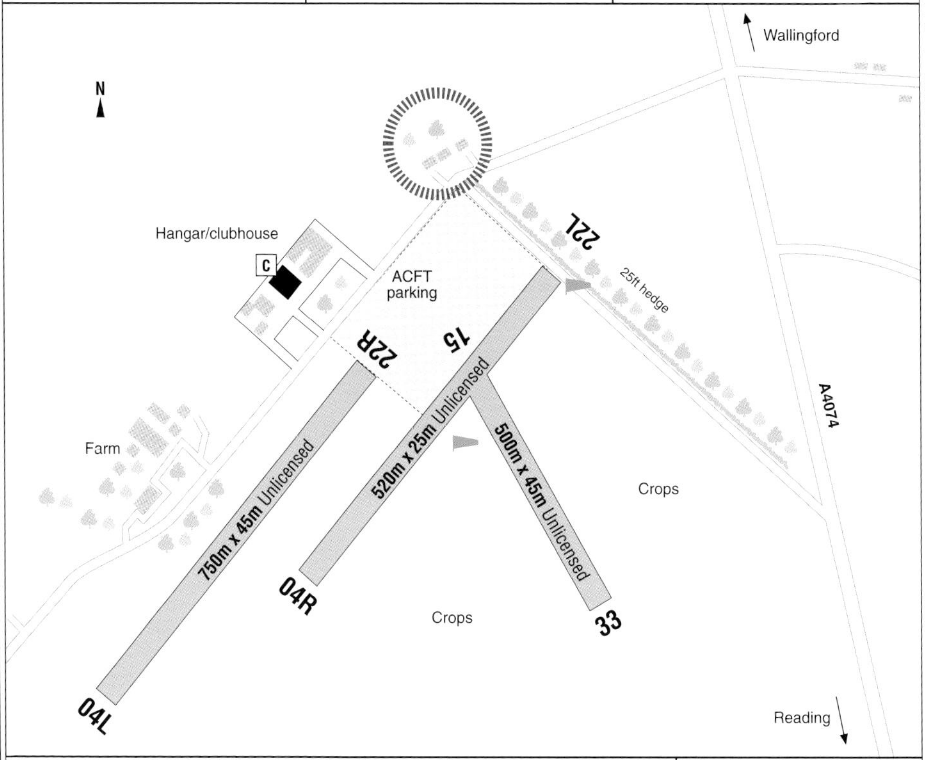

RWY	SURFACE	TORA	LDA	U/L	LIGHTING
04L/22R	Grass			750x45	Nil
04R/22L	Grass			520x25	Nil
15/33	Grass			500x45	Nil

RNAV			
CPT	114.35	056	5.6

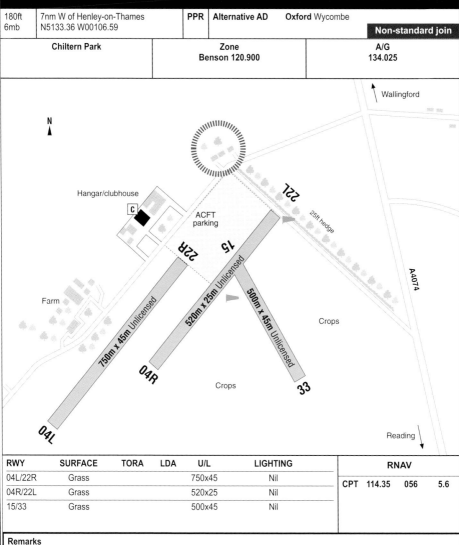

Remarks

PPR by telephone. Primarily a Microlight AD but suitable light ACFT, helicopters and gliders welcome at pilots own risk. Join on permanent deadside to E of AD at 1000ft, descend to circuit height.

Warnings

AD located within the Benson MATZ, inbound ACFT call Benson APP. Benson has intensive helicopter activity during weekdays but may operate at weekends for exercises.

Noise: Avoid all local habitation, Arr/Dept via SSW.

Operating Hrs Mon-Sat SR-SS Sun 1100-SS

Circuits All circuits to W 700ft

Landing Fee Fixed wing £5
Helicopters £10
Gliders £10

Maintenance Nil

Fuel Nil

Disabled Facilities

Restaurants Local Pub 2.5 miles from AD

Taxis **Tel:** 01491 837022

Car Hire Nil

Weather Info Air SE MOEx

Operator Dennis Pearson
Chiltern Aero Club
Chiltern Park Aerodrome
Ipsden, Wallingford
Oxon, OX10 6AS
Tel: 01491 875200
Tel: 07739 802010
dennis@chiltern.aero
www.chiltern.aero

Effective date:25/09/08 OP 08

XCHI CHIRK

448ft 14mb	1nm E of Chirk N5257.00 W00303.00	PPR	Alternative AD Hawarden Sleap

Non-standard join

Non-radio	LARS Shawbury 120.775	Safetycom 135.475

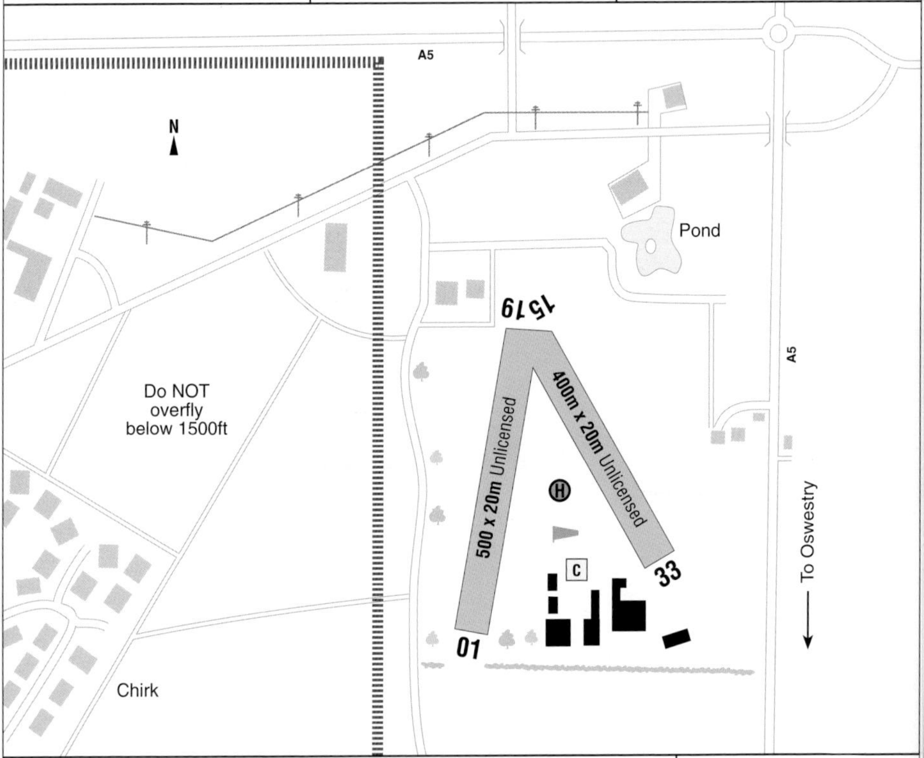

RWY	SURFACE	TORA	LDA	U/L	LIGHTING
01/19	Grass			500x20	Nil
15/33	Grass			400x20	Nil

RNAV			
SWB	116.80	308	16.8

Remarks

PPR essential. Primary a microlight AD but STOL ACFT welcome at pilots own risk. Rwys have no designator markings or edge marks.

Visual aid to location: AD is easily identifiable by white concrete 'H' in the centre of AD.

Warnings

Rwy01 has slight down slope. Sheep may be grazing if microlights are not active.

Noise: Area to W of AD is particularly noise sensitive and should not be over flown below 1500ft.

Operating Hrs	PPR AD Closed Apr-Nov Sat 1200 – Mon 0900
Circuits	15, 19 LH, 01, 33 RH, 600ft QFE
Landing Fee	Nil
Maintenance	BMAA & LAA types
Fuel	Nil
Disabled Facilities	Nil
Restaurants	Cafe on AD Mon-Fri
Taxis/Car Hire	Nil
Weather Info	Air Cen MOEx

Operator Mr R Everitt (Operator)
Tel: 01691 774137
Tel: 07974 952118
Mr J Pierce (Owner)
Tel: 01691 772659

C

27ft 1mb	4nm NW Barnstaple N5105.23 W00409.02	PPR MIL	**Alternative AD**	**Cardiff** Eaglescott

Chivenor *	A/G 130.200 *When gliders operate	C/S Alpha Charlie Base

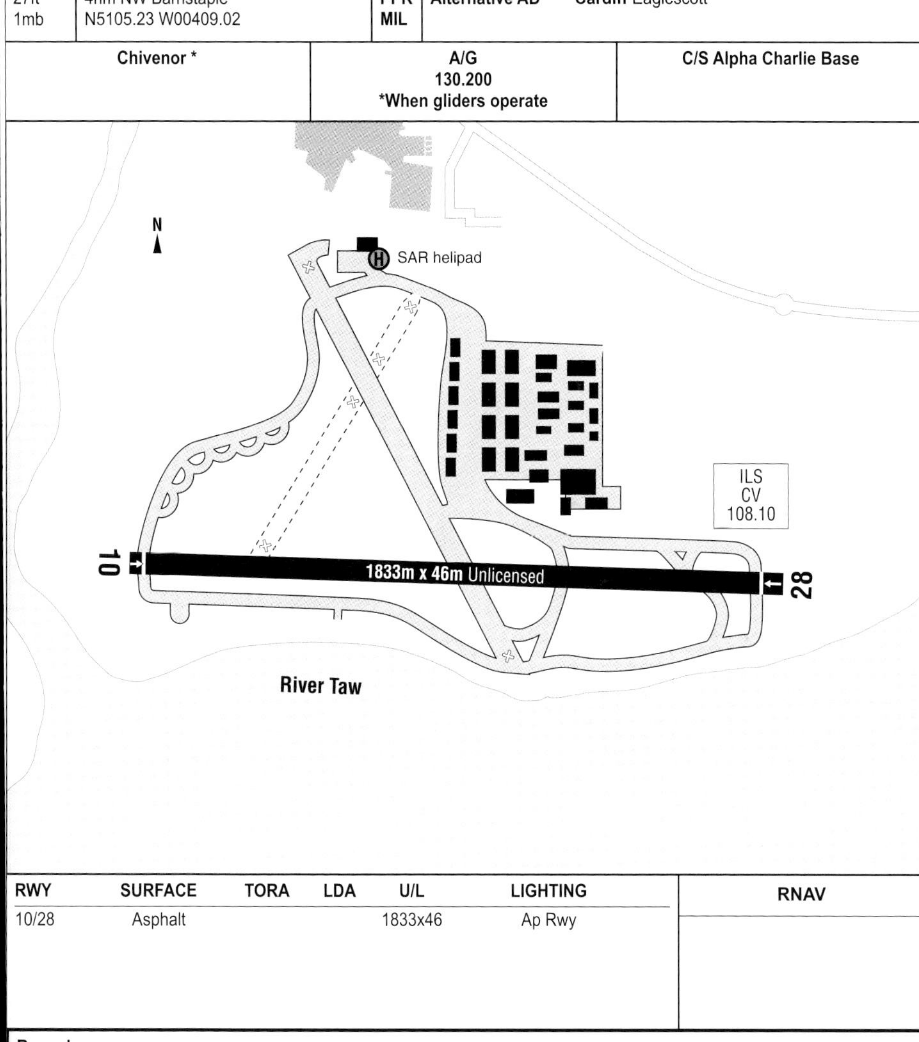

RWY	SURFACE	TORA	LDA	U/L	LIGHTING
10/28	Asphalt			1833x46	Ap Rwy

RNAV

Remarks
PPR with 24Hrs notice required. Applications should be made during office hours. Helicopters only not available to fixed wing ACFT. Military SAR helicopter activity H24. Powered gliders operate WE, PH and some evenings.

Warnings
AD Disused. Rwy and AD lighting maintained for SAR helicopter use and obstacles are frequently placed on Rwy and Twys.

Operating Hrs	SAR Helis H24 Training 0800-2300 (L)
Circuits	To S 1000ft QFE
Landing Fee	Charges in accordance with MOD policy Contact Station Ops for details
Maintenance	Nil
Fuel	Not available for visitors
Disabled Facilities	Nil
Restaurants	Nil
Taxis/Car Hire	Nil
Weather Info	Air SW MOEx

Operator
Royal Marines
Royal Marines Barracks Chivenor
Barnstable
Devon
EX31 4AZ
Tel: 01271 857220 (PPR)
Fax: 01271 813662

EGXG CHURCH FENTON

29ft 1mb	10nm SW of York N5350.06 W00111.73	PPR MIL	Alternative AD Diversion AD	**Leeds Bradford** Sherburn in Elmet

Fenton	LARS	APP	PAR	TWR	GND
	Linton 118.550	126.500	123.300	122.100	121.950

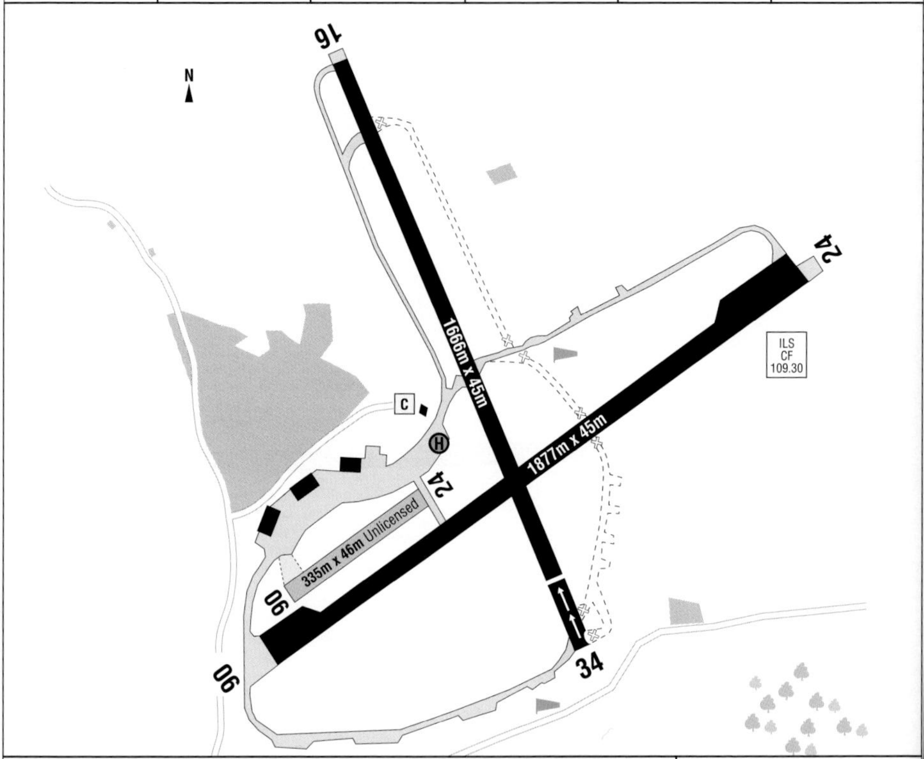

16
N
1666m x 45m
24
ILS CF 109.30
C
H
1877m x 45m
24
335m x 46m Unlicensed
06
06
34

RWY	SURFACE	TORA	LDA	U/L	LIGHTING
06/24	Asph/Conc	1711	1711		Ap Thr Rwy PAPI 3°
16	Asphalt	1666	1666		Thr Rwy PAPI 3°
34	Asphalt	1666	1467		Thr Rwy PAPI 3°
06/24	Grass			335x46	Nil

Displaced Thr Rwy06/34 Asphalt

RNAV

Remarks
PPR by telephone 24Hrs notice required. Satellite AD to Linton-on-Ouse. Intensive flying at this AD due to the flying training school.
Visual aids to location: Ibn CF Red.

Warnings
Public road (controlled by traffic lights) crosses final APP Rwy06 225m from Thr. Civil AD – Sherburn-in-Elmet –3nm to SW.

Operating Hrs Mon-Thu 0830-1715 Fri-Sun 0830-1700 (L) & by arr

Circuits 24, 34 RH, 06, 16 LH
1000ft QFE, 800ft Light ACFT

Landing Fee Charges in accordance with MOD policy
Contact Station Ops for details

Maintenance Nil
Fuel Nil

Disabled Facilities

Restaurants Nil

Taxis
Windmill **Tel:** 01937 232979

Car Hire
National (Leeds) **Tel:** 01132 777957

Weather Info Air N MOEx

Operator RAF Church Fenton
Tadcaster
North Yorkshire, LS24 9SE
Tel: 01347 848261 Ex 7901
(PPR Linton-on-Ouse)
Fax: 01347 848261 Ex 7936

C

37ft 1mb	2nm W of Clacton N5147.10 E00107.80	PPR	**Alternative AD** **Diversion AD**	**Southend** Elmsett

Clacton	LARS Southend 130.775	A/G 118.150

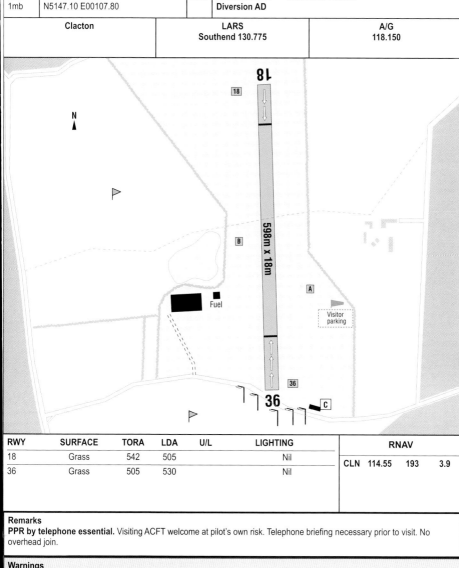

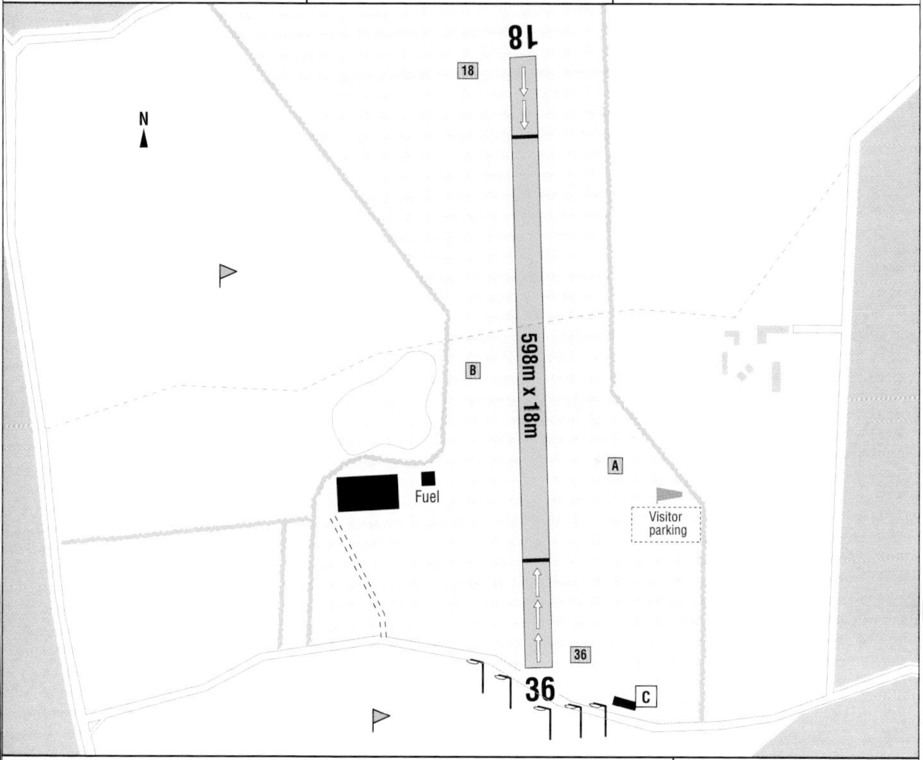

18
18
N
B
598m x 18m
A
Fuel
Visitor parking
36
36
C

RWY	SURFACE	TORA	LDA	U/L	LIGHTING
18	Grass	542	505		Nil
36	Grass	505	530		Nil

RNAV			
CLN	114.55	193	3.9

Remarks

PPR by telephone essential. Visiting ACFT welcome at pilot's own risk. Telephone briefing necessary prior to visit. No overhead join.

Warnings

There is a line of lamp posts 16ft agl on the public Rd crossing APP Rwy36 just before the AD boundary. A public footpath crosses the AD.

Operating Hrs 0900-1730 or SS (Summer)
1000-1600 or SS (Winter)

Circuits 18 RH, 36 LH, 1000ft QFE

Landing Fee Single £10

Maintenance
CAS Engineering **Tel:** 01255 222224

Fuel Nil

Disabled Facilities

Restaurants Refreshments available at AD

Taxis
George Won **Tel:** 01255 220050/270630
AJ **Tel:** 01255 474444

Car Hire Nil

Weather Info Air S MOEx

Operator Clacton Aero Club
Clacton Aerodrome
West Road
Clacton-On-Sea
Essex, CO15 1AG
Tel: 01255 424671
Fax: 01255 475364

Effective date:25/09/08 OP 08

623ft 20mb	2nm S of Marlborough N5123.37 W00143.94	PPR	Alternative AD	**Oxford** Thruxton

Clench Common	Zone Lyneham 123.400	Safetycom 135.475

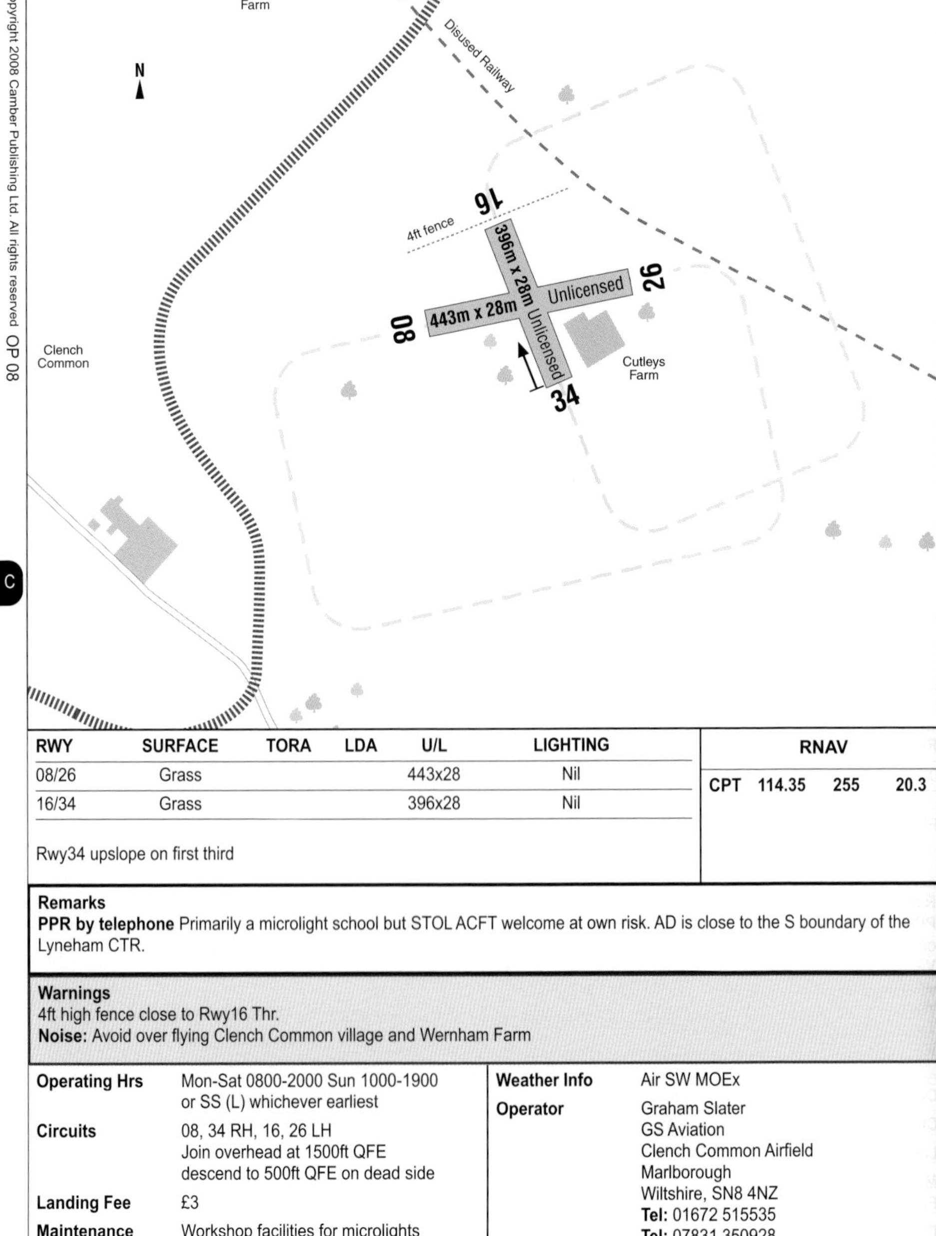

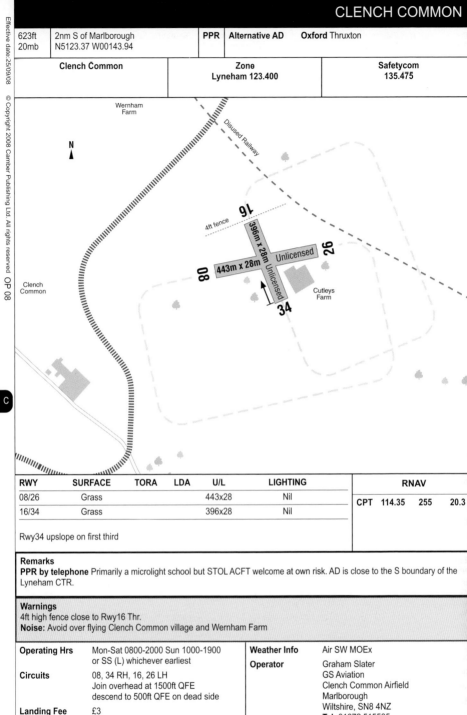

RWY	SURFACE	TORA	LDA	U/L	LIGHTING
08/26	Grass			443x28	Nil
16/34	Grass			396x28	Nil

Rwy34 upslope on first third

RNAV			
CPT	114.35	255	20.3

Remarks

PPR by telephone Primarily a microlight school but STOL ACFT welcome at own risk. AD is close to the S boundary of the Lyneham CTR.

Warnings

4ft high fence close to Rwy16 Thr.

Noise: Avoid over flying Clench Common village and Wernham Farm

Operating Hrs	Mon-Sat 0800-2000 Sun 1000-1900 or SS (L) whichever earliest
Circuits	08, 34 RH, 16, 26 LH Join overhead at 1500ft QFE descend to 500ft QFE on dead side
Landing Fee	£3
Maintenance	Workshop facilities for microlights
Fuel	MOGAS (local garage by arr)
Disabled Facilities	
Restaurants	Hot drinks available
Taxis/Car Hire	**Tel:** 01672 511088

Weather Info	Air SW MOEx
Operator	Graham Slater GS Aviation Clench Common Airfield Marlborough Wiltshire, SN8 4NZ **Tel:** 01672 515535 **Tel:** 07831 350928 **Fax:** 01672 511574 info@gsaviation.co.uk

CLIPGATE

406ft 13mb	6nm SSE of Canterbury N5111.11 E00109.30	PPR	**Alternative AD** **Manston** Rochester

Non-Radio	LARS Manston 126.350	Safetycom 135.475

N

20

490m x 30m Unlicensed

ACFT parking

C

02

7ft hedge

RWY	SURFACE	TORA	LDA	U/L	LIGHTING
02/20	Grass			490x30	Nil

Rwy02 slight downslope

RNAV			
DVR	**114.95**	**282**	**7.9**

Remarks
PPR by telephone essential. Visiting ACFT welcome at pilots own risk. Visitors are requested to complete AD log before dept. Short field experience is helpful.
Visual aid to location: Golf course 0.5nm ENE.

Warnings
Trees border strip to E and N, may generate turbulence. Low hedge by Rwy02 Thr. Trees on short final Rwy20.
Noise: No over flight of local villages. No local flying.

Operating Hrs SR-SS
Circuits 20 RH, 02 LH, 1000ft QFE
Landing Fee Nil
Maintenance Nil
Fuel Nil
Disabled Facilities

Restaurants
Accommodation Caravans and camping on site
Taxis Nil
Car Hire Nil

Weather Info Air SE MOEx
Operator
Mr R G Akehurst
Clipgate Farm
Lodge Lees
Barham
Canterbury
Kent, CT4 6NS
Tel: 01227 831327
Fax: 01227 832906
Tel: 07973 176879
bob@clipgate.co.uk
www.clipgate.co.uk

Effective date:25/09/08 OP C8

C

 OP 03

600ft 20mb	5nm WSW of Bath N5120.57 W00231.22	PPR	Alternative AD **Bristol Filton** Kemble

Non-standard join

Non-radio	ATIS Bristol 126.025	APP Bristol 125.650	Safetycom 135.475

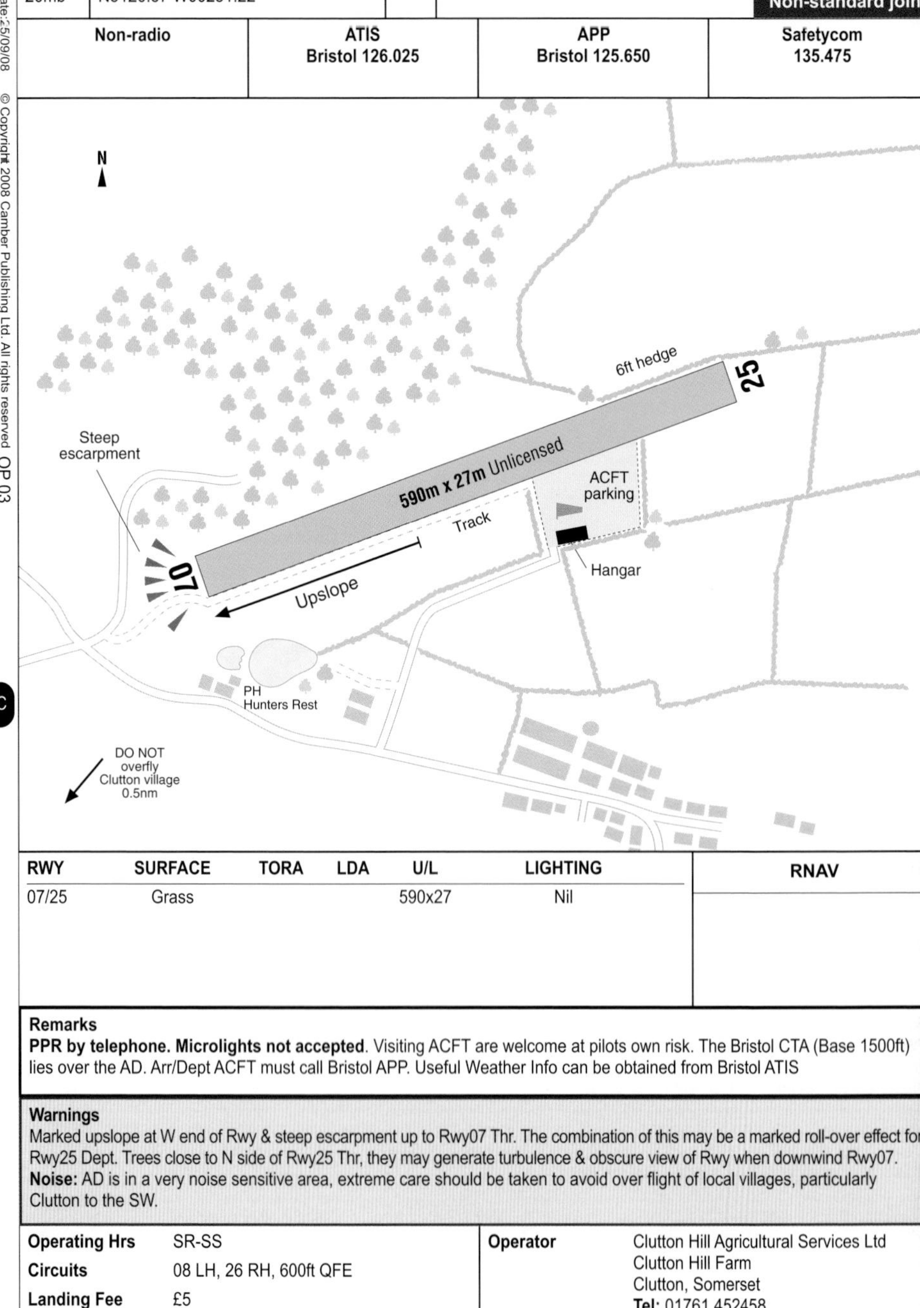

RWY	SURFACE	TORA	LDA	U/L	LIGHTING
07/25	Grass			590x27	Nil

RNAV

Remarks

PPR by telephone. Microlights not accepted. Visiting ACFT are welcome at pilots own risk. The Bristol CTA (Base 1500ft) lies over the AD. Arr/Dept ACFT must call Bristol APP. Useful Weather Info can be obtained from Bristol ATIS

Warnings

Marked upslope at W end of Rwy & steep escarpment up to Rwy07 Thr. The combination of this may be a marked roll-over effect for Rwy25 Dept. Trees close to N side of Rwy25 Thr, they may generate turbulence & obscure view of Rwy when downwind Rwy07.
Noise: AD is in a very noise sensitive area, extreme care should be taken to avoid over flight of local villages, particularly Clutton to the SW.

Operating Hrs SR-SS
Circuits 08 LH, 26 RH, 600ft QFE
Landing Fee £5
Maintenance Nil
Fuel Nil
Disabled Facilities Nil
Restaurants
Hunters Rest **Tel:** 01761 452303
Taxis **Tel:** 01761 417166
Car Hire Nil
Weather Info Air SW MOEx

Operator Clutton Hill Agricultural Services Ltd
Clutton Hill Farm
Clutton, Somerset
Tel: 01761 452458
Tel: 07751 673369

C

COAL ASTON

720ft 24mb	5nm S of Sheffield N5318.28 W00125.83	PPR	Alternative AD	East Midlands Retford

Non-radio	APP Doncaster Sheffield 126.225	Safetycom 135.475

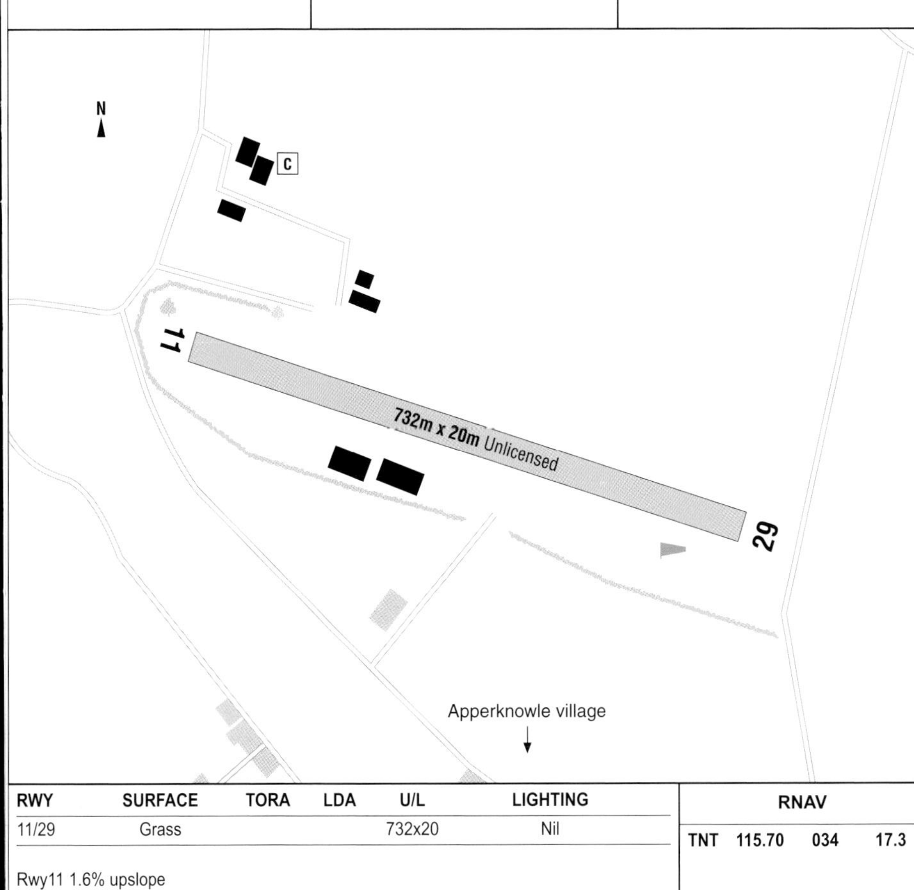

RWY	SURFACE	TORA	LDA	U/L	LIGHTING
11/29	Grass			732x20	Nil

Rwy11 1.6% upslope

RNAV			
TNT	115.70	034	17.3

Remarks
PPR strictly by telephone.

Warnings
Located on the edge of Doncaster Sheffield CTA.

Operating Hrs	SR-SS
Circuits	Nil
Landing Fee	On application
Maintenance	Nil
Fuel	Nil
Disabled Facilities	Nil
Restaurants	Nil
Taxis/Car Hire	Nil
Weather Info	Air Cen MOEx

Operator
Mr W H Valle
Bentley Farm
Summerley, Apperknowle
Sheffield
Tel: 01246 412305 (AD)

COLEMORE COMMON

610ft 20mb	4nm SSE of Alton N5103.76 W00100.58	PPR	**Alternative AD** **Southampton** Goodwood **Non-standard join**

Colemore Common	**LARS** **Farnborough West 125.250**	**A/G** **129.825** **Microlight freq**

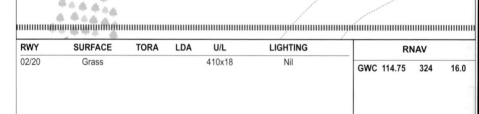

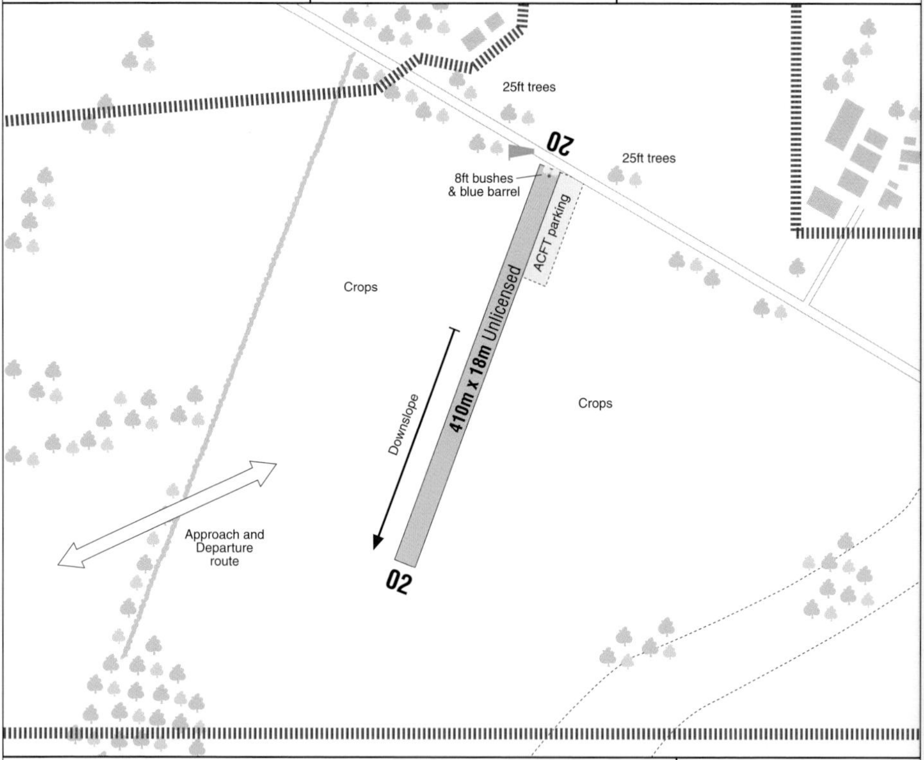

25ft trees
20
25ft trees
8ft bushes & blue barrel
ACFT parking
Crops
410m x 18m Unlicensed
Crops
Downslope
Approach and Departure route
02

RWY	SURFACE	TORA	LDA	U/L	LIGHTING
02/20	Grass			410x18	Nil

RNAV			
GWC	114.75	324	16.0

Remarks
PPR by telephone for non-members. Visiting ACFT welcome at pilots own risk. Well maintained strip in quiet area. Home of Hampshire Microlight Club. It is mandatory to book in and out.

Warnings
Downslope from midpoint Rwy20. Public road Rwy20 Thr.
Noise: Please Arr/Depart along track marked on map. Avoid over flying marked areas. Avoid over flying any neighbouring properties near AD.

Operating Hrs	SR-SS
Circuits	02 RH 20 LH 600ft QFE
Landing Fee	Donations in blue barrel by windsock
Maintenance	Nil
Fuel	Nil
Disabled Facilities	Nil
Restaurant	Nil
Taxi/Car Hire	Nil
Weather Info	Air SW MOEx

Operator
Hampshire Microlight Club
c/o 20 Bacon Lane
Hayling Island
Hampshire
PO11 0DN
Tel: 023 9246 8806 (PPR)
Tel: 078 3475 2083 (PPR)
www.hmfclub.com

C

EGEL COLL

20ft 0mb	5nm WSW of Arinagour N5636.07 W00637.04	PPR	**Alternative AD** **Benbecula** Tiree

Coll	FIS	AFIS	A/G
	Scottish 127.275	Tiree 122.70	125.00

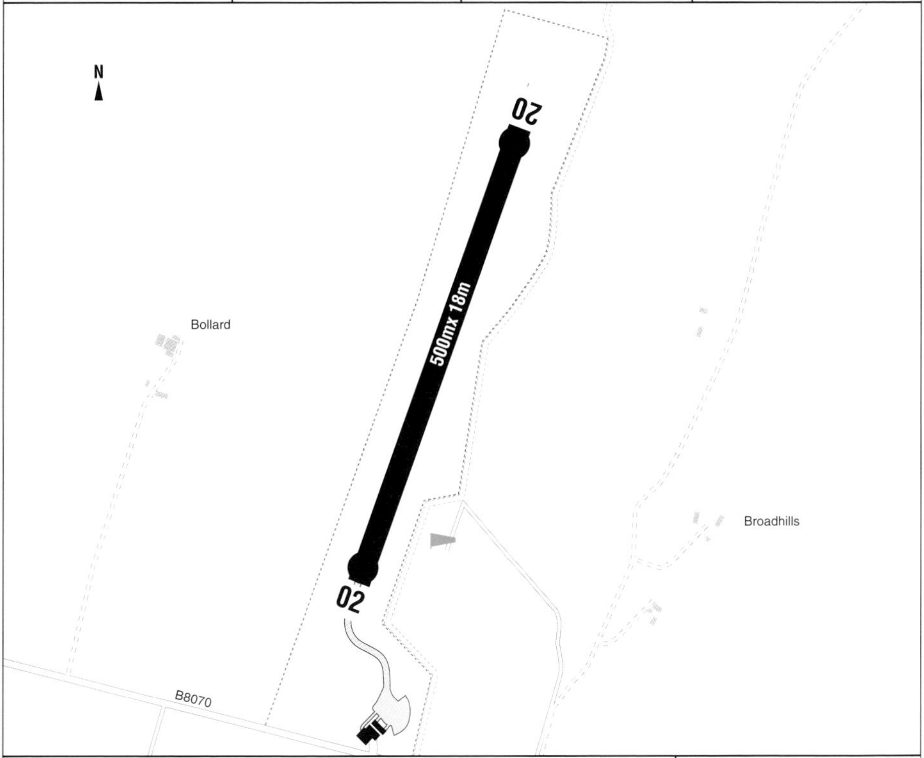

N

20

500mx 18m

Bollard

Broadhills

02

B8070

RWY	SURFACE	TORA	LDA	U/L	LIGHTING
02/20	Asphalt	500	500		Rwy

RNAV			
TIR	117.7	055	10.5

Remarks
PPR strictly by telephone. Hi-vis. Use minimum power whilst manoeuvering on the apron as front of terminal and personnel subject to propwash. AD can be used for training PPR from Oban Airport administration. Arr/Dept ACFT must contact Tiree AFIS. Unofficial IFR APP to Rwy23 at Tiree passes close to Coll. APP is not available to ACFT other than Loganair scheduled/ambulance ACFT.

Warnings
Concentrations of Greylag geese may be encountered on and around AD at any time of the year.

Operating Hrs	Mon & Wed 0800-0930 1530-1700 (Summer) Mon & Wed 0900-1030 and 1430-1600 (Winter) & by arr
Circuits	LH 1000ft
Landing Fee	On application
Maintenance	Nil
Fuel	Nil
Disabled Facilities	Nil
Restaurant	Café & restaurant in Arinagour 2.5 miles away
Island Café	**Tel:** 01879 230262 www.firstportofcoll.com/islandcafe.htm
Nic's Burger van	**Tel:** 01879 230359 www.visitcoll.co.uk/eatingout.php
Accomodation	
Coll Hotel:	**Tel:** 01879 230334 www.collhotel.com

Taxi	
Barritts	**Tel:** 01879 230402
Car Hire	Nil
Cycle Hire	
Post Office	**Tel** 01879 230395
Weather Info	Air Sc GWC
Oban	ATIS **Tel:** 01631 710830
Operator	Argyll & Bute Council Oban Airport North Connel Oban Argyll PA37 1SX **Tel:** 01631 710910 (Admin) **Tel:** 01631 710830 (ATC) **Fax:** 01631 710916 (Admin) **Fax:** 01631 710716 (ATC)

Effective date:25/09/08 OP 08

C

593ft 19mb	7nm E of Bath N5126.45 W00216.80	PPR MIL	Alternative AD Diversion AD	Bristol Filton Kemble

Colerne	Zone Lyneham 123.400	APP Bristol 125.650	APP 120.075	TWR/GND 120.075

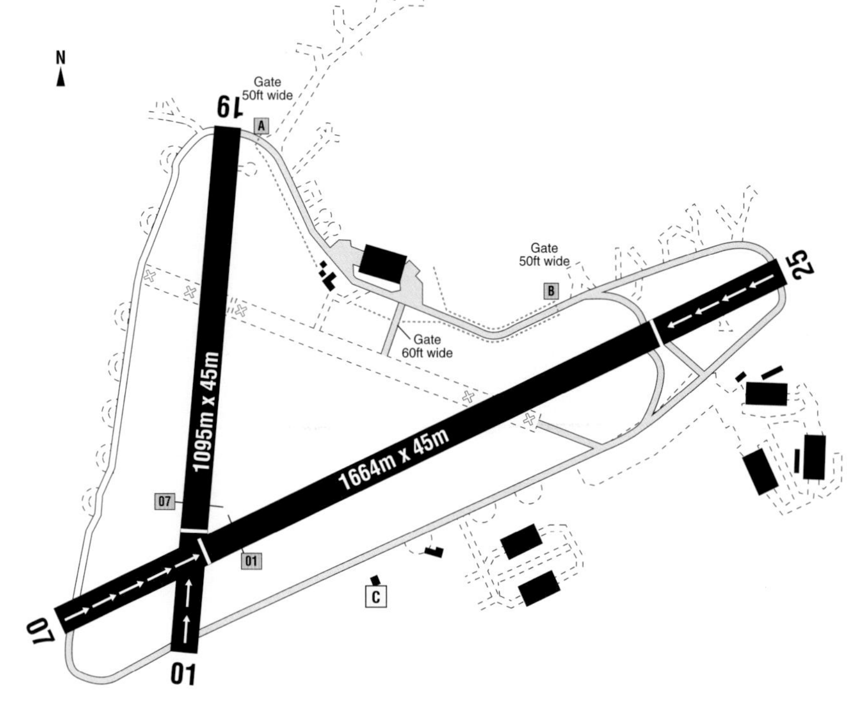

RWY	SURFACE	TORA	LDA	U/L	LIGHTING
07	Asphalt	1664	1422		Nil
25	Asphalt	1664	1344		Nil
01	Asphalt	1095	895		Nil
19	Asphalt	1095	1086		Nil

Displaced Thr Rwy01, 07 & 25

RNAV

Remarks
Strict PPR by telephone. Pilot training on AD. Special Arr procedures for helicopters details sought with PPR. Rwy01 only used for take-off.

Warnings
Rwy07/25/01 have displaced landing Thr. Obstructions are within APP areas up to 604ft amsl. No traffic lights on AD. Obstructions in the circuit are not lit. HIRTA D1616 may affect avionics within ATZ. Twy between A & B has reduced wing tip clearance due to security fencing and two gates 50ft wide. Turbulence expected in any wind conditions. AD borders on W edge of Lyneham CTR. ACFT Arr/Dept from/to S call Bristol APP. Garston Farm AD, Lucknam Park Hotel and Star Farm Heli site within AD circuit.
Caution: ACFT manoeuvring in unusual positions above ATZ.

Operating Hrs	As required by RAF operations
Circuits	As instructed by ATC at 800ft QFE
Landing Fee	Charges in accordance with MOD policy Contact Station Ops for details
Maintenance	Nil
Fuel	AVGAS 100LL strictly by prior arrangement
Disabled Facilities	Nil
Restaurants	Nil
Taxi Grahams	**Tel:** 0785 0874141

Car Hire	Nil
Weather Info	Air SW MOEx
Operator	BUAS Colerne Azimghur Barracks Colerne Airfield Chippenham Wiltshire SN14 8QY **Tel**: 01225 745338 **Fax:** 01225 745265

39ft 1mb	W side of Colonsay Island N5603.45 W00615.58	**PPR**	**Alternative AD** **Islay** Tiree

Colonsay	**FIS** **Scottish 127.275**	**AFIS** **Tiree 122.700**	**A/G** **123.800**

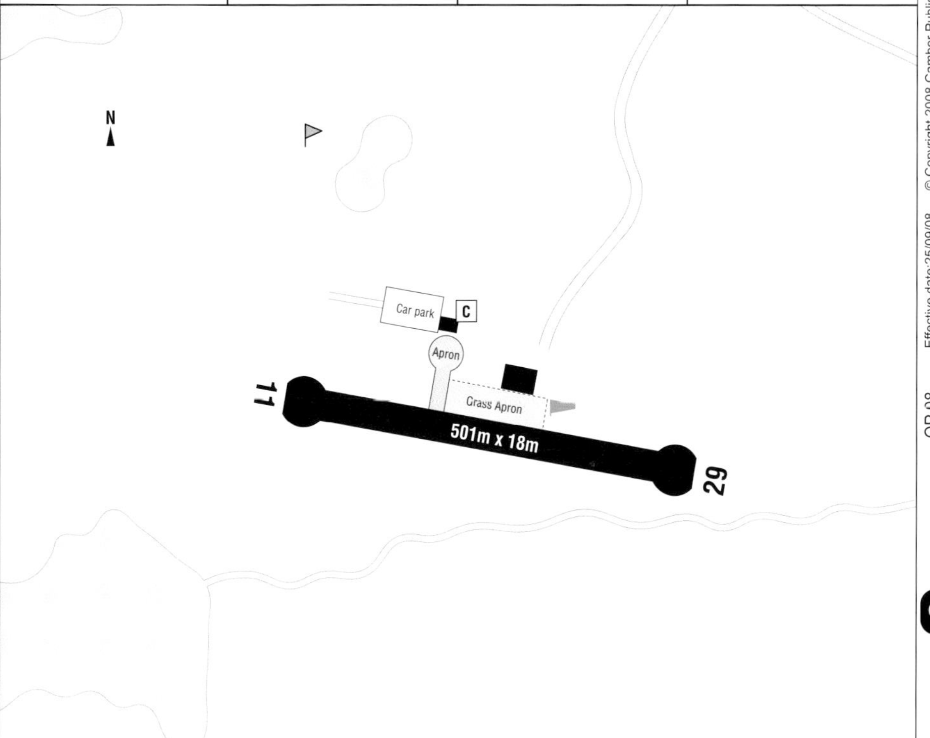

RWY	SURFACE	TORA	LDA	U/L	LIGHTING	RNAV
11/29	Asphalt	501	501		Nil	

Remarks
Strict PPR by telephone or fax to Oban Airport. Hi-vis. Visiting light ACFT at pilot's own risk. All circuits to the S to minimise domestic and wildlife disturbance.

Warnings
Noise: Avoid over-flying bird sanctuaries which extend along the coast to N of AD

Operating Hrs	Tue & Thu 0730-0900 1545-1715 (Summer) Tue & Thu 0830-1000 1430-1600 (Winter) & by arr
Circuits	All circuits to S
Landing Fee	Available with PPR
Maintenance	Nil
Fuel	Nil
Disabled Facilities	
Taxis/Hire Car	Transport on request
Weather Info	Air Sc GWC
Operator	Argyll & Bute Council

c/o Oban Airport
North Connel
Oban
Argyll, PA37 1PX
Tel: 01631 710830 (ATS)
Tel: 01631 710910 (Adminstration)
Fax: 01631 710916 (Administration)
Fax: 01631 710716 (ATS)
peter.jackson@argyll-bute.gov.uk
barry.mccaig@argyll-bute.gov.uk

811ft 27mb	2.7nm S of Shaftesbury N5058.03 W00209.22	PPR	**Alternative AD** **Diversion AD**	**Bournemouth** Old Sarum

Compton	LARS Bournemouth 119.475	LARS Boscombe Down 126.700	LARS Yeovilton 127.350	A/G 122.700

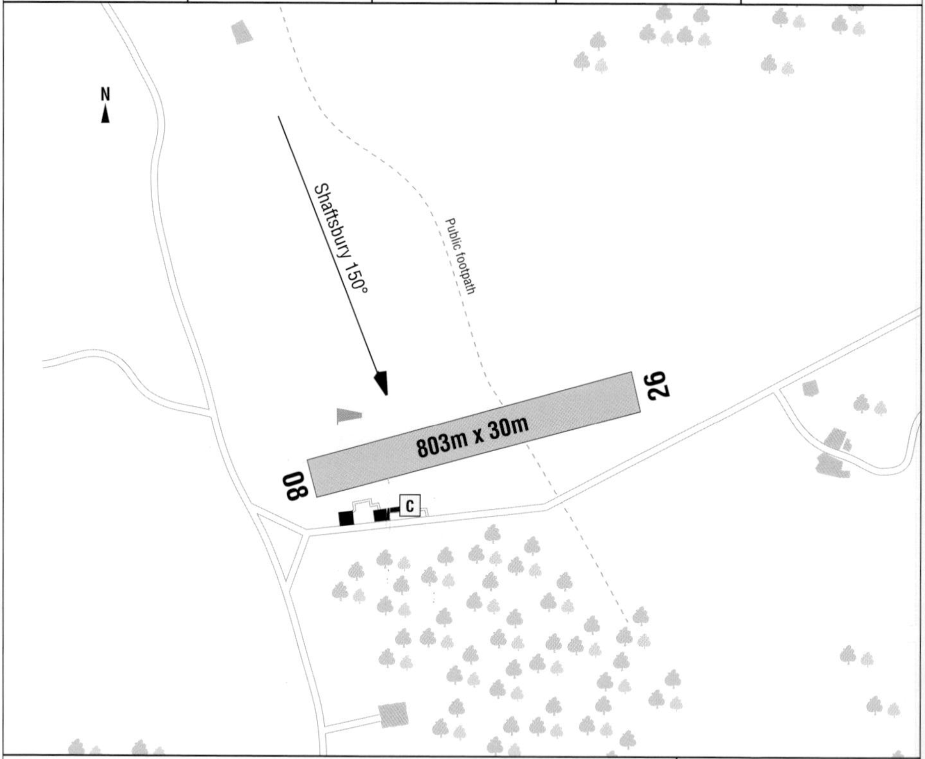

RWY	SURFACE	TORA	LDA	U/L	LIGHTING
08/26	Grass	799	803		Nil

RNAV			
SAM	113.35	276	30.0

Remarks
AD is not available at night by flights required to use a licensed AD. ACFT to clear left after landing on Rwy26 and right after landing on Rwy08. Over flights not below 3000ft altitude. RAD available Bournemouth (7 days), weekdays only from Boscombe Down LARS or Yeovilton LARS.
Visual aid to location: White strobe flashes during AD operating Hrs.

Warnings
Mast 55ft agl S of AD boundary. Check for aerobatics and formation flying taking place within ATZ. Due to prop wash, all ACFT to park E of flashing beacon. GND to the N of the Rwy has a steep slope gradient. Turbulence & wind shear will be experienced with southerly winds above 10kts.Particularly affected are Rwy08 Arr in SE winds & climb out Rwy26 with S or SW winds.
Noise: Avoid over-flying villages around the AD. Rwy26 Dept turn right to over fly Melbury Hill as soon after crossing AD boundary as safety permits. Noise abatement procedures must be obtained prior to Dept

Operating Hrs	Mon-Fri 0900-1800 Sat-Sun 0900-2000 (Summer) Mon-Sun 0900-SS (Winter)
Circuits	08 LH, 26 RH, 800ft QFE Microlights 500ft QFE inside Fixed wing circuit
Landing Fee	Single £8.50 Twin £12 Microlight £6
Maintenance Airtime	**Tel:** 01747 812791 Hangarage available
Fuel	AVGAS JET A1 100LL
Disabled Facilities	

Restaurant	Licensed restaurant & bar at AD 0930-1800 (Summer) 0930-1700 (Winter) Available for corporate entertainment
Taxis Hiltop	**Tel:** 01747 855555
Car Hire	Operator can arr on request
Weather Info	Air SW MOEx
Operator	Compton Abbas Airfield Ltd Ashmore, Dorset, SP5 5AP **Tel:** 01747 811767 **Fax** 01747 811161 fly@abbasair.com www.abbasair.com

C

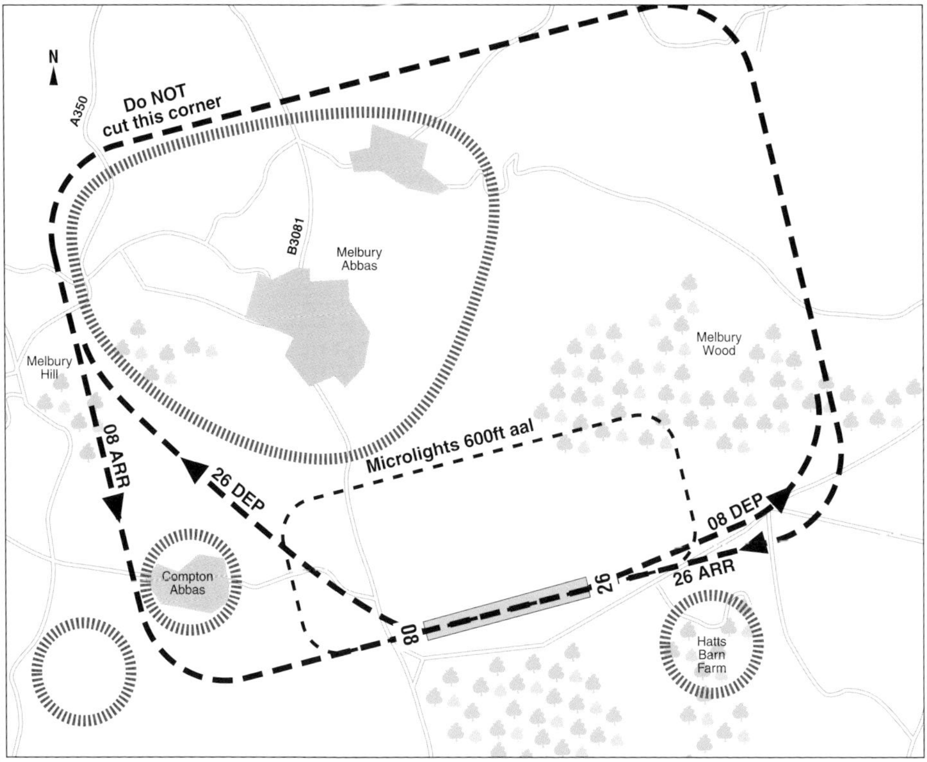

Arrivals:
Rwy08: APP normal, avoid low final APP or using excessive power settings. Avoid over flying Compton village
Rwy26: APP normal.

Departures:
Rwy08: As soon as possible on passing end of Rwy, turn left. Avoid over flying Hatts Barn Farmhouse.
Rwy26: As soon as possible on passing end of Rwy, turn right, crossing the top of Melbury Hill. Avoid over flying any part of Compton village.

24ft 1mb	8nm NW of Boston N5305.58 W00009.95	PPR MIL	**Alternative AD** **Diversion AD**	**East Midlands** Wickenby

Non-standard join

Coningsby	LARS	APP	TWR	GND
	Waddington 127.350	120.800	124.675	122.100

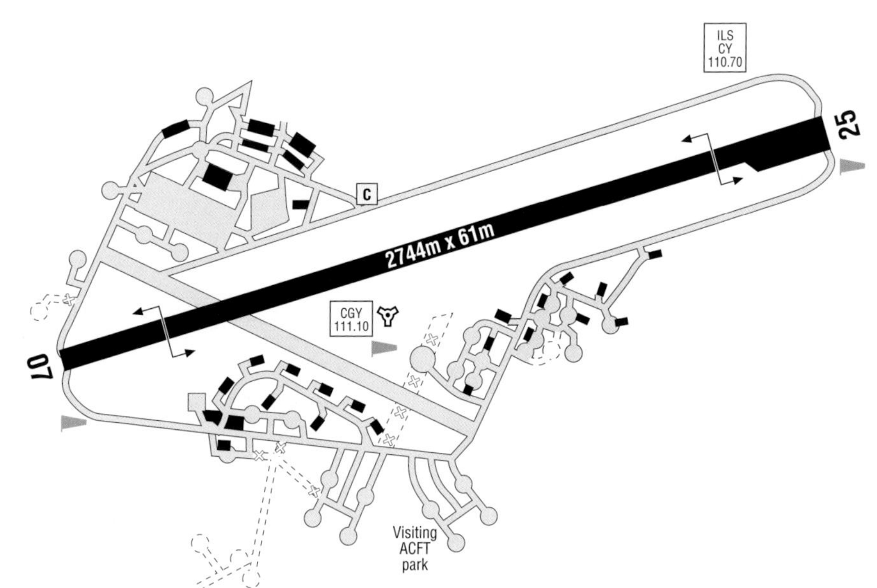

RWY	SURFACE	TORA	LDA	U/L	LIGHTING
07/25	Asph/Conc	2744	2744		Ap Thr Rwy PAPI 3°

Arrestor gear cables 396m from both Thrs, Rwy25 APP down, overrun up
Rwy07 both up, Arrestor cables up outside operating hrs

RNAV

Remarks
PPR strictly by telephone. RAF AD within active MATZ. Based jet ACFT carry out high energy manoeuvres within the vicinity of the AD. Civil visiting ACFT accepted only by telephone permission, may be subject to refusal or specified arrival conditions. Traffic is particularly severely restricted when Rwy07 in use. Frequent weekend movements, contact Waddington LARS for AD status.
Visual Aid to location: I Bn CY Red

Warnings
Vintage ACFT of the Battle of Britain Memorial Flight (BBMF) fly circuits to N of main Rwy and grass strip between 500 – 1000ft QFE. The grass strip is not available to visiting ACFT. Harrier ACFT conduct VSTOL manoeuvres at various locations on AD.
Caution: Arrester cables. Be sure you have identified their position and land beyond. Danger of severe turbulence
Noise: Do not over fly Engine de-tuner in SW dispersal when notified as active, avoid by 1000ft agl by 0.6nm radius. Light ACFT and helicopters may turn on route above 1000ft agl.

Operating Hrs	0800-1700 Mon-Fri (L). ATZ operational H24
Circuits	25 LH, 07 RH, 1000ft QFE
Landing Fee	Charges in accordance with MOD policy Contact Station Ops for details
Maintenance	Not normally available to Civil visitors
Fuel	AVGAS 100LL JET A1 strictly by prior arr
Disabled Facilities	

Restaurants	Nil
Taxis/Car Hire	Nil
Weather Info	Air S MOEx
Operators	RAF Coningsby Lincoln Lincolnshire LN4 4SY **Tel**: 01526 342581 **Tel:** 01526 347716/347959 (Ops) **Tel:** 01526 347443 (ATC)

EGWC COSFORD

272ft 9mb	7nm E of Telford N5238.40 W00218.33	PPR MIL	Alternative AD Diversion AD	Birmingham Wolverhampton

Cosford	LARS Shawbury 120.775	APP 135.875	GND 128.650	TWR 128.650	A/G BFC Base 135.875

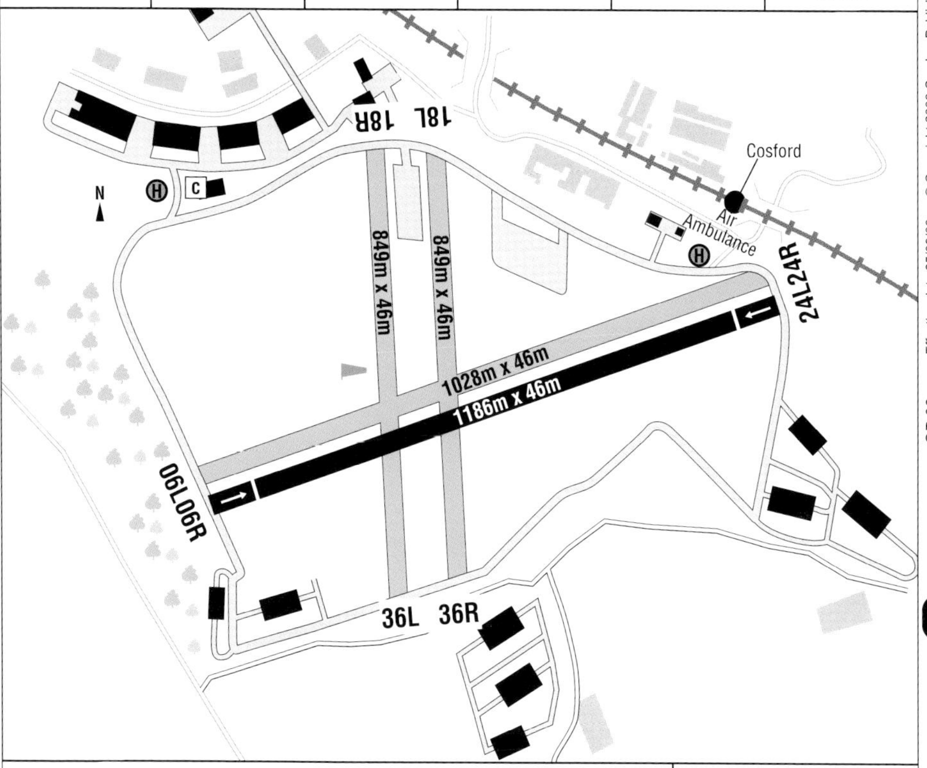

RWY	SURFACE	TORA	LDA	U/L	LIGHTING
06R/24L	Asphalt	1166	1132		Nil
06L/24R	Grass	1028	1028		Nil
18R/36L	Grass	849	849		Nil
18L/36R	Grass	849	849		Nil

RNAV			
SWB	116.80	130	16.1

Remarks

PPR. Ab initio pilot training takes place here. No civil ACFT accepted Sat/Sun. AD may close at indeterminate times if not required by station based training ACFT. ATZ remains active H24. Visiting civil ACFT will not be accepted if visibility is <5km. Air ambulance operations daily. Cosford Flying Club operations until dusk

Warnings

Glider and powered glider activity outside published Hrs and at weekends. Railway embankment 20ft aal 274m before Rwy24 Thr. Ravine 91m before Rwy06 Thr. Air Ambulance activity H24. Grass Rwys used by light ACFT and gliders and are not available for use by civilian ACFT.

Caution: full obstacle clearance criteria not met on APP. Up to 12 light ACFT operating at any one time.

Noise: Avoid over flying Albrighton village 1nm SE.

Operating Hrs	Mon-Fri 0900-1700 (L) or as requested by OC flying
Circuits	All to S
Landing Fee	Charges in accordance with MOD policy Contact Station Ops for details
Maintenance	Nil
Fuel	Nil
Disabled Facilities	Nil
Restaurants	In Aerospace Museum
Taxis/Car Hire	Nil
Weather Info	Air Cen MOEx
Operator	RAF Cosford Wolverhampton West Midlands, WV7 3EX **Tel:** 01902 377567 **Tel:** 01902 337030 **Tel:** 01902 377582

390ft 13mb	5nm SE of Baldock N5157.50 W00006.00	PPR	Alternative AD	Cambridge Duxford

Non-Radio	ATIS Luton 120.575	APP Luton 129.550	Safetycom 135.475

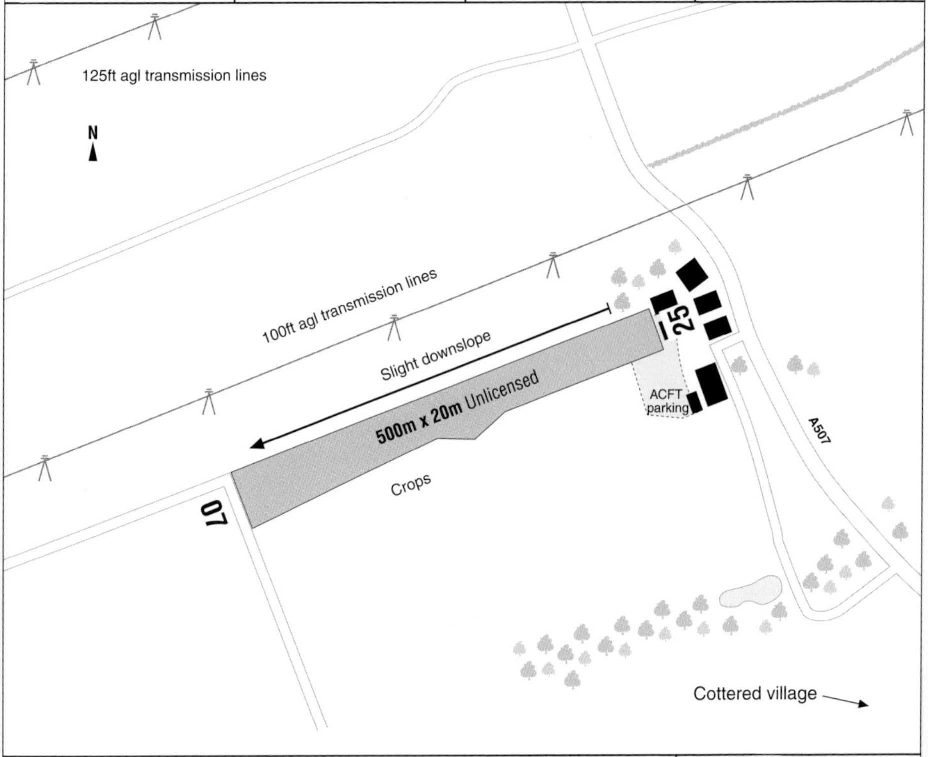

RWY	SURFACE	TORA	LDA	U/L	LIGHTING
07/25	Grass			500x20	Nil

Rwy25 slight downslope

RNAV			
BKY	116.25	251	6.5

Remarks
PPR by telephone. Visiting ACFT operate at own risk. Strip width is given as 20m there is a wider section at the midpoint and to the S Rwy07 Thr.

Warnings
AD is situated below Luton CTA (base 2500ft QNH). Trees and farm buildings close to Rwy25 Thr. Farm track runs down N side of strip and branches across Rwy07 Thr. 100ft agl transmission line parallel to AD 80m to N side with a second line 1000 metres further to the N. Crops are grown close to the strip edge.
Noise: Do not over fly Cottered village SE of AD

Operating Hrs SR-SS
Circuits 1000ft QFE
Landing Fee £6
Maintenance Nil
Fuel Nil
Disabled Facilities

Restaurants Bull Pub Cottered Village
Taxis/Car Hire Nil
Weather Info Air SE MOEx

Operator Kingsley Brothers
Childs Farm
Cottered, Buntingford,
Herts, SG9 9PU
Tel: 01763 281256
Fax: 01763 281652
colinbayles@hotmail.com

EGXJ COTTESMORE

461ft 15mb	5nm NE of Oakham N5244.14 W00038.93	PPR MIL	Alternative AD Diversion AD	East Midlands Leicester

Cottesmore	Zone/APP	TWR/GND
	130.200	122.100

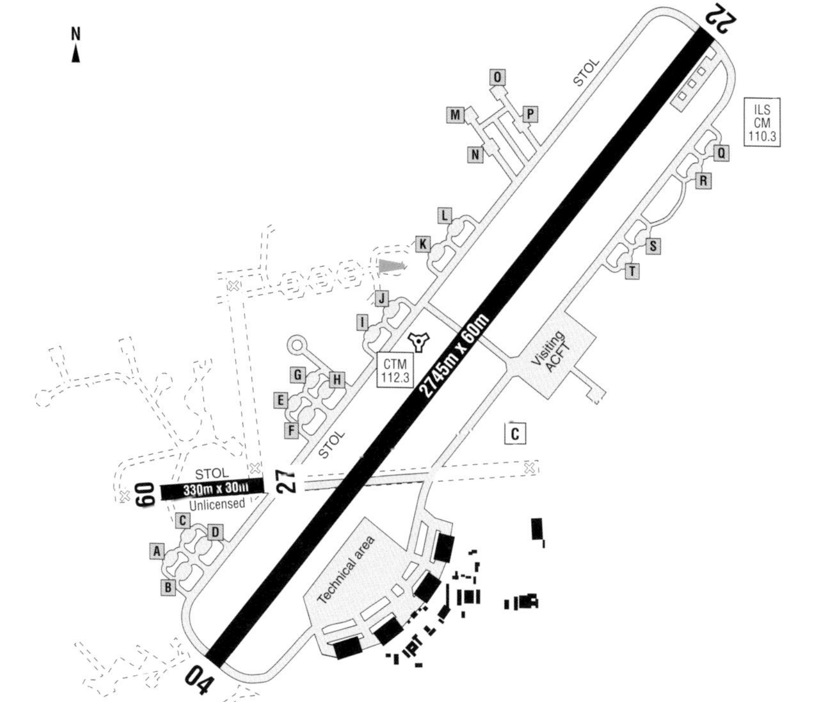

RWY	SURFACE	TORA	LDA	U/L	LIGHTING
22/04	Asph/Conc	2745	2745		Ap Thr Rwy PAPI 2.5°
09/27	Asphalt			300x30	Nil

RNAV

Remarks

24Hrs PPR by telephone essential. RAF AD with intensive fast jet operations. AD situated within CMATZ with RAF Wittering, Cottesmore is controlling authority. Inbound ACFT/Helicopters contact Cottesmore not less than 15nm before the MATZ boundary.

Warnings

N Twys have non-standard markings for use as STOL strips by based ACFT only. Based ACFT will carry out variable circuits. There is a significant bird hazard on AD. Visiting ACFT may be required to operate under RAD control to comply with local noise restrictions/ be sequenced in traffic. Visiting ACFT prohibited before 0830 (L). Due to restricted wing tip clearance visiting ACFT with wingspan exceeding 16m will not be permitted to use S Twy between Rwy04 Thr and the technical area. **Noise**: Visiting ACFT to climb to 1000ft QFE or higher to leave the local area. Over flight of local villages within 10nm of Cottesmore is to be avoided.

Operating Hrs	Mon-Fri 0800-1700 (L) ATZ active H24
Circuits	Variable but visiting ACFT should expect 22 RH, 04 LH, 1200ft QFE
Landing Fee	Charges in accordance with MOD policy Contact Station Ops for details
Maintenance	Nil for civil visitors
Fuel	JET A1 by prior arr
Disabled Facilities	

Restaurants	Nil
Taxis/Car Hire	Nil
Weather Info	M T Fax MOEx ATIS **Tel:** 01572 812241 Ex 7602 Met Office **Tel:** 01572 812241 Ex 7337
Operator	RAF Cottesmore Oakham Leicestershire LE15 7BL **Tel:** 01572 812241 Ex 7330/7270

Effective date:25/09/08 OP 08

267ft 9mb	3nm SSE of Coventry N5222.18 W00128.78	PPR	Alternative AD Diversion AD	Birmingham Wellesbourne Mountford

Coventry	ATIS	APP	RAD
	126.050	119.250	123.825

TWR	GND	FIRE
119.250 118.175	121.700	121.600

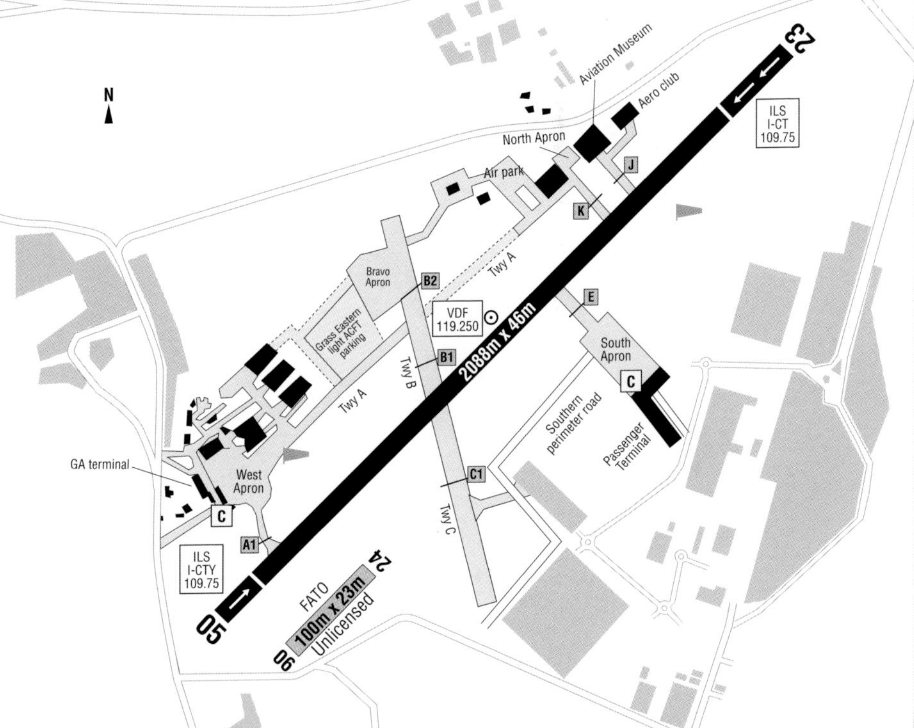

RWY	SURFACE	TORA	LDA	U/L	LIGHTING
05	Asphalt	1615	1795		Ap Thr Rwy PAPI 3° LHS
23	Asphalt	1825	1615		Ap Thr Rwy PAPI 3° LHS
FATO 06/24	Grass			100x23	Nil

RNAV			
HON	113.65	087	6.7

Remarks

PPR essential ACFT <500kgs not permitted. Circuit and instrument training is to be pre-booked with ATC. Non-radio ACFT join overhead at 1500ft QNH. Helicopter training flights operating at 700ft QFE and below might not comply with normal R/T procedure. Helicopter circuits will normally operate from a grass area (as directed by ATC) circuit height 700ft QFE (except at night when main Rwy is used). Pilots required to book-out by telephone. An ATC GMC service in use during busy periods when notified by NOTAM. GMC is for booking out. A careful lookout should be maintained at all times. ATC instructions will specify the taxi route to be followed. Light ACFT are to self manoeuvre for parking only if instructed by ATC.

Aids to Navigation: NDB CT 363.50

Warnings

Turbulence on short finals Rwy23 in SW winds. Helicopter Ops N Rwy23 APP 3.5nm from touchdown. Adhere to standard RTF procedures. Regular bird scaring. Due to close proximity of Birmingham AD, pilots must ensure their flight remains clear of Birmingham CTR/CTZ, unless ATC clearance is issued.

Operating Hrs H24

Circuits 05 RH, 23 LH
Circuits to SE 1000ft QFE

Landing Fee £12 per tonne or part there of
Circuit & Instrument training
50% discount for PPR/Training

Maintenance
Aerotech **Tel:** 02476 306888

Fuel AVGAS JET A1 100LL

Disabled Facilities Available

Restaurants Refreshments available in passenger & GA terminal

Taxis	
PABT	**Tel:** 02476 304777
Car Hire	
Avis	**Tel:** 02476 225500
National	**Tel:** 02476 677042
Hertz	**Tel:** 02476 251741
Weather Info	M T9 Fax 266 MWC ATIS **Tel:** 024 7633 2668

Operator West Midlands International Airport Ltd
Coventry Airport South
Coventry, CV8 3AZ
Tel: 02476 308600 (Admin)
Tel: 02476 308638 (ATC)
Fax: 02476 882669 (ATC)
info@coventryairport.co.uk
www.coventryairport.co.uk

Visual Reference Points (VRP)

Bitteswell Industrail Estate	N5227.47 W00114.78
Cement Works	N5216.35 W00123.07
Draycott Water	N5219.57 W00119.58
Nuneaton (Disused AD)	N5233.90 W00126.88

Coventry Noise Procedures

The tracks are to be flown by all departing jet ACFT and all other ACFT of more than 5700kg MTWA, unless instructed by ATC. After take-off all ACFT must ensure they are at a minimum heights of 500ft aal before starting any turn.
Rwy05: Climb on track to CT, after passing CT, turn on track or as instructed by ATC.
Training ACFT in circuit as above, then turn right cross wind
Rwy23 southerly depts: Climb straight ahead to 500ft aal, turn left onto150° (M), on reaching 1000ft aal turn onto track or as instructed by ATC.
Rwy23 northerly depts: Climb straight ahead to 500ft aal, turn left onto 215° (M). After crossing HON 115° (HON DME 5.5) turn on track or as instructed by ATC.
Training ACFT in circuit: As southerly depts, but continue on150° (M), until 1500ft aal, then complete left turn downwind.

All pilots must avoid over flying Binley Woods and Stoneleigh.

Effective date:25/09/08

71ft 2mb	10nm S of St Andrews N5616.08 W00236.33	PPR	Alternative AD	Dundee Fife

Non-Radio	LARS Leuchars 126.500	Safetycom 135.475

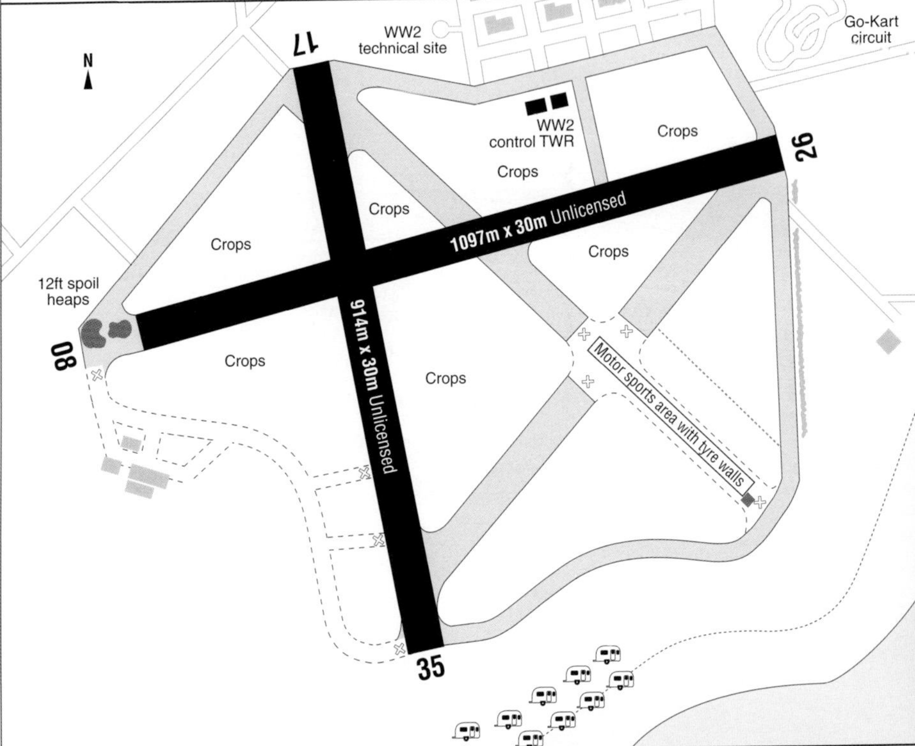

RWY	SURFACE	TORA	LDA	U/L	LIGHTING
08/26	Asphalt			1097x30	Nil
17/35	Asphalt			914x30	Nil

Rwy22/04 914x30m & Rwy31/13 914x30m are useable but normally obstructed by motorsport

RNAV			
SAB	112.50	333	25.6

Remarks

PPR by telephone essential. Visiting ACFT welcome at pilots own risk. AD was WW2 FAA base and Rwys are in good condition. There are many historically interesting AD buildings. AD has a coastal location. AD is used for location shoots for feature films

Warnings

AD has many uses unconnected with aviation, many of which are motor sport related. This often results in the closure or restriction in length of Rwy at short notice. Rwys shown on AD diagram as useable cannot be guaranteed without a briefing on day of visit.
Caution: Parachuting at Kingsmuir 3.5nm W

Operating Hrs	SR-SS
Circuits	LH 1000ft QFE
Landing Fee	£15
Maintenance	Nil
Fuel	Nil

Disabled Facilities

Restaurants	Nil
Taxis/Car Hire	Nil
Weather Info	Air Sc GWC

Operator
William Robertson
Balcomie Road
Crail, Fife, KY10 3XL
Tel: 01333 451839
Fax: 01333 451842
m3@sol.co.uk
www.crailthrash.co.uk

C

EGTC CRANFIELD

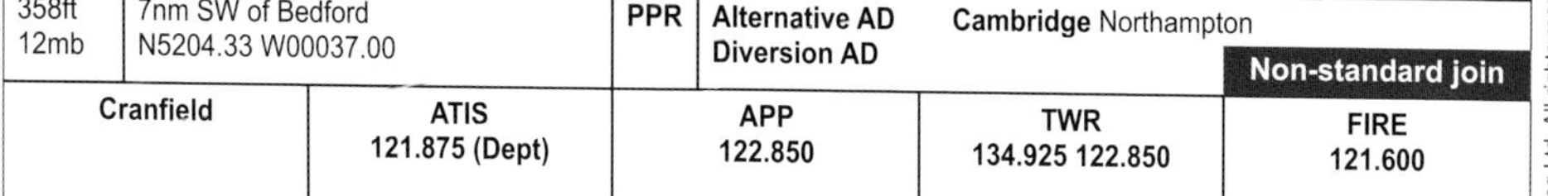

358ft 12mb	7nm SW of Bedford N5204.33 W00037.00	PPR	Alternative AD Diversion AD	Cambridge Northampton Non-standard join

Cranfield	ATIS	APP	TWR	FIRE
	121.875 (Dept)	122.850	134.925 122.850	121.600

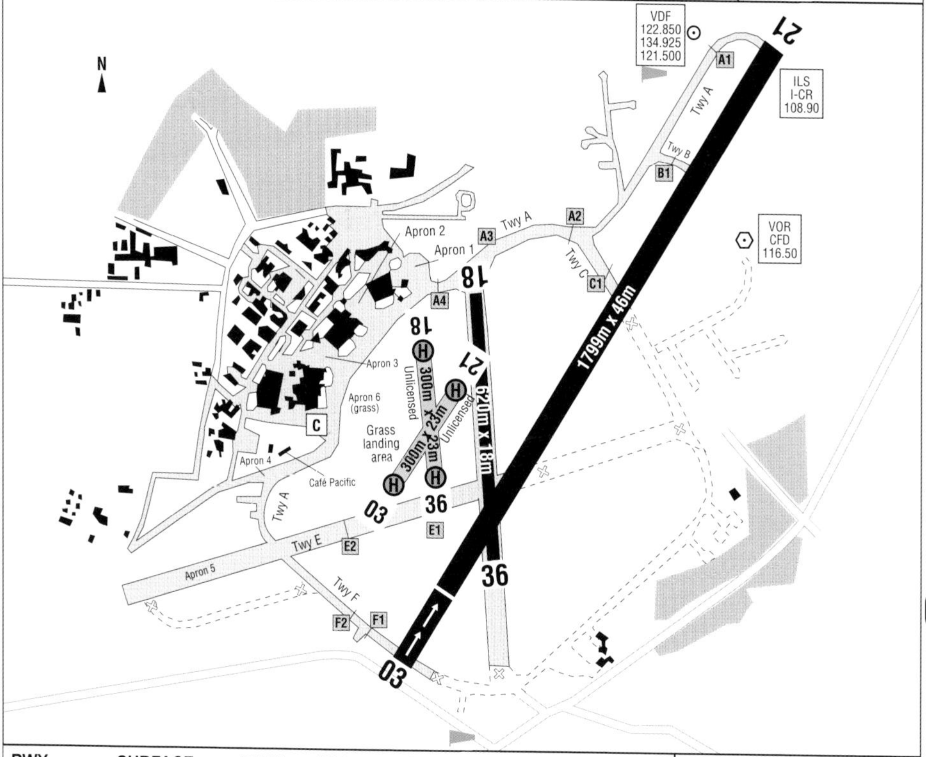

RWY	SURFACE	TORA	LDA	U/L	LIGHTING
03	Asphalt	1799	1594		Nil
21	Asphalt	1672	1672		Ap Thr Rwy PAPI 3° LHS
18/36	Asphalt	620	620		Nil
03/21	Grass			300x23	Nil
18/36	Grass			300x23	Nil

Rwy21 licensed for night use

RNAV		
CFD	116.50	On AD

Remarks

PPR to instrument training, instrument test & circuit training flights. Non-radio ACFT not permitted. Hi-Vis. Slots allocated by ATC must be adhered to. PPR day of flight only. No standard overhead joins, no dead side due heli circuits all Rwys. Instrument training: ACFT no go-around below 400ft agl without ATC clearance, especially Rwy03 active opposite direction. VFR traffic join via VRP. Rwy18 light ACFT day only. All helis must request start-up clearance. 12 Hrs notice Customs, details to ATC only.

Aids to Navigation: NDB CIT 850.00

Warnings

Intensive flight training AD. S 300m of Rwy18/36 unfit-use. Helicopter operations on grass area NW of main Rwy intersection. All fixed wing ACFT entering/exiting the grass via N Twy to use concrete entry/exit points. Windshear may be experienced Dept Rwy36, Arr Rwy18.

Caution: Twy E congested with parked ACFT, min wing tip clearance may not be available

Noise: Avoid over flying all buildings and structures 1500m W of disused Rwy below 500ft QFE.

Operating Hrs	Mon-Fri 0830-1900 Sat-Sun & PH 0900-1800 Extensions by arr **Tel:** 01234 754784
Circuits	Fixed wing day 800ft QFE Night 1200ft QFE
Landing Fee	On application
Maintenance	Various
Fuel	AVGAS 100LL JET A1

Disabled Facilities

Handling	**Tel:** 01234 752220/754789 **Fax:** 01234 752221/754785	**Operator**	Cranfield University Cranfield Beds, MK43 0AL **Tel:** 01234 754784 (Admin) **Tel:** 01234 754761 (ATC) **Fax:** 01234 754785 (ATC) **Fax:** 01234 751805 (Admin) airport@cranfield.ac.uk www.cranfieldairport.co.uk
Restaurants	Café Pacific Restaurant/Bar Mon-Fri 0800-1700 Sat 0900-1600 Sun 1000-1400 **Tel:** 01234 754611		
Taxis	**Tel:** 01234 750005		
Car Hire			
Budget	**Tel:** 01908 373111		
Hertz	**Tel:** 01908 374492		
Weather Info	M T9 Fax 268 A MOEx		
Visual Reference Points (VRP)			
Olney Town (Rwy03, 18 & 36 only)	N5209.20 W00042.10		
Stewartby Brickworks	N5204.40 W00031.05		
Woburn Town	N5159.40 W00037.15		

C

218ft 7mb	3nm N of Sleaford N5301.82 W00028.99	PPR MIL	**Alternative AD** East Midlands Syerston **Diversion AD**

Cranwell	ATIS 131.175	Zone/APP 119.375	TWR 125.050

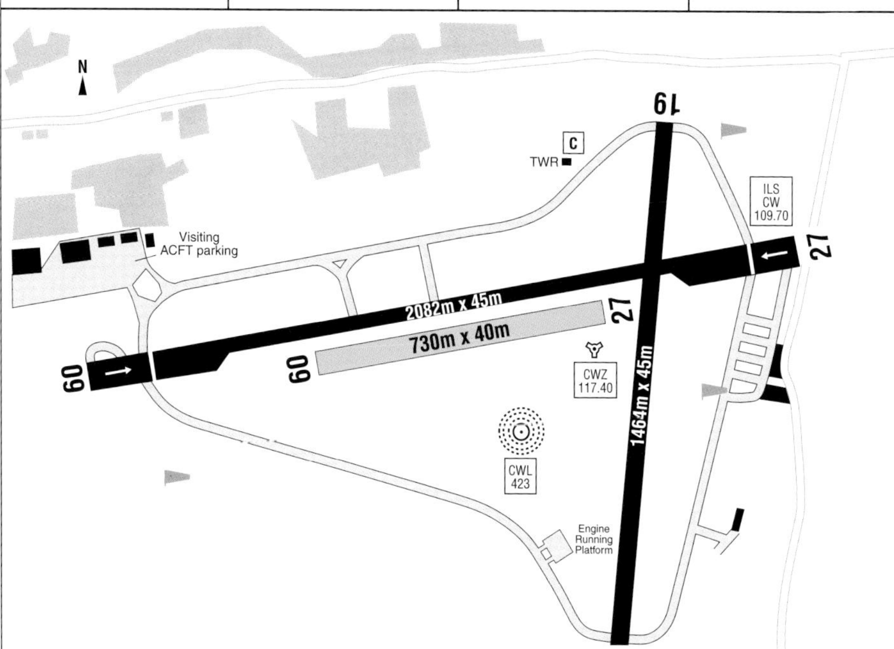

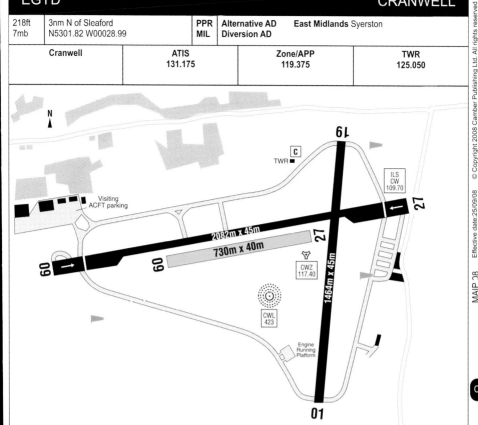

RWY	SURFACE	TORA	LDA	U/L	LIGHTING
09	Asph/Conc	2082	1918		Ap Thr Rwy PAPI 3°
27	Asph/Conc	2082	1989		Ap Thr Rwy PAPI 3°
01/19	Asph/Conc	1464	1464		Thr Rwy PAPI 3°
09/27	Grass			730x40	Nil

RNAV			
GAM	112.80	136	22.5

Remarks

Grass AD N of main AD is for glider ops only. ACFT inbound to either Cranwell or Barkston Heath are to call Cranwell APP at least 5nm before the boundary of the Cranwell/Barkston Heath CMATZ. ACFT must adhere to slot times. Light ACFT may operate outside normal operating times using A/G. Visiting ACFT note there is a grass strip S of and parallel to Rwy09/27 active with ACFT not using RTF.

Visual aid to location: Abn White; Ibn CW Red.

Warnings

Public roads cross APP to all Rwys. Motorised glider towing up to 3000ft and winch launching up to 2000ft takes place on the grass AD to N of main AD during daylight Hrs evenings & weekends. ATZ active H24.

Noise: On Dept climb straight ahead to 1000ft QFE before turning, avoiding all local villages.

Operating Hrs As required
ATZ active H24

Circuits 27 LH, 09 RH, 01 & 19 variable
CCT 1000ft QFE, Light ACT 800ft AFE

Landing Fee Charges in accordance with MOD policy
Contact Station Ops for details

Maintenance Nil

Fuel AVGAS 100LL AVTUR FS11
By arr min notice of 24Hrs
& max uplift of 500Imp Galls

Disabled Facilities

Restaurants Nil

Taxis/Car Hire Nil

Weather Info Air Cen MOEx

Operator RAF Cranwell College
Sleaford
Lincs NG34 8HB
Tel: 01400 267377
Fax: 01400 267339

190ft 6mb	2.75nm SSE of Cromer N5253.30 E00119.06	PPR	**Alternative AD** **Norwich** Old Buckenham **Diversion AD**

Cromer	ATIS Norwich 128.625	LARS Norwich 119.350	A/G 129.825

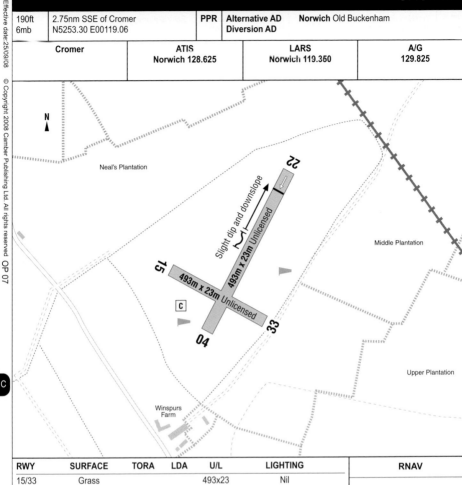

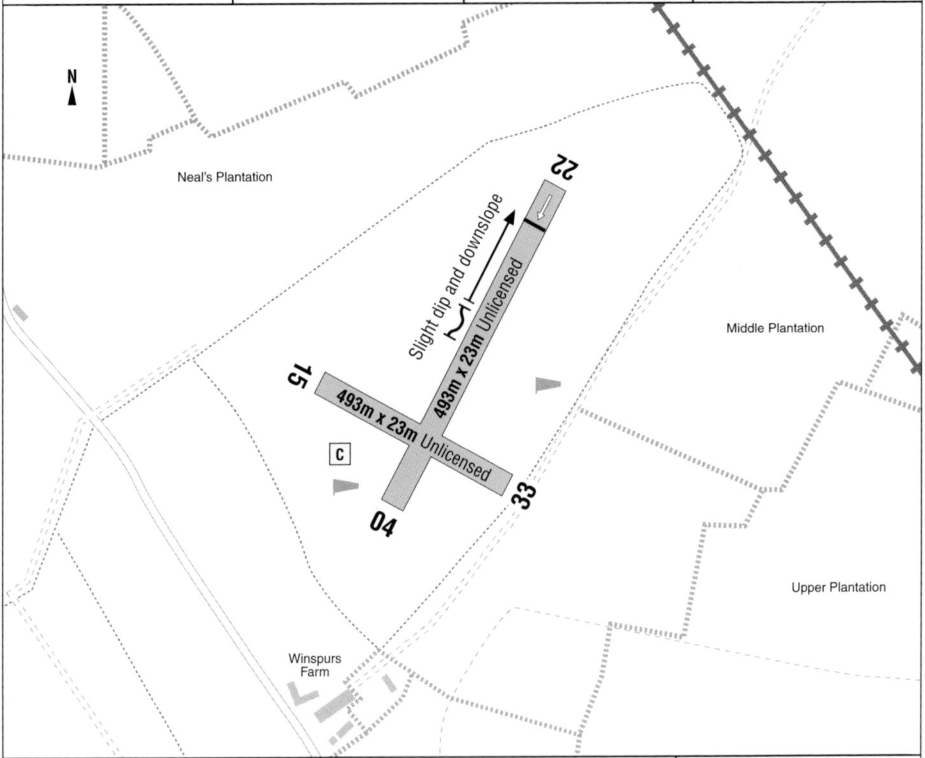

RWY	SURFACE	TORA	LDA	U/L	LIGHTING
15/33	Grass			493x23	Nil
04/22	Grass			493x23	Nil
Displaced Thr Rwy22 125m					

RNAV

Remarks
PPR essential for briefing required. Light flying machines welcome at pilots own risk. Extensive microlight and paramotor activity at AD. Military and civil helicopter training may take place at short notice. Any training is by strict arrangement only. Intensive military & civil low flying in the area including off-shore civil helicopters, Model ACFT flying may take place weekdays. All visiting ACFT must book each flight in and out. Ample parking and camping space.

Warnings
A public footpath runs E/W along S airfield boundary. There are cables on the railway line to E of field. Cables marked with day-glow markers. SAR helicopters may operate from AD. Heavy SAR helicopters landing area on Rwy04/22. Civil and military helicopter under slung load training may take place on weekdays.
Noise: No known sensitive areas, avoid over flying the farm SW of AD and the local area below 500ft QFE.

Operating Hrs	SR-SS & by arrangement
Circuits	Available
Landing Fee	Private £5 Microlights £4 Private Twin/Heli £10 Commercial on application
Maintenance	Nil
Fuel	MOGAS
Disabled Facilities	Nil
Restaurants	Snacks available on AD, Pub in village
Accomodation	Camping and B&B available on AD
Taxis	
A1 Cabs	**Tel:** 01263 513371
ACE	**Tel:** 01263 511749

Car Hire	Available in Cromer
Bike Hire	Available in Northreps
Weather Info	Air S MOEx
Operator	Chris Gurney Heath Cottage Northrepps, Cromer Norfolk, NR27 9LB **Tel:** 01263 513015 **Tel:** 07886 264992 **Fax:** 01263515516 northrepps@hotmail.com www.northreppsaerodrome.co.uk

201ft 7mb	4nm ESE of Stowmarket N5210.27 E00106.66	PPR	Alternative AD Diversion AD	Cambridge Elmsett

Non-standard join

Crowfield	APP Wattisham 125.800	A/G 122.775

RWY	SURFACE	TORA	LDA	U/L	LIGHTING
13/31	Grass			768x27	Nil

RNAV			
CLN	114.55	359	19.4

Remarks

PPR by telephone only. No multi engined ACFT. No singles more than 148kw/1200kgs AUW. No Gliders, Microlights or Helicopters. Total daily movements restricted. Arr must contact Wattisham APP when at least 15nm from Wattisham. Dept unless otherwise instructed ACFT must fly not above 800ft QFE while under Wattisham MATZ. Contact Wattisham before take-off if possible or ASAP after take-off.

Warnings

Noise: Please operate with consideration, this AD is in a noise sensitive area, avoid all local villages.

Operating Hrs 0800-1900 (Summer)
0900-1800 or SS (Winter)

Circuits LH 800ft QFE

Landing Fee £10

Maintenance Nil

Fuel AVGAS 100LL
Oils W100 W80 100 80 W15W-50

Disabled Facilities

Restaurants Coffee & tea available

Taxis Stowmarket — By arr or **Tel:** 01449 677777

Car Hire By arr

Weather Info Air S MOEx

Operator Mr A C Williamson
Crowfield Aerodrome
Coddenham Green, Ipswich
Suffolk, IP6 9UN
Tel: 01449 711017
Fax: 01449 711054

10ft 0mb	4nm S of Spalding (On Crowland Rd) N5242.53 W00008.57	PPR	Alternative AD	Cambridge Fenland

Non-standard join

Crowland	LARS Cottesmore 130.200	A/G 129.975

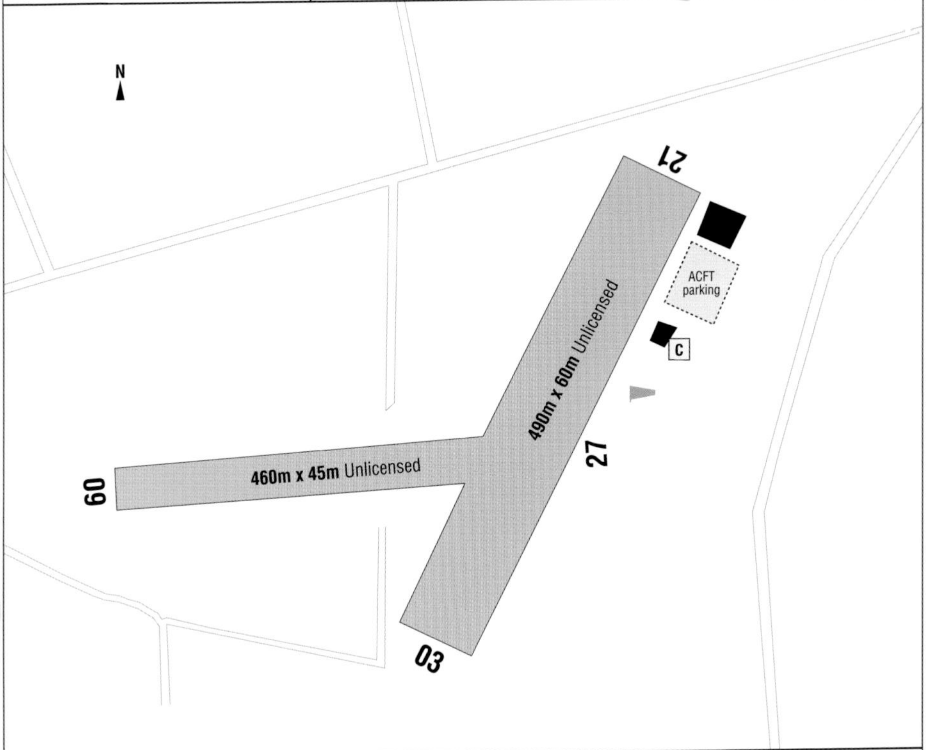

N
21
ACFT parking
C
490m x 60m Unlicensed
27
460m x 45m Unlicensed
09
03

RWY	SURFACE	TORA	LDA	U/L	LIGHTING
03/21	Grass			490x60	Nil
09/27	Grass			460x45	Nil

RNAV

Remarks

PPR by telephone. Visitors welcome at pilot's own risk. Good APP. Frequent aero-tow glider flying. RAF Wittering MATZ panhandle begins 5nm WSW of Crowland.

Warnings

Intensive military low-flying activity Mon-Fri in the vicinity. Mast 200 ft agl situated S of Crowland. AD surface rough in places.

Operating Hrs	SR-SS
Circuits	Variable 800-1000 QFE
Landing Fee	Nil
Maintenance	Nil
Fuel	Nil
Disabled Facilities	Nil
Restaurants	Light refreshments when gliding in progress
Taxis/Car Hire	**Tel:** 01775 711122
Weather Info	Air S MOEx

Operator Peterborough & Spalding Gliding Club
Postland, Crowland
Lincs, PE6 0JW
Tel: 07913 945634
www.psgc.co.uk

C

CUCKOO TYE FARM

240ft 8mb	2nm N of Sudbury N5204.50 E00045.50	PPR	Alternative AD	Southend Elmsett

Non-Radio	APP Wattisham 125.800	Safetycom 135.475

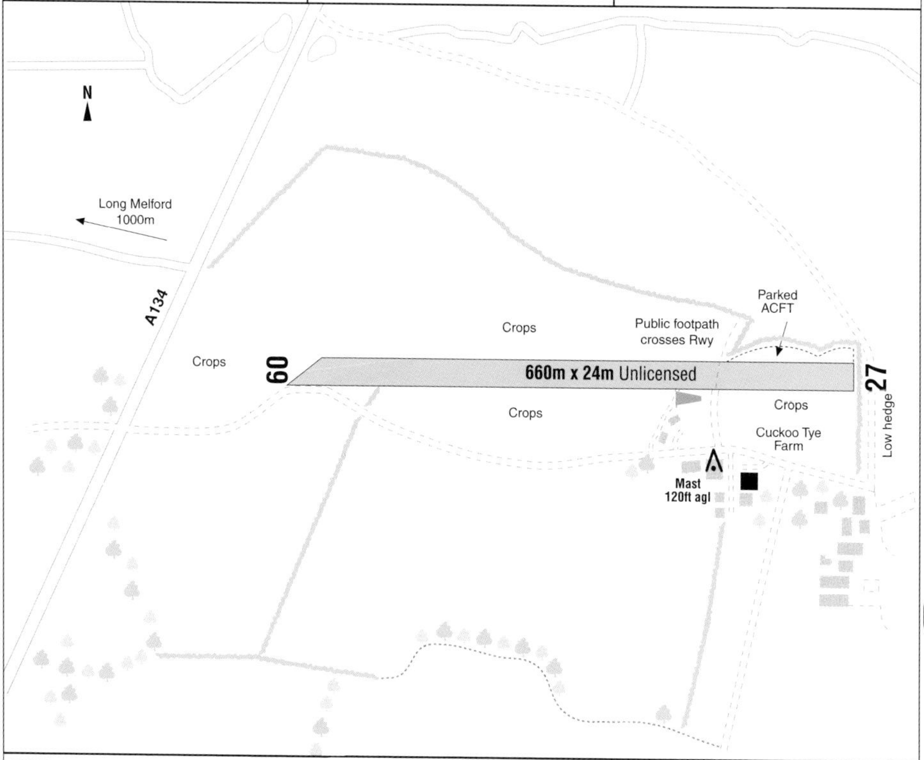

N
Long Melford
1000m
A134
Crops
09
660m x 24m Unlicensed
27
Crops
Public footpath crosses Rwy
Parked ACFT
Crops
Crops
Cuckoo Tye Farm
Low hedge
Mast
120ft agl

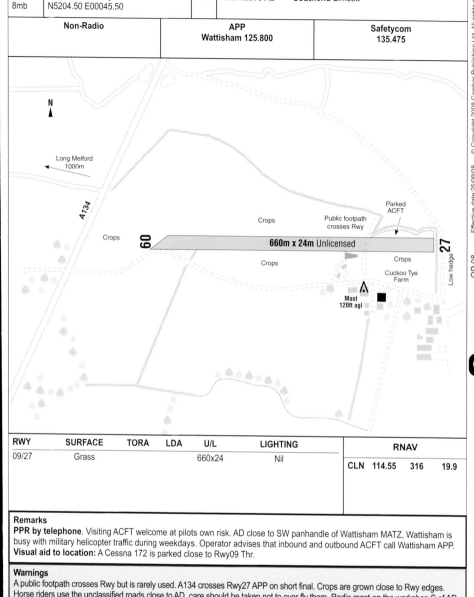

RWY	SURFACE	TORA	LDA	U/L	LIGHTING
09/27	Grass			660x24	Nil

RNAV			
CLN	114.55	316	19.9

Remarks
PPR by telephone. Visiting ACFT welcome at pilots own risk. AD close to SW panhandle of Wattisham MATZ, Wattisham is busy with military helicopter traffic during weekdays. Operator advises that inbound and outbound ACFT call Wattisham APP.
Visual aid to location: A Cessna 172 is parked close to Rwy09 Thr.

Warnings
A public footpath crosses Rwy but is rarely used. A134 crosses Rwy27 APP on short final. Crops are grown close to Rwy edges. Horse riders use the unclassified roads close to AD, care should be taken not to over fly them. Radio mast on the workshop S of AD.
Noise: Avoid local houses, particularly Long Melford.

Operating Hrs	SR-SS
Circuits	LH 1000ft QFE
Landing Fee	Nil
Maintenance	Nil
Fuel	Nil
Disabled Facilities	Nil
Restaurants	Nil
Taxi SCC	 **Tel:** 01787 373222
Car Hire	Nil
Weather Info	Air Cen MOEx

Operator
Mr P J Miller
Cuckoo Tye Farm
Acton, Sudbury
Suffolk, CO10 0AE
Tel: 01787 377233
Tel/Fax: 01787 881706
peter@cuckootye.co.uk

EGDR CULDROSE

267ft 9mb	1nm SE of Helston N5005.17 W00515.34	PPR MIL	Alternative AD Diversion AD	St Mawgan Lands End

Non-standard join

Culdrose	LARS	APP	RAD	TWR	GND
	134.050	134.050	123.300 122.100	122.100 123.300	122.100

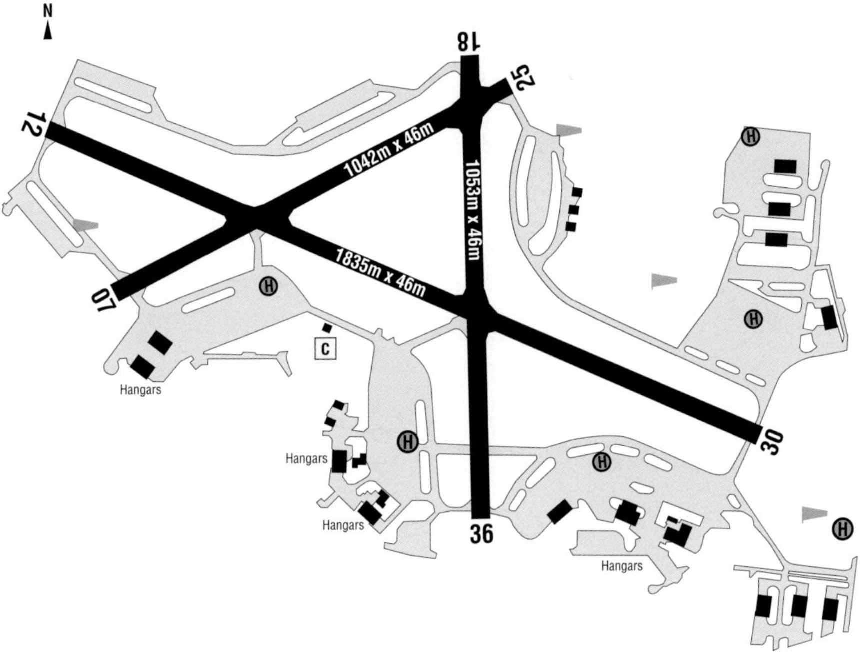

N
18
25
12
1042m x 46m
1053m x 46m
1835m x 46m
07
30
36
C
Hangars
Hangars
Hangars
Hangars

RWY	SURFACE	TORA	LDA	U/L	LIGHTING
07/25	Asphalt	1042	1042		Ap Rwy PAPI 3°
12/30	Asphalt	1835	1832		Ap Rwy PAPI 3°
18/36	Asphalt	1053	1053		Ap Rwy PAPI 3°

RNAV			
LND	114.20	106	15.0

Remarks
PPR 24Hrs required. Inbound ACFT to contact Culdrose APP at 20nm.
Visual aid to location: Ibn CU Red.

Warnings
High intensity fixed wing and helicopter operations in the area and at Preddannack. Glider launching at weekends and evenings. More than one Rwy may be used simultaneously. No visual signals.
Noise: Avoid over flying Helston

Operating Hrs Mon-Thu 0830-1700 Fri 0830-1400 or SS (L)
Circuits Variable 1000ft AFE
No dead side
Landing Fee Charges in accordance with MOD policy
Contact Station Ops for details
Maintenance Nil
Fuel AVGAS 100LL JET A1
By arr

Disabled Facilities

Restaurants Nil
Taxis/Car Hire Nil

Weather Info M T Fax 272 MOEx
Operator RNAS Culdrose
Helston
Cornwall
TR12 7RH
Tel: 01326 574121 Ex 2415 (ATC)
Tel: 01326 574121 Ex 2417 (PPR)
Tel: 01326 574121 Ex 2201 (OPS)

350ft 13mb	16nm NE of Glasgow N5558.48 W00358.53	PPR	**Alternative AD** **Diversion AD**	**Glasgow** Fife

Cumbernauld	A/G 120.600

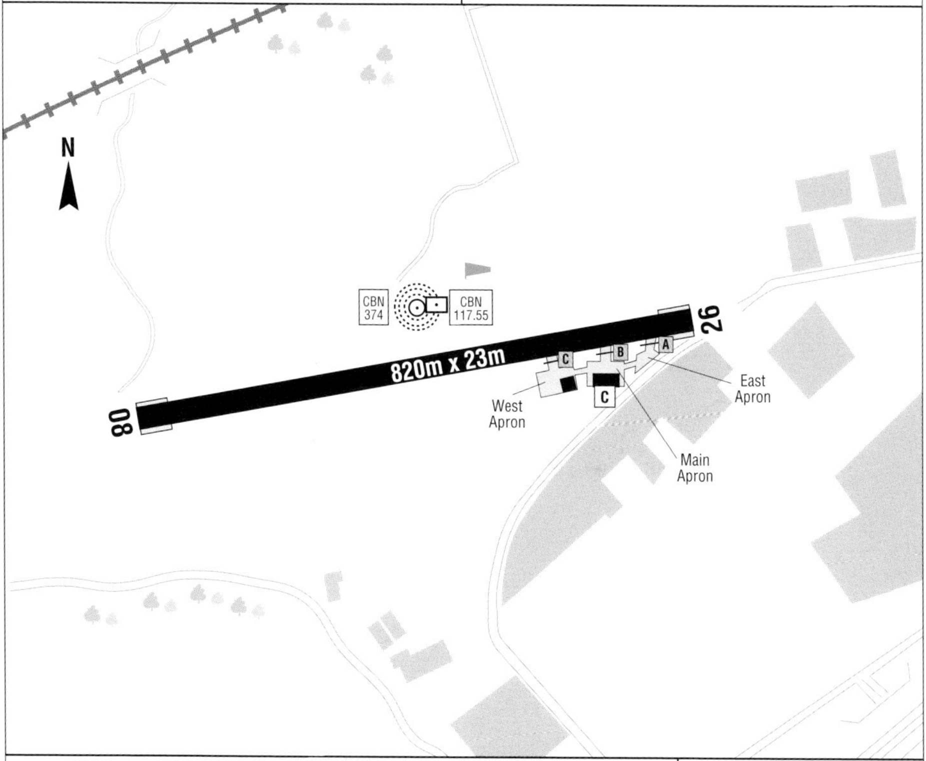

N
CBN 374
CBN 117.55
820m x 23m
08
26
A
B
C
C
West Apron
East Apron
Main Apron

RWY	SURFACE	TORA	LDA	U/L	LIGHTING
08	Asphalt	820	820		Thr Rwy APAPI 4° LHS
26	Asphalt	820	820		Thr Rwy APAPI 3.5° LHS

RNAV			
GOW	115.40	074	17.0

Remarks
Certain customs facilities available. In IFR, suitably equipped ACFT may let down at Edinburgh and proceed to Cumbernauld VMC.
Visual aids to location: White strobe on roof of Control TWR, available on request. If no reply on A/G observe signal square, proceed with overhead join and make A/G standard calls.

Warnings
AD is situated under Scottish TMA. Traffic in transit should anticipate local circuit activity at this AD. Microlight flying takes place at AD.
Noise: Avoid over flying the villages of Dullatur 0.75nm W of AD, Banton, High Banton and Kelvinhead all N of AD.

Operating Hrs 0800-1900 (Summer)
0900-1700 (Winter) & by arr

Circuits 26 RH, 08 LH, 1000ft QFE
Join overhead 2000ft QFE
descend on dead side to join circuit

Landing Fee Visitors < 3000kgs: Single £18.75 Twin 46.89
Local Club: Single £11.40
Other ACFT/helicopters call for rates

Maintenance Cormack Aircraft Services Ltd
Tel: 01236 457777
info@cormackaircraft.com

Fuel AVGAS JET A1 100LL available operating hrs
All major credit cards accepted

Disabled Facilities

Restaurant Coffee Shop 1000-1600 (L)

Taxis
Central **Tel:** 01236 722772

Car Hire
Arnold Clark **Tel:** 01236 731856

Weather Info Air Sc GWC

Operator Cumbernauld Airport Ltd
216 Duncan Macintosh Road
Cumbernauld
Glasgow
Lanarkshire G68 0HH
Tel: 01236 722100 (AD)
Tel: 01236 722822 (ATC)
Fax: 01236 781646
info@cumbernauldairport.org

XCUR CURROCK HILL

800ft 26mb	8nm SW of Newcastle Airport N5456.03 W00150.73	PPR	Alternative AD	Newcastle Eshott

Non-standard join

Currock Base	APP Newcastle 124.375	A/G 130.125

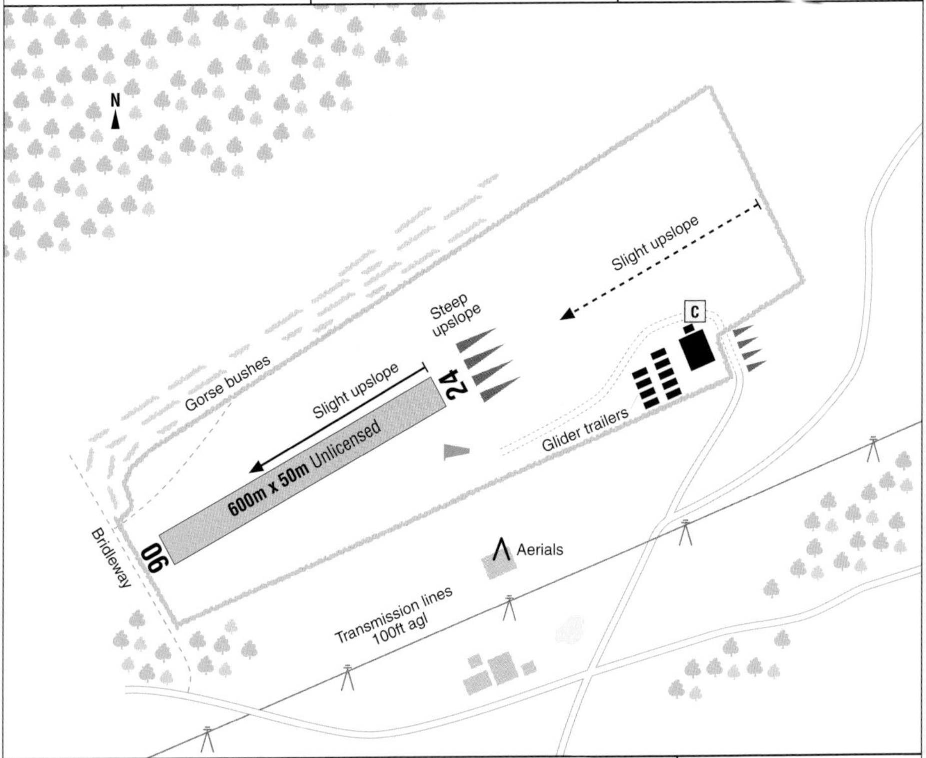

RWY	SURFACE	TORA	LDA	U/L	LIGHTING
06/24	Grass			600x50	Nil

RNAV			
NEW	114.25	223	8.1

Remarks

PPR and briefing by telephone. Primarily a gliding site but light ACFT welcome at pilot's own risk. The whole of the field (90 acres) is used for gliding but only the strip shown is recommended for visitors. AD is situated within Newcastle CTR, clearance to enter must be obtained from Newcastle APP.

Warnings

When Rwy24 in use do not land short of the windsock due to steep upslope to Thr and possible wind shadow effect. Slight upslope to Rwy24. Gliders launch with winch and aero tow. Launch positions may not be co-located.

Operating Hrs Sat-Sun & Wed 0900-SS (L) & by arr

Circuits Powered ACFT to S 800ft QFE gliders variable

Landing Fee Private £5 Commercial £10

Maintenance Nil

Fuel AVGAS 100LL by prior arr

Disabled Facilities Nil

Restaurants

Tea, coffee & snacks available when gliding in progress

Four Seasons **Tel:** 01207 561208 (10 min walk)

Taxis **Tel:** 0191 4131143

Car Hire Nil

Weather Info Air N MOEx

Operator

Northumbria Gliding Club Ltd
Currock Hill
Chopwell
Newcastle
Northumberland NE17 7AX
Tel: 01207 561286
info@northumbria.flyer.co.uk
www.northumbria-gliding-club.co.uk

DAMYNS HALL

56ft 2mb	2nm S of Upminster N5131.77 E00014.73	PPR	Alternative AD	**Southend** Stapleford

Hornchurch Radio	LARS Farnborough East 123.225	APP Thames Radar 132.700	A/G 119.550

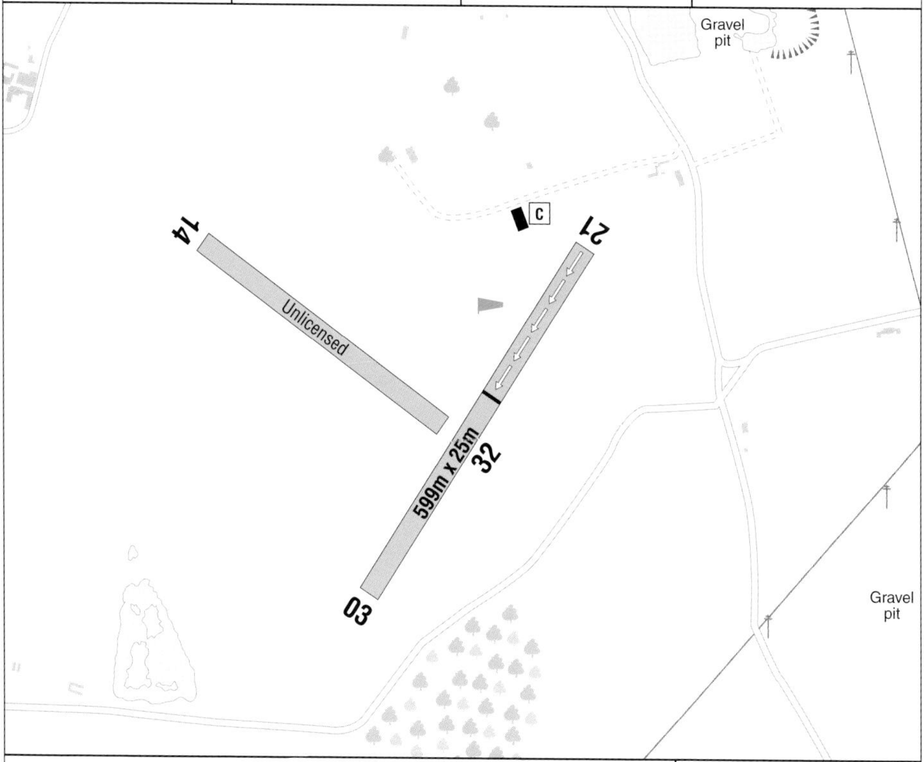

RWY	SURFACE	TORA	LDA	U/L	LIGHTING
03	Grass	341	595		Nil
21	Grass	595	341		Nil
14/32	Grass				Nil

RNAV

Remarks

Strict PPR by telephone. Visitors welcome at own risk. Helicopter joining procedures available with PPR. Hangar space available on request.

Warnings

Uphill slope Rwy03, prefered landing in light winds. AD close to London City CTA Class D Airspace – 1nm W of AD. London City CTR Class D Airspace 2.3nm W of AD. ACFT must contact London City APP before entering the ATZ. Gerpins Farm Airfield 0.6nm W of AD. Thurrock 4.6nm E of AD. Keep good look out for ACFT using these AD.
Noise: Avoid over flying the following villages surrounding the AD. Rainham SW of AD. South Ockendon SE of AD. Hornchurch NW of AD. Aveley S of AD. Upminster N of AD.

Operating Hrs	Thu-Sun 1000-1700 (Summer) Fri-Sun 1000-1600 (Winter)
Circuits	21 LH, 03 RH 1000ft QFE
Landing Fee	Available with PPR
Maintenance	Nil
Fuel	AVGAS JET A1

Disabled Facilities

Restaurants	Café on AD open daily
Taxi/Car Hire	Nil
Weather Info	Air SE MOEx
Operator	Damyns Hall Aerodrome Aveley Road Hornchurch Essex RM14 2TN **Tel:** 01708 556000

Effective date:28/08/08 OP 08

XDAV — DAVIDSTOW MOOR

969ft 33mb	3nm ENE of Camelford N5038.25 W00437.13	PPR	**Alternative AD** **Plymouth** Bodmin **Diversion AD**

Non radio	LARS St Mawgan 128.725	A/G 129.825 (Microlight freq)	Safetycom 135.475

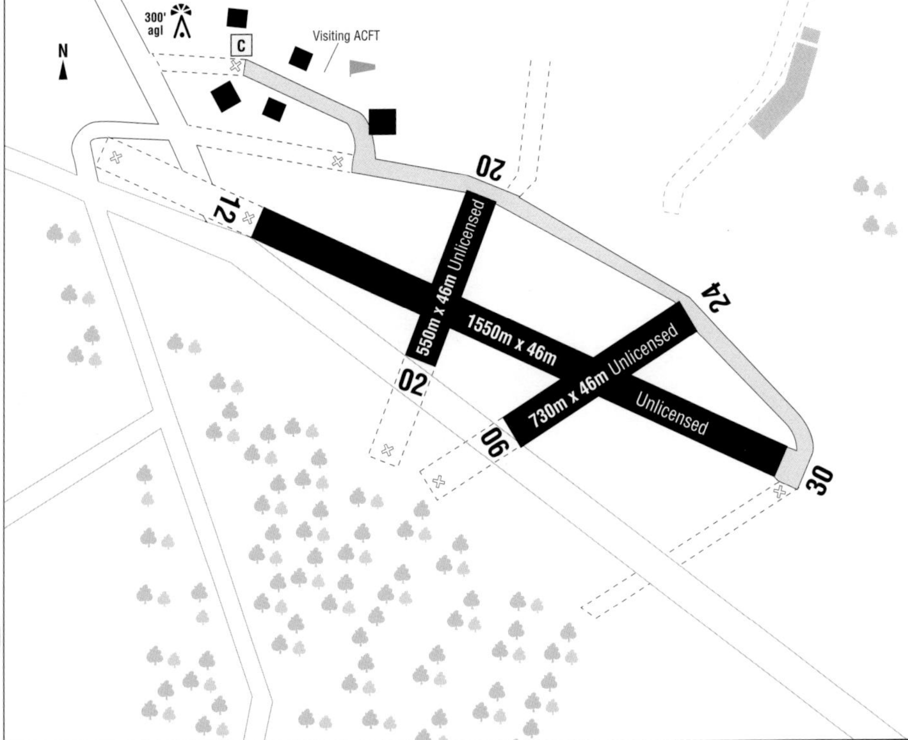

RWY	SURFACE	TORA	LDA	U/L	LIGHTING
12/30	Concrete			1550x46	Nil
06/24	Concrete			730x46	Nil
02/20	Concrete			550x46	Nil

RNAV

Remarks
Strict PPR by telephone. Microlights and SLMG's only, no light ACFT. Situated on unfenced moorland. Windsock displayed when flying in progress. Beware of livestock and people on Rwys. Gliding site. Microlight activity at any time, using Rwy12/30.

Warnings
A road running SE/NW bisects the AD. Only Rwy to NE of road are useable. Radio TWR 236ft aal in NW corner of AD, 200m from signals square.
Noise: Avoid over flying villages and factory NW and wood to S of AD.

Operating Hrs	0800-1700 (Summer) +1Hr (Winter)
Circuits	All S
Landing Fee	£5 for temporary membership
Maintenance	For microlights
Fuel	Nil
Disabled Facilities	Nil
Restaurants	Available in Camelford 1m NW
Taxis	**Tel:** 01840 213867
Car Hire	Nil
Weather Info	Air SW MOEx

Operator
Davidstow Flying Club Ltd
Davidstow Airfield
Camelford
Cornwall PL32 9YF
Tel: 01840 261517

60ft 2mb	5nm E of Lewes N5052.73 E00009.38	**PPR**	**Alternative AD** **Shoreham** Lashenden

Non-standard join

Deanland	A/G 129.725 (not always manned)

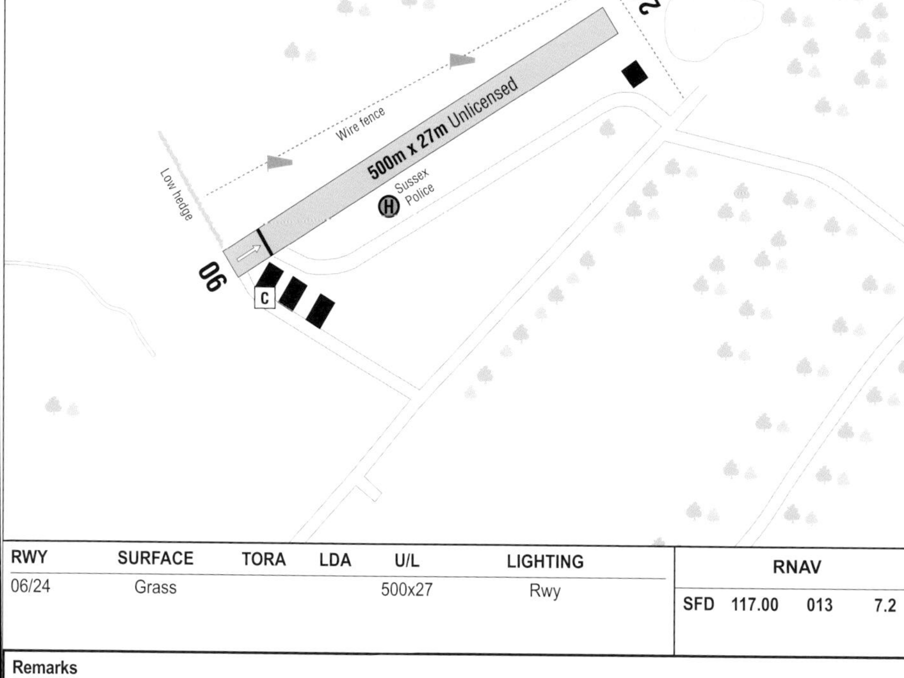

RWY	SURFACE	TORA	LDA	U/L	LIGHTING
06/24	Grass			500x27	Rwy

RNAV			
SFD	**117.00**	**013**	**7.2**

Remarks
PPR by telephone. No flexwing microlights. Available for single-engined ACFT only. Considerate pilots welcome at own risk but ACFT performance must be compatible with the length of the strip and pilot must have short field experience. Please enter flight details in movements book at the 'Control Point'. ACFT insurance must cover operational risks at strips. No local or training flights. **Arr:** large circuits with a minimum of 1.5nm final maintaining the Rwy centre line. **Under no circumstances cut the corners. Dept:** Climb accurately maintaining Rwy centre line for 1.5nm before turning on track. **Under no circumstances make early turns.**

Warnings
After prolonged or heavy rainfall the Rwy will become water logged, please check by phone. Make blind calls if radio unmanned. Model ACFT flying takes place on AD. Police helicopter operations may occur at any time
Caution: Private strip 1nm from end of Rwy24 to SW.
Noise: Do not over fly any local houses, the caravan park and village of Ripe

Operating Hrs SR-SS
Circuits O6 LH, 24 RH, 1000ft QFE
Landing Fee Private £10
Over night park £5, Commercial by arr.
Maintenance
David Hockings **Tel:** 07710 329369
Fuel Nil
Disabled Facilities Nil
Restaurant Nil
Taxis
Becks **Tel:** 01273 483838
Car Hire Nil

Weather Info Air SE MOEx
Operator Messrs Brook & Price
Deanland Airfield
c/o DJ Brook, BCL House
Gatwick Road, Crawley
Sussex RH10 9AX
Tel: 01323 811410 (AD)
Tel: 07785 316368
Tel: 01323 811858
Tel: 01903 774379
Fax: 01293 429836
david@gatwick-group.co.uk
www.deanland-airfield.co.uk

Effective date:28/08/08 OP 08

DEBACH

180ft 6mb	3nm NW of Woodbridge N5208.11 E00116.16	PPR	Alternative AD	**Norwich** Crowfield

Non-Radio	APP Wattisham 125.800	Safetycom 135.475

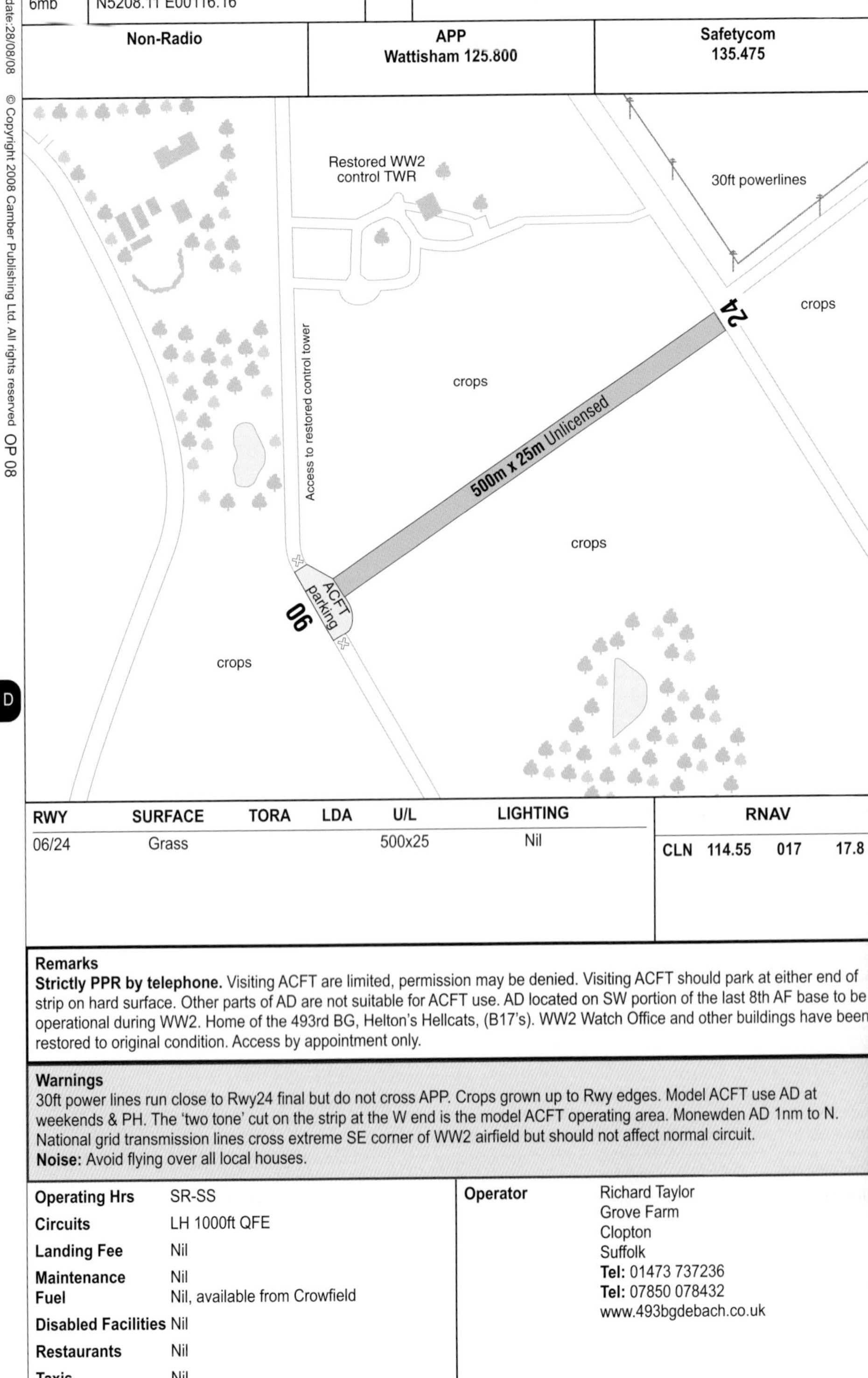

RWY	SURFACE	TORA	LDA	U/L	LIGHTING
06/24	Grass			500x25	Nil

RNAV			
CLN	114.55	017	17.8

Remarks

Strictly PPR by telephone. Visiting ACFT are limited, permission may be denied. Visiting ACFT should park at either end of strip on hard surface. Other parts of AD are not suitable for ACFT use. AD located on SW portion of the last 8th AF base to be operational during WW2. Home of the 493rd BG, Helton's Hellcats, (B17's). WW2 Watch Office and other buildings have been restored to original condition. Access by appointment only.

Warnings

30ft power lines run close to Rwy24 final but do not cross APP. Crops grown up to Rwy edges. Model ACFT use AD at weekends & PH. The 'two tone' cut on the strip at the W end is the model ACFT operating area. Monewden AD 1nm to N. National grid transmission lines cross extreme SE corner of WW2 airfield but should not affect normal circuit.
Noise: Avoid flying over all local houses.

Operating Hrs	SR-SS
Circuits	LH 1000ft QFE
Landing Fee	Nil
Maintenance	Nil
Fuel	Nil, available from Crowfield
Disabled Facilities	Nil
Restaurants	Nil
Taxis	Nil
Car Hire	Nil
Weather Info	Air SE MOEx

Operator Richard Taylor
Grove Farm
Clopton
Suffolk
Tel: 01473 737236
Tel: 07850 078432
www.493bgdebach.co.uk

328ft 11mb	4nm E of Corby N5230.37 W00035.35	PPR	Alternative AD	**Cambridge** Peterborough Conington

Non-Radio	LARS Cottesmore 130.200	Safetycom 135.475

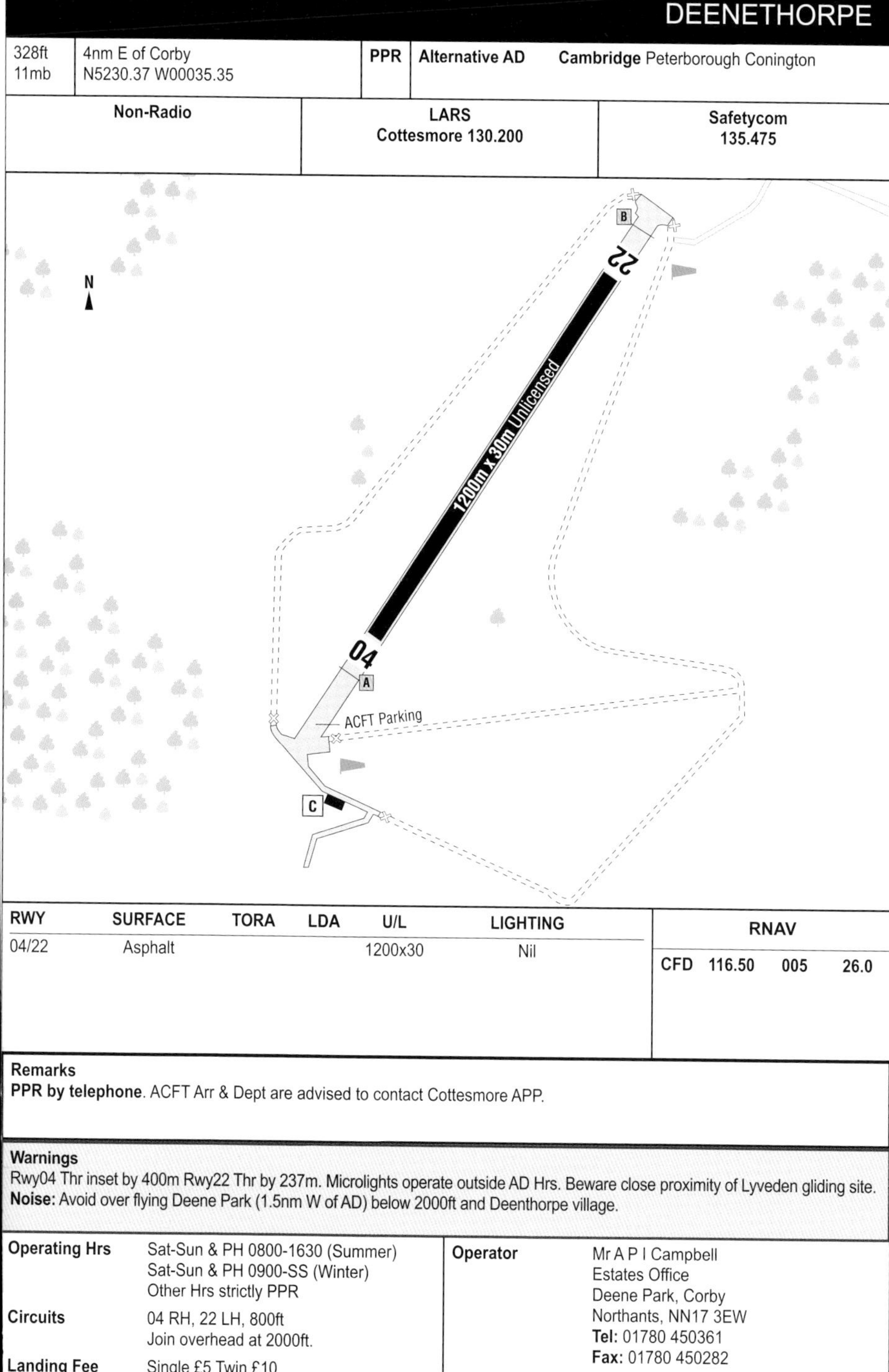

RWY	SURFACE	TORA	LDA	U/L	LIGHTING
04/22	Asphalt			1200x30	Nil

RNAV			
CFD	116.50	005	26.0

Remarks

PPR by telephone. ACFT Arr & Dept are advised to contact Cottesmore APP.

Warnings

Rwy04 Thr inset by 400m Rwy22 Thr by 237m. Microlights operate outside AD Hrs. Beware close proximity of Lyveden gliding site.
Noise: Avoid over flying Deene Park (1.5nm W of AD) below 2000ft and Deenthorpe village.

Operating Hrs	Sat-Sun & PH 0800-1630 (Summer) Sat-Sun & PH 0900-SS (Winter) Other Hrs strictly PPR
Circuits	04 RH, 22 LH, 800ft Join overhead at 2000ft.
Landing Fee	Single £5 Twin £10 penalty for no PPR
Maintenance	Nil
Fuel	Nil
Disabled Facilities	Nil
Restaurants	Nil
Taxis/Car Hire	Nil
Weather Info	Air Cen MOEx

Operator	Mr A P I Campbell Estates Office Deene Park, Corby Northants, NN17 3EW **Tel:** 01780 450361 **Fax:** 01780 450282

Effective date:28/08/08 OP 06

70ft 2mb	0.5nm SE of Defford Disused AD N5205.13 W00208.15	PPR	Alternative AD	Gloucestershire Wellesbourne Mountford

Defford	A/G 119.100 Please make routine circuit calls

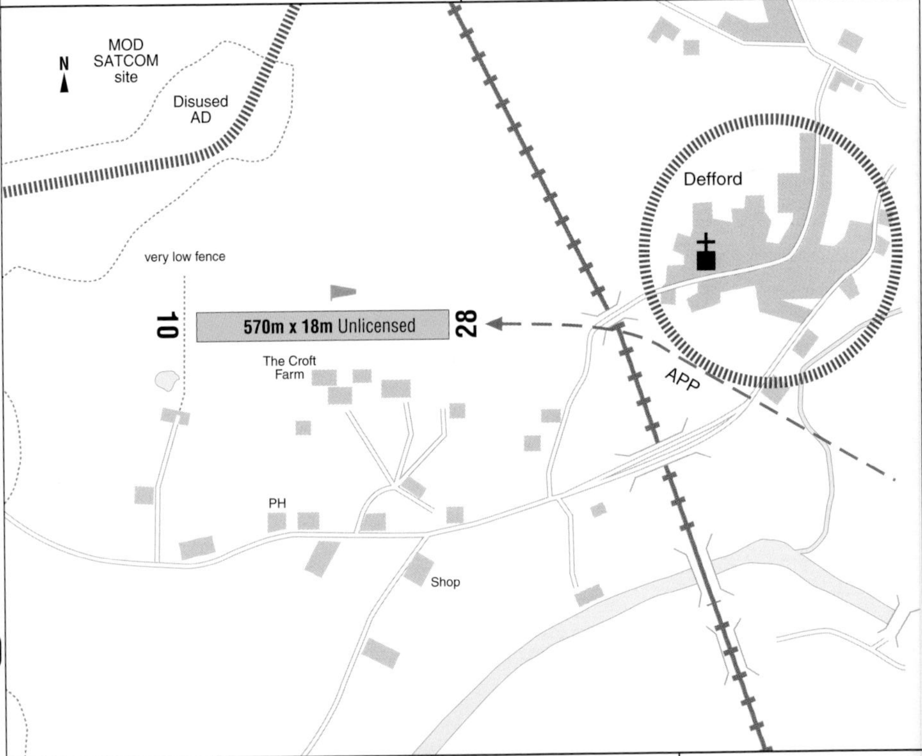

RWY	SURFACE	TORA	LDA	U/L	LIGHTING
10/28	Grass			570x18	Nil

RNAV			
HON	113.65	231	23.8

Remarks

PPR by telephone. Visiting ACFT and helicopters welcome at pilots own risk. Strip marked by reflective edge markings

Warnings

Strip may be soft in winter after heavy rain. Low fence by Rwy10 Thr.

Noise: Avoid over flying Satellite Communication Site N of AD and the villages of Defford and Eckington.

Operating Hrs	SR-SS
Circuits	1000ft QFE
Landing Fee	£5 minimum donation to Mission Aviation Fellowship gratefully received
Maintenance	Nil
Fuel	Nil
Disabled Facilities	
Restaurants	Pub 400m from AD Farm shop tea room 400m from AD

Taxis	
Pershore Private Hire	**Tel:** 08706 093526 **Tel:** 07710 164 679
Call-a-Car	**Tel:** 07803 663 387
Car Hire	
PJ Nichols	**Tel:** 01386 555555
Bredon Motors	**Tel:** 0800 614809
Weather Info	Air Cen MOEx
Operator	Mr C H Porter The Croft Farm Defford, Worcs, WR8 9BN **Tel:** 07767 606172 **Tel:** 07767 796355 clive.porter@farming.co.uk www.defford-croftfarm.co.ul

EGLD DENHAM

249ft 8mb	1.5nm E of Gerrards Cross N5135.30 W00030.78	PPR	Alternative AD Diversion AD	London Luton Elstree

Non-standard join

Denham	LARS	AFIS	APP	A/G
	Farnborough West 125.250	130.725	Northolt 126.450	130.725

N
12
24
546m x 18m
775m x 18m
30
06
C

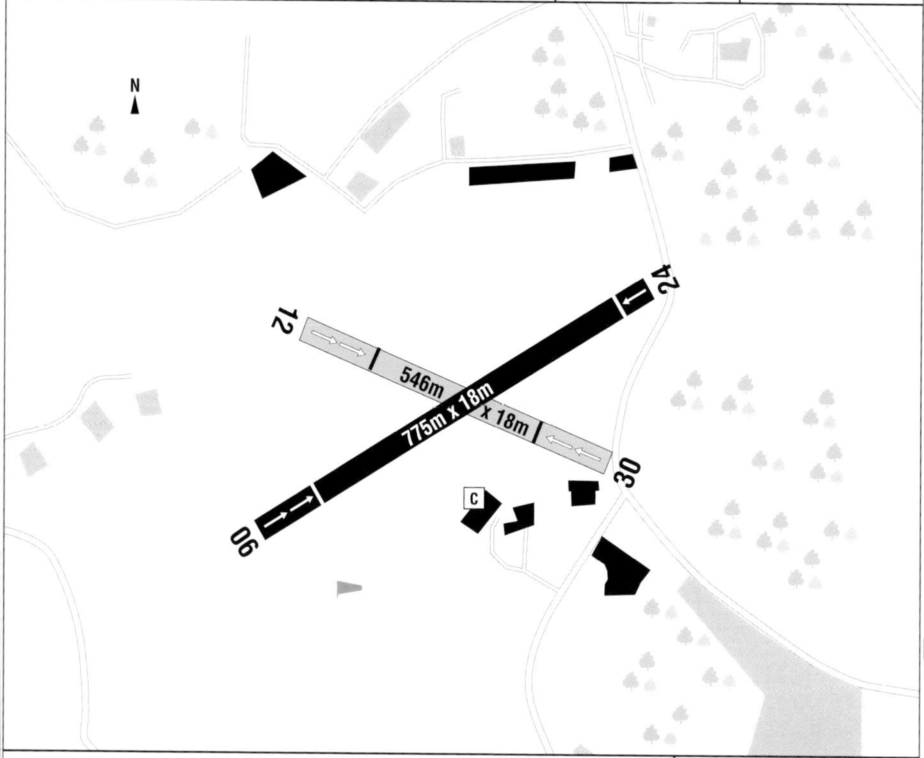

RWY	SURFACE	TORA	LDA	U/L	LIGHTING
06	Asphalt	686	706		Thr Rwy APAPI 4.5° LHS
24	Asphalt	728	670		Thr Rwy APAPI 4.5° LHS
12	Grass	363	419		Nil
30	Grass	432	363		Nil

RNAV			
LON	113.60	347	6.4

Remarks
PPR. Non-radio ACFT not accepted.
Visual aid to location: ID beacon green DN.

Warnings
A public road, adjacent to the AD boundary, crosses the extended centre line of Rwy24. Do not descend below the glide-path, or touchdown before the Thr. Visual glide slope guidance signals for Rwy06 are visible to the left of the extended centre line where normal obstacle clearance is not guaranteed. They should not be used until the ACFT is aligned with the Rwy.

Operating Hrs Licensed Hrs 0800-1630 or SS (Summer) 0900-1730 or SS (Winter). AD available 0900-1900 (Summer) 0800-1800 (Winter) & by arr

Circuits 06 LH, 24 RH, 12 30 variable
Max 750ft QFE (1000ft QNH)
No overhead joins

Landing Fee Up to 1 tonne £12

Maintenance Ltd

Fuel AVGAS 100LL JET A1 by arr

Disabled Facilities Available

Restaurant Restaurant & club facilities available

Taxis
Cabline **Tel:** 01895 270001

Car Hire
National **Tel:** 01753 534442
Lordship Motors **Tel:** 01753 883120

Weather Info Air SE MOEx

Operator Bickerton's Aerodromes Ltd
Denham Aerodrome
Uxbridge, Middlesex, UB9 5DE
Tel: 01895 832161 (ATS)
Fax: 01895 833486
www.egld.com

Effective date:28/08/08

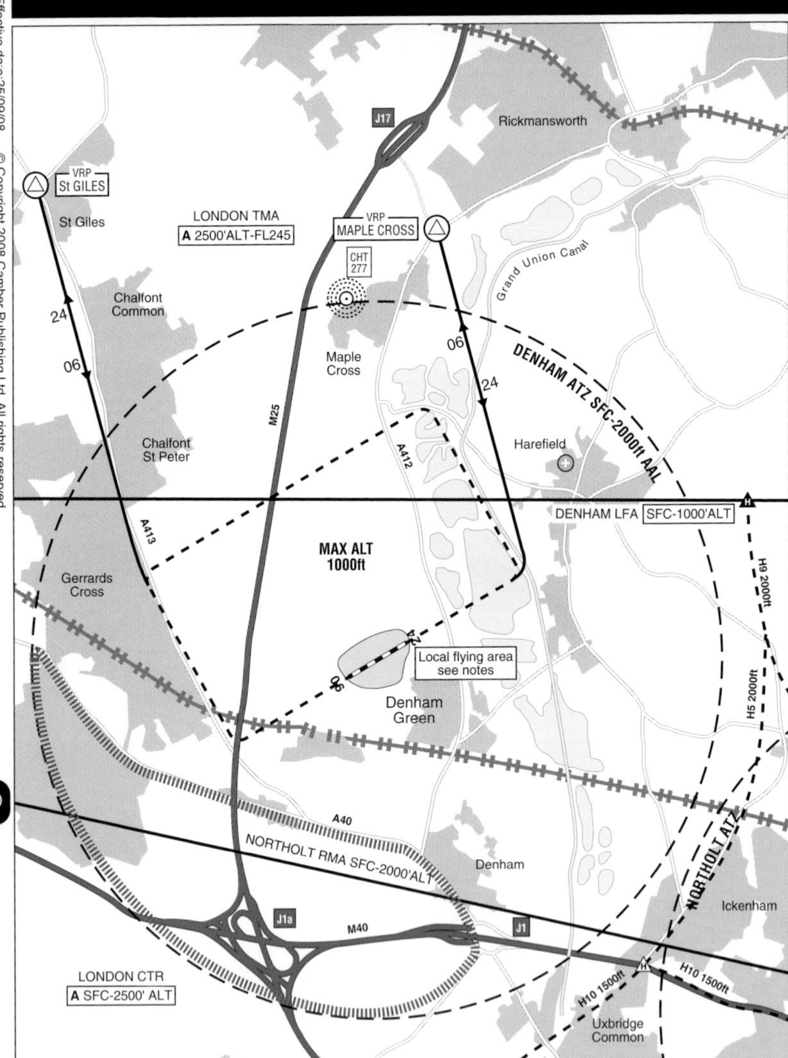

Circuit Traffic
Circuit traffic should stay south of Chalfont St Peter. Additional restrictions apply to twin engined ACFT & helicopters.

Flights without compliance to IFR within the Denham ATZ are permitted subject to the following conditions:
1 ACFT must remain clear of cloud and in sight of the surface.
2 Maximum Alt 1000ft QNH, with a minimum visibility of 3km.
3 The Area to the south of the A40 must be avoided at all times.

Arrivals:
Rwy06 Join via Chalfont St Giles (N5138.02 W00034.02) directly to base leg to the E of the A413 to avoid Gerrards Cross.
Rwy24 Join via Maple Cross (N5137.77 W00030.25) directly to base leg over the lakes to avoid Harefield.

Deptartures:
Rwy06 Turn left over the lakes to avoid Harefield.
Rwy24 After take-off continue straight ahead until past the houses on the right, then turn right before the A413 to avoid over flying Gerrards Cross.

Visual Reference Point (VRP)

	VOR/DME	VOR/DME	NDB
Maple Cross N5137.77 W00030.25	BNN 166°/6nm	BPK 247°/17nm	CHT 057°
Chalfont St Giles N5138.02 W00034.02	BNN 189°/6nm	BPK 250°/19nm	CHT 292°

EGBD DERBY

175ft 6mb	6nm SW of Derby N5251.58 W00137.05	PPR	**Alternative AD** **East Midlands** Tatenhill **Diversion AD**

Non-standard join

Derby	APP East Mids 134.175	A/G 118.350

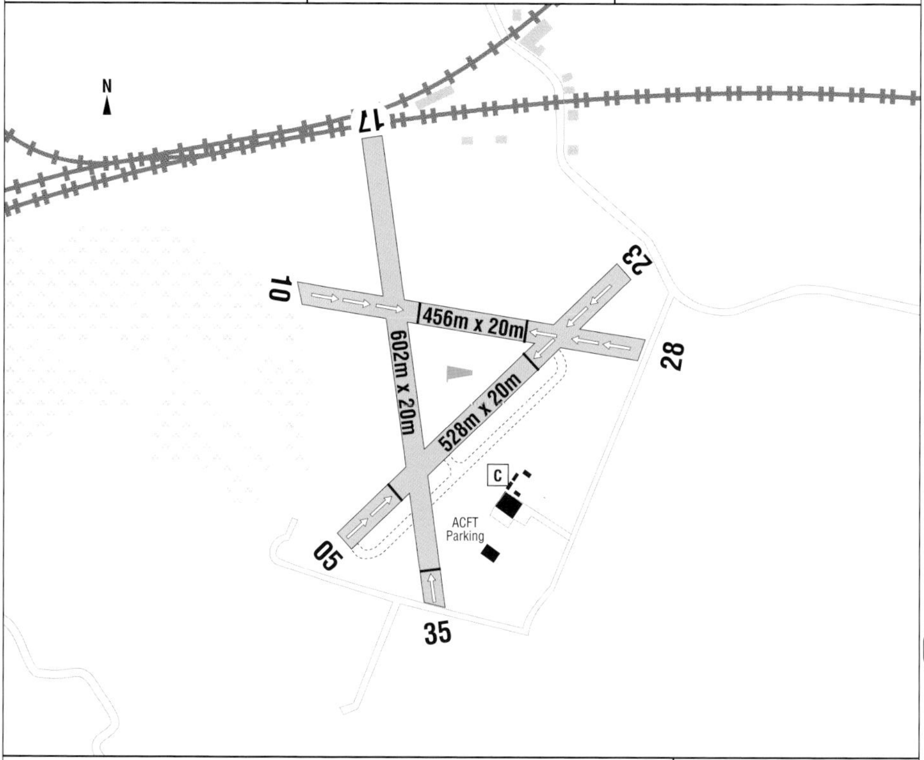

N

17

10

456m x 20m

23

28

602m x 20m

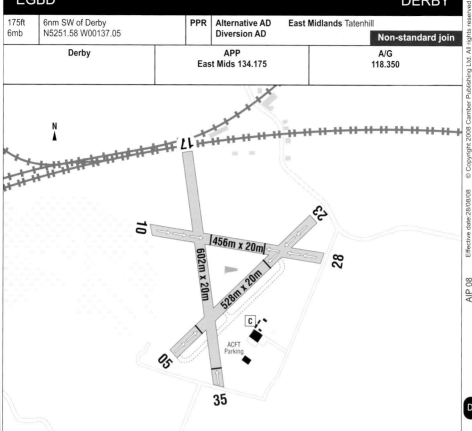

528m x 20m

C

ACFT Parking

05

35

RWY	SURFACE	TORA	LDA	U/L	LIGHTING
23	Grass	445	341		Nil
05	Grass	356	430		Nil
10	Grass	276	315		Nil
28	Grass	300	291		Nil
17	Grass	513	No Landing		Nil
35	Grass	No Take-Off	528		Nil

Displaced Thr Rwy05 83m, Displaced Thr Rwy23 172m, Displaced Thr Rwy10 120m, Displaced Thr Rwy28 146m, Displaced Thr Rwy35 44m

RNAV			
TNT	115.70	175	11.7

Remarks

PPR. Non-radio ACFT not accepted. Overhead joins are not permitted. Not available at night or to Public Transport flights required to use a licensed AD. Special Arr & Dept procedures apply, which can be obtained when telephoning for PPR. Derby is under the East Midlands CTA (base 1500ftAMSL over the AD). Rwy10/28 is only to be used for instruction when a QFI acts as pilot in command.

Warnings

Power line 100ft aal crosses Rwy23 APP 1200m from touchdown. Trees on the APP Rwy23 may cause turbulence and block the view of APP ACFT to ACFT on the GND. There are no QDM marks on the Rwys. Due to short LDA's on Rwy28/10 and Rwy23/05 an early go around decision is vital. DO NOT attempt to land long. Displaced Thr Rwy05, 23 & 35 are marked by black and white wing bars. Displaced Thr Rwy10 & 28 are marked by orange and white wing bars. Intentional touch and goes not permitted.
Noise: Avoid over flying local villages.

Operating Hrs	Mon-Sat 0900-1800 Sun & PH 0930-1800 (Summer) Mon-Sat 0900-SS Sun & PH 0930-SS (Winter)
Circuits	05 LH 1000ft QFE, 23 RH, 1000ft QFE 17, 10 LH 800ft QFE, 28 RH 800ft QFE
Landing Fee	Single £6, Twin/Heli £10
Maintenance	Airspeed Aviation Ltd **Tel:** 01283 733803
Fuel	AVGAS 100LL
Disabled Facilities	Nil

Restaurants	Tea & Coffee in club house
Taxis	
Stretton	**Tel:** 01283 511876
A1	**Tel:** 01283 838383
Car Hire	
Hertz	**Tel:** 01332 205215
National	**Tel:** 01332 382251
Weather Info	Air Cen MOEx

Operator	Derby Aero Club Derby Aerodrome Hilton Road Egginton Derby Derbyshire DE65 6GU **Tel:** 01283 733803 **Fax:** 01283 734829 www.derbyaeroclub.com

Derby Circuit Procedures

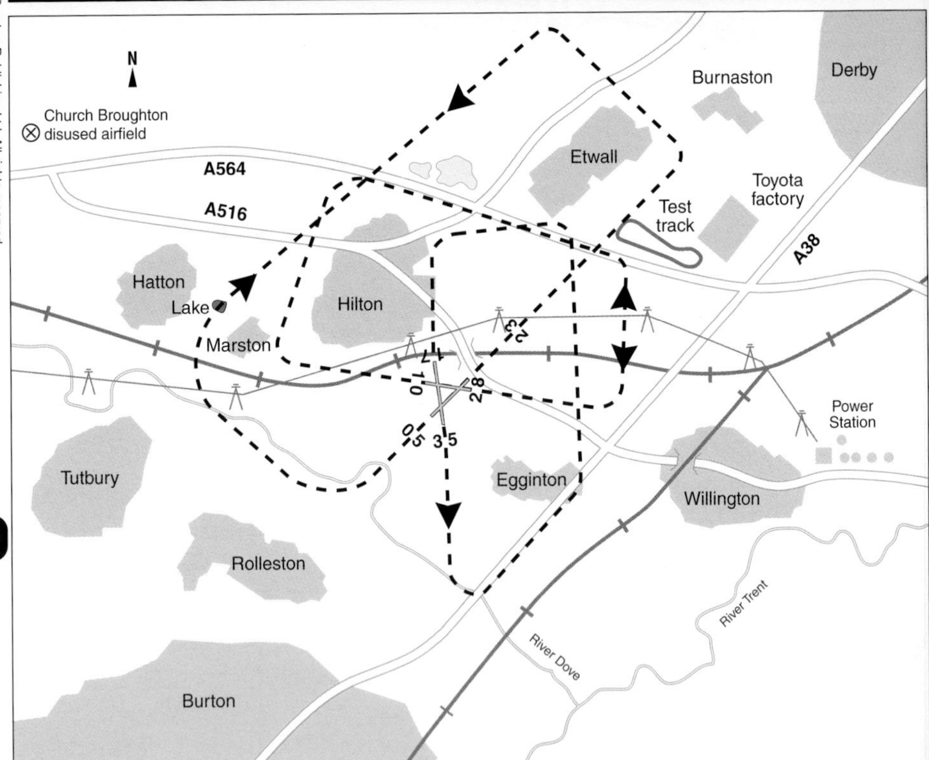

D

Rwy23
Turn crosswind S of river Dove but before Rolleston. Turn downwind at small lake between Hatton & Marston
Turn base leg between Burnaston & Etwall. Final APP will over fly Toyota test track

Rwy05
Turn crosswind abeam Toyota factory pass between Burnaston & Etwall. Turn downwind to remain W of Hilton. Turn base leg by initially turning at small lake to remain clear of Hatton & Marston, then follow course of river Dove to final remaining clear of Rolleston

Rwy28
Turn crosswind before Marston but remain W of Hilton. Turn downwind following course of A564. Turn base leg at Toyota test track. Continue to final

Rwy10
Turn crosswind abeam Toyota test track. Turn downwind following course of A564. Turn base leg W of Hilton & E of Marston
Continue to final

Rwy17 (Dept Only)
Turn crosswind at river Dove, intercept A38 to avoid Egginton. Turn downwind to Toyota test track. Continue onto base leg

Rwy35 (Arr Only)
Turn crosswind to avoid Etwall. Turn downwind at Toyota test track. Then leave the circuit

117ft 4mb	3nm NW of Borroughbridge N5408.23 W00125.22	PPR MIL	Alternative AD Diversion AD	Durham Tees Valley Sherburn in Elmet Non-standard join

Dishforth	LARS	APP	TWR/GND	A/G
	Leeming 127.750	Topcliffe 125.000	122.100	130.100 Glider Ops

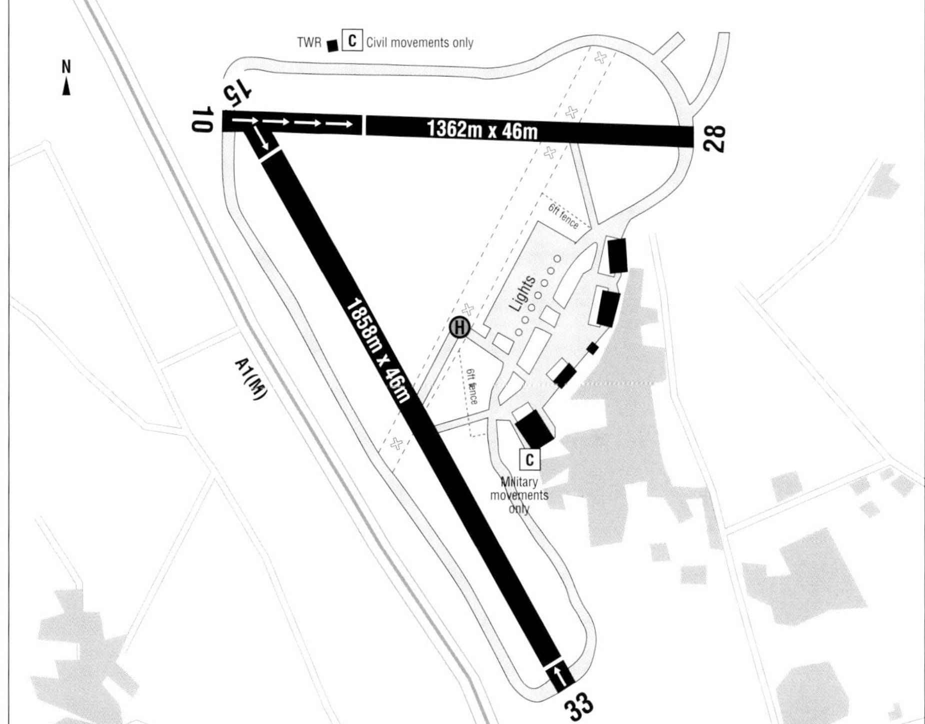

RWY	SURFACE	TORA	LDA	U/L	LIGHTING
15	Asphalt	1858	1636		Nil
33	Asphalt	1858	1782		Nil
10	Asphalt	1362	936		Nil
28	Asphalt	1362	1362		Nil

Rwy15 first 142m sterile, Rwy33 first 96m sterile, Rwy10 first 426m sterile

RNAV

Remarks
Pilots should contact Leeming LARS before entering the area. Army helicopter operations take place at any time

Warnings
Rwy10/28 not available for fixed wing ACFT. High intensity military flying during operational Hrs. Winch launched glider flying outside AD hrs, evenings and weekends.
Noise: Avoid over flying Boroughbridge, Kirby Hill and Dishforth.

Operating Hrs	Mon-Fri 0930-1700 (L) & as required
Circuits	10, 15 RH, 28, 33 LH, 1000ft QFE
Landing Fee	Charges in accordance with MOD policy Contact Station Ops for details
Maintenance	Nil
Fuel	JET A1 (not normally available to civil visitors)
Disabled Facilities	Nil
Restaurants	Nil
Taxis/Car Hire	Nil
Weather Info	Air N MOEx

Operator
British Army
Dishforth
York
North Yorkshire
YO7 3EZ
Tel: 01423 321633 (PPR Dishforth TWR)
Tel: 01423 321561 (Army Ops)
Fax: 01423 321664 (Dishforth TWR)
Fax: 01423 321560 (Army Ops)

DONAGHCLONEY

180ft 6mb	0.5nm S of Donaghcloney N5424.19 W00615.61	PPR	Alternative AD	**Belfast Aldergrove** Newtownards

Non-Radio	FIS Scottish 119.875	APP Aldergrove 128.500*	*If operating below or in proximity to the Belfast TMA	Safetycom 135.475

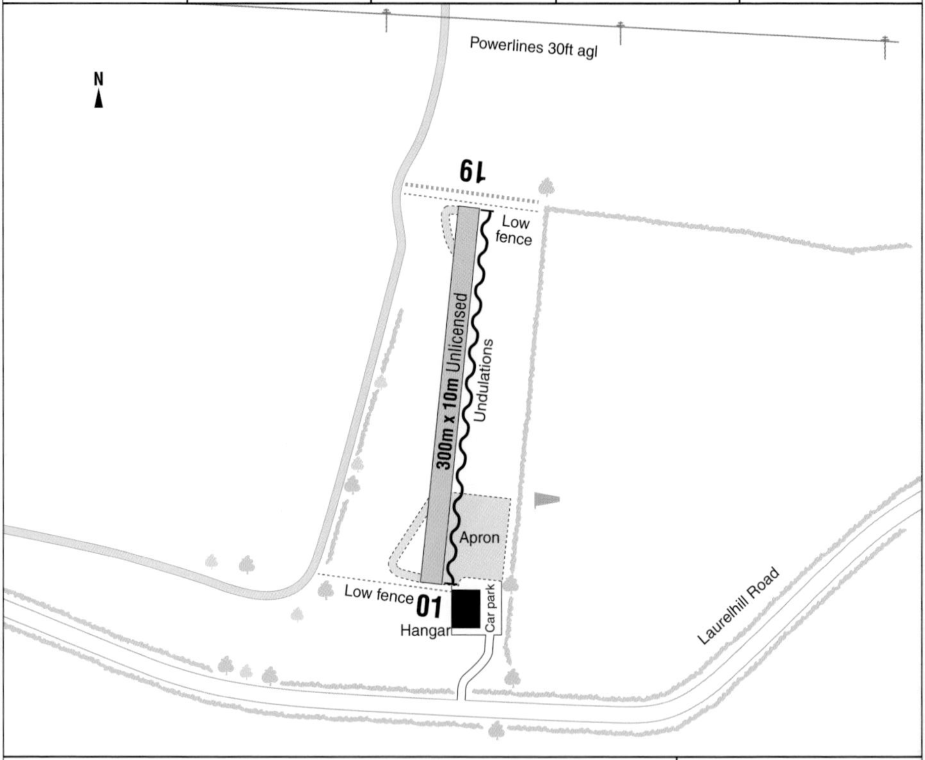

Powerlines 30ft agl
N
19
Low fence
300m x 10m Unlicensed
Undulations
Apron
Low fence
01
Hangar
Car park
Laurelhill Road

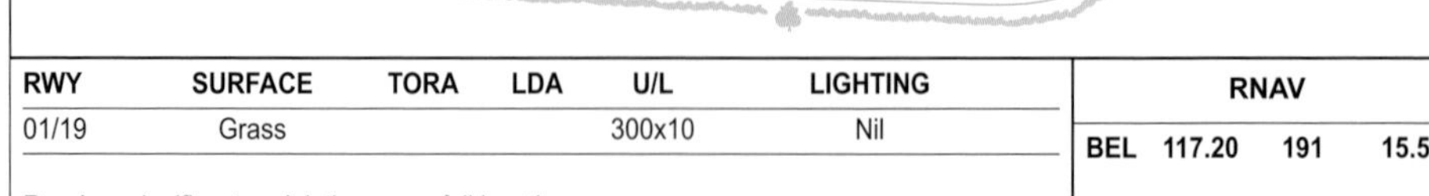

RWY	SURFACE	TORA	LDA	U/L	LIGHTING
01/19	Grass			300x10	Nil

Rwy has significant undulations over full length

RNAV			
BEL	117.20	191	15.5

Remarks
PPR by telephone. Visiting ACFT/Microlights welcome at pilots own risk. AD is not notified as a designated point of entry/exit for Northern Ireland under the prevention of Terrorism act but this can be arranged via The Police Service of Northern Ireland. Hangarage is limited, visiting Microlights can be accommodated with prior arrangement.

Warnings
First time visiting pilots should obtain a telephone briefing. Rwy has significant undulations over full length. Low fences adjacent to both Rwy Thr. Powerlines 30ft agl, cross Rwy19 APP on short final. AD situated just to S of Belfast TMA, base altitude 2000ft QNH. **Noise:** Avoid over flying houses to E of AD.

Operating Hrs	SR-SS
Circuits	19 RH 01 LH
Landing Fee	Nil
Maintenance	Microlights only **Tel:** 02897 532558
Fuel	MOGAS avail by prior arr
Disabled Faciities	Nil
Restaurants	Nil
Taxis	**Tel:** 02840 624794
Car Hire	Nil
Weather Info	Air N MOEx

Operator Fred Cameron
Tel: 07880 504626
Tel: 02890 650222 (PSNI)
Fax: 02840 621915
fly@euroflight.co.uk

EGCN — DONCASTER SHEFFIELD

55ft 2mb	3nm SE of Doncaster N5328.48 W00100.27	PPR	**Alternative AD**	**Gamston** Sandtoft **Non-standard join**

Doncaster	ATIS	APP	TWR	FIRE
	134.950	126.225	128.775	121.600

RWY	SURFACE	TORA	LDA	U/L	LIGHTING
02	Asphalt	2893	2743		Ap Thr Rwy PAPI 3.1°
20	Asphalt	2756	2604		Ap Thr Rwy PAPI 3°

RNAV			
GAM	112.80	354	11.8

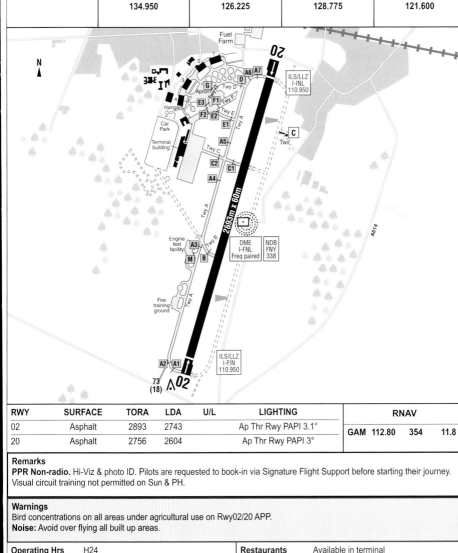

Remarks
PPR Non-radio. Hi-Viz & photo ID. Pilots are requested to book-in via Signature Flight Support before starting their journey. Visual circuit training not permitted on Sun & PH.

Warnings
Bird concentrations on all areas under agricultural use on Rwy02/20 APP.
Noise: Avoid over flying all built up areas.

Operating Hrs H24

Circuits 02 RH 1000ft QFE
20 LH 1000ft QFE
No overhead joins

Landing Fee Available on request

Maintenance Limited

Fuel AVTUR JET A1

Disabled Facilities

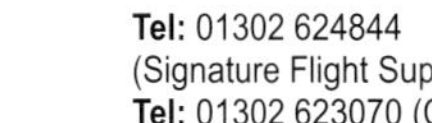

Handling **Tel:** 01302 624844
(Signature Flight Support)
Tel: 01302 623070 (Cargo)
Fax: 01302 624846
(Signature Flight Support)
Fax: 01302 623073 (Cargo)

Restaurants Available in terminal

Taxi/Car Hire Available in terminal

Weather Info M T9 MOEx
ATIS **Tel:** 0870 8332210 (External)
ATIS **Tel:** Ex 4854 (Internal)

Operator Robin Hood Airport Doncaster Sheffield
Heyford House
First Avenue
Doncaster
South Yorkshire DN9 3RH
Tel: 01302 801010
Tel: 01302 625022 (AD Ops)
Tel: 01302 625642 (ATC)
Fax: 01302 801011
Fax: 01302 625023 (AD Ops)
Fax: 01302 625641 (ATC)
www.robinhoodairport.com

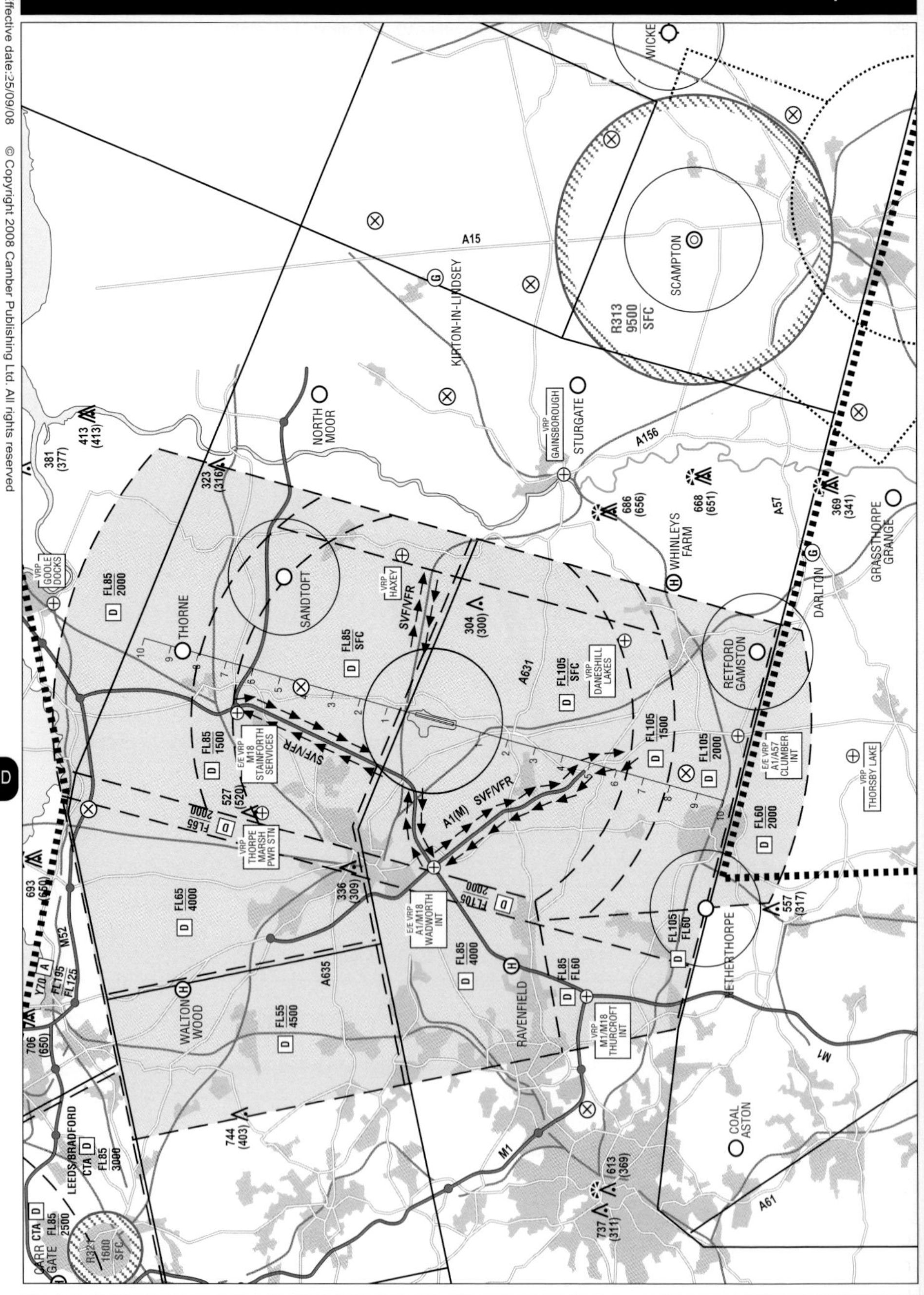

CTR/CTA – Class D Airspace
Normal CTR/CTA Class D Airspace rules apply. Transit Alt 5000ft

Visual Reference Points (VRP)

VRP	VOR/DME	VRP	VOR/DME
A1/A57 Clumber Interchange N5317.78 W00101.90	GAM 289°/3nm	Haxey N5329.42 W00050.62	GAM 019°/13nm
A1/M18 Wadworth Interchange N5328.75 W00108.90	GAM 332°/14nm	M1/M18 Thurcroft Interchange N5323.57 W00116.72	GAM 302°/14nm
Gainsborough N5323.55 W00046.25	GAM 046°/9nm	M18 Stainforth Services N5335.48 W00059.25	GAM 358°/19nm
Goole Docks N5341.82 W00052.67	GAM 008°/25nm	Thorpe Marsh Power Station N5334.88 W00105.33	GAM 347°/19nm

3ft 0mb	1nm S of Dornoch N5752.14 W00401.32	PPR	Alternative AD Diversion AD	Inverness Wick

Non radio	LARS Lossiemouth 118.900	DAAIS Tain Range 122.750	Safetycom 135.475

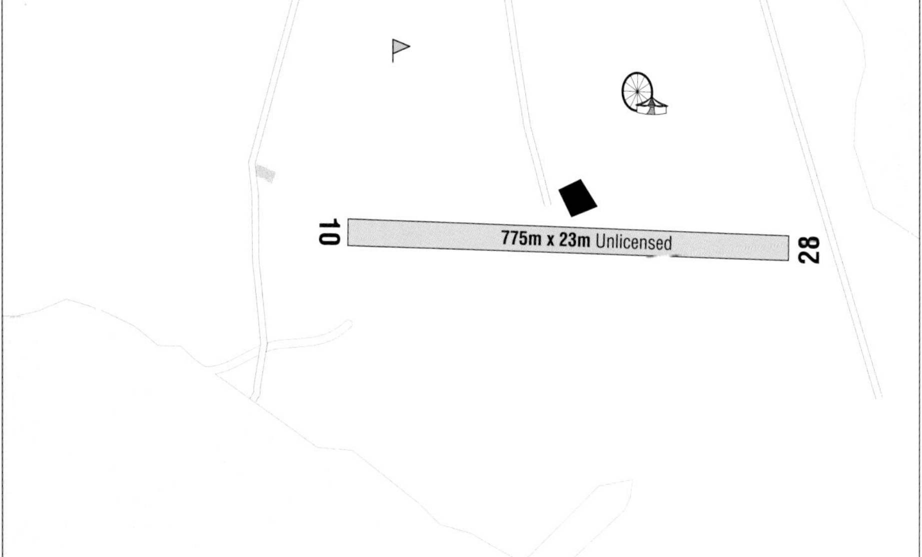

RWY	SURFACE	TORA	LDA	U/L	LIGHTING
10/28	Grass			775x23	Nil

RNAV			
INS	109.20	008	19.7

Remarks
PPR prospective visitors must telephone Council Offices, Brora during office Hrs. An entry/exit lane is established from the Danger Area boundary S to the AD via Embo from the surface to 1000ft amsl. Clearance to enter the Danger Area is required prior to Arr & Dept. Telephone available at AD.

Warnings
AD situated near W edge of Danger Area D703. DAAIS Tain Range. Landing strip is marked by 3ft high posts 90m either side of Rwy centreline and across ends.

Operating Hrs SR-SS
Circuits Nil
Landing Fee On application
Maintenance Nil
Fuel Nil
Disabled Facilities Nil
Restaurants
Royal Golf Hotel **Tel:** 01862 810283
Matlin House **Tel:** 01862 810335
Taxis/Car Hire
Hugh MacKay **Tel:** 01862 810612
Weather Info Air Sc GWC

Operator
The Highland Council
Area Roads & Community Works Manager
Drummuie
Golspie
Highland KW10 6TA
Tel: 01408 635307
Fax: 01408 534041

Effective date:28/08/08 OP 08

525ft 17mb	5nm S of Swindon N5129.75 W00144.62	PPR	**Alternative AD** **Oxford** Kemble

Non-Radio	**Zone** **Lyneham 123.400**	**Safetycom** **135.475**

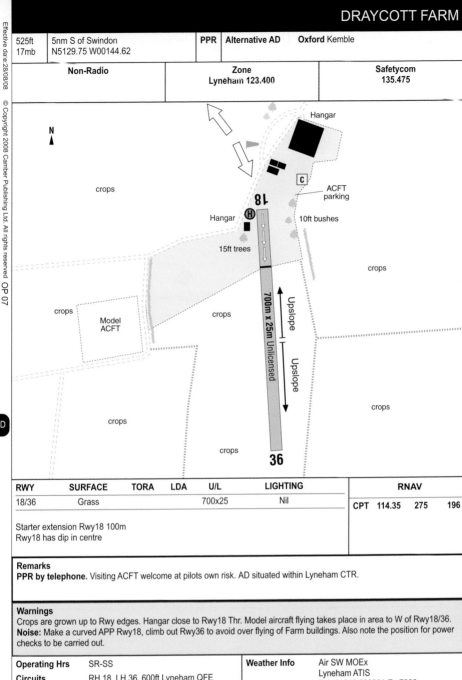

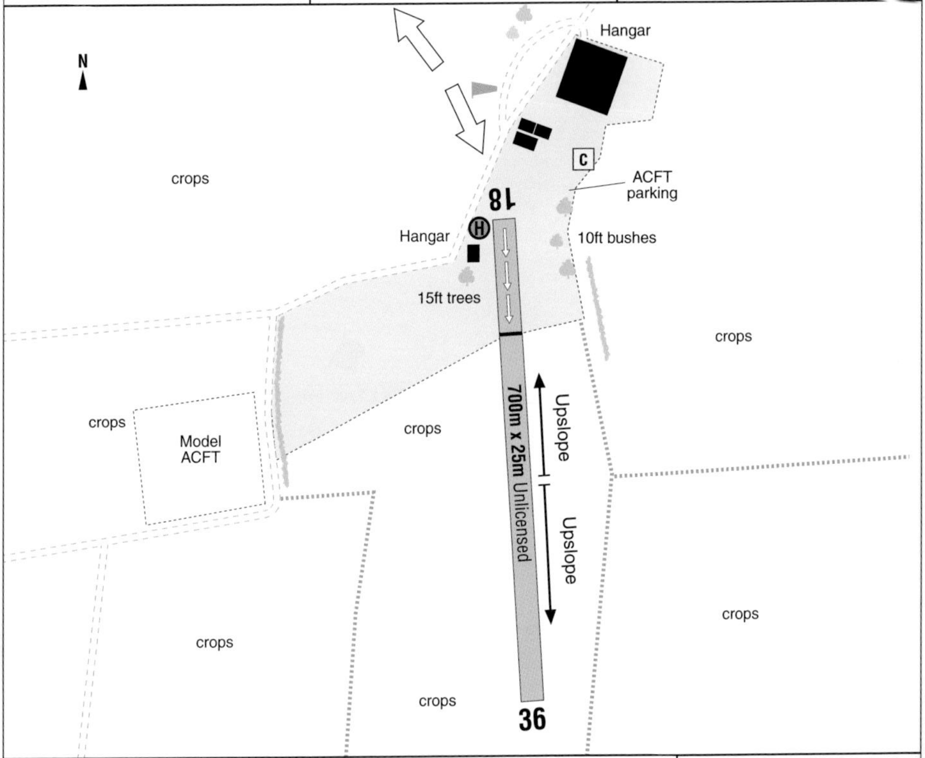

RWY	SURFACE	TORA	LDA	U/L	LIGHTING
18/36	Grass			700x25	Nil

Starter extension Rwy18 100m
Rwy18 has dip in centre

RNAV			
CPT	**114.35**	**275**	**196**

Remarks
PPR by telephone. Visiting ACFT welcome at pilots own risk. AD situated within Lyneham CTR.

Warnings
Crops are grown up to Rwy edges. Hangar close to Rwy18 Thr. Model aircraft flying takes place in area to W of Rwy18/36.
Noise: Make a curved APP Rwy18, climb out Rwy36 to avoid over flying of Farm buildings. Also note the position for power checks to be carried out.

Operating Hrs	SR-SS
Circuits	RH 18, LH 36, 600ft Lyneham QFE No Circuit training
Landing Fee	£10
Maintenance	Nil
Fuel	100LL JET A1 Fuel accounts available
Hangarage	Available
Disabled Facilities	Nil
Restaurants	Ops Room 'Summer House'
Taxis/Car Hire	Nil

Weather Info	Air SW MOEx Lyneham ATIS **Tel:** 01249 890381 Ex 7308
Operator	Draycott Flight Centre Chiseldon Swindon Wilts, SN4 0HX **Tel:** 01793 741527

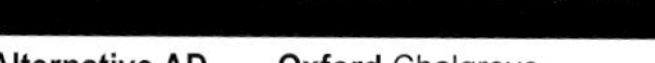

DRAYTON St LEONARD

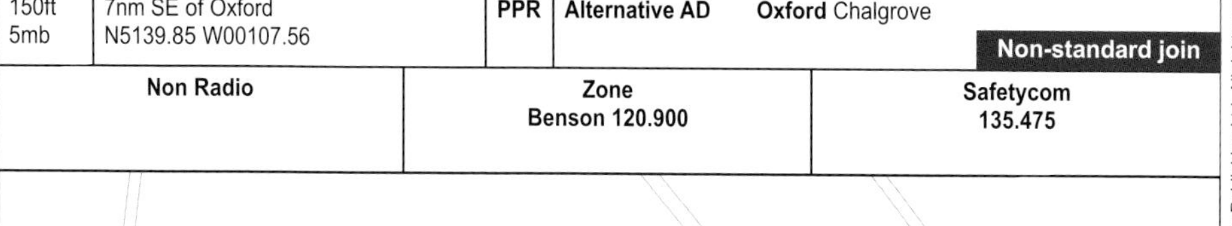

150ft 5mb	7nm SE of Oxford N5139.85 W00107.56	**PPR**	**Alternative AD** **Oxford** Chalgrove **Non-standard join**

Non Radio	**Zone** **Benson 120.900**	**Safetycom** **135.475**

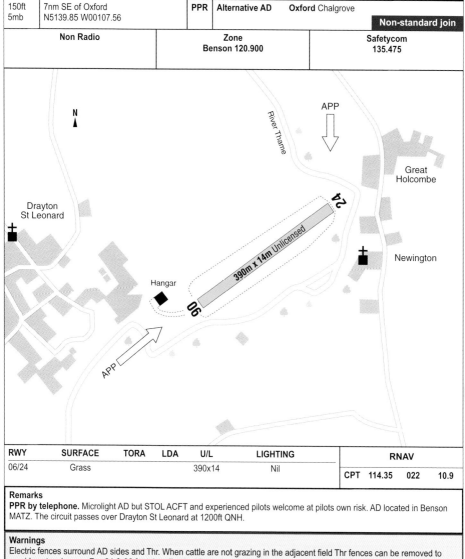

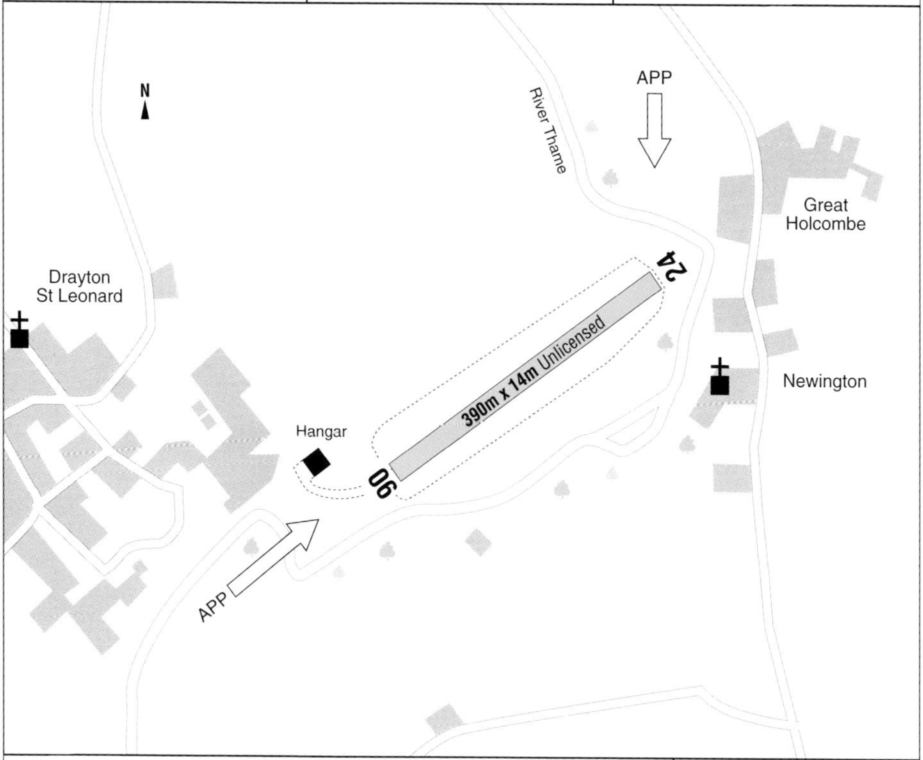

N
River Thame
APP
Great Holcombe
Drayton St Leonard
24
390m x 14m Unlicensed
Newington
Hangar
06
APP

RWY	SURFACE	TORA	LDA	U/L	LIGHTING
06/24	Grass			390x14	Nil

RNAV			
CPT	**114.35**	**022**	**10.9**

Remarks

PPR by telephone. Microlight AD but STOL ACFT and experienced pilots welcome at pilots own risk. AD located in Benson MATZ. The circuit passes over Drayton St Leonard at 1200ft QNH.

Warnings

Electric fences surround AD sides and Thr. When cattle are not grazing in the adjacent field Thr fences can be removed to provide extensions on Rwy24 & 06 for take-off only. AD is prone to flooding after heavy precipitation.

Caution: parachuting takes place at Chalgrove, 2nm ENE.

Local procedures/Noise: Inbound ACFT should contact Benson APP before entering the MATZ or telephone Benson ATC. Dept telephone Benson before take-off.

Noise: To avoid local sensitive areas avoid conflict with Benson circuit Arr are to follow these procedures. Do not carry out overhead joins or circuits. If safety allows carry out a direct APP from a long final. APP Rwy24 offset to N to avoid Newington, The farm to the W, & the farm on the hill. APP Rwy06 should be slightly right of centreline to avoid Drayton St Leonard. Dept Rwy06 ASAP after take-off turn left onto N. Rwy24 ASAP after take-off turn left onto 220° to avoid Drayton St Leonard.

Operating Hrs	SR-SS
Circuits	See Local procedures/Noise
Landing Fee	Nil
Maintenance	Nil Limited outside parking available by arr
Fuel	Nil
Disabled Facilities	Nil
Restaurants	Nil
Taxis/Car Hire	Nil
Weather Info	Air SE MOEx

Operator
George Farrant
Manor Farm
Drayton St Leonards
Wallingford
Oxon, OX10 7BE
Tel: 01865 890223
Fax: 01865 400064
Tel: 01491 837766 Ex 7555/7487
(Benson ATC)

17ft 0mb	0.5nm S of Dundee N5627.15 W00301.55	PPR	Alternative AD	Edinburgh Perth

Dundee	LARS	APP	TWR	FIRE
	Leuchars 126.500	122.900	122.900	121.600

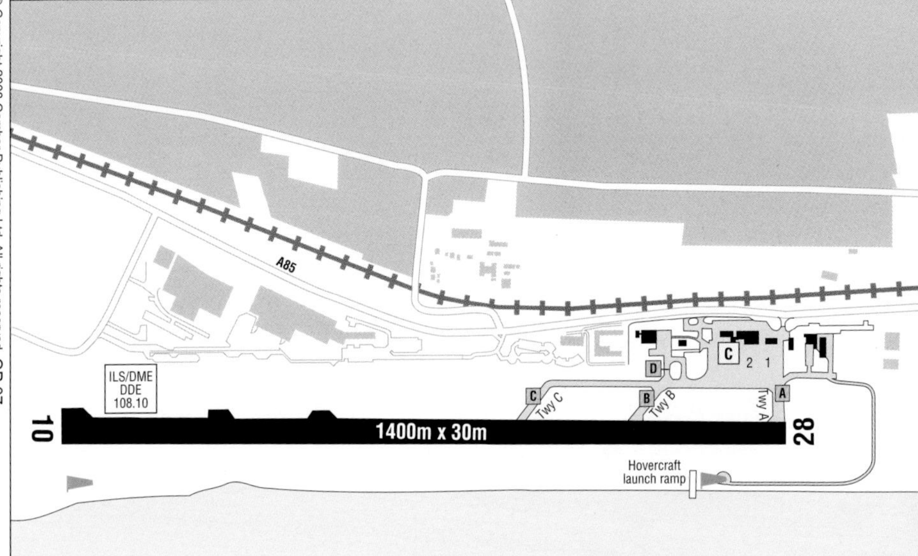

RWY	SURFACE	TORA	LDA	U/L	LIGHTING
10	Asphalt	1319	1400		Ap Thr Rwy PAPI 3.0° LHS
28	Asphalt	1319	1400		Thr Rwy PAPI 3.75° LHS

RNAV			
PTH	110.40	093	11.3

Remarks
PPR to non-radio ACFT and all training flights. Because view from Control TWR is restricted local movements to the N of the AD are not permitted. Link C only available to ACFT 5700kgs or less. Parachuting takes place at Errol.
Aids to Navigation: NDB DND 394.00

Warnings
AD is in the vicinity of Leuchars MATZ. Birds are a constant hazard at this AD particularly during autumn months.
Noise: ACFT Dept to N on either Rwy are to climb straight ahead to 2000ft before setting course or as directed by ATC. Pilots should avoid flying over Nine-Wells Hospital which is 1.2nm bearing 306° from the AD.

Operating Hrs Mon-Fri 0545-2100 Sat 0645-1600 Sun 0800-2100 (Summer) +1Hr (Winter) & by arr

Circuits 10 RH, 28 LH, 1000ft QFE

Landing Fee Single £9, Twin £12.34 per tonne

Maintenance Tayside Aviation
Tel: 01382 644577
Fax: 01382 644531

Fuel AVGAS JET A1 100LL

Disabled Facilities

Restaurant Coffee & licenced snack bar in Terminal
The Hungry Horse restaurant/bar
200m W of terminal

Taxis **Tel:** 01382 203020

Car Hire
National **Tel:** 01382 224037
Arnold Clark Tel: 01382 225382
Mitchells **Tel:** 01382 223484

Weather Info M* T9 GWC
ATIS Tel: 01382 662222

Visual Reference Points (VRP)
Broughty Castle N5627.75 W00252.18

Operator Dundee Airport Ltd
Dundee Airport
Riverside Drive
Dundee, DD2 1UH
Tel: 01382 662200 (AD)
Tel: 01382 643242 (Enq)
Tel: 01382 662220 (ATC)
Fax: 01382 641263 (AD)
Fax: 01382 662221 (ATC)

EGTU DUNKESWELL

839ft 28mb	14nm NE of Exeter N5051 60 W00314.08	PPR	Alternative AD Exeter Eaglescott

Non-standard join

Dunkeswell	A/G 123.475

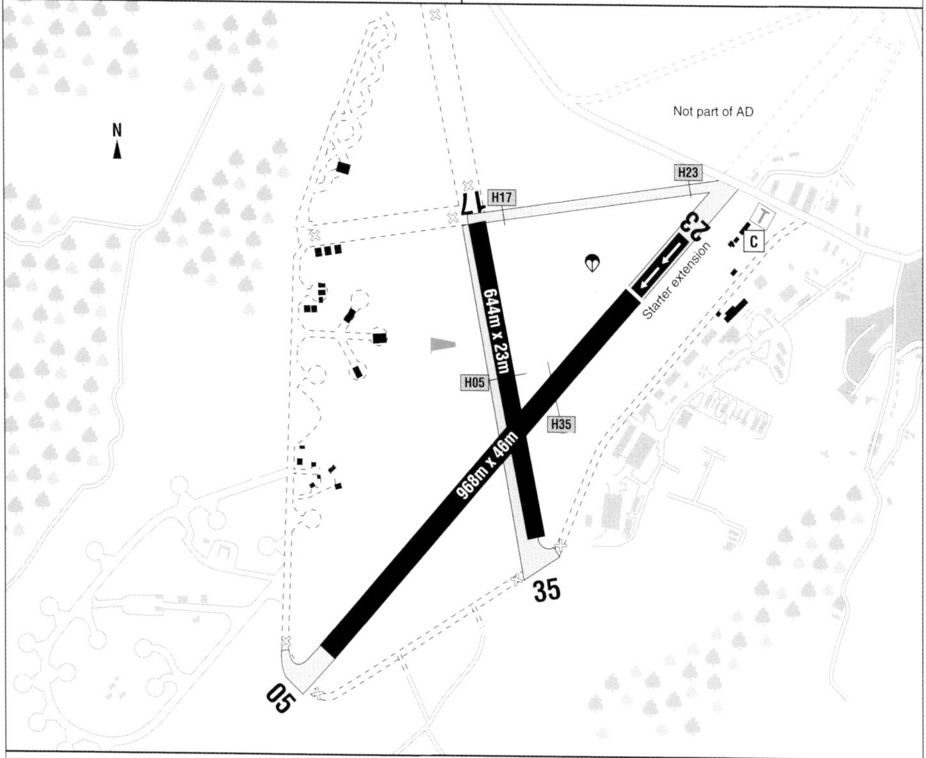

RWY	SURFACE	TORA	LDA	U/L	LIGHTING
05/23	Asphalt	968	968		Rwy
17/35	Asphalt	644	644		Nil

Starter extension Rwy23 150m

RNAV			
BHD	112.05	024	29.4

Remarks

Warnings
Gliders WSW of AD. Free-fall parachuting from up to FL150 on AD. Pilots should positively identify Rwy23 displaced Thr before committing ACFT to finals. Only use established Twys or Rwys for taxi, peri-track is unsuitable. Large paved area to NE not part of AD.
Noise: Avoid over flying Dunkeswell below 500ft QFE.

Operating Hrs 0830-1830 (L) & by arr

Circuits 05, 35 RH, 17, 23 LH
No overhead joins

Landing Fee Single £10, Twins £20

Maintenance Flymoore Aircraft Engineering
Tel: 01404 891504
Also limited hangerage available

Fuel AVGAS JET A1 100LL

Disabled Facilities

Restaurants Fully licenced bar & Restaurant open 24/7

Taxis/Car Hire
Honiton Garage **Tel:** 01404 42036

Weather Info T9 MOEx

Operator Air Westward Ltd Dunkeswell
Honiton Devon EX14 4LG
Tel: 01404 891643 (AD info)
Fax: 01404 891465
dsftltd@btconnect.com
www.dsft.co.uk

EGTD DUNSFOLD

172ft 5mb	8nm S of Guildford N5107.02 W00032.18	PPR	Alternative AD	Shoreham Goodwood

Dunsfold	ATIS Gatwick 136.525	LARS Farnborough West 125.250	A/G 119.100

N
Link Twy
1880m x 45m
07
25
C

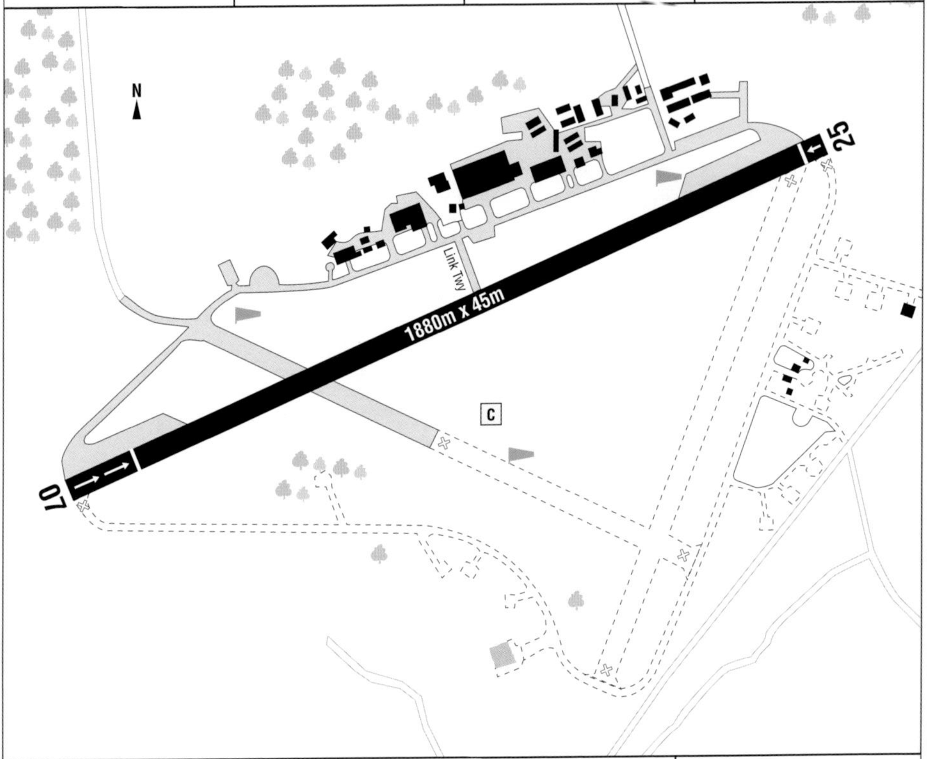

RWY	SURFACE	TORA	LDA	U/L	LIGHTING
07/25	Asphalt			1880x45m	App Thr Rwy

RNAV			
MID	114.00	045	5.5

Remarks
PPR by telephone. AD available by appointment only. Special events limit operational availability. Inbound ACFT should call Dunsfold Radio at the earliest opportunity when within 10nm of AD.

Warnings
High performance ACFT operate from AD. Gatwick CTR is close to the NE. LTMA base is 2500ft above the AD.

Operating Hrs	By appointment
Circuits	07 RH 25 LH 1000ft QNH
Landing Fee	Advised with PPR
Maintenance	Nil
Hangarage	Available
Fuel	AVGAS JET A1 100LL
Disabled Facilities	Nil
Restaurant	Nil
Taxi/Car Hire	Nil
Weather Info	Air SE MOEx

Operator
Dunsfold Park Ltd
Cranleigh
Surrey
GU6 8TB
Tel: 01483 200900 (PPR)
Tel: 01483 299899
Fax: 01483 299555
dmcallister@rutland.co.uk
dunsfoldaerodrome.com

D

DUNNYVADDEN

490ft 16mb	2nm ESE of Ballymena N5450.87 W00612.38	PPR	Alternative AD	Belfast Aldergrove Newtownards

Dunnyvadden	ATIS Aldergrove 128.200	APP Aldergrove 128.500	A/G 122.300

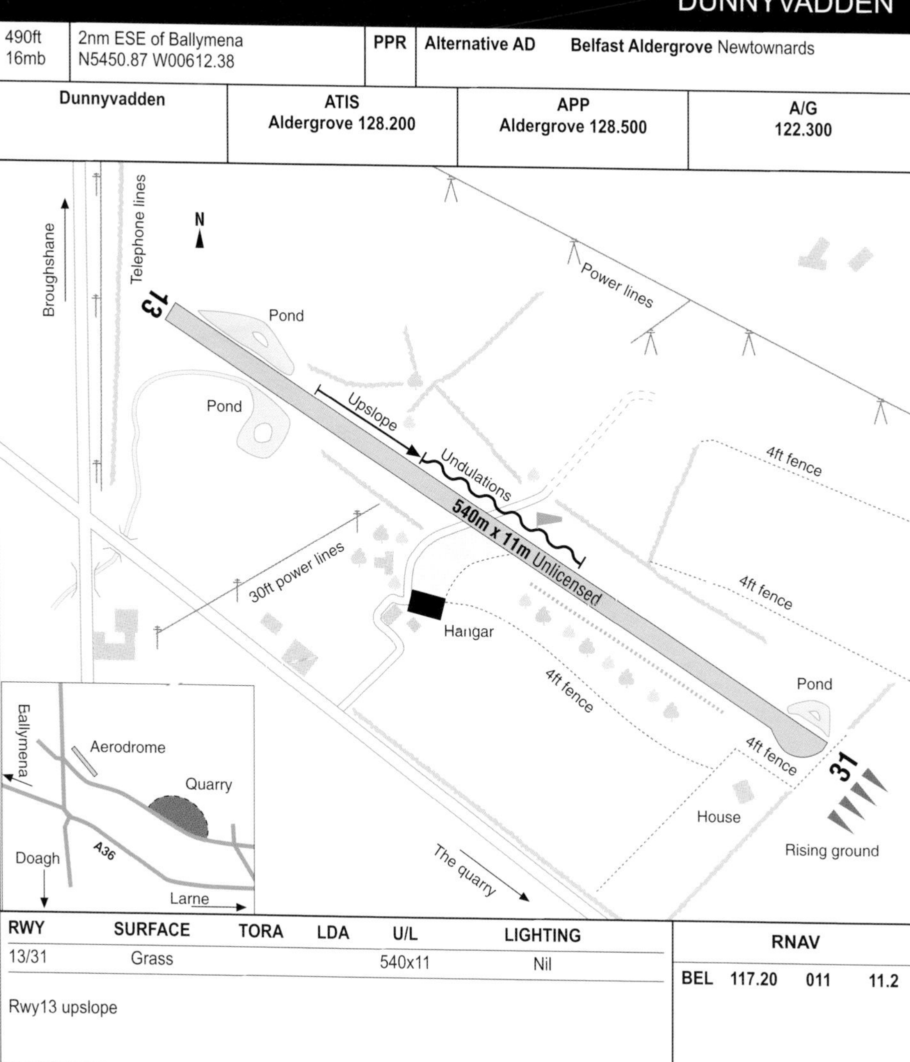

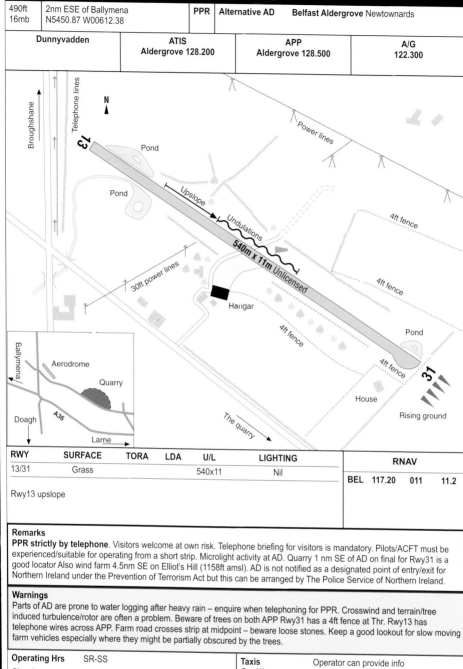

RWY	SURFACE	TORA	LDA	U/L	LIGHTING
13/31	Grass			540x11	Nil

Rwy13 upslope

RNAV			
BEL	117.20	011	11.2

Remarks
PPR strictly by telephone. Visitors welcome at own risk. Telephone briefing for visitors is mandatory. Pilots/ACFT must be experienced/suitable for operating from a short strip. Microlight activity at AD. Quarry 1 nm SE of AD on final for Rwy31 is a good locator Also wind farm 4.5nm SE on Elliot's Hill (1158ft amsl). AD is not notified as a designated point of entry/exit for Northern Ireland under the Prevention of Terrorism Act but this can be arranged by The Police Service of Northern Ireland.

Warnings
Parts of AD are prone to water logging after heavy rain – enquire when telephoning for PPR. Crosswind and terrain/tree induced turbulence/rotor are often a problem. Beware of trees on both APP Rwy31 has a 4ft fence at Thr. Rwy13 has telephone wires across APP. Farm road crosses strip at midpoint – beware loose stones. Keep a good lookout for slow moving farm vehicles especially where they might be partially obscured by the trees.

Operating Hrs SR-SS
Circuits Standard overhead join LH 1000ft QFE
Landing Fee Nil
Maintenance Nil possible hangarage by prior arr
Fuel MOGAS limited supplies by prior arr
Disabled Facilities
Restaurants Nil

Taxis Operator can provide info
Car Hire Nil
Weather Info Air N MOEx
Operator Christine Goodwin
Dunnyvadden Aerodrome
Craigadoo Rd, Ballymena
Co Antrim, BT42 4RS
Tel: 028 2565 0002
Tel: 028 9065 0222 (PSNI)
radiochristine@hotmail.com

Effective date:28/08/08 OP 07

120ft 4mb	4.7nm SE of Darlington N5430.55 W00125.77		Alternative AD	Newcastle Fishburn **Non-standard join**

Durham	ATIS 136.200	LARS/APP 118.850	TWR 119.800	FIRE 121.600

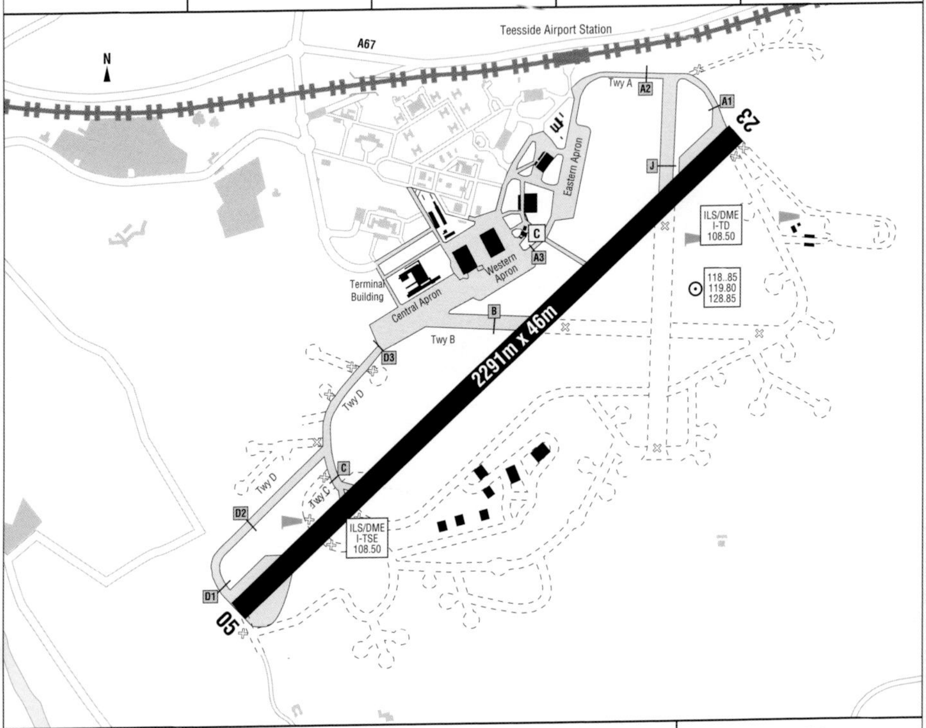

RWY	SURFACE	TORA	LDA	U/L	LIGHTING
05	Asphalt	2291	2291		Ap Thr Rwy PAPI 3° LHS
23	Asphalt	2291	2291		Ap Thr Rwy PAPI 3° RHS

RNAV

Remarks
Not available to non-radio ACFT. HI-Vis. Aerobatics and other unusual flight manoeuvres prohibited within ATZ except with prior written permission from AD MD. Training flights require prior arr with DO. Heli training is PPR from ATC. Unless otherwise instructed by ATC, ACFT using ILS in IMC or VMC shall not descend below 1800ft aal before intercepting the glide path, nor thereafter fly below it. ACFT APP without assistance from RAD or ILS must not fly lower than the ILS glide path or RAD APP procedure. Booking-out details will not be accepted on RT. Mandatory handling for all ACFT.
Aids to Navigation: NDB TD 347.50

Warning
Both ends of Rwy05/23 width is twice that of the associated edge lights take care to line up correctly, especially at night or in poor visibility. Deer hazard, report sightings to ATC.
Noise: Avoid over flying local villages, Middleton St George, Yarm, Middleton Oncrow and Eaglescliffe.

Operating Hrs 0500-2100 (Summer)
+1Hr (Winter) & by arr

Circuits Variable Light ACFT 1000ft QFE
Large ACFT minimum 1500ft QFE

Landing Fee £15.39 per metric tonne. Singles up to 2MT 25% discount if paid at the time

Maintenance Nil

Fuel AVGAS JET A1 100LL

Disabled Facilities

Handling **Tel:** 01325 333125 (Servisair)
Tel: 01325 332342 (Aviance)
Tel: 01325 337733 (Midwest Exec (GA))

Restaurant Restaurant & buffet at Terminal
St George Hotel **Tel:** 01325 332631 (on AD)

Taxis Available at terminal

Buses available at Terminal to: Darlington, Stockton, Middlesborough & Redcar

Car Hire
Avis **Tel:** 01325 332091
Hertz **Tel:** 01325 332600
Europcar **Tel:** 01325 333329

Weather Info M T9 Fax 436 VN MWC

Operator Durham Tees Valley Int Airport Ltd
Darlington,
Co Durham, DL2 1LU
Tel: 01325 332811
Fax: 01325 332810

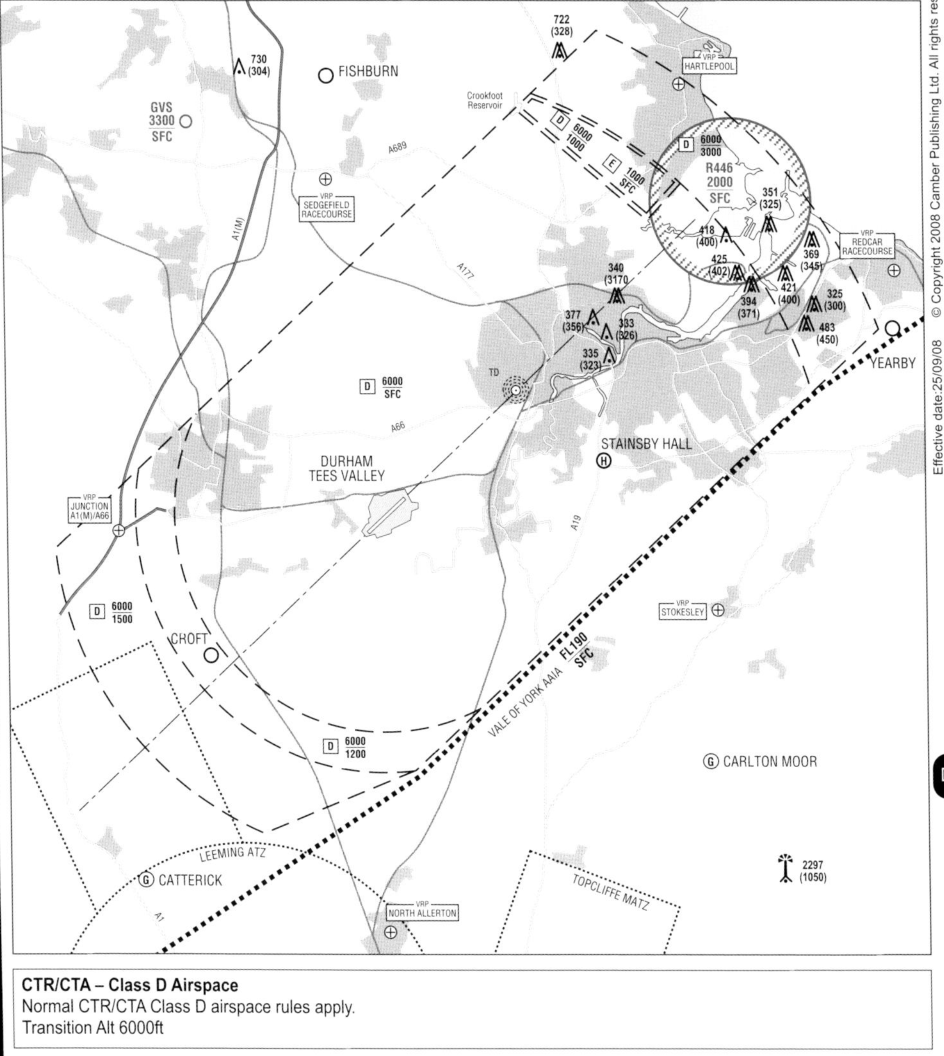

CTR/CTA – Class D Airspace
Normal CTR/CTA Class D airspace rules apply.
Transition Alt 6000ft

Visual Reference Points (VRP)

VRP	VOR/NDB	VOR/DME
Hartlepool N5441.00 W00112.83	NEW 144°/TD 033°	NEW 144°/27nm
Motorway Jct A1(M) & A66(M) N5430.00 W00137.60	NEW 179°/TD 255°	NEW 179°/32nm
Northallerton N5420.33 W00125.92		NEW 170°/43nm
Redcar Racecourse N5436.43 W00103.85	NEW 142°/TD 077°	NEW 142°/34nm
Sedgefield Racecourse N5438.75 W00128.10		NEW 164°/25nm
Stokesley N5428.18 W00111.68		NEW 156°/38nm

Effective date:25/09/08

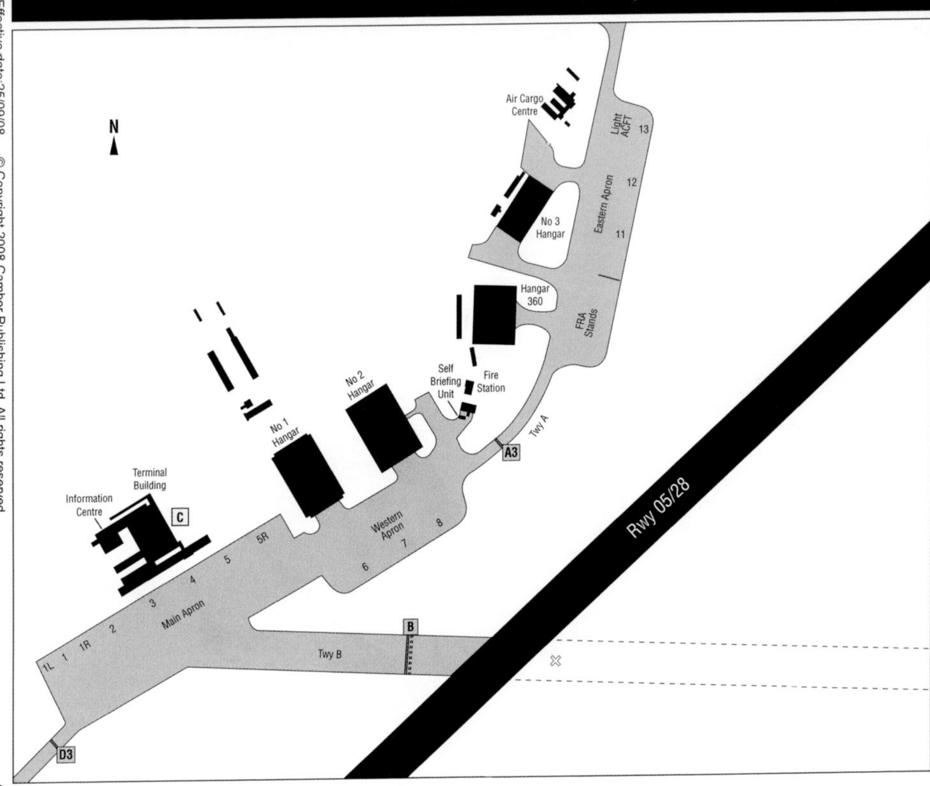
N
Air Cargo Centre
Light ACFT
13
12
11
Eastern Apron
No 3 Hangar
Hangar 360
FRA Stands
Self Briefing Unit
Fire Station
No 2 Hangar
No 1 Hangar
Twy A
A3
Terminal Building
Information Centre
C
5R
5
4
3
2
1R
1
1L
Main Apron
Western Apron
6
7
8
Rwy 05/28
B
Twy B
D3

D

EGSU DUXFORD

125ft 4mb	8nm S of Cambridge N5205.45 E00007.92	PPR	**Alternative AD** **Diversion AD**	**Cambridge** Bourn

Duxford	LARS Farnborough North 132.800	AFIS 122.075

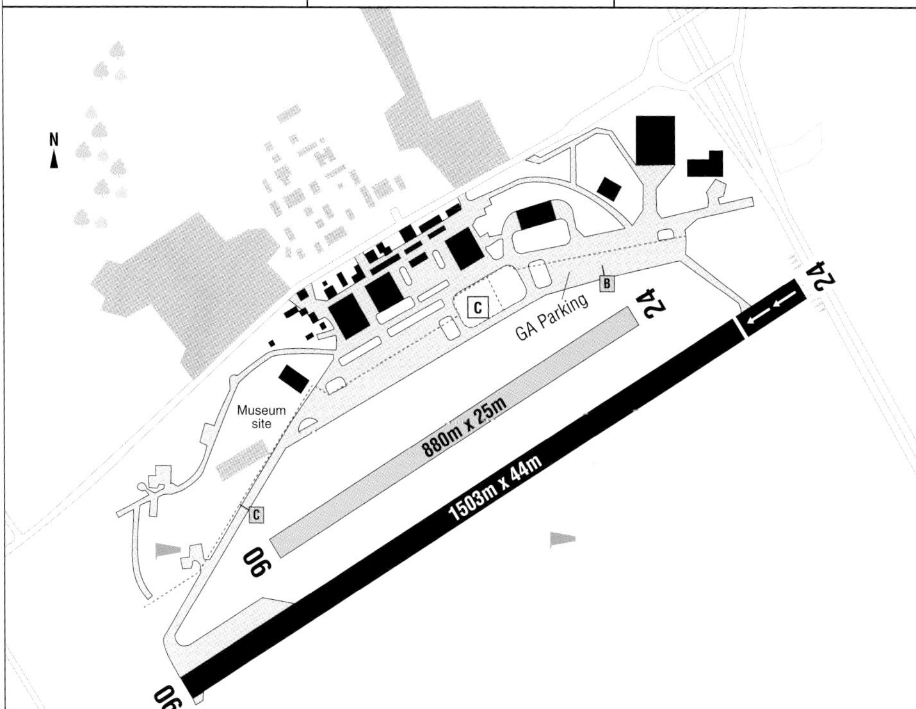

RWY	SURFACE	TORA	LDA	U/L	LIGHTING
06	Asphalt	1222	1222		Nil
24	Asphalt	1319	1219		Nil
06/24	Grass	880	880		Nil

Displaced Thr Rwy24 150m

RNAV			
BKY	116.25	025	6.6

Remarks
Strictly PPR by telephone. It is essential to obtain a briefing whether in or out bound. Powered ACFT circuits (from grass or paved Rwys) are to the S. The first 50m of Rwy24 (asphalt) is sterile and marked with yellow chevrons. Certain customs facilities available.

Warnings
AD may be closed due to adverse weather conditions. Wethersfield glider site to be avoided (Op Height 2000ft agl). Linton Zoo has birds of prey flying up to 2500ft.
Noise: Avoid over-flying the nearby villages of Duxford, Thriplow, Whittlesford and Fowlmere and adjacent bird sanctuary. Do not over fly Gas Venting Station to SE below 3200ft

Operating Hrs	1000-1800 (Summer) 1000-1600 (Winter)
Circuits	All to S 1000ft QFE No overhead/dead side joins
Landing Fee	On application
Maintenance	Aircraft Restoration Co **Tel:** 01223 835313
Fuel	JET A1 AVGAS 100LL 1000-1700 (L) & by arr
Disabled Facilities	Available
Restaurant	Restaurant at AD

Taxis	
Phil's Taxis	**Tel:** 01223 521918
Mick's Taxis	**Tel:** 01223 833613
Car Hire	
Willhire Veh Rental	**Tel:** 01223 414600
Weather Info	Air Cen MOEx
Operator	Imperial War Museum Cambridgeshire County Council Duxford Airfield, Cambs, CB2 4QR **Tel:** 01223 833376 (ATC) **Tel:** 01223 835000 Ex 236 (Switchboard) **Fax:** 01223 830410 (ATC) airtraffic@iwm.org.uk www.iwm.org.uk

N

Whittlesford

Newtown

Heathfield

Foxton

24

06

D

Arrivals

Rwy06 Dept – continue straight ahead 2nm (BP roundabout) before turning on course
Rwy24 Dept – LH circuit, Continue on Rwy, Do not turn right until passing Royston or 2000ft QNH
Rwy24 Arr – LH circuit, join downwind, position for 2nm final (BP roundabout)
Rwy06 Arr – RH circuit, join downwind

Inbound routes to avoid Stansted Controlled Airspace
Inbound from S to pass W of Stansted – Route LAM VOR – BPK VOR – BKY VOR – Duxford AD
Inbound from S to pass E of Stansted – Route Chelmsford VRP – Braintree VRP – Haverhill VRP – Duxford AD
Inbound from E – Route CLN VOR – Haverhill VRP – Duxford AD
Inbound from N to Rwy06 – Route via Sawston to join downwind
Inbound from N to Rwy24 – Route via Royston to join downwind

EGHU EAGLESCOTT

655ft 22mb	6nm ESE of Torrington N5055.72 W00359.37	PPR	**Alternative AD** **Diversion AD**	**Exeter** Dunkeswell

Eaglescott	**A/G** **123.000** **make blind calls**

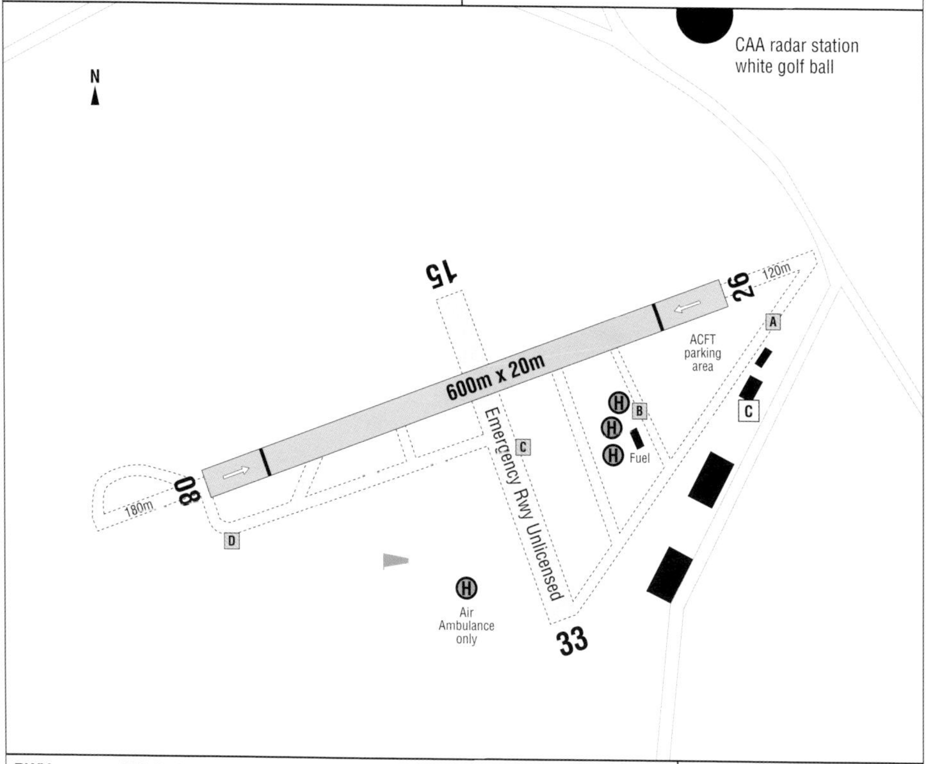

CAA radar station white golf ball

N

15

26

120m

A

ACFT parking area

600m x 20m

B

C

Emergency Rwy Unlicensed

C

Fuel

08

180m

D

Air Ambulance only

33

RWY	SURFACE	TORA	LDA	U/L	LIGHTING	RNAV
08/26	Grass	600	600		Nil	

Starter extension Rwy08 180m, Starter extension Rwy26 120m
Rwy15/33 (320m) available for light ACFT but is U/L

Remarks
PPR by telephone. AD licensed Sat-Sun & by arr. Not available at night for flights required to use a licensed AD or for public transport passenger flights required to use a licensed AD. Non-radio ACFT must contact AD prior to visit. If no response from A/G proceed with standard overhead join at 2000ft. H24 operations by Air Ambulance.

Warnings
Gliding by aerotow takes place at the AD using the area to the right of the Rwy in use. Microlight and model ACFT (SW corner) flying takes place at AD. All ACFT advised to hold over AD or on downwind leg if air ambulance calls 'starting' on an emergency call out. If on Base/Final leg continue to land.

Operating Hrs	0700-2000 (Summer) 0800-SS (Winter)
Circuit	All arriving ACFT LH. All Rwys 800ft Based gliders & Microlights RH
Landing Fee	Single £5, Heli £7.50 Twins £10
Maintenance	Nil
Fuel	AVGAS JET A1 MOGAS 100LL
Hangarage	Available

Disabled Facilities

Restaurants
Golf Club restaurant village cafe/restaurant in Atherington

Taxis	
Barum Cabs	**Tel:** 01271 24444
Car Hire	**Tel:** 01271 42746
Weather Info	Air SW MOEx
Operator	Devon Airsports Ltd Eaglescott Airfield Burrington, Umberleigh Devon, EX379LH **Tel:** 01769 520404 **Tel:** 07763 791834 www.eaglescott-airfield.com

Effective date:25/09/08

227ft 8mb	3nm SE of Halstead N5154.87 E00040.95	PPR	Alternative AD	Cambridge Andrewsfield

Earls Colne	LARS Southend 130.775 Farnborough North 132.800	A/G 122.425

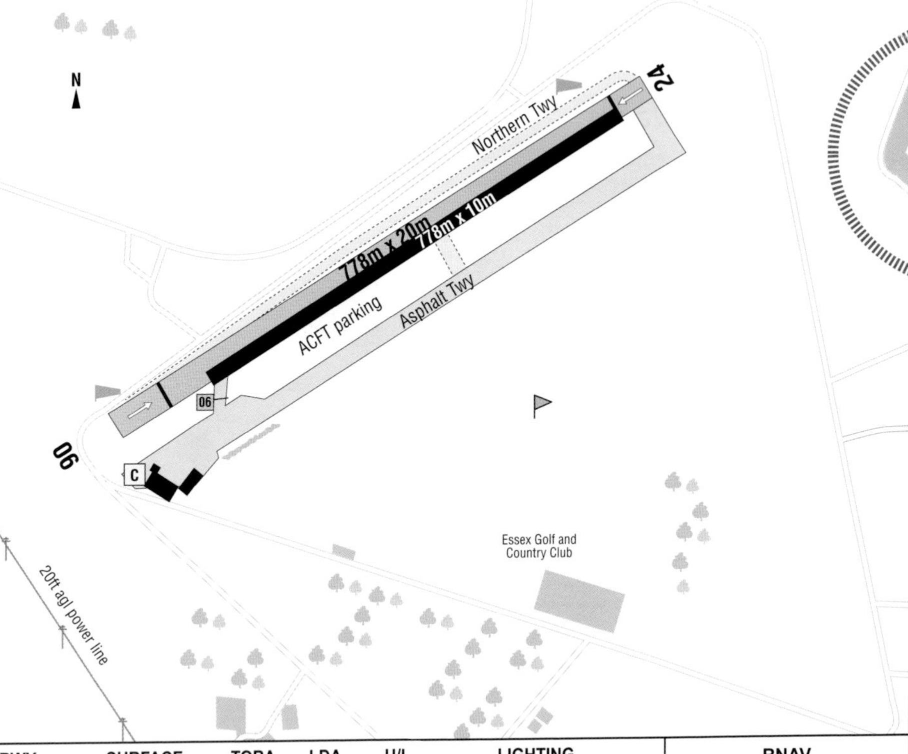

RWY	SURFACE	TORA	LDA	U/L	LIGHTING
06	Grass/Asph	877	778		Thr Rwy By Arr
24	Grass/Asph	840	778		Thr Rwy By Arr

Displaced Thr Rwy06 99m, Displaced Thr Rwy24 62m

RNAV			
CLN	114.55	286	17.8

Remarks
PPR essential for helicopters. Not available at night for flights required to use a licensed AD. Pilots are advised that the single 20m Rwy is 10m asphalt/20m grass and should select which surface to use and align appropriately.

Warnings
Power lines cross Rwy06 APP. Pilots should not land before displaced Thr. Customs facilities available 4hr PNR. Intense gliding at Wormingfield AD 4.5nm NE of AD. Winch launch up to 3000ft agl.
Noise: Rwy24 Dept climb ahead to 750ft QNH. Rwy06 Dept turn right after wooded area and mobile phone mast. Pilots are to obtain noise abatement brief prior to Dept. Avoid over flying Earls Colne village on Rwy06 dept and not below 500ft agl over Earls Colne village on Rwy24 APP.

Operating Hrs 0900-1800 (L)
Circuits 24 LH, 06 RH 1000ft QFE
Landing Fee Single £12, Twin £17, Heli £25
Maintenance Nil
Fuel AVGAS 100LL
Disabled Facilities

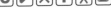

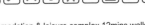

Restaurant
Restaurant accomodation & leisure complex 12mins walk from AD. 18 hole golf course & driving range
Tel: 01787 223676

Taxis/Car Hire By arr
Weather Info Air Cen MOEx
Operator Bulldog Aviation Ltd
Earls Colne Airfield
Colchester, Essex, CO6 2NS
Tel/Fax: 01787 223943 (AD Ops)
Tel: 01787 223676 (Flying School)
www.anglianflightcentres.co.uk

E

EAST FORTUNE

115ft 4mb	2.5nm S of North Berwick N5600.07 W00243.99	PPR	**Alternative AD** **Edinburgh** Fife

East Fortune Micro	**A/G** **118.750**

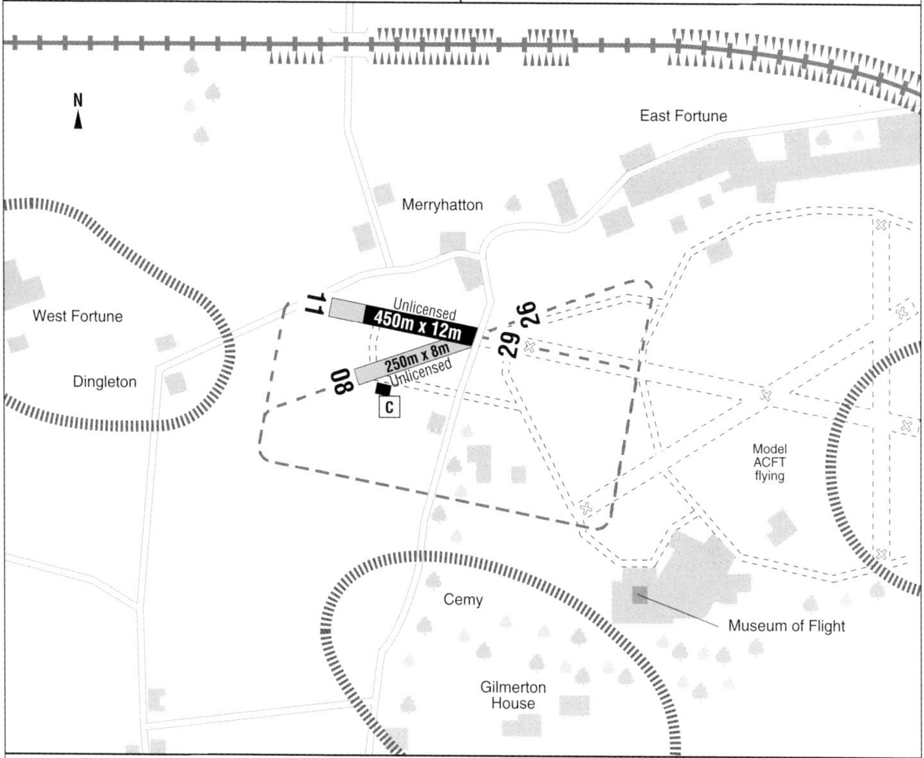

RWY	SURFACE	TORA	LDA	U/L	LIGHTING
11/29	Grass/Conc			450x12	Nil
08/26	Grass/Conc			250x8	Nil

RNAV			
SAB	112.50	292	18.7

Remarks
PPR by telephone. Primarily a microlight AD, light ACFT welcome. During Sunday Market PPR may be refused to visitors. The useable portion of WWII AD is clearly marked out in NW corner. Do not use other parts of AD which are the property of other landowners. AD is home of Museum of Flight which is a short walk down the perimeter track.

Warnings
Public road crosses WWII Rwy close to Rwy29 Thr. There is considerable military low flying in the vicinity. Model ACFT flying takes place on E portion of AD.
Noise: Please follow circuit pattern marked on AD chart. Do not over fly Sunday market on E portion of AD

Operating Hrs SR-SS

Circuits Join overhead 1500ft QFE
S 500ft QFE. Please follow tight circuit procedure on diagram

Landing Fee Nil donations gratefully received

Maintenance Nil

Fuel MOGAS available in emergency

Disabled Facilities

Restaurants Tea, coffee & biscuits available most days
Restaurant in museum complex and local garden centre

Taxis/Car Hire
Jim's Taxi **Tel:** 01620 894900
Johnny's Cab **Tel:** 01620 826222

Weather Info Air Sc GWC

Operator Mr G Douglas
East of Scotland Microlights
East Fortune
East Lothian
Tel: 01620 880332 (AD)
Tel: 01875 820102 (Mr Douglas)
gordon@eosm.co.uk
www.eosm.co.uk

50ft 1mb	7nm NE of RAF Coningsby N5308.25 E00000.75	PPR	Alternative AD	**Doncaster Sheffield** Wickenby

Non Radio	LARS Coningsby 120.80	LARS Waddington 127.350	Safetycom 135.475

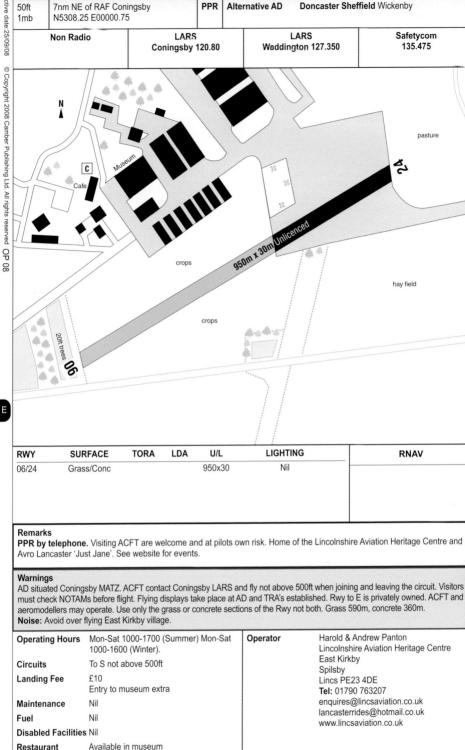

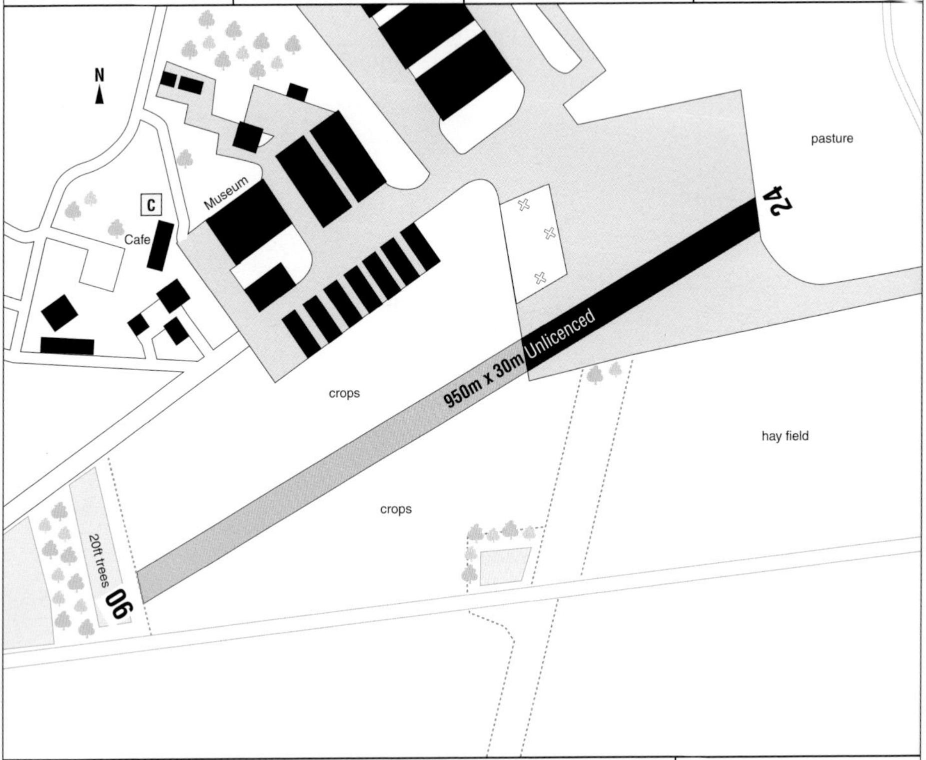

N
Museum
C
Cafe
pasture
24
Unlicenced
950m x 30m
crops
hay field
crops
20ft trees
06

RWY	SURFACE	TORA	LDA	U/L	LIGHTING	RNAV
06/24	Grass/Conc			950x30	Nil	

Remarks
PPR by telephone. Visiting ACFT are welcome and at pilots own risk. Home of the Lincolnshire Aviation Heritage Centre and Avro Lancaster 'Just Jane'. See website for events.

Warnings
AD situated Coningsby MATZ. ACFT contact Coningsby LARS and fly not above 500ft when joining and leaving the circuit. Visitors must check NOTAMs before flight. Flying displays take place at AD and TRA's established. Rwy to E is privately owned. ACFT and aeromodellers may operate. Use only the grass or concrete sections of the Rwy not both. Grass 590m, concrete 360m.
Noise: Avoid over flying East Kirkby village.

Operating Hours	Mon-Sat 1000-1700 (Summer) Mon-Sat 1000-1600 (Winter).
Circuits	To S not above 500ft
Landing Fee	£10 Entry to museum extra
Maintenance	Nil
Fuel	Nil
Disabled Facilities	Nil
Restaurant	Available in museum
Taxi/Car Hire	Nil
Weather Info	Air N MOEx

Operator
Harold & Andrew Panton
Lincolnshire Aviation Heritage Centre
East Kirkby
Spilsby
Lincs PE23 4DE
Tel: 01790 763207
enquires@lincsaviation.co.uk
lancasterrides@hotmail.co.uk
www.lincsaviation.co.uk

306ft 10mb	7nm SE of Derby N5249.87 W00119.68	PPR	Alternative AD **Birmingham** Leicester **Non-standard join**

East Midlands	ATIS	APP	RAD
	128.225	134.175	120.125

TWR	GND	FIRE
124.000	121.900	121.600

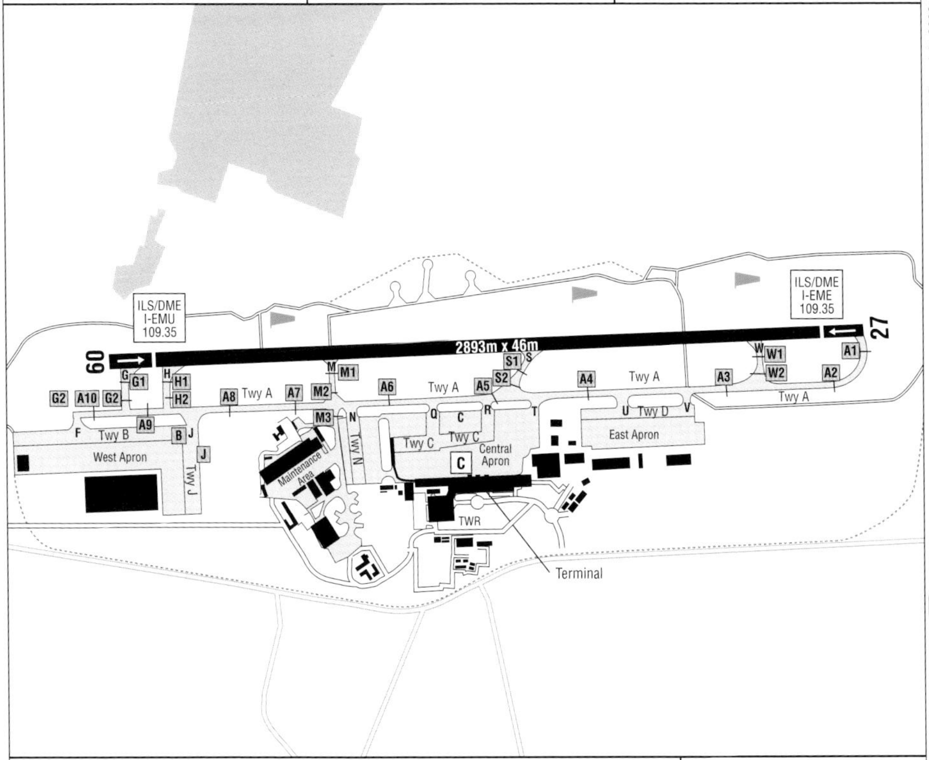

RWY	SURFACE	TORA	LDA	U/L	LIGHTING
09	Asphalt	2893	2713		Ap Thr Rwy PAPI 3° LHS
27	Asphalt	2893	2763		Ap Thr Rwy PAPI 3° LHS

7m shoulders either side of Rwy

RNAV			
TNT	115.70	141	18.1

Remarks

PPR to non-radio ACFT. Hi-Vis. Over night parking on the central apron is limited and requirements should be notified early to handling agents. Training flights are subject to approval and acceptance by ATC, but permission will not be given for any such flights by any type of ACFT 2200-0800 (weekdays). Training flights on Sun & PH only permitted for ACFT <17000kgs MTOW. Operators wishing to take advantage of rebated fees and charges for training must make an application for training rebates in advance to the Airport Authority. Use of a handling agent is mandatory when using all 3 aprons. Handling services available from: Donington Aviation, Servisair and Execair.

Aids to Navigation: NDB EME 353.50. NDB EMW 393.00

Warnings

Interference to magnetic compasses may be experienced by ACFT taxiing on Rwy N of final 100m of Twy A S of the Thr of Rwy27 in the areas of W2/W1. Carry out any pre take-off check of Heading Indicator against magnetic compass elsewhere. April-September when grass cutting is taking place in the areas immediately adjacent to the Rwy, circuit flying by light ACFT may be restricted at certain times. In Spring and Autumn bird concentrations maybe present on all areas under agricultural use on the APP to Rwy09/27. A pyrotechnic factory is situated approximately 3nm N of the AD. Rockets, carrying flares of up to 150,000 candela deployed on parachutes, may be tested up to a height on 1000 ft agl by day and night. A flare stack is situated at Chellaston. The stack is 36ft agl and the flare is 20 ft in length. ACFT must not descend below ILS GP on final APP. When landing Rwy09 in strong S winds, turbulence and windshear possible.

Noise: Pilots must ensure that as far as practicable ACFT are operated in a manner calculated to cause the least disturbance in areas surrounding the AD. Avoid making final turn on APP Rwy27 over Kegworth village.

Operating Hrs H24

Circuits Variable at the discretion of ATC

Landing Fee On application
Reduced rates for light ACFT handled by Execair

Maintenance Donington Aviation
East Midlands Flying School

Fuel AVGAS AVTUR W80 W100 available from Donington Aviation & Simon Aviation

Disabled Facilities

Handling
Tel: 01332 852204 (British Midland)
Tel: 01332 812278 (Servisair)
Tel: 01332 811004 (Donington Aviation)
Tel: 01332 811179 (Signature)
Fax: 01332 853584 (Servisair)
Fax: 01332 811139 (Signature)
Fax: 01332 852316 (British Midland)
Fax: 01332 812726 (Donington Avistion)

Restaurants Refreshments available in AD
Restaurants at Donington Thistle Hotel

Taxis Available at terminal
Airport **Tel:** 01332 814225
Donnington **Tel:** 01332 810146

Car Hire
Avis **Tel:** 01332 811403
National **Tel:** 01332 853551
Hertz **Tel:** 01332 811726

Weather Info MT9 T18 Fax247 A VM VN MOEx
Tel: 0891 517567

Operator
East Midlands Int Airport Ltd
East Midlands Airport
Castle Donington
Derby, DE74 2SA
Tel: 01332 852852
Tel: 01332 810444 (Donair Flying Club)
Fax: 01332 852823 (ATC)
atsm@eastmidlandsairport.com

E

Helicopter Arrival VFR
Helicopters must APP from N or S, remaining clear of the APP and climb-out of Rwy09/27. Do not over fly Castle Donington to N or Diseworth to S.
Arr from N must obtain specific clearance to cross Rwy09/27 prior to crossing AD boundary, and on crossing boundary are to descend towards the allocated apron stand without over flying equipment or occupied stands
Arr from S must join close base leg, (RB09, LB27) or as directed by ATC. Descend along Rwy or safe path parallel S of Rwy or as directed by ATC. GND or air taxi to parking areas as instructed, following Twys.

Helicopter Dept VFR
Dept as cleared by ATC. Dept must obtain specific clearance to cross Rwy09/27, which must be made at right angle to Rwy. Dept to S must GND or air taxi to Rwy, then on ATC clearance, climb above Rwy, turning S only when clear of all airport buildings. On reaching AD boundary comply with ATC instructions regarding heading/route & height/altitude.

Entry/Exit lanes are established to permit ACFT to operate to and from East Midlands Airport in IMC, but not under IFR.
1 Long Eaton Lane
2 Shepshed Lane
(Both are 3nm wide centered on the M1)
Use of the lanes is subject to SVFR clearance. ACFT must remain clear of cloud and in sight of the surface not above 2000ft (QNH). Also recommended for VFR arr and dept.

CTA/CTR Class D Airspace
Normal CTA/CTR Class D Airspace rules apply
Transition Alt 4000ft

Visual Reference Points (VRP)

VRP	VOR/VOR	VOR/NDB	VOR/DME
Bottesford	TNT 102°/HON 044°	TNT 102°/EME 065°	TNT 102°/33nm
N5257.88 W00046.90	DTY 017°		GAM 165°/20nm
Church Broughton	TNT 188°/HON 001°	TNT 188°/EME 283°	TNT 188°/10nm
N5253.17 W00141.90	DTY 336°	EMW 294°	
Markfield (M1 J22)	TNT 150°/HON 036°	DTY 351°/EME 206°	HON 036°/24nm
N5241.73 W00117.55	DTY 351°		DTY 351°/32nm
Measham (M42 J11)	TNT 171°/HON 015°	HON 015°/EME 239°	HON 015°/20nm
N5241.33 W00132.88	DTY 335°		DTY 335°/34nm
Melton Mowbray	TNT 126°/HON 053°	HON 053°/ DTY 016°	HON 053°/36nm
N5244.37 W00053.57	DTY 016°	EME 120°	DTY 016°/35nm
Trowell (M1 Services)	TNT 113°/HON 024°	TNT 113°/EME 344°	TNT 113°/16nm
N5257.70 W00116.50	DTY 356°	EMW 043°	GAM 214°/22nm

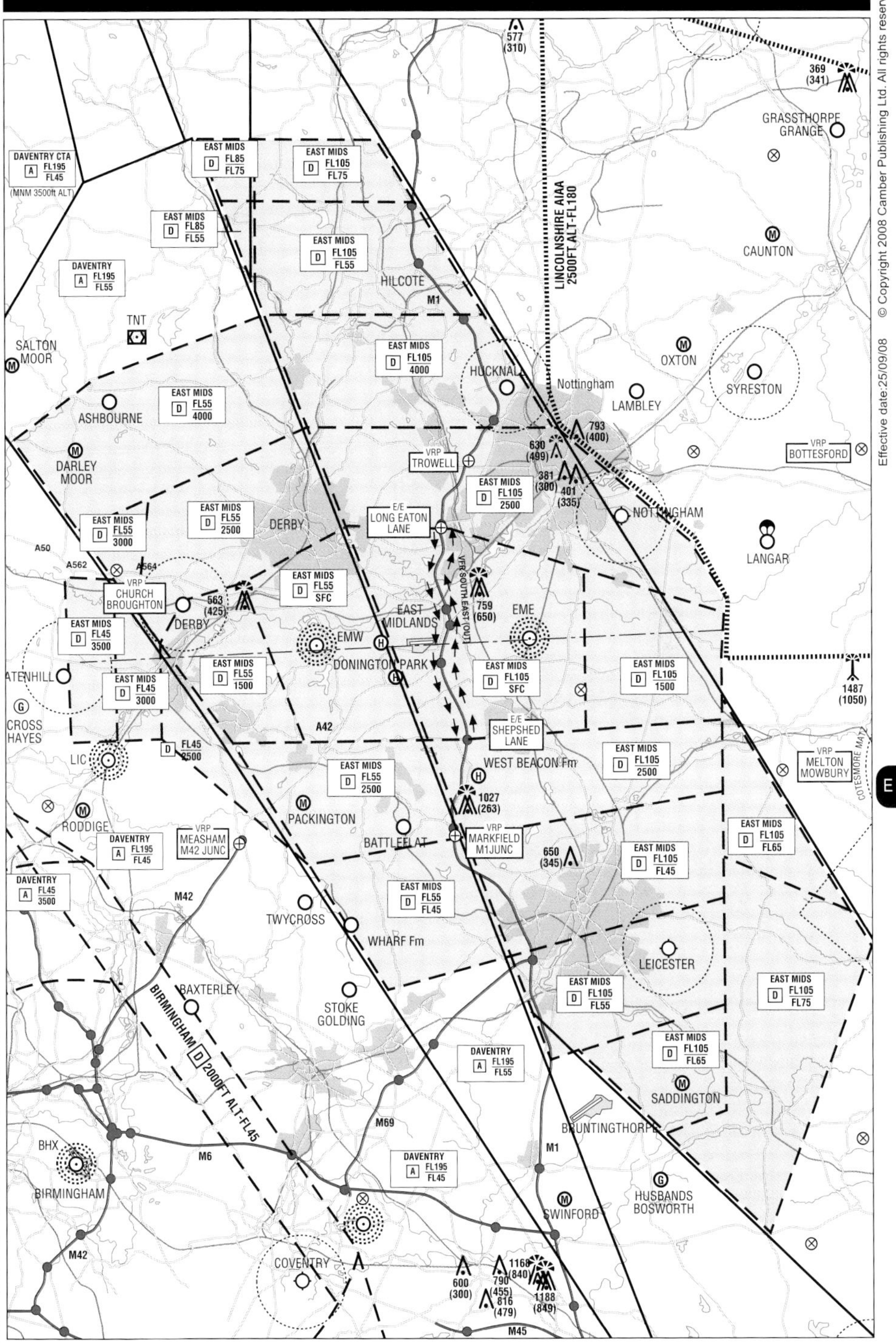

Effective date:25/09/08

E

600ft 20mb	6nm S of Ross on Wye N5150.13 W00235.98	PPR	Alternative AD **Gloucestershire** Shobdon

Non-Radio	APP Gloucester 128.550	LARS Brize 124.275	Safetycom 135.475

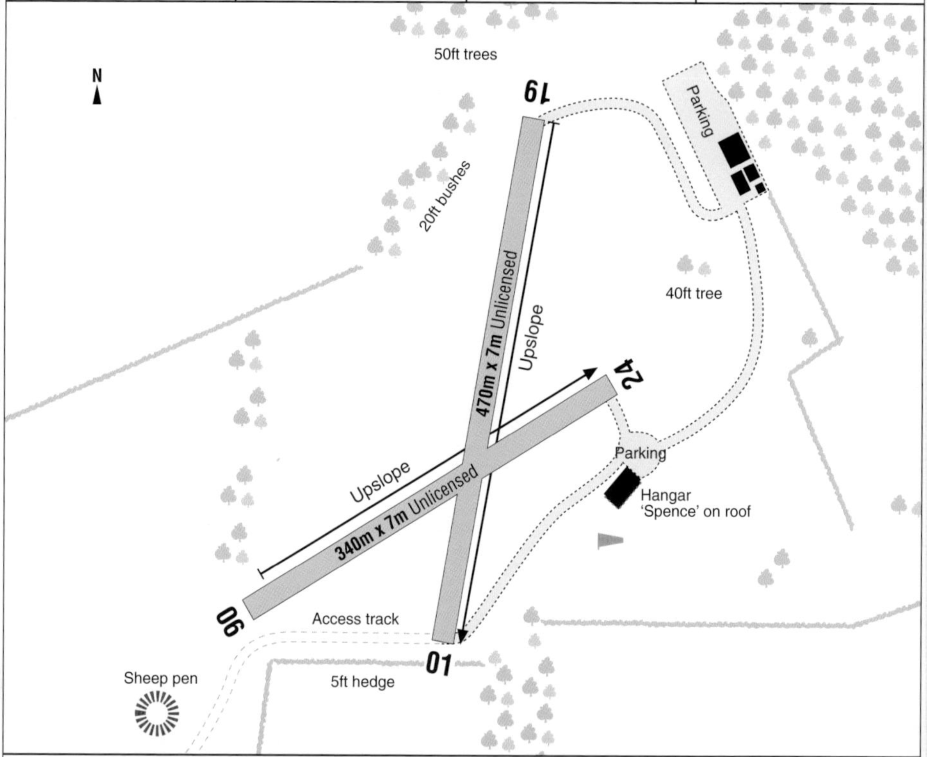

RWY	SURFACE	TORA	LDA	U/L	LIGHTING
01/19	Grass			470x7	Nil
06/24	Grass			340x7	Nil

RNAV			
BCN	117.45	079	25.8

Remarks

PPR by telephone. Visiting STOL ACFT welcome at pilot's own risk. AD situated on a hilltop. There is an upslope on Rwy 06 & 19. Visiting ACFT should land only on Rwy06 or 19, and Dept only on Rwy01 or 24. Very well maintained site with deep wooded escarpments to the NE & E.

Warnings

Because of the close proximity of woodland and escarpments pilots should be aware of rollover and turbulence even in light wind conditions. There is a copse of 50ft trees just right of short final Rwy19. Please use mown Twy. Windsock displayed on bank behind hangar in SE corner of AD. Access track crosses Rwy01 Thr.

Noise: Avoid over flying large house to the S of AD.

Operating Hrs	SR-SS
Circuits	LH 1000ft QFE
Landing Fee	Nil
Maintenance	Nil
Fuel	MOGAS by arr
Disabled Facilities	Nil
Restaurants	Nil
Taxis/Car Hire	Nil
Weather Info	Air Cen MOEx

Operator

Spence Airfield Associates Ltd
Holtar Bungalow
4 Albert Road
Coleford
Gloucester
Gloucestershire GL16 8DZ
Tel: 01594 562653 (Graham Vaughan)
Tel: 07768 746055 (Mark Taylor)
steveatholtar@tiscali.co.uk
www.spenceairfield.co.uk

EASTON MAUDIT

300ft 10mb	7nm ESE of Northampton N5212.80 W00042.10	**PPR**	**Alternative AD** **Cranfield** Northampton

Non-Radio	**ATIS** **Cranfield 121.875 (Dept)**	**Safetycom** **135.475**

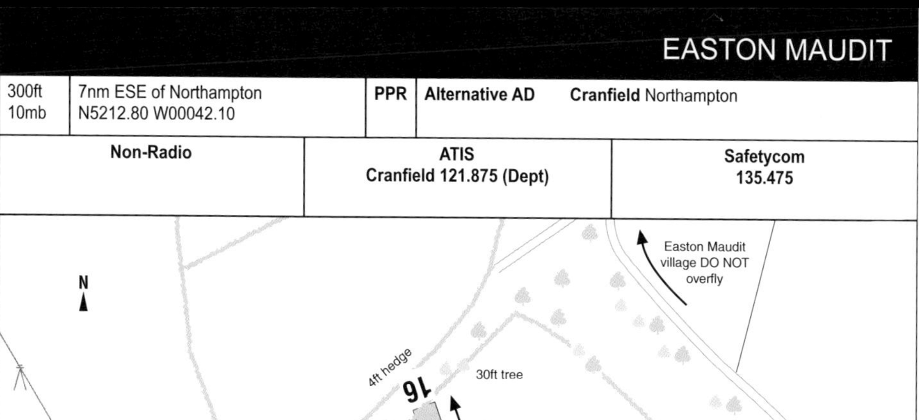

RWY	SURFACE	TORA	LDA	U/L	LIGHTING
16/34	Grass			604x23	Nil

Rwy16 recommended in light winds due to down slope at N end

RNAV			
DTY	**116.40**	**087**	**15.4**

Remarks
PPR by telephone. Authorised visitors welcome at pilot's own risk. Fuel available from Northampton Sywell 7nm NNW.

Warnings
Power lines run close to W of AD but do not obstruct APP/Dept. Low hedges at both Thrs. Crops grown close to Rwy edge.
Noise: Do not over fly Easton Maudit village and Farmhouse 0.5nm S of AD

Operating Hrs SR-SS
Circuit 1000ft QFE
Landing Fee Nil
Maintenance Nil
Fuel Nil
Disabled Facilities

Restaurant Nil
Taxis/Car Hire Nil
Weather Info Air Cen MOEx

Operator
Tim Allebone
The Limes
Easton Maudit
Northants NN29 7NR
Tel: 01933 663225
Tel: 07973 147143
tim.allebone@virgin.net

Effective date:25/09/08

20ft 1mb	On Isle of Eday N5911.43 W00246.34	PPR	Alternative AD Diversion AD	Kirkwall Sanday

Non-radio	APP Kirkwall 118.300	Safetycom 135.475

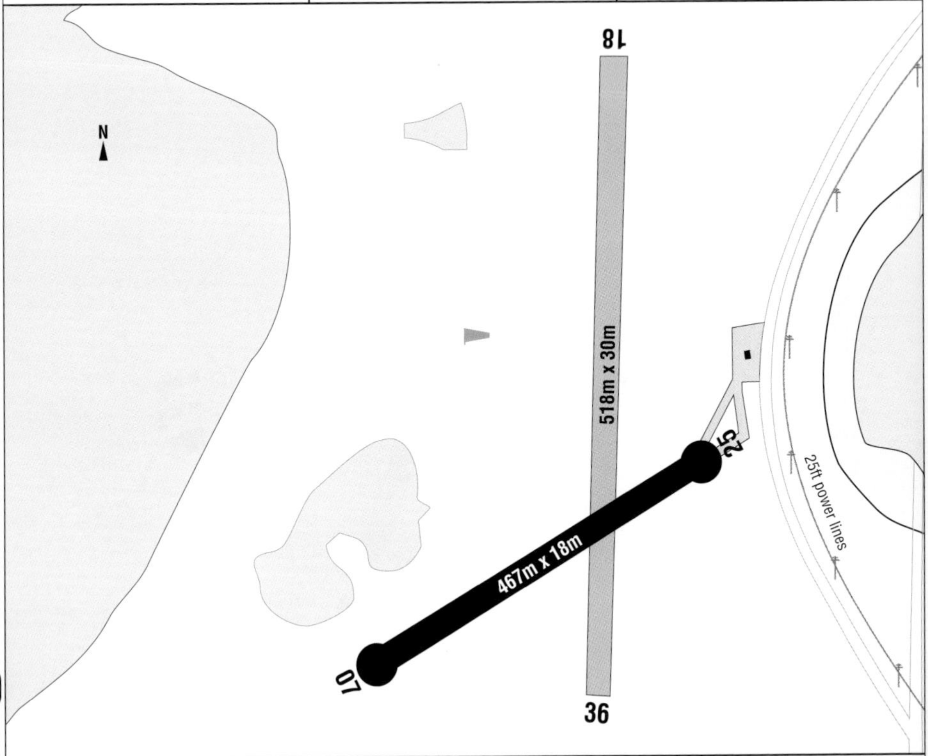

N
18
518m x 30m
36
07
467m x 18m
25
25ft power lines

RWY	SURFACE	TORA	LDA	U/L	LIGHTING
18/36	Grass	518	518		Nil
07	Graded Hardcore	462	462		Nil
25	Graded Hardcore	467	462		Nil

RNAV

Remarks
PPR for all ACFT. Licensed for day use only. RT contact with Kirkwall is recommended.

Warnings
Rwy18/36 may become soft and waterlogged after periods of continuous rainfall, particularly at W end.

Operating Hrs By arr
Circuits Nil
Landing Fee Nil
If fire cover provided then £36.95
Maintenance Nil
Fuel Nil
Disabled Facilities

Restaurants
Blett Boathouse **Tel:** 01857 622248
Papley House **Tel:** 01857 622282
Taxis
Mr A Stewart **Tel:** 01857 622206
Mrs E Thompson **Tel:** 01857 622256
Car Hire Nil

Weather Info Air Sc GWC
Operator Orkney Islands Council Council Offices
Kirkwall
Orkney
Scotland
Tel: 01856 873535 Ex 2305
Fax: 01856 876094

500ft 17mb	7nm N of Driffield N5406.42 W00027.26	PPR	Alternative AD Humberside Beverley Non-standard join

Eddsfield	LARS Humberside 119.125	A/G 134.000 (Not always manned)

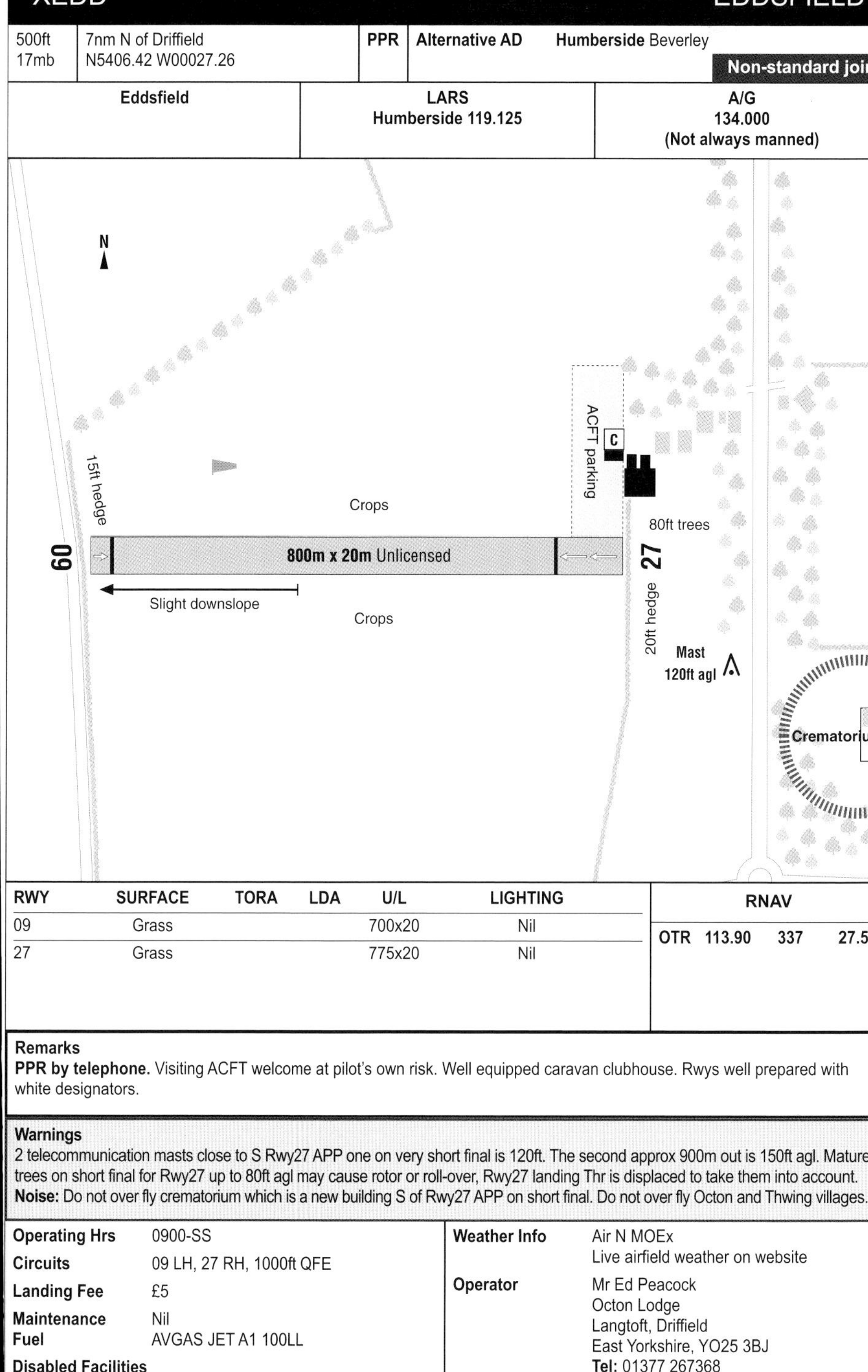

RWY	SURFACE	TORA	LDA	U/L	LIGHTING
09	Grass			700x20	Nil
27	Grass			775x20	Nil

RNAV			
OTR	113.90	337	27.5

Remarks
PPR by telephone. Visiting ACFT welcome at pilot's own risk. Well equipped caravan clubhouse. Rwys well prepared with white designators.

Warnings
2 telecommunication masts close to S Rwy27 APP one on very short final is 120ft. The second approx 900m out is 150ft agl. Mature trees on short final for Rwy27 up to 80ft agl may cause rotor or roll-over, Rwy27 landing Thr is displaced to take them into account. **Noise:** Do not over fly crematorium which is a new building S of Rwy27 APP on short final. Do not over fly Octon and Thwing villages.

Operating Hrs 0900-SS
Circuits 09 LH, 27 RH, 1000ft QFE
Landing Fee £5
Maintenance Nil
Fuel AVGAS JET A1 100LL
Disabled Facilities
Restaurants The Old Mill 0.5nm from AD
Taxis **Tel:** 01723 815815
Tel: 07852 407145
Car Hire Nil

Weather Info Air N MOEx
Live airfield weather on website

Operator Mr Ed Peacock
Octon Lodge
Langtoft, Driffield
East Yorkshire, YO25 3BJ
Tel: 01377 267368
Tel: 07792 398320
airfield@eastyorkshire.co.uk
www.eastyorkshire.co.uk/eddsfield

Effective date:25/09/08 OP 08

EGPH EDINBURGH

136ft 5mb	5nm W of Edinburgh N5557.00 W00322.35	PPR	Alternative AD **Glasgow** Fife Diversion AD

Non-standard join

Edinburgh	ATIS	APP	RAD
	131.350	121.200	128.975

TWR	GND	FIRE
118.700	121.750	121.600

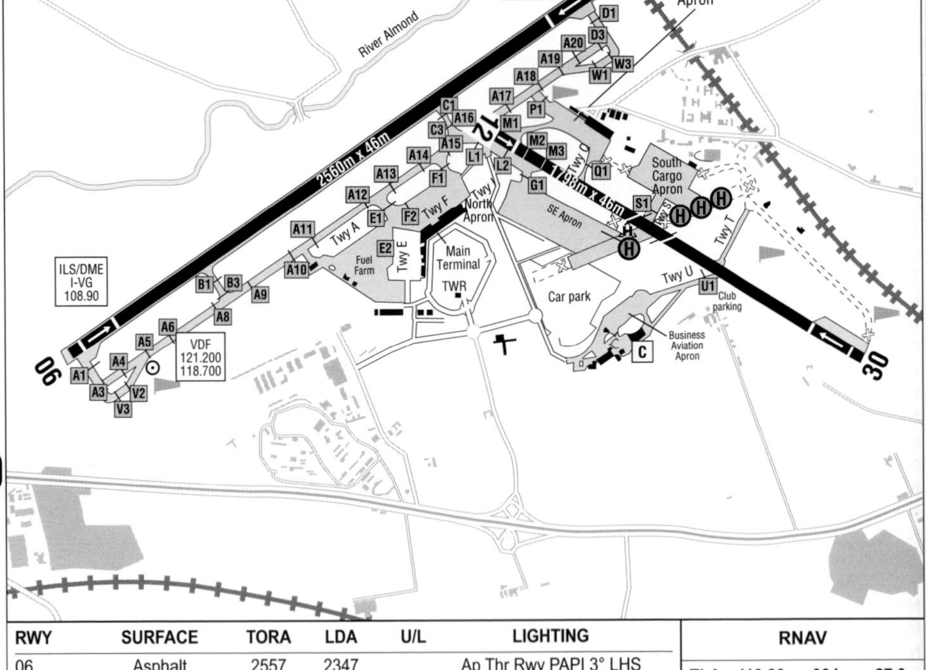

RWY	SURFACE	TORA	LDA	U/L	LIGHTING
06	Asphalt	2557	2347		Ap Thr Rwy PAPI 3° LHS
24	Asphalt	2555	2347		Ap Thr Rwy PAPI 3° LHS
12	Asphalt	1798	1798		Ap Thr Rwy PAPI 3° LHS
30	Asphalt	1798	1746		Ap Thr Rwy PAPI 3.5° LHS

Displaced Thr Rwy06 213m, Displaced Thr Rwy24 213m

RNAV			
TLA	113.80	004	27.0

Remarks

PPR to non-radio ACFT. Rwy06/24 PPR 0800-1000 for training flights. All GA must make prior Arr with a handling agent for GND handling of all flights. All movements on GA apron must be marshalled. Due to Ltd parking space ALL ACFT are PPR with their handling agent. All other GA ACFT may be required to go directly to GA terminal for off-loading/loading of passengers. Permission may be given for parking on the main apron for off-loading passengers interlining etc. But ACFT must move to GA apron ASAP. Transport to & from the main terminal is via your handing agent. All telephone calls are recorded.
Aids to Navigation: NDB EDN 341.00. NDB UW 368.00

Warnings

There is a large bird population around the AD and hence increased bird activity in the lower airspace, together with visible evidence of deterrent activity in the form of shell crackers being fired. All ACFT must be operated in a manner calculated to cause the least disturbance practicable in areas surrounding the AD. For visual APP Rwy06/24: Propeller driven ACFT whose MTWA does not exceed 5700kg will not join final below 1000ft QFE. Rwy12/30 sometimes unavailable for ACFT ops.

Operating Hrs	H24	**Maintenance**	Aeroscot Engineering **Tel:** 0131 344 3349
Circuits	As directed by ATC	**Fuel**	AVGAS JET A1 100LL Signature or Greer Aviation
Landing Fee	BAA Rates		

Disabled Facilities	
Handling	**Tel:** 0131 317 7447 (Signature) **Tel:** 0131 339 1010 (Greer Aviation) **Fax:** 0131 317 7484 (Signature) **Fax:** 0131 339 1020 (Greer Aviation) egph@greeraviation.com
Restaurant	Restaurants/buffet/bars available at Terminal
Taxis	Available at Terminal
Car Hire	
Avis	**Tel:** 0131 333 1866
Europcar	**Tel:** 0131 333 2588
Hertz	**Tel:** 0131 333 1019
Alamo	**Tel:** 0131333 5100
Weather Info	M T9 T18 Fax 276 A VSc GWC ATIS **Tel:** 0131 333 6216 Met Office **Tel:** 0131 339 7950

Operator	Edinburgh Airport Ltd Edinburgh Airport Lothian EH12 9DN **Tel:** 0131 344 3139 (OPS) **Tel:** 0131 333 6239 (ATC) **Fax:** 0131 317 7638 (ATC) **Fax:** 0131 333 5055 (EAL)

Visual Reference Points (VRP)

VRP	VOR/VOR	VOR/NDB	VOR/DME
Arthur's Seat N5556.63 W00309.70	GOW 088°/TLA 018°	TLA 018°/EDN 121°	SAB 278°/32nm
Bathgate N5554.17 W00338.42	TLA 342°/GOW 090°	TLA 342°/EDN 254°	GOW 090°/27nm
Cobbinshaw Reservoir N5548.47 W00334.00	TLA 343°/GOW 101°	TLA 343°/EDN 227°	TLA 343°/19nm
Dalkeith N5553.60 W00304.10	TLA 026°/SAB 272°	TLA 026°/EDN 129°	TLA 026°/26nm
Forth Road Bridge (N TWR) N5600.37 W00324.23	GOW 081°/TLA 001°	PTH 187°/EDN 297°	SAB 282°/41nm
Hillend Ski Slope N5553.30 W00312.50	TLA 016°/SAB 272°	SAB 272°/EDN 159°	TLA 016°/24nm
Kelty N5608.08 W00323.25	TLA 002°/SAB 293°	SAB 293°/EDN 344°	GOW 068°/39nm
Kirkcaldy Harbour N5606.83 W00309.00	TLA 015°/SAB 295°	SAB 295°/EDN 034°	GOW 075°/46nm
Kirkliston N5557.33 W00324.18	TLA 001°/GOW 085°	GOW 085°/EDN 255°	GOW 085°/36nm
Kirknewton N5553.25 W00325.08	GOW 092°/TLA 359°	GOW 092°/EDN 224°	GOW 092°/35nm
Musselburgh N5556.83 W00302.42	TLA 025°/SAB 279°	TLA 025°/EDN 107°	TLA 025°/29nm
Penicuik N5549.92 W00313.42	GOW 097°/TLA 016°	GOW 097°/EDN 171°	GOW 097°/41nm
Philipstoun (M9 J2) N5558.90 W00330.72	GOW 082°/TLA 354°	GOW 082°/UW 276°	GOW 082°/32nm
Polmont N5559.33 W00341.00	TLA 343°/SAB 280°	TLA 343°/EDN 277°	GOW 078°/27nm
West Linton N5545.17 W00321.45	TLA 004°/SAB 260°	SAB 260°/EDN 195°	TLA 004°/15nm

CTR – Class D Airspace

Normal CTA/CTR Class D Airspace rules apply

Transition Alt 6000ft

1 SVFR flight clearance may be given in the Edinburgh CTR subject to traffic limitations; normally when the MET reports indicate IMC within the zone or when the pilot is unable to maintain VMC.

2 Due to the nature of the terrain in the vicinity, a RAD service will not normally be provided.

3 Pilots are reminded that SVFR clearances only apply to flight within the CTR.

4 Entry/Exit lanes are established to permit ACFT to operate to and from Edinburgh in IMC but not under IFR. These are:

a Polmont lane

b Kelty lane

Both these lanes are 3nm wide and use is subject to ATC clearance, irrespective of weather conditions. ACFT must remain clear of cloud, insight of the surface and not above 2000ft QNH. Minimum visibility is 3km. ACFT using the lanes shall keep the centre-line on the left.

Pilots are responsible for maintaining adequate clearance from the ground and other obstacles.

SVFR clearances may not be confined to the Entry/Exit lanes described above.

5 During the day, non-radio ACFT may fly in the CTR provided they have previously obtained permission and maintain VFR.

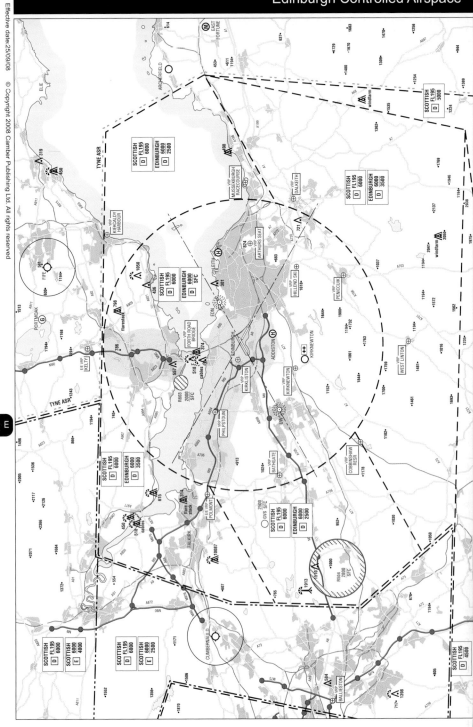

516ft 17mb	4nm E of Winkleigh (Disused AD) N5052.13 W00352.13	**PPR**	**Alternative AD**	**Exeter** Eaglescott

Eggesford	**LARS** **Exeter 128.975**	**A/G** **123.500** **(Not always manned)**

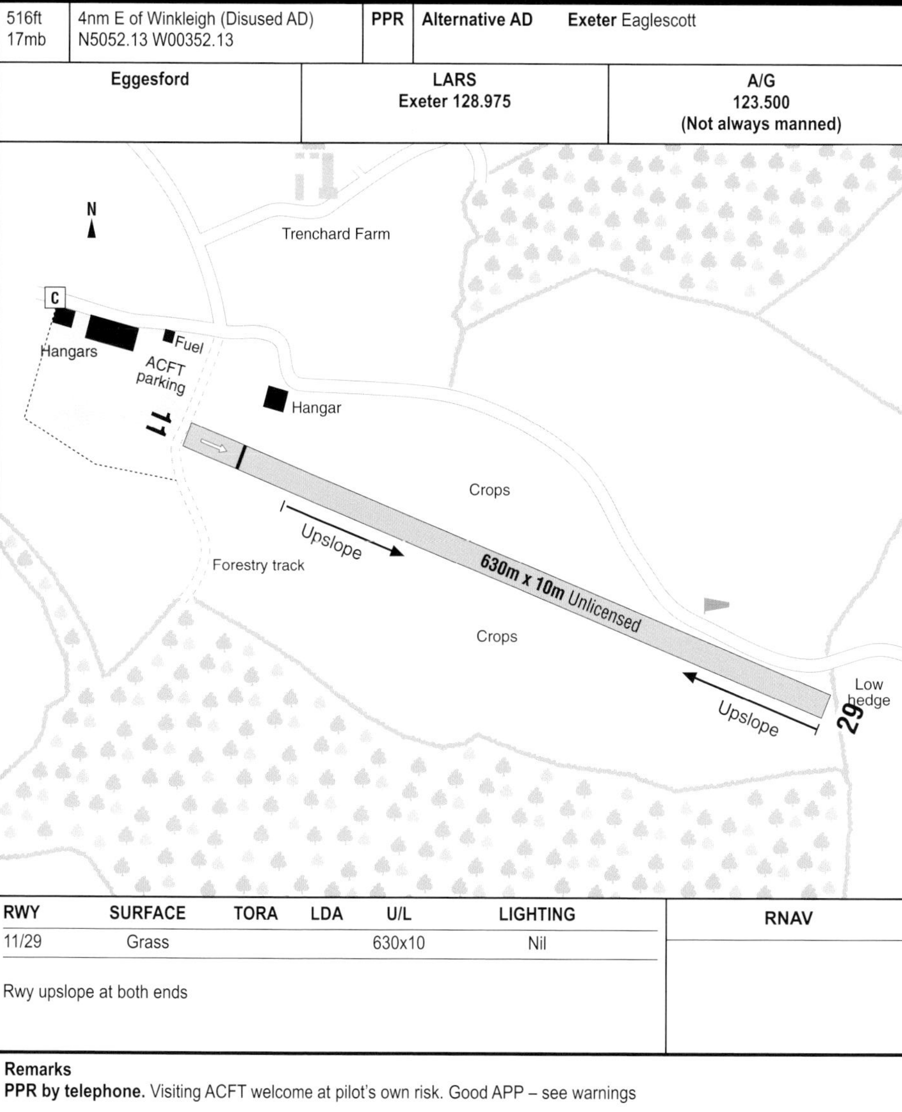

RWY	SURFACE	TORA	LDA	U/L	LIGHTING
11/29	Grass			630x10	Nil

Rwy upslope at both ends

RNAV

Remarks

PPR by telephone. Visiting ACFT welcome at pilot's own risk. Good APP – see warnings

Warnings

Sheep may be grazing so PPR essential. Forestry track crosses Rwy11 Thr, be alert to vehicles or pedestrians. There is a low hedge at the Rwy29 Thr. Woodland to the N & S of AD may cause turbulence, Windshear, or Rotor effects, particularly from a SW wind. **Noise:** Avoid village 1nm to the S and cottages 0.5nm to the N of AD.

Operating Hrs	0900-SS (L) & by arr
Circuits	29 LH, 11 RH800ft QFE
Landing Fee	Nil
Maintenance	Nil
Fuel	100LL available by arr
Disabled Facilities	Nil
Restaurants	Country hotel & garden centre within 1 mile of AD
Taxis	**Tel:** 01769 573636
Car Hire	Nil
Weather Info	Air SW MOEx

Operator

Nigel Skinner
Trenchard Farm
Eggesford, Chumleigh
Devon, EX18 7QY
Tel: 01363 83746
Fax: 01363 83746
nigel.skinner@talk21.com
www.eggesfordairfield.co.uk

246ft 7mb	3nm S of RAF Wattisham N5204.53 E00058.67	PPR	Alternative AD Diversion AD	Southend Earls Colne Non-standard join

Elmsett	APP Wattisham 125.800	A/G 130.900

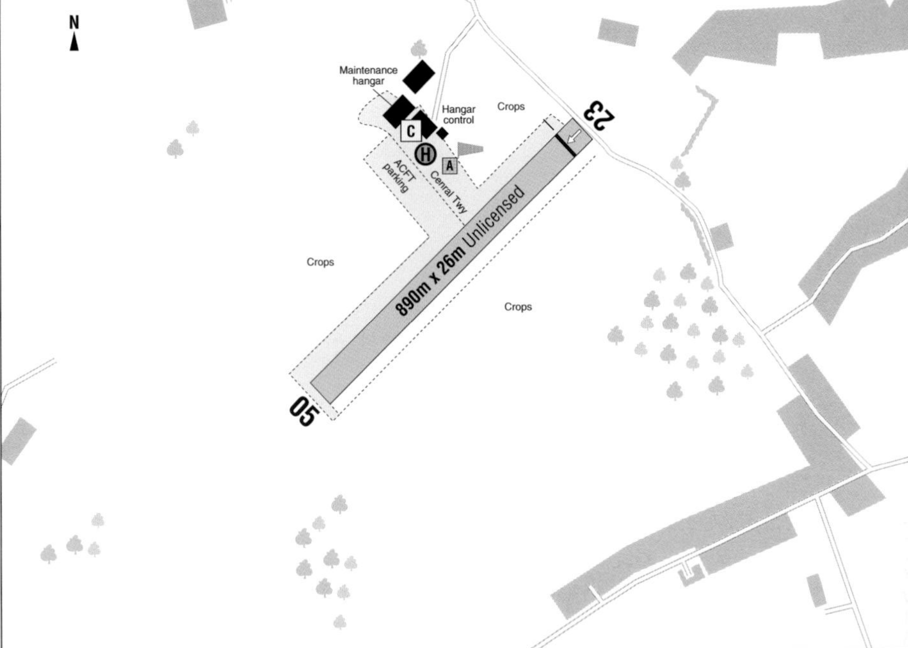

RWY	SURFACE	TORA	LDA	U/L	LIGHTING
05	Grass			890x26	Thr Rwy APAPI 3.75° LHS
23	Grass			890x26	Thr Rwy APAPI 4.0° LHS

Rwy05 1.8% upslope

RNAV			
CLN	114.55	338	15.0

Remarks

Strictly PPR by telephone. Arr Procedures: Contact Wattisham APP at least 15nm from Wattisham & obtain clearance. If unable to establish radio contact, route not above 800ft agl via VRP's at Raydon Disused AD or Copdock Jct A12/A14. Yak 50/52 ACFT must use Rwy23. Keep to circuit pattern to minimise noise. If no contact on ground, try ASAP after Dept. If no contact remain not above 800ft agl and Dept from circuit via Raydon or Copdock VRP's.

Warnings

Rwy lighting stands proud of surface exercise caution vacating Rwy. Crops up to edge of Rwy S side. Public right of way crosses APP Rwy23 70m from Thr. Taxiing beyond hold A not permitted when ACFT are taking-off or landing. Power checks Holding Point A only. **Noise:** Keep well clear of all towns and villages marked. Avoid over flying villages within 5nm of AD, leave local area ASAP. Do not fly inside circuit pattern shown, especially on Dept.

Operating Hrs	0700-2100 (L)
Circuits	05 RH, 23 LH, 800ft QFE
Landing Fee	On application
Maintenance	Aero Anglia
Fuel	AVGAS 100LL
Disabled Facilities	Nil
Restaurant	Hot drinks available
Taxis/Car Hire	By arr
Weather Info	Air S MOEx

Operator

Mr T D Gray
Poplar Aviation Ltd
Poplar Hall, Whatfield Road
Elmsett, Ipswich
Suffolk, IP7 6LN
Tel: 01473 824116
Fax: 01473 822896
tony@poplarhall.co.uk
www.poplaraviation.co.uk

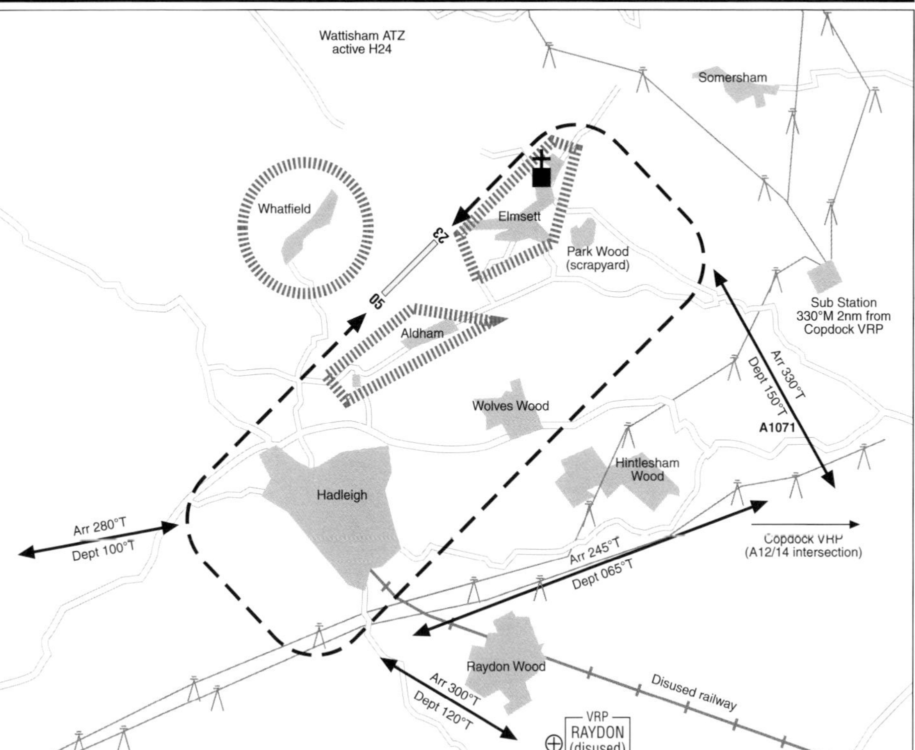

Arrival:

Contact Wattisham APP at least 15nm inbound, obtain clearance. Route inbound to AD not above 800ft agl via Copdock (Jct A12/A14), Raydon Disused AD or Sudbury Disused AD VRP unless instructed.

If unable to contact Wattisham, pilots should: Transmit blind on Wattisham APP. Remain VFR at or below 800ft agl within Wattisham MATZ/Elmsett ATZ.

From Copdock VRP track 330°T to join left base Rwy23 or track 245°T to join at Raydon Disused AD for Rwy05

From Raydon Disused AD VRP track 300°T to join right base to join right base for Rwy05 or downwind Rwy23.

From Sudbury Disused AD VRP track 100°T to join finals Rwy05 or join circuit Rwy23.

Departure

Contact Wattisham APP before dept to obtain clearance.

If unable to contact Wattisham, pilots should: Transmit blind on Wattisham APP. Dept VFR in noise abatement circuit not above 800ft agl routing outbound via Copdock (Jct A12/A14), Raydon Disused AD VRP or Sudbury Disused AD VRP.

Rwy05: Copdock dept – Maintain Rwy track 050°T, climb to circuit height ASAP. Turn crosswind before Middle Wood, fly parallel to power lines, track 140°T till overhead electricity sub-station, track 150°T to VRP.

Rwy05: Raydon Dept – Maintain Rwy track 050°T, climb to circuit height ASAP. Turn crosswind before Middle Wood, fly parallel to power lines, track 140°T aiming for electricity sub-station. Turn downwind when between Wolves Wood and Hintlesham Wood, track 230°T. When S of Hadleigh track 140°T to VRP.

Rwy05: Sudbury dept – Maintain Rwy track 050°T, climb to circuit height ASAP. Turn crosswind before Middle Wood, fly parallel to power lines, track 140°T aiming for electricity sub-station. Turn downwind when between Wolves Wood and Hintlesham Wood, track 230°T. Turn right base S of Hadleigh, track 320°T keeping clear of town. When clear to SW track 280°T to VRP.

Rwy23: Copdock dept – Dept as for Raydon, track 065°T to VRP.

Rwy23: Raydon dept – Maintain Rwy track 230°T, climb to circuit height ASAP. Turn crosswind when SW of Hadleigh, track 140T keeping clear of twon. When S of Hadleigh track 120°T to VRP.

Rwy23: Sudbury dept – Maintain Rwy track 050°T, climb to circuit height ASAP. When W of Hadleigh track 280°T to VRP.

E

EGTR ELSTREE

332ft 11mb	2.6nm E of Watford N5139.35 W00019.55	PPR	**Alternative AD** **Diversion AD**	**London Luton** Denham **Non-standard join**

Elstree	**A/G** **122.400**	**AFIS** **122.400**

N
Public footpath
26
651m x 30m
08
Twy B
Twy A
Twy C
Twy D
61ft trees agl
Reservoir

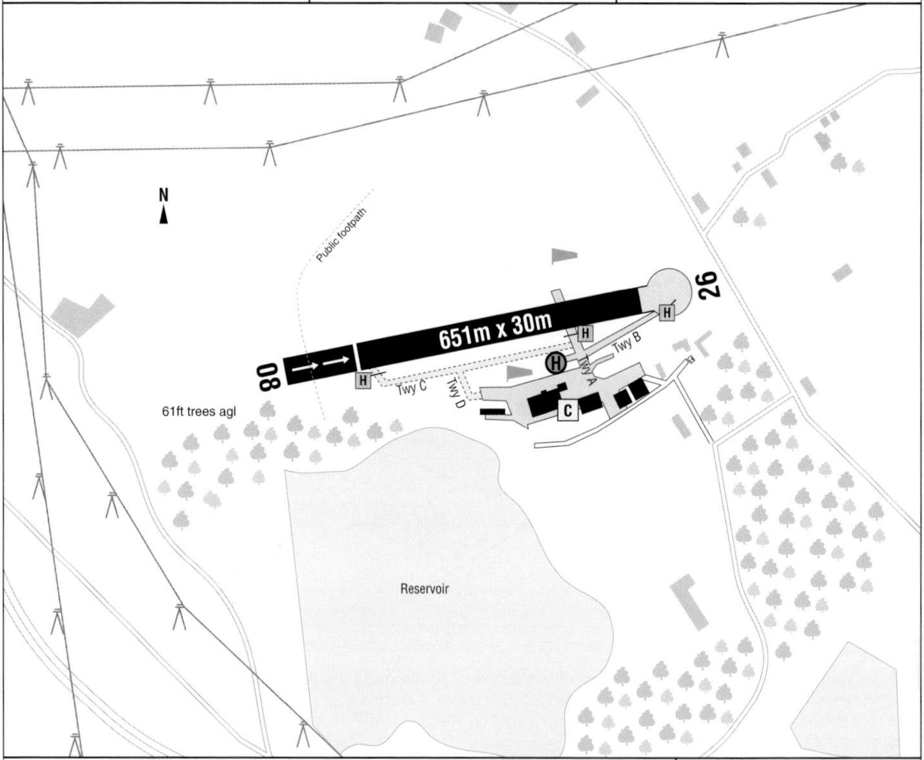

RWY	SURFACE	TORA	LDA	U/L	LIGHTING
08	Asphalt	651	651		Rwy
26	Asphalt	651	651		Thr Rwy LITAS 4.5° LHS

Pavement at W end provides 174x18 U/L stop way

RNAV			
BPK	**117.50**	**239**	**10.0**

Remarks
Strictly PPR by telephone. Not available to non-radio ACFT. Licensed night use Rwy26 only. ACFT must not join overhead. APP must be straight in from 4nm, reporting at the VRP's. Terms & conditions use available on request from AD operator. Specific Dept Routes.
Visual aids to location: Ibn Green EL, Abn White flashing.

Warnings
Distance between Twy centre line & parked ACFT 10.5m, but 8.5m on aprons. Taxi with extreme caution.
Noise: Obtain Noise Abatement dept instructions from Watch Office.

Operating Hrs As required

Circuits Reserved for flying training by Cabair and Firecrest

Landing Fee On application

Maintenance
Cabair **Tel:** 0208 953 3586
Metair **Tel:** 0208 2073702

Fuel JET A1 AVGAS 100LL

Disabled Facilities

Restaurants Licensed restaurant at AD

Taxis
Allied **Tel:** 01923 232505

Car Hire Available on request
National **Tel:** 01923 233340

Weather Info Air SE MOEx

Operator Montclare Shipping Co Ltd
Elstree Aerodrome
Borehamwood
Hertfordshire, WD6 3AR
Tel: 0208 953 7480 (ATC)
Fax: 0208 207 3691
www.egtr.net

Helicopter Approach/Departures

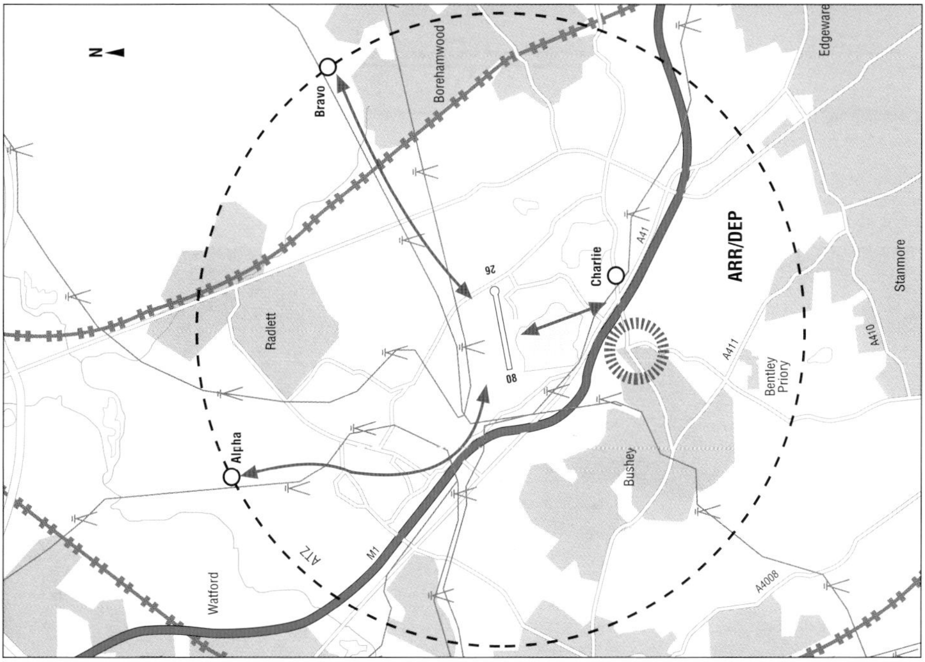

N
Bravo
Borehamwood
Edgeware
ARR/DEP
Charlie
26
08
A41
Radlett
Stanmore
A410
A411
Bentley Priory
Alpha
Bushey
ATZ
M1
Watford
A4008

Fixed Wing Approach/Departures

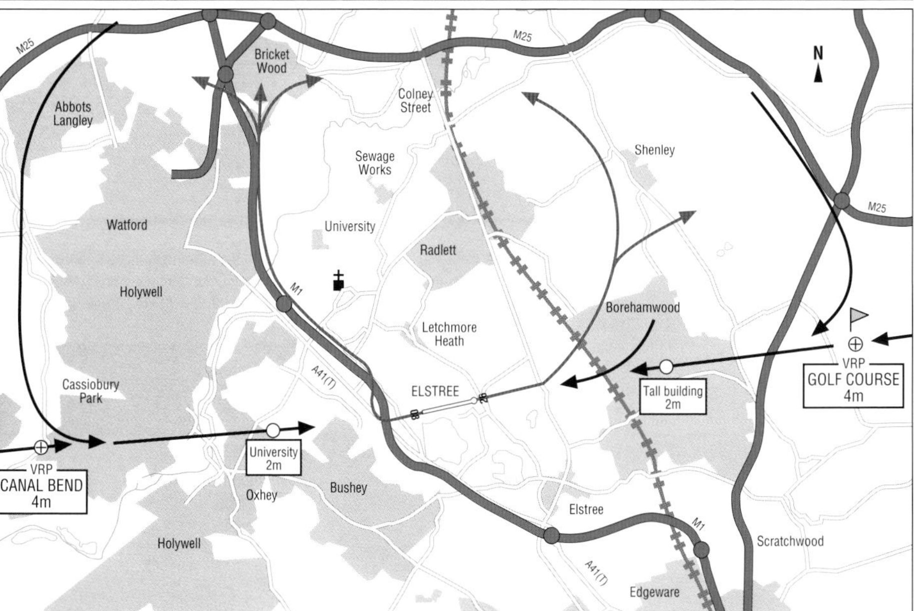

Visual Reporting Points (VRP)
Rwy08 Canal Bend
N5139.03 W00025.62 (4nm) University (2nm)
Rwy26 Golf Course
N5140.00 W00012.93 (4nm) Tall Building (2nm)

47ft 1mb	4nm SE of York N5355.28 W00059.55	PPR	**Alternative AD** **Leeds Bradford** Sherburn in Elmet

York Radio	APP	A/G
	Fenton 126.500	119.625

N
B1228
Ops/ATC
Hangar
(subject to planning)
26
Yorkshire Air Museum
C
3018m x 60m Unlicensed
08
233AGL
H

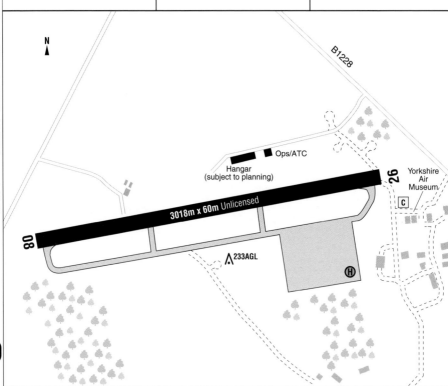

RWY	SURFACE	TORA	LDA	U/L	LIGHTING
08/26	Asph/Conc			3018x60	Nil

RNAV

Remarks

PPR strictly by telephone. Visitors welcome at pilots own risk. ACFT parking is by direction from the follow-me truck or by radio. Adjacent Yorkshire Air Museum has no authority to approve or deny ACFT movements. AD is used for events other than aviation activity. The museum has many interesting exhibits including an intact HP Halifax bomber from WW2. New hangar to be built on AD subject to planning permission.

Warnings

AD located under Church Fenton MATZ. 233ft agl radio mast S of Rwy mid point.
Noise: Avoid over flying all local habitation

Operating Hrs SR-SS
Circuits 26 LH, 08 RH, 1000ft QFE
Landing Fee On Application
Maintenance Nil
Fuel AVGAS JET A1 100LL
Disabled Facilities

Restaurants Café in Yorkshire Air Museum
Taxis
Crest Taxi **Tel:** 01904 608322
Car Hire Nil

Weather Info Air N MOEx
Operator Elvington Park Ltd
Halifax Way
Pocklington Ind Estate
Pocklington
North Yorkshire YO42 1NP
Tel: 01904 607081
aviation@elvington.biz
www.elvington.biz

EGAB ENNISKILLEN

Effective date:25/09/08 OP 08

155ft 5mb	4.5nm N of Enniskillen N5423.93 W00739.12	PPR	Alternative AD Diversion AD	**Belfast Aldergrove** Sligo

Enniskillen	A/G 123.200

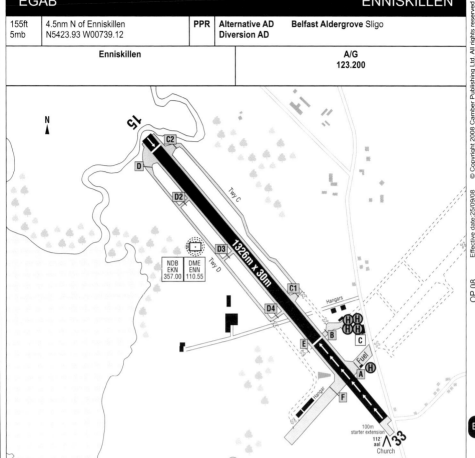

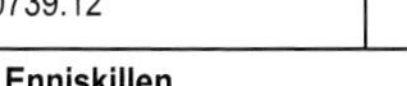

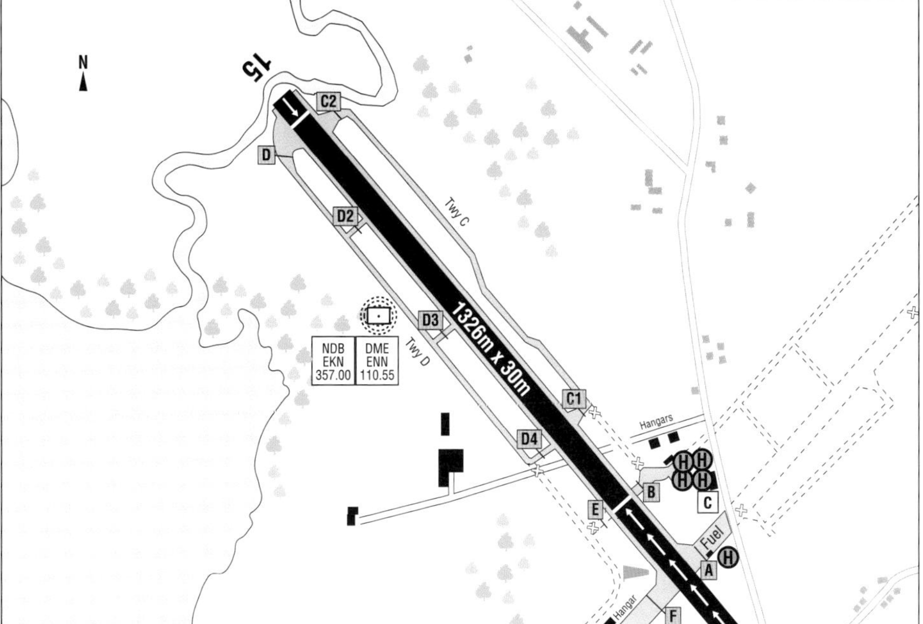

RWY	SURFACE	TORA	LDA	U/L	LIGHTING
15	Asphalt	1236	1286		Rwy PAPI 3.5° LHS
33	Asphalt	1337	1004		Rwy PAPI 4.5° LHS

Displaced Thr Rwy15 100m, Displaced Thr Rwy33 330m

RNAV

Remarks
PPR. Not available to ACFT unable to communicate by radio unless the pilot has obtained a specific prior permission.
Rwy33 PAPIS not to be used for APP slope guidance unless aligned with Rwy.

Warnings
Twys C & D available to ACF with wingspan <12m. No turns below 300ft QFE. Low level circuits only permitted for practice bad weather flying.

Operating Hrs 0900-1700 (L) & by arr

Circuits 15 RH, 33 LH 1000ft QFE
Microlights & Helicopters 800ft QFE

Landing Fee On application

Maintenance
London Helicopters **Tel:** 028 6632 3606
Sloane Helicopters **Tel:** 028 6632 6322

Fuel JET A1 AVGAS 100LL

Hangarage Limited

Disabled Facilities

Restaurants Café St Angelo on AD

Taxis/Car Hire Available on request

Weather Info Air N MOEx

Operator Enniskillen Airport Ltd
Trory
Enniskillen
Co Fermanagh
Northern Ireland
BT94 2FP
Tel: 0286 6329000
Fax: 0286 6329100
info@enniskillen-airport.co.uk
www.enniskillen-airport.co.uk

E

550ft 18mb	4.5nm E of Chipping Norton N5155.69 W00125.71	PPR	**Alternative AD** **Diversion AD**	**Oxford** Turweston

Enstone	**A/G** **129.875**

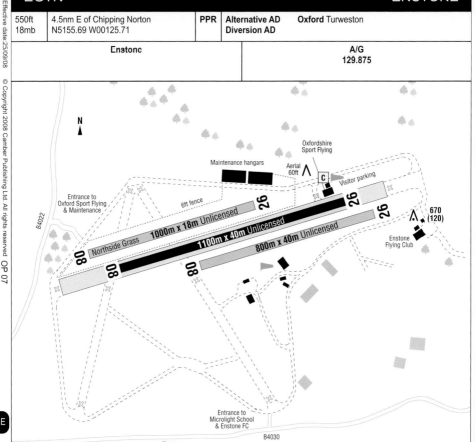

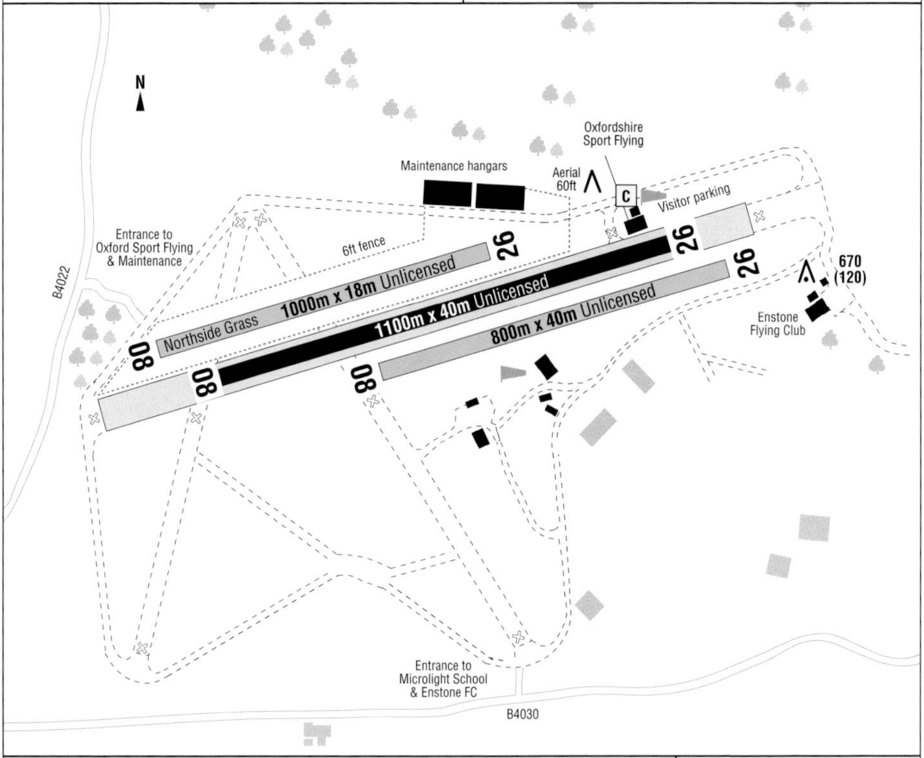

N
Oxfordshire Sport Flying
Maintenance hangars
Aerial 60ft
C
Visitor parking
Entrance to Oxford Sport Flying & Maintenance
6ft fence
26
B4022
Northside Grass 1000m x 18m Unlicensed
1100m x 40m Unlicensed
800m x 40m Unlicensed
08
670 (120)
Enstone Flying Club
Entrance to Microlight School & Enstone FC
B4030

RWY	SURFACE	TORA	LDA	U/L	LIGHTING
08/26	Asphalt			1100x40	Nil
08/26	Grass			800x40	Nil

RNAV			
DTY	116.40	222	19.1

Remarks
PPR by telephone or radio. No Dept before 0800 or after 1930 or SS whichever is earlier. Gliding no longer takes place on AD, Grass Rwy S of main Rwy available to ACFT. N side grass strip operated by maintenance organisation. Use at own risk

Warnings
Rwys15/33 and 02/20 are not usable. Motor Gliders, Light ACFT and Microlights operate from this AD. Radio mast 120ft aal (670ft amsl) in SE corner of the AD.
Noise: Avoid over flying the noise sensitive villages of Great Tew, Little Tew, Ledwell, Sandford St Martin, Enstone and Church Enstone and Heythrop College.

Operating Hrs 0800-SS (L)
Last dept 1930 (L)

Circuits 08 LH, 26 RH
Motor gliders 600ft QFE
Microlights 600ft QFE
ACFT 800ft QFE

Landing Fee Single £8.50 Microlights £5
Twin £17

Maintenance Available **Tel:** 01608 683625
Fuel AVGAS 100LL

Disabled Facilities

Restaurants
Snacks on AD inc home made cakes @ OSF
Little Chef on A44 & the Crown Inn Church Enstone

Accommodation
Swan Lodge **Tel:** 01608 678736
Pretty Bush **Tel:** 01608 738262
Cotswold View **Tel:** 01608 810314

Taxis
Aston Cars **Tel:** 01869 340460

Car Hire
Europcar **Tel:** 01295 51787

Weather Info Air Cen MOEx

Operator Oxfordshire Sport Flying Club Ltd
Enstone Aerodrome
Church Enstone
Oxon OX7 4NP
Tel: 01608 677208 (Oxfordshire Sport Flying)
Tel: 01608 678204 (Enstone Flying Club)
Tel: 01608 678741 (Microlights)
Fax: 01608 677808
(Oxfordshire Sport Flying)
osf@enstoneaerodrome.co.uk
www.enstone-aerodrome.co.uk

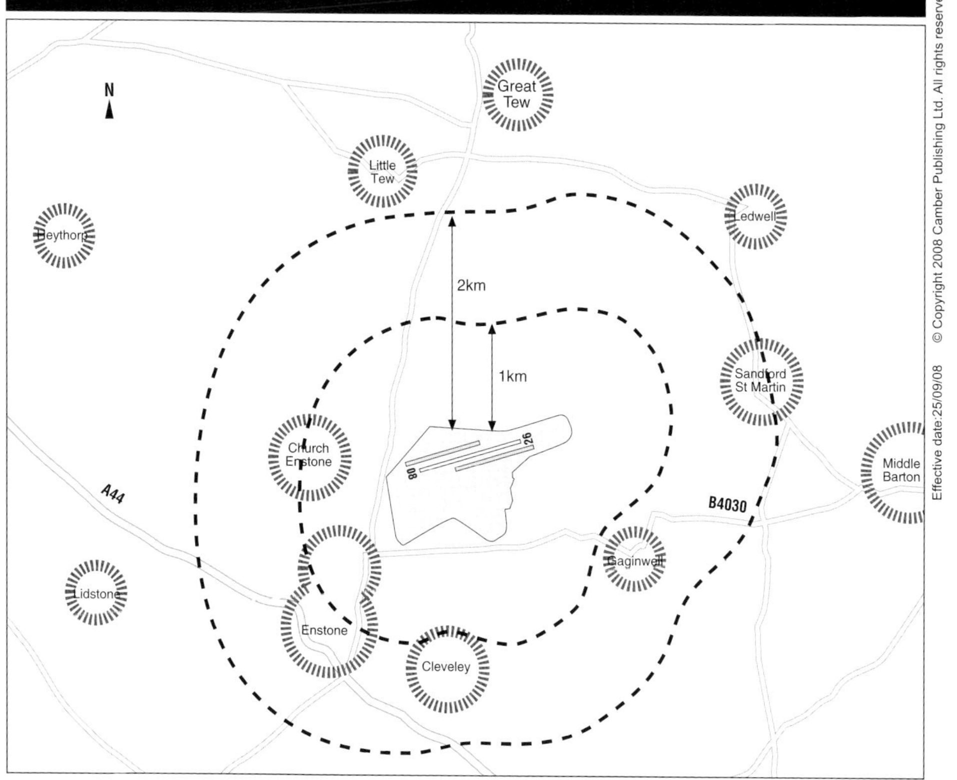
N
Great Tew
Little Tew
Heythorp
Ledwell
2km
1km
Sandford St Martin
Church Enstone
26
08
Middle Barton
A44
B4030
Gaginwell
Lidstone
Enstone
Cleveley

197ft 7mb	7nm N of Morpeth N5516.84 W00142.82	PPR	Alternative AD	Newcastle Peterlee

Non-standard join

Eshott	APP Newcastle 124.375	A/G 122.850

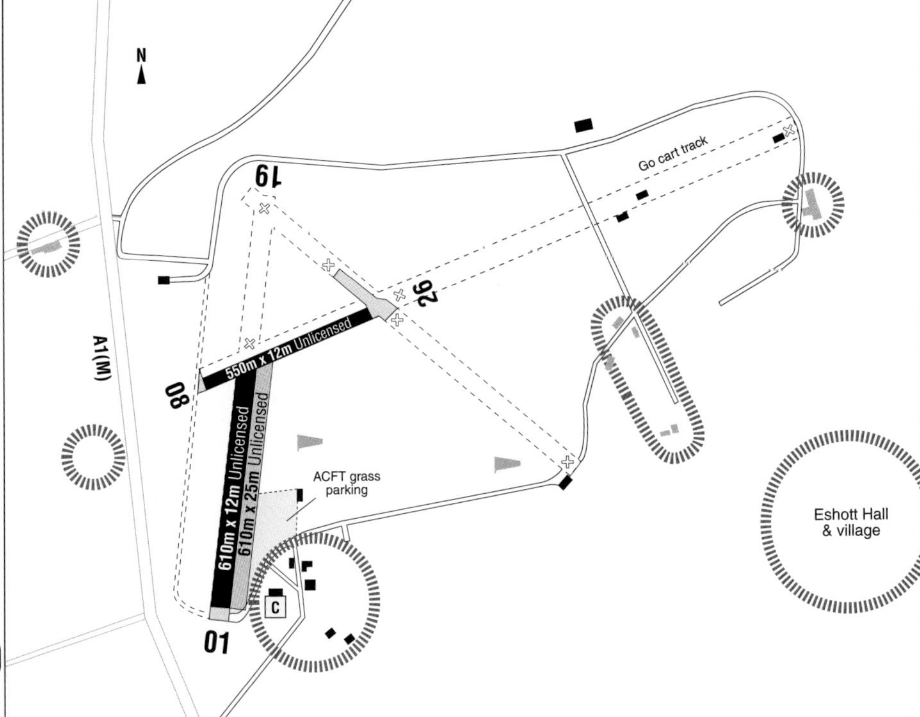

RWY	SURFACE	TORA	LDA	U/L	LIGHTING
01/19	Asphalt			610x12	Nil
01/19	Grass			610x25	Nil
08/26	Asphalt			550x12	Nil

RNAV			
NEW	114.25	002	14.6

Remarks
PPR only, essential for joining instructions. Please pay landing fee, if no one around, leave in box.

Warnings
Rwy08/26 has been resurfaced with Asphalt to a width of 12m. Asphalt E of the disused Rwy14/32 intersection is a go-kart racing track and not useable by ACFT. Intense ACFT activity keep a good lookout, contact Newcastle APP for information.
Noise: Avoid over flying Felton village to N and farm buildings and houses in the immediate area

Operating Hrs 0900-1900 (L)
No operations outside these Hrs

Landing Fee Microlight £5, Overnight parking £5
ACFT £7, Overnight parking £10
£50 fine if outside operating Hrs

Circuits 01, 08 RH, 19, 26 LH

Maintenance By arr

Fuel AVGAS

Disabled Facilities Nil

Restaurants Cafe on AD at weekends

Taxis/Car Hire AD operator will advise

Weather Info Air N MOEx

Operator Eshott Airfield Ltd
Bockenfield
Felton
Northumberland, NE65 9QJ
Tel: 01670 787881 (Operator)
Tel: 01670 787881 (AD)
Tel: 07798 771415
www.eshottairfield.co.uk

102ft 3mb	4nm NE of Exeter N5044.07 W00324.83		**Alternative AD** **Plymouth** Dunkeswell

Non-standard join

Exeter	ATIS	LARS	APP	RAD	TWR
	119.325	128.975	128.975	119.050	119.800

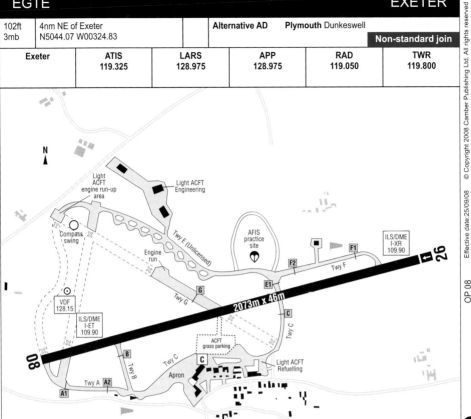

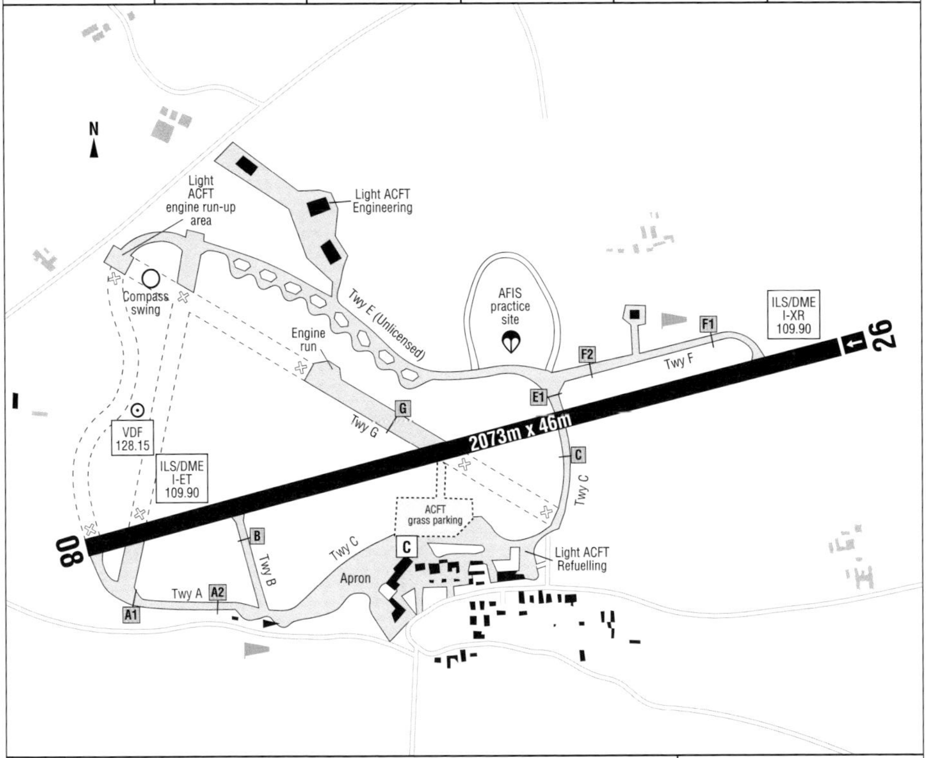

RWY	SURFACE	TORA	LDA	U/L	LIGHTING
08	Asphalt	2047	2037		Ap Thr Rwy PAPI 3° LHS
26	Asphalt	2073	2037		Ap Thr Rwy PAPI 3.5° LHS

Displaced Thr Rwy08 10m, Displaced Thr Rwy26 36m

RNAV			
BHD	112.05	013	20.4

Remarks

PPR to all ACFT >9m long via AD Ops. Non-radio ACFT not accepted. Hi-vis. Light ACFT pilots beware of elevated Rwy lights and PAPI 08/26. Twys except bravo are only 15m wide and thus not suitable for use by ACFT whose wheel base >18m and wheel span >9m. Twy E has green reflective centre line studs and blue edge studs from E1 to a line of amber studs across Twy. This Twy is limited to ACFT with wheel base <7.5m, wingspan <30m. The remainder of Twy is not suitable for ACFT with wheel base >7.5m and wingspan >15m. Twy F is not licensed, only 8m strip on Twy is useable by ACFT. Twy is only suitable for ACFT with <7.5m wheel base and <15m wingspan. Twy F is unlit, available in day light Hrs only. ACFT requiring apron parking must book with AD Ops prior to Arr. Pedestrians access on S of AD from/to grass or non-parking apron must be via airside barrier adjacent to fire section.
Fuelling: AVGAS pumps only. Max of 3 ACFT at fuelling apron at any one time. ACFT must call ATC prior to leaving fuelling apron.
Aids to Navigation: NDB EX 337.00

Warnings

ACFT APP without assistance from RAD shall follow a descent path no lower than the normal APP path indicated by the PAPIs. Restrictions on use for single engine ECFT – Rwy08 new displaced Thr not marked. Rwy08 not available for single engine ACFT precision APP and night use. Rwy26 900m available for single engine ACFT dept.
Noise: Pilots must ensure at all times that ACFT are operated to cause the least disturbance practicable in areas surrounding the AD, particularly the City of Exeter and Clyst Honiton village.

Operating Hrs	Mon-Fri 0700-1900 Sat 0700-1800 Sun 0800-1900 (Summer), Mon 0001-0100 0700-2359 Tue-Fri 0001-0200 0700-2359 (PPR before 0800, after 1900) Sat 0001-0200 0800-1700 Sun 0830-2359 (PPR before 0900, after 1700) (Winter)	**Circuits**	Variable
		Landing Fee	On application from ATC or via website Circuits variable
		Maintenance	Iscavia Eng **Tel:** 01392 362415 (Iscavia Eng)
		Fuel	AVGAS JET A1 100LL

Disabled Facilities

Handling	**Tel:** 01392 354943 (Executive Handling)
Restaurant	Bar/Buffet facilities available
Taxis	
Corporate Cars	**Tel:** 01392 362000
Car Hire	
Avis	**Tel:** 01392 360214
Weather Info	M T9 Fax 278 MOEx **Tel:** 01392 354915

Visual Reference Points (VRP)

Axminster	N5046.90 W00259.90
Crediton	N5047.43 W00339.08
Cullompton	N5051.47 W00323.63
Exmouth	N5037.48 W00324.13
Topsham	N5041.38 W00328.82

Operator

Exeter International Airport
Exeter, Devon, EX5 2BD
Tel: 01392 354915 (ATC)
Tel: 01392 447433 (Ops)
Fax: 01392 447422 (Ops)
Fax: 01392 354967 (ATC)
www.exeter-airport.co.uk

E

FADMOOR

780ft 26mb	4.5nm N of Wombleton N5418.52 W00058.43	PPR	Alternative AD	**Durham Tees Valley** Full Sutton

Fadmoor	LARS Linton 129.150	A/G 123.225 not manned

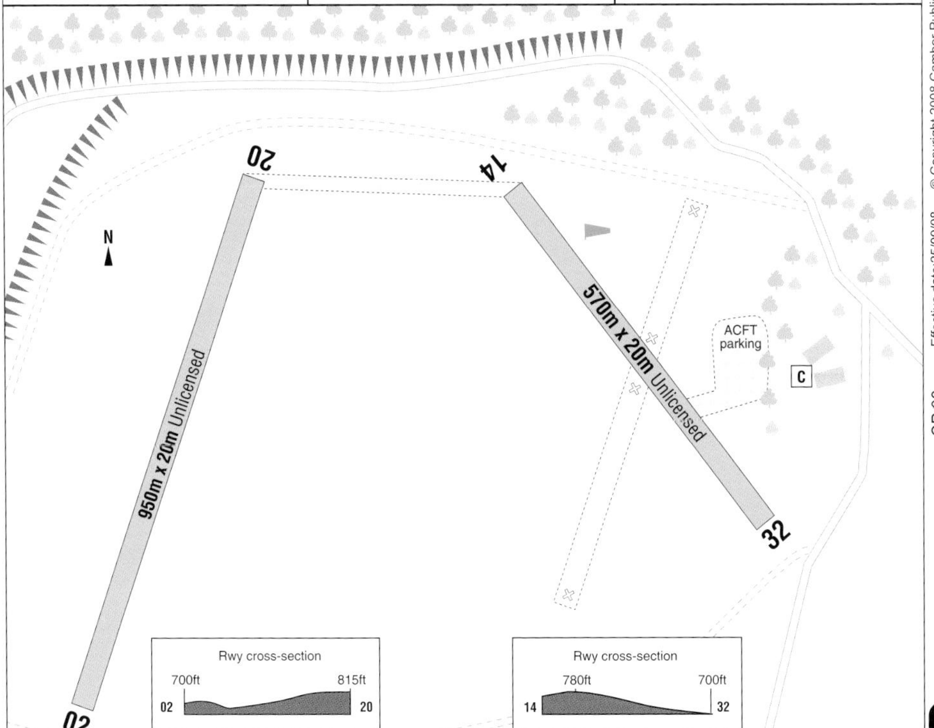

RWY	SURFACE	TORA	LDA	U/L	LIGHTING
02/20	Grass			950x20	Rwy
14/32	Grass			570x20	Rwy

Rwy02 or 32 preferred for landing

RNAV

Remarks

PPR visiting ACFT accepted on agricultural business to purchase farm pork. AD subject to planning regulations. Pilots should have experience in grass field landings. AD situated on crown of hill, on edge of escarpment, at S edge of moorland. GND slopes away from all Thr. Self contained holiday flat available for rent from operator on AD phone number.

Warnings

Beware of low flying military ACFT above and below AD level.

Operating Hrs Mon-Sat SR-SS Closed Sundays

Circuits Nil

Landing Fee On application

Maintenance Nil Ltd hangerage

Fuel AVGAS 100LL

Disabled Facilities Nil

Restaurants

Plough **Tel:** 01751 431515 (1 mile)

Royal Oak **Tel:** 01751431414 (1 mile)

Taxis/Car Hire On request

Weather Info Air N MWC

Operator

P H Johnson
Fadmoor
Kirkbymoorside
West Yorkshire YO62 7JH
Tel: 01751 431171 (AD)
Tel: 07989 383562
Fax: 01751 432727

INTENTIONALLY LEFT BLANK

EGVA FAIRFORD

286ft 7mb	8.7nm N of Swindon N5140.90 W00147.30	PPR MIL	**Alternative AD** **Oxford** Kemble

Non-standard join

Fairford	RAD Brize 134.300	TWR 119.150

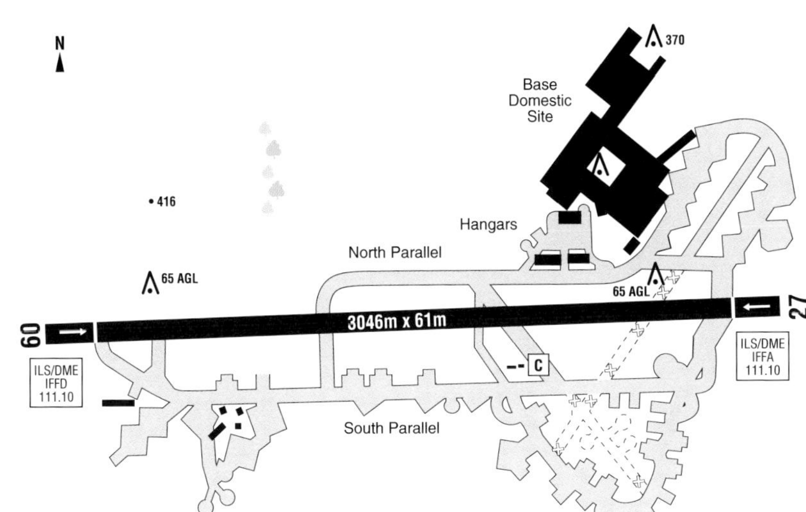

RWY	SURFACE	TORA	LDA	U/L	LIGHTING
09/27	Asphalt	3046	3046		Ap Thr Rwy PAPI 2.75°

RNAV			
CPT	114.35	302	24.2

Remarks
PPR 24Hrs notice required. Helicopters operate from main Rwy.

Warnings
Located in Brize Zone, all ACFT must call Brize at least 10 mins prior to ETA. Intense military activity in area. Bird hazard on AD.
Noise: Avoid over flying all local towns and villages. Rwy27 preferred for noise abatement.

Operating Hrs	As required by USAF
Circuits	Variable
Landing Fee	In accordance with USAF policy Contact Station Ops for details
Maintenance	Nil
Fuel	Nil
Disabled Facilities	Nil
Restaurants	Nil
Taxi/Car Hire	Nil
Weather Info	Air SW MOEx **Tel:** 01285 714805 Ex 4554

Operator
United States Air Force
RAF Fairford
Fairford
Glos
GL7 4DL
Tel: 01285 714805
Fax: 01285 714805 Ex 4048

F

223ft 7mb	On Fair Isle N5932.15 W00137.68	PPR	**Alternative AD** **Diversion AD**	**Sumburgh** Sanday

Fair Isle	**APP** **Sumburgh 131.300**	**A/G** **118.025**

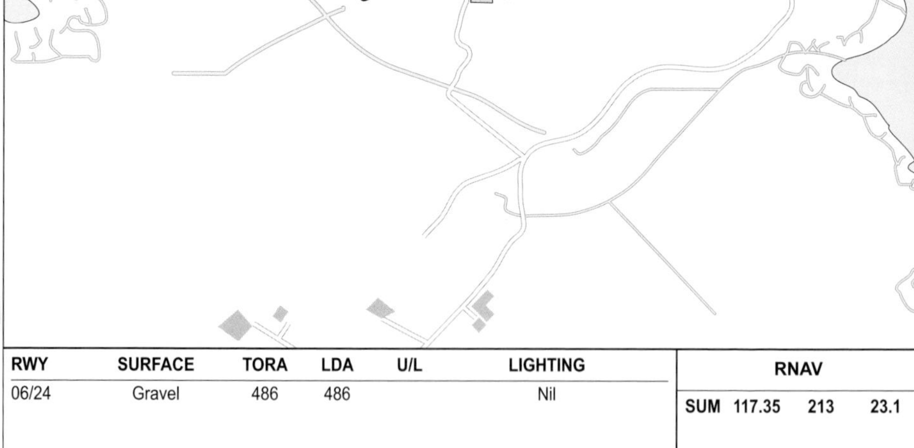

RWY	SURFACE	TORA	LDA	U/L	LIGHTING
06/24	Gravel	486	486		Nil

RNAV			
SUM	117.35	213	23.1

Remarks
PPR. GND falls away very steeply approx 30m beyond each Rwy end. Care should betaken to anticipate sudden wind changes which might result in a touch down short of Thr. Rwy surface prone to moss growth almost exclusively on E end and may be slippery, particularly when wet. Accommodation available at Fair Isle Observatory Lodge, E of AD. A/G is SR-SS only subject to PPR and as required for emergency use.

Warnings
Turbulence can be expected with a W wind. Avoid low flying over islands or cliffs. Rwy is banked above surrounding land. Weather conditions can change rapidly. Pilots can arrive, having had a favourable met. report, to find the Isle shrouded in fog/low cloud. Bird hazard, May-Aug particularly on Rwy06 APP.

Operating Hrs SR-SS

Circuits 06 RH, 24 LH

Landing Fee Single £10 Twin £15

Maintenance Nil

Fuel Nil

Disabled Facilities

Restaurants Food & accomodation available at the Fair Isle Observatory Lodge
Tel: 01595 760258

Taxis/Car Hire
J Stout **Tel:** 01595 760222

Weather Info Air Sc GWC

Operator The National Trust for Scotland
FairIsle
Shetland, ZE2 9JU
Tel: 01595 760224 (Mr D Wheeler)
Fax: 01595 760210
dave.wheeler@fairisle.org.uk
www.fairisle.org.uk/egrf

EGTF FAIROAKS

80ft 3mb	2nm N of Woking N5120.88 W00033.52	PPR	**Alternative AD** **Diversion AD**	**Farnborough** White Waltham **Non-standard join**

Fairoaks	LARS Farnborough West 125.250	AFIS 123.425	A/G 123.425

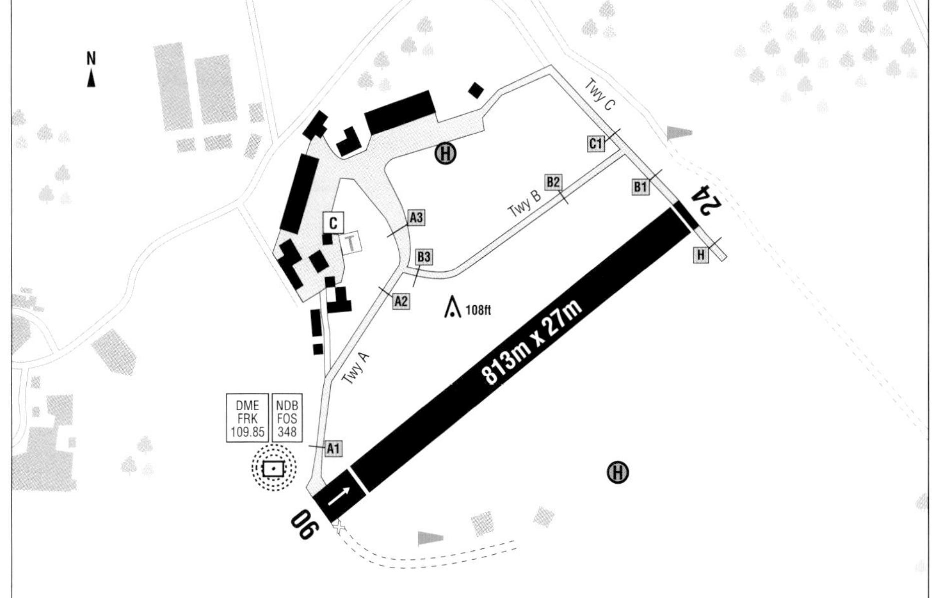

RWY	SURFACE	TORA	LDA	U/L	LIGHTING
06	Asphalt	813	760		Thr Rwy APAPI 3.5° LHS
24	Asphalt	813	800		Thr Rwy APAPI 4.0° LHS

Displaced Thr Rwy06 53m, Displaced Thr Rwy24 13m

RNAV			
OCK	115.30	304	5.0

Remarks
PPR. Not available to non-radio ACFT. Weight shift microlights not accepted. Airside passengers are pilots responsibility. New visitors should obtain a telephone briefing.
Visual aid to location: Abn flashing white.

Warnings
AD located inside S boundary of London Control Zone – special procedures apply. Due to a hump on Rwy Rwy24 red end lights are visible only for the last 150m of LDA. The last 3 Rwy edge lights are cautionary yellow. Exercise caution when taxiing through the apron/parking areas due to reduced wing tip clearances. Pilots of ACFT whose wingspan >15m should satisfy themselves that they have adequate clearance. Twy to SE of Rwy24 Thr is not available to ACFT required to use a licensed AD. Other ACFT should only use this Twy with the permission of AD management. Grass areas are subject to water logging. Public footpath crosses AD close to Rwy24 Thr. Helicopter training takes place on AD. AD is frequently used outside published Hrs, pilots in the vicinity should call Fairoaks to determine if it is active.
Noise: Inbound, do not over fly Knaphill below 1500ft QNH & avoid properties to NE of AD below 1000ft QFE.

Operating Hrs Mon-Sat 0700-1700 Sun 0800-1700 (Summer) Mon-Sat 0800-1800 Sun & PH 0900-1700 (Winter)

Circuits Variable

Landing Fee On application

Maintenance
Mann Aviation **Tel:** 01276 857441

Fuel AVGAS JET A1 100LL
All aviation oils

Disabled Facilities

Restaurants Hangar Café **Tel:** 01276 855446

Taxis		**Operator**	Fairoaks Airports Ltd Fairoaks Airport Chobham, Woking Surrey, GU24 8HX **Tel:** 01276 857700 (Admin) **Tel:** 01276 857300 (ATC) **Fax:** 01276 856898 **Telex:** 859033 FKSATC www.alanmann.co.uk
Five Star	**Tel:** 01483 755555		
Boomerang	**Tel:** 01483 714062		
Car Hire			
UK Airport Cars	**Tel:** 0208 8180102		
Weather Info	M* Air SE MOEx		

Fairoaks ATZ and Local Flying Area
Within the Local Flying Area (2nm radius centred on AD) flights may take place without compliance with IFR requirements subject to the following conditions.
1 ACFT to remain below cloud and in sight of the GND.
2 Maximum altitudes 800ft (QNH) when London Heathrow Rwy23 is in use. Otherwise maximum altitude is 1500ft (QNH).
3 Minimum visibility is 3km.
4 ACFT must not enter the Fairoaks ATZ without permission, even if operating on an SVFR clearance in the London CTR.
5 Inbound traffic APP from the S must remain W of the M25 whilst within the Fairoaks Local Flying Area.
6 Pilots of ACFT flying in the Local Flying Area are responsible for providing their own separation from other ACFT operating in the same airspace.

EGLF FARNBOROUGH

238ft 8mb	1nm NNW of Aldershot N5116.55 W00046.58	PPR	Alternative AD **Southampton** Blackbushe Diversion AD

Non-standard join

Farnborough	ATIS	APP	RAD
	128.400	134.350	125.250

TWR	FIRE	OPS
122.500	121.600	\130.375

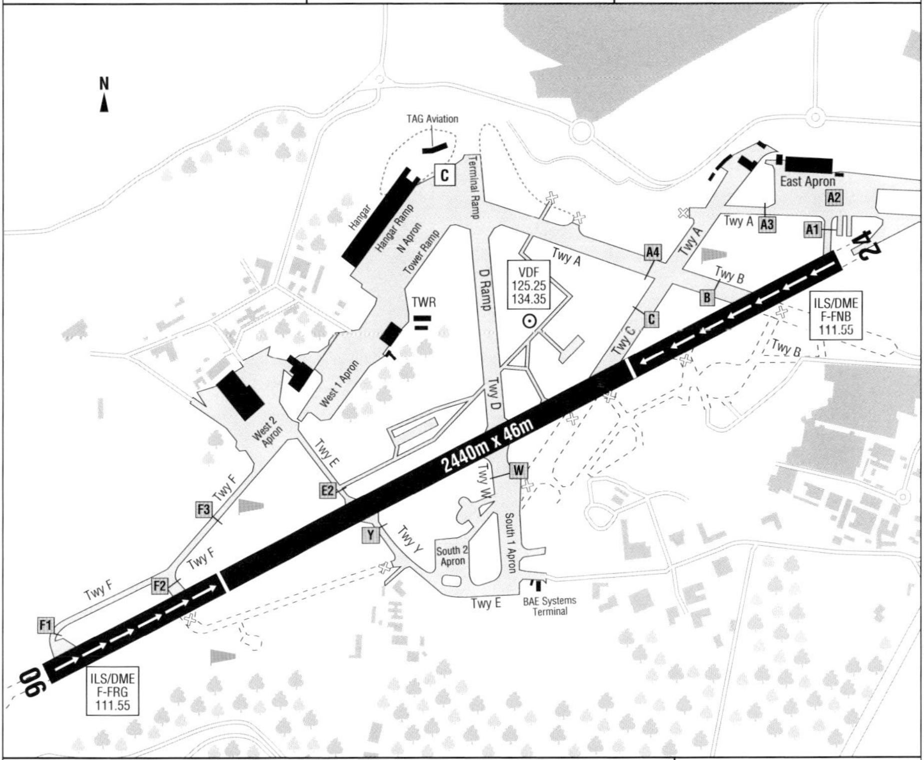

RWY	SURFACE	TORA	LDA	U/L	LIGHTING
06	Con/Asph	2000	1800		Ap Thr Rwy PAPI 3.5° LHS
24	Con/Asph	2063	1800		Ap Thr Rwy PAPI 3.5° LHS

Starter extension Rwy06 170m mandatory for all depts
Rwy06/24 friction surface no tight turns on asphalt section

RNAV			
OCK	115.30	265	12.6

Remarks
PPR. Pilots must book out by phone. All visiting ACFT must arrange handling and parking with TAG Aviation. Training available for home based ACFT only.
Visual aid to location: Flashing Green FH.

Warnings
Minimum obstacle clearance Rwy06/24 is not provided by PAR or PAPIs at less than 1nm from Thr. Danger Areas D132, D133A and D133 are within 3nm E of AD boundary. Traffic carrying out instrument APP Rwy28 at Odiham will pass approximately 1.5nm S of Farnborough AD at 1900ft QNH or lower. ATC brief available. Twy C and L the outer edges marked with yellow chevrons are not suitable for ACFT use. Single engine jet ACFT may not Dept Rwy06. AD will close prior to 2200 Mon-Fri when no operations expected.
Noise: All Dept are to use maximum climb until ACFT reaches initial clearance level.

Operating Hrs	Mon-Fri 0600-2100 Sat-Sun & PH 0700-1900 (Summer) +1Hr (Winter)	**Landing Fee**	Minimum charge including Nav & handling £50
Circuits	ACFT >2730Kg not below 1700ft QNH before turning base leg ACFT <2730Kg not below 1200ft QNH before turning base leg Avoid congested area 2nm W of AD unless ATC authorise	**Maintenance**	Farnborough Aviation Services **Tel:** 01252 524440
		Fuel	AVGAS 100LL JET A1 by arr with TAG Aviation
		Disabled Facilities	Available

Restaurants	Many pubs within walking distance
Taxis/Car Hire	Can be arranged on Arr at AD
Weather Info	M T9 Fax 282 MOEx METAR/TAF **Tel:** 09063 800400 Ex 282

Visual Reference Points (VRP)

Alton	N5109.12 W00057.97
Bagshot	N5120.95 W00041.95
Guildford	N5114.37 W00035.10
Hook	N5116.77 W00057.72
Nokia Factory	N5117.55 W00047.88

Operator TAG Aviation
Farnborough Airport
Hampshire, GU14 6XA
Tel: 01252 526015 (ATC RAD)
Tel: 01252 526017 (ATC VIS)
Tel: 01252 524440 (TAG Aviation PPR)
Fax: 01252 518771 (TAG Aviation)

Farnborough Helicopter VFR Arrival Routes

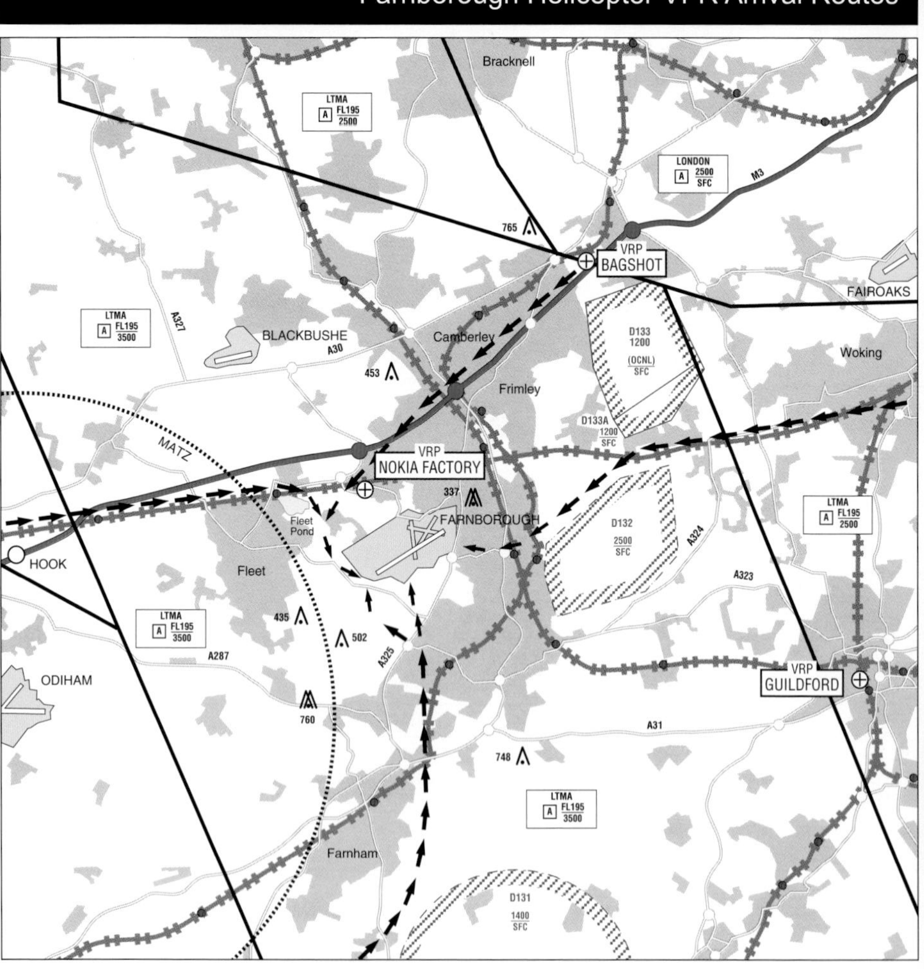

F

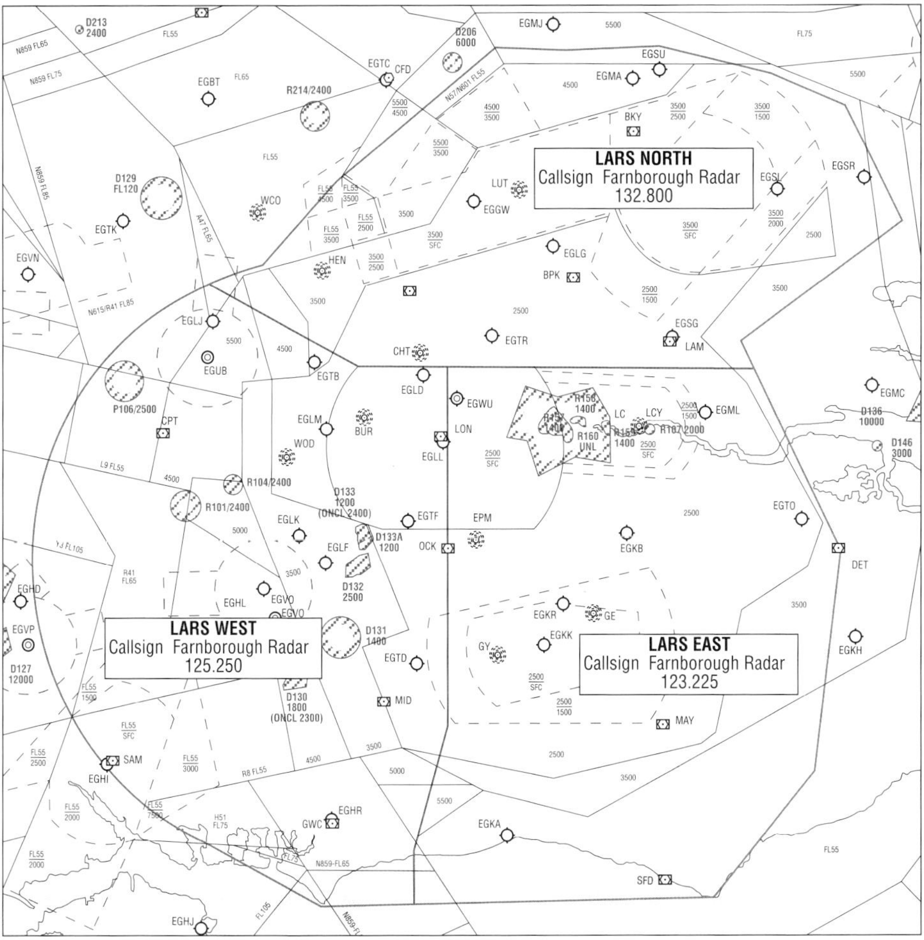

LARS NORTH
Callsign Farnborough Radar
132.800

LARS WEST
Callsign Farnborough Radar
125.250

LARS EAST
Callsign Farnborough Radar
123.225

Call Farnborough Lars on the appropriate frequency, turn on transponder, selecting Mode C.

CTR/CTA – Class D Airspace
Normal CTR/CTA Class D Airspace rules apply
Transition Alt 6000ft

FARTHING CORNER

420ft 14mb	4nm S of Gillingham N5119.83 E00036.07	PPR	**Alternative AD**	**Southend** Rochester

Non-radio	APP Rochester 122.250	Safetycom 135.475

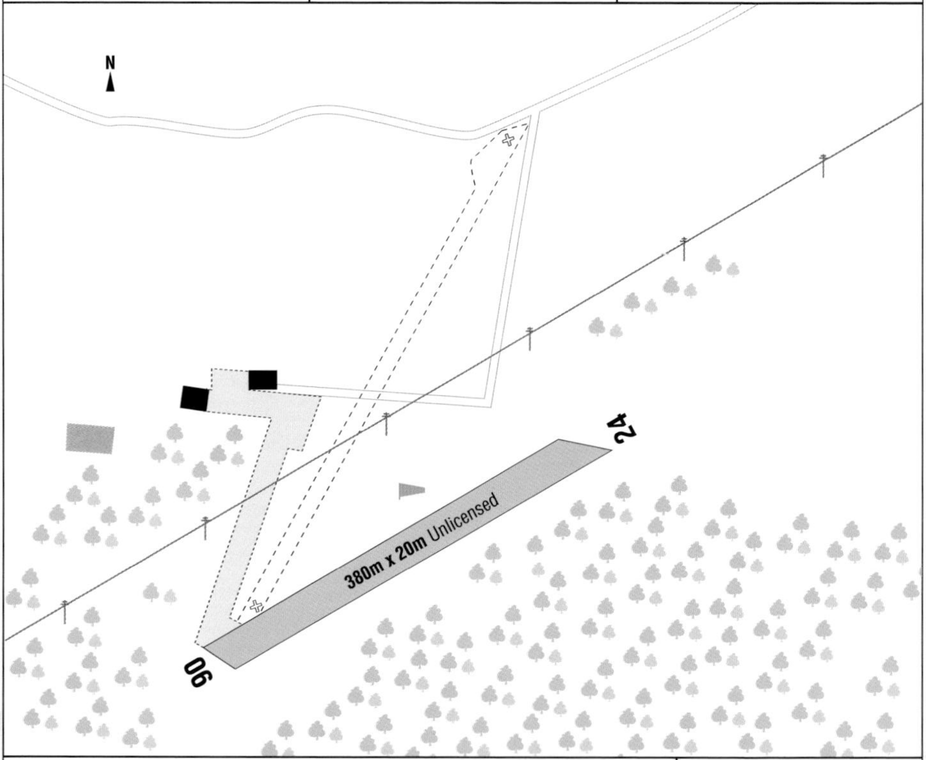

N
24
380m x 20m Unlicensed
06

F

RWY	SURFACE	TORA	LDA	U/L	LIGHTING
06/24	Grass			380x20	Nil

RNAV			
DET	117.30	007	1.6

Remarks
PPR essential.

Warnings
Turbulence on APP to both ends of Rwy. Detling VOR 1.25nm to S. Power lines up to 110ft agl run parallel to the strip 80-100m NW of strip. GND in the immediate undershoot area of Rwy06 falls away steeply.
Noise: Avoid over flying farmhouse 400 yards to E of Rwy. Final APP Rwy24 to be made between farmhouse and Thr.

Operating Hrs PPR
Circuits 24 LH, 06 RH
Landing Fee £2 (£50 without PPR)
Maintenance Nil
Fuel Nil
Disabled Facilities

Restaurants Nil
Taxis/Car Hire Nil
Weather Info Air SE MOEx

Operator SBC
Stoneacre Farm
Matts Hill Road, Hartlip
Sittingbourne, Kent ME97XA
Tel: 01634 264011

FARWAY COMMON

771ft 25mb	4nm NE of Sidmouth N5044.15 W00311.46	PPR	**Alternative AD** **Diversion AD**	**Exeter** Dunkeswell

Farway Radio	**LARS** **Exeter 128.975**	**Safetycom** **135.475**

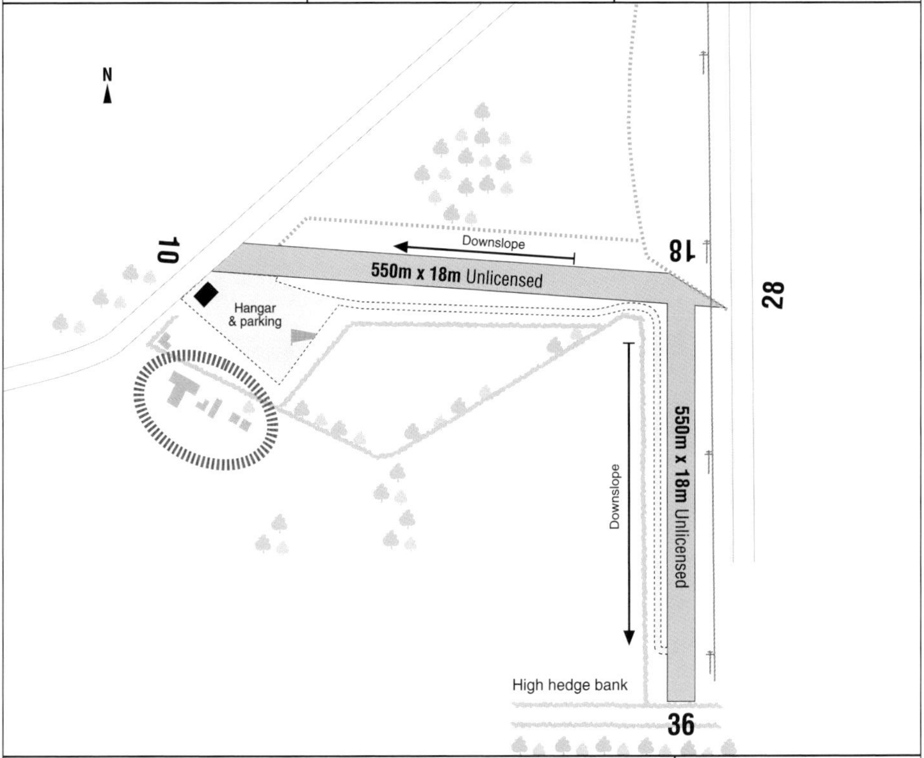

N
10
18
28
36
Downslope
550m x 18m Unlicensed
Hangar & parking
Downslope
550m x 18m Unlicensed
High hedge bank

RWY	SURFACE	TORA	LDA	U/L	LIGHTING
10/28	Grass			550x18	Nil
18/36	Grass			550x18	Nil

RNAV			
BHD	112.05	034	23.3

Remarks
PPR. Contact Exeter LARS on arr & dept. There is an annual fly-in associated with Devon PFA Strut which is well worth a visit. See aviation press for details and Devon PFA Strut website.

Warnings
Sheep may be grazing. There are numerous hazards (mostly minor) relating to most Rwys which should be considered. Please study the AD diagram closely.
Noise: Avoid local habitation, particularly area SW of AD

Operating Hrs SR-SS
Circuits 10, 18 LH. 28, 36 RH. 800ft AGL
Landing Fee Microlights £5 ACFT £10 Helicopters £25
Maintenance Nil
Fuel Nil
Disabled Facilities

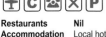

Restaurants Nil
Accommodation Local hotels & B&B
Taxis/Car Hire Locally by arr
Weather Info Air SW MOEx

Operator Terry Case
Moorlands Farm
Sidbury, Sidmouth
Devon, EX10 0QW
Tel/Fax: 01395 597535
Tel: 07779 538991
www.farwaycommon.com

226ft 7mb	2nm NE of Thirsk N5415.11 W00117.93	PPR	Alternative AD	Durham Tees Valley Bagby

Non Radio	LARS Leeming 127.750	APP Topcliffe 125.0	Safetycom 135.475

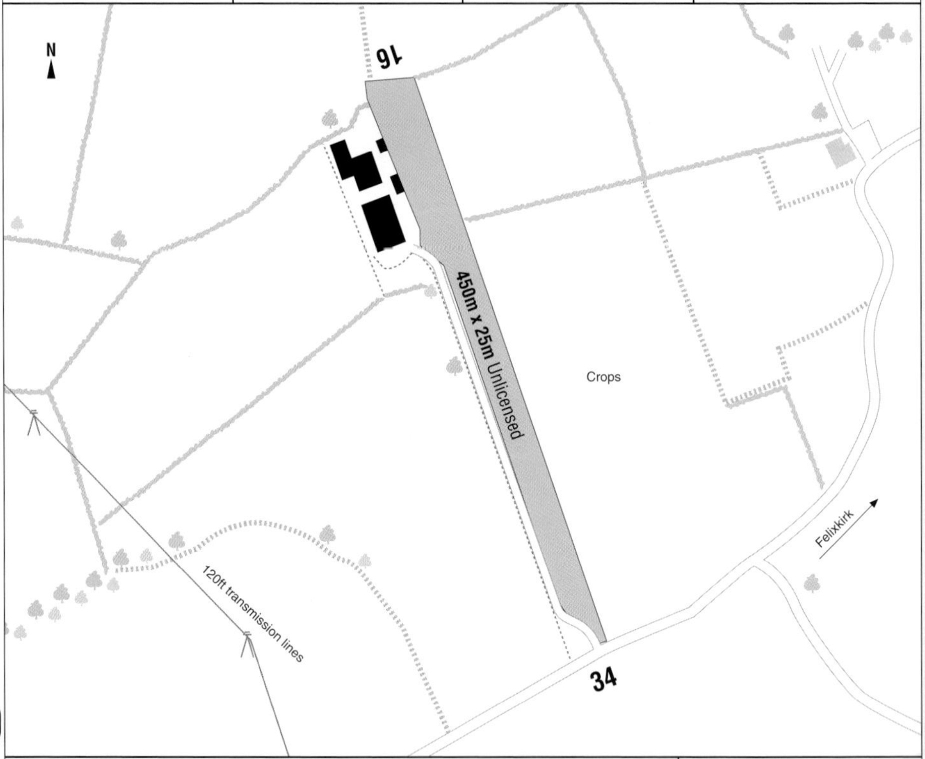

RWY	SURFACE	TORA	LDA	U/L	LIGHTING
16/34	Grass			450x25	Nil

RNAV

Remarks

Landing prohibited unless specific PPR obtained. Situated within the Topcliffe MATZ. Arr ACFT should contact Leeming initially and may be transferred to Topcliffe APP. Dept ACFT should attempt to contact Topcliffe APP on the GND. If no contact then ASAP after airborne.

Warnings

Rwy occasionaly obstructed by agricultural vehicles and equipment. Rwy may be soft after prolonged rain. Pylons close to W of AD.
Noise: Avoid over flying all local habitation, particularly Felixkirk village ESE of AD.

Operating Hours	By arrangement
Circuits	LH
Landing Fee	Nil
Maintenance	Nil
Fuel	Nil
Disabled Facilities	Nil
Restaurant	Carpenter Arms, Felixkirk
Taxi/Car Hire	Nil
Weather Info	Air N MOEx

Operator Mr G McDill
The Airfield
Felixkirk
Thirsk
North Yorkshire YO7 2DR

FELTHORPE

120ft 4mb	4nm NW of Norwich Airport N5242.35 E00111.57	PPR	**Alternative AD** **Norwich** Old Buckenham **Non-standard join**

Felthorpe	APP Norwich 119.350	A/G 123.500 (Not always manned)

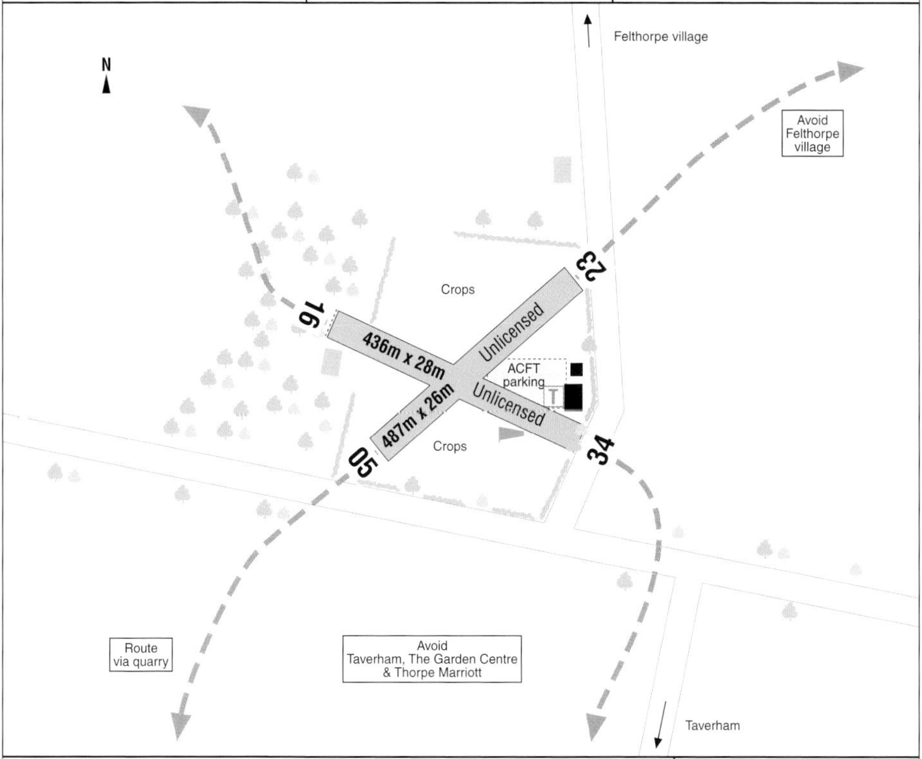

Felthorpe village

N

Avoid Felthorpe village

Crops

16

23

436m x 28m Unlicensed

487m x 26m Unlicensed

ACFT parking

T

Crops

05

34

Route via quarry

Avoid Taverham, The Garden Centre & Thorpe Marriott

Taverham

RWY	SURFACE	TORA	LDA	U/L	LIGHTING
16/34	Grass			436x28	Nil
05/23	Grass			487x26	Nil

RNAV

Remarks

PPR by telephone. Visiting ACFT welcome at pilots own risk. Windsock and landing T displayed. Due to close proximity of Norwich AD all ACFT call Norwich APP. New 1.5m high fence across Rwy16 Thr. Club house open weekends.

Warnings

Trees at boundary may cause turbulence, even in light wind and also obscure view of ACFT in circuit when Dept. Space between Rwys cultivated, agricultural workers & machinery may be present. Busy public Rd on 2 sides of AD. New 1.5m high fence accross Rwy16 Thr.

Noise: Avoid over flying Felthorpe village to NE & Taverham to SSE, also Taverham nursery between AD & village.

Operating Hrs SR-SS

Circuits 05 16 RH, 23 34 LH, 500ft QFE
Over head joins 1000ft QFE

Landing Fee Nil

Maintenance Nil

Fuel Nil

Disabled Facilities

Restaurant Norwich approx 15mins drive

Taxis
Olivers Travels **Tel:** 01603 261010
HP Private Hire **Tel:** 01603 897261

Car Hire
National **Tel:** 01603 631912

Weather Info Air S MOEx

Operator Felthorpe Flying Group Ltd
Kevin Day, The Field Cottage
King Street, Neathshield
Norfolk NR12 8BW
Tel: 01603 867691 (AD)
Tel: 01692 630942 (Secretary)
Tel: 07900 162459 (Secretary)
Tel: 01483 746500 (Secretary Office)

Effective date:25/09/08

OP 02

6ft 0mb	6nm SE of Spalding N5244.37 W00001.80	PPR	**Alternative AD** **Diversion AD**	**Cambridge** Peterborough Conington

Fenland	A/G 122.925	AFIS 122.925 (weekends & by arr)

Holbeach St Johns

South Holland Drain

Noise Abatement

N

18 W E Hangar RVP FNL 401 Fuel AVGAS C Tower Hangar Clubhouse & flying school Fuel JET A1 ACFT parking A

594m x 30m

Crops

B 26 670m x 18m Unlicensed 36 C 08

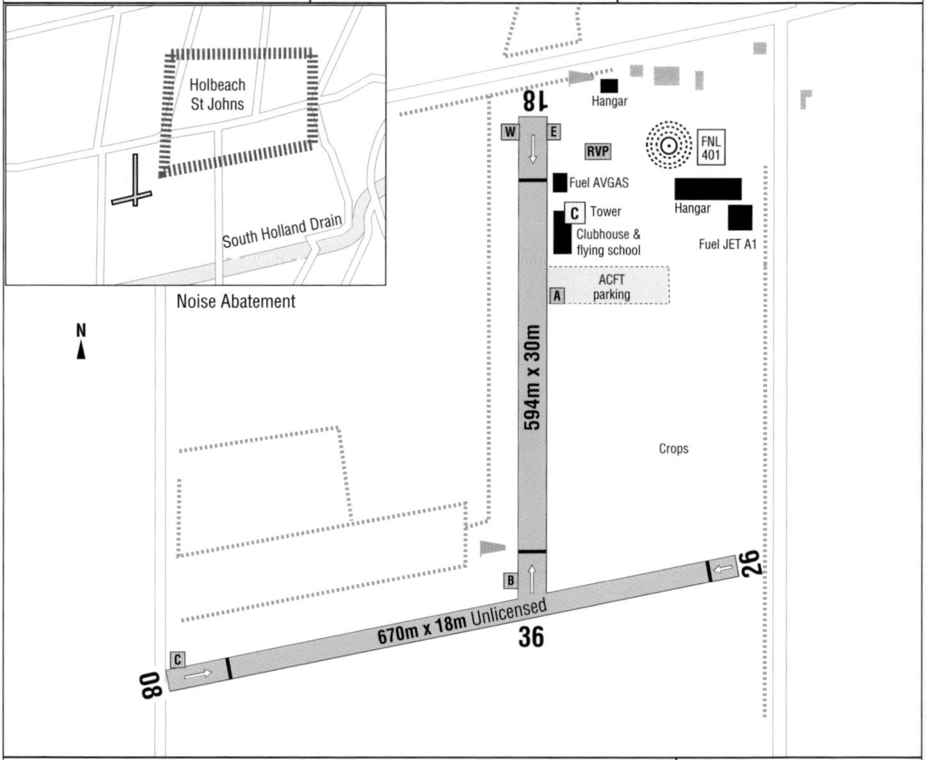

RWY	SURFACE	TORA	LDA	U/L	LIGHTING
18	Grass	594	512		Thr Rwy LITAS 4.25°
36	Grass	594	591		Nil
08/26	Grass			670x18	Nil

Rwy18 lighting PPR

RNAV

Remarks
PPR. AD not available for use by public transport passenger flights required to use a licensed AD. Certain customs facilities available.
Visual aid to location: Ibn FE Green

Warnings
AD is in a low flying military training area. All ACFT movements confined to marked grass strips and Rwy. Caution – Rwy08/26 may appear longer from the air than the actual usable length indicated on charts. Beware of drainage channels close to AD.
Noise: Rwy18 LH in use downwind is wide of the village to E of AD Do not fly between the village and AD, keep well wide to E.

Operating Hrs Closed Monday
Tue-Sun & PH 0900-SS (L) & by arr

Circuits 08, 18 RH, 36, 26 LH, 1000ft QFE

Landing Fee Single £8 Twin £12 Helicopter £8 Micro £6
Overnight parking £5
Free landing with >100 ltrs fuel uplift

Maintenance Fenland AeroServices Ltd (Tue-Sun)

Fuel AVGAS JET A1 100LL
available during operating Hrs

Disabled Facilities

Restaurant Fully licensed restaurant open Tue-Sun

Taxis
Phoenix Taxi Ser. **Tel:** 01406 22807

Car Hire
4 Star **Tel:** 01406 370882

Weather Info Air S MOEx

Operator Fenland Aero Club Ltd
Fenland Aerodrome
Jekylls Bank
Holbeach St Johns
Lincolnshire, PE128RQ
Tel: 01406 540330 (Clubhouse/ATC)
Tel: 01406 540461 (Flying School)
www.fenlandairfield.co.uk

F

XFES FESHIEBRIDGE

860ft 28mb	1.5nm SE of Loch Insh N5706.00 W00353.08	PPR	Alternative AD Inverness Perth

Non-standard join

Feshiebridge	A/G 130.100 (Glider freq)

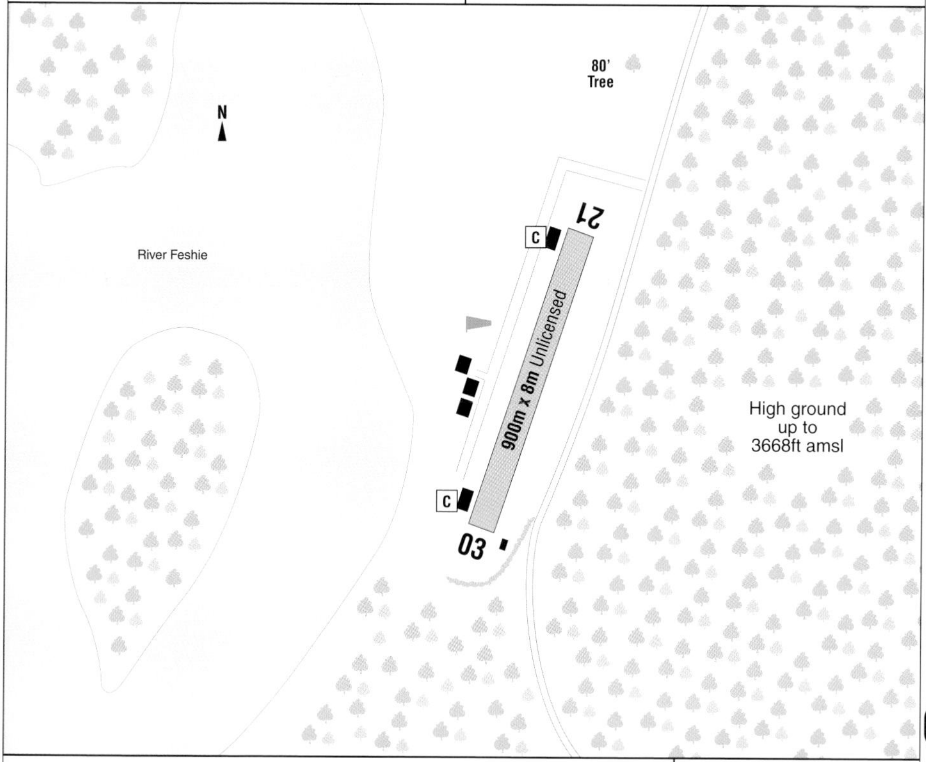

80' Tree

N

River Feshie

21

C

900m x 8m Unlicensed

C

03

High ground up to 3668ft amsl

RWY	SURFACE	TORA	LDA	U/L	LIGHTING
03/21	Grass			900x8	Nil

Rwy21 slight upslope in last 25%

RNAV			
INS	109.20	176	26.8

Remarks

PPR by telephone. Primarily a gliding field with both winch and aerotow. Powered ACFT welcome. AD situated in stunning countryside but due consideration should be given for mountain weather and turbulence. Parking by the control caravan parked at appropriate landing Thr. Pilots are welcome to camp on AD.

Warnings

Caution turning off strip: Rwy smooth but lower than surrounding land with varying 'kerb effect' up to approx. 15cm (6"). There is an 80ft tree on centre line approx. 250m Rwy21 Thr, also low fence crosses 25m away from Rwy21 APP Thr. Give priority to gliders, they may block the Rwy for short periods during launch and retrieval. Information is passed by control on glider common freq. Make normal circuit calls on this freq. High GND up to 3668ft immediately to E and heavily wooded areas close to E & SE.

Operating Hrs	SR-SS
Circuits	21 RH, 03 LH Gliders use L & R circuit on both Rwys
Landing Fee	£10 inc day membership to club
Maintenance	Nil
Fuel	Nil
Disabled Facilities	Nil
Restaurant	Tea & coffee available at control TWR Aviemore Tourist Board **Tel:** 01479 810363 (for restaurants/accommodation etc)

Taxis	**Tel:** 01479 810118
Car Hire	
Budget	**Tel:** 01463 713333
Weather Info	Air Sc GWC
Operator	Cairngorm Gliding Club Miss J Williamson Balnespick, Kincraig Kingussie, Inverness Highland **Tel:** 01540 651246 (Landowner) **Tel:** 01540 651317 (AD) **Tel:** 07770 454593

Effective date:25/09/08 OP 06

F

270ft 9mb	1nm NW of Houbie Isle of Fetlar N6036.23 W00052.33	**PPR**	**Alternative AD** **Scatsta** Unst

Non-radio	**APP** **Sumburgh 131.300**	**Safetycom** **135.475**

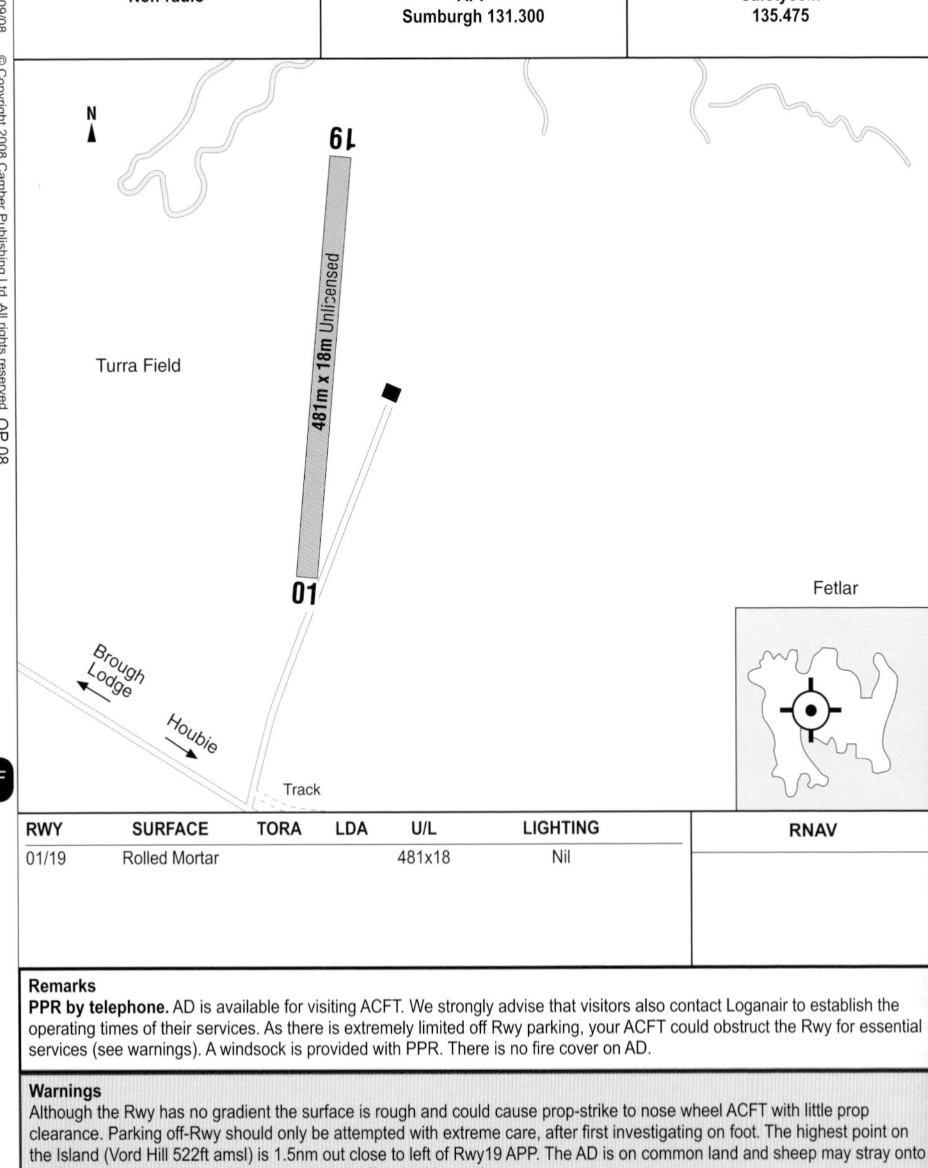

RWY	SURFACE	TORA	LDA	U/L	LIGHTING
01/19	Rolled Mortar			481x18	Nil

RNAV

Remarks

PPR by telephone. AD is available for visiting ACFT. We strongly advise that visitors also contact Loganair to establish the operating times of their services. As there is extremely limited off Rwy parking, your ACFT could obstruct the Rwy for essential services (see warnings). A windsock is provided with PPR. There is no fire cover on AD.

Warnings

Although the Rwy has no gradient the surface is rough and could cause prop-strike to nose wheel ACFT with little prop clearance. Parking off-Rwy should only be attempted with extreme care, after first investigating on foot. The highest point on the Island (Vord Hill 522ft amsl) is 1.5nm out close to left of Rwy19 APP. The AD is on common land and sheep may stray onto the Rwy at any at any time. Moss growth may affect braking action.

Operating Hrs	SR-SS
Circuits	1000ft QFE
Landing Fee	Nil
Maintenance	Nil
Fuel	Nil
Disabled Facilities	

Restaurants/Accomodation

B&B **Tel:** 01957 733227 (Mrs L Boxall)
Tel: 01957 733242 (P Kelly)

Taxis/Car Hire	Nil Mr Leaper can provide transport by arr
Weather Info	Air Sc GWC
Operator	Fetlar Development Group Fetlar Aerodrome Shetland, ZE2 9DJ **Tel:** 01957 733267 (Mr R Leaper) **Tel:** 01595 840246 (Loganair)

F

399ft 13mb	2nm W of Glenrothes N5611.00 W00313.22	PPR	**Alternative AD** **Diversion AD**	**Edinburgh** Perth

Fife	A/G 130.450

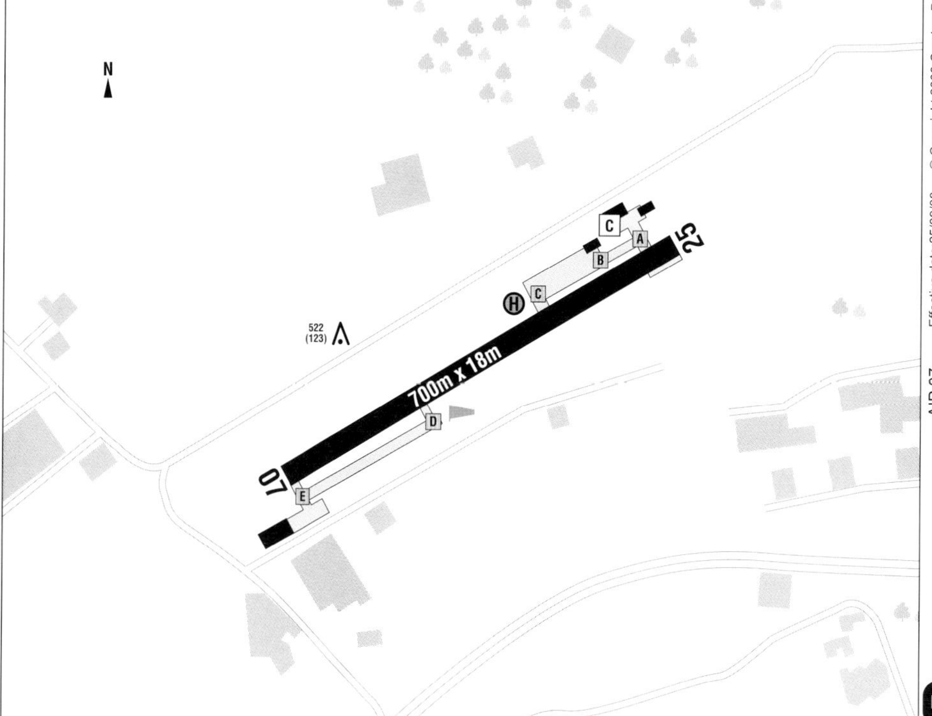

RWY	SURFACE	TORA	LDA	U/L	LIGHTING
07	Asphalt	700	700		Thr Rwy APAPI 4° RHS
25	Asphalt	700	700		Rwy APAPI 4.25° LHS

RNAV			
PTH	110.40	169	16.3

Remarks
PPR. Pilots should avoid flying over the town of Glenrothes and are advised when taking off from Rwy07 to turn right on reaching 300ft aal.

Warnings
Caution: Road close to Rwy07 Thr
Noise: Avoid over flying Kinglasie SW of AD. Dept Rwy25 climb straight ahead until W of Kinglassie village before turning left into circuit. Rwy07 extend downwind leg to turn base leg W of Kinglassie village. Overhead rejoin if circuit busy. When turning finals for Rwy25 at 300ft avoid all houses.

Operating Hrs	Mon-Sat 0700-2100 Sun 0830-2030 (L)
Circuits	25 LH, 07 RH
Landing fees	Single £8 Twin £16 Commercial Twin £32 Light Commercial Twin £16 £5 voucher issued per landing, redeemable in Tipsy Nipper on day of landing Hangarage available on request
Maintenance	Nil
Fuel	AVGAS 100LL
Disabled Facilities	Available

Restaurant	Tipsy Nipper fully licensed restaurant refreshments & club facilities
Taxis/Car Hire	By arrangement on arrival
Weather Info	Air Sc GWC
Operator	Tayside Aviation Ltd Fife (Glenrothes) Airport Fife, KY6 2SL **Tel:** 01592 753792 **Fax:** 01592 612812 enquiries@taysideaviation.co.uk www.taysideaviation.co.uk

405ft 14mb	2.5nm WSW of Buckingham N5159.13 W00103.36	PPR	Alternative AD Diversion AD	Cranfield Turweston

Non-standard join

Non Radio	Safetycom 135.475

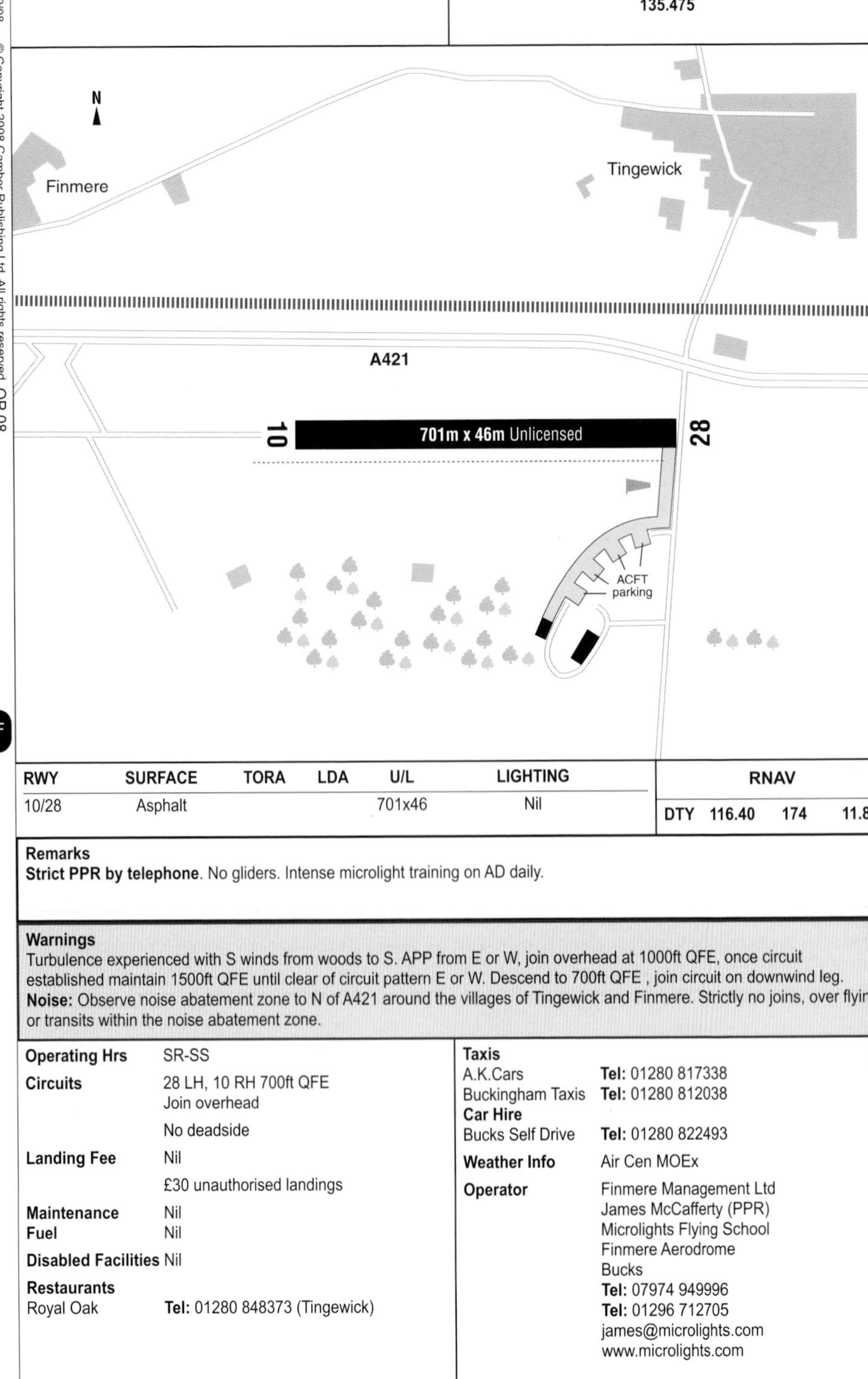

RWY	SURFACE	TORA	LDA	U/L	LIGHTING
10/28	Asphalt			701x46	Nil

RNAV			
DTY	116.40	174	11.8

Remarks
Strict PPR by telephone. No gliders. Intense microlight training on AD daily.

Warnings
Turbulence experienced with S winds from woods to S. APP from E or W, join overhead at 1000ft QFE, once circuit established maintain 1500ft QFE until clear of circuit pattern E or W. Descend to 700ft QFE , join circuit on downwind leg.
Noise: Observe noise abatement zone to N of A421 around the villages of Tingewick and Finmere. Strictly no joins, over flying or transits within the noise abatement zone.

Operating Hrs SR-SS
Circuits 28 LH, 10 RH 700ft QFE
Join overhead
No deadside
Landing Fee Nil
£30 unauthorised landings
Maintenance Nil
Fuel Nil
Disabled Facilities Nil
Restaurants
Royal Oak **Tel:** 01280 848373 (Tingewick)

Taxis
A.K.Cars **Tel:** 01280 817338
Buckingham Taxis **Tel:** 01280 812038
Car Hire
Bucks Self Drive **Tel:** 01280 822493
Weather Info Air Cen MOEx
Operator Finmere Management Ltd
James McCafferty (PPR)
Microlights Flying School
Finmere Aerodrome
Bucks
Tel: 07974 949996
Tel: 01296 712705
james@microlights.com
www.microlights.com

F

FINNINGLEY VILLAGE

5ft 0mb	3nm NE of Doncaster Sheffield AD N5330.71 W00056.27	PPR	Alternative AD	Humberside Sandtoft
				Non-standard join

Non-Radio	APP Doncaster Sheffield 126.225	Safetycom 135.475

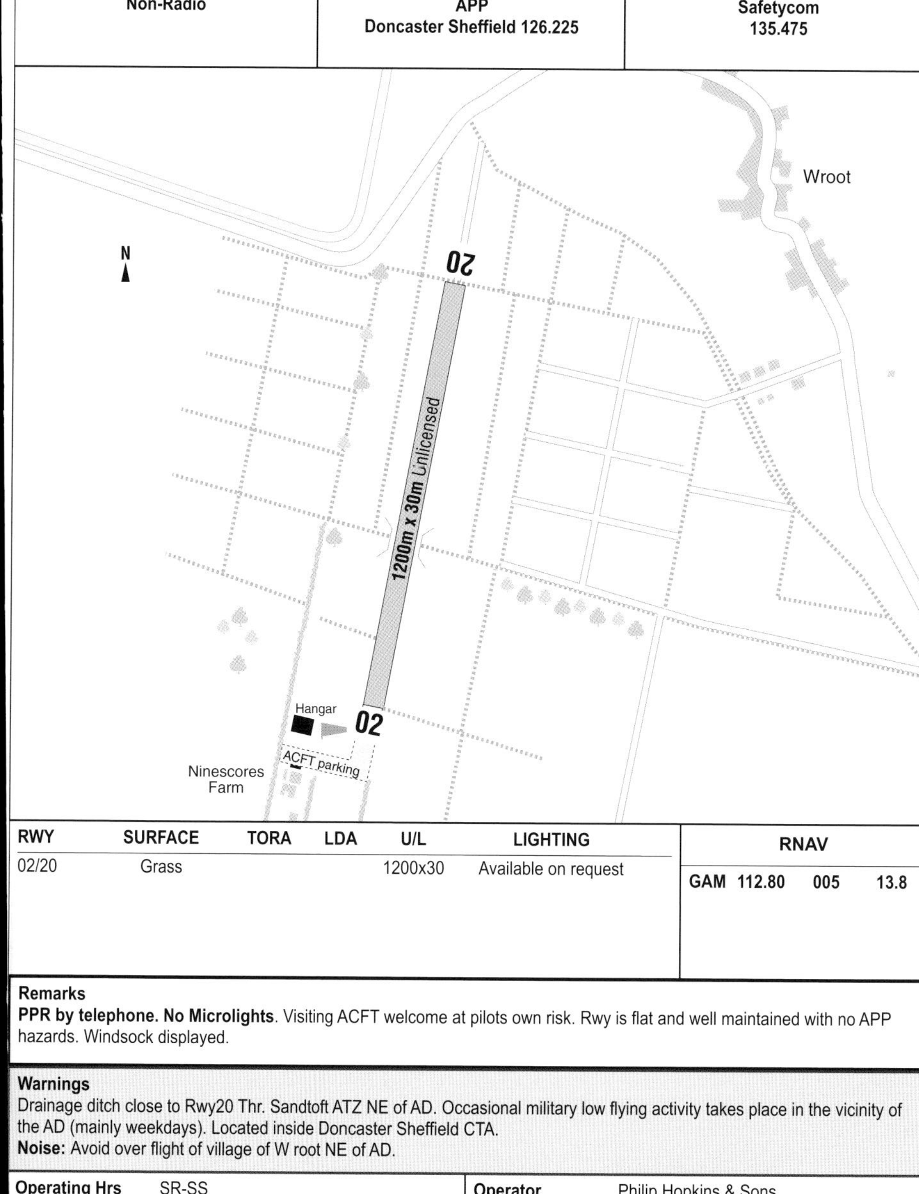

RWY	SURFACE	TORA	LDA	U/L	LIGHTING
02/20	Grass			1200x30	Available on request

RNAV			
GAM	112.80	005	13.8

Remarks
PPR by telephone. No Microlights. Visiting ACFT welcome at pilots own risk. Rwy is flat and well maintained with no APP hazards. Windsock displayed.

Warnings
Drainage ditch close to Rwy20 Thr. Sandtoft ATZ NE of AD. Occasional military low flying activity takes place in the vicinity of the AD (mainly weekdays). Located inside Doncaster Sheffield CTA.
Noise: Avoid over flight of village of W root NE of AD.

Operating Hrs	SR-SS
Circuits	LH 1000ft QFE
Landing Fee	Nil
Maintenance	Nil
Fuel	Nil
Disabled Facilities	Nil
Restaurants	Bawtry or Epworth
Taxi	
Axholme Hire	**Tel:** 01427 871486
Taxi & Mini Cab Co	**Tel:** 01427 533335
Car Hire	Nil
Weather Info	Air N MOEx

Operator
Philip Hopkins & Sons
Ninescores Farm
Finningley
South Yorkshire DN9 3DY
Tel: 01302 770274
Tel: 07836 659322
Fax: 01302 772800

377ft 12mb	2.5nm NNW of Sedgefield N5441.30 W00127.85	PPR	Alternative AD	**Durham Tees Valley** Peterlee

Fishburn	APP Durham 118.850	A/G 118.275

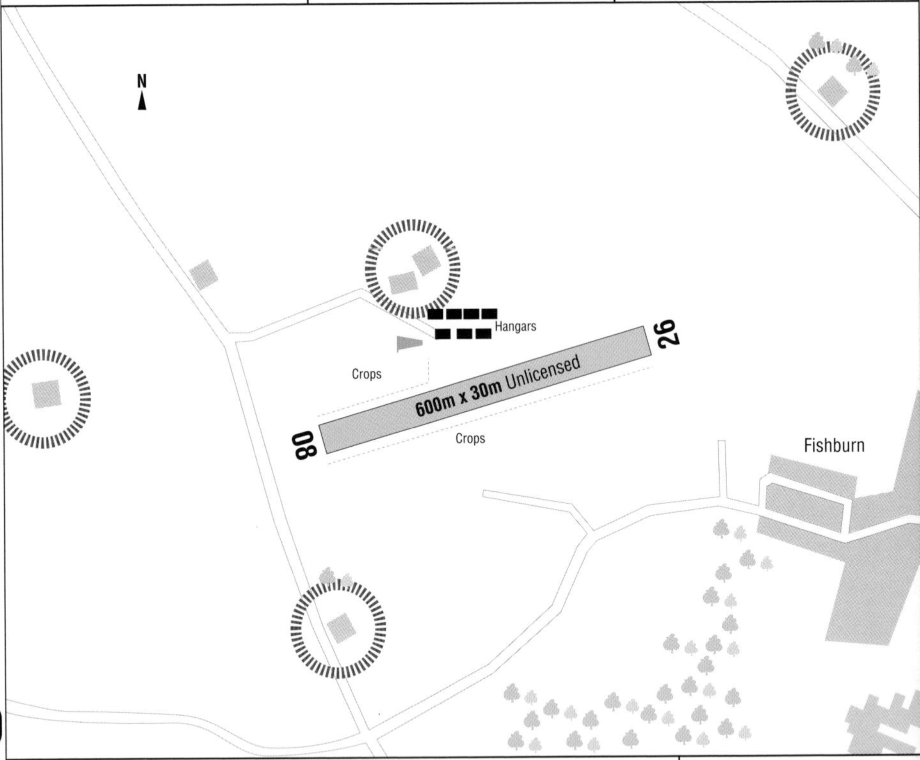

N
Hangars
26
Crops
600m x 30m Unlicensed
08
Crops
Fishburn

RWY	SURFACE	TORA	LDA	U/L	LIGHTING
08/26	Grass			600x30	Nil

Rwy26 1.6% upslope

RNAV			
NEW	114.25	163	22.5

Remarks
PPR by telephone. Situated N of the Teesside CTR. Helicopters accepted.

Warnings
Join circuit from N only. Crops grown right up to Rwy edge.
Noise: Avoid over flying local habitation.

Operating Hrs	Mon-Sat 0800-2030 Sun 0930-2030 (L) (Last take-off 2000)
Circuits	08 LH, 26 RH, 800ft QFE
Landing Fee	Single £3 Twin £5 Overnight parking £5 Cheques £1 surcharge
Maintenance	In emergency
Fuel	AVGAS 100LL Cheques £1 surcharge No credit cards taken

Disabled Facilities

Restaurants
Snacks & hot drinks available in clubhouse

Taxis	
Ron's	**Tel:** 01740 621862
Turners	**Tel:** 01740 620338
Car Hire	
Turners	**Tel:** 01742 620338
Weather Info	Air N MOEx
Operator	Beryl Morgan Airfield Cottage West House Farm Bishop Middleham Co Durham DL17 9DY **Tel:** 0191 3770137 (Airfield) **Tel:** 0191 3778430 (Home) **Tel:** 07785 786710

150ft 5mb	Hametown, Isle of Foula N6007.33 W00203.12	PPR	Alternative AD	**Lerwick** Scatsta

Non-radio	APP Sumburgh 131.300	Safetycom 135.475

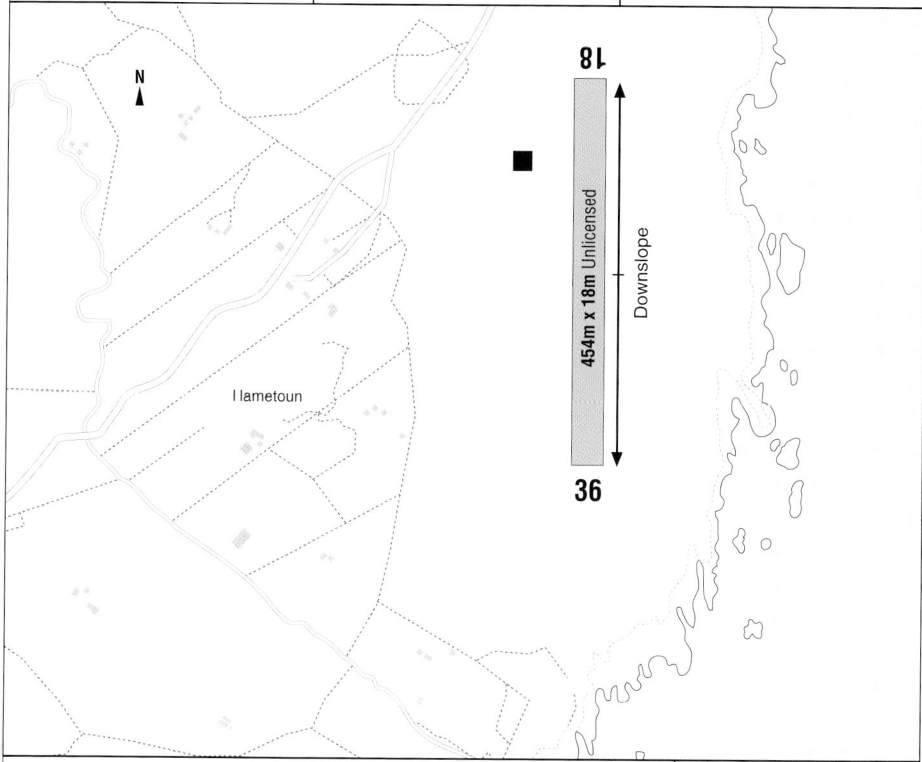

18

454m x 18m Unlicensed

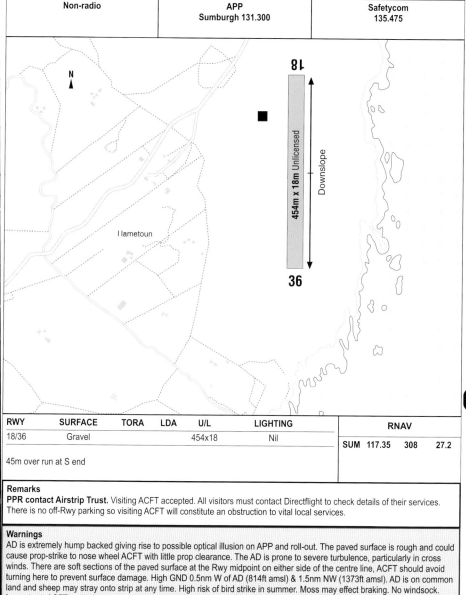

Downslope

Hametoun

36

RWY	SURFACE	TORA	LDA	U/L	LIGHTING
18/36	Gravel			454x18	Nil

45m over run at S end

RNAV			
SUM	117.35	308	27.2

Remarks
PPR contact Airstrip Trust. Visiting ACFT accepted. All visitors must contact Directflight to check details of their services. There is no off-Rwy parking so visiting ACFT will constitute an obstruction to vital local services.

Warnings
AD is extremely hump backed giving rise to possible optical illusion on APP and roll-out. The paved surface is rough and could cause prop-strike to nose wheel ACFT with little prop clearance. The AD is prone to severe turbulence, particularly in cross winds. There are soft sections of the paved surface at the Rwy midpoint on either side of the centre line, ACFT should avoid turning here to prevent surface damage. High GND 0.5nm W of AD (814ft amsl) & 1.5nm NW (1373ft amsl). AD is on common land and sheep may stray onto strip at any time. High risk of bird strike in summer. Moss may effect braking. No windsock.
Important: ACFT parked on strip restrict scheduled & ambulance services – consult with Directflight.

Operating Hrs	SR-SS
Circuits	1000ft QFE
Landing Fee	£30 per landing
Maintenance	Nil
Fuel	Nil
Disabled Facilities	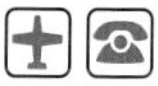
Restaurants	Nil
Taxis/Car Hire	Nil
Weather Info	Air Sc GWC

Operator
Mrs Isobel Holbourn
Foula Airstrip Trust
Isle of Foula
Shetland Isles
Tel: 01595 753233 (Airstrip Trust)
Tel: 01957 753235 (Fire Service)
Tel: 01595 840246 (Directflight)

17ft 4mb	7.5nm SSW of Cambridge N5204.65 E00003.70	PPR	Alternative AD Diversion AD	Cambridge Duxford

Non-standard join

Fowlmere	LARS	APP	AFIS	A/G
	Farnborough North 132.800	Essex RAD 120.625	Duxford 122.075	135.700

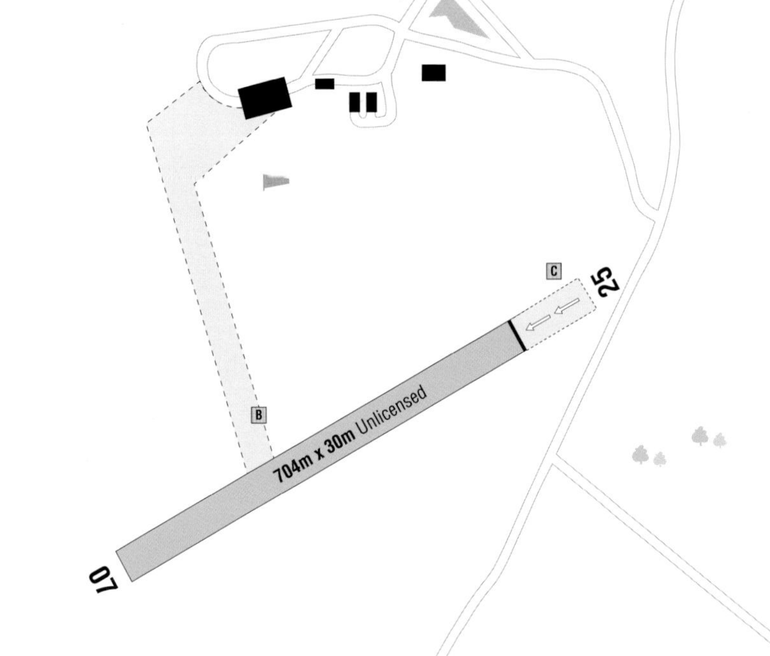

RWY	SURFACE	TORA	LDA	U/L	LIGHTING
07/25	Grass			704x30	Nil

Rwy25 150m of unmarked Rwy is available at E end for take-offs
Rwy07 150m of unmarked Rwy is available for landings & take-offs

RNAV			
BKY	116.25	002	5.3

Remarks
PPR strictly by telephone for briefing. Fowlmere is close to Duxford AD, 2.5nm WSW. Contact Duxford info prior to joining for Wy25 or dept Rwy07. Join via Royston Rwy25: follow railway NE between Melbourn & Meldrith keep N of bird sanctuary, turn right base between Fowlmere & Thirplow. Rwy07: Royston direct to long final.

Warnings
Back tracking is necessary for entry/exit on Rwy07/25. Pilots should not take-off or land while this is in progress. ACFT holding at the marked holding points will be clear of the Rwy and strips.
Noise: Strict compliance with noise abatement. Avoid making a low APP Rwy25 due public Rd, flying over Fowlmere village & built up areas in the vicinity. Bird reserve 700m NW of AD.

Operating Hrs Tue-Fri & PH 0800-1200
Sat-Sun 0800-1200 (L)

Circuits 07 LH, 25 RH, 800ft QFE
No overhead joins

Landing Fee Single £10 Twin £15

Maintenance Modern Air
Fuel AVGAS 100LL by arr

Disabled Facilities

☎

Restaurants
Sheen Mill **Tel:** 01763 261393 (Melbourne)
The Chequers **Tel:** 01763 208369 (Fowlmere)

Taxis
Meltax **Tel:** 01763 244444
Car Hire
Kirkham Cars **Tel:** 01763 261116
Ford **Tel:** 01763 242084

Weather Info Air S MOEx

Operator Modern Air (UK) Ltd
Fowlmere Aerodrome
Royston, Herts, SG8 7SJ
Tel: 01763 208281 (AD)
Tel: 01223 833376 (Duxford ATC)
Fax: 01763 208861

EGNU FULL SUTTON

86ft 3mb	7nm E of York N5358.83 W00051.88	PPR	Alternative AD Diversion AD	Humberside Sherburn in Elmet Non-standard join

Full Sutton	A/G 132.325

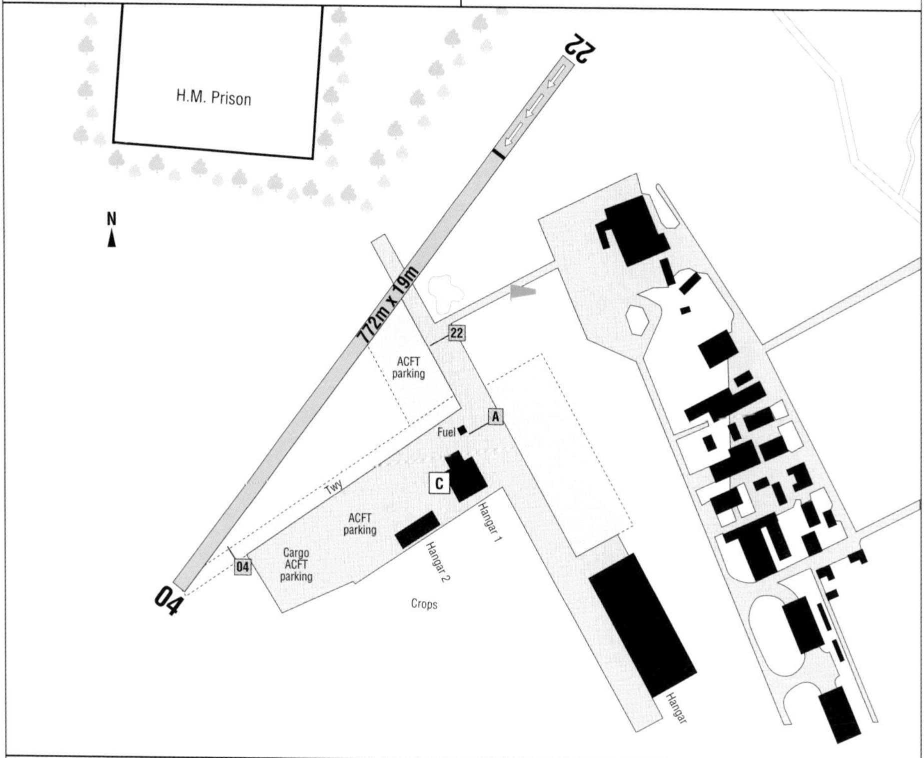

RWY	SURFACE	TORA	LDA	U/L	LIGHTING
04	Grass	772	772		Nil
22	Grass	772	715		Nil

Displaced Thr Rwy22 79m

RNAV

Remarks
PPR. Non–radio ACFT not accepted. Radio use is mandatory. AD not available to Public Transport flights which require a licensed AD.
Visual aid to location: 4 large grain silos E of AD.

Warnings
AD is within Restricted Area R315 (applies to helicopters only). Do not land short of displaced Thr. Intensive gliding at Pocklington, 4nm SE of AD. High GND up to 807ft amsl 4nm E of AD.When wind >240° windshear my be experienced Rwy22 Thr.
Noise: Do not over fly the prison on N side of AD under any circumstances. Dept Rwy22, fly over pig farm on climb out.

Operating Hrs Tue-Fri 0800-1800 Sat-Sun 0900-SS (Summer) Tue-Fri 0900-1700 Sat-Sun 0900-SS (Winter)

Circuits 04 LH, 22 RH, 800ft QFE

Landing Fee Single £5, Twin £10

Maintenance
RH Aviation **Tel:** 01759 372849

Fuel AVGAS 100LL available by arr

Disabled Facilities

Restaurants Tea & coffee in clubhouse

Taxis
Central **Tel:** 01759 302146
Kumar **Tel:** 07949 574508

Car Hire
Premier **Tel:** 01759 306910

Weather Info Air N MOEx

Operator Full Sutton Flying Centre Ltd
Full Sutton Airfield
Stamford Bridge
East Yorkshire YO4 1HS
Tel: 01759 372717
Tel: 01759 373277 (Club)
Fax: 01759 37299

200ft 6mb	6.9nm W of Sherburn-in-Elmet N5347.30 W00121.50	PPR	Alternative AD	**Leeds Bradford** Sherburn in Elmet

Non-Radio	ATIS Leeds 118.025	APP Fenton 126.500	APP Leeds 123.750	Safetycom 135.475

N
18
Public footpath
Public footpath
700m x 20m Unlicensed
A656
Garforth village DO NOT overfly
ACFT parking by hangar
Crops
Slight upslope
750m x 40m Unlicensed
36
28
175ft agl powerlines 500m from 28 Thr
Railway in deep cutting

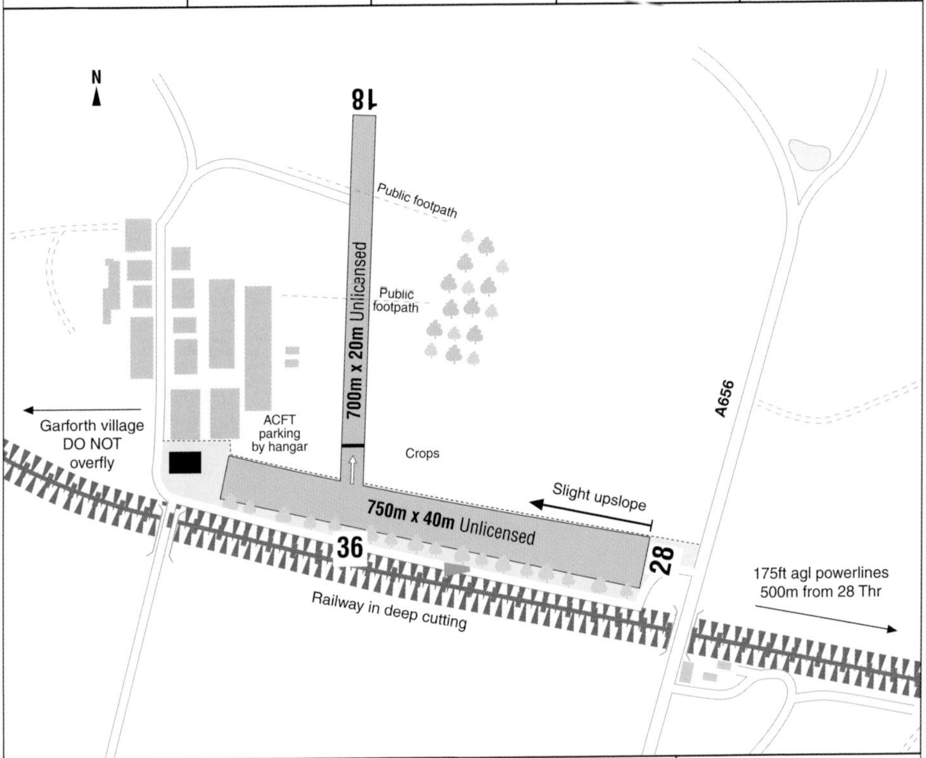

RWY	SURFACE	TORA	TODA	U/L	LIGHTING
28	Grass			750x40	Nil
18/36	Grass			700x20	Nil

Rwy36 banked on either side for first 350m, Displaced Thr Rwy36 200m

RNAV			
POL	112.10	088	26.5

Remarks
PPR by telephone. Microlights not accepted. Visitors welcome at pilots own risk. Rwy S edge is slightly curved. Operator advises pilots keep to line of A1 to remain clear of Church Fenton MATZ then follow railway line in on Rwy28 APP.
Visual aid to location: Railway cutting and industrial buildings to the W.

Warnings
AD situated between Church Fenton MATZ (usually closed weekends), and Leeds CTR/CTA (H24).
Caution: National Grid pylons & transmission lines 175ft agl cross Rwy28 APP 500m from Thr. A656 crosses short final Rwy28. 2 public footpaths cross Rwy18/36.
Noise: Do not over fly Garforth village close to W.

Operating Hrs	SR-SS
Circuits	28 36 RH, 18 LH
Landing Fee	Advised with PPR
Maintenance	Nil
Fuel	AVGAS 100LL

Disabled Facilities

Restaurants	The Swan, Aberford (3nm from AD) The Hilton Hotel, Garforth

Taxi

Garforth Cars	**Tel:** 0113 2872866
D+D Services	**Tel:** 0113 2860114

Car Hire

Central Self Drive	**Tel:** 01977 603280
L C H Leeds	**Tel:** 01132 468989 (Free delivery to AD)
Weather Info	Air N MOEx
Operator	Chris Makin Sturton Grange Michlefield, Leeds West Yorkdhire LS25 4DZ **Tel:** 0113 2862631 **Fax:** 0113 2873747 chris@makins.co.uk

600ft 20mb	1nm NNW of Colerne AD N5127.60 W00218.10	PPR	Alternative AD **Bristol Filton** Kemble **Non-standard join**

Non-radio	LARS Bristol 125.650	APP Colerne 120.075	Safetycom 135.475

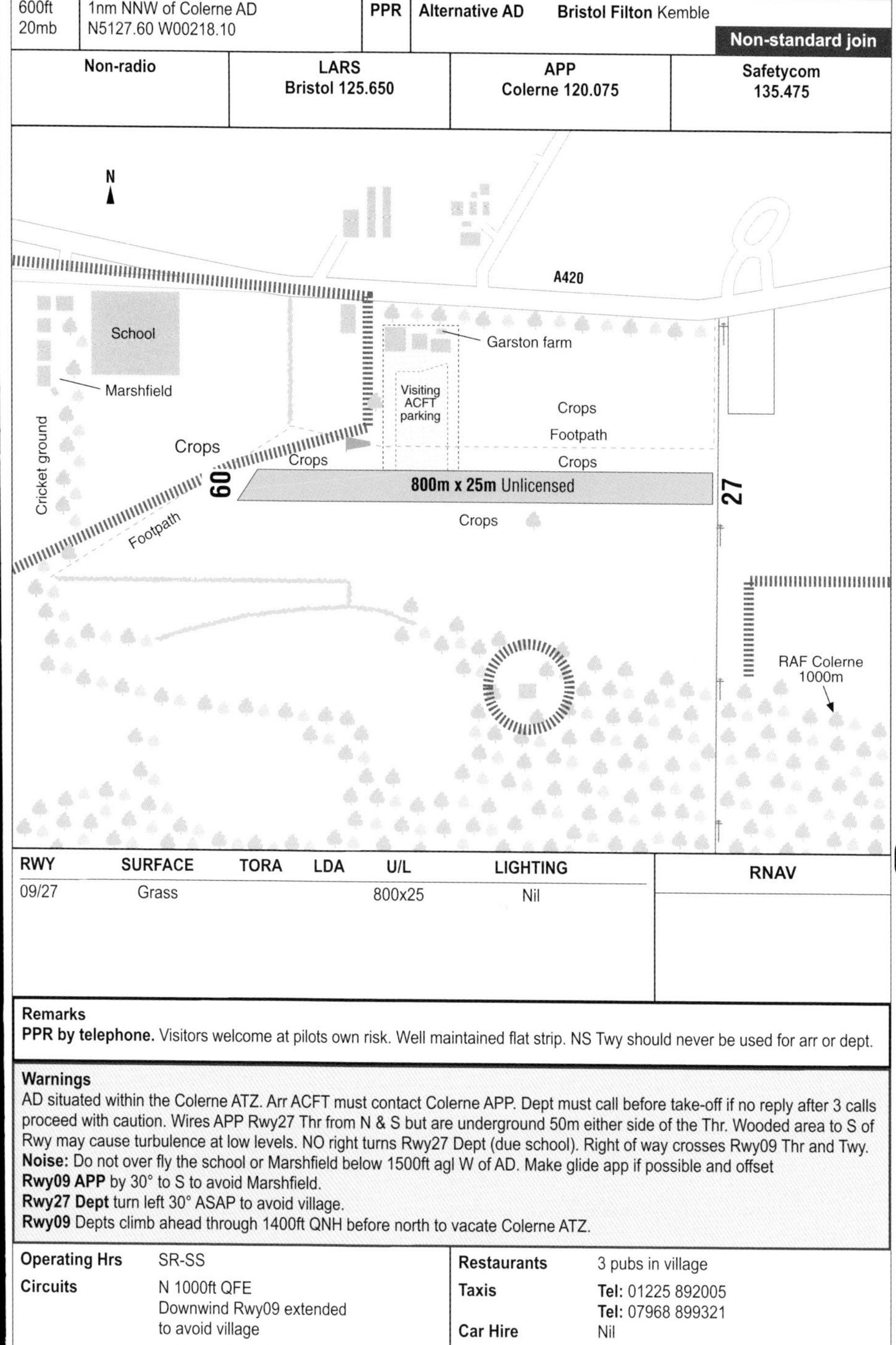

RWY	SURFACE	TORA	LDA	U/L	LIGHTING
09/27	Grass			800x25	Nil

RNAV

Remarks

PPR by telephone. Visitors welcome at pilots own risk. Well maintained flat strip. NS Twy should never be used for arr or dept.

Warnings

AD situated within the Colerne ATZ. Arr ACFT must contact Colerne APP. Dept must call before take-off if no reply after 3 calls proceed with caution. Wires APP Rwy27 Thr from N & S but are underground 50m either side of the Thr. Wooded area to S of Rwy may cause turbulence at low levels. NO right turns Rwy27 Dept (due school). Right of way crosses Rwy09 Thr and Twy.
Noise: Do not over fly the school or Marshfield below 1500ft agl W of AD. Make glide app if possible and offset
Rwy09 APP by 30° to S to avoid Marshfield.
Rwy27 Dept turn left 30° ASAP to avoid village.
Rwy09 Depts climb ahead through 1400ft QNH before north to vacate Colerne ATZ.

Operating Hrs	SR-SS
Circuits	N 1000ft QFE Downwind Rwy09 extended to avoid village
Landing Fee	Advised with PPR
Maintenance	Nil
Fuel	Nil
Disabled Facilities	

Restaurants	3 pubs in village
Taxis	**Tel:** 01225 892005 **Tel:** 07968 899321
Car Hire	Nil
Weather Info	Air SW MOEx
Operator	Mr M Ball Garston Farm, Marshfield Chippenham, Wilts, SN14 8LH **Tel:** 07901 755312 **Tel:** 01225 891284 www.garstonfarm.flyer.co.uk

GARTON FIELD

39ft 1mb	6.5nm NW of Withernsea N5347.40 W00005.16	PPR	Alternative AD	**Humberside** Beverley

Garton	**LARS** **Humberside 119.125**	**A/G** **122.075** **Available on request**

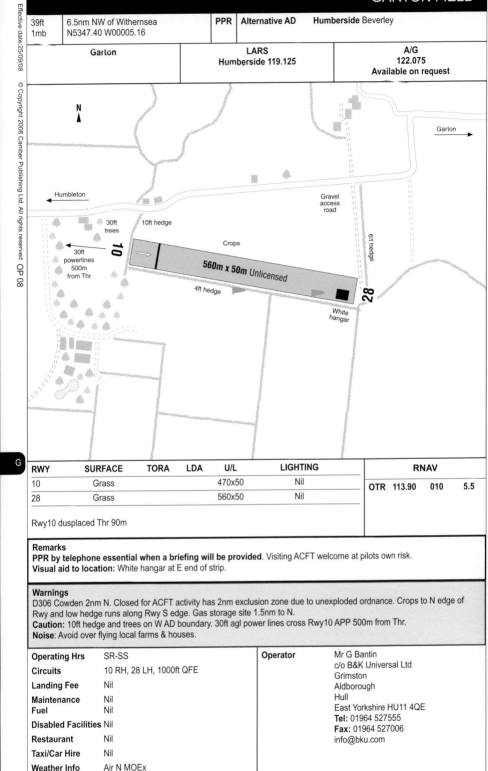

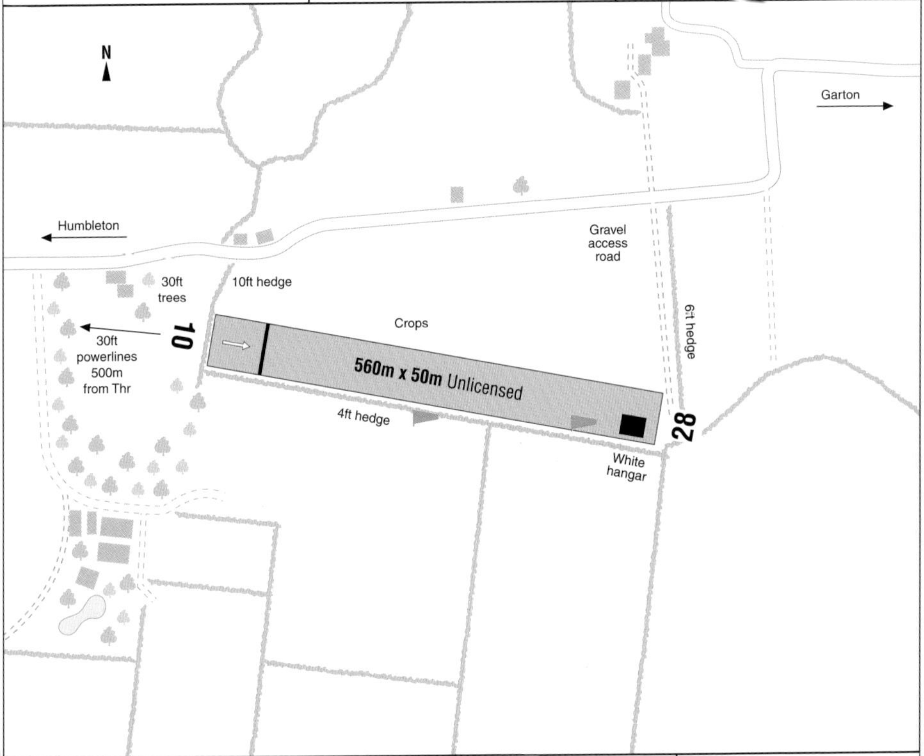

RWY	SURFACE	TORA	LDA	U/L	LIGHTING
10	Grass			470x50	Nil
28	Grass			560x50	Nil

Rwy10 dusplaced Thr 90m

RNAV			
OTR	**113.90**	**010**	**5.5**

Remarks
PPR by telephone essential when a briefing will be provided. Visiting ACFT welcome at pilots own risk.
Visual aid to location: White hangar at E end of strip.

Warnings
D306 Cowden 2nm N. Closed for ACFT activity has 2nm exclusion zone due to unexploded ordnance. Crops to N edge of Rwy and low hedge runs along Rwy S edge. Gas storage site 1.5nm to N.
Caution: 10ft hedge and trees on W AD boundary. 30ft agl power lines cross Rwy10 APP 500m from Thr.
Noise: Avoid over flying local farms & houses.

Operating Hrs	SR-SS
Circuits	10 RH, 28 LH, 1000ft QFE
Landing Fee	Nil
Maintenance	Nil
Fuel	Nil
Disabled Facilities	Nil
Restaurant	Nil
Taxi/Car Hire	Nil
Weather Info	Air N MOEx

Operator
Mr G Bantin
c/o B&K Universal Ltd
Grimston
Aldborough
Hull
East Yorkshire HU11 4QE
Tel: 01964 527555
Fax: 01964 527006
info@bku.com

90ft 3mb	1nm S of Upminster N5131.80 E00014.78	PPR	Alternative AD	Southend Stapleford

Non-Radio	APP Thames 132.700	Safetycom 135.475

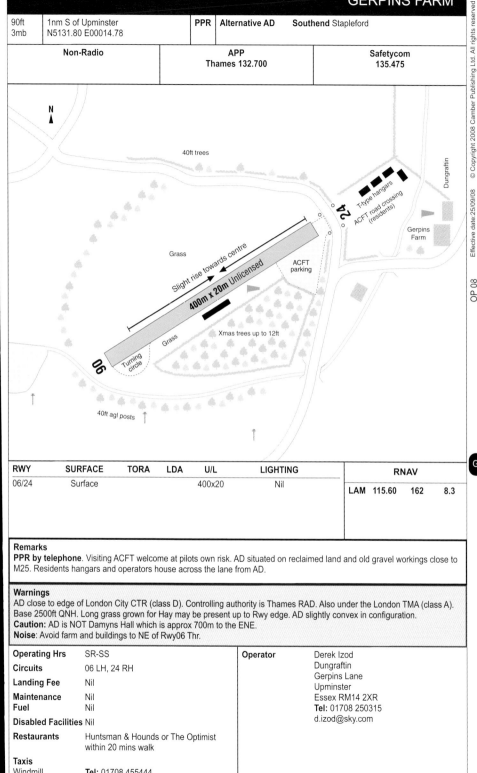

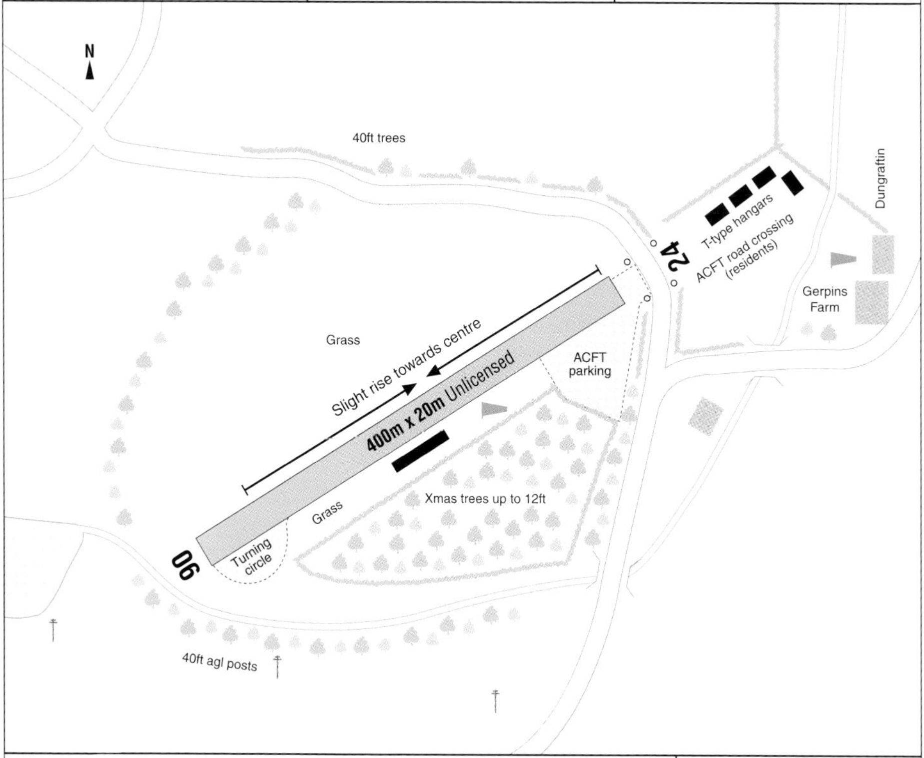

N
40ft trees
Dungraftin
T-type hangars
ACFT road crossing (residents)
24
Gerpins Farm
Grass
Slight rise towards centre
400m x 20m Unlicensed
ACFT parking
Xmas trees up to 12ft
Grass
Turning circle
06
40ft agl posts

RWY	SURFACE	TORA	LDA	U/L	LIGHTING
06/24	Surface			400x20	Nil

RNAV			
LAM	115.60	162	8.3

Remarks
PPR by telephone. Visiting ACFT welcome at pilots own risk. AD situated on reclaimed land and old gravel workings close to M25. Residents hangars and operators house across the lane from AD.

Warnings
AD close to edge of London City CTR (class D). Controlling authority is Thames RAD. Also under the London TMA (class A). Base 2500ft QNH. Long grass grown for Hay may be present up to Rwy edge. AD slightly convex in configuration.
Caution: AD is NOT Damyns Hall which is approx 700m to the ENE.
Noise: Avoid farm and buildings to NE of Rwy06 Thr.

Operating Hrs	SR-SS
Circuits	06 LH, 24 RH
Landing Fee	Nil
Maintenance	Nil
Fuel	Nil
Disabled Facilities	Nil
Restaurants	Huntsman & Hounds or The Optimist within 20 mins walk
Taxis	
Windmill	**Tel:** 01708 455444
Car Hire	Nil
Weather Info	Air SE MOEx

Operator
Derek Izod
Dungraftin
Gerpins Lane
Upminster
Essex RM14 2XR
Tel: 01708 250315
d.izod@sky.com

46ft 2mb	1.5nm S of Village N5539.20 W00545.47	PPR	Alternative AD Diversion AD	Prestwick Campbeltown

Non-radio	FIS Scottish 127.275	Safetycom 135.475

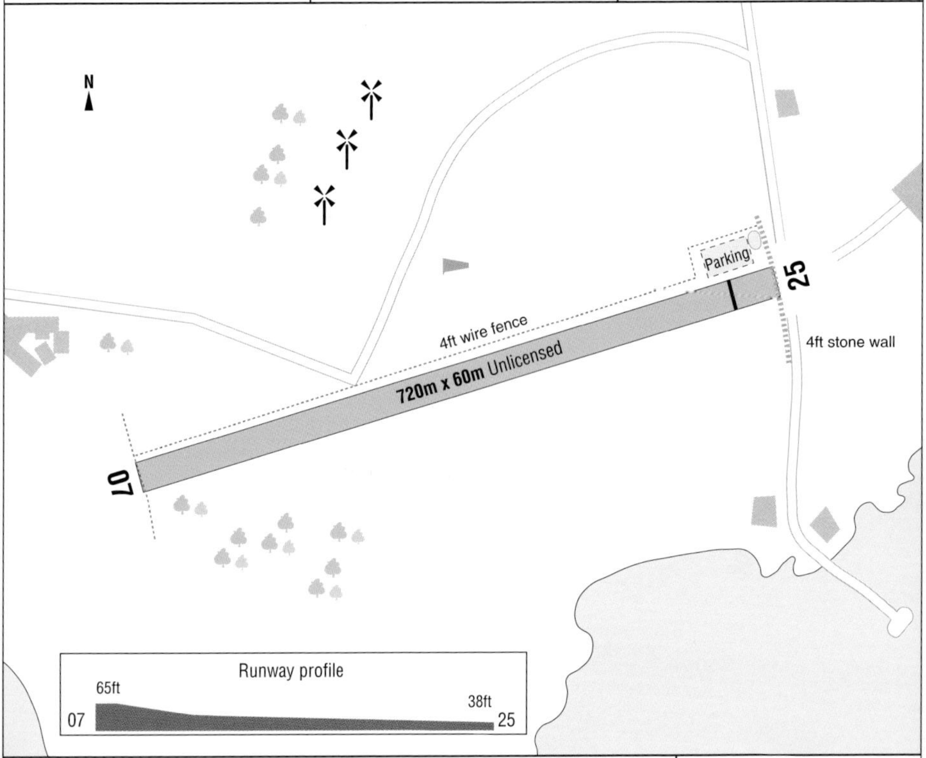

N
4ft wire fence
Parking
25
4ft stone wall
720m x 60m Unlicensed
07

Runway profile
65ft
38ft
07
25

RWY	SURFACE	TORA	LDA	U/L	LIGHTING
07/25	Grass			720x60	Nil

RNAV			
MAC	116.00	351	13.9

Remarks
PPR by telephone. Visiting ACFT welcome. Tie-downs available N side of Rwy25 Thr. Guests of the Gigha Hotel (1.5m N) can be provided with transport to and from the hotel.

Warnings
Rwy has marked step down at Rwy07 Thr. See profile diagram. Shallow dyke on N side of apron. Access Twy is clearly visible as the grass is cut. Use mown entrance to apron only. The un-mown areas are bad ground containing rocks.
Noise: Avoid over flying the village on Sundays between 1100-1200 (L).

Operating Hrs SR-SS
Circuits Nil
Landing Fee Single £15 Twin £25
£5 discount if staying overnight at Gigha Hotel
Maintenance Nil
Fuel MOGAS by arr with Gigha Stores
Disabled Facilities Nil
Restaurants
Gigha Hotel **Tel:** 01583 505254 (Same as PPR)
Taxis/Bike Hire
Gigha Hotel **Tel:** 01583 505254
Gigha Stores **Tel:** 01583 505251

Weather Info Air Sc GWC
Operator Gigha Trading Ltd
Gigha Hotel
Isle of Gigha
Argyll, PA41 7AA
Tel: 01583 505254
Fax: 01583 505244
www.gigha.org.uk

G

EGPF GLASGOW

26ft 1mb	6nm W of Glasgow N5552.32 W00425.98		Alternative AD Diversion AD	Prestwick Cumbernauld

Non-standard join

Glasgow	ATIS 129.575	APP 119.100	RAD 119.300 121.300
TWR 118.800	GND 121.700	FIRE 121.600	Signature 122.350

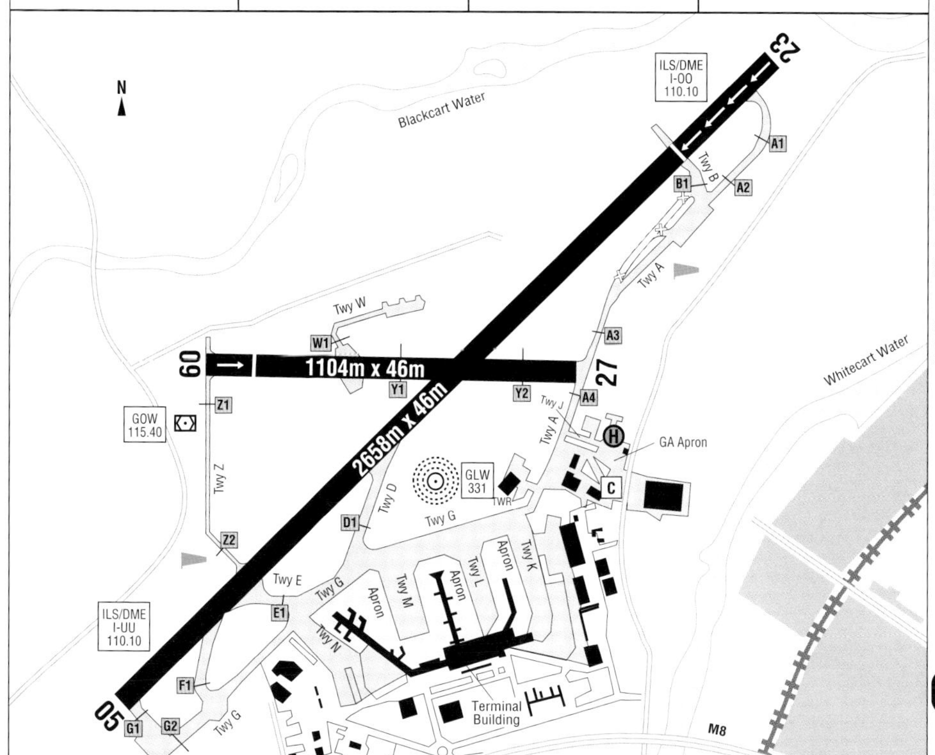

RWY	SURFACE	TORA	LDA	U/L	LIGHTING
05	Asphalt	2658	2658		Ap Thr Rwy PAPI 3° LHS
23	Asphalt	2658	2353		Ap Thr Rwy PAPI 3° LHS
09	Asphalt	1104	1042		Thr Rwy PAPI 3° LHS
27	Asphalt	1104	1104		Thr Rwy PAPI 3° LHS

RNAV
GOW 115.40 on AD

Remarks

Use governed by Scottish CTR regulations. Filing a flight plan does not constitute permission to use Glasgow AD. All pleasure, training & non-business GA traffic subject to prior notification to ATC. Operators must make prior arr with handling agent for GND handling all flights. Use of AD for training purposes is subject to Operations Directors permission, Glasgow AD Ltd ATC. Visiting GA ACFT including international Arr will be parked on GA Park Stand 35. Pilots of international Arr and Dept GA ACFT are responsible for presenting their passengers to Customs and Immigration. Transport to and from the Customs Office will be provided by a Handling Agent.

Warnings

No GND signals except light signals. Large Whooper swans up to 12kgs are present around the AD from Sept-April. Flocks of up to 100 birds may fly at heights up to 500ft. The main flying activity of the swans is usually confined to short periods around dawn and dusk and ATC will endeavour to advise their presence when airborne. Hang Gliding takes place within the Glasgow CTR up to 2500ft amsl (occasionally 3000ft with ATC permission) and sites are considered active during all daylight Hrs. Pilots inbound to or outbound from the AD must operate ACFT so as to cause the least disturbance practicable to the areas in and around the AD.

Operating Hrs	H24 All flights subject to approval
Circuits	Nil
Landing Fee	BAA rates
Maintenance	Available
Fuel	AVGAS JET A1 100LL arr via mandatory handling agent

Disabled Facilities	Available
Handling	**Tel:** 0141 887 8348 (Signature)
Restaurant	Restaurant buffet & bars in Terminal
Taxis	Available at Terminal
Car Hire	
Avis	**Tel:** 0141 887 2261
Hertz	**Tel:** 0141 887 2541

Weather Info	M T9 T18 Fax 286 A VSc GWC ATIS **Tel:** 0141 877 7449	**Operator**	Glasgow Airport Ltd Paisley, Strathclyde, PA3 2ST **Tel:** 0141 887 1111 (AD) **Tel:** 0141 840 8000 (NATS) **Tel:** 0141 840 8029 (ATC) **Tel:** 0141887 9319 (AIS) **Fax:** 0141 848 4354 (AD)

Helicopter Operations
Helicopters are not to move out of the alighting and parking area with out obtaining taxi instructions from ATC. Glasgow-based helicopters will park on the old Loganair Twy. Visiting helicopters will normally be allocated a stand on the W apron (Stands 31-34). Helicopters, inbound and outbound, are to avoid over flying AD buildings whenever possible. Inbound helis (other than large) will be routed to the helicopter app point – Rwy27 Thr. CASEVAC helicopters will be directed by ATC to alight on the main apron Twy, then to GND taxi to an ACFT stand.

Use Of Rwys
Rwy09/27 may be used at night by ACFT up to ATP size but only when the cross wind component on Rwy05/23 is greater than that specified in the ACFT's operations data manual. A Rwy lighting system including PAPI set at 5.25° can be made available at thirty minutes notice. Rwy09/27 is not available when low visibility procedures are in force.

GND Movement Control
GMC is responsible for:
The surface movement of all ACFT on the Manoeuvring area excluding the Rwy in use.
Passing Air Traffic Control clearances to ACFT.
Passing parking instructions to all ACFT. All ACFT making requests for taxiing or towing clearance on the GND freq should state their location in the initial call.

Visual Reference Points (VRP)

VRP	VOR/VOR	VOR/NDB	VOR/DME
Alexandria N5559.33 W00434.58	GOW 332°/TRN 014°	TRN 014°/GLW 331°	GOW 332°/8nm TRN 014°/41nm
Ardmore Point N5558.28 W00441.95	GOW 310°/TRN 009°	TRN 009°/GLW 309°	GOW 310°/10nm
Baillieston N5551.17 W00405.37	TLA 315°/GOW 099°	TLA 315°/GLW 100°	GOW 099°/12nm
Barrhead N5548.00 W00423.50	TRN 029°/TLA 302°	TRN 302°/GLW 166°	GOW 161°/5nm TRN 029°/32nm
Bishopton N5554.13 W00430.10	GOW 320°/TUR 020°	TRN 020°/GLW 315°	GOW 320°/3nm
Dumbarton N5556.67 W00434.10	GOW 321°/TRN 015°	TRN 015°/GLW 319°	GOW 3221/6nm TRN 015°/39nm
East Kilbride N5545.83 W00410.33	TRN 042°/TLA 304°	TRN 042°/GLW 130°	GOW 129°/11nm
Erskine Bridge N5555.22 W00427.77	GOW 353°/TRN 021°	TRN 021°/GLW 347°	GOW 353°/3nm
Greenock N5556.83 W00445.08	GOW 298°/TRN 006°	TRN 006°/GLW 298°	GOW 298°/11nm
Inverkip Power Stn N5553.90 W00453.20	GOW 281°/TRN 359°	TRN 359°/GLW 281°	GOW 281°/15nm
Kilmacolm N5553.67 W00437.65	TRN 013°/GOW 287°	TRN 013°/GLW 288°	GOW 287°/6nm TRN 013°/35nm
Kilmarnock N5536.75 W00429.90	GOW 191°/TRN 033°	GOW 191°/NGY 341°	GOW 191°/16nm
Kingston Bridge N5551.37 W00416.18	GOW 102°/TRN 032°	TRN 032°/GLW 103°	GOW 102°/6nm TRN 032°/37nm

CTR-Class D Airspace
Normal CTA/CTR Class D Airspace rules apply
Transition Alt 6000ft
1 These rules do not apply to non-radio ACFT by day provided they have obtained permission and maintain 5km visibility 1500m horizontally and 1000ft vertically away from cloud.
2 SVFR clearances may be given that are not confined to Entry/Exit lanes.
3 When operating on a SVFR clearance, pilots must remain clear of cloud insight of the surface and remain in flight conditions that will ensure they can determine their flight path and remain clear of obstacles.
4 Due to the nature of the terrain, a RAD service will not normally be provided to ACFT on a SVFR clearance.
5 SVFR clearance only applies to the CTR.
6 Entry/Exit lanes are established to permit ACFT to operate to and from Glasgow in IMC, but not under IFR these are
a) Clyde lane
b) Alexandria lane
c) Barrhead E Kilbride Lane.
All these lanes are 3nms wide and use of the lanes is subject to ATC clearance and radio contact with Glasgow App. ACFT must remain clear of cloud and in sight of the surface not above 2000ft. Minimum visibility is 3km.ACFT must keep the lane centre line on the left, unless other wise instructed.

G

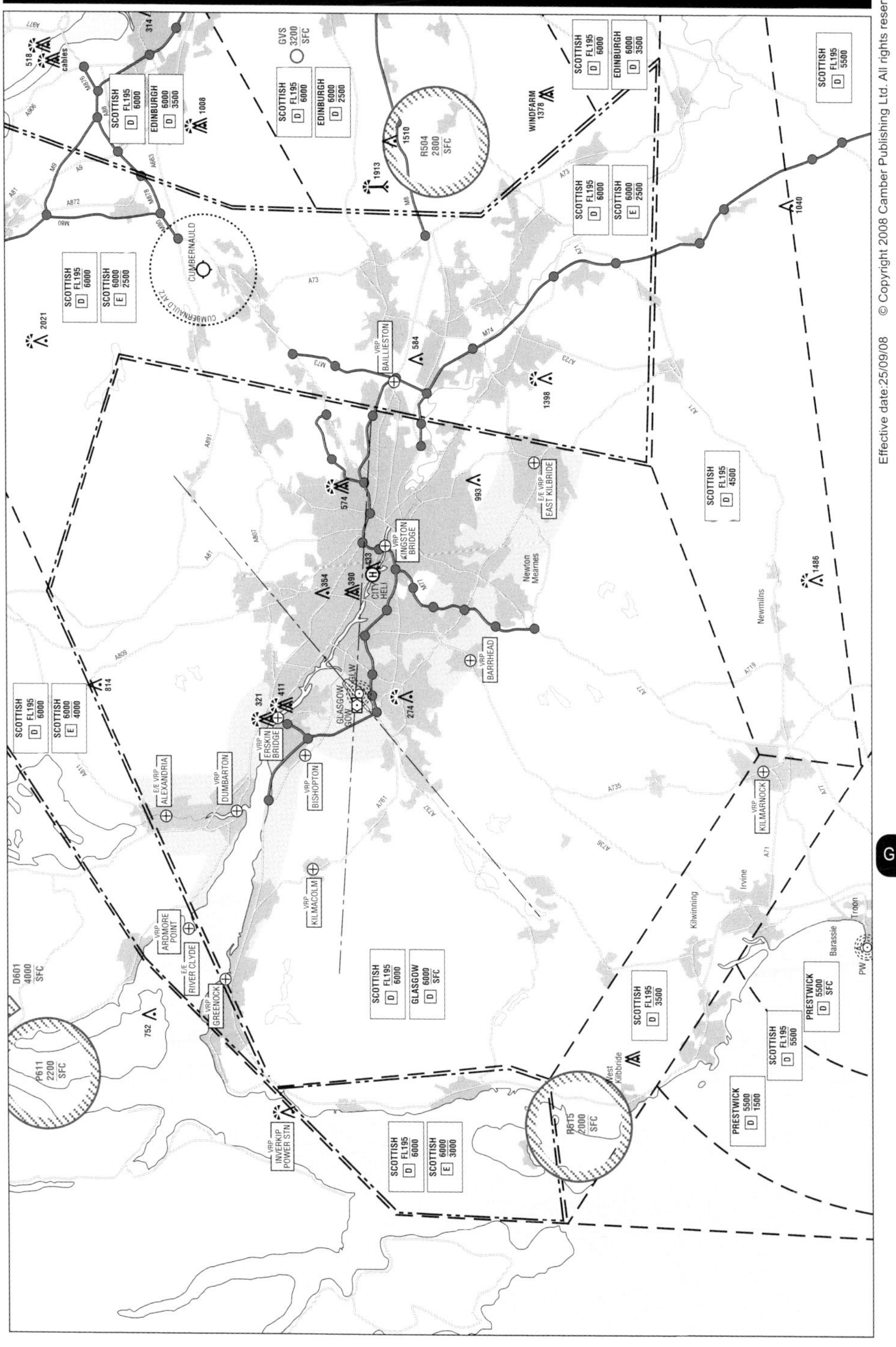
SCOTTISH D FL195 6000
EDINBURGH D 6000 3500
SCOTTISH D FL195 6000
EDINBURGH D 6000 2500
GVS 3200 SFC
R504 2800 SFC
WINDFARM 1378
SCOTTISH D FL195 6000
EDINBURGH D 6000 3500
SCOTTISH D FL195 5500
SCOTTISH D FL195 6000
SCOTTISH E 6000 2500
CUMBERNAULD
CUMBERNAULD ATZ
SCOTTISH D FL195 6000
SCOTTISH E 6000 2500
VRP BAILLIESTON
VRP KINGSTON BRIDGE
E/E VRP EAST KILBRIDE
Newton Mearnes
CITY HELI
SCOTTISH D FL195 4500
Newmilns
VRP BARRHEAD
GLASGOW
GLW
SCOTTISH D FL195 6000
SCOTTISH E 6000 4000
E/E VRP ALEXANDRIA
VRP DUMBARTON
VRP ERSKIN BRIDGE
VRP BISHOPTON
VRP KILMARNOCK
VRP KILMACOLM
Irvine
Kilwinning
Troon
Barassie
PW
VRP ARDMORE POINT
E/E RIVER CLYDE
VRP GREENOCK
D601 4000 SFC
SCOTTISH D FL195 6000
GLASGOW D 6000 SFC
SCOTTISH D FL195 3500
PRESTWICK D 5500 SFC
SCOTTISH D FL195 5500
P611 2200 SFC
West Kilbride
R615 2000 SFC
PRESTWICK D 5500 1500
VRP INVERKIP POWER STN
SCOTTISH D FL195 6000
SCOTTISH E 6000 3000

G

600ft 20mb	7nm NE of Penrith N5444.28 W00239.12	**PPR**	**Alternative AD** Carlisle **Non-standard join**

Glassonby	**A/G** **129.825** **Not always manned**

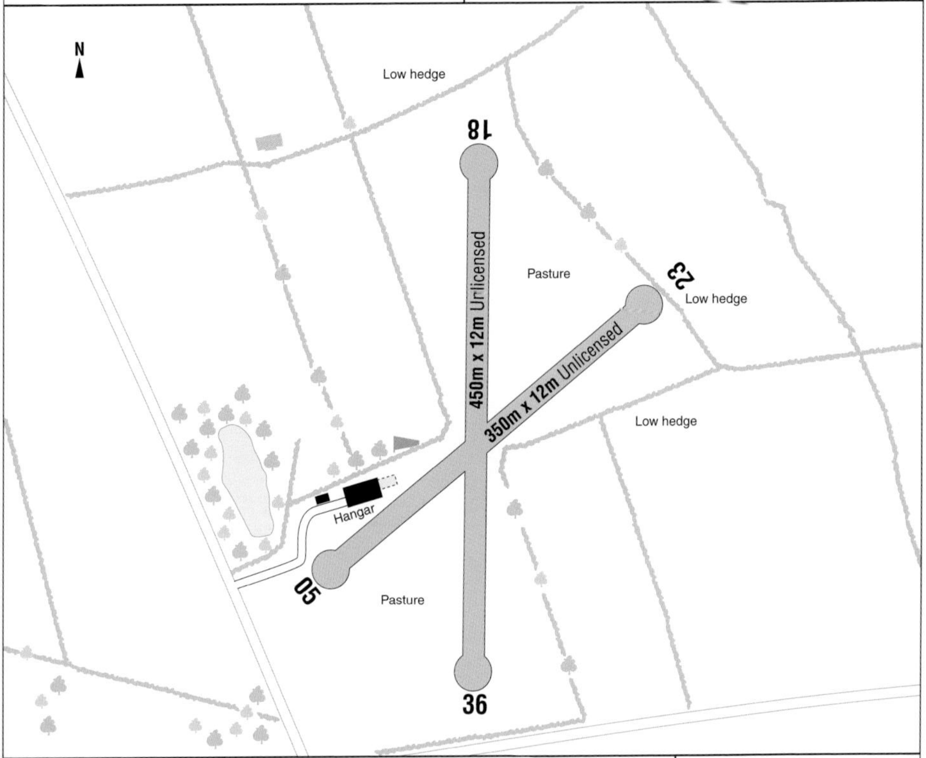

RWY	SURFACE	TORA	LDA	U/L	LIGHTING
18/36	Grass			450x12	Nil
05/23	Grass			350x12	Nil

Rwy35 preferred In light or variable winds

RNAV			
DCS	115.20	090	24

Remarks
Strictly PPR by telephone. AD is not normally manned. AD is available for both Microlights and Light aircraft. Hangarage may be available for visiting aircraft

Warnings
Windsock displayed near hangar but no other GND signals displayed. Sheep may be grazing in winter period.
Noise: There are nearby noise sensitive areas. See map.

Operating Hrs	SR-SS
Circuits	23 & 18 LH 05 & 36 RH 500ft QFE Join overhead at 1000ft QFE Descend while in the circuit. No deadside
Landing Fee	Donations welcome
Maintenance	Nil
Fuel	By arrangement
Disabled Facilities	Nil
Restaurant	Tea & Coffee available
Accomodation	Local B&B's available
Taxi/Car Hire	Nil
Weather Info	Air N MOEx

Operator
Robin Rowley
Glassonby Lodge
Penrith
Cumbria CA10 1DT
Tel: 01768 898382

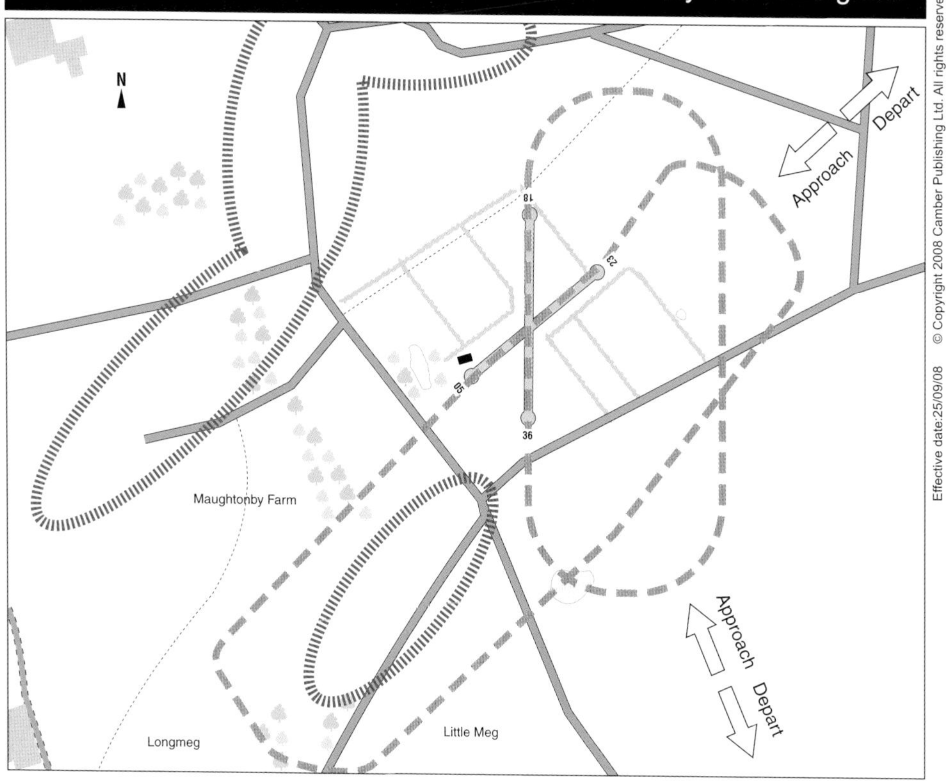
N
18
36
05
23
Approach
Depart
Approach
Depart
Maughtonby Farm
Longmeg
Little Meg

GLENFORSA

15ft 0mb	1nm E of Salen on Isle of Mull N5631.04 W00554.85	PPR	**Alternative AD** **Diversion AD**	**Glasgow** Tiree

Non-radio	**FIS** **Scottish 127.275**	**Safetycom** **135.475**

N

Sound of Mull

Perimeter Fence

730m x 18m Unlicensed

25

07

House

Hotel

ACFT parking

H

RWY	SURFACE	TORA	LDA	U/L	LIGHTING
07/25	Grass			730x18	Nil

RNAV

Remarks

PPR essential. All ACFT welcome at pilots own risk. AD open daily 1st May – 30th September, every Sat-Sun throughout the year.. AD clear of livestock on these days. April – October telephone before 1600hrs for livestock to be removed. For advisory WX actuals and info on state of strip call AD. On rare occasions pilots are not met at the AD; please leave flight details at the adjacent cabin.

Warnings

Rwy07 requires a curved APP to keep clear of high GND to W. There is also high GND to the SE close to the AD. Sheep graze from Oct-Apr on the strip, removed at weekends. Keep a lookout for microlight activity at any time. Due to prolonged wet weather, permission to use AD may be suspended especially during the winter months.

Noise: Avoid over flying Glenforsa Hotel and village of Salen, also large new structure S of Rwy25 Thr

Operating Hrs	By arrangement
Circuits	Over sea 800ft QFE
Landing Fee	<500kg MTWA £8.82 501-1000kg MTWA £11.75 1001-1500kg MTWA £17.63 Others on application
Maintenance	Nil
Fuel	Oban from Paul Keegan **Tel:** 01631 710888 **Tel:** 07770 620988

Disabled Facilities

Restaurants

Glenforsa Hotel	**Tel:** 01680 300377
Salen Hotel	**Tel:** 01680 300324

Taxis

R Atkinson	**Tel:** 01680 300441

Car Hire

Mull Car Hire	**Tel:** 01680 300402 **Tel:** 07799 744908

Weather Info	Air Sc GWC
Operator	Argyll and Bute Council Mr D S Howitt Aerodrome Bungalow Glenforsa, Isle of Mull Argyll, PA72 6JN **Tel:** 01680 300402 (D S Howitt) **Tel:** 07799 744908 (D S Howitt) **Tel:** 01631 710384 (Oban AD)

EGBJ GLOUCESTERSHIRE

101ft 3mb	3.5nm W of Cheltenham N5153.65 W00210.03		Alternative AD **Bristol Filton** Kemble

Gloster	ATIS	APP	RAD	TWR	FIRE
	127.475	128.550	120.975	122.900	121.600

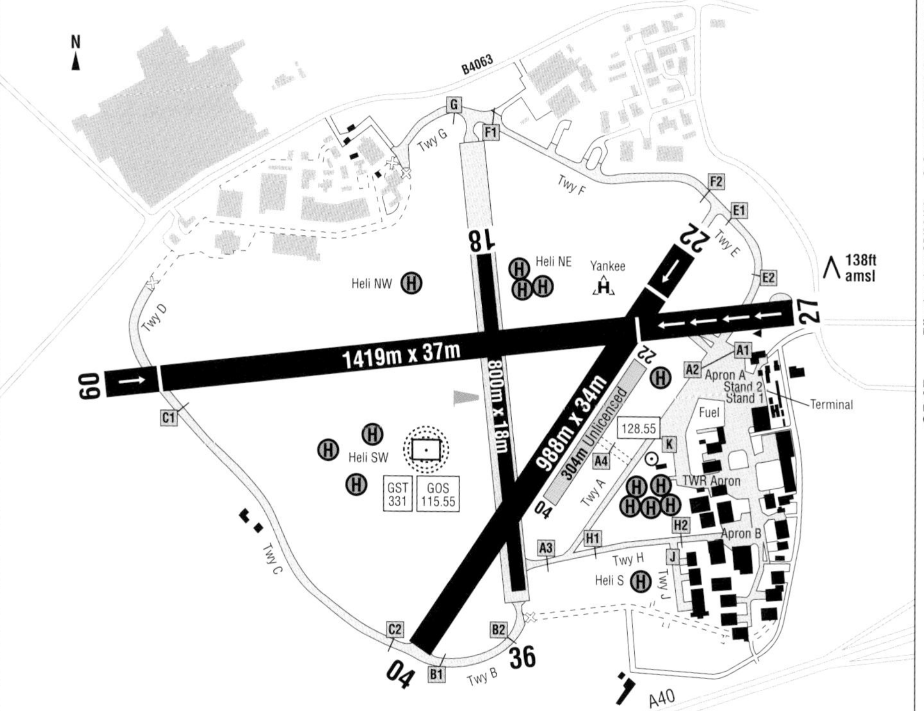

RWY	SURFACE	TORA	LDA	U/L	LIGHTING
04	Asphalt	988	988		APAPI 4.5° LHS
22	Asphalt	988	900		APAPI 3.5° LHS
09	Asphalt	1271	1153		Thr Rwy PAPI 3° LHS
27	Asphalt	1317	997		Ap Thr Rwy PAPI 3.5° LHS
18/36	Asphalt	799	799		Nil
04/22	Grass	304	304		Nil

Displaced Thr Rwy22 88m, Displaced Thr Rwy09 118m, Displaced Thr Rwy27 312m

RNAV

Remarks

PPR at all times for instrument training. Non-radio ACFT not accepted. Hi-vis. Permission to use AD outside scheduled Hrs to be obtained from ATC. APP will only provide FIS to ACFT within 10nm of AD, if traffic conditions permit. VFR ACFT outside this radius are requested not to call Gloucester. All pilots must book out at the Flight Briefing Unit via telephone.
Visual aid to location: Ibn Green Go.

Warnings

Twy C between Rwy09 & 04 Thr is edge-marked white reflective discs. Entry/exit curves to Rwys are marked by green reflective studs. Due to extensive standing water Rwy04/22 may not be usable after periods of heavy/prolonged rain. Use extreme caution when using Twy in maintenance area due vehicles & pedestrians. Caution: Bird hazzard, flocks of gulls may be encountered over AD at dawn /dusk.
Noise: Dept Rwy18 turn left 20°after passing upwind end of Rwy. Dept Rwy27 turn right 10° on crossing upwind end of Rwy to avoid housing estate, a left turn can be made after passing 700ft QFE. Dept Rwy22 no left turns until after passing Chosen Hill. Avoid over flying all adjacent villages to AD.

Operating Hrs	Mon-Fri 0730-1830 Sat-Sun 0800-1830 (Summer) Mon-Fri 0830-1930 Sat-Sun 0900-1800 (Winter) & by arr	Circuits	04, 09, 18 LH, 22, 27, 36 RH Fixed wing >1000ft QFE Heli 750ft QFE max

Landing Fee	£10 <750kg, £17.63 751-1500kg, £11.75 with 50L fuel <1500kg		**Operator**	Gloucestershire Airport Ltd Gloucestershire Aerodrome Cheltenham Glos, GL516SR **Tel:** 01452 857700 Ex 223 (ATC/Briefing) **Tel:** 01452 857700 Ex 227 (Admin) **Fax:** 01452 715174 briefing@gloucestershireairport.co.uk (ATC) www.gloucestershireairport.co.uk
Maintenance	Available + hangarage			
Fuel	AVGAS JET A1 100LL			
Disabled Facilities				

Handling	Tel: 01452 856333 ops@jet1.co.uk			
Restaurants	Cafe & Club facilities at AD			
Taxis/Car Hire National	Available from Ops **Tel:** 01452421133			
Weather Info	M T9 Fax 288 A MOEx			

G

GORREL FARM

520ft 17mb	14nm SW of Barnstaple N5056.70 W00423.20	PPR	**Alternative AD** **Exeter** Eaglescott **Non-standard join**

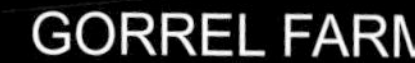

Non Radio	LARS Exeter 128.975	Safetycom 135.475

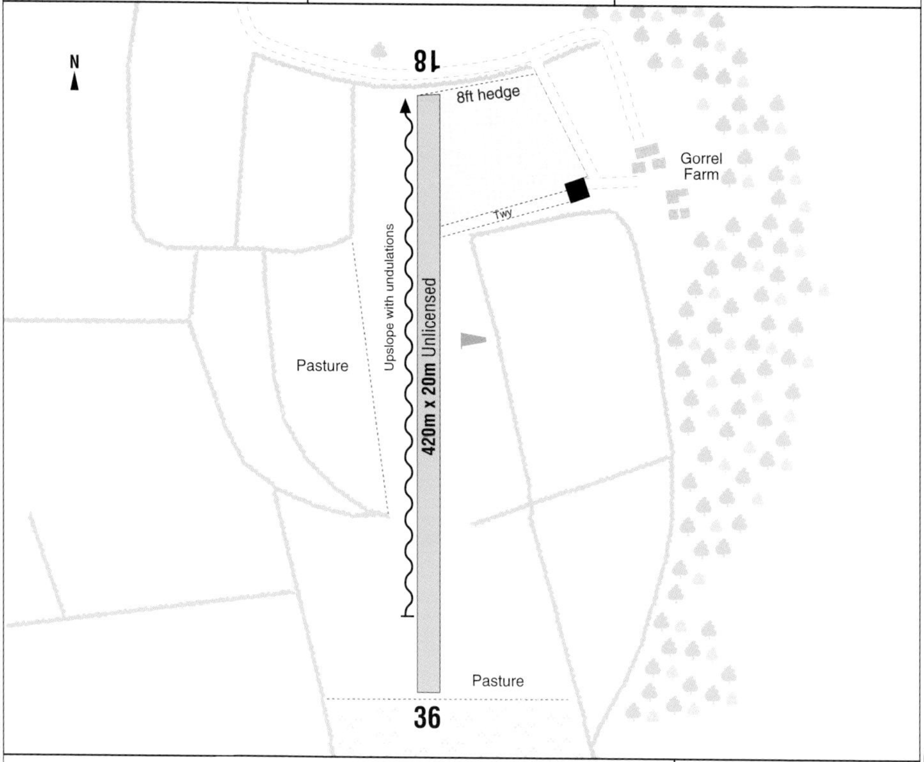

RWY	SURFACE	TORA	LDA	U/L	LIGHTING
18/36	Grass			420x20	Nil

RNAV

Remarks
PPR by telephone essential. Experienced strip flyers welcome at own risk. AD is located on a working farm and sheep may graze the Rwy at any time.

Warnings
Rwy is undulating and has a marked Upslope from S to N. ACFT land uphill Rwy36, take-off Rwy18. S end may become waterlogged after prolonged rain. High GND up to 771ft amsl surrounds the AD.
Noise: Avoid over flying of local farms and fields containing livestock.

Operating Hrs SR-SS daily
Circuits LH 1500ft QNH
Landing Fee Nil
Maintenance Nil
Fuel Nil
Disabled Facilities Nil
Taxi/Car Hire
Sams **Tel:** 01237 471800
Weather Info Air SW MOEx

Operator Frank Cox
Gorrel Farm
Woolfardisworthy
Bideford
Devon
EX39 5QZ
Tel/Fax: 01237 431503
coxs.gorrel@virgin.net

Effective date:25/09/08 OP 08

GRASSTHORPE GRANGE

35ft 1mb	5nm N of Newark on Trent N5311.70 W00048.40	PPR	Alternative AD	Doncaster Sheffield Retford

Non Radio	APP Doncaster Sheffield 126.225	LARS Waddington 127.350	Safetycom 135.475

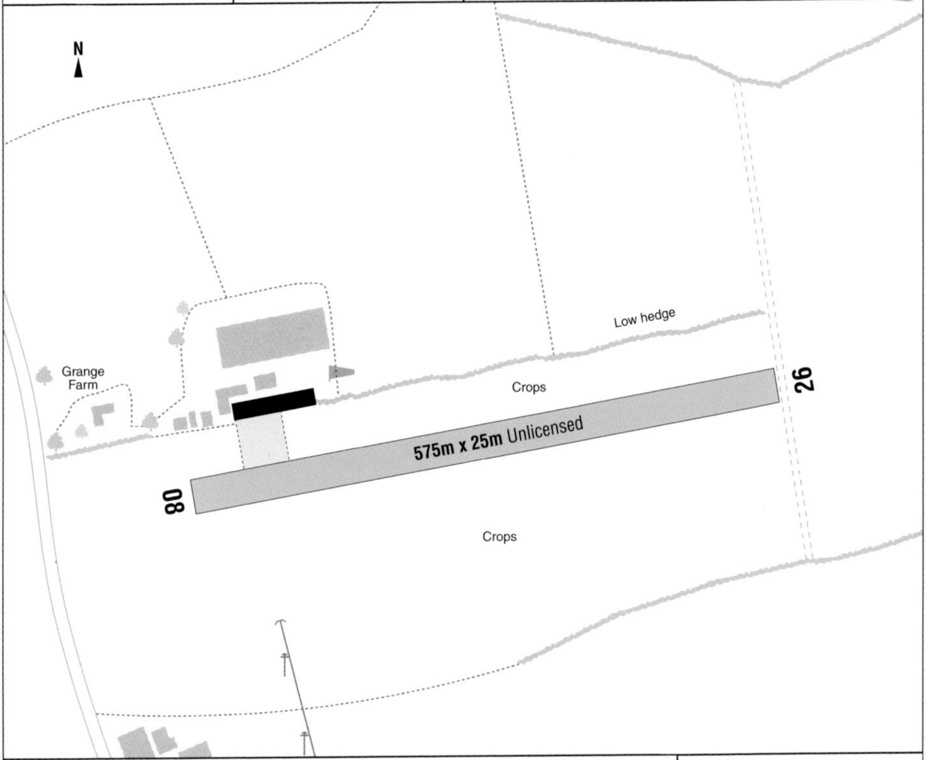

RWY	SURFACE	TORA	LDA	U/L	LIGHTING
08/26	Grass			575x25	Nil

RNAV			
GAM	112.8	139	7.5

Remarks
Strictly PPR by telephone. Well maintained strip with windsock close to buildings on the N side.

Warnings
AD is close to the Scampton/Waddington MATZ and Doncaster Sheffield CTA. Power lines APP strip from S but go underground to cross the strip.
Noise: Avoid over flying all local habitation.

Operational Hrs	SR-SS
Circuits	To N at 800ft QFE
Landing Fee	Nil
Maintenance	Nil
Fuel	Nil
Disabled Facilities	Nil
Restaurant	Nil
Taxi/Car Hire	Nil
Weather Info	Air Cen MOEx

Operator
Bob Beard
Grange Farm
Grassthorpe
Newark
Notts NG23 6QX
Tel: 01636 822140
Tel: 07708 248571
bobatgrangefarm@hotmail.co.uk

300ft 10mb	3nm SE of Hitchin N5156.45 W00012.10	PPR	Alternative AD	Luton Cranfield

Non-standard join

Non-Radio	ATIS	APP	Safetycom
	Luton 120.575	Luton 129.550	135.475

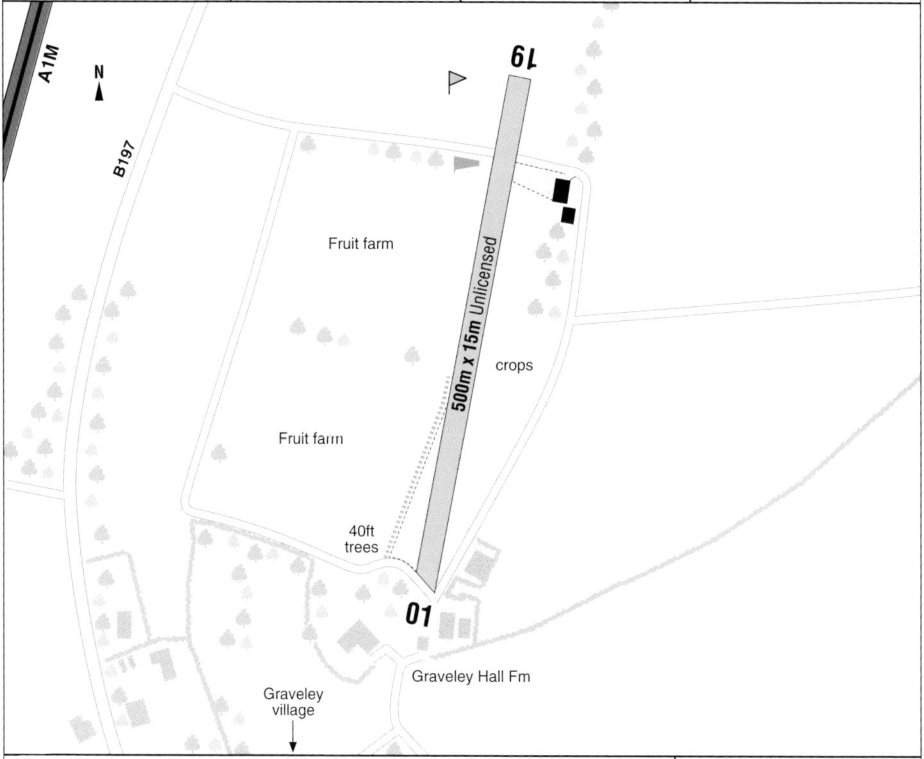

RWY	SURFACE TORA	LDA	U/L	LIGHTING
01/19	Grass		500x15m	Nil

RNAV			
BKY	116.25	254	10.3

Remarks

PPR by telephone. Primarily a microlight site, light ACFT welcome at pilots own risk. There is a 'pick your own' fruit farm adjacent to AD which is owned by the airfield operator. (Usually available Jun-Sept).

Warnings

AD situated within Luton CTR. Clearance to enter CTR must be obtained from Luton APP. Non-Radio ACFT both inbound and outbound should telephone Luton ATC before take-off.

Noise: Avoid low over flying of the houses to NW of AD and Graveley village to the S & SW. This is a very noise sensitive area.

Operating Hrs	SR-SS
Circuits	Join from N or E into overhead Circuit to E 500ft QFE
Landing Fee	Nil
Maintenance	Nil
Fuel	Nil
Disabled Facilities	Nil
Restaurants	Tea shop at farm during fruit picking season
Taxis	**Tel:** 01438 317777
Car Hire	Nil
Weather Info	Air S MOEx

Operator

Mr T Franklin
Graveley Hall Farm
Hitchin
Herts, SG4 7LY
Tel: 01438 317112
Tel: 07770 572 927
Tel: 01582 395029 (Luton ATC)

295ft 10mb	10nm E of Kings Lynn N5246.73 E00040.35	PPR	**Alternative AD** **Norwich** Old Buckenham

Non radio	LARS Marham 124.150	Safetycom 135.475

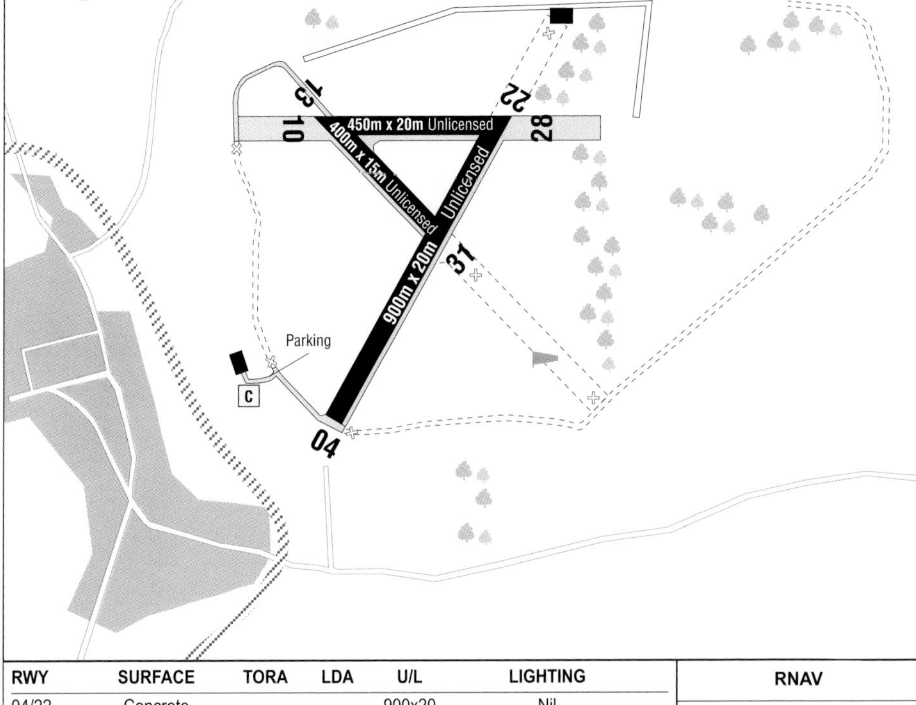

RWY	SURFACE	TORA	LDA	U/L	LIGHTING
04/22	Concrete			900x20	Nil
10/28	Concrete			450x20	Nil
13/31	Concrete			400x15	Nil

RNAV

Remarks
PPR by telephone, non-radio ACFT not accepted. AD is unmanned. AD used by military for training. WW II AD. Radio contact with Marham essential (when open) due to proximity to Marham MATZ. No signals square. AD used by microlights, who may use short Rwy because of wind direction. ACFT parking next to hangar at SW corner of AD. Visiting pilots requested to complete movements book in control hut adjacent to hangar. No training flights permitted.

Warning
Agricultural operations may temporarily block Rwys.
Caution: pedestrians – perimeter track is a public footpath. ACFT using Rwy04/22 keep a good look out for microlights.
Noise: Avoid over flying Gt Massingham and other local villages. Dept Rwy22 turn left 20° to avoid houses.

Operating Hrs	SR-SS
Circuits	04 RH, 22 LH
Landing Fee	Single £8, Twin £12 Overnight parking £4
Maintenance	Nil
Fuel	Nil
Disabled Facilities	Nil
Restaurants	The Dabbling Duck in the village
Taxis	
Silverlink	**Tel:** 01485 520938
Car Hire	Nil

Weather Info	Air S MOEx
Operator	Mr O C Brun Leicester House Great Massingham Kings Lynn, Norfolk PE32 2HB **Tel:** 01485 520257 **Fax:** 01485 520234

G

60ft 2mb	3.5nm SW of Harwich N5154.00 E00110.30	**PPR**	**Alternative AD**	**Southend** Clacton

Non-Radio	**LARS** **Southend 130.775**	**A/G** **123.200**

N
crops
22
15ft tree
crops
27
800m x 40m Unlicensed
09
Slight upslope
600m x 22m Unlicensed
Twy
crops
crops
Twy
04
crops
ACFT parking
Twy
Hangar
Great Oakley Lodge

RWY	SURFACE	TORA	LDAK	U/L	LIGHTING
04/22	Grass			600x22	Nil
09/27	Grass			800x40	Nil

Displaced Thr Rwy09 70m. Displaced Thr Rwy27 70m

RNAV			
CLN	**114.55**	**017**	**3.2**

Remarks
PPR by telephone. Visiting ACFT welcome at pilots own risk. Coarse fishing available in 2 lakes, day tickets available. New clubhouse open.
Visual aid to location: Group of 3 small lakes SSE of AD.

Warnings
Crops grown up to strip edge. Tractor path crosses Rwy04 Thr. 15ft tree to S of Rwy22 Thr. Powerline 30ft agl crosses Rwy22 APP 350m from Rwy Thr.
Noise: Avoid over flight of local habitation, particularly Great Oakley village SSE of AD.

Operating Hrs	0830-2100 (L)
Circuits	22 27 RH, 04 09 LH, 1000ft QFE
Landing Fee	£5
Maintenance	Nil Hangarage available on monthly basis
Fuel	AVGAS 100LL
Disabled Facilities	
Restaurant	Tea & Coffee available on request Cold drinks in the clubhouse

Taxi		
Harwich Taxis	**Tel**: 01255 551111	
Car Hire	Nil	
Weather Info	Air S MOEx	
Operator	Tim Spurge Great Oakley Lodge Harwich Essex, CO12 5AE **Tel:** 01255 880045 **Fax:** 01255 880244 **Tel:** 07770 880145 tim.spurge@btconnect.com www.greatoakleyairfield.co.uk	

Effective date:25/09/08

588ft 19mb	4nm WSW of Holywell N5317.40 W00319.50	PPR	**Alternative AD** **Hawarden** Caernarfon **Non-standard join**

Greenlands	A/G 129.825 (Microlight freq)	A/G 129.975 (Glider freq)	A/G Bryngwyn 118.325

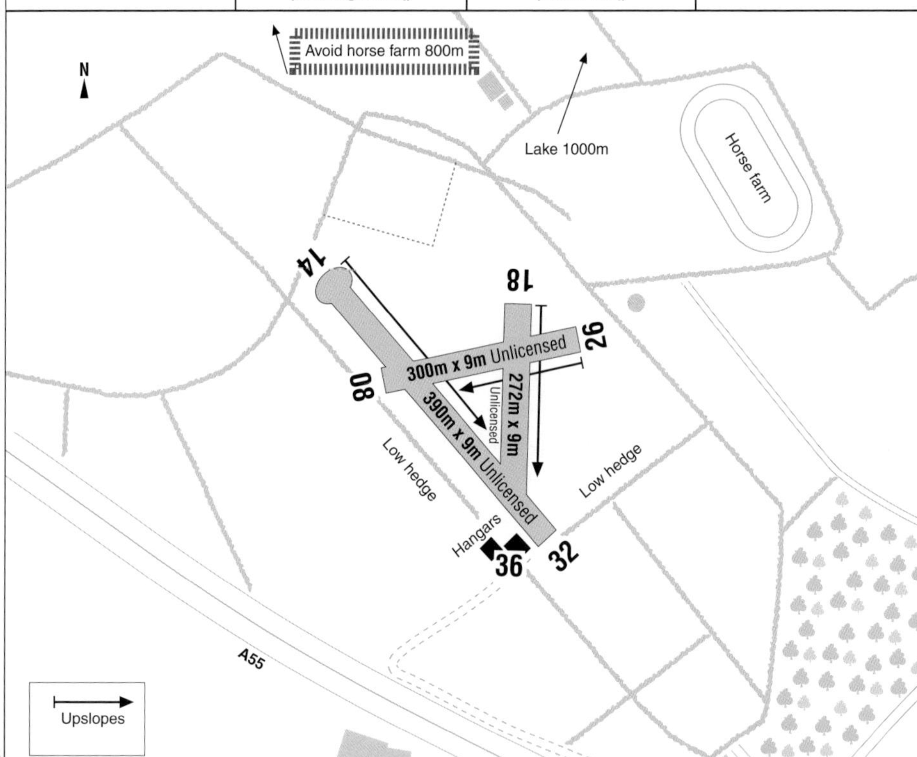

RWY	SURFACE	TORA	LDA	U/L	LIGHTING
14/32	Grass			390x9	Nil
08/26	Grass			300x9	Nil
18/36	Grass			272x9	Nil

Rwy14/26/18 upslope
Rwy14 Thr marked with red square

RNAV			
WAL	114.10	233	9.2

Remarks
PPR by telephone essential. Microlights operate from AD. Visiting ACFT welcome at pilots own risk. Windsock occasionally displayed on S AD boundary. Sheep and cattle graze on AD.
Visual aid to location: small lake to N and A55 dual carriageway to S.

Warnings
AD is convex, this may cause turbulence/roll-over on APP. Rwys become waterlogged during winter months and after heavy rain. Vintage military ACFT operate from strip to S of A55. Visitors are requested to call Bryngwyn to ascertain if strip is active.
Noise: Avoid over flying local habitation, particularly the Farmhouse & horse farm track 800m N of AD.

Operating Hrs	SR-SS
Circuits	Overhead join N 500ft QFE
Landing Fee	Nil
Maintenance	Nil
Fuel	MOGAS provided in cans by prior arr
Disabled Facilities	☎

Restaurant/Accommodation

Travellers Inn	**Tel:** 01352 720251 (200m from AD)
White House Hotel	**Tel:** 01745 582155
Taxi/Car Hire	Nil
Weather Info	Air N MOEx
Operator	Richard Emlyn Jones Rhedyn Coch Rhuallt St Asaph Denbighshire LL17 0TT **Tel:** 01745 584051 **Tel:** 07880 733274

G

EGJB GUERNSEY

336ft 11mb	2.5nm WSW of St Peter Port N4926.10 W00236.12	PPR	Alternative AD: **Jersey** Alderney; Diversion AD

Non-standard join

Guernsey	ATIS	APP	RAD
	109.40 (GUR VOR)	128.650	118.900 124.500

TWR	GND	FIRE
119.950	121.800 (Jul-Sep)	121.600

RWY	SURFACE	TORA	LDA	U/L	LIGHTING
09	Asphalt	1453	1453		Ap Thr Rwy PAPI 3° LHS
27	Asphalt	1463	1453		Ap Thr Rwy PAPI 3° LHS

RNAV		
GUR	109.40	On AD

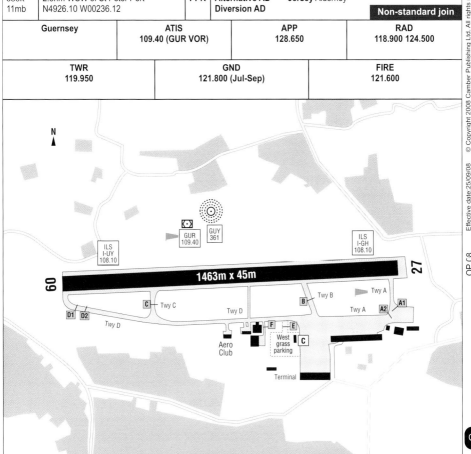

Remarks

PPR. Hi-Vis. On Arr all GA pilots must report to the FBU for Special Branch and Customs Clearance. Use governed by regulations applicable to Channel Islands CTR. IMC flight to Guernsey by ACFT not equipped with VOR is by prior permission only. Model ACFT flying at Chouet Headland takes place up to 400ft amsl on any day of the year during daylight hours. All training must be booked in advance with ATC. Light ACFT grass parking to W of control TWR. Parking on hard apron PPR except schedule ACFT. Access to the terminal is via the public Rd or by arrangement with AD security. There is no access to the terminal from airside, access only via handling agents. All commercial flights and ACFT with MTOW >4 tonnes must use designated handling agent.

Warnings

Flight is not permitted at height less than 2000ft agl within 3nm of N4952.83 W00221.67 on Sark except with permission of States Guernsey Public Services Department. All ACFT are to avoid over flying the Princess Elizabeth hospital (2nm ENE of AD) at less than 1000ft agl. Light ACFT grass parking areas on W side of control TWR. All chocks and picketing blocks should be removed to edge of parking area after use. Down draught or turbulence may be experienced on APP to either Rwy in strong winds from any direction due to local terrains cliffs and valleys. Landing Rwy27 in strong SE-SW winds, buildings induce turbulence & windshear. All air crew & passengers must carry a means of identification to gain access airside. Due to coastal location birds are a hazard most of year, particularly during migration season. Firing at Fort le Marchant small arms range N4930.20 W00231.07, takes place seaward within 347-069°, radius 3000m. ACFT proceeding to and from stands 1, 2, A, B and the E apron must not cross Rwy27 holding point without clearance.

Noise: Rwy09/27 climb straight ahead thru 1500ft agl before turning on course. If on SVFR/VFR clearance not above 1000ft proceed to coast before turning on course. Rwy09/27 Arr join final APP not less than 500ft, maintain until intercepting glide path PAPI on directions.

Operating Hrs 0530-2000 (Summer)
+1Hr (Winter) & by arr

Circuits 700ft QFE

Landing Fee Available on request

Maintenance
ACFT Servicing **Tel:** 01481 265750 (Guernsey)
Fuel AVGAS JET A1 100LL
Purchasing fuel may result in reduced landing fees

Disabled Facilities

Handling **Tel:** 01481 239544 (Aigle)
Tel: 01481 263965 (ASG Flt Support)
Fax: 01481 235008 (Aigle)
Fax: 01481 265633 (ASG Flt Support)

Restaurant Buffet at Terminal

Taxis
Taxi Rank **Tel:** 01481 235283
Car Hire
Harlequin **Tel:** 01481 239511
Value Rent A Car **Tel:** 01481 236344
Cycle Hire
Rent-a-bike **Tel:** 01481 249311
W Coast **Tel:** 01481-253654

Weather Info M T9 Fax 292 A JER
ATIS **Tel:** 01481 238957

Operator States of Guernsey Airport
Guernsey Channel Islands
Tel: 01481 237766
Tel: 01481 237766 Ex 2130 (APC)
Tel: 01481 237766 Ex 2131 (TWR)
Tel: 01481 235791 (Fuel)
Fax: 01481 239595
Fax: 01481 239440 (FBU)
www.guernsey-airport.gov.gg

Guernsey Control Zone
Unless other wise authorised, a pilot who intends to fly in the Guernsey CTR must:
1 Contact Jersey Zone for entry into the Channel Islands Control Zone, giving details of the ACFT position, level and track.
2 Maintain a listening watch on the appropriate freq.
3 Comply with any instructions from ATC.
4 An ACFT shall not fly below 2000ft within 5nm of the AD, unless permission has been obtained.
5 SSR transponder equipment is mandatory within the Channel Islands Control Zone (Mode A).
6 In the event of radio failure the pilot should leave the Control Zone by maintaining track 225°T from overhead Guernsey Airport at 2000ft.
7 A VFR lane is established between GUR & ALD for traffic routing between the AD. The lane is 5nm either side of a line joining the AD, with a maximum alt of 2000ft, subject to ATC clearance.

G

Channel Island Visual Reference Points (VRP)

VRP	VOR/DME	VOR/DME
Carteret Lighthouse N4922.00 W00148.00	JSY 051°/13nm	GUR 101°/32nm
Casquets Lighthouse N4943.00 W00222.00	JSY 340°/32nm	GUR 032°/19nm
Corbiere Lighthouse N4911.00 W00215.00	JSY 257°/8nm	GUR 141°/21nm DIN 353°/36nm
Heauville N4934.60 W00148.06	JSY 026°/24nm	GUR 078°/33nm
NE Point of Guernsey N4930.42 W00230.52	JSY 317°/25nm	GUR 045°/6nm
NW corner of Jersey N4915.30 W00214.50	JSY 289°/8nm	GUR 131°/18nm
Point de Rozel N4928.60 W00150.60	JSY 029°/18nm	GUR 088°/30nm
St. Germain N4914.00 W00138.00	JSY 091°/16nm	GUR 111°/40nm DIN 028°/43nm
SE Corner of Jersey N4910.00 W00202.00	JSY 176°/3nm	GUR 130°/28nm DIN 007°/35nm
W of Cap de la Hague N4943.00 W00200.00	JSY 008°/30nm	GUR 058°/29nm

See Channel Islands Transit Corridor – Jersey

EGWN HALTON

370ft 12mb	3.5nm SE of Aylesbury N5147.55 W00044.27	PPR MIL	Alternative AD Diversion AD	Cranfield Wycombe

Non-standard join

Halton	A/G 130.425

N

20

780m x 45m

07

25

1130m x 45m

02

H1

H2

C

RWY	SURFACE	TORA	LDA	U/L	LIGHTING
02	Grass	1130	1100		Nil
20	Grass	1130	840		Nil
07/25	Grass	780	780		Nil

Rwys have white sideline markers

RNAV			
BNN	113.75	303	8.1

Remarks
PPR 24 Hrs notice required via RAF. Pilots of visiting ACFT are to obtain Arr procedure briefing by telephone before Dept. Inbound ACFT will be requested to route via VRPs.

Warnings
Intensive light ACFT and glider, tug, motor and winch. Cables up to 2000ft QFE. Mirror circuits with no dead side. Powered ACFT to NW and gliders to SE. Extensive soaring over ridge 5nm SE.
Noise: Dept routes for all Rwys.

Operating Hrs Mon-Fri 0800-2000 Sat-Sun & PH 0900-2000 (L)

Circuits 20, 26 RH, 02, 08 LH, 1000ft QFE

Landing Fee Charges in accordance with MOD policy Contact Station Ops for details

Maintenance Nil

Fuel Nil

Disabled Facilities

Restaurants Nil

Taxis/Car Hire Nil

Weather Info Air Cen MOEx

Visual Reference Points (VRP)

Lakes 2nm NE Rwy20/26

Terrick 2nm SW min height 1500ft QFE

Operator RAF Halton
Aylesbury
Bucks, HP22 5PG
Tel: 01296 656367
(PPR 0800-1700 Mon-Fri)

645ft 21mb	12nm NW of Worcester N5217.98.W00228.22	PPR	Alternative AD **Birmingham** Shobdon

Non Radio	APP Birmingham 118.050	LARS Brize 124.275	Safetycom 135.475

N

23

600m x 30m Unlicensed

C

05

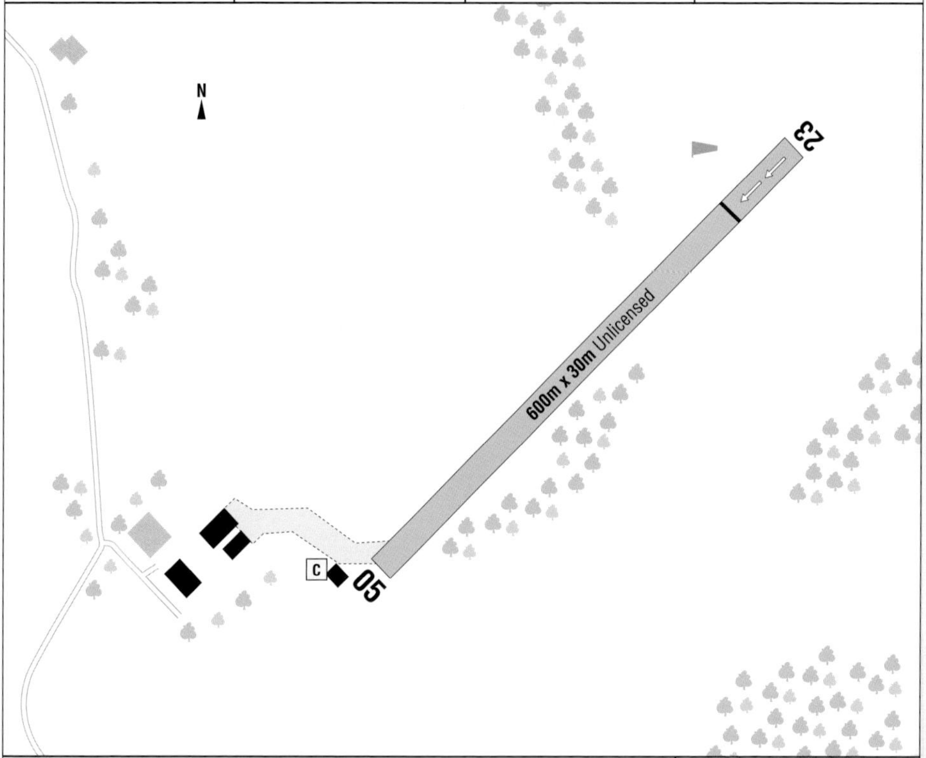

RWY	SURFACE	TORA	LDA	U/L	LIGHTING
05/23	Grass			600x30	Nil

Displaced Thr Rwy23 100m due to 18% upslope
Displaced end marked by 2 white chevrons

RNAV			
HON	113.65	267	29.8

Remarks
PPR by telephone. AD on top plateau with steep upslope E end Rwy. Surface slightly undulating. Considerate visitors welcome at own risk.

Warnings
Strong S winds can cause turbulence Rwy23 APP due to local geography.
Noise: Please be considerate of local habitants, avoid over flying all local houses & maintain Rwy centreline on APP/dept.

Operating Hrs 0900-SS
Circuits LH 800ft QFE but can vary
Landing Fee £7.50
Maintenance Nil
Fuel Nil
Disabled Facilities

Restaurants Light refreshments on site
The Fox Inn **Tel:** 01886 853189
Tally Ho Inn **Tel:** 01886 853241
The Baiting House **Tel:** 01886 853201
Upper Sapey Golf Club **Tel:** 01886 853506

Taxis/Car Hire
Swan Cabs **Tel:** 01584 810310
Weather Info Air N MOEx
Operator Geoff & Angela Bunyan
Hanley House Farm
Hanley William
Tenbury Wells
Worcs, WR15 8QT
Tel/Fax: 01886 853410
www.hwas.orangehome.co.uk

HARDWICKE

450ft 15mb	3nm ENE of Hay on Wye N5205.22 W00303.95	**PPR**	**Alternative AD** **Gloucestershire** Shobdon **Non-standard join**

Non Radio	FIS London 124.750	Safetycom 135.475

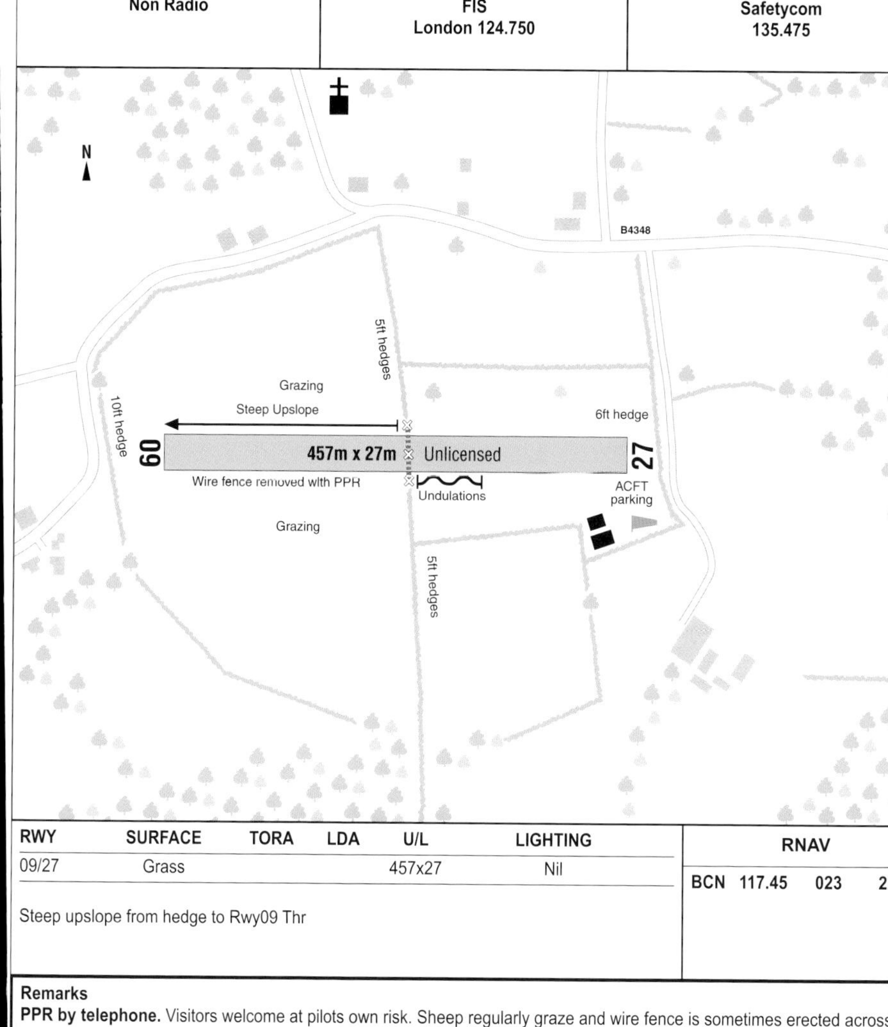

RWY	SURFACE	TORA	LDA	U/L	LIGHTING
09/27	Grass			457x27	Nil

Steep upslope from hedge to Rwy09 Thr

RNAV			
BCN	117.45	023	22.9

Remarks

PPR by telephone. Visitors welcome at pilots own risk. Sheep regularly graze and wire fence is sometimes erected across strip making PPR essential.

Visual aid to location: Large Orange windsock close to hangars and caravan.

Warnings

Not recommended for novice pilots. Rwy passes through gap in 5ft hedge at Rwy midpoint. Portion of Rwy between hedge gap & Rwy09 Thr rises 100ft: Land Rwy27 & dept Rwy09 unless very experienced with AD. See notes above reference the essential nature of PPR. AD is located within the Wye valley on the S on rising GND. Highest point is 4nm S 2306ft amsl. High GND up to1044ft amsl 1.5nm to E. 6ft hedge close to Rwy27 Thr. 10ft hedge on short finals Rwy09.

Operating Hrs	SR-SS
Circuits	N 1000ft QFE
Landing Fee	Nil
Maintenance	Nil
Fuel	MOGAS available by prior arr
Disabled Facilities	Nil
Restaurants	Nil
Taxis/Car Hire	Nil
Weather Info	Air N MOEx

Operator
Graham & Judy Pritchard
New House Farm
Hardwicke
Hay on Wye
Herefordshire
Tel/Fax: 01497 831259
Tel: 07774 001446
flyers@dsl.pipex.com

Effective date:25/09/08 OP 08

159ft 5mb	2nm N of Haverfordwest N5149.98 W00457.67	PPR	**Alternative AD**	**Swansea** West Wales

Haverfordwest	**A/G** **122.200**

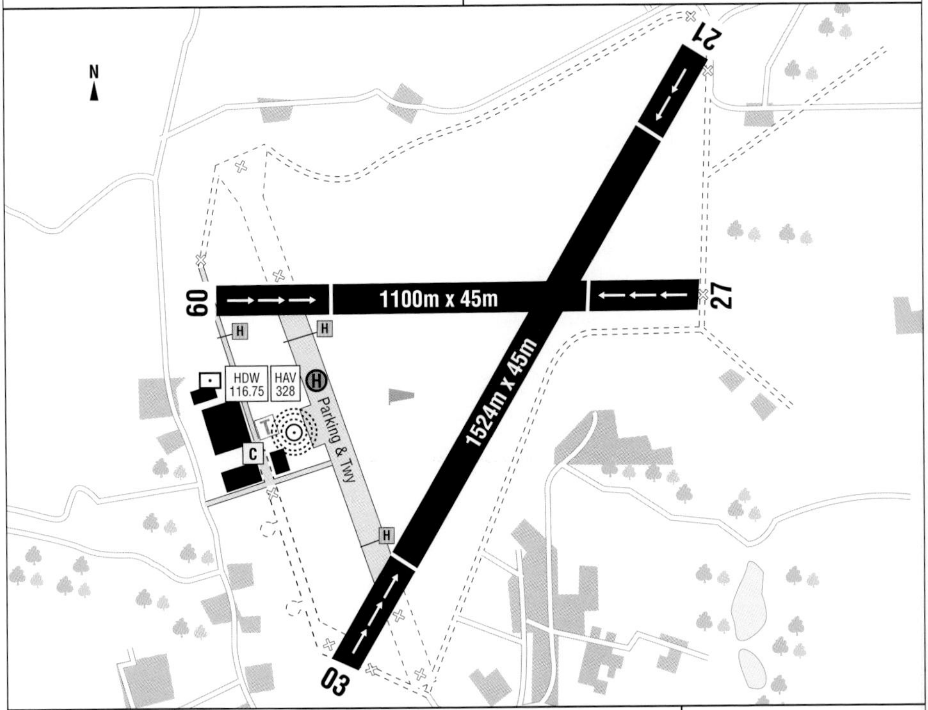

RWY	SURFACE	TORA	LDA	U/L	LIGHTING
03	Asphalt	1199	1202		Thr Rwy APAPI 3.5° LHS
21	Asphalt	1199	1269		Thr Rwy APAPI 3.5° LHS
09	Asphalt	1040	800		Nil
27	Asphalt	1010	800		Nil

Displaced Thr Rwy03 227m, Displaced Thr Rwy21 255m, Displaced Thr Rwy09 240m
Displaced Thr Rwy27 210m,

RNAV			
STU	**113.10**	**169**	**10.1**

H

Remarks
PPR essential. AD U/L Weekends. Microlight flying takes place on AD.
Visual aid to location: Ibn HW Green.

Warnings
A 3rd disused Rwy not available except as Twy between Rwy03 & 09 Thrs and as ACFT parking area. Rwy03/21 & 09/27 intersection liable to flooding during/after heavy rain.
Noise: Avoid local riding stables and residences N Rwy09/27, maintain circuit position on down wind leg.

Operating Hrs Mon-Fri 0815-1530 (Summer)
Mon-Fri 0915-1630 (Winter)
except PH & by arr

Circuits Fixed Wing LH
Microlights RH
1000ft QFE

Landing Fee Single £10

Maintenance
Prestige **Tel:** 01437 766126

Fuel AVGAS JET A1 100LL & Oil

Disabled Facilities

Restaurants Propellers Cafe

Taxis
Rocky's Taxis **Tel:** 01437 764822
Tel: 0800 074 8838

Car Hire
Days Drive **Tel:** 01437 760860

Weather Info Air S MOEx

Operator Pembrokeshire County Council
Fishguard Road
Haverfordwest
Dyfed SA62 4BN
Tel: 01437 764551 (Licensee)
Tel: 01437 764841 (out of Hrs)
Tel: 01437 765283 (PPR)
Tel: 01437 760822 (Club/AOC Ops)
Fax: 01437 769246(ATC)
hwest.airport@pembrokeshire.gov.uk
www.pembrokeshire.gov.uk

EGNR HAWARDEN

45ft 1mb	3.5nm WSW of Chester N5310.68 W00258.67	PPR	**Alternative AD** **Diversion AD**	**Liverpool** Sleap

Hawarden	APP	RAD	TWR	FIRE
	123.350	130.250	124.950	121.600

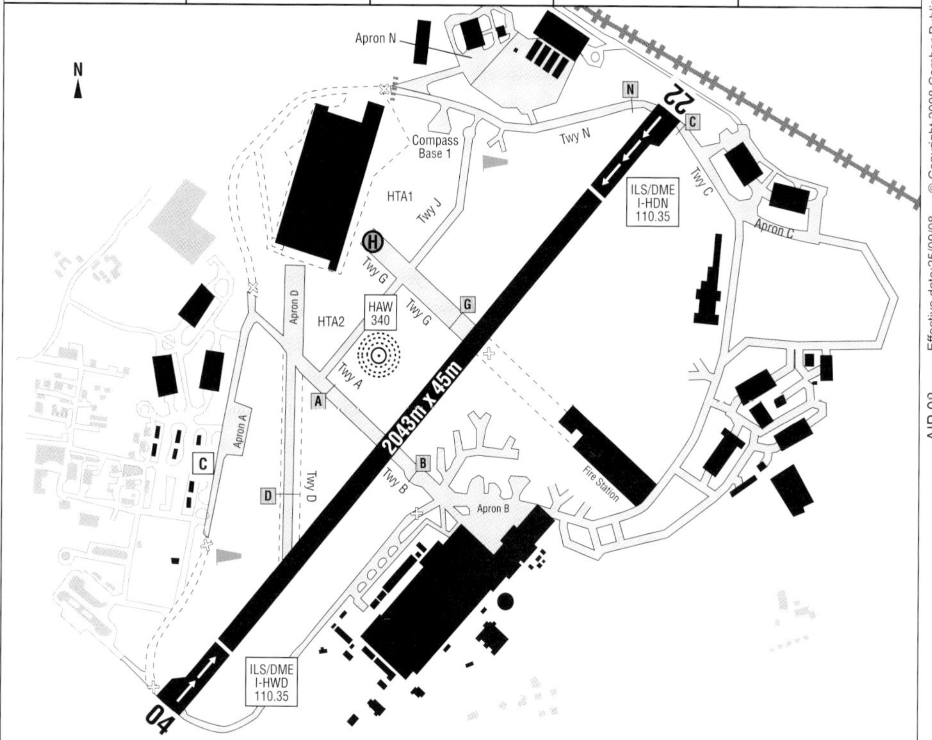

RWY	SURFACE	TORA	LDA	U/L	LIGHTING
04	Asph/Conc	1962	1663		Ap Thr Rwy PAPI 3.5° RHS
22	Asph/Conc	2043	1743		Ap Thr Rwy PAPI 3°LHS

Displaced Thr Rwy04 300m, Displaced Thr Rwy22 300m

RNAV			
WAL	**114.10**	**162**	**14.0**

Remarks

PPR (24 Hrs). Non-radio ACFT not accepted. Hi-Vis.

Warnings

Test flying takes place (including outside promulgated Hrs of ATC). Pilots are reminded of the proximity of Restricted Area R311 5nm N of AD. Compass deviation likely on new portion Rwy04/22 due to steel reinforcement. SFC winds over 15kts from E or W may cause turbulence from buildings. Apron N restricted to ACFT <17m wingspan. Apron N and parts of Twy N are not visible from ATC. Glider activity at Sealand 3nm NNW weekends up to 3000ft agl.

Noise: All ACFT are to climb ahead to 1.5nm before turning onto course or downwind into the circuit. Avoid over flight of local habitation below 1500ft.

Operating Hrs	Mon 0530-1800 Tue-Fri 0630-1800 Sat-Sun 0830-1500 (Summer) +1Hr (Winter)
Circuits	04 RH, 22 LH, 1000ft QFE
Landing Fee	<1500kgs £17.48 1500-2000kgs £28.40 2000-3000kgs £42.03 ACFT >3000kgs requires Handling Agent Weekend excess applied
Maintenance	Hawarden Air Services **Tel:** 01244 538568
Fuel	AVGAS JET A1 100LL By prior arr only 48Hrs notice required at weekends
Disabled Facilities	Nil
Handling	**Tel:** 01244 536853 (Chester Handling)

Restaurants	Nil
Taxis	
Airport Service	**Tel:** 01244 346550
Abbey Taxis	**Tel:** 01244 311804
Dee Cars	**Tel:** 01244 671671
Car Hire	
Avis Rent-a-Car	**Tel:** 01244 311463
National	**Tel:** 01244 390008
Weather Info	M T9 MOEx
Operator	Airbus UK Ltd Chester Hawarden Airport Broughton, Chester Flintshire CH4 ODR **Tel:** 01244 522012 (ATC) **Tel:** 01244 522013 (PPR) **Fax:** 01244 523035

11ft 0mb	12.5nm E of Doncaster N5329.42 W00049.79	PPR	Alternative AD	Humberside Sandtoft

Non Radio	LARS Waddington 127.350	APP Doncaster Sheffield 126.225	Safetycom 135.475

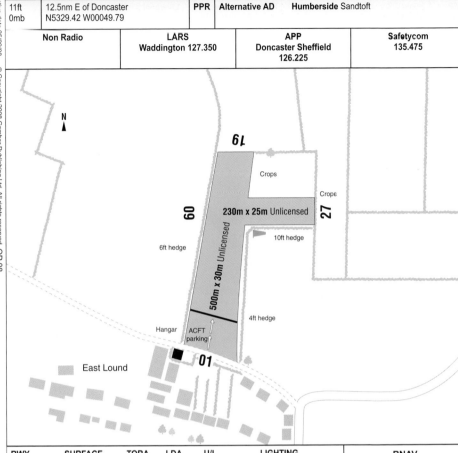

RWY	SURFACE	TORA	LDA	U/L	LIGHTING
01	Grass			500x30	Nil
19	Grass			400x30	Nil
27/09	Grass			230x25	Nil

Displaced Thr Rwy01, Rwy09 not available for take-off or landing

RNAV			
GAM	112.80	025	13.4

Remarks
PPR essential by telephone. All ACFT to contact Doncaster Sheffield ATC en-route and before dept.

Warnings
Located inside Doncaster Sheffield CTR. AD slightly undulating. Avoid obstructing farm track which crosses extreme S edge of AD.
Noise: Avoid over flying local villages and houses on short final on APP Rwy01 or Dept Rwy19

Operating Hrs SR-SS
Circuits Overhead join
01 LH, 19 27 RH
Landing Fee On application
Maintenance Nil
Fuel Can be arranged
Disabled Facilities Nil
Restaurant Various good pubs
Taxi/Car Hire
Epworth Taxi **Tel:** 01427 874569
Weather Info Air N MOEx

Operator Mr J D Bingham
Haxey Airfield
East Lound
Doncaster
South Yorkshire DN9 2LR
Tel: 01427 752291
Tel: 01427 754077
Tel: 07702 039625
Tel: 07926 809527
fly.gassf@btinternet.com

80ft 2mb	4nm NNW of Warrington N5328.53 W00237.30	PPR	**Alternative AD** **Liverpool** Manchester Barton **Non-standard join**

Non-radio	ATIS Manchester 128.175 (Arr)	APP Manchester 135.000	Safetycom 135.475

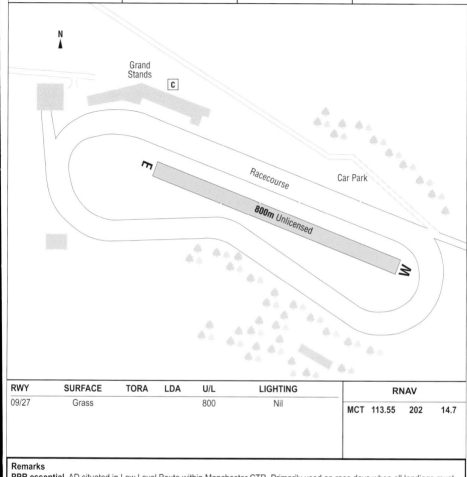

N
Grand Stands
C
E
Racecourse
Car Park
800m Unlicensed
W

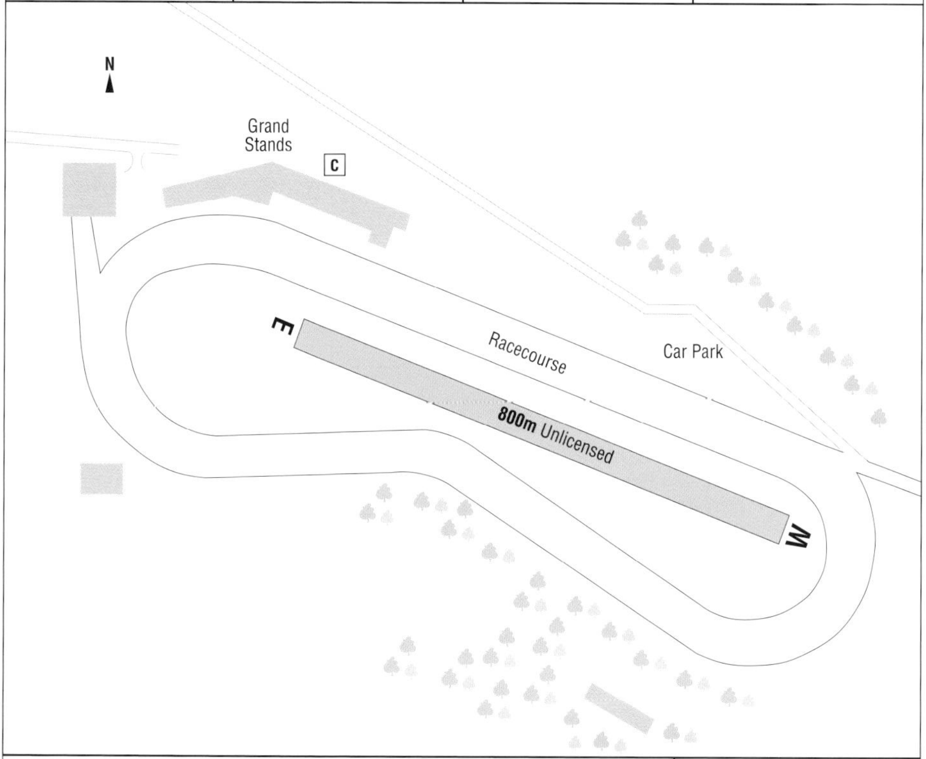

RWY	SURFACE	TORA	LDA	U/L	LIGHTING
09/27	Grass			800	Nil

RNAV			
MCT	113.55	202	14.7

Remarks
PPR essential. AD situated in Low Level Route within Manchester CTR. Primarily used on race days when all landings must be made 30mins before the first race. Light ACFT may be accepted on non race days at pilot's own risk. Windsock displayed on race days and when given sufficient prior notice. Limited helicopter servicing on race days.

Warnings
Care should be taken over rough GND, particularly at each end of Rwy. Parasending on race days.

Operating Hrs Available on request
Circuits Nil
Landing Fee Light ACFT £25
Nil on race days
Maintenance Limited helicopter facilities race days
Ground Zero **Tel:** 0161 7996967
Fuel Helicopter fuel available on race days
Disabled Facilities Nil
Restaurants Nil
Taxis/Car Hire Nil
Weather Info Air Cen MOEx

Operator The Haydock Park Racecourse Ltd
Newton-Le-Willows
Merseyside, WA12 0HQ
Tel: 01942 725963 Ex 208
(0900-1700 Mon-Fri)
Fax: 01942 270879

170ft 5mb	4nm N of Hitchin N5201.17 W00018.10	PPR MIL	**Alternative AD** **Diversion AD**	**Cranfield** Little Gransden

Henlow	**APP** **Luton 129.550**	**A/G** **121.100**	**If no contact transmit normal calls blind & proceed with caution**

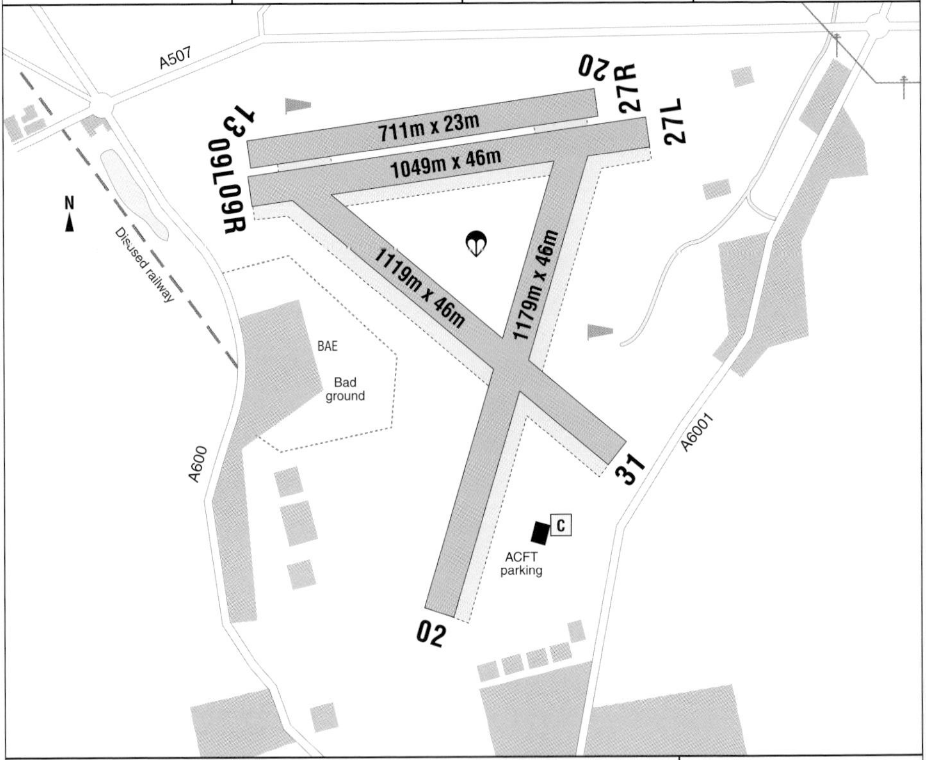

A507
20
27R
27L
13
09L
09R
711m x 23m
1049m x 46m
N
Disused railway
1119m x 46m
1179m x 46m
BAE
Bad ground
A600
A6001
31
C
ACFT parking
02

RWY	SURFACE	TORA	LDA	U/L	LIGHTING
02/20	Grass	1179	1052		Nil
09L/27R	Grass	711	711		Nil
09R/27L	Grass	1049	949		Nil
13/31	Grass	1119	1016		Nil

Rwys have white edge markings

RNAV			
BKY	**116.25**	**280**	**13.6**

Remarks

PPR 48Hrs notice by telephone. Civil flying training organisation operating on an RAF AD. Visitors PPR OC flying, or station duty officer 48Hrs beforehand and must obtain Arr briefing from flying club. Arr Standard OH join. During gliding operations route via local VRPs.

Warnings

Considerable ATC flying, some model ACFT flying & free-fall parachuting. Grass area consolidated with metal tracking that protrudes in places, remain within Rwys & Twys. Do not over fly the BAE complex.

Noise: Dept Normal procedure except Rwy02 No left turns before 700ft QFE. Rwy31 at 300ft QFE, turn left, track 295° until clear of ATZ.

Operating Hrs 0830-SS (L)

Circuits LH except 13 RH 27R (variable) 1000ft QFE

Landing Fee Charges in accordance with MOD policy

Maintenance Nil

Fuel AVGAS 100LL

Disabled Facilities

Restaurant Cafe & pub food in Henlow village

Taxis/Car Hire By arrangement

Weather Info Air Cen MOEx

Visual Reference Points (VRP)

Blue Lagoon (Brick pit with blue water)	140°/2.25nm
Chick Sands (Aerial farm NW Shefford)	300°/2.5nm
Water TWR (Light concrete structure)	060°/3.5nm

Operator RAF Henlow
Beds
Tel: 01462 851515 Ex 6150 (PPR)
Tel: 01462 851936

H

184ft 6mb	5nm SSE of Wincanton N5059.30 W00221.52	PPR	**Alternative AD** **Diversion AD**	**Bournemouth** Compton Abbas

Henstridge	LARS Yeovilton 127.350	A/G 130.250

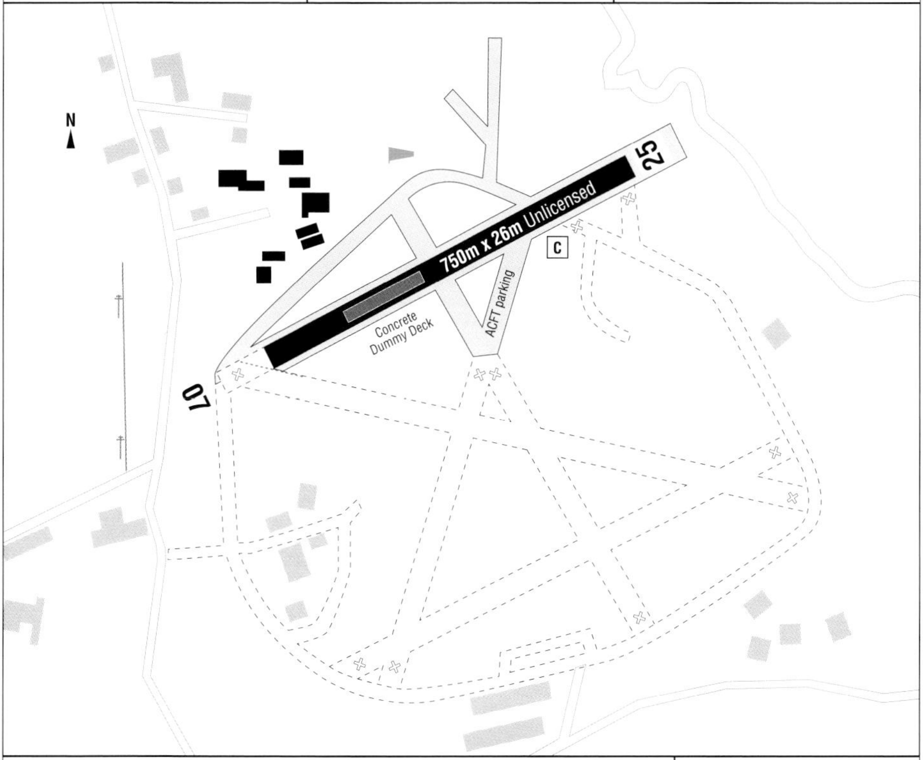

N
25
750m x 26m Unlicensed
C
ACFT parking
Concrete Dummy Deck
07

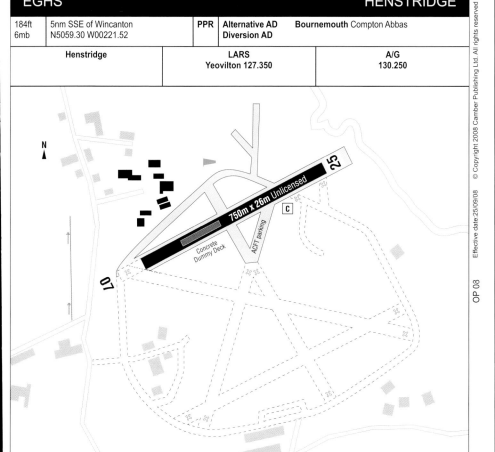

RWY	SURFACE	TORA	LDA	U/L	LIGHTING
07/25	Asph/Conc			750x26	Nil

RNAV

Remarks

PPR non radio ACFT. Visiting ACFT welcome. Situated close to Yeovilton MATZ, call Yeovilton LARS.
Visual aid to location: Rwy07/25 identified by the Concrete 'dummy deck' in the middle

Warnings

Keep a good lookout for high speed military ACFT and high intensity helicopter operations associated with Yeovilton.
Caution: Power cables 20ftagl cross Rwy07 final APP 230m from Thr. Fence 50m from Rwy07 Thr.
Noise: Avoid over flying near by villages and dwellings. Visit website for more noise abatement instructions and up to date notice board.

Operating Hrs	0900-1700 or SS whichever earlier
Circuits	Variable 800ft QFE
Landing Fee	£9 Microlight & Gyro £4.50
Maintenance	Nil
Fuel	AVGAS JET A1 100LL

Disabled Facilities

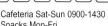

Restaurant	Cafeteria Sat-Sun 0900-1430 Snacks Mon-Fri

Taxis
Bill **Tel:** 01963 362754

Car Hire	Nil
Weather Info	Air SW MOEx
Operator	EGHS Ltd Henstridge Airfield Somerset, BA8 0TN **Tel:** 01963 364231 **Fax:** 01963 364351 www.henstridgeairfield.com

Effective date:25/09/08 OP 08

XHIN HINTON IN THE HEDGES

505ft 17mb	2nm W of Brackley N5201.75 W00112.48	PPR	**Alternative AD** **Diversion AD**	**Oxford** Turweston

Non-standard join

Hinton	A/G 119.450

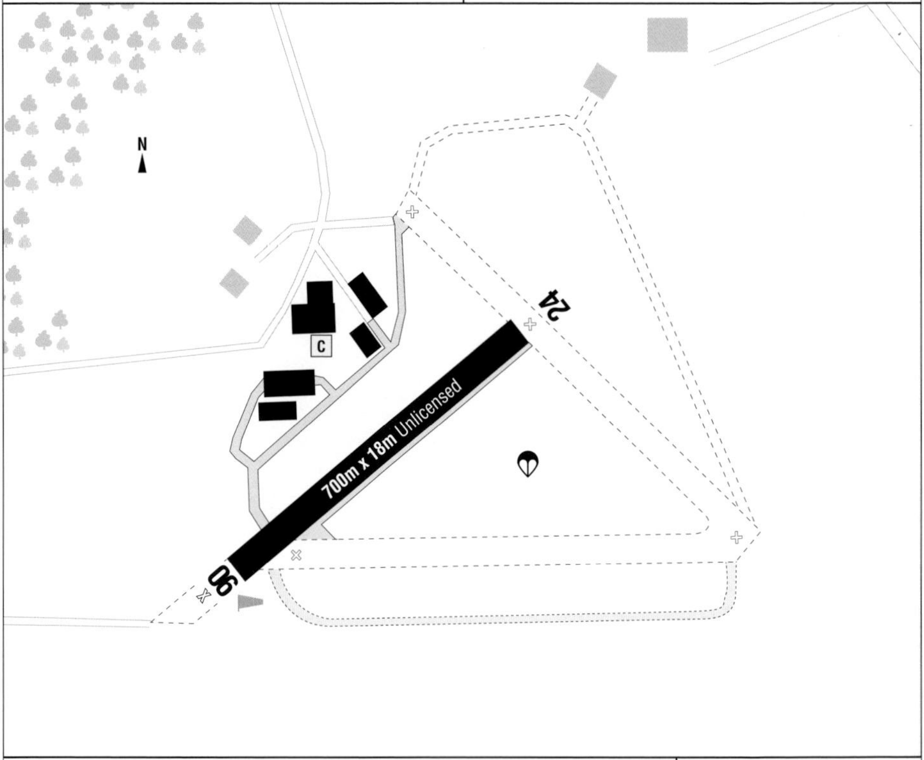

N

24

700m x 18m Unlicensed

06

C

RWY	SURFACE	TORA	LDA	U/L	LIGHTING
06/24	Asphalt			700x18	Nil

RNAV			
DTY	116.40	205	9.7

Remarks
PPR by telephone. Visitors welcome. Gliding and parachuting daily throughout the year. All ACFT must call at least 5nm away.

Warnings
Rwy06/24 has new surface. Strip on N side of original centre line. Gliding and parachuting daily throughout the year.
Noise: Avoid over flying villages and habitation in vicinity of AD.

Operating Hrs SS

Circuits Variable
No over head or cross wind joins

Landing Fee Donations welcome

Maintenance Holdcroft Aviation
Tel: 01295 810287
Fax: 01295 812247

Fuel AVGAS 100LL

Disabled Facilities

Restaurants Light refreshments in club house

Taxis
PJ Cars **Tel:** 01280 704330

Car Hire Nil

Weather Info Air Cen MOEx

Operator Mr R B Harrison
Walltree House Farm
Steane, Brackley, Northants
harrison@walltreehousefarm.co.uk
Tel: 01295 811235 (PPR)
Tel: 01295 812300 (Hinton Skydiving)
info@skydive.co.uk
Tel: 01295 811056 (Gliding club)
Tel: 01295 812775
(Flight Training Tom Eagles)
Fax: 01295 811147 (Owner)
Fax: 01295 812400 (Hinton Skydiving)

H

HOLMBECK FARM

420ft 14mb	2.6nm W of Leighton Buzzard N5154.62 W00043.77	PPR	**Alternative AD** **Cranfield** Turweston

Non Radio	ATIS Luton 120.575	Safetycom 135.475

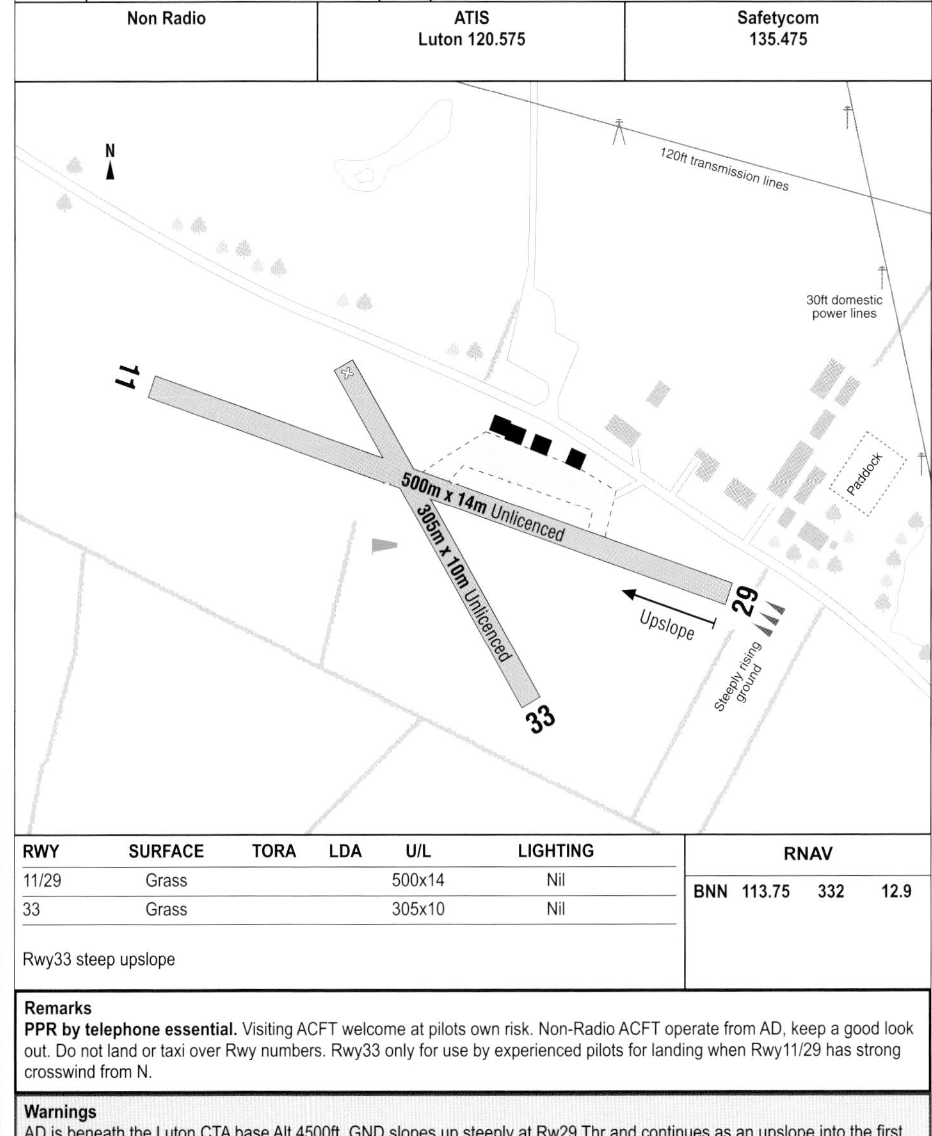

RWY	SURFACE	TORA	LDA	U/L	LIGHTING
11/29	Grass			500x14	Nil
33	Grass			305x10	Nil

Rwy33 steep upslope

RNAV			
BNN	113.75	332	12.9

Remarks
PPR by telephone essential. Visiting ACFT welcome at pilots own risk. Non-Radio ACFT operate from AD, keep a good look out. Do not land or taxi over Rwy numbers. Rwy33 only for use by experienced pilots for landing when Rwy11/29 has strong crosswind from N.

Warnings
AD is beneath the Luton CTA base Alt 4500ft. GND slopes up steeply at Rw29 Thr and continues as an upslope into the first 100m of Rwy.
Caution: Power lines to the N of the AD
Circuits: Inbound ACFT are requested to call blind their position and intentions 3nm from AD, overhead, downwind and on final APP.
Noise: Avoid over flying all local habitation and note particularly sensitive areas on noise diagram.

Operating Hours	SR-SS
Circuits	N 800ft QFE Standard overhead join requested
Landing Fee	£3
Maintenance	Nil
Fuel	Nil
Disabled Facilities	Nil
Restaurant	Local pubs within walking distance.
Taxi/Car Hire	Nil
Weather Info	Air Cen MOEx

Operator
Rita Perkins
Holmbeck Farm
Burcott
Wing
Leighton Buzzard
LU7 0JW
Tel: 01296 681925/681816
Tel: 07748 557202
www.users.globalnet.co.uk/~dartdirx/holmbeck_farm_airfield.html

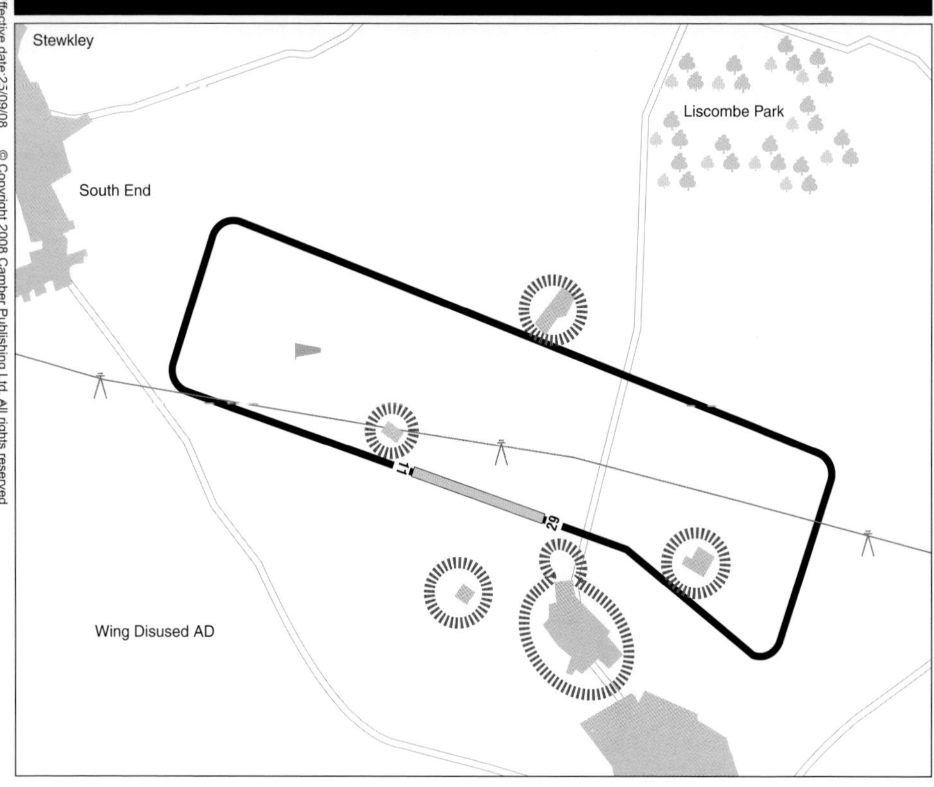
Stewkley
Liscombe Park
South End
11
29
Wing Disused AD

HOLLYM

50ft 1mb	1nm S of Withernsea N5342.63 E00002.22	PPR	Alternative AD **Humberside** Beverley **Non-standard join**

Hollym	ATIS Humberside 124.125	LARS Humberside 119.125	A/G 129.825 (Microlight freq) Make blind calls

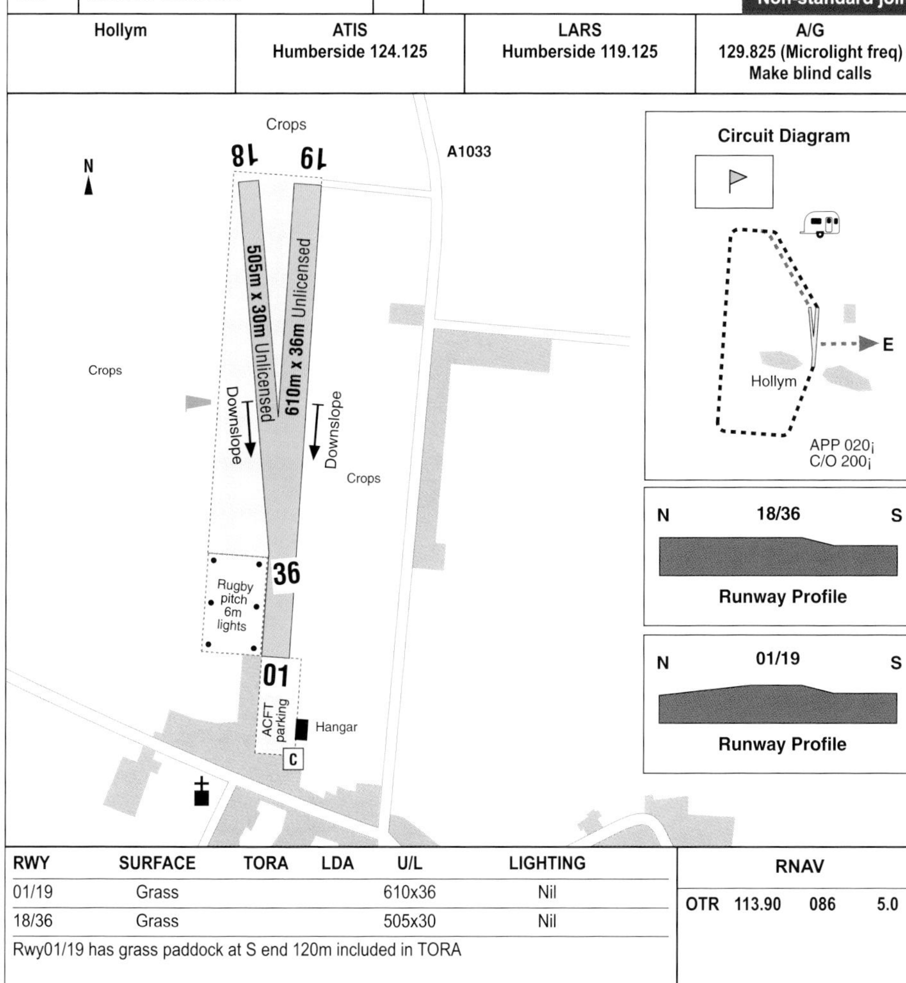

RWY	SURFACE	TORA	LDA	U/L	LIGHTING
01/19	Grass			610x36	Nil
18/36	Grass			505x30	Nil

Rwy01/19 has grass paddock at S end 120m included in TORA

RNAV			
OTR	113.90	086	5.0

Remarks
PPR by telephone. ACFT welcome with PPR and at pilots own risk. A slight down slope for 20m portion of both Rwy. Strip is kept close mown and is in excellent condition. Rwy lighting installation is planned for 01/19. Rwy01/19 dimensions are planned to be altered to 690x36m (TORA 690 LDA 690) for both Rwy. Confirm with operator on obtaining PPR.
NB: An additional rugby pitch is established during the season (Winter). Rwy18/36 is closed on match days.

Warnings
Rugby pitch with floodlight stancions 6m high at S end of AD on W side. Large model ACFT use AD. There is an annual fly-in for ACFT & models, some models are up to half size and may be jet powered! Be aware of gulls which congregate on land around AD.
Noise: See circuit diagram showing avoidance areas. ACFT Dept Rwy19 or 18 with sufficient performance may turn E to avoid Hollym village.

Operating Hrs	0900-SS (L)
Circuits	W 1000ft QFE See circuit diagram
Landing Fee	Nil but donations towards grass cutting welcome
Maintenance	Microlight maintenance available from KWS aviation
Fuel	Nil
Disabled Facilities	Nil
Restaurants	Small cafe in village
Taxis/Car Hire	Nil
Bicycles	Operator plans to have two loan bikes

Weather Info	Air N MOEx www.hollym.org.uk
Operator	Ken Wootton KWS Aviation Green Linnet Northside Rd, Hollym East Yorkshire, HU19 2RS **Tel:** 01964 615622 **Tel:** 07941 698088 steve@hollymairfield.co.uk www.hollymairfield.co.uk

EGXH HONINGTON

174ft 5mb	6nm NE of Bury St Edmunds N5220.50 E00046.44	PPR MIL	Alternative AD	Norwich Old Buckenham

Honington	RAD Lakenheath 128.900	APP 123.300	TWR 122.100

2747m x 61m

09

27

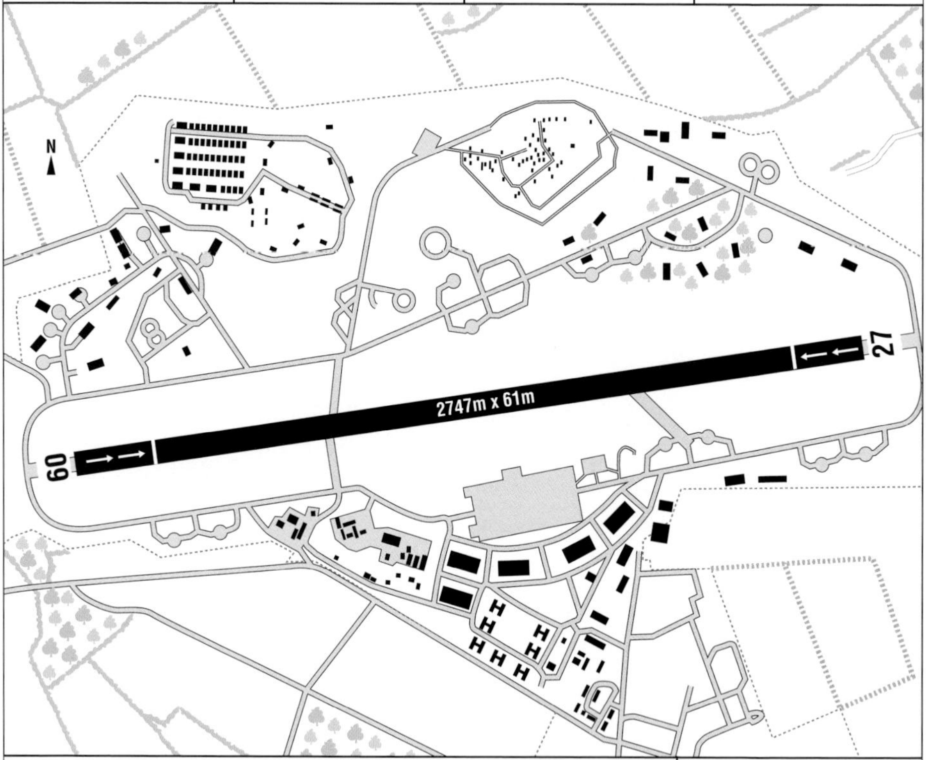

RWY	SURFACE	TORA	LDA	U/L	LIGHTING
09	Asphalt	2747	2739		PAPI 3°
27	Asphalt	2747	2747		PAPI 3°

RNAV

Remarks
PPR essential 24Hrs notice required.

Warnings

Operating Hrs	See NOTAMs for active times
Circuits	Variable
Landing Fee	Charges in accordance with MOD policy Contact Station Ops for details
Maintenance	Nil
Fuel	Nil
Disabled Facilities	Nil
Restaurants	Nil
Taxi/Car Hire	Nil
Weather Info	Air SE MOEx

Operator
RAF Honington
Bury St Edmunds
Suffolk
IP31 1EE
Tel: 01359 237118
Fax: 01359 269082

H

100ft 3mb	5nm SE of Newark N5300.35 W00041.35	PPR	**Alternative AD** **Humberside** Retford

Hougham	**LARS** **Waddington 127.350**	**APP** **Cranwell 119.375**	**A/G** **129.825** **(Microlight freq)**

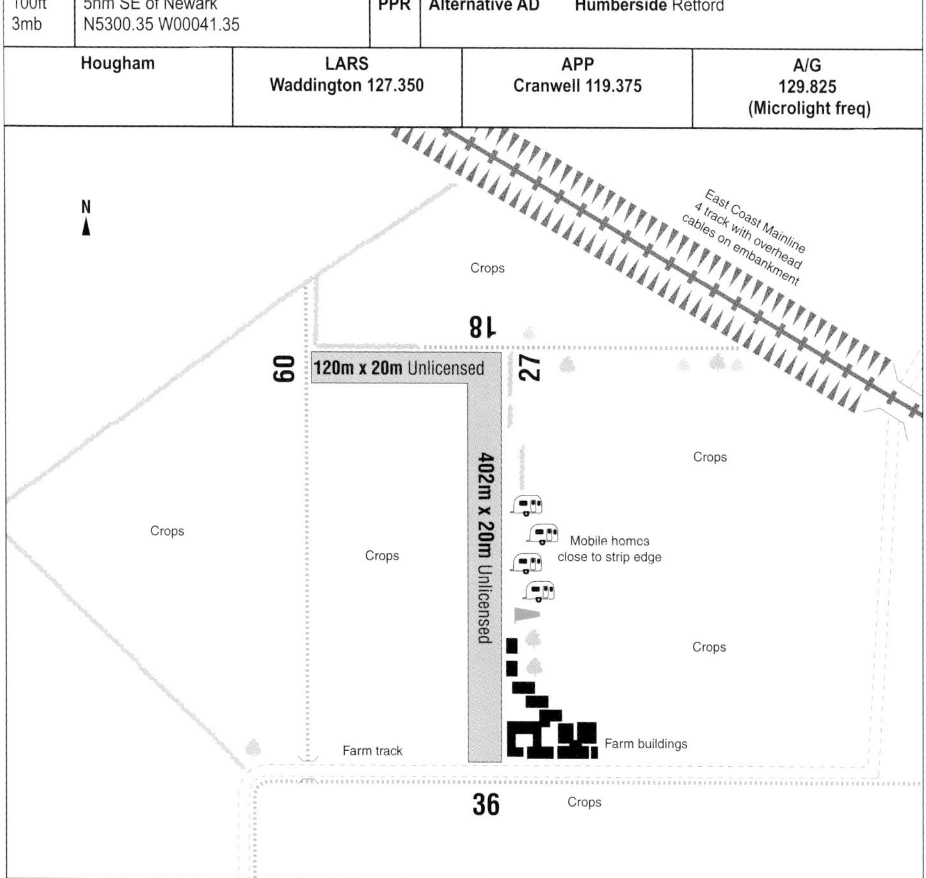

RWY	SURFACE	TORA	LDA	U/L	LIGHTING
18/36	Grass			402x20	Nil
09/27	Grass			120x20	Nil

RNAV			
GAM	112.80	155	18.9

Remarks
PPR by telephone. Visiting ACFT & Microlights welcome at pilots own risk.

Warnings
AD is situated close to the boundaries of Cranwell & Barkston Heath CMATZ. Cranwell APP is the controlling authority. Both AD are not normally active at weekends. Care should be taken as E coast mainline with 25kv overhead lines runs on embankment 400m N of Rwy18 Thr. Domestic power cables cross Rwy36 APP 400m S of Thr. Drainage ditch crosses Rwy18/09 Thr. Farm track crosses Rwy36 Thr – pedestrians and farm vehicles. 5ft hedge crosses Rwy27 Thr. Mobile homes are parked along Rwy18/36 E edge.
Noise: Avoid over flying farms & houses in the vicinity.

Operating Hrs	SR-SS
Circuits	18, 36 E, 09, 27 N, 800ft QFE
Landing Fee	Donation appreciated
Maintenance	Nil
Fuel	Nil
Disabled Facilities	
Restaurants	Nil
Taxi/Car Hire	Nil
Weather Info	Air Cen MOEx

Operator
Mike Barnatt-Millns
The Old Coach House
Coach Road
Hougham, Grantham
Lincs, NG32 2JF
Tel: 01400 250293
mike.hougham@virgin.net

Effective date:25/09/08 OP 07

EGNA HUCKNALL

281ft 9mb	5nm NNW of Nottingham N5300.87 W00113.10	PPR	Alternative AD	East Midlands Nottingham

Hucknall	A/G 130.800

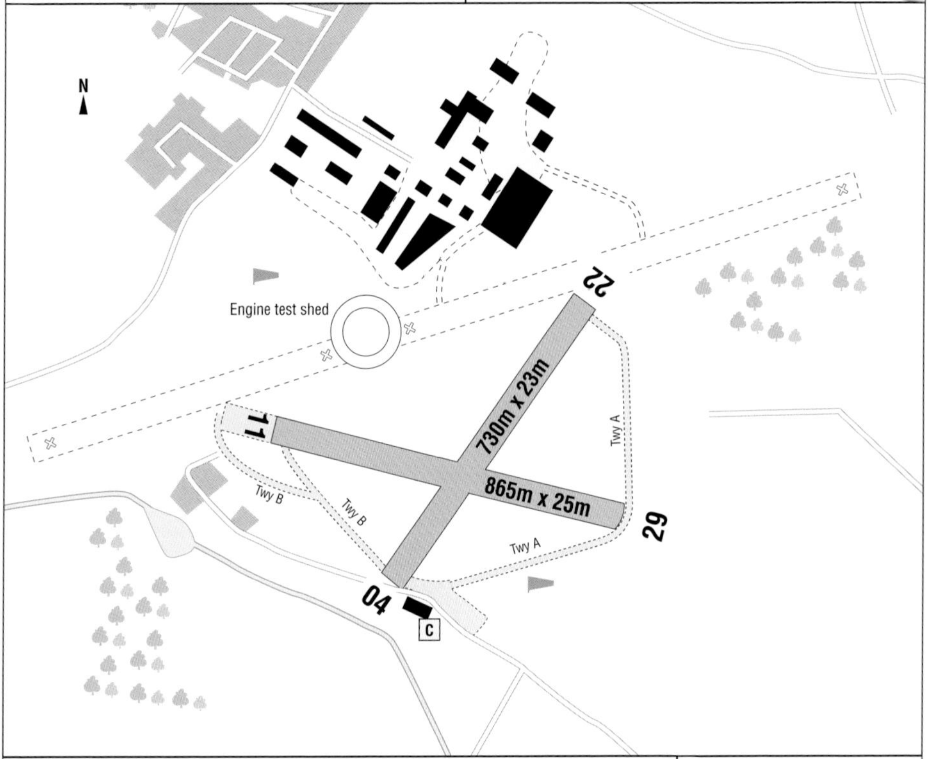

RWY	SURFACE	TORA	LDA	U/L	LIGHTING
04/22	Grass	730	730		Nil
11	Grass	799	776		Nil
29	Grass	776	776		Nil

Starter extension Rwy11 89m

RNAV			
TNT	115.70	102	16.4

Remarks

PPR by telephone. Open weekends only to visiting ACFT. AD available Sat-Sun only. AD is not available for public transport passenger flights required to use a licensed AD.

Warnings

Hard Rwy08/26 is disused. Mast 530ft amsl.280°/1.4nm. Mast 530ft amsl 275°/1.9nm. Rwy29 Thr low fence.

Operating Hrs Mon-Fri closed to visiting ACFT
Sat-Sun 1000-1800 or SS (Winter)
Sat-Sun 0900-1700 or SS (Summer)

Circuits Nil

Landing Fee £3

Maintenance Nil

Fuel AVGAS 100LL
Available by prior arr only

Disabled Facilities Nil

Restaurants Tea & coffee available

Taxis
Streamline **Tel:** 0115 947 3031

Car Hire
National **Tel:** 0115 950 3385

Weather Info Air Cen MOEx

Operator Merlin Flying Club
Rolls Royce Ltd
Aero Division
Hucknall
Nottingham, NG15 6EU
Tel: 0115 975 5153
Tel: 0115 964 2269

825ft 28mb	1.5nm of Huddersfield N5337.28 W00149.72	PPR	Alternative AD	**Leeds Bradford** Sherburn in Elmet

Huddersfield	APP Leeds 123.750	APP Manchester 135.000	A/G 128.375

RWY	SURFACE	TORA	LDA	U/L	LIGHTING
07/25	Asph/Grass			790x22	Nil

Rwy 550m asphalt 250m grass

RNAV			
POL	112.10	131	12.2

Remarks
PPR by telephone. Use restricted to ACFT <2730kg AUW. Whenever possible land and take-off of Rwy25. When Rwy25 is in use pilots are advised to land well beyond the Thr. Fuel available to club ACFT only.

Warnings
Emley Moor TV mast (concrete) 1924ft amsl 6nm to E. Holme Moss TV mast 2490ft amsl 5nm to S. Radio masts 1614ft amsl 2.5nm to NW. Rwy gradient 2.6% down on Rwy07 from start of asphalt. Possible down drafts over head quarry very close to Thr 25.
Noise: Avoid low flying over houses and hospital 0.5m from Thr of Rwy25.

Operating Hrs SR-SS
Circuits LH 1000ft QFE
Landing Fee Single £5, Twin £10
Maintenance Nil
Fuel Limited
Disabled Facilities

Restaurants Light refreshments available

Taxis
GT **Tel:** 01484 534565

Car Hire
National **Tel:** 01484 455050
Eurocar **Tel:** 01484 513353

Weather Info Air Cen MOEx

Operator
J Whitham
Huddersfield Aviation Ltd
The Airfield
Crossland Moor
Huddersfield
West Yorkshire HD47AG
Tel: 01484 645784/654473
Tel: 07767 483373

121ft 3mb	10nm W of Grimsby N5334.47 W00021.05	PPR	Alternative AD	Leeds Bradford Sandtoft Non-standard join

Humberside	ATIS	APP	TWR	FIRE
	124.125	119.125	124.900	121.600

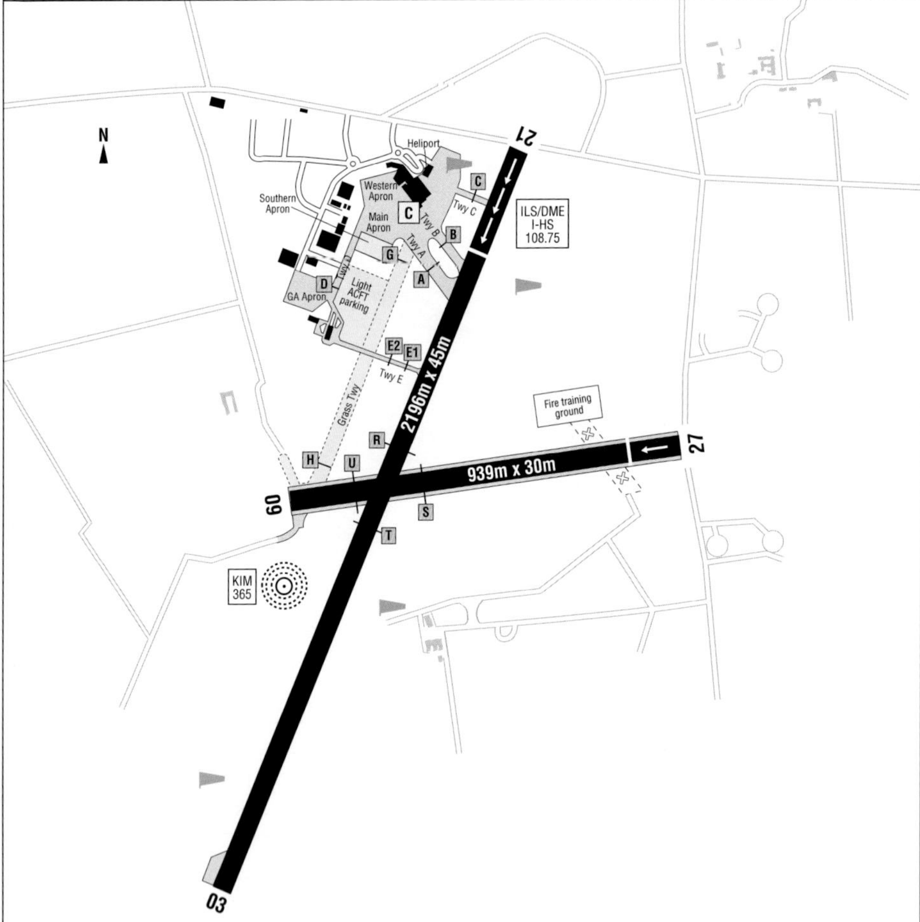

RWY	SURFACE	TORA	LDA	U/L	LIGHTING
03	Asph/Conc	2070	2070		Ap Thr Rwy PAPI 3.5° LHS
21	Asph/Conc	2196	1950		Ap Thr Rwy PAPI 3° LHS
09	Asphalt	939	933		Nil
27	Asphalt	939	865		Nil

RNAV

Remarks

PPR only. Non-radio ACFT NOT accepted. Hi-vis. Training flights subject to ATC approval. Helicopters to land as instructed by ATC. Helicopters operating to and from main apron must avoid over-flying buildings on S edge of apron. Twy to light ACFT parking area and maintenance area is routed behind apron area and marked with a single yellow centre line, exercise caution in this area due to movement of vehicles and personnel. Non handled visiting ACFT are to report to vehicle control post adjacent to the apron. Handling by Servisair.

Warnings

Light ACFT pilots should be aware of the possible effect of rotor down wash generated by large helicopters operating through the main apron area.

Caution: Parachuting takes place at Hibaldstow U/L AD between FL150 and GND.

Noise: Avoid over flying Barnetby, Brocklesby and Kirmington villages

Operating Hrs	0530-2015 (Summer) +1Hr (Winter)
Landing Fee	On application
Maintenance	
Eastern Airways	**Tel:** 01652 681059
Hangar 9	**Tel:** 01652 688062
Fuel	AVGAS JET A1 100LL **Tel:** 01652 682044
Hangarage	
Hangar 9	**Tel:** 01652 688062

Disabled Facilities

Handling	
Servisair	**Tel:** 01652 688864
Restaurant	Licensed buffet in Terminal
Taxis	Available at Terminal
Car Hire	
Avis	**Tel:** 01652 680325
Europcar	**Tel:** 01652 680338
Weather Info	M T9 Fax 296 A MOEx VN ATIS **Tel:** 01652 682020

Visual Reference Points (VRP)

Immingham Docks	N5337.70 W00011.60
N Tower Humber Bridge	N5342.85 W00027.03
Caistor	N5329.77 W00019.10
Brigg	N5333.20 W00029.20
Laceby Crossroads	N5332.12 W00010.82
Elsham Wolds	N5336.52 W00025.68

Operator

Humberside International Airport Ltd
Kirmington
Ulcerby
Humberside
DN39 6YH
Tel: 01652 688456 (Admin)
Tel: 01652 682022 (ATC)
Fax: 01652 680244 (ATC)
Fax: 01652 680524 (Admin)
admin@humbersideairport.com

H

254ft 8mb	2nm NW of Harlow N5148.58 E00004.18	PPR	Alternative AD	Southend Stapleford Non-standard join

Hunsdon Microlight traffic	ATIS Stansted 127.175	APP Essex 120.625	A/G 129.825 (microlight freq)

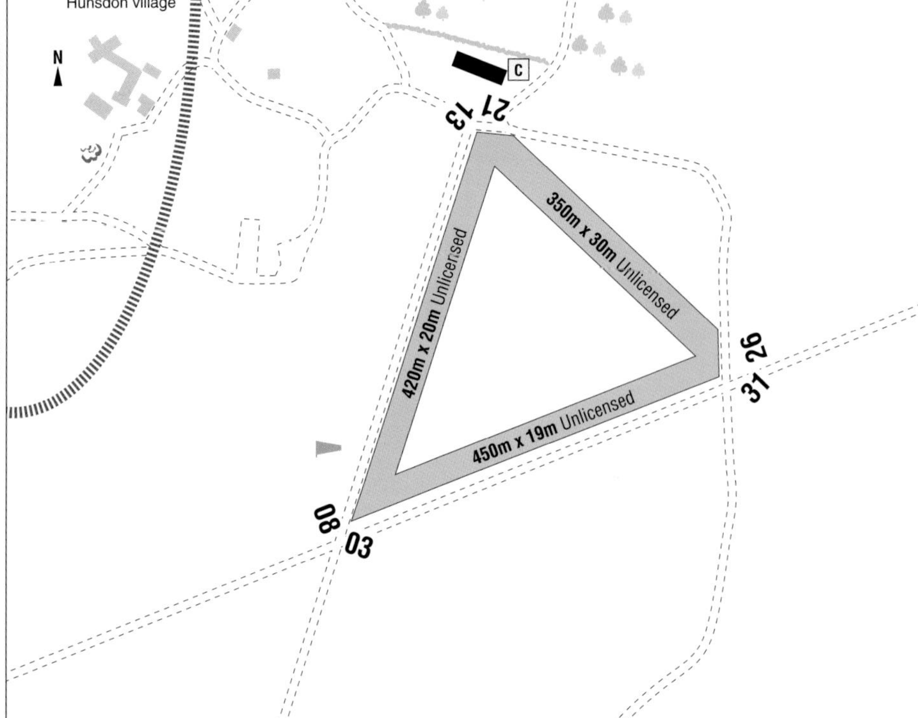

RWY	SURFACE	TORA	LDA	U/L	LIGHTING
08/26	Grass			450x19	Nil
03/21	Grass			420x20	Nil
13/31	Grass			350x30	Nil

RNAV			
BPK	117.50	065	6.9

H

Remarks
PPR by telephone essential. Microlight ACFT only accepted. Visitors welcome at own risk. AD situated within Stansted CTR. Flying activities can only be carried out when Essex RAD have been notified AD active daily, it is not a blanket approval. PPR essential for briefing on APP & Dept procedures, routes and noise sensitive areas. Unless requesting transit Stansted CTR do not call Essex RAD but monitor frequency. AD mainly used for microlight training.

Warnings
When entering circuit do not enter Stansted CTR more than 0.5nm to W and S. Stansted CTA base 1400ft QNH.
Noise: Do not over fly Hunsdon & Hunsdonbury. Route clear of all local habitation, and avoid glide descents whenever possible. All APP to AD from the S.

Operating Hrs	Mon-Sat 0800-1900 Sun 0900-1900 (L)
Circuits	To N or E 800ft QFE
Landing Fee	Weekdays £2 Weekends £4
Maintenance	Nil
Fuel	Nil
Disabled Facilities	Nil
Restaurants	Nil
Taxis/Car Hire	Nil
Weather Info	Air Cen MOEx

Operator
Jay Airsports
116 Mount Pleasant
New Barnet
Herts, EN4 9HQ
Tel: 07956 434958
Tel: 07904 244035
Tel: 07967 091908

N
HUNSDON
21
13
26
31
08
03

XHUS HUSBANDS BOSWORTH

505ft 16mb	8.5nm NE of Rugby N5226.43 W00102.63	PPR	Alternative AD	East Midlands Leicester

Non-standard join

Husbands Bosworth	Launch point 129.975

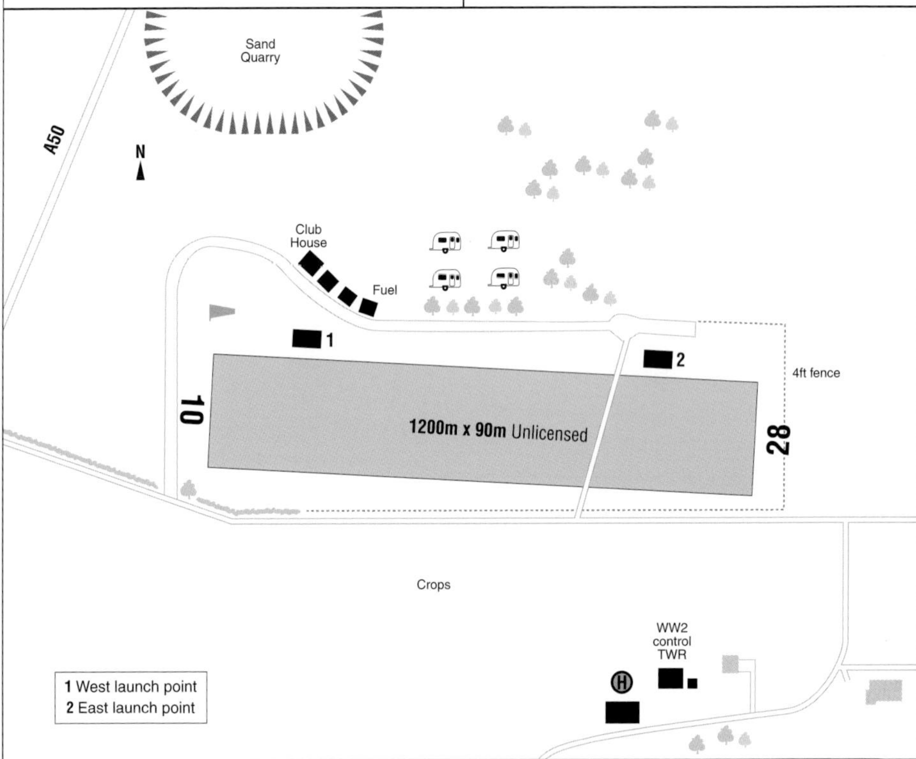

RWY	SURFACE	TORA	LDA	U/L	LIGHTING
10/28	Grass			1200x90	Nil

RNAV			
DTY	116.40	013	15.8

Remarks
PPR by telephone. Primarily gliding site with winch & aerotow launching. Cables up to 3000ft agl.

Warnings
Use extreme vigilance – intensive gliding. Although launch point may not acknowledge, please make circuit calls, give preference to aerotow ACFT. Concrete track crosses AD. Police helicopter may lift from helipad on old S portion of AD without warning.
Noise: Dept Rwy28 turn left towards lake & climb to lake before turning on course. Dept Rwy10 turn on course before Sibbertoft village but do not overfly farmhouses E of AD.

Operating Hrs SR-SS
Circuits 28 LH, 10 RH 1000ft QFE
Landing Fee £10
Maintenance Nil
Fuel AVGAS 100LL by arr only
Disabled Facilities

Restaurants Refreshments & comprehensive
Accomodation list available at AD
Local B+B's in Sibbertoft village (2 miles)
Mary Hart **Tel:** 01858 880886

Taxis
A&B Murphy's **Tel:** 01858 410210/410776/434935
ACE Cabs **Tel:** 01858 462233
Car Hire Nil
Weather Info Air Cen MOEx
Operator The Gliding Centre
Husbands Bosworth Airfield
Lutterworth, Leics
Tel: 01858 880429 (AD)
Tel: 01858 880521 (Office)
office@theglidingcentre.co.uk

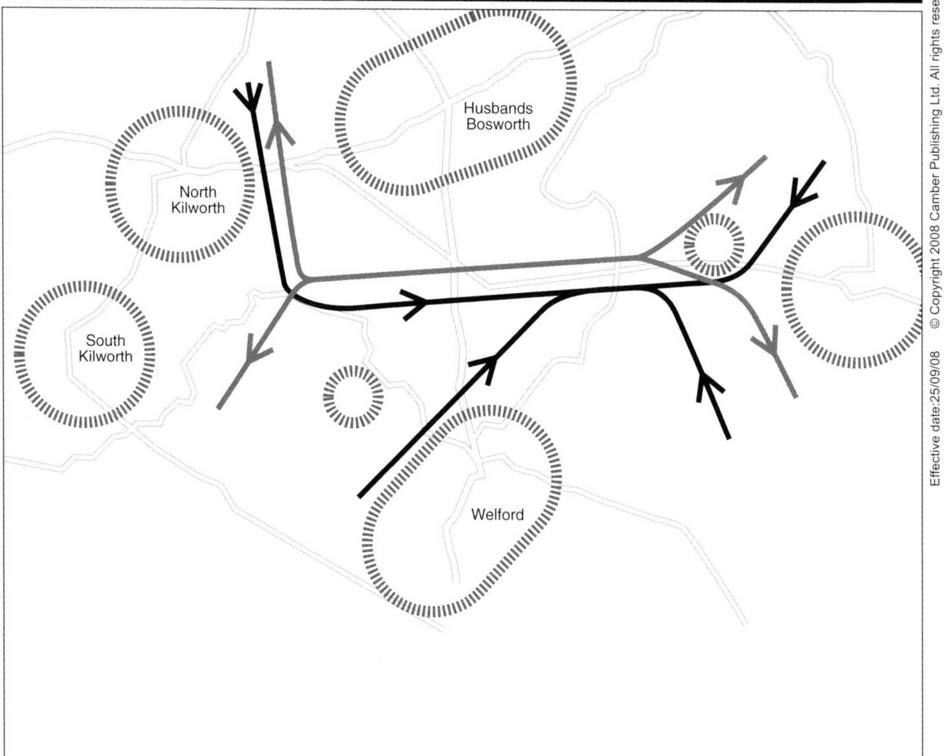

Please avoid over flying any of the areas highlighted on the map.
Towing ACFT will generally fly low level circuits to S of AD.
Dept Rwy27 to W: Hold Rwy heading until reaching the canal, dept to N turn R keeping the canal on your left until passing abeam North Kilworth, then turn on track.
Dept Rwy09 to E: ASAP after take off but not before passing AD boundary, turn L or R to avoid over flying The Wrongs Farm, then after passing abeam the village turn on track.
Arr ACFT from NE: Keep a good look out as you will be passing very close to AD circuit on N side of AD., please use SE arrival preference to help prevent conflicts.

INCE

10ft 0mb	3nm SSE of RAF Woodvale N5332.30 W00302.25	PPR	Alternative AD	**Liverpool** Blackpool

Ince	LARS Warton 129.525	APP Woodvale 121.000	APP Liverpool 119.850	A/G 121.075 Make blind calls

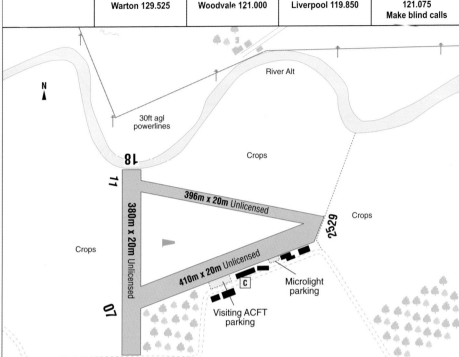

River Alt

N

30ft agl powerlines

Crops

18

11

396m x 20m Unlicensed

380m x 20m Unlicensed

Crops

2529

Crops

410m x 20m Unlicensed

C

Microlight parking

07

Visiting ACFT parking

36

Access track crosses Thr

Ince Blundell village 3/4nm
DO NOT overfly

RWY	SURFACE	TORA	LDA	U/L	LIGHTING
07/25	Grass			410x20	Nil
11/29	Grass			396x20	Nil
18/36	Grass			380x20	Nil

RNAV			
WAL	114.10	029	9.3

Remarks
PPR by telephone. Primarily a Microlight AD but suitable visiting ACFT are welcome at pilots own risk. Be considerate of ab-initio trainees.

Warnings
Power cables cross Rwy18 APP on short final. An access track crosses the Rwy36 Thr. AD is close to RAF Woodvale ATZ boundary which is 1nm NNW and the Liverpool CTR is 3.5nm to S. University Air Squadron light ACFT carry out general handling exercises in the vicinity.
Noise: Please pay careful attention to the Circuit diagram.

Operating Hrs SR-SS

Circuits 29, 07, 18 RH, 11, 25, 36 LH
Please obtain details with PPR and have circuit diagram to hand.
Usual requirement is an overhead join at 1500ft QFE with descent on the deadside to 500ft QFE. (Usual microlight circuit height)

Landing Fee £2

Maintenance Nil

Fuel MOGAS available by arr from garage 2miles

Disabled Facilities

Restaurants The Weld Ince, Blundell
The Red Squirrel, Blundell

Taxis/Car Hire Nil

Weather Info Air Cen MOEx

Operator John North
West Lancashire Microlight School
Ince Blundell, Formby
Merseyside, L38 6JJ
Tel: 0151 9293319
Tel: 07850 882309
Tel: 07970 234933
www.wlms.co.uk

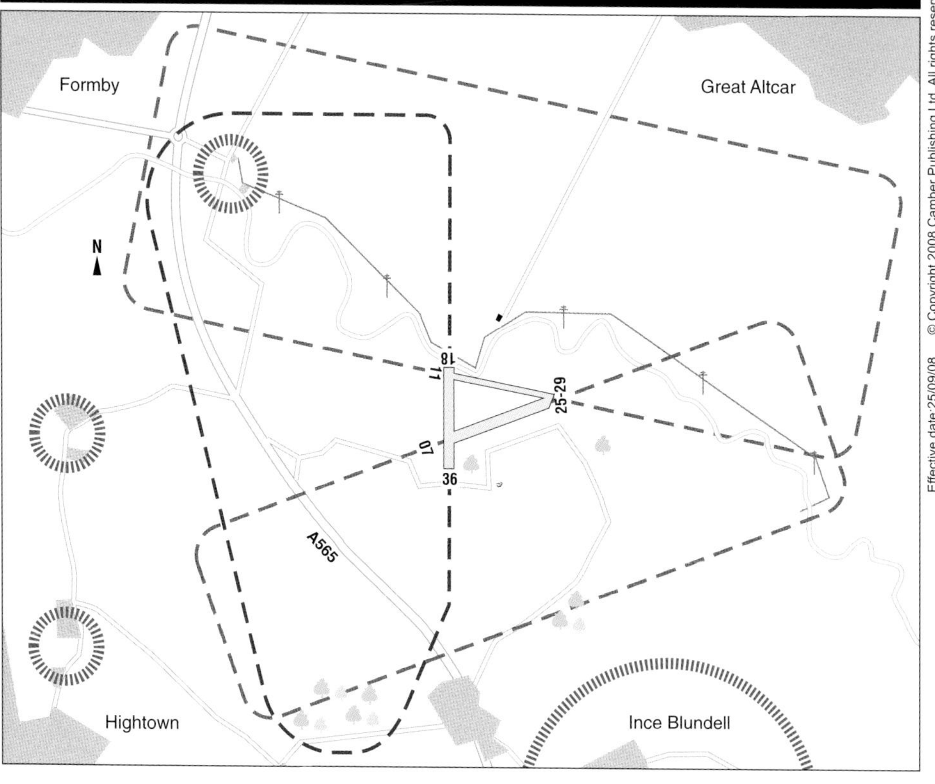

Effective date:25/09/08

500ft 17mb	2nm SW of Insch N5718.68 W00238.80	PPR	**Alternative AD**	**Aberdeen** Inverness

Insch	APP Aberdeen 119.050	A/G 129.825

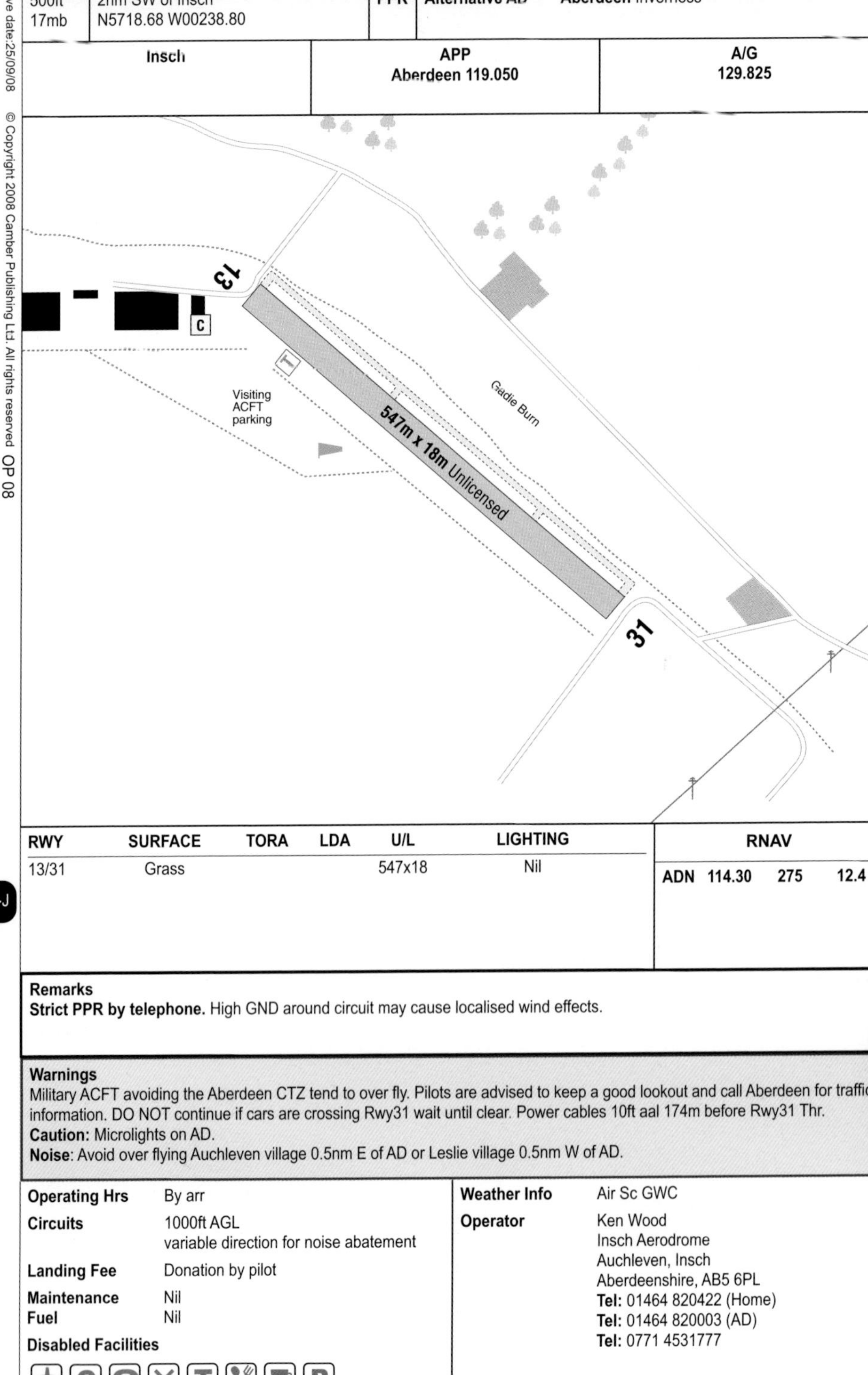

RWY	SURFACE	TORA	LDA	U/L	LIGHTING
13/31	Grass			547x18	Nil

RNAV			
ADN	**114.30**	**275**	**12.4**

Remarks

Strict PPR by telephone. High GND around circuit may cause localised wind effects.

Warnings

Military ACFT avoiding the Aberdeen CTZ tend to over fly. Pilots are advised to keep a good lookout and call Aberdeen for traffic information. DO NOT continue if cars are crossing Rwy31 wait until clear. Power cables 10ft aal 174m before Rwy31 Thr.

Caution: Microlights on AD.

Noise: Avoid over flying Auchleven village 0.5nm E of AD or Leslie village 0.5nm W of AD.

Operating Hrs	By arr
Circuits	1000ft AGL variable direction for noise abatement
Landing Fee	Donation by pilot
Maintenance	Nil
Fuel	Nil
Disabled Facilities	
Restaurants	Local pub
Taxis/Car Hire	Available via AD

Weather Info	Air Sc GWC
Operator	Ken Wood Insch Aerodrome Auchleven, Insch Aberdeenshire, AB5 6PL **Tel:** 01464 820422 (Home) **Tel:** 01464 820003 (AD) **Tel:** 0771 4531777

I-J

31ft 1mb	7nm NE of Inverness N5732.55 W00402.85	PPR	Alternative AD Aberdeen Diversion AD

Inverness	ATIS	LARS	APP	TWR	FIRE
	109.200 (INS VOR)	Lossiemouth 118.900	122.600	118.400	121.600

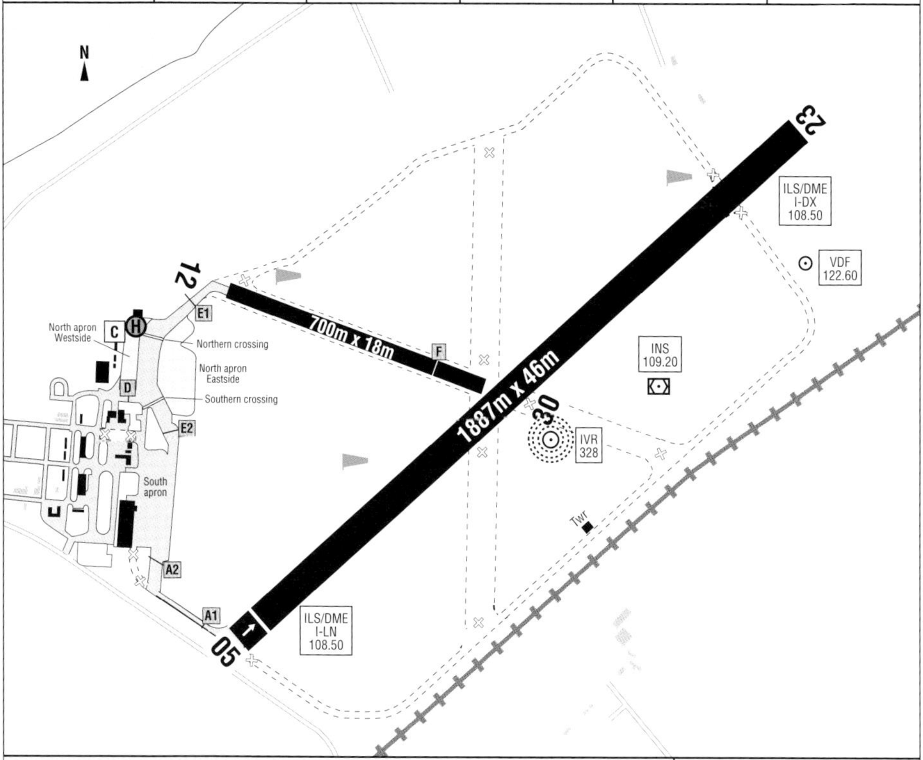

RWY	SURFACE	TORA	LDA	U/L	LIGHTING
05	Asphalt	1887	1827		Ap Thr Rwy PAPI 3° LHS
23	Asphalt	1820	1820		Ap Thr Rwy PAPI 3° LHS
12/30	Asphalt	700	700		Thr Rwy

RNAV		
INS	109.20	On AD

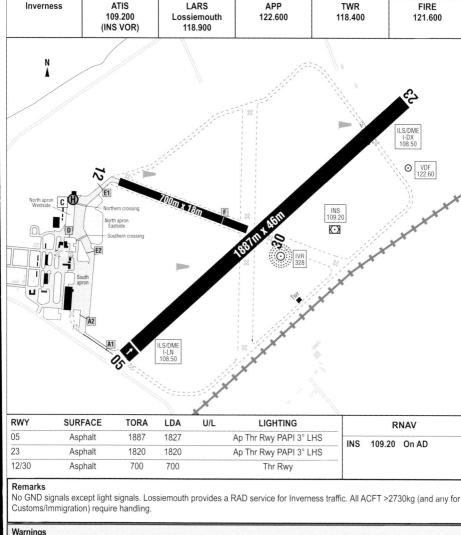

Remarks
No GND signals except light signals. Lossiemouth provides a RAD service for Inverness traffic. All ACFT >2730kg (and any for Customs/Immigration) require handling.

Warnings
Agricultural work takes place on grass areas throughout year. Exercise caution taxiing to hangars No.1 & 2 due close proximity of adjacent security fence. Twy between N end of S apron & Thr12 available for use only by ACFT with wingspan <36m. Grass apron for parking of single piston engined ACFT <1500kg MAUW. Entry to apron E2. AD has constant deer hazard, particularly around dawn/dusk. Patrols mounted whenever the presence of deer is known or anticipated, pilots requested to report to ATC the location of any animals on AD. Birds are constant hazard especially during migration. No hover taxing permitted W of Hold D. All GND movement W of Hold D is at pilots discretion. TV Masts 1074ft amsl 5.6nm to N & 1495ft amsl 8nm WNW. High GND to S 1500ft amsl.

Operating Hrs	Mon-Sat 0530-2030 Sun 0545-2030 (Summer) Mon-Fri 0630-2130 Sat 0630-1915 Sun 0815-2130 (Winter)
Circuits	Nil
Landing Fee	£11.15 ACFT under 3MT VFR cash/cheque on day if PPR obtained
Maintenance	Nil
Fuel	AVGAS 100LL 0730-1800 (L) **Tel:** 01667 462360 JET A1 0600-2000 (L) Fuel available out of Hrs on payment of surcharge

Disabled Facilities

Handling	**Tel:** 01667 461122 (Signature) **Fax:** 01667 461133 (Signature)
Restaurants	Refreshments & Bar
Taxis	Available at the terminal
Car Hire	
AVIS	**Tel:** 01667 462787
Hertz	**Tel:** 01667 462652
Weather Info	M T9 Fax 298 VSc GWC ATIS **Tel:** 01667 464255

Visual Reference Points (VRP)		**Operator**	HIAL Inverness
Invergordon	N5741.53 W00410.05		Inverness Aerodrome
Lochindorb	N5724.17 W00342.95		Inverneshire
Tomatin	N5720.03 W00359.50		Highland IV1 2JB
Dores	N5722.92 W00419.92		**Tel:** 01667 464000/464293 (ATC)
Dingwall	N5735.97 W00425.88		**Fax:** 01667 462041 (Admin)
			Fax: 01667 462586 (ATC)
			www.highlands-and-islands-airports.uk.com

IPSWICH MONEWDEN

180ft 6mb	8nm NNE of Ipswich N5210.06 E00115.60	PPR	Alternative AD	**Norwich** Elmsett

Ipswich Radio	APP Wattisham 125.800	A/G 121.000

N
40ft tree
22
Crops
C
Hangar
ACFT parking
60ft tree
Twy
Downslope
Crops
800m x 20m Unlicensed
Downslope
Crops
Crops
50ft tree
04
50ft tree

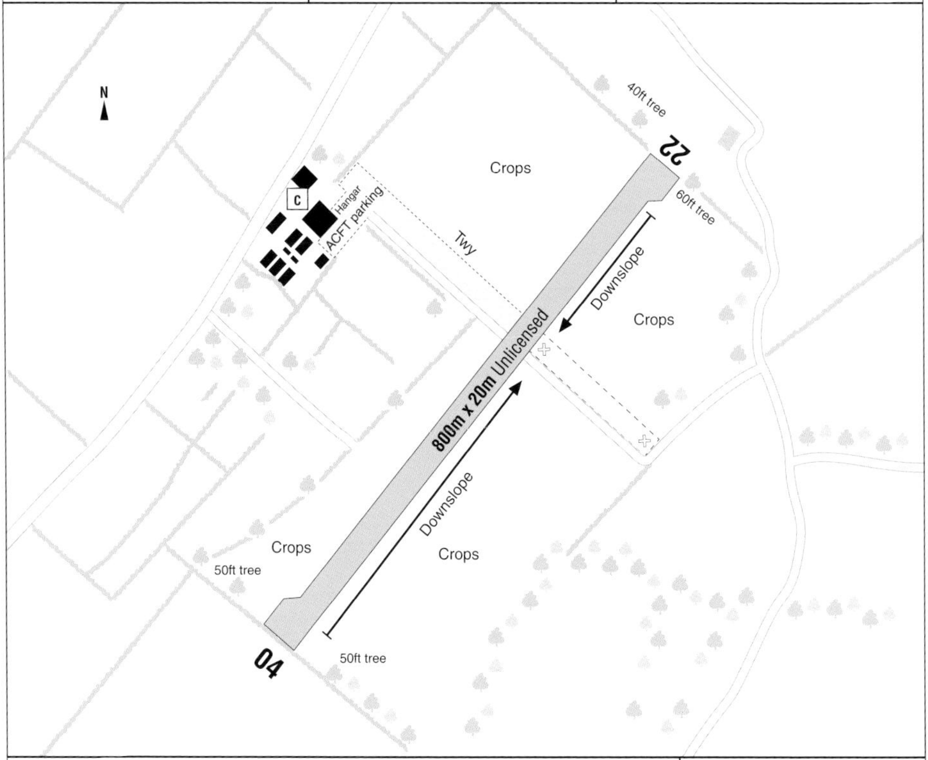

RWY	SURFACE	TORA	LDA	U/L	LIGHTING
04/22	Grass			800x20	Nil

Rwy has undulations

RNAV			
CLN	**114.55**	**015**	**20.1**

I-J

Remarks
PPR by telephone. Visiting ACFT welcome at pilots own risk. Caravan available for hire on AD

Warnings
APP to Rwys clear, but trees at Thr which may cause turbulence. Crops are grown close to S of strip and N of first third Rwy04/22. Irrigation pipes present in summer.
Noise: Do not carry out power checks at Rwy22 Thr due to close proximity of house. Do not over fly village church on Sundays.
Arr – No tight circuits. Position for 1.5nm final, keeping to R of church on Rwy22 APP.
Dept – Rwy22 climb straight ahead to 1000ft before turning. Rwy04 climb straight ahead keeping church on R. Do not turn below 500ft avoiding Crettingham village.

Operating Hrs	SR-SS
Circuits	LH 1000ft QFE
Landing Fee	£5 Overnight parking £5
Maintenance	Nil
Fuel	Nil
Disabled Facilities	Nil
Restaurant	Nil
Taxis	**Tel:** 01728 685883 **Tel:** 07836 676656
Car Hire	**Tel:** 01728 685883 **Tel:** 07836 676656
Weather Info	Air S MOEx
Operator	John F Wright Cherry Tree Farm Monewden, Woodbridge Suffolk **Tel:** 01473 737223 **Tel:** 01473 737677 (Horizon Flying Club/PPR) **Tel:** 07813 105071 (Horizon Flying Club)

56ft 2mb	4.5nm NNW of Port Ellen N5540.92 W00615.40	PPR	Alternative AD	**Prestwick** Campbeltown

Islay	FIS Scottish 127.275	AFIS 123.150	FIRE 121.600

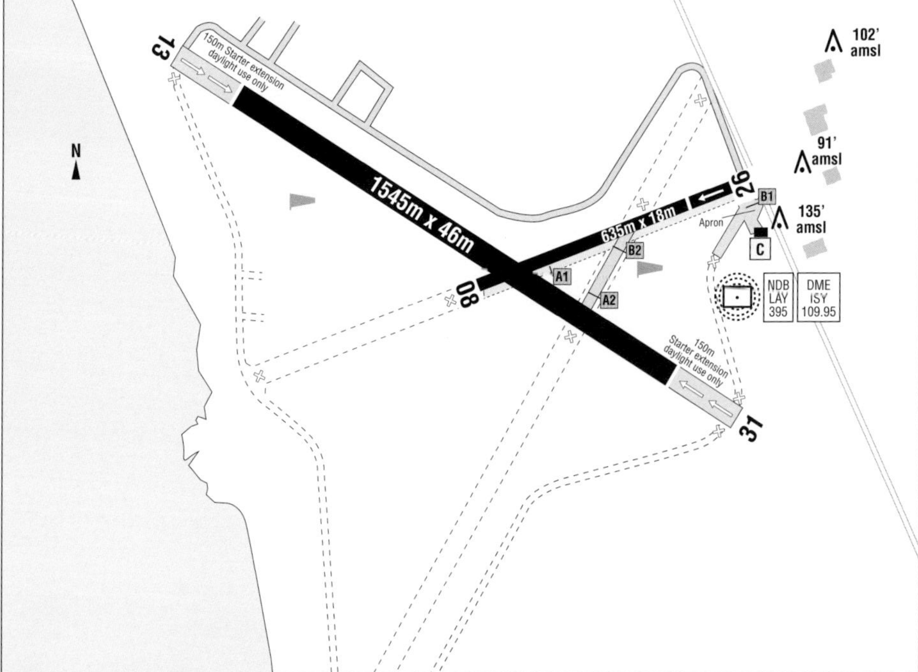

RWY	SURFACE	TORA	LDA	U/L	LIGHTING
13	Asphalt	1245	1245		Ap Thr Rwy APAPI 3° LHS
31	Asphalt	1230	1230		Thr Rwy APAPI 4° LHS
08	Asphalt	635	635		Thr Rwy
26	Asphalt	635	575		Thr Rwy

Displaced Thr Rwy13 150m, Displaced Thr Rwy31 150m, Displaced Thr Rwy26 60m

RNAV			
MAC	116.00	313	25.5

Remarks

PPR by telephone. Pilots should only call Islay Information when within 10nm radius of AD and below 3000ft.

Warnings

No GND signals. Increased numbers of deer and large flocks of geese possible on AD between the months of Oct-Mar. Uncontrolled public road 700m from the start of Rwy08. Do not park or taxi on grass areas adjacent to Rwys unless marshalled by AD staff. Link Twy between Rwy13/31 & Rwy08/26 available for light single engine ACFT. Grass areas soft and unsafe. Poor load bearing characteristics maybe found on Rwy/Twy strips and area adjacent to apron. Only marked Twy to be used. Mobile obstructions in undershoot Rwy31. Farm track E of Rwy31 Thr and uncontrolled public track NE of Rwy13/31 outside AD boundary.

Operating Hrs Mon-Fri 0800-1730 Sat 0800-0900
Sun 1630-1730 (Summer) +1Hr (Winter)

Landing Fee £16 ACFT under 3MT
VFR cash/cheque on day

Maintenance Nil

Fuel AVGAS Limited stock available

Disabled Facilities

Restaurants Café in terminal

Taxis **Tel:** 01496 302155
Tel: 07899 756159

Car Hire **Tel:** 01496 302300

Bike Hire **Tel:** 01496 810366

Weather Info M* T9 GWC

Visual Reference Points (VRP)

Mull of Oa	N5535.50 W00620.30
North Coast	N5556.00 W00609.90
Port Ellen	N5538.00 W00611.40
Rhinns Point	N5540.40 W00629.10

Operator
HIAL Islay Aerodrome
Isle of Islay
Argyll, PA42 7AS
Tel: 01496 302361
Fax: 01496 302096
islayapm@hial.co.uk
www.highlands-and-islands.airports.uk.com

I-J

EGNS ISLE OF MAN

52ft 2mb	6nm SW of Douglas N5405.00 W00437.43	PPR	**Alternative AD** **Belfast City** Newtownards **Non-standard join**

Ronaldsway	ATIS 123.875	APP 120.850	RAD 120.850

TWR 118.900	FIRE 121.600	FIS Scottish 119.875

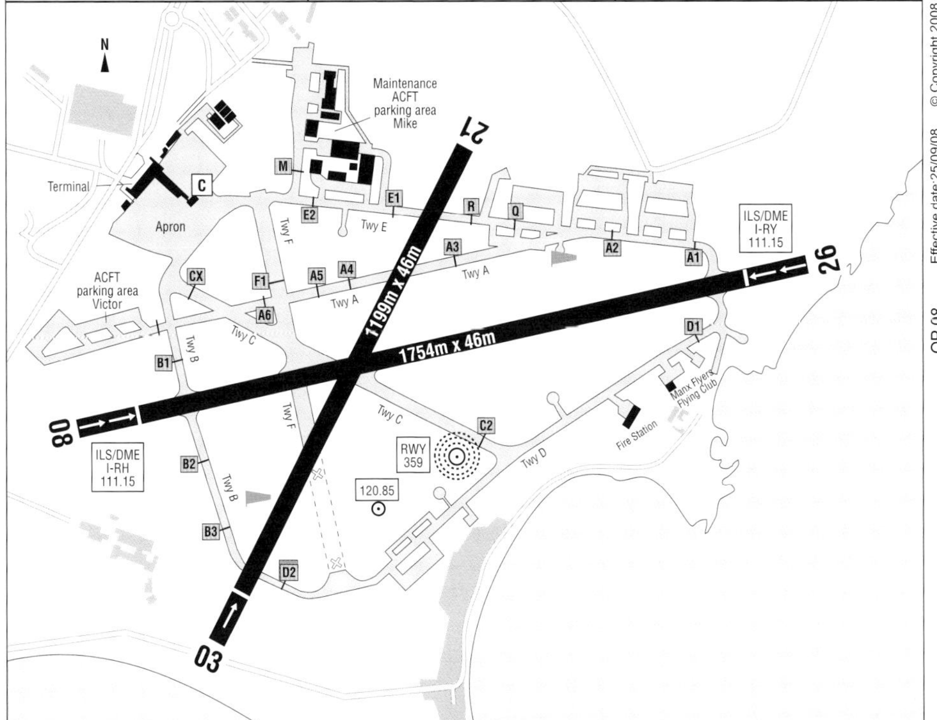

RWY	SURFACE	TORA	LDA	U/L	LIGHTING
03	Asphalt	1199	1104		Thr Rwy PAPI 3° LHS
21	Asphalt	1104	1104		Ap Thr Rwy PAPI 3.5° RHS
08	Asph/Conc	1631	1463		Ap Thr Rwy PAPI 3.5° LHS
26	Asph/Conc	1736	1613		Ap Thr Rwy PAPI 3° LHS

RNAV			
IOM	112.20	084	5.0

Remarks

PPR for non-radio ACFT. Use governed by regulations applicable to the Isle of Man CTR/CTA. Instrument training is subject to prior permission from ATC. Extensions to AD Hrs are frequent, pilots intending to transit Isle of Man CTR outside published AD Hrs must contact Ronaldsway APP. Pilots of helicopters should APP & land in accordance with ATC instructions. Radio communications N of IOM control zone are restricted at low level (<3000ft amsl) due to screening by high GND. Pilots take note of limitations when planning any flight. Ensuring they do not enter IOM controlled airspace without ATC clearance. FIS is available from Scottish Info. Light ACFT are to land and take off on the Rwy, no other landing area is available. In very strong winds into wind parking may be requested with assistance of a marshal. Marshaller available on request. Simulated engine failure Dept Rwy26 not permitted. Handling is compulsory for ACFT needing access to the restricted zone (main apron). Self briefing FBU available

Warnings

No GND signals except light signals. Wind shear exists on short final Rwy08 in SE winds. There is a possibility of turbulence on all Rwys during strong wind conditions. Rwy21due to high GND to the left of the APP for Rwy21, pilots must establish on the Rwy centre line before descending on the PAPI glide path. Due to the presence of an uncontrolled public road Rwy03 APP, Rwy not permitted for use when PAPI's are out of service. The apron flood lighting to the W of the apron area is 7m from the edge of the useable paved apron area. If self parking in this area exercise extreme caution in respect of wing tip clearance. Bird scaring takes place using pyrotechnics.

Noise: Pilots must ensure that ACFT are operated in a manner calculated to cause the least disturbance practicable in areas surrounding the AD, particularly near Castletown and Ballasalla.

Operating Hrs	Mon-Sat 0515-1945 Sun 0600-1945 (Summer) +1Hr (Winter) & by arr	**Operator**	The Isle of Man Dept of Transport-Airports Division Isle of Man Airport Ballasalla Isle of Man, IM9 2AS **Tel:** 01624 821600 (AD) **Tel:** 01624 439098 (Customs) **Tel:** 01624 822926 (Manx Flyers FC) **Fax:** 01624 821611 (AD) **Fax:** 01624 821627 (ATC) **Fax:** 01624 821650 (Customs)
Circuits	By arr with ATC		
Landing Fee	£19.17 <1999kgs £38.64 2000-3000kgs > 3000kgs on application (cash on day)		
Maintenance	Woodgate Aviation		
Hangerage	By arr with local companies		
Fuel	AVGAS JET A1 100LL W100 W80 Available 0630-2030 (L) & by arr with		
Manx Petroleums	**Tel:** 01624 821681		
Disabled Facilities	Available		
Handling	**Tel:** 01624 824300 (Island Aviation) **Fax:** 01624 824946 (Island Aviation) **Tel:** 01624 822926 (Light ACFT – Manx Flyers)		
Restaurants	Buffet & bar at terminal Club facilities @ Manx Flyers		
Taxis	Available at terminal		
Car Hire			
Athol Car Hire	**Tel:** 01624 822481		
Mylchreests	**Tel:** 01624 823533		
Weather Info	M T9 Fax 322 VN IOM		

Isle of Man Control Zone (CTR) & Control Area (CTA) are notified as Class D Airspace
Normal CTA/CTR Class D Airspace rules apply
SVFR within the zone in IMC or night will be given subject to traffic conditions.

Visual Reference Points (VRP)

VRP	VOR/NDB	VOR/DME
Laxey N5413.75 W00424.10	IOM 057°/CAR 036°	IOM 057°/16nm
Peel N5413.33 W00441.50	IOM 017°/CAR 310°	IOM 017°/10nm

I-J

34ft 1mb	On the Isle of Skye N5715.19 W00549.68	PPR	Alternative AD	Benbecula Barra

Non-radio	FIS Scottish 127.275	Heli Ops 130.650

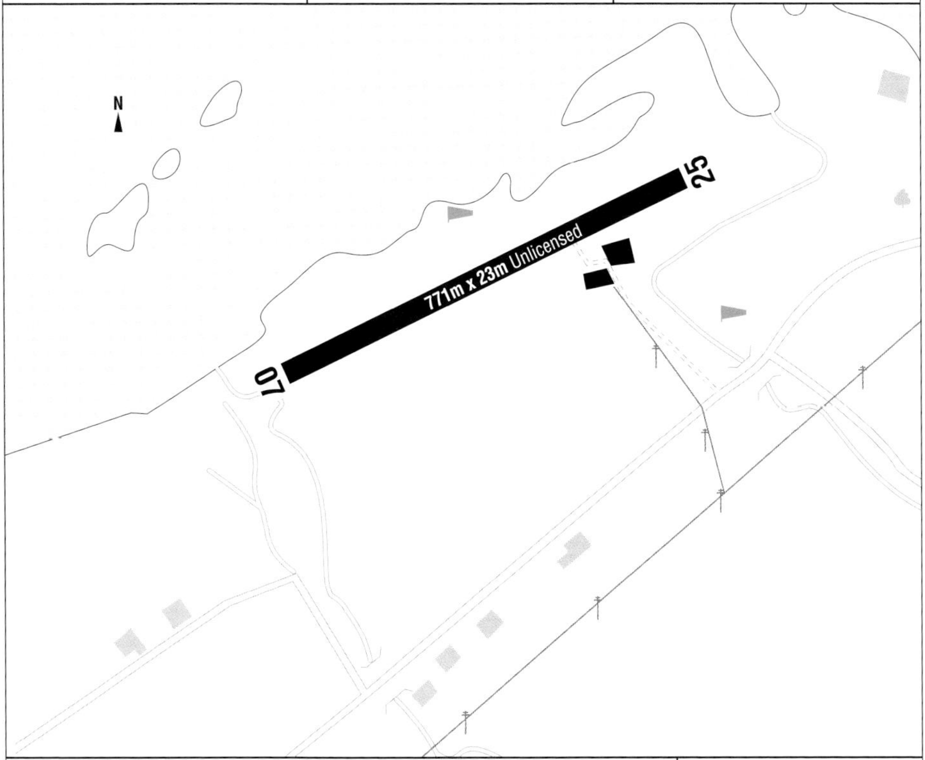

N

25

771m x 23m Unlicensed

07

RWY	SURFACE	TORA	LDA	U/L	LIGHTING
07/25	Asphalt			771x23	Emergency Only

RNAV

Remarks
PPR 24Hrs notice required.

Warnings
Helicopter operations take place at AD and local areas up to 2000ft within a radius of 25nm. High GND up to 2405ft to E & W of AD.

Operating Hrs SR-SS
Circuit Nil
Landing Fee On application
Maintenance Nil
Fuel Nil
Disabled Facilities Nil

Restaurants
Broadford Hotel **Tel:** 01471 822204 (Bar meals)
Claymore Restaurant **Tel:** 01471 882333 (Broadford)

Taxis
Waterloo **Tel:** 01471 822630 (Broadford)

Car Hire
Sutherland's Garage **Tel:** 01471 822225 (self drive)

Weather Info Air Sc GWC

Operator Highland Regional Council
TEC Services
Glenurguhart Road
Inverness
Highland IV3 5NX
Tel: 01478 612727 (R&T Portree)
Tel: 01463 702604 (HQ Inverness)
Fax: 01478 612255 (R&T Portree)
Fax: 01463 702606 (HQ Inverness)

EGHN ISLE OF WIGHT

55ft 2mb	5nm SE of Newport N5039.18 W00110.92	PPR	Alternative AD	Southampton Bembridge

Sandown	A/G 119.275

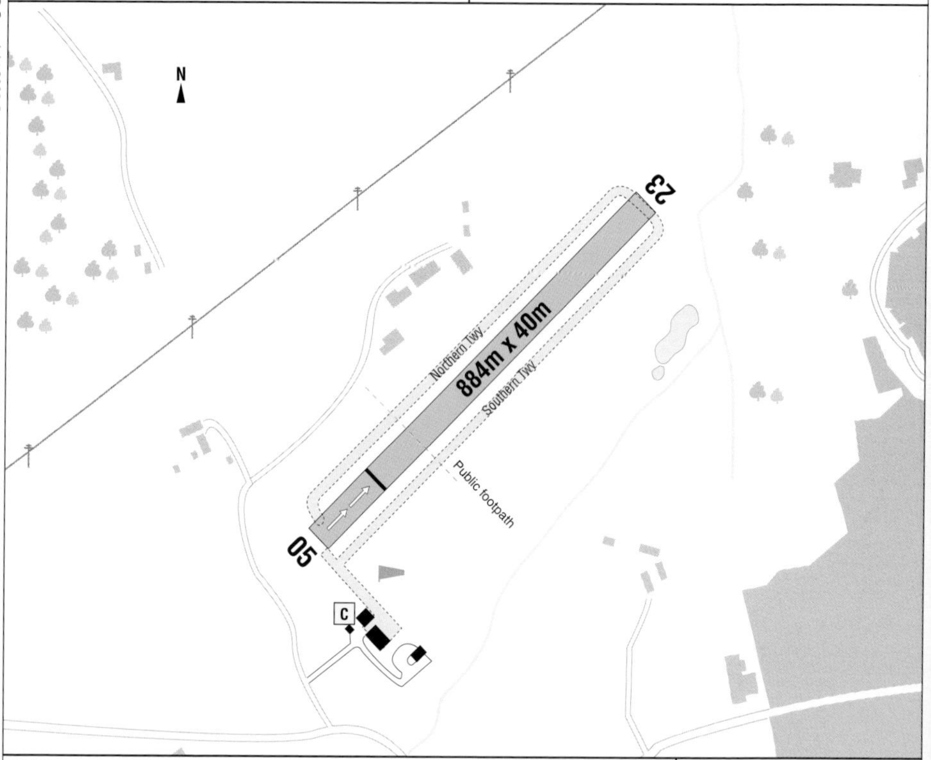

N
23
884m x 40m
Northern Twy
Southern Twy
Public footpath
05
C

RWY	SURFACE	TORA	LDA	U/L	LIGHTING
05/23	Grass	799	799		Nil

RNAV			
SAM	113.35	163	19.3

Remarks
PPR by telephone.

Warnings
Either Rwy or Twy maybe withdrawn or dimensions changed at short notice. Black & white wing bars mark the landing Thr. Taxi with care at all times due to undulating GND in some parts of Twy, active public foot path crosses Rwy 200m upwind of Rwy05 Thr. ATZ over laps Bembridge ATZ, it may be necessary to contact Bembridge after Dept/Arr for transit clearance. Maintain Rwy heading 1nm before turn en-route.
Caution: High sided vehicles cross Rwy05 APP. Rising GND and high trees to SW of AD.
Noise: Avoid over flying local towns & villages below 1500ft QNH

Operating Hrs	0800-1700 (Summer) 0900-1700 or SS whichever is earlier (Winter) & by arr
Circuit	05 LH, 23 RH, 1000ft QFE
Landing Fee	Single £10 Twin £15
Maintenance	Vectis Aviation Services **Tel:** 07929 241546
Fuel	AVGAS 100LL
Disabled Facilities	Nil
Restaurant	Aviator bar adjacent to TWR **Tel:** 01983 408471

Taxis	
Lake	**Tel**: 01983 402641
Car Hire	
Wilton Car Hire	**Tel:** 01983 864414
SW Rentals	**Tel:** 01983 864263
Weather Info	Air S MOEx
Operator	Isle of Wight Aviation Ltd Isle of Wight Airport Sandown, Isle of Wight, PO36 0JP **Tel:** 01983 405125 **Tel:** 01983 404838 **Fax:** 01983 406117 tower@isleofwightairport.co.uk

I-J

250ft 8mb	2.5nm SSW of Horsham N5101.90 W00019.88	PPR	Alternative AD	**Shoreham** Goodwood

Non-Radio	ATIS Gatwick 136.525	APP Gatwick Director 126.825	Safetycom 135.475

45ft trees
Gap in 30ft trees
21
Pasture
Downslope
550m x 11m Unlicensed
Pasture
Hangars amongst 40ft trees
35ft mast
03
6ft hedge
Caravan site

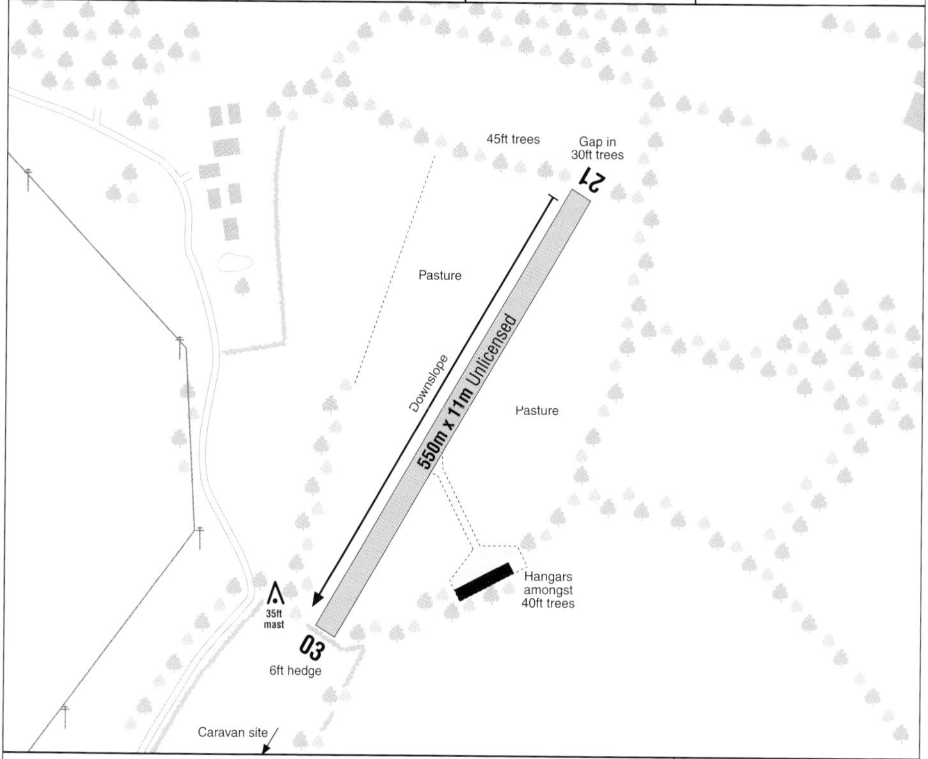

RWY	SURFACE	TORA	LDA	U/L	LIGHTING
03/21	Grass			550x11	Nil

RNAV			
MID	114.00	098	11.5

Remarks
PPR Strictly by email to obtain APP map and detailed info to avoid other strips close by. Visiting ACFT welcome at pilots own risk. Visitors are requested to complete movement book by hangars.

Warnings
Downslope on Rwy21. Recommended land Rwy03. Depart Rwy21. Obstacles at Rwy21 Thr. No windsock displayed except when flexwing microlights fly. Stay on cut surfaces of Rwy and Twy all other surfaces are grass crop.
Caution: There are six other strips in close proximity. One prominent with its own windsock 350m SW of Jackrells Farm close by the Southwater bypass. Airfield is beneath the Gatwick CTA and close to CTR.
Noise: Avoid over flying local houses, particularly to N of AD.

Operating Hrs	SR-SS
Circuits	To E 600ft QFE
Landing Fee	Nil
Maintenance	Nil
Fuel	Nil
Disabled Facilities	
☎	
Restaurant	Nil
Taxi/Car Hire	Nil

Weather Info	Air SE MOEx
Operator	Mike Hallam Birches Ashmore's Lane Rusper Horsham West Sussex RH12 4PS mikehallam@bluebottle.com mikehallam@onetel.com

Effective date:25/09/08 OP 08

277ft 10mb	4nm WNW of St Helier N4912.48 W00211.73	Alternative AD Diversion AD	Guernsey Alderney

Non-standard join

Jersey	ATIS 129.725 112.200 (VOR)	ZONE 125.200	APP 120.300
RAD 118.550	TWR 119.450	GND 121.900	FIRE 121.600

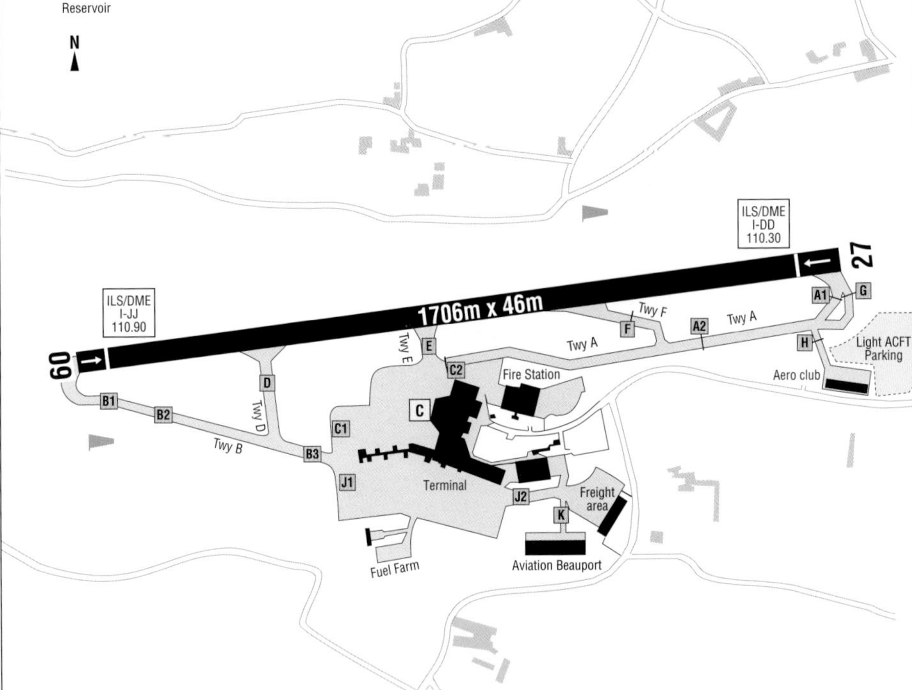

RWY	SURFACE	TORA	LDA	U/L	LIGHTING
09	Asphalt	1706	1645		Ap Thr Rwy PAPI 3° LHS
27	Asphalt	1645	1554		Ap Thr Rwy PAPI 3° RHS

RNAV			
JSY	112.20	266	5.9

Remarks

PPR essential for permit ACFT and microlights. Use governed by regulations applicable to Channel Islands CTR. Proof of insurance should be available for inspection. GND signals other than light signals and letter C not displayed. Only use designated Twy to access Jersey Aero Club. Access from H to light ACFT park does not meet Twy standards. The centre line is for assistance only, it does not provide the usual clearances. Helicopters are to use the main Rwy for all Arr/Dept as no specific helicopter landing area exists. Visiting ACFT under 3 metric tonne will be parked as directed by ATC and will be handled by Jersey Aero Club. ACFT over 3 metric tonnes will be parked as directed by ATC and handled by Aviation Beauport. If passengers need to be conveyed to the main terminal building for customs/immigration, the handling agents will provide transport. For propeller-driven ACFT: Rwy27: Take-off; Climb to at least 500ft aal before turning on to a heading and avoid over-flying land below 1000ft aal. Landing; Maintain at least 1000ft aal until intercepting the ILS glide path or PAPI indication and thereafter descend on the facility. If under 5700kg and making a visual APP, land must not be over flown below 500ft agl until on final APP. Rwy09: Take-off; Climb straight ahead to a minimum of 500ft aal before turning and climb as rapidly as safe to not less than 1000ft agl. Landing. Maintain at least 1000ft aal until intercepting the ILS glide path or PAPI indication and there after descend on the facility. If under 5700kg and making a visual APP land must not be over flown below 500ft agl until on final APP.

Aids to Navigation: NDB JW 329.00

Warnings

All surface movement of ACFT subject to ATC authority, including start-up, push-back and taxi clearance. Turbulence and variable wind conditions may be caused by nearby cliffs on final APP and landing Rwy09. Blasting takes place infrequently on any weekday at quarries adjacent to AD bearing 042° 1.36nm from the VRP. Turning on Rwy for back-tracking only allowed from the Rwy ends with ATC permission.

Caution: Manoeuvring on grass parking areas due to wet and uneven surfaces.

Operating Hrs	0600-2030 (Summer) 0700-2100 (Winter) & by arr
Circuits	When ever cloud base permits maintain at least 1000ft QFE and make the majority of the circuit over the sea.
Landing Fee	On application
Maintenance	Jersey Aircraft Maintenance **Tel:** 01534 496405 Channel Islands Aero Services **Tel:** 01534 742373
Fuel	AVGAS 100LL AVTUR JET A1 Refuelling not available after 1930 (L) for AVGAS100LL or after 2000 (L) for JET A1 except by special arrangement through AD switchboard
Handling	**Tel:** 01534 499970 (Jersey Aero Club) **Tel:** 01534 496496 (Aviation Beauport) **Fax:** 01534 496497 (Aviation Beauport)

Disabled Facilities

Restaurant	Restaurant in arrivals terminal & Aero club
Taxis/Car Hire	Available at terminal
Weather Info	M T9 Fax 324 A VS JER **Tel:** 0905 807 7777

Operator

States of Jersey
States of Jersey Airport
Jersey
Channel Islands, JE1 1BY
Tel: 01534 446109 (Admin)
Tel: 01534 466086/466087 (ATC)
Tel: 01534 446108 (Ops)
Tel: 01534 498073 (ATIS)
Fax: 01534 466082 (Admin)
Fax: 01534 466108 (Ops)
Fax: 01534 466076 ATC)
information@jerseyairport.com
atc@jerseyairport.com
www.jerseyairport.com

Channel Islands Control Zone (Class A) & Jersey Control Zone (Class D)

Normal CTA/CTR Class D Air space rules apply

In the event of RAD failure whilst within the Jersey Zone, the ACFT should proceed to overhead Jersey AD at 2000ft and then leave the Zone tracking 225°T.

Carriage of SSR transponders is mandatory within the Channel Islands Control Zone. Mode 'A' for SVFR, Mode 'A+C' for IFR flights.

Channel Island Visual Reference Points (VRP)

VRP	VOR/DME	VOR/DME	VOR/DME
Carteret Lighthouse N4922.00 W00148.00	JSY 048°/13nm	GUR 101°/31nm	
Casquets Lighthouse N4943.00 W00222.00	JSY 340°/33nm	GUR 031°/19nm	
Corbiere Lighthouse N4911.00 W00215.00	JSY 256°/8nm	GUR 142°/21nm	DIN 352°/36nm
Heauville N4934.60 W00148.06	JSY 026°/24nm	GUR 078°/33nm	
NE Point of Guernsey N4930.42 W00230.52	JSY 317°/25nm	GUR 045°/6nm	
NW corner of Jersey N4915.30 W00214.50	JSY 289°/8nm	GUR 131°/18nm	
Point de Rozel N4928.60 W00150.60	JSY 029°/18nm	GUR 088°/30nm	
St. Germain N4914.00 W00138.00	JSY 091°/16nm	GUR 111°/40nm	DIN 028°/43nm
SE Corner of Jersey N4910.00 W00202.00	JSY 176°/3nm	GUR 130°/28nm	DIN 007°/35nm
W of Cap de la Hague N4943.00 W00200.00	JSY 008°/30nm	GUR 058°/29nm	

I-J

RT Frequencies

Brest Info	134.200
Deauville	119.825
Jersey Zone	125.200
London Info	124.750
Plymouth	124.150
Solent Approach	120.225

SOUTHHAMPTON CTA D 2000 SFC
SAM
SOLENT CTA D FL55 3000
SOLENT CTA D FL55 2000
SOLENT CTA D FL55 2000
BOURNEMOUTH CTR D
BIA
SOLENT CTA D FL55 2000
SOLENT CTA D FL55 2000
SOLENT CTA D FL55 3500
SOLENT CTA D FL55 3500
D015 3600 SFC
P 047 1000 SFC
H51 A FL195 FL125
D012 1800 (OCNL 25000) SFC
D014 5000 (OCNL 15000) SFC
D026 15000 SFC (ONCL20000) SFC
D031 15000 SFC
N63 A FL195 FL165
D021 15000 SFC
A FL195 FL105
D037 55000 SFC
D013 16000 SFC
D038 55000 SFC
D017 2200 (OCNL 55000) SFC
D023 22000 (OCNL 55000) SFC
Recommended VFR route 185(M) 005(M)
D036 19000 (OCNL 55000) SFC
D036 19000 (OCNL 55000) SFC
LONDON FIR
CHANNEL ISLANDS CTR A FL195 SFC
CHANNEL ISLANDS A FL195 FL35
BREST FIR
D FL195 FL115
LONDON FIR
BREST FIR
CHANNEL ISLANDS CTR A FL195 SFC
VRP WEST OF CAP DE LA HAGUE
LA HAGUE 3900 SFC
VRP CASQUETS LIGHTHOUSE
ALDERNEY
ALDERNEY D 2000 SFC
P81 FL195 SFC
VAUVILLE
DEAUVILLE E FL45 1500
D575 FL110 SFC
CHERBOURG MP
E 1500 SFC
VRP HEAUVILLE
D82 FL600 SFC
VRP NORTH EAST POINT
FLAMVILLE 500ASFC SFC
FLAMVILLE 3400 500ASFC
VRP POINTE DE ROZEL
R10 FL105 FL195
GUR
GUY
Guernsey
R095 2400 SFC
GUERNSEY D 2000 SFC
VRP CARTERET LIGHTHOUSE
VRP NORTH WEST CORNER
VRP ST GERMAIN
CHANNEL ISLANDS A FL195 SFC
JSY
VRP CORBIERE LIGHTHOUSE
VRP SOUTH EAST CORNER
JERSEY D 2000 SFC

NOTE:
ATS routes outside the French TMA/CTA are classified as follows:
E from lower limit to FL115
D from FL115 to FL195

RENNES TMA D FL115 2500

Controlled airspace with an upper vertical limit of FL195 and above is not shown

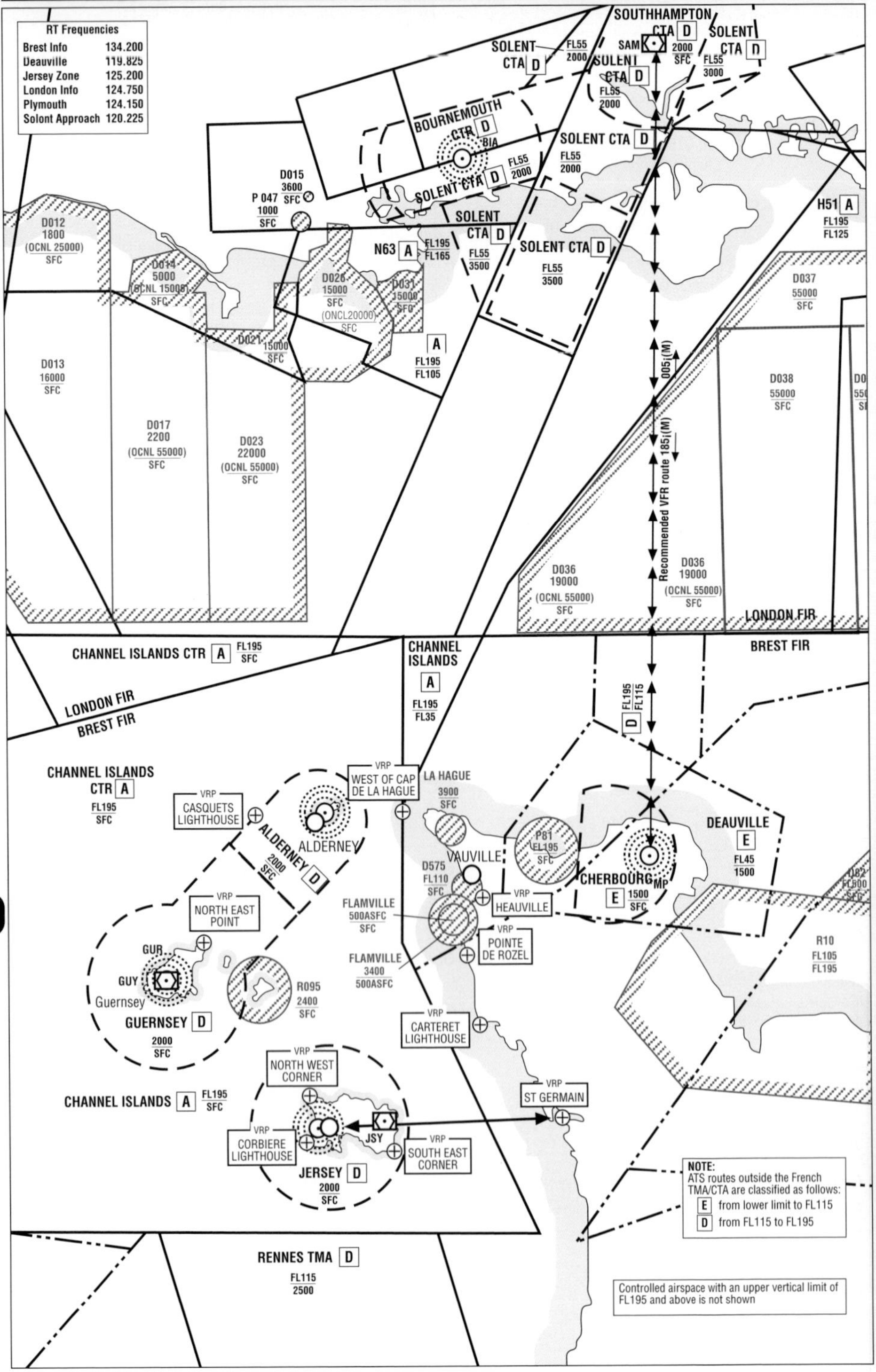

I-J

5ft 0mn	4.5nm SW of Wisbech N5238.00 E00003.89	PPR	**Alternative AD Cambridge** Fenland

Non Radio	LARS Marham 124.150	Safetycom 135.475

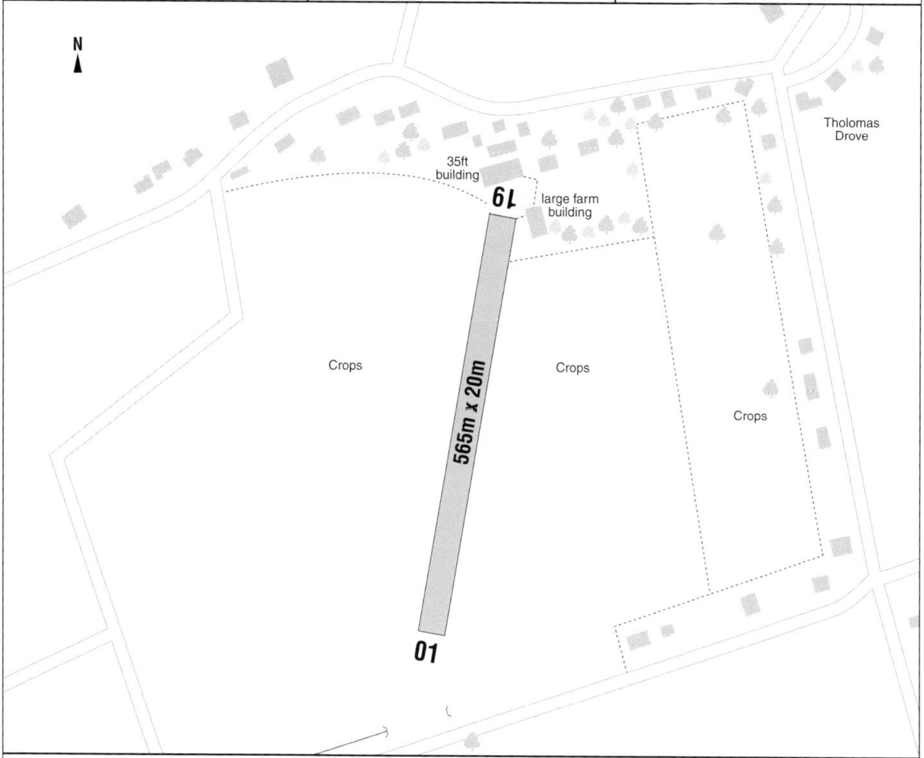

N

Tholomas Drove

35ft building

19

large farm building

Crops

565m x 20m

Crops

Crops

01

RWY	SURFACE	TORA	LDA	U/L	LIGHTING	RNAV
01/19	Grass			565x20	Nil	

Remarks
Strictly PPR by telephone. Flat strip.

Warnings
Large farm buildings adjacent to Rwy19 Thr which may cause turbulence as well as constituting a hazard. Low flying military AVFT may be encountered mainly during weekdays.
Noise: Avoid over flying all local habitation. Particularly to the E of the AD.

Operating Hrs	SR-SS	**Operator**	Frank Ball Jubilee Farm Tholomas Drove Wisbech St. Mary Cambridgeshire PE13 4SP **Tel:** 01945 410261
Circuits	01 LH 19 RH 1000ft QFE.		
Landing Fee	Nil		
Maintenance	Nil		
Fuel	Nil		
Disabled Facilities	Nil		
Restaurant	Nil		
Taxi/Car Hire	Nil		
Weather Info	Air S MOEx		

433ft 14mb	5nm SW of Cirencester N5140.08 W00203.42	PPR	**Alternative AD Diversion AD**	**Gloucestershire** Oxford

Kemble	LARS Brize 124.270	Zone Lyneham 123.400	AFIS 118.900

RWY	SURFACE	TORA	LDA	U/L	LIGHTING
08	Asphalt	1759	1778		Ap Thr Rwy PAPI 3°LHS
26	Asphalt	1799	1594		Ap Thr Rwy 3°LHS
08/26	Grass			450x20	Available on request

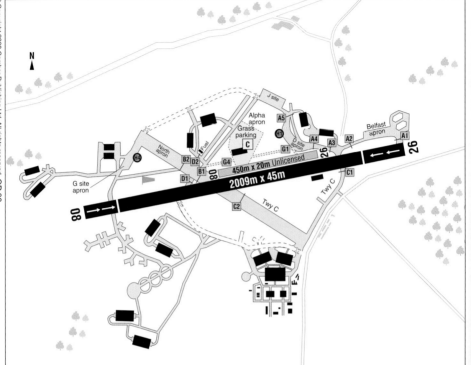

Rwy08/26 Grass U/L movements only

RNAV

Remarks

PPR. Non Radio ACFT not accepted. Hi-Vis. AD is multi-use including non-aviation use. Look out for microlights & model ACFT. All visitors welcome. Please book-in and pay landing fees in the TWR. Fees not settled before Dept will incur an admin charge. All fuel uploads must be paid for on the day. The ACFT commander or person nominated by the ACFT commander is responsible for passenger safety whilst airside. Straight in APP are not encouraged, standard overhead joins preferable.

Warnings

Pilots should avoid Aston Down 3.5nm NW, active cable launch glider site to 3000ft, often mistaken for Kemble. Oaksey Park AD 2.5nm to SE, South Cerney (parachuting) 5nm to ENE, keep good lookout for traffic. AD may close for special events, telephone for information.

Caution: Turbulence likely on APP Rwy26 with N or S wind.

Noise: Do not over fly any of the local villages. Kemble AD welcomes careful, noise conscious pilots. APP Rwy26 offset to S of Kemble village. APP to Rwy08 offset to N.

Operating Hrs 0800-1700 (Summer) 0900-1700 or SS whichever earlier (Winter) & by arr

Circuits LH all Rwys unless advised
Fast Jets 1500ft QFE
ACFT 1000ft QFE
Microlights 600ft QFE
Helicopters 700ft QFE
Paramotors 300ft QFE

Landing Fee See website for latest prices

Maintenance
Delta Jets **Tel:** 01285 771494

Fuel AVGAS 100LL JET A1 0900-1700 (L) by prior arr
Tel: 01285 771177

Disabled Facilities

Handling	**Tel:** 01285 771047 (Kemble Exec Handling Ops) **Tel:** 07824 311603 **Fax:** 01285 771498	**Operator**	Kemble Air Services Ltd The Control Tower, Kemble Airfield Cirencester, Glos, GL7 6BA **Tel:** 01285 771177 (Switchboard) **Fax:** 01285 771414 (TWR) ops@kemble.com www.kemble.com
Restaurant	AV8 **Tel:** 01285 771188		
Taxis/Car Hire	Info available **Tel:** 01285 771177		
Weather Info	Air SW MOEx		

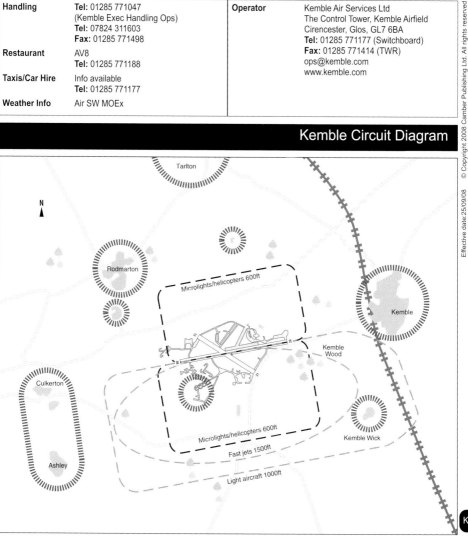

Kemble Circuit Diagram

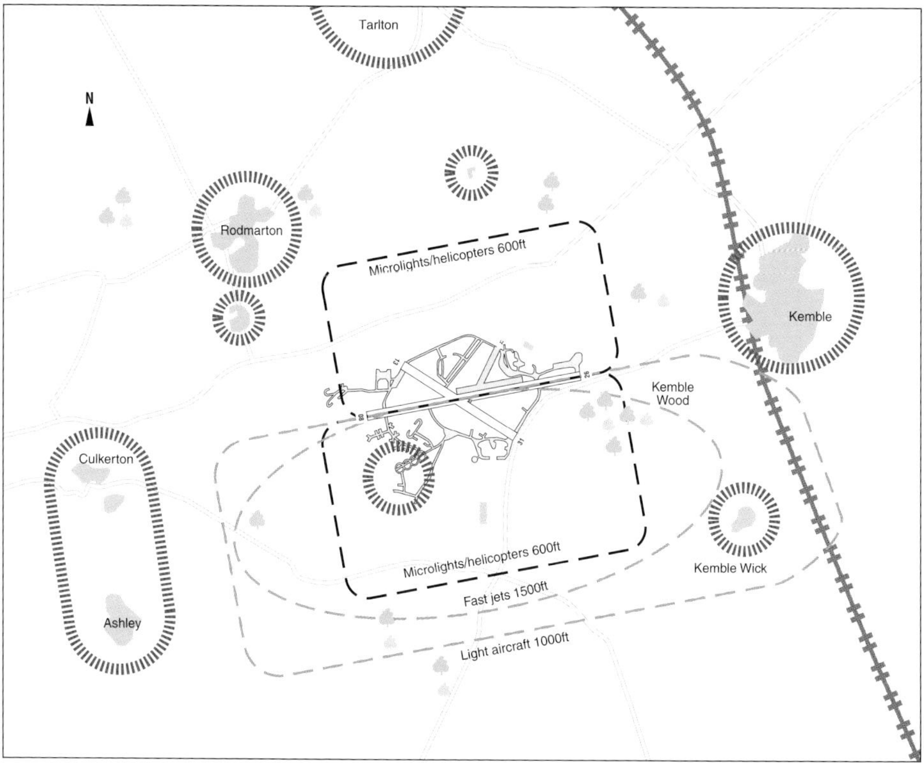

Tarlton
N
Rodmarton
Microlights/helicopters 600ft
Kemble
Kemble Wood
Culkerton
Microlights/helicopters 600ft
Kemble Wick
Fast jets 1500ft
Ashley
Light aircraft 1000ft

K

246ft 8mb	1nm W of Grafham Water N5218.98 W00022.75	PPR	Alternative AD	**Northampton** Peterborough Conington

Non Radio	LARS Cottesmore 130.200	Safetycom 135.475

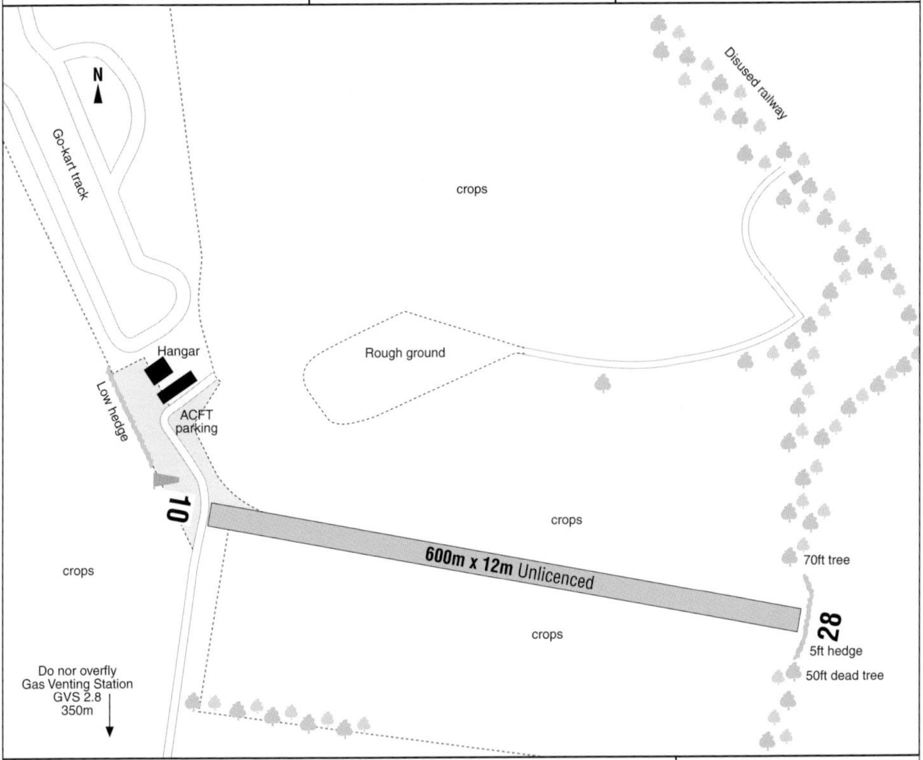

RWY	SURFACE	TORA	LDA	U/L	LIGHTING
10/28	Grass			600x12	Nil

RNAV			
BKY	116.25	322	25.5

Remarks
PPR by telephone. Visiting ACFT welcome subject to PPR at pilots own risk. Well maintained strip situated on SE corner of WWII AD.
Visual aid to location: Go-cart track to NW.

Warnings
Gas venting site SW of AD, max alt 28000ft. Do not over fly. Tree on Rwy28 APP which generate turbulence. Crops grown up to edge of Rwy.
Noise: Avoid over flying all local houses and villages.

Operating Hrs	SR-SS
Circuits	28 RH, 10 LH 1000ft QFE
Landing Fee	Nil
Maintenance	Nil
Fuel	Nil
Disabled Facilities	Nil
Restaurant	Nil
Taxi/Car Hire	Nil
Weather Info	Air Cen MOEx

Operator
Mr R C Convine
Yendis
Stow Longa
Huntingdon
Cambs
Tel: 01480 860300

K

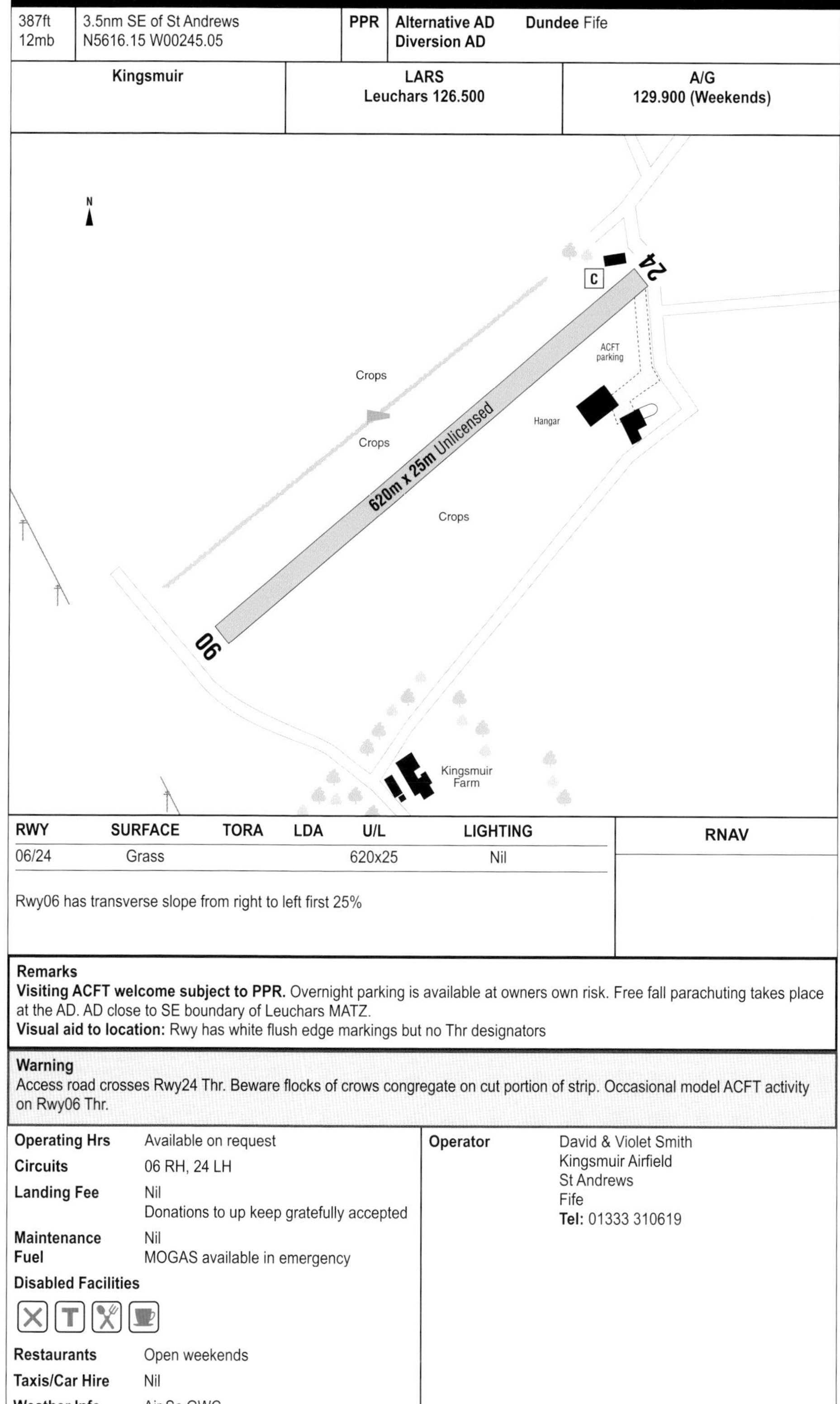

KINGSMUIR

387ft 12mb	3.5nm SE of St Andrews N5616.15 W00245.05	**PPR**	**Alternative AD** **Dundee** Fife **Diversion AD**

Kingsmuir	**LARS** **Leuchars 126.500**	**A/G** **129.900 (Weekends)**

RWY	SURFACE	TORA	LDA	U/L	LIGHTING
06/24	Grass			620x25	Nil

Rwy06 has transverse slope from right to left first 25%

RNAV

Remarks
Visiting ACFT welcome subject to PPR. Overnight parking is available at owners own risk. Free fall parachuting takes place at the AD. AD close to SE boundary of Leuchars MATZ.
Visual aid to location: Rwy has white flush edge markings but no Thr designators

Warning
Access road crosses Rwy24 Thr. Beware flocks of crows congregate on cut portion of strip. Occasional model ACFT activity on Rwy06 Thr.

Operating Hrs	Available on request
Circuits	06 RH, 24 LH
Landing Fee	Nil Donations to up keep gratefully accepted
Maintenance	Nil
Fuel	MOGAS available in emergency

Disabled Facilities

Restaurants	Open weekends
Taxis/Car Hire	Nil
Weather Info	Air Sc GWC

Operator
David & Violet Smith
Kingsmuir Airfield
St Andrews
Fife
Tel: 01333 310619

Effective date:25/09/08

22ft 0 mb	3nm NE of Forres N5738.96 W00333.64	PPR MIL	**Alternative AD** **Diversion AD**	**Inverness** Wick

Kinloss	APP	DEPS	TWR
	118.950	119.350	122.100

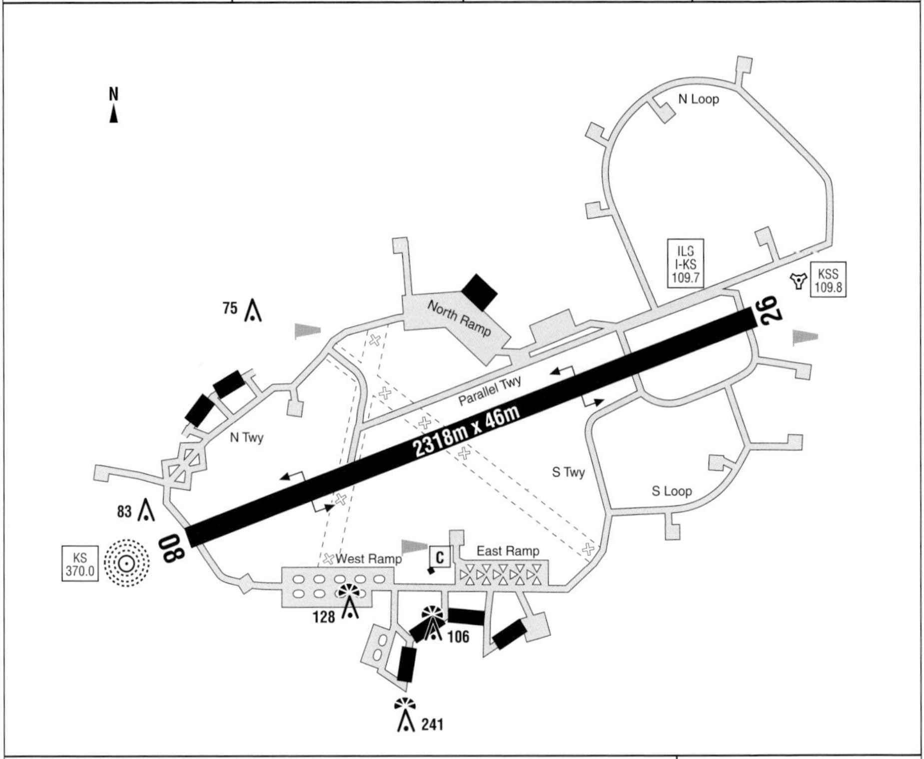

RWY	SURFACE	TORA	LDA	U/L	LIGHTING
08/26	Asph/Conc	2318	2318		Ap Thr Rwy PAPI 3° LH

Arrester gear normal ops: APP cable down overun cable up
Arrester gear Rwy26 704m from landing Thr, Arrester gear Rwy08 498m from landing Thr

RNAV			
INS	109.20	074	16.8

Remarks
PPR by telephone essential. RAF AD used by heavy ACFT situated in combined MATZ with Lossiemouth. Lossie also provide LARS service within the local area of Intense aerial activity. Civil ACFT not accepted on weather diversion.

Warnings
Parallel Twy used as Rwy in emergency. Inbound ACFT must contact Lossie APP at 50nm if APP at medium/high level and at 20nm when APP from low level.
Caution: Bird hazard, Geese activity may be encountered within 10nm of the AD from Sept-Apr. Glider flying activity on AD Sat-Sun & PH.
Noise: Do not over fly Langcot House (N side Rwy08 Thr), Binsness House (270°/2.5nm), Forres and Findhorn. Rwy26 all Dept maintain Rwy heading to 1000ft QFE before turning.

Operating Hrs	H24
Circuits	Normally LH
Landing Fees	Charges in accordance with MOD policy Contact Station Ops for details
Maintenance	Not normally available to civil visitors
Fuel	AVGAS JET A1 100LL by prior arr

Disabled Facilities

Taxi/Car Hire	Nil

Weather Info	M T Fax326 GWC
Operator	RAF Kinloss Forres Morrayshire IV36 3UH **Tel:** 01309 672161 Ex 7608 **Fax:** 01309 672161 Ex 7656

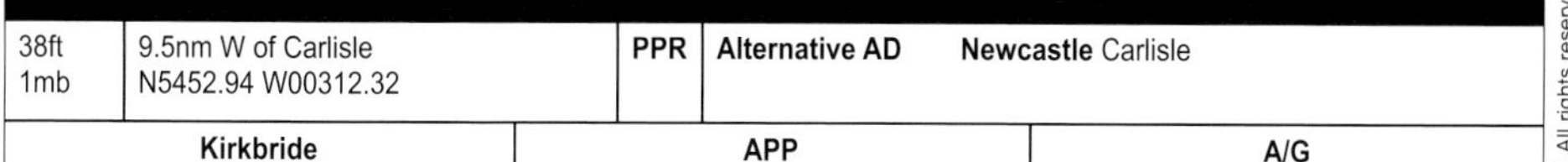

KIRKBRIDE

38ft 1mb	9.5nm W of Carlisle N5452.94 W00312.32	PPR	**Alternative AD**	**Newcastle** Carlisle

Kirkbride	APP Carlisle 123.600	A/G 124.400 (call at 10nm)

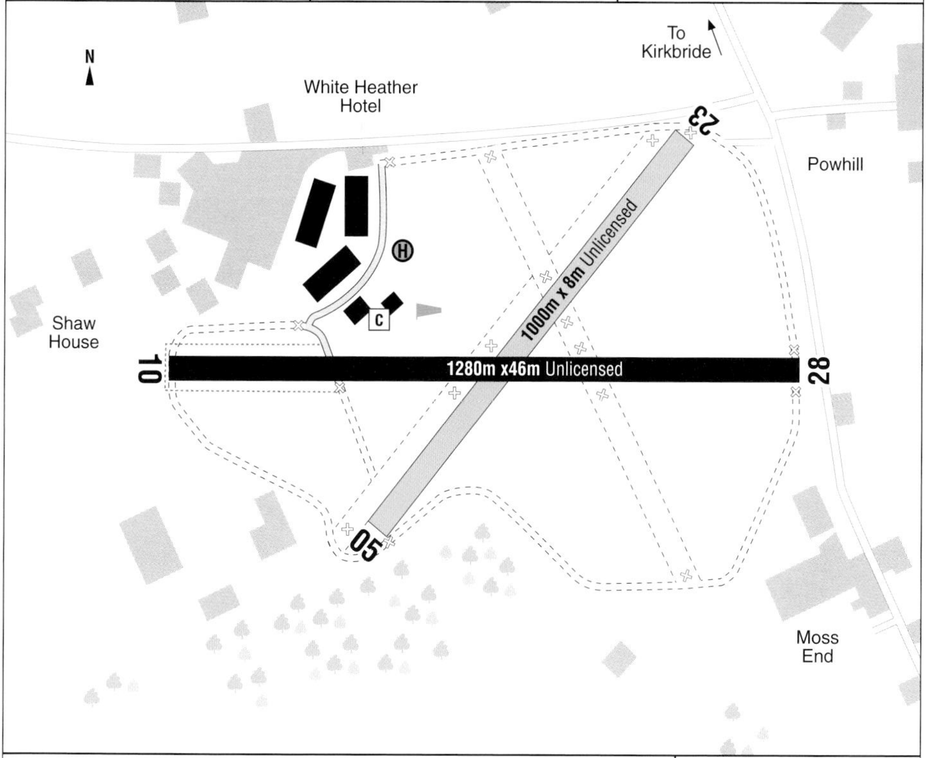

N
To Kirkbride
White Heather Hotel
Powhill
Shaw House
Moss End
C
H
10
28
05
23
1280m x46m Unlicensed
1000m x 8m Unlicensed

RWY	SURFACE	TORA	LDA	U/L	LIGHTING
05/23	Grass			1000x8	Nil
10/28	Asphalt			1280x46	Nil

RNAV			
DCS	115.20	031	10.7

Remarks
PPR by telephone. Visiting ACFT welcome at own risk. Microlight and autogyro activity at all times. Book in at white control tower. Parking on grass outside hangars.

Warnings
Considerable military low flying activity weekdays. HGV's may use AD manoeuvring area to access storage facilities on AD. Masts: TV 3nm SE of AD 1985ft amsl, 1034ft agl. 3.5nm S 1753ft amsl, 561ft agl & Anthorn Disused AD 2.5nm NW 778ft amsl, 561ft agl. Only one Twy useable. A wire fence 4ft high runs across Thr Rwy10 on both sides of Rwy up to first Twy intersection.
Noise: Do not over fly Kirkbride village.

Operating Hrs AD manned at weekends but available during week

Circuits All circuits to S 1000ft QFE

Landing Fee Nil

Maintenance Nil

Hangarage Available upon request

Fuel Nil

Disabled Facilities

Restaurants White Heather Hotel on AD
Tea & Coffee available in TWR

Taxis **Tel:** 01697 343148

Car Hire Nil

Weather Info Air N MOEx

Operator Solway Light Aviation Ltd
Kirkbride, Cumbria
CA7 5LF
Tel: 01697 342142
Tel; 07710 672087
Tel: 07796 955805

Effective date:25/09/08

135ft 4mb	1nm S of Kirkbymoorside N5415.00 W00057.00	PPR	**Alternative AD** **Durham Tees Valley** Full Sutton **Non-standard join**

Slingsby	LARS Linton 118.550	A/G 129.900

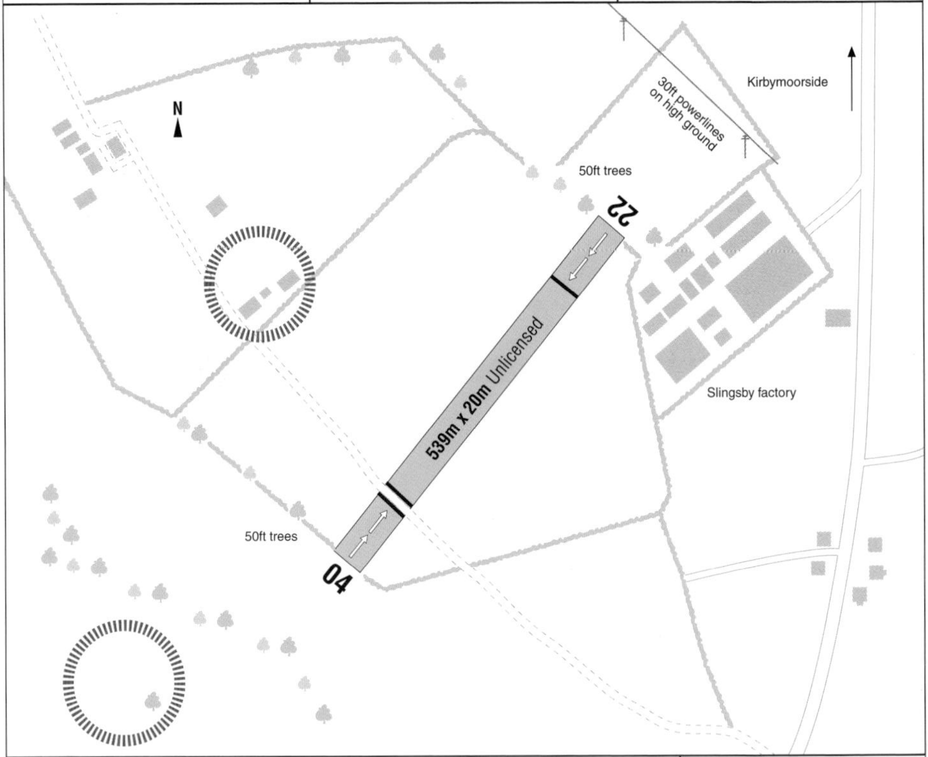

RWY	SURFACE	TORA	LDA	U/L	LIGHTING
04/22	Grass			539x20	Nil

RNAV

Remarks
PPR by telephone. Use of AD is restricted to visitors to Slingsby Aviation and company flight tests or by prior arr. Operations at pilots own risk.

Warnings
Domestic power lines on high GND on short final Rwy22. Trees close to APP may cause turbulence. After heavy/prolonged precipitation AD may be boggy. Considerable military low-level activity in the area. Wombleton AD is 1.5nm to SW.
Noise: Avoid over flight of local habitation.

Operating Hrs	PPR
Circuits	04 RH, 22 LH
Landing fee	Advised with PPR
Maintenance	Slingsby Aviation
Fuel	AVGAS 100LL by arr only

Disabled Facilities

Restaurant/Accomodation

George & Dragon	**Tel:** 01751 433334 (Hotel)
Kings Head	**Tel:** 01751 431340 (Hotel)
Fox & Hounds	**Tel:** 01751 731577 (Hotel, Sinnington approx 3nm from factory)

Taxi	**Tel:** 01751 431670
Car Hire	**Tel:** 01751 431214
Weather Info	Air N MOEx
Operator	Slingsby Advanced Composites Ltd Kirkbymoorside North Yorkshire YO62 6EZ **Tel:** 01751 432474 **Fax:** 01751 431173 sal5@slingsby.co.uk

KIRKNEWTON

652ft 21mb	5nm SW of Edinburgh AD N5552.45 W00324.00	PPR	Alternative AD	Edinburgh Cumbernauld

Non-standard join

Kirknewton	ATIS Edinburgh 131.350	APP Edinburgh 121.200	A/G 129.975

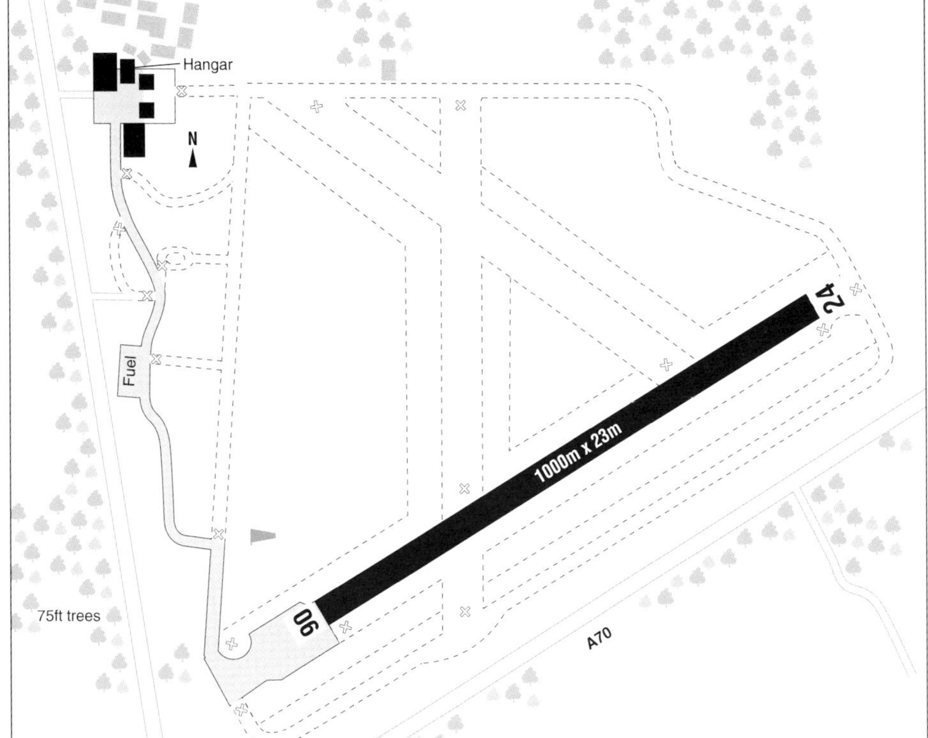

RWY	SURFACE	TORA	LDA	U/L	LIGHTING
06/24	Asphalt			1000x23	Nil

RNAV			
TLA	113.80	001	22.5

Remarks
Strict PPR via RAF Cranwell. Visiting ACFT welcome at pilots own risk. Strip on WWII AD, see map for usable sections of AD. Pilots must follow Arr/Dept procedures.

Warnings
AD situated inside Edinburgh CTA, Class D airspace. ATC gliding takes place on AD.
Noise: Avoid over flying houses to N of Rwy24 on dept.

Operating Hrs	SR-SS
Circuits	S 1000ft QFE
Landing Fee	Available with PPR
Maintenance	Nil
Fuel	Nil
Disabled Facilities	Nil
Restaurant	Nil
Taxi/Car Hire	Nil
Weather Info	Air Sc GWC

Operator
HQ Air Cadets
RAF Cranwell
Sleaford
Lincs
NG34 8HB
Tel: 01400 267612 (PPR)
Tel: 07771 942452 (PPR)

Effective date:25/09/08 OP 08

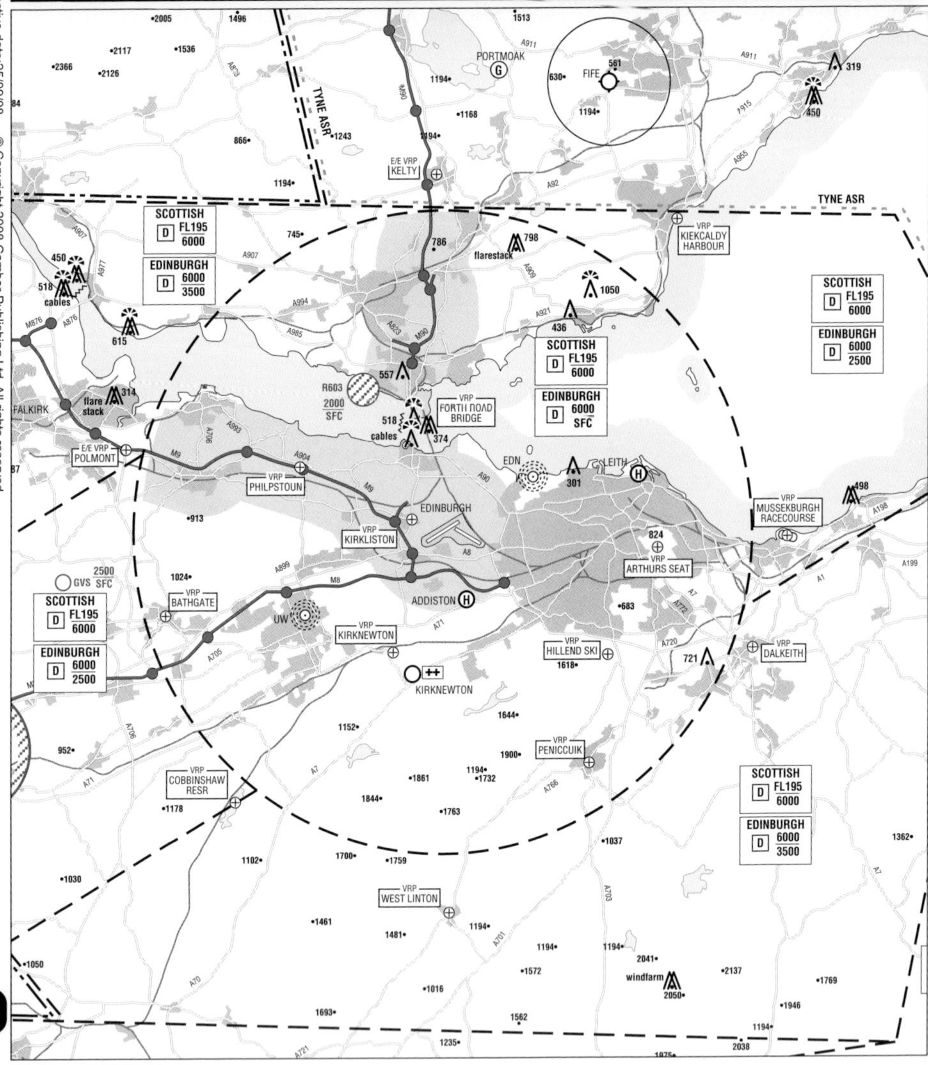

Arrivals

1 Standard VFR Cobbinshaw
Via Cobbinshaw Reservoir not above 2000ft. Follow A70.

2 Standard VFR Hillend/Dalkeith
Via Hillend or Dalkeith not above 2000ft.

3 Standard Kelty
Via Edibugh overhead at 1500-2000ft, as directed by ATC. Then into Kelty lane.

Departures
Rwy24 Dept must turn left and route overhead AD before turning towards the Edinburgh overhead.
All ACFT dept Kirknewton must book out with Edinburgh APP and establish contact with Edinburgh ATC before Dept.
All ACFT must contact Edinburgh APP at least 5mins before edge of boundary.

Edinburgh CTR – Class D Airspace
Normal CTA/CTR Class D Airspace rules apply.
Transition Alt 6000ft

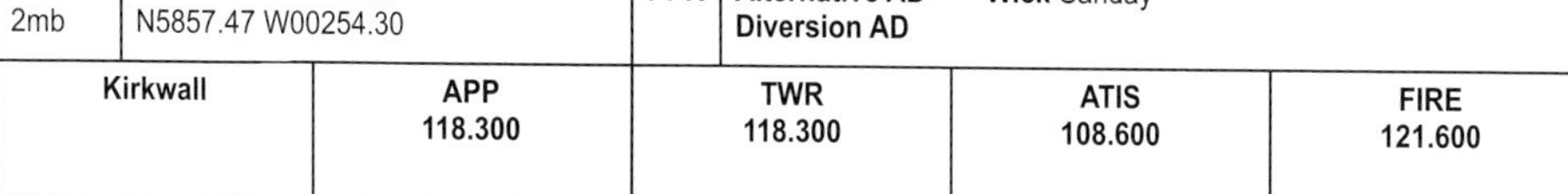

58ft 2mb	2.5nm SE of Kirkwall N5857.47 W00254.30	PPR	Alternative AD Diversion AD	Wick Sanday

Kirkwall	APP	TWR	ATIS	FIRE
	118.300	118.300	108.600	121.600

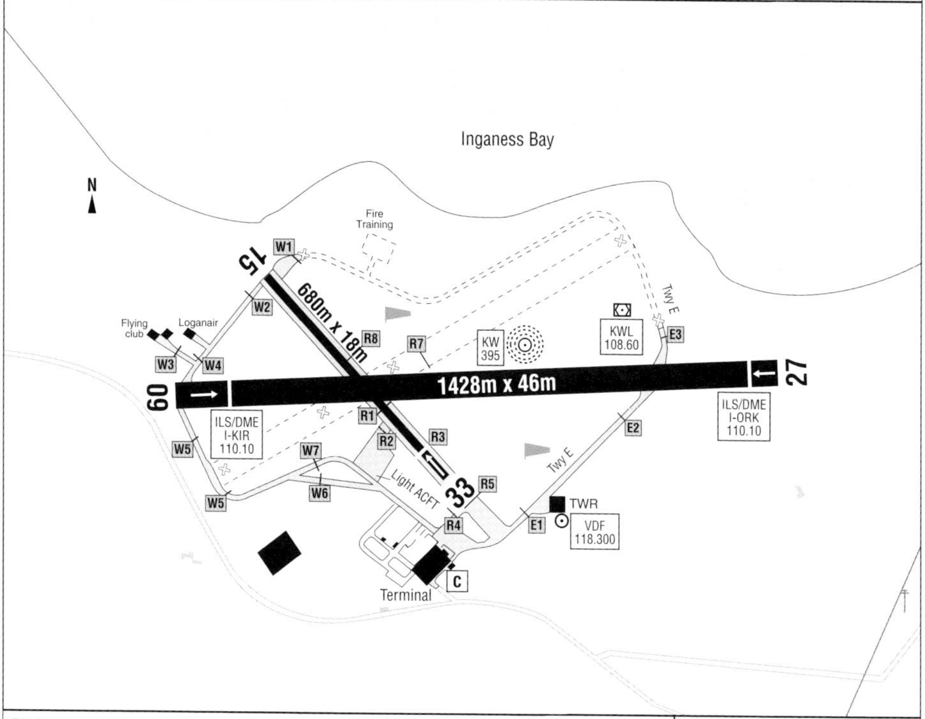

Inganess Bay
N
Fire Training
W1 W2 W3 W4 W5 W6 W7
15 680m x 18m 33
R1 R2 R3 R4 R5 R7 R8
Flying club
Loganair
KW 395
KWL 108.60
E1 E2 E3
Twy E
09 1428m x 46m 27
ILS/DME I-KIR 110.10
ILS/DME I-ORK 110.10
Light ACFT
TWR
VDF 118.300
C
Terminal

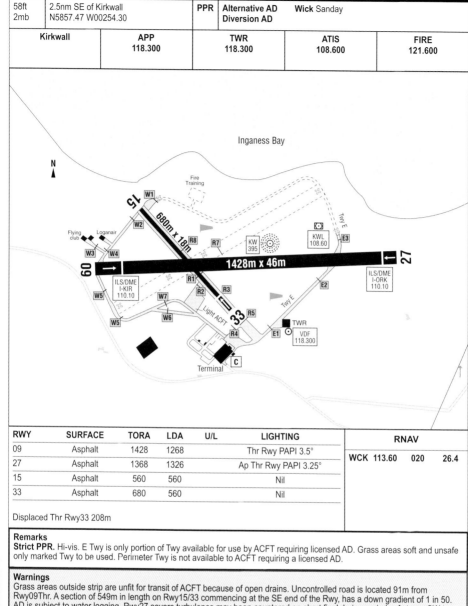

RWY	SURFACE	TORA	LDA	U/L	LIGHTING
09	Asphalt	1428	1268		Thr Rwy PAPI 3.5°
27	Asphalt	1368	1326		Ap Thr Rwy PAPI 3.25°
15	Asphalt	560	560		Nil
33	Asphalt	680	560		Nil

Displaced Thr Rwy33 208m

RNAV			
WCK	113.60	020	26.4

Remarks
Strict PPR. Hi-vis. E Twy is only portion of Twy available for use by ACFT requiring licensed AD. Grass areas soft and unsafe only marked Twy to be used. Perimeter Twy is not available to ACFT requiring a licensed AD.

Warnings
Grass areas outside strip are unfit for transit of ACFT because of open drains. Uncontrolled road is located 91m from Rwy09Thr. A section of 549m in length on Rwy15/33 commencing at the SE end of the Rwy, has a down gradient of 1 in 50. AD is subject to water logging. Rwy27 severe turbulence may been countered on short final during periods of strong SW to NW winds. Security post 3m high at edge of apron adjacent to passenger gate.

Operating Hrs Mon-Fri 0630-1845 Sat 0630-1745 Sun 0800-1845 (Summer) +1Hr (Winter) & by arr

Circuits Nil

Landing Fee ACFT up to 3MT £11.79. Payable on Arr

Maintenance Ltd engineering facilities available from Loganair on request

Fuel AVGAS JET A1 100LL Oil
Tel: 01856 872415

Disabled Facilities

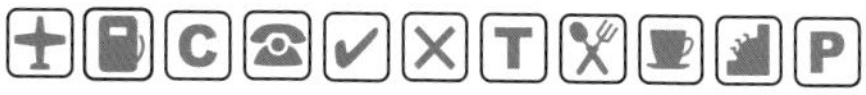

Restaurants Light refreshments at AD

Taxis Available at taxi rank outside terminal

Car Hire
W R Tullock **Tel:** 01856 875500

Weather Info M T9 Fax 328 GWC
ATIS **Tel:** 01856 878476

Visual Reference Points (VRP)
Foot N5901.72 W00248.38
Lamb Holm Island N5853.23 W00253.60
Stromberry N5901.82 W00256.02

Operator HIAL Kirkwall Airport
Kirkwall
Orkney, KW15 1TH
Tel: 01856 872421
Tel: 01856 886205 (ATC)
Fax: 01856 875051
www.highlands-and-islands-airports.co.uk

290ft 9mb	4.5nm SE of Oswestry N5248.27 W00259.45	PPR	Alternative AD	Hawarden Sleap

Non-radio	LARS Shawbury 120.775	Safetycom 135.475

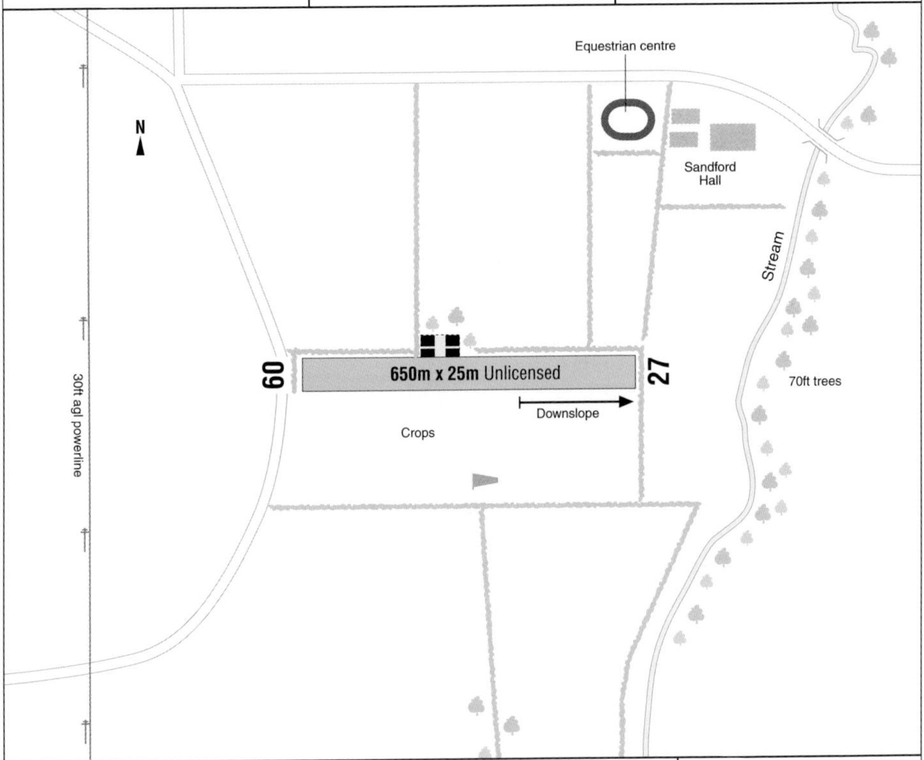

Equestrian centre
N
Sandford Hall
Stream
09
650m x 25m Unlicensed
27
Downslope
70ft trees
Crops
30ft agl powerline

RWY	SURFACE	TORA	LDA	U/L	LIGHTING
09/27	Grass			650x25	Nil

RNAV			
SWB	116.80	281	11.9

Remarks
PPR by telephone. Well prepared grass strip. Light ACFT visitors welcome at own risk. AD used by RAF Shawbury for helicopter training (weekdays).

Warnings
6ft hedgerow runs along N edge of strip & crosses both Thr. Conifer tree on N edge of strip adjacent to hangars. Down slope in final 1/3rd Rwy09. A copse of mature trees bordering a stream crosses Rwy27 APP 250m from Thr. Power cables 30ft cross Rwy27 APP 400m from Thr. RAF Shawbury helicopter activity in vicinity.

Operating Hrs	SR-SS
Circuits	As you wish, avoid local habitation
Landing Fee	Nil
Maintenance	Nil
Fuel	Nil
Disabled Facilities	Nil
Restaurants	Nil
Taxis	**Tel:** 01691 650651
Car Hire	Nil
Weather Info	Air N MOEx

Operator
Mr T R Jones
Sandford Hall
West Felton
Oswestry
Shropshire, TF11 4EX
Tel: 01691 610889
(PPR during office Hrs)
Tel: 01691 610206 (PPR evenings)
Fax: 01691 690699

50ft 1mb	5nm E of Tonbridge N5111.60 E00024.80	PPR	**Alternative AD**	**Manston** Rochester

Non-Radio	**LARS** **Southend 130.775**	**Safetycom** **135.475**

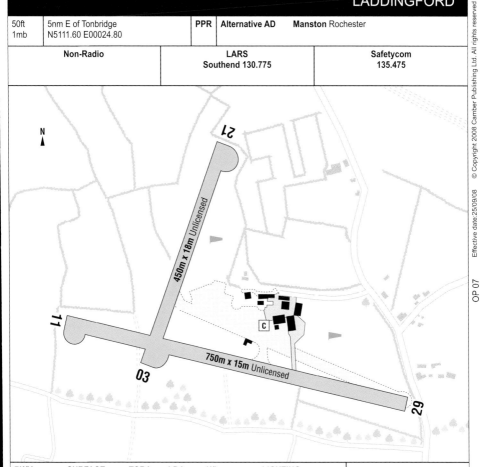

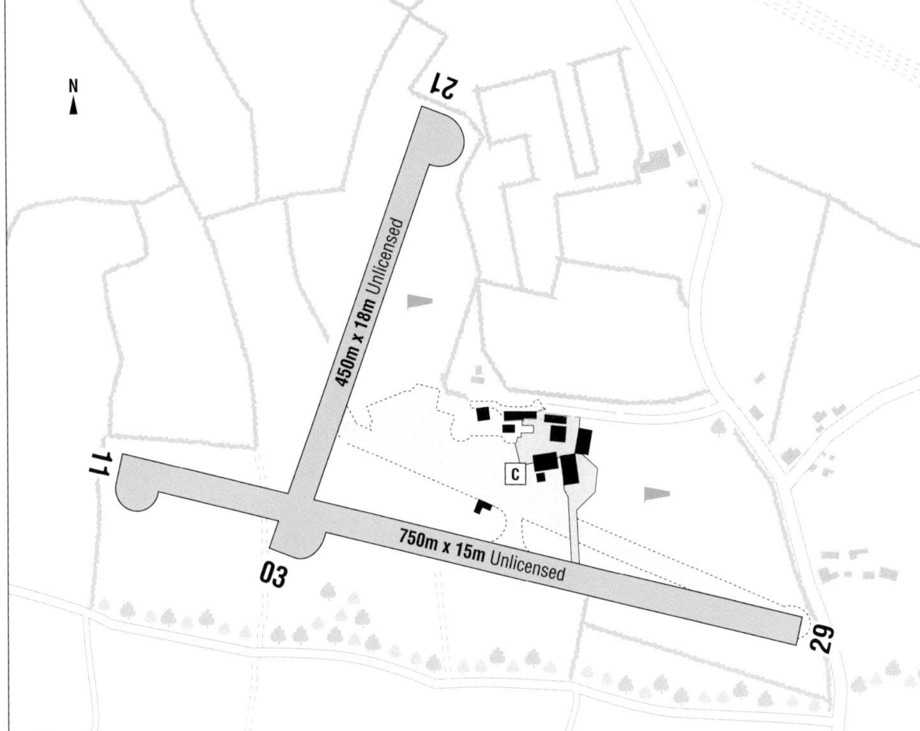

RWY	SURFACE	TORA	LDA	U/L	LIGHTING
11/29	Grass			750x15	Nil
03/21	Grass			450x18	Nil

RNAV			
DET	**117.30**	**229**	**9.6**

Remarks
PPR. Visiting ACFT welcome at pilots own risk.

Warnings
ACFT must keep to well-prepared mown strip and manoeuvring areas. Heavy wet land may prevail during the winter months making AD unusable.
Noise: Avoid over flying the villages of Laddingford and Paddock Wood.

Operating Hrs SR-SS

Circuits 11, 21 LH, 29, 03 RH 1000ft QFE

Landing Fee £5

Maintenance Nil

Fuel Nil

Disabled Facilities

Restaurants Pubs in Laddingford village, 1 mile N

Taxis **Tel:** 01892 837799
Tel: 01892 835050
Tel: 01892 838383

Car Hire Nil

Weather Info Air SE MOEx

Operator Laddingford Aero Club
T/A Laddingford Farm Ltd
c/o Badger Cottage
Sham Farm Road
Eridge Green
Tunbridge Wells
Kent TN3 9JD
Tel: 07712 502030
Tel: 07801 721128
2pk@peterkember.co.uk

Effective date:25/09/08

EGUL LAKENHEATH

32ft 1mb	2.5nm SW of Brandon N5224.56 E00033.66	PPR MIL	Alternative AD Diversion AD	**Cambridge** Old Buckenham **Non-standard join**

Lakenheath	APP	APP	TWR	DEPT
	128.900 (Civil)	136.500 (Military)	122.100	137.250

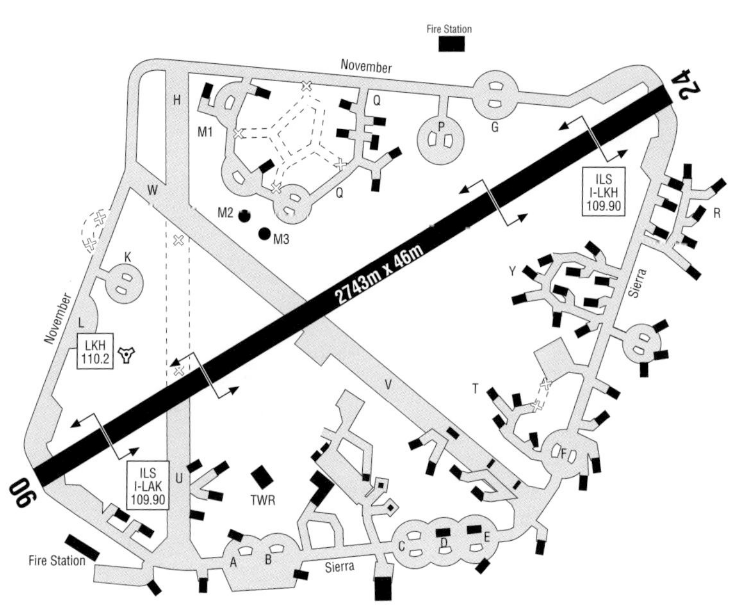

RWY	SURFACE	TORA	LDA	U/L	LIGHTING
06/24	Asph/Conc	2743	2743		Ap Thr Rwy PAPI 3° LH

Lighting strobe lead in
Arrestor cables strung at 762m, 1981m & 2378m from Thr

RNAV

L

Remarks
Official business only. 72Hrs PPR by telephone essential. Non-military visitors accepted after approval process has been completed. AD operated by USAF.

Warnings
Rwy equipped with arrestor gear. Visiting Piston engined pilots are advised to obtain information on advisability of trampling this equipment with PPR request. All inbound ACFT should contact APP in good time to ascertain state of EGD203, situated 7-12nm finals for Rwy24. High performance jet operations on AD.
Noise: ACFT should avoid over flying all local towns

Operating Hrs	Mon-Thu 0600-2200 Fri 0600-1800 (Summer) +1Hr (Winter) Sat-Sun & US PH AD closed unless PPR obtained. ATZ 24Hrs
Circuits	To N
Landing Fee	Charges in accordance with USAF policy Contact AD Ops for details
Maintenance	Nil
Fuel	JET A1 strictly by prior arr
Disabled Facilities	Nil
Restaurants	Nil
Taxis/Car Hire	Nil
Weather Info	Air S MOEx
Operator	48 FW USAF RAF Lakenheath Brandon Suffolk IP27 9PN **Tel:** 01638 524186/522439 (AD Ops)

65ft 2mb	4nm S of Kirkwall Airport N5853.18 W00253.60	PPR	**Alternative AD** **Kirkwall** Wick **Diversion AD**

Lamb Holm	**APP** **Kirkwall 118.300**	**A/G** **129.825** **Microlight Ops**

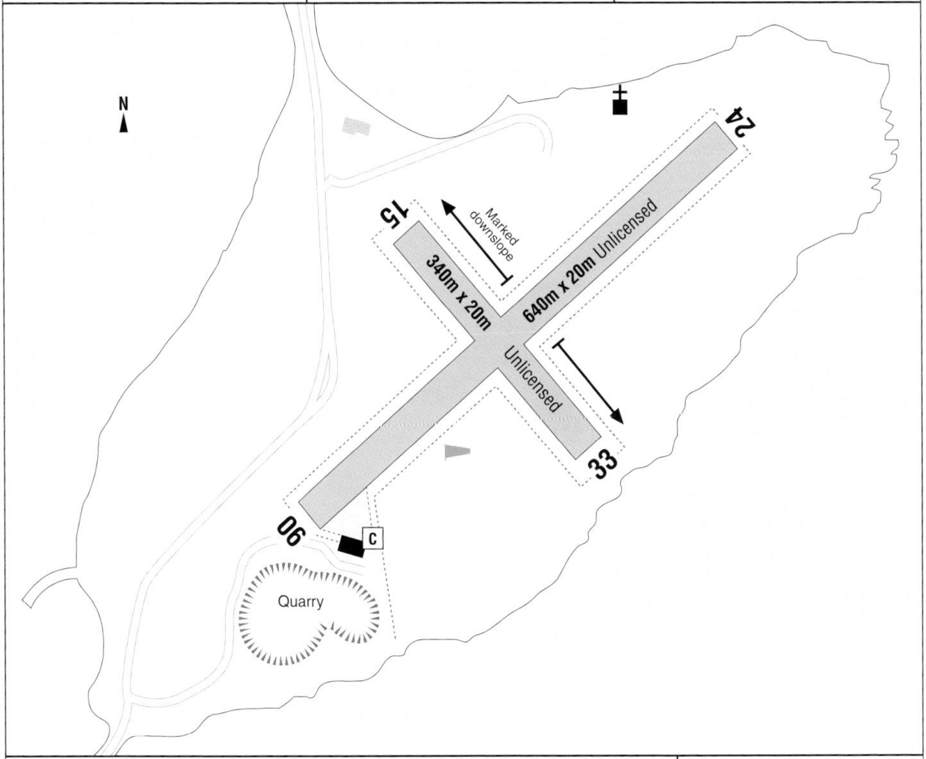

N
24
15
Marked downslope
340m x 20m
640m x 20m Unlicensed
Unlicensed
33
06
C
Quarry

RWY	SURFACE	TORA	LDA	U/L	LIGHTING
06/24	Grass			640x20	Nil
15/33	Grass			340x20	Nil

Rwy06/24 fence to fence distance 658m
Rwy15/33 severe hump-back only use when strong winds preclude

RNAV			
KWL	**108.60**	**186**	**4.4**

Remarks
PPR by telephone. Visiting ACFT welcome own risk. AD close to S boundary Kirkwall ATZ, keep good look out for commercial traffic operating low level VFR in the area. Inbound make initial call to Kirkwall. Kirkwall town centre approx 7 miles by road. Italian chapel (hand painted to resemble a basilica by Italian prisoners of War) is short walk.

Warning
Width of strip between fencing is 40m, 20m Rwy & 10m each side rough grass. 20ft electricity pole (no wires) 120m from Rwy15 Thr. 4ft boundary fence, wooden poles & barbed wire surrounds AD.
Caution: Turbulence near the quarry.
Noise: Avoid over flying St. Mary's village 1nm NW of AD.

Operating Hrs	SR-SS
Circuits	06, 15 RH, 24, 33 LH
Landing Fee	Nil Donation accepted
Maintenance	Nil
Fuel	Mogas by arr
Disabled Facilities	Nil
Restaurants	15min walk across causeway food & accomodation
Commodore Motel	**Tel:** 01856 781319
Taxis	**Tel:** 01856 876543

Car Hire	**Tel:** 01856 872866
National	**Tel:** 01856 875500 **Fax:** 01856 874458
Weather Info	M T9 Fax 328 GWC
Operator	Tom Sinclair Tighsith, Holm Orkney Islands, KW17 2RX **Tel:** 0780 3088938 (Days) **Tel/Fax:** 01856 781310 (Home/Evenings)

Effective date:25/09/08 OP 07

300ft 10mb	4nm NE of Nottingham N5300.55 W00103.48	PPR	Alternative AD	East Midlands Syerston

Lambley Radio	APP East Mids 134.175	A/G Hucknall 130.800	A/G 123.050 Only occasionally manned

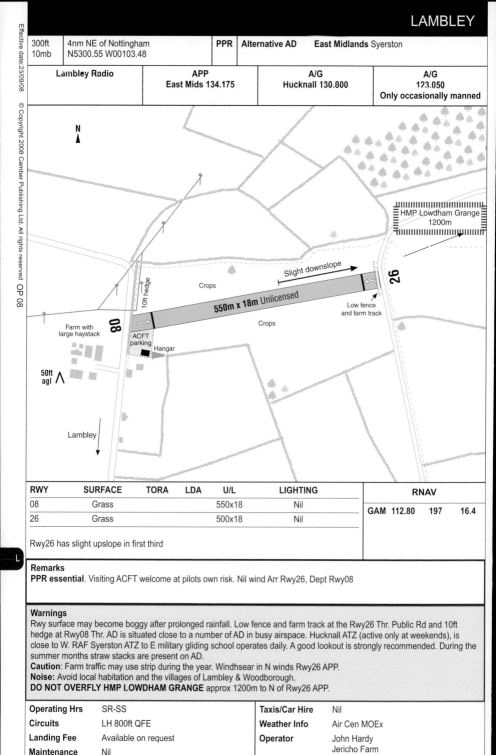

RWY	SURFACE	TORA	LDA	U/L	LIGHTING
08	Grass			550x18	Nil
26	Grass			500x18	Nil

Rwy26 has slight upslope in first third

RNAV			
GAM	112.80	197	16.4

Remarks
PPR essential. Visiting ACFT welcome at pilots own risk. Nil wind Arr Rwy26, Dept Rwy08

Warnings
Rwy surface may become boggy after prolonged rainfall. Low fence and farm track at the Rwy26 Thr. Public Rd and 10ft hedge at Rwy08 Thr. AD is situated close to a number of AD in busy airspace. Hucknall ATZ (active only at weekends), is close to W. RAF Syerston ATZ to E military gliding school operates daily. A good lookout is strongly recommended. During the summer months straw stacks are present on AD.
Caution: Farm traffic may use strip during the year. Windhsear in N winds Rwy26 APP.
Noise: Avoid local habitation and the villages of Lambley & Woodborough.
DO NOT OVERFLY HMP LOWDHAM GRANGE approx 1200m to N of Rwy26 APP.

Operating Hrs	SR-SS
Circuits	LH 800ft QFE
Landing Fee	Available on request
Maintenance	Nil
Fuel	AVGAS in emergency
Disabled Facilities	

Restaurant	Pub 800yds in village
Taxis/Car Hire	Nil
Weather Info	Air Cen MOEx
Operator	John Hardy Jericho Farm Green Lane Lambley, Notts, NG4 4QE **Tel**: 0115 9313530 (Home/Office) **Tel**: 0115 9313639 (Hangar) **Tel**: 07768 726279 JW.Hardy@farmline.com

401ft 13mb	5nm W of Penzance N5006.17 W00540.23	PPR	**Alternative AD** **Diversion AD**	**St Mawgan** Perranporth

Lands End	LARS Culdrose 134.050	TWR 120.250 (Mon-Sat)	A/G 120.250 (Sun)

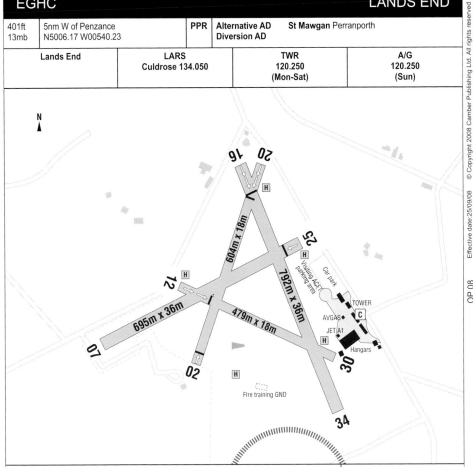

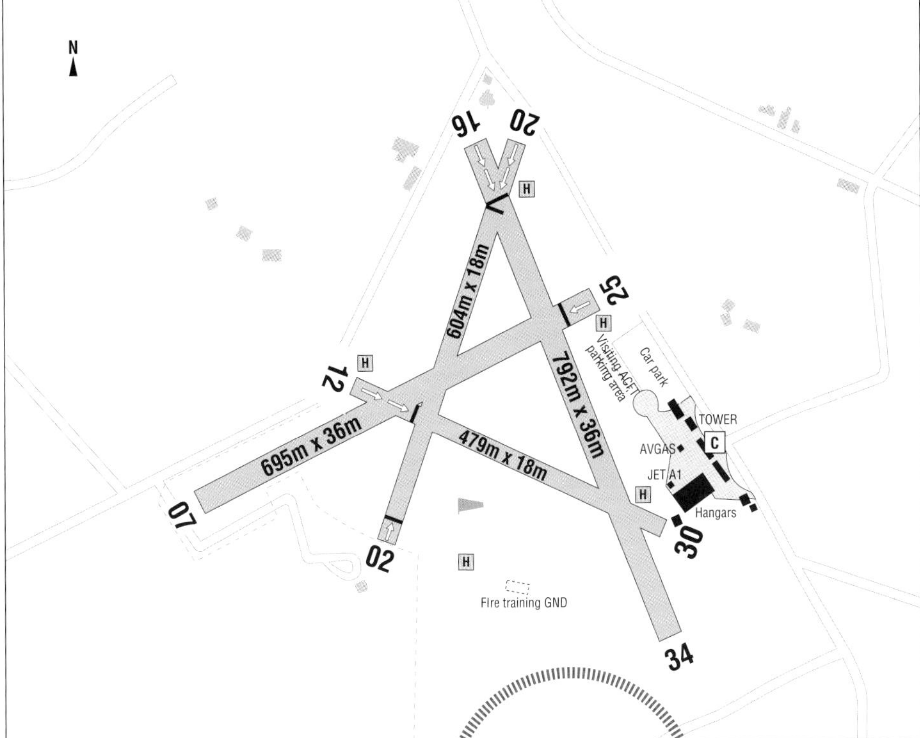

RWY	SURFACE	TORA	LDA	U/L	LIGHTING
07	Grass	677	677		Nil
25	Grass	695	630		Nil
16	Grass	792	707		Nil
34	Grass	778	778		APAPI 4° LHS
12	Grass	479	417		Nil
30	Grass	506	–		Nil
02	Grass	574	544		Nil
20	Grass	574	436		Nil

Displaced Thr Rwy16 85m, Displaced Thr Rwy02 30m, Displaced Thr Rwy12 62m
Displaced Thr Rwy25 65m, Displaced Thr Rwy20 138m, Starter extension Rwy30 27m
Rwy30 not available for ACFT requiring a licensed Rwy for landing

RNAV			
LND	114.20	219	2.3

Remarks

Strict PPR by telephone. Non radio ACFT not accepted. Hi-vis. Entire grass area is maintained and useable. Rwy16/34 & 07/25 are sufficiently wide to allow differential use of each side of Rwy to conserve grass surfaces. Pilots may be asked to use Rwy (left or right) in order to achieve this. Passengers are not permitted on the refuelling area. Schedule flights to the Scillies operate using the Lands End Transit Corridor SFC-2000ft QNH.

Warning

AD prone to rapid weather changes. When parachuting in progress permission must be obtained before starting engines or engaging rotors. ACFT may be held outside the ATZ until all canopies have landed. Parts of the manoeuvring area are undulating. Public footpath crosses Rwy02 Thr. Turning circle used extensively by helicopters lifting loads.

Noise: Avoid over flying St Just village N of AD and houses S of AD.

Effective date:25/09/08 OP 08

Operating Hrs	
TWR	Mon-Sat 0730-1700 (Summer) Mon 0800-1200, 1330-1700 Tue-Fri 0800-1700 Sat 0900-1200, 1330-1700 (Winter)
A/G	Sun 0800-1700 (Summer) Mon & Sat 1200-1330 Sun 0900-1700 (Winter)
Circuits	LH & RH 1000ft QFE
Landing Fee	Single £13 Twin £18 Microlight £6
Maintenance	
Westward	**Tel:** 01736 788771
Fuel	AVGAS JET A1 Oil 80 W80 W100
Disabled Facilities	
Restaurant	Restaurant, club facilities & garden viewing area available
Taxis	
Country Cars	**Tel:** 01736 333919
Rosevale Cars	**Tel:** 01736 810751
Village Cars	**Tel:** 07703 112031
Car Hire	
Enterprise	**Tel:** 01736 332000
Weather Info	Air SW MOEx

Operator
Westward Airways Ltd
Land's End Aerodrome
St Just, Cornwall, TR19 7RL
Tel: 01736 788771 (Operator)
Tel: 01736 788944 (ATC)
Fax: 01736 788366
Fax: 01736 786450 (ATC)
flyingschool@isleofscilly-travel.co.uk
www.landsendairport.co.uk

L

Lands End Transit Corridor

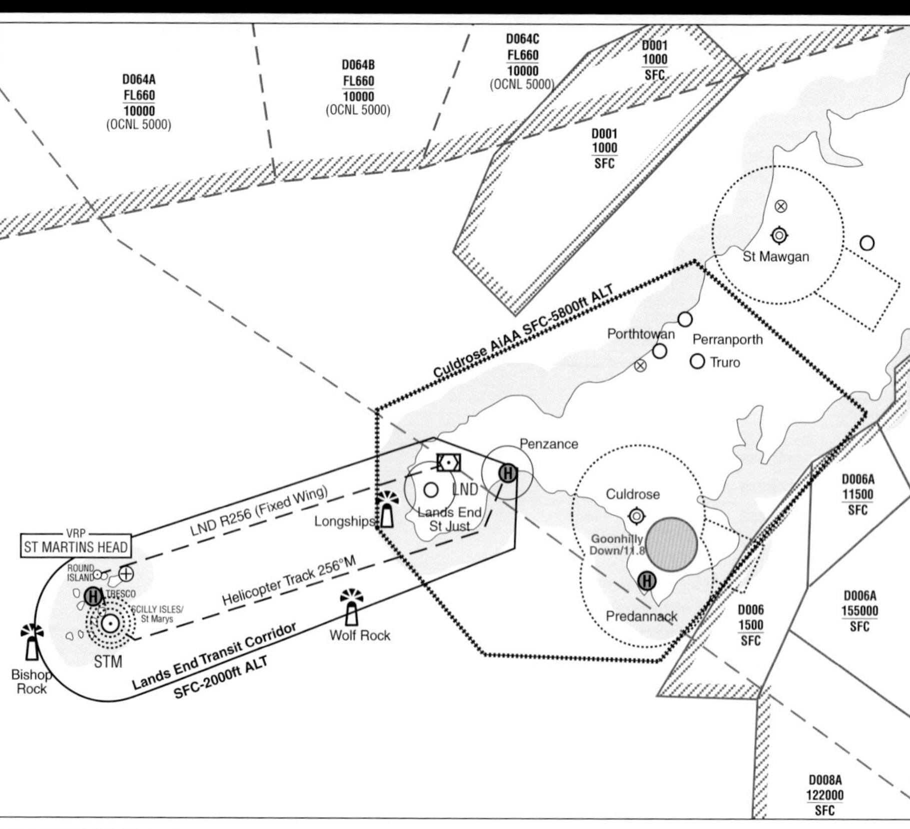

Reporting Points – all nm to run to St Mary's Airport (Scillies)

	LND VOR/DME	
1 Charlie	10 DME	18nm to run
2 Midpoint	17 DME	11nm to run
3 25	25 DME	3.5nm to run

109ft 4mb	10nm ESE of Nottingham N5253.63 W00054.27	PPR	Alternative AD Diversion AD	East Midlands Nottingham

Non-standard join

Langar	LARS Cottesmore 130.200	Para Base 129.900

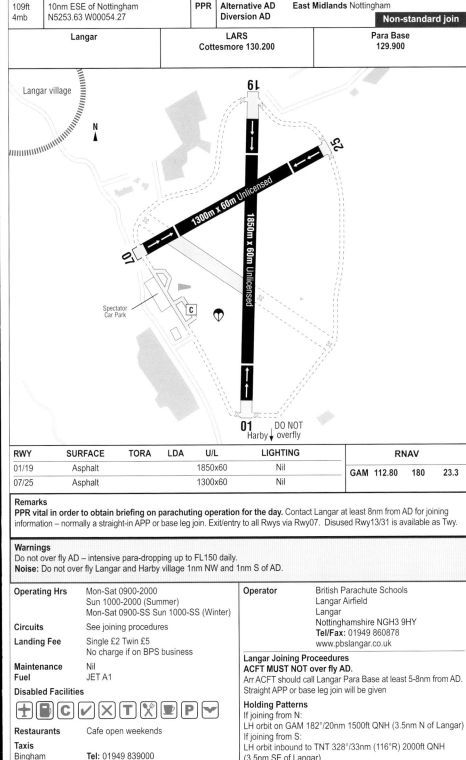

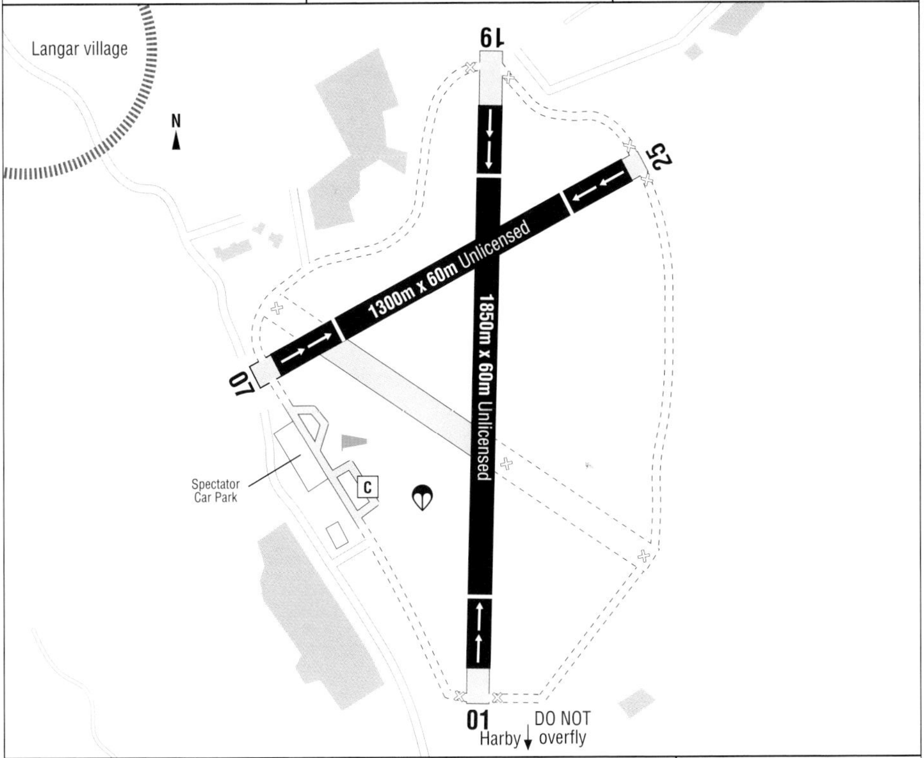

Langar village
N
19
25
1300m x 60m Unlicensed
1850m x 60m Unlicensed
07
Spectator Car Park
C
01
Harby
DO NOT overfly

RWY	SURFACE	TORA	LDA	U/L	LIGHTING
01/19	Asphalt			1850x60	Nil
07/25	Asphalt			1300x60	Nil

RNAV			
GAM	112.80	180	23.3

Remarks

PPR vital in order to obtain briefing on parachuting operation for the day. Contact Langar at least 8nm from AD for joining information – normally a straight-in APP or base leg join. Exit/entry to all Rwys via Rwy07. Disused Rwy13/31 is available as Twy.

Warnings

Do not over fly AD – intensive para-dropping up to FL150 daily.
Noise: Do not over fly Langar and Harby village 1nm NW and 1nm S of AD.

Operating Hrs Mon-Sat 0900-2000
Sun 1000-2000 (Summer)
Mon-Sat 0900-SS Sun 1000-SS (Winter)

Circuits See joining procedures

Landing Fee Single £2 Twin £5
No charge if on BPS business

Maintenance Nil

Fuel JET A1

Disabled Facilities

Restaurants Cafe open weekends

Taxis
Bingham **Tel:** 01949 839000

Car Hire Nil

Weather Info Air Cen MOEx

Operator British Parachute Schools
Langar Airfield
Langar
Nottinghamshire NGH3 9HY
Tel/Fax: 01949 860878
www.pbslangar.co.uk

Langar Joining Proceedures
ACFT MUST NOT over fly AD.
Arr ACFT should call Langar Para Base at least 5-8nm from AD. Straight APP or base leg join will be given

Holding Patterns
If joining from N:
LH orbit on GAM 182°/20nm 1500ft QNH (3.5nm N of Langar)
If joining from S:
LH orbit inbound to TNT 328°/33nm (116°R) 2000ft QNH (3.5nm SE of Langar)

Effective date:25/09/08 OP 08

L

618ft 21mb	5nm SE of Basingstoke N5111.17 W00101.83	PPR	**Alternative AD** **Diversion AD**	**Farnborough** Blackbushe **Non-standard join**

Lasham	LARS Farnborough West 125.250	A/C 131.025

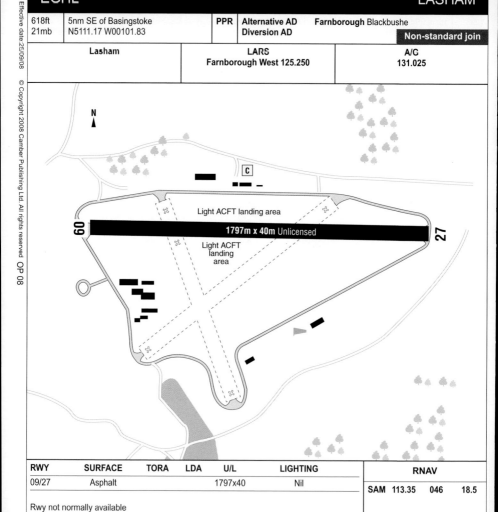

N
C
Light ACFT landing area
09
1797m x 40m Unlicensed
27
Light ACFT landing area

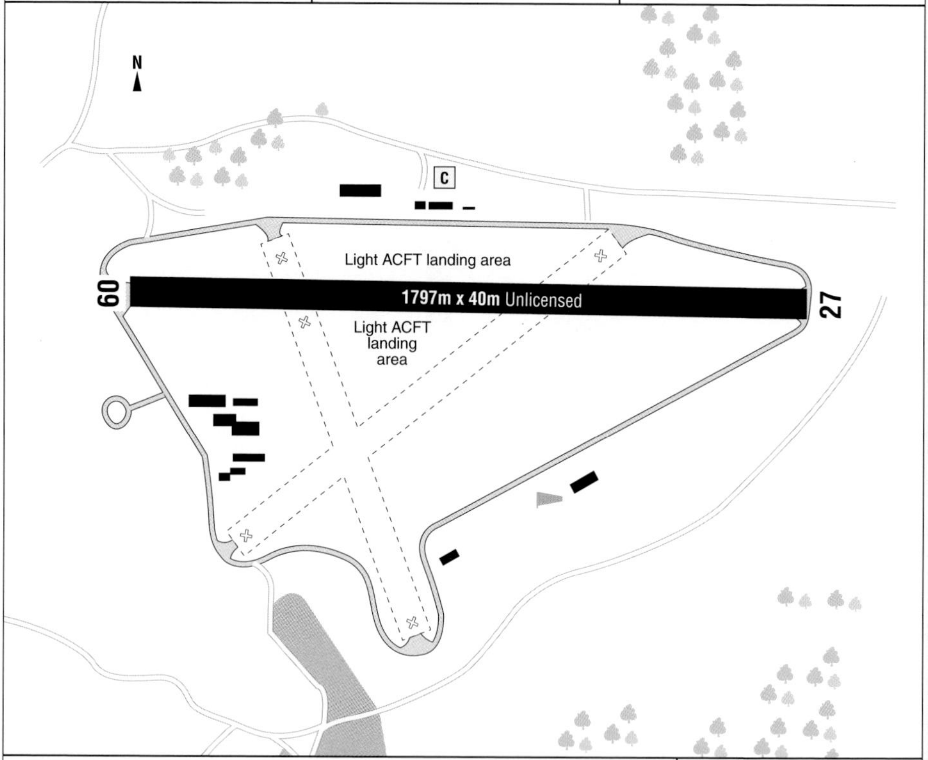

RWY	SURFACE	TORA	LDA	U/L	LIGHTING
09/27	Asphalt			1797x40	Nil

Rwy not normally available
Landing on grass only

RNAV			
SAM	113.35	046	18.5

L

Remarks
PPR strictly by telephone. AD is only available to persons having business with Lasham Gliding Society. Light ACFT must use grass area N of main Rwy or centre triangle dependent on Rwy in use. Visiting pilots & passengers are required to become temporary members, indemnifying the society of all liability.

Warnings
Extreme caution due to cables winch launching to 3000ft agl. Parts of AD surfaces are unsuitable for the movement of ACFT. Intense gliding activity takes place on AD. Occasionally AD used by heavy ACFT for maintenance. Contact Farnborough LARS for clearance in Odiham MATZ.

Operating Hrs Strictly PPR
Gliding business only
Circuits Nil
Landing Fee N/A
Maintenance Nil
Fuel Nil
Disabled Facilities

Adapted K21 Glider available
Restaurant Clubhouse facilities available at AD

Taxis
Alton **Tel:** 01420 84455
Ames **Tel:** 01420 83309
Car Hire
National **Tel:** 01256 477777
Weather Info Air SE MOEx
Operator Lasham Gliding Society Ltd
Lasham Aerodrome
Lasham, Alton
Hants, GU34 5SS
Tel: 01256 384900

EGKH LASHENDEN

72ft 2mb	8nm S of Maidstone N5109.42 E00038.50	PPR	**Alternative AD** **Manston** Rochester **Diversion AD**

Non-standard join

Lashenden	A/G 122.000

N
River Beult
11
840m x 30m
29
21
312m x 29m Unlicensed
03
T
C
HLS 115.95
LSH 115.95

RWY	SURFACE	TORA	LDA	U/L	LIGHTING
11/29	Grass	840	840		Nil
03/21	Grass			312x29	Nil

Rwy03/21 Tiger Moth training & microlights

RNAV			
DET	117.30	173	8.9

Remarks
PPR. Not available for use at night by flights required to use a licensed AD. Rwy03/21 not available to ACFT flying for public transport or flying instruction.

Warnings
Helicopters must obtain clearance before engaging rotors. Free-fall parachuting takes place up to FL150. Helicopters may not operate & no overhead joins when parachuting in progress. No marked Twys. Taxi to S of Rwy, due to poor condition & undulating surface of AD.
Noise: Avoid over flying local villages

Operating Hrs	0900-SS (L) & by arr
Circuits	Fixed Wing LH 1000ft QFE Rotary 11 LH 700ft QFE, 29 RH 1000ft QFE
Landing Fee	Single £10 Twin £15 Free with 40lts of fuel or lamb from farm
Maintenance	Available
Fuel	AVGAS Jet A1 Oil 80 W80 100 W100 W100+15W 50

Disabled Facilities

Restaurant	
Cafe at AD	**Tel:** 01622 890671
Chequers	**Tel:** 01233 770217
Taxis	
MTC	**Tel:** 01622 890003
Car Hire	
Nathan	**Tel:** 01622 684844
Weather Info	Air SE MOEx
Operator	Shenley Farms (Engineering) Ltd Headcorn Aerodrome Ashford, Kent, TN27 9HX **Tel:** 01622 890226 **Tel:** 01622 890236 (Out of Hrs) **Fax:** 01622 890876 **Telex:** 966127 www.headcornaerodrome.co.uk

Effective date:25/09/08 OP 08

250ft 8mb	3nm SW of Ledbury N5200.17 W00228.50	Alternative AD	**Gloucestershire** Shobdon

Non-radio	LARS Brize 124.275	Safetycom 135.475

N
Please do not obstruct hangars
ACFT parking
830m x 28m Unlicensed
Crops
Crops
07
25

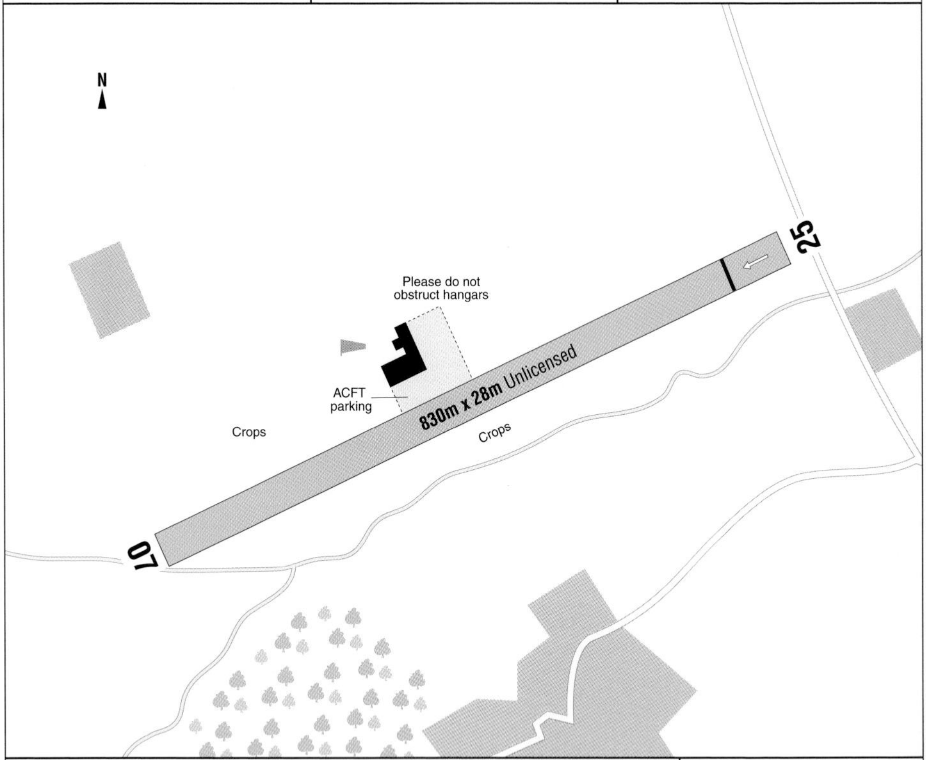

RWY	SURFACE	TORA	LDA	U/L	LIGHTING
07/25	Grass			830x28	Nil

RNAV

Remarks
PPR by telephone. AD unmanned. Visitors welcome at own risk. Smooth surface on regularly cut Rwy.

Warnings
Rwy25 Thr displaced to avoid high sided vehicles on main road. Crops grow to edge of strip. Sheep graze AD.30ft power lines cross Rwy25 APP 300m from Thr. Trees SW of Rwy07 can cause turbulence on final in SE wind. TV mast 1210amsl, (540agl) 2nm W AD. Hangar close to mid point of strips N edge. Please do not block access to the hangar.

Operating Hrs SR-SS
Circuits LH 1000ft QFE
Landing Fee £5 Pls register visit
Maintenance Nil
Fuel Nil
Disabled Facilities Nil
Restaurant Nil
Taxis
Wyvern (Ledbury) **Tel:** 01531 633001
Ames **Tel:** 01420 83309
Car Hire Nil
Weather Info Air SW MOEx

Operator Preston Cross Airstrip Ltd
c/o R Chapman
The Dower House
Preston Cross
Ledbury
Herefordshire
HR8 2LJ
Tel: 01531 660258

L

EGNM LEEDS BRADFORD

681ft 23mb	6nm NW of Leeds N5351.95 W00139.63	PPR	Alternative AD Durham Tees Valley Sherburn in Elmet

Non-standard join

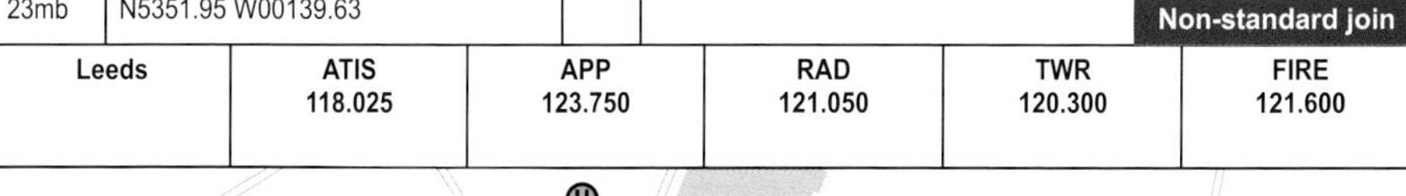

Leeds	ATIS	APP	RAD	TWR	FIRE
	118.025	123.750	121.050	120.300	121.600

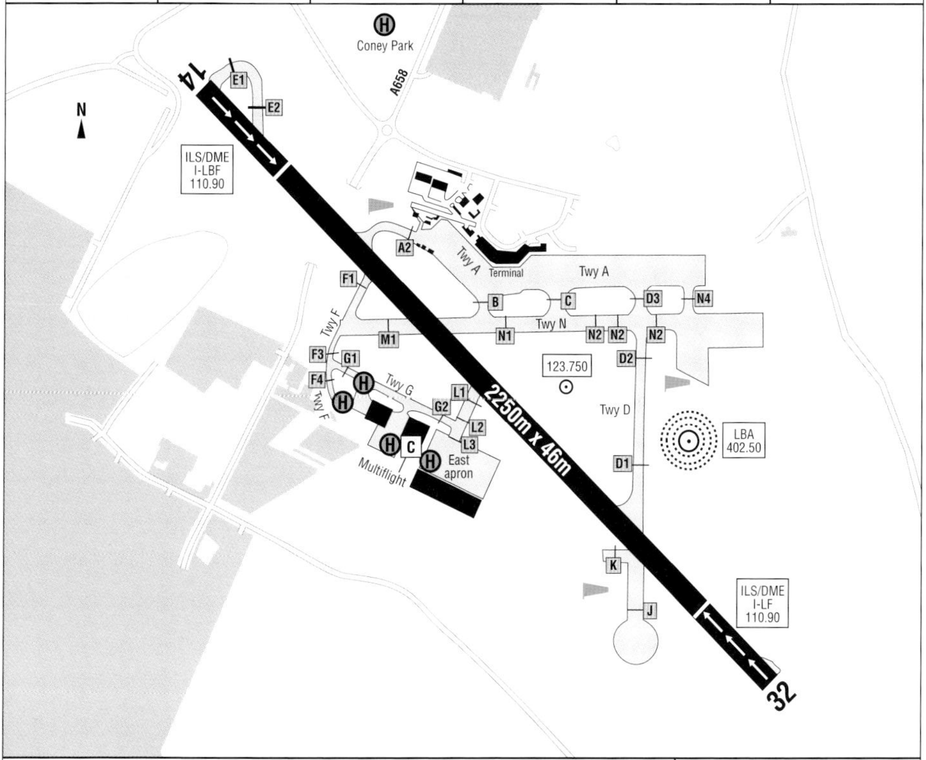

RWY	SURFACE	TORA	LDA	U/L	LIGHTING
14	Concrete	2113	1802		Ap Thr Rwy PAPI 3.5° RHS
32	Concrete	2190	1916		Ap Thr Rwy PAPI 3° LHS

RNAV			
POL	112.10	069	17.3

Remarks

PPR to all GA ACFT. Microlights NOT accepted. All public transport ACFT must designate a handling agent in advance if operating from the main N side apron. Helicopters to land as instructed by ATC. Rebated fees for training flights subject to prior written approval from the AD Authority. A booking slot system is in operation for ACFT using the AD for training. Pilots transiting the Vale of York AIAA, use LARS offered by Linton or Leeming. Helicopter training is permitted dual only, no circuits. All GA and non-based ACFT must co-ordinate parking with Multiflight.

Handling agents: Northside – Servisair & Aviance. Southside – Multiflight. Customs during AD Ops Hrs.

Warnings

Bird activity noted at this AD – large flocks of Lapwings. ACFT may be delayed while flocks are cleared. The S Twy is restricted to use by ACFT with a wingspan <17m. Windshear my be experienced on APP 190-240° >24kts.

Operating Hrs H24
PPR 2200-0600 (Summer) +1Hr (Winter)

Circuits Variable

Landing Fee On application

Maintenance
Multiflight **Tel:** 0113 2387100

Fuel AVGAS JET A1 100LL
Fuel available by prior arr AVGAS only available 0800-1800 or by prior arr. AVGAS not available to ACFT with wingspan >17m

Disabled Facilities

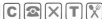

Handling **Tel:** 0113 2503251 (Servisair)
Tel: 0113 3913382 (Aviance)
Tel: 0113 2387140 (Multiflight)

Restaurant Restaurant buffet & bar available at Terminal

Taxis Available at Terminal
Telecabs **Tel:** 0113 2792222

Car Hire
Avis **Tel:** 0113 2503880
Europcar **Tel:** 0113 2509066
Hertz **Tel:** 0113 2504811

Weather Info M T9 Fax 334 A VN MOEx

Visual Reference Points (VRP)

VRP	VOR/DME
Dewsbury N5341.50 W00138.10	POL 105°/17nm
Eccup Reservoir N5352.27 W00132.60	POL 073°/21nm
Harrogate N5359.50 W00131.60	POL 058°/25nm
Keighley N5352.00 W00154.60	POL 047°/10nm

Operator Leeds Bradford Int Airport Ltd
Yeadon, Leeds
West Yorkshire, LS19 7TU
Tel: 0113 2509696 (Admin)
Tel: 0113 3913282 (ATC)
Tel: 0113 3913231 (AD Ops)
Fax: 0113 2505426 (Admin)
www.lbia.co.uk

CTR/CTA – Class D Airspace
Normal CTR/CTA Class D Airspace rules apply
Transition Alt 5000ft

L

EGXE LEEMING

132ft 5mb	4.5nm SW of Northallerton N5417.54 W00132.11	PPR MIL	Alternative AD Diversion AD	Durham Tees Valley Full Sutton **Non-standard join**

Leeming	LARS/Zone 127.750	TWR 120.500 122.100

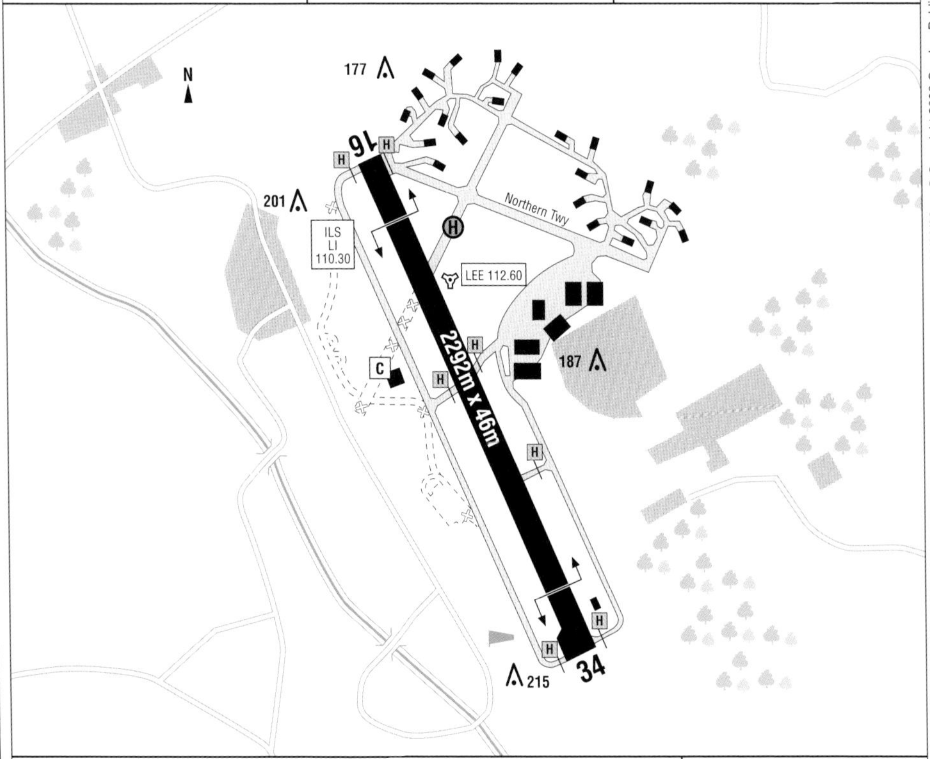

RWY	SURFACE	TORA	LDA	U/L	LIGHTING
16/34	Asphalt	2292	2292		Ap Thr Rwy PAPI 3°
Arrester gear 390m from Thr, APP cable down and overrun cable up					

RNAV

Remarks
PPR 24Hrs required. Resident jet ACFT have priority for take-off, visiting ACFT may have to break-off APP to permit Dept. Limited parking and handling facilities. AD often active at weekends, ATZ active H24. Station based light ACFT operate outside normal Hrs.
Visual aid to location: IBn LI Red.

Warnings
Strong possibility of wind shear on Rwy16 APP when wind is more than 10 knots in sector 210°-250°. Glider flying at Catterick and Dishforth outside normal Hrs.
Noise: All ACFT are to avoid over flying towns and villages within MATZ unless weather or flight conditions dictate otherwise.

Operating Hrs Mon-Thu 0800-1800 Fri 0800-1700
Sat 0830-1730
ATZ H24

Circuits Large ACFT 1000ft QFE
Small ACFT 800ft QFE

Landing Fee Charges in accordance with MOD policy
Contact Station Ops for details

Maintenance Nil
Fuel AVGAS Jet A1 100LL

Disabled Facilities

Restaurants In Northallerton
Taxis/Car Hire Nil
Weather Info M T Fax 336 MOEx
ATIS **Tel:** 01677 423041 Ex 7770

Operator RAF Leeming
Northallerton
North Yorkshire DL7 9NJ
Tel: 01677 423041 Ex 7749 (Ops)
Fax: 01677 423041 Ex 7094 (Ops)

Leeming Noise Procedures
All helicopters and light ACFT are not to fly below 500ft QFE within the MATZ, unless weather or operational reasons dictate. Fixed wing ACFT other than light ACFT are not to fly below 1000ft QFE within the MATZ, unless joining the visual circuit. All ACFT must avoid over flying towns and villages within the MATZ – see map for details.
Avoid over flying the local areas of Bedale, Northallerton, Leeming Bar, Leeming village, Laidonderry, Gatenby, Scruton, Scorton Hospital, Breckenborough, Theakeston Hall, Sion Hall. Medium/heavy helicopters msut also avoid, Cross Lanes farm, Grewelmarpe village and Kirkby Mabeard.

469ft 16mb	4nm ESE of Leicester N5236.47 W00101.92	PPR	**Alternative AD** **Diversion AD**	**East Midlands** Northampton

Leicester	**A/G** **122.125**

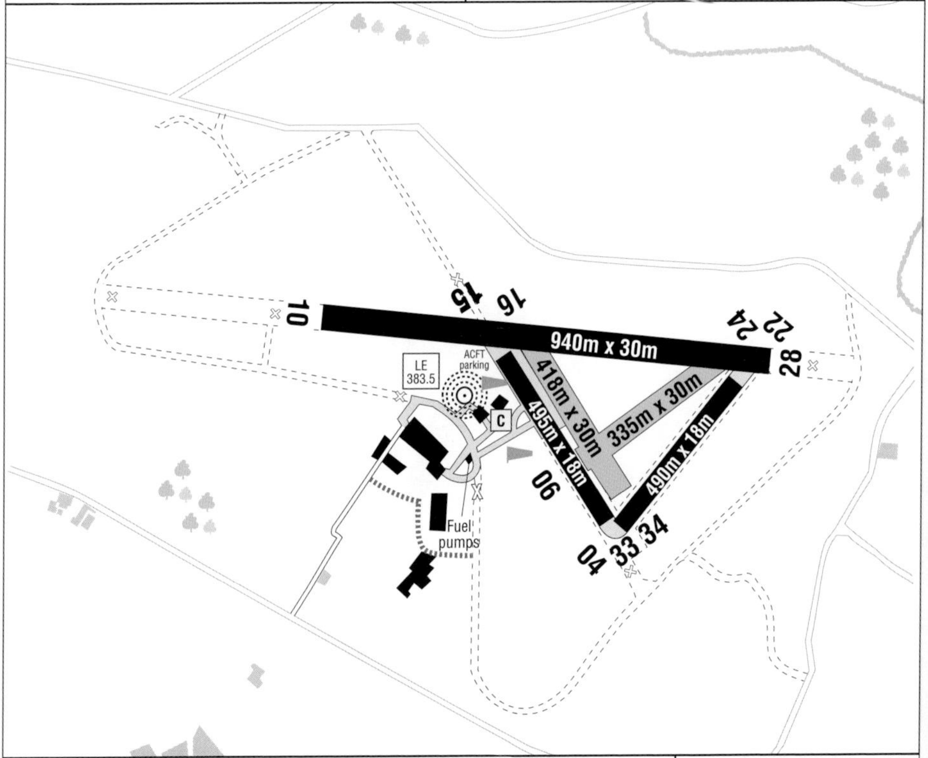

940m x 30m
418m x 30m
335m x 30m
495m x 18m
490m x 18m
10 28 15 33 16 34 04 22 06 24
LE 383.5
ACFT parking
C
Fuel pumps

RWY	SURFACE	TORA	LDA	U/L	LIGHTING
10/28	Asphalt	940	940		Thr Rwy APAPI 3.25° LHS
06/24	Grass	335	335		Nil
16/34	Grass	418	418		Nil
04/22	Asphalt	490	490		Nil
15/33	Asphalt	495	495		Nil

RNAV			
HON	**113.65**	**061**	**27.5**

L

Remarks
PPR. When using Rwy28, provided the glide clear, requirement of the ANO is maintained at all times, all ACFT to climb straight ahead maintaining Rwy centre line to 1000ft QFE before turning.
Visual aids to location: Ibn, Green, LE.

Warnings
Rwy15/33 used for parking when not active. Helicopters to join circuit not above 500ft. Grass Rwys and Twy are subject to water logging, especially in winter.

Operating Hrs	0800-1600 (Summer) +1Hr (Winter) & by arr
Circuits	LH
Landing Fee	Single £12 Twin £24 Weekends free with 50l of fuel
Maintenance	
R N Aviation	**Tel:** 01162 593629
Fuel	AVGAS JET A1 100LL

Disabled Facilities

Restaurant
Club facilities & bar meals available at AD

Taxis	
ABC	**Tel:** 01162 555111
Car Hire	
National	**Tel:** 01162 510455
Europcar	**Tel:** 01162 538531
Weather Info	Air Cen MOEx
Operator	Leicestershire Aero Club Ltd Leicester Airport Gartree Road, Leicester, LE2 2FG **Tel:** 01162 592360 **Fax:** 01162 592712

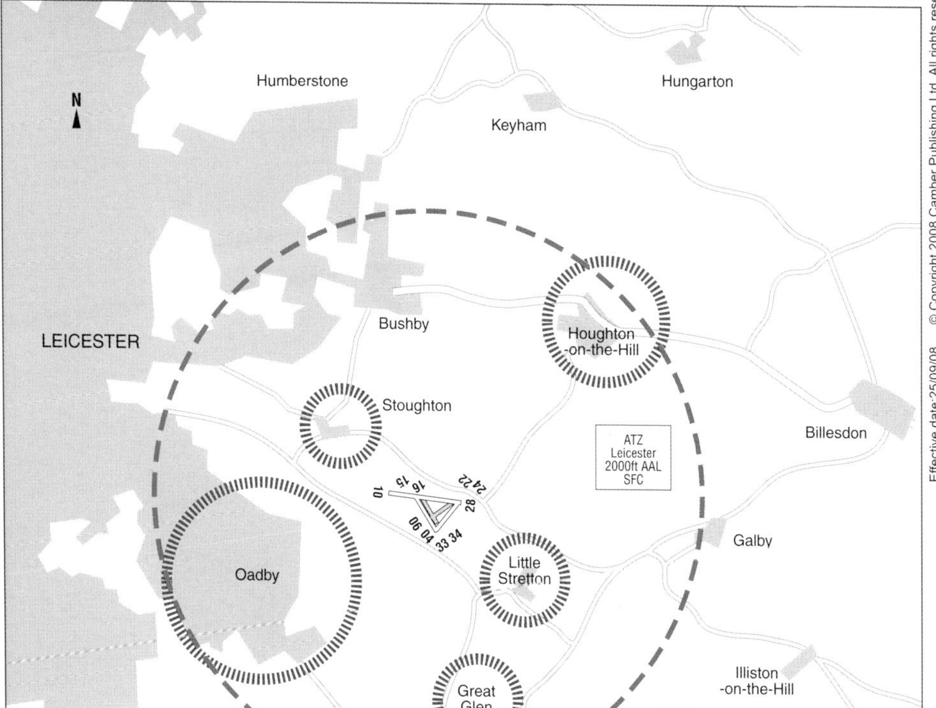

Noise: On Dept please avoid over flying Houghton-on-the-Hill, Little Stretton, Stoughton and Oadby where possible.

45ft 1mb	4nm NW of Lerwick N6011.53 W00114.62	PPR	Alternative AD	Sumburgh Scatsta

Tingwall	APP Sumburgh 131.300	AFIS 125.300

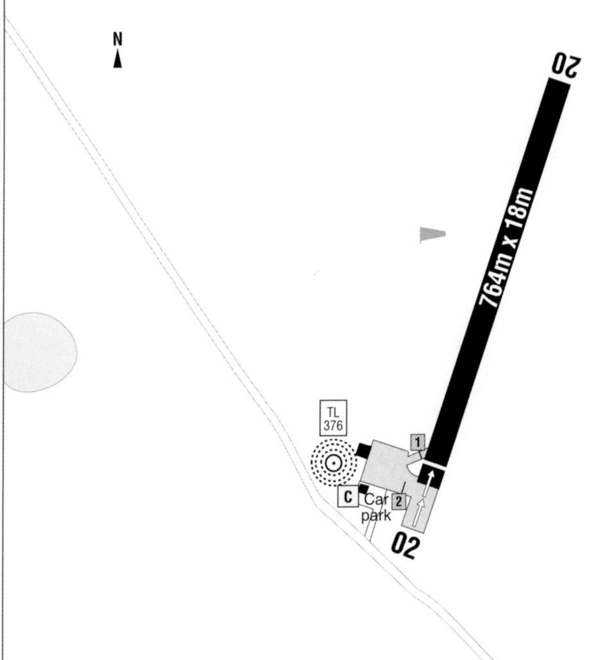

RWY	SURFACE	TORA	LDA	U/L	LIGHTING
02	Asphalt	764	764		Ap Thr Rwy APAPI 4° LHS
20	Asphalt	764	764		Thr Rwy APAPI 4° LHS

Displaced Thr Rwy02

RNAV			
SUM	117.35	010	18.7

L

Remarks
PPR

Warnings
High GND 449ft aal 1.25nm to NW. High GND 274ft aal 1nm to NE. High GND 407ft aal 1nm to ESE. High GND from S through to W up to 420ft aal within 1.5nm od AD. 5 wind turbines 246ft aal situated on high GND S of AD.

Operating Hrs Mon-Fri 0730-1600 Sat 1030-1500 (May-Oct)
Mon-Fri 0830-1700 (Winter)

Circuits Nil

Landing Fee £17 per tonne
Parking fees: £5 per tonne or part there of for each 24Hrs or part thereof

Maintenance Nil

Fuel AVGAS 100LL

Disabled Facilities

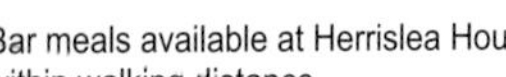

Restaurants Bar meals available at Herrislea House within walking distance

Taxis
L Sinclair **Tel:** 01595 694617
R Greenwald **Tel:** 01595 692080

Car Hire
Bolts Car Hire **Tel:** 01595 692855

Weather Info Air Sc GWC

Operator Shetland Islands Council
20 Commercial Road
Lerwick
Shetland ZE1 0LX
Tel: 01595 840306 (AD)
Fax: 01595 744869

EGQL LEUCHARS

38ft 1mb	5nm NW of St Andrews N5622.37 W00252.11	PPR MIL	Alternative AD **Edinburgh** Fife Diversion AD

Non-standard join

Leuchars	LARS 126.500	APP 123.300	TWR/GND 122.100

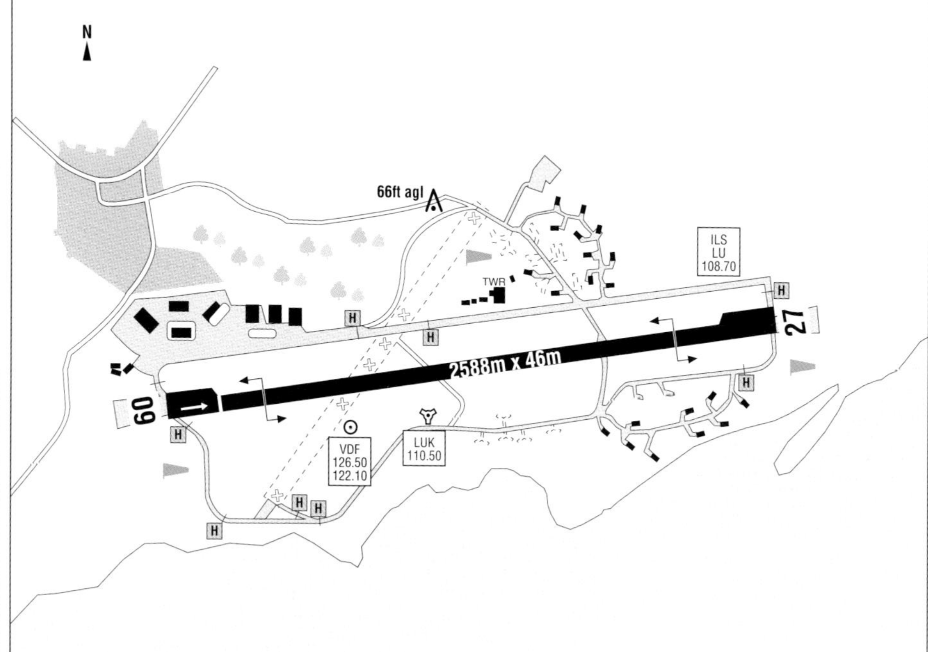

RWY	SURFACE	TORA	LDA	U/L	LIGHTING
09	Asphalt/Conc	2588	2317		Ap Thr Rwy PAPI 3°
27	Asphalt/Conc	2588	2588		Ap Thr Rwy PAPI 2.5°

Displaced Thr Rwy09 275m

RNAV			
PTH	110.40	110	17.1

Remarks

PPR. All ACFT inbound to Leuchars to call APP before 40nm, unless prior permission has been obtained. All ACFT to avoid St Andrews by 2000ft/2nm. Light ACFT circuits up to 800ft QFE. Airways traffic request start on 122.10. Tutor hold 800ft live side N of N Twy and inside Rwy09/27 Thrs. Helicopters not to hover or taxi in the vicinity of the Watchman RAD TWR 66ft agl W Rwy22 Thr.

Warnings

Arrester gear is fitted 396m from Rwy09/27/22 Thr. There is a possible radiation hazard W Rwy22 Thr. Increased bird hazard on Rwy27 APP, 30 mins either side of sunset (Sep-Mar).
Caution: Windshear on finals Rwy27 when wing 210-240 >15kts.
Noise: Avoid flying over local villages when ever possible.

Operating Hrs	Mon-Fri 0800-2300 (L)
Circuits	09 LH, 27 RH Jet ACFT 1200ft Light ACFT 800ft Gliders 1500ft
Landing Fee	Charges in accordance with MOD policy Contact Station Ops for details
Maintenance	Nil
Fuel	AVGAS JET A1 100LL
Disabled Facilities	Nil
Restaurants	Nil
Taxis/Car Hire	Local taxi by private arr
Weather Info	M T Fax 338 GWC
Operator	RAF Leuchars Fife St Andrews KY16 0JX **Tel:** 01334 839471 Ex 6602 (Ops) **Tel:** 01334 839471 Ex 7283 (ATC) **Fax:** 01334 839471 Ex 7807 (Ops)

L

EGXU LINTON-ON-OUSE

53ft 2mb	9nm NW of York N5402.95 W00115.17	PPR MIL	Alternative AD Diversion AD	**Leeds Bradford** Full Sutton

Non-standard join

Linton	LARS	APP	RAD	TWR	A/G 118.550 (Weekends & evenings)
	118.550	118.550	118.550	122.100	

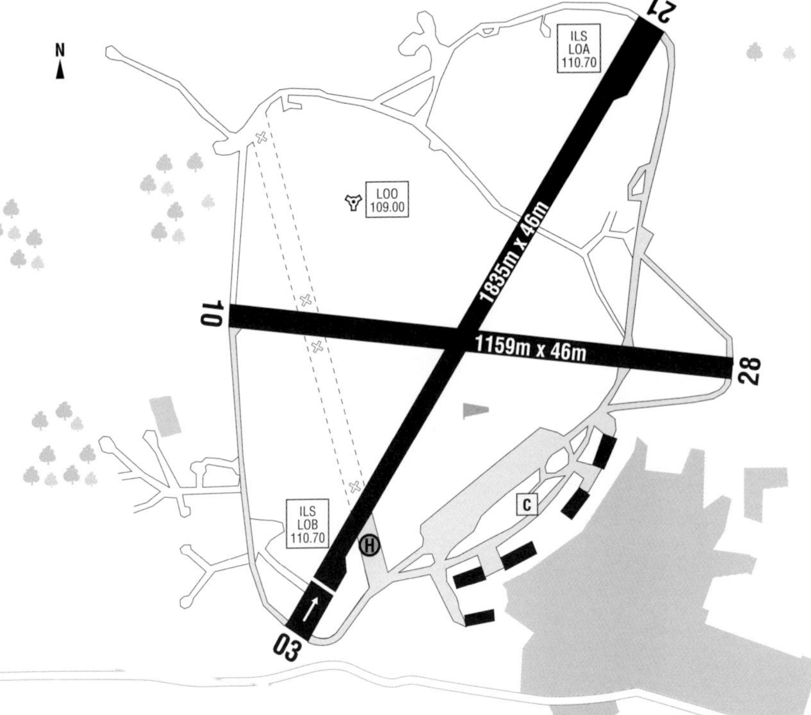

RWY	SURFACE	TORA	LDA	U/L	LIGHTING
03	Asphalt	1835	1681		Ap Thr Rwy PAPI 3°
21	Asphalt	1835	1833		Ap Thr Rwy PAPI 3°
28	Asphalt	1159	1159		Thr Rwy PAPI 3°
10	Asphalt	Emergency landings only			

First 152m Rwy04 sterile

RNAV

Remarks
A third Rwy17/35 closed.
Visual aid to Location: Ibn LO Red.

Warnings
Linton is a high intensity flying training school. 2 Rwys may be in use at the same time. Glider launching at AD takes place in the evenings and weekends.
Caution: Rwy28 trees 110ft 130m from Thr 88m left of centre line. Rwy10 only available for landing in an emergency – High trees within APP area.

Operating Hrs	Mon-Thu 0630-1615 Fri 0630-1600 (Summer) +1Hr (Winter)
Circuits	03, 21, 28 RH, 10 LH
Landing Fee	Charges in accordance with MOD policy Contact Station Ops for details
Maintenance	Nil
Fuel	Ltd quantities PNR AVGAS JET A1 100LL

Disabled Facilities

Restaurants	Nil
Taxis/Car Hire	Nil
Weather Info	Air N MOEx ATIS **Tel:** 01347 847467
Operator	OC Ops Wing RAF Linton on Ouse York North Yorkshire YO30 2AJ **Tel:** 01347 847511 (ATC) **Tel:** 01347 847491/2 (Ops/PPR) www.raf.mod.uk/raflintononouse

L

EGMJ LITTLE GRANSDEN

250ft 8mb	5nm SE of St Neots N5210.00 W00009.23	PPR	Alternative AD Diversion AD	Cambridge Bourn

Little Gransden	A/G 130.850

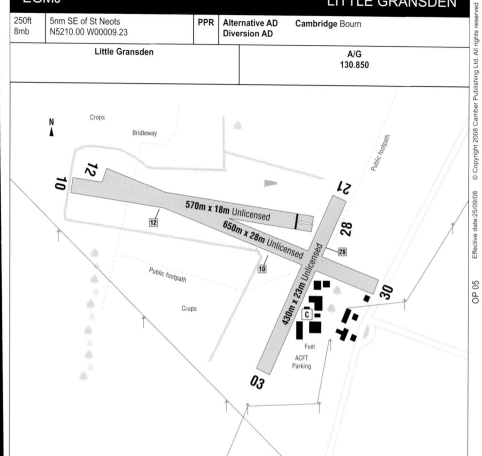

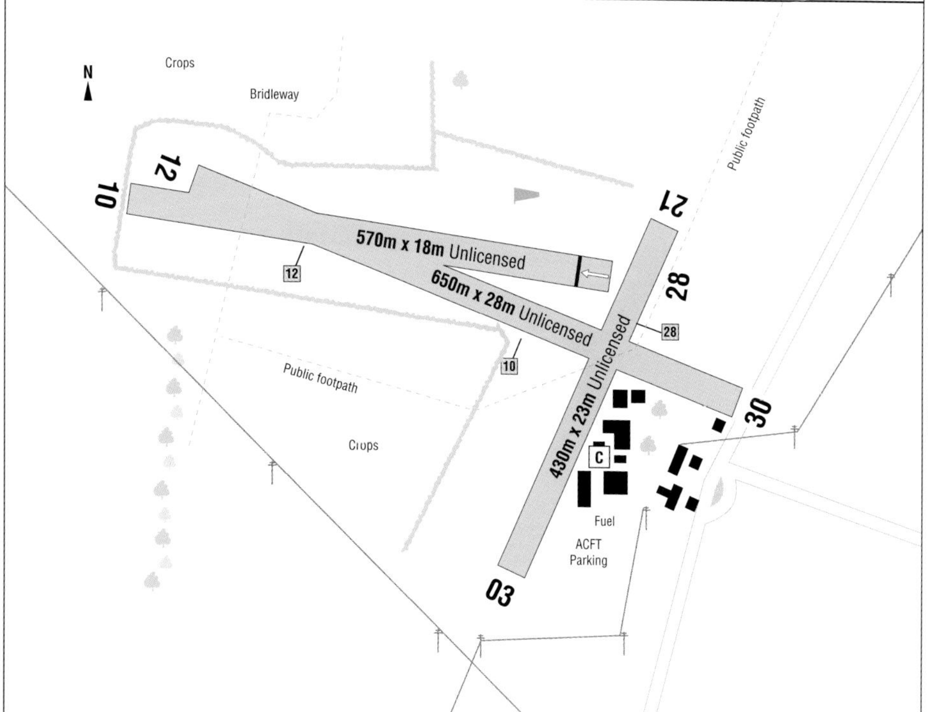

RWY	SURFACE	TORA	LDA	U/L	LIGHTING
12/30	Grass			650x28	Nil
10/28	Grass			570x18	Nil
03/21	Grass			430x23	Nil

Starter extension Rwy28 240m

RNAV			
BKY	116.25	326	13.3

Remarks
PPR by telephone essential. Non-radio ACFT not accepted. In the absence of A/G facility, make normal calls. No dead side, all ACFT join downwind to the S or W of AD. Pilots equipped with constant speed propellers should at safest opportunity set power and propellers to cruise climb configuration.

Warnings
Gransden Lodge Gliding AD is located 2500m to the NE. Rwy03/21 is only for use by experienced pilots, marked power lines cross Thr of Rwys03 & 28.Bridle-path crosses Rwy10/28. Rwy03/21 is unmarked and also used as Twys. Rwy designators positioned in front of Thr.
Noise: Avoid over flying The Gransdens, Gamlingay, Hatley Estate and Waresley.

Operating Hrs	Mon-Sat 0700-1900 Sun 0700-1900 (L)
Circuit	03, 28, 30 LH, 10, 12, 21 RH 800ft QFE
Landing Fee	Single £5 Free with 50ltr fuel
Maintenance	YAK UK Ltd **Tel:** 01767 651156 **Fax:** 01767 651157
Fuel	AVGAS 100LL
Disabled Facilities	Nil
Restaurants	Tea & coffee available at AD

Taxis	
Dereks	**Tel:** 01767 260430
Sandy Cars	**Tel:** 01767 682634
Andys	**Tel:** 01767 260288
Car Hire	
Budget	**Tel:** 01223 323838
Weather Info	Air Cen MOEx
Operator	Skyline School of Flying Fullers Hill, Little Gransden Cambridgeshire SG19 3BP **Tel:** 01767 651950 **Fax:** 01767 651575

730ft 24mb	N5151.30 W00142.06 8nm NW of RAF Brize Norton	PPR	**Alternate AD** **Oxford** Enstone **Non-standard join**

Non-radio	LARS Brize 124.275	Safetycom 135.475

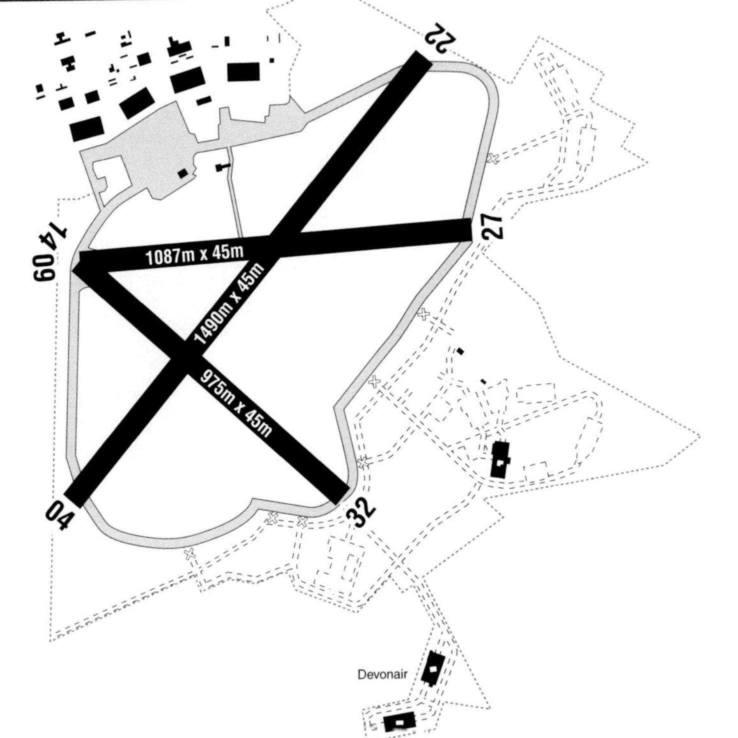

RWY	SURFACE	TORA	LDA	U/L	LIGHTING
04/22	Tarmac			1490x45m	Nil
09/27	Tarmac			1087x45m	Nil
14/32	Tarmac			975x45m	Nil

RNAV

Remarks
PPR essential. All visitors welcome at pilots own risk. WWII AD. Active RAF gliding site. Home of Devonair. If VGS gliders are operating a separate Brize frequency will be allocated to them on a daily basis this should be regarded as an AFISO service, (callsign:Rissington Radio). Devonair will advise if gliders are operating, it is then essential that PPR be obtained from the VGS DI. The VGS DI must also be advised before visiting acft depart. All visiting pilots must read the Flying Order Book, accessible on Devonair website.

Warnings
AD located close to Brize Zone and situated within Oxford AIAA. Helicopters must arr/dept 500ft agl.
Noise: Avoid over flying the villages of Great Rissington, Little Rissington, Idbury, Chruch Westcote, Westcote and Fifield.

Operating Hrs	SR-SS First take-off should not be before 0800 local or 1030 (L) on Sun if 05 is in use. Circuit flying must cease at 1830 (L).
Circuits	14, 22, 27, 32 LH, 04, 09 RH 800ft Join over head 1000ft
Landing Fee	Single £7
Maintenance	Devonair Tel 07836 561073 ACFT < 5700kgs
Fuel	AVGAS
Hangarage	Available
Disabled Facilities	Nil
Restaurants	Nil

Taxi/Car Hire	Nil
Weather Info	Air SW MOEx
Operator	Devonair Hangar 102-103 RAF Little Rissington Airfield Upper Rissington Glos GL54 2LR **Tel:** 07836 561073 (Devonair) **Tel:** 01451 810078 (PPR) **Tel:** 07786 504892 (PPR) martin@devonair.net www.devonair.net

L

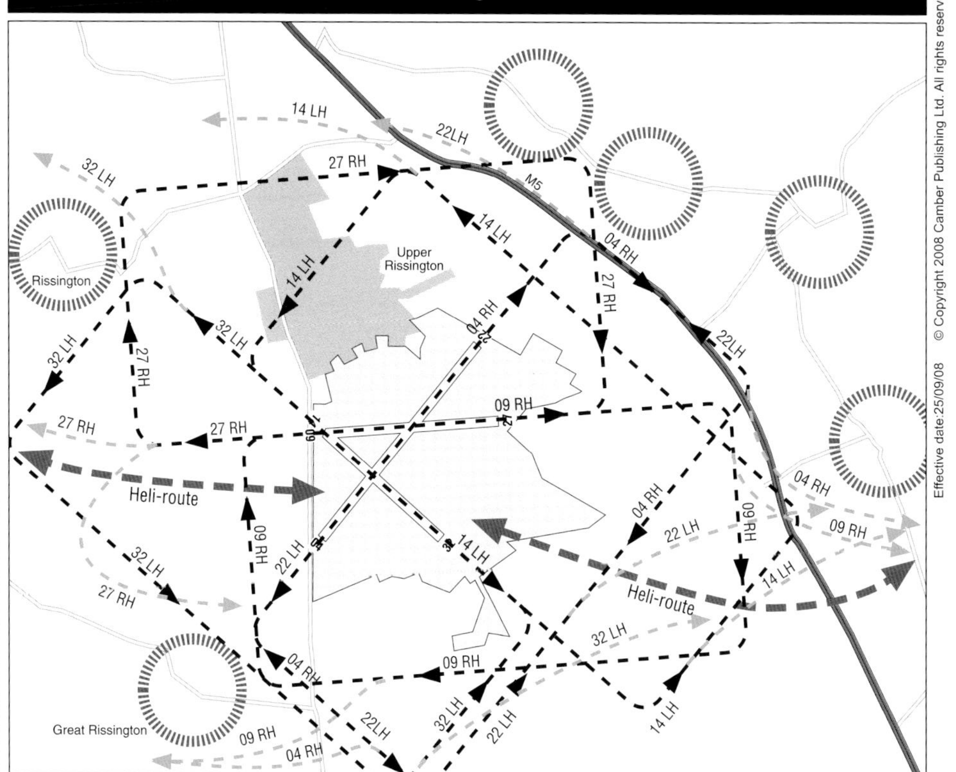

Effective date:25/09/08

INTENTIONALLY LEFT BLANK

LITTLE SNORING

196ft 7mb	3nm NE of Fakenham N5251.65 E00054.57	PPR	**Alternative AD**	**Norwich** Old Buckenham

Little Snoring	LARS Marham 124.150	A/G 118.125

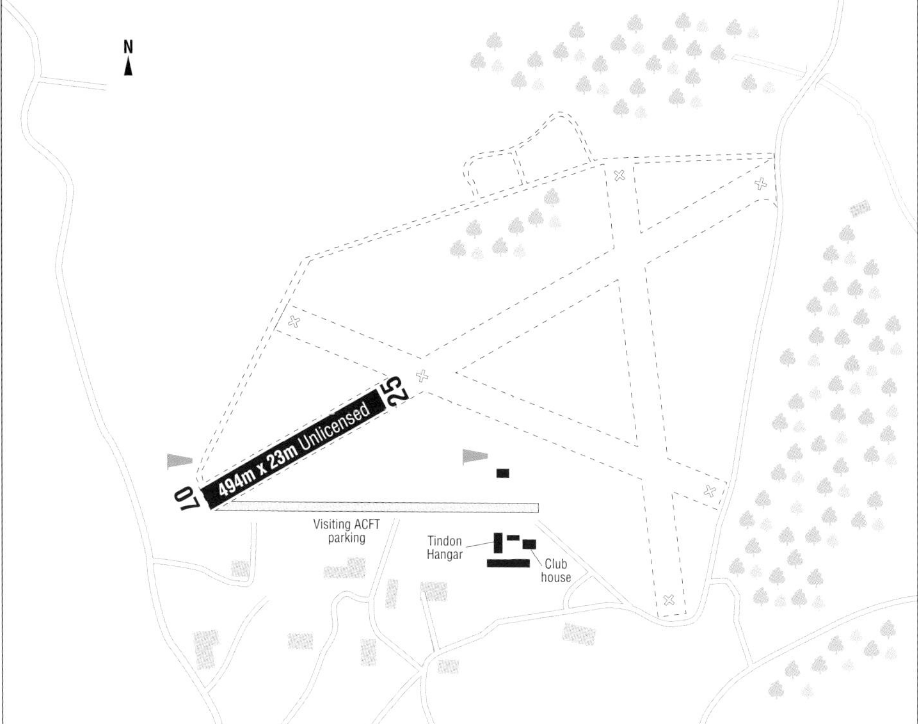

RWY	SURFACE	TORA	LDA	U/L	LIGHTING
07/25	Asphalt			494x23	Nil

RNAV

Remarks
Strict PPR. Visiting ACFT welcome at owners risk. All fly-ins do not require PPR.

Warnings
Uncontrolled vehicles often on AD.
Noise: Avoid over flying villages and habitation in vicinity of AD.

Operating Hrs	SR-SS
Circuits	LH 800ft QFE
Landing Fee	Donations please box at visiting ACFT parking
Maintenance	Nil
Fuel	AVGAS available when Flying Group memebrs present
Disabled Facilities	Nil
Restaurants	Good place for a picnic
Taxis	
Courtesy Cabs	**Tel:** 01328 855500
Car Hire	
Candy	**Tel**: 01328 855348

Weather Info	Air S MOEx
Operator	McAully Flying Group Little Snoring Aerodrome Little Snoring Fakenham Norfolk, NR21 0JR **Tel:** 01328 878470 (Mr T Cushing)

225ft 7mb	10nm NE of Bedford N5214.57 W00021.85	PPR	Alternative AD	Cranfield Little Gransden

Little Staughton	A/G 123.925 Make blind calls

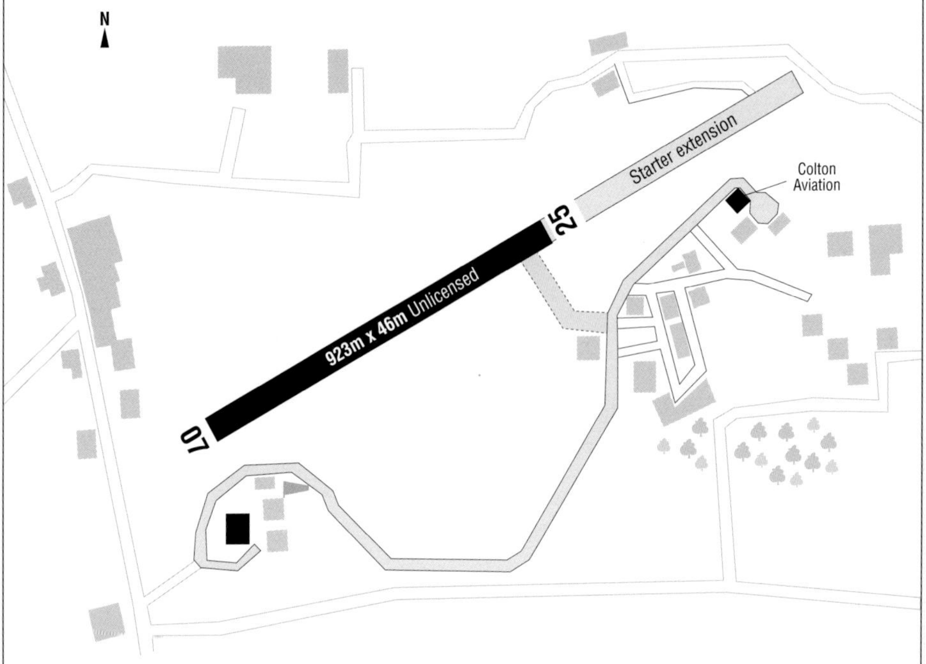

N

Starter extension

Colton Aviation

25

923m x 46m Unlicensed

07

RWY	SURFACE	TORA	LDA	U/L	LIGHTING
07/25	Asphalt			923x46	Nil

Starter extension Rwy25 500m

RNAV			
CFD	116.50	043	13.9

Remarks
Strictly PPR. Visiting ACFT should proceed to Colton Aviation.

Warnings
Twy leads to perimeter road which acts as an access track. Mast 171ft agl 331ft amsl, 1500m from Rwy25 Thr.
Caution: Vehicles on perimeter road. Gliders may be operating at weekends from Sackville Farm strip 3nm WNW, and from Thurleigh AD.
Noise: Avoid over flight of local villages.

Operating Hrs 0900-2000 (Summer) 0900-SS (Winter)
Circuits 07 RH, 25 LH
Landing Fee Single £5 Twin £10
No charge if in for maintenance
Maintenance Colton Aviation (M3)
Fuel AVGAS 100LL
Disabled Facilities

Restaurants Local pub in village 20mins walk

Taxis
A1 (Bedford) **Tel:** 01234 364444
Steve (St Neots) **Tel:** 01480 471111
Car Hire
National **Tel:** 01234 269565
Weather Info Air Cen MOEx
Operator Colton Aviation Ltd
Little Staughton Airfield
Bedfordshire MK44 2BN
Tel: 01234 376775/376705
Fax: 01234 376544

L

EGGP LIVERPOOL JOHN LENNON

80ft 3mb	6.5nm SE of Liverpool N5320.02 W00251.00	PPR	**Alternative AD** **Diversion AD**	**Hawarden** Manchester Barton **Non-standard join**

Liverpool	ATIS 124.325	APP 119.850	RAD 118.450
TWR 126.350	GND 121.950	FIRE 121.600	Handling LAS131.750

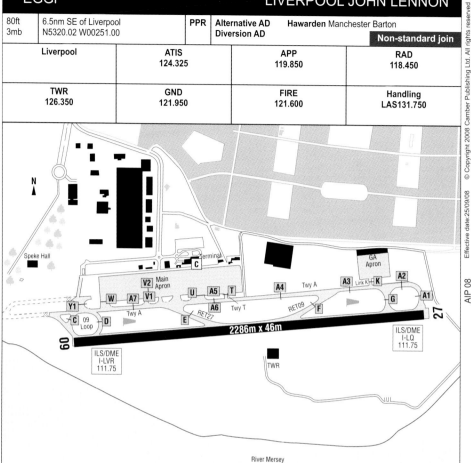

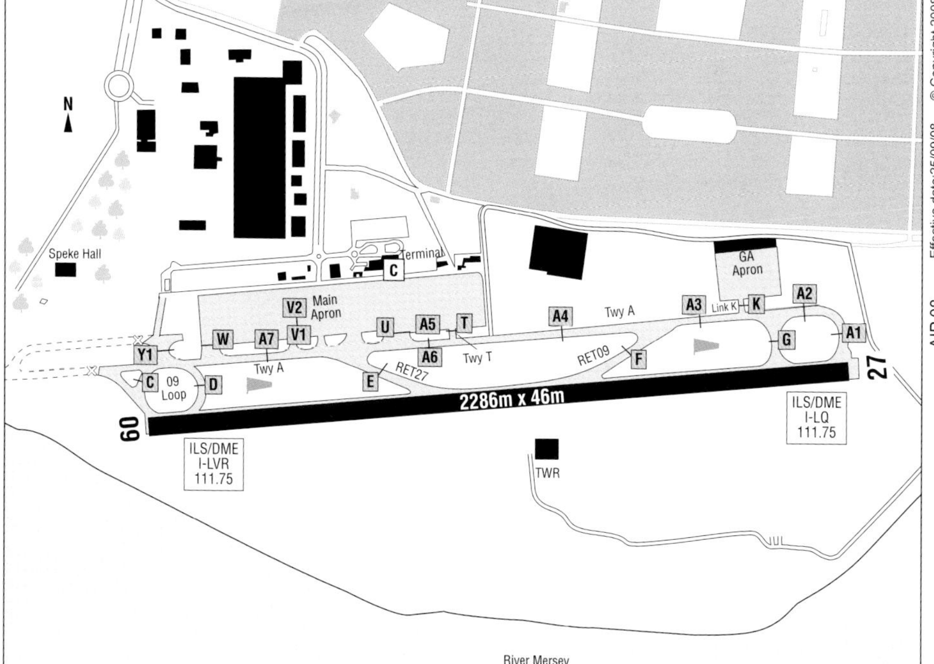

RWY	SURFACE	TORA	LDA	U/L	LIGHTING
09	Asphalt	2286	2225		Ap Thr Rwy PAPI 3° LHS
27	Asphalt	2286	2286		Ap Thr Rwy PAPI 3° LHS

RNAV			
WAL	114.10	114	10.7

Remarks
PPR non-radio ACFT & non-based ACFT via Handling Agent. Mandatory handling for all visiting ACFT. Await signals from marshaller before proceeding on to main apron. Failure to make a booking may result in the ACFT being refused use of the facilities. Payment of landing fees does not constitute booking out. Landing and taxiing on grass area not permitted. All ACFT to enter main apron via Twy V, unless directed by ATC. Hold B only available to ACFT <5700kgs. Twy A abeam holding point C and Twy Y only available for use by Code B ACFT or smaller. Not available at night or in LVP's. Circuit training for non-Liverpool based operators is only available by prior arr with ATC and is subject to local circuit traffic. ACFT without PPR could be refused landing permission except in an emergency. For training flights, a booking system is now in operation by ATC. ACFT repositioning on the apron require marshaller guidance. Visiting aircrew not to walk across apron without escort. Inform TWR of any special requests on APP to AD. GA parking area is limited to ACFT <5700kgs.
Aids to Navigation: NDB LPL 349.50

Warnings
Positively identify Rwy27/09 before committing to landing. Be aware of Restricted Area R311, 5nm to the SW. Take care when leaving the main apron not to enter the rapid exit turn off for Rwy09/27. Bird activity on Rwy09/27 APP. Radio controlled ACFT <75 kgs in weight operate 11nm WNW (Arrowe Park) up to 400ft agl (daylight only). Twy A from A3 to Rwy27 Thr is restricted to ACFT with wingspan less than 52m. Overhead join of the CCT is not available. Pilots join as directed by ATC.

Operating Hrs H24
Circuits Variable at the discretion of ATC
Landing Fee Available on application
Maintenance
LAS **Tel:** 0151 486 6161

Fuel AVGAS JET A1 100LL
Tel: 0151 486 7084 (Depot)
Fax: 0151 486 7720
Payment by cash cheque Esso Exxon carnet 3rd Party cards by prior arr or credit card

Effective date:25/09/08
AIP 08
L

Disabled Facilities	Available	**Operator**	Liverpool Airport PLC Liverpool Airport Liverpool Merseyside L24 1YD **Tel:** 0870 750 8484 (AD) **Tel:** 0151 907 1541 (ATC) **Tel:** 0151 907 1501 (Admin) **Tel:** 0151 907 1551 (AD Ops & PPR) **Tel:** 0151 907 1531 (Flt Plans) **Fax:** 0151 907 1520 (ATC) **Fax:** 0151 907 1500 (Admin) **Fax:** 0151 907 1550 (AD Ops & PPR) **Fax:** 0151 907 1540 (Flt Plans)
Handling	**Tel:** 0151 486 6161 (LAS) **Fax:** 0151 486 5151 (LAS) ops@liverpoolhandling.co.uk www.liverpoolhandling.co.uk		
Restaurants	Restaurant refreshments in terminal		
Taxis	Taxi Rank outside Terminal		
Car Hire			
Eurocar	**Tel:** 0151 448 1652		
Hertz	**Tel:** 0151 486 7111		
Weather Info	M T9 T18 Fax 342 VN MWC		

Noise Abatement Procedures

ACFT must be operated in a manner calculated to cause the least disturbance practicable in areas surrounding the AD. Inbound ACFT, other than light ACFT flying under VFR or SVFR, shall maintain a height of at least 2000ft aal until cleared to descend for landing. ACFT requiring to hold S of AD to minimise flight over Stanlow Oil Refinery (4nm S). ACFT APP without assistance from ILS or RAD must not fly lower than the ILS glide path. Between 2300-0700 (Winter) 2200-0600 (Summer), Rwy09 will only be available for take off when over-riding operational considerations necessitate its use. Avoid over flying Speke Hall.

Liverpool Standard Entry/Exit Routes:

Rwy27 Outbound

To N – Route via River Mersey, leave CTR via Seaforth, not above 1500ft

To S – Cross River Mersey, follow M53, leave via Chester, remaining E of Capenhurst, not above 1500ft

Rwy27 Inbound

From N – Enter via Kirkby, route E of M57, as directed by ATC, not above 1500ft

From S – Enter via Oulton Park, route W of Helsby, as directed by ATC, not above 1500ft

Rwy09 Outbound

To N – Route E of M57, leave via Kirkby, not above 1500ft

To S – Cross River Mersey, leave CTR via Oulton Park, not above 1500ft

Rwy09 Inbound

From N – Enter via Seaforth, route via River Mersey, as directed by ATC, not above 1500ft

From S – Enter via Chester, follow M53 to Outlet Village, as directed by ATC, not above 1500ft

L

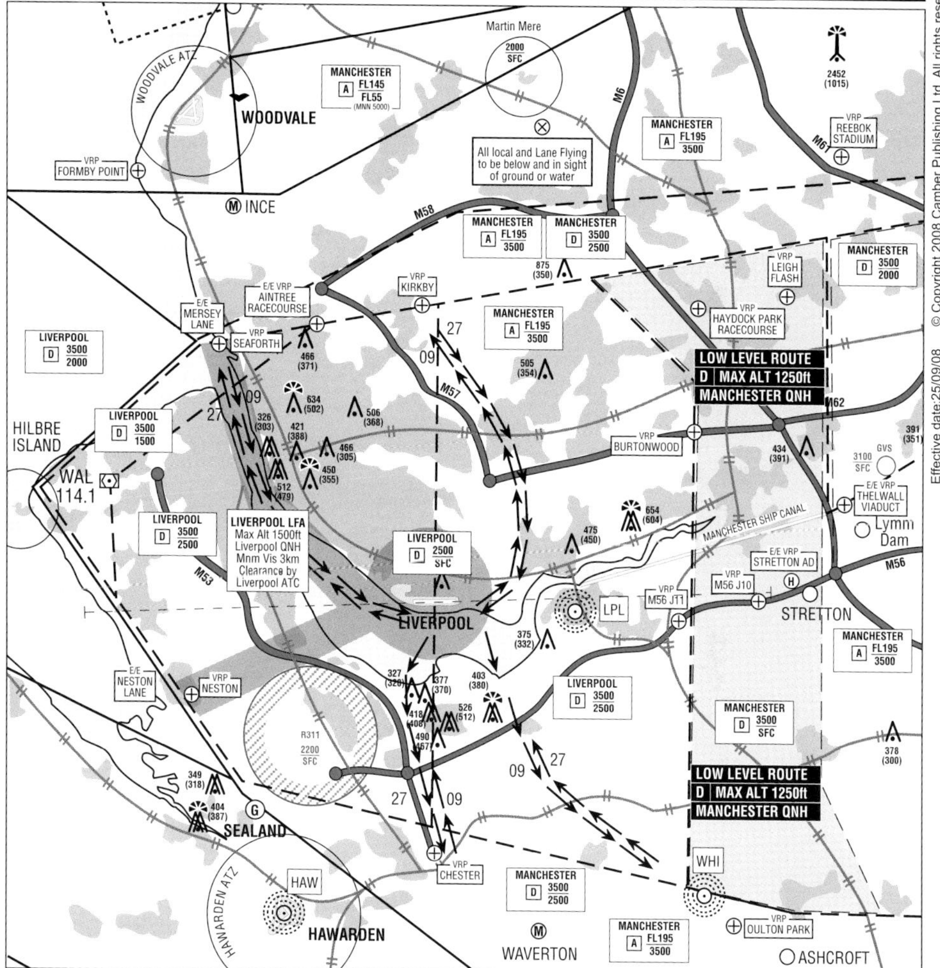

Visual Reference Points (VRP)

VRP	VOR/DME	VOR/DME
Aintree Racecourse N5328.60 W00256.58	WAL 057°/9nm	
Burtonwood Services N5325.00 W00238.28	WAL 088°/18nm	MCT 288°/14nm
Chester (A55 (T)/A5 (T)) N5311.70 W00250.63	WAL 142°/15nm	MCT 248°/23nm
Haydock Park Racecourse N5328.80 W00237.33	MCT 302°/15nm	WAL 080°/23nm
Kirby N5328.80 W00252.90	WAL 063°/11nm	MCT 292°/23nm
M56 J11 N5319.63 W00238.62	MCT 266°/14nm	WAL 106°/18nm
Neston N5317.50 W00303.60	WAL 159°/7nm	MCT 265°/29nm
Oulton Park N5310.57 W00236.80	MCT 232°/17nm	WAL 128°/23nm
Seaforth N5327.68 W00302.08	WAL 044°/6nm	
Stretton AD N5320.77 W00231.58	WAL 100°/22nm	MCT 269°/10nm

Notes: Burtonwood/M56 J11: Remain to E of these VRPs to remain clear of Liverpool CTR.
Stretton AD: Remain to W of this VRP to remain clear of Manchester CTR.

Effective date:25/09/08

19ft 1mb	6nm E of City of London N5130.32 E00003.32	PPR	Alternative AD **Biggin Hill** Stapleford **Non-standard join**

London City	LARS Farnborough East 123.225	ATIS 136.350	APP Thames RAD 132.700 (0630-2230 L)	APP Heathrow Director 119.725 (2230-0630 L

TWR 118.075	GND 121.825	RAD Thames 132.700	FIRE 121.600

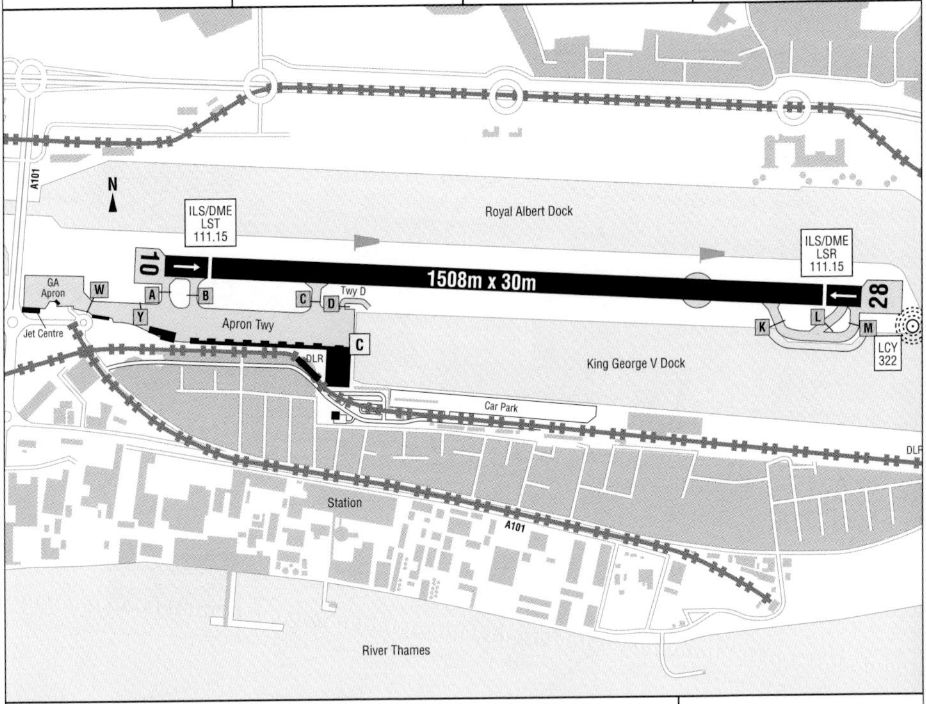

RWY	SURFACE	TORA	LDA	U/L	LIGHTING
10/28	Concrete	1199	1319		Ap Thr Tdz Rwy PAPI 5.5° LHS

Starter extension Rwy10 75m. Starter extension Rwy28 186m

RNAV			
LAM	**115.60**	**207**	**9.2**

Remarks
PPR essential. Non-radio and single engine ACFT not accepted. AD is licensed only for ACFT that have in their Flight Manual data and procedures for APP path angles of 5.5°. The use of AD is subject to prior permission of the AD Director. Operators to provide Noise Certificate details on request. AD not available for use by helicopters, single engined ACFT or for recreational flights. Only training necessary for the operation of ACFT at the AD will be permitted. All training is subject to approval. ACFT landing Rwy28 are not permitted to exit via A unless instructed by ATC. No ACFT to self park without marshaller guidance.

Warnings
Possibility of building induced turbulence and/or wind shear when landing in strong wind conditions. Compass drift can be experienced on Rwy28 hold.

Operating Hrs	Mon-Fri 0530-2005 Sat 0530-1135 Sun 1130-2000 (Summer) +1Hr (Winter)
Circuits	Nil
Landing Fee	Available on request
Maintenance	Scot Airways & BA
Fuel	AVTUR JET A1
Disabled Facilities	Available
Handling	**Tel:** 0207 6460400 (The Jet Centre)
Restaurants	Restaurant buffet bar
Taxis/Car Hire	Available at Terminal
Weather Info	M T9 Fax 344 MOEx ATIS **Tel:** 0207 6460224

Operator
London City Airport Ltd
Royal Dock Silvertown
London, E16 2PX
Tel: 0207 6460000 (Admin)
Tel: 0207 6460205 (ATC)
Fax: 0207 5111040 (Admin)
www.londoncityairport.com

CTR – Class D Airspace
Normal CTR/CTA Class D Airspace rules apply
Transition Alt 6000ft

London City Controlled Airspace Noise Abatement Procedures

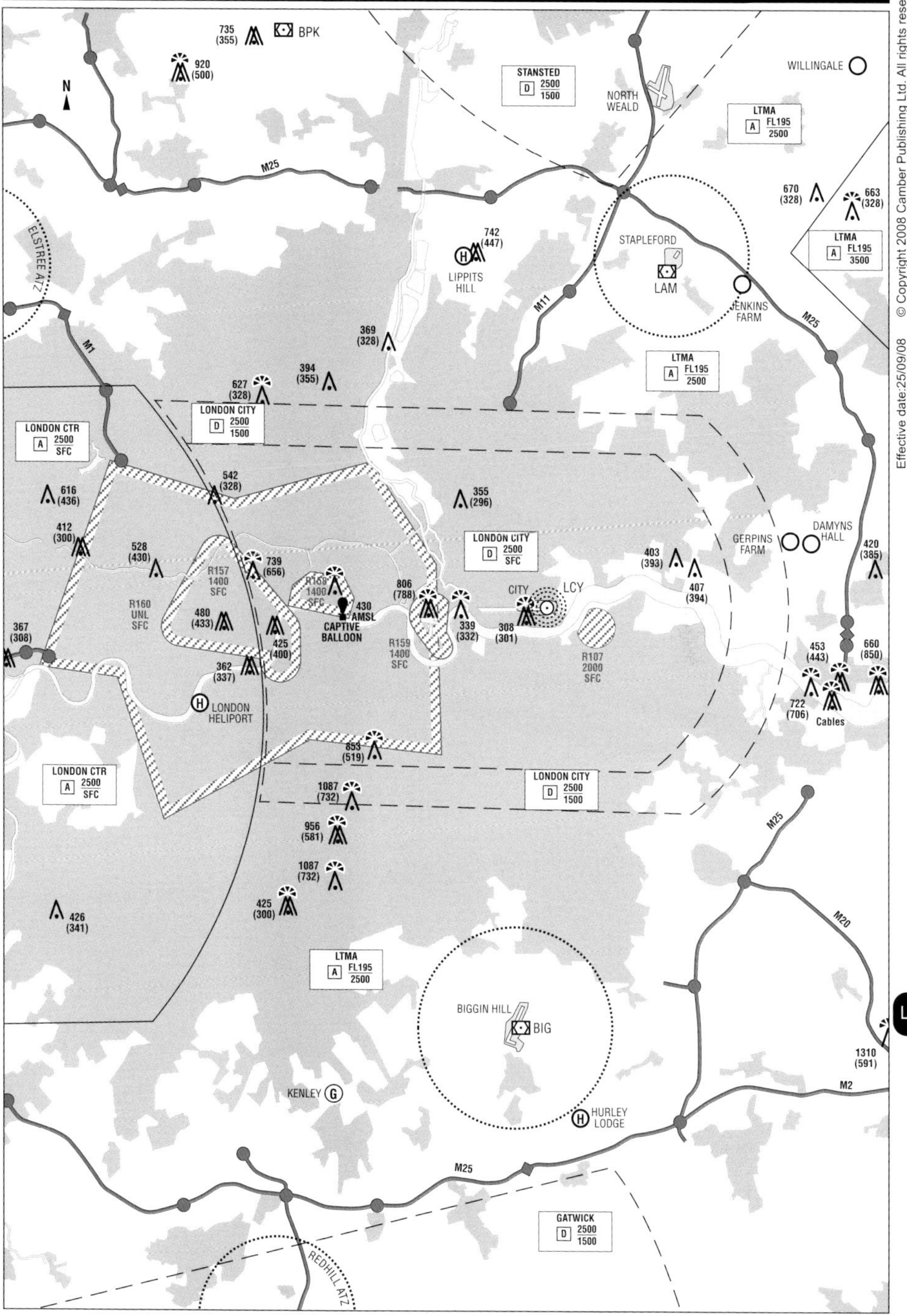

Noise abatement procedures for ACFT Dept London City and joining Controlled Airspace are included in the appropriate Standard Instrument Dept (SID) instructions. ACFT Dept London City CTR into the FIR or Dept on training flights within the London City CTR are to climb straight ahead to a minimum of 1000ft aal before turning on track unless otherwise instructed by ATC. ACFT making APP to London City without assistance from the ILS shall follow a descent path not lower than the ILS glide path. Pilots of ACFT carrying out visual APP to either Rwy or carrying out training circuits visually shall fly at a height of not less than 1500ft QFE until established on the final APP. To reduce noise impact on the local community, ACFT should use the full length of the Rwy for take-offs. ACFT manoeuvring visually (circling) to one Rwy after making ILS APP to the other Rwy shall do so at as high Alt as possible, compatible with the cloud base, retaining visual contact and appropriate published visual manoeuvring (circling) height minima.

Effective date:25/09/08

L

EGKK LONDON GATWICK

202ft 6mb	2.7nm N of Crawley N5108.88 W00011.42	PPR	Alternative AD Farnborough Redhill

Non-standard join

Gatwick	ATIS 136.525	APP 126.825	TWR 124.225
LARS Farnborough East 123.255	GND 121.800	DEL 121.950	FIRE 121.600

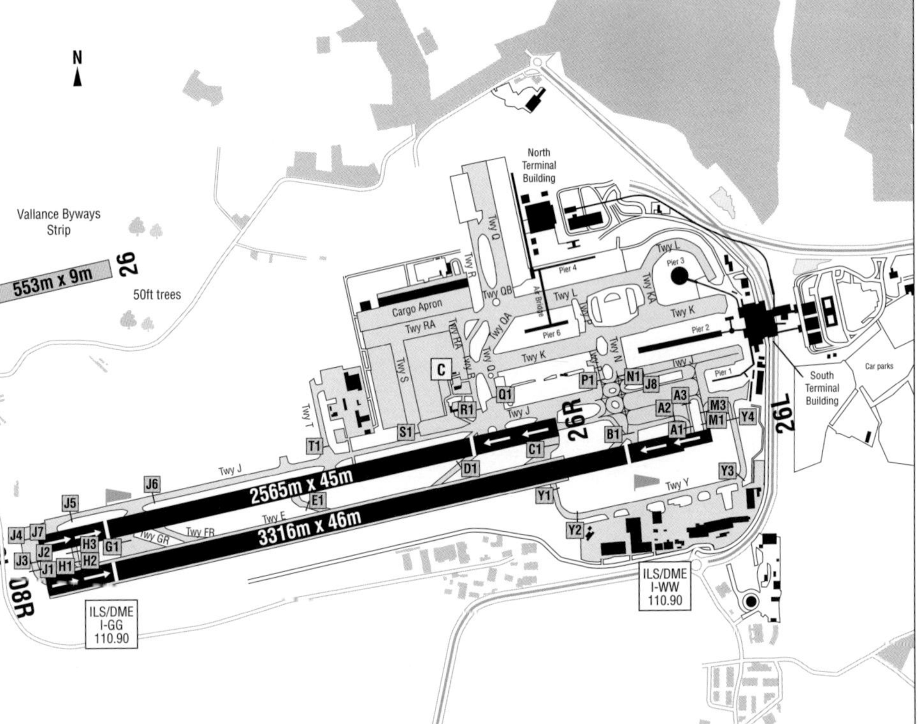

RWY	SURFACE	TORA	LDA	U/L	LIGHTING
08R	Asph/Conc	3159	2766		Ap Thr Rwy PAPI 3° RH
26L	Asph/Conc	3255	2831		Ap Thr Rwy PAPI 3° LH
08L	Asph/Conc	2565	2243		Ap Thr Rwy PAPI 3° LH
26R	Asph/Conc	2565	2148		Ap Thr Rwy PAPI 3° LH

RNAV			
BIG	115.10	221	13.8

Remarks

PPR mandatory. Non-radio ACFT not accepted. Use governed by regulations applicable to Gatwick CTR. AD may be used by executive and private ACFT GA subject to the following conditions. GA operators must notify details of each flight in advance to their nominated handling agent who will obtain permission from apron control. Operators are advised that before selecting Gatwick as an alternate, prior arr for GND handling should have been agreed with one of the nominated handling agents. The use of this AD for training is prohibited. Helicopter operations: There are no helicopter alighting areas at AD, all helicopters use Rwys. Handling agents to obtain slots. Helicopters may not carry out direct APP to or from apron areas or Twys. After landing helicopters will GND/air taxi to parking slot. Extreme caution to be used due to wing tip clearance whilst helicopters are taxiing. Operator to provide Noise Certificate details on request. All telephones to ATC may be recorded.

Warnings

In low visibility at night the apron and car park flood lighting may be seen before APP lights on Rwy26L and Rwy26R APP. Except for light signals, GND signals are not displayed. When landing on Rwy26L/R in strong S/SW winds, there is the possibility of building induced turbulence and windshear.

Operating Hrs	H24
Circuits	Nil
Landing Fee	Available on request
Maintenance	Available by arr with local operators
Fuel	AVTUR JET A1
Disabled Facilities	Available
Handling	GA handling **Tel:** 01293 503201 (Interflight)

Restaurants
Restaurants buffets & bars in N & S terminals

Taxis	Available at N & S Terminals	**Operator**	Gatwick Airport Ltd London Gatwick Airport West Sussex, RH6 0NP **Tel:** 0870 000 2468 (GAL) **Tel:** 01293 503089 (Apron Control) **Tel:** 01293 601042 (NATS/FBU) **Fax:** 01293 601033 (NATS) **Fax:** 01293 505149 (Apron Control) www.gatwickairport.com
Car Hire			
Avis	**Tel:** 0870 0104 068		
Hertz	**Tel:** 0870 8460 003		
Weather Info	M T9 T18 Fax 346 A VM VN MOEx		

CTA/CTR Class D Airspace

Normal CTA/CTR Class D Airspace rules apply

1 VFR ACFT should, whenever possible, avoid flying below 3000ft over towns and other populated areas within the zone. ACFT must also avoid over-flying Crawley.

2 SVFR clearances for flights within the Gatwick CTR can be requested and will be given whenever traffic conditions permit. SVFR clearances will not be granted if the flight visibility is less than 3km or the cloud base is less than 1000ft.

3 ACFT may be given a RAD service within the zone, if ATC consider it advisable. However pilots must be able to determine their flight path at all times and comply with the low flying rules.

Visual Reference Points (VRP)

VRP	VOR/VOR	VOR/NDB	VOR/DME
Billingshurst N5100.90 W00027.00	MID 113°/GWC 053°	MID 113°/GY 219°	MID 113°/7nm
Dorking N5113.62 W00020.10	BIG 248°/LON 165°	BIG 248°/GY 356°	BIG 248°/15nm LON 165°/16nm
Guildford N5114.37 W00035.10	MID 010°/BIG 260°	MID 010°/GY 305°	MID 010°/11nm
Handcross N5103.17 W00012.13	MID 094°/SFD 327°	MID 094°/GE 220°	MID 094°/16nm MAY 283°/12nm
Haywards Heath N5100.45 W00005.77	MID 101°/SFD 333°	MID 101°/GE 189°	MID 101°/20nm MAY 269°/8nm
Tunbridge Wells N5108.00 E00015.90	BIG 146°/DET 234°	BIG 146°/GE 101°	BIG 146°/15nm MAY 042°/9nm

L

83ft 3mb	12nm W of London N5128.65 W00027.68	PPR	Alternative AD	Farnborough Denham Non-standard join

Heathrow	LARS Farnborough West 125.2560	ATIS 121.850 (Arr)	ATIS 121.935 128.075 (Dept)	APP 119.725
RAD 125.625 (SVFR & Heli in CTR)	TWR 118.500 118.700	GND 121.900 121.700	DEL 121.975	FIRE 121.600

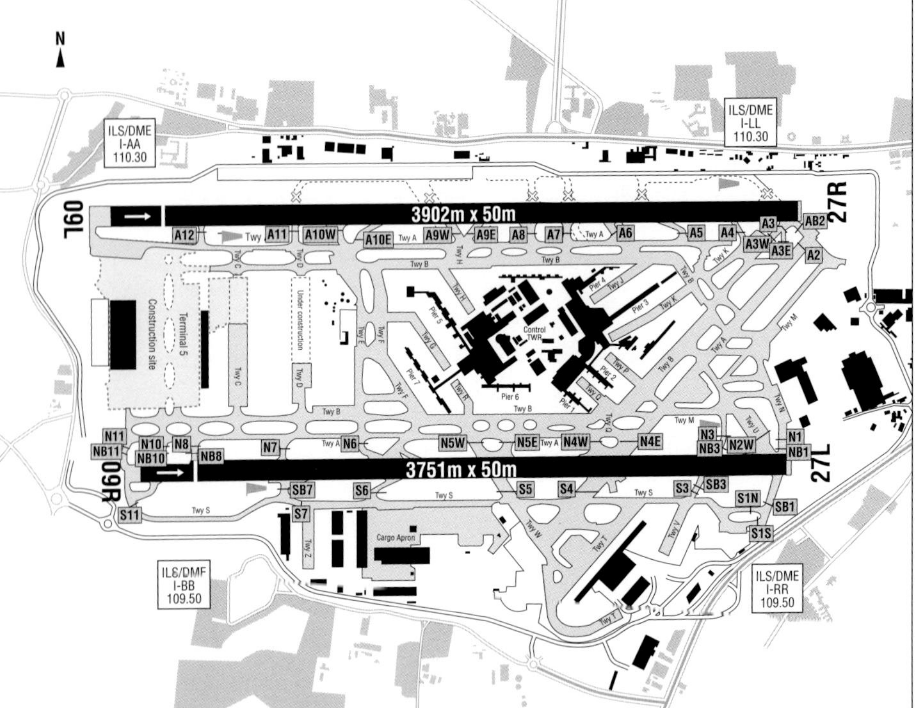

RWY	SURFACE	TORA	LDA	U/L	LIGHTING
09L	Conc/Asph	3901	3595		Ap Thr Rwy PAPI 3°
27R	Conc/Asph	3884	3884		Ap Thr Rwy PAPI 3°
09R	Asphalt	3660	3353		Ap Thr Rwy PAPI 3°
27L	Asphalt	3660	3660		Ap Thr Rwy PAPI 3°

RNAV			
LON	113.60	180	1.0

Remarks

PPR mandatory not more than 10 days not less than 24Hrs. Use governed by regulations applicable to London CTR. IFR procedures apply in all weather conditions. Light single and twin engined ACFT may not use the AD. General and business aviation movements permitted subject to the following conditions. GA operators must notify details of each flight in advance to the Manager Operations Centre. Before selecting Heathrow as an alternate, prior arr for GND handling should have been agreed with one of the nominated handling agents. The use of this AD for training is prohibited. The Arr ATIS is broadcast on the Bovingdon, Biggin, Ockham and Lambourne VOR's.

Helicopter operations

Helicopter aiming point is located at NE end of Block97. Helicopters alighting at the aiming point will GND or air taxi to parking areas as directed by ATC. The following conditions and procedures apply to single-engined and light twin-engined ACFT not fully equipped with radio apparatus (including ILS receiver) as specified in the RAC Section but carrying at least the VHF RT frequencies to allow communication with London Heathrow AD APP/Director, TWR and GND Movement Control: The flight must be made on Special VFR clearance under the weather conditions and along the routes specified in the RAC Section. Operator to provide Noise Certificate details on request. All flights (inc Helicopters) are at all times subject to PPR.

Warnings

When landing on Rwy27R in strong S/SW winds, beware of the possibility of building induced turbulence and large wind shear effects.

Operating Hrs	H24	**Operator**	London Heathrow Airport Heathrow Point Middlesex, UB3 5AP **Tel:** 0870 000 0123 (HAL) **Tel:** 0208 750 2615 (FBU) **Tel:** 0208 750 2560 (NATS) **Tel:** 0208 759 4871 (Manager Ops Centre) **Tel:** 0208 745 3228 (Heli route ATC NATS) **Fax:** 0208 745 3491 (NATS) **Fax:** 0208 750 2617/2618 (FBU) **Fax:** 0208 745 4290 (HAL)
Circuits	Nil		
Landing Fee	BAA Plc Airports Rates		
Maintenance	Available by arr		
Fuel	AVTUR JET A1		
Disabled Facilities	Available		
Restaurants	Restaurants buffets & bars in Terminals		
Taxis	Available at Terminals		
Car Hire			
Avis	**Tel:** 0208 897 9321		
Hertz	**Tel:** 0208 679 1799		
Alamo	**Tel:** 0208 897 0536		
Weather Info	M T9 T18 Fax 348 A VM VSc MOEx		

Effective date:25/09/08

CTR – Class A Airspace

Transition Alt 6000ft

1 SVFR clearances for flights within the London CTR can be requested and will be given whenever traffic conditions permit. ACFT must be able to communicate on the relevant RT freq

2 SVFR will be restricted to ACFT having an all up weight of <5700kg wishing to proceed to an AD within the CTR, or transit the zone at lower levels.

3 SVFR clearance below 1500ft will not be given in the sector enclosed by bearings 020° & 140° from LHR, unless otherwise approved.

4 SVFR clearances will not be granted when the visibility is less than10km or the cloud base is less than 1200ft.

5 ACFT will be given a RAD service within the zone. However, pilots must remain in conditions such that a flight path can be determined visually. At the same time due regard must be given to the low flying rules, especially the ability to land clear of a built-up area in the event of engine failure.

6 SVFR flights may be subject to delay, and pilots must therefore ensure they have adequate fuel reserves and are able to divert if necessary.

L

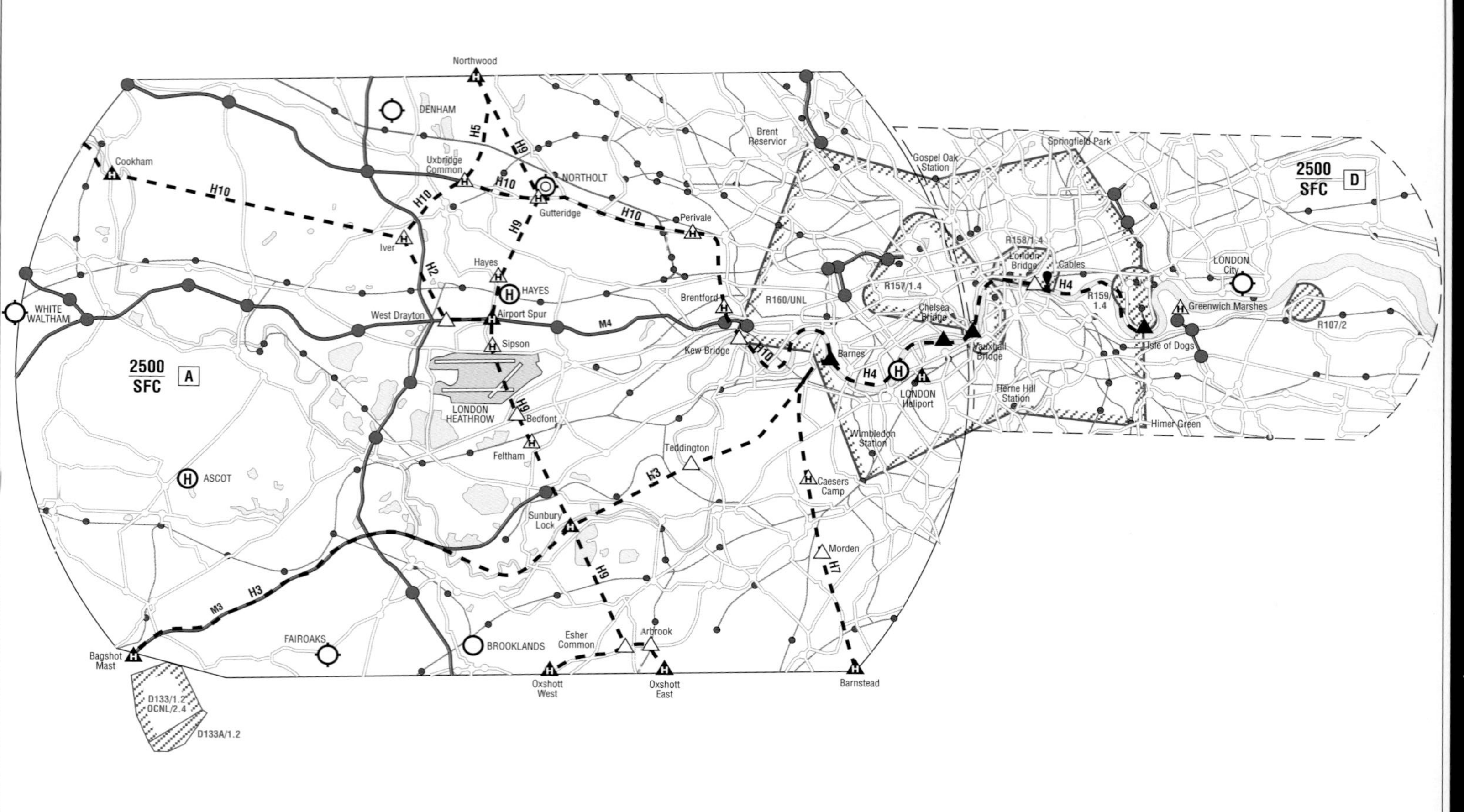

2500
SFC
D
R107/2
LONDON City
Greenwich Marshes
Isle of Dogs
Himer Green
Springfield Park
Cables
R159/1.4
H4
R158/1.4
London Bridge
Herne Hill Station
Vauxhall Bridge
Gospel Oak Station
Chelsea Bridge
R157/1.4
LONDON Heliport
Wimbledon Station
Barnes
Caesers Camp
Morden
H7
Barnstead
Brent Reservior
R160/UNL
H10
Kew Bridge
Brentford
Perivale
Teddington
H3
Arbrook
Oxshott East
H9
Esher Common
Oxshott West
Sunbury Lock
NORTHOLT
Gutteridge
HAYES
Hayes
Airport Spur
Sipson
Bedfont
Feltham
LONDON HEATHROW
M4
Northwood
H5
Uxbridge Common
DENHAM
H2
Iver
West Drayton
BROOKLANDS
FAIROAKS
ASCOT
M3
D133A/1.2
D133/1.2
OCNL/2.4
Bagshot Mast
Cookham
A
WHITE WALTHAM

L

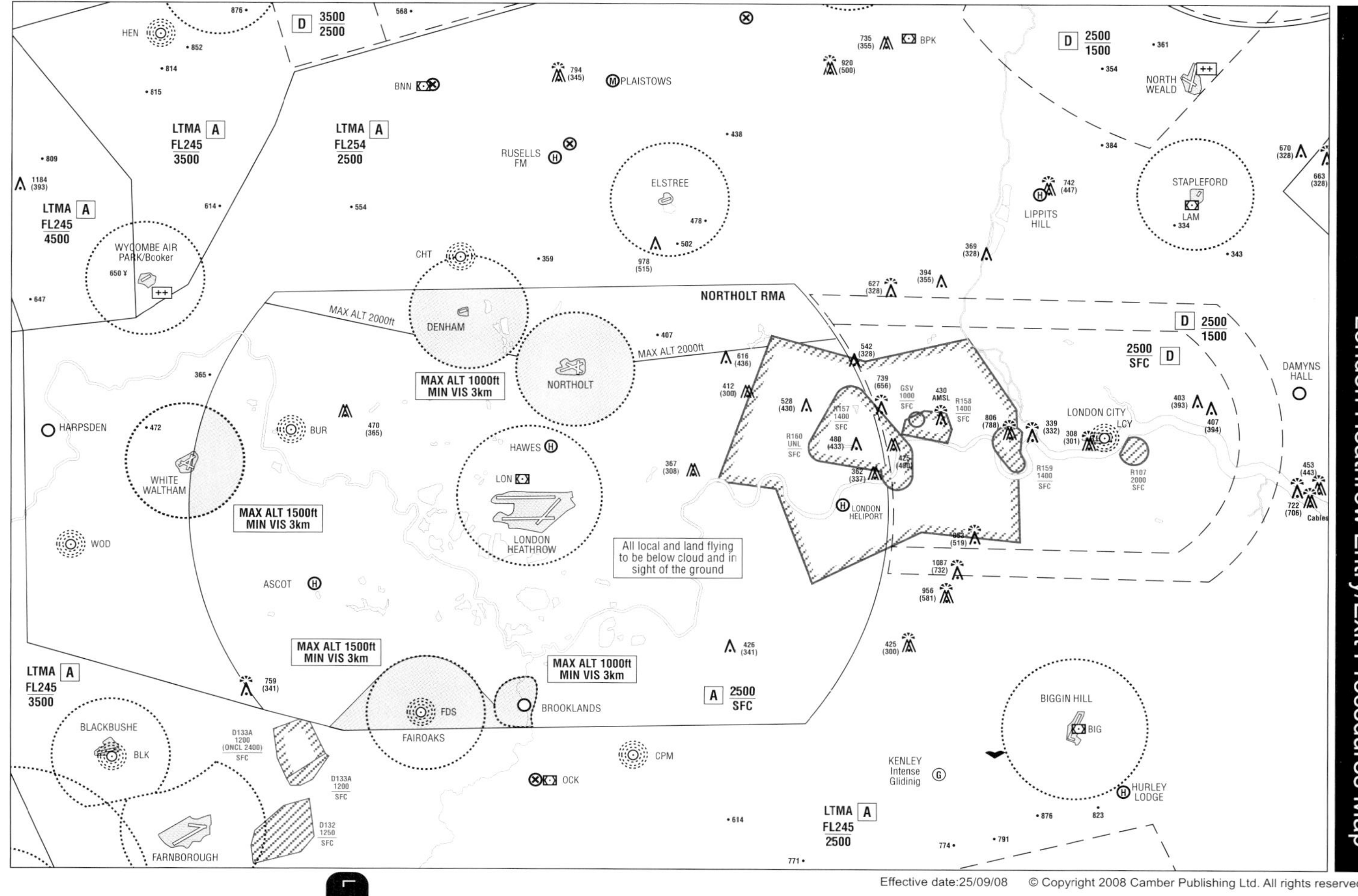

HEN
D 3500 2500
BNN
PLAISTOWS
BPK
D 2500 1500
NORTH WEALD
LTMA A FL245 3500
LTMA A FL254 2500
RUSELLS FM
ELSTREE
LIPPITS HILL
STAPLEFORD
LAM
LTMA A FL245 4500
WYCOMBE AIR PARK/Booker
CHT
NORTHOLT RMA
MAX ALT 2000ft
DENHAM
NORTHOLT
D 2500 1500
2500 SFC D
DAMYNS HALL
MAX ALT 1000ft MIN VIS 3km
GSV 1000 SFC
R157 1400 SFC
R158 1400 SFC
R160 UNL SFC
LONDON CITY
LCY
HARPSDEN
BUR
WHITE WALTHAM
HAWES
LON
R159 1400 SFC
R107 2000 SFC
LONDON HELIPORT
MAX ALT 1500ft MIN VIS 3km
WOD
LONDON HEATHROW
All local and land flying to be below cloud and in sight of the ground
ASCOT
MAX ALT 1500ft MIN VIS 3km
MAX ALT 1000ft MIN VIS 3km
LTMA A FL245 3500
A 2500 SFC
FDS
BROOKLANDS
BIGGIN HILL
BIG
BLACKBUSHE
BLK
FAIROAKS
D133A 1200 (ONCL 2400) SFC
CPM
D133A 1200 SFC
OCK
KENLEY Intense Glidinig
HURLEY LODGE
LTMA A FL245 2500
D132 1250 SFC
FARNBOROUGH

EGGW LONDON LUTON

526ft 18mb	1.5nm E of Luton N5152.48 W00022.10	PPR	Alternative AD **Cranfield** Panshanger

Non-standard join

Luton	LARS Farnborough North 132.800	ATIS 120.575	APP 129.550
TWR 132.550	**DEL 126.725**	**GND 121.750**	**FIRE 121.600**

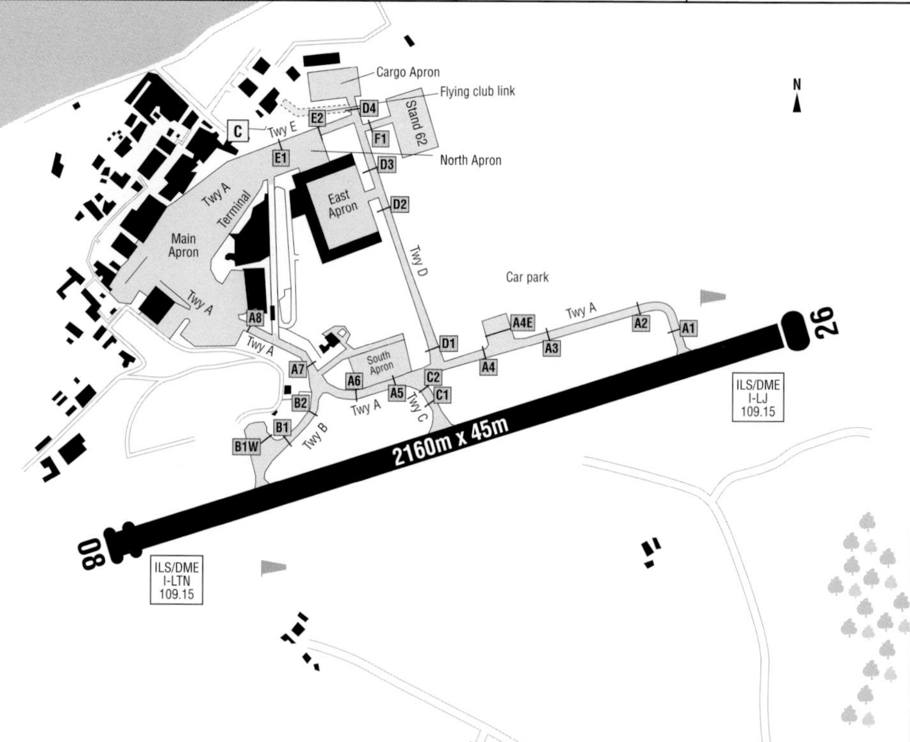

RWY	SURFACE	TORA	LDA	U/L	LIGHTING
08	Asphalt	2160	2160		Ap Thr Rwy PAPI 3°
26	Asphalt	2160	2075		Ap Thr Rwy PAPI 3°

Displaced Thr Rwy26 85m

RNAV			
BNN	113.75	040	11.2

Remarks
Use governed by regulations applicable to Luton CTR. Non-scheduled commercial executive and private ACFT are subject to PPR. All flight training PPR. When taking off from Rwy26 if able to turn cross wind by the end of the Rwy confine circuit to E of London/Luton railway line. To assist parking Arr, details of each flight must be notified in advance to the ATC Watch Manager. All flights using the AD must have a handling agent. AD is available only to qualified pilots. Minimum circuit height for ACFT whose MTWA <5700kg (12500lbs) is 1000ft QFE in the vicinity of AD. Pilots of visiting ACFT to contact apron control before Dept and/or after Arr. Booking out of flights by RTF is not accepted. Booking out must be made with ATC by telephone.
Aids to Navigation: NDB LUT 345.00

Warnings
Pilots of ACFT APP B1, should exercise extreme caution due to the unusual alignment of Twy and Rwy entry point. Grass cutting takes place as required during the summer months. The flying club link is not part of the manoeuvring area, uncontrolled vehicles operate on and close to link, use is at pilots discretion.

Operating Hrs	H24
Circuits	See Remarks
Landing Fee	On application, mandatory handling
Maintenance	**Tel:** 01582 724182 (Signature Flight Support)

Fuel	AVGAS 100LL (0600-2359 Other times by arr with surcharge) AVTUR JET A1 Out of Hrs contact
Shell UK Ltd	**Tel:** 01582 417659
Disabled Facilities	Available

L

Handling	**Tel:** 01582 488410 (Air Foyle) **Tel:** 01582 402040 (Allied Signal) **Tel:** 01582 724182 (Signature) **Tel:** 01582 700900 (Aviance) **Tel:** 01582 618603 (Servisair) **Tel:** 01582 589317 (Harrods Business Aviation)	**Operator**	London Luton Airport Ltd Navigation House Airport Way Luton, Bedfordshire, LU2 9LY **Tel:** 01582 405100 (Switchboard) **Tel:** 01582 395299 (ATC) **Tel:** 01582 395525 (PPR) **Tel:** 01582 395029 (NATS) **Tel:** 01582 395029 (Booking Out) **Tel:** 01582 395355 (Booking Out) **Fax:** 01582 395141 (ATC) **Fax:** 01582 395399 (NATS)
Restaurant	Restaurant refreshments & Club facilities available at AD		
Taxis	Available at Terminal		
Car Hire			
Alamo	**Tel:** 01582 468414		
National	**Tel:** 01582 417723		
Europcar	**Tel:** 01582 413438		
Weather Info	M T9 T18 Fax 358 A VS MOEx ATIS **Tel:** 0906 4744474		

Effective date:25/09/08

Helicopter Operations

VFR helicopters inbound to/dept from Luton AD will normally be required to route via TR, joining the following VRP, in order to minimise noise impact and to ensure integration with arr/dept flights. Dept VFR helicopters should identify their preferred routeing when booking out.

To/from N: Pirton: N5158.30 W00019.90 Offley N5156.02 W00020.50
To/from S and SE: A1(M) J4 N5146.75 W00013.47 Kimpton Hall N5150.75 W00017.80 Hyde N5150.63 W00021.97
To/from S and SW: M1 J8 N5145.37 W00024.97 M1 J9 N5149.22 W00025.08 Hyde N5150.63 W00021.97
To/from London Stansted: Puckeridge N5153.10 E00000.27 Kimpton Hall N5150.75 W00017.80 Hyde N5150.63 W00021.97

Helicopters will typically be issued with VFR clearances not above 1500ft amsl. However, pilots are requested to maintain the highest possible level in accordance with the clearance to minimise noise impact on the gnd.

CTA/CTR Class D Airspace

Normal CTA/CTR Class D Airspace rules apply.
1 Clearances may be requested for SVFR flights within Stansted and Luton Control Zone whenever the traffic situation permits.
2 RAD service maybe given whilst within the zone if ATC consider it advisable. However, pilots must remain in conditions such that a flight path can be determined visually. At the same time, due regard must be given to the low flying rules, especially the ability to alight clear of a built-up area in the event of engine failure.
3 To permit ACFT to operate to and from Luton in IMC, but not IFR, the following Entry/Exit lanes have been established:
a N Lane
b S Lane
4 Both lanes are only 1.5nm wide and use is subject to an SVFR clearance from Luton. ACFT must remain clear of cloud and in sight of the surface, not above 1500ft QNH.
5 Pilots are responsible for their own separation from other ACFT within the lanes and are also responsible for maintaining adequate ground clearance.
SVFR is not compulsory. ACFT can fly VFR in the Luton CTR, subject to ATC clearance.

Visual Reference Points (VRP)

VRP	VOR/DME	VOR/DME	NDB
A1 (M) J4 N5146.75 W00013.47	BPK 292°/5nm	BNN 077°/13nm	LUT 174°
A1 (M) J8 N5145.37 W00024.97	BPK 274°/12nm	BNN 072°/5nm	LUT 218°
Hyde N5150.65 W00021.97	BPK 303°/11nm	BNN 046°/10nm	LUT 237°
Kimpton Hall N5150.75 W00017.80	BPK 311°/9nm	BNN 057°/12nm	LUT 207°
M1 J9 N5149.22 W00025.08	BPK 293°/12nm	BNN 043°/7nm	LUT 236°
Offley N5156.02 W00020.50	BPK 325°/14nm	BNN 035°/15nm	LUT 309°
Pirton N5158.30 W00019.90	BPK 330°/16nm	BNN 031°/17nm	LUT 331°

L

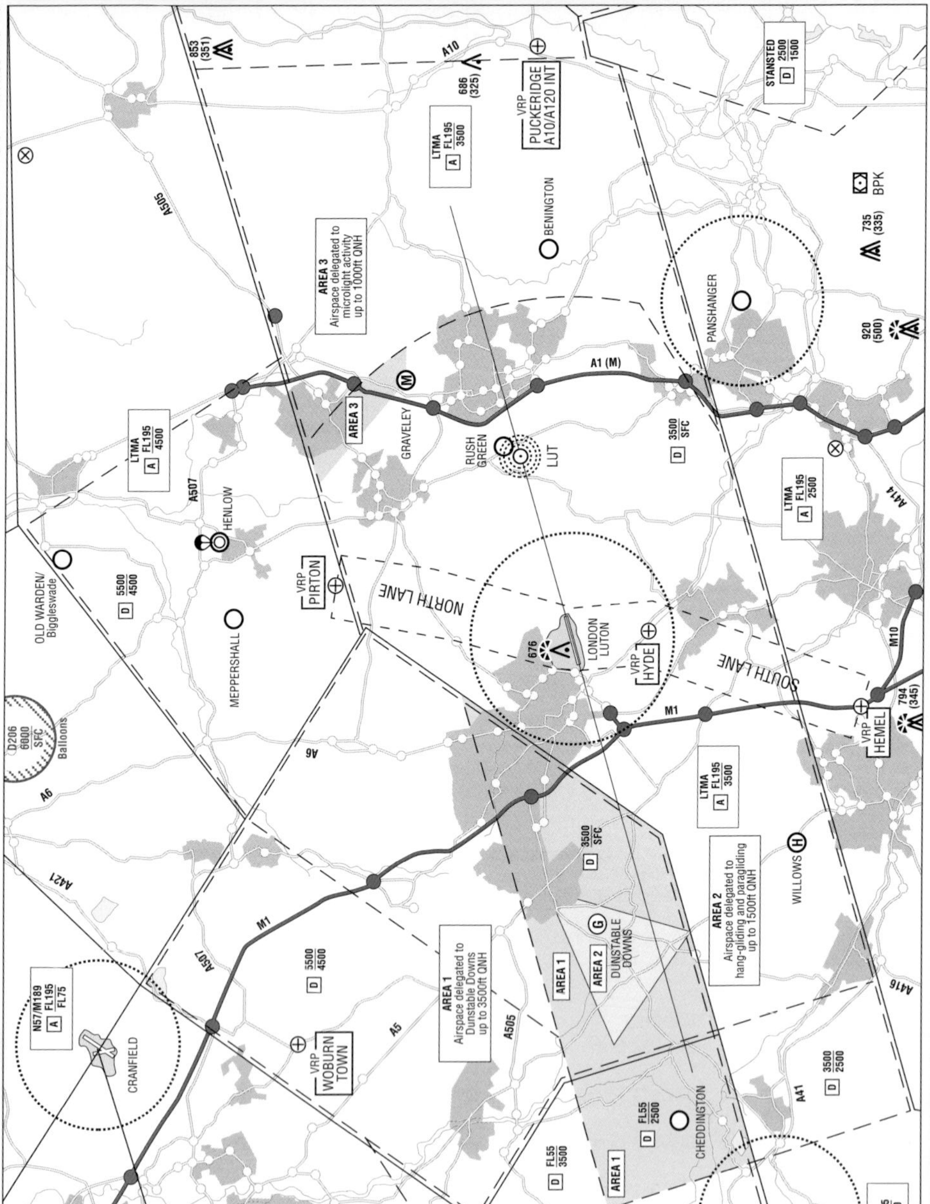

AREA 3
Airspace delegated to
microlight activity
up to 1000ft QNH

AREA 1
Airspace delegated to
Dunstable Downs
up to 3500ft QNH

AREA 2
Airspace delegated to
hang-gliding and paragliding
up to 1500ft QNH

Effective date:25/09/08

L

EGSS LONDON STANSTED

348ft 11mb	2.5nm ENE of Bishops Stortford N5153.10 E00014.10	PPR	Alternative AD Diversion AD	Cambridge Andrewsfield Non-standard join

Stansted	ATIS 127.175	APP Essex 120.625	RAD 126.950
TWR 123.800	GND 121.725	DEL 121.950	FIRE 121.600

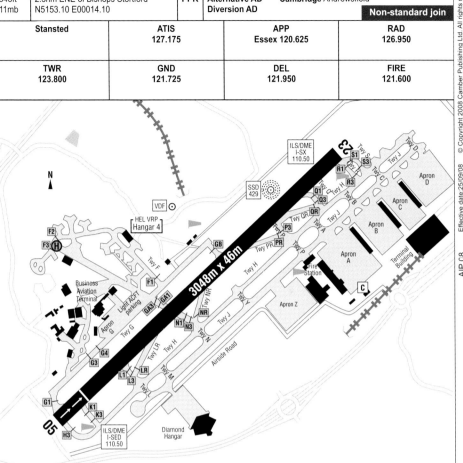

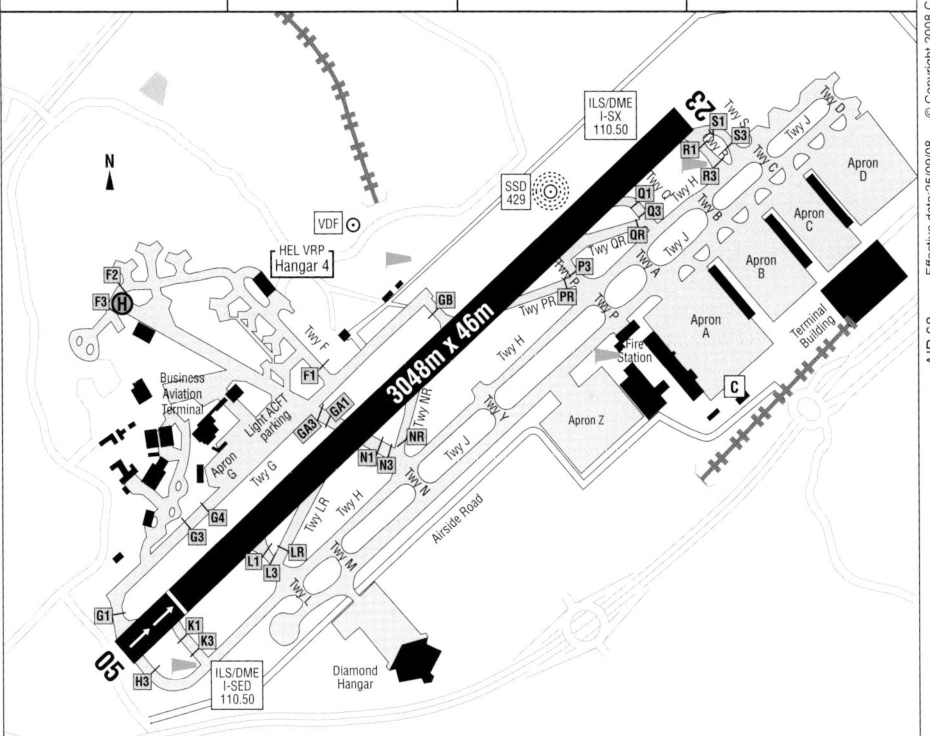

RWY	SURFACE	TORA	LDA	U/L	LIGHTING
05	Asphalt	3048	2748		Ap Thr Rwy PAPI 3° LHS
23	Asphalt	3048	3048		Ap Thr Rwy PAPI 3° LHS

RNAV			
BKY	116.25	137	9.0

L

Remarks
PPR not less than 4Hrs before intended movement. Non-radio ACFT not accepted. Use governed by regulations applicable to Stansted CTR. Use of a handling agent is mandatory. Pilots of non-commercial (GA) flights Arr from abroad are required to report to Customs at the designated Customs Clearance Office in the Business Aviation Terminal. The Business Aviation Terminal is manned 0700-2300 (L) daily & available outside Hrs by Arr with Harrods Business Aviation. The use of the AD for training is subject to prior permission, contact Stansted ATC before Dept. On PH flying training is permitted only by ACFT whose MTWA <9000kg.0700-2300 HAP F available for use located Twy F. During poor weather conditions helicopters will be instructed to use Rwys. APP HAP F from W passing N of Bury Lodge Hotel, remaining clear of Burton End. Helicopter inbound from E pass over Thr not below 500ft before commencing APP from W. Helicopters may Arr/Dept from the aiming point and air or GND taxi as directed by ATC. Twy E & W cul de sac taxi lanes ltd to ACFT with wingspan of <34.5m. Flying training is extremely limited. Make requests to ACL. Dept ACFT to call GND/DEL 10mins before start up. All telephone calls are recorded

Warnings
Noise: ACFT using AD must maintain as high an altitude as practicable. Avoid over flying Bishops Stortford, Sawbridgeworth and Stansted Mount Fitchet below 2500ft amsl and St. Elizabeth's Home below 4000 ft amsl.

Operating Hrs	H24	**Maintenance**	Available by arr
Circuits	Do not descend below 2000ft QNH down wind. Avoid over flying Gt Dunmow & Takeley	**Fuel**	JET A1 Water/Meth 45/55/30 N side JET A1 available 0700-2300 (L). At other times a call out charge of £100.00 will be levied unless fuel is required for medical flight or prior arr has been made
Landing Fee	BAA Plc Airport Rates	Esso	**Tel:** 01279 663178/9

Effective date:25/09/08   AIP C8

Disabled Facilities	Available	**Operator**	Stansted Airport Ltd Stansted Essex CM24 1QW **Tel:** 08700 000303 (AD) **Tel:** 01279 669328 (NATS) **Fax:** 01279 662066 (AD) **Fax:** 01279 669336 (NATS/FBU) www.baa.com/stansted
Handling	**Tel:** 01279 665312 (Harrods Aviation) **Tel:** 01279 831000 (Inflite Ltd) **Tel:** 01279 680349 (Universal Aviation UK) **Fax:** 01279 681367 (Harrods Aviation) **Fax:** 01279 837900 (Inflite Ltd) **Fax:** 01279 680372 (Universal) (Universal Aviation UK)		
Restaurants	Buffets & bars in Terminal		
Taxis/Car Hire	Available at Terminal		
Weather Info	M T9 T18 Fax 352 A VM MOEx ATIS **Tel:** 01279 669325		

CTA/CTR Class D Airspace
Transition Alt 6000ft
Normal CTA/CTR Class D Airspace rules apply
1 Clearances may be requested for SVFR flights within the Stansted and Luton Control Zone and will be given when ever the traffic situation permits.
2 RAD service may be given whilst within the zone if ATC consider it advisable. However, pilots must remain in conditions such that a flight path can be determined visually. At the same time due regard must be given to the low flying rules, especially in the event of engine failure.
3 Stansted VFR and SVFR Arr/Dept are cleared normally not above 1500ft QNH by the following routes:
a Audley End Railway Station via M11
b Gt Dunmow via A120
c Puckeridge via A120 avoiding Bishops Stortford
d Nuthampstead VRP
4 VFR traffic wishing to transit the Stansted zone can expect a clearance via the routes detailed in 3 a-d Gt Dunmow and either Puckeridge or Nuthampstead routing via the Stansted overhead not above 2000ft QNH. NB Beware of ACFT in the Nuthampstead circuit up to 1500ftQNH.
5 The following areas are notified for the purposes of the low flying rule:
a Within 1nm of the A10 and the river Lea from the Ware (VRP) to the intersection with the M25.
b Within 1nm of the M25 from its intersection with the A10 clockwise to its intersection with the M11
c Within 1nm of the track between Ware and Epping (VRP) where the route lies beneath the CTR/CTA.
6 a For clearance contact Essex RAD giving at least 5min notice. Do not enter controlled airspace without clearance.
b Clearance may be subject to delay or re-routing.
c Pilots are reminded of the close proximity of busy minor AD adjacent to CTA/CTR periphery.

Visual Reference Points (VRP)

VRP	VOR/VOR	VOR/DME
Audley End Stn N5200.25 E00012.42	BKY 083°/LAM 007°	BKY 083°/5nm
Braintree N5152.70 E00033.23	BKY 113°/LAM 048°	LAM 048°/20nm
Chelmsford N5144.00 E00028.40	BKY 138°/LAM 068°	LAM 068°/13nm
Epping N5142.00 E00006.67	BKY 177°/BNN 095°	BNN 095°/25nm
Gt Dunmow N5152.30 E00021.75	BKY 125°/LAM 032°	BKY 125°/13nm
Haverhill N5204.95 E00026.07	BKY 070°/LAM 023°	LAM 023°/28nm
Nuthampsted (Disused AD) N5159.40 E00003.72	BKY VOR site	LAM 353°/21nm
Puckeridge (A10/A120) N5153.10 E00000.27	BKY 201°/LAM 341°	BKY 201°/7nm
Ware N5148.70 W00001.60	BKY 200°/LAM 329°	LAM 329°/12nm

L

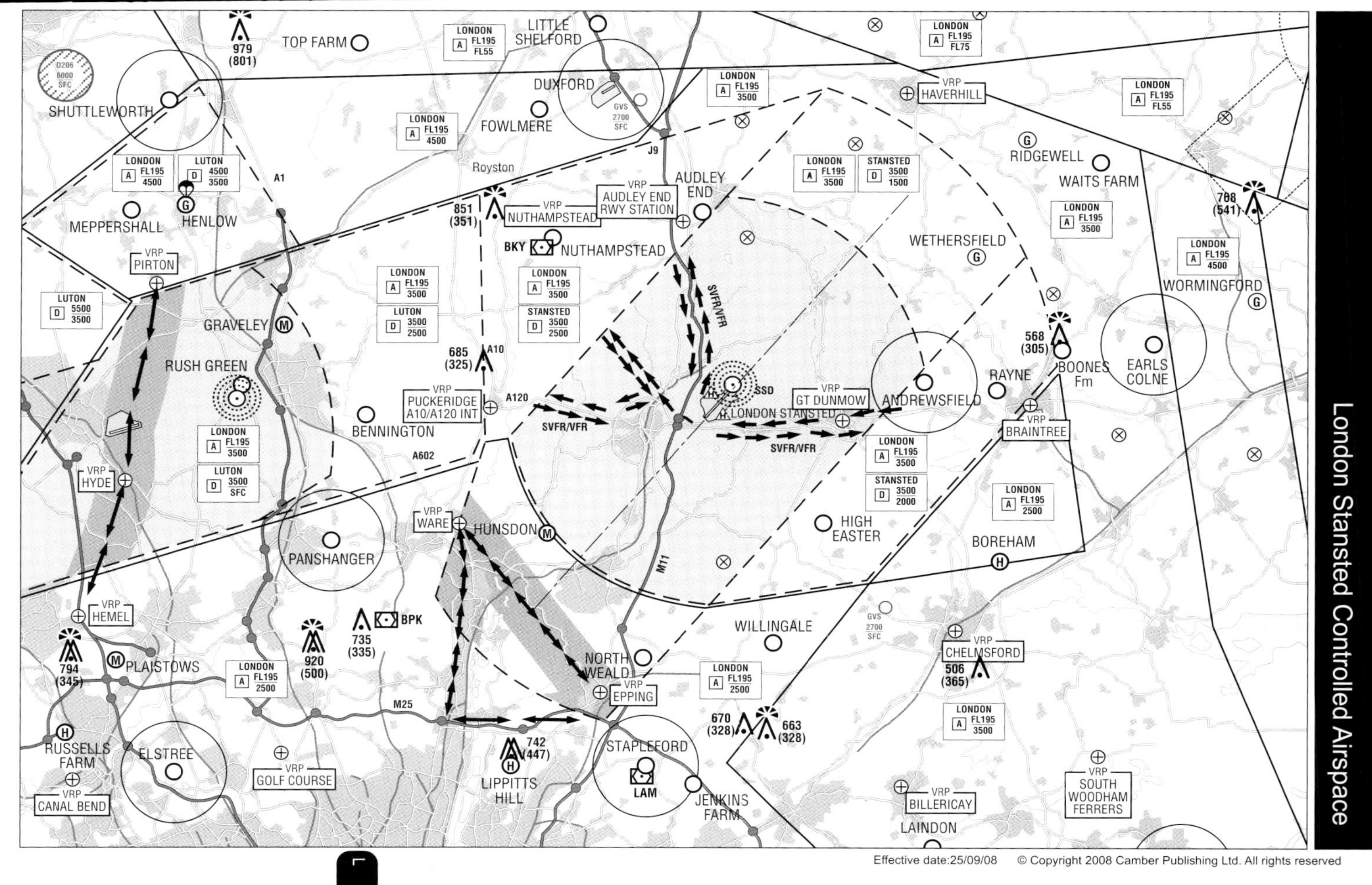

Effective date:25/09/08

L

EGAE LONDONDERRY

22ft 1mb	7nm ENE of Londonderry N5502.57 W00709.67	Alte rnat	ive AD Diversion AD	Belfast Aldergrove

Non-standard join

City of Derry	APP 123.625	TWR 134.150	FIRE 121.600

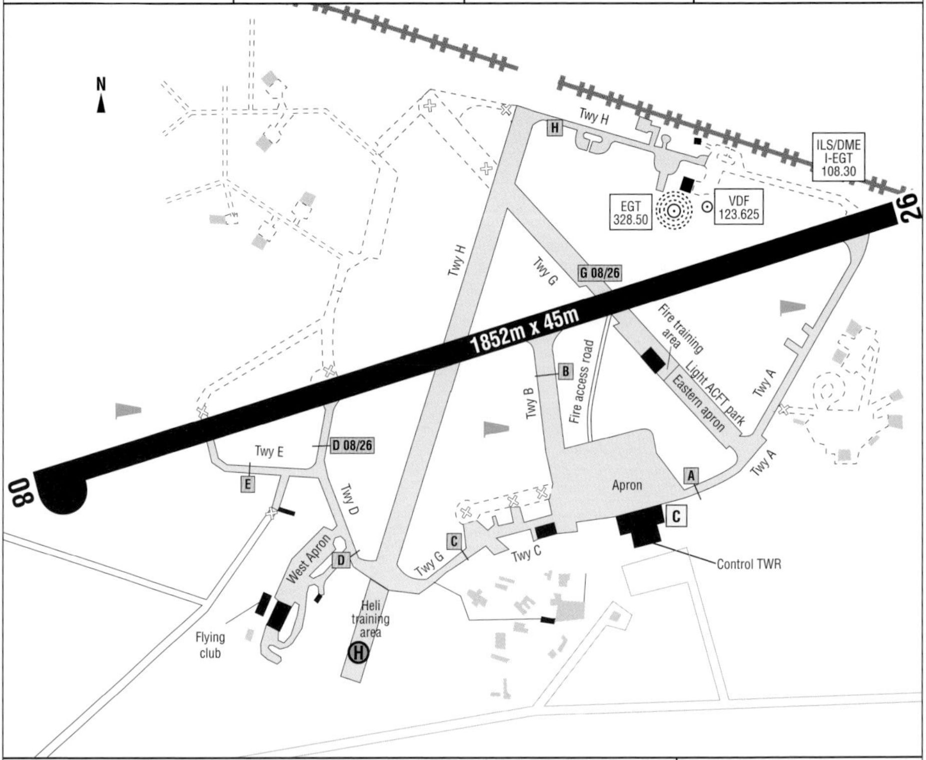

RWY	SURFACE	TORA	LDA	U/L	LIGHTING
08	Asphalt	1812	1690		Thr Rwy PAPI 3° LHS
26	Asphalt	1817	1817		Thr Rwy PAPI 3° LHS

RNAV

L

Remarks

PPR. Hi-Vis. Rwy26 sequenced strobe APP lighting. Railway crosses undershoot Rwy26. No ACFT movements Rwy08 Dept/Rwy26 Arr 5 mins prior train. Delays possible. No-radio ACFT subject to ATC approval. Single engine ACFT avoid over-flying chemical plant 2-3nm W of AD below 1500ft. Training – book with ATC. Rwy08/26 no training after 2359 (L). ACFT must not execute in-flight turns within AD boundary unless instructed by ATC. Use of AD subject published terms & conditions, (on request). ACFT to/from destinations outside N Ireland use main terminal building customs, Special Branch & Immigration. ACFT minimise noise disturbance. ACFT must not fly below visual glide path indicated by PAPIS.
Visual aid to location: Abn, white flashing.

Warnings

Large congregations of sea-birds in APP area Rwy26. Close proximity Ballykelly 5nm ENE AD, close to the final APP centre line to Rwy26 &, Rwy lighting may be displayed there. Pilots should positively identify Eglington before committing to land.

Operating Hrs Mon-Fri 0630-2100 Sat 0630-1630
Sun 1030-2130 (Summer) + 1Hr (Winter)

Circuits 08 1000ft LH
26 LH 1200ft & 1000ft RH. Night 1500ft

Landing Fee Available on request

Maintenance Available

Fuel AVGAS JET A1 100LL

Disabled Facilities

Restaurant Snack bar in main Terminal

Taxis Available at Terminal

Car Hire
Avis **Tel:** 02871 811708
Hertz **Tel:** 02871 811994
Eurocar **Tel:** 02871 812773
Ford Rent a Car **Tel:** 02871 367137

Weather Info M T9 Fax 354 BEL

Visual Reference Points (VRP)		**Operator**	
Buncrana	N5508.00 W00727.40		Derry City Council
Coleraine	N5507.90 W00640.30		City of Derry Airport
Dungiven	N5455.70 W00655.50		Airport Road, Eglinton
Moville	N5511.40 W00702.40		Londonderry, BT47 3GY
New Buildings	N5457.50 W00721.50		**Tel:** 02871 812152
			Tel: 02871 811246
			Tel: 02871 810784 Ex 208 (Ops)
			Tel: 02871 811099 (ATC)
			Fax: 02871 811426 (Admin)
			Fax: 02871 812152 (ATC)

80ft 2mb	By A1 close to W of Sandy N5207.44 W00018.35	PPR	**Alternative AD**	**Cranfield** Little Gransden

Sandy	**A/G 129.825 (Microlight freq) make blind calls**

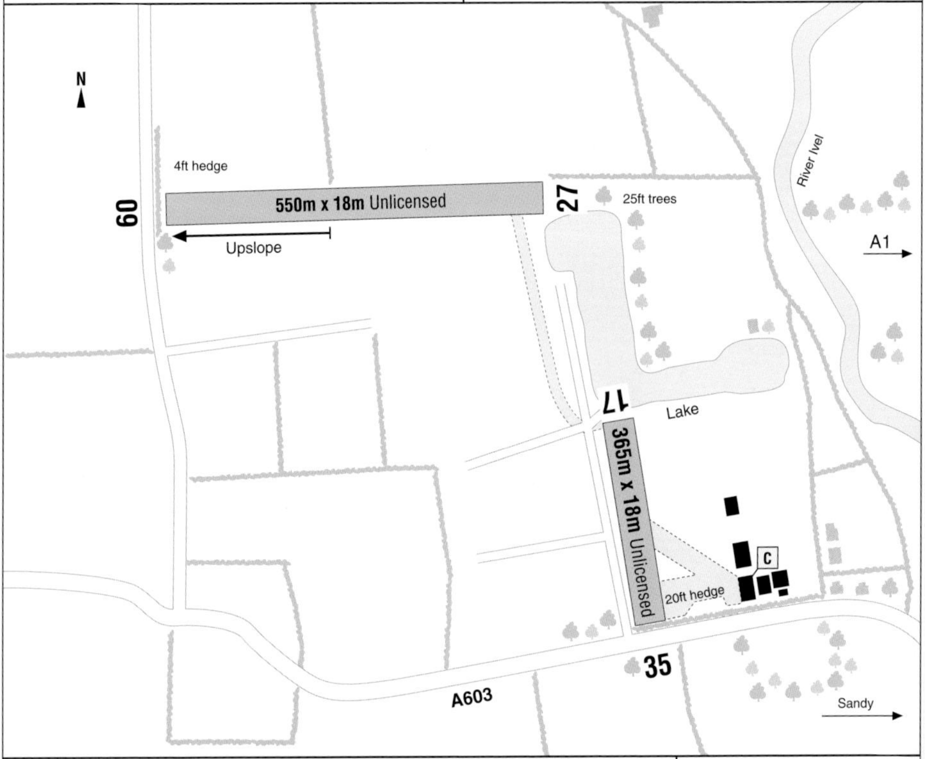

N
4ft hedge
09
550m x 18m Unlicensed
27
Upslope
25ft trees
River Ivel
A1
17
Lake
365m x 18m Unlicensed
C
20ft hedge
35
A603
Sandy

RWY	SURFACE	TORA	LDA	U/L	LIGHTING
17/35	Grass			365x18	Nil
09/27	Grass			550x18	Nil

Rwy27 upslope final third

RNAV			
CFD	116.50	080	11.7

Remarks
PPR by telephone. Briefing essential. Microlight AD with Ab-initio training but suitable STOL ACFT welcome at pilots own risk.

Warnings
Considerable road traffic crosses Rwy35 short final using A603. 25ft trees adjacent to lake on short final Rwy27. 4ft hedge close to Rwy09 Thr. Sandy TV mast 972ft amsl (790ft agl) 2.5nm E of AD. Shuttleworth AD 2.5nm SSW of AD has regular air displays during the summer period, particularly at weekends.
Noise: Do not over fly Sandy E of AD.

Operating Hrs SR-SS
Circuits 35 LH, 27, 17, 09 RH
No dead side
Landing Fee Nil
Maintenance Microlight maintenance available
Fuel MOGAS available from nearby garage
Disabled Facilities Nil
Restaurants Tea & Coffee available at AD
Little Chef within walking distance adjacent to A1
Taxis
Sandy Taxis **Tel:** 01767 683333

Car Hire Nil
Weather Info Air Cen MOEx
Operator Snowy Barton
Long Acres Farm
Mogerhanger Road
Sandy, Beds, SG19 1ND
Tel: 01767 691616

L

154ft 5mb	3.5nm SW of Stratford-on-Avon N5208.44 W00145.18	PPR	Alternative AD	Birmingham Wellesbourne Mountford

Non-standard join

Long Marston	ATIS	APP	A/G
	Birmingham 136.025	Coventry 119.250	129.825 (Microlight freq)

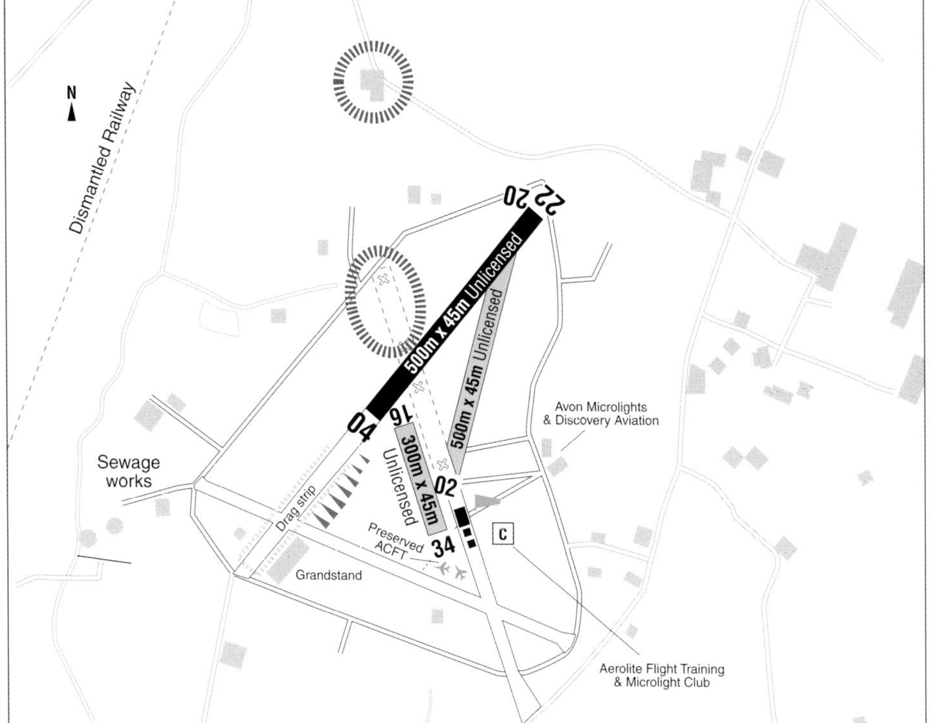

RWY	SURFACE	TORA	LDA	U/L	LIGHTING
02/20	Grass			500x45	Nil
04/22	Asphalt			500x45	Nil
16/34	Grass			300x45	Nil

RNAV			
HON	113.65	199	13.2

Remarks
PPR by telephone. Visiting ACFT welcome. AD used for microlighting and occasional motor sport.

Warnings
Wellesbourne Mountford ATZ 3nm NE.
Noise: Avoid over flying HMP Long Lartin (R204), 8nm WSW of AD, Long Marston village to W & farm

Operating Hrs	0900-SS (L)
Circuits	02, 22 RH, 04, 20 LH 600ft QFE 04, 22 500ft QFE
Landing Fee	Nil £25 without PPR
Maintenance	Microlight available
Fuel	Nil
Disabled Facilities	Nil
Restaurant	Tea & coffee making facilities
Taxis/Car Hire	Can be arr locally
Weather Info	Air Cen MOEx

Operator
H G Hodges & Son Ltd
Long Marston Airfield
Stratford on Avon
Warwickshire
CV37 8LL
Tel: 01789 414119
Tel: 07768 525567
Fax: 01789 262030

Effective date:25/09/08 OP 04

172ft 5mb	11.5nm SW of Norwich AD N5229.30 E00113.00	PPR	**Alternative AD** **Norwich** Seething

Cheqair Ops	**LARS** **Norwich 119.350**	**LARS** **Marham 124.150**	**A/G** **122.950**

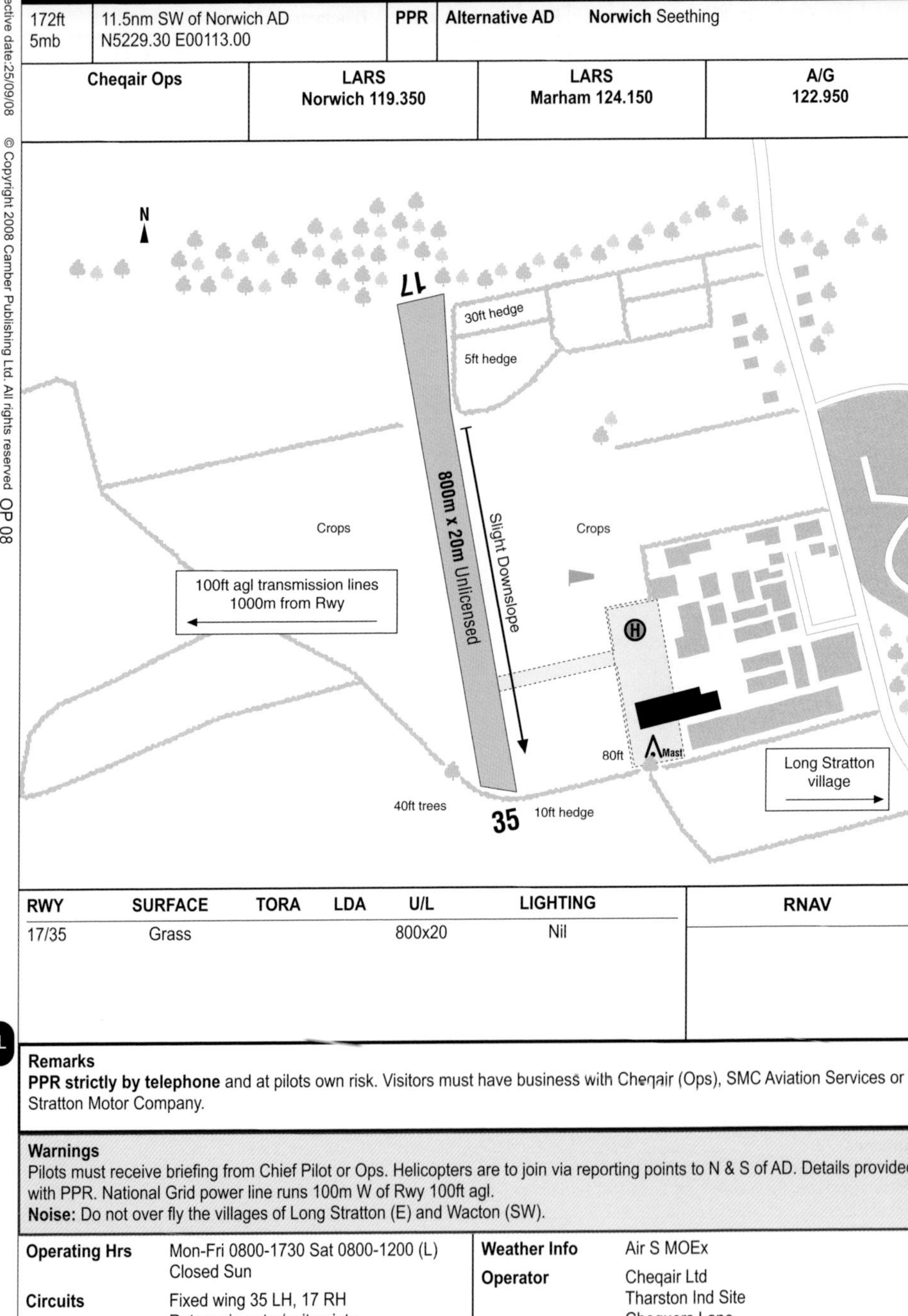

RWY	SURFACE	TORA	LDA	U/L	LIGHTING	RNAV
17/35	Grass			800x20	Nil	

Remarks
PPR strictly by telephone and at pilots own risk. Visitors must have business with Cheqair (Ops), SMC Aviation Services or Stratton Motor Company.

Warnings
Pilots must receive briefing from Chief Pilot or Ops. Helicopters are to join via reporting points to N & S of AD. Details provided with PPR. National Grid power line runs 100m W of Rwy 100ft agl.
Noise: Do not over fly the villages of Long Stratton (E) and Wacton (SW).

Operating Hrs Mon-Fri 0800-1730 Sat 0800-1200 (L)
Closed Sun

Circuits Fixed wing 35 LH, 17 RH
Rotary via entry/exit points

Landing Fee £15

Maintenance Nil

Fuel JET A1

Hangarage Subject to availability

Disabled Facilities

Restaurant Nil

Taxis/Car Hire Available from Operator by arr

Weather Info Air S MOEx

Operator Cheqair Ltd
Tharston Ind Site
Chequers Lane
Long Stratton
Norwich, NR15 2PE
Tel: 01508 531144 (PPR)
Fax: 01508 531670
ops@cheqair.com
www.cheqair.com

L

EGQS LOSSIEMOUTH

41ft 2mb	3nm NW of Elgin N5742.31 W00320.35	PPR MIL	Alternative AD Inverness Wick Diversion AD

Non-standard join

Lossiemouth	LARS/DEPT	APP/DIR	TWR/GND
	119.350	123.300	118.200

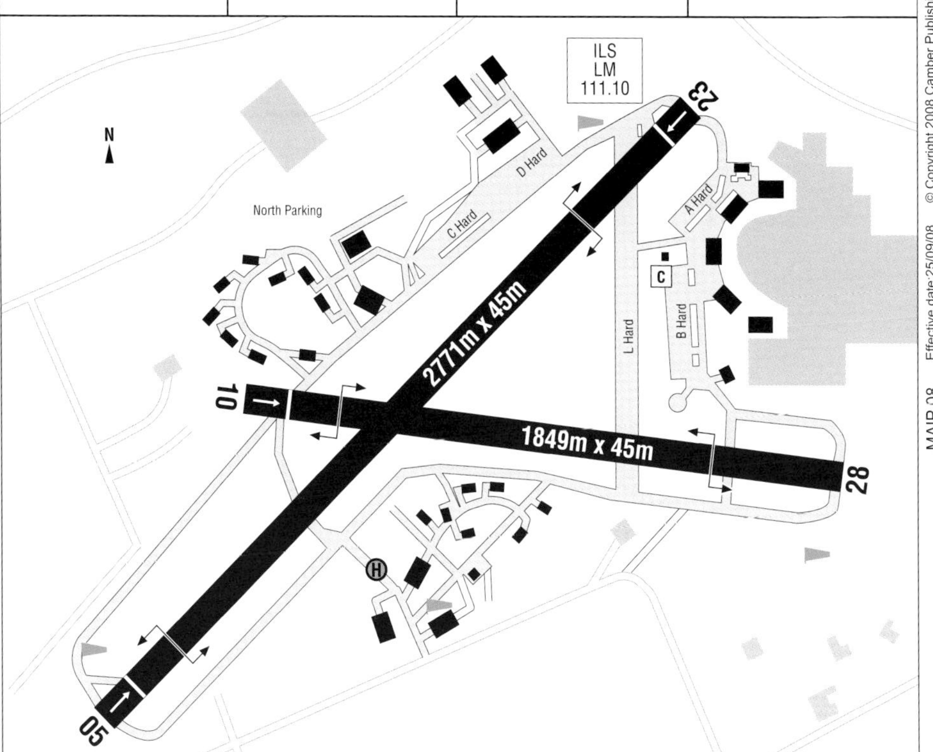

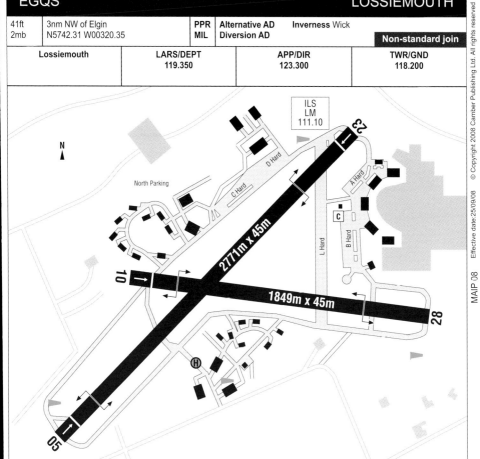

RWY	SURFACE	TORA	LDA	U/L	LIGHTING
23	Asphalt	2771	2678		Ap Thr Rwy PAPI 2.5° RH
05	Asphalt	2771	2771		Ap Thr Rwy PAPI 2.5° RH
10	Asphalt	1849	1751		Ap Thr Rwy PAPI 3.0° LH
28	Asphalt	1849	1849		Ap Thr Rwy PAPI 2.5 RH

Displaced Thr Rwy05 76m
Arrester Gear Rwy23/28 426m from Thr
Arrester Gear Rwy05 396m from Thr
Arrester Gear Rwy10 61m from Thr

RNAV			
INS	109.20	073	24.6

Remarks
PPR required 24Hrs. ATZ active H24. Aerial farm at Mill town Disused AD 4nm SE of AD.
Visual aid to location: IBn LM Red

Warnings
Noise: Avoid over flying Elgin, Lossiemouth & Gordonstoun school.

Operating Hrs	Mon-Thu 0800-1800 Fri 0800-1700 (L)
Circuits	Join not below 1000ft QFE All circuits LH
Landing Fee	Charges in accordance with MOD policy Contact Station Ops for details
Maintenance	Nil
Fuel	JET A1
Disabled Facilities	Nil
Restaurants	Nil
Taxis/Car Hire	Nil
Weather Info	M T Fax 356 GWC ATIS **Tel:** 01343 817666
Operator	RAF Lossiemouth Lossiemouth Morayshire IV31 6SD **Tel:** 01343 817426 (ATC) **Tel:** 01343 816872 (OPS) **Fax:** 01343 817148 (ATC)

60ft 2mb	1.5nm SE of Louth N5321.50 E00002.00	PPR	**Alternative AD**	**Humberside** Wickenby

Non Radio	LARS Waddington 127.350	LARS Coningsby 120.800	Safetycom 135.475

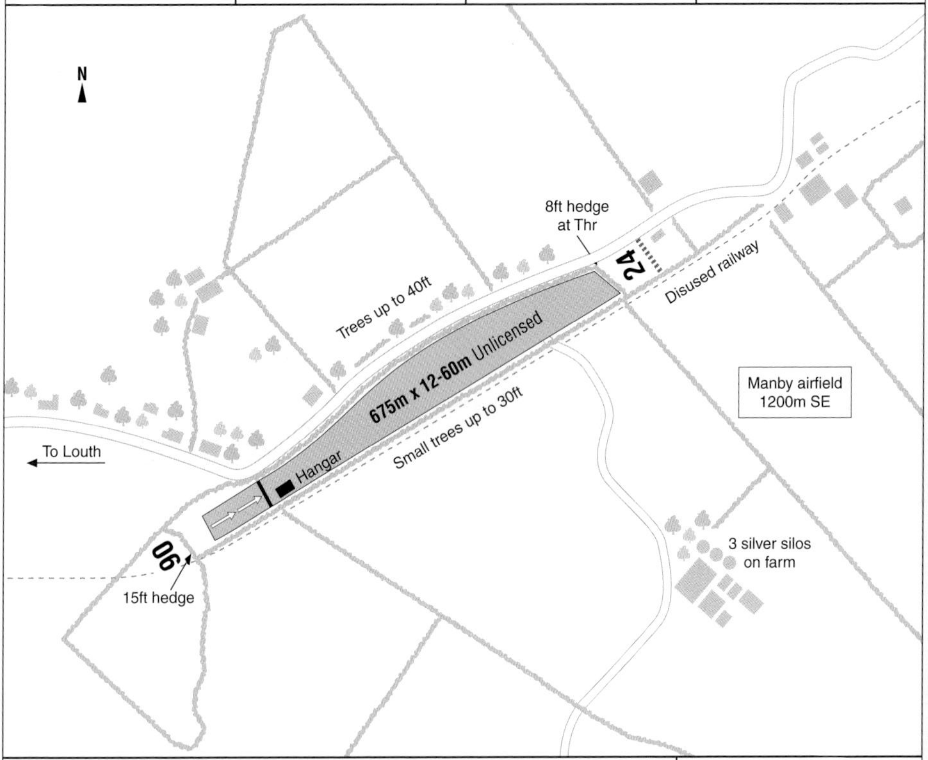

RWY	SURFACE	TORA	LDA	U/L	LIGHTING
06/24	Grass			675x12-60	Nil

Rwy06 grass run off 100m

RNAV

Remarks
PPR by telephone. AD of variable width between the Louth to Stewton road and the disused, (and removed), Louth to Mablethorpe railway. The witness marks of the old railway track are clearly visible. Visiting pilots are welcome at pilots own risk. AD is unusual in its location and great care should be taken.

Warnings
AD is bordered by mature hedges and trees which may cause turbulence. AD has undulations in the centre. Identification of the Thr is particularly important. Rwy24 Thr the adjoining field is used for paddocks and a hedge across it. Rwy is to the W of the hedge.

Operating Hrs	SR-SS
Circuits	As you wish Avoid local habitation 1000ft QFE
Landing Fee	Nil
Maintenance	Nil
Fuel	Nil
Disabled Facilities	Nil
Restaurant	Nil
Taxi/Car Hire	Operator can provide help/assistance
Weather Info	Air N MOEx

Operator Douglas Electronic Industries Ltd
55 Eastfield Road
Louth, Lincs, LN11 7AL
Tel: 01507 603643

 OP 07

L

50ft 1mb	11nm ENE of Norwich City Centre N5243.10 E00133.07	PPR	**Alternative AD** **Diversion AD**	**Norwich** Seething

Non radio	LARS Norwich 119.350	Safetycom 135.475

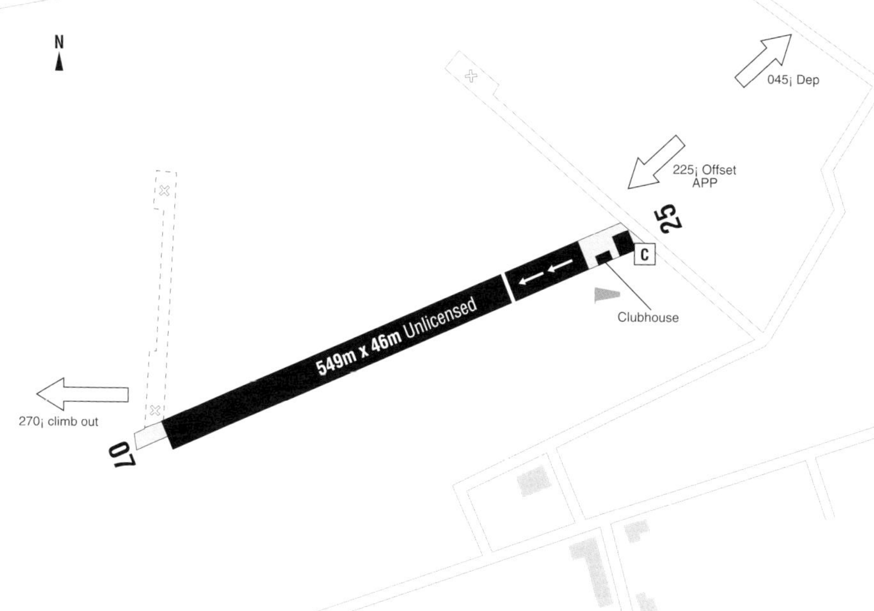

RWY	SURFACE	TORA	LDA	U/L	LIGHTING
07	Concrete			420x46	Nil
25	Concrete			549x46	Nil

RNAV

Remarks
PPR essential. No microlights. Visiting ACFT and vehicle parking on S side of Rwy to W of clubhouse.

Warnings
Hangar at E end of Rwy necessitates an off-set APP Rwy25. Loose stones on Rwy. Large commercial helicopters operate at low altitudes to the E of AD following defined helicopter routes.
Noise: AD situated in the heart of Broadland, please fly with consideration.

Operating Hrs	Available on request
Circuits	Nil
Landing Fee	Single £10 Light commercial £30
Maintenance	Nil
Fuel	Nil
Disabled Facilities	Nil
Restaurant	Nil
Taxis/Car Hire	Nil
Weather Info	Air S MOEx

Operator
Ludham Airield Ltd
c/o Musicbank Ltd
Lefevre Way
Gapton Hall Ind Estate
Gt Yarmouth
Norfolk NR31 0NW
Tel: 07787 554389 (Tony Walsh)
Tel: 01493 369969 (Tony Walsh)
Tel: 07899 915103 (Mark Tingle)
Tel: 07747 535135 (Don Sargant)
www.ludhamairfield.org

Effective date:25/09/08 OP 08

L

455ft 15mb	11nm NW of Hartland Point N5110.20 W00440.23	PPR	Alternative AD	Swansea Pembrey

Non-radio	FIS London 124.750	Safetycom 135.475

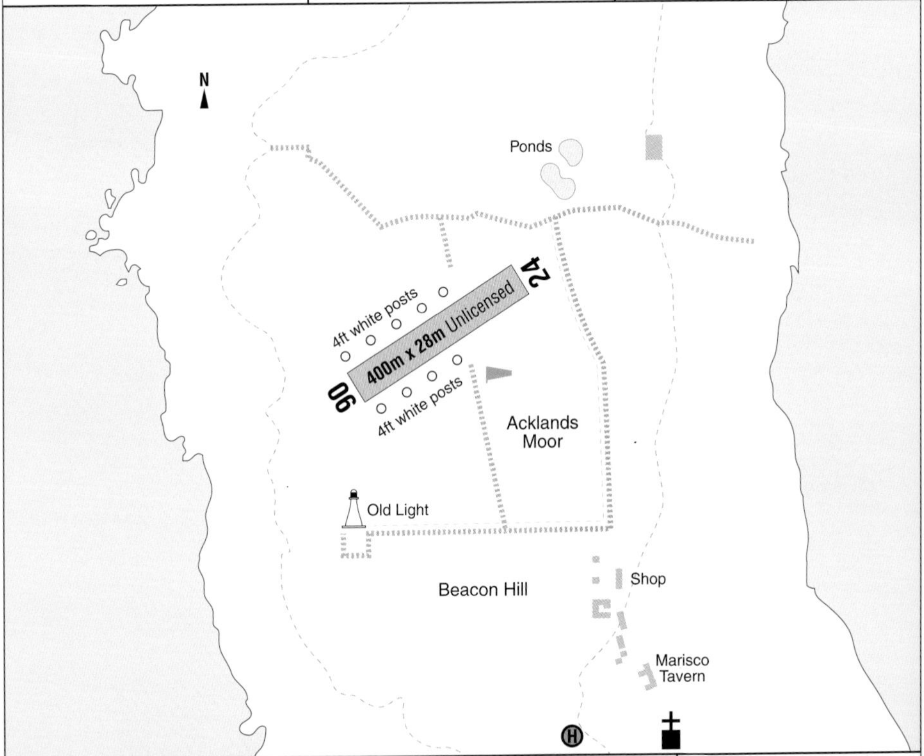

N
Ponds
4ft white posts
400m x 28m Unlicensed
24
06
4ft white posts
Acklands Moor
Old Light
Beacon Hill
Shop
Marisco Tavern

RWY	SURFACE	TORA	LDA	U/L	LIGHTING	RNAV
06/24	Grass			400x28	Nil	

Remarks
PPR by telephone. Light ACFT welcome at pilots own risk. Rwy has no designators but is marked by 4ft white posts at its edges on SW part only. The island has many interesting buildings and much wildlife. The Old Lighthouse is close to SW of strip.

Warnings
This is a difficult strip and for the experienced pilot only. The Rwy is convex in configuration. PPR is essential so that livestock may be moved. Advise land Rwy06 if wind conditions allow, the strip is bumpy and undulating and is only suitable for landing in good weather conditions.
Noise: Please do not low fly in the vicinity of the island to avoid disturbance to bird colonies and possibility of bird strike. However a fly by is advised to examine strip prior to landing.

Operating Hrs Available on request
Circuits 1000ft QFE
Landing Fee Administered by the National Trust Landing fee is £12 + £5 National Trust admission per person (waived on production of NT membership card)
Maintenance Nil
Fuel Nil
Disabled Facilities

Restaurants
Marisco Tavern (within easy walking distance of the strip) B&B sometimes available contact the operator for more info

Taxis/Car Hire Nil
Weather Info Air SW MOEx
Operator The Lundy Island Company
The Lundy Shore Office
The Quay
Bideford
Devon, EX39 2LY
Tel: 01237 470074
Fax: 01237 477779
admin@lundyisland.co.uk
www.lundyisland.co.uk

 OP 08

L

13ft 0mb	1.2nm E of Lydd N5057.37 E00056.35	PPR	Alternative AD **Manston** Lashenden

Non-standard join

Lydd	APP	TWR	ATIS
	120.700	120.700 128.525	129.225

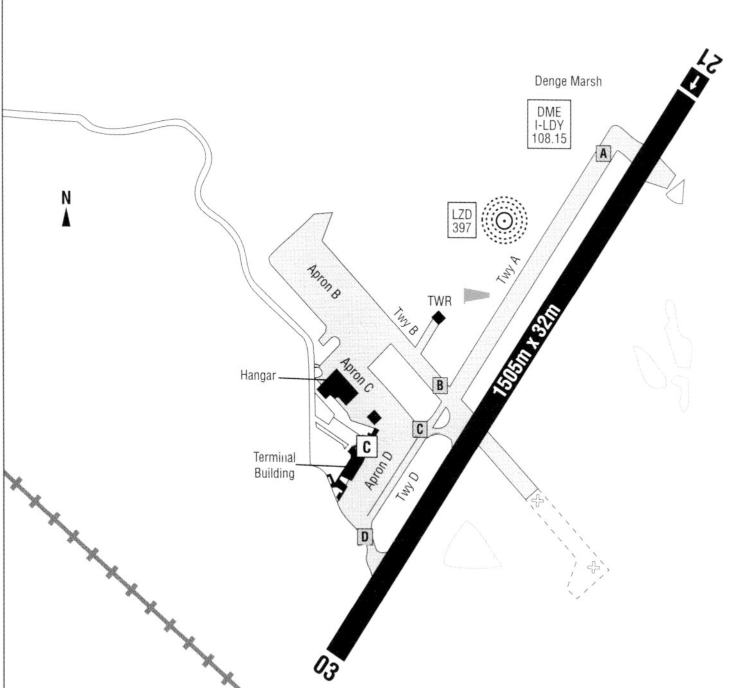

RWY	SURFACE	TORA	LDA	U/L	LIGHTING
03	Asphalt	1470	1470		Ap Thr Rwy PAPI 3° LHS
21	Asphalt	1505	1470		Ap Thr Rwy PAPI 3.5° LHS

RNAV			
LYD	114.05	141	3.4

Remarks

PPR microlights. Hi-vis. Non radio ACFT not accepted. Power checks hold B or C, then as instructed. Handling madatory for ACFT >6000kg.

Visual aid to location: Flashing white strobe.

Warnings

Caution: D084, D141 & R063 within vicinity of AD. DAAIS available on Lydd APP during Ops Hrs, outside Hrs from London Info.

Noise: Rwy03/21: Climb straight ahead to 500ft before turning left or right. Training Dept involving engine failure practice Not allowed Rwy03. VFR Arr position overhead 1500ft QNH downwind at 1000ft QNH. Do not descend deadside.

Operating Hrs 0830-1900 (L) & by arr

Circuits 03 RH, 21 LH

Landing Fee 0-1500kg £12 Circuits £6
1501-2500 £22 Circuits £8
2501-4000kg £35 Circuits £10
4001-6000kg £60 Circuits £15
Instrument Trn £16 per approach

Maintenance
Phoenix **Tel:** 01797 322430

Fuel AVGAS JET A1 100LL Water/Meth

Disabled Facilities

Handling **Tel:** 01797 322480 (FAL)
Fax: 01797 322481 (FAL)
info@falaviation.com
www.falaviation.com

Restaurant
Biggles **Tel:** 01797 322440 (bar & restaurant)

Taxis/Car Hire Arranged at front desk

Weather Info Air SE MOEx
ATIS **Tel:** 01797 322422
www.lydd-airport.co.uk

Operator London Ashford Airport Ltd
Lydd Airport, Lydd
Romney Marsh, Kent, TN29 9QL
Tel: 01797 320881(ATC)
Tel: 01797 322400 (Switchboard)
Fax: 01797 321964 (ATC)
Fax: 01797 322419 (Switchboard)
info@lydd-airport.co.uk
www.lydd airport.co.uk

Effective date:25/09/08
OP 08

L

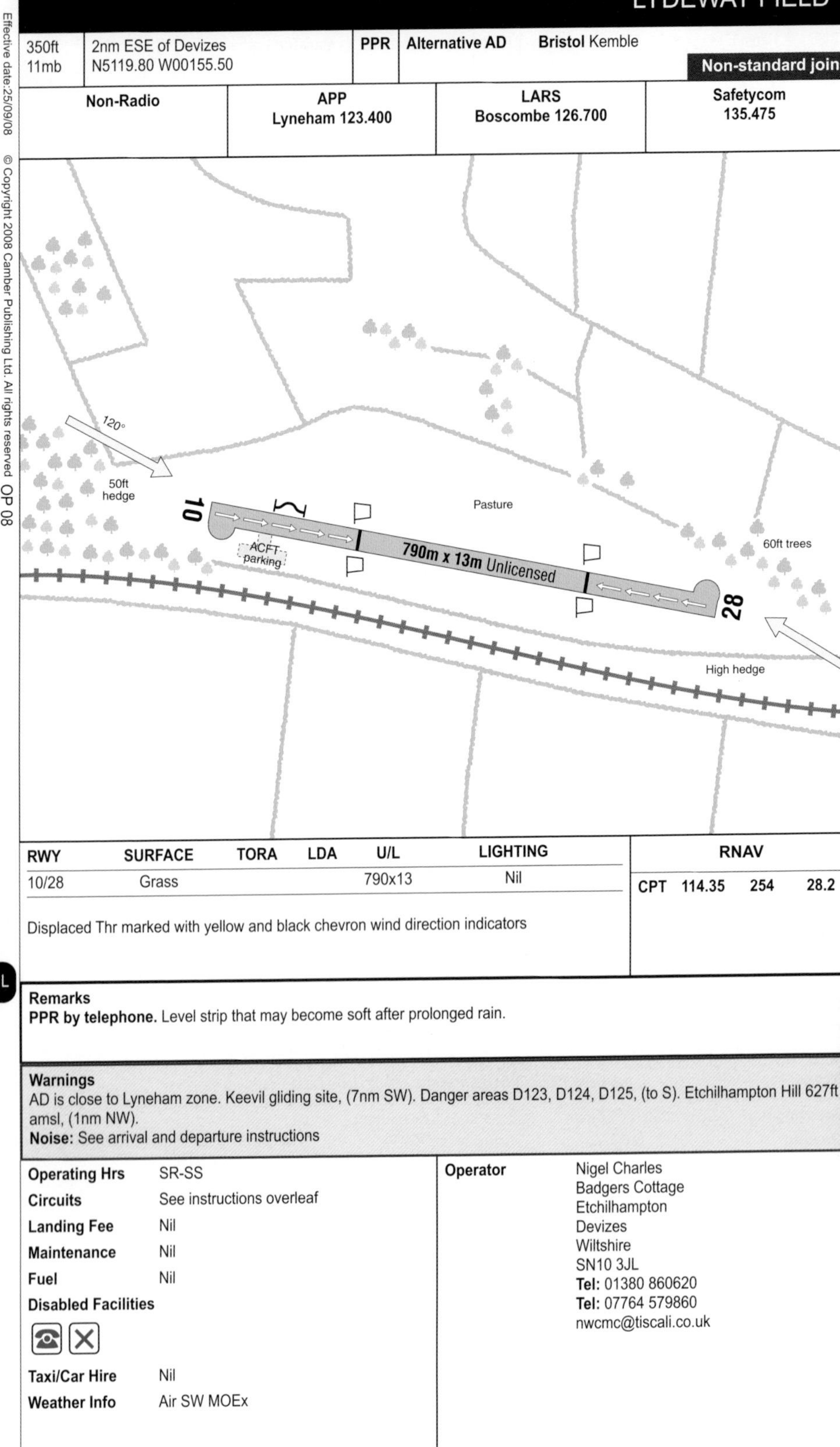

LYDEWAY FIELD

350ft 11mb	2nm ESE of Devizes N5119.80 W00155.50	PPR	Alternative AD	**Bristol** Kemble **Non-standard join**

Non-Radio	APP Lyneham 123.400	LARS Boscombe 126.700	Safetycom 135.475

RWY	SURFACE	TORA	LDA	U/L	LIGHTING
10/28	Grass			790x13	Nil

Displaced Thr marked with yellow and black chevron wind direction indicators

RNAV			
CPT	114.35	254	28.2

Remarks
PPR by telephone. Level strip that may become soft after prolonged rain.

Warnings
AD is close to Lyneham zone. Keevil gliding site, (7nm SW). Danger areas D123, D124, D125, (to S). Etchilhampton Hill 627ft amsl, (1nm NW).
Noise: See arrival and departure instructions

Operating Hrs	SR-SS
Circuits	See instructions overleaf
Landing Fee	Nil
Maintenance	Nil
Fuel	Nil
Disabled Facilities	
Taxi/Car Hire	Nil
Weather Info	Air SW MOEx

Operator
Nigel Charles
Badgers Cottage
Etchilhampton
Devizes
Wiltshire
SN10 3JL
Tel: 01380 860620
Tel: 07764 579860
nwcmc@tiscali.co.uk

L

Effective date:25/09/08

Etchilhampton

Wabi Farm

Hatfield Farm

120°

10

28

295°

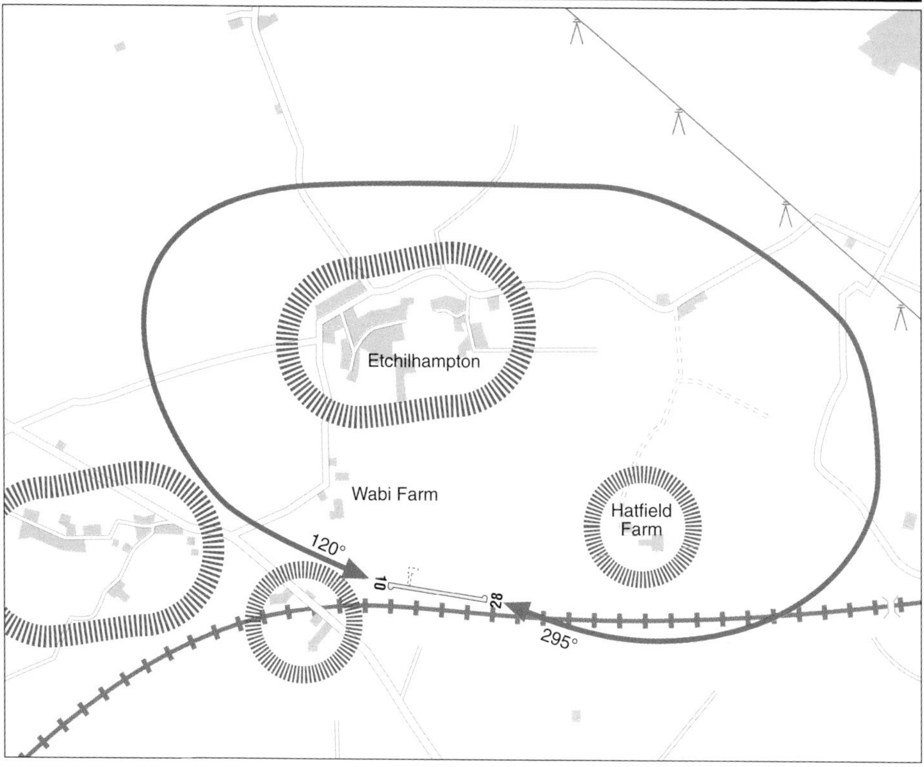

Arrival

Contact with Lyneham APP is recommended for traffic information (or zone transit). Their surface wind and QNH is useful if Lydeway is unmanned.
Call LYDEWAY TRAFFIC using Safetycom to make circuit reports.
This is a noise sensitive area so please avoid over flying villages during approach. The circuit pattern optimises flight path for both noise abatement and obstruction avoidance.
A slow flypast ensures the strip is clear of deer and walkers.
Strong S winds generate turbulence from hedges along the S AD boundary.

Rwy 10: Beware rising ground on base leg. Turn final over Rwy.

Rwy28: 15° offset final APP allows better view and offset from high trees on short final. Due to low crossing altitude of railway line discontinue approach if a train is coming. Full Rwy length is available with care but displaced Thr is marked.

Departure

Caution: Trees on both APP may obscure ACFT on final check well before committing to backtrack.

Rwy10: Caution slight hump before Twy which can ski-jump ACFT prematurely into the air. Climb out N of the railway until above 500ft QFE.

Rwy28: As soon as altitude permits TURN RIGHT and fly just W of Wabi Farm. The farmer here likes ACFT and this will avoid noise sensitive areas.

LYMM DAM

250ft 5mb	1nm S of Lymm N5322.00 W00228.00		**Alternative AD**	**Liverpool** Manchester Barton
				Non-standard join

Non-Radio	**ATIS** **Manchester** **128.175 (Arr)**	**APP** **Manchester 135.00**	**Safetycom** **135.475**

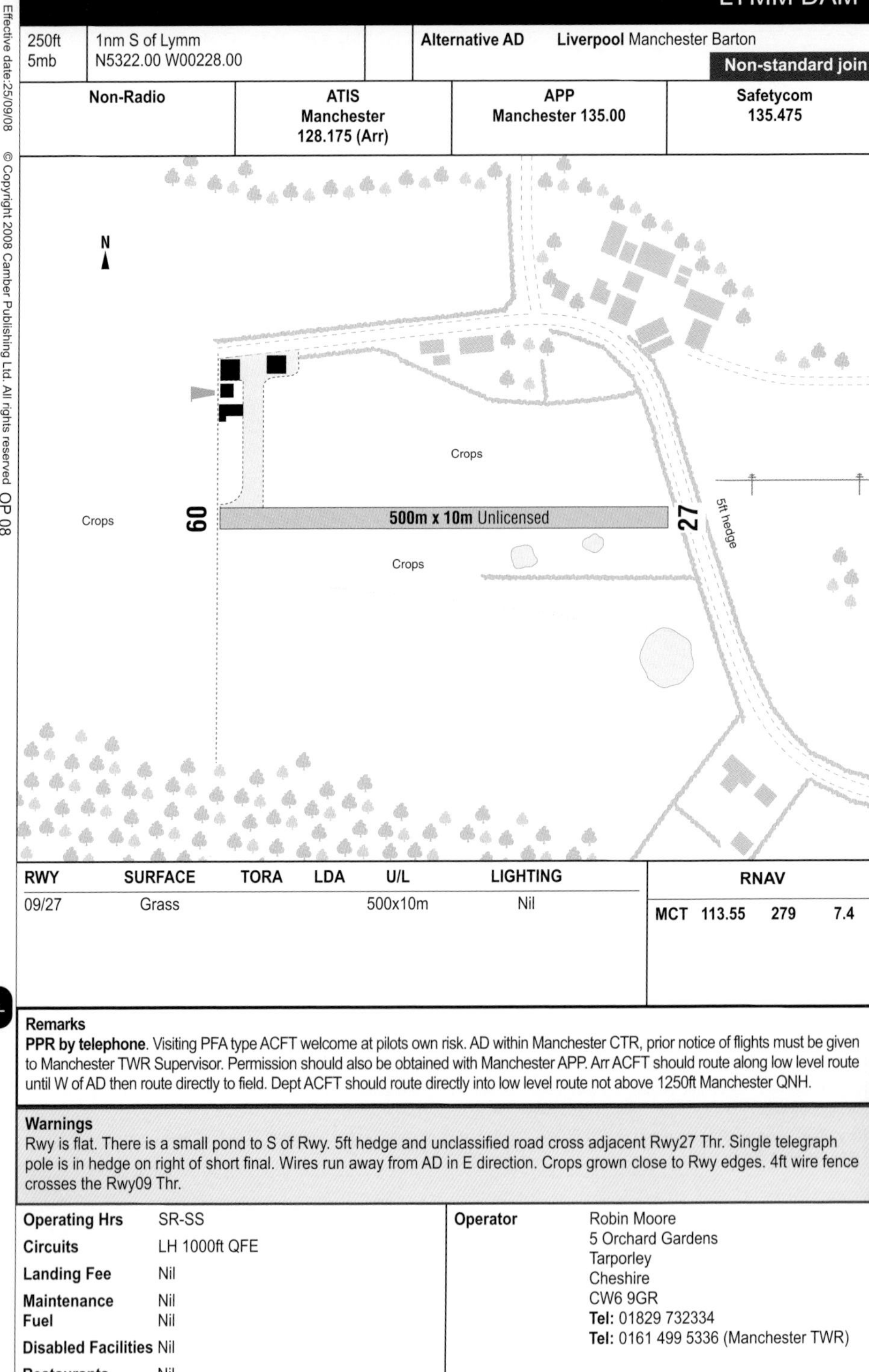

RWY	SURFACE	TORA	LDA	U/L	LIGHTING
09/27	Grass			500x10m	Nil

RNAV			
MCT	**113.55**	**279**	**7.4**

L

Remarks

PPR by telephone. Visiting PFA type ACFT welcome at pilots own risk. AD within Manchester CTR, prior notice of flights must be given to Manchester TWR Supervisor. Permission should also be obtained with Manchester APP. Arr ACFT should route along low level route until W of AD then route directly to field. Dept ACFT should route directly into low level route not above 1250ft Manchester QNH.

Warnings

Rwy is flat. There is a small pond to S of Rwy. 5ft hedge and unclassified road cross adjacent Rwy27 Thr. Single telegraph pole is in hedge on right of short final. Wires run away from AD in E direction. Crops grown close to Rwy edges. 4ft wire fence crosses the Rwy09 Thr.

Operating Hrs SR-SS

Circuits LH 1000ft QFE

Landing Fee Nil

Maintenance Nil

Fuel Nil

Disabled Facilities Nil

Restaurants Nil

Taxis

Jolly's **Tel:** 01925 755631

Car Hire Nil

Weather Info Air Cen MOEx

Operator

Robin Moore
5 Orchard Gardens
Tarporley
Cheshire
CW6 9GR
Tel: 01829 732334
Tel: 0161 499 5336 (Manchester TWR)

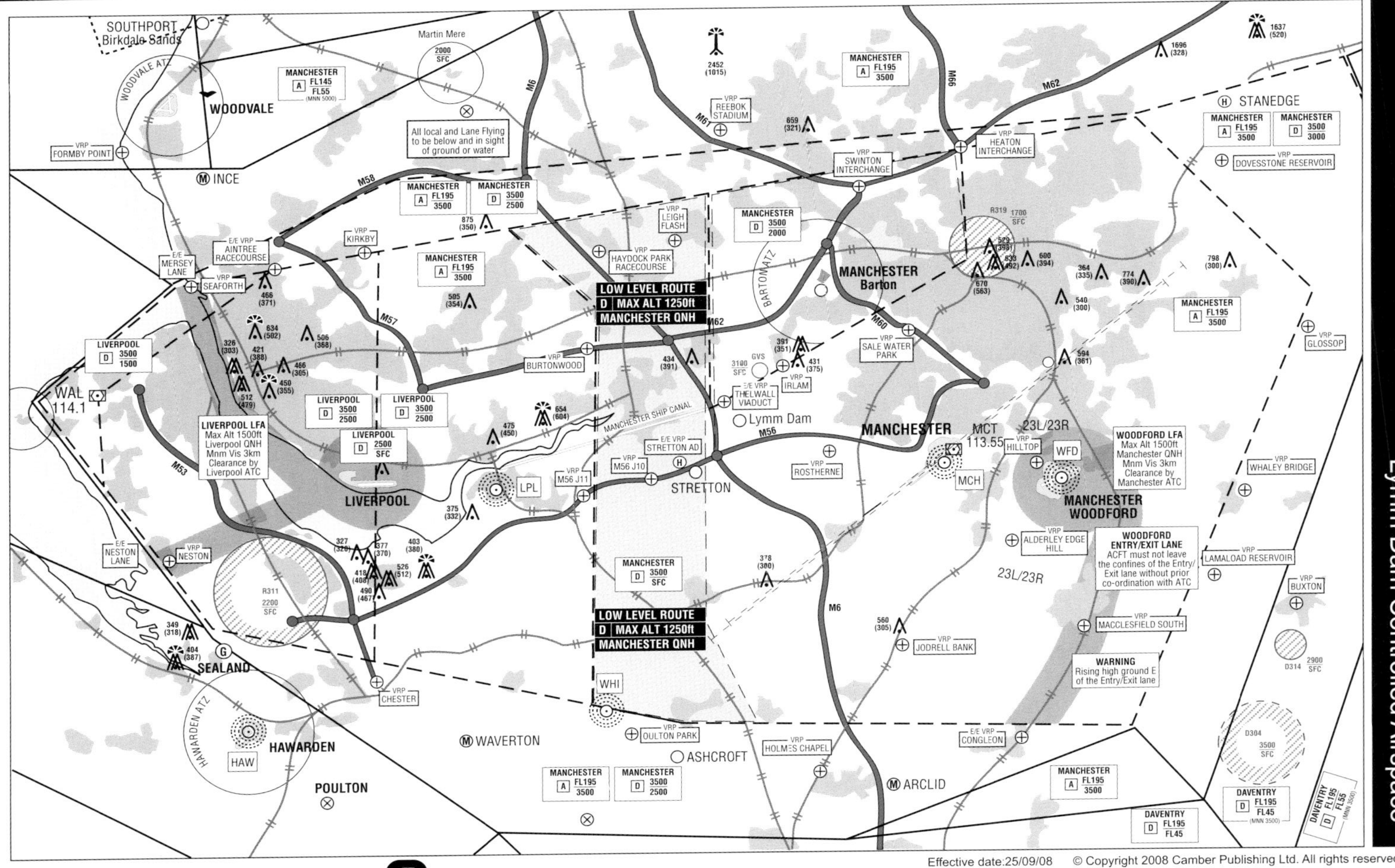

SOUTHPORT Birkdale Sands
WOODVALE ATZ
WOODVALE
Martin Mere
All local and Lane Flying to be below and in sight of ground or water
INCE
STANEDGE
MANCHESTER
Barton
BARTON ATZ
Lymm Dam
STRETTON
MCT 113.55
23L/23R
WOODFORD LFA
Max Alt 1500ft
Manchester QNH
Mnm Vis 3km
Clearance by
Manchester ATC
MANCHESTER WOODFORD
WOODFORD
ENTRY/EXIT LANE
ACFT must not leave the confines of the Entry/Exit lane without prior co-ordination with ATC
WARNING
Rising high ground E of the Entry/Exit lane
LOW LEVEL ROUTE
D MAX ALT 1250ft
MANCHESTER QNH
LIVERPOOL
LIVERPOOL LFA
Max Alt 1500ft
Liverpool QNH
Mnm Vis 3km
Clearance by
Liverpool ATC
WAL 114.1
MANCHESTER SHIP CANAL
HAWARDEN
HAWARDEN ATZ
SEALAND
POULTON
WAVERTON
ASHCROFT
ARCLID
DAVENTRY
M6
M56
M57
M58
M60
M61
M62
M66
M53
VRP FORMBY POINT
E/E MERSEY LANE
VRP SEAFORTH
E/E VRP AINTREE RACECOURSE
VRP KIRKBY
VRP LEIGH FLASH
VRP HAYDOCK PARK RACECOURSE
VRP BURTONWOOD
VRP REEBOK STADIUM
VRP SWINTON INTERCHANGE
VRP HEATON INTERCHANGE
VRP DOVESSTONE RESERVOIR
VRP GLOSSOP
VRP SALE WATER PARK
VRP IRLAM
E/E VRP THELWALL VIADUCT
E/E VRP STRETTON AD
VRP M56 J10
VRP M56 J11
VRP ROSTHERNE
VRP HILLTOP
VRP ALDERLEY EDGE HILL
VRP WHALEY BRIDGE
VRP LAMALOAD RESERVOIR
VRP BUXTON
VRP MACCLESFIELD SOUTH
VRP JODRELL BANK
E/E VRP CONGLEON
VRP HOLMES CHAPEL
VRP OULTON PARK
VRP CHESTER
VRP NESTON
E/E NESTON LANE

EGDL — LYNEHAM

513ft 17mb	8nm WSW of Swindon N5130.31 W00159.60	PPR MIL	Alternative AD Diversion AD	Oxford Kemble

Non-standard join

Lyneham	ZONE	APP/DIR	TWR	GND
	123.400	118.425	119.225 122.100	129.475 122.100

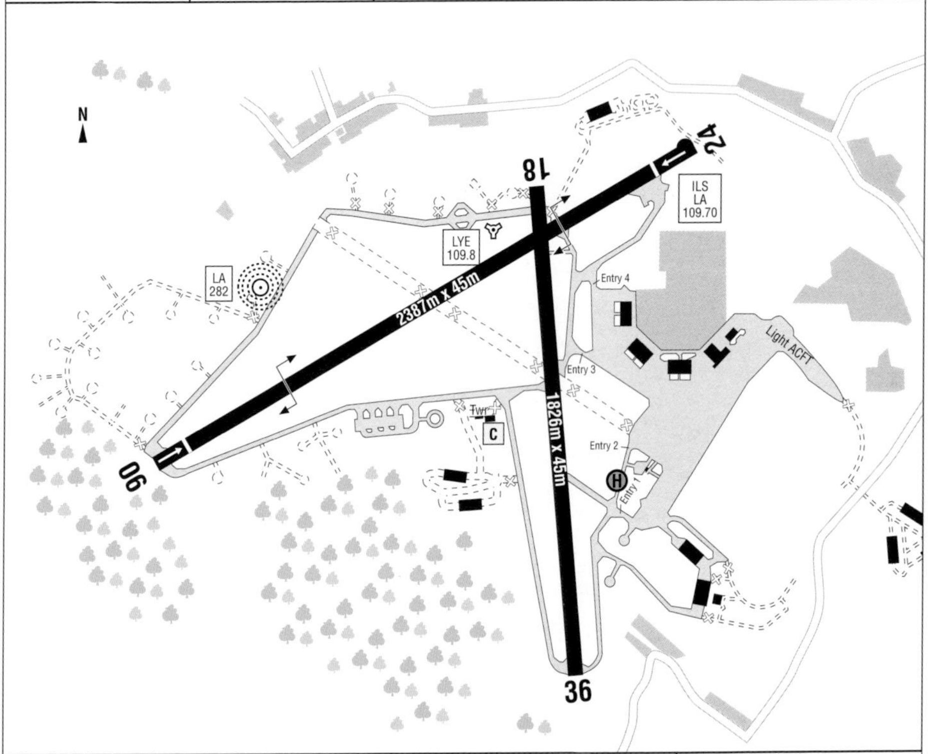

RWY	SURFACE	TORA	LDA	U/L	LIGHTING
06	Asphalt/Conc	2356	2359		Ap Thr Rwy PAPI 3°
24	Asphalt/Conc	2387	2202		Ap Thr Rwy PAPI 3°
18/36	Asphalt/Conc	1826	1825		Ap Thr Rwy PAPI 3°

Rwy06 LDA 2235m (Night), Arrester Gear Rwy24 480m from Thr
Arrester Gear Rwy06 510m from Thr

RNAV			
CPT	114.35	276	29.1

Remarks

PPR 24Hrs notice required. Military Emergency Diversion AD. No night stopping for visiting ACFT. ACFT to contact Lyneham APP at 20nm unless under control of another agency who should be asked to advise Lyneham of the ETA. Instrument APP may be mandatory. ACFT are not to request start-up unless RAF starter crew are present. After landing and before take-off pilots must report personally to Operations.

Warnings

GND rises sharply from 300ft below AD to Rwy06 Thr which may cause turbulence and windshear on APP. Vehicles/pedestrians may be present on the apron not under the control of ATC. Heavy bird concentration in the area at dawn and dusk.

Operating Hrs H24

Circuits 06 variable 1000ft
Low level 500ft

Landing Fee Charges in accordance with MOD policy
Contact Station Ops for details

Maintenance Nil

Fuel JET A1

Disabled Facilities

Restaurant Nil

Taxis
Bradies **Tel:** 01249 890794
Calne Taix **Tel:** 01249 821111

Car Hire Nil

Weather Info M T Fax 364 MOEx
ATIS **Tel:** 01249 897308

Operator RAF Lyneham
Chippenham
Wiltshire, SN15 4PZ
Tel: 01249 894004/5/6 (ATC)
Tel: 01249 896536 (Operations)
Tel: 01249 894008 (ATC Supervisor)
Tel: 01249 896214 (Duty Met Observer)
Fax: 01249 894007 (ATC)

Class D Airspace
Normal CTA/CTR Class D Airspace rules apply
Transition Alt 3000ft
1 To assist Lyneham RAD in ensuring access to its airspace pilots should make an R/T call when 20nm or 5 minutes flying time from the zone boundary, whichever is the earlier.

Visual Reference Points (VRP)

VRP	VOR/VOR	VOR/NDB	VOR/DME
Avebury N5125.68 W00151.28	CPT 263°/SAM 329°	CPT 263°/LA 134°	CPT 263°/24nm
Blakehill Farm N5137.00 W00153.10	CPT 289°/SAM 336°	CPT 289°/LA 038°	CPT 289°/26nm
Calne N5126.20 W00200.30	CPT 266°/SAM 322°	CPT 266°/LA 182°	CPT 266°/30nm
Chippenham N5127.60 W00207.40	CPT 269°/SAM 319°	CPT 269°/LA 240°	CPT 269°/34nm
Clyffe Pypard N5129.40 W00153.70	CPT 272°/SAM 330°	CPT 272°/LA 107°	CPT 272°/25nm
Devizes N5120.80 W00159.30	CPT 256°/SAM 317°	CPT 256°/LA 179°	CPT 256°/30nm
M4 J15 N5131.60 W00143.48	CPT 279°/SAM 340°	CPT 279°/LA 087°	CPT 279°/19nm
M4 J16 N5132.70 W00151.25	CPT 280°/SAM 334°	CPT 280°/LA 072°	CPT 280°/24nm
M4 J17 N5130.88 W00207.30	CPT 275°/SAM 322°	CPT 275°/LA 278°	CPT 275°/34nm
Malmesbury N5135.10 W00206.20	CPT 283°/SAM 326°	CPT 283°/LA 325°	CPT 283°/33nm
Marlborough N5125.20 W00143.70	CPT 260°/SAM 335°	CPT 260°/LA 120°	CPT 260°/19nm
Melksham N5122.50 W00208.30	CPT 261°/SAM 313°	SAM 314°/LA 215°	CPT 261°/35nm
S Marston N5135.40 W00144.10	CPT 290°/SAM 342°	CPT 290°/LA 067°	CPT 290°/20nm
Wroughton N5130.55 W00147.98	CPT 275°/SAM 335°	SAM 336°/LA 023°	CPT 275°/22nm

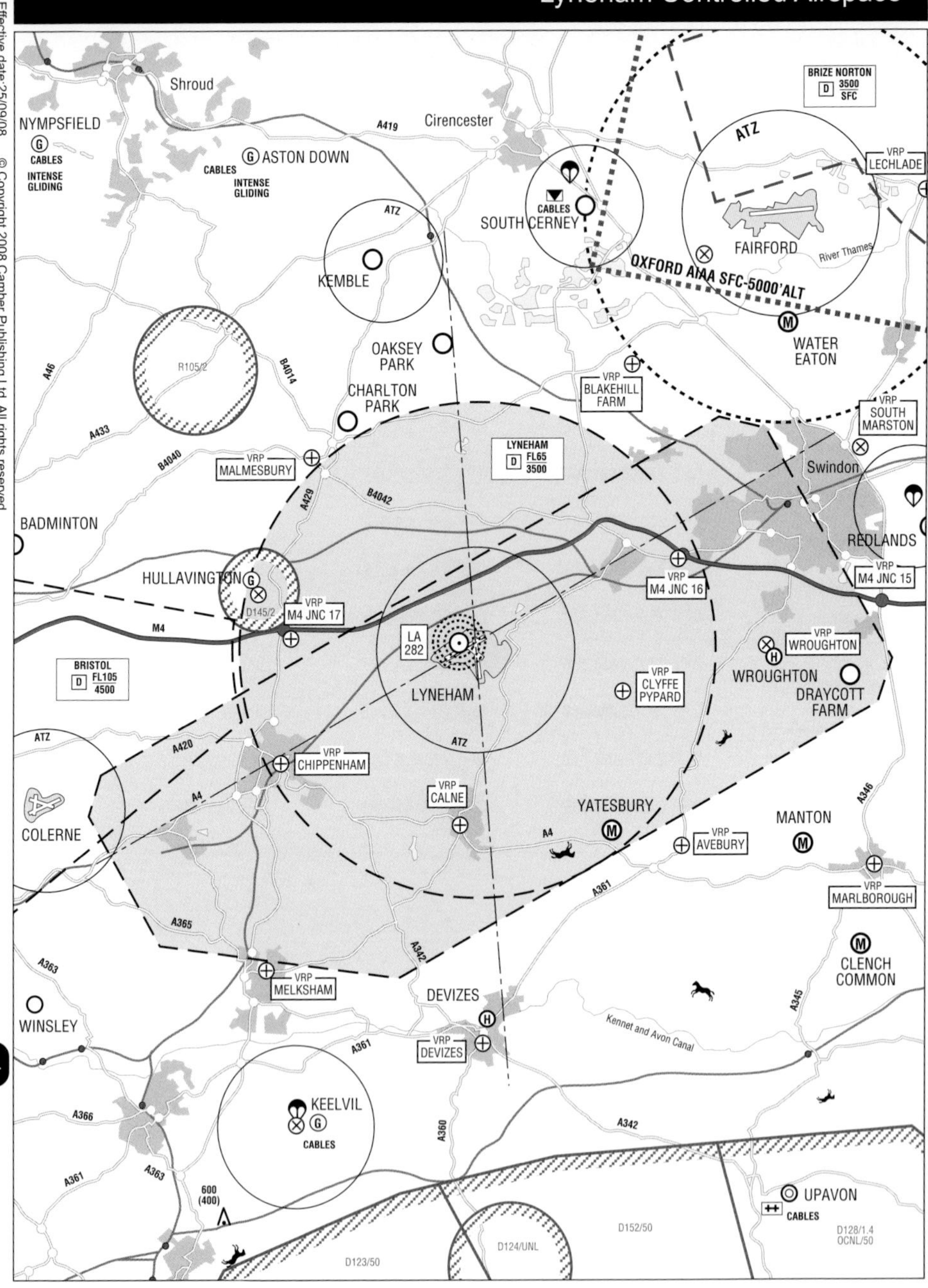
Shroud
NYMPSFIELD
CABLES
INTENSE GLIDING
A419
Cirencester
ASTON DOWN
CABLES
INTENSE GLIDING
BRIZE NORTON
D 3500 SFC
ATZ
VRP LECHLADE
CABLES
SOUTH CERNEY
ATZ
KEMBLE
FAIRFORD
River Thames
OXFORD AIAA SFC-5000'ALT
WATER EATON
OAKSEY PARK
R105/2
B4014
A46
CHARLTON PARK
VRP BLAKEHILL FARM
VRP SOUTH MARSTON
A433
LYNEHAM
D FL65 3500
VRP MALMESBURY
B4040
A429
B4042
Swindon
BADMINTON
REDLANDS
HULLAVINGTON
D145/2
VRP M4 JNC 17
VRP M4 JNC 16
VRP M4 JNC 15
M4
LA 282
VRP WROUGHTON
BRISTOL
D FL105 4500
LYNEHAM
WROUGHTON
DRAYCOTT FARM
VRP CLYFFE PYPARD
ATZ
ATZ
A420
VRP CHIPPENHAM
VRP CALNE
A4
YATESBURY
MANTON
A346
COLERNE
A4
VRP AVEBURY
A361
VRP MARLBOROUGH
A365
A342
A363
VRP MELKSHAM
DEVIZES
CLENCH COMMON
WINSLEY
A345
Kennet and Avon Canal
A361
VRP DEVIZES
KEELVIL
CABLES
A366
A360
A342
A363
A361
600 (400)
UPAVON
CABLES
D152/50
D128/1.4 OCNL/50
D124/UNL
D123/50

L

63ft 2mb	5nm SE of Huntingdon N5216.18 W0004.15	PPR	Alternative AD	Cambridge Bourn

Non-Radio	ATIS Cambridge 134.600	APP Cambridge 123.600	APP Wyton 134.050	Safetycom 135.475

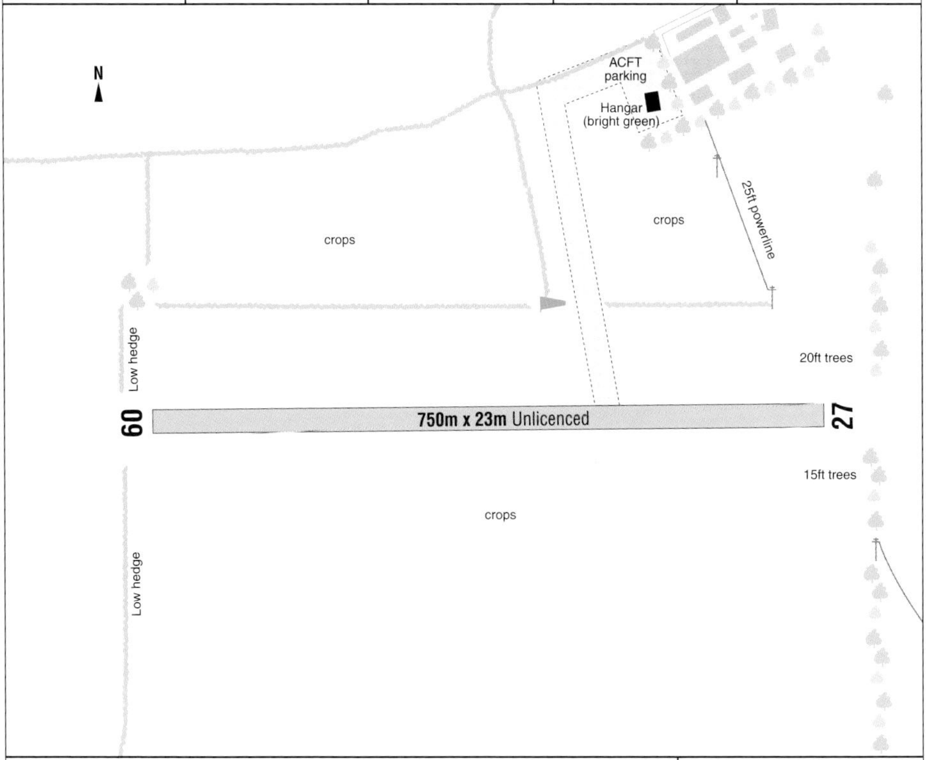

N
ACFT parking
Hangar (bright green)
25ft powerline
crops
crops
Low hedge
20ft trees
09
750m x 23m Unlicenced
27
15ft trees
crops
Low hedge

RWY	SURFACE	TORA	LDA	U/L	LIGHTING
09/27	Grass			750x23	Nil

RNAV			
BKY	116.250	345	17.5

Remarks
PPR by telephone. Well maintained strip. Wyton ATZ to the N of AD.

Warnings
Farm vehicles operate on AD, crops grown up to Rwy edge. Powerlines to NW/SE of Rwy27 Thr. Cables go underground to cross Rwy.
Noise: Avoid over flying all local habitation. After take-off climb straight ahead through 1000ft before turning.

Operating Hrs SR-SS
Circuits LH 1000ft QFE
Landing Fee Nil
Donations towards grass-cutting gratefully received
Maintenance Nil
Fuel Nil
Restaurant Nil
Taxi/Car Hire Nil
Weather Info Air Cen MOEx

Operator
Charles Papworth
Hall Farm
Conington
Cambridgeshire
CB23 4LR
Tel: 01954 267215
Tel: 07860 578146
charles@papworth-air.com

Effective date:25/09/08
OP 08
M

EGCC MANCHESTER

257ft 9mb	7.5nm SW of Manchester N5321.23 W00216.50	PPR	Alternative AD	Liverpool Manchester Barton **Non-standard join**

Manchester	ATIS	APP	RAD	TWR
	128.175 (Arr) 121.975 113.550 (Dept)	135.000	135.000 118.575	118.625 (23R/05L) 119.400 (23L/05R)
DEL	**DIR**	**GND**	**FIRE**	**Handling**
121.700	121.350	121.850	121.600	Oceansky 130.650

23R
ILS/DME
I-NN
109.50

MCT
113.55

3048m x 46m

23L

05L

3047m x 45m

ILS/DME
I-MC
111.55

05R

M

RWY	SURFACE	TORA	LDA	U/L	LIGHTING
05L	Conc/Asph	3048	2621		Ap Thr Rwy PAPI 3° RHS
23R	Conc/Asph	3048	2865		Ap Thr Rwy PAPI 3° LHS
05R	Conc/Asph	3047	2864		Ap Thr Rwy PAPI 3° LHS
23L	Conc/Asph	3050	2864		Ap Thr Rwy PAPI 3° LHS

Starter extension Rwy23L 150x30m

RNAV

MCT 113.55 on AD

Remarks

PPR essential. Hi-Vis. All flights are at all times subject to PPR. The filling of a Flight Plan does not constitute PPR. Operation of business and GA ACFT require permission from AD operator in advance of each movement, obtained as follows: During office Hrs contact ACL. Outside office Hrs contact AD Ops. Include following info ACFT owner/operator, type & registration. Flight number (if any), requested time of Arr/Dept at Manchester and nominated handling agent. Use governed by regulations applicable to Manchester CTR. Applications for PPR must be made not more than 10 days and not less than 24Hrs before the proposed flight Before filing Manchester as an alternate, make arr for GND handling. Training flights by all ACFT are subject to the approval of AD Ops. All initial calls to ATC for dept should be made on Manchester Del between 0530-2100 (Summer) +1Hr Winter. Outside these Hrs call Manchester GND. At all times ACFT must be operated in a manner calculated to cause the least disturbance practicable in areas surrounding the AD. Unless otherwise instructed by ATC, ACFT shall not descend below 2000ft before intercepting the glide path. ACFT APP without assistance from the ILS shall follow a descent path no lower than that of the ILS glide path. Dept Rwy23R/L 4 bright lights from golf driving range 1500m left of Rwy23R Thr (SS-2030 Summer SS-2130 Winter).

Warnings

GND signals other than light signals are not displayed. The hard shoulders outboard of the Rwy side stripes have only 25% of Rwy bearing strengths and should not be used by ACFT turning on the Rwy or when backtracking. Only grass parking area is suitable for ACFT – avoid all other grass surfaces.

Caution: Turbulence Rwy23R in strong NW winds. Flocks of racing pigeons cross AD below 100ft April-September.

Noise: Avoid over flying Knutsford.

Operating Hrs	H24
Circuits	Nil
Landing Fee	On application
Maintenance	Up to B747 by arr
Fuel	JET A1 100LL Arranged via mandatory handling agent
Disabled Facilities	Available
Handling	**Tel:** 061 436 6666 (Oceansky) **Fax:** 0161 436 3450 (Oceansky)
Restaurants	Restaurants buffets & bars (24Hr)
Taxis	Available at Terminal
Car Hire	
Avis	**Tel:** 0161 934 2300
Europcar	**Tel:** 0161 436 2200
Hertz	**Tel:** 0161 437 8208
Sixt Kenning	**Tel:** 0161 489 2666

Weather Info	M T9 T18 Fax 368 A VM VN MOEx ATIS **Tel:** 0161 499 2324
Operator	Manchester Airport Plc Manchester Airport Manchester Greater Manchester M90 1QX **Tel:** 0161 489 3000 (AD) **Tel:** 0161 489 3331 (AD Duty Manager) **Tel:** 0161 499 5502 (FPRS) **Fax:** 0161 499 5504 (Flight plans) **Fax:** 0161 493 1853 (ACL)

Low Level Route Through Manchester Control Zone

This low level route allows ACFT to transit the Manchester CTR without compliance with full IFR procedures. Additionally, to allow ACFT to transit to and from Barton AD, there is a branch route to Barton from the low level corridor.

The rules governing flight within the low level route are as follows:

1 Remain clear of cloud and in sight of the surface.

2 Maximum altitude 1250ft (Manchester QNH).

3 Minimum flight visibility 4km.

4 ACFT must be transiting the CTR, or proceeding directly to or from an AD within the CTR.

5 Pilots using the corridor are responsible for their own separation from other ACFT.

6 The corridor is not aligned with the M6 motorway or railway line. The M6 should not be used as a navigational line feature. To the NW or SE of the route stubs are alined to the M6 along the Crewe/Winsford railway line to enable pilots to access the route accurately.

VFR/SVFR Flights

Transition Alt 5000ft

VFR and Special VFR clearance for flights within the control zone may be requested and will be given whenever traffic conditions permit. These flights are subject to the general conditions for VFR and Special VFR flight and will normally be given only to helicopters or aeroplanes other than microlights which can communicate with ATC on the appropriate freq.

The use of VFR/SVFR clearance is intended to be for the following types of flight:

Light ACFT (less than 5700kg MTOW) which cannot comply with full IFR and wish to transit the zone or proceed to or from an AD within the zone. ACFT using the low level corridor will be considered as complying with a VFR/SVFR clearance.

Special VFR clearance to operate within the Manchester CTR will not be granted to fixed-wing ACFT when:

1 Proceeding inbound to Manchester AD, if the reported weather conditions at AD are at below 2800m visibility or a cloud ceiling of less than 1000ft.

2 Wishing to Dept Manchester AD if the reported weather conditions at AD are at below 1800m visibility or a cloud ceiling of less than 600ft.

M

Visual Reference Points (VRP)

VRP	**VOR/DME**
Alderley Edge Hill	MCT 157°/4nm
N5317.72 W00212.73	
Burtonwood	WAL 089°/18nm
N5325.00 W00238.28	MCT 288°/14nm
Buxton	MCT 119°/14nm
N5315.35 W00154.77	
Congleton	MCT 169°/12nm
N5309.90 W00210.85	TNT 293°/20nm
Dovestoves Reservoir	MCT 047°/15nm
N5332.15 W00158.12	
Glossop	MCT 071°/13nm
N5326.26 W00155.04	
Haydock Park Racecourse	MCT 302°/15nm
N5328.70 W00237.33	WAL 080°/23nm
Hilltop	MCT 109°/3nm
N5320.50 W00210.45	TNT 316°/25nm
Holmes Chapel	MCT 203°/11nm
N5310.55 W00222.07	
Irlam	MCT 315°/7nm
N5326.20 W00224.47	
Jodrell Bank	MCT 196°/7nm
N5314.18 W00218.55	
Lamaload Reservoir	MCT 126°/9nm
N5316.20 W00202.33	
Leigh Flash	MCT 310°/13nm
N5329.38 W00233.58	
M56 J10	MCT 266°/11nm
N53200.07 W00234.28	
M56 J11	MCT 266°/14nm
N5319.63 W00238.62	WAL 106°/18nm
M60/M62/M66 Interchange	MCT 003°/11nm
N5333.00 W00215.40	
Macclesfield South	MCT 150°/8nm
N5314.10 W00208.05	
Reebok Stadium	MCT 327°/17nm
N5334.83 W00232.13	
Rostherne	MCT 271°/4nm
N5321.23 W00223.12	
Sale Water Park	MCT 345°/5nm
N5326.00 W00218.17	
Stretton AD	MCT 269°/10nm
N5320.77 W00231.58	WAL 101°/22nm
Swinton Interchange	MCT 344°/11nm
N5331.40 W00221.60	
Thelwall Viaduct	MCT 286°/9nm
N5323.43 W00230.35	
Whalley Bridge	MCT 104°/9nm
N5319.35 W00159.30	
Winsford Flash	MCT 224°/14nm
N5311.10 W00230.73	

Standard Inbound Visual Routes

Entry point	Rwy	Max Alt (QNH)	Route
Stretton	05L/05R	1250ft	From Stretton AD VRP route via M56 keep motorway on left join left base Rwy06L
		Remarks:	**1** Out bound traffic operates N of M56 **2** ACFT may be held at Stretton VRP or Rostherne VRP
Congleton	23R	2500ft	From CTR Boundary E of Congleton VRP, route via the Woodford Entry/Exit Lane (Notes 1 & 4) (keep railway line on left) to Woodford AD. Join left base for Rwy23R
		Remarks:	**1** Maximum altitudes 2500ft between CTR Boundary & N edge of Macclesfield 1500ft N of Macclesfield to Woodford ATZ S Boundary **2** ACFT may be held at Hilltop VRP. Pilots must hold by visual reference to ensure that the holding pattern does not deviate to the N, which would come in to conflict with Rwy23R final instrument APP, particularly in a S wind. **3** The Entry/Exit Lane may be under Woodford Control. Pilots should contact Woodford APP initially then, if no contact Manchester APP. **4 Warning:** High GND to the E of the Entry/Exit Lane. **5** ACFT must not leave confines of Entry/Exit Lane without prior ATC co-ordination **6** ACFT with radio failure inbound to Manchester in Woodford Entry/Exit Lane, or holding at Hilltop, carry out RAD Communication Failure procedure.

Standard Outbound Visual Routes

Entry point	Rwy	Max Alt (QNH)	Route Designator Route
Thelwall	05L	1250ft	**Thelwall 1 Vis.** Cross M56. Route N of M56 to Thelwall Viaduct VRP thence via the low level route.
		Remarks:	**1** Avoid over flying Lymm. **2** Inbound traffic operates S of M56for Rwy05L. **3 Warning:** Traffic in Low Level Route is unknown to ATC.
Congleton	23R/23L	2500ft	**Congleton 3 Vis.** Left turn towards Alderley Edge VRP. Route W then S of Alderley Edge Hill and join the Woodford entry/exit lane at Prestbury station. Keep railway line on left and leave CTR via Congleton VRP.
		Remarks:	**1** Max alt 1500ft between Manchester & N edge of Macclesfield, 2500ft S of N edge to CTR Boundary. **2 Warning:** High GND to the E of Entry/Exit Lane. **3** Entry/Exit Lane may under Woodford or Manchester control. **4** ACFT may be routed direct from Manchester to Prestbury Station, or via Woodford. **5** ACFT must not leave the Entry/Exit Lane without ATC prior co-ordination. **6 Caution:** Alderley Edge 650ft amsl.

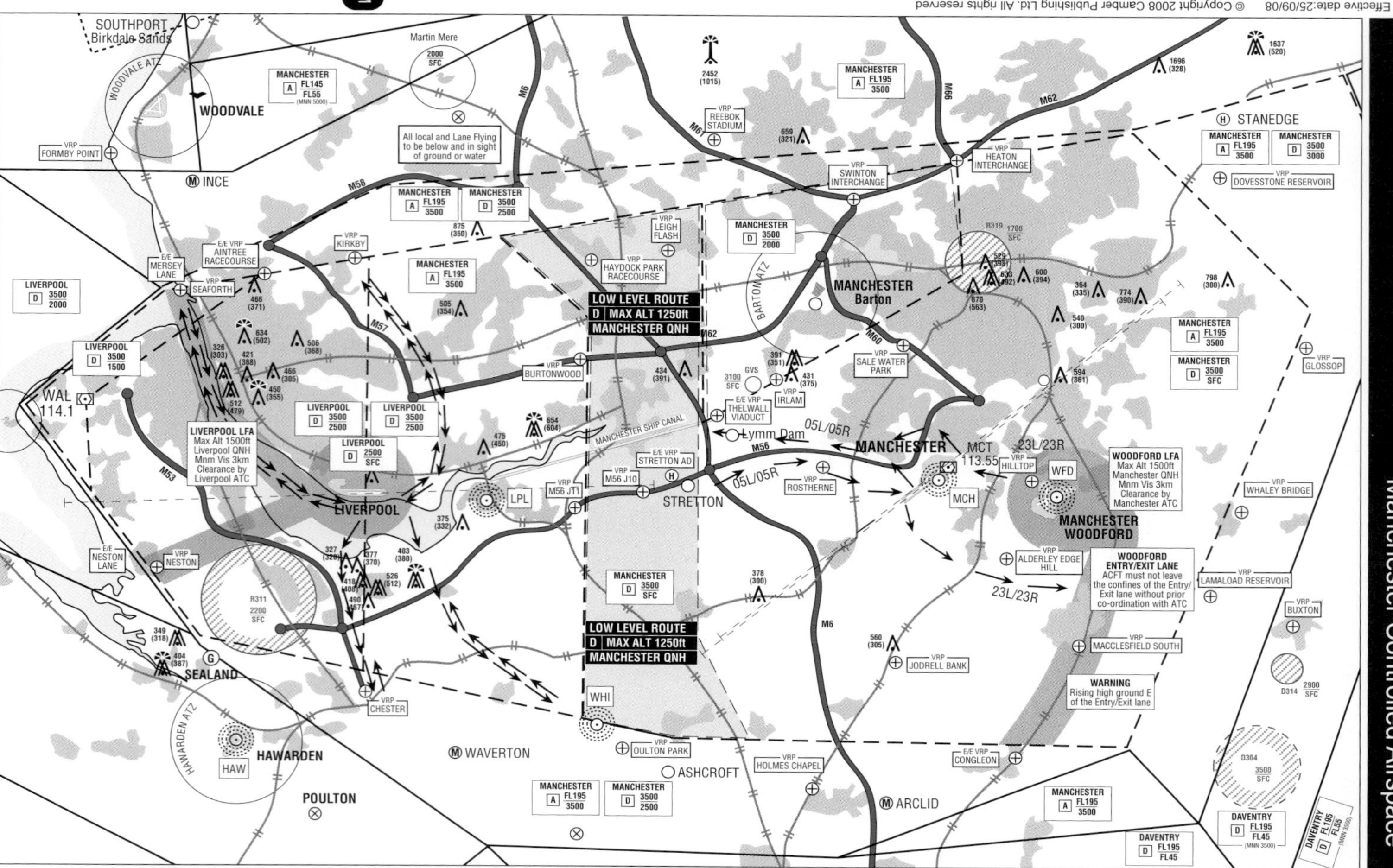

SOUTHPORT
Birkdale Sands
Martin Mere
WOODVALE
WOODVALE ATZ
FORMBY POINT
INCE
All local and Lane Flying to be below and in sight of ground or water
MANCHESTER A FL145 FL55 (MNN 5000)
LOW LEVEL ROUTE
D MAX ALT 1250ft
MANCHESTER QNH
LIVERPOOL LFA
Max Alt 1500ft
Liverpool QNH
Mnm Vis 3km
Clearance by
Liverpool ATC
WOODFORD LFA
Max Alt 1500ft
Manchester QNH
Mnm Vis 3km
Clearance by
Manchester ATC
WOODFORD
ENTRY/EXIT LANE
ACFT must not leave the confines of the Entry/Exit lane without prior co-ordination with ATC
WARNING
Rising high ground E of the Entry/Exit lane
MANCHESTER
MANCHESTER Barton
BARTON ATZ
MANCHESTER WOODFORD
LIVERPOOL
HAWARDEN
HAWARDEN ATZ
SEALAND
STANEDGE
WAVERTON
POULTON
ASHCROFT
ARCLID
STRETTON
WAL 114.1
MCT 113.55
23L/23R
05L/05R
Lymm Dam
MANCHESTER SHIP CANAL
REEBOK STADIUM
HEATON INTERCHANGE
SWINTON INTERCHANGE
DOVESTONE RESERVOIR
GLOSSOP
WHALEY BRIDGE
LAMALOAD RESERVOIR
BUXTON
MACCLESFIELD SOUTH
JODRELL BANK
CONGLEON
HOLMES CHAPEL
OULTON PARK
CHESTER
NESTON
NESTON LANE
MERSEY LANE
SEAFORTH
AINTREE RACECOURSE
KIRKBY
LEIGH FLASH
HAYDOCK PARK RACECOURSE
BURTONWOOD
SALE WATER PARK
IRLAM
THELWALL VIADUCT
STRETTON AD
M56 J10
M56 J11
ROSTHERNE
HILLTOP
ALDERLEY EDGE HILL
M6
M56
M62
M66
M60
M61
M57
M58
M53

M

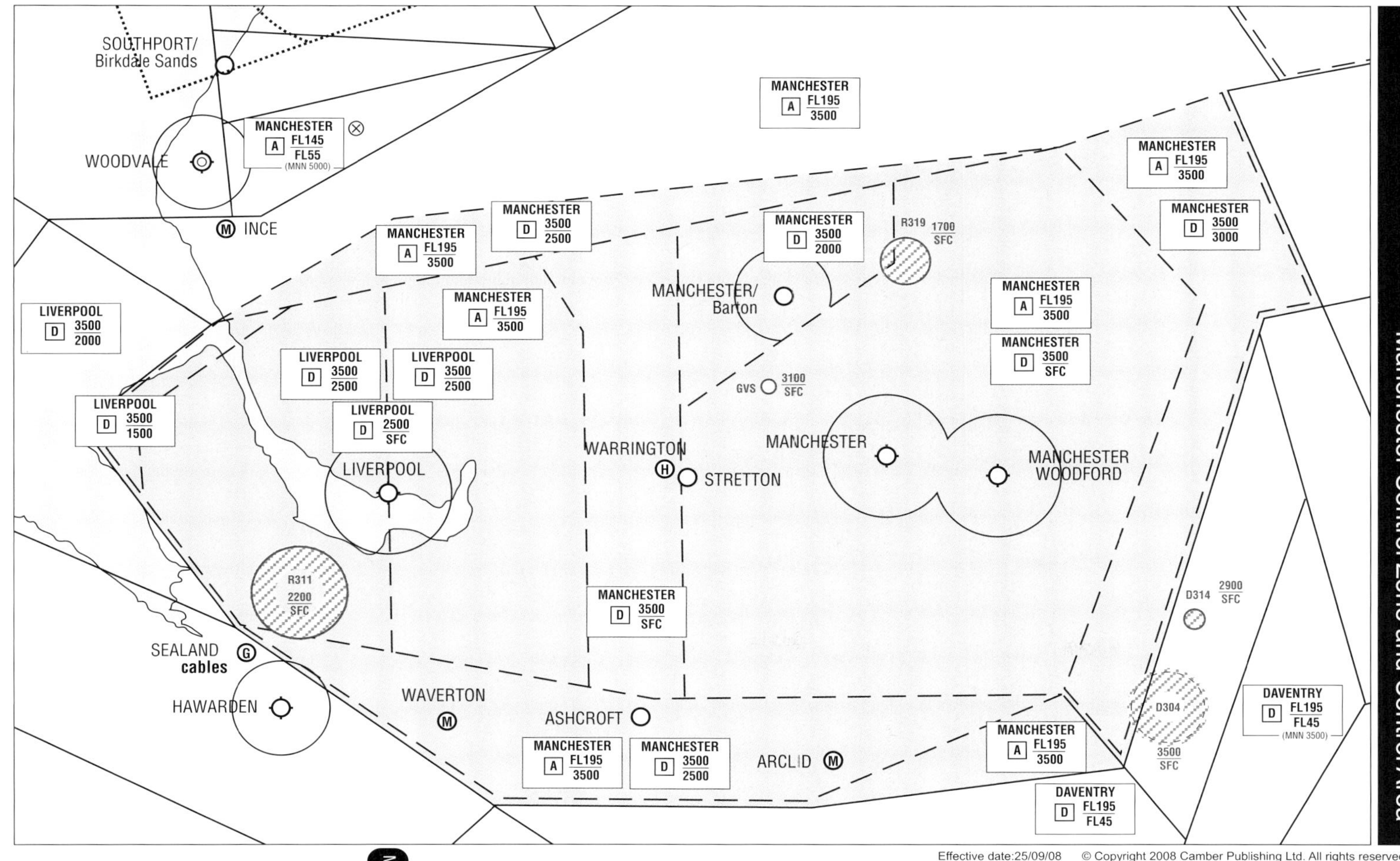
SOUTHPORT/ Birkdale Sands
MANCHESTER A FL195 3500
MANCHESTER A FL145 FL55 (MNN 5000)
WOODVALE
MANCHESTER A FL195 3500
MANCHESTER D 3500 3000
INCE
MANCHESTER D 3500 2500
MANCHESTER A FL195 3500
MANCHESTER D 3500 2000
R319 1700 SFC
MANCHESTER/ Barton
MANCHESTER A FL195 3500
MANCHESTER A FL195 3500
MANCHESTER D 3500 SFC
LIVERPOOL D 3500 2000
LIVERPOOL D 3500 2500
LIVERPOOL D 3500 2500
GVS 3100 SFC
LIVERPOOL D 3500 1500
LIVERPOOL D 2500 SFC
WARRINGTON
MANCHESTER
MANCHESTER WOODFORD
LIVERPOOL
STRETTON
R311 2200 SFC
MANCHESTER D 3500 SFC
D314 2900 SFC
SEALAND cables
HAWARDEN
WAVERTON
ASHCROFT
D304 3500 SFC
DAVENTRY D FL195 FL45 (MNN 3500)
MANCHESTER A FL195 3500
MANCHESTER A FL195 3500
MANCHESTER D 3500 2500
ARCLID
DAVENTRY D FL195 FL45

M

Effective date:25/09/08

INTENTIONALLY LEFT BLANK

EGCB MANCHESTER BARTON

73ft 2mb	5nm W of Manchester N5328.30 W00223.38	PPR	Alternative AD Diversion AD	Liverpool Blackpool Non-standard join

Barton	APP Manchester 135.000	AFIS 120.250

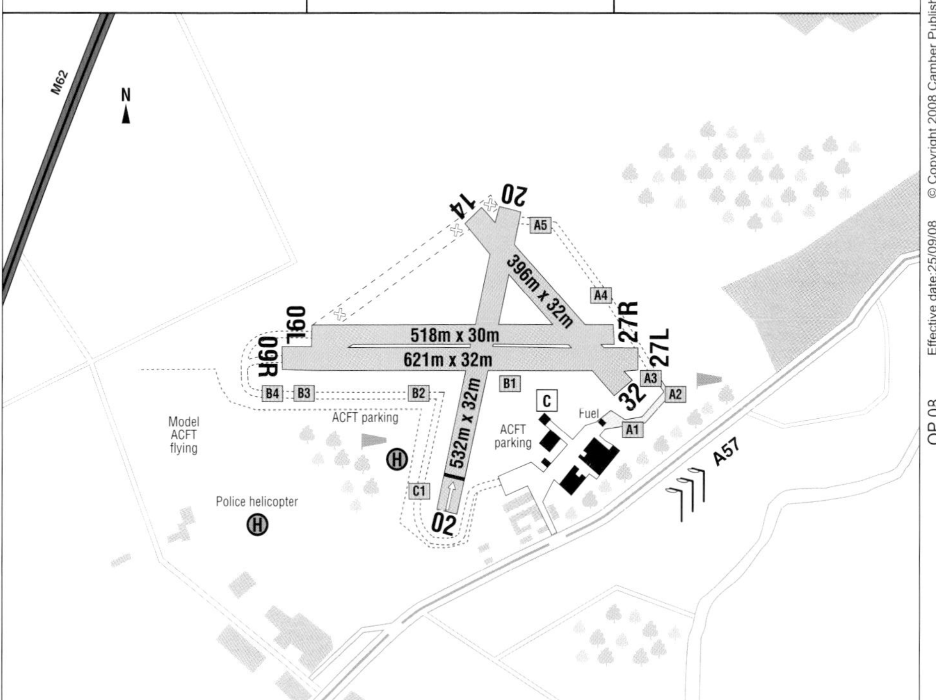

RWY	SURFACE	TORA	LDA	U/L	LIGHTING
09R/27L	Grass	621	621		Nil
09L/27R	Grass	518	518		Nil
14/32	Grass	396	396		Nil
20	Grass	532	532		Nil
02	Grass	532	464		Nil

RNAV			
MCT	113.55	330	8.3

Remarks

PPR essential. Hi Viz. Barton LFA is shown on Manchester Controlled Airspace map. It is Class G airspace and up to 2000ft alt. Manchester QNH. W edge of the LFA abuts the low level route. Fixed wing twin engined ACFT and fixed wing ACFT >1500kg must obtain PPR via telephone with ATS prior to flight. Non-radio ACFT must obtain PPR via telephone with ATS prior to flight. During adverse weather conditions the AD and associated services may be withdrawn. A computer ATIS display is provided for Dept ACFT. A full copy of the Aerodrome Rules and Procedures (Pilot Handbook) is available on request or can be downloaded from the website. Operating Hrs extensions available on request 0700-2345 (L) (Helicopters).

Warnings

35ft high lights on the A57 SE and SW of AD. Clay pigeon and game shooting takes place NW of AD within ATZ, helicopters must avoid this area below 500ft agl. Red/white marker boards or non standard markings (cones) may be used to indicate areas of soft GND. Pilots must exercise extreme caution as not all soft areas may be indicated. Surface undulating in places and soft after heavy rain. Rwy14/32 closed at times for ACFT parking. Rwy09/27 pilots must ensure that they have identified the correct Rwy in use. Bird hazard – Herons regularly fly across the aerodrome at 100-500ft. Gulls and pigeon activity increases during period of wet weather and grass seeding. All bird strikes must be reported.

Operating Hrs	0800-SS (Summer) +1Hr (Winter)	**Landing Fee**	See website for details
Circuits	Fixed Wing 14, 20, 27L, 27R RH, 02, 09L, 09R, 32 LH, 1000ft QFE Overhead joins at 1800ft QFE Helicopter circuits flown in fixed wing circuit at 500ft	**Maintenance**	Ravenair **Tel:** 0161 707 8644
		Fuel	AVGAS JET A1 100LL Fuel not available before 0900 and 15mins prior to last landing

Disabled Facilities		**Operator**	City Airport Manchester Ltd City Airport Manchester Liverpool Road, Eccles Manchester Greater Manchester M30 7SA **Tel:** 0161 789 1362 (Admin/ATC/PPR) **Fax:** 0161 787 7695 (Admin) **Fax:** 0161 789 7731 (ATC) admin@cityairportmanchester.com ops@cityairportmanchester.com www.cityairportmanchester.com
Restaurant	Restaurant facilities available at AD		
Taxis Passsenger Cars	Arranged on Arr or **Tel:** 0161 747 8000		
Car Hire National	 **Tel:** 0161 834 3020		
Weather Info	Air Cen MOEx www.cityairportmanchester.com		

Noise Abatement Procedures
Pilots should avoid flying low over the farm buildings on the NW corner of AD boundary. These building are directly under Rwy09L APP.
Helicopters must avoid over flying the built up areas S and E of AD.
Except for safety reasons, turns after take off should not be made below 500ft agl. Advise FISO before Dept.
Fixed wing ACFT standard join is overhead at 1800ft QFE. Pilots should inform ATS if performing a non-standard join prior to entering the ATZ.
Orbits within the circuit are not permitted unless required for safety reasons.

Go-around Procedure
Above 200ft – If safe, manoeuvre the ACFT to the dead side of AD keeping any other ACFT in sight, climb on Rwy heading, parallel to Rwy in use to circuit height.
Below 200ft – Climb straight ahead unless avoiding action must be taken, to circuit height. Do not climb above 500ft until you have passed the upwind numbers on Rwy in use.
ACFT should not continue APP below 200ft if Rwy is occupied.
Pilots must not carry out run and break manoeuvres within circuit.

Helicopter Procedures
Helicopters must not fly above 500ft whilst joining/leaving the AD or circuit unless practising emergency procedures.
All helicopters must arrive via specific entry/exit points, reporting prior to reaching and at the point.
Hovering training takes place on AD. All helicopters must ensure that adequate safety clearance is given for down wash when operating close to Rwy in use remaining at least 50m from Rwy in use.
All helicopter hover training must obtain PPR from ATS prior to flight.

Helicopter Arrivals
See Helicopter entry/exit points and circuits
Astley: Helicopters to enter circuit not above 500ft agl and position to N boundary of AD, landing at Rwy20 or Rwy14 Thr as instructed by ATS.
Worsley: Helicopters to enter circuit not above 500ft agl routing direct to N AD boundary, landing at Rwy20 or Rwy14 Thr as instructed by ATS.
Irlam: Helicopters to route along the Manchester Ship Canal not above 500ft agl, landing at Rwy02 or Rwy32 Thr as instructed by ATS.

Helicopter Departures
Request to start rotors from ATS must be acquired.
Helicopters must not lift until clearance has been given.
Traffic dependant, helicopters may be requested to Dept direct or via a specified Rwy.
Helicopters must not over fly SW corner of AD below 200ft due to model flying.

Manchester Barton ATZ Heli Entry/Exit Points & Circuits

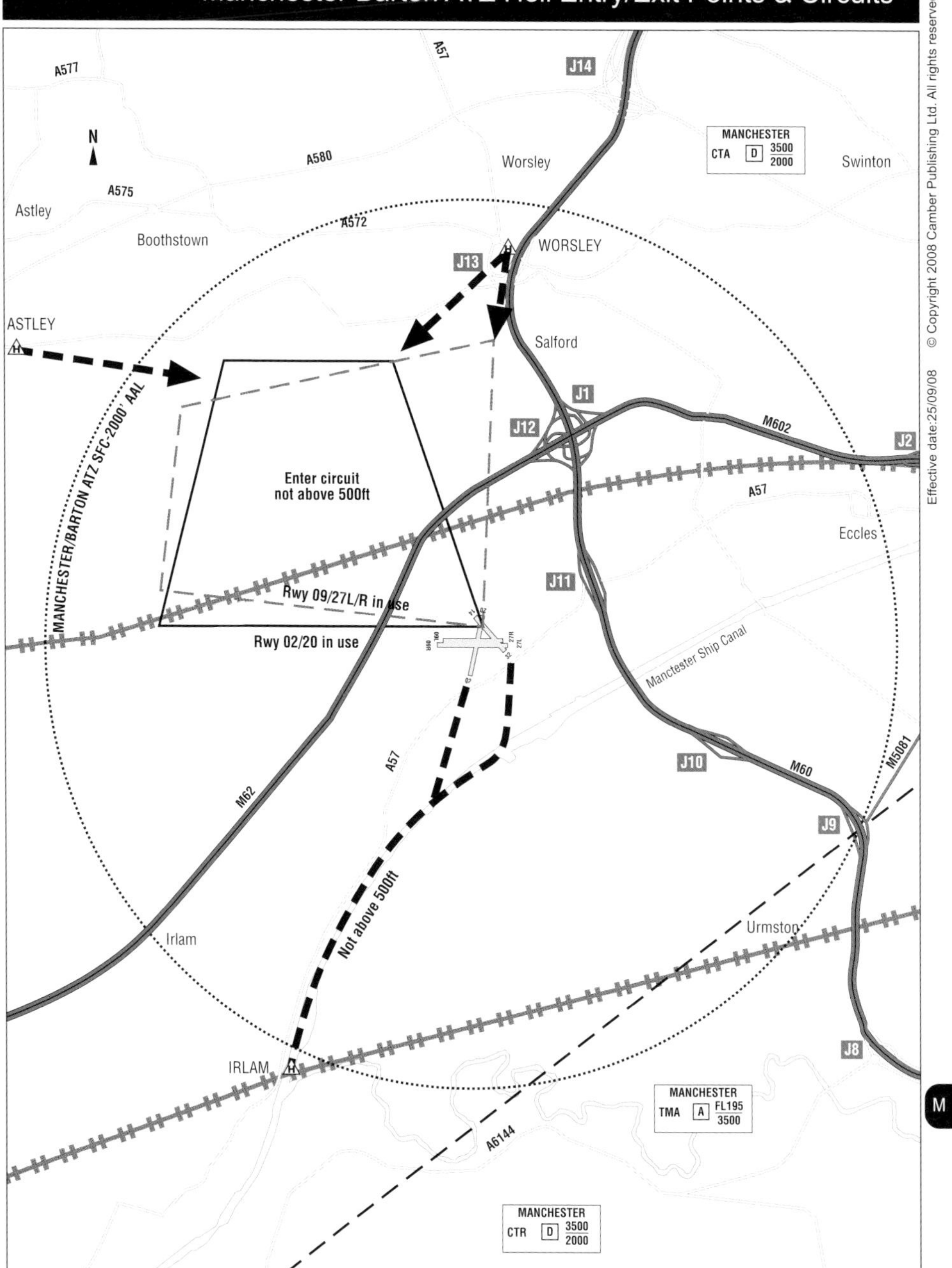

M

EGCD MANCHESTER WOODFORD

295ft 10mb	6nm N of Macclesfield N5320.26 W00208.93	PPR	Alternative AD	**Manchester** Manchester Barton
				Non-standard join

Woodford	ATIS Manchester 128.175 (Arr)	APP Manchester 135.000	APP 120.700	TWR 120.700	FIRE 121.600

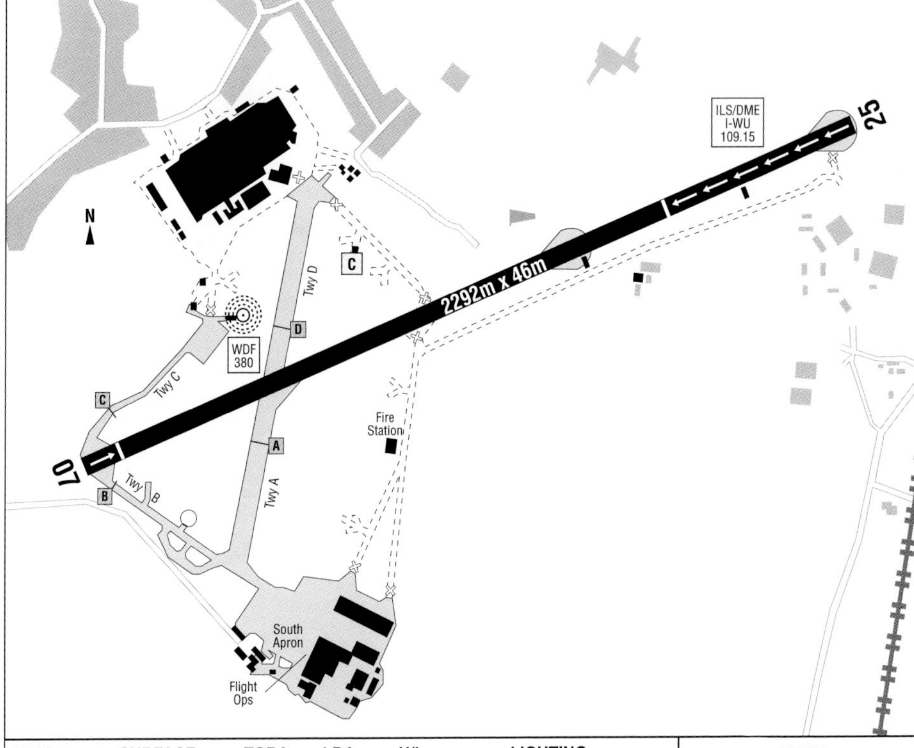

RWY	SURFACE	TORA	LDA	U/L	LIGHTING
07	Asphalt	2167	2061		Thr Rwy PAPI 3° LHS
25	Asphalt	2217	1671		Thr Rwy PAPI 3.6° LHS

Displaced Thr Rwy07 106m, Displaced Thr Rwy25 546m

RNAV			
MCT	**113.55**	**109**	**4.2**

Remarks
AD currently only available to BAE Systems ACFT. No visiting ACFT accepted. Twy B & C not available to public transport ACFT.

Warnings
AD located inside Manchester Control Zone. An additional set of PAPI on Rwy25, 360m prior to the displaced Thr are solely for test flying purposes. Broken yellow lines are for calibration purposes. The use of mobile phones on the apron area is strictly prohibited.

Operating Hrs	Mon-Thu 0750-1525 Fri 0750-1430 (Summer) +1Hr (Winter)
Circuits	07 RH, 25 LH
Landing Fee	Available on request
Maintenance	Nil
Fuel	JET A1
Disabled Facilities	Nil
Restaurants	Nil
Taxis	**Tel:** 0161 456-7099 **Tel:** 0161 440-9769 **Tel:** 0161 439-9056
Car Hire	Bramhall Self Drive Hire **Tel:** 0161 439 5826
Weather Info	M* Air Cen MOEx

Operator
BAe Systems
Manchester Woodford Aerodrome
Chester Road, Bramhall
Greater Manchester SK7 1QR
Tel: 0161 439 5050 Ex 3294 (PPR)
Tel: 0161 439 3383 (ATC)
Fax: 0161 955 3316

M

Woodford Local Flying Area
Within a local flying area of 1.5nm radius, centred on the AD VFR/SVFR flights may take place subject to ATC clearance from Manchester/Woodford ATC.

Entry-Exit Lane
An Entry-Exit lane is established 1nm wide aligned on the Congleton-Macclesfield railway from the boundary of the LFA to the S boundary of Manchester CTR. VFR/SVFR flights may take place subject to ATC clearance & compliance with the following conditions.
1 ACFT using the lane must remain clear of cloud and in sight of the GND & in a flight visibility of **at least 3km.**
2 ACFT using the lane **must comply with the left hand rule** when following the railway line unless otherwise instructed by ATC for separation purposes.
3 Pilots are responsible for maintaining adequate clearance from the GND and other obstacles, & are warned of **high GND to the E** of the lane.
4 ACFT **must not** leave the confines of the lane unless authorised by ATC.
5 Inbound ACFT should make their first call to Woodford APP to ascertain the controlling agency at the time they wish to join.
It is essential that inbound ACFT follow the flight profile detailed below
Fly not above 2500ft QNH from Congleton to Macclesfield
Fly not above 1500ft QNH from N of Macclesfield to LFA

Woodford Standard VFR Dept
To assist in reducing RTF Workload, Woodford ATC will use the following abreviated phraseology to issue the following Dept clearances.
Congleton One VFR Dept Rwy25
A left turn out towards Macclesfield to intercept the Macclesfield-Congleton railway then remain within the confines of the Entry-Exit lane unless other wise instructed by ATC.
Flight Profile ACFT MUST
Fly not above1500ft QNH to the N edge of Macclesfield
Fly not above 2500ft QNH to the Congleton VRP
Congleton Two VFR Dept Rwy07
A right turnout towards Macclesfield & then as the procedure above.
The Woodford Entry-Exit lane is notified for the purpose of Rule 5 (2)(a). That is it is NOT obligatory to comply with the '1500ft rule' but essential that the ACFT be flown at such a height that would enable the ACFT to alight clear of the congested area in the event of failure of a power unit.

Visual Reference Points (VRP)

VRP	VOR/VOR	VOR/NDB	VOR/DME
Congleton N5309.90 W00210.85	MCT 169°/TNT 293°	MCT 169°/WHI 099°	MCT 169°/12nm TNT 293°/20nm

M

643ft 21mb	9nm S of Marlborough N5118.30 W00140.00	PPR	**Alternative AD**	**Southampton** Thruxton

Non Radio	LARS Boscombe 126.700	DACS Salisbury Ops 122.750	Safetycom 135.475

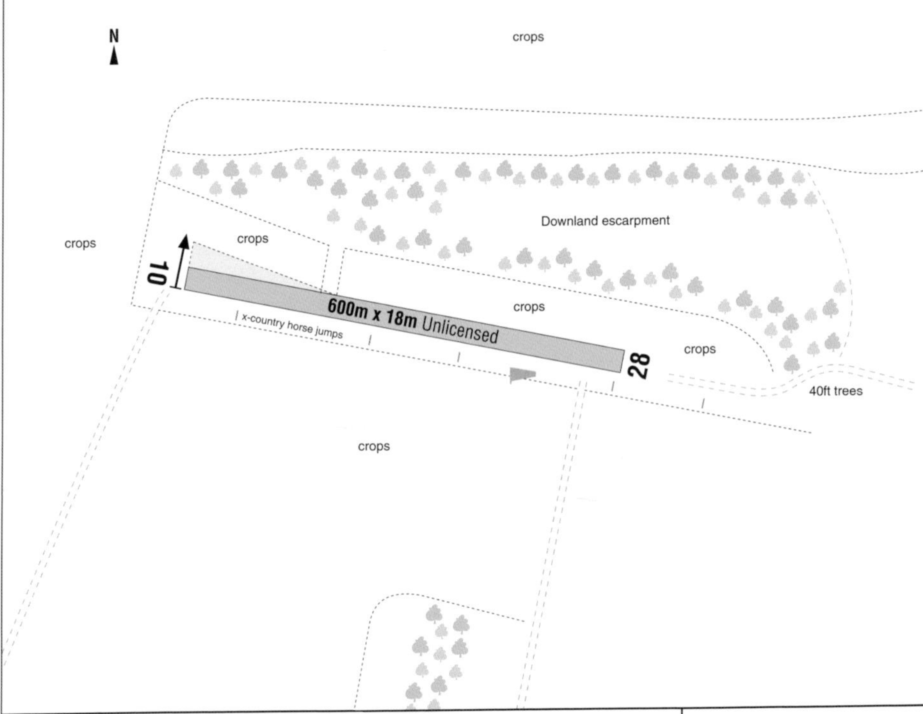

RWY	SURFACE	TORA	LDA	U/L	LIGHTING	RNAV
10/28	Grass			600x18	Nil	

Remarks
Strictly PPR by telephone, preferably with 24hrs notice as stock may need to be moved . Usually only available to guests staying at Manor Farm B&B. AD well prepared and well drained on top of chalk escarpment. Windsock displayed with PPR. Operator will meet visiting ACFT to help with ground handling to ensure a safe operation. Due to close proximity of D128, visiting pilots are advised to contact Salisbury Plain Ops.

Warnings
Be aware of close proximity of Salisbury Plain Danger area complex to the S & W. C130 para dropping acft regularly operate in close proximity to the AD. Public footpath and solid cross-country horse jumps on the southern edge of the strip. Watch out for people and horses on the strip! Farm machinery may be parked close to the strip.
Noise: App Rwy28. Curved noise abatement approach and departure required between Aughton Farm and Aughton, (Operator can provide information). Please fly with consideration for our neighbours.

Operating Hrs	By arrangement
Circuits	To N at 1000ft QFE Join downwind
Landing Fee	Nil
Maintenance	Nil
Fuel	Nil
Disabled Facilities	Nil
Accomodation	4 star B & B Manor Farmhouse www.manorfm.com **Tel:** 01264 850859
Taxi/Car Hire	Operator can assist
Weather Info	Air SW MOEx

Operator
James Macbeth
Manor Farm
Collingbourne Kingston
Wiltshire
SN8 3SD
Tel/Fax: 01264 850859
Tel: 01980 674710 (Salisbury Ops)
Tel: 01980 674730 (Salisbury Ops)
stay@manorfm.com
www.manorfm.com

178ft 6mb	2.5nm W of Ramsgate N5120.53 E00120.77	PPR	Alternative AD Diversion AD	Southend Rochester

Non-standard join

Manston	ATIS	LARS/APP	TWR	FIRE
	133.675	126.350	119.925	121.600

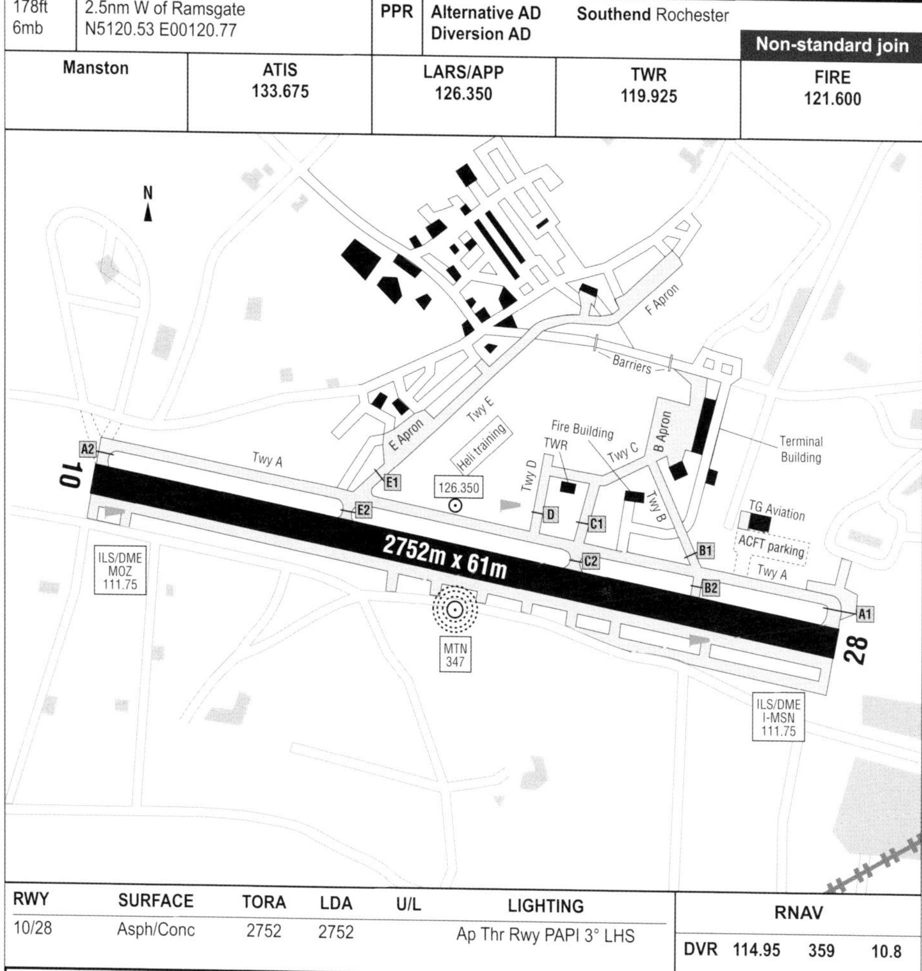

RWY	SURFACE	TORA	LDA	U/L	LIGHTING
10/28	Asph/Conc	2752	2752		Ap Thr Rwy PAPI 3° LHS

RNAV			
DVR	114.95	359	10.8

Remarks
Strict PPR inc training. Hi-vis. All ACFT must be handled by agent – ACFT <4 tonnes TG Aviation, ACFT >4 Tonnes AD Ops. Captains of visiting ACFT are responsible for the escort and safety of their passengers whilst airside. LARS available (0900-1700 L Daily). Helicopter training on grass area N Twy A between Apron E & Twy D.
Visual aid to location: Ibn MN Green.

Warnings
Twy B 23m wide, all other 15m wide with sharp turns. Short Twy links Twy A with TG Aviation. Pilots entering Apron B must do so with caution under marshallers instructions. The Y shaped pans off Twy C & D are also used.
Caution: Rwy28 short finals turbulence may be encountered with NW or S winds. Bird concentrations may be present on Rwy APP.

Operating Hrs Available by prior arrangement. Minimum 30mins notice required

Circuits Jets & ACFT 5700kg 1800ft QFE
All other ACFT 1000ft QFE
Circuits may be varied

Landing Fee On application

Maintenance
TG Aviation **Tel:** 01843 823656

Fuel AVGAS 100LL (TG Aviation)
JET A1 (AD Ops)

Disabled Facilities Nil

Handling **Tel:** 01843 823600/825063 (AD Ops)
Tel: 01843 823656 (TG Aviation)
Fax: 01843 821386 (AD Ops)
Fax: 01843 822024 (TG Aviation)

Restaurants Refreshments available

Taxis
Minicabs **Tel:** 01843 581581

Car Hire
Budget **Tel:** 01843 860310

Weather Info M T15 Fax 372 MOEx

Operator Infratil Ltd
Kent International Airport Manston
Manston
Ramsgate, Kent, CT12 5BP
Tel: 01843 823600 (Switchboard)
Fax: 01843 821386 (AD)

Effective date:25/09/08 AIP 07

Manston Noise Procedures
Unless other wise instructed by ATC or unless deviations are required in the interests of safety, all jet ACFT and all ACFT >5700kgs MTWA dept AD are subject to the following noise preferential routings:
Rwy10: Climb straight ahead until 3000ft QNH, then as directed by ATC.
Rwy28: Climb straight ahead to 1.5nm DME I-MSN, then track 310° until 3000ft QNH and passing 5nm DME I-MSN, then as directed by ATC.
Rwy28: Dept joining airways at DVR VOR: Initially as above, but subject to traffic, after passing 5nm DME I-MSN, R turn on track DVR VOR and arrange flight to pass 4000ft QNH by 15nm DME VOR.

VFR ACFT subject to noise preferential routings will not jeopardise their VFR status, and will be asked where possible to avoid large areas of population.

Flying near Manston
Manston regularly generates ACFT in the medium/heavy vortex wake categories, therefore ACFT flying within 20nm of Manston are advised to call Manston APP for traffic info.

VRP

Canterbury (A2 Harbledown Jct)	N5116.92 E00102.10
Deal	N5113.44 E00124.30
Whistable	N5121.80 E00101.60

M

EGYM MARHAM

77ft 2mb	5nm SE of Kings Lynn N5238.90 E00033.04	PPR MIL	Alternative AD Diversion AD	Norwich Old Buckenham

Non-standard join

Marham	LARS/APP 124.150	TWR 122.100

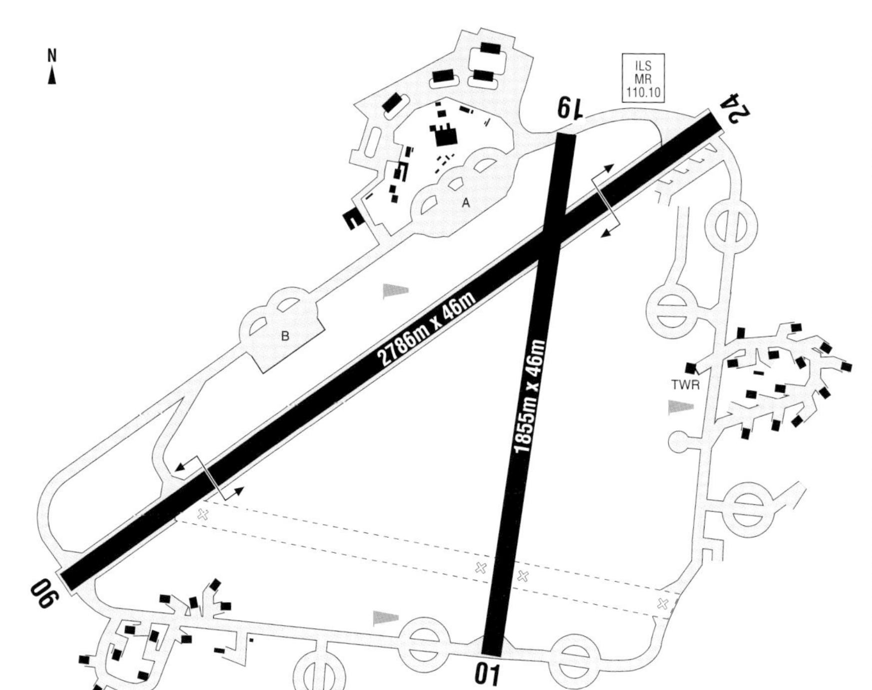

RWY	SURFACE	TORA	LDA	U/L	LIGHTING
06/24	Asph/Conc	2786	2786		Ap Thr Rwy PAPI 2.5°
01/19	Concrete	1855	1799		Rwy PAPI 3°

Rwy01/19 emergency use only
Arrester gear Rwy06 640m from Thr
Arrester gear Rwy24 487m from Thr
Rwy06/24 widths displaced By 50m
Normal ops: app cable down over run cable up

RNAV

Remarks
PPR strictly by telephone, 24Hrs notice required. Active RAF AD. Intensive fast Jet operations. Civil visitors may be subject to refusal or individual Arr conditions. Inbound ACFT call Marham APP at least 20nm from AD.
Visual aid to Location: I Bn MR red.

Warnings
Considerable bird activity in vicinity of AD. Glider flying takes place outside normal operating Hrs. Under normal operations the APP arrester gear is down trampling of the wires by light ACFT constitutes a hazard.

Operating Hrs	0800-2359 Mon-Thu 0800-1800 Fri (L) ATZ active 24Hrs
Circuits	24, 01 LH, 06, 19 RH, 1000ft QFE
Landing Fee	Charges in accordance with MOD policy Contact Station Ops for details
Maintenance	Not available to Civil visitors
Fuel	JET A1 by prior arr
Disabled Facilities	Nil
Restaurants	Nil
Taxis/Car Hire	Nil
Weather Info	M T Fax374 Air S MOEx ATIS **Tel:** 01760 337261 Ex 7888
Operator	RAF Marham Kings Lynn Norfolk PE33 9NP **Tel:** 01760 337261 Ex 6244/6240 (Ops) **Fax:** 01760 337261 Ex 6018 (Ops)

-6ft 0mb	5nm ESE of Wisbech N5239.50 E00018.00	PPR	Alternative AD Cambridge Fenland

Herbert Operations	LARS Marham 124.150	A/G 130.375 Not normally manned

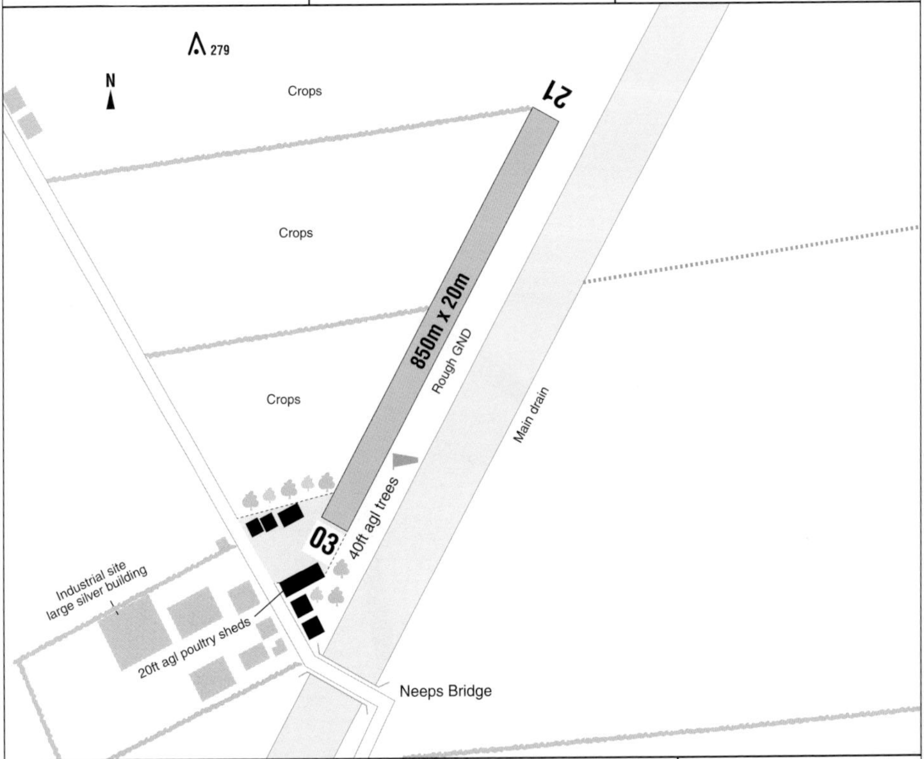

RWY	SURFACE	TORA	LDA	U/L	LIGHTING
03/21	Grass			850x20	Rwy

RNAV

Remarks
PPR by telephone. Visiting ACFT welcome at pilots own risk. AD is suitable for light twin ACFT with a good level surface.
Visual aid to location: Close proximity to main drain and industrial site with large silver roofed building.

Warnings
AD may be soft after prolonged rain or snow. Rwy03 APP is over group of buildings and trees. Crops are grown up to Rwy on W side. 82m test mast 800m NNW Rwy21 Thr.

Operating Hrs	SR-SS
Circuits	LH
Landing Fee	Nil
Maintenance	Nil
Fuel	AVGAS 100LL by arr
Disabled Facilities	
Restaurant	Nil
Taxis/Car Hire	Available on request
Weather Info	Air S MOEx

Operator
R J Herbert
Harps Hall
Walton Highway
Wisbech, Cambs
Tel: 01945 430365 (Evenings)
Tel: 01945430666 (Daytime/weekend)
Fax: 01945 430487
sales@rjherbert.co.uk

 OP 07

M

EGHB — MAYPOLE

110ft 3mb	3nm NE of Canterbury N5120.31 E00109.34	PPR	Alternative AD	Manston Lashenden

Non-standard join

Maypole	LARS Manston 126.350	A/G Maypole 119.400 make blind calls

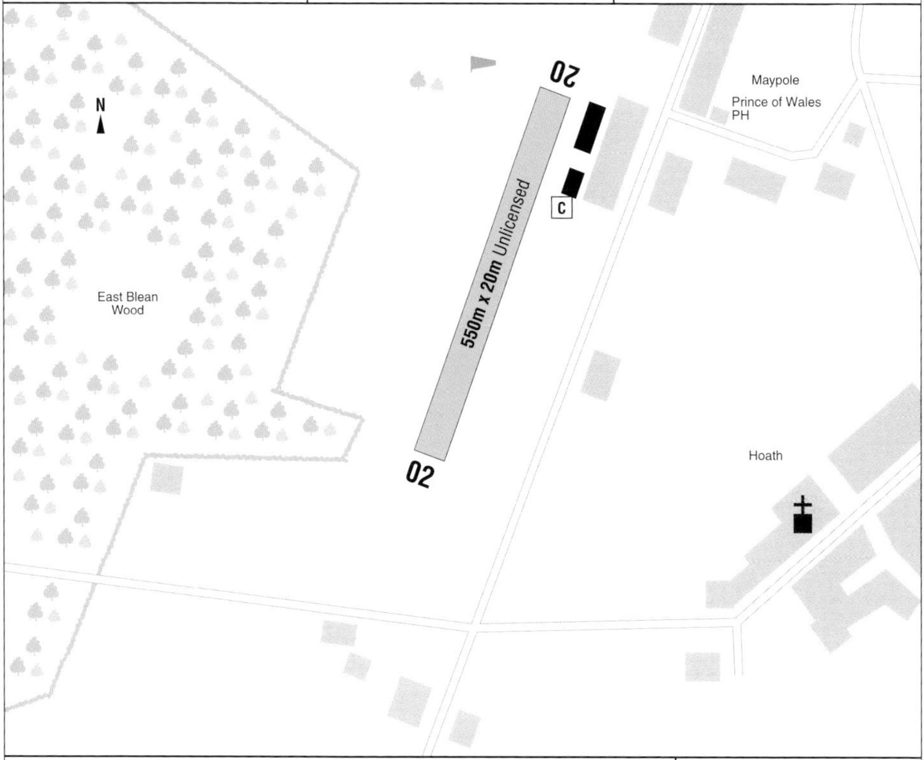

RWY	SURFACE	TORA	LDA	U/L	LIGHTING
02/20	Grass			550x20	Nil

RNAV			
DVR	114.95	326	13.1

Remarks
Strictly PPR by telephone only & at pilots own risk. ACFT call Maypole Radio when inbound. Planning restraints mean that permission to visit this AD may be denied.

Warnings
Buildings on short final Rwy02. Windsock at N of Rwy. Turbulence possible from trees in woodland to W of AD.
Noise: Do not over fly the villages of Maypole & Hoath, avoid all other local habitation.

Operating Hrs 0800-2100 (L) or dusk if earlier

Circuits All circuits to W 800ft
Do not fly E of centreline
Join downwind
No overhead joins

Landing Fee Single £10 Helicopter £15

Maintenance
General Aero Services **Tel:** 01375 891165

Fuel AVGAS (Cash only)

Disabled Facilities

Restaurants Refreshments in clubhouse.
Food available at Prince of Wales pub
Tel: 01227 860338, Maypole village
Nearest accommodation in
Herne Bay (2miles)

Taxis **Tel:** 01227 369999

Car Hire Nil

Weather Info Air SE MOEx

Operator Mr & Mrs Haigh
Maypole Farm, Maypole
Canterbury
Kent CT3 4LN
Tel: 01227 860374/860375 (PPR)
Tel: 07768 658153 (PPR)
Tel: 07778 787447 (PPR)
Tel/Fax: 01227 860150 (Clubhouse)
www.maypoleairfield.com

Effective date:25/09/08 OP 08

MEASHAM COTTAGE FARM

350ft 10Mb	2nm S of Measham N5240.12 W00131.46	PPR	**Alternative AD** **East Midland** Leicester **Non-standard join**

Cottage Farm	ATIS East Midlands 128.225	APP East Midlands 134.175	AG 129.825

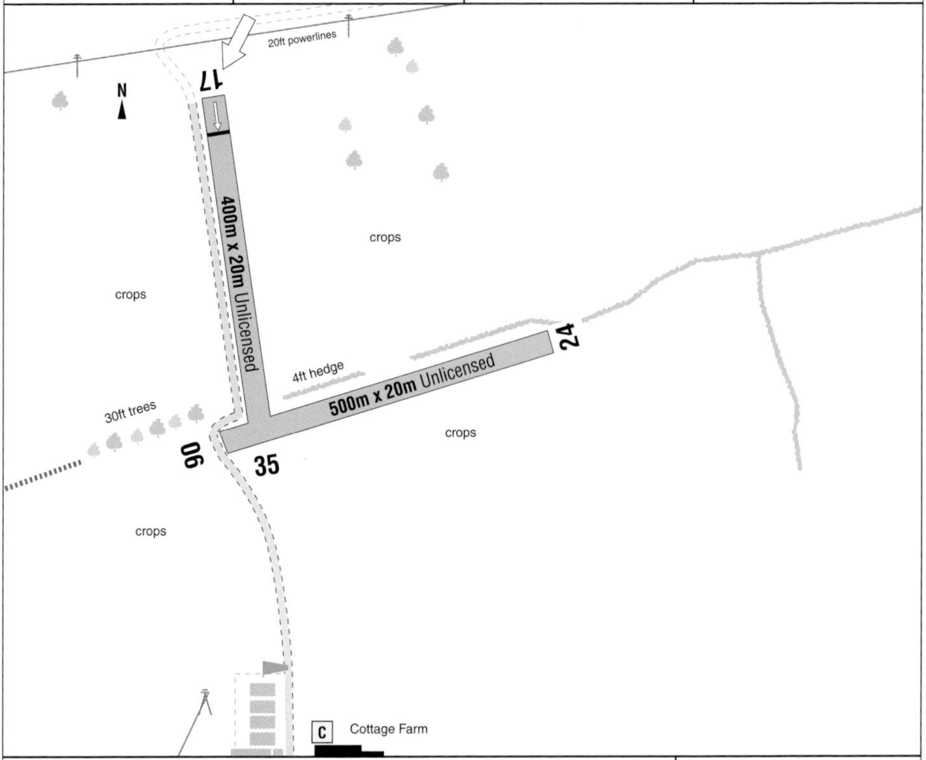

20ft powerlines
17
N
400m x 20m Unlicensed
crops
crops
4ft hedge
500m x 20m Unlicensed
24
30ft trees
06
35
crops
crops
C Cottage Farm

RWY	SURFACE	TORA	LDA	U/L	LIGHTING
06/24	Grass			500x20	Nil
17/35	Grass			400x20	Nil

RNAV			
HON	113.65	019	19.5

M

Remarks
PPR by telephone, if no answer then AD closed. Mircrolights only due to planning restrictions. Home of Four Counties microlights. Rwys flat and well prepared. Windsock by hangars to S of Rwys.

Warnings
AD close to NEMA CTR. 20ft power line close to Rwy17 Thr .
Noise: Follow the entry/exit lanes marked on chart. Dept ACFT must climb overhead to 1500ft QFE before setting course. Avoid all local habitation. Rwy17– 45° offset final **must** be flown to avoid neighbouring land to the N/NW.

Operating Hrs	SR-SS
Circuits	24 06 to S, 17 35 to E. Join downwind 1500ft QNH Descend in the pattern No deadside
Landing Fee	Nil
Maintenance	Nil
Fuel	Nil
Disabled Facilities	Nil
Restaurant	Nil
Taxi/Car Hire	Nil
Weather Info	Air Cen MOEx

Operator William Corbett Farm Ltd
c/o Mick Moulton
6 Launceston Drive
Hugglescote
Leicestershire LE67 2HW
Tel: 07712 773601

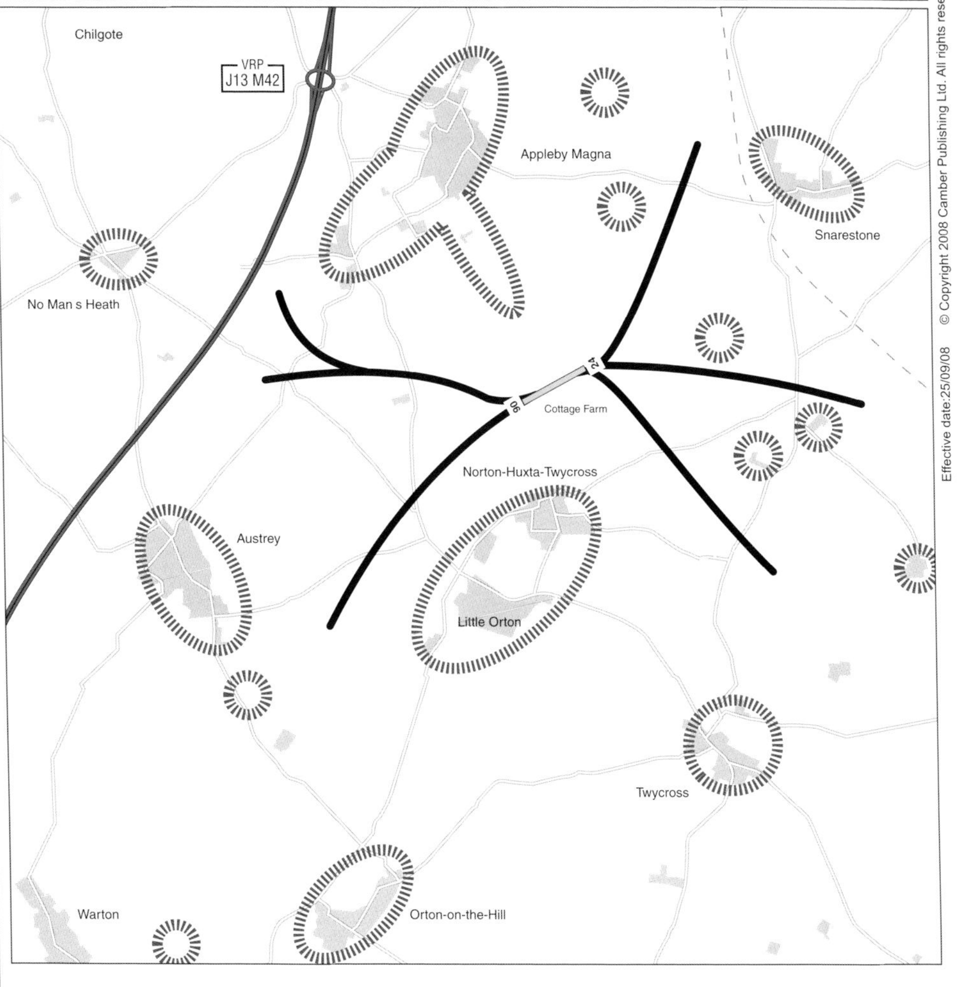

Effective date:25/09/08

164ft 4mb	2nm S of Ilminster N5057.75 W00256.14	PPR MIL	Alternative AD **Exeter** Dunkeswell **Non-standard join**

Merryfield	APP Yeovilton 127.350	TWR 122.100

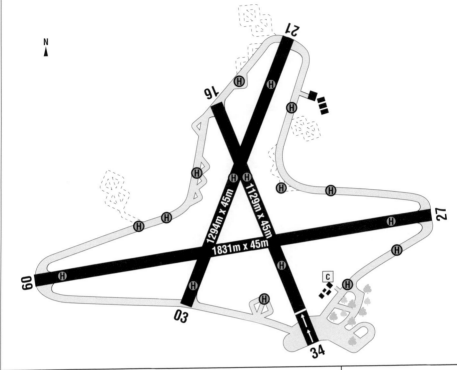

RWY	SURFACE	TORA	LDA	U/L	LIGHTING
09/27	Asphalt	1831	1831		Nil
03/21	Asphalt	1294	1294		Nil
16/34	Asphalt	1129	1129		Nil

RNAV

Remarks
Strictly PPR by telephone. Operated by Royal Navy as a satellite landing area for Yeovilton

Warnings
Helicopter operations normally Mon-Fri as required by Yeovilton. ATZ active H24. Glider flying outside Op Hrs. Rwys have non-standard markings associated with helicopter training. Intensive military helicopter activity within 3nm of AD.

Operating Hrs	Mon-Thu 0900-1630 Fri 0900-1200 ATZ Active H24
Circuits	Helicopters may fly variable circuits No deadside
Landing Fee	Charges in accordance with MOD policy Contact Station Ops for details
Maintenance	Nil
Fuel	Nil

Disabled Facilities

Restaurant	Nil
Taxis/Car Hire	Nil

Weather Info	MT Fax 456 MOEx Tel: 01935 455456
Operator	RNAS Merryfield Ilton Somerset TA19 9HN **Tel:** 01935 840551 Ex 5497/5498 (PPR) **Tel:** 01460 52018 (AD)

M

EGVP MIDDLE WALLOP

288ft 10mb	10nm NE of Salisbury N5108.57 W00134.05	PPR MIL	Alternative AD **Southampton** Thruxton

Non-standard join

Wallop	LARS Boscombe 126.700	TWR 118.275	RAD 123.300

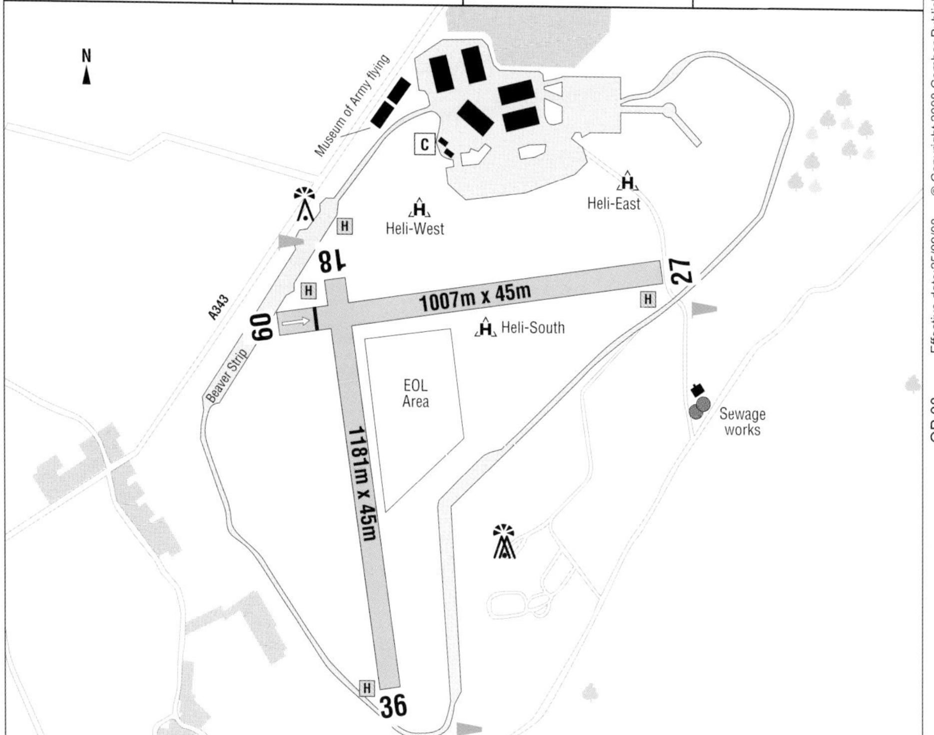

RWY	SURFACE	TORA	LDA	U/L	LIGHTING
09	Grass	1096	1007		Nil
27	Grass	1096	972		Nil
18/36	Grass	1181	1181		Nil

RNAV			
SAM	113.35	329	13.8

Remarks

PPR by telephone essential 24Hrs notice required. Visitors will be allowed only if the planned military use is low due to the complicated circuit procedures. Intensive helicopter & fixed wing activity, special procedures apply. Flying may take place at W/E, parascending W/E & PH. Frequent night flying. ATZ active H24. Helicopters Arr/Dept to heli W, E, S while fixed wing circuit is active. Helicopters Arr/Dept Rwy09/27 will pass beneath the fixed wing circuit. Helicopter engine off landing (EOL) circuit will be opposite direction to fixed wing. Visiting ACFT will be held to enable military training to be completed. It is imperative that all visitors are briefed by ATC. DAIS available during working Hrs.

Visual aid to location: IBn MW Red.

Warnings

Operating Hrs	Mon-Fri 0830-1700 or SS + 15mins (L) ATZ active H24 Weekends AD active
Circuits	Helicopters 500ft QFE Fixed Wing 1000ft QFE
Landing Fee	Charges in accordance with MOD policy Contact Station Ops for details
Maintenance	Not available to civil ACFT
Fuel	JET A1
Disabled Facilities	Nil
Restaurants	In Museum of Army Flying

Taxis/Car Hire	Nil
Weather Info	Air SW MOEx ATIS **Tel:** 01264 784142
Operator	Army School of Aviation Middle Wallop Stocksbridge Hamps SO20 8DU **Tel:** 01264 784380 **Fax**: 01264 784145

600ft 20mb	5nm SE of Galashiels N5532.00 W00244.00	PPR	Alternative AD	Edinburgh Carlisle

Non-standard join

Non-Radio	FIR Scottish 119.875	Safetycom 135.475

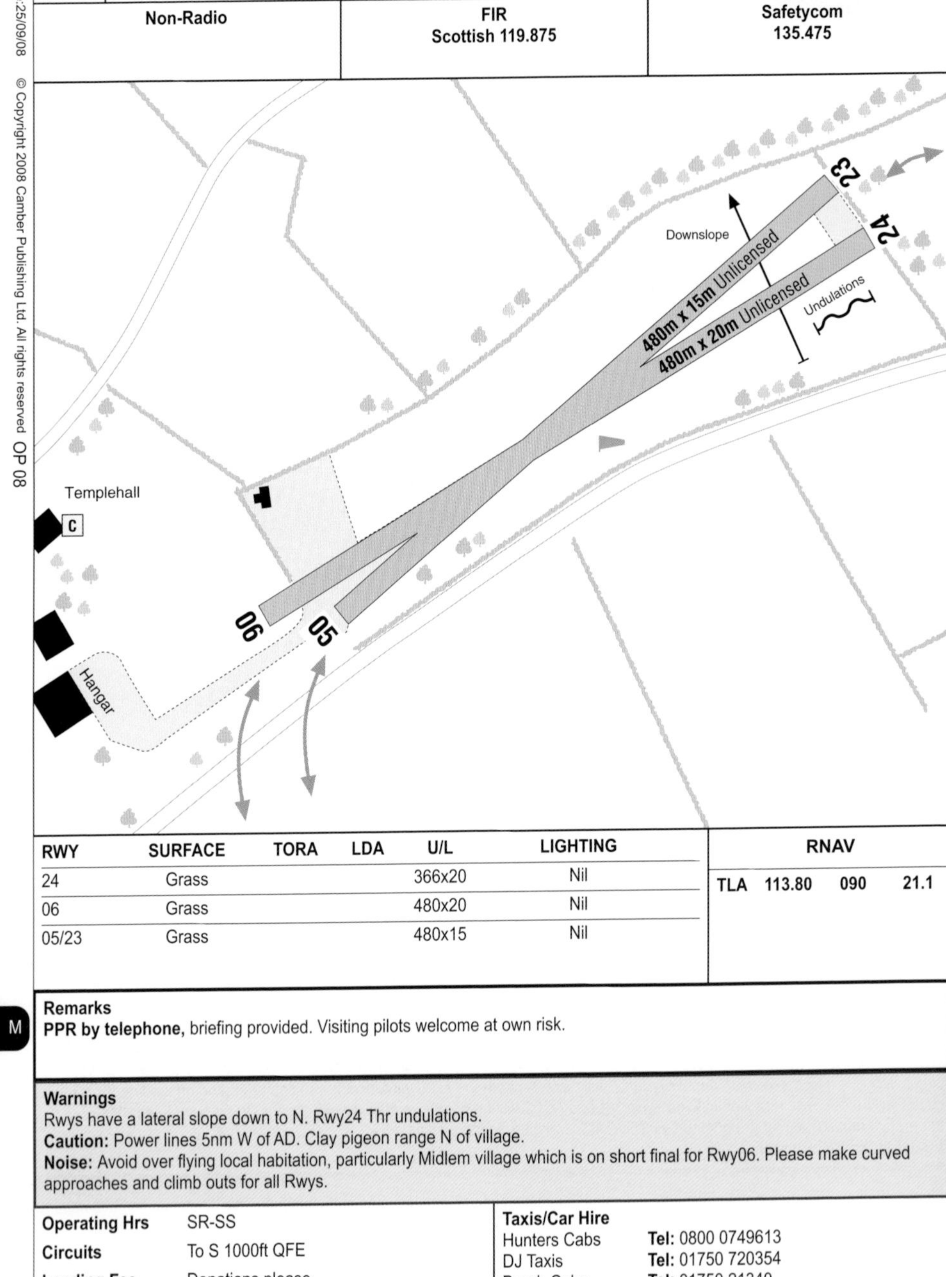

RWY	SURFACE	TORA	LDA	U/L	LIGHTING
24	Grass			366x20	Nil
06	Grass			480x20	Nil
05/23	Grass			480x15	Nil

RNAV			
TLA	113.80	090	21.1

Remarks
PPR by telephone, briefing provided. Visiting pilots welcome at own risk.

Warnings
Rwys have a lateral slope down to N. Rwy24 Thr undulations.
Caution: Power lines 5nm W of AD. Clay pigeon range N of village.
Noise: Avoid over flying local habitation, particularly Midlem village which is on short final for Rwy06. Please make curved approaches and climb outs for all Rwys.

Operating Hrs SR-SS
Circuits To S 1000ft QFE
Landing Fee Donations please
Maintenance Nil
Fuel MOGAS by arr
Disabled Facilities
☎
Restaurants Nil

Taxis/Car Hire
Hunters Cabs **Tel:** 0800 0749613
DJ Taxis **Tel:** 01750 720354
Burgh Cabs **Tel:** 01750 21340
Weather Info Air Sc GWC
Operator Mr R M Johnson
Templehall
Midlem
Selkirk
Borders TD7 4QB
Tel/Fax: 01835 870361
robinJ100@aol.com

EGUN MILDENHALL

33ft 1mb	2nm N of Mildenhall N5221.72 E00029.18	PPR MIL	Alternative AD Diversion AD	Cambridge Bourn

Non-standard join

Mildenhall	LARS Lakenheath 128.900	APP 128.900	TWR 122.550

N
218
Controlled ramp
Base Ops
C
Flight Terminal
Base Ops
ILS I-MIL 110.15
Navy Ops
H
A
D
A
TWR
C
A
11
2810m x 61m
MLD 115.90
A
D
B
Controlled ramp
C
29
Hangars
B
B
B
ILS I-MLD 110.15

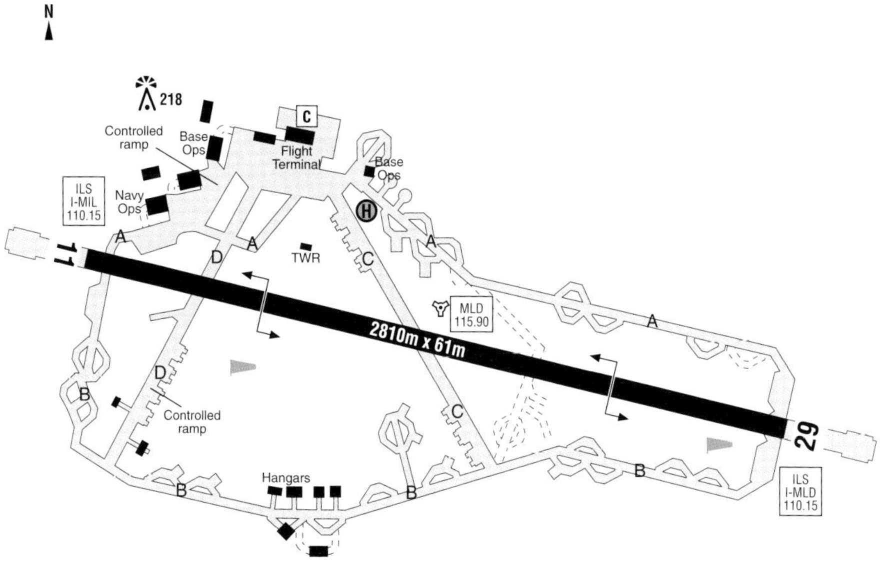

RWY	SURFACE	TORA	LDA	U/L	LIGHTING
11/29	Asph/Conc	2810	2810		Ap Thr Rwy PAPI 3° LHS

RNAV			
BKY	116.25	08	27.1

Remarks

PPR 24Hrs in advance. Military AD operated by USAF. Heavy jet movements may be encountered at any time. ILS for both Rwy29 & 11 uses DME element of TACAN MLD to provide distance from touchdown info.

Warnings

All movements under IFR. Ltd parking for visiting ACFT. Engine start for Dept must be requested from TWR. Rwy11 Dept are to commence turn on course at 1.8 DME MLD or 1nm from the AD boundary.

Operating Hrs	Mon-Thu 0600-2300 Fri-Sun 0600-1800 (L) ATZ active H24
Circuits	As instructed by ATC
Landing Fee	Charges in accordance with MOD policy Contact Station Ops for details
Maintenance	Nil for visiting civil ACFT
Fuel	JET A1 only by arr to visiting civil ACFT
Disabled Facilities	Nil
Restaurants	Nil
Taxis/Car Hire	Nil
Weather Info	Air S MOEx

Operator
RAF Mildenhall
Bury St Edmunds
Suffolk
IP28 8NG
Tel: 01638 547777/544130 (Ops)
Fax: 01638 542304 (Ops)

MAIP 08 Effective date:25/09/08

160ft 5mb	4nm NW of Wooler N5535.35 W00205.10	PPR	Alternative AD **Newcastle** Charterhall **Non-standard join**

Milfield	**A/G 130.100**	**Manned during operating Hrs only**

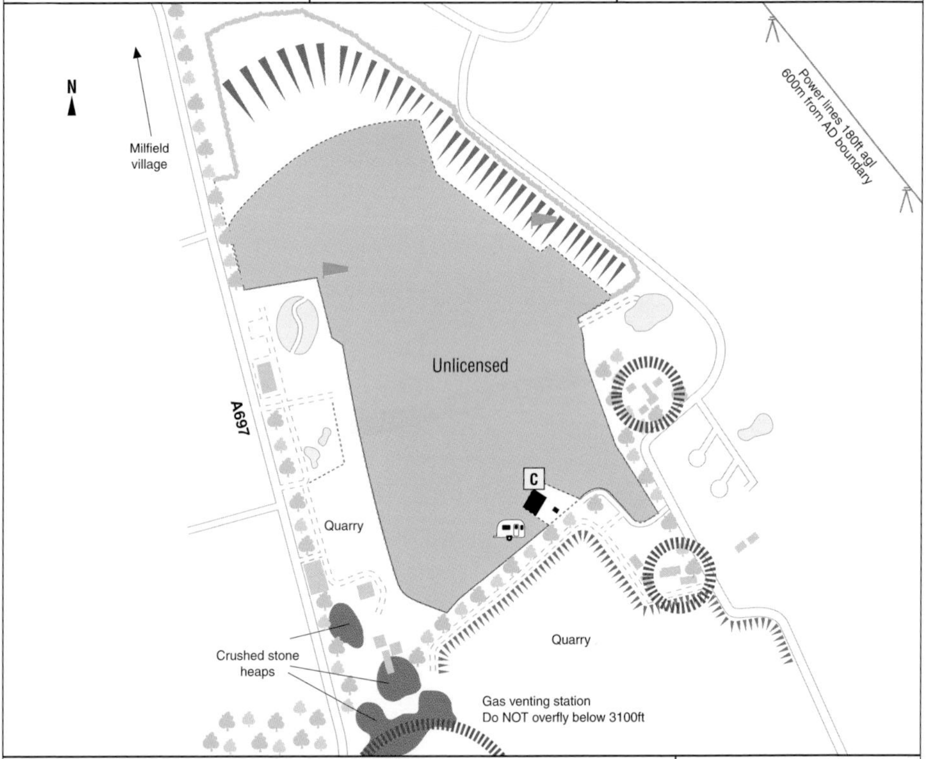

N

Milfield village

Power lines 180ft agl 600m from AD boundary

A697

Unlicensed

C

Quarry

Quarry

Crushed stone heaps

Gas venting station
Do NOT overfly below 3100ft

RWY	SURFACE	TORA	LDA	U/L	LIGHTING	RNAV

Maximun length 900m on Rwy31/13
All grass surface is useable

Remarks

PPR essential.No visiting ACFT accepted unless directly involved in Gliding Operations or in emergency. All landings at owners risk after radio contact with A/G.

Warnings

Do not over fly GVS on SSW corner of AD under any circumstances. AD is WW2 RAF Milfield, it is now a reclaimed gravel quarry and is 20ft below the surrounding terrain. This, and the slopes into AD at NW & NE boundary, may give an incorrect aspect of surface on APP. Surface is undulating but fairly smooth with well maintained grass surfaces. Wind gradient is severe in a strong S to SW wind with the possibility of MTW rotor down to the surface giving severe turbulence in the circuit and APP. **Noise**: Do not over fly Milfield village or any other settlement on the airfield boundary whilst landing or taking off.

Operating Hrs	Fri-Sun SR-SS & by arr
Circuits	Advised by radio on Arr Join overhead 1500ft QFE
Landing Fee	Private ACFT £10
Maintenance	Nil
Fuel	Nil except in emergency (AVGAS 100LL)
Restaurants	Tea Coffee and light snacks when gliding in progress. Local Cafes Restaurants and Pubs
Taxis	By arr
Car Hire	Nil
Weather Info	Air N MOEx
Operator	The Borders (Milfield) Gliding Club Ltd Milfield Airfield Wooler Northumberland, NE71 6HD **Tel:** 01668 216284 www.bordersgliding.co.uk

500ft 16mb	3nm WSW of Cleobury Mortimer N5221.69 W00232.74	PPR	Alternative AD	Birmingham Wolverhampton

Non-radio	ATIS Birmingham 126.275	APP Birmingham 118.050	LARS Shawbury 120.775	Safetycom 135.475

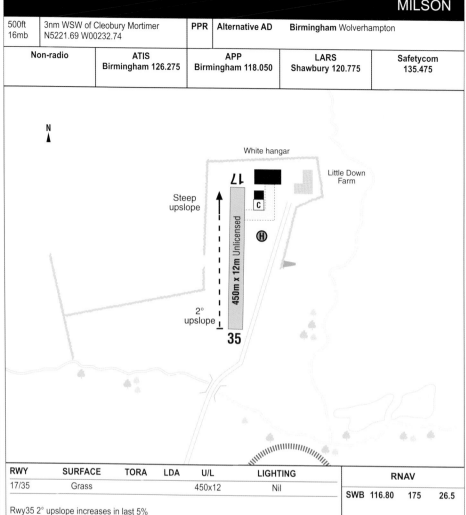

RWY	SURFACE	TORA	LDA	U/L	LIGHTING
17/35	Grass			450x12	Nil

Rwy35 2° upslope increases in last 5%

RNAV			
SWB	116.80	175	26.5

Remarks
PPR by telephone essential. Pilot/ACFT must be capable of operating from a short strip. Please sign visiting ACFT movement book situated in the caravan. Occasional military helicopter movements weekdays.
Visual aid to location: 2 white hangars & farm house at N end of strip.

Warnings
Rwy35 has up slope which increases markedly in last portion, Arr Rwy35, Dept Rwy17 unless wind is extreme. Rwy17 APP area has obstructions & high GND, a long final is recommended for accurate Arr.
Caution: Clee Hill 1750ft amsl 2nm NW. Cross winds & terrain induced turbulence are often a problem. Model rocket launching Sundays pm.
Noise: Avoid over flying white house SE of AD.

Operating Hrs	10 flights a day is max permissible under planning consent. Arr only (no Dept) 1400-1700 (L) on Sun (April-Sept)
Circuits	35 LH, 17 RH
Landing Fee	£2
Maintenance	Nil
Fuel	Ltd AVGAS/MOGAS by arr
Disabled Facilities	

Restaurants	Nil Toilet facilities available
Taxis/Car Hire	Nil
Weather Info	Air N MOEx
Operator	Chris Jones Little Down Farm Milson, Kidderminster Worcs, DY14 OBD **Tel:** 01584 890486 (AD PPR) **Tel:** 0777 5582023 www.milsonairstrip.co.uk

OP 08 Effective date:25/09/08

MITCHELLS FARM

10ft 0mb	8nm N of Cambridge Airport N5220.42 E00011.04	PPR	**Alternative AD**	**Cambridge** Bourn

Non-Radio	LARS Lakenheath 128.900	APP Cambridge 123.600	Safetycom 135.475

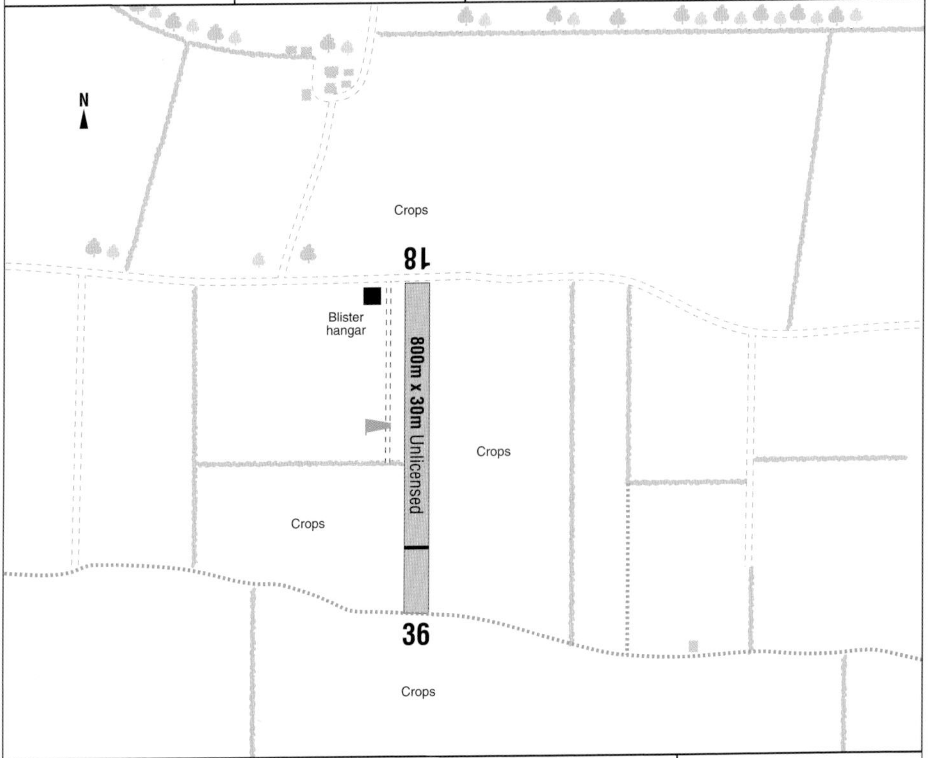

RWY	SURFACE	TORA	LDA	U/L	LIGHTING
18/36	Grass			800x30	Nil

RNAV			
BKY	116.25	015	21.5

Remarks
PPR by telephone is essential for safety reasons. Rwy flat and well maintained with clear APP. Rwy can be difficult to identify due to crop strip colours. Please sign movements book and leave details.
Visual aid to location: Small blister hangar to W of Rwy18 Thr.

Warnings
AD situated very close to boundary of Lakenheath/Mildenhall/ Honington CMATZ. Arr & Dept ACFT are advised to contact Lakenheath APP. Crops are grown up to the strip edge and a drainage ditch crosses Rwy36 Thr.
Noise: Avoid over flight of local habitation, particularly the village of Wilburton to N of AD

Operating Hrs	SR-SS
Circuits	LH 800ft QFE
Landing Fee	Nil
Maintenance	Nil
Fuel	AVGAS 100LL by arr
Disabled Facilities	Nil
Restaurants	
Kings Head	**Tel:** 01353 741029
Taxis/Car Hire	Nil
Weather Info	Air Cen MOEx

Operator Mr A Furness
Mitchells Farm, Millfield Lane
Wilburton, Cambs, CB6 3SD
Tel: 01353 740361
Tel: 07831 148084

 OP 07

M

202ft 7mb	2nm W of Llangefni Anglesey N5315.52 W00422.40	PPR MIL	Alternative AD Diversion AD	Liverpool Caernarfon

Non-standard join

Mona	LARS	APP	A/G	TWR
	Valley 125.225	125.225	118.950 (Flying Club)	119.175

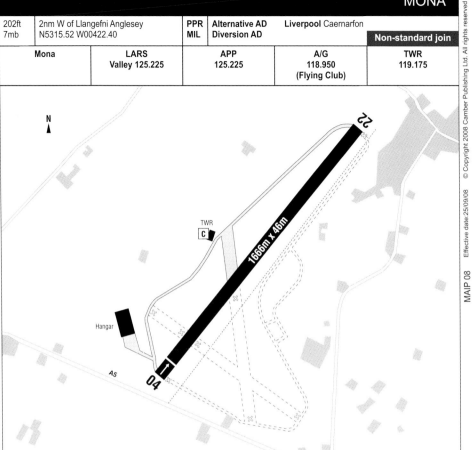

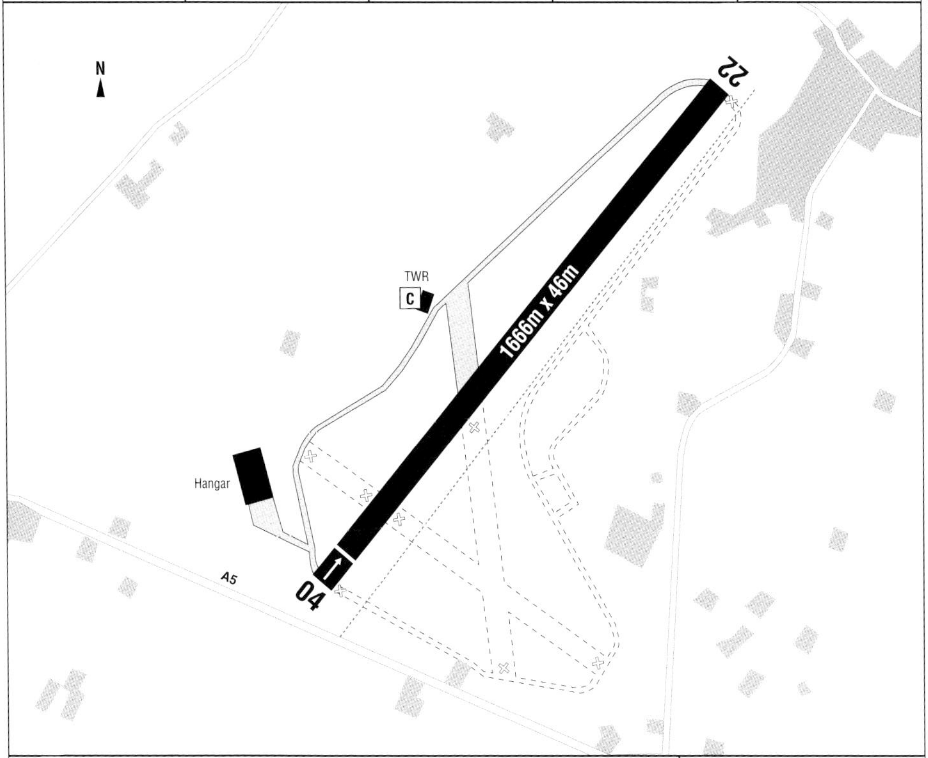

RWY	SURFACE	TORA	LDA	U/L	LIGHTING
04	Asphalt	1579	1524		Ap Thr Rwy PAPI 3°
22	Asphalt	1579	1579		Ap Thr Rwy PAPI 3°
Arrester gear Rwy04 Thr & Rwy22 Thr					

RNAV

Remarks

PPR during RAF operating Hrs through Valley Ops. Relief AD to RAF Valley. PPR obtained through Mona Flying Club evenings & W/E during BST. PPL/IMC/Night rating training available through flying club. Visiting pilots report to flying club near hangar.

Warnings

Visiting ACFT contact Valley before entering MATZ. Valley will transfer to Mona. If Valley does not answer contact Mona direct. DO NOT enter Valley MATZ or attempt to land if Valley or Mona cannot be contacted.
Noise: Avoid over flying Bodffordd, particularly downwind & base leg Rwy22.

Operating Hrs As per RAF Valley requirements
Mona Flying Club: Mon-Fri 1830-SS Sat-Sun 0900-SS (L)

Circuits 04 RH, 22 LH, 800ft QFE
Join dead side not below 2000ft QFE
On APP Rwy04 cross A5 not below 200ft QFE

Landing Fee Members: free
Visitors: Charges in accordance with MOD policy. Contact Station Ops for details

Maintenance Nil
Hangarage Available
Fuel Nil

Disabled Facilities

Restaurants Nil
Taxis/Car Hire Info in clubhouse
Weather Info Air N MOEx
Operator RAF Mona
Holyhead
Gwynedd LL65 3NY
Tel: 01407 762241 Ex 7450
(PPR RAF Ops Hrs)
Tel: 01407 720581
(PPR Mona Flying Club Hrs)
Fax: 01407 762241
www.flymona.com

180ft 6mb	4nm NW of Kilrea Northern Ireland N5459.25 W00638.81	PPR	Alternative AD Londonderry

Non-standard join

Movenis Drop Zone	A/G 129.900

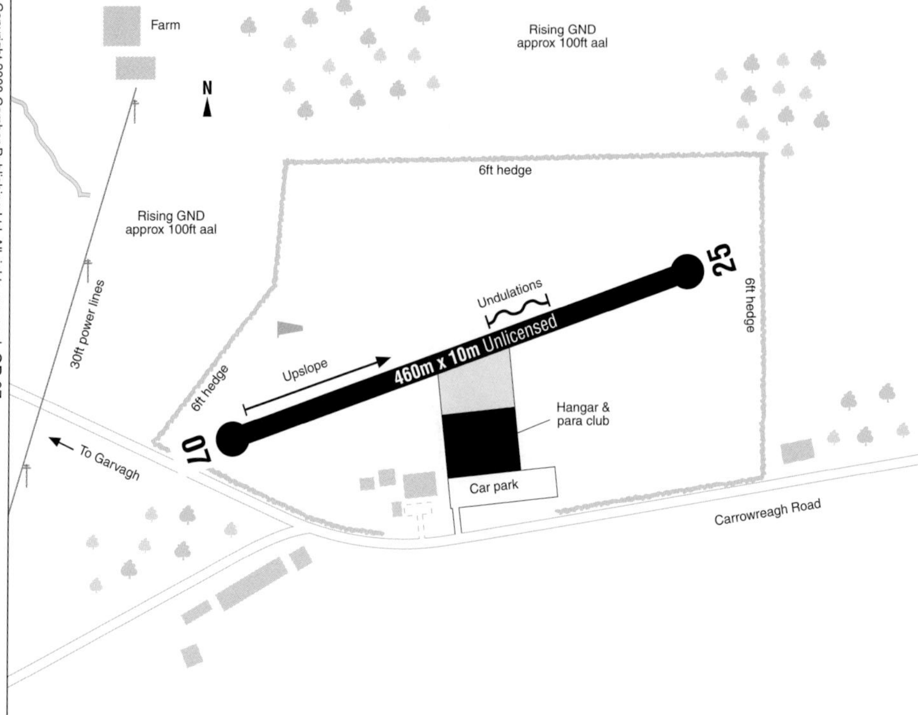

RWY	SURFACE	TORA	LDA	U/L	LIGHTING
07/25	Asphalt			460x10	Nil

RNAV			
BEL	117.20	331	24.3

Remarks

PPR by telephone. Primarily a parachute centre but light ACFT & microlights welcome. Rwy has undulating surface. No Rwy designators. The AD is situated in a very scenic rural area, Although this AD is not notified as a point of entry/exit under the terms of the Prevention of Terrorism Act permission will normally be granted after contact with The Police Service of Northern Ireland.

Warnings

Inbound ACFT should call Movenis to ascertain parachuting status; free fall parachuting takes place up to FL120. Parachutists use the nearby drop zone at Garvagh. Visiting pilots are requested to avoid transiting this area. AD is surrounded by a hedge and rolling hills.

Operating Hrs SR-SS

Circuits Standard overhead join
LH both Rwys

Landing Fee Nil

Maintenance Nil

Fuel Nil

Disabled Facilities Nil

Restaurants/Accomodation
Tea & Coffee at AD.
Restaurants & hotel at Garvagh
Accommodation can be provided in the parachute clubhouse for £5 per night
Neighbouring hotels & B&B's can be recommended

Taxis/Car Hire Nil

Weather Info Air N MOEx

Operator
Wild Geese Skydiving Centre
Movenis Airfield
Garvagh
Coleraine
Co Londonderry
BT51 5LQ
Tel: 02829 558609 (PPR)
Tel: 02890 650222 (PSNI)
Fax: 02829 557050
jump@skydivewildgeese.com
www.skydivewildgeese.com

NAYLAND

180ft 6mb	5nm NW of Colchester N5158.29 E00051.03	PPR	Alternative AD	**Southend** Earls Colne

Non-radio	LARS Southend 130.775	APP Wattisham 125.800	Safetycom 135.475

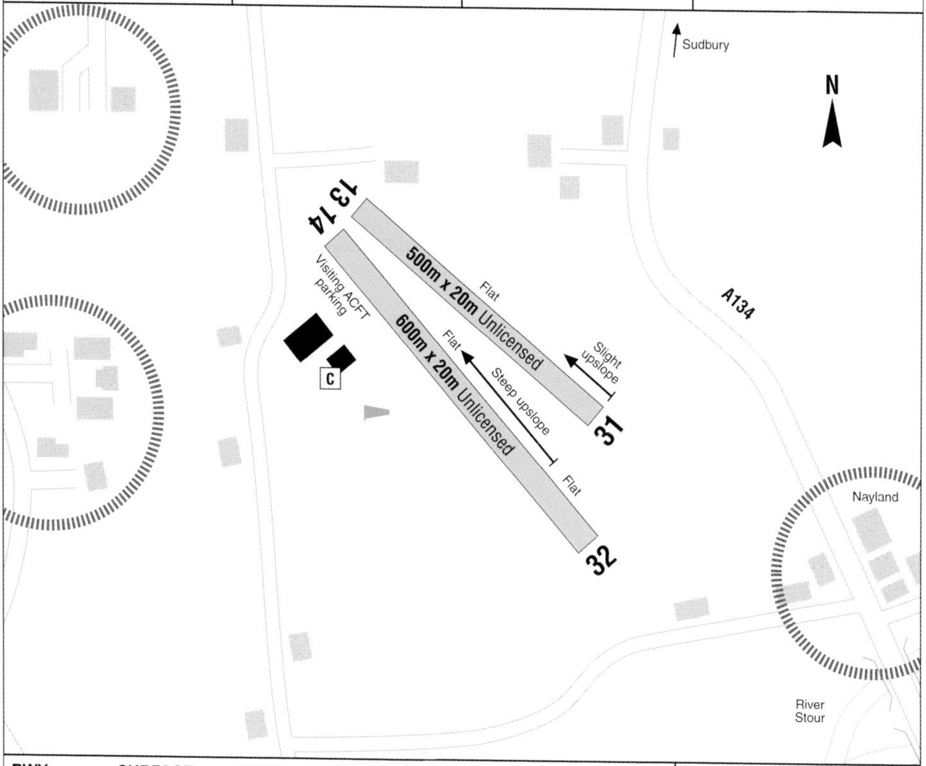

RWY	SURFACE	TORA	LDA	U/L	LIGHTING
14/32	Grass			600x20	Nil
13/31	Grass			500x20	Nil

RNAV			
CLN	114.55	307	13.5

Remarks
PPR by telephone for briefing essential. Visitors welcome at own risk. Rwy is delineated with white edge markers. Steep up slope Rwy32. Unless in extreme conditions land Rwy32 Dept Rwy14

Warnings
Noise: Avoid over flying Nayland to SE, hospital to W and large house to NW.

Operating Hrs	SR-SS
Circuits	LH 800ft QFE
Landing Fee	£2
Maintenance	**Tel:** 01206 263178 (Clubroom) **Tel:** 01206 230333
Fuel	AVGAS 100LL Cash only
Disabled Facilities	Nil
Restaurants	Light refreshments available at weekends
Taxis	**Tel:** 01206 262049
Car Hire	**Tel:** 07979 640040
Weather Info	Air S MOEx

Operator
Mr R Harris
Nayland Flying Group
Hill Farm
Wiston
Nayland
Essex CO6 4NL
Tel: 01206 262298
Tel: 07887 594355

455ft 15mb	11nm N of Salisbury N5114.83 W00145.25	PPR MIL	Alternative AD Diversion AD	Southampton Thruxton

Non-standard join

Netheravon	A/G Salisbury Plain 122.750	A/G 128.300

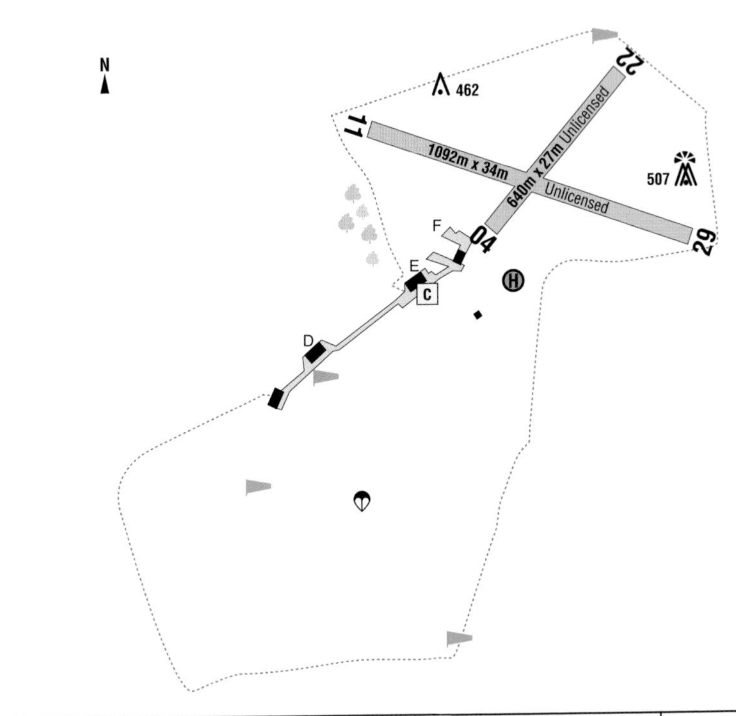

RWY	SURFACE	TORA	LDA	U/L	LIGHTING
11/29	Grass			1092x34	Thr Rwy
04/22	Grass			640x28	Rwy

RNAV			
SAM	113.35	323	23.1

Remarks
PPR essential due to special procedures associated with D128. Military AD. Inbound pilots to contact Salisbury Plain to ascertain range status at least 10nm from the Danger Area boundary before contacting Netheravon.

Warnings
AD used for parachuting up to FL150. Outside ATC Ops Hrs parachute Drop zone will operate using call sign Drop Zone. All ACFT must call for start up clearance.

Operating Hrs Mon-Fri 0800-1700 (L)
Military useage may be outside these times

Circuits 11, 22 LH, 29, 04 RH, 1000ft QFE
Remaining outside Boscombe MATZ

Landing Fee Charges in accordance with MOD policy
Contact Station Ops for details

Maintenance Nil
Fuel Nil
Disabled Facilities Nil
Restaurants Nil
Taxis/Car Hire Nil
Weather Info Air SW MOEx

Operator MOD (Army)
Netheravon Airfield
Salisbury Plain
Wiltshire
SP4 9SF
Tel: 01980 628289
Fax: 01980 678247

EGNF NETHERTHORPE

254ft 8mb	2.5nm WNW of Worksop N5319.02 W00111.78	PPR	Alternative AD Diversion AD	Doncaster Sheffield Retford

Netherthorpe	APP Doncaster Sheffield 126.225	A/G 123.275

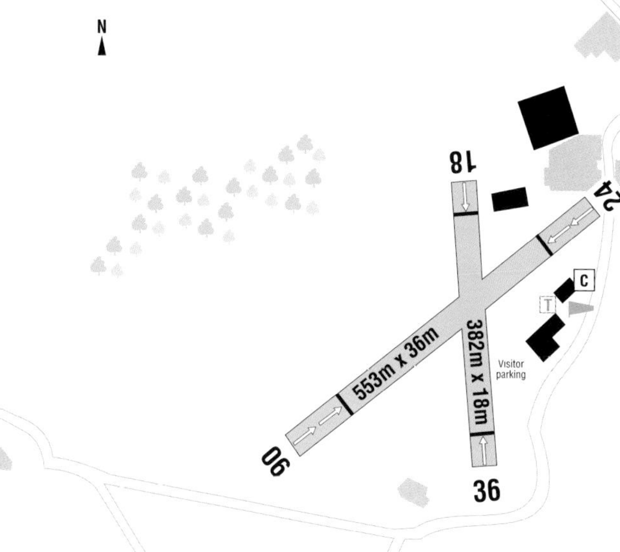

RWY	SURFACE	TORA	LDA	U/L	LIGHTING
06	Grass	476	407		Nil
24	Grass	490	370		Nil
18	Grass	382	357		Nil
36	Grass	382	309		Nil

Starter extension Rwy06 38m 1.9% down, Displaced Thr Rwy06 92m
Displaced Thr Rwy24 120m, Displaced Thr Rwy18 25m, Displaced Thr Rwy36 73m

RNAV			
GAM	112.80	287	9.3

Remarks
Strict PPR by telephone. ACFT Arr/Dept from N or E contact Doncaster APP. Inexperience pilots are to phone for advice before arrival and are to contact a member of Flying Staff for short briefing before dept.

Warnings
Located inside Doncaster Sheffield CTA. When Rwy06/24 in use, ACFT may be parked at S end of Rwy18/36. Pilots whose APP would result in being below 20ft crossing the road must initiate an immediate missed APP.
Noise: Avoid over flying the villages of Shireoaks, Thorpe Salvin and Whitwell.

Operating Hrs Mon 0930-1700 or SS whichever earlier 0930-2000 or SS (Summer) 0900-1700 or SS (Winter) & by arr

Circuits 06 36 RH, 18 24 LH, 800ft QFE

Landing Fee Single £8.50 Helicopters £17. Free with >20L fuel uplift

Maintenance
Dukeries Aviation **Tel:** 01909 481802

Fuel AVGAS 100LL by arr

Disabled Facilities

Restaurant Restaurant facilities available at AD Closed Monday

Taxis
Nunns **Tel:** 01909 500005

Car Hire
Hertz **Tel:** 01142 796644
National **Tel:** 01142 754111

Weather Info Air Cen MOEx

Operator Sheffield Aero Club Ltd
Netherthorpe Aerodrome
Thorpe Salvin
South Yorkshire
Tel: 01909 475233
Fax: 01909 532413
info@sheffieldaeroclub.net
www.sheffieldaeroclub.net

9ft 0mb	1.5nm S of RAF Coningsby N5304.03 W00009.16	PPR	Alternative AD **East Midlands** Fenland **Non-standard join**

Non-Radio	LARS Waddington 127.350	APP Coningsby 120.800	Safetycom 135.475

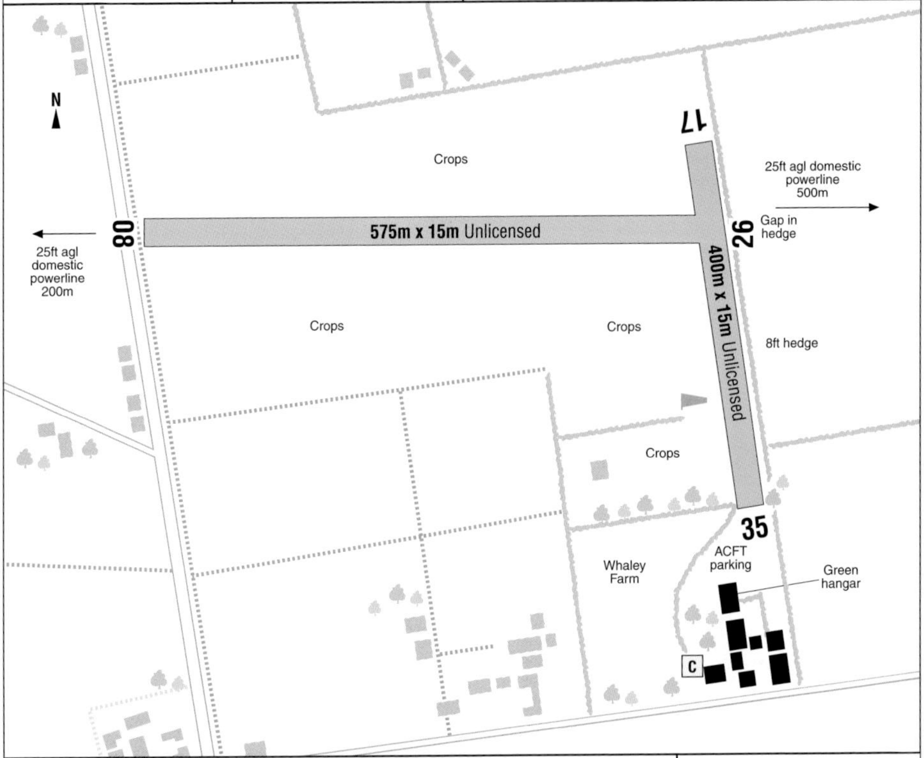

N
17
Crops
25ft agl domestic powerline 500m
08
575m x 15m Unlicensed
26
Gap in hedge
25ft agl domestic powerline 200m
400m x 15m Unlicensed
Crops
Crops
8ft hedge
Crops
35
ACFT parking
Whaley Farm
Green hangar
C

RWY	SURFACE	TORA	LDA	U/L	LIGHTING
08/26	Grass			575x15	Nil
17/35	Grass			400x15	Nil

Rwy17/35 primary used as Twy

RNAV

Remarks
PPR by telephone. Visiting ACFT welcome at pilots own risk. AD is inside Coningsby ATZ which is notified active H24. Arr/Dept ACFT MUST contact Coningsby APP if no answer try TWR. Arr ACFT, if no reply on either Coningsby freq, status can be obtained from Waddington APP. High performance military ACFT based at Coningsby. Circuit passes directly overhead AD. Before take-off contact Coningsby APP or TWR then after take-off make early turn S, leave ATZ NOT ABOVE 500ft QFE. Arr should, after contact with Coningsby position for a straight-in APP for appropriate Rwy. Local attractions including the BBMF at Coningsby, Lincolnshire Aviation Heritage Centre at East Kirkby and Tattershall Castle.

Warnings
25ft agl power lines cross Rwy09 APP 200m from Thr. Drainage dyke across Rwy09 Thr. Rwy17/35 only use as Rwy with permission from operator & in extreme wind conditions.
Noise: Avoid over flight of local habitation. Horses are kept on the Farm.

Operating Hrs SR-SS
Circuits See Remarks
Landing Fee Optional
Maintenance Nil
Hangarage Available
Fuel Nil
Disabled Facilities

Restaurants/Accommodation
Tea & Coffee available for visiting pilots

Taxi
Coningsby Taxis **Tel:** 01526 342069
Car Hire Nil
Weather Info Air S MOEx
Operator Walter Shaw
Whaley Farm
New York, Lincs
Tel: 01205 280329
Tel: 01526 347443 (Coningsby ATC)
Tel: 07860 386340
Waltershaw2@aol.com

N

NEWBURY RACECOURSE

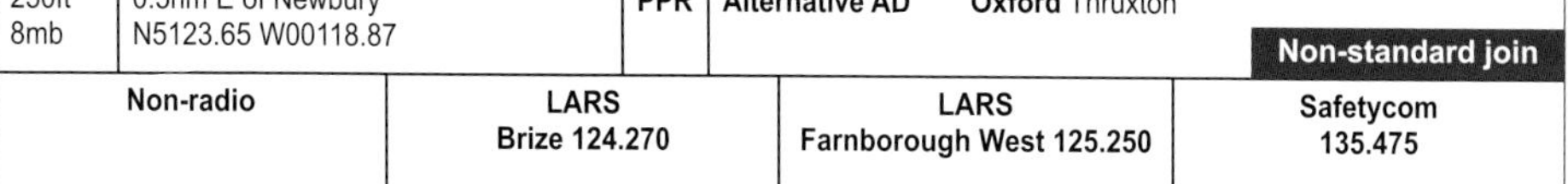

250ft 8mb	0.5nm E of Newbury N5123.65 W00118.87	PPR	Alternative AD	Oxford Thruxton

Non-standard join

Non-radio	LARS Brize 124.270	LARS Farnborough West 125.250	Safetycom 135.475

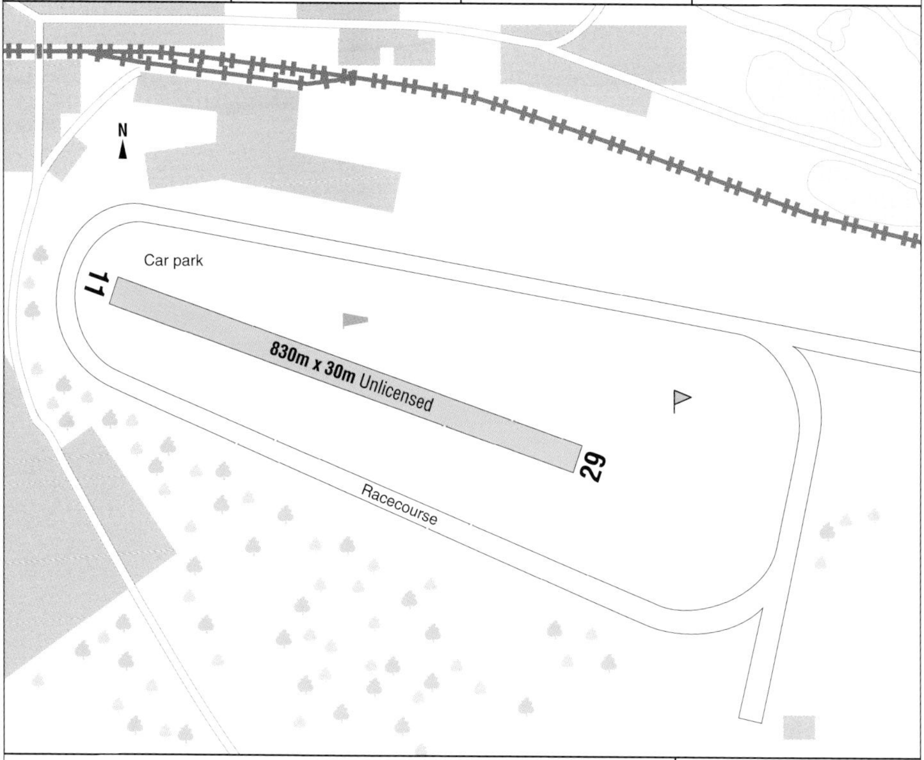

N
Car park
11
830m x 30m Unlicensed
29
Racecourse

RWY	SURFACE	TORA	LDA	U/L	LIGHTING
11/29	Grass			830x30	Nil

Rwy29 Arrivals, Rwy11 Depts
Rwy has white corner & edge markers

RNAV			
CPT	114.35	216	6.9

Remarks

PPR by telephone. Visiting ACFT and helicopters welcome at pilots own risk. AD is strictly ONLY available to those involved or attending race meetings. Open race days only. **Pilots should book in & out at the race course office**. Comprehensive briefing notes are essential before Arr and Dept. The strip may be closed from time to time, please check with PPR.

Warnings

Situated in the middle of golf course but play is suspended race days. **ACFT movements are not allowed** 30min before the first race until 30min after the final race or **when horses are on the track**. Copse of mature trees 200m W of Rwy11 Thr. When white X is in place on W end, do not land and all engines are to be shut down. This is changed to a white T when landing appropriate. **AD is periodically closed to fixed wing ACFT**. Helicopters may land when Rwy closed.
Noise: Avoid built-up areas to W, N & S.

Operating Hrs	Race days only PPR 1st race 2 Hrs until SS
Circuits	N 1000ft QFE Orbit N for best views of racecourse
Landing Fee	Nil Groundsman fund donations gratefully appreciated (box in racecourse office)
Maintenance	Nil
Fuel	Nil
Disabled Facilities	Nil
Restaurant	Extensive facilities in racecourse stands

Taxis	
Baileys of Newbury	**Tel:** 01635 40661
Car Hire	Nil
Weather Info	Air SW MOEx
Operator	Newbury Racecourse PLC Newbury, Berks, RG14 7NZ **Tel:** 01635 40015 (PPR/Racecourse Office) **Fax:** 01635 528354 info@newbury-racecourse.co.uk

Effective date:25/09/08

EGNT NEWCASTLE

266ft 9mb	5nm NW of Newcastle-upon-Tyne N5502.25 W00141.50	PPR	Alternative AD Diversion AD	Durham Tees Valley Eshott **Non-standard join**

Newcastle	ATIS	LARS	APP	RAD
	118.375	124.375	124.375	118.500

GND	TWR	FIRE	Handling
121.725	119.700	121.600	130.650

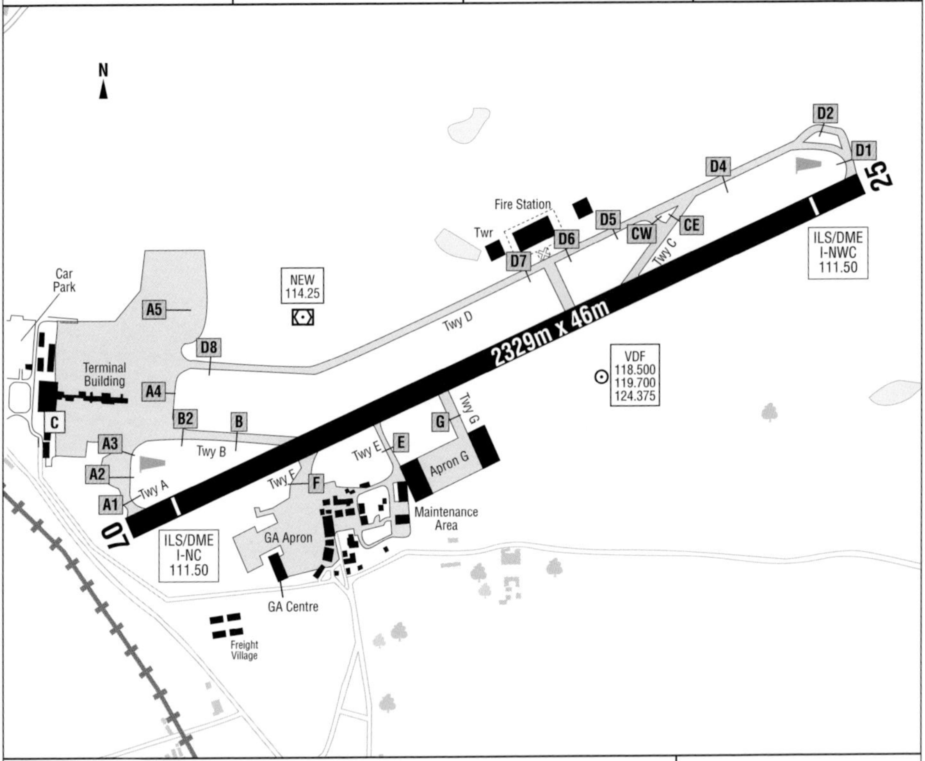

N
D2
D1
25
D4
Fire Station
D5
CE
Twr
D6
CW
D7
Twy C
ILS/DME I-NWC 111.50
Car Park
NEW 114.25
A5
Twy D
2329m x 46m
D8
VDF 118.500 119.700 124.375
Terminal Building
A4
Twy G
C
B2
B
G
A3
Twy B
Twy E
E
Apron G
A2
Twy A
Twy E
F
A1
Maintenance Area
07
GA Apron
ILS/DME I-NC 111.50
GA Centre
Freight Village

RWY	SURFACE	TORA	LDA	U/L	LIGHTING
07	Asphalt	2329	2209		Ap Thr Rwy PAPI 3° RHS
25	Asphalt	2262	2125		Ap Thr Rwy PAPI 3° LHS

RNAV
NEW 114.25 On AD

Remarks

PPR to non-radio ACFT. Hi-Vis. ACFT towing banners may not operate to or from AD. The grass verges along the sides of the Rwy and Twys are soft in many places. Hangar entrances should remain unobstructed. In association with the Fire Station and Rwy link road located mid-way along the parallel Twy, to Twy holding points D6 and D7 are introduced to hold ACFT for AFS deployment. Booking out details should be passed by telephone. (including those inbound from or returning to the EU) are required to nominate a handling agent. For GA flights Samson Aviation operates a full GA Terminal and will arrange any necessary clearances Helicopter Ops 1). As directed by ATC 2) Helicopters must use the Rwy for take-off & landing 3) Helicopters parking on the S apron at positions Papa W or Papa E are restricted to Jet Ranger size and below 4). Handling is provided by Swissport UK NE & Servisair.

Aids to Navigation: NDB NT 352.00

Warnings

Gliding may take place at Currock Hill gliding site, 8nm SW of Newcastle AD from dawn to dusk. ATC will advise when active. ACFT using the ILS in IMC or VMC shall not descend on APP to Rwy25 below 1500ft QFE and on Rwy07 below 2300ft QFE before intercepting the glide path and shall not thereafter fly below it. ACFT APP without assistance from RAD or ILS shall follow a descent path not lower than the ILS glide path. ACFT must not join the final APP track to either Rwy at a height of less than 1500ft QFE (1800ft QNH) unless they are a propeller driven ACFT whose MTWA <5700kg when the minimum height shall be 1000ft QFE (1300ft QNH). The portion of Twy E to the W of the Belman hangar has a wing span clearance <17m. When Rwy25 is in use and wind direction is from 160-190° expect turbulence and possible negative gradient. Model ACFT flying takes place at Gosforth Racecourse 2.5nm SE of AD. Bird activity from nature reserve N of NT beacon 1.2nm from Rwy25.

Operating Hrs	H24
Circuits	Variable as advised by ATC
Landing Fee	ACFT <2 tonnes £29.38
Maintenance	
M3 GA Terminal	**Tel:** 0191 286 4156
Fuel	Check availability with fuelling companies
	AVGAS 100LL
Samson Av	**Tel:** 0191 286 4156
	JET A1
Swissport Ltd	**Tel:** 0191 214 4562

Disabled Facilities

Handling	Samson Aviation **Tel:** 0191 286 4156 **Tel:** 0191 214 5916 (Out of Hrs) **Fax:** 0191 286 5347
Restaurant	Restaurant & Club facilities available at AD
Taxis	Available at Main & GA Terminals Metro link to Newcastle GA Terminal has courtesy coach
Car Hire	
Hertz	**Tel:** 0870 1221488 Ex 4281
Budget	**Tel:** 0870 1221488 Ex 4393
Europcar	**Tel:** 0870 1221488 Ex 4382
Avis	**Tel:** 0191 286 0815
Weather Info	M T9 T18 Fax 376 A VN MOEX ATIS **Tel:** 0191 214 3400/3401

Operator	Newcastle Int Airport Ltd Newcastle Airport Woolsington Newcastle upon Tyne Northumberland NE13 8BZ **Tel:** 0871 882 1121 (Switchboard) **Tel:** 0871 882 1121 Ex 3244 (ATC) **Fax:** 0191 214 3254 (ATC) www.newcastleinternational.co.uk

CTR-Class D Airspace

Normal CTA/CTR Class D Airspace rules apply

Transition Alt 6000ft

These rules do not apply by day to non-radio ACFT provided they have obtained permission and maintain 5km visibility, 1500m horizontally and1000ft vertically away from cloud, or for gliders provided they maintain 8km visibility, 1500m horizontally and 1000ft vertically away from cloud.

Visual Reference Points (VRP)

VRP	VOR/DME
Blaydon N5458.10 W00141.62	NEW 181°/4nm
Blyth Wind Farm N5507.40 W00129.62	NEW 057°/9nm
Bolam lake N5507.88 W00152.47	NEW 316°/8nm
Derwent Reservoir N5420.00 W00158.47	NEW 226°/16nm
Durham N5446.43 W00134.60	NEW 168°/16nm
Hexham N5458.25 W00206.17	NEW 257°/15nm
Morpeth Rly Station N5509.75 W00140.97	NEW 007°/7nm
Ouston (Disused AD) N5501.50 W00152.52	NEW 266°/6nm
Stagshaw Masts N5502.00 W00201.42	NEW 272°/11nm
Sunderland Harbour N5455.06 W00121.30	NEW 124°/14nm
Tyne Bridges N5458.05 W00136.42	NEW 146°/5nm

N

Effective date:25/09/08

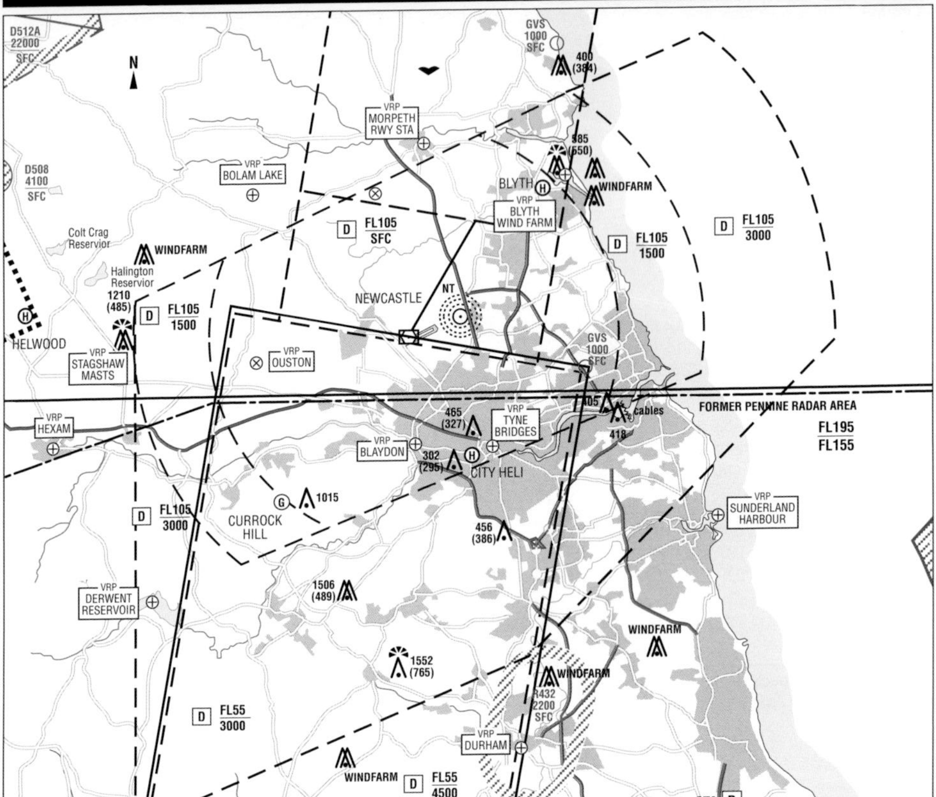

D512A
22000
SFC
N
GVS
1000
SFC
400
(384)
VRP
MORPETH
RWY STA
385
(550)
D508
4100
SFC
VRP
BOLAM LAKE
BLYTH
WINDFARM
VRP
BLYTH
WIND FARM
D FL105 SFC
D FL105 3000
D FL105 1500
Colt Crag
Reservior
WINDFARM
Halington
Reservior
1210
(485)
D FL105 1500
NEWCASTLE
NT
HELWOOD
VRP
STAGSHAW
MASTS
VRP
OUSTON
GVS
1000
SFC
VRP
HEXAM
405
cables
418
FORMER PENNINE RADAR AREA
FL195
FL155
465
(327)
VRP
TYNE
BRIDGES
VRP
BLAYDON
302
(295)
CITY HELI
1015
D FL105 3000
CURROCK
HILL
456
(386)
VRP
SUNDERLAND
HARBOUR
VRP
DERWENT
RESERVOIR
1506
(489)
WINDFARM
1552
(765)
WINDFARM
R432
2200
SFC
D FL55 3000
VRP
DURHAM
WINDFARM
D FL55 4500
CTA D
6000
1000
CTR E
1000
SFC
CTA D
6000
3000
VRP
HARTLEPOOL
730
(304)
FISHBURN
D FL75 6000
GSV
3000
SFC
VRP
S FIELD R CSE
DURHAM TEES VALLEY CTR D
6000
SFC
R446
2000
SFC
351
(325)
418
(400)
434
(385)
cables
425
(402)
421
(400)
335
(323)
TD
DURHAM TEES
VALLEY
VRP
M WAY JUNC
VRP
STOKESLEY
R408
2500
(ONCL 5600)
SFC

EGSW NEWMARKET HEATH

100ft 3mb	1.5nm W of Newmarket N5214.50 E00022.33	PPR	Alternative AD Cambridge Duxford **Non-standard join**

Non-radio	APP Cambridge 123.600	APP Lakenheath 128.900	Safetycom 135.475

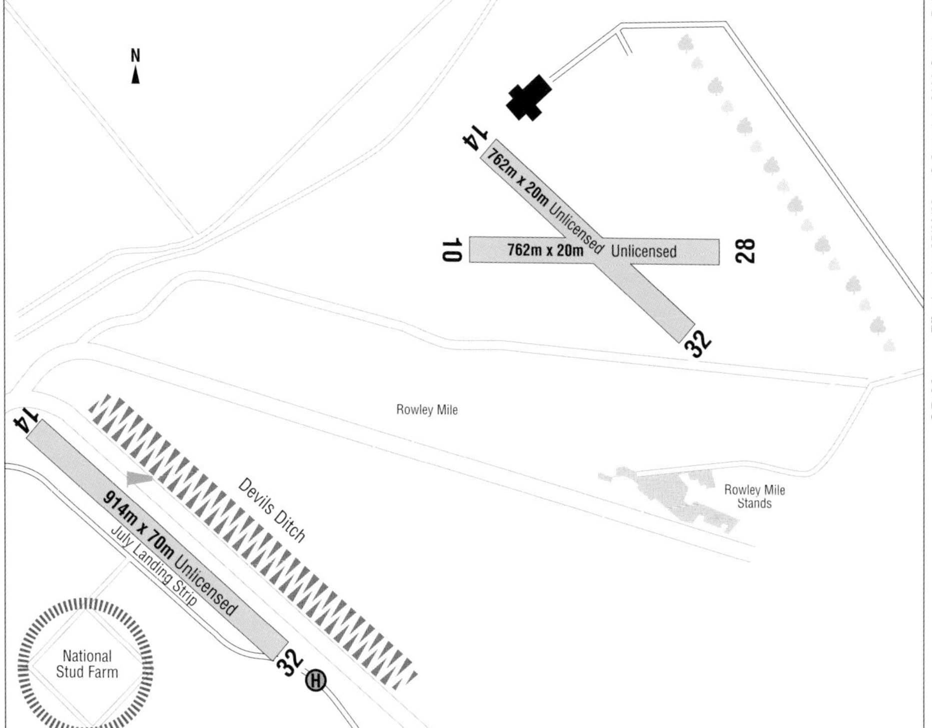

RWY	SURFACE	TORA	LDA	U/L	LIGHTING
10/28	Grass			762x20	Nil
14/32	Grass			762x20	Nil
14/32	Grass	July Strip		914x70	Nil

RNAV			
BKY	116.25	040	18.9

Remarks

PPR open race days only. Visits at pilots own risk. Two separate strips on race course. No flights 30mins before first race until 30mins after last race, unless extreme circumstances, via racecourse manager if horses are within parade ring. Non race days July strip is only available, strictly PPR through Jockey Club Estates.

Rowley mile landing area: Available when racing Rowley mile course 1200-1800 (L) PPR.

July Strip: Restricted use both race & non-race days. PPR, briefing sheet MUST be obtained prior to Arr. Rwy14 arrivals, Rwy32 depts.

All landing & take-offs banned when yellow or white cross is displayed at S end of strip.

Warnings

Noise: Stud farms & training facilities in local area. Correct adherence to local restrictions essential. ACFT are prohibited to fly over the crowd/grandstands on race days.

Operating Hrs Available on request

Circuits Nil

Landing Fee Nil Race days
£23.50 non-race days

Maintenance Nil

Fuel Nil

Disabled Facilities Nil

Restaurants Racecourse facilities

Taxis
NewTax **Tel:** 01638 561561

Car Hire
Godfrey Davis **Tel:** 01223 48198

Weather Info Air S MOEx

Operator Jockey Club Estates
Jockey Club Offices, 101 High Street
Newmarket, Suffolk, CB8 8JL
Tel: 01638 664151 (Non Race Day)
Tel: 01638 662762 (Race Day)
Tel: 01638 662758 (PPR Race Day)
Tel: 01638 663482 (Racecourse Office)
Tel: 01638 664151 (Jockey Club Office)
newmarket@rht.net
www.newmarketracecourses.co.uk

Effective date:25/09/08 OP 08

N

200ft 6mb	2.5nm N of Baldock N5201.42 W00009.45	PPR	Alternative AD	Cambridge Little Gransden

Non-Radio	APP Luton 129.550	Safetycom 135.475

RWY	SURFACE	TORA	LDA	U/L	LIGHTING
09/27	Grass			750x15	Nil

Rwy27 first 75% slight down slope

RNAV

Remarks
Strict PPR only. Visiting ACFT and Microlights welcome at pilots own risk.

Warnings
Hedge & hangars in undershoot Rwy27. Crops are grown close to strip S edge.
Caution: Farm vehicles may use tracks which run along N of AD and across Rwy09 Thr.
Noise: Avoid over flying Newnham village 1nm to WSW.

Operating Hrs SR-SS
Circuits N 800ft QFE
Landing Fee £5 without PPR
Maintenance Nil
Fuel MOGAS by prior arr
Lift can be provided to local garage
Disabled Facilities
P
Restaurants Nil
Taxis/Car Hire Nil
Weather Info Air S MOEx

Operator Kevin Woods
15 Rectory Lane
Somersham
Cambs, PE28 3EL
Tel: 01487 840539
Tel: 07941 325992
kwskr1@tiscali.co.uk

N

NEWTON PEVERIL

120ft 4mb	4nm SE of Blandford Forum N5047.38 W00206.03	PPR	Alternative AD	Bournemouth Compton Abbas

Non-Radio	ATIS Bournemouth 133.725	LARS Bournemouth 119.475	Safetycom 135.475

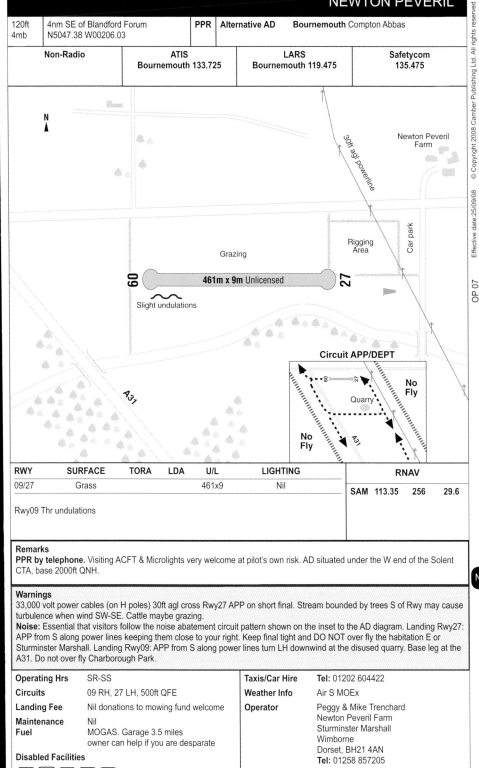

RWY	SURFACE	TORA	LDA	U/L	LIGHTING
09/27	Grass			461x9	Nil

Rwy09 Thr undulations

RNAV			
SAM	113.35	256	29.6

Remarks
PPR by telephone. Visiting ACFT & Microlights very welcome at pilot's own risk. AD situated under the W end of the Solent CTA, base 2000ft QNH.

Warnings
33,000 volt power cables (on H poles) 30ft agl cross Rwy27 APP on short final. Stream bounded by trees S of Rwy may cause turbulence when wind SW-SE. Cattle maybe grazing.
Noise: Essential that visitors follow the noise abatement circuit pattern shown on the inset to the AD diagram. Landing Rwy27: APP from S along power lines keeping them close to your right. Keep final tight and DO NOT over fly the habitation E or Sturminster Marshall. Landing Rwy09: APP from S along power lines turn LH downwind at the disused quarry. Base leg at the A31. Do not over fly Charborough Park.

Operating Hrs	SR-SS
Circuits	09 RH, 27 LH, 500ft QFE
Landing Fee	Nil donations to mowing fund welcome
Maintenance	Nil
Fuel	MOGAS. Garage 3.5 miles owner can help if you are desparate
Disabled Facilities	

Restaurants	Black Horse Pub 0.25 mile

Taxis/Car Hire	**Tel:** 01202 604422
Weather Info	Air S MOEx
Operator	Peggy & Mike Trenchard Newton Peveril Farm Sturminster Marshall Wimborne Dorset, BH21 4AN **Tel:** 01258 857205

Effective date:25/09/08 OP 07

EGAD NEWTOWNARDS

9ft 0mb	8.5nm E of Belfast N5434.87 W00541.52	PPR	Alternative AD Diversion AD	Belfast Aldergrove Belfast City Non-standard join

Newtownards	ATIS Belfast Aldergrove 128.200	ATIS Belfast City 136.625	APP Belfast City 130.850	A/G 128.300

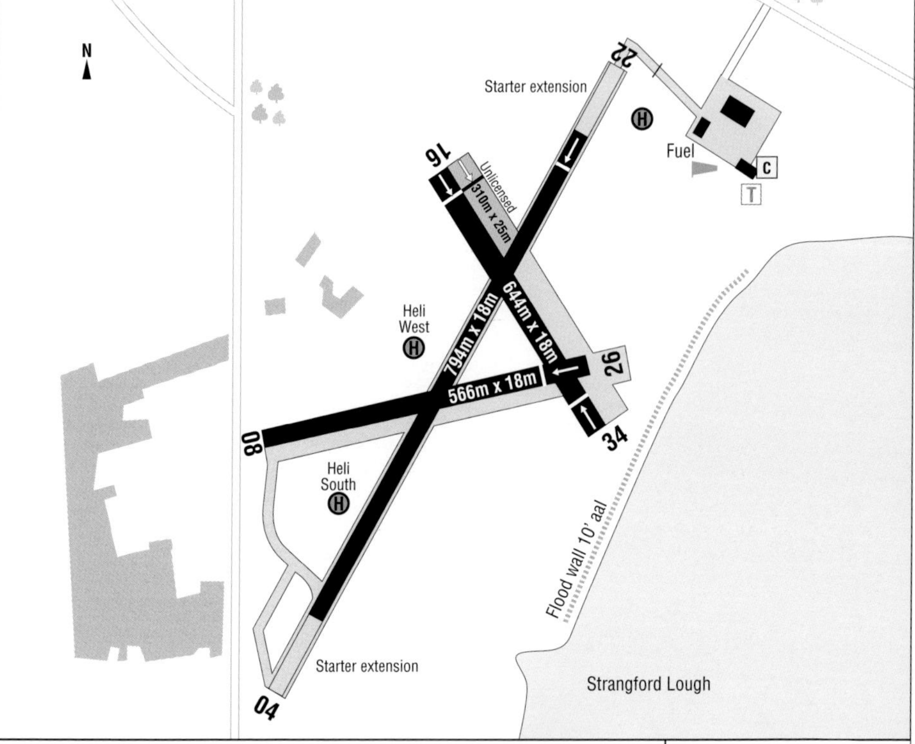

RWY	SURFACE	TORA	LDA	U/L	LIGHTING
04	Asphalt	794	794		Thr Rwy APAPI 4.5°
22	Asphalt	794	720		Thr Rwy APAPI 4.5°
16	Asphalt	566	533		Nil
34	Asphalt	559	566		Nil
08	Asphalt	566	N/A		Nil
26	Asphalt	N/A	566		Nil
16/34	Grass			310x25	Nil

Starter extension Rwy04 150x12m, Starter extension Rwy22 80x12m
Displaced Thr Rwy26 60m, Displaced Thr Rwy22 74m
Displaced Thr Rwy16 85m, Displaced Thr Rwy34 75m
Rwy08 Dept only, Rwy26 landing only
Rwy26 not available to solo students

RNAV			
BEL	117.20	111	19.3

Remarks

PPR. Visiting ACFT welcome, not a designated AD under the Prevention of Terrorism Act. ACFT operating under restrictions of the act must contact The Police Service of Northern Ireland. AD U/L for ACFT >2730kgs.

Warnings

Situated on the shore of Strangford Lough with high GND & obstructions to W & N. Belfast City CTZ boundary close to N & W. No helicopter APP to Rwy08. **Obstructions:** Monument (lit) 591ft amsl 267°/0.9nm. HT cables on high GND 232ft aal within 0.5nm Rwy22 APP. Hill 705ft amsl 314°/2.8nm. High GND infringing Rwy26 climb out. Lamp stands on road may affect ACFT making a late decision to go-around on Rwy26.Turbulence may be experienced on a missed APP Rwy26. Pilots APP Rwy26 should satisfy themselves at or above 300ft that they will be able to land and stop. If any doubt exists pilots are advised to carry out a missed APP and early left turn to avoid high GND. ACFT landing Rwy26 without wheels firmly on the GND by Rwy22 intersection are advised to carry out a missed APP. Rwy34 possible pedestrian/vehicle traffic on sea wall, carry out missed APP if necessary.
Noise: Avoid over flying bird sanctuary at Castle Espie.

N

Operating Hrs	0800-1600 (Summer) +1Hr (Winter) Late flying Tues & Thur 2000 (L) & by arr	**Operator**	Ulster Flying Club (1961) Ltd Newtownards Aerodrome Portaferry Road, Newtownards County Down Northern Ireland BT23 8SG **Tel:** 02891 813327 **Fax:** 02891 814575
Circuits	04 RH, 22, 16, 34 LH, 1000ft QFE Microlights 700ft QFE No circuits 26		
Landing Fee	<2000kg Single £12, Light Twin £25		
Maintenance	Nil		
Fuel	AVGAS 100LL JET A1		
Disabled Facilities			

Restaurants	Nil		
Taxis			
Ards Cabs	**Tel:** 02891 81111		
Car Hire	Lindsay Car Rental **Tel:** 02891 474700		
Weather Info	Air N MOEx ATIS **Tel:** 02890 734847 (Belfast City)		

N

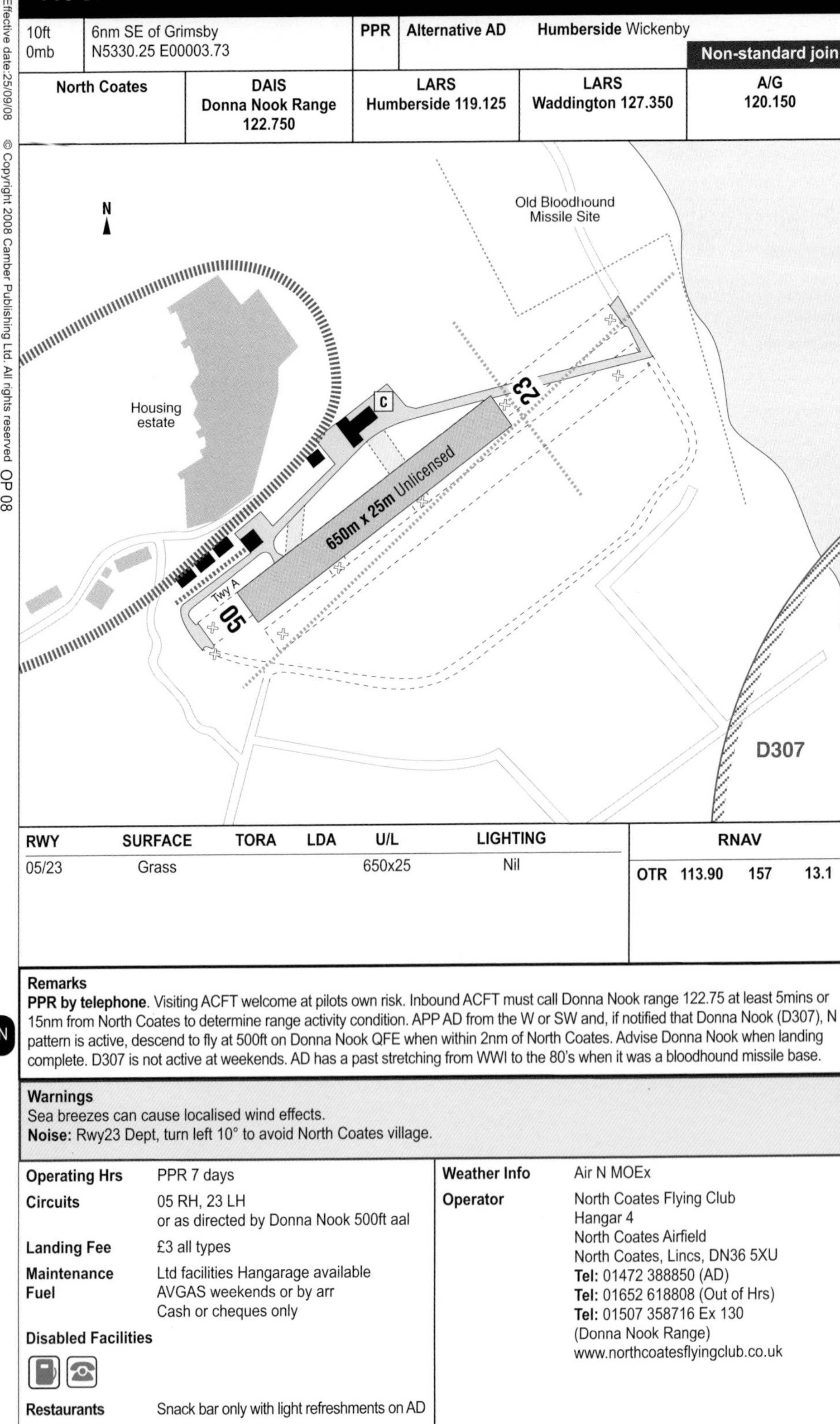

10ft 0mb	6nm SE of Grimsby N5330.25 E00003.73	PPR	Alternative AD	**Humberside** Wickenby **Non-standard join**

North Coates	DAIS Donna Nook Range 122.750	LARS Humberside 119.125	LARS Waddington 127.350	A/G 120.150

RWY	SURFACE	TORA	LDA	U/L	LIGHTING
05/23	Grass			650x25	Nil

RNAV			
OTR	113.90	157	13.1

Remarks
PPR by telephone. Visiting ACFT welcome at pilots own risk. Inbound ACFT must call Donna Nook range 122.75 at least 5mins or 15nm from North Coates to determine range activity condition. APP AD from the W or SW and, if notified that Donna Nook (D307), N pattern is active, descend to fly at 500ft on Donna Nook QFE when within 2nm of North Coates. Advise Donna Nook when landing complete. D307 is not active at weekends. AD has a past stretching from WWI to the 80's when it was a bloodhound missile base.

Warnings
Sea breezes can cause localised wind effects.
Noise: Rwy23 Dept, turn left 10° to avoid North Coates village.

Operating Hrs PPR 7 days
Circuits 05 RH, 23 LH
or as directed by Donna Nook 500ft aal
Landing Fee £3 all types
Maintenance Ltd facilities Hangarage available
Fuel AVGAS weekends or by arr
Cash or cheques only
Disabled Facilities
Restaurants Snack bar only with light refreshments on AD
Taxis/Car Hire By arrangement

Weather Info Air N MOEx
Operator North Coates Flying Club
Hangar 4
North Coates Airfield
North Coates, Lincs, DN36 5XU
Tel: 01472 388850 (AD)
Tel: 01652 618808 (Out of Hrs)
Tel: 01507 358716 Ex 130
(Donna Nook Range)
www.northcoatesflyingclub.co.uk

N

22ft 0mb	3.5nm SSW of Scunthorpe N5332.09 W00040.85	PPR	**Alternative AD** **Diversion AD**	**Humberside** Sandtoft

Non-standard join

North Moor	LARS	APP	A/G
	Humberside 119.125 Waddington 127.350	Doncaster Sheffield 126.225	119.275

N
90ft agl powerlines
ACFT parking
crops
12ft ditch
Twy
Twy 1
Twy 2
Clubhouse
5ft hedge
09
550m x 50m Unlicensed
27
25m
25m
Cables 270m from threshold
Gas venting station
500m from airfield
350m radius exclusion area

RWY	SURFACE	TORA	LDA	U/L	LIGHTING
09/27	Grass			550x20	Nil

Rwy27 25m run-off area at each end

RNAV			
GAM	112.80	036	17.9

Remarks
PPR by telephone. Visiting ACFT welcome at pilots own risk. Due to planning restrictions Helicopters and ACFT >2300kgs MAUW cannot be accepted. Distance to go markers adjacent to Rwy show 200 & 400m points. Tie downs are available for visitors.

Warnings
Located on the edge of Doncaster Sheffield CTA. 90ft agl transmission lines cross Rwy27 APP 270m from Thr. 5m deep irrigation ditch runs along S AD boundary and crosses W boundary marked by orange & white boards. Gas compressor station 500m S of AD which has an exclusion zone 350m radius up to 3100ft QNH. **THIS MUST NOT BE OVERFLOWN.**
Noise: Avoid over fly Messingham village 1nm E of AD.

Operating Hrs 0730-1930 or SS (L)
Circuits Variable 1000ft QFE
Wide circuits must be flown
Landing Fee Donations please
Maintenance Nil
Fuel Nil
Disabled Facilities

Restaurants B & B, Pub lunches & Bar meals available in Messingham 1nm E of AD
Taxis Can be arr by operator
Tel: 01724 841000

Car Hire Nil
Weather Info Air N MOEx
Operator E W & A Chapman
North Moor Aero Club Ltd
Low Hill Farm
West Common North Road
off North Moor Road
Messingham, Scunthorpe
Lincs, DN17 3PS
Tel/Fax: 01724 851244
Tel: 07724 203764
www.northmoor.flyer.co.uk

Effective date:25/09/08

40ft 1mb	28nm NE by N of Kirkwall Airport N5922.05 W00226.07	**PPR**	**Alternative AD** **Diversion AD**	**Kirkwall** Sanday

Non-Radio	APP Kirkwall 118.300	Safetycom 135.475

Apron
21
14
10
467m x 18m
28
376m x 30m
330m x 18m
03
32

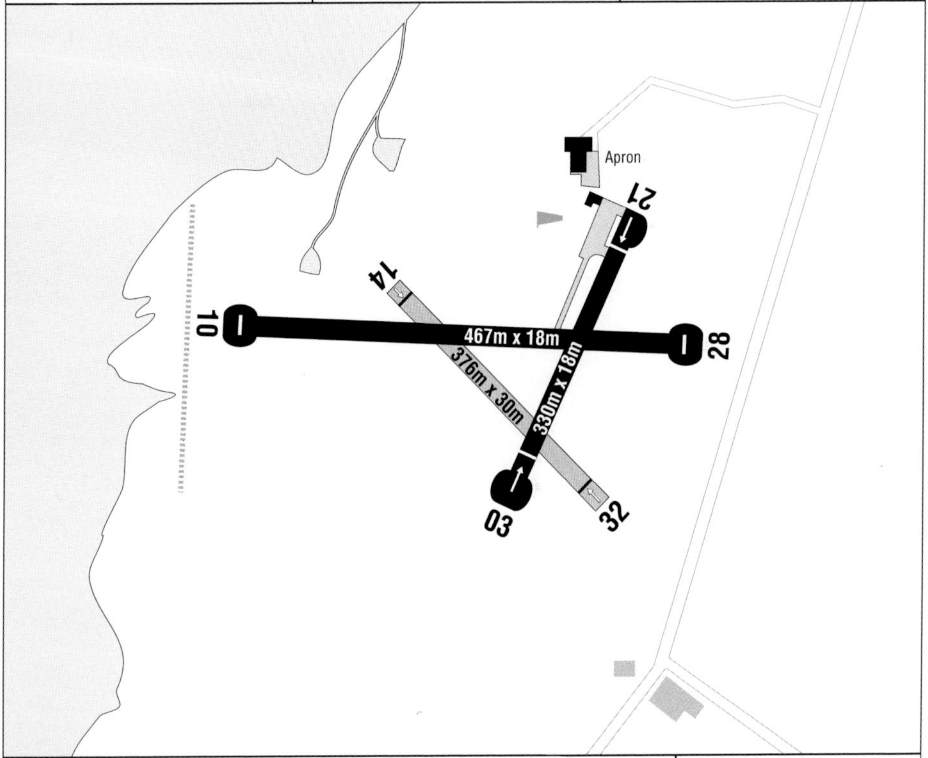

RWY	SURFACE	TORA	LDA	U/L	LIGHTING
10/28	Graded Hardcore	467	467		Rwy
14	Grass	336	356		Rwy
32	Grass	326	346		Nil
03	Graded Hardcore	310	276		Rwy
21	Graded Hardcore	314	314		Rwy

Starter extensions 15m available on all Rwys

RNAV			
KWL	108.60	036	28.2

N

Remarks
PPR for private pilots. AD is used at pilot's own risk. Licensed AD (day use only).

Warnings
Lighthouse 100ft aal/140ft amsl 2.0nm 051° from APP.

Operating Hrs SR-SS
Circuits Nil
Landing Fee Nil
Fire cover £36.95 if required
Maintenance Nil
Fuel Nil
Disabled Facilities

Restaurants Meals & accomodation at North Ronaldsay Bird Sanctuary
Tel: 01857 633200
alison@nrbo.prestel.co.uk

Taxis/Car Hire
Garso **Tel:** 01857 633244
AD Goods & Svcs **Tel:** 01857 633220
Weather Info Air Sc GWC
Operator Orkney Islands Council Offices
Kirkwall, Orkney
Tel: 01856 873535 Ex 2305
Fax: 01856 876094

EGSX NORTH WEALD

321ft 11mb	3.5nm SE of Harlow N5143.30 E00009.25	PPR	**Alternative AD** **Diversion AD**	**Cambridge** Stapleford **Non-standard join**

North Weald	APP Essex RAD 120.625	A/G 123.525

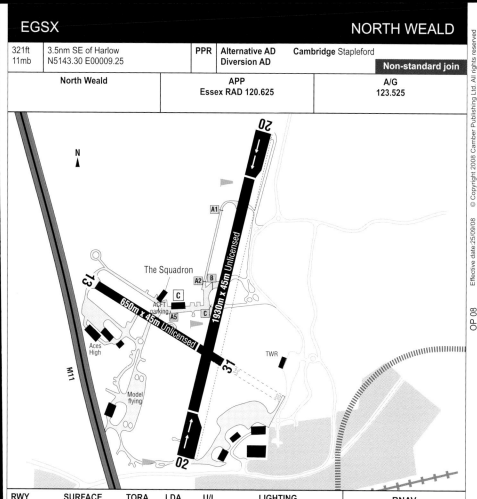

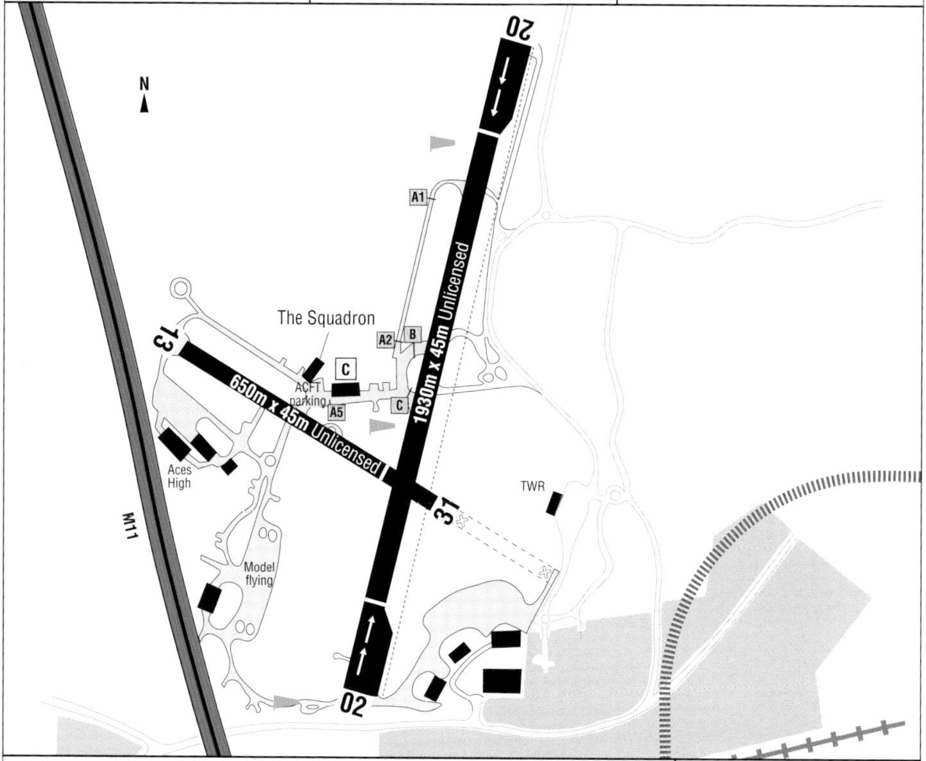

N
20
A1
The Squadron
A2
B
C
ACFT parking
A5
C
1930m x 45m Unlicensed
13
650m x 45m Unlicensed
Aces High
31
TWR
M11
Model flying
02

RWY	SURFACE	TORA	LDA	U/L	LIGHTING
02/20	Asphalt			1930x45	Nil
13/31	Asphalt			650x45	Nil

RNAV			
LAM	115.60	004	4.6

Remarks

PPR by telephone. Visitors welcome at pilots own risk. Entry to Rwy20 is via either A1 or B. Exit from Rwy20 is via C or Rwy31. AD is situated below the Stansted CTA 1500-2500ft ALT. Contact Essex RAD prior to entering Controlled Airspace at 1500ft. Flights without reference to Essex RAD may be subject to remaining VFR and/or remain below 1500ft ALT. Rwy13 is to be used only when strong winds preclude the use of Rwy02/20. During Special Event days contact with Essex RAD is not required except for permission to enter controlled airspace or in an emergency. ACFT Dept AD must continue ahead until 500ft agl, until outside AD boundary.

Warnings

Model ACFT flying take place on AD. Masts up to 304ft agl/625ft amsl 1nm E of AD. Rwy02/20 PCN varies from 5 at 02 Thr 09 at 20 Thr. High performance ACFT may be encountered in the area and circuit, pilots to keep good look out, contact A/G for info. **Noise**: Avoid over flying local villages and houses within the vicinity of AD, obtain briefing. Depts continue ahead until 500ft agl and outside AD boundary.

Operating Hrs 0900-1900 or SS if earlier than 1900 (L)

Circuits 02 LH, 20 RH 800ft aal
Jets 1000ft aal
No circuits on Rwy13/31

Landing Fee Nil

Maintenance North Weald Flying Services (M5/Part 145)
Tel: 01992 524510

Fuel AVGAS JET A1 100LL

Disabled Facilities

Restaurants The Squadron on AD bar & restaurant

Taxis Can be arranged via The Squadron or
Bassett Car Services **Tel:** 01992 524242

Car Hire Can be arranged via The Squadron or
Hertz **Tel:** 01279 433316

Weather Info Air SE MOEx

Operator Epping Forest District Council
25 Hemnall Street, Epping
Essex, CM16 4LX
Tel: 01992 524740 (ATC)
Tel: 01992 564200 (Ops)
Tel: 01992 524510 (The Squadron)
Fax: 01992 522238 (The Squadron)
Fax: 01992 524047 (ATC)

EGBK NORTHAMPTON

419ft 15mb	5nm NE of Northampton N5218.32 W00047.58	PPR	**Alternative AD** **Diversion AD**	**Cranfield** Leicester

Sywell	**AFIS** **122.700**

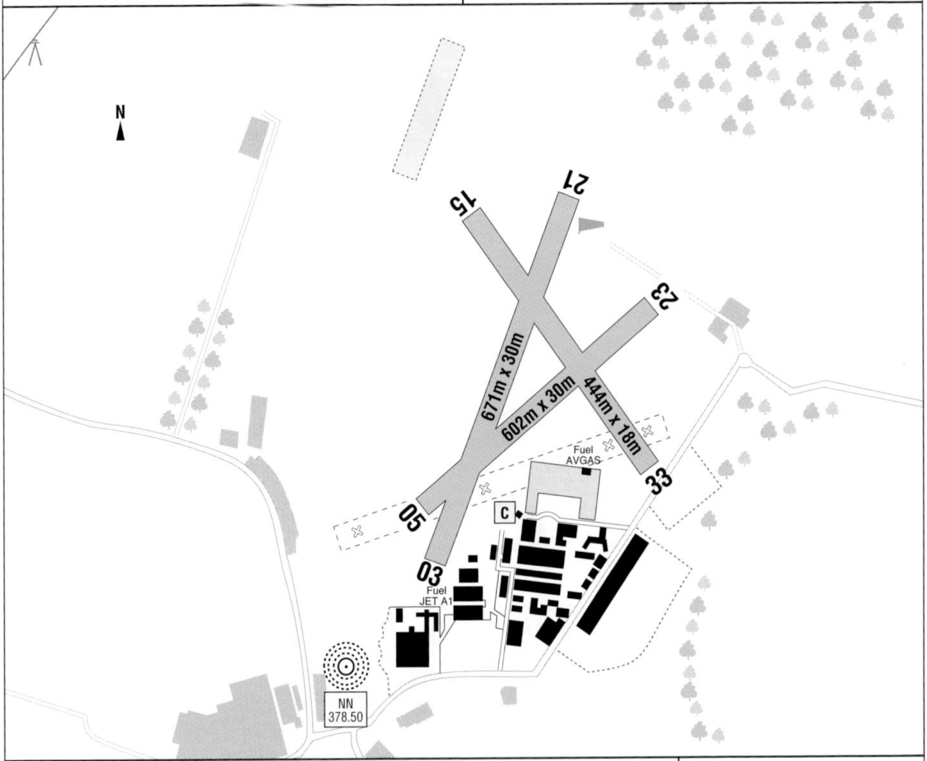

N

15
21
23
33
05
03
671m x 30m
602m x 30m
444m x 18m
Fuel AVGAS
Fuel JET A1
C
NN 378.50

RWY	SURFACE	TORA	LDA	U/L	LIGHTING
03/21	Grass	671	671		Nil
15/33	Grass	528	528		Nil
05/23	Grass	602	602		Nil

RNAV			
DTY	**116.40**	**061**	**13.9**

Remarks

PPR by telephone. Non-radio ACFT permitted after obtaining briefing. PPR can be obtained via radio. All visiting helicopters to Sloane Helicopters, Strict PPR. Helicopter training circuits are opposite to fixed wing circuits and are flown up to 700ft agl on the dead side of the active Rwy. Resident aerobatic team regular practice and corporate displays upto 5000ft 3nm radius.
Visual aid to location: Ibn NN Green.

Warnings

Public road runs along the SE, S and SW boundaries. N edge of Rwy15/33 are marked by a number of 2m square white GND markers for helicopter operations; fixed wing pilots should disregard. All Rwys have non-standard white centreline markings.

Operating Hrs	0900-1800 (Summer) 0900-1700 or SS (Winter)
Circuits	Fixed Wing 05, 21, 33 RH, 03, 15, 23 LH 1000ft Helicopters see Remarks
Landing Fee	Single/Heli £12, Twin £20, Microlight £10 Special rates at certain times
Maintenance	Brooklands Engineering
Fuel	AVGAS 100LL JET A1 MOGAS Rotors running refuel avail published Hrs from:
Sywell Aerodrome	**Tel:** 01604 644917 **Fax:** 01604 499210

Disabled Facilities

Restaurants	Restaurants & refreshments available
Aviator Hotel	**Tel:** 01604 642111
Pilots Mess	**Tel:** 01604 671131
Taxis	
Northampton	**Tel:** 01604 754444
Wellingborough	**Tel:** 01933 441666
Car Hire	
National	**Tel:** 01604 259101
Weather Info	Air Cen MOEx www.sywellaerodrome.co.uk www.skylink-pro.com/airfields/sywell/index.php
Operator	Sywell Aerodrome Ltd Sywell Aerodrome Northampton, NN6 0BT **Tel:** 01604 644917 (ATC) **Tel:** 01604 491112 (Admin) **Tel:** 01604 817146 (PPR Helicopters) **Fax:** 01604 499210 (ATC)

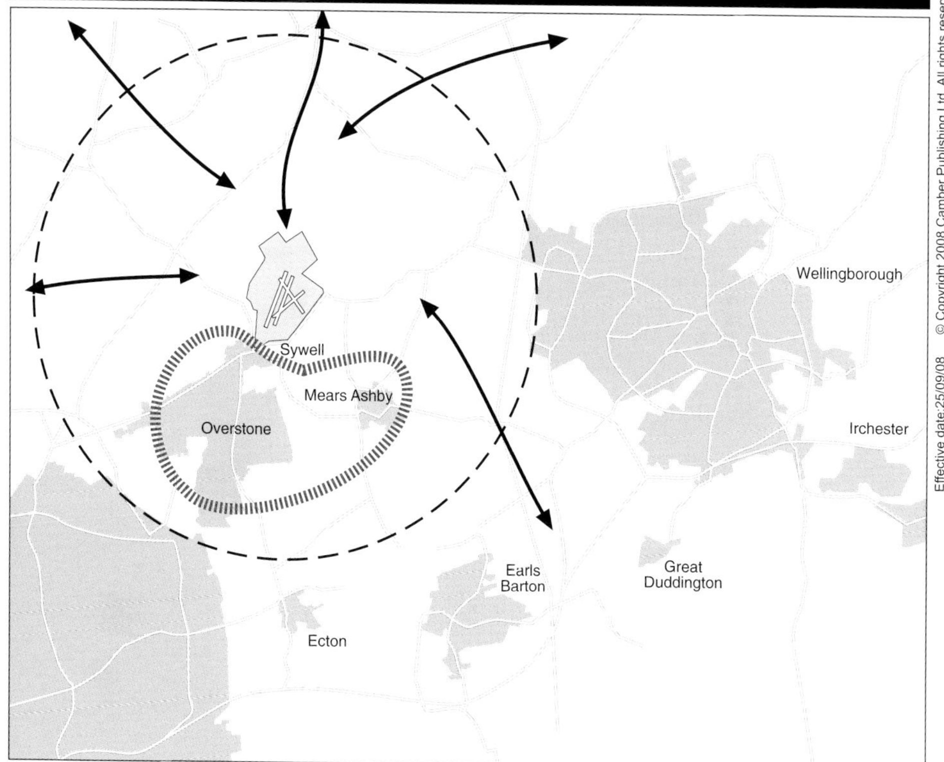

Effective date:25/09/08

All pilots and ACFT operators must comply to the following to reduce the impact of ACFT noise.
1 Avoid over flight of properties and villages close to SE, S and SW AD boundaries, and must not fly on Rwy03 & 33 APP.
2 Multi-engine helicopters arr from S sector, join via overhead at 2000ft QNH, descend dead side, before hover taxi to alight.
3 Helicopters may arr and dept in any direction other than the S.

Helicopter Routes
Helicopters dept to S must initially depart to the E or W avoiding Sywell, Overstone and Mears Ashby. Turn onto So can be made once clear of these villages.
NB: When using either Rwy21L or Rwy03R circuit, it is permissible to enter the large hatched area to use the normal circuit pattern. Do not over fly Mears Ashby village. A109 & B206 ACFT are asked to Arr & Dept via the overhead whenever possible. Dept to W, NW, N, NE & E remain unaffected. Avoid over flying villages

124ft 4mb	2nm E by N of Uxbridge N5133.18.W00025.10	PPR MIL	Alternative AD Diversion AD	London Luton Denham Non-standard join

Northolt	ATIS	LARS	APP	DIR	TWR	OPS
	125.125	Farnborough East 123.225	126.450	130.350	120.675	132.650

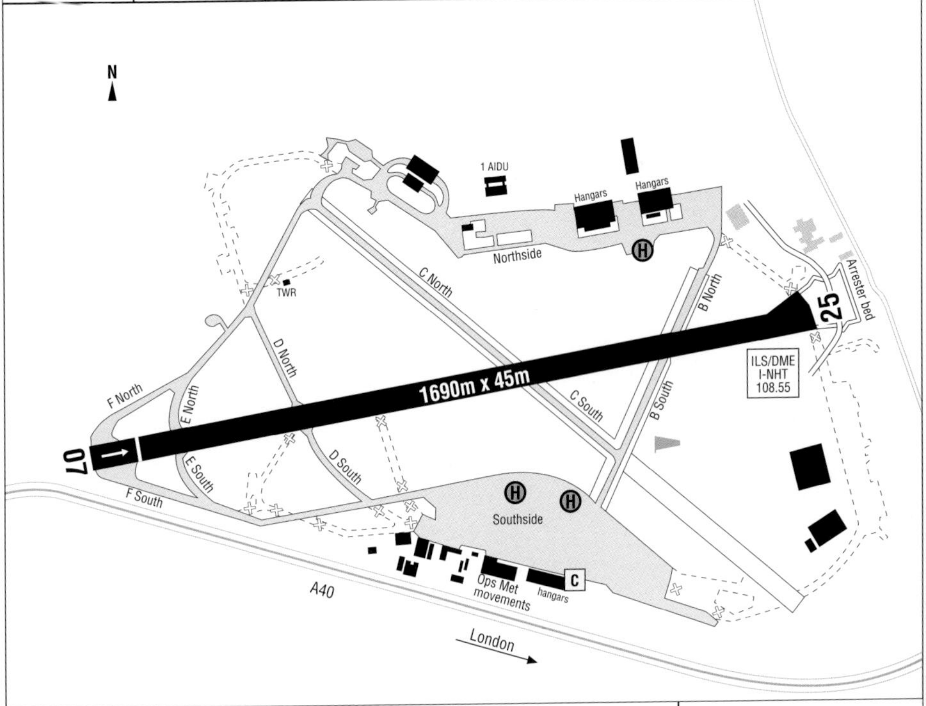

RWY	SURFACE	TORA	LDA	U/L	LIGHTING
07	Asphalt	1684	1592		Ap Thr Rwy PAPI 3°
25	Asphalt	1687	1684		Ap Thr Rwy PAPI 3.5°

RNAV			
LON	113.60	027	4.3

Remarks
PPR (before 1300 (Summer) +1 Hr (Winter) for all private, executive and charter flights 24Hrs notice required for all flights. Hi-vis. Animals are not permitted to transit through RAF Northolt at any time. Between 0800-2000 Sat Sun civil ACFT will only be accepted when AD is planned to be open for military movements. Flight plans showing previously arranged alternatives are to be filed for each flight. Civilian movements at Northolt are limited to 28 per day. Single-engined ACFT are not permitted to land at Northolt. Located within the London CTR. Non Awy inbound to Northolt should work from NW: London RAD from NE: Essex RAD. Pilots are to exercise caution on Echo S at night or during low visability as the Twy is unlit. Exercise caution on the parking areas as wing tip clearance is not assured. Pilots are to make initial call on TWR for start and ATC clearance. No tight turns on Rwy07/25 friction course. Visiting Helicopters to use intersection of disused Rwy for land and takeoff. A Northolt marshaller must be in attendance before any engine start will be approved. Crews are not to remove their own chocks. Chocks must only be removed by a Northolt marshaller. The full crew of civil flights arr at AD must report to Ramp Control with photo ID. Passports required for flights from outside UK.
Visual aid to location: Ibn NO Red.

Warnings
Rwy usage dictated by Heathrow. In certain circumstances pilots may have to accept a tailwind. Moderate wind turbulence/wind shear on APP Rwy25 in strong NW wind. Heavy bird activity Oct-Mar adjacent to Rwy25 Thr.
Noise: Pilots must be familiar with the Northolt procedures.

Operating Hrs 0800-2000 (L)
PPR by 1400 previous day

Circuits 25 RH, 07 LH, 1000ft QNH

Landing Fee Charges in accordance with MOD policy
Contact Station Ops for details

Maintenance Nil

Fuel JET A1 Air BP via:
Foster Aviation **Tel/Fax:** 0208 842 1611
Tel: 07850 118359 (H24)
gary.forster@bp.com

Disabled Facilities

Handling **Tel:** 0208 845 2797
Fax: 0208 845 6803

Restaurants Light refreshments at cafeteria in terminal

Taxis/Car Hire Nil

Weather Info Air SE MOEx
Tel: 0208 845 2300 Ex 8937

Operator RAF Northolt
West End Road
Ruislip
Middx, HA4 6NG
Tel: 0208 833 8930 (OPS)
Fax: 0208 833 8923 (OPS)

EGSH NORWICH

117ft 4mb	2.8nm N of Norwich N5240.55 E00116.97	PPR	**Alternative AD** **Cambridge** Seething

Non-standard join

Norwich	ATIS	LARS	RAD	TWR	FIRE
	128.625	119.350	119.350 128.325	124.250	121.600

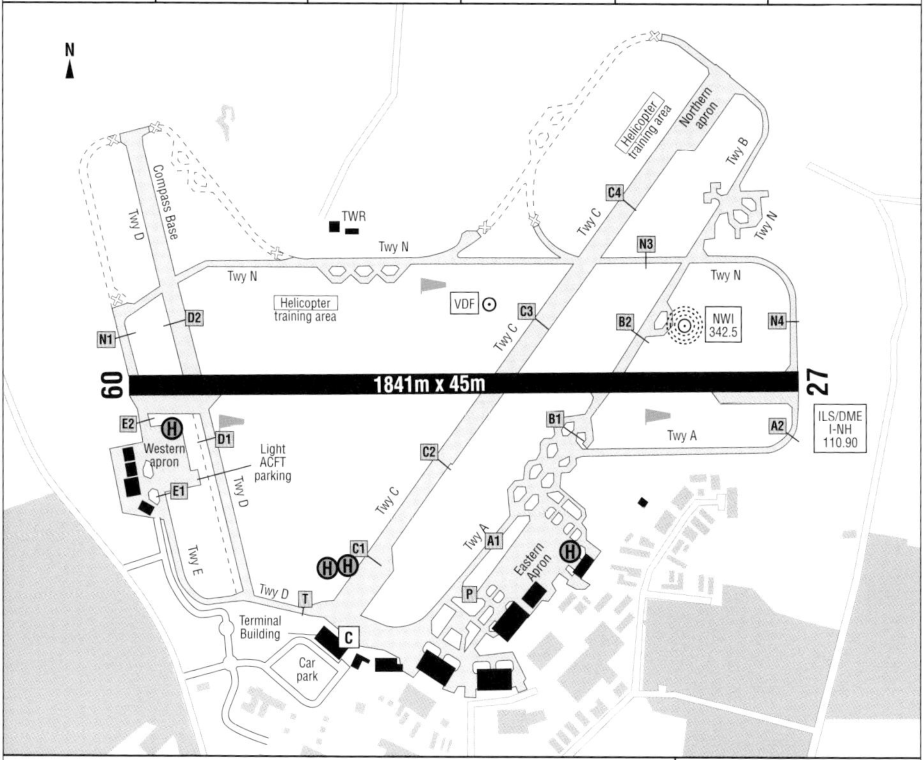

N
Compass Base
Twy D
TWR
Twy N
Helicopter training area
Northern apron
Twy B
Twy C
C4
N3
C3
VDF
B2
NWI 342.5
N4
N1
D2
09
1841m x 45m
27
E2
B1
Twy A
A2
ILS/DME I-NH 110.90
Western apron
D1
Light ACFT parking
C2
E1
Twy E
C1
A1
Eastern Apron
Twy D
T
P
Terminal Building
C
Car park

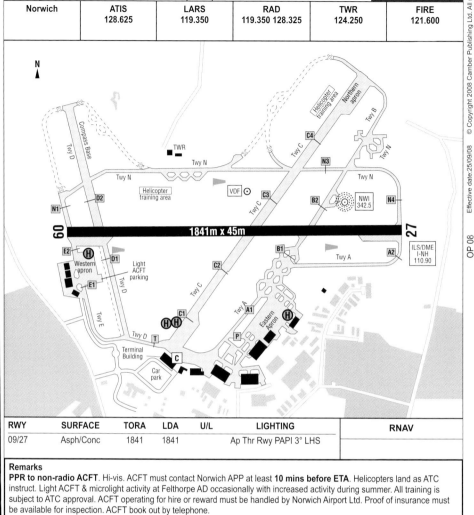

RWY	SURFACE	TORA	LDA	U/L	LIGHTING	RNAV
09/27	Asph/Conc	1841	1841		Ap Thr Rwy PAPI 3° LHS	

Remarks

PPR to non-radio ACFT. Hi-vis. ACFT must contact Norwich APP at least **10 mins before ETA**. Helicopters land as ATC instruct. Light ACFT & microlight activity at Felthorpe AD occasionally with increased activity during summer. All training is subject to ATC approval. ACFT operating for hire or reward must be handled by Norwich Airport Ltd. Proof of insurance must be available for inspection. ACFT book out by telephone.

Visual aids to location: Ibn NH Green

Warnings

Both ends Rwy09/27 width is twice that of associated edge lights due to extra pavement on one side. Rwy centre line lighting is installed, pilots should ensure they are correctly lined up, especially at night.

Operating Hrs Sun-Fri 0530-2115 Sat 0530-2100 (Summer) +1Hr (Winter) & by arr

Circuits As instructed by ATC Rwy27/09 only

Landing Fee On application

Maintenance Available

Fuel AVGAS JET A1 100LL

Disabled Facilities

Restaurants Restaurant/bar & cafeteria services available in terminal

Taxis Available during AD opening Hrs

Car Hire

Avis **Tel:** 01603 416719

Europcar **Tel:** 01603 400280

Hertz **Tel:** 01603 404010

Weather Info M T9 Fax 378 VS MOEx
ATIS **Tel:** 01603 420640

Operator Norwich Airport Ltd
Amsterdam Way
Norwich, NR6 6JA
Tel: 01603 411923 (Admin)
Tel: 01603 420641 (ATC)
Tel: 01603 420642 (Ops)
Tel: 01603 420645 (Duty Manager)
Fax: 01603 487523 (Admin)
dam@norwichinternational.com
www.norwichinternational.com

Effective date:25/09/08 OP 08

Norwich Noise Abatement Procedures

Departures: Avoid turning from extended Rwy centre line until at or passing 1000ft. Avoid over flying built up areas.
Arrivals: Arrange flight to avoid over flying built up areas, hold descent from circuit height until within Rwy APP funnel.
Helicopter: Route around built up areas. Avoid low flying, use Rwy APP funnels to move into/out of AD as per fixed wing. If practical and subject to ATC climb to planned cruise alt within AD boundaries.
Circuit: Circuits only Rwy27/09. Circuits will be to N when Coltishall closed/inactive. Otherwise to S.

138ft 5mb	3nm SE of Nottingham N5255.20 W00104.75	**PPR**	**Alternative AD** **Diversion AD**	**East Midlands** Leicester

Nottingham	**APP** **East Mids 134.175**	**A/G** **134.875**

RWY	SURFACE	TORA	LDA	U/L	LIGHTING
03/21	Asphalt	821	821		Nil
09	Asph/Conc	989 (Day)	837 (Day)		Nil
09	Asph/Conc	837 (Night)	837 (Night)		Thr Rwy LITAS 3.5°
27	Asph/Conc	970 (Day)	929 (Day)		Nil
27	Asph/Conc	837 (Night)	837 (Night)		Thr Rwy LITAS 3.75°

RNAV			
GAM	**112.80**	**197**	**22.2**

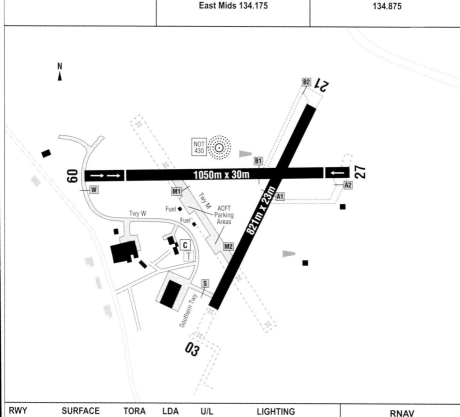

Remarks
PPR to non-radio ACFT. Hi-viz. AD is situated close to the East Midlands CTR and under the East Midlands CTA (base 2500ft AMSL). Contact East Midlands APP for transit. Public transport or instructional flights exceeding 2730kgs not accepted.
Visual aids to location: Ibn NT Green.

Warnings
Chimney 205ft aal/343 ft amsl 1.4nm 285° from the APP. Rwy end lights for Rwy27 are located at the end of the declared TORA. In an emergency pilots should be aware that there is a further 150m of usable Rwy beyond the lighting.

Operating Hrs	Mon-Fri 0800-1700 Sat 0800-1800 Sun 0900-1800 (Summer) Mon-Sat 0900-1700 Sun 1000-1700 Wed 1700-2000 (Winter) & by arr with 24Hrs notice
Circuits	800ft QFE
Landing Fee	Single £10 Twin £14
Maintenance Truman	**Tel:** 0115 982 6090
Fuel	AVGAS JET A1 100LL

Disabled Facilities

Restaurant	Club facilities at AD
Taxis	Arranged locally
Car Hire National	**Tel:** 0115 9503385
Weather Info	Air Cen MOEx
Operator	Truman Aviation Ltd Nottingham City Airport Tollerton, Nottingham NG12 4GA **Tel:** 0115 9811327 (ATC) **Tel:** 0115 9815050 (AD) **Fax:** 0115 9811444

Effective date:25/09/08 OP 08

460ft 15mb	4nm SE of Royston N5159.40 E00004.07	PPR	**Alternative AD** **Cambridge** Duxford

Non-Radio	**APP** **Essex RAD 120.625**	**APP** **Luton 129.550**	**Safetycom** **135.475**

Old go-kart track
N
Clay Pigeon Range
Crops
Upslope
23
Low hedge
5ft hedge
Hangar & ACFT parking
700m x 35m Unlicensed
Crops
Pond
50ft agl
Farm track
05
Crops
WW2 Rwy witness marks
BKY 115.80

RWY	SURFACE	TORA	LDA	U/L	LIGHTING
05/23	Grass			700x35	Nil

Rwy23 upslope first 100m

RNAV		
BKY	**116.25**	**On AD**

Remarks
PPR by telephone. Visiting ACFT welcome with PPR & at pilot's own risk. Situated on WW2 AD, Rwy established on site of wartime hard Rwy with BKY VOR/DME on extended centre line.

Warnings
AD situated beneath the Stansted CTA, base 2500ftQNH. ATZ's of Fowlmere & Duxford are close to N. Vehicles & Pedestrians may use the 6m wide concrete tracks that parallel the Rwy and actually cross it at the mid point. ACFT must operate within the strip markers, as the rest of AD is not consolidated for aviation use. There is a low mast 50ft agl 150m N Rwy05 Thr and a 120ft agl mast approx 1000m 270° from the Rwy05 Thr.

Operating Hrs	SR-SS
Circuits	05 RH, 23 LH 800ft QFE
Landing Fee	Nil
Maintenance	Nil
Fuel	Nil
Disabled Facilities	Nil
Restaurants	Woodman Pub in Northampstead village
Taxis	
Drayton's	**Tel:** 01763 848233
Car Hire	Nil
Weather Info	Air S MOEx

Operator
Nuthampstead Airfield Associates Ltd
Keffords Barley
Royston
Herts, SG8 8LB
Tel: 01763 848287
Fax: 01763 849616

N

OAKLANDS

370ft 12mb	3nm WNW of Kidlington N5150.51 W00126.44	PPR	Alternative AD	**Oxford** Enstone

Non Radio	ATIS Oxford 136.225	LARS Brize 124.275	Safetycom 135.475

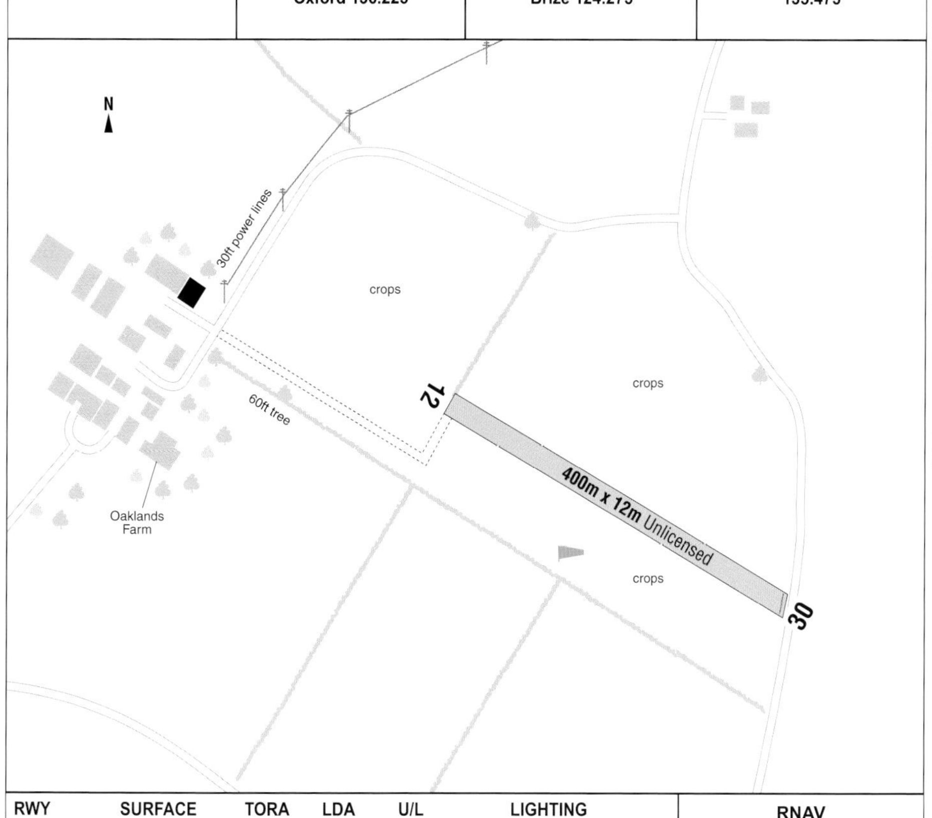

RWY	SURFACE	TORA	LDA	U/L	LIGHTING
12/30	Grass			400x12	Nil

RNAV			
CPT	114.35	342	23.0

Remarks
PPR by telephone. Visiting ACFT welcome at own risk. Level but narrow strip. Twy to hangar is very restricted in width.

Warnings
Tall crop growth may make the strip unusable for low wing ACFT during certain periods of the farming year. Pole laid across Rwy30 Thr stop vehicle access to strip from the public road which crosses end of Rwy.
Noise: Avoid over flying of local villages and farms.

Operating Hrs	SR-SS
Circuits	S 600ft QFE
Landing Fee	Nil
Maintenance	Nil
Fuel	Nil
Disabled Facilities	Nil
Restaurant	Nil
Taxi/Car Hire	Nil
Weather Info	Air Cen MOEx

Operator
Robert J Stobo
Oaklands Farm
Stonesfield
Oxford
OX29 8DW
Tel: 01993 891226
robstobo@stonesfield.f9.co.uk

INTENTIONALLY LEFT BLANK

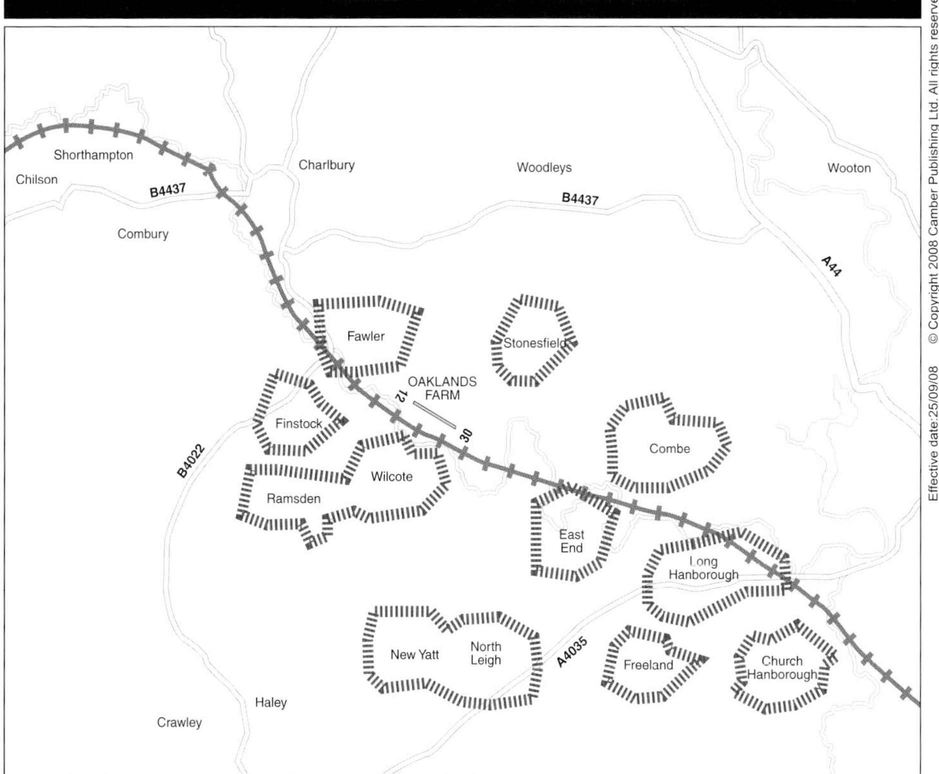
Shorthampton
Chilson
B4437
Charlbury
Woodleys
B4437
Wooton
Combury
A44
Fawler
Stonesfield
OAKLANDS
FARM
12
30
Finstock
Combe
B4022
Wilcote
Ramsden
East
End
Long
Hanborough
New Yatt
North
Leigh
A4035
Freeland
Church
Hanborough
Haley
Crawley

O

250ft 8mb	5nm SSE Cirencester N5137.95 W00200.92	**PPR**	**Alternative AD** **Diversion AD**	**Bristol Filton** Kemble

Oaksey Park	**Zone** **Lyneham 123.400**	**A/G** **132.225**

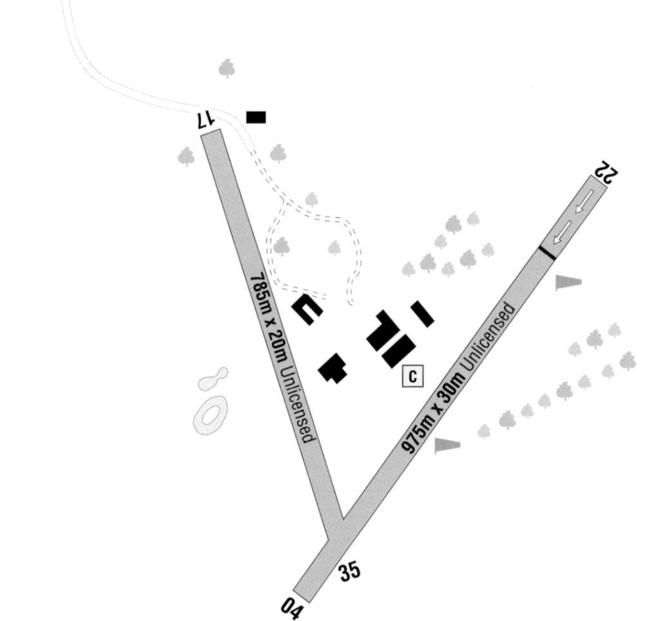

RWY	SURFACE	TORA	LDA	U/L	LIGHTING
17/35	Grass			785x20	Nil
22/04	Grass			975x30	Nil

Rwy17/35 emergency use only

RNAV

Remarks
Visitors welcome at own risk. ACFT must be kept to the mown strips and manoeuvring areas. Heavy wet land may prevail during some winter months making AD unusable. No low flying or beat-ups.

Warnings
200Kv national grid power line 1.75km E of AD on Rwy22 APP. White markers barrels on Rwy22. Land between to avoid bump. **Noise:** Visiting pilots must avoid noise sensitive areas of local villages and avoid over flying local farms and houses. Standard circuit joining and Dept must be obeyed at all times.

Operating Hrs 0700-2100 or SR-SS
Circuits 04 RH, 22 LH, 1000ft QNH
Landing Fee Single £12 Twin/Heli £23
Maintenance **Tel:** 01666 575111
Fuel AVGAS JET A1 100LL
Disabled Facilities

Restaurants Good pubs in Oaksey village
Taxis **Tel:** 01285 650850
Car Hire Nil
Weather Info Air SW MOEx

Operator Mr B & Mrs E Austen
Oaksey Park Airfield
The Green
Oaksey
Wiltshire
SN16 9SD
Tel: 01666 577130 (Manager)
Tel: 01666 577152 (Clubhouse)

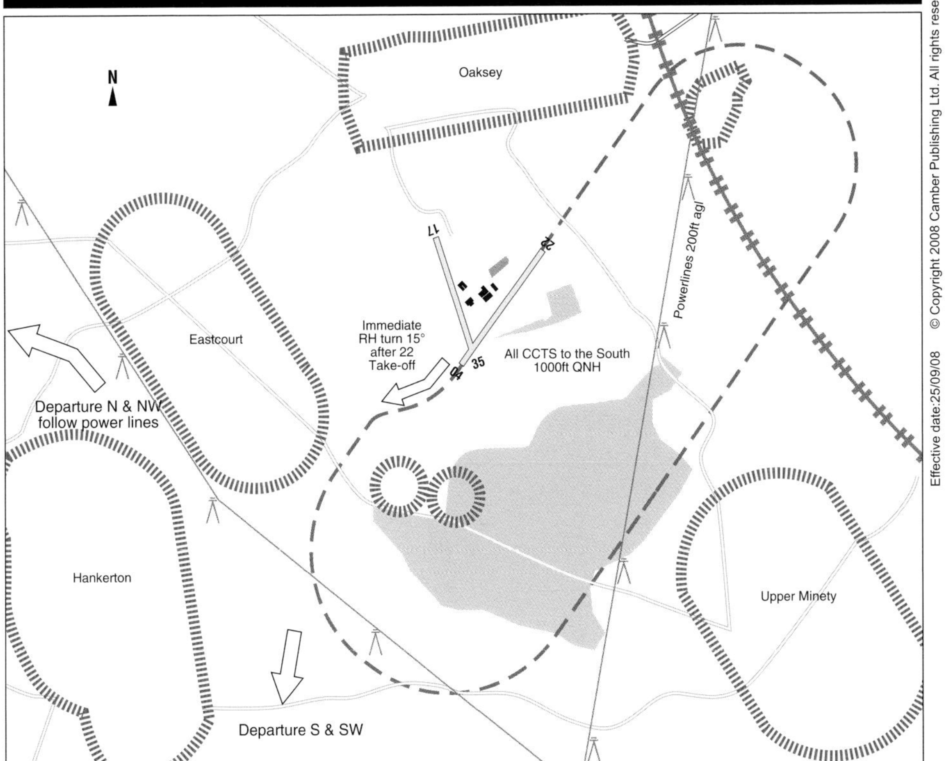
N
Oaksey
Eastcourt
Immediate
RH turn 15°
after 22
Take-off
17
22
04
35
All CCTS to the South
1000ft QNH
Powerlines 200ft agl
Departure N & NW
follow power lines
Hankerton
Upper Minety
Departure S & SW

22ft 1mb	5nm NE of Oban N5627.82 W00524.00	PPR	Alternative AD Diversion AD	Glasgow Glenforsa

Oban Radio	FIS Scottish 127.275	A/G 118.050

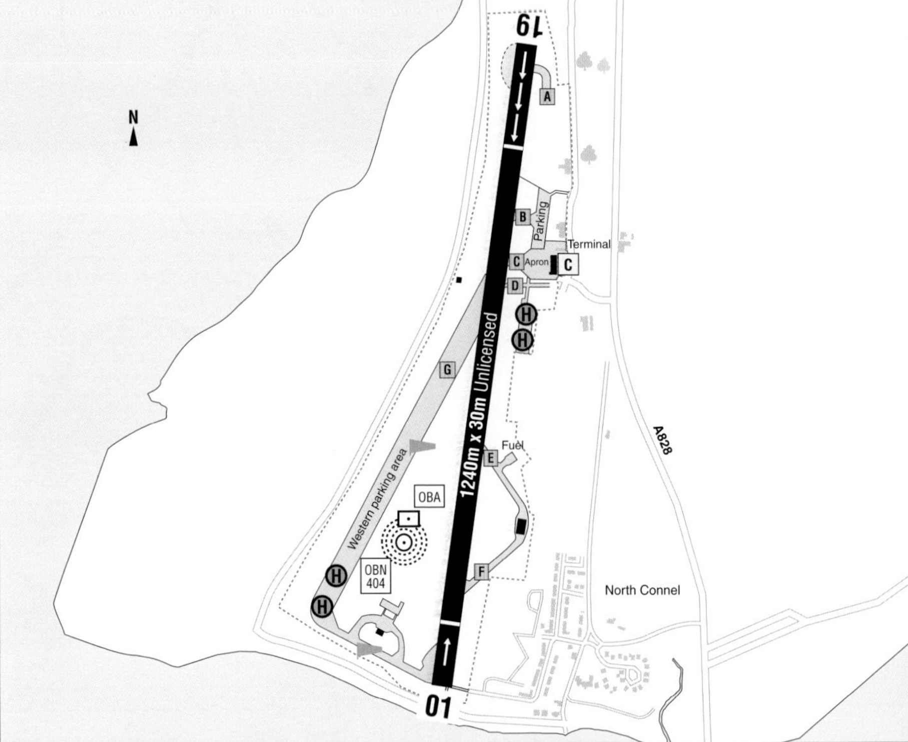

RWY	SURFACE	TORA	LDA	U/L	LIGHTING
01	Asphalt	1064	1110		Thr Rwy PAPI 4.25° LHS
19	Asphalt	1141	993		Thr Rwy PAPI 4.25° LHS

RNAV

Remarks
PPR. Hi-vis. AD is increasingly active with light ACFT & light/heavy helicopters.

Warnings
Glider launching and microlight flying takes place at AD. High GND 990ft aal/1010ft amsl 1nm to N and NNE of AD respectively. Gliders are operating on AD.

Operating Hrs 0730-1730 (Summer) + 1Hr (Winter)

Circuits 01 LH, 19 RH

Landing Fee Single £10 Twin £15
Public transport £5.75 per 500kgs AUW

Maintenance Nil

Fuel AVGAS 100LL JET A1 H24 7 days
Tel: 01631 710384 (AD)
Tel: 01631 710888
Tel: 07770 620988
Tel: 07796 473670

Disabled Facilities Nil

Restaurants Light refreshments at AD
Lochnell Arms **Tel:** 01631 710408
Falls of Lora **Tel:** 01631 710483
The Ferryman **Tel:** 01631 710666

Taxis **Tel:** 01631 710100
Tel: 01631 562834
Tel: 01631 563784

Car Hire **Tel:** 01631 566553
Tel: 01631 566476

Weather Info Air Sc GWC
Also observed actuals from AD
Tel: 01631 710384/710888

Operator Oban Airport
Oban, Argyll
Scotland, PA37 1SX
Tel: 01631 710910 (Admin)
Tel: 01631 710830 (ATC)
Fax: 01631 710916 (Admin)
Fax: 01631 710716 (ATC)
Fax: 01631 710888 (Fuel)

EGVO ODIHAM

405ft 14mb	6nm ESE of Basingstoke N5114.05 W00056.57	PPR MIL	Alternative AD Diversion AD	Farnborough Blackbushe **Non-standard join**

Odiham	LARS	APP	TWR
	Farnborough West 125.250	131.300	122.100

N
North Dispersal LIMA
Eastern 1
Eastern Dispersal
23
497m x 46m Helicopters Unlicenced
North Dispersal CHARLIE
Heliland
Eastern 2
ILS/DME I-ODH 109.55
05
905m x 46m Helicopters Unlicenced
27
09
1838m x 45m
27
Tactical heli circuits aligned when heliland in use
ODH 109.60
Compass Base
Southern Dispersal
Southern Specs
TWR

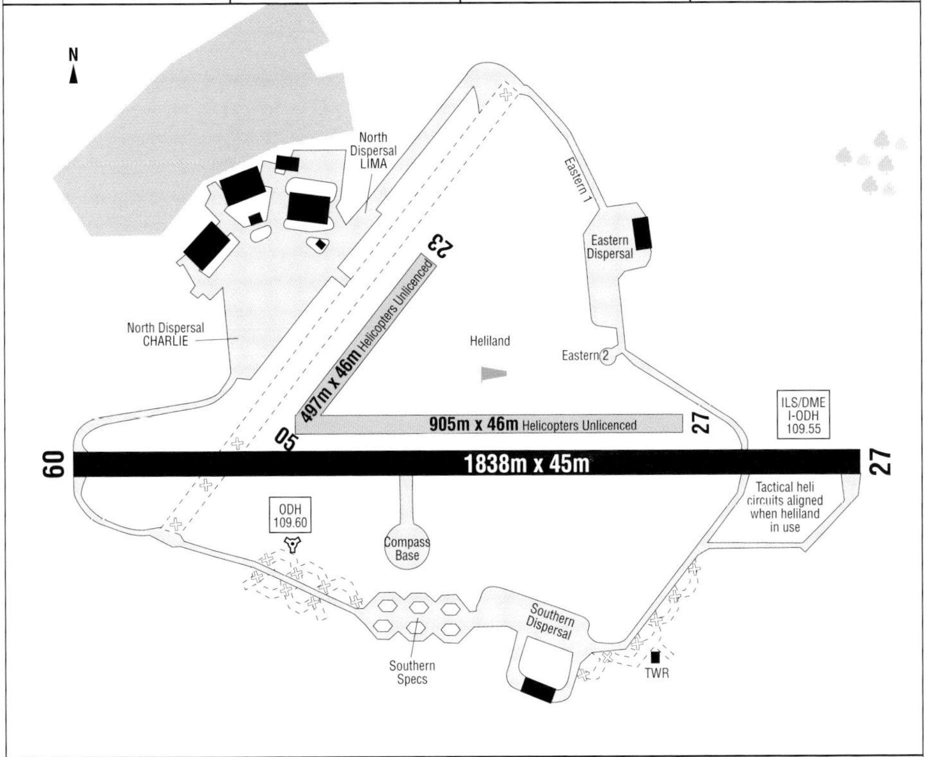

RWY	SURFACE	TORA	LDA	U/L	LIGHTING
09	Asphalt	1838	1836		Ap Thr Rwy PAPI 3°
27	Asphalt	1838	1838		Ap Thr Rwy PAPI 3°
05/23	Grass			497x46	Nil
09/27	Grass			905x46	Nil

Rwy 05/23 & Rwy 09/27 Helicopter use only

RNAV			
MID	114.00	315	16.1

Remarks

PPR 24Hrs notice required. Intensive helicopter activity, special procedures apply. Inbound helicopters if flying below 2000ft VFR London/Farnborough QNH, call Odiham APP when inbound before 10nm with details of which cardinal sector they wish to recover from. Variable helicopter circuits, no dead side. All fixed wing visual circuits to S of Rwy. ATZ active H24.

Visual aid to location: IBn Ol Red.

Warnings

Glider flying weekends, PH & summer 1700 till dusk. Full bird control measures at not implemented on AD. ACFT to remain outside the MATZ boundary until given clearance and height to fly to join the visual circuit.

Operating Hrs HO PPR
ATZ H24

Circuits Variable for heli 500ft QFE
Fixed wing to S

Landing Fee Charges in accordance with MOD policy
Contact ATC for details

Maintenance Nil

Fuel AVTUR Jet A1 by arr

Disabled Facilities Nil

Restaurants Nil

Taxis/Car Hire Nil

Weather Info M T 382 MOEx

Operator RAF Odiham
Hampshire
Tel: 01256 367276 (ATC)
Tel: 01256 367254 (OPS)

194ft 6mb	12nm SW of Norwich N5229.85 E00103.12	PPR	Alternative AD	Norwich Seething

Non-standard join

Old Buckenham	Civil Transit Lakenheath 128.900 (Mon-Fri)	A/G 124.400

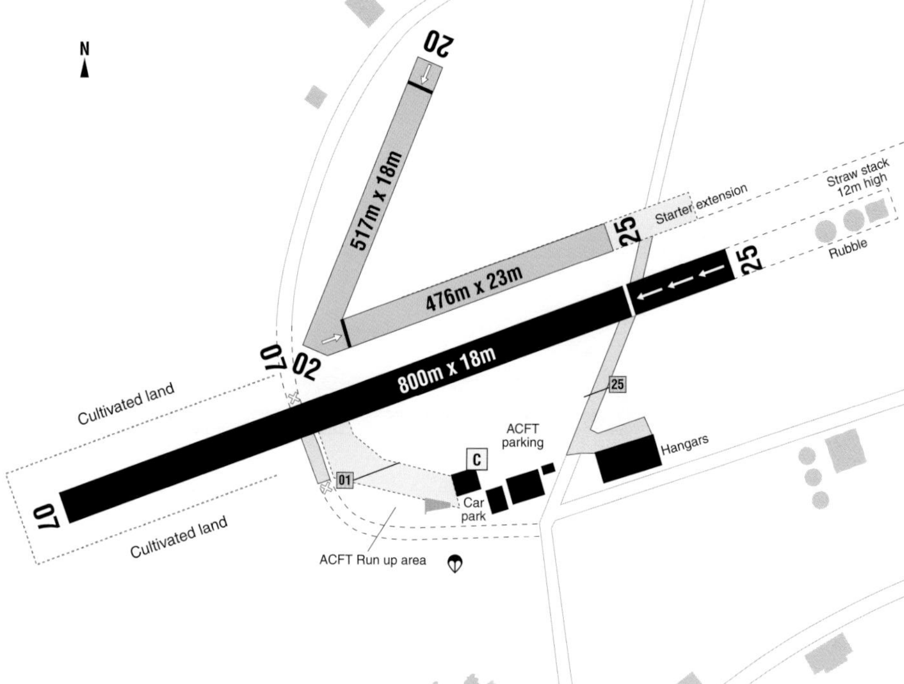

RWY	SURFACE	TORA	LDA	U/L	LIGHTING
07	Tarmac	640	640		Thr Rwy
25	Tarmac	799	640		Thr Rwy
07	Grass	442	442		Nil
25	Grass	472	409		Nil
02	Grass	361	451		Nil
20	Grass	451	361		Nil

Starter extension Rwy25 (Tarmac) 160m Concrete

RNAV

Remarks

PPR by telephone. Helicopters and Microlights not accepted. AD U/L Mon-Thur 0900-SS. Tarmac Rwy constructed on WWII Rwy & partly beyond old perimeter track. Flying training, ACFT hire & sales avail. No mobile phones air side. Passengers are the pilots responsibility airside.

Warnings

No ACFT movements 2000-0700 (L) on any day. Tacolneston TV mast (735ft amsl) 3nm ENE. Considerable gliding activity at Tibenham 4nm SE & Watton 5nm NNW. Disused section short of Rwy25 starter extension, rubble piles & up to 12m high straw stacks. Free-fall parachuting SR-SS Sun-Mon & PH up to FL150. Strictly no ACFT movements within ATZ or running engines on AD when parachuting in progress. All Dept pilots must contact Buckenham Radio for start clearance during para operations. **Noise:** Rwy07 LH Arr – Either via downwind N Attleborough or straight in from Snetterton Race track. Dept – Climb straight ahead 1500ft or Tacolneston Mast. Rwy25 RH Arr – Either via downwind N Attleborough or straight in from Tacolneston Mast. Dept – After take-off track 270 to the railway line. In any event avoid over flying Old Buckenham & Attleborough. No ATZ entry without positive RT contact (non-radio ACFT PPR required). Permission must be obtained from Buckenham A/G to enter the ATZ. If not possible, ACFT must remain clear of ATZ and wait permission to enter zone. During dark all ACFT to access Rwy via Rwy25 Thr hold. Twy centre line delineated by green reflective studs.

Operating Hrs	Fri-Sun 0800-1900 (Summer) Fri-Sun 0900-SS (Winter) & by arr AD licensed Fri-Sun	Circuits	07 LH, 25 RH, 1000ft QFE No overhead joins No deadside

Landing Fee Single £10 Twins £15.00
Members Free

Maintenance Scanrho Aviation **Tel:** 01953 861351
Fuel AVGAS JET A1 100LL

Disabled Facilities

Restaurants Restaurant & bar in clubhouse
Hot meals, snacks & Sunday lunches available.
Open Fri-Sun & PH

Taxis
A+G **Tel:** 01953 453134
Car Hire
Dingles **Tel:** 01953 452274 (AD pick-up)

Weather Info Air S MOEx

Operator Touchdown Aero Centre ltd
Old Buckenham Airfield
Abbey Road
Old Buckenham
Norfolk, NR171PU
Tel: 01953 860806
Fax: 01953 860606
flying@oldbuck.com
www.oldbuck.com

Effective date:25/09/08

Old Buckenham Circuit Procedures

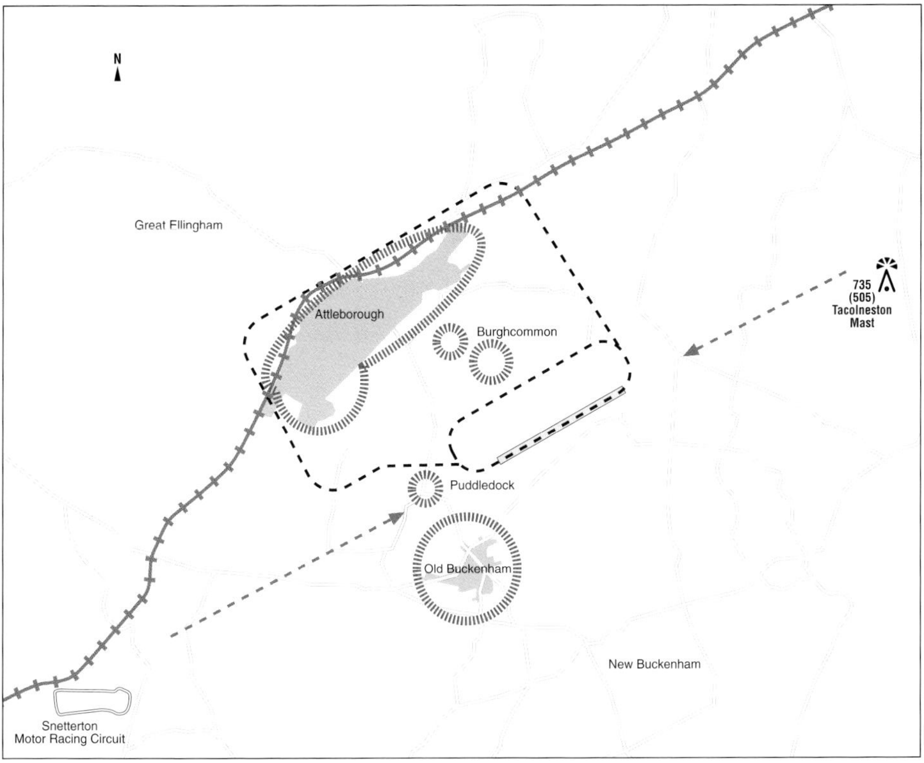

N
Great Ellingham
Attleborough
Burghcommon
735
(505)
Tacolneston
Mast
Puddledock
Old Buckenham
New Buckenham
Snetterton
Motor Racing Circuit

O

55ft 1mb	2nm W of Paddock Wood N5110.00 E00026.30	PPR	Alternative AD	Biggin Hill Lashenden

Old Hay	A/G 119.500 Not always manned

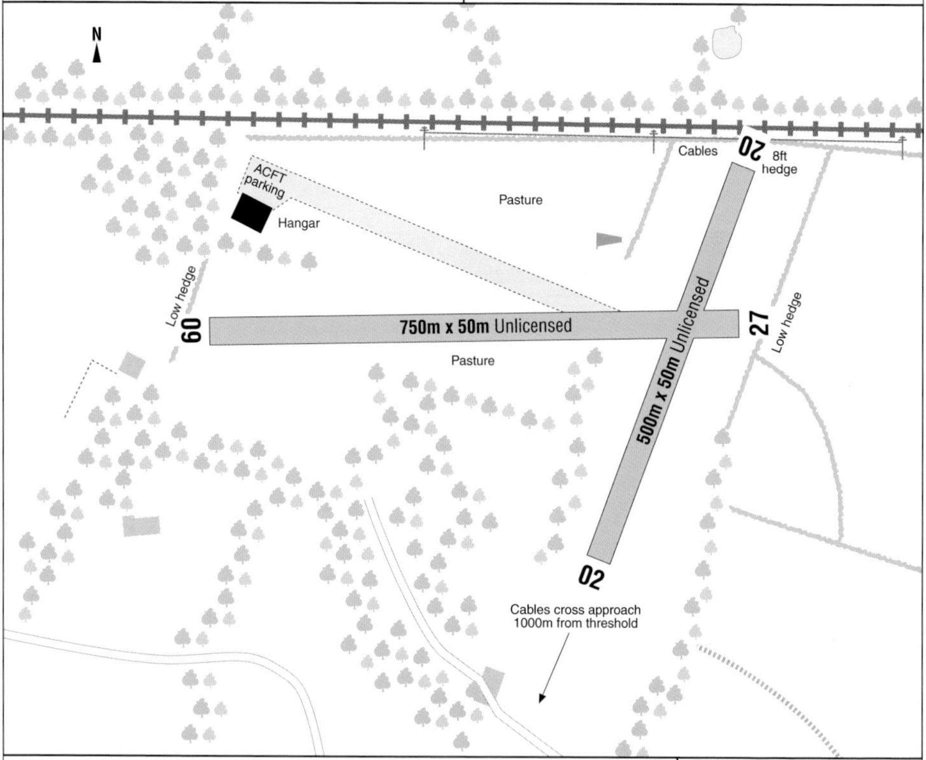

N
ACFT parking
Hangar
Pasture
Cables
20
8ft hedge
Low hedge
09
750m x 50m Unlicensed
27
Low hedge
500m x 50m Unlicensed
Pasture
02
Cables cross approach 1000m from threshold

RWY	SURFACE	TORA	LDA	U/L	LIGHTING
09/27	Grass			750x50	Nil
02/20	Grass			500x50	Nil

Rwy20 emergency use only

RNAV			
MAY	117.9	054	15

Remarks
Strictly PPR by telephone. AD is not normally manned. Rwys in very good condition with clear APP to Rwy09/27. Do not confuse with Laddingford AD, close to NW with a similar layout. No road access as locked gate is maintained unless owner is on site.

Warnings
HT wires on Rwy02 APP. Cables on Rwy20 Thr parallel to railway. Rwy20 only to be used in emergencies.
Noise: Avoid over flying Paddock Wood village.

Operating Hrs	SR-SS
Circuits	To S 1000ft QFE.
Landing Fee	Donations welcome
Maintenance	Nil
Fuel	Nil
Disabled Facilities	Nil
Restaurant	Nil
Taxi/Car Hire	Nil
Weather Info	Air SE MOEx

Operator Old Hay Farms Ltd
PO Box 39
Rye
East Sussex TN31 6ZT
Tel: 01892 832216

285ft 9mb	2nm NNE of Salisbury N5105.93 W00147.05	PPR	**Alternative AD** **Diversion AD**	**Southampton** Thruxton

Old Sarum	LARS Boscombe 126.700	A/G 123.200

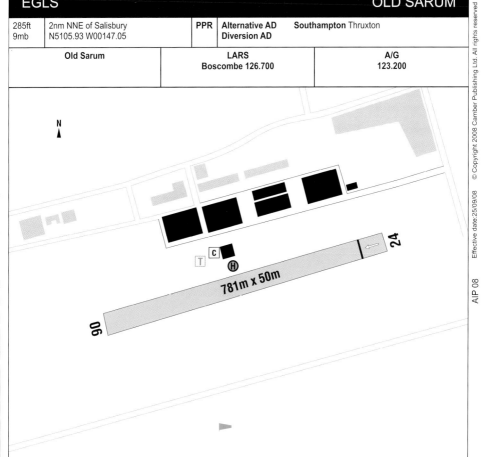

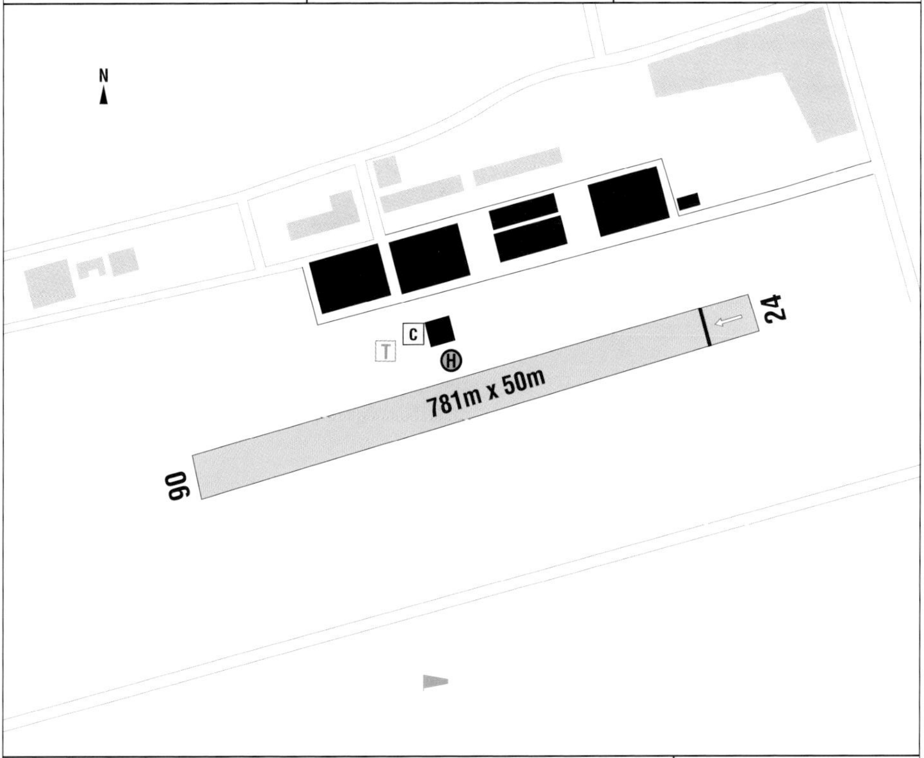

N

24

781m x 50m

06

RWY	SURFACE	TORA	LDA	U/L	LIGHTING
06	Grass	781	781		Nil
24	Grass	781	731		Nil

Displaced Thr Rwy24 50m

RNAV			
SAM	113.35	302	18.3

Remarks
PPR to non-radio ACFT. AD is not available at night or by ACFT required to use a licensed AD or for public transport passenger flights.

Warnings
AD is located within the Boscombe Down MATZ, ATZ H24. Danger Area D127 is located 2nm to the E of the AD. Due to a hump on the Rwy, pilots of ACFT with low eye level should exercise caution. Helicopters may operate to the S of the Rwy.

Operating Hrs Mon-Sun 0830-1830 or SS (L)
AD U/L after 2000 Tue-Sun

Circuits Variable dependent on Boscombe Zone
800ft QFE

Landing Fee Single £11.75 Twin £18.80 Microlights £7.05

Maintenance Nil

Fuel AVGAS JET A1 100LL

Disabled Facilities

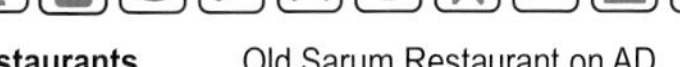

Restaurants Old Sarum Restaurant on AD
Various others in Salisbury within 2 miles

Taxis/Car Hire On request

Weather Info Air SE MOEx

Operator Blanefield Airfield Operations Ltd
The Control Tower
Old Sarum Airfield
Old Sarum, Salisbury
Wilts, SP4 6DZ
Tel: 01722 322525
Fax: 01722 323702
ops@aoldsarumairfield.co.uk
www.oldsarumairfield.co.uk

Effective date:25/09/08 AIP 08

O

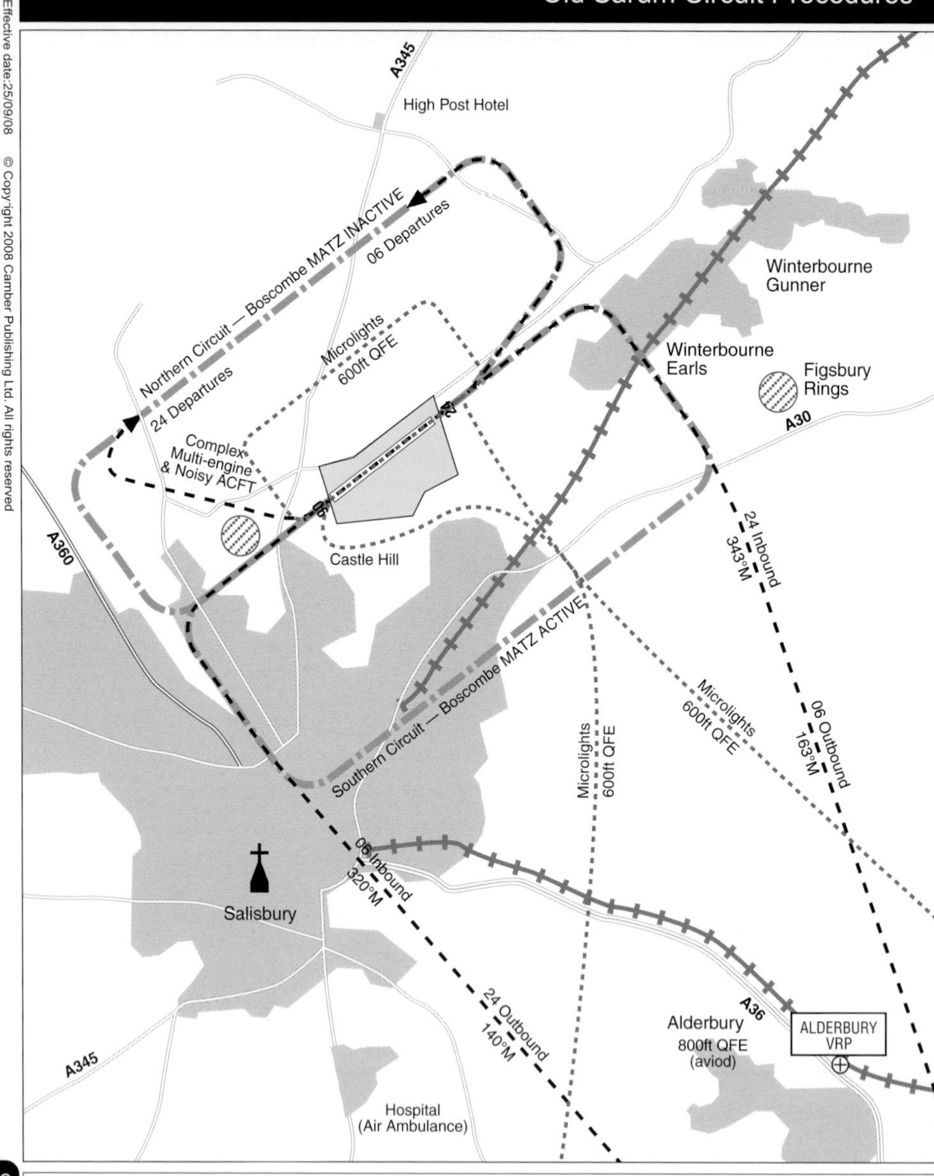

O

Visual Reference Points (VRP)

Alderbury	N5102.90 W00143.90

Arr pilots must establish contact with Boscombe Down before entering the MATZ at VRP Alderbury 155° 4nm from AD.
When Boscombe Zone is closed standard overhead join at Old Sarum.
Circuit direction when Boscombe Zone is open Rwy06 RH, Rwy24 LH.
Circuit direction when Boscombe Zone is closed Rwy06 LH, Rwy24 RH.

Noise: Avoid flying low level over Salisbury & local villages. Please avoid over flying local habitation
Microlight ACFT operate at 600ft, avoiding all built up areas.

OTHERTON

340ft 11mb	1.5nm SE of Penkridge N5242.49 W00205.56	PPR	Alternative AD	**Birmingham** Wolverhampton

Otherton	A/G 129.825 (Microlight freq)

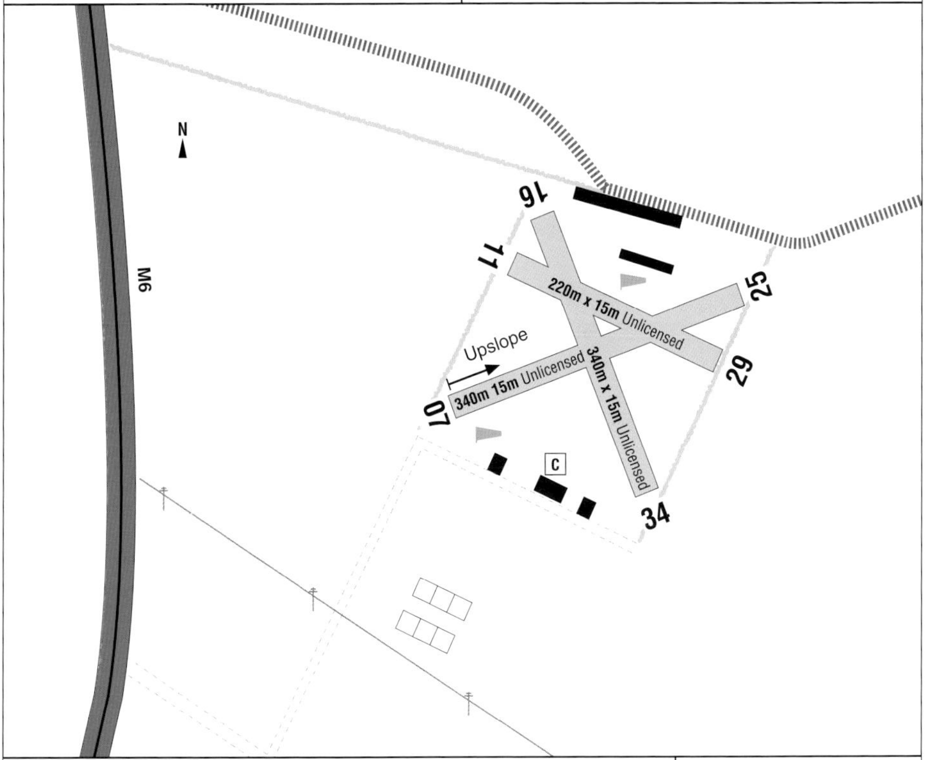

N
M6
16
34
07
25
11
29
220m x 15m Unlicensed
340m 15m Unlicensed
340m x 15m Unlicensed
Upslope
C

RWY	SURFACE	TORA	LDA	U/L	LIGHTING
07/25	Grass			340x15	Nil
11/29	Grass			220x15	Nil
16/34	Grass			340x15	Nil

RNAV			
SWB	116.80	109	21.3

Remarks
PPR by telephone small light ACFT ONLY. Microlight training school on AD. A/G only occasionally manned mainly W/E. Visitors should keep a good look out for non-radio ACFT in circuit.

Warnings
Noise: All Arr into overhead at 1000ft QFE from at least 2nm out from E or W. All circuits S only at 500ft QFE. Direction; Rwy07/11 16 RH Rwy25/29/34 LH. Keep circuits tight. Dept: Climb in overhead to min 1200ft QFE then Dept to E or W maintaining heading until at least 2nm from AD before turning on course. Do not over fly Penkridge town, the village, farm buildings to N of AD, or Gailey lake wildlife reserve and farm to S. Rwy25 2% down slope over final 80m.

Operating Hrs Mon-Sat 0800-2000 Sun 0900-1700 (L)
Circuits See Warnings
Landing Fee Nil donations appreciated
Maintenance Available on AD
Fuel MOGAS by arr with the operator (Not Mondays)

Disabled Facilities

Restaurant Self-service hot drinks available in the clubhouse most days

Taxi
Penkridge Cabs **Tel:** 01785 712589
Car Hire Nil
Weather Info Air Cen MOEx
Operator Staffordshire Microlight Centre
Otherton Airfield
Micklewood Lane
Penkridge
Staffs, ST19 5NX
Tel: 07973 339108
rob@staffordshiremicrolights.co.uk
www.staffordshiremicrolights.co.uk

20ft 0mb	Bruary, Out Skerries, Shetland N6025.54 W00044.80	PPR	Alternative AD	Sumburgh Scatsta

Skerries	APP Sumburgh 131.300	A/G 130.650

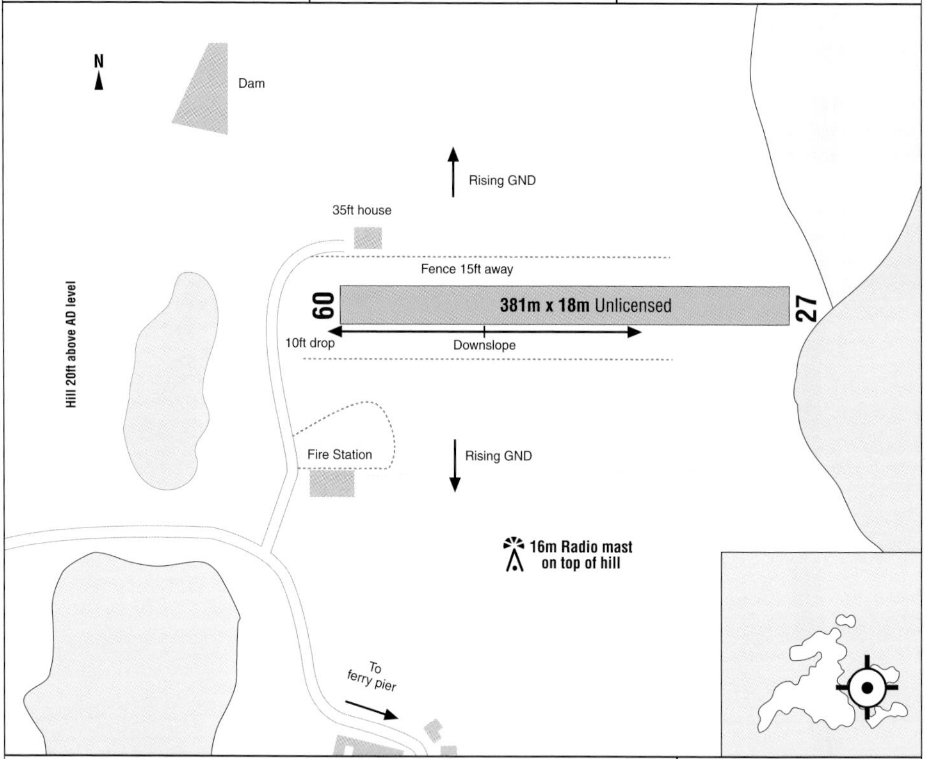

RWY	SURFACE	TORA	LDA	U/L	LIGHTING
09/27	Gravel/Asphalt			381x18	Rwy

Lighting available for emergency night landings

RNAV

Remarks
PPR by telephone essential. Visiting ACFT accepted. Visitors to contact Loganair to ascertain when their service operates. There is no off-Rwy parking visiting ACFT will constitute an obstruction to vital local services.

O

Warnings
Rwy surface is poor & uneven fenced on both sides. Due to uneven surface there is danger of prop-strike to nose wheel ACFT with little prop clearance. Rwy profile is hump-backed. The hamlet of Bruray is close to SW of AD. Moss may affect braking action.
Important: ACFT parked on strip restrict scheduled & ambulance services – consult with Loganair.

Operating Hrs	SR-SS
Circuits	1000ft QFE
Landing Fee	£6.50
Maintenance	Nil
Fuel	Nil
Disabled Facilities	Nil
Restaurants	
Accomodation	Alice Arthur can provide B&B
Taxis/Car Hire	Nil
Weather Info	Air Sc GWC

Operator Alice Arthur
Out Skerries Airfield
Bruary
Out Skerries
Shetland
Tel: 01806 515253 (Alice Arthur PPR)
Tel: 01595 840246 (Directflight)

OXENHOPE

1150ft 38mb	4nm SW of Keighley N5348.00 W00155.00	PPR	Alternative AD	**Leeds** Huddersfield **kNon-standard join**

Non Radio	ATIS Leeds 118.025	APP Leeds 123.750	Safetycom 135.475

N
11
Downslope with undulations
250m x 15m Unlicensed
24
Rough GND
Rough GND
Moorland
06
400m x 15m Unlicensed
Hangar
29

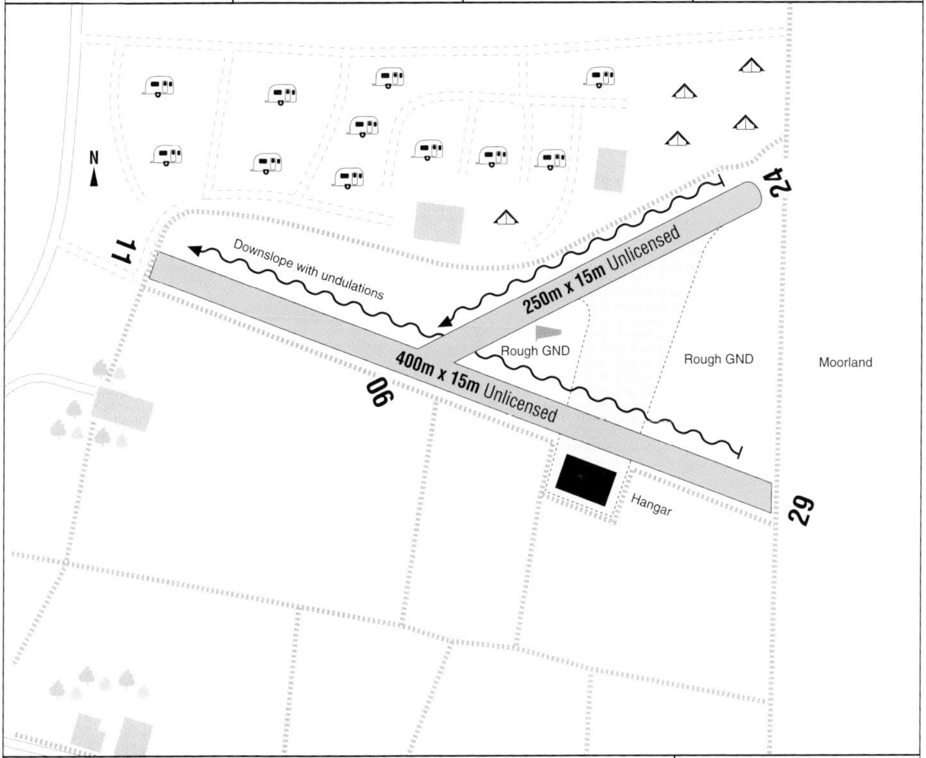

RWY	SURFACE	TORA	LDA	U/L	LIGHTING
11/29	Grass			400x15	Nil
06/24	Grass			250x15	Nil

Rwys undulate, Rwy29 downslope

RNAV			
POL	112.10	058	7.5

Remarks
PPR by telephone. Helicopters not accepted. AD situated on high GND. Worth Valley steam railway is located W of AD and is a short taxi ride away.

Warning
AD situated beneath Leeds CTA, (base 3000ft QNH). Rwys can become waterlogged during winter months. Stone walls at all Thrs.
Noise: Avoid over flying local houses and farms, particularly the caravan site to N of AD.

Operating Hrs	SR-SS
Circuits	LH 600ft QFE
Landing Fee	Donation please
Maintenance	Nil
Fuel	Nil
Disabled Facilities	
Taxi/Car Hire	Nil
Weather Info	Air Cen MOEx

Operator
Mr J R Heaton
Hawksbridge Farm
Oxenhope
Keighley
West Yorkshire
BD22 9QU
Tel: 01535 644863
rodney.heaton@btinternet.com

Effective date:25/09/08
OP 08

EGTK OXFORD

270ft 9mb	6nm NW by N of Oxford N5150.22 W00119.20	PPR	**Alternative AD** **Diversion AD**	**Gloucestershire** Turweston

Oxford	ATIS	LARS	APP	TWR	GND
	136.225 (Arr)	Brize 124.270	125.325	133.425	121.950

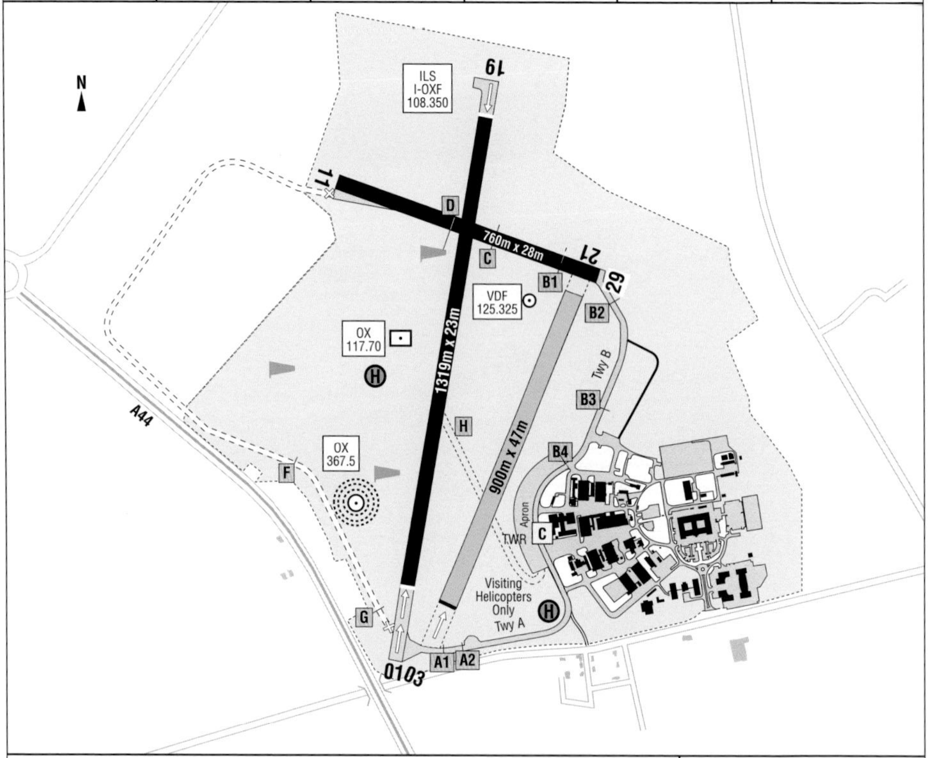

RWY	SURFACE	TORA	LDA	U/L	LIGHTING
01	Asphalt	1319	1319		Thr Rwy PAPI 3.5° LHS
19	Asphalt	1319	1319		Thr Rwy PAPI 3.0° LHS
03/21	Grass	880	880		Nil
11/29	Asphalt	760	760		Nil

RNAV			
DTY	116.40	204	22.0

Remarks
PPR via Ops. Hi-Vis. Customs parking area N of TWR is for short term use only.
Visual aid to location: Ibn KD Green.

O

Warnings
Helicopter training takes place in designated areas on AD. Jet fuel installation N of tower, infringes W Twy B, ACFT wingspan >15m; exercise caution. D129 is 4.5nm NE of AD.

Operating Hrs Mon-Fri 0530-2130 Sat-Sun & PH 0730-1700 (Summer) +1Hr (Winter) & by arr

Circuits Variable fixed-wing ACFT 1200ft QFE

Landing Fee Single £15
Twin on application

Maintenance Nil

Fuel AVGAS JET A1 100LL

Disabled Facilities

Restaurants Restaurant/refreshments available at AD

Taxis
Ox Air Trans **Tel:** 07864 928566

Car Hire
Godfrey Davis **Tel:** 01865 246373
Hertz **Tel:** 01865 319972

Weather Info M* A Air Cen MOEx

Operator Oxford Aviation Services
Oxford Airport
Kidlington
Oxford, OX5 1RA
Tel: 01865 290650 (ATC)
Tel: 01865 290660 (PPR/Ops)
Fax: 01865 290661
www.oxfordairport.co.uk

AFE **Tel:** 01865 841441
Fax: 01865 842495

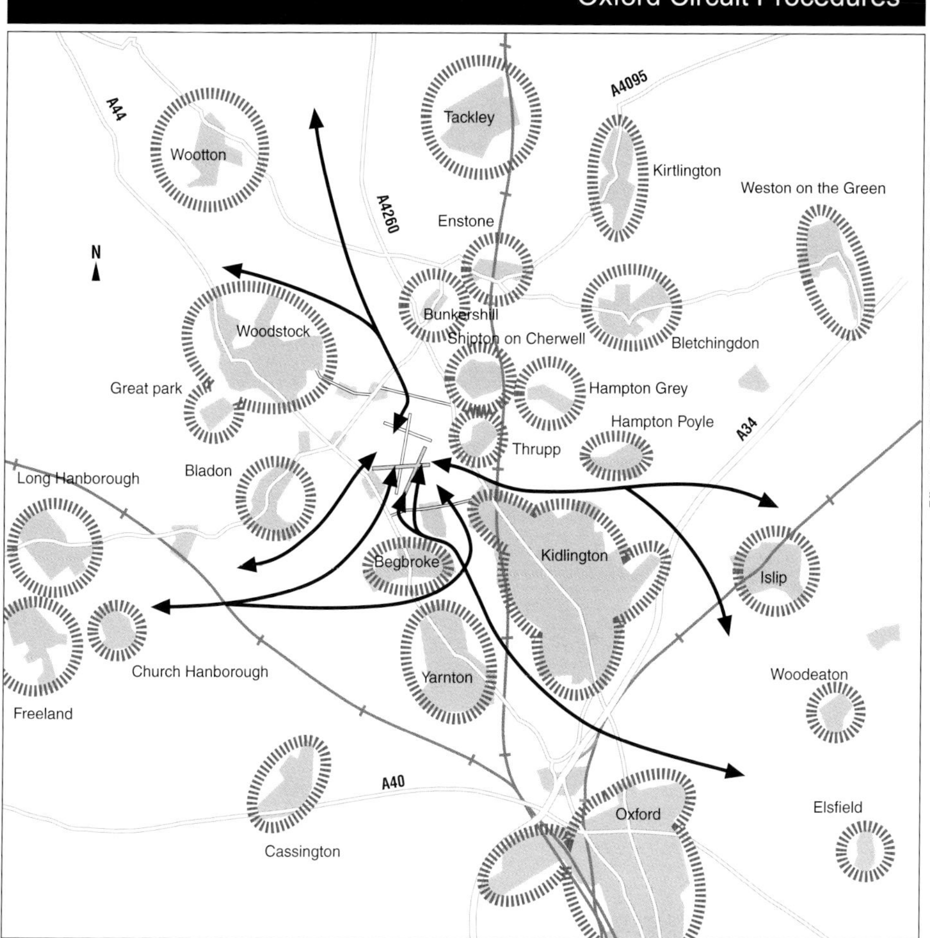

Effective date:25/09/08

Noise Abatement Procedures

All Dept fixed-wing ACFT climb straight ahead to 1000ft QNH before turning crosswind, endeavour to complete this before the Mercury satellite station. Rwy19 visual Dept turning left should climb ahead until clear to S of Yarnton village, remaining clear of the Brize CTR. Subject to Rwy & circuit direction pilots should avoid noise sensitive areas as shown on map.

ACFT joining the circuit will join over head unless they request a non-standard join, which will be approved subject to traffic.

ACFT joining will give way to ACFT in the circuit.

Helicopters must avoid built up areas as shown on map or should follow marked track

EGLG PANSHANGER

250ft 8mb	2.5nm W of Hertford N5148.12 W00009.50	PPR	**Alternative AD** **London Luton** Elstree

Panshanger	LARS	APP	A/G
	Farnborough North 132.800	Luton 129.550	120.250

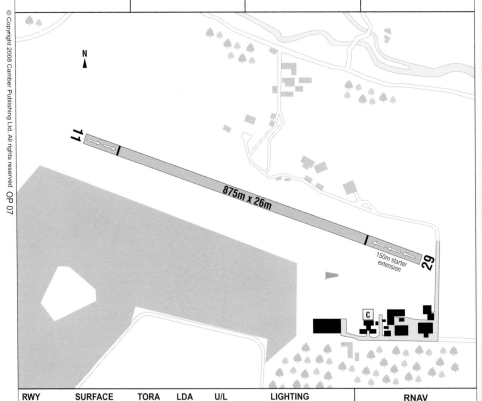

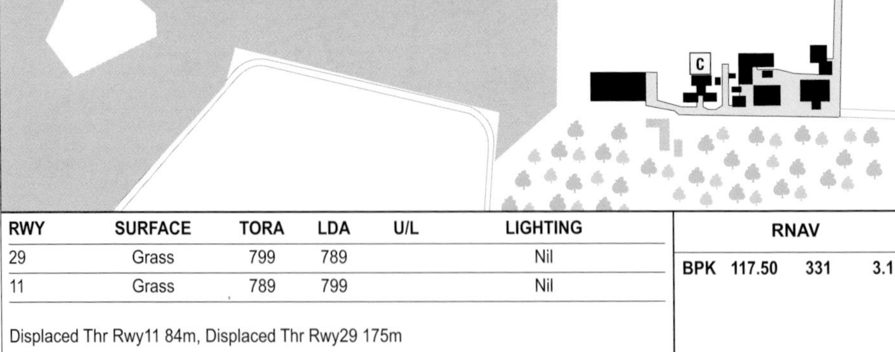

RWY	SURFACE	TORA	LDA	U/L	LIGHTING
29	Grass	799	789		Nil
11	Grass	789	799		Nil

Displaced Thr Rwy11 84m, Displaced Thr Rwy29 175m

RNAV			
BPK	117.50	331	3.1

Remarks
AD strictly PPR. No visitors at weekends.

Warnings
Luton CTR is 1nm to N and ATZ passes into Luton CTR.
Noise: Pilots are to obtain a Dept briefing to avoid noise sensitive areas. Rwy29 After take-off turn right over fly golf clubhouse, turn to Rwy QDM until passing prominent white building (school). Turn right, fly to square wood approx 0.5nm, turn downwind between Tewin and Tewin Wood.

P

Operating Hrs	0900-1900 (Summer) 0900-SS (Winter)
Circuits	11 LH, 29 RH, 800ft QFE Heli 1000ft QFE standard overhead joins
Landing Fee	Singles/Heli £10 Twins £10 Commercial £25
Maintenance	P F Maintenance (M3 & FAA)
Fuel	AVGAS 100LL

Disabled Facilities

Restaurants
Blue Sky **Tel:** 01707 395593 Closed Monday

Taxis	**Tel:** 01707 333333
Castle	**Tel:** 01992 501002
County	**Tel:** 01992 504111
Car Hire	
Europcar	**Tel:** 01438 715888
Hertz	**Tel:** 01707 331433
Weather Info	Air SE MOEx
Operator	Professional Flight Management Ltd Panshanger Airfield, Cole Green Hertford, Herts, SG14 2NH **Tel:** 01707 391791 **Fax:** 01707 392792 eastherts.flyingschool@virgin.net

82ft 2mb	Isle of Papa Stour Shetland Isles N6120.13 W00145.18	PPR	**Alternative AD** **Sumburgh** Scatsta

Papa Stour	APP Sumburgh 131.300	APP Scatsta 123.600	A/G 130.650 (monitored when flights expected)

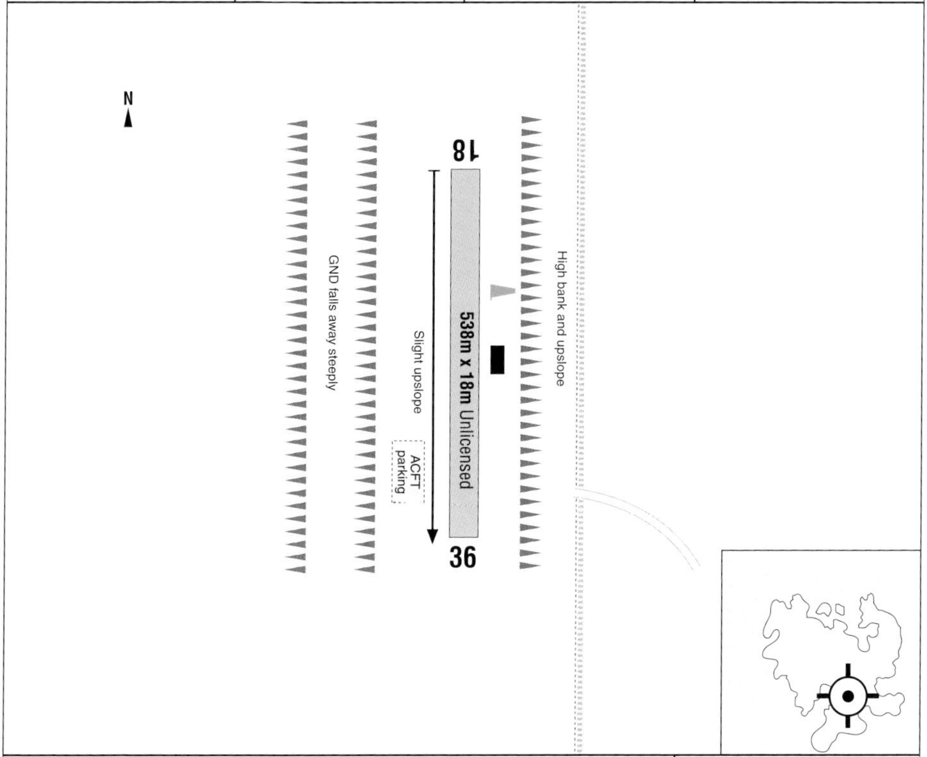

N
18
36
538m x 18m Unlicensed
Slight upslope
ACFT parking
GND falls away steeply
High bank and upslope

RWY	SURFACE	TORA	LDA	U/L	LIGHTING
18/36	Grass/Stones			538x18	Thr

RNAV			
SUM	117.35	340	30.0

Remarks

PPR by telephone. Visiting ACFT accepted. We recommend visitors seek up to date AD condition advice from A S Glover.

Warnings

Rwy surface is rough & could cause prop-strike to nose wheel ACFT with little prop clearance. Rwy profile has a slight up gradient from Rwy18 to Rwy36 Thr. Rwy is constructed on the side of a hill with an up slope to E & down slope to W. Expect severe turbulence on short finalRwy18 as you cross the cliffs. AD is common land & sheep may stray across the strip at any time.
Important: ACFT parked on strip restrict scheduled & ambulance services – consult Operator.

Operating Hrs	SR-SS
Circuits	1000ft QFE
Landing Fee	Nil
Maintenance	Nil
Fuel	Nil
Disabled Facilities	Nil
Restaurants	Nil
Accomodation	Hurdiback **Tel:** 01595 873229
Taxis/Car Hire	Nil
Weather Info	Air Sc GWC

Operator Papa Stour Airstrip Committee
Tel: 01595 873236 (A S Glover)
airstrip@papastour.shetland.co.uk
www.papastour.shetland.co.uk/airstrip.html

OP 03 Effective date:25/09/08

EGEP — PAPA WESTRAY

91ft 3mb	22nm N of Kirkwall Airport N5921.10 W00254.02	PPR	**Alternative AD** **Diversion AD**	**Kirkwall** Sanday

Non-radio	**APP** **Kirkwall 118.300**	**Safetycom** **135.475**

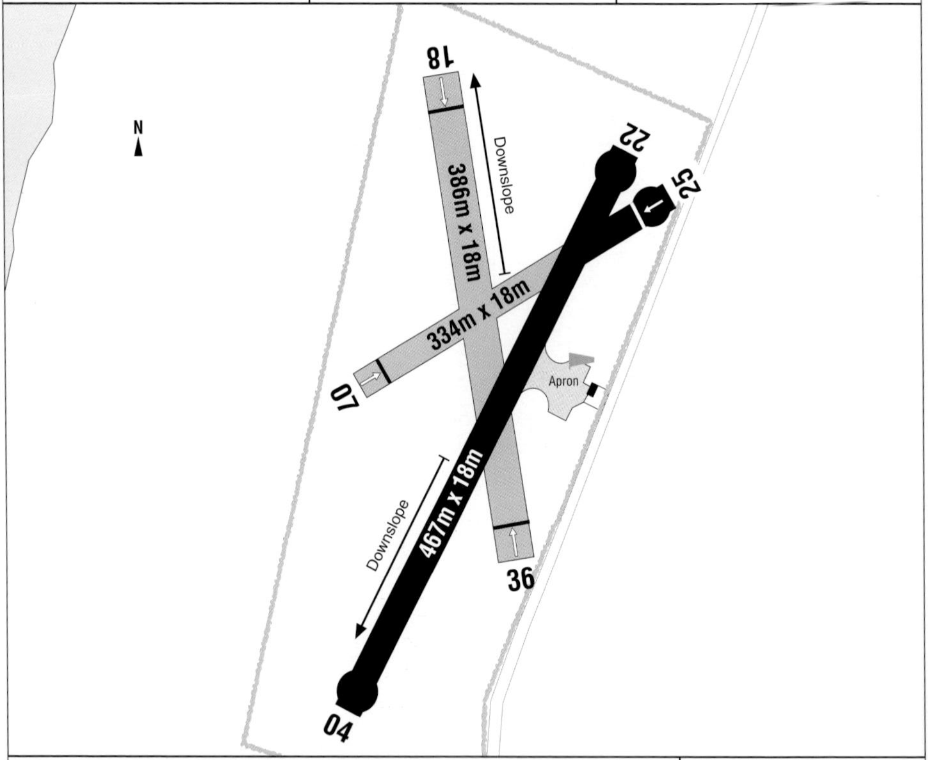

RWY	SURFACE	TORA	LDA	U/L	LIGHTING
04/22	Graded Hardcore	467	467		Nil
18	Grass	383	323		Nil
36	Grass	386	323		Nil
07/25	Grass/Graded Hardcore	292	250		Nil

Starter extension Rwy18 40m
Starter extension Rwy36 43m

RNAV			
KWL	108.60	006	23.5

Remarks
PPR from OIC. AD available at pilot's own risk. Rwy conditions contact AD Manager.

P

Warnings

Operating Hrs	SR-SS
Circuits	Nil
Landing Fee	Nil Fire cover £36.95 if req
Maintenance	Nil
Fuel	Nil

Disabled Facilities

Restaurants
Beltane House **Tel:** 01857 644321 (Hotel)

Taxis
Beltane House **Tel:** 01857 644321 (Hotel)

Car Hire	Nil
Weather Info	Air Sc GWC
Operator	Orkney Islands Council Offices Kirkwall Orkney, KW15 1NY **Tel:** 01856 873535 Ex 2305 **Fax:** 01856 876094

EGFP PEMBREY

15ft 0mb	6nm WNW of Llanelli N5142.48 W00418.44	PPR	**Alternative AD** **Swansea** Haverfordwest

Pembrey	**DAAIS** **Pembrey Range 122.750**	**A/G** **124.400**

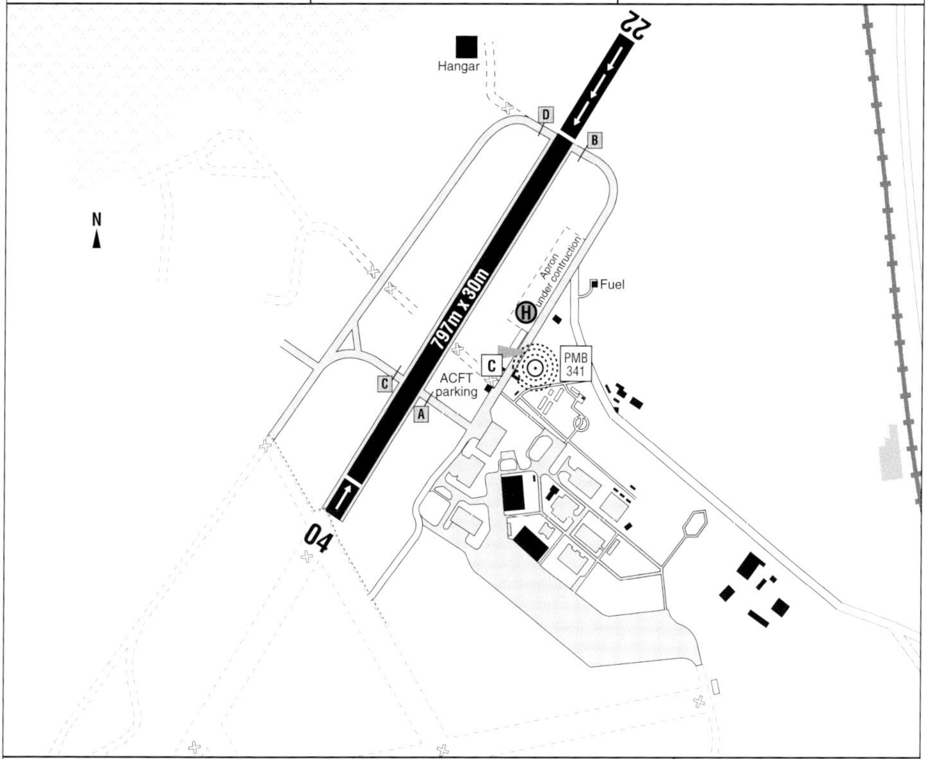

RWY	SURFACE	TORA	LDA	U/L	LIGHTING
04	Concrete	797	731		Nil
22	Concrete	731	767		Nil

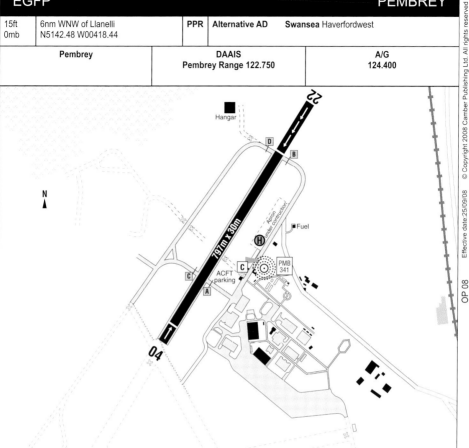

Displaced Thr Rwy04 66m

RNAV

Remarks
PPR by telephone weekdays only. 24Hrs notice required. Non-radio ACFT not accepted. Located within D118. Special procedures apply. Active portion is the NE corner of ex-RAF AD. Visitors welcome. Many local attractions of natural & historical significance. Cefn Sidan Beach (Blue flag 20min walk) & Ashburnham Golf Club 2 miles.

Warnings
Access to Pembrey penetrates D118 active Mon-Thu 0830-1700 Fri 0830-1400. All ACFT must call RAF range 24Hrs in advance for permission and slot allocation. All movements during these times must be to E of Rwy centreline. Inbounds must call Pembrey Range 10nm before DA boundary. In-bounds may be instructed to hold if the range is active. Vehicles cross at mid-point.

Operating Hrs PPR Mon-Fri 24hrs before flight
Sat-Sun 0800-1730 (L) & by arr

Circuits 22 LH, 04 RH

Landing Fee On application

Maintenance Available also hangarage

Fuel AVGAS JET A1 100LL
Cash or cheque only

Disabled Facilities

Restaurants Meals served daily inc Sunday lunch
Tel: 07968 867116

Hotel accommodation
Gwenllian Court **Tel:** 01554890217
Ashburnham Hotel **Tel:** 01554 834455
Diplomat Hotel **Tel:** 01554 756156
Stady Park Hotel **Tel:** 01554 758171

Taxis **Tel:** 01269 861936
Car Hire **Tel:** 01554 753040

Weather Info Air S MOEx

Operator Cpt Winston Thomas
Pembrey Airport
Pembrey, Carms, SA16 0HZ
Tel: 01554 891534
Tel: 01554 890420 (PPR)
Tel: 01554 890420 (Pembrey Range)
Fax: 01554 891388
www.pembreyairport.com

Effective date:25/09/08 OP 08

222ft 7mb	5nm S of Market Drayton N5248.36 W00229.52	PPR	Alternative AD	Hawarden Sleap

Non-Radio	LARS Shawbury 120.775	Safetycom 135.475

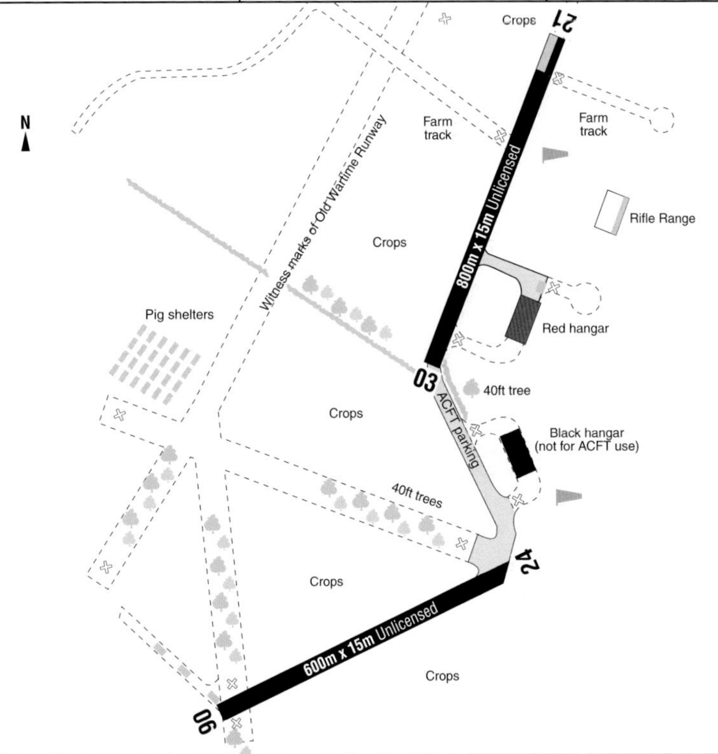

N
Crops
21
Farm track
Farm track
Witness marks of Old Wartime Runway
800m x 15m Unlicensed
Rifle Range
Crops
Pig shelters
Red hangar
03
40ft tree
Crops
ACFT parking
Black hangar (not for ACFT use)
40ft trees
24
Crops
600m x 15m Unlicensed
Crops
06

RWY	SURFACE	TORA	LDA	U/L	LIGHTING
03/21	Asph/Grass			800x15	Nil
06/24	Asphalt			600x15	Nil

Rwy21 has small portion of grass/asphalt at Thr

RNAV			
SWB	116.80	090	6.2

Remarks
PPR by telephone. Visiting ACFT welcome at pilots own risk. AD established using E side perimeter tracks of WW2 AD. All other parts of AD are not available for ACFT use.

Warnings
Farm vehicles use Rwy, pilots should keep good lookout and beware of debris. Crops grown up to Rwy edges. AD is within Shawbury/Ternhill CMATZ, controlling authority is Shawbury APP. Visiting ACFT call Shawbury when inbound and ASAP after take-off. Weekdays there is considerable military helicopter training at low level.
Noise: Avoid over flying all local habitation.

P

Operating Hrs SR-SS
Circuits 03, 21 RH, 06, 24 LH, 1000ft QFE
Landing Fee Nil
Maintenance Nil
Fuel Nil
Disabled Facilities

Restaurants
Four Alls **Tel:** 01630 652995

Taxis/Car Hire
Newport Cars **Tel:** 01952 8204077

Weather Info Air Cen MOEx

Operator Mr D R Williams
Standford Service Station
Standford Bridge, Newport
Shropshire, TF10 8BA
Tel: 01952 550261

EGTP PERRANPORTH

330ft 11mb	1.5nm SW of Perranporth N5019.90 W00510.65	PPR	**Alternative AD** **St Mawgan** Lands End **Diversion AD**

Non-standard join

Perranporth	LARS Culdrose 134.050	LARS St Mawgan 128.725	A/G 119.750

RWY	SURFACE	TORA	LDA	U/L	LIGHTING
05/23	Asphalt	940	940		Nil
09/27	Asphalt	750	750		Nil
01/19	Asphalt			600x27	Nil

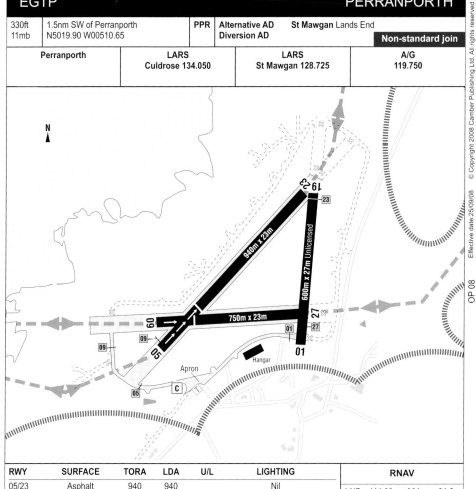

Starter extension Rwy05 204m, Starter extension Rwy09 129m

RNAV			
LND	114.20	061	21.2

Remarks

Strictly PPR. ACFT under the control of Culdrose are by agreement permitted to fly in the ATZ at 2000ft QFE & above during Culdrose ATC Hrs of watch. Accordingly ACFT should not fly within the Perranporth ATZ above 1000ft without clearance from either Culdrose ATC orvia relay from Perranporth. Some parts of the manoeuvring area prone to loose gravel. It is also used for taxiing by ACFT using other Rwys

Warnings

Gliding takes place at AD. When gliding is taking place fixed wing ACFT should make wide circuits. Tandem paarchute jumps take place from 10,000ft in overhead. AD is located within the Culdrose AIAA. Rwy 01/19 is available for ACFT not required to use a licensed AD. Only the hard Twys from the apron to the Rwy05 hold and Rwy27 hold are useable. Beware of windshear and severe turbulence on Rwy27 in strong NW winds.

Operating Hrs	0900-1700 or SS Daily
Circuits	N of AD No deadside join
Landing Fee	Minimum £6 there after £0.010p/kg gross weight +VAT
Maintenance	By arr
Fuel	AVGAS 100LL
Disabled Facilities	

Restaurants	Hotels in Perranporth
Taxis Atlantic	**Tel:** 01872 572126
Car Hire	Available on request
Weather Info	Air SW MOEx
Operator	Perranporth Airfield Ltd The Airfield, Higher Trevellas St Agnes, Cornwall, TR5 0XS **Tel:** 01872 552266 (AD) **Fax:** 01872 552261 (AD) www.perranporthairfield.co.uk

Effective date:25/09/08

Perranporth Noise Abatement Procedure

Land Rwy19 and take-off Rwy01 – beware of windshear in NW wind. Pilots should avoid flying directly over St Agnes, Perranporth & villages S of AD. Areas are particularly noise sensitive. After take-off, when practicable, reduce to climb power and turn to track out over the sea to at least 1500ft QNH before proceeding on course. Pilots Arr from E should make contact with St Mawgan.

397ft 13mb	3nm NE of Perth N5626.35 W00322.33	PPR	**Alternative AD** **Dundee** Fife

Perth	**A/G** **119.800**

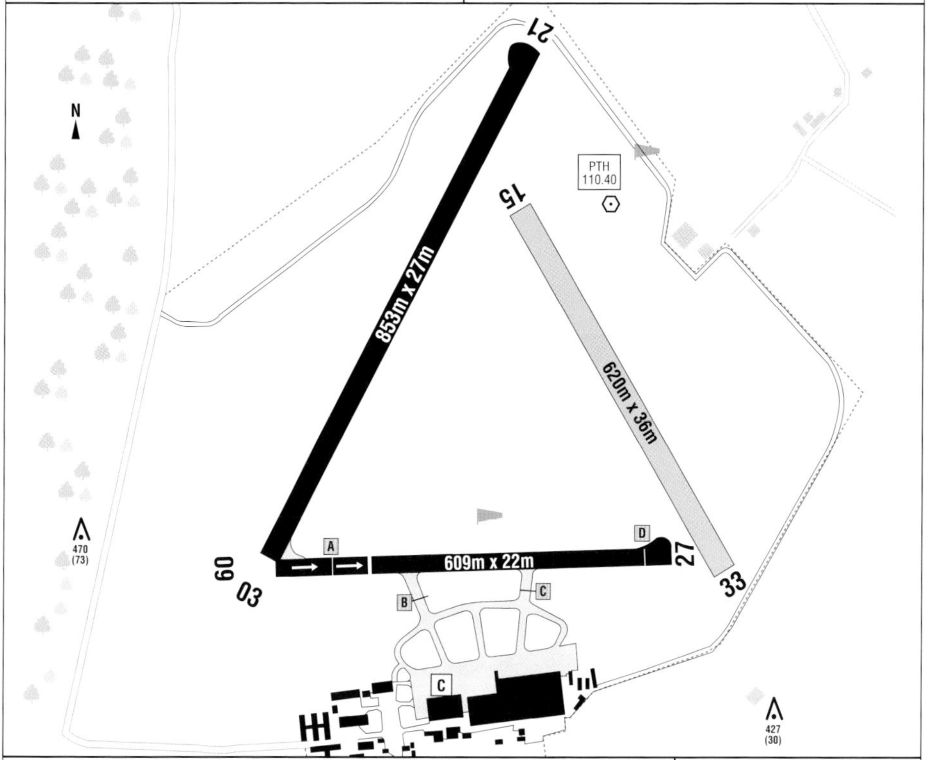

RWY	SURFACE	TORA	LDA	U/L	LIGHTING
03/21	Asphalt	853	853		Thr Rwy PAPI 3°
09	Asphalt	609	466		Nil
27	Asphalt	466	609		Nil
15/33	Grass	620	620		Nil

RNAV		
PTH	**110.40**	**On AD**

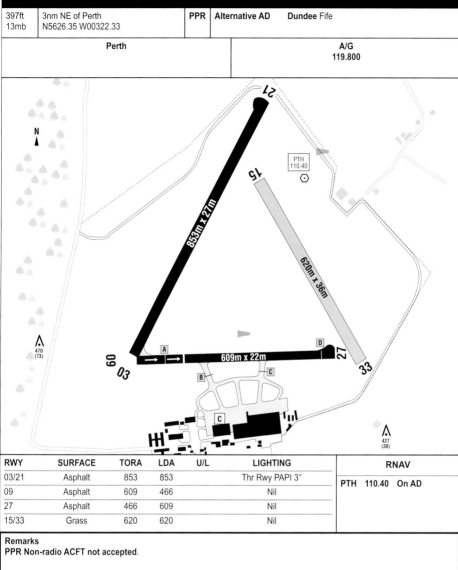

Remarks
PPR Non-radio ACFT not accepted.

Warnings
When landing Rwy03 with the wind from NW, turbulence can be expected from the tree line during the final APP.

Operating Hrs 0800-1600 (Summer) 0900-1700 (Winter) & by arr

Circuits 03, 09, 15 LH, 21, 27, 33 RH

Landing Fee Single <1000kg £12
Twin <2000kg £19.86
Others available on request

Maintenance
ACS **Tel:** 01738 550112

Fuel AVGAS JET A1 100LL

Disabled Facilities

Restaurants Restaurant & Club facilities available

Taxis
A & B Taxis **Tel**: 01738 634567

Car Hire
Thrifty **Tel:** 01738 633677

Weather Info Air Sc GWC

Operator ACS Aviation Ltd
Perth Airport
Scone, PH2 6PL
Tel: 01738 551631
Tel: 01738 550112
Tel: 01738 551631 (ATC)
Fax: 01738 554846

Effective date:25/09/08 OP 08

26ft 1mb	7nm S of Peterborough N5228.08 W00015.05	PPR	Alternative AD	Cambridge Fenland

Conington	A/G 129.725

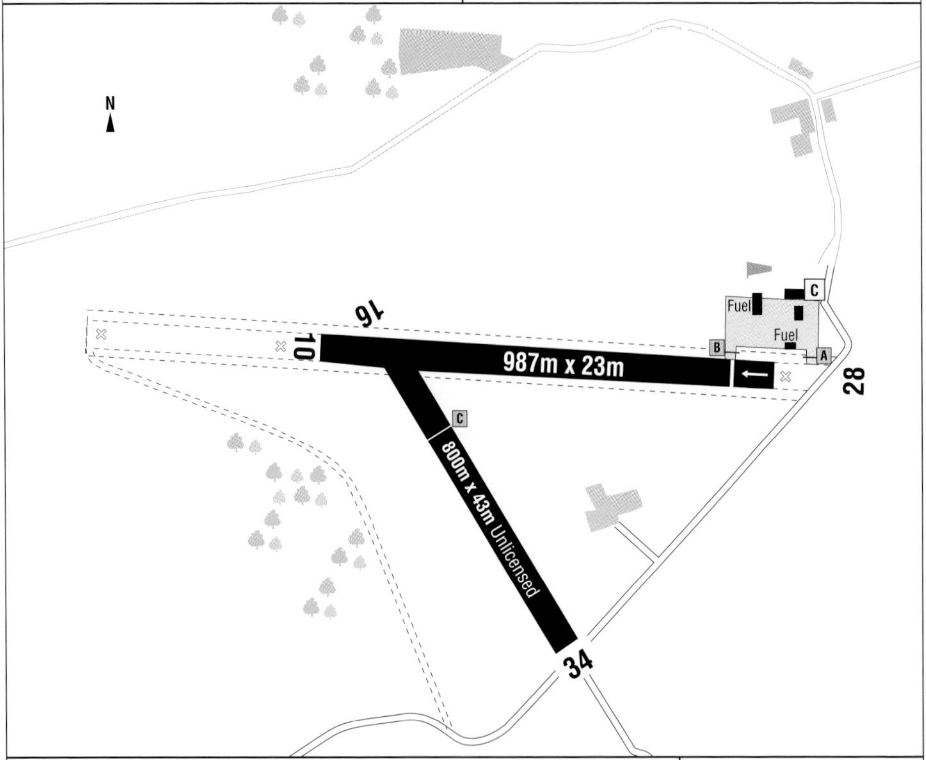

N
16
10
987m x 23m
Fuel
Fuel
C
B
A
28
C
800m x 43m Unlicensed
34

RWY	SURFACE	TORA	LDA	U/L	LIGHTING
10	Asphalt	957	957		Thr Rwy LITAS 3.25°
28	Asphalt	987	876		Thr Rwy LITAS 3.25°
16/34	Asphalt			800x43	Nil

Displaced Thr Rwy28 111m

RNAV

Remarks
PPR. Non-radio ACFT not accepted. AD is 1nm E of A1M.
Visual aid to location: Ibn PB Green.

Warnings
Avoid Sibson AD (parachuting) 7nm NW of AD. For Pilots of ACFT with wingspan >15m – clearance from obstacles through Hold A is reduced due to AVGAS tank and possible parked ACFT. Rwy lights are at 35m spacing, Rwy is 23m wide.
Noise: All pilots must avoid over flying all local villages.

Operating Hrs Mon-Fri 0830-1800
Sat-Sun & PH 0900-1800 (Summer).
Mon-Fri 0830-1700
Sat-Sun & PH 0900-1700 (Winter)

Circuits 1000ft QFE. Direction may be varied to suit local requirements at any time

Landing Fee Single & R22 £10 Light Twins £15.
Free landings with 40ltr AVGAS per engine or 120ltrs AVTUR.
Prices for large twins available on request

Maintenance Aerolease CAA M3 Approved
Tel: 01487 834161

Fuel AVGAS JET A1 100LL
Oil W80, W100, S80, S100, 15W50

Disabled Facilities

Restaurants Club facilities with members bar. Snacks & hot meals available 7 days a week 1100-1500

Taxis **Tel:** 01733 244400
Tel: 07971 189242

Car Hire On request

Weather Info Air Cen MOEx

Operator Aerolease Ltd
Peterborough Business Airfield
Holme, Peterborough, Cambs PE7 3PX
Tel: 01487 834161
Fax: 01487 834246
info@flying-club-conington.co.uk
www.flying-club-conington.co.uk

P

130ft 3mb	6nm W of Peterborough N5233.35 W00023.18	PPR	Alternative AD Diversion AD	Cambridge Peterborough Conington Non-standard join

Sibson	LARS Cottesmore 130.200	A/G 120.325

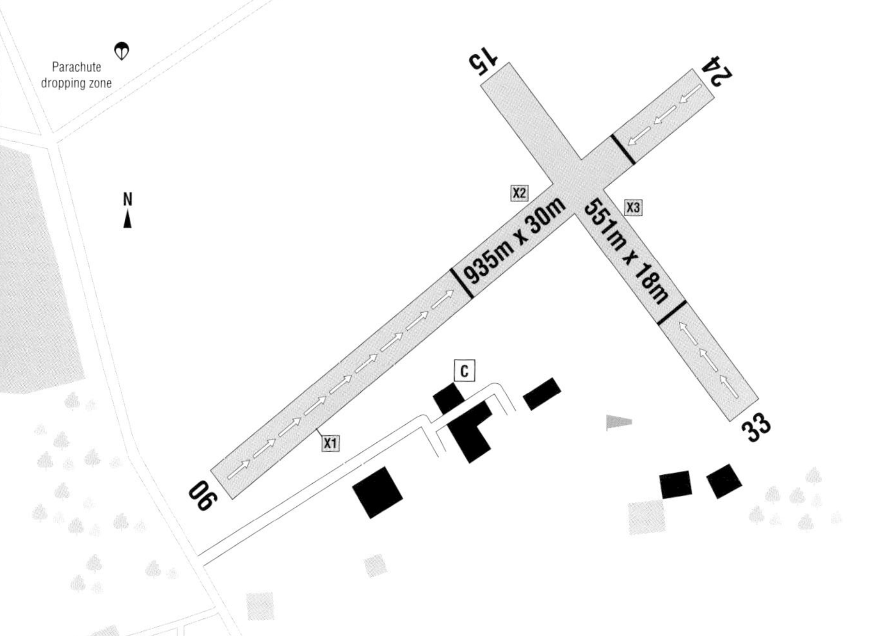

RWY	SURFACE	TORA	LDA	U/L	LIGHTING
15	Grass	551	551		Thr Rwy APAPI 4° LHS
33	Grass	551	424		Thr Rwy APAPI 4° LHS
06	Grass	676	468		Nil
24	Grass	468	676		Nil

Displaced Thr Rwy33 127m, Displaced Thr Rwy24 259m, Displaced Thr Rwy06 467m

RNAV

Remarks

PPR by telephone Non-radio ACFT not accepted. Not available to public transport passenger flights required to use a licensed AD. Inbound ACFT to call Cottesmore MATZ/LARS when no less than 15nm from Wittering. If no R/T contact is made during opening Hrs for Wittering, ACFT must avoid the Wittering MATZ except for that part which lies S of Sibson, and must descend to the Sibson circuit height before entering. Transiting fixed & rotary wing ACFT may not penetrate the ATZ whilst parachuting is in progress. Helicopters may not operate in the ATZ whilst parachuting is in progress.

Warnings

Free-fall parachuting up to FL130. Visiting pilots to contact A/G station to ascertain the latest situation. Do not over fly the AD. Power lines on ARR Rwy25. Surface can become boggy in winter.
Noise: Avoid over flying Eton village downwind Rwy06/24 and Stibbington village left base Rwy15 and climb out Rwy33.

Operating Hrs	0800-2000 (Summer) 0800-SS (Winter) & by arr
Circuits	15, 24 LH, 06, 33 RH, 1000ft QFE No over head joins. No dead side
Landing Fee	Single £10, Twin £20, Microlights £5
Maintenance	Available (CAA-approved)
Fuel	AVGAS 100LL Oils W80 80 W100/100
Disabled Facilities	

Restaurants	Bar and Restaurant on AD
Taxis	**Tel:** 01733 555344 (facility for wheelchairs) **Tel:** 01733 566661 **Tel:** 01733 775555
Car Hire	
Avis	**Tel:** 01733 349489
Hertz	**Tel:** 01733 273543
Weather Info	Air Cen MOEx
Operator	Modi Aviation T/A Sibson Flying School Sibson Aerodrome Wansford Peterborough, Cambs PE8 6NE **Tel:** 01832 280289 **Fax:** 01832 280675

450ft 15mb	1.5nm W of Peterlee Co Durham N5446.10 W00123.00	**PPR**	**Alternative AD**	**Newcastle** Durham Tees Valley

Peterlee Drop Zone	**APP** **Newcastle 124.375**	**APP** **Durham 118.850**	**A/G** **129.900**

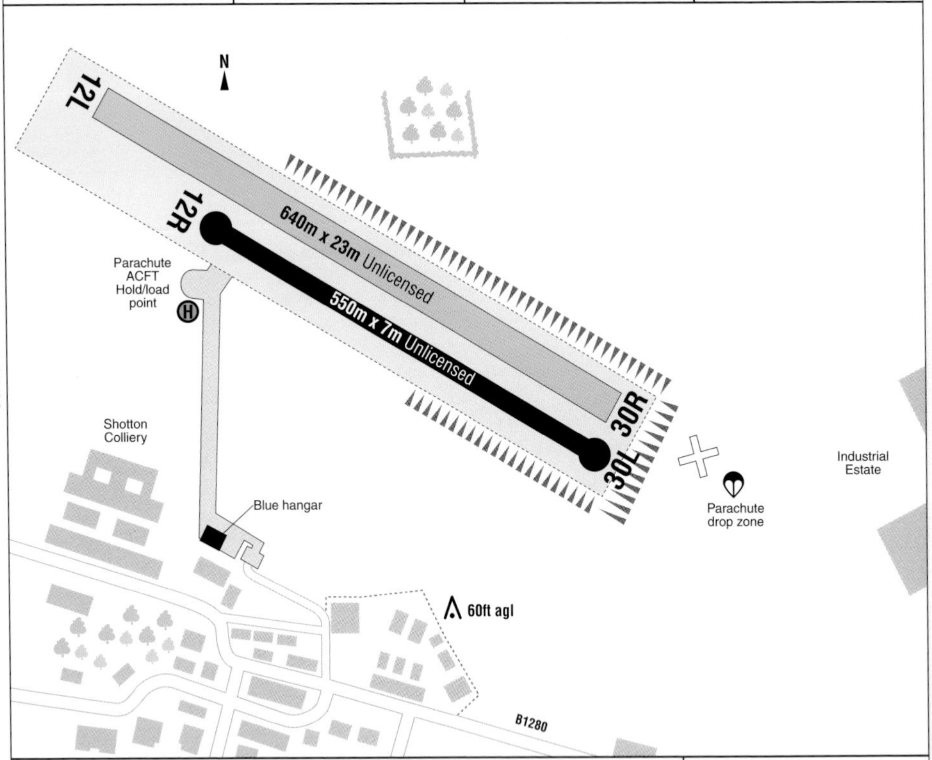

RWY	SURFACE	TORA	LDA	U/L	LIGHTING
12L/30R	Grass			640x23	Nil
12R/30L	Tarmac			550x7	Nil

RNAV			
NEW	**114.25**	**150**	**19.5**

Remarks
PPR by telephone. AD operated primarily as parachute centre with free-fall operations up to FL150. Visiting ACFT welcome with PPR & at own risk. AD constructed on a disused colliery site with slight down slopes E side of Rwy & S end. Rwy has white edge markers & Rwy designators.

Warnings
AD situated on reclaimed land may be water logged after heavy rain. Circuits to N only. AD situated close to N edge of Teeside CTZ, Teeside APP.
Noise: Avoid over flying Peterlee & the village of Shotton Colliery.

Operating Hrs 0830-2030 (L) daylight Hrs only
Circuits 12 LH, 30 RH, 1000ft N of AD only
Landing Fee £2.50 per seat
Overnight parking £1 per seat
Maintenance Nil
Fuel AVGAS JET A1 100LL
Mon-Fri 0930-1500
(phone to book mid week)
Disabled Facilities

Restaurants Canteen Fri-Sun & PH

Taxis **Tel:** 0191 517 2222
Tel: 0191 586 2244
Tel: 0191 587 2624
Car Hire Nil
Weather Info Air N MOEx
Operator Peterlee Parachute Centre
The Airfield, Shotton Colliery
Co Durham, DH6 2NH
Tel: 0191 5171234

330ft 11mb	South Shore of Pitsford Water N5219.00 W00053.50		**Alternative AD**	**Cranfield** Northampton

Non Radio	**AFIS** Northampton 122.700	**Safetycom** 135.475

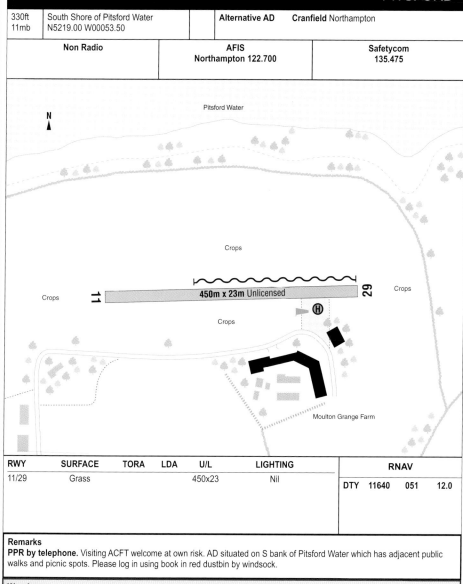

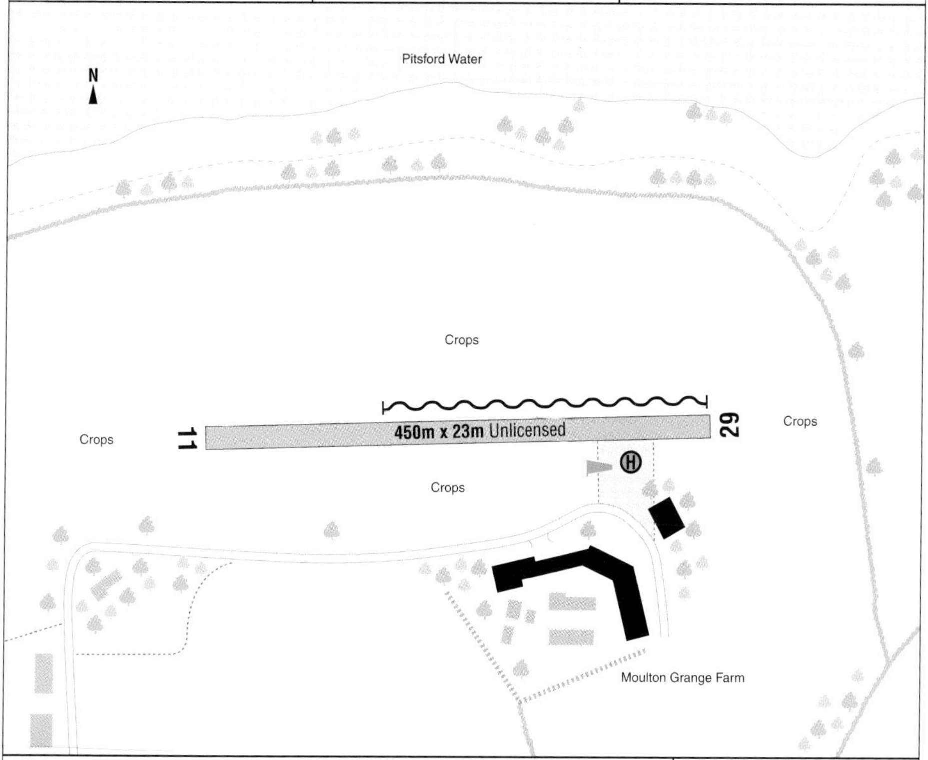

Pitsford Water

N

Crops

450m x 23m Unlicensed

11

29

Crops

Crops

Crops

Moulton Grange Farm

RWY	SURFACE	TORA	LDA	U/L	LIGHTING
11/29	Grass			450x23	Nil

RNAV			
DTY	11640	051	12.0

Remarks

PPR by telephone. Visiting ACFT welcome at own risk. AD situated on S bank of Pitsford Water which has adjacent public walks and picnic spots. Please log in using book in red dustbin by windsock.

Warnings

Northampton Sywell ATZ to E of AD and may be contacted if required. AD is well cut and there are undulations for the first two thirds Rwy29.

Noise: Turn N after take-off or climb straight ahead. Avoid over flight of local habitation.

Operating Hrs SR-SS

Circuits To N 1000ft QFE

Landing Fee Donations to local Air Ambulance fund

Maintenance Nil

Fuel Nil

Disabled Facilities

Restaurant Pub in village

Taxi/Car Hire By arrangement

Weather Info Air Cen MOEx

Operator

Richard Stanley
Moulton Grange Farm
Grange Lane
Pitsford
Northampton
NN6 9AN
Tel: 01604 645656
inbox@moultongrangefarm.org.uk

Effective date:25/09/08 OP 08

P

395ft 13mb	2nm SE of Hemel VRP N5143.70 W00022.71		**Alternative AD**	**London Luton** Elstree

Plaistows	**ATIS Luton 120.575**	**APP Luton 129.550**	**A/G Elstree 122.400**	**A/G 129.825 (Microlight freq)**

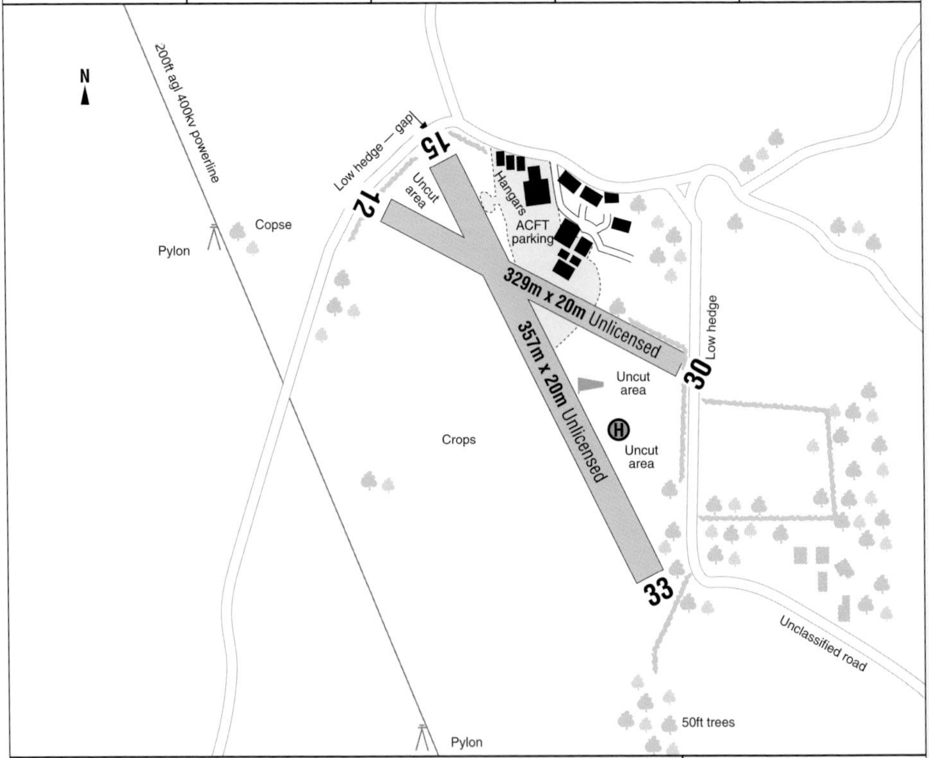

N
200ft agl 400kv powerline
Pylon
Copse
Low hedge — gap
15
12
Uncut area
Hangars
ACFT parking
329m x 20m Unlicensed
357m x 20m Unlicensed
Low hedge
30
Uncut area
Crops
Uncut area
33
Unclassified road
50ft trees
Pylon

RWY	SURFACE	TORA	LDA	U/L	LIGHTING
15/33	Grass			357x20	Nil
12/30	Grass			329x20	Nil

RNAV			
BNN	113.75	091	6.3

Remarks
PPR is not required. Primarily a Microlight AD but suitable STOL ACFT welcome and at pilot's own risk. Rwy always well cut. Please call downwind and on finals.

Warnings
Small copse of trees 50ft high on very short final Rwy33 may cause turbulence in W to NW wind. Power lines 200ftagl run approx 200m W of AD and cross Rwy12 APP. Rwy30 climb out approx 300m from Rwy12 Thr. AD close to S boundary of Luton CTR (Class D) and 2.5nm N of the N boundary of the Elstree ATZ.
Noise: Please avoid over flying all local habitation.

P

Operating Hrs SR-SS Dept restricted to between Mon-Sat 0800-1900 Sun 0900-1900

Circuits 30, 33 LH, 12, 15 RH

Landing Fee Donations to Royal Marsden Hospital gratefully received

Maintenance Nil

Fuel MOGAS

Disabled Facilities

Restaurants The Three Hammers Chiswell Green 1nm E of AD

Taxis/Car Hire Nil

Weather Info Air SE MOEx

Operator Mr Derrick Brunt
Plaistows Farm
Chiswell Green Lane
St Albans, Herts, AL2 3NT
Tel: 01727 851642

250ft 8mb	3.5nm NE of Kyle of Lochalsh N5720.12 W00540.32	PPR	**Alternative AD** **Inverness** Isle of Skye

Plockton	**A/G** **130.650** **make blind calls**

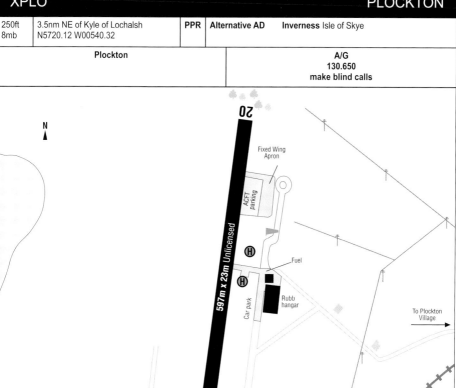

N
20
Fixed Wing Apron
ACFT parking
597m x 23m Unlicensed
Fuel
Rubb hangar
Car park
To Plockton Village
Plockton Station
02

RWY	SURFACE	TORA	LDA	U/L	LIGHTING
02/20	Asphalt			597x23	Nil

RNAV

Remarks
Strictly PPR. Visitors welcome at pilots own risk. Fixed wing ACFT parking near windsock or on the short grass between the apron and Rwy. Use Twy to get to both locations.

Warnings
Ridge of high GND up to 140ft amsl 500m to E and up to 400ft amsl 500m to SE. High trees Rwy20 APP. Helicopter operations (Air Ambulance & Coast Guard) take place at AD and local areas up to 2000ft within a radius of 25nm.
Noise: Fly all circuits to W of AD, over the sea, to avoid flying over Plockton village and Plockton High School.

Operating Hrs H24
Circuits 02 LH, 20 RH
No dead side
Landing Fee TBN
Maintenance Nil
Fuel AVTUR JET A1 self service
Check availability
Hangarage Limited
Disabled Facilities

Restaurants/Accomodation
Plockton Shores **Tel:** 01599 544263
www.plocktonshoresrestaurant.co.uk
The Haven **Tel:** 01599 544223
www.havenhotelplockton.co.uk
Plockton Hotel **Tel:** 01599 544274
www.plocktonhotel.co.uk
Plockton Inn **Tel:** 01599 544222
www.plocktoninn.f9.co.uk

Taxis
Kyle Taxi **Tel:** 01599 534323
Boat Trip **Tel:** 01599 544306
www.calums-sealtrips.com

Weather Info Air Sc GWC

Operator PDG Helicopters (Kyle)
BUTEC, Kyle of Lochalsh,
Highland IV40 8AJ
Tel/Fax: 01599 534926 (Pete Rawling)
Tel: 07899 936455 (Pete Rawling)
Tel: 07748 656553 (Hugh Vowles)
pdgkyle@btconnect.com
www.pdg-helicopters.co.uk

Effective date:25/09/08
OP 08
P

EGHD PLYMOUTH CITY

476ft 16mb	3.5nm NNE of Plymouth N5025.22 W00406.21	PPR	Alternative AD Exeter Bodmin Diversion AD	Non-standard join

Plymouth	APP 133.550	TWR 118.150	FIRE 121.600

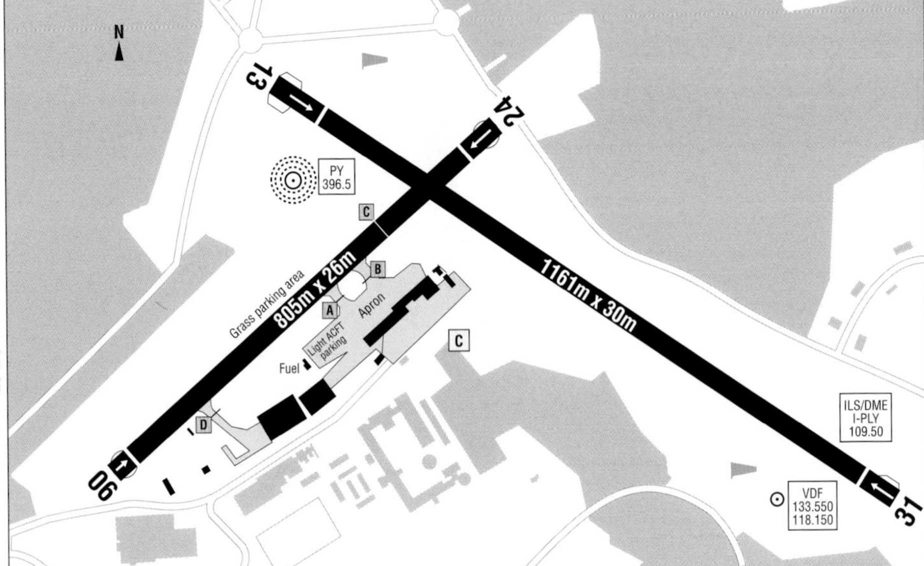

RWY	SURFACE	TORA	LDA	U/L	LIGHTING
06	Asphalt	680	680		Thr Rwy APAPI 3.75° RHS
24	Asphalt	740	708		Thr Rwy PAPI 4° LHS
13	Asphalt	1109	1027		Thr Rwy Apapi 3.75° LHS
31	Asphalt	1102	1045		Ap Thr Rwy PAPI 3.5° LHS

RNAV			
BHD	112.05	279	23.4

Remarks

Strict PPR at all times. Non-radio ACFT not accepted. Rescue & Police heli flights may take place any time outside Hrs. Rwy31 preferential Rwy in zero wind conditions. Light ACFT parking normally W end main apron subject ATC requirements. Light ACFT & helicopters may be directed park adjacent grass areas. ACFT must cause least disturbance in areas surrounding AD. Aerobatic manoeuvres & low fly pasts prohibited unless ACFT participating organised flying display. ACFT parking tarmac light ACFT area or stand 5 use & return chocks provided, due sloping GND. Use caution taxiing, wing tip clearance not assured. Grass parking area telephone provided, contact ATC for permission to use pedestrian route across Rwy06/24. Route marked by green lines. Helicopter parking circles on grass between apron & Rwy06/24. Slot time arrangement for training by arrangement with ATC.

Visual aid to location: White Strobe.

Warnings

Rwy06 signals visible at night N of extended centre line where normal obstacle clearance is not guaranteed. No APP slope guidance until ACFT is aligned with Rwy. Surface gradients in excess of 2.4% in S W corner of AD. Strong wind windshear & turbulence may be experienced on APP and climb out all Rwys. Downdraughts & sudden changes in W/V possible in light winds. Small flocks wood pigeons up to 2000ft in vicinity Rwy31 TDZ.

P

Operating Hrs 0530-2130 (Summer) +1Hr (Winter)
See remarks for PPR periods

Circuits 06,13 LH, 24,31RH 1000ft QFE
or as directed by ATC

Landing Fee Available on request from ATC. Out of Hrs surcharges after 1900 (Summer) 2000 (Winter)

Maintenance Nil

Fuel AVGAS JET A1 100LL

Disabled Facilities

Restaurants Available in terminal

Taxis Available at terminal

Car Hire
Hertz **Tel:** 01752 207206

Weather Info M T9 Fax 386 MOEx

Visual Reference Points (VRP)

Avon Estuary	N5017.00 W00353.00
Ivy Bridge	N5023.08 W00355.10
Saltash	N5025.13 W00414.08
Yelverton	N5029.52 W00405.22

Operator Plymouth City Airport Ltd
North QuayHouse
Sutton Harbour, Plymouth
Devon, PL4 0RA
Tel: 01752 515341 (ATC/PPR)
atc.plymouth@btconnect.com
www.plymouthairport.com

XPOC POCKLINGTON

87ft 3mb	10nm ESE of York N5355.50 W00047.77	PPR	Alternative AD Humberside Full Sutton **Non-standard join**

Pocklington	LARS Linton 118.550	A/G Glider Ops 130.100	GND to GND 129.900

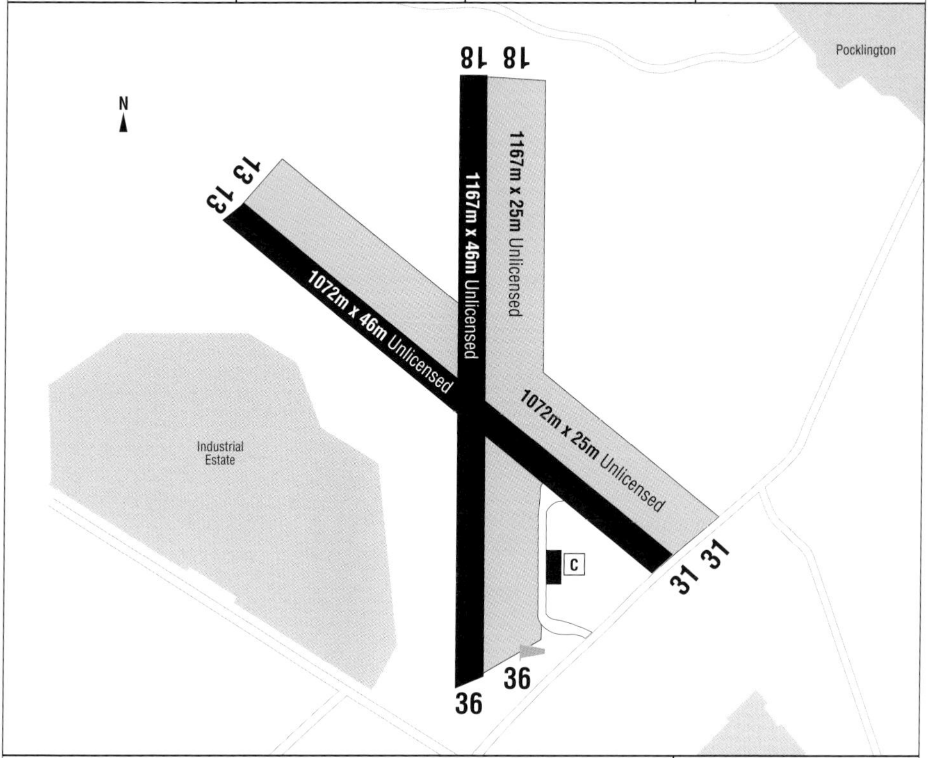

RWY	SURFACE	TORA	LDA	U/L	LIGHTING
13/31	Asphalt			1072x46	Nil
13/31	Grass			1072x25	Nil
18/36	Asphalt			1167x46	Nil
18/36	Grass			1167x25	Nil

Asphalt Rwys in poor condition but safe for landing & take-off

RNAV			
OTR	113.90	303	28.1

Remarks
Operated by the Wolds Gliding Club Ltd. Primary used for gliding operations. Situated within Vale of York AIAA, pilots are advised to use the LARS of Linton APP. Joining Instructions: During gliding activity plan circuit on Rwy in use by gliders regardless of wind direction. Orbit AD at about 1000ft aal, keeping well outside the traffic pattern, to indicate intention to land. When the Rwy & APP are clear of gliders, land on asphalt or grass Rwy & backtrack to glider launch point. With no glider activity, check windsock, select Rwy and land on either Rwy. Taxi to hangar area.

Warnings
Look out for gliders. DO NOT join overhead below 2000ft agl when gliding is in progress due to cables.
Noise: Avoid over flying the villages of Barmby Moor NW of AD & Pocklington.

Operating Hrs SR-SS
Circuits Variable no overhead joins
Landing Fee Private £10 Commercial £25
Maintenance Nil
Fuel AVGAS 100LL
Disabled Facilities

Restaurant
The Feathers **Tel:** 01759 303155

Taxis
Hessels **Tel:** 01759 303176
Car Hire
National **Tel:** 01904 612141
Weather Info Air N MOEx
Operator Wolds Gliding Club Ltd
The Airfield, Pocklington
East Yorkshire, YO4 2NR
Tel: 01759 303579
Office Hrs Wed, Sat & Sun 1000-1600
Answer phone at other times

P

550ft 18mb	8.5nm NNE of Winchester N5111.66 W00114.17	PPR	Alternative AD Diversion AD	Farnborough Thruxton

Popham	LARS Farnborough West 125.250	A/G 129.800

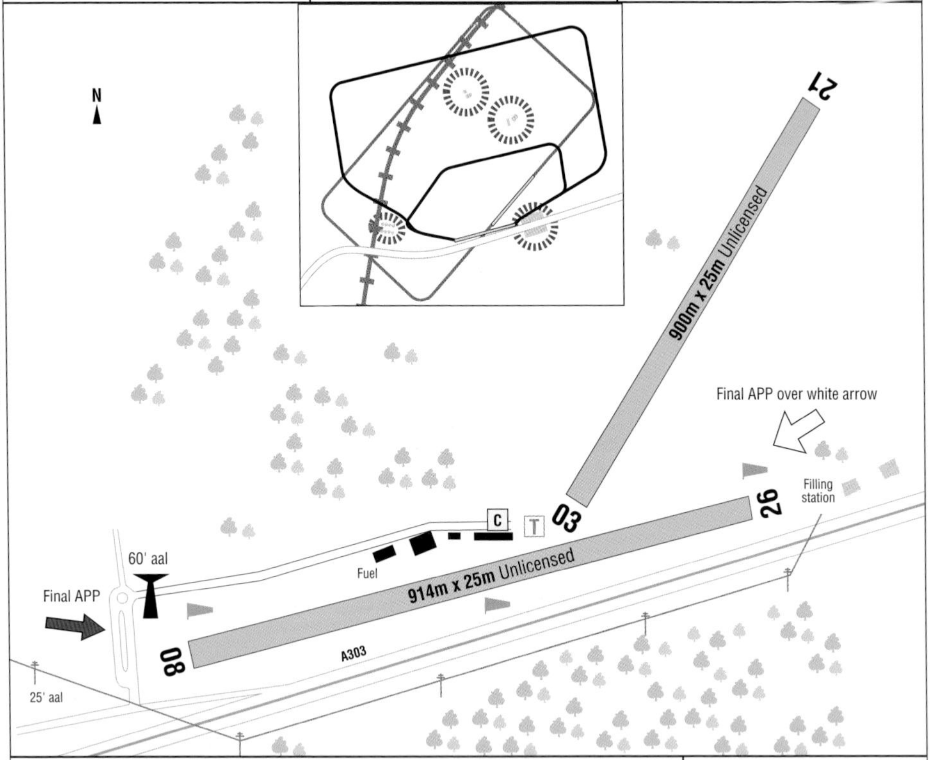

N
21
900m x 25m Unlicensed
Final APP over white arrow
Filling station
26
03
C
T
60' aal
Fuel
914m x 25m Unlicensed
Final APP
08
A303
25' aal

RWY	SURFACE	TORA	LDA	U/L	LIGHTING
08/26	Grass			914x25	Nil
03/21	Grass			900x25	Nil

Rwy03/21 use restricted to certain dates check in advance
Rwy08 thr down slopes 1%, Rwy26 thr down slopes 3.3%

RNAV			
SAM	113.35	021	15.1

Remarks
PPR to non-radio ACFT. ACFT within 4500lbs MAUW welcome at pilots own risk

Warnings
Caution: Water tower 60ft aal close N of Rwy08 Thr. Microlight activity at AD. During week extensive military flying in local area, mainly helicopters & C130 ACFT often low level & very close to the AD.
Noise: Rwy08/26 APP offset, Rwy26 over white arrow avoiding bungalow & filling station, Rwy08 over silver grain silos avoiding houses W of AD.

P

Operating Hrs 0800-1700 (L)
Circuits N 800ft QFE
Landing Fee £5 non-members
Free to Members
Maintenance Wiltshire ACFT Maintenance
Tel: 01256 398372
Fuel AVGAS 100LL
Aeroshell Oils
(cash/cheque only)

Disabled Facilities

Restaurants Sat-Sun hot & cold refreshment
Mon-Fri light snacks

Taxis
Grassbys Taxis **Tel:** 01256 464212
Car Hire
Contract Self Drive **Tel:** 01256 322400
Weather Info Air SE MOEx
Operator Charles Church (Spitfires) Ltd
Popham Airfield, Winchester
Hants, SO21 3BD
Tel: 01256 397733
Fax: 01256 397114
pophamairfield@btconnect.com
www.popham-airfield.co.uk

PORTMOAK

360ft 12mb	0.5nm E of Loch Leven N5611.21 W00319.45	PPR	**Alternative AD** Fife **Non-standard join**

Portmoak	LARS Leuchars 126.500	A/G 129.975

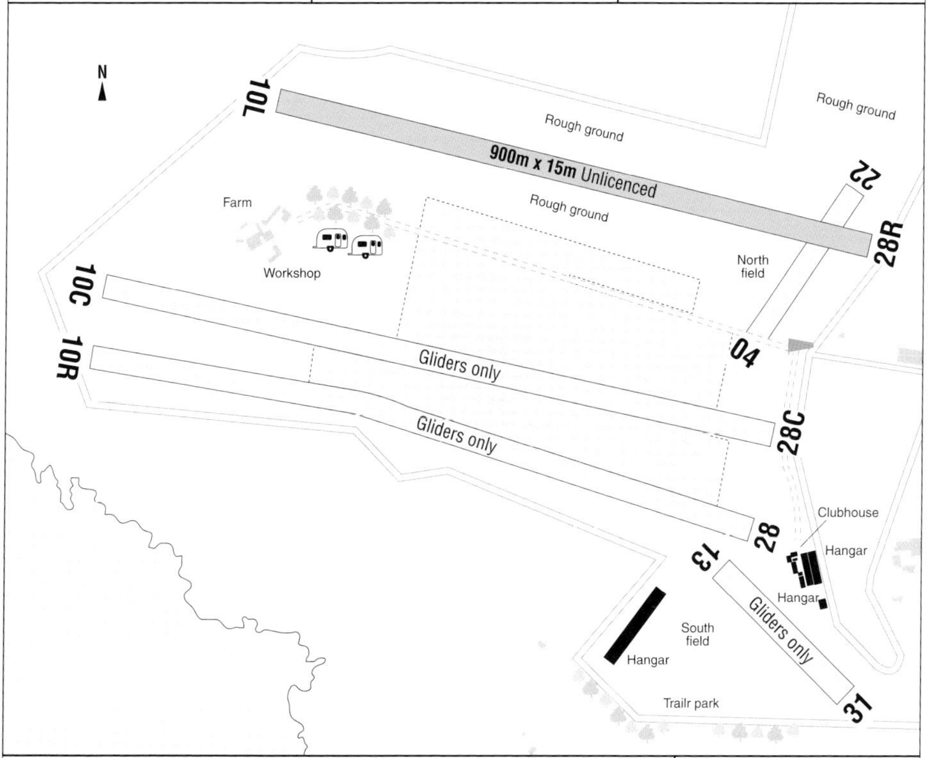

N
10L
900m x 15m Unlicenced
28R
Rough ground
Rough ground
Rough ground
22
04
North field
Farm
Workshop
10C
10R
Gliders only
Gliders only
28C
28
Clubhouse
Hangar
Hangar
13
31
Gliders only
South field
Hangar
Trailr park

RWY	SURFACE	TORA	LDA	U/L	LIGHTING
10L/28R	Grass			900x15	Nil

RNAV			
PTH	110.400	174	15

Remarks

Strictly PPR by telephone. Request circuit info with PPR. Primarily a gliding site with both winch launch and aerotow. AD active 7 days per week. Inbound ACFT must contact Leuchars and advise inbound to Portmoak. When 5nm from AD make blind calls on A/G.

Warnings

Pilot's of nosewheel ACFT should exercise extreme caution. Rough gnd on both edges of Rwy28R/10L. Although AD has a number of Rwys, it is essential that visiting ACFT use the aerotow strip Rwy28R/10L on N AD only.

Caution: Winch cables. Large bird concentrations may be encountered on AD at any time of the year. Keep a good lookout for gliders at any altitude.

Noise: Do not over fly the AD or the villages of Scotlandwell, Kinneswood or the Vane RSPB centre on the S side of Loch Leven.

Operating Hours	SR-SS daily
Circuits	Request briefing on the day with PPR No overhead joins
Landing Fee	Single £8 Microlight £4
Maintenance	Nil
Fuel	Nil
Restaurant	Café on AD
Taxi/Car Hire	Nil
Weather Info	Air SC GWC

Operator

Scottish Gliding Centre
Portmoak Airfield
Scotlandwell
Kinross
KY13 9JJ
Tel: 01592 840543 (Office)
Tel: 01592 840243 (Clubhouse)
Fax: 08707 626543
office@scottishglidingcentre.co.uk
www.scottishglidingcentre.co.uk

360ft 12mb	5nm NW of Kidderminster N5224.01 W00220.30	PPR	Alternative AD	**Birmingham** Wolverhampton **Non-standard join**

Pound Green Micro	ATIS	APP	LARS	A/G
	Birmingham 136.025	Birmingham 118.050	Shawbury 120.775	129.825

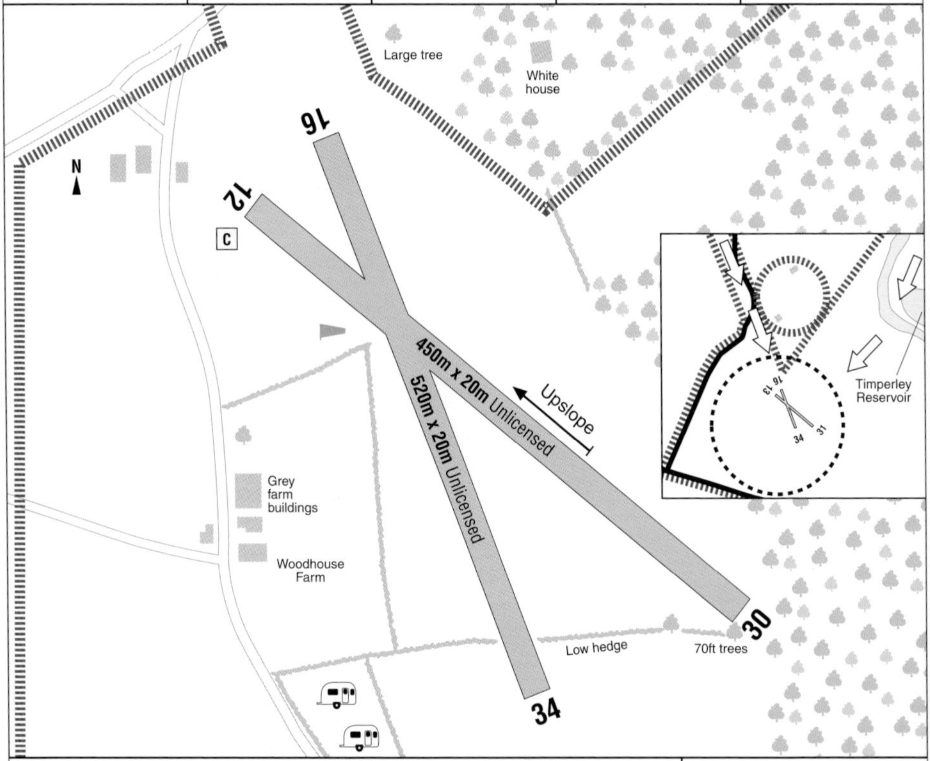

Large tree
White house
16
12
C
N
450m x 20m Unlicensed
520m x 20m Unlicensed
Upslope
Grey farm buildings
Woodhouse Farm
Low hedge
70ft trees
30
34
16 13
34 31
Timperley Reservoir

RWY	SURFACE	TORA	LDA	U/L	LIGHTING
12/30	Grass			450x20	Nil
16/34	Grass			520x20	Nil

RNAV			
HON	113.65	280	24.9

Remarks

PPR by telephone essential. Microlight ACFT only. Briefing given with PPR. AD located 1nm W of Trimpley Reservoir.

Warning

Sheep may be grazing. Power cables before Rwy16 Thr.

Noise: Avoid over flying local houses and keep circuit within farm boundary whenever possible. When APP Rwy16 fly straight in from 3km out. This is a narrow corridor, pilots must avoid white houses to E of APP. Inbound ACFT should follow E bank of River Severn to Trimpley Reservoir. Then fly directly to the field 1km to WSW. Plan circuit using Woodhouse Farm as a guide, (grey sheds are good guide). Keep circuit within farm boundary which is marked by triangle made by roads to S & W. Do not cross these roads.

Operating Hrs	Mon-Sat 0900-2030 Sun 0930-2030 (L)
Circuits	500ft QFE 34 RH from Trimpley Reservoir 16 2nm long final 12/30 use after inspection only
Landing Fee	Reciprocal
Maintenance	Nil
Fuel	Petrol available on request
Disabled Facilities	
Restaurants	Burton Oak Pub & New Inn 0.5mile away
Taxi/Car Hire	Nil
Weather Info	Air Cen MOEx
Operator	Mr E Gatehouse Pinewood Lodge Pound Green Arley Bewdley Worcs DY12 3LE **Tel/Fax:** 01299 401447

P

EGDO PREDANNACK

295ft 9mb	2nm SE of Million N5000.07 W00513.85	PPR MIL	Alternative AD St Mawgan Lands End Non-standard join

Predannack	LARS Culdrose 134.050	TWR 122.100

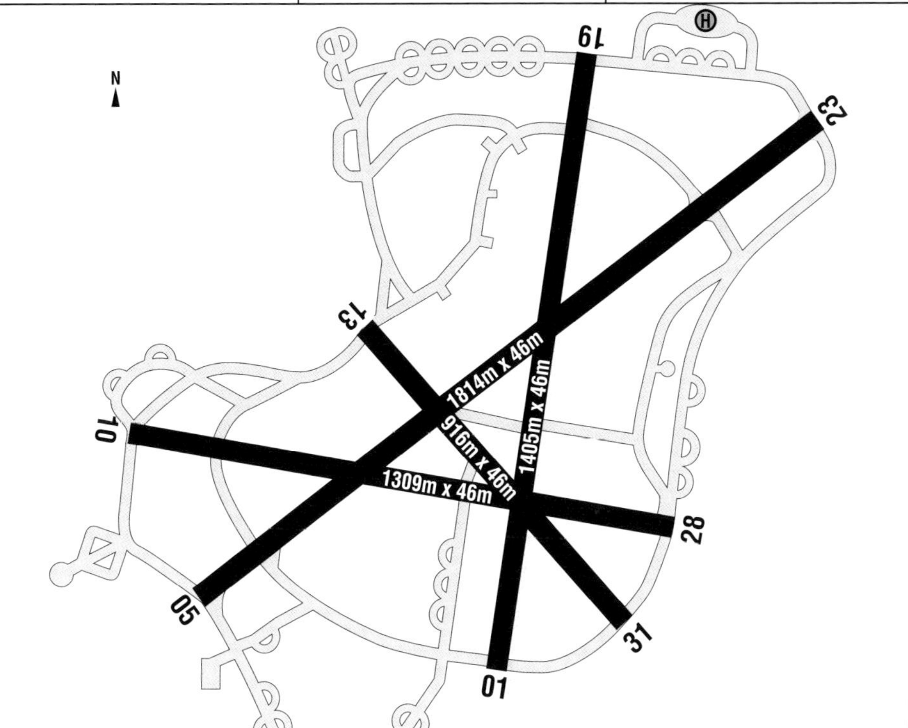

RWY	SURFACE	TORA	LDA	U/L	LIGHTING
05/23	Asphalt	1814	1814		Nil
01/19	Asphalt	1405	1405		Nil
10/28	Asphalt	1309	1309		Nil
13/31	Asphalt	916	916		Nil

Twy & Rwy01/19 10/28, 13/31 maintained to road standard

RNAV		
LND	122	17.5

Remarks

Strictly PPR only. Satellite airfield for RNAS Culdrose. ATZ H24. AD ops are only as required by Culdrose. Landings not authorised. Rwy05/23 designated as emergency fixed wing ACFT Rwy.

Warnings

Intensive military helicopter ops at AD and vicinity. Goonhilly Down HIRTA to NE of AD, intrudes into ATZ. Glider and Model ACFT activity outside normal op hrs as required by RNAS Culdrose. Rwys have non-standard markings associated with helicopter training. Vehicles my use perimeter track without warning. Winch launch gliding up to 2000ft SR-SS sat-Sun & PH

Noise: Avoid over flying all local habitation.

Operating Hrs	Mon-Fri as required by RNAS Culdrose
Circuits	As instructed
Landing Fee	Charges in accordance with MOD policy Contact Station Ops for details
Maintenance	Nil
Fuel	Nil
Disabled Facilities	Nil
Restaurants	Nil
Taxi/Car Hire	Nil
Weather Info	M T Fax 272 MOEx

Operator

Royal Navy
RNAS Culdrose
Helston
Cornwall, TR12 7RH
Tel: 01326 574121 Ex 2417 (Culdrose/PPR)
Tel: 01326 574121 Ex 2319 (AD)

EGPK PRESTWICK

65ft 2mb	1nm NE of Prestwick N5530.47 W00435.20	PPR	**Alternative AD** **Diversion AD**	**Glasgow** Cumbernauld **Non-standard join**

Prestwick	ATIS	APP	TWR
	121.125	120.550	118.150

RAD	FIRE	Handling
120.550	121.600	120.500 (Greer Aviation) 129.700 (Ocean Sky)

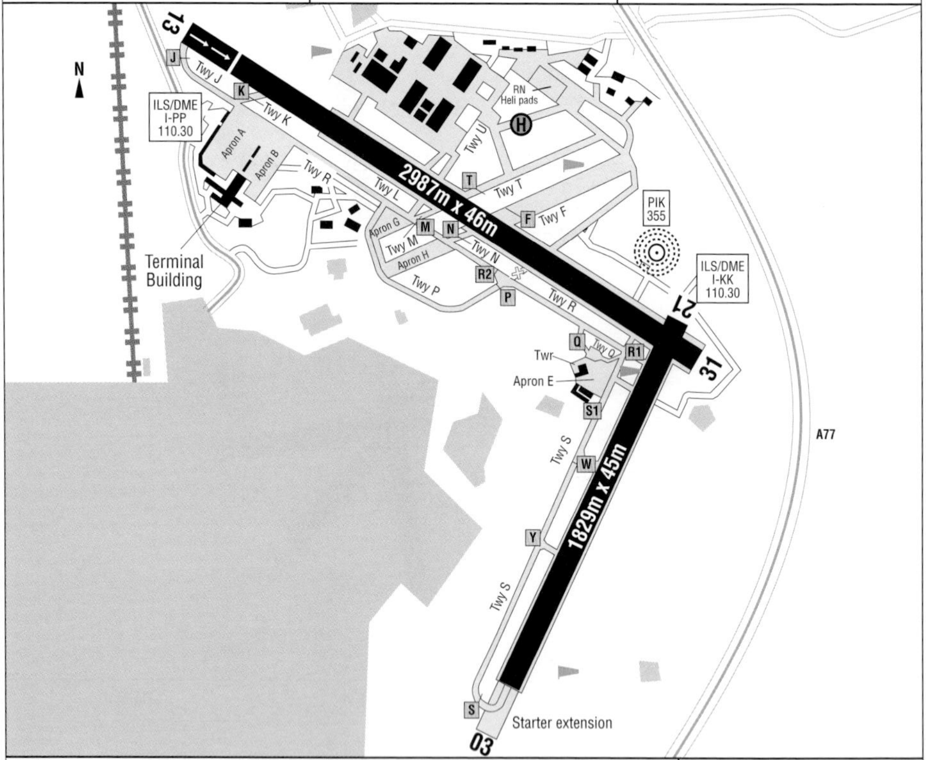

N
13
J
Twy J
K
Twy K
ILS/DME
I-PP
110.30
Apron A
Apron B
Twy R
Twy L
2987m x 46m
Terminal Building
RN Heli pads
Twy U
T
Twy T
F
Twy F
Apron G
M
N
Twy M
Apron H
Twy N
R2
Twy P
P
Twy R
PIK
355
ILS/DME
I-KK
110.30
21
Q
Twy Q
R1
31
Twr
Apron E
S1
Twy S
W
1829m x 45m
A77
Y
Twy S
S
Starter extension
03

RWY	SURFACE	TORA	LDA	U/L	LIGHTING
13	Conc/Asph	2987	2743		Ap Thr Rwy PAPI 3° LHS
31	Conc/Asph	2987	2987		Ap Thr Rwy PAPI 3.5° LHS
03	Asphalt	1829	1829		Thr Rwy PAPI 3° LHS
21	Asphalt	1829	1829		Ap Thr Rwy PAPI 3.5° LHS

Starter extension Rwy03 160m

RNAV			
TRN	117.50	036	13.5

P

Remarks

PPR via ATC. Handling mandatory. Training flights PPR from ATC. In VMC or when following a non-standard instrument Dept avoid flying over Troon. ACFT shall maintain as high an altitude as practicable. If APP without assistance from ILS or RAD fly not lower than the ILS glide path. Only marked Twys to be used. Helicopter operations: Civil helicopters normally allocated apron stand. Helicopters to route to apron by APP Rwy13/31 or Rwy03/21 as instructed. Helicopters may air/GND taxi between this area and military parking circles. Apron C only marked designated Twy routes to be used.

Aids to Navigation: NDB PW 426.00.

Warnings

If carrying out circuits on Rwy03/21 be warned of rising GND to the NE. Bird hazard assessed as 'moderate' and severe during migratory periods Oct/Nov and Mar/Apr. Except for light signals, GND signals are not displayed. Traffic flow management of inbound, outbound & local ACFT may be applied without notice. Twys N not to be used at night or in low vis.

Operating Hrs	H24	**Maintenance**	Available
Circuits	See Warnings	**Fuel**	AVGAS JET A1 100LL
Landing Fee	Light ACFT £35 min charge	**Disabled Facilities**	Available

 OP 07

Handling	**Tel:** 01292 678252 (Greer Aviation **Fax:** 01292 678222 (Greer Aviation) ops@greeraviation.com **Tel:** 01292 478961 (Ocean Sky) **Fax:** 01292 479616 (Ocean Sky) pikops@oceansky.com **Tel:** 01292 511260 (PIK Handling) **Fax:** 01292 511259 (PIK Handling) prestwick_handling@glasgowprestwick.com	**Operator**	Glasgow Prestwick Airport Ltd Aviation House Prestwick South Ayrshire Scotland KA92PL **Tel:** 01292 511000 (Switchboard) **Tel:** 01292 511107 (ATC) **Fax:** 01292 475464 (ATC) www.glasgowprestwick.com
Restaurants	Restaurant buffet & bar in terminal		
Taxis	Available at terminal or on request		
Car Hire			
Avis	**Tel:** 01292 77218		
Hertz	**Tel:** 01292 79822 Ex 3080		
Weather Info	M T9 T18 Fax 388 A VSc GWC		

Effective date:25/09/08

Prestwick Controlled Airspace

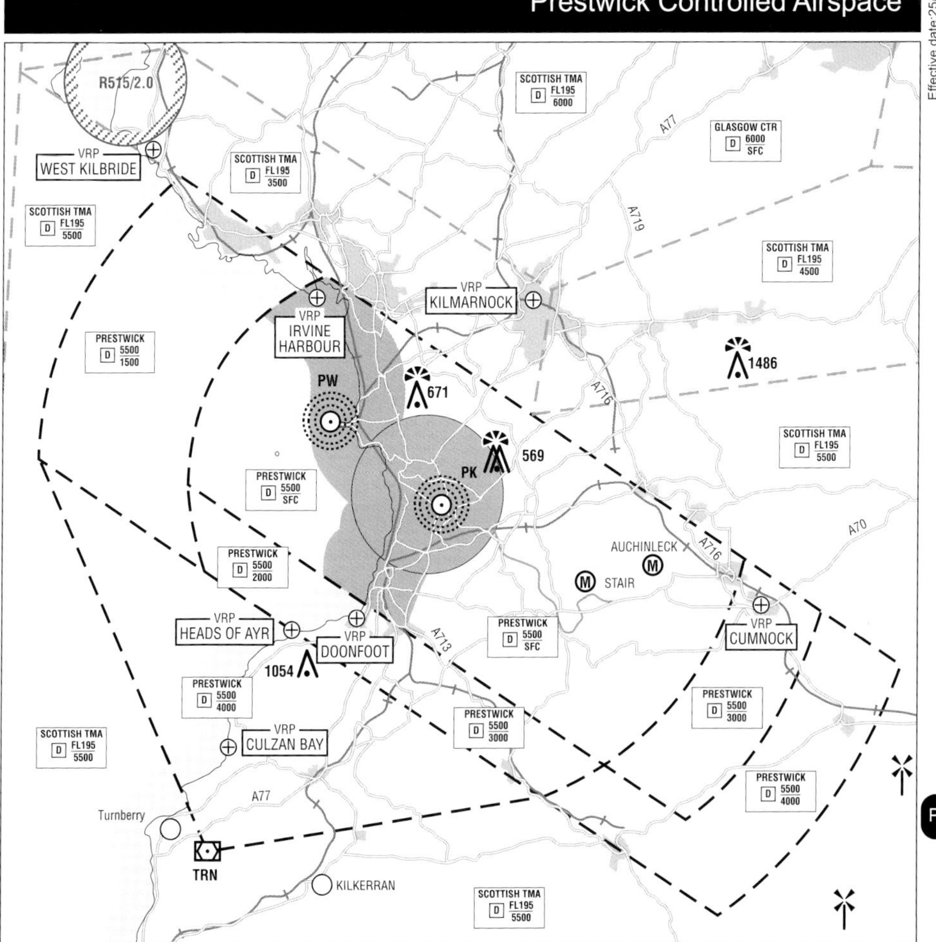

Prestwick CTZ and CTA Class D Airspace. Pilots must flight plan in/out by contacting ATC with brief details of flight.

Visual Reference Points (VRP)

Culzean Bay/Castle	N5522.17 W00446.08
Cumnock	N5527.33 W00415.45
Doonfoot	N5526.42 W00439.05
Heads of Ayr	N5525.97 W00442.78
Irvine Harbour	N5536.65 W00441.92
Kilmarnock	N5536.75 W00429.90
Pladda	N5525.58 W00507.07
West Kilbride	N5541.13 W00452.08

P

RAYDON WINGS

170ft 5mb	2.5nm SE of Hadleigh N5200.00 E00100.24	PPR	**Alternative AD** **Clacton** Elmsett

Non-standard join

Non-Radio	MATZ Wattisham 125.800	LARS Southend 130.775	Safetycom 134.475

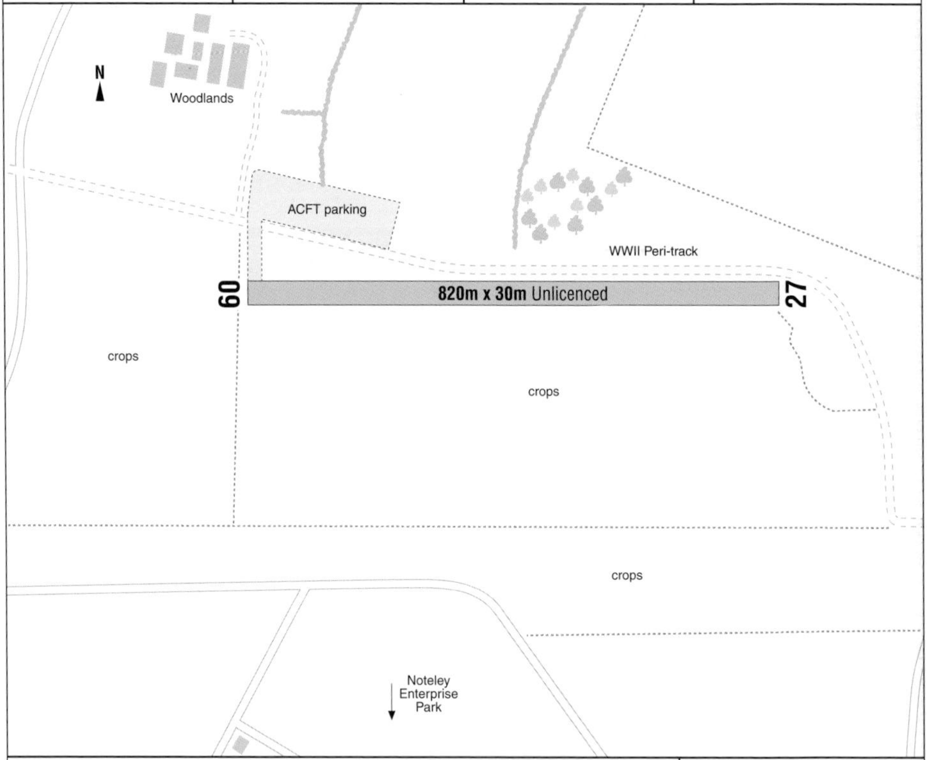

RWY	SURFACE	TORA	LDA	U/L	LIGHTING
09/27	Grass			820x30m	Nil

RNAV

CLN	114.55	336	11

Remarks
PPR by telephone. Visiting ACFT welcome at pilot's own risk. AD situated on NE corner of WW2 AD. Parts of WW2 hard surfaces not useable by ACFT. AD was base for the 357th & 358th FG (P47 & P51).

Warnings
Wattisham MATZ to N of AD. Powerlines running E-W 1nm N of AD.
Noise: Avoid over fling all neighbouring properties. Fly curved approach to Rwy27.

R

Operating Hrs	SR-SS
Circuits	09 RH 27 LH Join from the S 800ft QFE. (Fly curved approach)
Landing Fee	Nil
Maintenance	Nil
Fuel	Nil
Disabled Facilities	Nil
Restaurant	Nil
Taxi/Car Hire	Nil
Weather Info	Air Cen MOEx

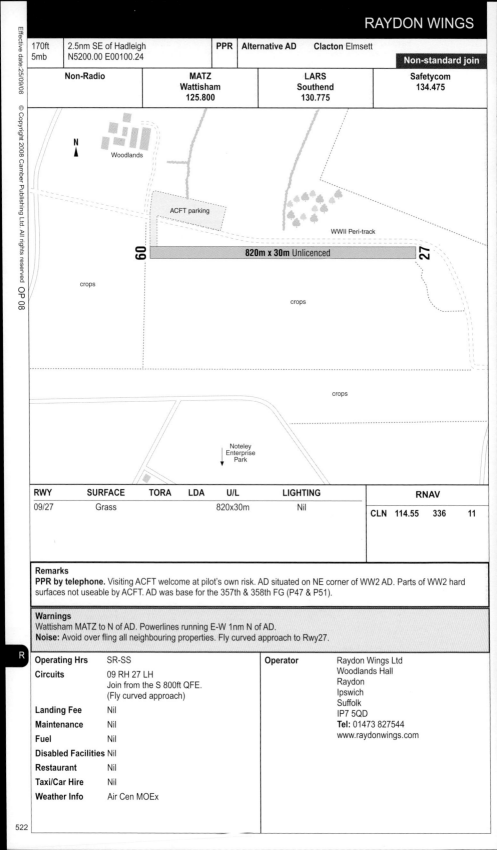

Operator
Raydon Wings Ltd
Woodlands Hall
Raydon
Ipswich
Suffolk
IP7 5QD
Tel: 01473 827544
www.raydonwings.com

225ft 7mb	1.3nm W of Braintree N5153.23 E00031.42	PPR	Alternative AD	**Southend** Andrewsfield

Rayne	ATIS Stansted 127.175	APP Essex RAD 120.625	A/G 125.050

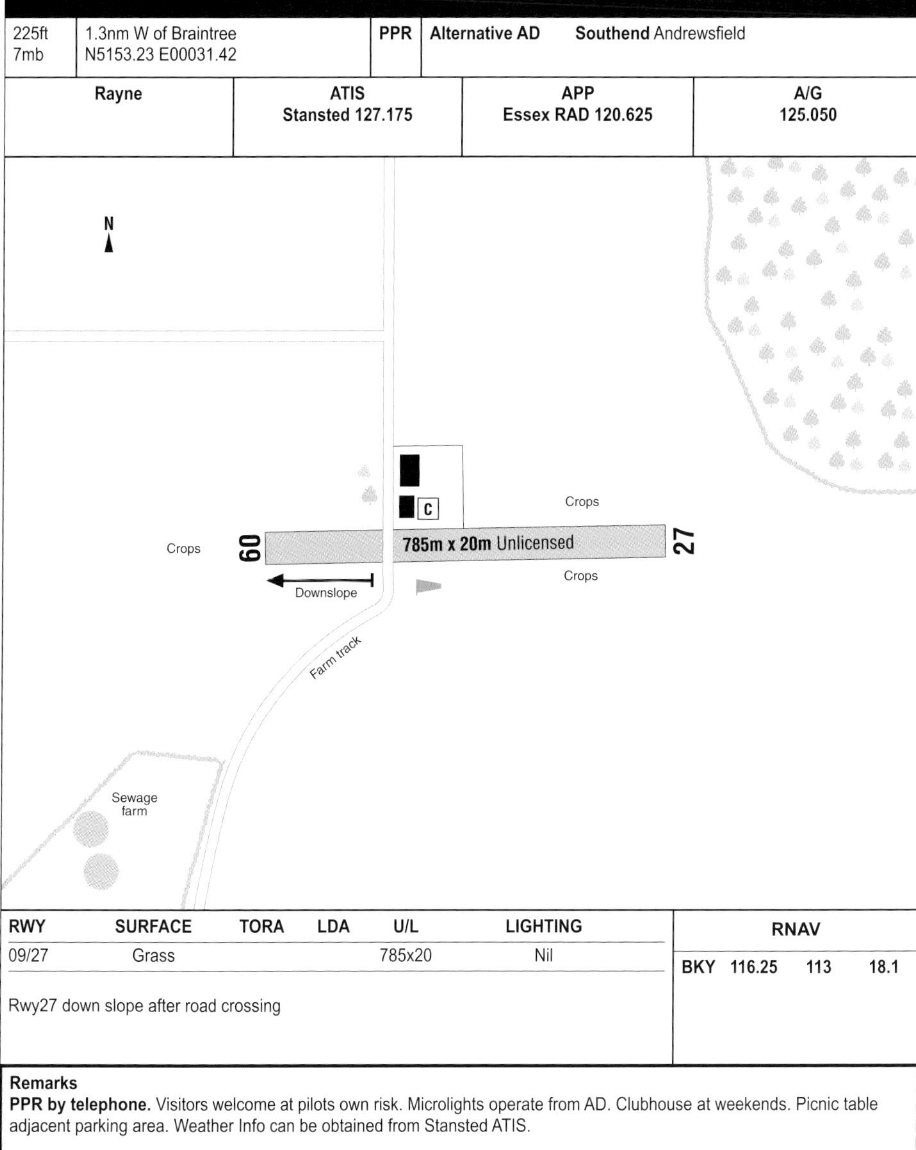

RWY	SURFACE	TORA	LDA	U/L	LIGHTING
09/27	Grass			785x20	Nil

Rwy27 down slope after road crossing

RNAV			
BKY	116.25	113	18.1

Remarks
PPR by telephone. Visitors welcome at pilots own risk. Microlights operate from AD. Clubhouse at weekends. Picnic table adjacent parking area. Weather Info can be obtained from Stansted ATIS.

Warnings
Situated under Stansted CTA (base 2000ft QNH). Andrewsfield ATZ boundary close to E of AD.
Caution: Crops grow up to edge of strip. Farm road crosses Rwy midpoint loose stones may be encountered when crossing the road.
Noise: Avoid over flying local habitation.

Operating Hrs Available on request
Circuits N 1000ft QFE
Landing Fee £5
Maintenance Nil
Fuel Nil
Disabled Facilities Nil
Restaurants Nil
Taxis
T&M Taxis **Tel:** 01376 347888
Car Hire Nil
Weather Info Air Cen MOEx

Operator Mr D S McGregor
Rayne Hall Farm, Braintree
Essex, CM77 6BT
Tel/Fax: 01376 321899 (Operator)
Tel: 07850 921961
megregordavidmac@tiscali.co.uk

Effective date:25/09/08 OP 08

222ft 7mb	1.5nm SE of Redhill N5112.82 W00008.32	PPR	Alternative AD Diversion AD	Biggin Hill Fairoaks

Redhill	LARS Farnborough East 123.225	ATIS 136.125	TWR 119.600

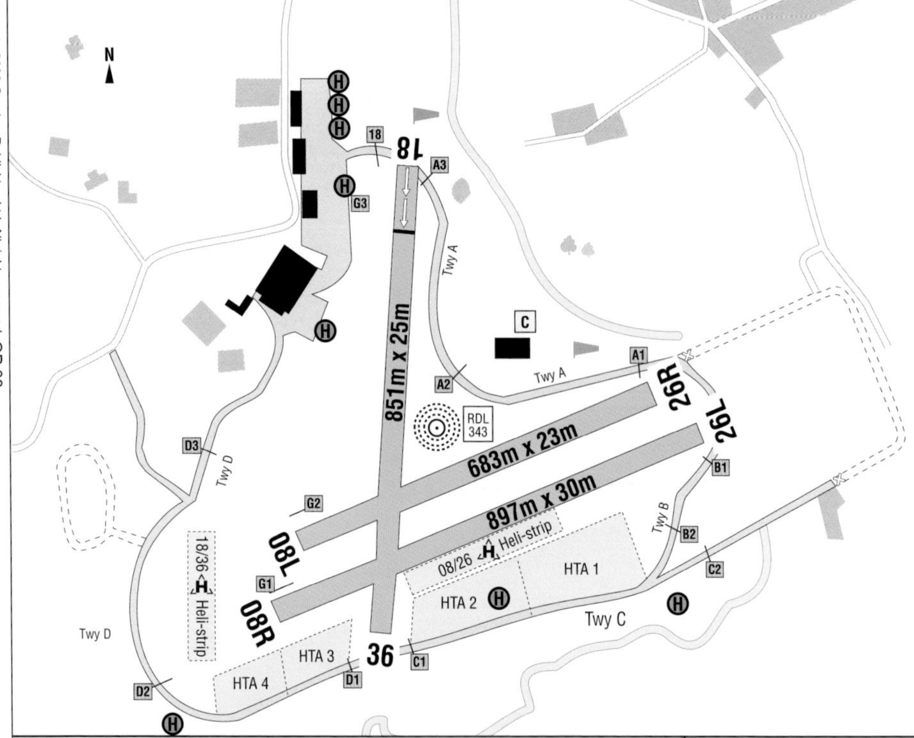

RWY	SURFACE	TORA	LDA	U/L	LIGHTING
36	Grass	851	851		Nil
18	Grass	851	699		Nil
08R	Grass	897	897		Thr Rwy APAPI 4.25° LHS
26L	Grass	897	897		Thr Rwy APAPI 3.5° LHS
08L/26R	Grass	683	683		Nil

Displaced Thr Rwy18 151m

RNAV			
BIG	115.10	226	9.6

Remarks

PPR by telephone. AD based Microlights only. Rwy08R/26L licensed for night use by all ACFT. Fixed wing ACFT ops restricted to marked Rwys and Twys N of Rwy08R/26L. Unmarked Twys not to be used without ATC permission. Training restricted to base Ops and approved helicopter ops. AD has a fixed lighted helipad.
Visual aid to location: Abn white flashing.

Warnings

AD subject to water logging. Surface slopes up 10ft from centre to W boundary. Intensive helicopter ops. Helicopters may not comply with standard R/T procedures. Care must be taken on APP and Dept not to drift into helicopter circuit area. Do not vacate any Rwy until instructed by ATC. Caution down wash from taxiing helicopters. When Rwy36/18 is in use it is not possible to provide separation between helicopters and fixed wing ACFT therefore significant delays will occur.

Operating Hrs 0800-1800 (Summer) 0700-0800 & 1800-1900 24 Hr PNR

Circuits Variable Fixed wing/Heli 1000ft QFE. See helicopter & fixed wing joining procedures. Helicopters will fly cct pattern opposite to fixed wing ACFT

Landing Fee Single £12
Twin <1500kg £16
<2000kg £22
<2500kg £30

Maintenance
Redhill Engineering **Tel:** 01737 822959

Fuel AVGAS JET A1 100LL

 OP 08

R

Disabled Facilities

Restaurant	Cafe in Redhill Aviation
Taxis	
Bellfry Cars	**Tel:** 01737 766111
Roadrunners	**Tel:** 01737 760076
Car Hire	See companies listed for London Gatwick
Weather Info	Air SE MOEx ATIS **Tel:** 01737 832947

Operator

Redhill Aerodrome Ltd
Terminal Building, Redhill Aerodrome
Surrey, RH1 5YP
Tel: 01737 821801 (Admin)
Tel: 01737 821805 (Fuel)
Tel: 01737 821802 (ATC)
atc@redhillaerodrome.com
www.redhillaerodrome.com

Visual Reporting Points (VRP)

Junction (Jct M23/M25)	N5115.83 W00007.68
Godstone (Jct A25/B2236)	N5114.83 W00004.02
Reigate Rlwy Station	N5114.52 W00012.25
Godstone Rlwy Station	N5113.08 W00003.07

Joining Procedures

ATC will require all VFR ACFT to enter and leave the ATZ via a VRP.

Fixed wing ACFT join at 1300ft QFE. If required to join overhead – enter the ATZ on Rwy QDM remaining within the fixed wing circuit area (N Rwy08/26 or E Rwy36/18). When instructed descend to circuit height and join the visual circuit pattern. Dept at 1500ft QNH.

Helicopters join at 1000ft QFE. When Rwy36/18 is in use helicopters joining from E may be instructed to route from Godstone Station to E AD boundary at500ft QFE. Dept at 1200ft QNH.

Noise:

Always use best rate of climb. Avoid over flying South Nutfield & East Surrey Hospital. Fixed wing – after Dept Rwy36/08/26 climb straight ahead to 1000ft QNH below turning. After Dept Rwy19 commence left turn at 500ft QNH. Avoid all built up areas within ATZ

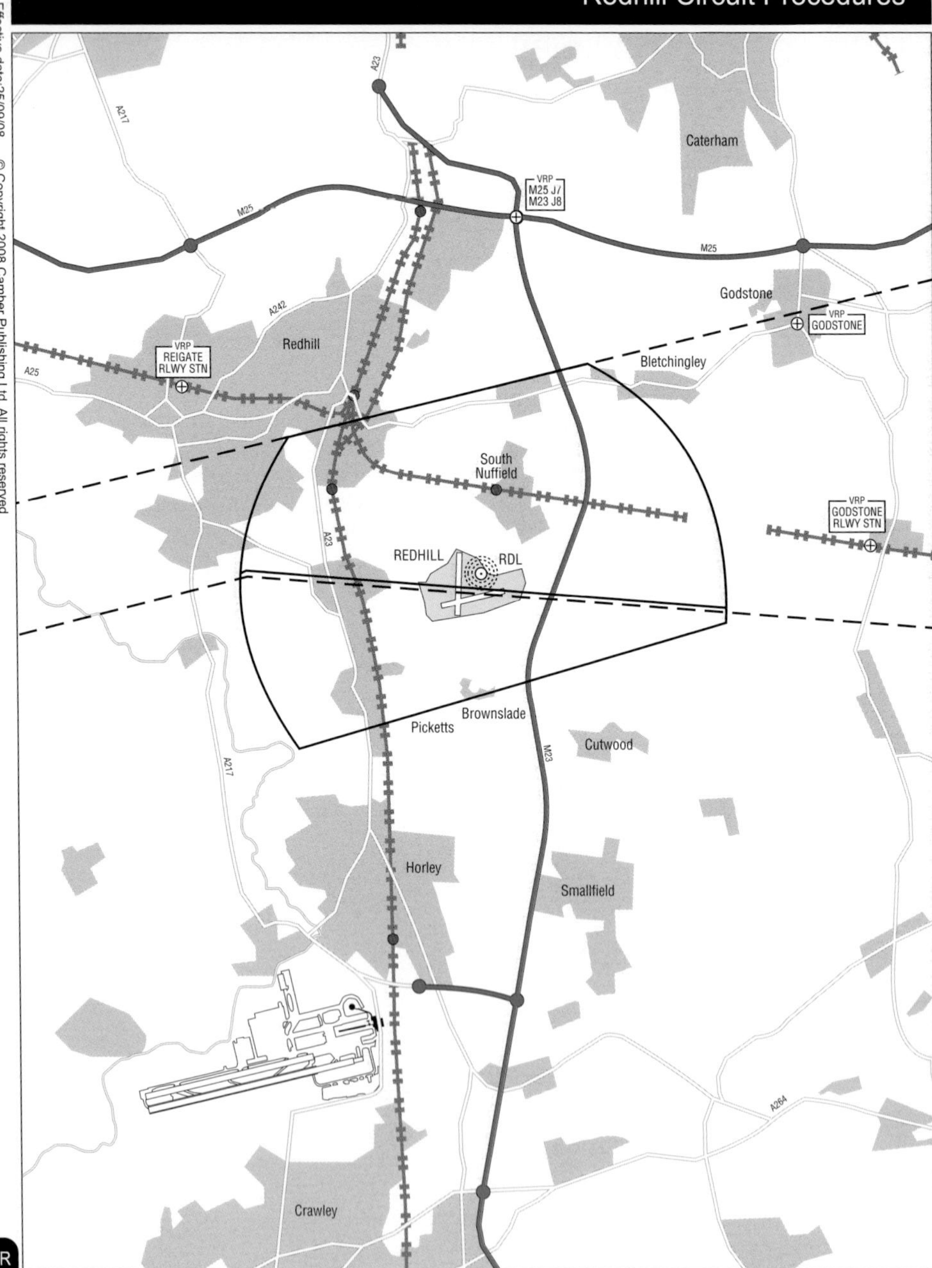

Redhill Circuit Diagram
Although the Redhill ATZ is within Gatwick CTR a local flying area has been established which permits ops within this area without reference to Gatwick ATC. Such flights may ONLY be made during the Hrs of watch of REDHILL ATC.

Area A

1 Clear of cloud & in sight of surface in minimum flight visibility (fixed wing ACFT) of 3km.

2 Fly not above 1500ftQNH.

Flight in circuit must not proceed beyond

W: A23 Redhill Horley road

E: Outwood Bletchingley road

S: Picketts & Brownslade farms

Area B

Fly NOT ABOVE 1500ft QNH

All ACFT must obtain clearance from Redhill ATC at least 5min before ETA. (This includes ACFT which have initially contacted Gatwick ATC)

Arr & Dept ACFT must do so N of Gatwick CTR.

Ensure you are familiar with joining/Dept procedures detailed in this section.

322ft 10mb	1nm E of Swindon N5133.65 W00142.27	PPR	Alternative AD	Oxford Kemble

Non-standard join

Redlands	Zone Lyneham 123.400	A/G 129.825

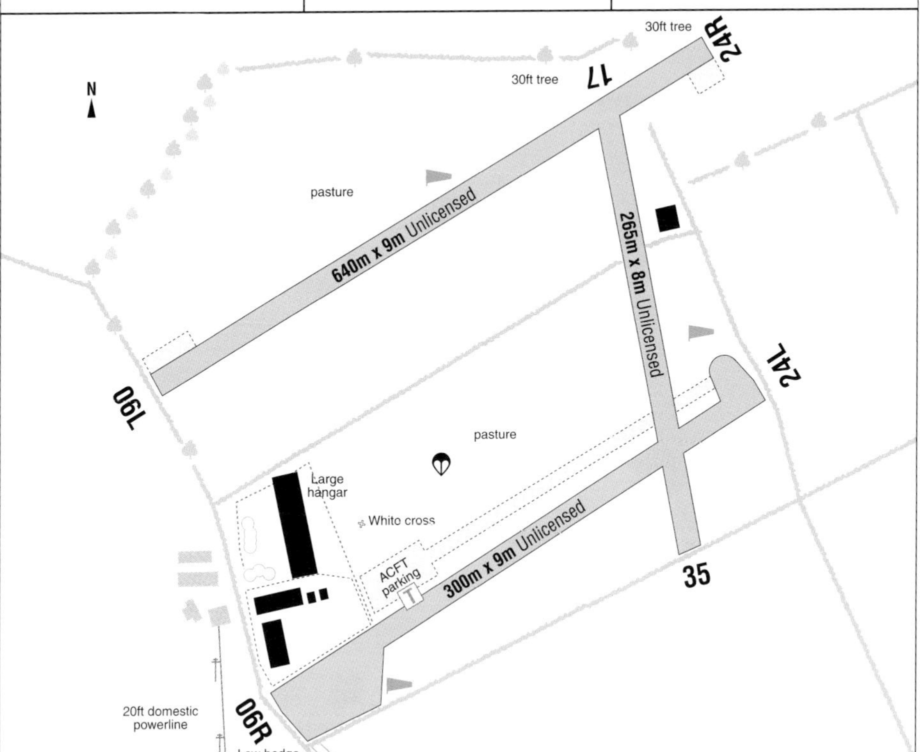

RWY	SURFACE	TORA	LDA	U/L	LIGHTING
06R/24L	Grass			300x9	Nil
17/35	Grass			265x8	Nil
06L/24R	Grass			640x9	Nil

RNAV			
CPT	114.35	287	18.6

Remarks

PPR by telephone essential. Microlight ACFT only accepted due to planning constraints. Visitors welcome at own risk. Beware parachute activity weekends & some weekdays. Redlands Radio give details of parachuting activity. See website for joining instructions and parachuting information. Observe signals square. Overnight camping available with toilets on site. **Visual aid to location:** 300ft hangar. Redlands painted on roof in yellow.

Warnings

AD is close to Lyneham CTR.
Noise: Arr/Dept via N corridor between the twin barns over AD and railway line. **Inbound ACFT:** Join downwind Rwy06&35, Right Base Rwy 24&17, avoiding over flying local habitation and Wanborough. **Outbound ACFT:** climb out N & turn over the barns to railway before setting course.

Operating Hrs	Mon-Sat SR-SS Sun 1000-2000 or SS (L)
Circuits	06, 35 LH, 24, 17 RH, 500ft aal
Landing Fee	£3.50
Maintenance	Nil
Fuel	MOGAS available by prior arrangement
Disabled Facilities	Nil
Restaurants	Help yourself Tea, Coffee & Biscuits Full catering facilities with Hot/cold snacks & lunches during weekends
Taxis/Car Hire	Can be arranged by operators

Weather Info	Air SW MOEx
Operator	Joe & Sarah Smith Redlands Airfield Redlands Farm Wanborough, Swindon Wilts, SN4 0AA **Tel:** 01793 791014 **Tel:** 07703 182756 sarah@redlandsairfield.co.uk www.redlandsairfield.co.uk

275ft 10mb	4.5nm SE of Oswestry N5250.50 W00255.83	PPR	**Alternative AD** **Hawarden** Sleap

Rednal	LARS Shawbury 120.775	Safetycom 135.475

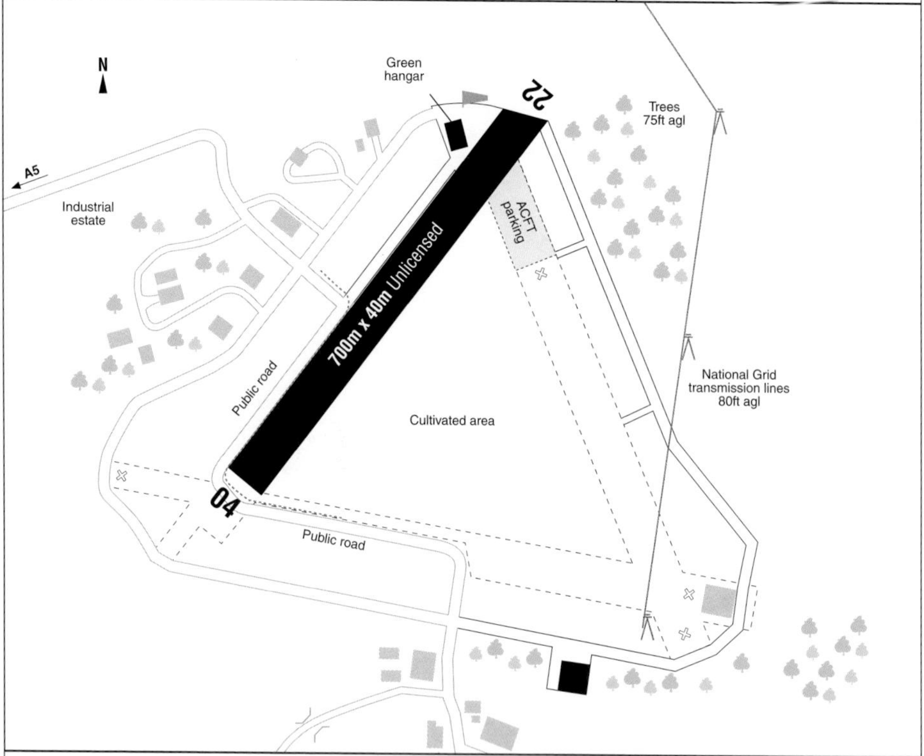

N
Green hangar
22
Trees 75ft agl
A5
Industrial estate
ACFT parking
700m x 40m Unlicensed
Public road
Cultivated area
National Grid transmission lines 80ft agl
04
Public road

RWY	SURFACE	TORA	LDA	U/L	LIGHTING
04/22	Asphalt			700x40	Nil

RNAV			
SWB	116.80	289	10.1

Remarks
PPR by telephone, fax or email. Established on W portion of WWII AD. All other Rwys are unavailable.

Warnings
National grid power lines & pylons cross APP Rwy22 80ft aal approx 0.5nm out. Public road crosses Rwy04 Thr & runs along W side for half Rwy length. 4ft wire fence divides the road from the active Rwy. A copse of mature trees, 25ft aal, encroach on the E side of Rwy22 final APP. Rwy surface gritty.
Noise: Avoid over flying all local habitation. No flying to W of AD.

R

Operating Hrs SR-SS

Circuits Join overhead 1500ft QFE
All circuits E 800ft QFE

Landing Fee Nil

Maintenance Nil
Fuel Nil

Disabled Facilities

Restaurants/Accomodation
Travelodge **Tel:** 01691 658178 (Oswestry 4m)
Queens Head1m good food (no accom)

Taxis
Berwin Cars **Tel:** 01691 652000
Car Hire Nil

Weather Info Air N MOEx

Operator Roger Reeves
Jupiter House
Tattenhall
Chester, CH3 9PX
Tel: 07747 618131 (AD)
Tel: 01829 771440 (Office)
Fax: 01829 771487
roger.reeves@goldford.co.uk

EGNE RETFORD

87ft 3mb	2nm S of Retford N5316.83 W00057.08	PPR	Alternative AD Diversion AD	Doncaster Sheffield Sandtoft

Gamston	APP Doncaster Sheffield 126.225	A/G 130.475

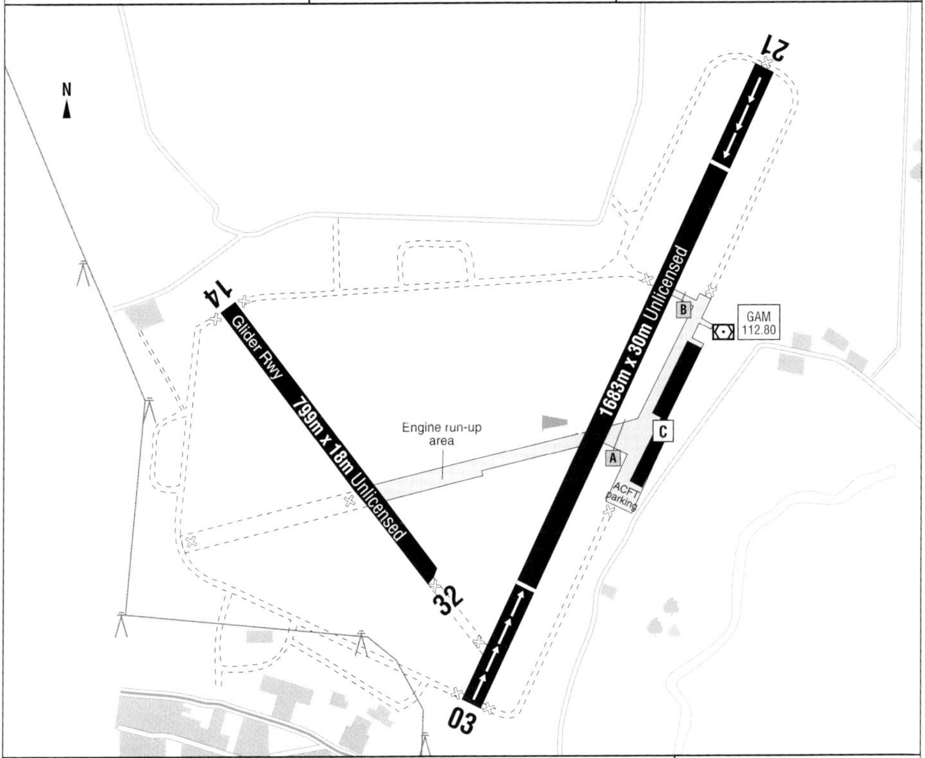

RWY	SURFACE	TORA	LDA	U/L	LIGHTING
03	Asphalt	1203	1203		Thr Rwy APAPI 3.5° LHS
21	Asphalt	1203	1203		Thr Rwy APAPI 3° LHS
14/32	Asphalt			799x18	Nil

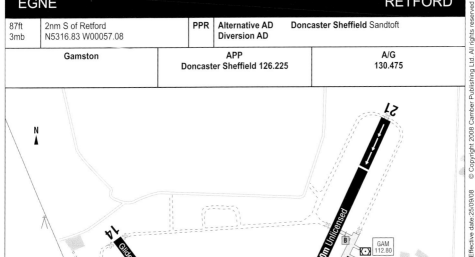

Starter extension Rwy03/21 240m, Starter extension Rwy14/32 50m

RNAV

GAM 112.80 On AD

Remarks

PPR by R/T acceptable. Non-radio ACFT accepted only with PPR. Pilots are to contact A/G 10 mins before ETA. Visiting ACFT asked to park on numbered stands marked by yellow boards on the Twy edges.

Warnings

Located inside Doncaster Sheffield CTR. Pilots taxiing for take-off on Rwy21 at night should not back track further than the red Rwy end lights. Rwy edge lights are positioned at edge of hard surface at a width of 46m. Rwy03/21 is side striped at 30m. Rwy14/32 available on request to powered ACFT. Access to and from Rwy03/21 is via points A and B only.

Operating Hrs Mon-Fri 0800-1800
Sat-Sun & PH 0900-1800 (L)

Circuits 1000ft QFE

Landing Fee Single £12
Heli £9.40 per half tonne
Twin £8.23 per half tonne

Maintenance
Diamond Aircraft **Tel:** 01777 839200
Kinch Aviation **Tel:** 01777 839159 (Jets & King Air)

Fuel AVGAS JET A1. All major credit cards accepted except Diners

Disabled Facilities

Restaurants Refreshments available at AD
Local pubs within 1.5 miles

Taxis
DJ Taxi **Tel:** 01777 701066
Hinchcliffe **Tel:** 01777 702049

Car Hire On request

Weather Info Air Cen MOEx

Operator Gamston Aviation Ltd
Retford/Gamston Airport
Retford, Nottingham, DN22 0QL
Tel: 01777 838593 (Ops/ATC)
Tel: 01777 838521 (Outside Ops Hrs)
Fax: 01777 838035
ops@retfordairport.co.uk
www.retfordairport.co.uk

Effective date:25/09/08 OP 08

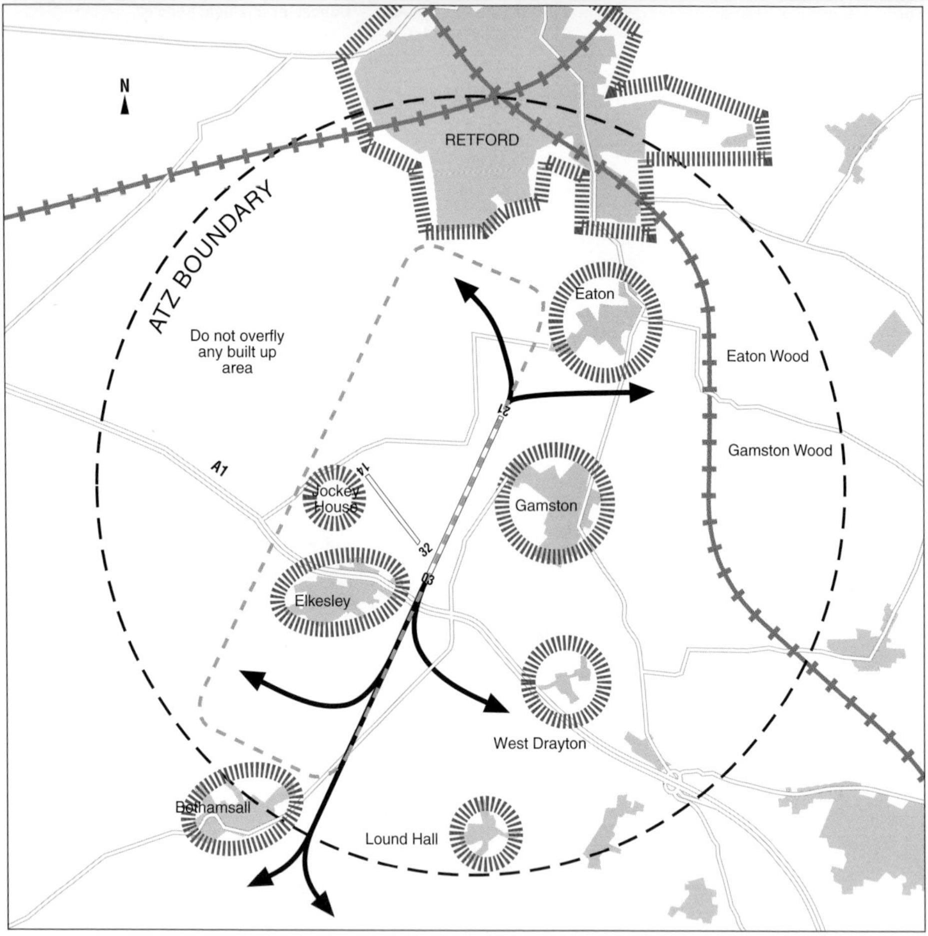

Noise Procedures

1 Do not over fly Bothamsall, Eaton, Elkesley, Gamston, Lound Hall or West Drayton.
2 Whenever possible, backtrack to use all available Rwy for take-off.
3 After take-off Rwy21 turn onto the crosswind leg to avoid over flying Elkesley or West Drayton.
4 Reduce power slowly.
5 Keep circuit flying to a minimum, especially at weekends.
6 Low approaches to land should be avoided.

Circuit Procedures

Rwy21 RH: Climb out – maintain Rwy heading and track to 1.2nm on GAM VOR. Turn crosswind heading 290°. Turn downwind heading 030°. Turn base leg heading 110°. Turn onto final APP heading 210°.

Rwy03 LH: Climb out and make early left turn onto crosswind heading 290°. Turn downwind heading 210°. Turn base leg heading 110°. Turn onto final APP heading 030°.

Arrivals: Join the circuit NOT BELOW 100ft QFE.

Departures: Use the circuit – leave the circuit NOT BELOW 1000ft QFE. Intersection departures are not permitted. The full length of the Rwy must be used on take off.

VRPs	**VOR/DME**
Thorsby Lake N5313.63 W00103.33	GAM 277°/5nm
Daneshill Lakes N5321.62 W00056.12	GAM 002°/5nm
Gainsborough N5323.57 W00046.25	GAM 046°/9nm
A1/A56 Cliumber Interchange N5317.78 W00101.93	GAM 289°/3nm

RHEDYN COCH

650ft 21mb	3nm SE of Prestatyn N5316.58 W00322.07	PPR	Alternative AD **Hawarden** Caernarfon

Rhedyn Coch	A/G 129.825 (Microlight freq)	A/G Bryngwyn 118.325 Make blind calls

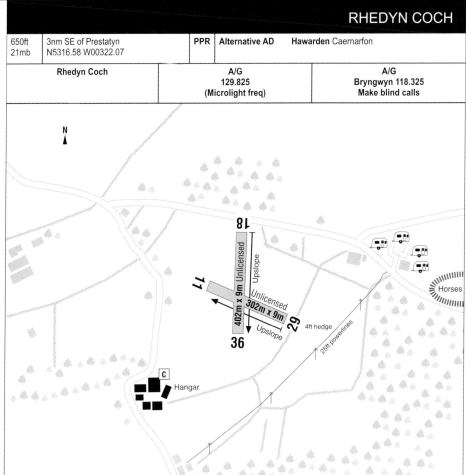

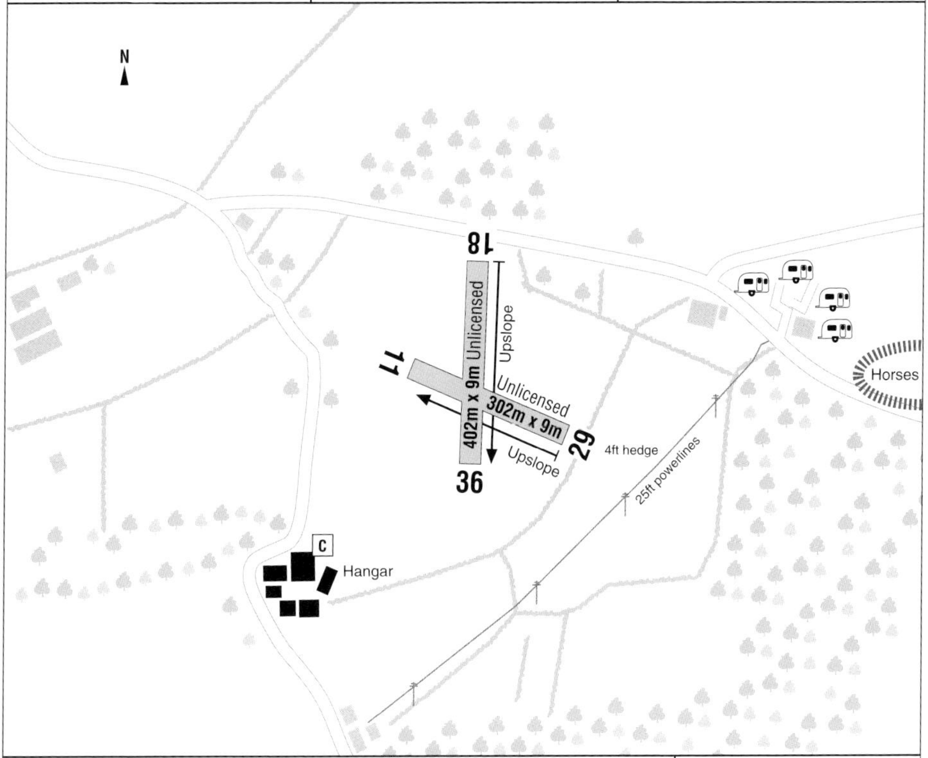

N
18
Unlicensed
402m x 9m
Upslope
11
Unlicensed
302m x 9m
29
Upslope
36
4ft hedge
25ft powerlines
Horses
C
Hangar

RWY	SURFACE	TORA	LDA	U/L	LIGHTING
18/36	Grass			402x9	Nil
11/29	Grass			302x9	Nil

Rwy have no markings, ID by witness marks on large field

RNAV			
WAL	114.10	236	10.9

Remarks

PPR by telephone. Visiting STOL ACFT and microlights welcome at pilots own risk. Rwys are large part of field which allows run off to either side.

Warnings

Difficult AD to locate, particularly during the winter when there is little aviation use. High GND up to 998ft amsl 0.25nm W of AD. Wood plantations close to AD, particularly on Rwy18 APP which may cause turbulence. There are up slopes on Rwy29 & 18.
Noise: Do not over fly local habitation.

Operating Hrs SR-SS

Circuits Join overhead 1500ft QFE
Descend quietly to 600ft QFE
36, 18, 11 LH, 29 RH

Landing Fee Nil

Maintenance Nil

Fuel MOGAS available in cans on request

Disabled Facilities

Restaurant Nil

Taxi/Car Hire By arrangement

Weather Info Air Cen MOEx

Operator
Mr Richard Emlyn Jones
Rhedyn Coch
Rhault, St Asaph, Denbighshire
Tel: 01745 584051 (Home)
Tel: 07880 733274

Effective date:25/09/08 OP 08

EGTO ROCHESTER

426ft 15mb	1.5nm S of Rochester N5121.12 E00030.17	PPR	Alternative AD Diversion AD	**Southend** Lashenden

Rochester	LARS Farnborough East 123.225	AFIS 122.250

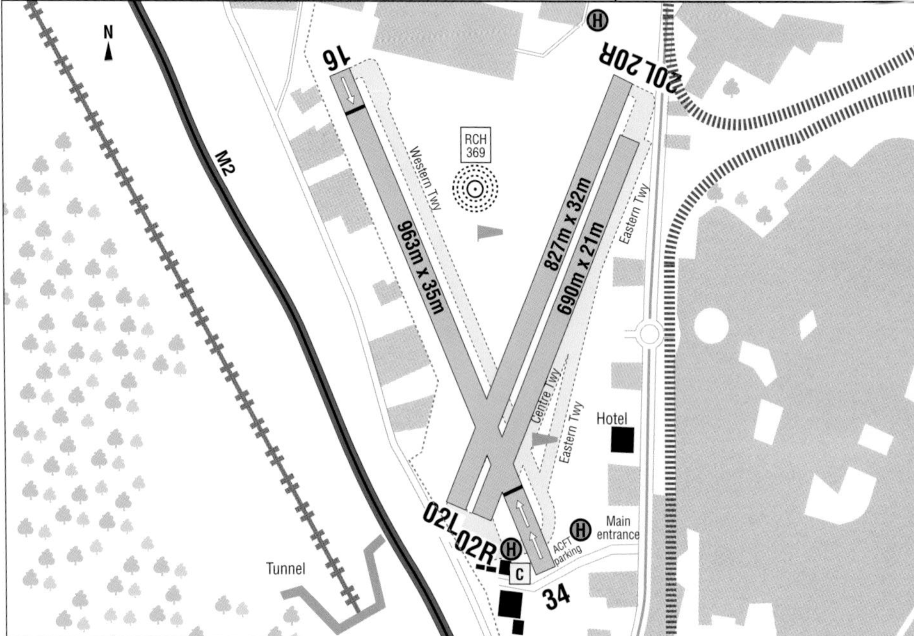

RWY	SURFACE	TORA	LDA	U/L	LIGHTING
02L	Grass	827	827		Thr Rwy APAPI 4° LHS
20R	Grass	827	827		Ap Thr Rwy APAPI 3.5° LHS
02R/20L	Grass	690	690		Nil
16	Grass	773	808		Nil
34	Grass	963	773		Nil

Rwy02R additional 35m available

RNAV			
DET	117.30	312	4.6

Remarks

PPR by telephone. Relief Rwy02R/20L has been established parallel to Rwy02/20 used when main Rwy under maintenance. Rwys & Twys may be restricted/withdrawn short notice due surface conditions. Pilots obtain latest info before Arr. Taxi prepared & marked areas only. AD based ACFT may use AD after Hrs in daylight. Police and Air Ambulance helicopters H24 operations.

Visual aid to location: Abn White flashing. AD name displayed.

Warnings

Road used by vehicular traffic runs E/W immediately S of take-off Rwy34 Thr. Rwy16 has non-standard markings. Designator located before landing Thr. Visual glide slope signals for Rwy20R are visible to E of extended Rwy centre line where normal obstacle clearance is not guaranteed. They should not be used until the ACFT is aligned with the extended Rwy centre line.

Caution: ACFT should taxi with caution due to uneven surfaces.

Noise: Circuits variable to avoid flying over built up noise sensitive areas.

R

Operating Hrs 0800-1800 (L)
ATZ may be active at other times

Circuits Fixed wing 1000 QFE
Heli 800ft QFE. 16, 20 RH, 02, 34 LH

Landing Fee Single £10, Twin £15

Maintenance RAS Ltd **Tel:** 01634 200008

Fuel AVGAS JET A1 100LL

Disabled Facilities

Restaurants Holiday Inn Hotel/Restaurant
Several pubs nearby
Airport Cafe

Taxis

Medway **Tel:** 01634 848848

Volkes **Tel:** 01634 222222/843601

Car Hire

Kenning **Tel:** 01634 845145

Weather Info Air SE MOEx

Operator Rochester Airport Plc
Rochester Airport, Chatham
Kent, ME5 9SD
Tel: 01634 861378 (ATC)
Tel: 01634 869969 (Admin)
Fax: 01634 861682 (ATC)
Fax: 01634 869968 (Admin)

RODDIGE

171ft 6mb	3nm NE of Lichfield N5242.80 W00144.63	PPR	**Alternative AD**	**Birmingham** Tatenhill

Roddige	**APP** **Birmingham 118.050**	**APP** **East Mids 134.175**	**A/G** **129.825**

RWY	SURFACE	TORA	LDA	U/L	LIGHTING
02/20	Grass			390x18	Nil
09/27	Grass			480x25	Nil

RNAV			
TNT	**115.70**	**192**	**20.4**

Remarks
PPR by telephone. Primarily a microlight training AD but light ACFT and pilots with STOL capability welcome at own risk.

Warnings
4ft hedge crosses Rwy27 Thr & 6.5ft embankment screening gravel workings on the opposite side of road from Thr.
Caution: Do not confuse Roddige with Sittles Farm strip to SW on opposite side of hedge.
Noise: Avoid over flying all local habitation.

Operating Hrs 0900-dusk (L)
Circuits 27 20 LH, 09 02 RH 500ft QFE
Join overhead 1500ft QFE
Landing Fee Nil
Maintenance Microlight only
Fuel MOGAS
Hangarage Microlight only
Disabled Facilities

Restaurants Tea & coffee available
Taxis **Tel:** 01543 254999
Car Hire **Tel:** 01543 254825

Weather Info Air Cen MOEx
Operator Mr Shea
The Microlight School
Roddige Lane
Fradley
Lichfield
Staffs WS13 8QS
Tel: 01283 792193
Tel: 07767 474847
www.microlightschool.org.uk

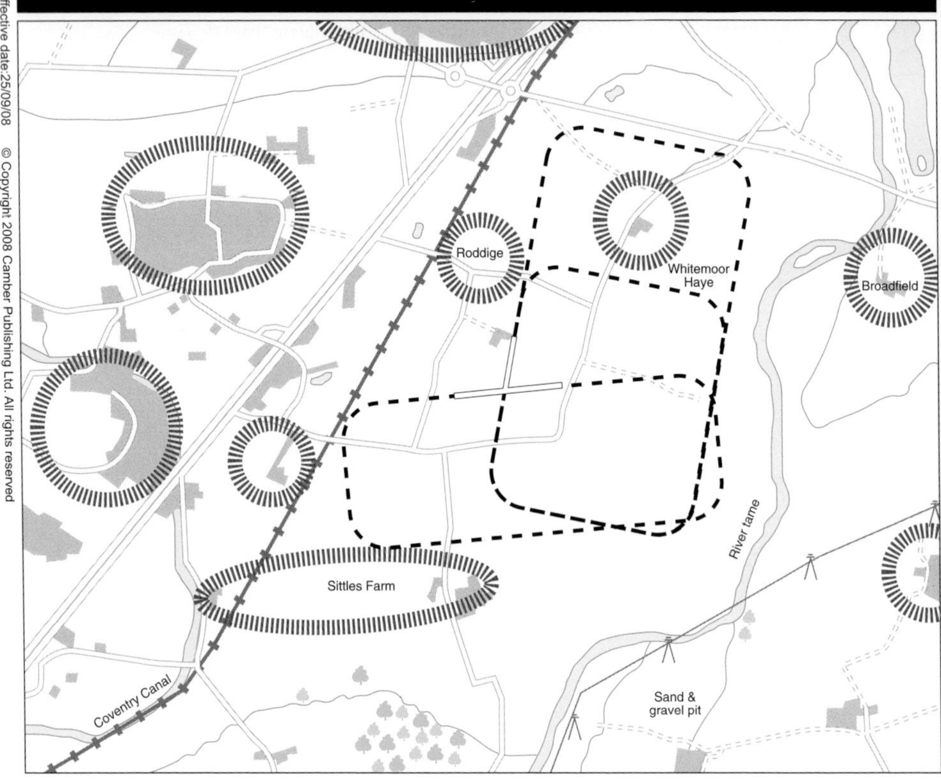
Roddige
Whitemoor
Haye
Broadfield
River tame
Sittles Farm
Coventry Canal
Sand &
gravel pit

130ft 4mb	1nm SE of Polzeath N5033.72 W00454.02	**PPR**	**Alternative AD** **St Mawgan** Lands End

Non-Radio	**LARS** **St Mawgan 128.725**	**Safetycom** **135.475**

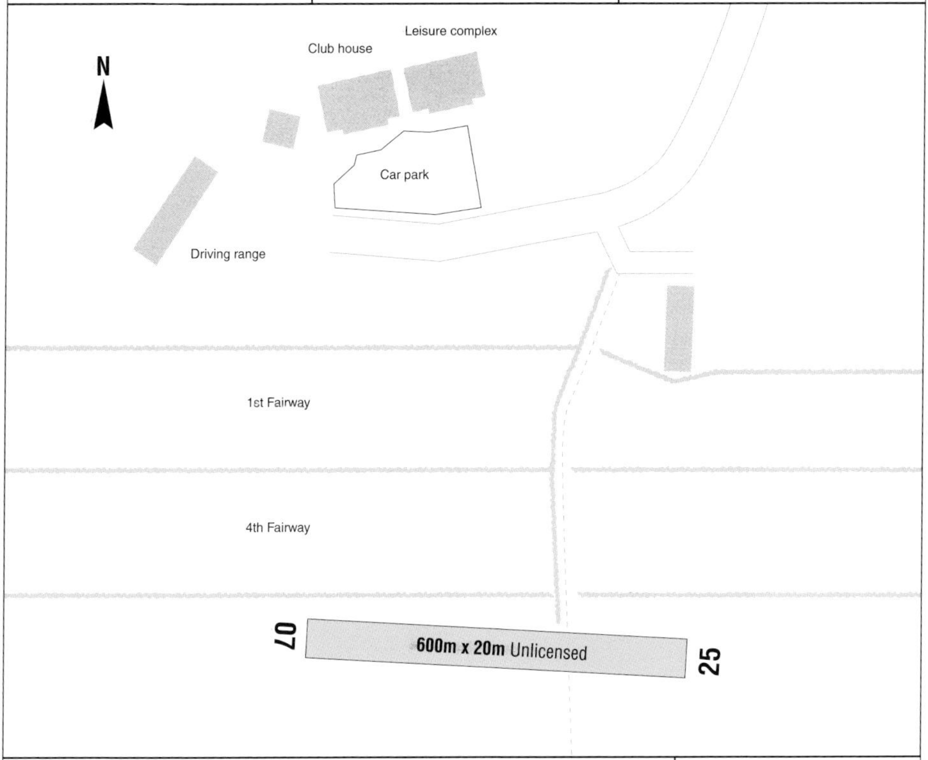

Leisure complex

Club house

N

Car park

Driving range

1st Fairway

4th Fairway

07

600m x 20m Unlicensed

25

RWY	SURFACE	TORA	LDA	U/L	LIGHTING
07/25	Grass			600x20	Nil

RNAV

Remarks

PPR by telephone is essential. Visiting ACFT are welcome at own risk. AD part of large golf course sports complex. Marked H for helicopter visitors. Overnight parking for fixed and rotary winged visitors is available by arr.

Warnings

AD is close to NW boundary of St Mawgan MATZ. Visiting ACFT are advised to contact St Mawgan APP. Para dropping at St Merryn AD, 3nm WSW of Roserrow, St Mawgan can advise on activity.

Operating Hrs SR-SS

Circuits Overhead join then Circuit LH 1000ft QFE

Landing Fee £12 Overnight parking £5

Maintenance Nil

Fuel Nil

Disabled Facilities Nil

Restaurants/Accomodation
Restaurant available in Golf Club & Complex. Accomodation available on site

Taxis/Car Hire Nil

Weather Info Air SW MOEx

Operator Roserrow Golf & Country Club
Roserrow, St.Minver, Wadebridge
Cornwall, PL27 6QT
Tel: 01208 863000
Fax: 01208 863002
www.roserrow.co.uk

Effective date:25/09/08

15ft 0mb	7nm SSW of Lancaster N5356.30 W00250.50	PPR	Alternative AD	Blackpool Manchester Barton Non-standard join

Rossall	ATIS Blackpool 127.200	LARS Warton 129.525	APP Blackpool 119.950	A/G 129.825 (microlight freq) make blind calls

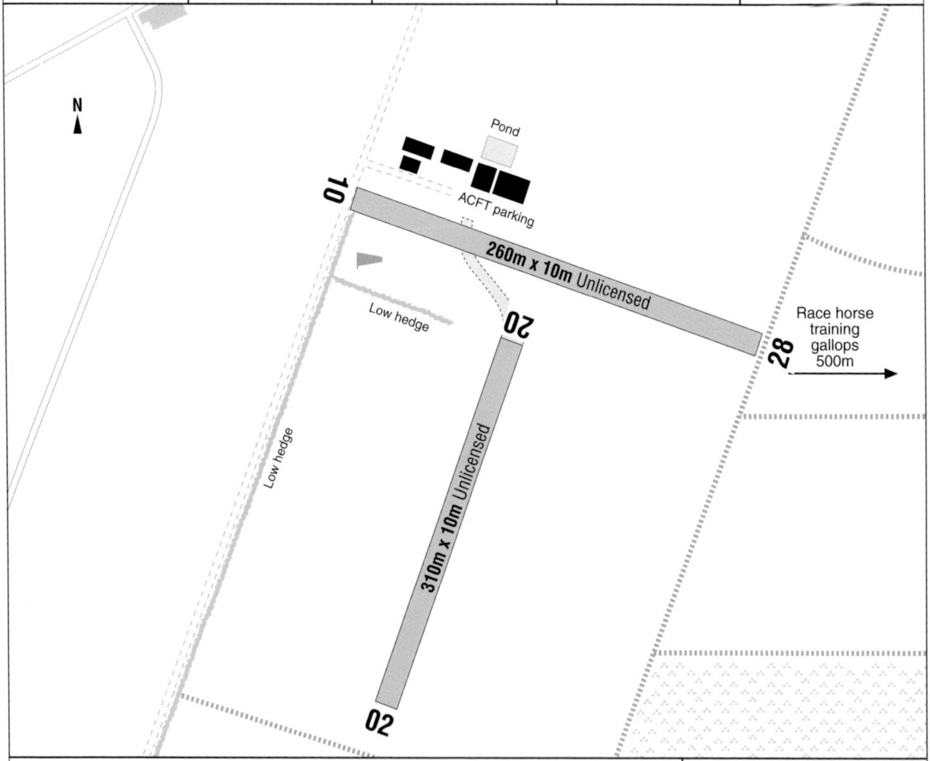

RWY	SURFACE	TORA	LDA	U/L	LIGHTING
02/20	Grass			310x10	Nil
10/28	Grass			260x10	Nil

RNAV			
POL	112.10	297	28.6

Remarks
PPR by telephone. Visiting suitable STOL ACFT welcome at pilot's own risk. Primarily Microlight AD. Be considerate of ab-initio pilots in circuit. Rwy Thr marked with brown designators burned into grass surface.

Warnings
Sheep graze AD when microlights not active. Parachuting takes place at Cockerham 1.5nm NE of AD mainly at weekends. Do not transit this area without ascertaining whether parachutist are active. (Warton or Blackpool can advise).
Noise: Avoid over flying all local habitation W of AD

R

Operating Hrs Mon-Sat 0800-2100 or SS
Sun/PH 1000-2100 or SS (L)

Circuits 02, 10 RH, 20, 28 LH, 500ft QFE
Join overhead at 1000ft QFE
descend dead side

Landing Fee £3

Maintenance Keith Worthington
Tel: 01257453430

Fuel MOGAS available on request

Disabled Facilities

Restaurants The Manor Cockerham

Taxis/Car Hire Nil

Weather Info Air N MOEx

Operator The Bay Flying Club at Cockerham
CFI Ian Lonsdale
28 Sterling Court
Burnley, BB10 3QT
Tel: 01282 436280
Tel: 07946 547342
Tel: 01253 790522
(Tarn Farm Club House)

400ft 13mb	2nm W of Kettering N5224.70 W00047.40	PPR	**Alternative AD** **Cranfield** Northampton **Non-standard join**

Rothwell	LARS Cottesmore 130.200	A/G 129.900 (Glider freq) make blind calls

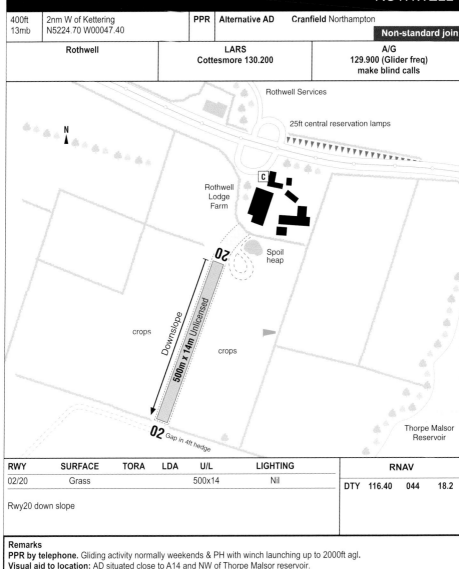

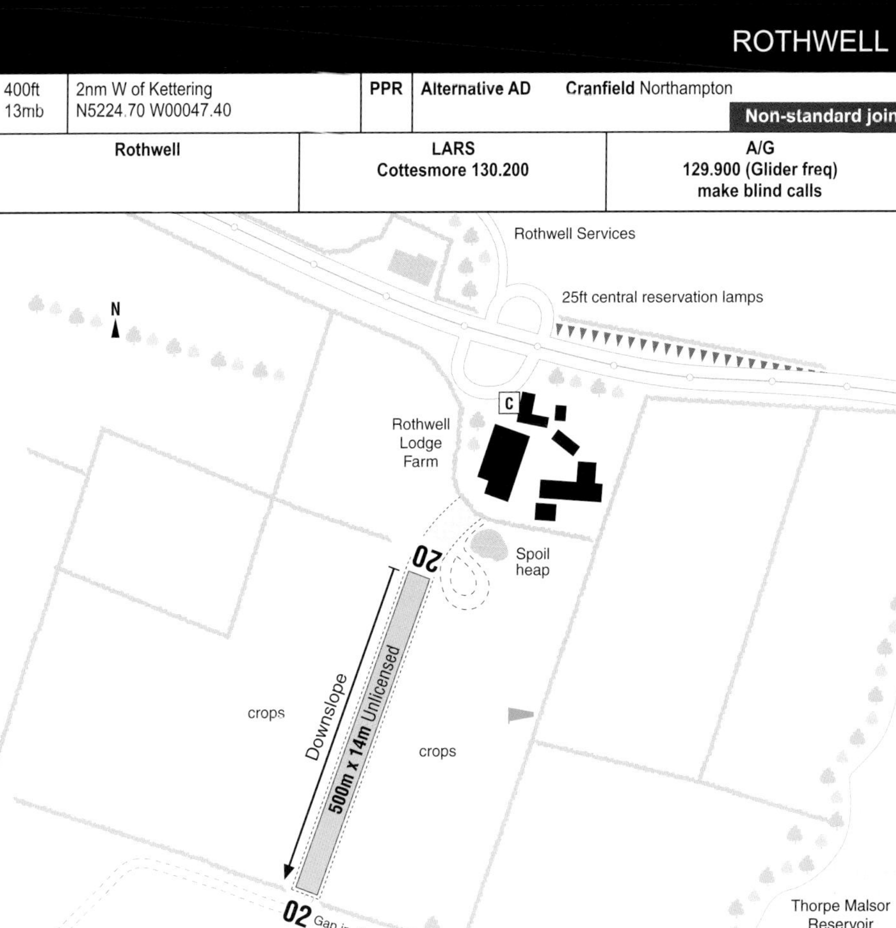

RWY	SURFACE	TORA	LDA	U/L	LIGHTING
02/20	Grass			500x14	Nil

Rwy20 down slope

RNAV			
DTY	116.40	044	18.2

Remarks
PPR by telephone. Gliding activity normally weekends & PH with winch launching up to 2000ft agl.
Visual aid to location: AD situated close to A14 and NW of Thorpe Malsor reservoir.

Warnings
25ft lamp standards on central reservation of A14 on short final Rwy20. Farm vehicles use Rwy for access to neighbouring fields. Low flying military ACFT may be encountered during weekdays. Crops are grown close to both Rwy edges. When gliders are operating exercise extreme caution and NO over head joins.
Noise: Avoid over flying Rothwell (NW) & Loddington (SW) villages.

Operating Hrs	SR-SS
Circuits	LH 1000ft QFE
Landing Fee	Nil
Maintenance	Nil
Fuel	Nil
Disabled Facilities	Nil
Restaurants	Nil
Taxis/Car Hire	Nil
Weather Info	Air Cen MOEx

Operator Mr G A Pentelow
Orton Lodge, Orton Lane
Loddington, Kettering
Northants, NN14 1LQ
Tel: 01536 711750

Effective date:25/09/08
OP 03
R

ROUGHAM

200ft 6mb	2nm E of Bury St.Edmunds N5214.79 E00046.23	PPR	Alternative AD **Cambridge** Elmsett **Non-standard join**

Rougham	APP Lakenheath 136.500	A/G 118.900

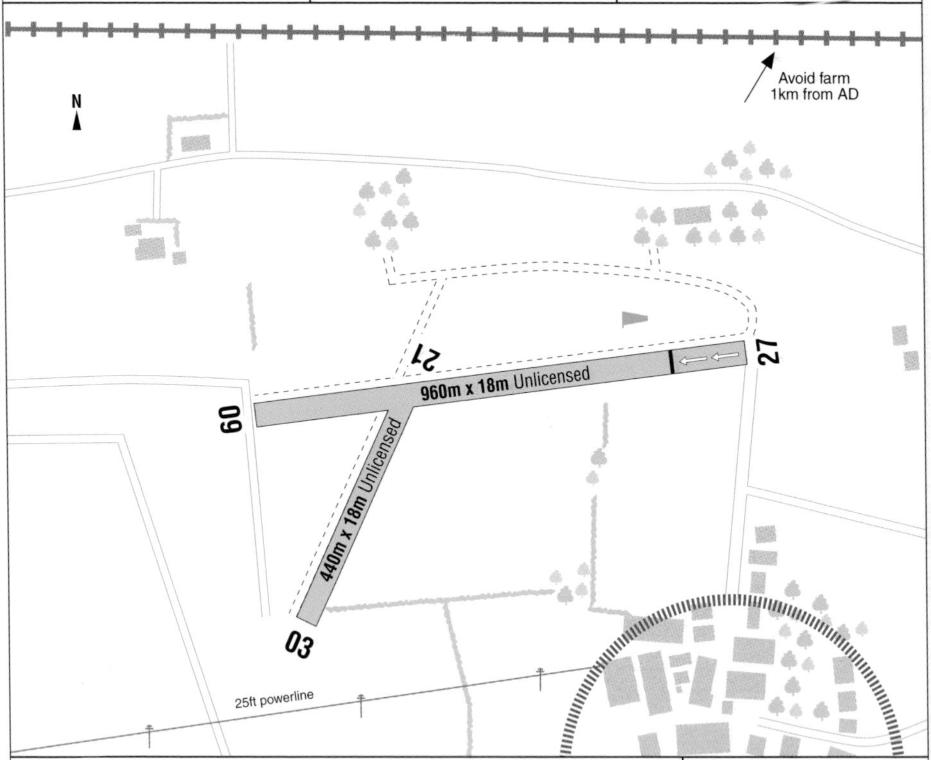

N

Avoid farm 1km from AD

21

27

09

960m x 18m Unlicensed

440m x 18m Unlicensed

03

25ft powerline

RWY	SURFACE	TORA	LDA	U/L	LIGHTING
09/27	Grass			960x18	Nil
03/21	Grass			400x18	Nil

RNAV			
CLN	114.55	332	27.7

Remarks

Strictly PPR by telephone. Visiting pilots welcome at own risk. Non-radio ACFT not accepted on event days. Grass Rwys located on part of old WW2 AD. Join through the overhead at 1500ft, to join circuit at 1000ft QNH. After landing clear Rwy by first exit. Taxi with caution as GND is uneven, (on event days) look out for marshal who will indicate parking spot. All Arr pilots must report to the 'C'. AD holds seasonal licence Jun-Nov.

Warnings

AD not manned on non-event days, pre-landing Rwy inspection essential. Rougham situated on S edge of Lakenheath MATZ which is activated by NOTAM. Lakenheath APP are controlling authority. See joining instructions in Remarks.

Noise: Avoid over flying farm 1km NE Rwy27 Thr. Downwind leg to S of A14 to avoid over flying industrial estate. Avoid over flying houses on base leg/final APP Rwy09.

Operating Hrs	0900-1800 (L) event days Other times by arrangement
Circuits	S 1000ft QNH
Landing Fee	Event days: Pilots & passengers to pay daily show fee Non-event days: All ACFT £5
Maintenance	Nil
Fuel	AVGAS by prior arr
Disabled Facilities	Nil
Restaurants	Tea & coffee at events

Taxis/Car Hire	**Tel:** 01284 766777
Weather Info	Air SE MOEx
Operator	Rougham Estate Office Rougham Bury St Edmunds Suffolk IP30 9LZ **Tel:** 07840 837952 (PPR Event days) **Tel:** 01359 270238 (PPR Non event days) **Fax:** 01359 271555 info@roughamairfield.org www.roughamairfield.org

R

RUSH GREEN

350ft 11mb	3nm S of Hitchin N5154.18 E00014.85	PPR	Alternative AD London Luton Henlow Non-standard join

Rush Green	ATIS Luton 120.575	APP Luton 129.550	A/G 122.350 by request only

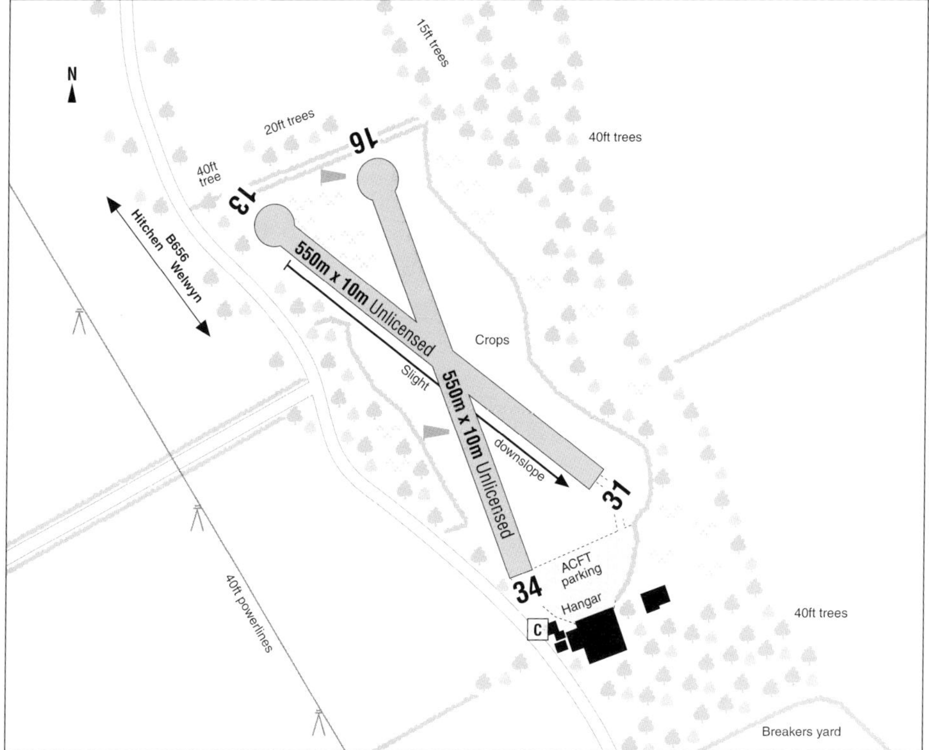

RWY	SURFACE	TORA	LDA	U/L	LIGHTING
16/34	Grass			550x10	Nil
13/31	Grass			550x10	Nil

Rwy13 has slight downslope

RNAV			
BPK	117.50	335	10.2

Remarks
PPR by telephone. Light ACFT welcome at pilots own risk. Visitors requested to book in at caravan by hangar.
Visual aid to location: Large scrapyard to S of AD.

Warning
AD situated within Luton CTR, clearance to enter zone must be obtained from Luton . Hay is grown up to Rwy edges. Area of rough GND to E of Rwy16 Thr. AD may be boggy after heavy rain. 40ft trees close to Rwy13 Thr on very short final.

Operating Hrs SR-SS
Circuits To E 500ft QFE
Landing Fee £5 for recreational visitors
Commercial landing fee on application
Maintenance Outside parking
Servicing & repairs available
Fuel Nil
Disabled Facilities Nil
Restaurants
Royal Oak **Tel:** 01438 820436
Taxis **Tel:** 01438 353562
Tel: 07785 347348
Car Hire Nil

Weather Info Air SE MOEx
Operator Mr Maurice Parker
Rush Green Aviation Ltd
Four Winds Industrial Park
Bedford Road
Haynes
Bedford, MK45 3QT
Tel: 07747 864216

Effective date:25/09/08 OP 08

163ft 6mb	3nm NW of Cardiff Airport N5124.29 W00326.15	PPR MIL	Alternative AD	Cardiff Swansea	Non-standard join

St Athan	ATIS	LARS	APP	TWR
	Cardiff 132.475	St Mawgan 128.725	Cardiff 125.850	118.125

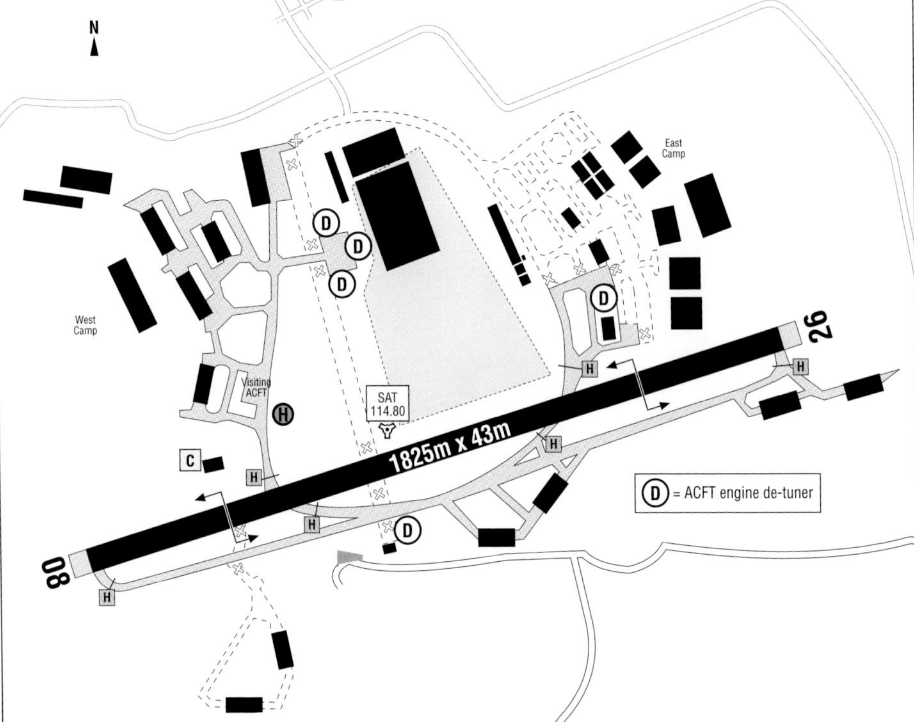

RWY	SURFACE	TORA	LDA	U/L	LIGHTING
08	Asphalt	1825	1825		Thr Rwy PAPI 2.5°
26	Asphalt	1825	1825		Ap Thr Rwy PAPI 2.5°

RNAV			
BCN	117.45	203	20.3

Remarks
PPR 24Hrs noticed required. AD within Cardiff CTR. Light ACFT & glider flying evening & weekends. ATZ active H24. Facilities and services for visiting ACFt are limited to refuelling and aircrew turnarounds only. Parking instructions as directed by ATC. Subject ot commitments the AD and ATC may be closed during published hrs.

Warnings
Beware mis-identifying AD, Cardiff AD (Rwy12/30 & 03/21) 3nm E of AD. Wind shear hazard Rwy26 in strong NW winds. No Twy lighting N of Rwy. Rwy slippy when wet due to limited friction. Visiting ACFT are to carry out RAD to straight in or TACAN APP to land only. Visual circuits are not permitted except in an emergency. Railway (282m from Thr) and road (300m from Thr) cross Rwy08 APP.
Noise: Avoid over flying St Athan village.

S

Operating Hrs	Mon-Thu 0830-1700 Fri 0830-1600 (Summer) +1Hr (Winter)
Circuits	Nil
Landing Fee	Charges in accordance with MOD policy Contact Station Ops for details
Maintenance	Nil
Fuel	AVGAS JET A1 100LL
Disabled Facilities	Nil
Restaurants	Nil
Taxis	
Major Cars	**Tel:** 01446 794545

Car Hire	Nil
Weather Info	Air S MOEx
Operator	MOD St Athan Barry Vale of Glamorgan CF62 4WA **Tel:** 01446 755696 (OPS) **Tel:** 01446 798889 (ATC) **Fax:** 01446 798257 **Fax:** 01446 755743 (Ops)

EGDG ST MAWGAN

391ft 13mb	3.5nm ENE of Newquay N5026.43 W00459.72	PPR MIL	**Alternative AD** **Plymouth** Perranporth

Non-standard join

St Mawgan	ATIS	LARS	APP	DIR	TWR
	122.550	128.725	128.725	125.550	123.400

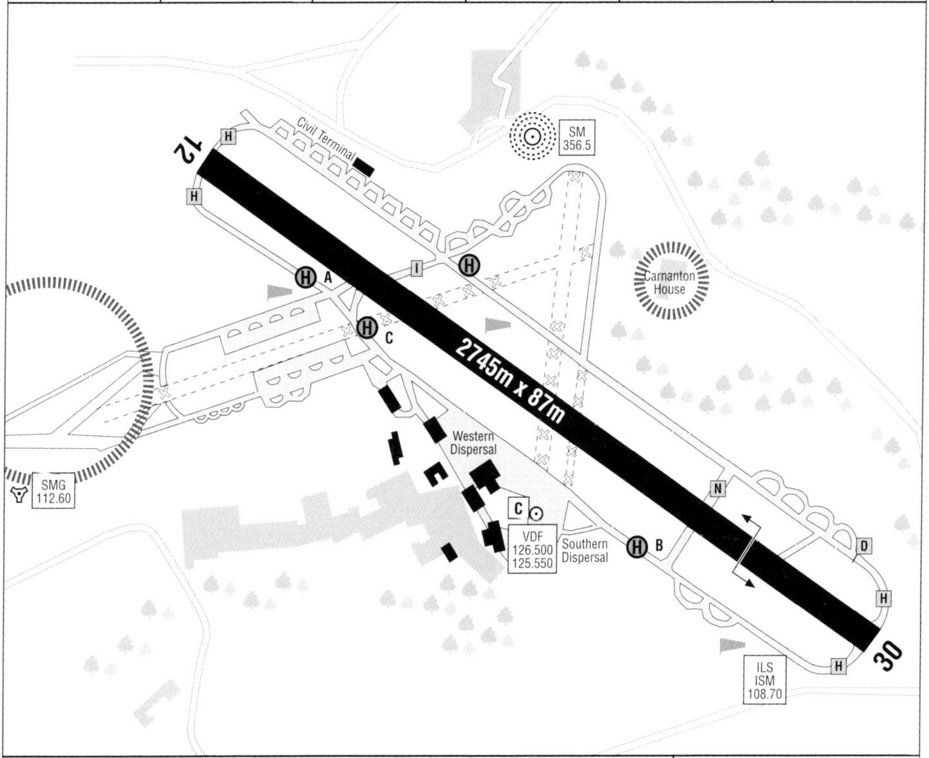

RWY	SURFACE	TORA	LDA	U/L	LIGHTING
12/30	Asph/Conc	2745	2745		Ap Thr Rwy PAPI 3°
Reduced dimensions for ACFT unable to trample arrester gear					
12	Asph/Conc	2230	2230		
30	Asph/Conc	2325	2325		

RNAV

Remarks
PPR 24Hrs civil ACFT wishing to operate at weekends must request PPR not later than 1700hrs Friday. Civil Flight Plans must be sent to Ops for processing EGDGYXYW. All inbound ACFT to contact St Mawgan APP at 20nm. RADAR APP may be mandatory.
Visual aid to location: Ibn SM Red.

Warnings
Risk of bird strikes. Pilots unfamiliar with the area should note that St Eval Disused AD lies 3nm N of St Mawgan. Standard arrester gear configuration is both cables down. There is no dead side when helicopters operate within the visual circuit N Rwy12/30. Fixed wing ACFT do not use dead side without ATC approval.
Helicopters use points N and S Twys and may operate to within 100m of edge of Rwy.
Noise: Avoid over flying Carnanton House 400m NE of AD

Operating Hrs 0700-2200 (L)
Closed to non-schedule traffic Sat-Sun 1515-1645

Circuits No dead side
Fixed wing S, Heli N, 1000ft QFE

Landing Fee Contact Midwest Exec
Tel: 01637 860551

Maintenance Nil

Fuel AVGAS JET A1

Disabled Facilities

Handling **Tel:** 01637 860551(Mid West Aviation)
Fax: 01637 860788 (Mid West Aviation)
nqy@midwestexec.com
www.midwestexec.com

Restaurants In terminal

Taxis/Car Hire Available in terminal

Weather Info M T Fax 392 MOEx

Operator RAF St Mawgan
Newquay, Cornwall TR8 4HP
Tel: 01637 860551
Fax: 01637 857556
www.newquay-airport.co.uk

Effective date:25/09/08 OP 08

16ft 0mb	7nm NNW of Preston N5350.71 W00246.96	PPR	Alternative AD	Liverpool Manchester Barton

St Michaels	ATIS Liverpool 124.325	LARS Warton 129.525	APP Liverpool 119.850	A/G 129.825 (Microlight freq)

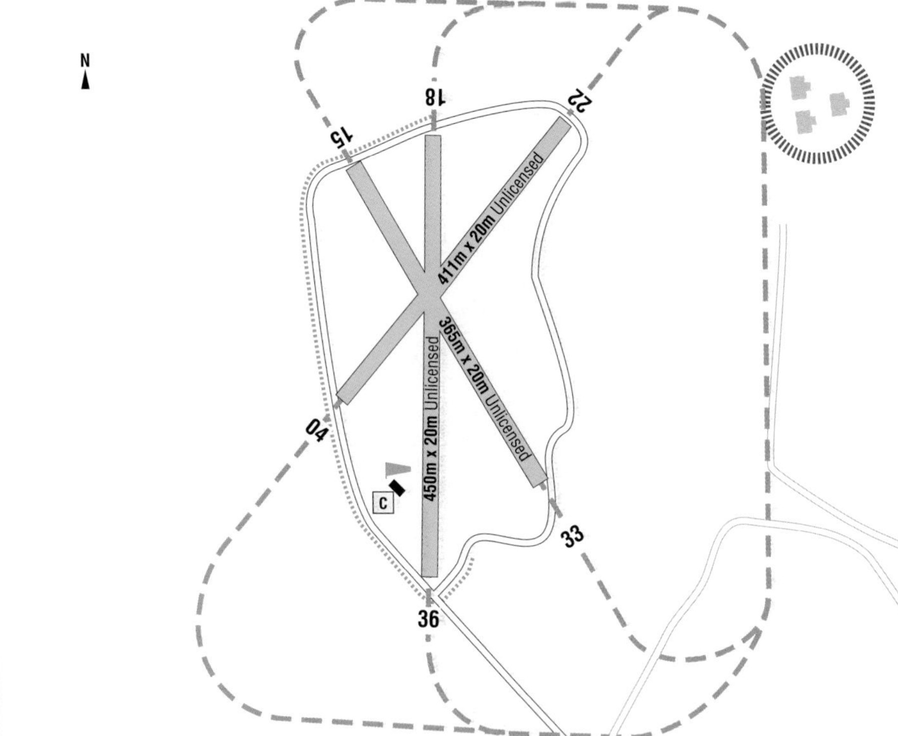

RWY	SURFACE	TORA	LDA	U/L	LIGHTING
04/22	Grass			411x20	Nil
18/36	Grass			450x20	Nil
15/33	Grass			365x20	Nil

RNAV			
POL	112.10	289	25.0

Remarks

PPR by telephone. Microlight school is particularly active at weekends. Please be considerate of ab-initio students. Although Rwys are marked by cut grass strips, all the field is useable. Take-offs are restricted to Rwys. Student pilots are encouraged to land into wind and not stick blindly to cut Rwys.

Warnings

Occassionaly waterlogged after heavy winter rain/snow. Grass may be long at sides of cut Rwys in summer.
Caution: Telephone poles and lines along N boundary of AD. Dyke 10ft W of AD.
Noise: Avoid over flying local habitation. Do not over fly the large houses in the trees to NE of AD 1nm.

S

Operating Hrs	SR-SS
Circuits	Join overhead 1500ft QFE Circuits E 500ft QFE
Landing Fee	£4 for as many landings as required in any 1 day
Maintenance	Nil Overnight parking available at owners risk
Fuel	MOGAS available by arr
Disabled Facilities	Nil
Restaurant	Self brew tea & coffee available
Taxis/Car Hire	Available by mobile phone
Weather Info	Air N MOEx

Operator

Graham Hobson
Northern Microlight School
2 Ashlea Cottage
St Michaels Road
Bilsborrow
Preston
PR3 0RT
Tel: 01995 641058 (Office)

250ft 8mb	2nm N of Bedford Thurleigh Disused AD N5215.87.W00029.08	PPR	Alternative AD	Cranfield Northampton

Sackville	APP Cranfield 122.850	A/G 119.200

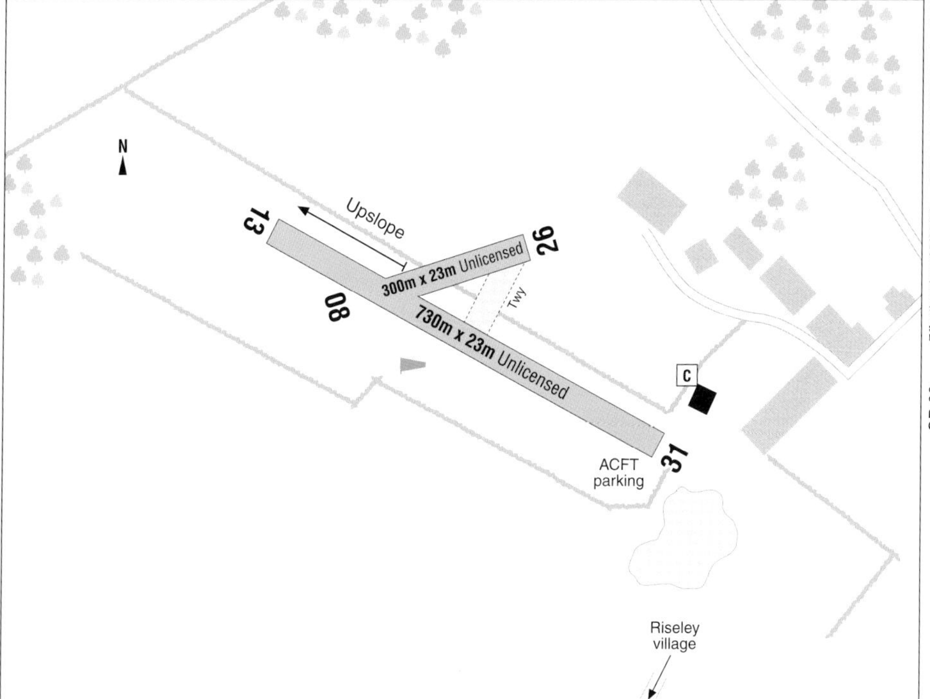

RWY	SURFACE	TORA	LDA	U/L	LIGHTING
13/31	Grass			730x23	Nil
08/26	Grass			300x23	Nil

Rwy31 upslope in final third

RNAV			
BKY	116.25	312	26.0

Remarks

PPR by telephone for briefing. All ACFT inc microlights welcome at own risk. Glider launching is carried out most weekends by winch & aerotow. Visitors are invited to try gliding.

Warnings

Rwy08/26 short, use only when strong cross winds on main Rwy. For use by microlights with limited cross wind limits.
Noise: Do not over fly Riseley village S of strip.

Operating Hrs	SR-SS
Circuits	1000ft agl
Landing Fee	Nil
Maintenance	Nil
Fuel	Nil
Hangarage	Available
Disabled Facilities	Nil
Restaurants	Tea coffee & snacks weekends Fox & Hounds in Riseley village approx 10mins walk
Taxis	**Tel:** 01234 750005
Car Hire	
National	**Tel:** 01234 269565 (Bedford)

Weather Info	Air Cen MOEx
Operator	Mr T Wilkinson Sackville Lodge Farm Riseley, Beds **Tel:** 01234 708877 (AD PPR) **Tel:** 07774 291283 **Tel:** 01933 311895 (Microlight School) **Fax:** 01234 708862 www.sackvilleflyingclub.co.uk

Effective date:25/09/08 OP 08

420ft 14mb	1nm SW of Salcombe N5013.65 W00348.50	PPR	Alternative AD	Plymouth Exeter

Non-Radio	LARS Plymouth Military 121.250	LARS Exeter 128.975	Safetycom 135.475

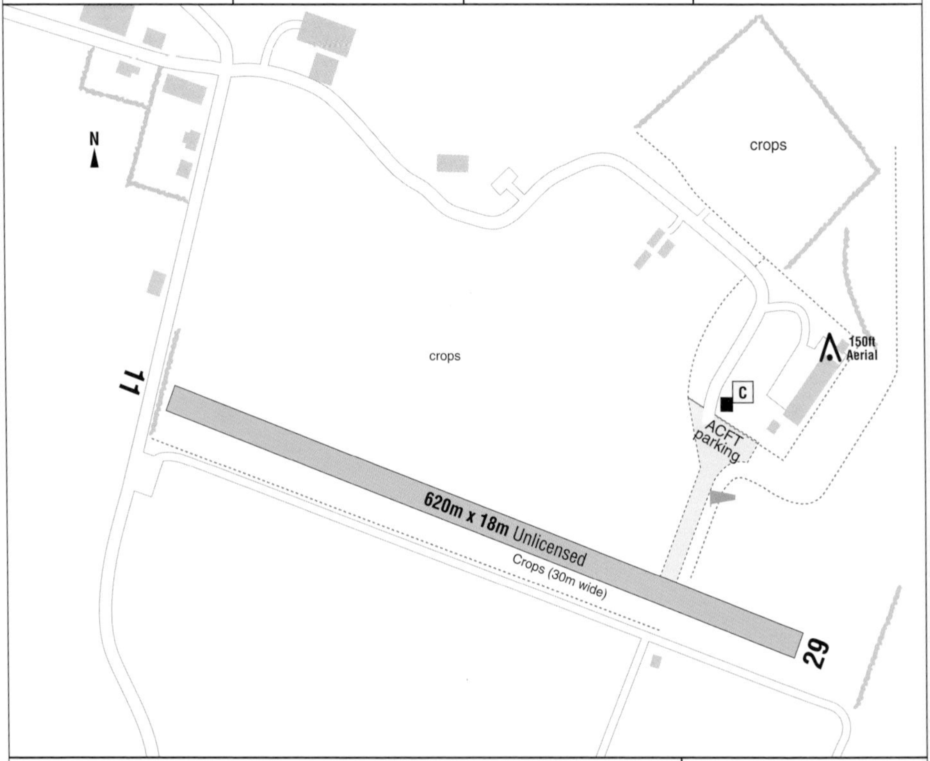

RWY	SURFACE	TORA	LDA	U/L	LIGHTING
11/29	Grass			620x18	Nil

RNAV

Remarks
PPR by telephone essential. Visiting pilots welcome at own risk. Rwy is well prepared. WW II AD. Campsite available at farm.
Visual aid to location: Large concrete bunker with 150agl aerial on roof.

Warnings
AD generally in good condition. Due to the proximity of sea and nearby cliffs coastal weather effects can be expected including sea mist and downdrafts Rwy29 APP. 4ft hedge Rwy11 Thr. 6ft fence along S side of Rwy. 4ft hedge Rwy29 Thr.
Noise: All Arr and Dept must avoid over flying all local properties. No over flying of Salcombe and Malborough or local villages.

S

Operating Hrs SR-SS
Circuits To seaward side 1000ft QFE
Landing Fee £10
Maintenance Nil
Fuel Nil
Disabled Facilities

Restaurant/ Accomodation Soar Mill Cove Hotel, 1nm from AD
Tides Reach Hotel, South Sands.
(Ferry service from South Sands to Salcombe Mar-Nov)
Salcombe TIC **Tel:** 01548 843927

Taxis
Clarke Cars **Tel:** 01548 842914
Moonraker Taxis **Tel:** 01548 560231
Car Hire Nil
Weather Info Air SW MOEx
Operator Squire Brothers
Higher Rew Farm
Malborough
Devon TQ7 3BW
Tel: 01548 842681
Tel: 07970 654662
www.higherrew.co.uk
Tel: 01548 843927 (Tourist Board)
www.salcombeinformation.co.uk

XSBY SALTBY

480ft 16mb	7nm NE of Melton Mowbray N5249.77 W00042.65	PPR	Alternative AD **East Midlands** Leicester **Non-standard join**

Saltby Base	LARS Cottesmore 130.200	A/G 129.975 Not always manned*	*If no answer make normal circuit calls

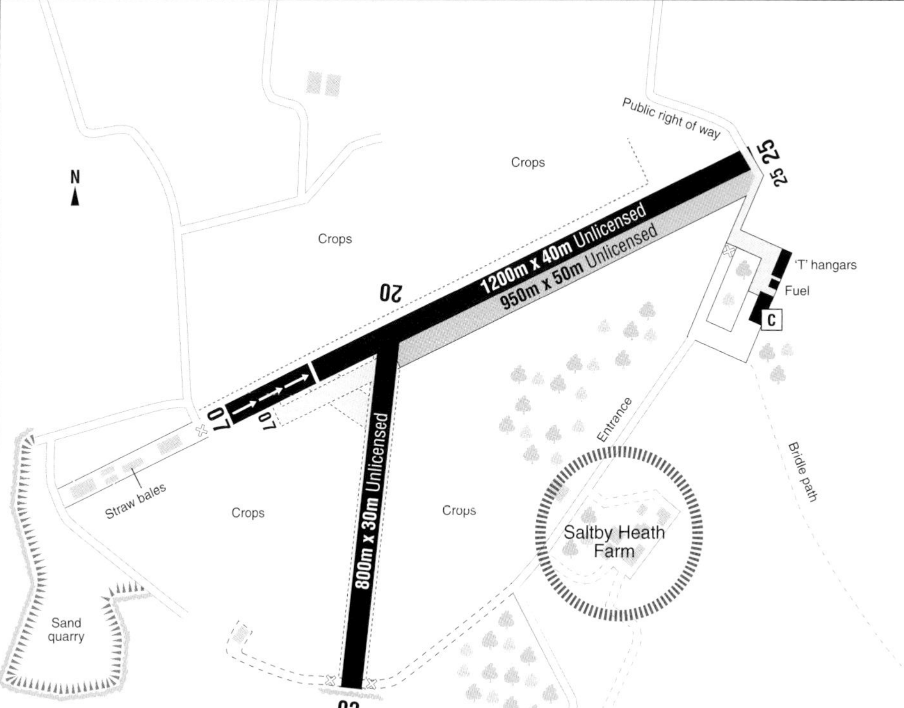

RWY	SURFACE	TORA	LDA	U/L	LIGHTING
07/25	Conc/Asph			1200x40	Nil
07/25	Grass			950x50	Nil
02/20	Concrete			800x30	Nil

Rwy20 surface rough

RNAV			
GAM	112.80	167	28.4

Remarks

PPR by telephone. Primarily a gliding site but light ACFT welcome at own risk. Operated by Buckminster Gliding Club on lease from Buckminster Estates. Due to rural nature/gliding tasks PPR may be denied. Gliders launch by aerotow & winch. Priority should be given to gliding activity. Keep a good lookout at all times. Considering Rwy07/25 surface dates to 1945 it is in excellent condition. A public right of way crosses Rwy25 Thr

Warnings

Wire fence along N side of hard Rwy07/25. Crops grow up to S edge of grass Rwy07/25. Waltham on the Wold TV mast (1487ft amsl, 1050ftagl) 3.5nm Rwy07 APP. Cottesmore MATZ 1.5nm SSE. Inbound/outbound ACFT call Cottesmore. Due to cables NO overhead joins (Mon-Fri 2000ft Weekends 3000ft).
Noise: Avoid over flying local villages.

Operating Hrs SR-SS

Circuits 07, 02, 25 LH, 07 RH, 1000ft QFE
No overhead joins. Join downwind.
Glider circuits variable

Landing Fee Contributions gratefully received

Maintenance Nil

Fuel Nil

Disabled Facilities

Restaurants Snacks tea & coffee at GC

Taxis/Car Hire Nil

Weather Info Air Cen MOEx

Operator Buckminster Gliding Club
Saltby Airfield
Sproxton Road, Skillington
Grantham, Lincs, NG33 5HL
Tel: 01476 860385
Tel: 01476 860947
Tel: 07769 955791
Fax: 01476 860947
office@buckminstergc.co.uk
www.buckminstergc.co.uk

Effective date:25/09/08 OP 08

66ft 2mb	20nm NNE of Kirkwall Airport N5915.02 W00234.60	PPR	**Alternative AD** **Diversion AD**	**Kirkwall** Eday

Non-Radio	APP Kirkwall 118.300	Safetycom 135.475

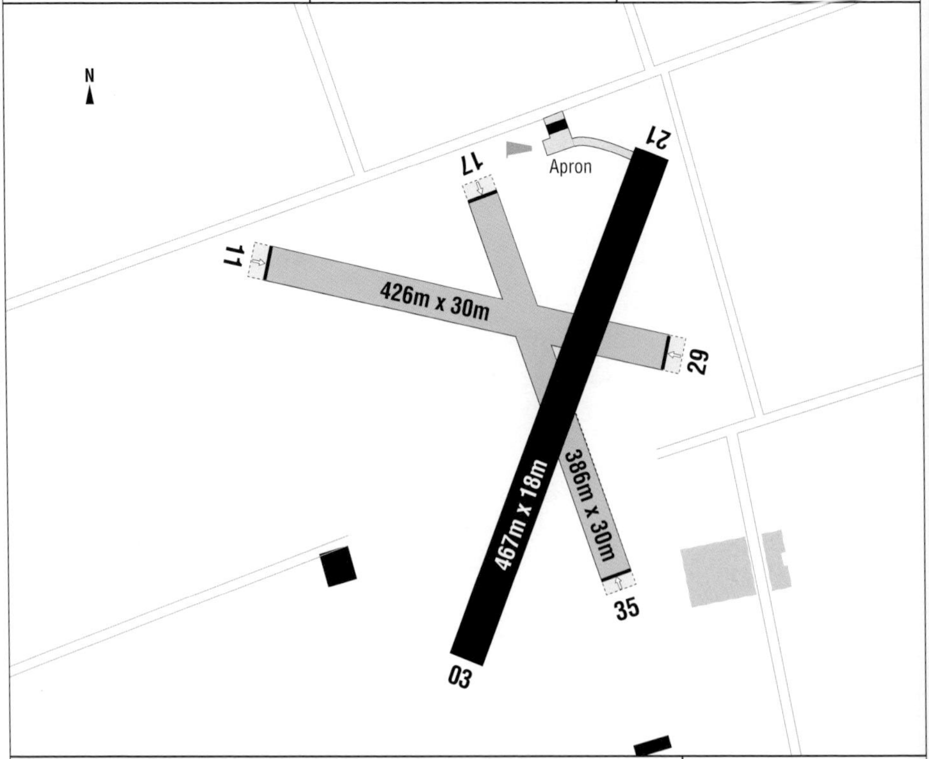

N

Apron

17

21

11

426m x 30m

29

386m x 30m

467m x 18m

35

03

RWY	SURFACE	TORA	LDA	U/L	LIGHTING
03/21	Graded Hardcore	467	467		Nil
11/29	Grass	426	396		Nil
17/35	Grass	378	366		Nil

Starter extension 15m on all Rwys

RNAV

KWL	108.60	035	19.9

Remarks
Visiting ACFT accepted at pilot's own risk. Scheduled Air Service daily Mon-Sat.

Warnings

Operating Hrs SR-SS
Circuits Nil
Landing Fee Nil
Maintenance Nil
Fuel Nil
Disabled Facilities

T

Restaurants
Belsair Hotel **Tel:** 01857 600206
Fax: 01857 600453
Ketteltoft Hotel **Tel:** 01857 600217

Taxis/Car Hire
Kettletoft Garage **Tel:** 01857 600321/600255
B Fleet **Tel:** 01857 600284
Weather Info Air Sc GWC

Operator Orkney Islands Council Offices
Sanday Aerodrome, Kirkwall
Orkney, KW15 1NY
Tel: 01856 873535 (PPR)
Fax: 01856 876094

S

XSAN SANDHILL FARM

350ft 11mb	4nm NE of Swindon N5136.14 W00140.30	PPR	Alternative AD Oxford Kemble **Non-standard join**

Non-Radio	Zone	LARS	Safetycom
	Lyneham 123.400	Brize 124.275	135.475

N

B4000

14

crops

Emergency use only

450m x 20m

07

21

23

25

700m x 20m Unlicensed

500m x 20m Unlicensed

500m x 20m Unlicensed

05

03

32

Glider trailers

C Hangars

Sandhill Farm

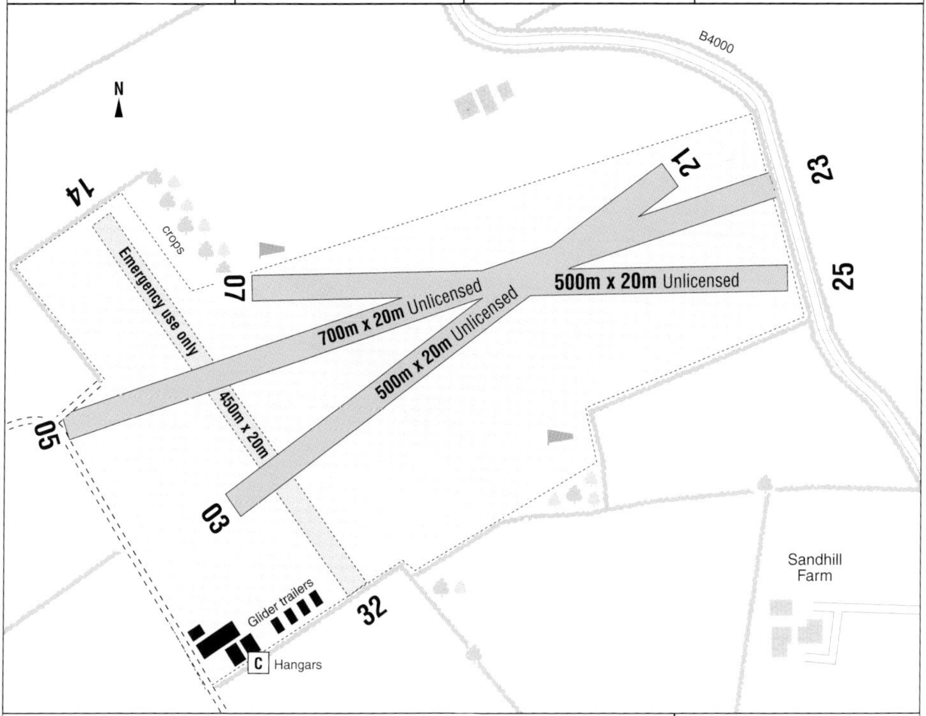

RWY	SURFACE	TORA	LDA	U/L	LIGHTING
03/21	Grass			500x20	Nil
05/23	Grass			700x20	Nil
07/25	Grass			500x20	Nil

Rwy03 up slope at narrowest point, Rwy21 down slope after narrowest point
Rwy05 up slope & undulations at narrowest point, Rwy23 down slope after narrowest point
Rwy07 up slope at narrowest point, Rwy25 down slope after narrowest point

RNAV			
CPT	114.35	295	18.2

Remarks

Strict PPR. AD is primarily a gliding site with winch and aerotow launches, beware cables. Powered ACFT circuits to the N of AD, glider circuits either side of AD. Rwys approx 20m wide, but most of year the whole AD can be used. In spring the 'off Rwy' grass may be too long.

Warnings

AD may become waterlogged in winter. Rwy23 or 25 in use gliders will be parked close to hedge adjacent to B4000. Rwy03 or 05 in use gliders will be parked close to boundary fence and adjacent to public footpath. Farm vehicles or pedestrians use farm track Rwy03 & 06 Thr.
Noise: Avoid over flying local villages, particularly two farms either side of B4000 0.5nm N of AD. Do not over fly less than 1000ft agl.

Operating Hrs	SR-SS Weekends only
Circuits	03, 05, 07 LH 21, 23, 25 RH 1000ft QFE No over head or dead side joins
Landing Fee	£6
Maintenance	Nil
Fuel	Nil
Disabled Facilities	Nil
Restaurants	Tea & Coffee available when gliding in progress
Taxi	**Tel:** 01793 766666

Car Hire	Nil
Weather Info	Air SW MOEx
Operator	Vale of White Horse Gliding Centre Sandhill Farm Shrivenham, Wilts **Tel:** 01793 783685 (AD) **Tel:** 01235 224308 (Secretary)

EGCF SANDTOFT

11ft 0mb	7nm SW of Scunthorpe N5333.58 W00051.50	PPR	**Alternative AD** **Diversion AD**	**Humberside** Retford

Sandtoft	APP Doncaster Sheffield 126.225	A/G 130.425

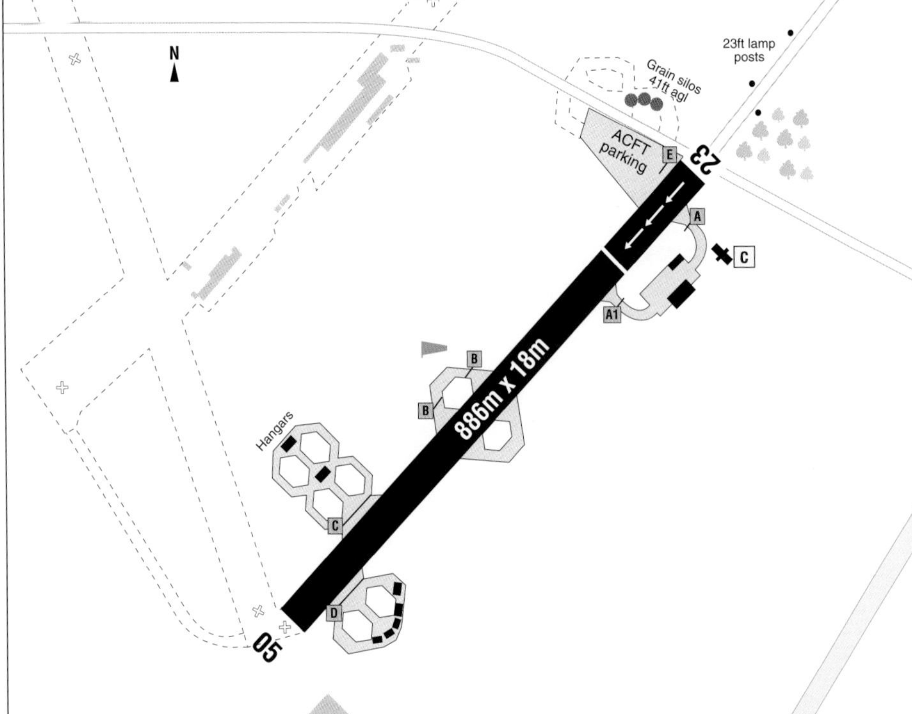

RWY	SURFACE	TORA	LDA	U/L	LIGHTING
05	Asphalt	786 (Day)	786 (Day)		Thr Rwy
23	Asphalt	799 (Day)	696 (Day)		Thr Rwy APAPI 4° LHS
05	Asphalt	696 (Night)	696 (Night)		Thr Rwy
23	Asphalt	696 (Night)	696 (Night)		Thr Rwy APAPI 4° LHS

RNAV			
GAM	112.80	015	17.0

Remarks
PPR for non-radio ACFT. Rwy05 is not licensed for night use.

Warnings
Street lights on road at Rwy23 Thr. 12.5m agl silos Rwy23 APP
Noise: Avoid over flying Belton village to E. Local flying area NE of AD, clear of built-up areas

Operating Hrs 0800-1700 (Summer) 0900-SS (Winter)

Circuits 05 LH, 23 RH, 1000ft QFE
Microlights 1000ft QFE
Helicopter 1000ft QFE

Landing Fee Single £5, Twin £10
Heli £10, Microlight £3

Maintenance Nil
Fuel AVGAS JET A1

Disabled Facilities Nil

Restaurant Restaurant & bar available at AD
0900-1800 (L)

Taxis
Alan **Tel:** 01427 875675
Epworth Taxi **Tel:** 01427 874569

Car Hire
Europcar **Tel:** 01724 840655/843239

Weather Info Air N MOEx

Operator Sheffield City Flying School
Sandtoft Aerodrome
Belton, Doncaster
South Yorkshire, DN9 1PN
Tel: 01427 873676 (AD)
Fax: 01427 874656

S

EGXP SCAMPTON

202ft 6mb	4nm N of Lincoln N5318.47 W00033.05	PPR	**Alternative AD** **Humberside** Wickenby **Diversion AD**

Non-standard join

Non-Radio	LARS Waddington 127.350

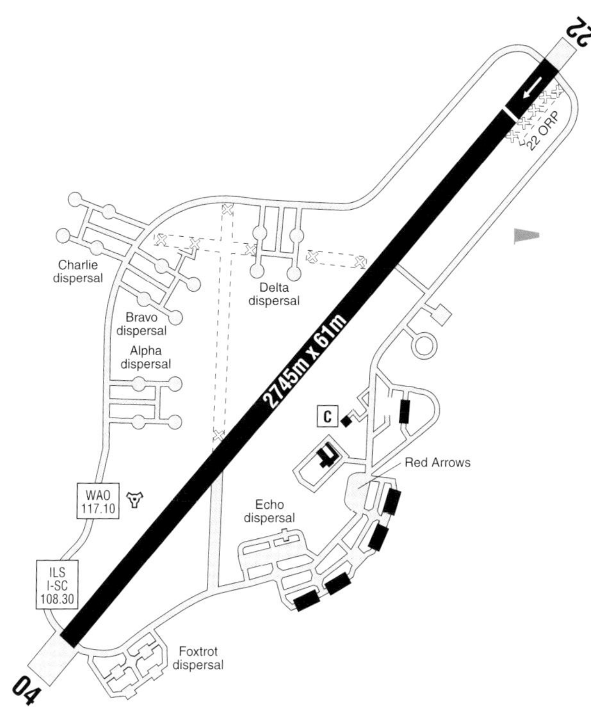

RWY	SURFACE	TORA	LDA	U/L	LIGHTING
04	Asphalt	2745	2740		Rwy App Thr PAPI 3° LHS
22	Asphalt	2745	2655		Rwy App Thr PAPI 3° LHS

RNAV			
GAM	112.80	088	14.2

Remarks

Strict PPR by telephone. RAF AD home of Red Arrows, also relief landing GND for RAF Cranwell. AD situated within R313/9.5 which is active when aerobatic practice in progress. Activity status obtained by RTF from Waddington APP, UK AIP ENR 5-1-2-5, or Waddington ATC.

Warnings

ACFT are advised to taxi on all Twy centrelines to ensure clearance from drainage covers, the integrity of which cannot be guaranteed.
Caution: Stadium lights up to 30m agl to W, S & E of Echo dispersal.

Operating Hrs As required for based/Cranwell Ops

Circuits 04 LH, 22 RH, 1000ft QFE

Landing Fee Charges in accordance with MOD policy Contact Scampton ATC for details

Maintenance Not available to visiting ACFT

Fuel Nil

Disabled Facilities

X T

Restaurants Nil

Taxis/Car Hire Nil

Weather Info Waddington M T Fax 446 MOEx
Tel: 01400 261201 Ex 7262 (Cranwell)
Tel: 01522 733051 (Scampton ATC)

Operator RAF Scampton
Lincoln
Lincolnshire
LN1 2ST
Tel: 01522 733055 (ATC)
Tel: 01400 261201 Ex 7377 (Cranwell Ops)
Fax: 01522 733058

81ft 2mb	17nm N of Lerwick N6025.97 W00117.77	PPR	Alternative AD	Sumburgh Lerwick

Scatsta	APP	TWR	RAD	FIRE
	123.600	123.600	122.400	121.600

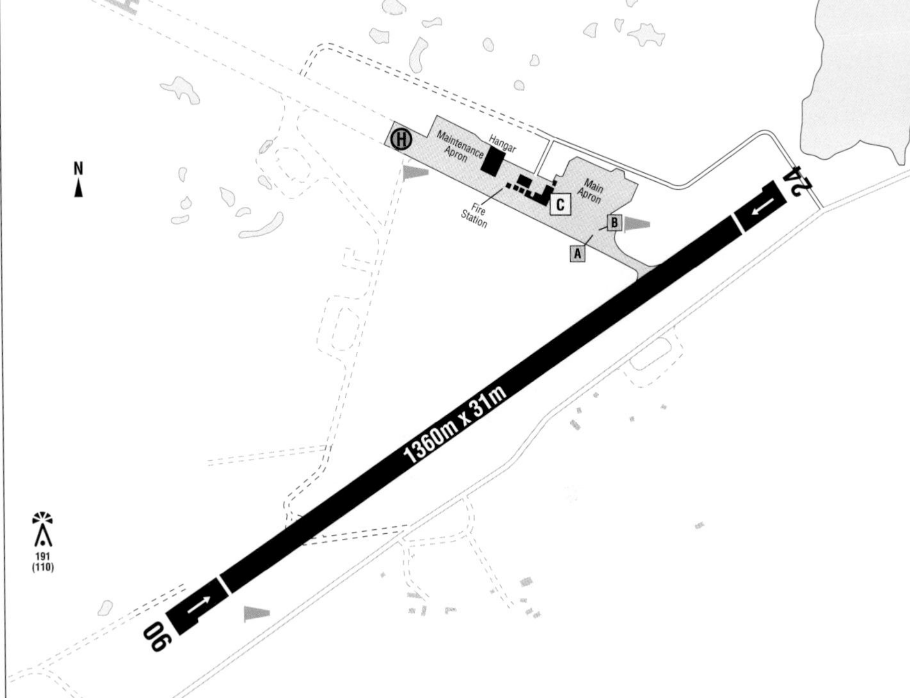

RWY	SURFACE	TORA	LDA	U/L	LIGHTING
06	Asphalt	1253	1138		Ap Thr Rwy PAPI 4° LHS
24	Asphalt	1262	1168		Ap Thr Rwy PAPI 3.25° LHS

RNAV

Remarks
Strict PPR 24Hrs notice required. Non-radio ACFT not accepted. No training flights.
Aids to Navigation: NDB SS 315.50
Visual aid to location: Strobe alignment beacons for Rwy06 APP.

Warnings
Area of poor GND in strip near Rwy06 Thr on S side suitably marked with 'bad GND' markers. Unpaved surfaces are liable to be soft, particularly after periods of heavy rain. High GND in vicinity of AD. Twy S side of main apron has semi-width of only 6.6m. Rwy lights 15in above agl.
Noise: Avoid over flying oil terminal area

Operating Hrs Mon-Fri 0630-2015 (Summer) +1Hr (Winter) & by arr
Circuits Nil
Landing Fee On application
Maintenance Nil
Fuel AVTUR JET A1 (2Hrs PNR)
Disabled Facilities Nil
Restaurants Nil
Taxis
W Hurson **Tel:** 01806 522550
G Johnson **Tel:** 01806 522443
Car Hire
Bolts Car Hire **Tel:** 01595 692855

Weather Info M T9 Fax 394 GWC

Visual Reference Points (VRP)

Brae	N6023.82 W00121.23
Fugla	N6026.95 W00119.43
Hillswick	N6028.55 W00129.32
Linga Island	N6021.40 W00121.58
Voe	N6021.00 W00115.97

Operator Serco Ltd on behalf of BP
Scatsta Aerodrome, Brae
Shetland, ZE2 9QP
Tel: 01806 242791
Tel: 01806 242257 (ATC)
Fax: 01806 242110

S

EGHE SCILLY ISLES

116ft 4mb	1nm E of Hugh Town N4954.80 W00617.50	**PPR**	**Alternative AD** **St Mawgan** Lands End **Diversion AD**

Scillies	**APP** **124.875**	**TWR** **124.875**	**FIRE** **121.600**

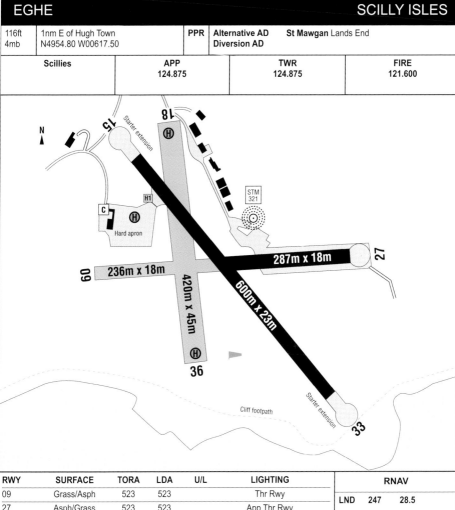

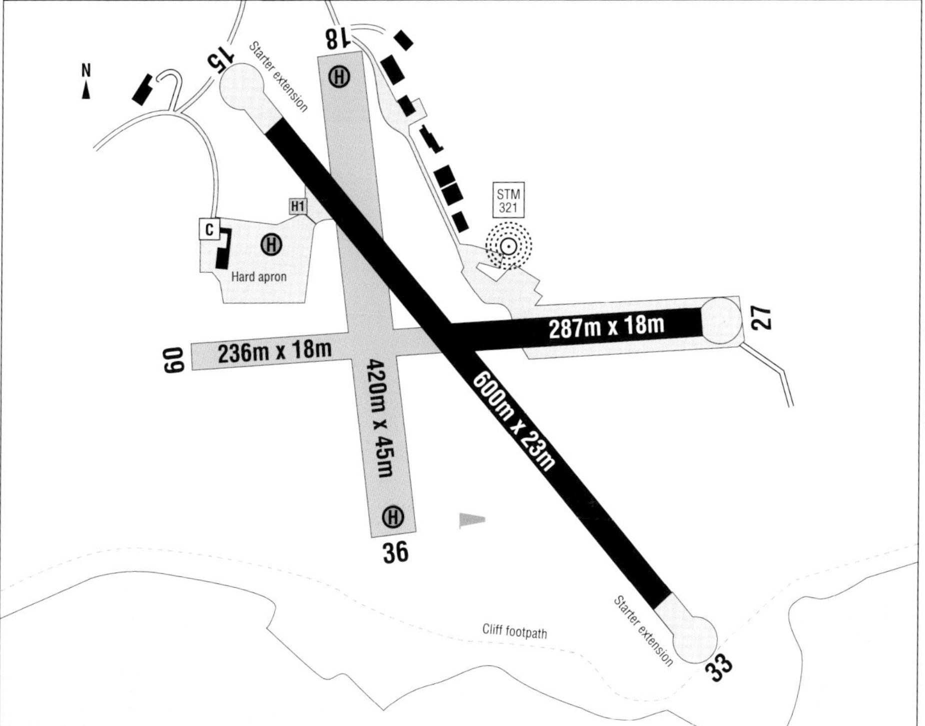

RWY	SURFACE	TORA	LDA	U/L	LIGHTING
09	Grass/Asph	523	523		Thr Rwy
27	Asph/Grass	523	523		App Thr Rwy
15/33	Tarmac	600	600		Thr Rwy PAPI 3.5° LHS
18/36	Grass	400	400		Helicopter Rwy

Starter extension Rwy15 13m. Starter extension Rwy33 38m

RNAV		
LND	**247**	**28.5**

Remarks
Strict PPR by telephone. Non-radio ACFT not accepted. Asphalt strips marked by white centre lines, grass strips have grass edge markings. AD is closed to all other ACFT Sundays. DO NOT attempt to land. Dept by arr 1500-1600 (L). Flight plans should be filed for all flights to and from Scilly Isles/St Mary's – SEE LANDS END TRANSIT CORRIDOR MAP.
Visual aid to location: Ibn Green SC.

Warnings
Caution: Landing/take-off AD is markedly hump-backed. Turbulence may be experienced at lower levels on all APP. The gradients increase to 1 in 13 at Rwy ends. Pilots – different braking characteristics of the grass/asphalt sections Rwy09/27. Perimeter road runs around N part of AD & vehicular traffic crosses Rwy15 APP. Coastal footpath crosses Rwy33 APP. Pilots exercise great care when using Rwy33 turning circle due reduced clearance SSE – granite outcrop present. SAR & local ACFT activity may take place outside published Hrs.

Operating Hrs Mon-Sat 0730-1900 (L)
Mon-Fri 0830-1230 1330-1700
Sat 0830-1230 (Nov-Feb), 1400-1700
(14 Feb-21 Mar) (Winter)

Circuits As directed by ATC

Landing Fee Single £19.55, Twin £28.72
Parking Fee Single £8.80 after 2Hrs
Twin £11.60 after 2Hrs

Maintenance Nil
Fuel Nil
Disabled Facilities

Restaurants Buffet & bar available at AD

Effective date:25/09/08 OP 08

S

Taxis	
Scilly Cabs	**Tel:** 01720 422901
St Mary's Taxis	**Tel:** 01720 422555
Island Taxis	**Tel:** 01720 422635
Car Hire	Nil
Weather Info	M T9 Fax 396 MOEx

Visual Reference Points (VRP)

Pendeen Lighthouse	N5009.92 W00540.32
St Martins Head	N4958.05 W00615.95

Operator

Council of the Isles of Scilly
St. Mary's Airport
St Mary's
Isles of Scilly, TR21 0NG
Tel: 01720 422677 (ATC)
Fax: 01720 424338 (AM)
Fax: 01720 424337 (ATC)

Lands End Transit Corridor

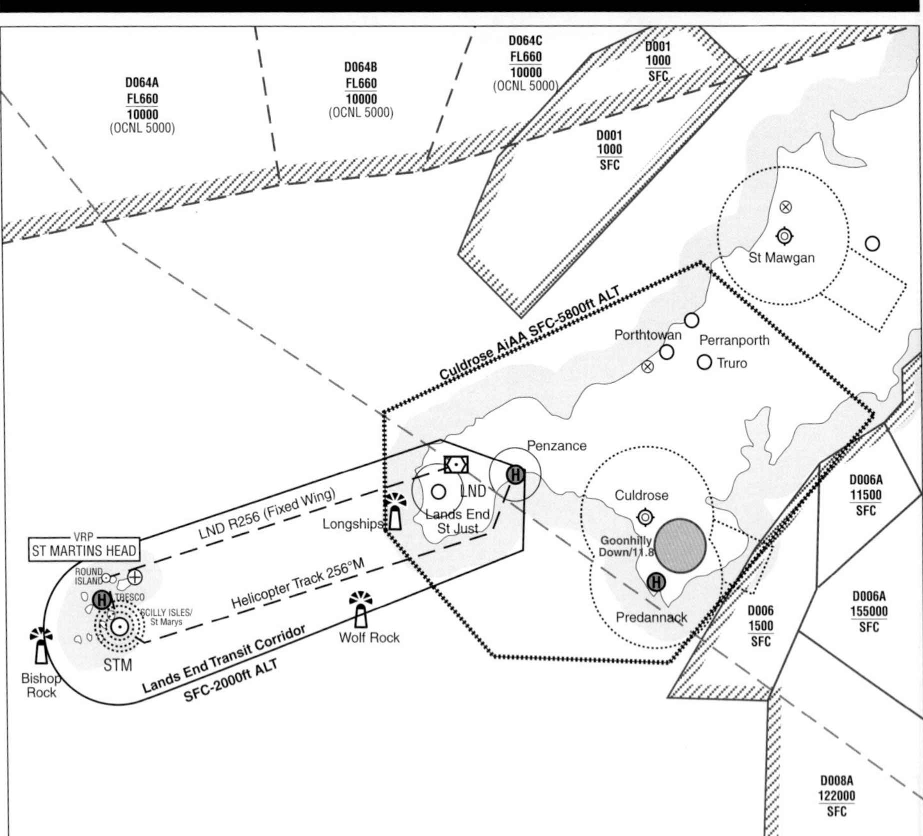

S

EGSJ SEETHING

130ft 4mb	9nm SSE of Norwich N5230.67 E00125.03		**Alternative AD** **Diversion AD**	**Norwich** Beccles

Seething	LARS Norwich 119.350	A/G 122.600

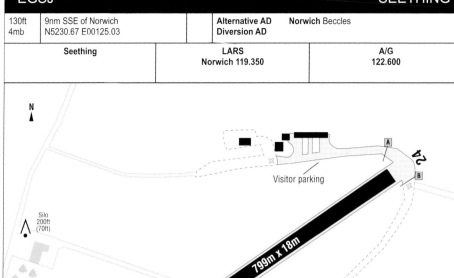

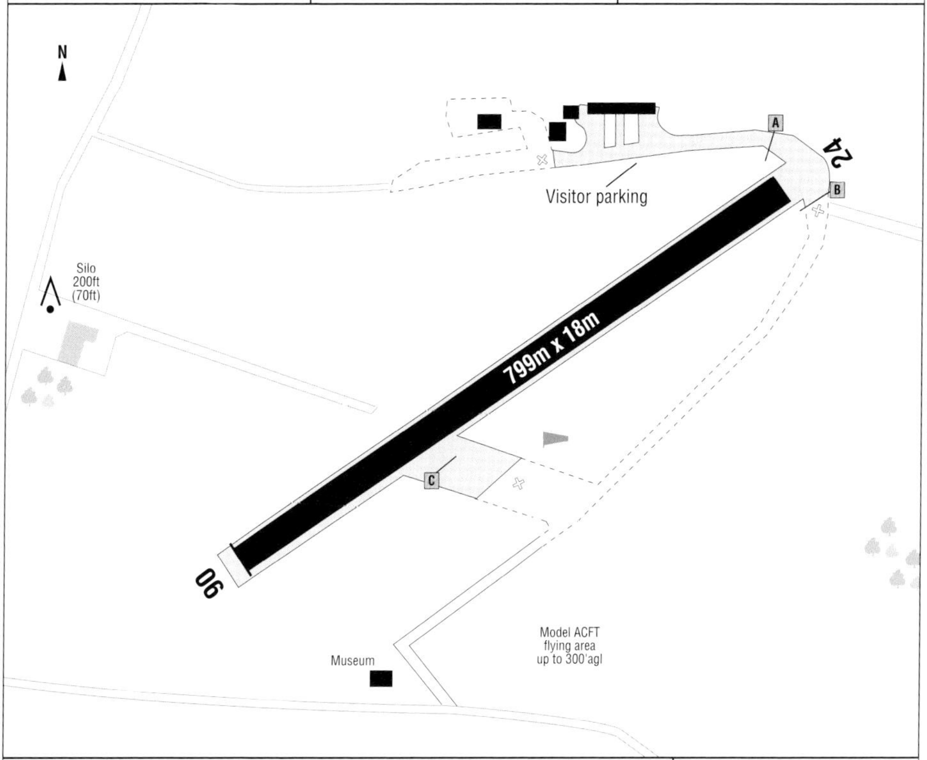

N

Silo
200ft
(70ft)

Visitor parking

A

B

C

24

06

799m x 18m

Museum

Model ACFT
flying area
up to 300'agl

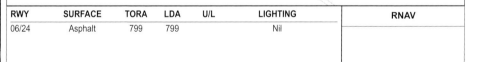

RWY	SURFACE	TORA	LDA	U/L	LIGHTING
06/24	Asphalt	799	799		Nil

RNAV

Remarks
Flying activity may take place outside published Ops Hrs.

Warnings
Agricultural vehicles and equipment may cross close to Rwy24 Thr. Silo 70ft aal/200ft amsl 0.13nm 277° from APP. Windshear may be experienced on Rwy24 APP with S winds. Model ACFT flying takes place on AD.
Caution: Distance between marked Twy centre line and parked ACT can be <8m
Noise: Avoid over flying surrounding villages below 1000ft. Pilots taking-off to leave the circuit from Rwy24 should climb straight ahead to 500ft before turning. Dept Rwy06, turn right 30°, climb to 1000ft before turning. ACFT must fly away from the village SE of AD. Also avoid small hamlet 1.24nm from Rwy.

Operating Hrs	0800-SS (Summer) 0900-SS (Winter)
Circuits	06 RH, 24 LH, 1000ft
Landing Fee	Business Flights: Single £6 Twin £12 GA ACFT: no landing fees but a donation to the group to assist in Rwy maintenance would be appreciated
Maintenance	Ltd
Fuel	AVGAS 100LL (Ltd)

Disabled Facilities

Restaurants	Snacks available at AD

Taxis	
Bungay	**Tel:** 01502 712625
Car Hire	
Godfrey Davis	**Tel:** 01603 45798
Weather Info	Air S MOEx
Operator	Wingtask 1995 Ltd Seething Aerodrome Brooke Norwich Norfolk NR15 1EL **Tel:** 01508 550453 (AD) **Tel:** 07778 592150 (PPR out of Hrs) **Fax:** 01508 558653 seethingairfield@linknorfolk.net www.seething-airfield.co.uk

EGOS SHAWBURY

249ft 8mb	6nm NNE of Shrewsbury N5247.89 W00240.08	PPR MIL	Alternative AD Diversion AD	Hawarden Sleap

Non-standard join

Shawbury	LARS	APP	RAD	TWR
	120.775	120.775	123.300	122.100

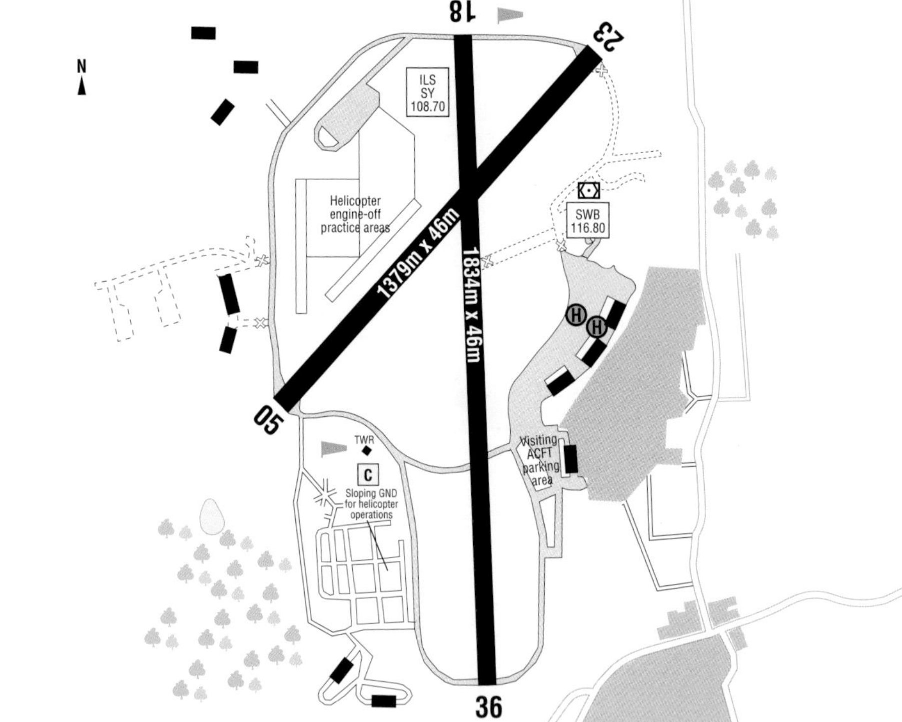

RWY	SURFACE	TORA	LDA	U/L	LIGHTING
18/36	Asph/Conc	1834	1834		Ap Thr Rwy PAPI 3°
05/23	Asph/Conc	1379	1379		Thr Rwy PAPI 3°

RNAV
SWB 116.80 On AD

Remarks
Visiting pilots wishing to operate out of Shawbury are to contact Shawbury Ops.
Visual aid to location: Ibn SY Red

Warnings
Helicopters operate within 50m of either side of the active Rwy below1500ft. Go-arounds to be made down the full length of Rwy. There is no dead side in AD. PAPI Rwy18 coincides with ILS touchdown only. PAR APP will result in incorrect PAPI indications. Visitors contact LARS at 20nm for instrument or RAD visual APP. All fixed wing ACFT to carry out instrument APP, subject to traffic and weather. A RAD vectored visual straight into land may be permitted, providing ACFT is visual and in line with Rwy at 5nm.

S

Operating Hrs	Mon-Thu 0830-1730 Fri 0830-1700 (L) ATZ H24
Circuits	05, 36 RH, 18, 23 LH, 1500ft QFE No dead side
Landing Fee	Charges in accordance with MOD policy Contact Station Ops for details
Maintenance	Nil
Fuel	AVTUR JET A1
Disabled Facilities	
Restaurants	Nil

Taxis/Car Hire	Nil
Weather Info	M T Fax 398 MOEx ATIS **Tel:** 01939 250351 Ex 7574
Operator	RAF Shawbury Shrewsbury Shropshire, SY4 4DZ **Tel:** 01939 250351 Ex 7232/7233

310ft 10mb	15nm E of Bude N5050.10 W00409.50	PPR	Alternate AD	**Exeter** Eaglescott

Non Radio	LARS Exeter 128.975	Safetycom 135.475

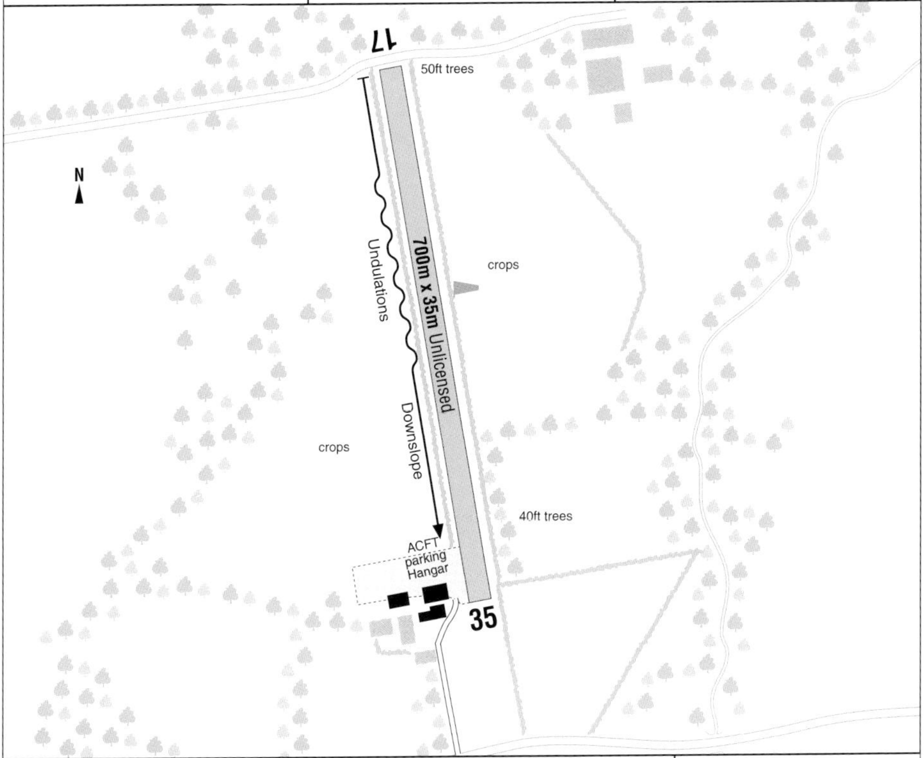

RWY	SURFACE	TORA	LDA	U/L	LIGHTING
17/35	Grass			700x35	Nil

Rwy17 downslope with undulations on mid section

RNAV

Remarks
PPR by telephone. Experienced pilots welcome at own risk.

Warnings
Rwy slope and undulations mean ALL landings must be on Rwy35. Take-off on Rwy17 only. Windshear and roll-over may be experienced. Large trees border AD. High tensile stock fences surround AD. Public footpath on E bounday of AD. Do not land if footpath in use.
Noise: Avoid over flying all local villages.

Operating Hrs SR-SS
Circuits 35 LH 17 RH 1000ft QFE
Join overhead
Landing Fee Donation to upkeep appreciated
Maintenance Nil
Fuel Nil
Disabled Facilities

Taxi/Car Hire NIl
Weather Info Air SW MOEx

Operator Roger Appleton
Westover
Sheepwash
Devon
EX21 5HQ
Tel: 01409 231619
roger@westover-sheepwash.co.uk
www.westover-sheepwash.co.uk

XSHN SHENINGTON

642ft 21mb	5nm NW of Banbury N5205.10 W00128.38	PPR	Alternative AD	**Oxford** Wellesbourne Mountford

Non-standard join

Shenington	A/G 129.975 make blind circuit calls

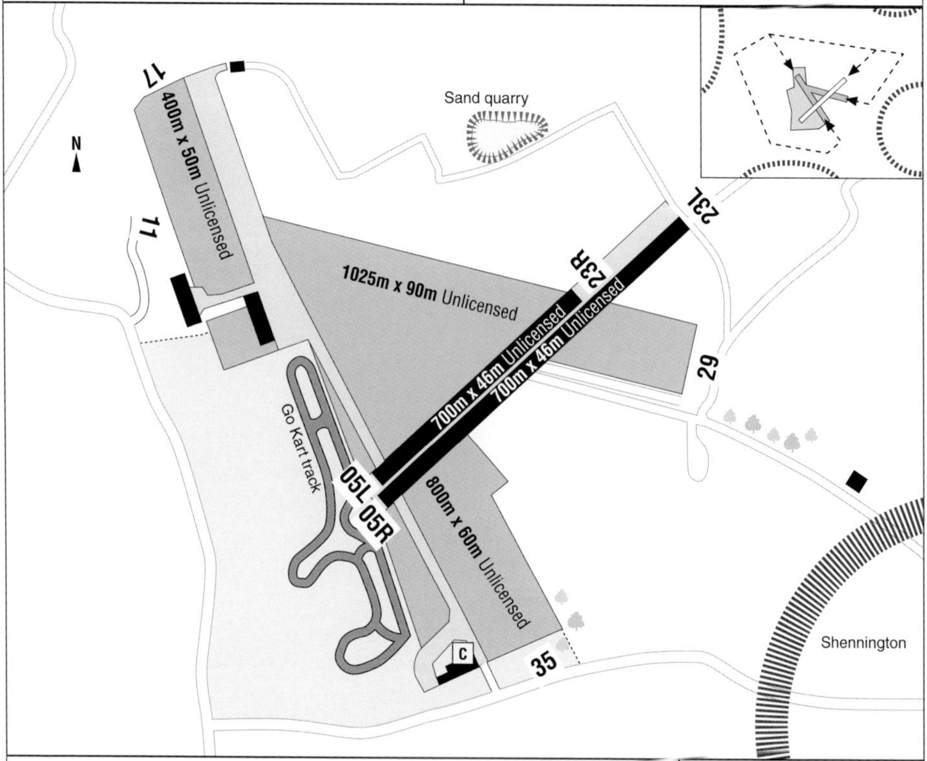

RWY	SURFACE	TORA	LDA	U/L	LIGHTING
17	Concrete			400x50	Nil
35	Tarmac			800x60	Nil
05L/23R	Concrete			700x46	Nil
05R/23L	Concrete			700x46	Nil
11/29	Grass			1025x90	Nil

RNAV			
DTY	116.40	250	14.3

Remarks

Strictly PPR by telephone for airfield briefing. Primarily a Gliding site. Visiting powered ACFT are welcome at pilots own risk. Telephone PPR is required to receive info on the days gliding operations or competitions. When in the local area stand-off for a while to assess the gnd operations, once assessed join normal glider circuit.

Warnings

Glider operations every day with simultaneous RH and LH circuits by gliders and tug ACFT on more than 1 Rwy. Beware of tractors and pedestrians associated with glider retrieval and farm operations.
Caution: Launch cables on the GND as well as in the air up to 2,000 aal, these must be avoided. Go-cart track Rwy05 Thr.
Noise: Avoid over flying all local villages. Avoid over flying the stud farm 1nm E of Shenington village.

S

Operating Hrs	SR-SS daily
Circuits	Variable advised with PPR No overhead joins
Landing Fee	Gliders £0, Singles £5, Twins £10, Helicopters £10
Maintenance	Nil
Fuel	Nil

Disabled Facilities

Restaurants	Refreshments available on AD
Taxis/Car Hire	Nil
Weather Info	Air Cen MOEx
Operator	Oxfordshire Shenington Gliding Club Shenington Airfield Shenington, Oxon **Tel:** 01295 688121

EGCJ SHERBURN-IN-ELMET

26ft 1mb	5.5nm W of Selby N5347.07 W00113.03	PPR	Alternative AD Diversion AD	Leeds Bradford Full Sutton

Sherburn	APP Fenton 126.500	LARS Linton 118.550	A/G 122.600

N

Disused runway used as vehicle test track

793m x 18m

585m x 18m

616m x 18m

830m x 18m

Cultivated area

Heli hovering area

ACFT parking

Fuel

ACFT parking

ACFT parking

Twy A

Twy B

Twy C

SBL 323

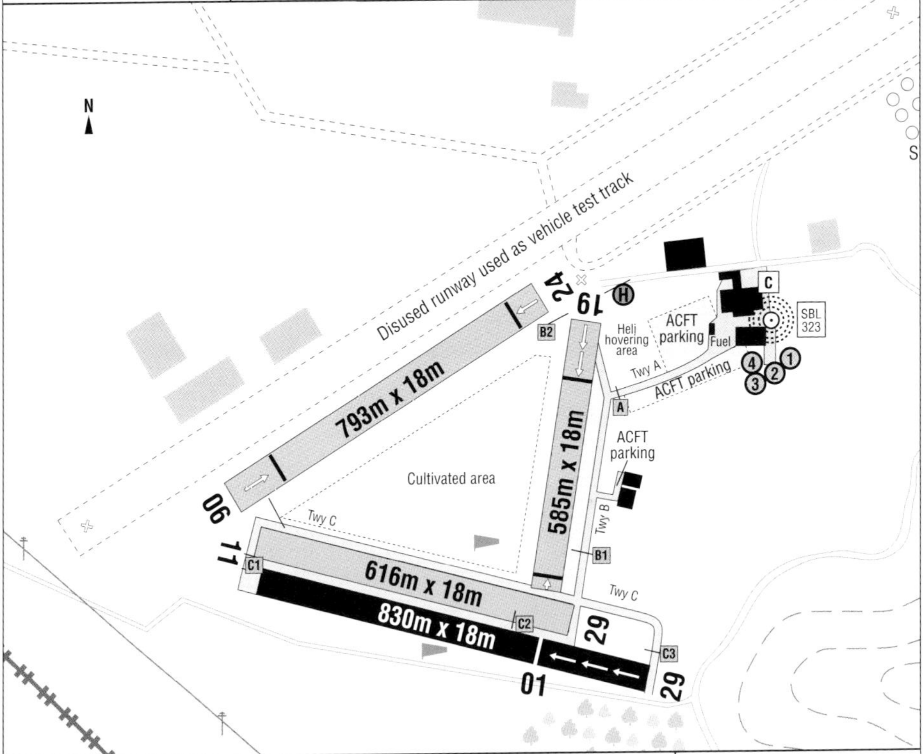

RWY	SURFACE	TORA	LDA	U/L	LIGHTING
01	Grass	553	553		Nil
19	Grass	553	521		Nil
11/29	Grass	616	616		Nil
06	Grass	723	676		Nil
24	Grass	696	703		Nil
11	Tarmac	616	830		Nil
29	Tarmac	830	616		Nil

Displaced Thr Rwy01 32m
Displaced Thr Rwy19 32m
Displaced Thr Rwy06 87m
Displaced Thr Rwy24 60m
Displaced Thr Rwy29 Tarmac 214m

RNAV

Remarks

PPR. AD situated within Church Fenton MATZ. AD not available for use by public transport passenger flights required to use licensed AD. Inbound ACFT contact Fenton MATZ when at 15nm or 5mins flying time from MATZ boundary and are to enter MATZ at 1500ft on Sherburn QFE. If unable to make contact with Fenton APP, pilots to contact Sherburn Radio or Linton MATZ and advise inability to contact Fenton. Dept ACFT are to contact Fenton MATZ before leaving Sherburn circuit and are to leave MATZ below 1500ft QFE.
Refuelling: Follow yellow line on Twy onto apron, then follow arrows anti-clockwise around the pump. DO NOT park nose to the pump.

Warnings

Paved Rwy N of grass Rwys is closed to ACFT. It is used as a vehicle test track. Inbound ACFT rwy29 use Rwy01 grass as Twy when opposing traffic in sight.
Noise: Avoid over flying the villages of Sherburn-in-Elmet, South Milford, Monk Fryston or Hambleton.

Operating Hrs	0830-SS (Summer) 0900-SS (Winter) Fri closed 1700	Circuits	01, 19 variable 1000ft QFE 24, 29 LH, 06, 11 RH 1000ft QFE

Effective date:25/09/08 OP 07

Landing Fee Single £10 Twin £20
Commercial rate available
No charge with fuel uplift >40l AVGAS, >80l JET A1

Maintenance Sherburn Engineering
Tel: 01977 685296

Fuel AVGAS JET A1 100LL
Sherburn Aero Club **Tel:** 01977 682674

Disabled Facilities

Restaurants Bar & Cafe

Taxis
A1 Private Hire **Tel:** 01977 681100
South Milford Private Hire **Tel:** 01937 689200

Car Hire
National **Tel:** 0113 277 7957

Weather Info Air N MOEx

Operator Sherburn Aero Club Ltd
Sherburn-in-Elmet Aerodrome
Lennerton Lane, Sherburn-in-Elmet
West Yorkshire, LB25 6JE
Tel: 01977 682674
Fax: 01977 683699

Sherburn-in-Elmet Circuit Procedures

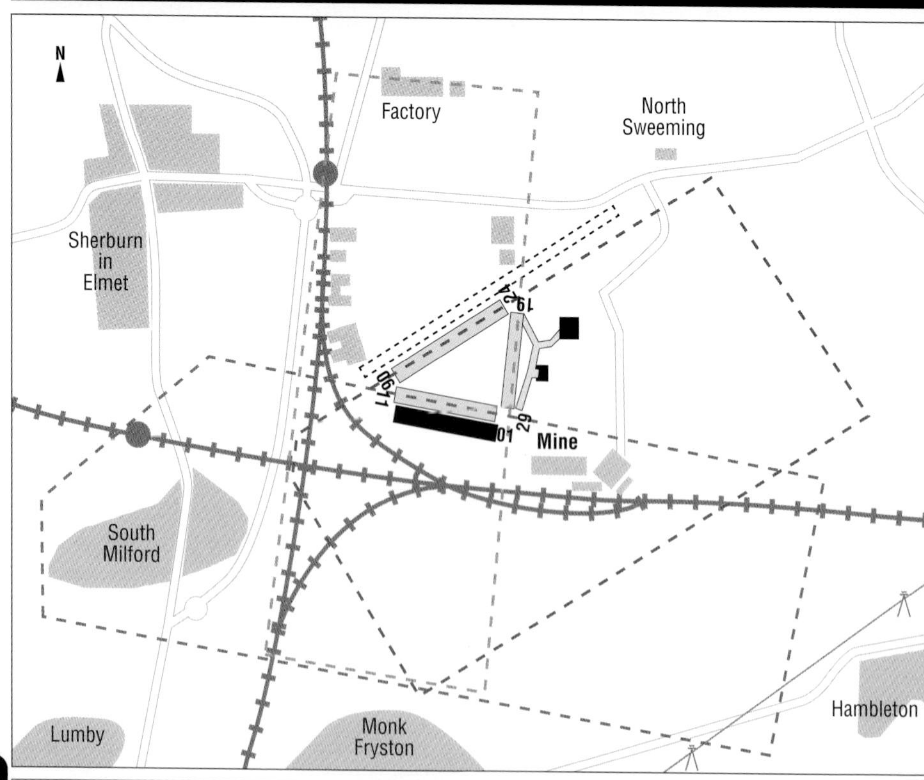

Rwy06 RH: Taxi out along Rwy29.After Dept turn right, not above 500ft QFE. Turn base leg before Monk Fryston. Turn final no further W than Sherburn by-pass. DO NOT over fly South Milford.
Rwy24 LH: Turn left onto 190°, when height & speed permit turn crosswind before South Milford. Turn downwind before Monk Fryston. DONOT extend downwind due to Church Fenton circuit. DO NOT over fly farmhouse at North Sweeming. After landing exit along grass.
Rwy11 RH: Taxi out along Rwy24. Turn crosswind before Hambleton. Turn downwind N of Monk Fryston. Turn base leg W of South Milford, DO NOT over fly built up areas on APP. Complete final turn not below 400ft QFE. DO NOT over fly South Milford or Lumby
Rwy29 LH: After Dept climb out between Sherburn & South Milford. DO NOT over fly South Milford or Lumby. Turn base leg before Hambleton. After landing exit along grass.
Rwy01 LH: After Dept turn left crosswind at 400ft or abeam factory (whichever is first). Continue to 700ft QFE max until downwind. DO NOT over fly Sherburn or South Milford downwind leg. Turn base leg before Monk Fryston.
Rwy19 RH: Turn crosswind before Monk Fryston. DO NOT over fly South Milford or Sherburn on downwind leg. Turn base leg no further N than abeam factory.

210ft 7mb	4.5nm SE of RAF Shawbury N5244.13 W00236.09	PPR	Alternative AD Hawarden Sleap Non-standard join

Sherlowe	LARS Shawbury 120.775	A/G 119.300 Not always manned

RWY	SURFACE	TORA	LDA	U/L	LIGHTING
15/33	Grass			680x25	Nil

Rwy33 2° upslope first 430m

RNAV			
SWB	116.80	153	4.4

Remarks
Strict PPR by telephone. Visiting ACFT welcome at own risk. AD located 1.5nm to SW of High Ercall disused AD. AD within Shawbury MATZ. Arr/Dept ACFT to contact Shawbury.

Warnings
Ditch at Rwy33 Thr. Farm track crosses Rwy keep a good lookout for farm traffic particularly on landing.
Noise: Pilots join at own discretion to avoid over flying local habitation. Avoid over flying High Ercall village 1nm N AD. Noise reduction routes on clubhouse notice board.

Operating Hrs	0800-2000 or SS (L) which ever earlier
Circuits	Nil
Landing Fee	Donations appreciated
Maintenance	Nil
Fuel	Nil
Disabled Facilities	Nil
Restaurants	Tea Coffee & Snacks available in clubhouse "Terminal 1"
Taxis	Operator can advise
Car Hire	Nil
Weather Info	Air Cen MOEx

Operator
Mr R F Pooler
Lower Grounds Farm
Sherlowe, High Ercall
Shropshire, TF6 6LT
Tel: 01952 770189
Fax: 01952 770762
Tel: 07768 333030
bob@sherlowe.com

420ft 14mb	5nm E of Telford N5240.74 W00224.10	PPR	Alternative AD	Birmingham Wolverhampton

Non-Radio	LARS Shawbury 120.775	Safetycom 135.475

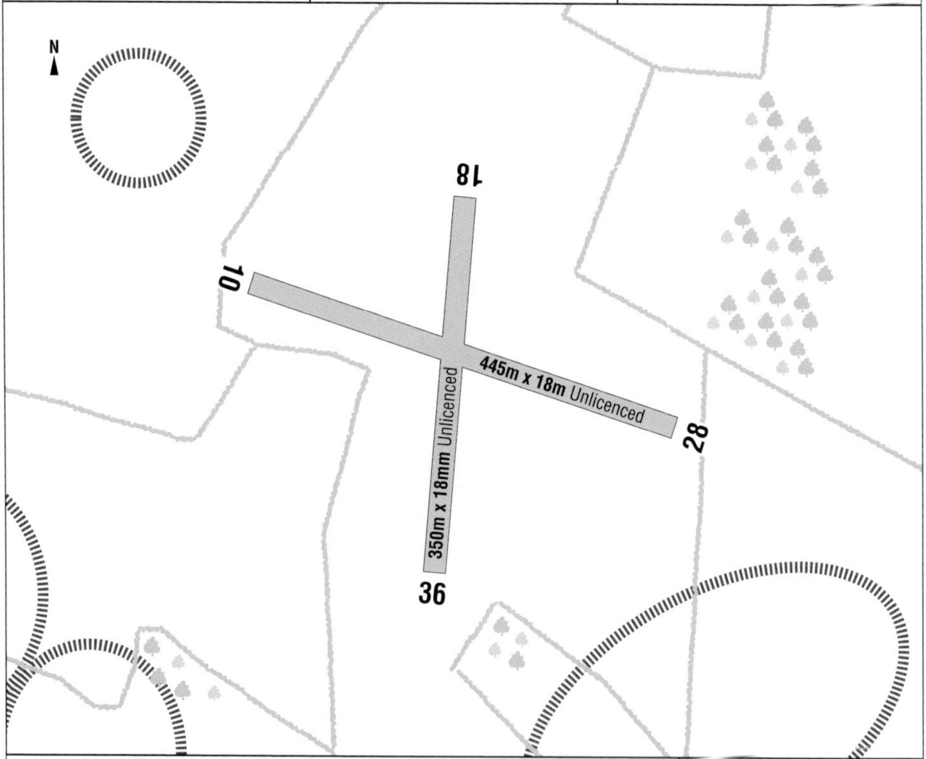

N

18

10

445m x 18m Unlicenced

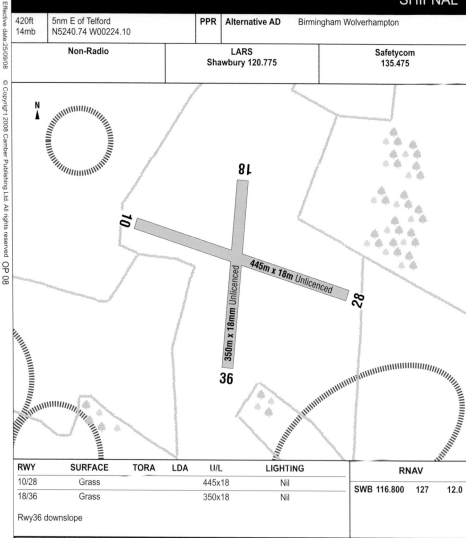

28

350m x 18mm Unlicenced

36

RWY	SURFACE	TORA	LDA	U/L	LIGHTING
10/28	Grass			445x18	Nil
18/36	Grass			350x18	Nil

Rwy36 downslope

RNAV		
SWB 116.800	127	12.0

Remarks
Strict PPR by telephone in order to advise RAF. Microlights only. AD within RAF AIAA and on the edge of Shawbury MATZ. Flying activities can only be carried out when RAF Cosford have been notified.

Warnings
Intense military activity during weekdays. AD used by RAF for helicopter pilot training. Use entry and exit points when joining the circuit. No not enter no fly zones. 4ft fence runs parallel on S side Rwy10/28 and E side going S from cross section.
Caution: Power cables within circuit.

S

Operating Hrs 0800-2000
Circuits 18, 28 RH 10, 36 LH 500ft
Join over head 1500ft AGL
No deadside
Landing Fee £2
Maintenance Nil
Fuel By prior arrangement
Disabled Facilities

Restaurant Pubs in Shifnal
Taxi Shifnal Taxis **Tel:** 01952 460044

Car Hire Nil
Weather Info Air Cen MOEx
Operator Wrekin Microlight Club
Shifnal Airfield
Shaw Lane
Shifnal
Shropshire
TF11 9PU
Tel: 07850 880351
Tel: 07882 832256
Tel: 07751 127979
Tel: 01952 619674

Industrial Estate
M54
Do NOT overfly while in circuit
18
10
28
36
Shifnal
Telford

210ft 7mb	3.5nm S of East Dereham N5237.77 E00055.68	PPR	Alternative AD Diversion AD	Norwich Old Buckenham Non-standard join

Shipdham	LARS Marham 124.150	A/G 132.250 make blind calls

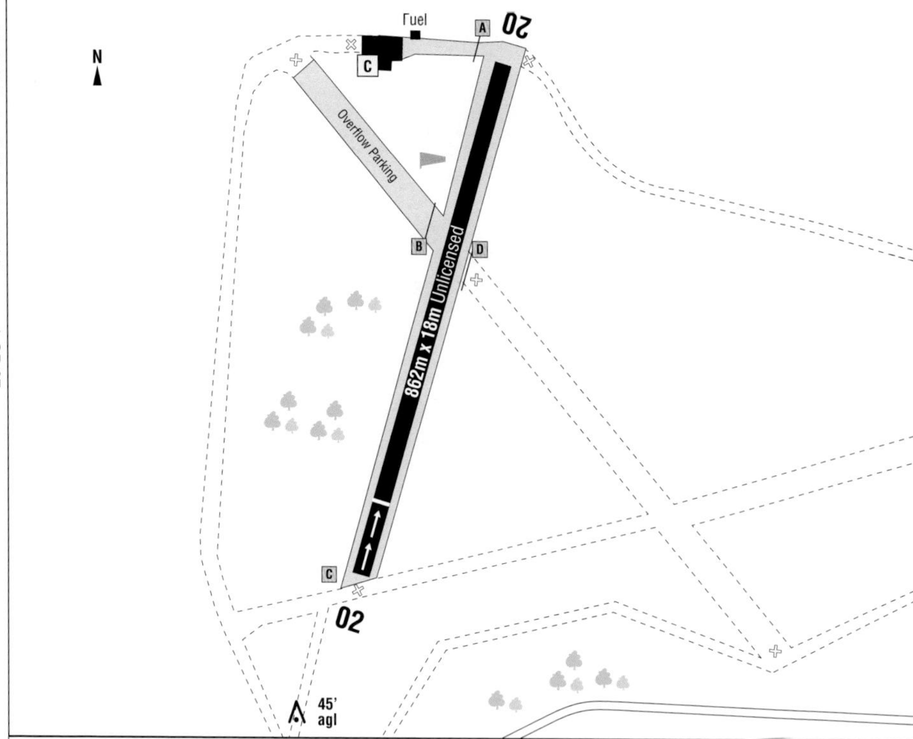

RWY	SURFACE	TORA	LDA	U/L	LIGHTING
02/20	Asphalt			862x18	Nil

RNAV

Remarks
PPR by telephone. Visiting ACFT welcome at own risk.

Warnings
All movement on AD is confined to the paved surfaces.
Noise: Avoid over flying Shipdham village 0.5nm W of AD

Operating Hrs	Sat-Sun 0900-1700 (L) Weekdays by arr
Circuit	1000ft QFE Powered ACFT to E of Rwy Gliders to W of Rwy
Landing Fee	Single £5
Maintenance	Nil
Fuel	AVGAS 100LL weekends only
Disabled Facilities	Nil
Restaurant	Cafe on AD at weekends
Taxis	
Anglia	**Tel:** 01362 690050
Car Hire	
Hertz	**Tel:** 01842 761362
Weather Info	Air SE MOEx

Operator
Shipdham Aero Club
Shipdham Aerodrome
Thetford, Norfolk, IP25 7SB
Tel: 01362 820709
www.shipdhamaeroclub.co.uk

S

EGBS SHOBDON

317ft 11mb	6nm W of Leominster N5214.50 W00252.88	PPR	Alternative AD Diversion AD	Gloucestershire Wolverhampton

Shobdon	AFIS 123.500	A/G 123.500

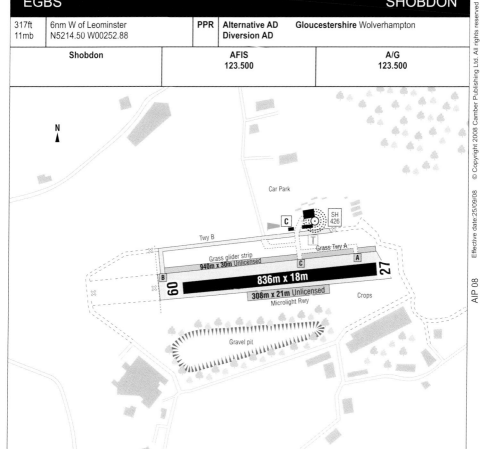

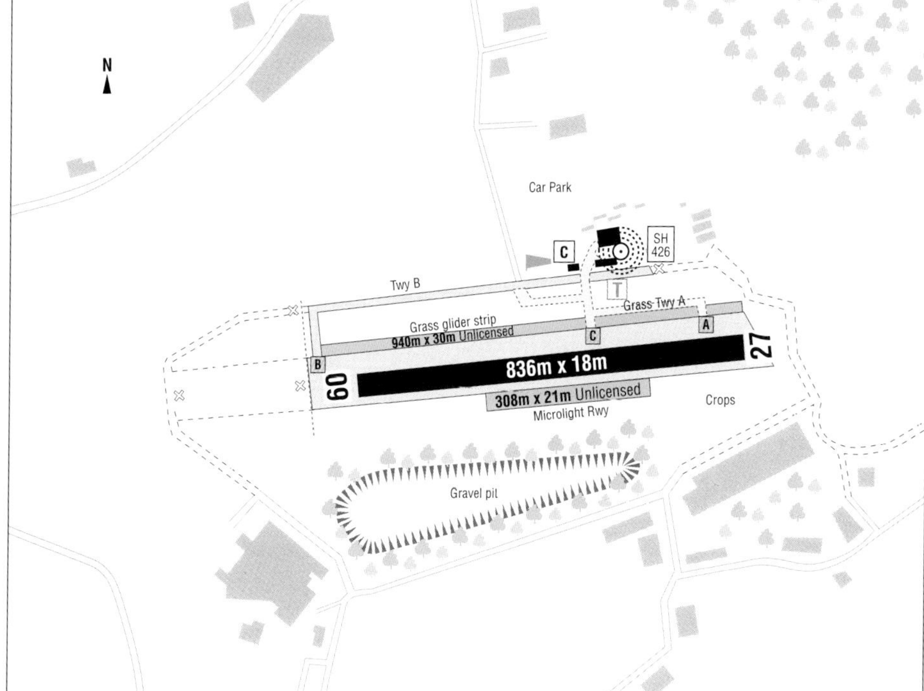

RWY	SURFACE	TORA	LDA	U/L	LIGHTING
09	Asphalt	799	836		Thr Rwy
27	Asphalt	799	836		Thr Rwy APAPI 3.5° LHS

RNAV

Remarks
PPR. Rwy09 not licensed for night use.

Warnings
Parallel asphalt Twy and W access Twy are suitable only for ACFT with a wing span <8m and wheel span <4.5m. Deviation from marked movement area can be hazardous. When Rwy27 is in use, gliders land on grass strip to N of Rwy. Grass microlight strip 280m S of main Rwy09/27. Fence 4.5ft high, 97m W of Rwy09Thr. During heavy rain the Rwy is liable to have patches of standing water. Pilots should use the centre of the Rwy at night as the outer sections are rough.

Operating Hrs Nov-Mar Fri-Wed 0900-1630
Thu 0900-2100 Apr 0800-1700
May-Aug 0800-1830
Sep-Oct 0800-1700 daily

Circuits Powered ACFT wide 09 RH, 27 LH, 1000ft QFE. Microlight/Heli using microlight strip tight 800ft QFE (Heli) 500ft QFE (Micro). Overhead joins 1500ft QFE min dead side. Descend to circuit height S of Rwy, see noise chart.

Landing Fee Single £8 Twin £16
Microlight £3

Maintenance Herefordshire Aero Club Maintenance
Tel: 01568 709170

Fuel AVGAS JET A1 100LL

Disabled Facilities Nil

Restaurants Café & bar on AD 0900-2100 (L)
Tel: 01568 708783
Camping and caravan site on AD

Taxis
Markham's **Tel:** 01568 708208

Car Hire
Watson's Leominster **Tel:** 01568 612060
Hereford Vehicle Rent **Tel:** 01432 277887

Weather Info Air N MOEx

Operator Herefordshire Aero Club Ltd
Shobdon Aerodrome, Leominster
Hereford, Herefordshire HR6 9NR
Tel: 01568 708369
Fax: 01568 708935
hac@aeroclub.co.uk
www.aeroclub.co.uk

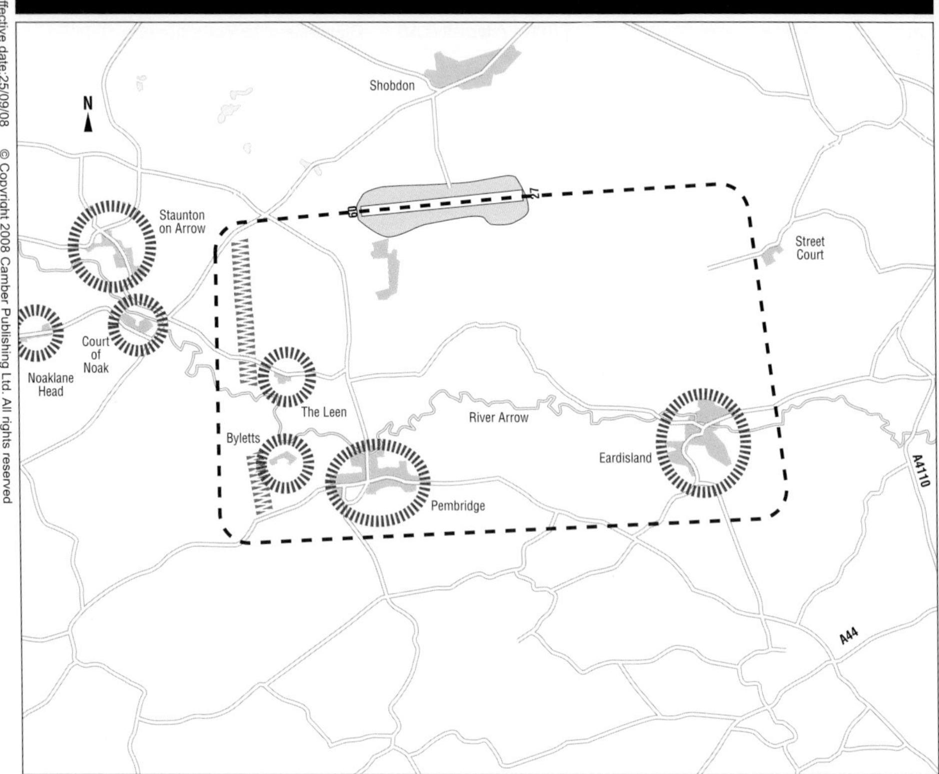
N
Shobdon
09
27
Staunton
on Arrow
Street
Court
Court
of
Noak
Noaklane
Head
The Leen
Byletts
River Arrow
Eardisland
Pembridge
A4110
A44

EGKA SHOREHAM

7ft 0mb	1nm W of Shoreham by Sea N5050.13.W00017.83	PPR	Alternative AD Diversion AD	Farnborough Chichester

Shoreham	ATIS	LARS	APP	TWR	A/G
	125.300	Farnborough East 123.225	123.150	123.150 125.400	123.150

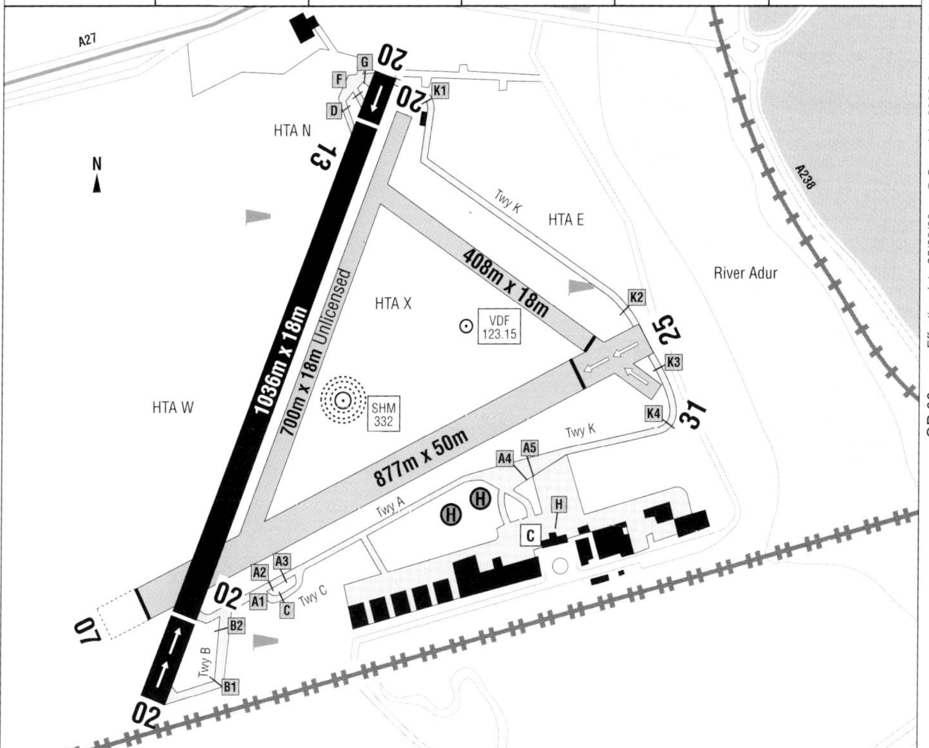

RWY	SURFACE	TORA	LDA	U/L	LIGHTING
02	Asphalt	960	871		Thr Rwy PAPI 3.5° LHS
20	Asphalt	916	865		Thr Rwy PAPI 4.5° RHS
02/20	Grass			700x18	Nil
07	Grass	877	877		Nil
25	Grass	877	794		Nil
13/31	Grass	400	400		Nil

Starter extension Rwy31 126m

RNAV			
SFD	117.00	289	16.5

Remarks

PPR for non-radio ACFT, Microlights, IR Training and qualifying cross-countries, (all of which may be refused at weekends), Hi-vis. Unless otherwise instructed, join circuit by over-flying AD at 2000ft aal, when instructed descend to circuit height on dead side of Rwy in use and join circuit by crossing upwind end. More than 1 Rwy may be in use at any one time.Rwy02/20 will always be preferred subject to operational limitations. ACFT Dept Rwy20 should avoid over-flying as much of built-up area to S as practical. Noise abatement techniques should be practised at all times, area to E & W being particularly sensitive. Training: Touch and go training is not permitted on Sundays or before 1000 and after 1800 local Mon-Sat. Rwy13/31 is not available for 'touch and go' landing. Only Rwy02/31 may be used for practice engine failures after take-off.
Contact ATC for customs details.

Helicopter Operations: Extensive helicopter training takes place in area W of **Rwy02/20 ('W') alongside E perimeter fence ('E') and N of VDF aerial ('X'). Helicopter circuits will vary in direction. Helicopter Arr & Dept should follow ATC instructions closely and will be subject to specific ATC authorisation to cross Rwys, more than one of which may be in use at any one time. Helicopters should avoid over-flying built up areas that are adjacent to the Arr/Dept routes.**

Radio failure procedures: In the event of an ACFT experiencing radio failure during daytime, join over head AD, fit into the traffic pattern, over fly Rwy in use at 500ft before positioning for landing. Standard light signals should be followed.

Visual aid to location: Ibn SH Green.

Warnings

Caution soft GND either side of Twy K. Enter/exit using marked points only. Caution on Twy A, ensure adequate wing tip separation from ACFT holding at Hold C. Mobile obstructions (up to 50ft) on adjacent roads and railways. ACFT APP Rwy02 (hard) are reminded of the displaced Thr due to the elevated railway line. Kite flying/Surfing between Shoreham beach up to 132ft daily during daylight Hrs. Model ACFT flying up to 100ft, approx 1nm from Rwy20 Thr.

Operating Hrs	Mon-Sat 0700-1900 or SS Sun 0730-1930 or SS (Summer) Mon 0800-1800 Tue-Sat 0800-1900 Sun 0830-1800 (Winter), & by arr
Circuits	Variable, normally LH ACFT 1100ft QFE Heli 600ft QFE
Landing Fee	500kgs-1.5MT £18 1.5MT-2.5MT £36
Maintenance	
AS Engineering	**Tel:** 01273 464791
MCA	**Tel:** 01273 464222
KB Air	**Tel:** 01273 453333
Apollo Aviation	**Tel:** 01273 440737
Fuel	AVGAS JET A1 100LL

Disabled Facilities

Restaurants	Restaurant refreshments & Club facilities available **Tel:** 01273 467373
Taxis	At terminal **Tel:** 01273 414141
Car Hire	
Europcar	**Tel:** 01273 329332
Avis	**Tel:** 01273 673738
Hertz	**Tel:** 01273 738227
Weather Info	M T9 Fax 422 A MOEx ATIS **Tel:** 01273 467372
Operator	Shoreham Airport Shoreham-by-Sea West Sussex BN43 5FF **Tel:** 01273 467377/78 (ATC) **Tel:** 01273 467374 (Reception) **Fax:** 01273 467370 admin@shorehamairport.co.uk www.shorehamairport.co.uk

Shoreham Arrival & Departures

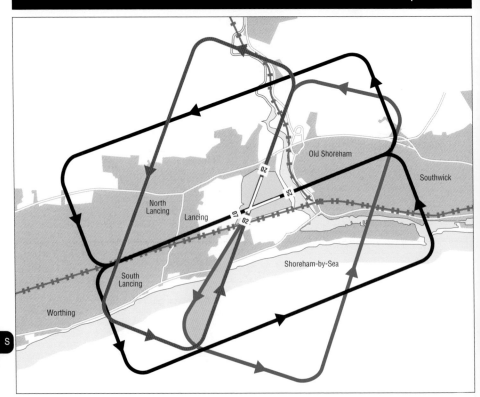

Visual Reference Points (VRP)

Brighton Marina	N5048.65 W00006.05
Lewes Intersection	N5051.87 W00001.45
Littlehampton	N5048.77 W00032.78
Washington Intersection	N5054.57 W00024.47

S

SHOTTESWELL

530ft 17mb	3nm N of Banbury N5206.25 W00122.80		**Alternative AD** **Cranfield** Wellesbourne Mountford

Non-radio	APP Birmingham 118.050	Safetycom 135.475

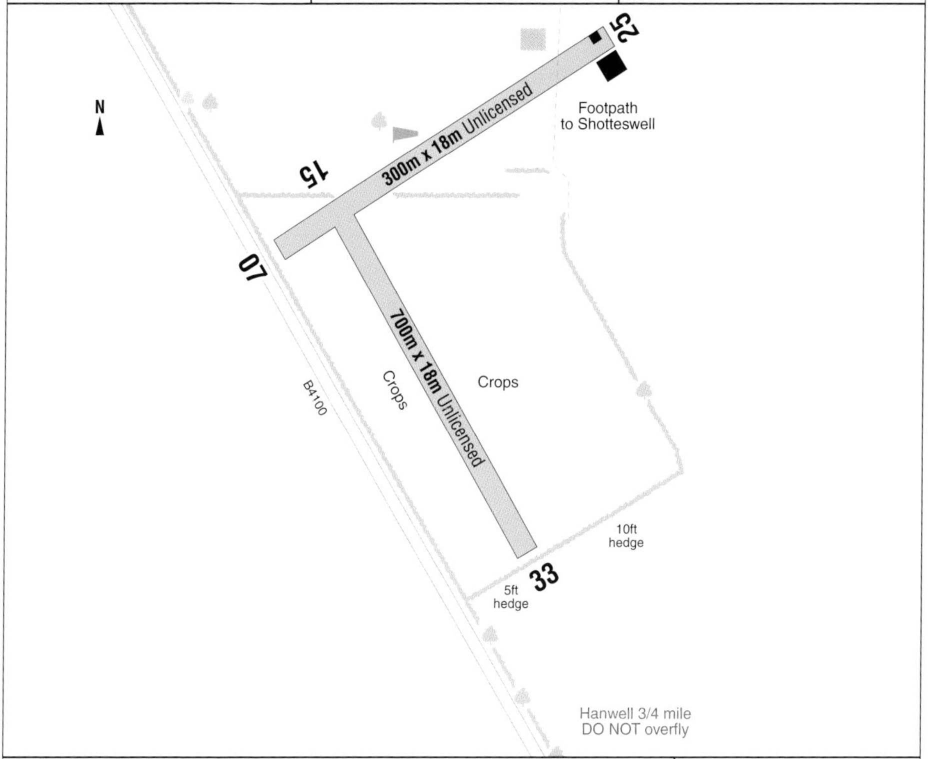

RWY	SURFACE	TORA	LDA	U/L	LIGHTING
15/33	Grass			700x18	Nil
07/25	Grass			300x18	Nil

RNAV			
DTY	116.40	247	10.5

Remarks
PPR not required, considerate visitors welcome at own risk. Rwy15/33 smooth slightly undulating surface. Rwy07/25 use only when crosswind precludes use of Rwy15/33. Orange windsock on N boundary. Rwy surface maintenance excellent.

Warnings
Hedge rows up to Thr all Rwys. Crops E edge Rwy15/33 & S edge Rwy07/25. Rwy07/25 only recommended for use by microlights, STOL ACFT& experienced pilots due to parked ACFT & hangars Rwy25 Thr. Also upslope from Rwy25 Thr.
Noise: Avoid over flying local villages particularly Hanwell on Rwy33 APP.

Operating Hrs	SR-SS
Circuits	1000ft QFE
Landing Fee	Nil
Maintenance	Nil
Fuel	Nil
Disabled Facilities	Nil
Restaurants	The Wobbly Wheel Motel 0.75 mile from AD
Shotteswell Hse	**Tel:** 01295 738227 (B&B)
Taxis	**Tel:** 01295 270011 **Tel:** 01295 264774
Car Hire	Nil
Weather Info	Air Cen MOEx

Operator
Chris O'Donnell
43 Trinity Close
Banbury
Oxon
OX16 0UB
Tel: 07971 719661
Fax: 01295 709174
chris@chervale.co.uk

Effective date:25/09/08 OP 08

110ft 4mb	6nm ESE of Bedford N5205.33 W00019.09	PPR	Alternative AD Diversion AD	**Cranfield** Little Gransden

Shuttleworth	A/G 130.700	AFIS 130.700 Display days & occasional events only

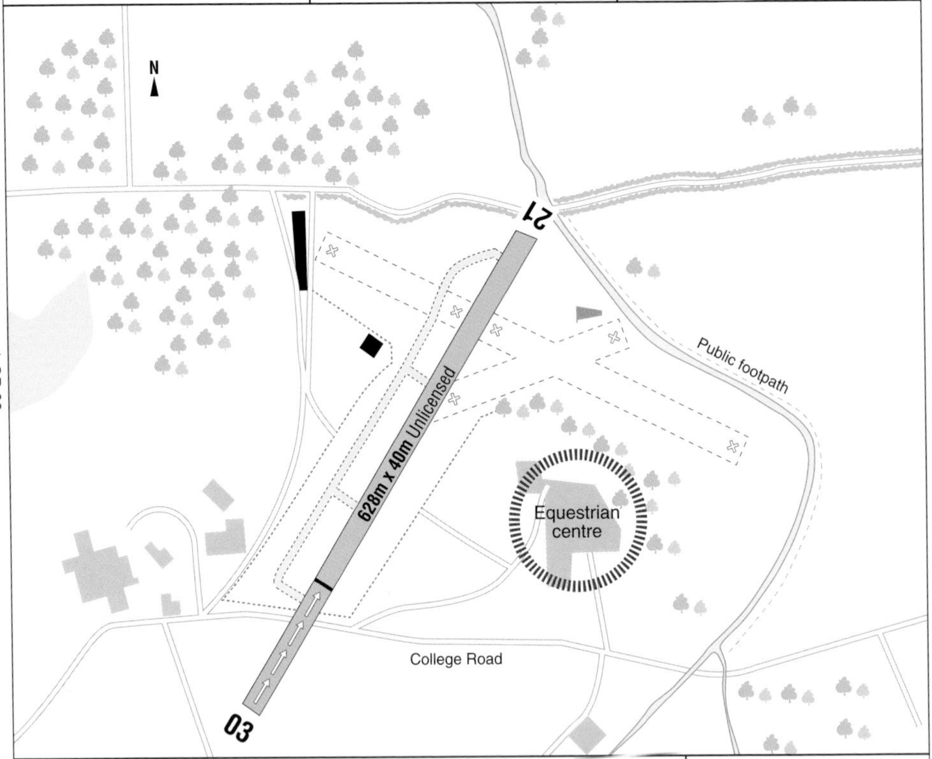

RWY	SURFACE	TORA	LDA	U/L	LIGHTING
03/21	Grass			628x40	Nil

Rwy03 has marked down slope
Rwy extension S of Rwy03 not available to visiting ACFT

RNAV			
BKY	116.25	296	15.3

Remarks
PPR by telephone essential. AD closed some days for public events, consult NOTAMs. On non-event days please book in at Shuttleworth shop. On flying days & for events parking is limited PPR should be obtained well in advance. A slot time will be issued. Special admission charges apply. Non-radio ACFT from the collection may be conducting flight trials or practice displays. Vacate Rwy03/21 to NW as directed by ATC.

Warnings
Do not backtrack on Rwy. High sided vehicles use College Rd keep good lookout. During winter months sheep may be grazing AD. Birds of pray fly over AD up to 500ft agl. Aero-modellers may be present, normal circuit should be flown to enable them to clear Rwy.

Operating Hrs	0900-1700
Circuits	Join overhead 21 LH, 03 RH, 800ft QFE
Landing Fee	See website
Maintenance	Available in emergency only
Fuel	AVGAS 100LL Flying days only must be requested immediately on Arr, cash payment only

Disabled Facilities

Restaurants	Full facilities avail until 1700 (1600 Nov-Mar)

S

Taxis	**Tel:** 01767 316438
Maurice	**Tel:** 01234 262222
Car Hire	On request or
Biggleswade Mtr Co	**Tel:** 01767 313788
Weather Info	Air Cen MOEx
Operator	The Shuttleworth Trust Old Warden/Biggleswade Aerodrome Northill, Biggleswade Beds, SG189EP **Tel:** 01767 627563 **Fax:** 01767 627949 enquiries@shuttleworth.org www.shuttleworth.org

Shuttleworth Arrival Procedure (Displays & Events)

1 On first contact state Booking ref & ACFT details. If unable to meet your slot time please advise early as others are keen to visit. Pilots should be aware that a practice display may be in progress using conflicting Rwy. ATC will advise and may request a delay.
2 Non-radio ACFT are required to Arr within +/-10 mins of slot time. Pilots should be aware that a practice display may be in progress using conflicting Rwy. LOOK OUT FOR LIGHT SIGNALS.
3 All ACFT to make a standard overhead join and visual circuit. Keep a good lookout for non-radio ACFT
4 After landing vacate Rwy to NW ASAP unless otherwise instructed by ATC. There are Twy but the whole of the AD is useable with care.
5 The LAST available time for arrival is 1Hr before start of the display
6 All movements on AD require ATC approval with specific reference to entering or crossing Rwys. Marshallers or the security team may provide additional supervision.
7 On display days pilots should book-in at the base of the TWR to receive an ID pass to allow pilot & passenger access airside solely to return to your ACFT. Prior to Dept ATC must be advised before you return to your ACFT

Departure Procedure (Displays & Events)
1 Visiting ACFT may not Dept before display has ended.
2 All movements on the manoevering area require approval from ATS. All Rwys must be treated as active and **only crossed with specific clearance.**
3 Exits from visiting ACFT park cross Rwys. Report when No 1 at the exit and obtain ATS permission to proceed. Please also satisfy yourself of no confliction. Also observe marshallers.
4 All visiting ACFT at any time should avoid low flying or aerobatics in the vicinity of the AD.

Effective date:25/09/08

190ft 6mb	3nm E of Lichfield N5242.30 W00144.50	PPR	Alternative AD **Birmingham** Tatenhill

Non Radio	APP Birmingham 118.050	A/G Roddige 129.825	Safetycom 135.475

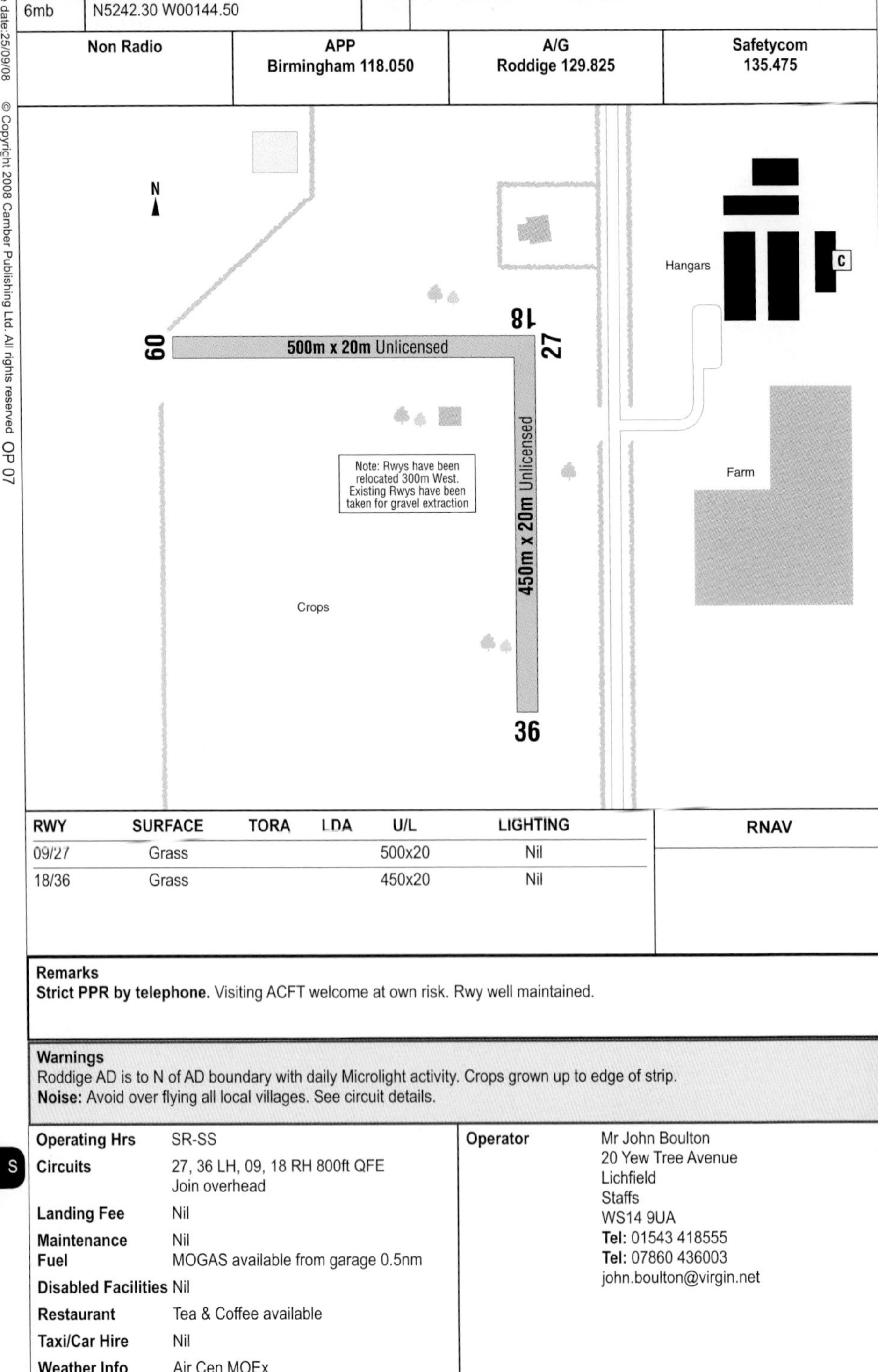

RWY	SURFACE	TORA	LDA	U/L	LIGHTING
09/27	Grass			500x20	Nil
18/36	Grass			450x20	Nil

RNAV

Remarks
Strict PPR by telephone. Visiting ACFT welcome at own risk. Rwy well maintained.

Warnings
Roddige AD is to N of AD boundary with daily Microlight activity. Crops grown up to edge of strip.
Noise: Avoid over flying all local villages. See circuit details.

Operating Hrs	SR-SS
Circuits	27, 36 LH, 09, 18 RH 800ft QFE Join overhead
Landing Fee	Nil
Maintenance	Nil
Fuel	MOGAS available from garage 0.5nm
Disabled Facilities	Nil
Restaurant	Tea & Coffee available
Taxi/Car Hire	Nil
Weather Info	Air Cen MOEx

Operator
Mr John Boulton
20 Yew Tree Avenue
Lichfield
Staffs
WS14 9UA
Tel: 01543 418555
Tel: 07860 436003
john.boulton@virgin.net

S

SKEGNESS

10ft 0mb	1.5nm N of Skegness N5310.40.E00020.00	PPR	Alternative AD	**Humberside** Wickenby

Non-standard join

Skegness	LARS Conningsby 120.800	LARS Waddington 127.350	A/G 132.425

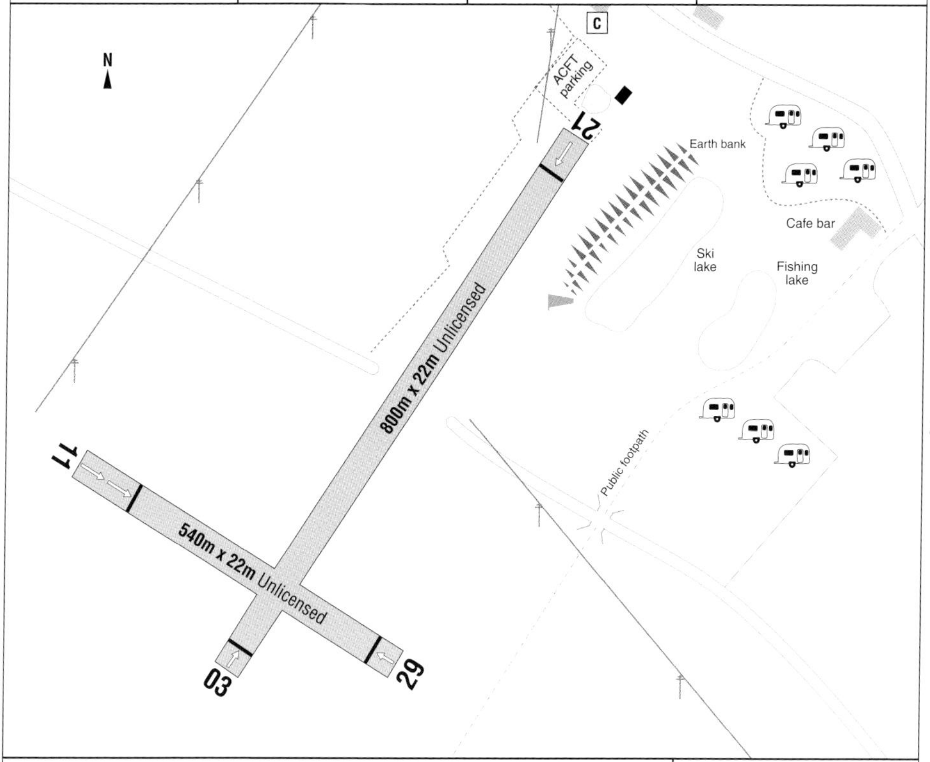

N
C
ACFT parking
21
Earth bank
Cafe bar
Ski lake
Fishing lake
800m x 22m Unlicensed
11
540m x 22m Unlicensed
Public footpath
03
29

RWY	SURFACE	TORA	LDA	U/L	LIGHTING
11/29	Grass			540x22	Nil
03/21	Grass			800x22	Nil

Starter extension Rwy11 192m, Starter extension Rwy29 45m

RNAV

Remarks
AD situated within Water Leisure Park complex 0.5nm from Butlins Fun Coast World (day tickets available).

Warnings
AD close to N boundary of the Wash AIAA. ACFT Arr from S must contact Coningsby during their Ops Hrs, other times Waddington. Rwy11 displaced Thr due to over head power lines on AD boundary.
Noise: Rwy03 ensure base leg turn is made before built up area of Skegness

Operating Hrs	Request only. Closed Mondays
Circuits	LH 800ft QFE
Landing Fee	£7 pay at hangar or site reception
Maintenance	
M3	**Tel:** 01754 611127 **Tel:** 07957 595835
Fuel	Nil
Disabled Facilities	Nil
Restaurants	Available in Water Leisure Park during summer season
Taxis	Nil
Car Hire	Available by arr
Weather Info	Air Cen MOEx

Operator
Mr F Ellis
Skegness Water Leisure Park
Walls Lane
Skegness
Links
Tel: 07957 595835
Fax: 01754 611127

Effective date:25/09/08 OP 08

EGCV SLEAP

275ft 9mb	10nm N of Shrewsbury N5250.03 W00246.30	PPR	Alternative AD Diversion AD	**Hawarden** Wolverhampton **Non-standard join**

Sleap	LARS Shawbury 120.775	A/G 122.450

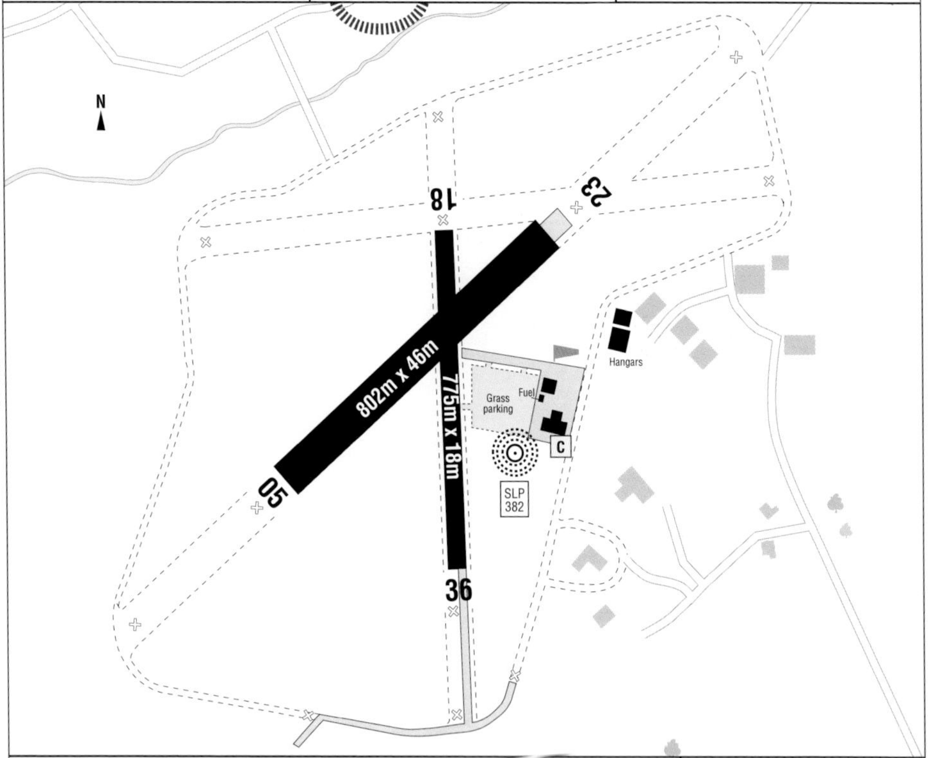

RWY	SURFACE	TORA	LDA	U/L	LIGHTING
05/23	Asphalt	802	802		Thr Rwy LITAS 3.5°
18/36	Asphalt	775	775		Nil

Starter extension Rwy23 50m (day only)

RNAV			
SWB	116.80	302	4.5

Remarks
Strict PPR by telephone. AD not available for public transport passenger flights and civil helicopter training flights or jet ACFT. Inbound ACFT are to contact Shawbury. ACFT not to be parked on grass parallel to Twy or opposite to fuel pumps. Used for helicopter training Mon-Fri visiting ACFT must obtain a telephone briefing.
Visual aid to location: Ibn Green SP

Warnings
Glider launching takes place on AD. Pilots are warned that deviation from the marked movement area can be hazardous. Circuits to W of AD are active with intense military rotary activity when RAF Shawbury are active.
Caution: RAF Shawbury entry /exit gates exist just to the SE of Sleap ATZ.

S

Operating Hrs Fri-Wed 0900-1700
Thu 0900-2015 (Summer) +1Hr (Winter)

Circuits Variable – See circuit procedures

Landing Fee Single £10, Twin £20

Maintenance Shropshire Light Aviation
Tel: 01939 290861

Fuel AVGAS Jet A1 100LL

Disabled Facilities

Restaurants Hot & cold food/drinks available

Taxis
Wem Taxis **Tel:** 01939 233673
Shawbury Taxis **Tel:** 01939 250777

Car Hire Nil

Weather Info Air Cen MOEx

Operator Shropshire Aero Club Ltd
Sleap Aerodrome
Harmer Hill
Shropshire, SY4 3HE
Tel: 01939 232882
Fax: 01939 235058
info@shropshireaeroclub.com
www.shropshireaeroclub.co.uk

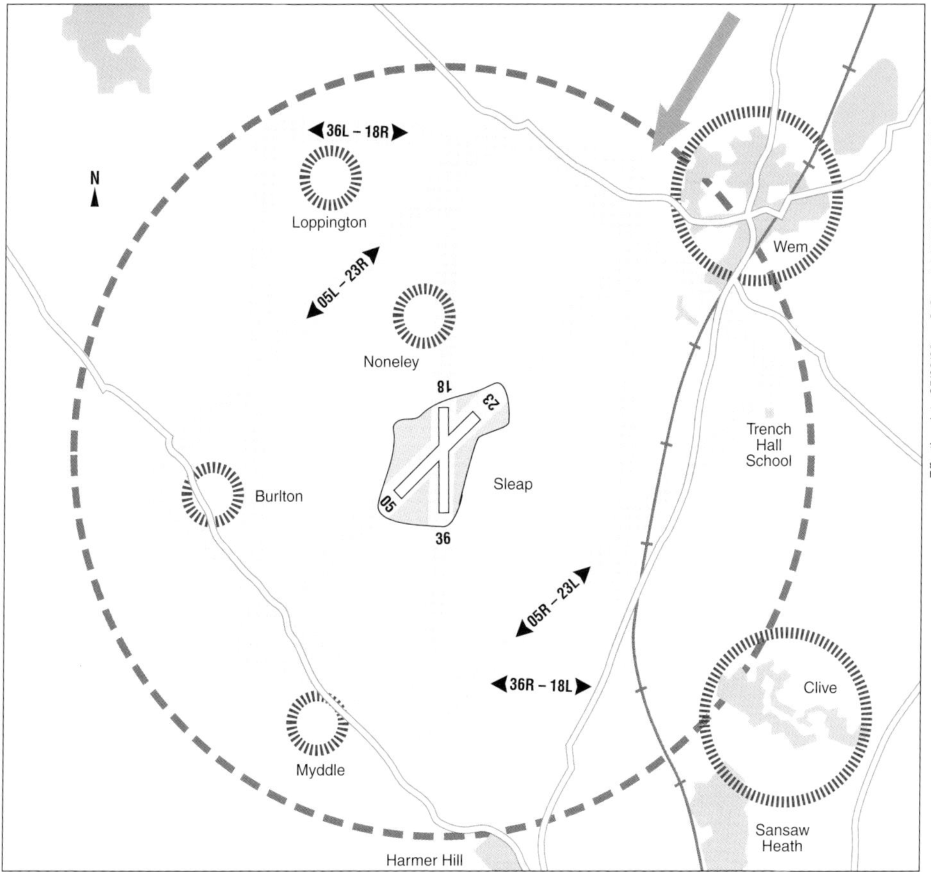

Joining procedures: Weekend standard joins 2000ft QFE. Weekdays ACFT should carry out non-standard centre line join 2000ft QFE. Call for briefing.

RAF Shawbury entry /exit gates exist just to the SE of Sleap ATZ.

Circuit Procedures:

Circuit Height 1000ft QFE

Circuits generally LH except when RAF Shawbury is active, when circuits will be E of AD.

Circuits should be contained within ATZ(large broken circle).

Circuit patterns shown are required maxima.

Avoid over flying Wem, Clive, Myddle, Loppington, Noneley & Burlton.

Arr ACFT should carry out standard 2000ft overhead joining procedure except when RAF Shawbury are active when ACFT should carry out a centre line join at 2000ft QFE. A full briefing on this procedure must be obtained by contacting the operator before dept.

ACFT APP Rwy23 on a straight-in or long final should keep to W of Wem (220°).

ACFT especially high-powered singles or twins Dept Rwy36 should make a10° right turn after take-off to avoid Noneley village.

0ft 0mb	1nm NE of Sollas village N5739.51 W00719.33	PPR	Alternative AD	Benbecula

Non-Radio	ATIS 113.950 (BEN VOR)	Benbecula APP 119.200	Scottish FIS 127.275	Safetycom 135.475

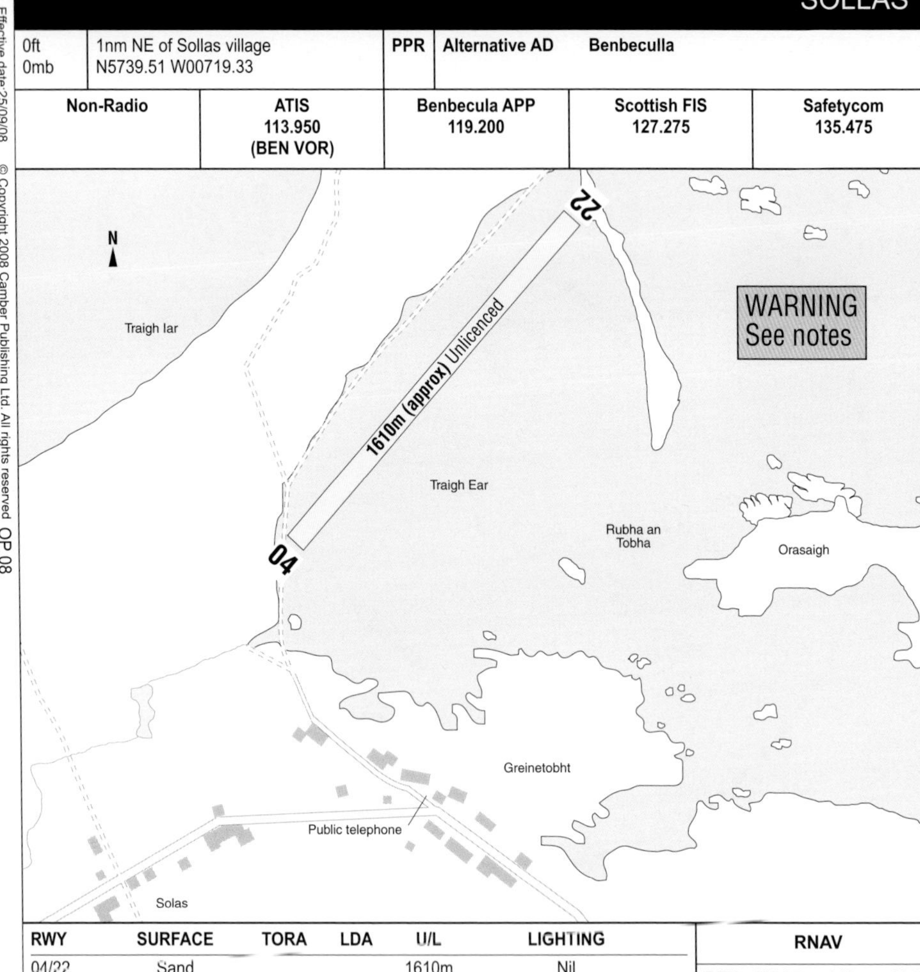

RWY	SURFACE	TORA	LDA	U/L	LIGHTING
04/22	Sand			1610m	Nil

RNAV			
BEN	113.95	013	10.5

Remarks
AD is a public beach. PPR is not required, pilots are strongly recommended to obtain local info from local PPL – See Operator. To calculate tide time use tables for Lochmaddy. There are no facilities at the beach. Annual fly-in is held in September.

Warnings
Beach flying operations can be dangerous, the information given is for guidance only. Pilots are welcome at their own risk. All dimensions and Rwy headings are approximate. The useable portion is below the high water mark. Pilots should exercise caution during the flare and hold-off as height judgement may be difficult over the feature less surface. Preferred landing technique is to use power down to touchdown.
Caution: S end of strip may be subject to ridgeing and standing water which will be clearly seen when flying over to inspect. Beach is used by agricultural vehicles as a route to a farm lane. Pilots must ensure that vehicles and pedestrians are clear of beach.

Operating Hrs SR-SS
Circuits N at 1000ft
Landing Fee Nil
Maintenance Nil
Fuel Nil
Disabled Facilities Nil
Restaurant Nil
Taxi
Buchanan **Tel:** 01870 602277
MacVicar **Tel:** 01870 602307
Maclennan **Tel:** 01870 602191
Car Hire Maclennan Tel: 01870 602191

Weather Info Air Sc GWC
Operator Mr J A Macleod (Local PPL)
17 Balallen
Isle of Lewis
H52 9PN
Tel: 01851 830366
Tel: 07778 673513
jaml.bal@tiscali.co.uk

460ft 15mb	8nm WNW of Hull N5346.30 W00034.62	PPR	Alternative AD	**Humberside** Beverley

Non-radio	LARS Humberside 119.125	Safetycom 135.475

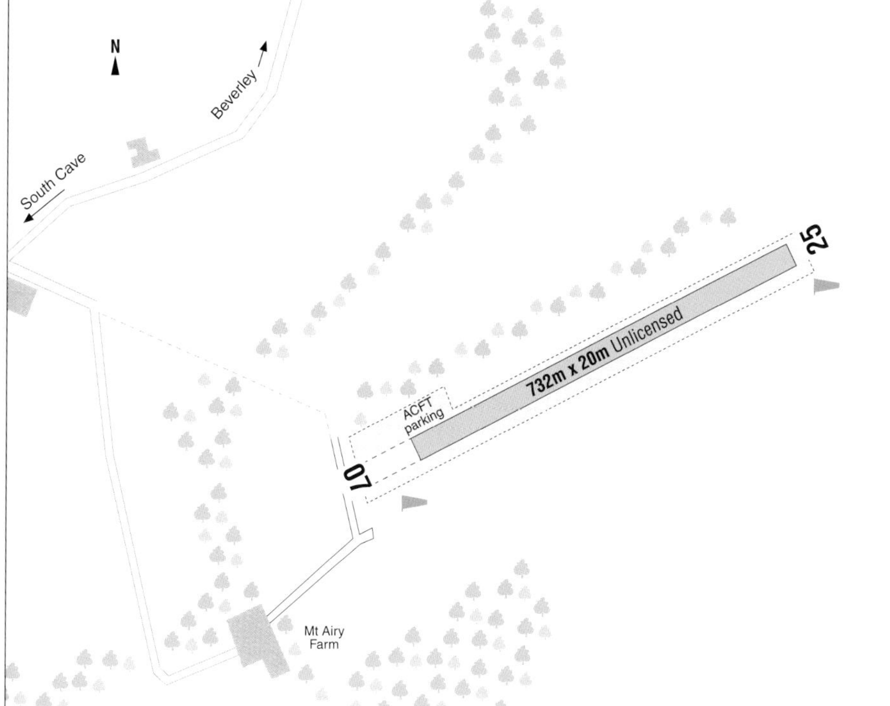

RWY	SURFACE	TORA	LDA	U/L	LIGHTING
07/25	Grass			732x20	Nil

Rwy25 2.3° down gradient

RNAV			
OTR	113.90	288	17.4

Remarks
PPR. Visitors welcome at pilots own risk. Pilots of visiting ACFT must obtain a briefing on landing and take-off procedures. Available by telephone from AD operator at weekends.

Warnings
Caution: Steeply rising GND and trees on W boundary produce roll-over which should be anticipated at any time, particularly with strong winds. Public footpath crosses undershoot of Rwy07 95m short of Thr. Radio masts 208ft agl close to N of Rwy25 APP 1300m from Thr. Low flying high speed military ACFT may be encountered in the vicinity of AD.
Noise: Avoid over flying village of South Cave W of AD.

Operating Hrs	No takeoff before 0800 or after 2000 (L) Landings are permitted
Circuits	07 RH, 25 LH 1000ft QFE
Landing Fee	Singles £5 Microlights £3 Twins & Business use £10
Maintenance	Can be arr on a call out basis
Fuel	Nil
Disabled Facilities	Nil
Restaurants	Food available in South Cave (1.25nm)
Taxis/Car Hire	Courtesy Car usually available or taxi arr
Weather Info	Air N MOEx

Operator
N & L May
Mount Airy Farm
South Cave
Brough, East Yorkshire, HU15 2BD
Tel: 01430 422395/422973 (Operator)
Fax: 01430 422395

Effective date:25/09/08

EGHI SOUTHAMPTON

44ft 2mb	3.5nm NNE of Southampton N5057.02 W00121.40	PPR	Alternative AD Diversion AD	Bournemouth Thruxton

Non-standard join

Southampton	ATIS 113.350 (SAM VOR)	ZONE Solent APP 120.225	APP 128.850
LARS Farnborough West 125.250	RAD 128.850	TWR 118.200	FIRE 121.600

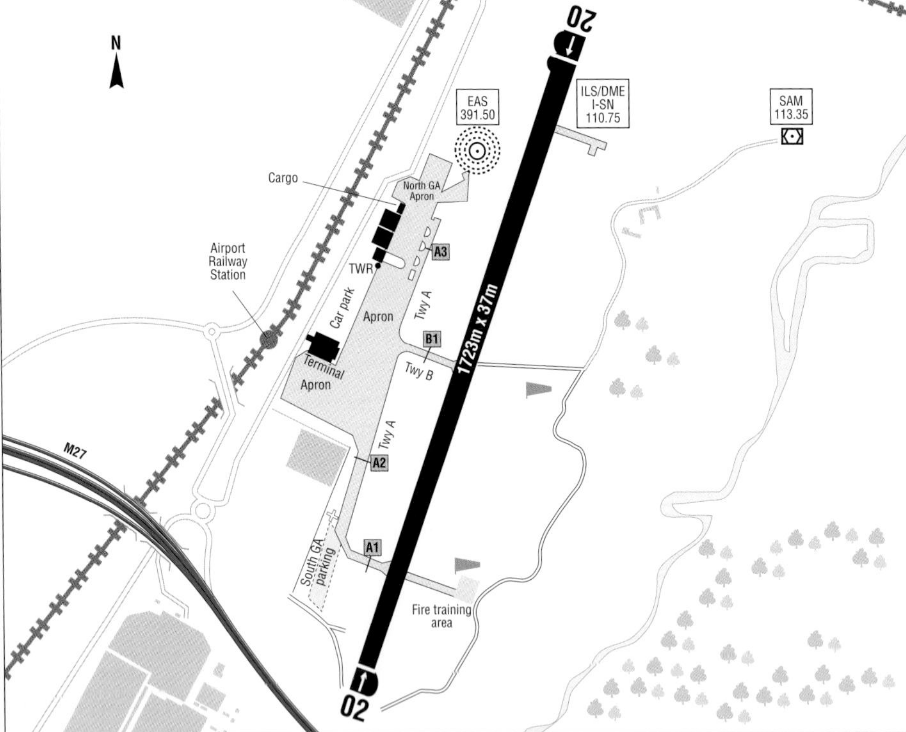

RWY	SURFACE	TORA	LDA	U/L	LIGHTING
02	Asphalt	1723	1650		Ap Thr Rwy PAPI 3°
20	Asphalt	1650	1605		Ap Thr Rwy PAPI 3.1°

Displaced Thr Rwy02 73m, Displaced Thr Rwy20 45m

RNAV

SAM 113.35 On AD

Remarks

PPR for visiting GA ACFT. Non-radio ACFT not accepted. Landing/taxiing grass areas prohibited. Use of AD by training flights subject approval from AD operator. Requests for approval to ATC briefing unit.

Warnings

GA ACFT parking stands 9-11, S/N GA aprons required to use AD GND transport. ACFT commanders responsible for safety of themselves, passengers/crew when airside. When GND transport not provided all passengers/crew to be escorted by ACFT commander, Circuit training by helis not permitted.

Noise Preferential Routes & Procedures: After take-off Rwy20 ACFT not below 500ft agl, turn right make good track of 218°M maintain track to 2000ft (Southampton AD QNH) or Southampton Water (compatible with ATC requirements), individual cases may be varied by ATC.

S

Operating Hrs	Mon-Fri 0530-2130 Sat 0530-1945 Sun 0630-2130 (Summer) + 1 Hr (Winter)
Circuits	Day 1000ft QNH, Night 1500ft QNH
Landing Fee	Available with PPR
Maintenance	
Signature Aviation	**Tel:** 02380 620727
Fuel	AVGAS JET A1 100LL

Disabled Facilities	Nil
Handling	**Tel:** 02380 616600 (Signature) **Fax:** 02380 629648 (Signature)
Restaurants	Cafe bar at AD
Taxis	
Airport Cars	**Tel:** 02380 627100
Car Hire	
Avis/Hertz/	**Tel:** 02380 629600

Weather Info	M T9 A Fax 424 VS MOEx ATIS **Tel:** 02380 627103	**Operator**	BAA Southampton, Southampton Airport, Southampton, Hamps SO18 2NL **Tel:** 02380 629600 (AD Switchboard) **Tel:** 02380 627113 (AD Duty Manager) **Tel:** 02380 627102 (AD Ops) **Tel:** 02380 627243 (ATC) **Fax:** 02380 629300 **Fax:** 02380 627104 (Duty Ops Mgr)

Effective date:25/09/08

Southampton Controlled Airspace

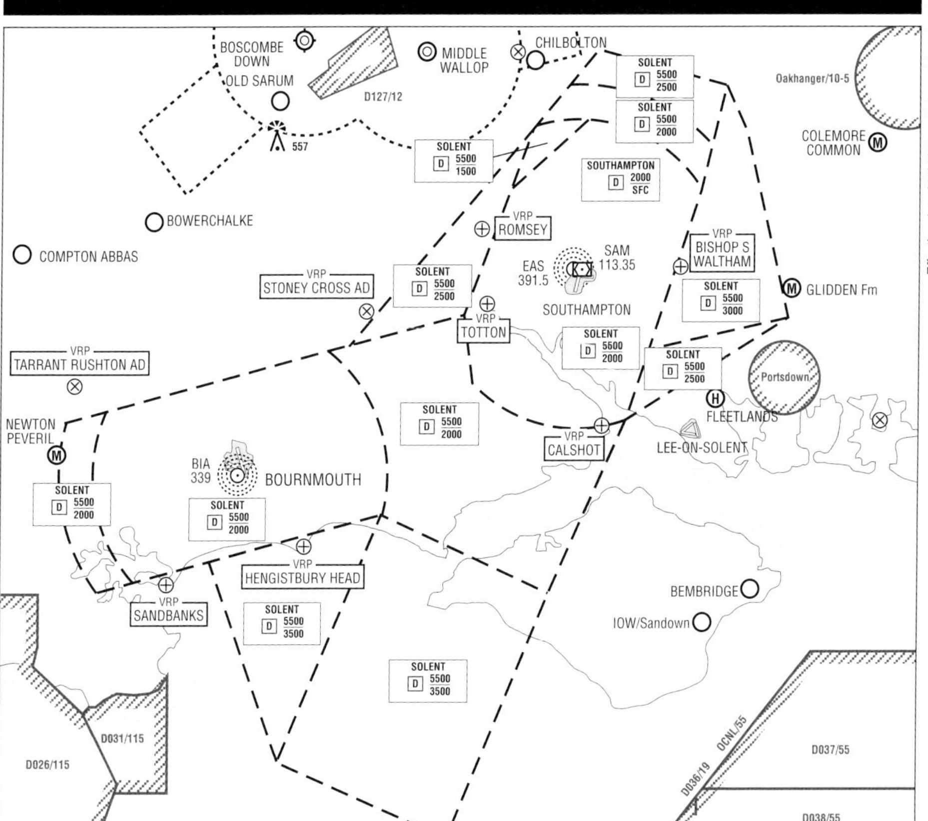

CTA/CTR Class D Airspace

Normal CTA/CTR Class D Airspace rules apply.
Transition Alt 6000ft. Outside the Solent CTA notified hours Transition Alt 3000ft.
These rules do not apply to non-radio ACFT by day provided they have obtained permission and maintain 5km visibility, 1500m horizontally and1000ft vertically away from cloud, or for gliders provided they maintain 8km visibility, 1500m horizontally and 1000ft vertically away from cloud.
Pilots are advised that Lower Upham and Roughay Farm have notified airspace within the Southampton Control Zone, within the arc of a circle of 2nm radius at N5056.25 W00113.88. daylight hrs, SFC-1500ft amsl. Pilots operating under VFR or Special VFR clearance are advised to avoid this area. Traffic information will not be passed by ATC.

S

VFR Transit Traffic

VFR traffic wishing to transit the Southampton CTR from the E or W should plan to route via ROMSEY-SAM Bishops Waltham or vice versa.

Visual Reference Points (VRP)

VRP	VOR/NDB	VOR/DME
Bishops Waltham N5057.28 W00112.58	SAM 093°/EAS 093°	SAM 093°/5nm
Calshot N5049.07 W00119.75	SAM 178°/BIA 086°	SAM 178°/8nm
Romsey N5059.45 W00129.75	SAM 293°/EAS 295°	SAM 293°/6nm
Totton N5055.20 W00129.33	SAM 251°/EAS 250°	SAM 250°/6nm

49ft 1mb	1.5nm N of Southend on Sea N5134.28 E00041.73		**Alternative AD** **Diversion AD**	**Biggin Hill** Rochester

Southend	ATIS	LARS	APP	RAD	TWR	Handling
	136.050	130.775	130.775	130.775	127.725	131.400

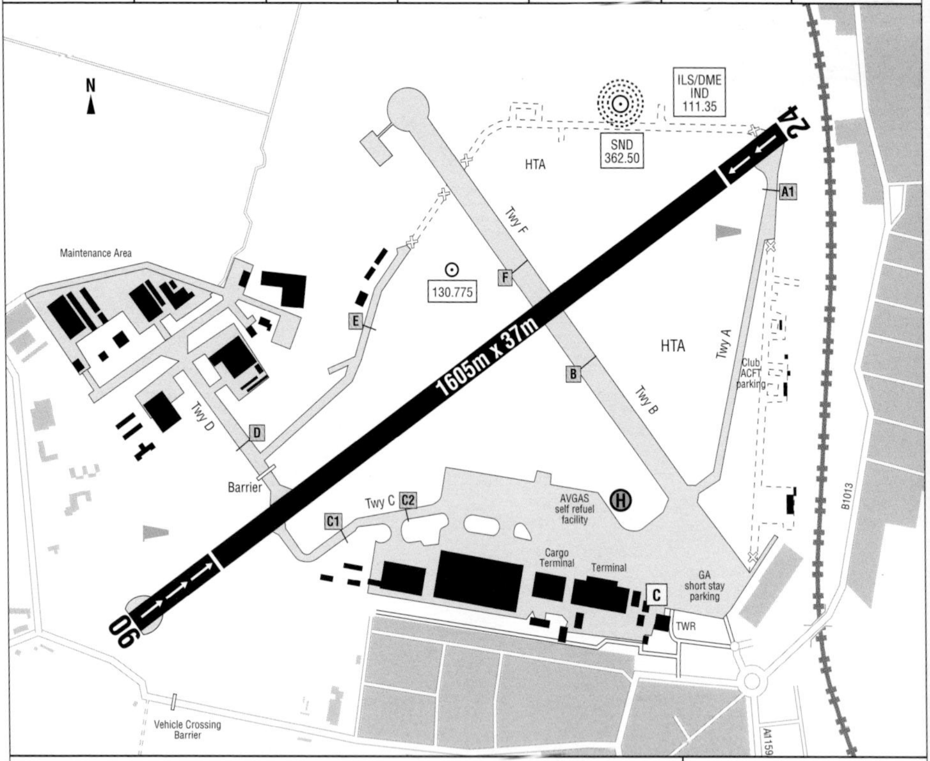

RWY	SURFACE	TORA	LDA	U/L	LIGHTING
06	Asphalt	1459	1285		Ap Thr Rwy PAPI 3° RHS
24	Asphalt	1531	1399		Ap Thr Rwy PAPI 3.5° LHS

Displaced Thr Rwy24 146m, Displaced Thr Rwy06 174m

RNAV			
DET	117.30	016	16.5

Remarks
PPR Instrument training, QXC's, examination flights & non-radio ACFT. Hi-Vis. Dept all propeller driven ACFT must climb straight ahead at least 600ft aal before turning. Dept Rwy24 propeller driven ACFT requiring a left turn shall, pass 600ft aal, maintain track 190° to N bank River Thames, or until Detling DME 13nm or less, before setting course. Busy public road crosses extended Rwy centreline at SW end Rwy06/24. APP Rwy06/24 in VMC intercept Rwy extended centreline min range 2nm from touchdown not below PAPI APP slope 3° Rwy06 or 3.5° Rwy24. Heli training S of Rwy between Twy A & B and N of Rwy. Heli circuits normally parallel fixed wing Rwy in use at 500ft/1000ft as advised by ATC. Twy barriers installed across Twy D S of Hold D max height 3ft agl. Barriers controlled by ATC and lit. AVGAS self-fuelling facility for Southend account card holders/Air BP holders only. GA park by TWR ACFT <PA31 self parking. ACFT nose wheel must be left on, but perpendicular to broken line. Pilots operating into AD must read and accept the terms and conditions of use. Slots required for instrument APP and circuit training, advise ATC of cancellations or delays of >10mins.
Visual aid to location: Abn White flashing.

Warnings
Not all Twy are available for use, ATC will advise. Deviation from marked movement area hazardous. Twy D is un-lit, use at pilots own discretion. Extensive instrument flying takes place 0800-2000.

Operating Hrs	H24
Circuits	Variable at the discretion of ATC
Landing Fee	£19.98 per 1000kg Discount for circuits & go-arounds
Parking Fee	<2.5 tonnes <2Hrs Free, 2-4 Hrs £6.46, 4-8 Hrs £12.04, 8-24 Hrs £14.69 Night surcharge £58.75 2300-0600 (L)

Maintenance	Available (major)
Fuel	AVGAS JET A1 100LL

Disabled Facilities

Handling **Tel:** 01702 608150
handling@southendairport.net

S

Restaurant	Restaurant in Terminal (Mon-Fri 0800-1530 Sat-Sun 1000-1500) **Tel:** 01702 608138 McDonalds 300m SE Terminal	Operator	Regional Airports Ltd London Southend Airport Southend-on-Sea Essex, SS2 6YF **Tel:** 01702 608125 (FBO) **Tel:** 01702 608120 (ATC) **Fax:** 01702 608128(ATC) fbo@southendairport.net www.southendairport.net
Taxis At terminal	**Tel:** 01702 334455		
Car Hire Budget Hertz	 **Tel:** 01268 772774 **Tel:** 01702 546666		
Weather Info	M T9 A Fax 426 VS MOEx		

Visual Reference Points (VRP)

Billericay	N5138.00 E00025.00
Maldon	N5143.70 E00041.00
Sheerness	N5126.50 E00044.90
St Marys Marsh	N5128.50 E00036.00
South Woodham Ferrers	N5139.00 E00037.00

Pilots are requested to contact APP prior to reaching abeam any of the VRP's when inbound or over flying the area.

Arrivals & Departures

VFR flights and over flight must establish communications with ATC at least 5 minutes before ETA overhead Southend and prior to reaching abeam any of the VRP's. Instructions may be issued with a restriction, this does not absolve pilots from any requirement they may have to remain in VMC at all times, pilots must advise ATC if they are unable to comply.
Arr or over flying VFR flights must avoid the instrument APP let down areas and dept climb outs at all times, unless ATC have indicated no traffic. ATC may specify a specific route or track requirement to assist pilots. Pilots wishing to make a standard overhead join are to request this on initial contact.

VFR Departures

Depts may be issued with a level and/or routing restrictions by ATC to assist in deconflicting traffic and is circuit integration. Pilots are advised that IAP's may be flown that do not conform to the Rwy in use.

335ft 11mb	6nm SW of RAF Wittering N5233.95 W00036.34	PPR	Alternative AD	East Midlands Peterborough Conington **Non-standard join**

Non-Radio	LARS Cottesmore 130.200	Safetycom 135.475

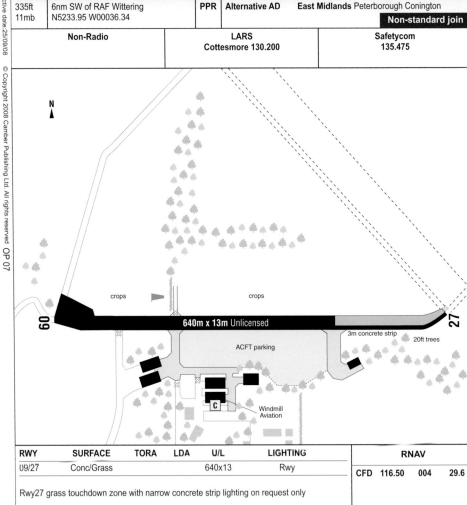

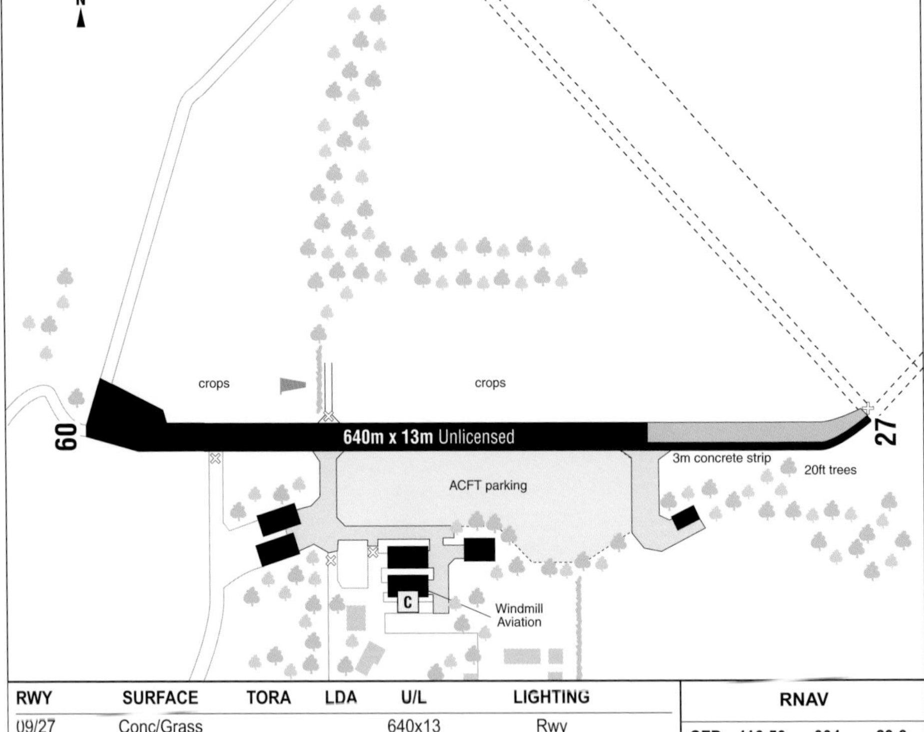

RWY	SURFACE	TORA	LDA	U/L	LIGHTING
09/27	Conc/Grass			640x13	Rwy

Rwy27 grass touchdown zone with narrow concrete strip lighting on request only

RNAV			
CFD	116.50	004	29.6

Remarks
Strictly PPR by telephone. Home of Windmill Aviation (M3). AD situated on S. perimeter track of WW2 AD, all other areas unsuitable for aviation use.

Warnings
AD situated beneath the SW MATZ stub of RAF Wittering, (controlling authority Cottesmore). Arr/Dept ACFT may be requested to contact Wittering TWR. Inbound ACFT contact Cottesmore and prior to Dept. Caution: Vehicles occasionally use Rwy.
Noise: Avoid over flight of local villages.

S

Operating Hrs Mon-Sat 0800-1900 (L) by arr
Closed Sunday

Circuits Variable 1000ft QFE

Landing Fee Advised with PPR

Maintenance
Windmill Aviation **Tel:** 01780 450205
Hangarage available for visiting ACFT by arr

Fuel AVGAS 100LL

Disabled Facilities Nil

Restaurants/Accomodation
Spanhoe Lodge **Tel:** 01780 450328
Guest House **Tel:** 01780 450328
White Swan **Tel:** 01572 747543 (Harringworth)

Taxis
Corby Cabs **Tel:** 01536 260033

Car Hire Nil

Weather Info Air Cen MOEx

Operator Windmill Aviation
Spanhoe Airfield
Laxton, Corby
Northants, NN17 3AT
Tel/Fax: 01780 450205

EGSG STAPLEFORD

185ft 6mb	4.5nm N of Romford N5139.15 E00009.35	PPR	**Alternative AD** **Diversion AD**	**Southend** Elstree

Stapleford	**APP** **Thames RAD** **132.700**	**APP** **Stansted 120.625**	**LARS** **Farnborough North 132.80**	**A/G** **122.800**

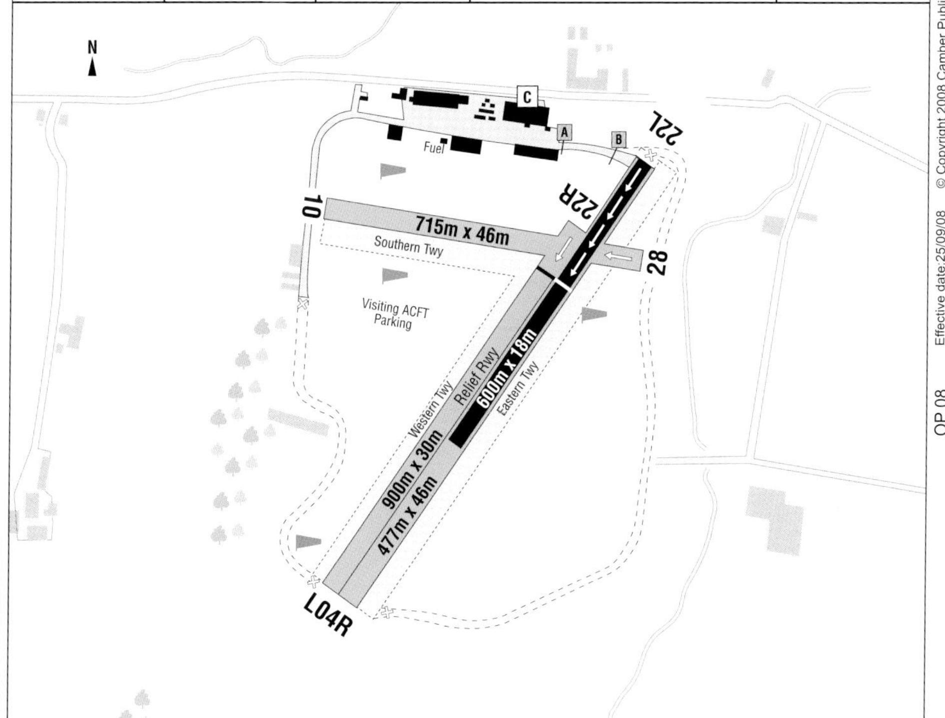

RWY	SURFACE	TORA	LDA	U/L	LIGHTING
04R	Grass/Asph	1127	1077		Ap Thr Rwy APAPI 4.5° RHS
22L	Asph/Grass	1100	900		Ap Thr Rwy APAPI 4.25° LHS
10	Grass	698	698		Nil
28	Grass	715	500		Nil
04L	Grass	900	900		Nil
22R	Grass	900	900		Nil

Rwy22L 600mx18m asphalt insert starts 17m after beginning of TORA
Starter extension Rwy04 50x44m, Starter extension Rwy22L 23x48m
Displaced Thr Rwy28 215m, Displaced Thr Rwy22L 177m

RNAV			
LAM	**115.60**	**010**	**1.0**

Remarks

PPR 2Hrs outside published Hrs of operation. Licensed relief Rwy has been established to W, parallel to and adjoining Rwy04/22. Rwy is marked with white corners and white painted edge markers. Pilots may be asked to use this Rwy at certain times.

Warnings

Radio mast 295ft aal SW of AD and 1.2nm from Rwy04 Thr in line withRwy04/22. Do not land short of displaced Rwy22L/22R Thr. Power cables 210ftagl running NW/SE 1nm NE of Rwy22 Thr. Not all Twys available for use during winter months, deviation from marked manoeuvring area can be hazardous. E Twy closed, clear right after landing Rwy22L.
Noise: Avoid over flying villages of Abridge and Lambourne below 1000ft agl. Rwy28 Dept ACFT should maintain Rwy heading until passing 1000ft agl. Rwy22Dept: No right turn below 1000ft agl.

Operating Hrs	0830-SS (L) & by arr	**Maintenance**	Stapleford Maintenance **Tel:** 01708 688449
Circuits	LH 1200ft QNH	**Fuel**	AVGAS JET A1 100LL with PPR
Landing Fee	Single £15 Twin/Heli £30 £5 per night parking Out of Hrs by arr		

Disabled Facilities

Restaurants	Cafe & bar at AD
Taxis	
Theydon Bois	**Tel:** 01992 814335
Car Hire	
Hertz	**Tel:** 01708 721882
Weather Info	Air SE MOEx

Operator

The Herts and Essex Aero Club Ltd
Stapleford Aerodrome
Stapleford, Romford
Essex, RM41SJ
Tel: 01708 688380
Fax: 01708 688421
www.flysfc.com

STOKE AIRFIELD

10ft 0mb	4nm W of Sheerness N5126.64 E00037.96		**Alternative AD** **Southend** Rochester

Stoke	**LARS** **Southend 130.775**	**A/G** **118.925**

A228
N
Middle Stoke
Stoke
200ft pylons
400m x 20m Unlicensed
06
24
Stoke Saltings

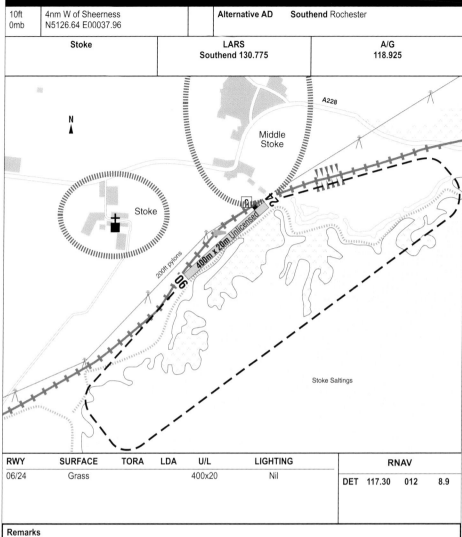

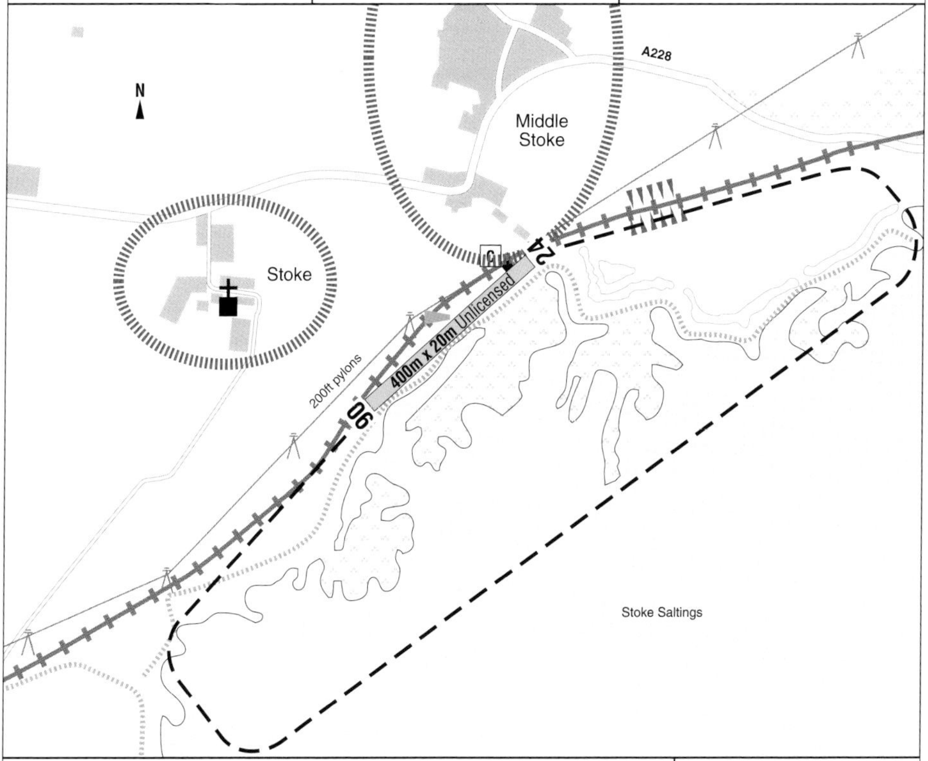

RWY	SURFACE	TORA	LDA	U/L	LIGHTING
06/24	Grass			400x20	Nil

RNAV			
DET	**117.30**	**012**	**8.9**

Remarks
PPR not required visiting ACFT & microlights welcome. Intense microlight training site please keep a good lookout & make blind calls if no reply. Strip has a very slight curve over its entire length. Taxi on the sea wall side of Rwy & park with propeller close to bushes, first 4 spaces used by school ACFT only. Visitors book in at club hut.

Warnings
National grid transmission lines 200ft high parallel to Rwy and final APP on land ward side. Railway passes along this side of AD between Rwy & pylons. The seaward marsh is SSSI do not over fly below 500ft QFE.
Noise: Do not over fly Stoke village or St Mary's Marsh to N of AD.

Operating Hrs	SR-SS Last permitted take-off 2000 (L)
Circuits	06 RH, 24 LH 800ft QFE Join overhead 1500ft QFE (Slightly offset final APP to avoid transmission lines)
Landing Fee	Mon-Fri £2 Sat-Sun & PH £4
Maintenance	Medway Microlight Factory 200 yds from AD Mon-Fri 0900-1700 sales service & maintenance
Fuel	MOGAS at local village 0800-1800 (L) 7-days (transport available with notice)
Hangarage	Available for de-rigged microlights & 3 axis
Disabled Facilities	Nil

Restaurants/Accomodation	Hot & cold drinks Mon-Fri Food available weekends Accomodation can be arr
Taxis	
Hoo Cabs	**Tel:** 01634 251234
Car Hire	Nil
Weather Info	Air SE MOEx
Operator	Medway Microlights Stoke Airfield Stoke, Rochester Kent, ME3 9RN **Tel:** 01634 270236 (AD) **Tel:** 01634 270780 (Factory)

Effective date:25/09/08 OP 08

STOKE GOLDING

300ft 10mb	4nm NE of Nuneaton N5234.82 W00125.72	PPR	Alternative AD	**Birmingham** Leicester

Stoke Golding Radio	A/G 127.925

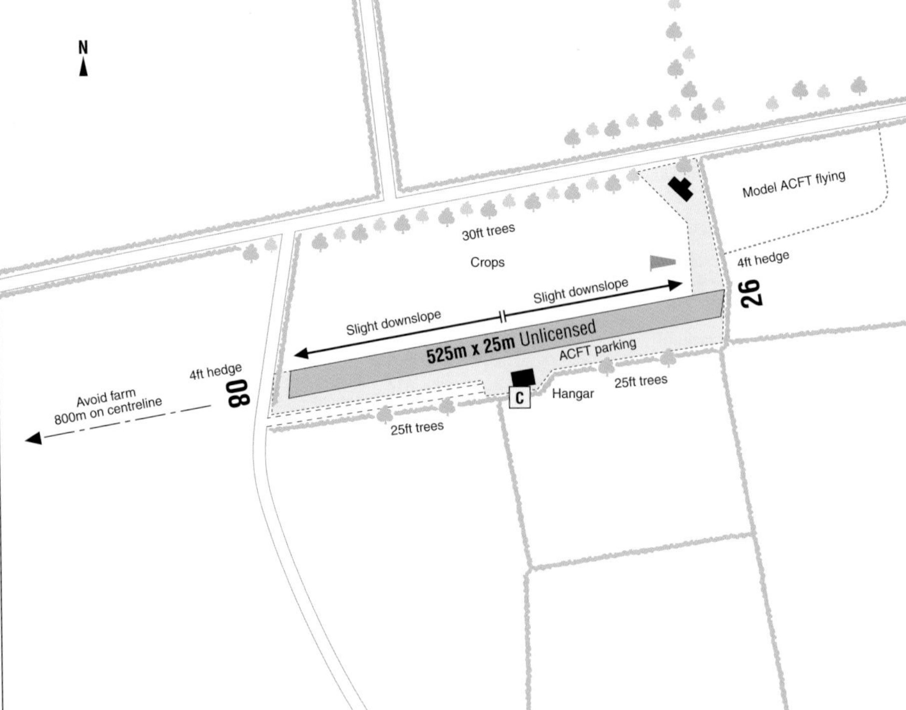

RWY	SURFACE	TORA	LDA	U/L	LIGHTING
08/26	Grass			525x25m	Nil

RNAV			
HON	113.65	036	15.8

Remarks
PPR by telephone or Website. Very friendly strip, visiting ACFT and microlights welcome at pilots own risk. Battle of Bosworth site and Shackerstone steam railway short distance from AD.

Warnings
Large model ACFT may operate at W/E, PH & some evenings. Modellers will land on observing ACFT making overhead join to circuit. Do not turn over head control line models.
Noise: Avoid over flying Stoke Golding village, and farms and houses in close vicinity to AD, particularly the farm 800m from Rwy08 Thr. Rwy26 depts make early turn to avoid farm.

S

Operating Hrs	SR-SS
Circuits	26 RH, 08 LH 1000ft QFE
Landing Fee	Donation to grass-cutting welcomed
Maintenance	Nil
Fuel	AVGAS available by prior arr
Disabled Facilities	Nil
Restaurant	Refreshments normally available at W/E
Dog & Hedgehog	**Tel:** 01455 212629 (Dadlington village)
Taxi/Car Hire	Operator can assist
Weather Info	Air Cen MOEx

Operator
Tim Jinks
Sminks Aviation
95 Main Road
Baxterley
Warwickshire, CV9 2LE
Tel: 01827 712706
Tel: 07771 701498
e-mail via website
www.stokegoldingairfield.co.uk

EGPO STORNOWAY

26ft 1mb	2nm E of Stornoway N5812.93 W00619.87		Alternative AD Diversion AD	Benbecula

Stornoway	ATIS 115.100 (on STN VOR)	APP 123.500	TWR/AFIS 123.500	FIRE 121.600

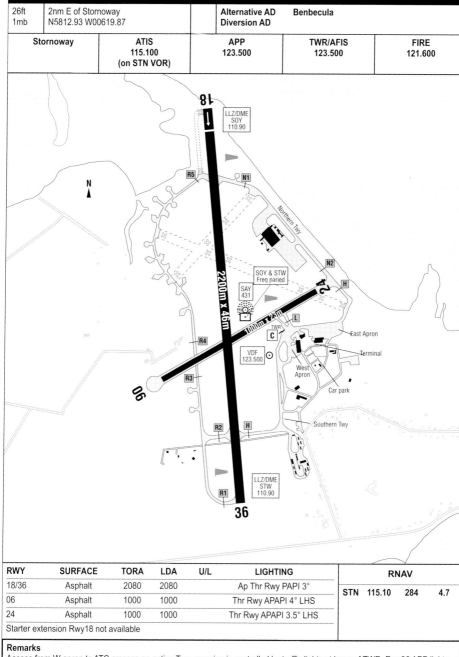

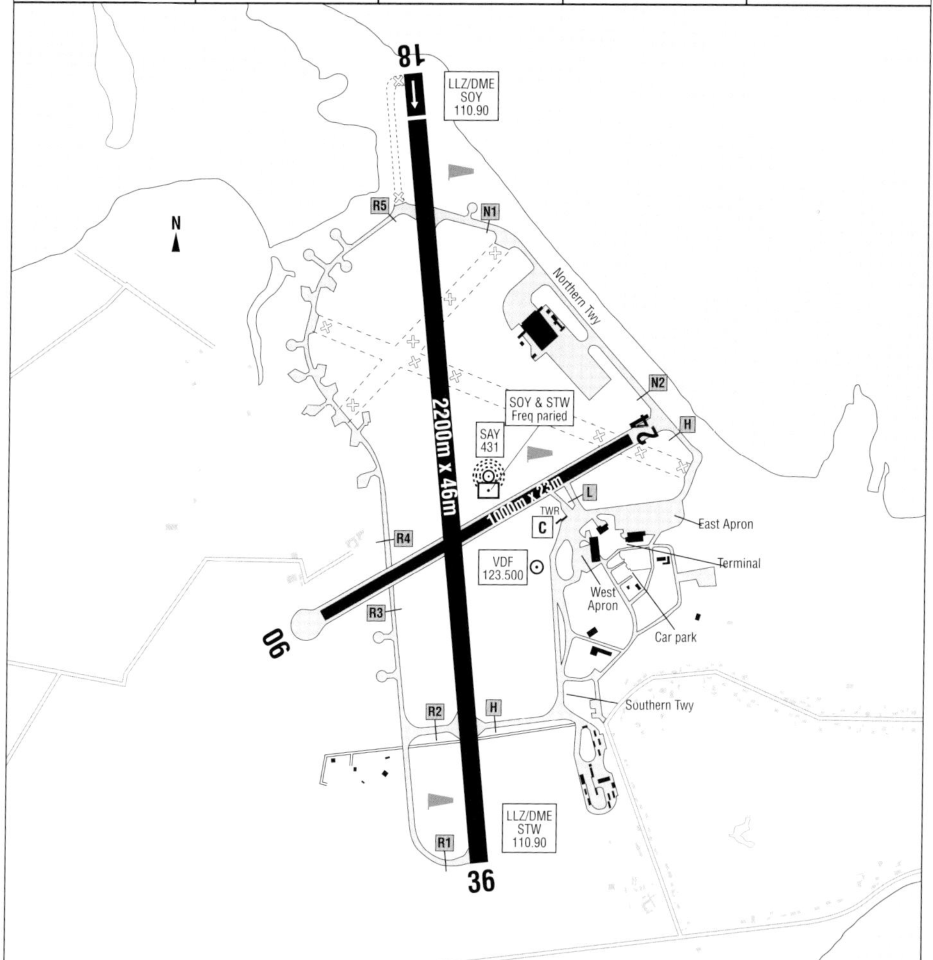

RWY	SURFACE	TORA	LDA	U/L	LIGHTING
18/36	Asphalt	2080	2080		Ap Thr Rwy PAPI 3°
06	Asphalt	1000	1000		Thr Rwy APAPI 4° LHS
24	Asphalt	1000	1000		Thr Rwy APAPI 3.5° LHS

Starter extension Rwy18 not available

RNAV			
STN	115.10	284	4.7

Remarks

Access from W apron to ATC crosses an active Twy, crossing is controlled by traffic lights at base of TWR. Rwy36 APP lights terminate 150m short Thr. Rwy06/24 no night landings. Flight clearance, Weather info and Customs (General Declaration) all available from ATC.

Warnings

Grass areas soft & unsafe. No GND signals except light signals. N & S Twys on E side of AD 15m wide. Use only marked Twys. Rwy36 Thr displaced a public road crosses APP. Use minimum APP angles of 3° as indicated by PAPI. 120m asphalt Rwy extending beyond Rwy36 Thr not avail for ACFT manoeuvring or starter extension. Western apron surface uneven, mashalling instructions must be complied with. SK61 Coast Guard helicopter operates priority over other traffic for SAR duties.

Operating Hrs	Mon-Fri 0645-1730 Sat 0645-1600 (Summer) +1Hr (Winter) & by arr	Circuits Landing Fee	18, 24 LH, 06, 36 RH £12 ACFT up to 3MT VFR cash, cheque or credit card on day

Maintenance Nil

Fuel AVGAS JET A1 100LL
Tel: 01851 703026
Available outside published Hrs
by arr with ATC

Disabled Facilities

Handling **Tel:** 01851 701282 (Highland Airways)
Tel: 01851 703673 (British Airways)

Restaurants Refreshments & bar
Pubs & restaurants in Stornoway

Taxis
Central **Tel:** 01851 706900

Car Hire
Stornoway Car Hire **Tel:** 01851 702658

Weather Info M T9 T18 Fax 428 VSc GWC
ATIS **Tel:** 01851 707444

Operator HIAL Stornoway Aerodrome
Isle of Lewis, HS2 0BN
Tel: 01851 707415 (ATC)
Tel: 01851 707400 (Admin)
Fax: 01851 707402 (ATC)
Fax: 01851 707401 (Admin)
stornatc@hial.co.uk
www.hial.co.uk

STRATHALLAN

120ft 4mb	4nm SE of Crieff N5619.50 W00344.91	PPR	**Alternative AD** **Dundee** Perth **Non-standard join**

Strathallan	A/G 129.900

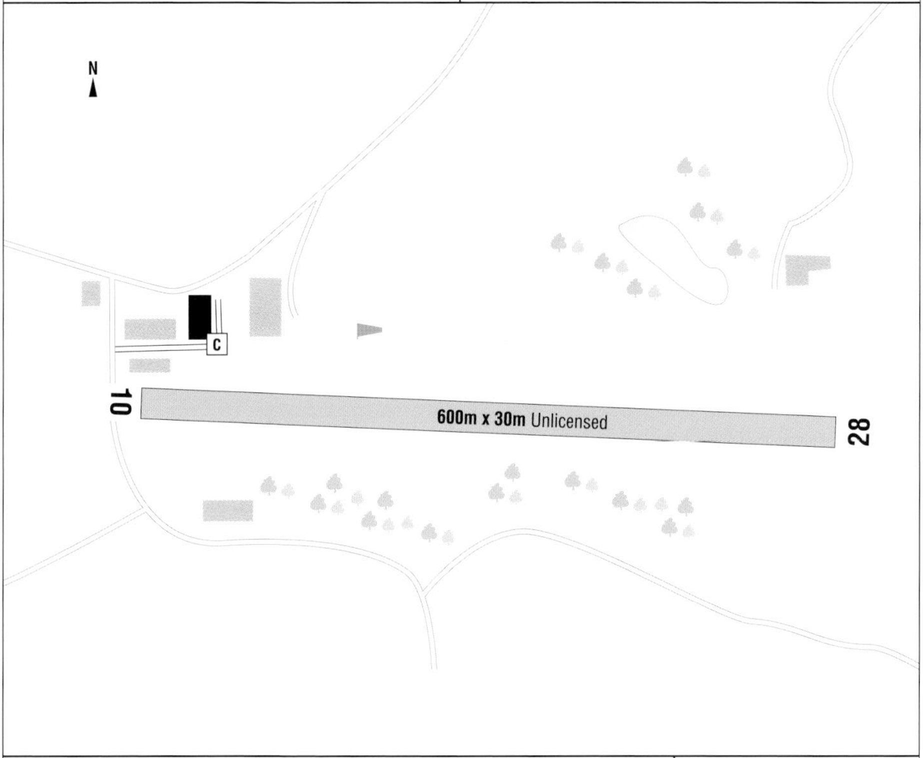

N

10

600m x 30m Unlicensed

28

C

RWY	SURFACE	TORA	LDA	U/L	LIGHTING
10/28	Grass			600x30	Nil

RNAV

Remarks
PPR by telephone. Non-radio ACFT not accepted. Call Strathallan, if no response, assume no parachuting. Para-dropping ACFT will advise. Before starting engines, obtain permission.

Warnings
Intensive free-fall parachuting takes place up to FL120. High GND 1225ft aal (1345ft amsl) 4nm SE of AD. Sheep may graze on AD. **Noise:** ACFT must not over fly AD.

Operating Hrs	Fri-Sun & PH 0900-2100 or SS (L)
Circuits	10 RH, 28 LH, 1000ft QFE No over head joins
Landing Fee	Nil
Maintenance	Nil
Fuel	Nil
Disabled Facilities	Nil
Restaurants	Cafe at weekends 0900-2100 (L)
Taxis/Car Hire	Available on request
Weather Info	Air Sc GWC

Operator
Scottish Parachute Club
Strathallan Aerodrome
Auchterarder
Perthshire PH3 1LA
Tel: 01764 662572 (Weekends)
Tel: 01698 832462
(Kieran Brady Weekdays)

847ft 28mb	19.5nm NE of Prestwick Airport N5540.80 W00406.33	PPR	Alternative AD	Prestwick

Non-Radio	ATIS Prestwick 121.125	FIS Scottish 119.875	Safetycom 135.475

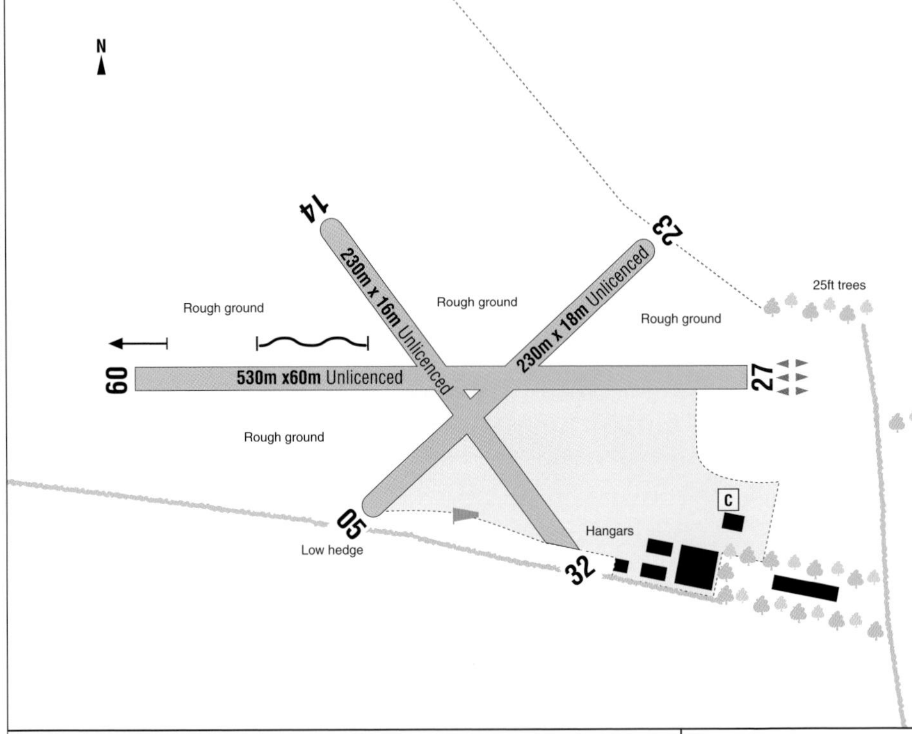

RWY	SURFACE	TORA	LDA	U/L	LIGHTING
09/27	Grass			530x60m	Nil
05/23	Grass			230x18m	Nil
14/32	Grass			230x16m	Nil

RNAV

Remarks
PPR by telephone. Visiting pilots welcome at own risk. Microlight training takes place at the AD.

Warnings
AD situated on high gnd close to SE corner of Glasgow CTR Class D Airspace. Rwys appear longer from the air than actual dimensions. Middle section of AD prone to waterlogging after heavy rain. Smoothest section is from Rwy27 Thr to secondary Rwy intersection.
Caution: Ridge close to Rwy27 Thr where there is a buried wall. Rwy09 slopes down 10ft within 25m W of Rwy markers.

Operating Hrs	SR-SS
Circuits	All circuits to the N
Landing Fee	£5 donation would be welcomed towards AD upkeep
Maintenance	Nil
Fuel	Nil
Disabled Facilities	Nil
Restaurant	Nil
Taxi/Car Hire	Nil
Weather Info	Air Sc GWC

Operator
The Scottish Flying Club LP
Strathaven Airfield
Strathaven
Highlands ML10 6RW
Tel: 07979 971301
(Colin MacKinnon, Microlight Scotland)
fly@microlightscotland.com
www.strathavenairfield.co.uk

39ft 1mb	15nm NE by N of Kirkwall Airport N5909.32 W00238.48	PPR	Alternative AD Diversion AD	Kirkwall Sanday

Non-Radio	APP Kirkwall 118.300	Safetycom 135.475

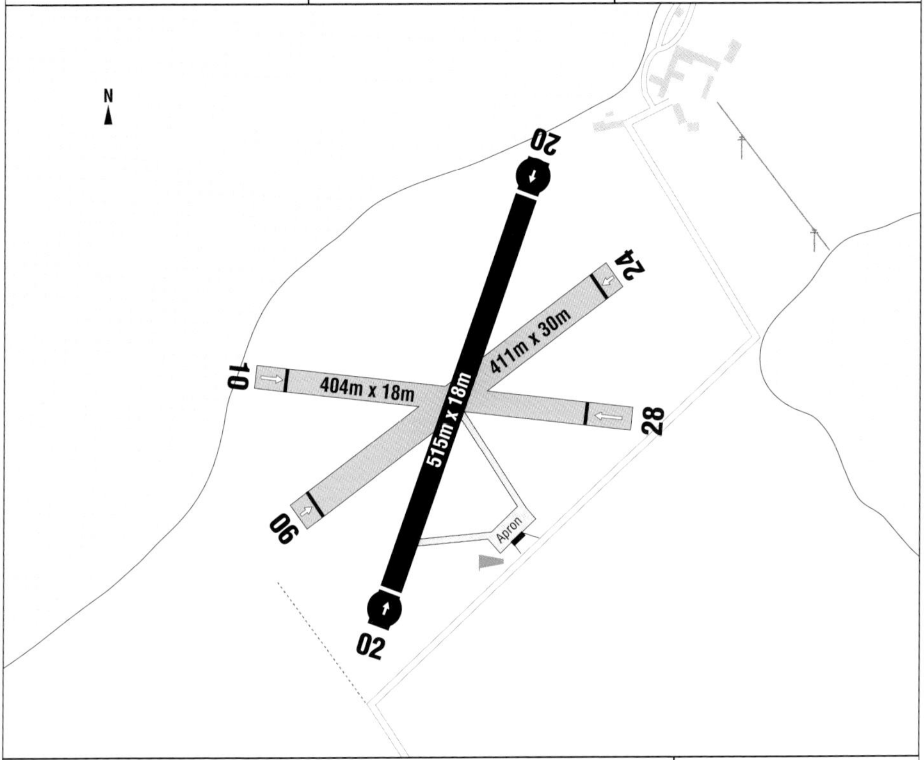

N

20

24

411m x 30m

10

404m x 18m

515m x 18m

28

06

Apron

02

RWY	SURFACE	TORA	LDA	U/L	LIGHTING
02	Graded Hardcore	495	480		Nil
20	Graded Hardcore	515	478		Nil
06/24	Grass	411	391		Nil
10	Grass	360	340		Nil
28	Grass	384	340		Nil

RNAV			
KWL	108.60	040	14.0

Remarks
Licensed AD (day use only). Visiting ACFT accepted at pilot's own risk. Scheduled Air Services daily Mon-Sat.

Warnings

Operating Hrs SR-SS
Circuits Nil
Landing Fee Nil
Maintenance Nil
Fuel Nil
Disabled Facilities Nil
Restaurants (Wed & Sat-Sun) Woodlea Restaurant & Takeaway **Tel:** 01857 616337

Taxis
Peace **Tel:** 01857 616335
Williamson **Tel:** 01857 616255

Car Hire
Peace **Tel:** 01857 616335

Weather Info Air Sc GWC

Operator
Orkney Islands Council
Stronsay Aerodrome, Kirkwall
Orkney, KW15 1N
Tel: 01856 873535
Fax: 01856 876094

S

47ft 1mb	4nm SW of Mablethorpe N5318.28 E00010.20	PPR	Alternative AD Humberside Wickenby Non-standard join

Strubby Base	DAIS Donna Nook 122.750	A/G 118.750	Gliders 130.100

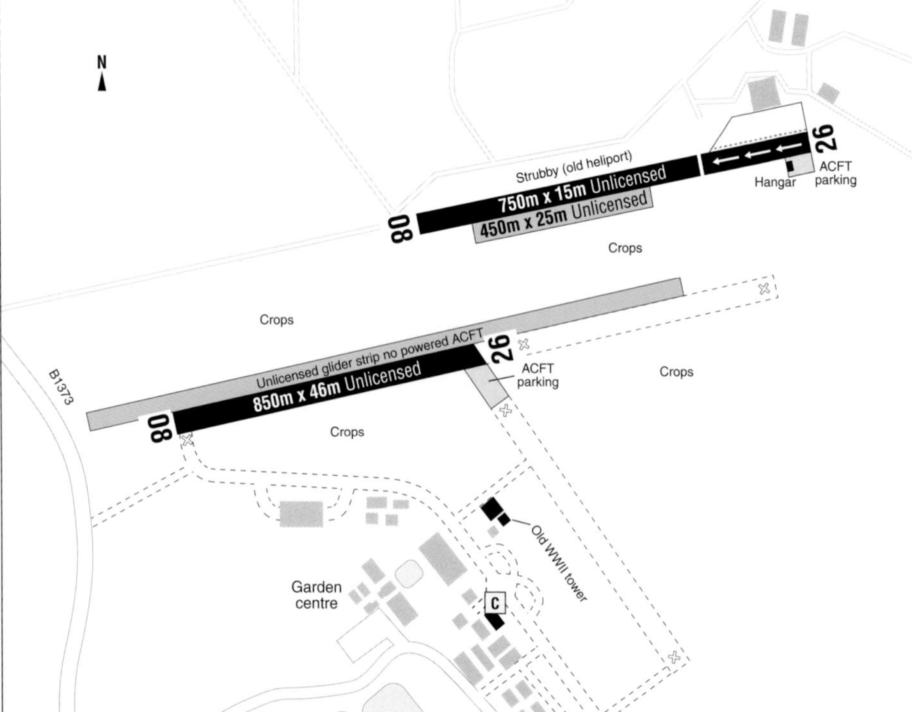

STRUBBY GLIDING

RWY	SURFACE	TORA	LDA	U/L	LIGHTING
08/26	Asph/Conc			850x46	Nil

Rwy surface rough. Grass section not suitable for powered ACFT

STRUBBY OLD HELIPORT

RWY	SURFACE	TORA	LDA	U/L	LIGHTING
08	Asphalt			650x15	Nil
26	Asphalt			750x15	Nil
08/26	Grass			450x25	Nil

Displaced Thr Rwy26

RNAV

Remarks

PPR. Both strips established on WW2 AD. Visiting ACFT are welcome at pilots own risk.
Strubby Gliding: Gliders operate mainly at WE & PH using Winch and Aerotow.
Strubby Old Heliport: Due to planning constraints is only available to ACFT <5700kgs MAUW.

Warnings

Strubby Gliding: Keep good lookout for Gliders and Winch cables. No overhead joins. Radio rarely manned but make blind circuit calls. Small manouvering area marked, all other hard surfaces not available for ACFT use.
Noise: Do not over fly villages of Strubby Maltby le Marsh or Withern.
Strubby Old Heliport: No circuit training, touch and goes, or intentional go arounds. Fence runs up to N side Rwy26 Thr and along N side of Twy to hangar and parking area. Visitors must transmit their intentions to Strubby Base, usually there will be no reply, in which case make blind calls and keep a good lookout because Gliders may launch from Rwy close to S by winch or aero tow. Gliders can and do operate over the Old Heliport. Most of the gliders do not carry radios, so although base may be able to inform you where they are, and will attempt to inform Dept pilots. Gliders already airborne will not normally be aware of you.
Noise: Do not over fly villages of Strubby, Maltby le Marsh or Withern.

Operating Hrs	
Strubby Gliding	SR-SS
Old Heliport	0830-2000 or SS whichever is earlier (L)
Circuits	
Strubby Gliding	Advised with PPR
Old Heliport	N 1000ft QFE
Landing Fee	
Strubby Gliding	£5
Old Heliport	ACFT £5 Microlights £2.50
Maintenance	Nil
Fuel	Nil
Disabled Facilities	Nil
Restaurants	Café at nearby Garden Centre is a short walk from Gliding field but some distance from Old Heliport
Taxi/Car Hire	Nil
Weather Info	Air N MOEx

Operators

Strubby Gliding
Lincolnshire Gliding Club Ltd
Strubby Airfield
Alford, Lincs, LN13 1AA
Tel: 01507 463726

Strubby Old Heliport
Strubby Aviation Club
C/o Mr Ron Larder
Orme Lane
Louth, Lincs
Tel: 01507 600588 (Work)
Tel: 01507 450498 (Home)

S

58ft 2mb	4nm SE of Gainsborough N5322.87 W00041.12	PPR	Alternative AD Diversion AD	Humberside Retford

Sturgate	LARS	APP	A/G
	Waddington 127.350	Doncaster Sheffield 126.225	130.300

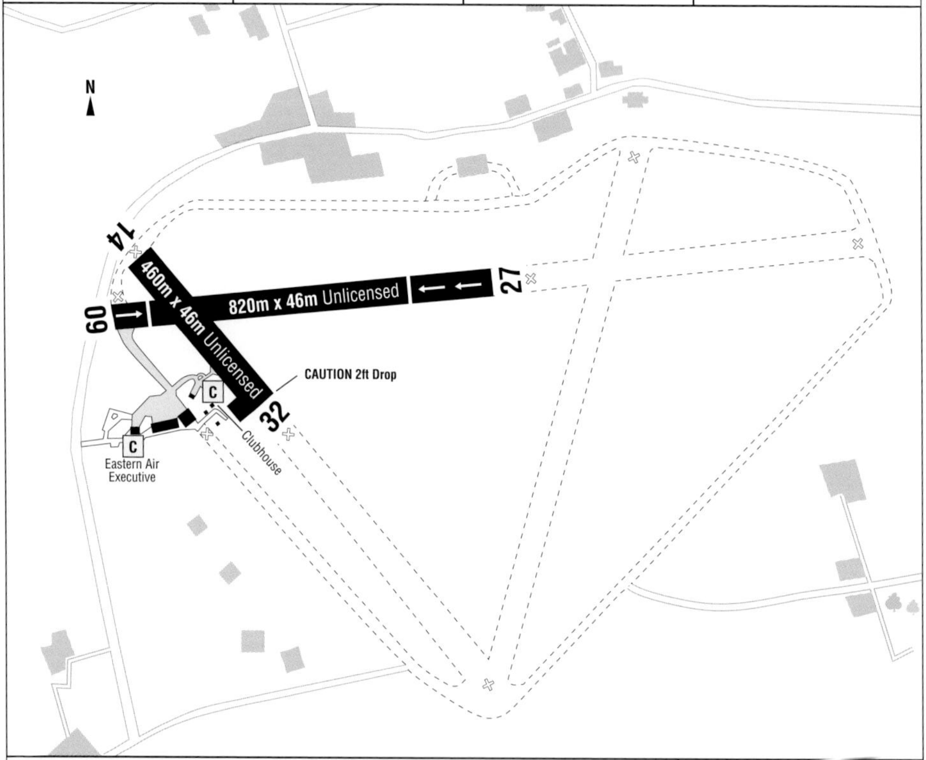

N
14
09
460m x 46m Unlicensed
820m x 46m Unlicensed
27
32
CAUTION 2ft Drop
C
Clubhouse
C
Eastern Air Executive

RWY	SURFACE	TORA	LDA	U/L	LIGHTING
09	Asphalt			805x46	Thr Rwy PAPI 3° RHS
27	Asphalt			790x46	Thr Rwy AVASIS 3°
14/32	Asphalt			460x46	Nil

Starter extension Rwy27 30m (day only)

RNAV			
GAM	112.80	061	11.1

Remarks
Microlights not accepted. AD is NOT available for public transport passenger flights required to use a licensed AD. Non-radio ACFT should remain well clear of the MATZ. Flights to Sturgate AD is limited to 1500ft aal unless prior arr has been made with Waddington. When within 10nm of Sturgate, pilots should use the MATZ altimeter setting.
Visual aid to location: Ibn SG Green.

Warnings
Located on edge of Doncaster Sheffield CTA. SE end Rwy14/32 ends abruptly in a 2ft drop indicated by a white line and a row of crosses. A road crosses the APP short of Rwy09 Thr. EG R313 Scampton abuts the S of ATZ. Home of the Red Arrows.

S

Operating Hrs Mon-Fri 0800-1600 (Summer)
Mon-Fri 0900-1600 (Winter) & by arr

Circuits Variable

Landing Fee Single £5 Twin £20

Maintenance
Eastern Air **Tel:** 01427 838280

Fuel AVGAS 100LL. No heli refueling available

Disabled Facilities

Restaurants Nil

Taxis/Car Hire Arr can be made via Eastern Executive Ops

Weather Info Air N MOEx

Operator Eastern Air Executive Ltd
Sturgate Aerodrome, Gainsborough
Lincs, DN21 5PA
Tel: 01427 838280 (Mon-Fri)
Tel: 01427 838305 (Sat-Sun)
Fax: 01427 838416

EGPB SUMBURGH

24ft 1mb	17nm S of Lerwick N5952.88 W00117.63	PPR	**Alternative AD** **Scatsta** Lerwick **Diversion AD**

Sumburgh	ATIS	APP	TWR	FIRE
	125.850	131.300	118.250	121.600

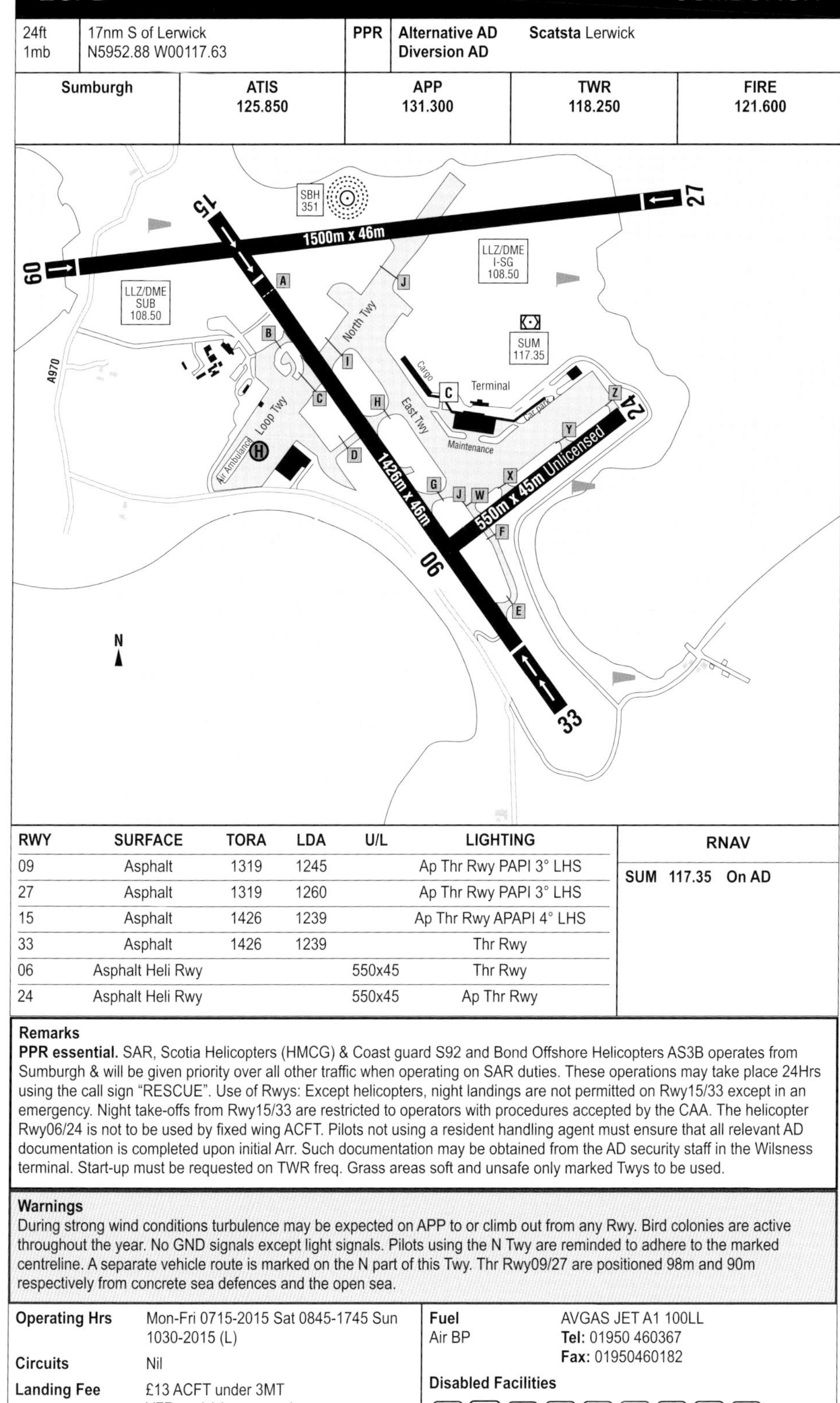

RWY	SURFACE	TORA	LDA	U/L	LIGHTING
09	Asphalt	1319	1245		Ap Thr Rwy PAPI 3° LHS
27	Asphalt	1319	1260		Ap Thr Rwy PAPI 3° LHS
15	Asphalt	1426	1239		Ap Thr Rwy APAPI 4° LHS
33	Asphalt	1426	1239		Thr Rwy
06	Asphalt Heli Rwy			550x45	Thr Rwy
24	Asphalt Heli Rwy			550x45	Ap Thr Rwy

RNAV		
SUM	**117.35**	**On AD**

Remarks

PPR essential. SAR, Scotia Helicopters (HMCG) & Coast guard S92 and Bond Offshore Helicopters AS3B operates from Sumburgh & will be given priority over all other traffic when operating on SAR duties. These operations may take place 24Hrs using the call sign "RESCUE". Use of Rwys: Except helicopters, night landings are not permitted on Rwy15/33 except in an emergency. Night take-offs from Rwy15/33 are restricted to operators with procedures accepted by the CAA. The helicopter Rwy06/24 is not to be used by fixed wing ACFT. Pilots not using a resident handling agent must ensure that all relevant AD documentation is completed upon initial Arr. Such documentation may be obtained from the AD security staff in the Wilsness terminal. Start-up must be requested on TWR freq. Grass areas soft and unsafe only marked Twys to be used.

Warnings

During strong wind conditions turbulence may be expected on APP to or climb out from any Rwy. Bird colonies are active throughout the year. No GND signals except light signals. Pilots using the N Twy are reminded to adhere to the marked centreline. A separate vehicle route is marked on the N part of this Twy. Thr Rwy09/27 are positioned 98m and 90m respectively from concrete sea defences and the open sea.

Operating Hrs	Mon-Fri 0715-2015 Sat 0845-1745 Sun 1030-2015 (L)
Circuits	Nil
Landing Fee	£13 ACFT under 3MT VFR cash/cheque on day
Maintenance	Nil

Fuel Air BP	AVGAS JET A1 100LL **Tel:** 01950 460367 **Fax:** 01950460182

Disabled Facilities

Effective date:25/09/08

OP 08

S

Restaurant	Terminal ground floor buffet	**Operator**	HIAL, Sumburgh Airport, Virkie, Shetland, ZE3 9JP **Tel:** 01950 460654 (HIAL) **Tel:** 01950 460173 (ATC) **Tel:** 01244 727199 (Sumburgh APP) **Tel:** 01224 727160 (Aberdeen Watch Manager) **Fax:** 01950 460218 (HIAL) **Fax:** 01950 460718 (ATC) sumbadmin@hial.co.uk www.hial.co.uk
Taxis	Available at Terminal		
Car Hire	Europcar & Avis agents		
Bolts Car Hire	**Tel:** 01950 460777		
Star Rentacar	**Tel:** 01950 460444		
Weather Info	M T9 Fax 432 A VSc GWC **Tel:** 01950 461037		

Visual Reference Points (VRP)

VRP	VOR/DME
Bodam N5955.10 W00116.10	SUM 017°/2.4nm
Mousa N6000.00 W00109.60	SUM 032°/8.2nm

CTA/CTR-Class D Airspace

Normal CTA/CTR Class D Airspace rules apply.
Helicopter operating VFR, or at night SVFR, may be routed via a VRP.
All ACFT intending to enter Sumburgh CTR/CTA must operate with a functioning transponder, Mode A & C. Any exemptions mut be aurthorised prior to the flight by Aberdeen Watch Manager

Helicopter Operations

Helicopter operations in support of N Sea oil rigs may take place outside the published Hrs of AD availability. Helicopters are treated as fixed wing traffic and should normally GND taxi, unless skid equipped, between the Rwys and parking areas. In adverse weather conditions and during snow-clearing operations, hover taxiing of wheeled helicopters may be permitted by ATC. 'Rotors running' refuelling of helicopters with passengers onboard is only permitted during exceptionally severe wind conditions and with the permission of ATC. Helicopter parking spots 1-9 are designated quick turn round spots and should not be occupied for more than 15 minutes. Long term parking spots 10-19.

Fixed Wing Parking

Stands 20-22 for schedule services
Stands 23-26 for all other fixed wing ACFT

SUTTON MEADOWS

8ft 0mb	5nm W of Ely N5223.12 E00003.84	PPR	Alternative AD Cambridge Bourn **Non-standard join**

Sutton Meadows	A/G 129.825 (Microlight Freq)

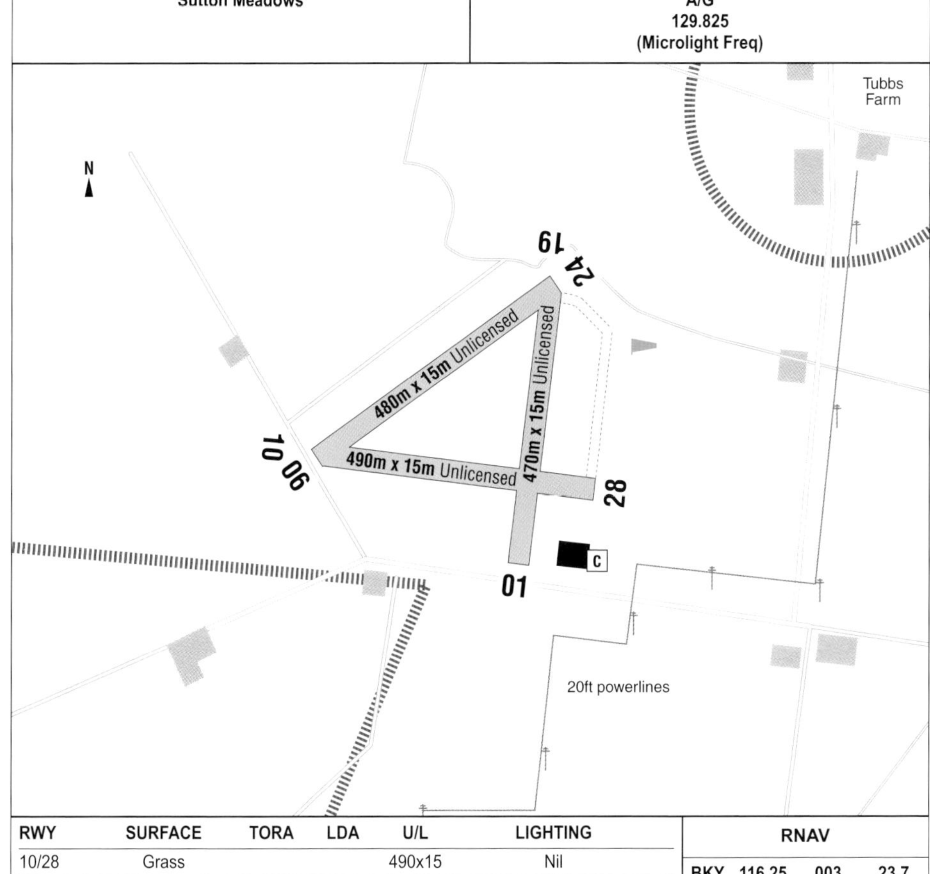

RWY	SURFACE	TORA	LDA	U/L	LIGHTING
10/28	Grass			490x15	Nil
06/24	Grass			480x15	Nil
01/19	Grass			470x15	Nil

RNAV			
BKY	116.25	003	23.7

Remarks
PPR by telephone. Visiting ACFT welcome at pilots own risk. Well maintained level grass strip. AD is primarily a microlight training field but is not challenging for fixed wing ACFT/pilots with reasonable short field performance. Signal square near clubhouse, gliding symbol near square when hang gliders active. Cambridgeshire Aerotow Club now on AD. Hang gliders and tug can be at any height, have the right of way both air and GND, may not be using the designated Rwy. All hang gliders circuits usually inside normal circuit.

Warnings
No radio service, make blind calls with intentions. Power lines 20ft agl S & E of AD.
Noise: Do not over fly Tubbs Farm. Be considerate of local habitation.

Operating Hrs	SR-SS
Circuits	Join overhead 1200ft QFE 06, 10, 19 LH, 01, 24, 28 RH, 700ft QFE
Landing Fee	PPR £2 otherwise £5 free with reciprocal arr
Maintenance	Nil
Fuel	MOGAS Ltd quantities by arr
Disabled Facilities	Nil
Restaurants	Clubhouse open for light refreshments when microlight flying is in progress
Taxis/Car Hire	Nil
Weather Info	Air Cen MOEx
Operator	Peter Robinson Argents Farm House 114 High Street Sutton, Ely, Cambs **Tel:** 01353 778446 (Operator) **Tel:** 01487 842360 (Pegasus Flight Training) www.cambsmicrolightclub.co.uk

Effective date:25/09/08 OP 08

N

Tubbs Farm

The Hundred Foot Washes

S

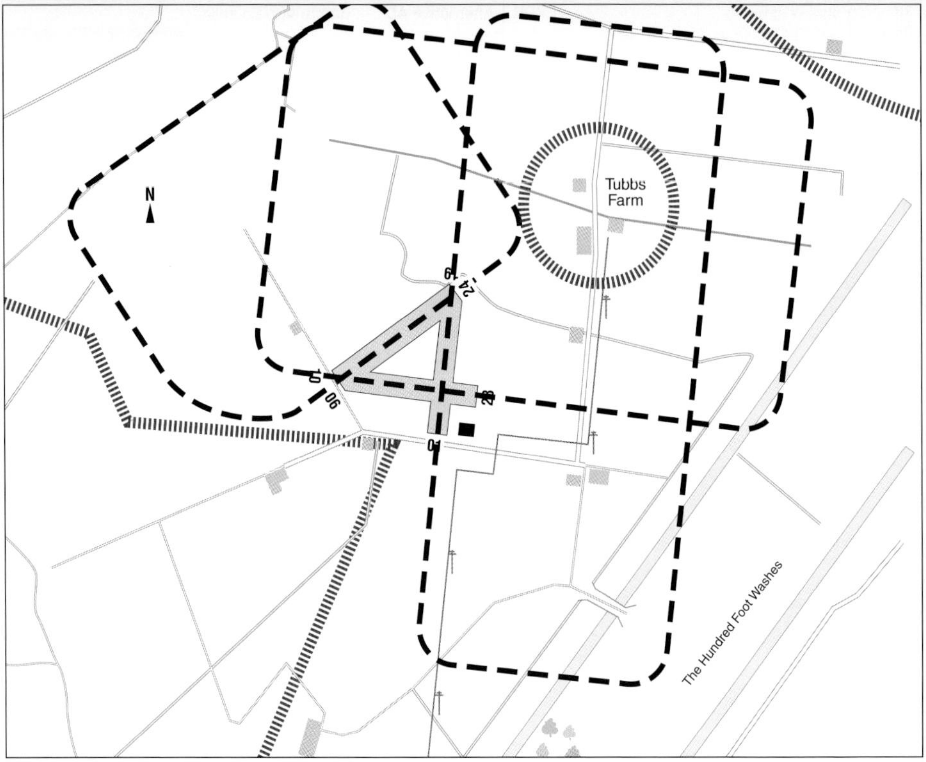

SWANBOROUGH FARM

10ft 0mb	2nm S of Lewes N5051.30 W00000.30	PPR	Alternate AD	**Shoreham** Lashenden

Swanborough Traffic	ATIS Shoreham 125.300	APP Shoreham 123.150	Safetycom 135.475

RWY	SURFACE	TORA	LDA	U/L	LIGHTING
06/24	Grass			650x25	Nil

Rwy06 downslope to midpoint

RNAV			
SFD	117.00	322	8.0

Remarks
PPR by telephone. Visiting ACFT welcome at pilots own risk. AD not suitable for inexperienced pilots. Windsock may be displayed at Rwy midpoint on S side. Day tickets available for angling lakes to N of AD (owned by operator).

Warnings
Low hedge and ditch Rwy24 Thr. Rwy may be waterlogged after heavy rain.
Noise: Avoid over flying all local habitation.

Operating Hrs SR-SS
Circuits S 1100ft QNH
Landing Fee Nil
Maintenance Nil
Fuel Nil
Disabled Facilities

Taxi/Car Hire Nil
Weather Info Air SE MOEx

Operator Mr Will Greenwood
Swanborough Farm
Lewes
East Sussex
BN7 3PF
Tel: 01273 477388
Tel: 07850 811704
will.greenwood@btconnect.com
www.swanboroughfarm.co.uk

Effective date:25/09/08 OP 08

EGFH — SWANSEA

299ft 10mb	5nm WSW of Swansea N5136.32 W00404.07		**Alternative AD** **Diversion AD**	**Cardiff** Pembrey

Swansea	A/G 119.700

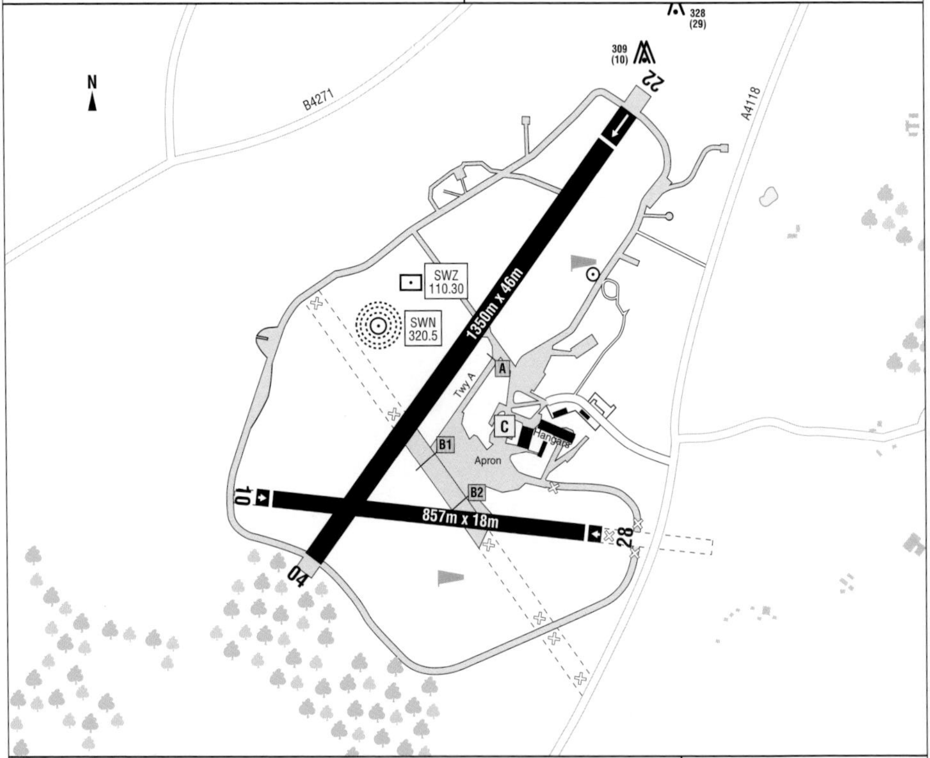

N
B4271
A4118
328 (29)
309 (10)
22
04
10
28
1350m x 46m
857m x 18m
SWZ 110.30
SWN 320.5
Twy A
A
B1
B2
C
Hangars
Apron

RWY	SURFACE	TORA	LDA	U/L	LIGHTING
04	Concrete	1199	1200		Ap Thr Rwy PAPI 3° LHS
22	Concrete	1199	1200		Ap Thr Rwy PAPI 3.25° LHS
10	Asphalt	799	824		Nil
28	Asphalt	799	794		Nil

RNAV

Remarks
Strict PPR. Non-radio ACFT not accepted. Hi-Vis. Light ACFT experiencing radio failure in VMC are to carry out the standard overhead join for Rwy in use as notified by either previous dept or joining information passed by A/G. Gliding operations by Air Training Corps at weekends. Operations by emergency service helicopters occur outside normal operating hrs.

Warnings
Unusable parts of Rwys short of Rwy10/28 and Rwy04/22 Thr are marked by white crosses. Not all Twy are usable. Road crosses near Rwy28 Thr and is marked by orange triangular markers outside the AD and orange/white circular markers on the AD side. Deviation from marked manoeuvring area can be hazardous.

S

Operating Hrs 0900-1730 (L) & by arr
Hrs available with PPR

Circuits 04, 28 LH, 10, 22 RH
Helicopters must conform with standard circuits

Landing Fee Private singles £11.00

Maintenance Nil

Fuel AVGAS JET A1 100LL

Disabled Facilities

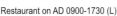

Restaurants Restaurant on AD 0900-1730 (L)

Taxis
Exec Travel Servcs **Tel:** 01792 203080

Car Hire
Europcar **Tel:** 01792 650526
Hertz **Tel:** 01792 587391

Weather Info M T9 Fax 434 MOEx

Operator Swansea Airport Ltd
Swansea Airport
Fairwood Common
Swansea, SA2 7JU
Tel: 01792 2 208182 (A/G)
Fax: 01792 207550 (ATC)

EGXY SYERSTON

228ft 7mb	5nm SW of Newark N5302.00 W00055.00	PPR MIL	**Alternative AD** **East Midlands** Nottingham **Non-standard join**

Syerston	**LARS** **Waddington 127.350**	**A/G** **125.425**

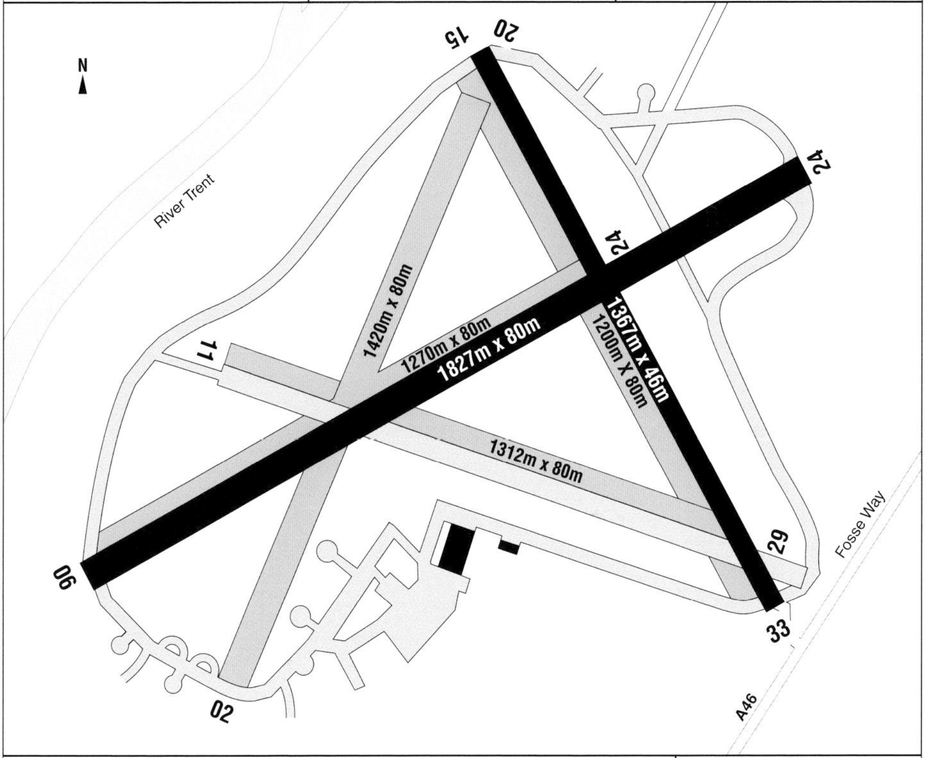

N
River Trent
15
20
24
24
11
1420m x 80m
1270m x 80m
1827m x 80m
1367m x 46m
1200m X 80m
1312m x 80m
06
29
33
02
Fosse Way
A46

RWY	SURFACE	TORA	LDA	U/L	LIGHTING
06/24	Asphalt	1827	1727		Nil
06/24	Grass	1100	1150		Nil
15/33	Asphalt	1347	1247		Nil
15/33	Grass	1200	1100		Nil
11/29	Grass	1292	1192		Nil
02/20	Grass	1400	1300		Nil

2 dayglo markers at Thr may mark grass Rwy in use, Rwy11/29 surface poor
Rwy02/20 used by gliders and motor gliders

RNAV

GAM 112.80 180 15.6

Remarks
Strict 48Hrs PPR required by telephone. RAF glider operations have priority at all times. WW2 AD with aged Asphalt surfaces, loose stones may be present.

Warnings
Intense cable launched (3000ft agl) and motor glider activity during operational hours. Full obstacle clearance criteria not met on APP to all Rwys. No fire cover available for visiting civil ACFT. Rwy markings becoming indistinct.
Noise: Avoid over flying Kneeton and Hoveringham villages to W of AD.

Operating Hrs	Mon-Fri 0830-1700 Sat-Sun 0630-SS (L)
Circuits	Full briefing must be obtained with PPR
Landing Fee	Charges in accordance with MOD policy Contact Station Ops for details
Maintenance	Nil
Fuel	Nil
Disabled Facilities	Nil
Restaurants	Nil
Taxi/Car Hire	Nil
Weather Info	Air Cen MOEx
Operator	RAF Syerston Fosse Road, Syerston Newark, Nottinghamshire NG23 5NG **Tel:** 01636 525467 Ex 4525 (General Office) **Tel:** 01636 525467 Ex 4523 (Officer Commanding)

S

40ft 1mb	1nm NE of Tywyn N5236.70 W00404.50	PPR	**Alternative AD** **Hawarden** Caernarfon **Non-standard join**

Talybont Micro Base	LARS Valley 125.225	A/G 129.825

N
Talybont
1.75nm
high ground
1027ft amsl
21
ACFT parking
5ft hedge
460m x 16m Unlicensed
Upslope
Crops
Afon Dysynni
Crops
Upslope
03
5ft hedge

RWY	SURFACE	TORA	LDA	U/L	LIGHTING
03/21	Grass			460x16	Nil

Rwy03 rises 10ft in first 200m then has down slope
Rwy21 rises 20ft in first 300m then has down slope

RNAV

Remarks
Strictly PPR by telephone. Gyros not accepted. Grass strip high GND close proximity must be treated with respect. Experienced pilots with STOL ACFT welcome at pilot's own risk. Sheep live on AD.

Warnings
Operator publishes AD bulletin identified by information code as ATIS broadcast. Visitors must obtain this by E-mail, phone, Fax, or post quote code letter on Arr overhead or no landing! Sheep graze AD will be kept off the field for 1Hr after notified ETA. AD suffers rotor in N & NW winds, particularly Rwy21. Pilots should also be aware of coastal wind effects. Grass can be very slippery when wet so please do not land long as Rwy gradient will not assist. Operator advises you be lightly loaded on first visit. Valley to NE rises 3000ft in 7nm should be treated with respect! Fast flying ACFT advised avoid slow-flying cormorants! **Noise:** Avoid over flying local habitation and do not 'Buzz' AD as noise sensitive neighbours will report offenders.

Operating Hrs SR-SS
Circuits 21 LH, 03 RH, 1200ft QNH
Join overhead 1200ft QNH
Landing Fee Nil with PPR
£500 without PPR
Maintenance Nil
Fuel MOGAS Ltd avail check with PPR
Microlight pilots must bring their own Oil
Disabled Facilities Nil
Restaurants B&B/Bar snacks at
Peniarth Arms **Tel:** 01654 711505 (0.5m)
Penhelig Arms **Tel:** 01654 767215 Aberdovey (6m)

Taxis/Car Hire **Tel:** 01654 711788
Weather Info Air N MOEx
Operator Mr William Williams-Wynne
Peniarth, Tywyn
Gwynedd, LL36 9UD
Tel: 01654 710101 (Day)
Tel: 01654 710102 (Evening)
Tel: 07831 131000
Fax: 01654 710103
www@wynne.co.uk

EGBM TATENHILL

439ft 15mb	4nm W of Burton on Trent N5248.38 W00146.17	PPR	**Alternative AD** **East Midlands** Wolverhampton **Diversion AD**

Tatenhill	APP East Mids 134.175	APP Birmingham 118.050	A/G 124.075

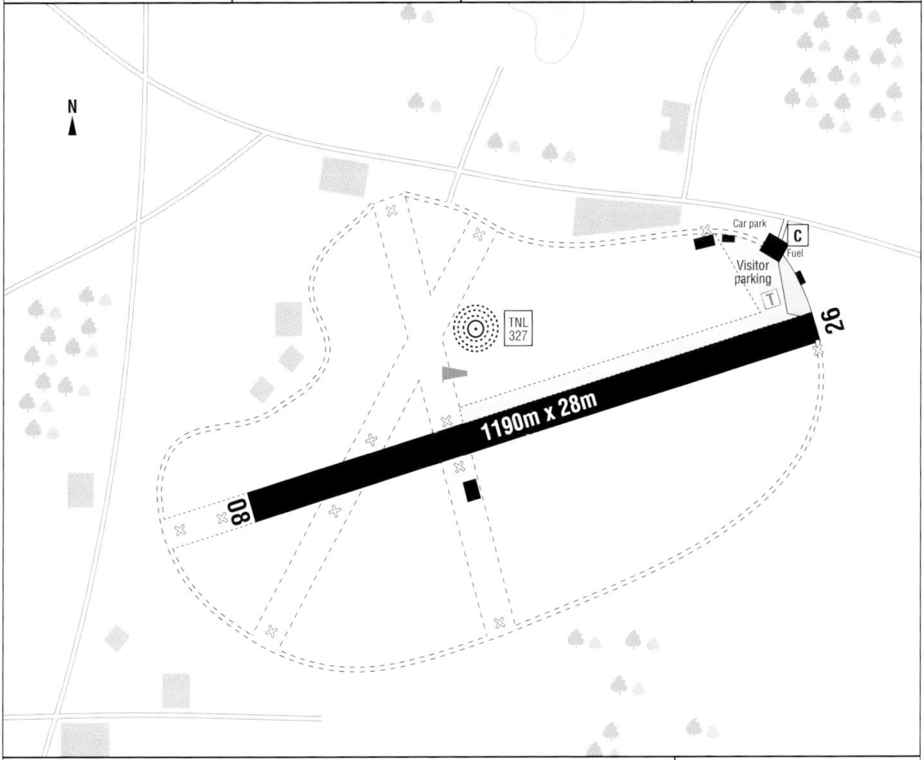

RWY	SURFACE	TORA	LDA	U/L	LIGHTING
08/26	Asphalt	1190	1190		by arr

RNAV			
TNT	115.70	198	14.8

Remarks
PPR. Non-radio ACFT not accepted. AD not available to weight shift microlights. Pilots should note proximity of Birmingham & East Midlands CTA and are advised to call Birmingham or East Midlands for traffic info before calling Tatenhill. Night flying by arr. Air Ambulance operations H24.

Warnings
Pilots are advised to keep a good lookout for military traffic. Gliding may take place at Cross Hayes (N5247.40 W00149.14)

Operating Hrs 0800-1600 (Summer) +1Hr (Winter)

Circuits 08 & 26 LH 1000ft QFE
Join overhead

Landing Fee Single £12 Twin £22

Maintenance Tatenhill Aviation Ltd
Tel: 01283 575283

Fuel AVGAS 100LL JET A1 (by arr)

Disabled Facilities

Restaurants Tea, coffee & sandwiches available
Catering at weekends only

Taxis/Car Hire By arr

Weather Info Air Cen MOEx

Operator Tatenhill Aviation Ltd
Tatenhill Airfield
Newborough Road, Needwood
Burton on Trent, Staffs, DE13 9PD
Tel: 01283 575283
Fax: 01283 575650
office@tatenhill.com
www.tatenhill.com

Effective date:25/09/08 OP 08

240ft 8mb	8nm S of Lincoln N5304.60 W00030.70	**PPR**	**Alternative AD** **Doncaster Sheffield** Retford

Non Radio	**APP** **Cranwell 119.375**	**LARS** **Waddington 127.350**	**Safetycom** **135.475**

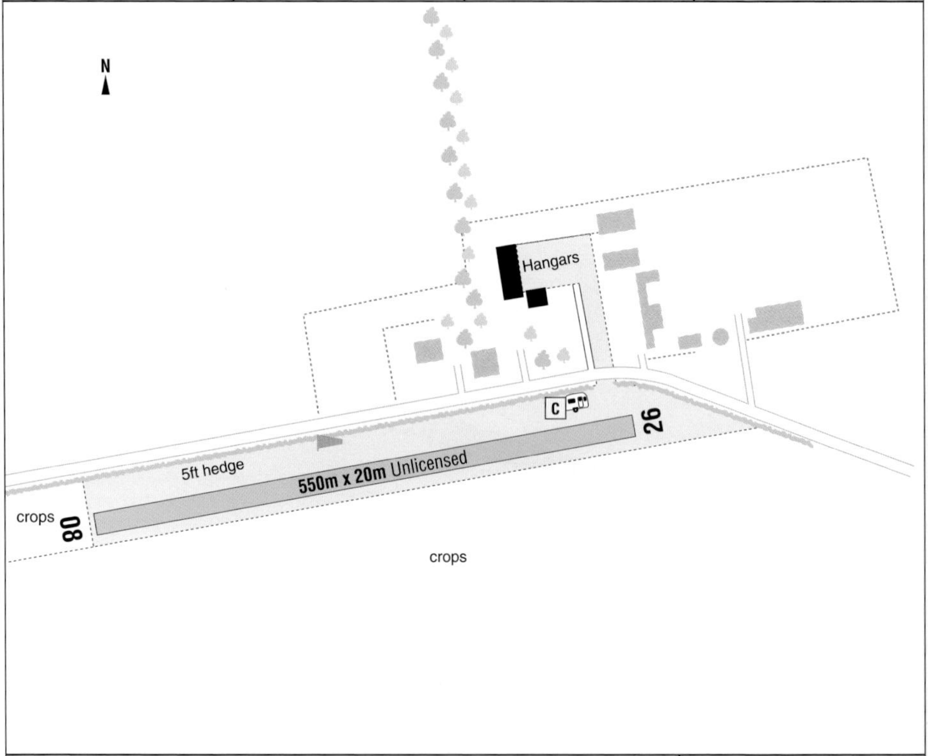

N
Hangars
C
26
5ft hedge
550m x 20m Unlicensed
crops
08
crops

RWY	SURFACE	TORA	LDA	U/L	LIGHTING
08/26	Grass			550x20	Nil

RNAV			
GAM	**112.80**	**129**	**20.0**

Remarks
PPR strictly by telephone. Briefing will be given. Planning limitations restrict visits to 5 per day, permission for visiting ACFT may be refused. Level strip with crops grown close to the S side.

Warnings
AD situated within Cranwell MATZ. Contact Waddington when Cranwell closed. Gliding takes place from Cranwell North, (2nm S of AD).

Operating Hrs	0800-SS
Circuits	LH 500ft QFE
Landing Fee	Single £5 Twin & Helicopter £10
Maintenance	Nil
Fuel	Nil
Disabled Facilities	Nil
Restaurant	Nil
Taxi/Car Hire	Nil
Weather Info	Air N MOEx

Operator
Mr D A Porter
The Old Granary
Holly Lane
Temple Bruer
Lincoln
Lincs LN5 0DF
Tel/Fax: 01522 810840
Tel: 07970 033618

T

272ft 9mb	2nm SW of Market Drayton N5252.27 W00232.01	PPR MIL	Alternative AD **Hawarden** Sleap **Non-standard join**

Ternhill	LARS Shawbury 120.775	TWR 122.100

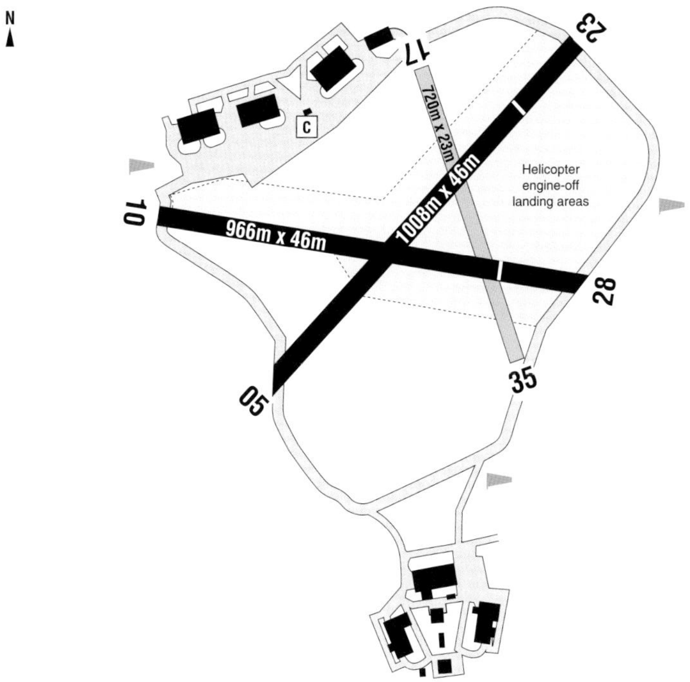

RWY	SURFACE	TORA	LDA	U/L	LIGHTING
05	Asphalt	1004	953		Nil
23	Asphalt	1004	766		Nil
10	Asphalt	966	903		Nil
28	Asphalt	966	744		Nil
17/35	Grass	720	720		Nil

RNAV			
SWB	116.80	051	6.4

Remarks
Strict PPR by telephone. **No fixed wing movements accepted.** RAF relief landing ground for Military helicopter training and ATC Glider/Motor glider activity. Master AD is RAF Shawbury.

Warnings
Intensive military training weekdays. Glider flying outside normal Hrs and weekends up to 3000ft. ACFT not to cross Rd adjacent to Rwy23/28 Thr below 50ft. Thr have non standard markings.

Operating Hrs	ATZ 24 Hrs AD active as required by RAF Shawbury
Circuits	Variable in direction & height
Landing Fee	Charges in accordance with MOD policy Contact Station Ops for details
Maintenance	Nil
Fuel	Nil
Disabled Facilities	Nil
Restaurants	Nil
Taxis/Car Hire	Nil
Weather Info	M T Fax 398 MOEx

Operator RAF Shawbury
Shrewsbury
Shropshire, SY4 4DZ
Tel: 01939 250351 Ex 7227
(Shawbury Ops)

Effective date:25/09/08 OP 08

319ft 11mb	4.5nm W of Andover N5112.63 W00136.00	PPR	Alternative AD Diversion AD	Southampton Old Sarum Non-standard join

Thruxton	LARS Boscombe 126.700	A/G 130.450

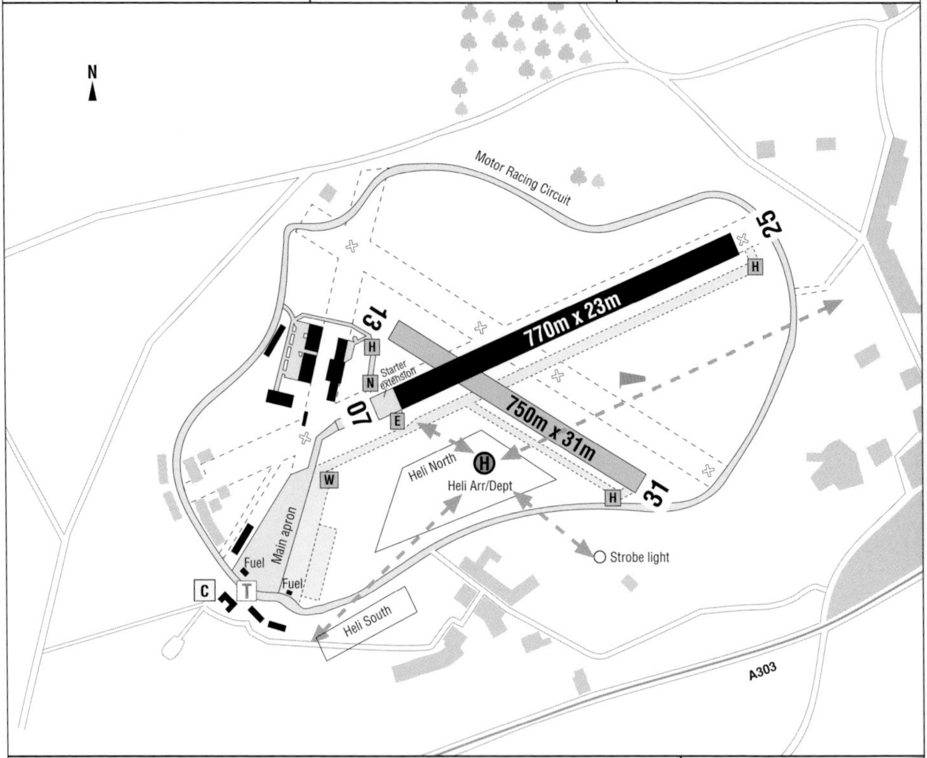

RWY	SURFACE	TORA	LDA	U/L	LIGHTING
07	Asphalt	770	760		Thr Rwy APAPI 4° LHS
25	Asphalt	770	770		Thr Rwy APAPI 4° LHS
13/31	Grass	750	750		Nil
Starter extension Rwy07 220m U/L					

RNAV			
SAM	113.35	333	17.8

Remarks
Certain Microlights not accepted. HI-Vis. Non radio ACFT PNR. Race days helicopters by arrangement only. No dead side Rwy07/25 due variable circuit directions Circuit joining height 1200ft QFE or 1500ft QFE when CMATZ not in operation. ACFT vacating Rwy13/31 must vacate to W. ACFT commanders responsible for passengers and crew members.

Warnings
APP Thruxton avoid Danger Areas D123, D125, D125A, D126 & D127. Middle Wallop AD 4nm S of Thruxton intensive rotary flying training. Instrument APP service operates 070°-080° up to 8nm from Middle Wallop & may be used for practice VMC conditions. Racing Track permanently obstructed not available for ACFT. Power cables cross final APP Rwy25 200m from Thr.

Operating Hrs 0800-1600 (Summer) +1Hr (Winter) & by arr

Circuits Fixed Wing 07/31 LH, 25/13 RH, 800ft QFE. Helicopter (via heli north) HA 07, 31 LH HA 25, 13 RH. HA 07/25 1000ft HA31/13 800ft. Circuit height 1000ft QFE when Boscombe MATZ is closed

Landing Fee Single £10 Twin £20. Free for qual cross countries. Consessions on fuel uplift

Maintenance
Aeromaritime **Tel:** 01264 771700 (Rotary)

Fuel AVGAS JET A1 100LL

Disabled Facilities

Restaurants
Jackaroo **Tel:** 01264 882217 (0900-1700 (L)

Taxis **Tel:** 01264 359000

Car Hire
Eurodollar **Tel:** 01264 338181

Weather Info Air SW MOEx

Operator Western Air (Thruxton) Ltd
Thruxton Aerodrome
Andover, Hampshire, SP11 8PW
Tel: 01264 772352 (TWR)
Tel: 01264 772171 (Admin)
Fax: 01264 773913
www.westernairthruxton.co.uk

T

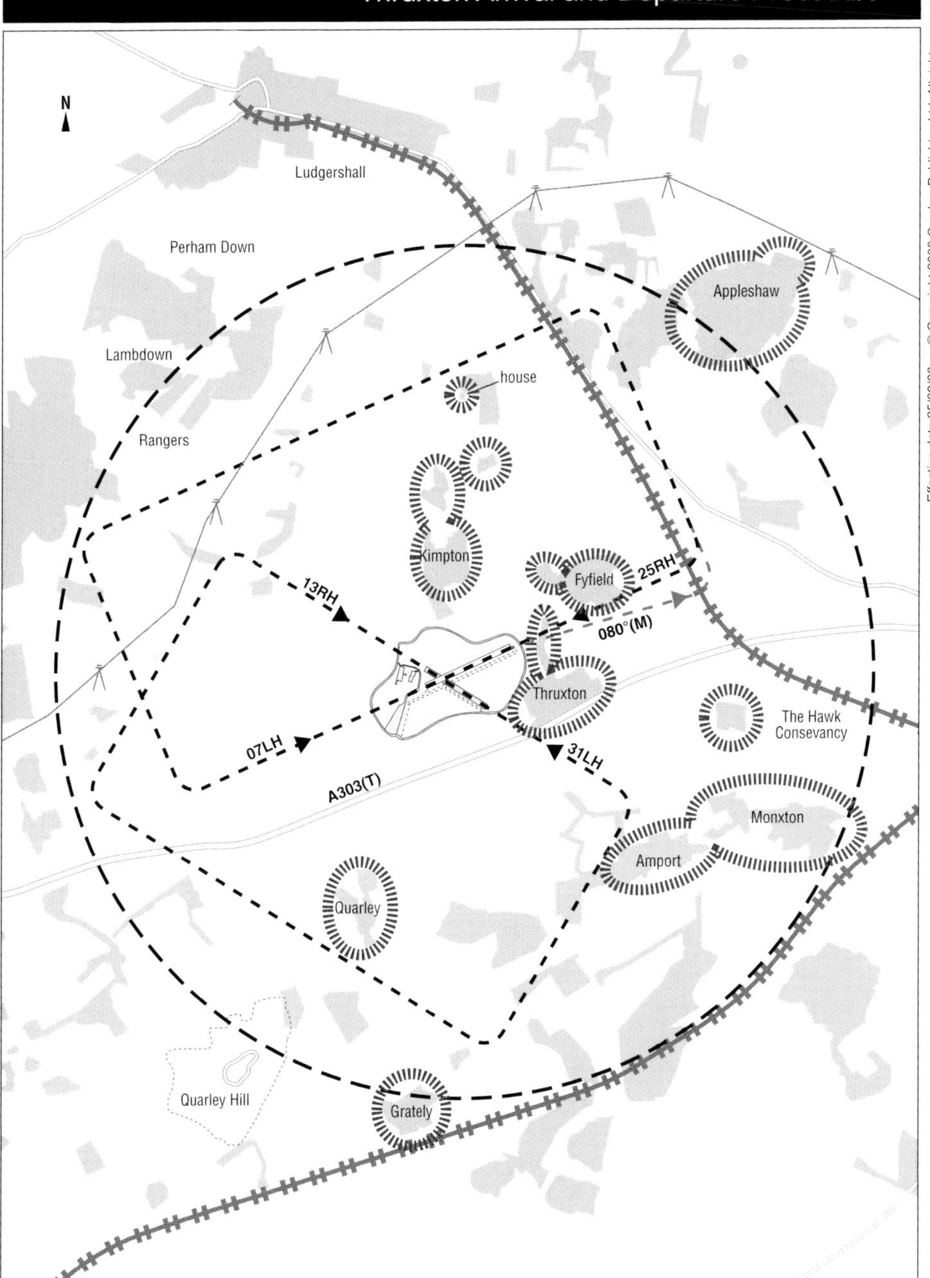

Arrivals:
When Boscombe MATZ is active, ACFT should call Boscombe Down for MATZ penetration. ACFT being provided ATS from Boscombe are not to enter the Thruxton ATZ unless contact has been established with Thruxton A/G and relevant information obtained.

Departures:
All ACFT should dept to E or NE.
Climb to 1200ft QNH or 900ft QFE or remain VMC before free calling Boscombe APP, or climb when clear from the CMATZ.
W bound depts should call Boscombe APP prior to take-off.

Noise: Avoid over flying the following villages– Kimpton, Fyfield, Thruxton, Quarley & Thruxton Down, also avoid Hawk Conservancy 1.5m SE of AD
Dept Rwy07: Fixed wing ACFT should turn R onto 080° on passing the AD boundary or when safe to do so.

25ft 0mb	5nm SW of Basildon N5132.17 E00022.00	PPR	**Alternative AD** **Southend** Stapleford

Non-Radio	LARS Farnborough East 123.225	LARS Southend 130.775	Safetycom 135.475

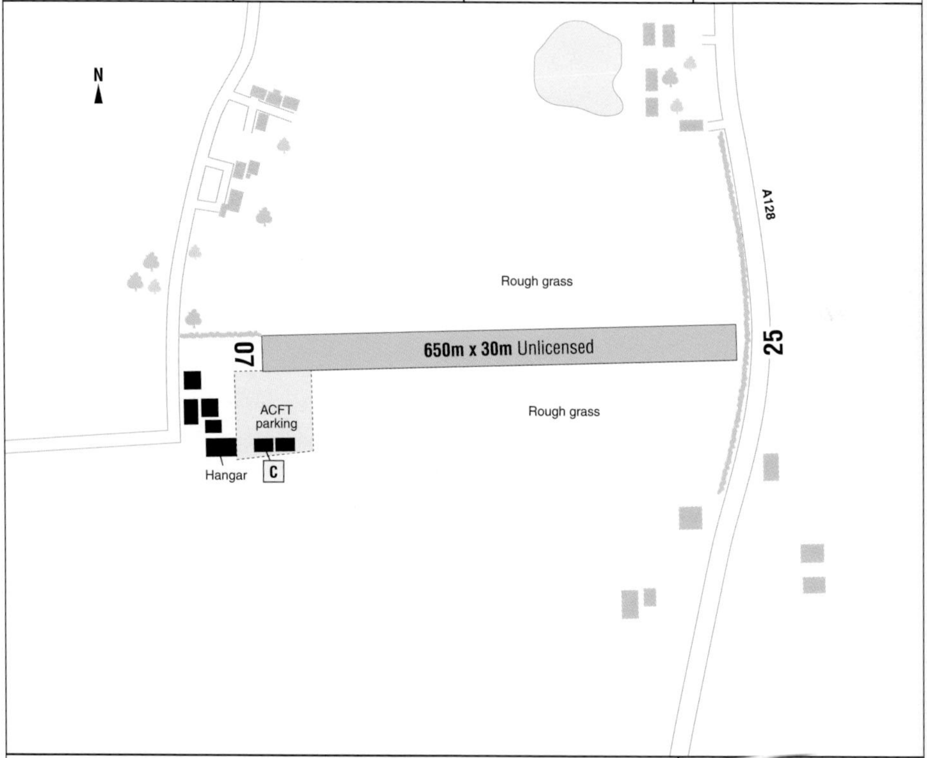

RWY	SURFACE	TORA	LDA	U/L	LIGHTING
07/25	Grass			650x30	Nil

Rwy is part of large field which allows run-off to S & N of strip

RNAV	
LAM	115.60
133	10.4

Remarks
PPR by telephone. Visitors welcome at pilots own risk. NO TRAINING.
Visual aid to location: Light ACFT parked on AD.

Warnings
High sided vehicles on A128 crosses Rwy25 Thr. 6ft hedge between road and Thr. Trees and hedge adjacent Rwy09 Thr.
Noise: Avoid over flying all local habitation.

Operating Hrs	SR-SS
Circuits	25 LH, 07 RH, 1000ft QFE
Landing Fee	Available with PPR
Maintenance	Hangarage & parking by arr
Fuel	AVGAS 100LL
Disabled Facilities	Nil
Restaurant	Nil
Taxis	
Abbey Cars	**Tel:** 01277 812812
Car Hire	Nil
Weather Info	Air SE MOEx

Operator Thurrock Leisure Ltd
Thurrock Airfield
Tilbury Road, Orsett, Essex
Tel: 01375 891165

TIBENHAM

186ft 6mb	12nm SW of Norwich N5227.40 E00109.25	PPR	**Alternative AD Norwich** Old Buckenham **Non-standard join**

Tibenham	ATIS Norwich 128.625	LARS Lakenheath 128.900	A/G 129.975

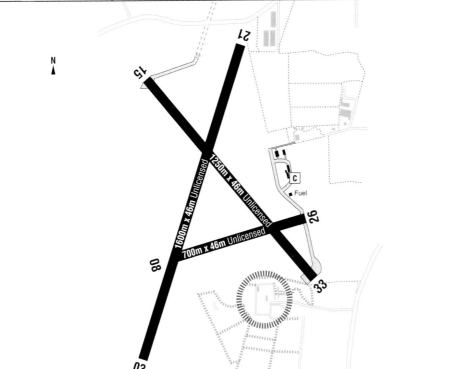

N

21
15
1250m x 46m Unlicensed
1600m x 46m Unlicensed
700m x 46m Unlicensed
C
Fuel
26
08
33
03

RWY	SURFACE	TORA	LDA	U/L	LIGHTING
03/21	Asphalt			1600x46	Nil
08/26	Asphalt			700x46	Nil
15/33	Asphalt			1250x46	Nil

RNAV

Remarks

PPR by telephone. Primarily a gliding site but powered ACFT welcome at pilots own risk. Rwy surfaces are in good condition. Excellent website also has local weather data.

Warnings

Glider launching by aerotow and winch up to 3200ft. Trees and possible turbulence Rwt33 Thr. Old Buckenham ATZ which is 4.5nm to NW where parachuting takes place up to 12000ft. Priory Fm AD is 1nm to the W of AD. Tacolneston TV mast (547agl/757 amsl) 354 degrees 4nm.
Noise: Avoid habitation in marked avoidance zone.

Operating Hrs SR-SS

Circuits Request information with PPR
No overhead joins

Landing Fee Donations welcomed

Maintenance Nil

Fuel AVGAS 100LL

Disabled Facilities

Restaurant Club facilities available

Taxi/Car Hire By arrangement

Weather Info Air S MOEx
Tel: 01603 420640 (Norwich ATIS)

Operator Norfolk Gliding Club
Tibenham Airfield
Norfolk
Tel: 01379 677207
manager@norfolkglidingclub.com
www.norfolkglidingclub.com

OP 07 Effective date:25/09/08

T

XTIB — TIBENHAM PRIORY FARM

186ft 6mb	1nm W of Tibenham AD N5227.00 E00107.00	PPR	Alternative AD	**Norwich** Old Buckenham

Priory	LARS Lakenheath 128.900	A/G 118.325 (Make blind calls)

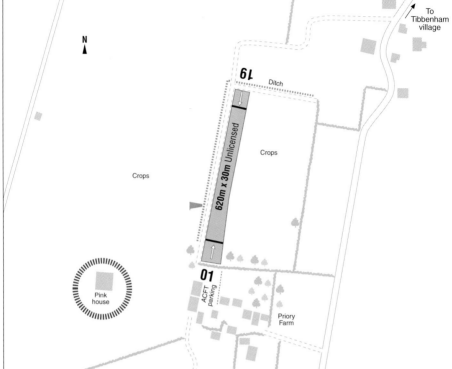

N
To Tibbenham village
19
Ditch
620m x 30m Unlicensed
Crops
Crops
01
ACFT parking
Pink house
Priory Farm

RWY	SURFACE	TORA	LDA	U/L	LIGHTING
01/19	Grass			620x30	Nil

RNAV

Remarks
PPR by telephone. Visiting ACFT welcome at own risk. Annual fly-in, check aviation press for details.

Warnings
Keep good lookout for glider activity from Tibenham AD 1nm to E. Rwy01 APP over farm buildings with group of trees to left of Thr. Low hedge extends across Rwy01 Thr from right. Use Rwy19 for landing when conditions permit. A ditch runs along full length of Rwy19 Thr. Crops grow up to edge of strip on E side.
Noise: Do not over fly the Pink House and Tibenham village NNE of AD.

Operating Hrs	1000-2000 (L)
Circuits	Overhead joins 01 LH, 19 RH, 500ft QFE
Landing Fee	Donation please
Maintenance	Nil
Fuel	AVGAS 100LL by arr
Hangarage	Available by prior arr

Disabled Facilities

Restaurants	By arr

Taxis	
Diss	**Tel:** 01362 696161
Car Hire	Nil
Weather Info	Air S MOEx
Operator	Bob Sage Priory Farm Tibenham Norwich Norfolk NR1 6NY **Tel/Fax:** 01379 677334 **Tel:** 07799 695144 bobs.airstrip@btinternet.com www.bobs.airstrip@btinternet.com

301ft 10mb	2nm SE of Whitchurch N5255.93 W00238.83	PPR	Alternative AD Hawarden Sleap Non-standard join

Tilstock	LARS Shawbury 120.775	TWR Shawbury 122.100	A/G 118.100

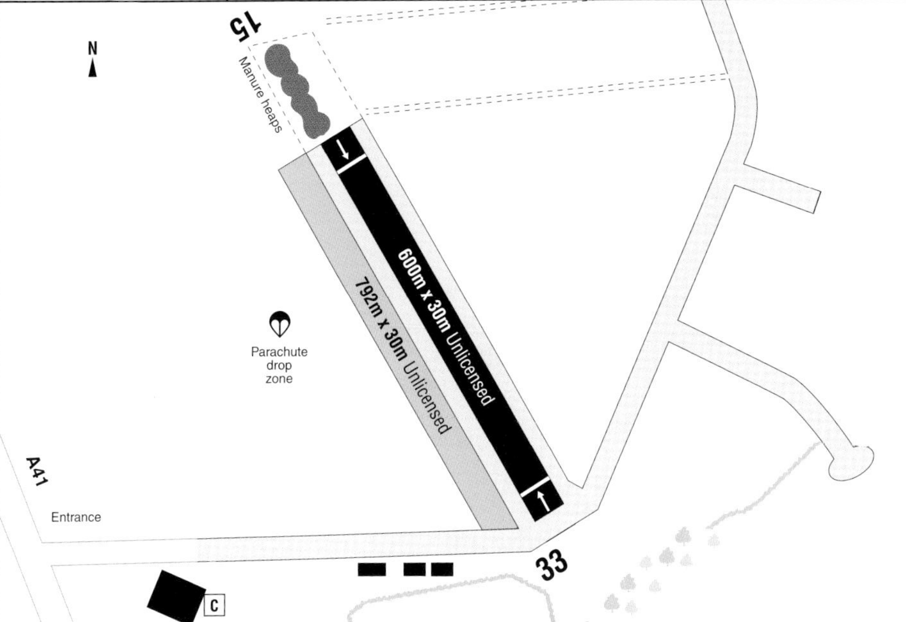

RWY	SURFACE	TORA	LDA	U/L	LIGHTING
15/33	Tarmac			600x30	Nil
15/33	Grass			792x30	Nil

RNAV			
SWB	16.80	008	7.9

Remarks
PPR by telephone closed Sunday. Visiting light ACFT welcome at owner's risk. Intensive parachute activity up to FL150. AD is situated under N portion of Shawbury MATZ

Warnings
No overhead joins or circuits. Narrow Twy between parking area & Rwy with no passing places. AD frequently closed for other activities. Manure piles up to 15ft high are often present on N end of Rwy.

Operating Hrs Available on request
Circuits Join downwind 1000ft QFE
Landing Fee £10 cash
Maintenance Nil
Fuel AVGAS 100LL available by prior arr
Disabled Facilities
Restaurants Snacks tea & coffee available at AD
Taxis
Halls **Tel:** 01948 662222
Car Hire Nil
Weather Info Air Cen MOEx
Operator The Parachute Centre
Tilstock Aerodrome, Whitchurch
Shropshire, SY13 2HA
Tel: 01948 841111 (Parachute Centre)
Tel: 01948 663239
(Landowner/PPR Mr Matson)
Tel: 01939 250351 Ex 7232
(Shawbury ATC)
skydive@theparachutecentre.com
www.theparachutecentre.com

Tilstock Arrival & Departure Procedures
Arrival
contact Shawbury when 20nm from Tilstock. Contact Tilstock when 5nm from Tilstock if no reply from Shawbury.
Departure
Telephone Shawbury ATC at least 10 mins before Dept stating "Tilstock Dept" with flight details. Then:
1 Maintain VMC & climb not above 1000ft Tilstock QFE until in contact Shawbury or well clear extended centreline Shawbury Rwy18/36.
2 After initial (or if no) contact turn heading 050°, remain VMC continue climb. After Shawbury contact turn onto agreed track, otherwise turn onto desired track after passing AUDLEM 050°/6.5nmTilstock.
3 W/E PH & evenings when Shawbury limited activity/LARS unavailable, call Shawbury TWR when airborne for info on Shawbury & Ternhill activity.

Effective date:25/09/08 OP 08

38ft 1mb	2.5nm NNE of Balemartin N5629.93 W00652.15	PPR	**Alternative AD** **Islay** Barra **Diversion AD**

Tiree	FIS Scottish 127.275	AFIS 122.700

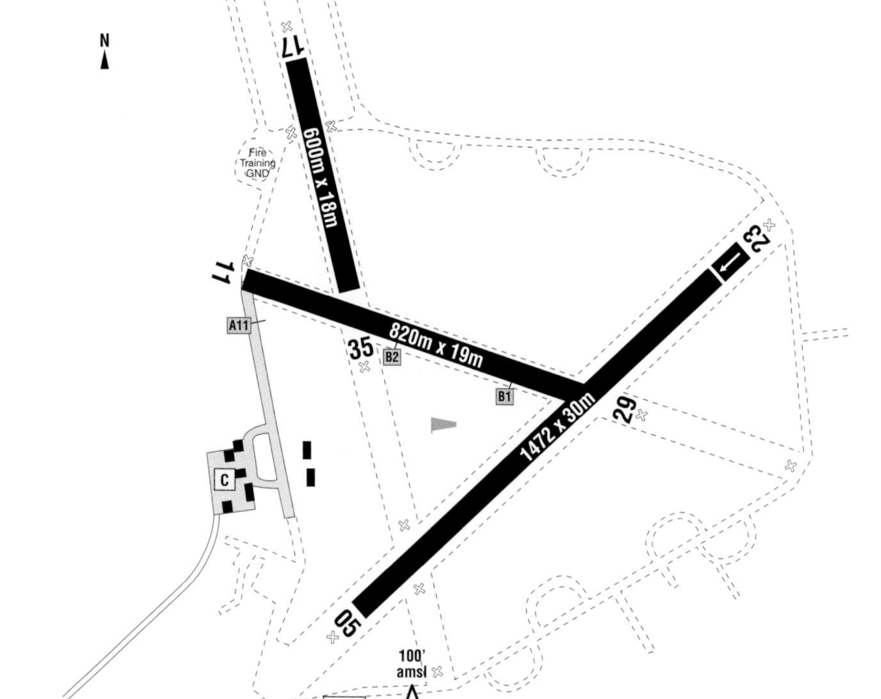

RWY	SURFACE	TORA	LDA	U/L	LIGHTING
05	Asphalt	1402	1402		Thr Rwy APAPI 3° LHS
23	Asphalt	1402	1350		Thr Rwy APAPI 3° LHS
11/29	Asphalt	820	820		Nil
17/35	Asphalt	600	600		Nil

Displaced Thr Rwy23 122m

RNAV		
TIR	117.70	On AD

Remarks
Grass areas soft and unsafe. Use marked Twys only.
Visual aid to location: Abn White flashing.

Warnings
All Twys are closed except between the control TWR & Rwy11 Thr. Unserviceable sections of Rwy are fenced off and marked with crosses. No GND signals except light signals. The useable portion of Rwy17/35 is marked with white sidelines. Windsurfing and kite surfing takes place on beaches near AD. Large flocks of geese in vicinity of AD Oct-Mar.

Operating Hrs	Mon-Fri 1000-1500 Sat 1115-1245 (L)
Circuits	Nil
Landing Fee	£15 under 3MT VFR cash/cheque
Maintenance	Nil
Fuel	Nil
Disabled Facilities	Nil
Restaurants	
Mart Café	200m from AD
Scarinish Hotel	**Tel:** 01879 220308
Lodge Hotel	**Tel:** 01879 220368 (Bar lunches)

Taxis	
A J Mackechnie	**Tel:** 01879 220419
Car Hire	
Tiree Motor Co	**Tel:** 01879 220469
A MacLennan Mtrs	**Tel:** 01879 220555
Weather Info	M T9 Fax 438 GWC
Operator	HIAL, Tiree Aerodrome Isle of Tiree, Argyll, PA77 6UW **Tel:** 01879 220456 **Fax:** 01879 220714 tireeapm@hial.co.uk

TOP FARM

200ft 6mb	7nm NW of Royston N5207.45 W00007.20	**PPR**	**Alternative AD** **Diversion AD**	**Cambridge** Little Gransden

Non-radio	**A/G** **Little Gransden 130.850**	**Safetycom** **135.475**

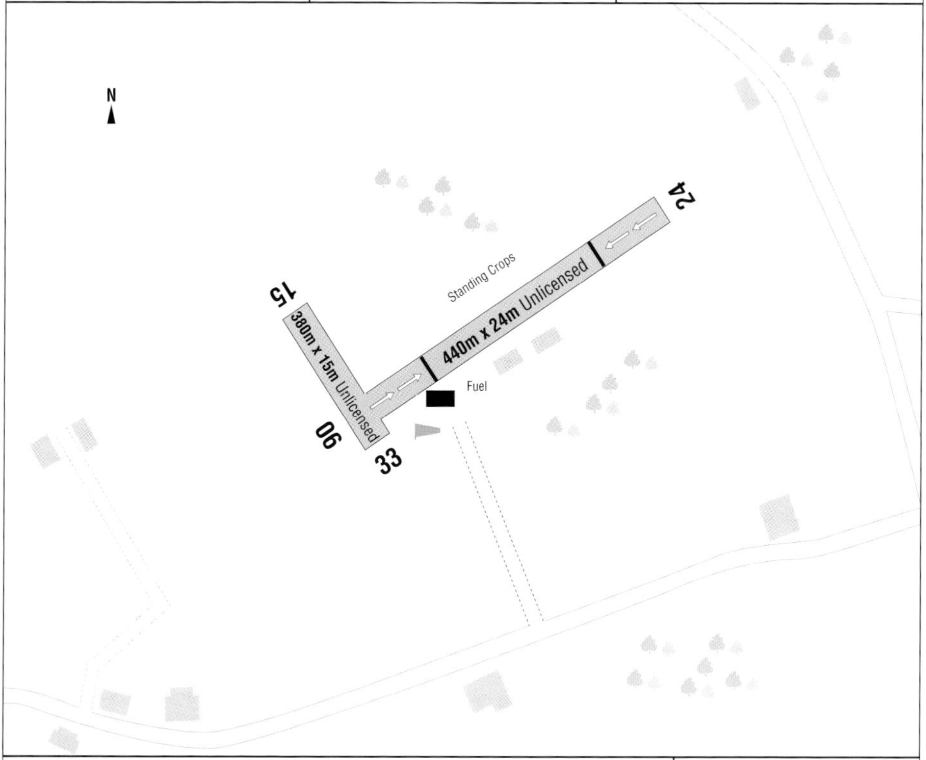

N
15
380m x 15m Unlicensed
06
33
Standing Crops
440m x 24m Unlicensed
24
Fuel

RWY	SURFACE	TORA	LDA	U/L	LIGHTING
06/24	Grass			440x24	Nil
15/33	Grass			380x15	Nil

Rwy06/24 over runs 230m at either end, Rwy15/33 only for use in strong winds
Rwy15 has marked upslope

RNAV			
BKY	**116.25**	**322**	**10.1**

Remarks
PPR by telephone. Visitors welcome at own risk. Well prepared strip. Rwy06/24 level and smooth. No take-offs after 1400 (L) on Sundays.

Warnings
Intense gliding activity at Gransden Lodge 2.5nm to N. Little Gransden ATZ boundary is 1nm to N and NW of Top Farm. Sandy TV mast (972ft amsl) is 3nm WNW.
Noise: Avoid over flying local habitation. Do not over fly house on 1nm final for Rwy06

Operating Hrs Available on request
No take-offs after 1400Hrs Sundays
Circuits 06 RH, 24 LH, 1100ft QFE
Landing Fee £5
Maintenance
Barmoor Aviation **Tel:** 01767 631377
Fuel AVGAS 100LL
Disabled Facilities Nil
Restaurants
Randall's **Tel:** 01223 207229 (B&B)
Queen Adelaide **Tel:** 01223 208278

Taxis
Mayalls **Tel:** 01763 243225
Car Hire Nil
Weather Info Air Cen MOEx
Operator David Morris
Barmoor House
Top Farm, Croydon, Royston
Herts, SG8 0EQ
Tel: 01767 631377
Tel: 07711 197738

Effective date:25/09/08

EGXZ TOPCLIFFE

92ft 3mb	2.5nm SW of Thirsk N5412.33 W00122.93	PPR MIL	**Alternative AD** **Diversion AD**	**Durham Tees Valley** Full Sutton **Non-standard join**

Topcliffe	LARS	APP	TWR	A/G
	Leeming 127.750	125.000	122.100	125.000 (Glider freq)

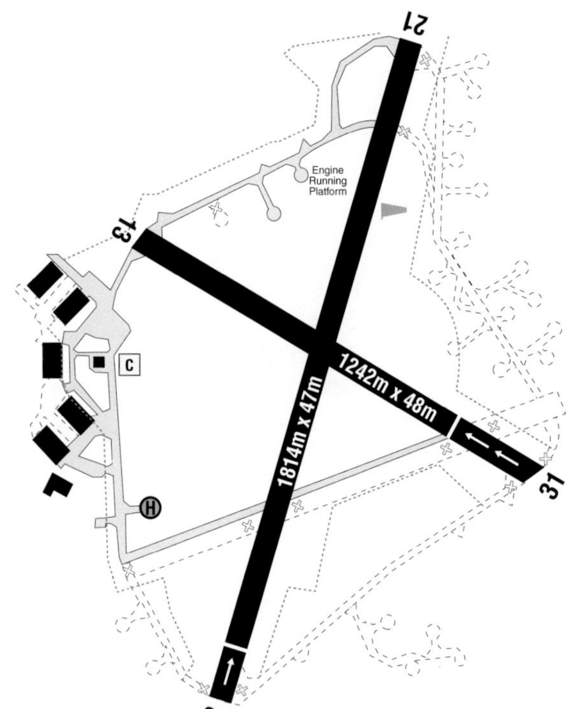

RWY	SURFACE	TORA	LDA	U/L	LIGHTING
03	Asphalt	1814	1434		Thr Rwy PAPI 3°
21	Asphalt	1814	1814		Ap Thr Rwy PAPI 3°
13	Asphalt	1242	1242		Thr Rwy PAPI 3°
31	Asphalt	1242	946		Thr Rwy PAPI 3°

Displaced Thr Rwy03 380m, Displaced Thr Rwy31 316m

RNAV

Remarks
PPR 24 Hrs notice required via Linton Ops. Satellite to Linton-on-Ouse

Warnings
Glider flying Mon-Fri evenings, Sat-Sun all day.

Operating Hrs Mon-Thu 0800-1715 Fri 0800-1700 (L) & as required by Linton-on-Ouse

Circuits 13, 21 RH, 03, 31 LH

Landing Fee Charges in accordance with MOD policy Contact Station Ops for details

Maintenance Nil
Fuel Nil

Disabled Facilities

Restaurants Topcliffe village 2 miles S

Taxis/Car Hire Nil

Weather Info Air N MOEx

Operator
RAF Topcliffe
Topcliffe
Thirsk
North Yorkshire
YO7 3QE
Tel: 01845 595340 (ATC)
Tel: 01347 848261 Ex 7491 (PPR)
Tel: 01347 848261 Ex 7491 (Linton Ops)
Fax: 01845 595227 (ATC)
Fax: 01845 595367 (Ops)

T

EGHY — TRURO

400ft 13mb	3nm WNW of Truro N5016.72 W00508.55	PPR	**Alternative AD** **Diversion AD**	**St Mawgan** Perranporth

Truro	APP Culdrose 134.050	APP St Mawgan 128.725	A/G 129.800

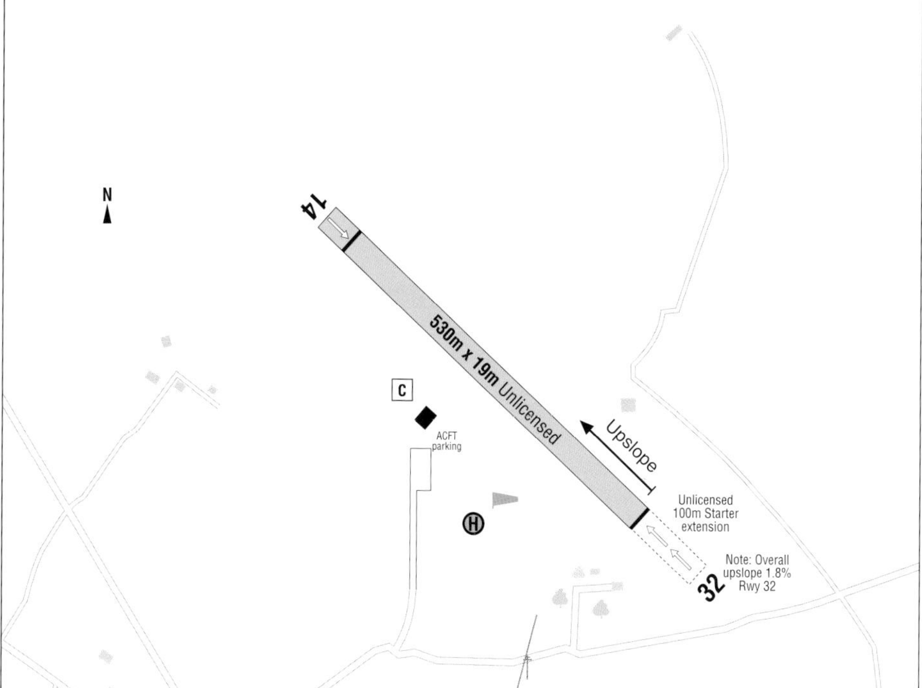

RWY	SURFACE	TORA	LDA	U/L	LIGHTING
14/32	Grass			530x19	Nil

Starter extension Rwy32 100m, Displaced Thr Rwy14 39m, Rwy32 Upslope 5.5%

RNAV			
LND	**114.20**	**070**	**20.6**

Remarks

PPR by telephone. Inbound & outbound ACFT to and from NE are requested to call St Mawgan. AD situated below Culdrose AAIA for info contact Culdrose.

Warnings

AD is located under RNAS Culdrose AIAA.
Noise: Climb straight ahead for 0.75nm after take-off before turning on-route.

Operating Hrs	0800-1900 or SS whichever earliest (Summer) +1Hr (Winter))
Circuits	To N 800ft QFE
Landing Fee	Single £8.81, Twin & Heli £11.75
Maintenance	Nil
Fuel	To be advised
Disabled Facilities	Nil
Restaurants	AD owner will advise
Taxis	
City Taxis	**Tel:** 01872 273053 **Tel:** 0800 318708
Avcab	**Tel:** 01872 241214

Car Hire	
Hertz	**Tel:** 01872 223638
Car Rental	**Tel:** 01872 676797
Weather Info	Air SW MOEx
Operator	Graham Barall Truro Aerodrome Truro, Cornwall TR4 9EX **Tel:** 01872 560488

448ft 15mb	2nm E of Brackley N5202.45 W00105.73	PPR	**Alternative AD** **Diversion AD**	**Oxford** Wellesbourne Mountford

Turweston	**A/G** **122.175**

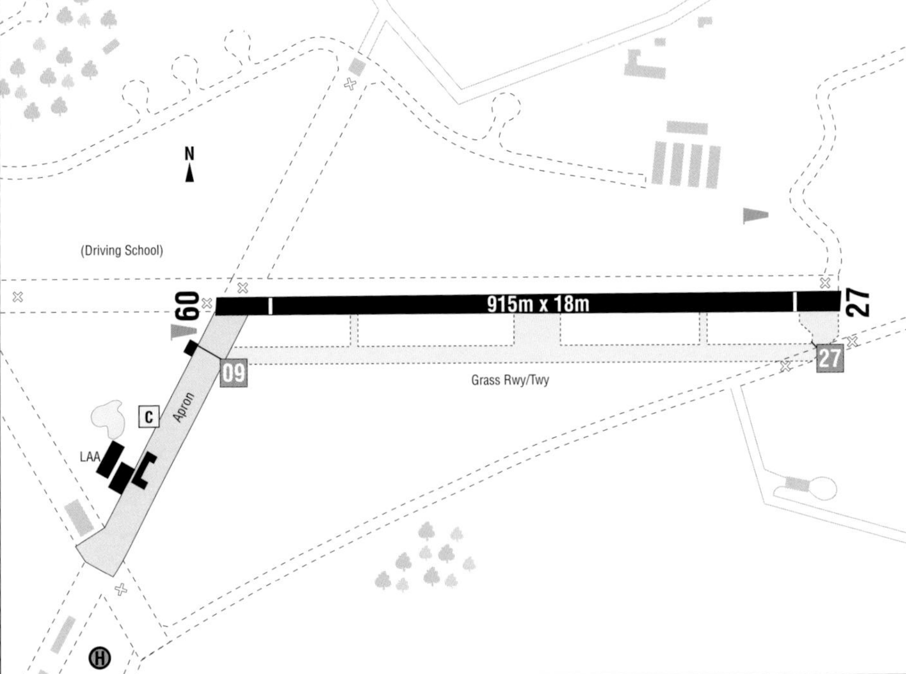

RWY	SURFACE	TORA	LDA	U/L	LIGHTING	RNAV			
09/27	Asphalt	915	800		Nil	DTY	116.40	180	8.3

Remarks
PPR by telephone or website form to all users. AD not available for use at night by flights required to use licensed AD. AD U/L on Sundays, no dept after 1600.Connecting service available to Silverstone Circuit during British Grand Prix weekend.

Warnings
Radio Masts 232° aal/680ft amsl 220°/3.5nm. Power cables run NW/SE 1nm W of AD. Not all Twys are available for use. Deviation from the marked manoeuvring area can be hazardous. Tail wheel ACFT may with prior permission land & take-off on the grass Twy. Parachuting and gliding at Hinton-in-the-Hedges 4nm SW of AD.
Caution: EG D129 Weston on the Green Active H24.
Helicopters: fly fixed wing circuit using reference points. Telephone AD for full procedure or website.

Operating Hrs	Mon-Fri 0900-1800 0800-2000 on request Sat 0900-1800 Sun 1000-1800 (L)
Circuits	09 LH, 27 RH, 1300ft QFE
Landing Fee	Single £12 (Free with up lift of fuel 60ltr) Twin £20 (Free with up lift of fuel 80ltr)
Maintenance	Akki Enterprises (JAR 145) **Tel:** 01280 706616 (Day) **Tel:** 01933 355127 (Evening) www.akkiavationservices.co.uk
Paint Shop	**Tel:** 01280 840661 (Mick Allen) **Fax:** 01280 840662 www.allenaircraftresprays.co.uk
Fuel	AVGAS 100LL
Disabled Facilities	Nil
Restaurants/Accomodation	
Wellington's Café	**Tel:** 07968 966241
Taxis	
R&R	**Tel:** 01280 823636
Car Hire	Budget will pick up at AD contact ATC for details
Weather Info	Air Cen MOEx
Operator	Turweston Flight Centre Ltd Turweston Aerodrome Brackley, Northants, NN13 5YD **Tel**: 01280 705400 (TWR/Admin) **Tel**: 01280 701167 (Flight Training Turweston) info@turwestonflight.com www.turweston.flight.com
LAA	**Tel:** 01280 846786 Office@laa.uk.com www.lightaircraftassociation.co.uk

T

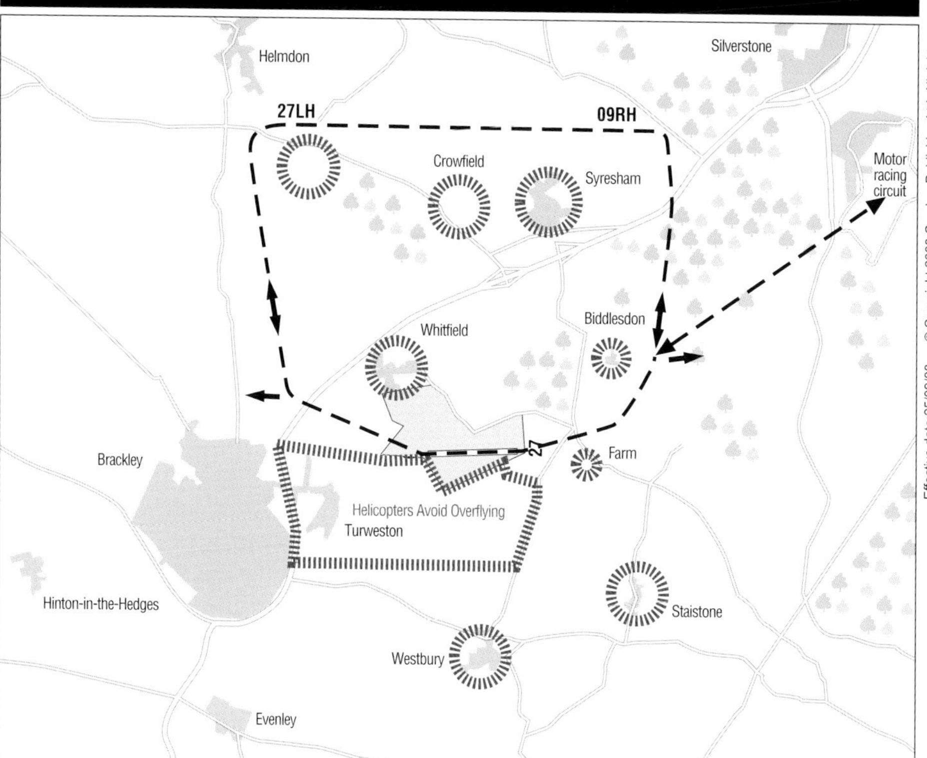

Effective date:25/09/08

Noise Procedures
Dept Rwy27: Turn right 20° at 200ft to pass midway between villages. Strictly no turns before crossing A43 and not below 1500ft. Avoid over flying settlements and houses. Keep north of Brackley.
Arr Rwy27: Follow fire break in wood to avoid farmhouse. No turn out below 1000ft QNH. Avoid over flying settlements and houses.
Arr Rwy27: Joining offset final Rwy27 via Silverstone (Rwy24).
Dept Rwy09: Follow fire break in wood to avoid farm house. No turn out below 1500ft QNH. Avoid over flying settlements and houses.

Additional Helicopter Procedures
Arrivals
Helicopters must fly the fixed wing circuit and from the threshold hover taxi to land at the H opposite the tower.
Depatrures
On departure helicopters must use max rate of climb and ensure 1000ft QNH at the airfield boundary.

INTENTIONALLY LEFT BLANK

62ft 2mb	On the Isle of Unst N6044.83 W00051.23	PPR	Alternative AD **Scatsta** Lerwick

Unst	APP Sumburgh 131.300	A/G 130.350

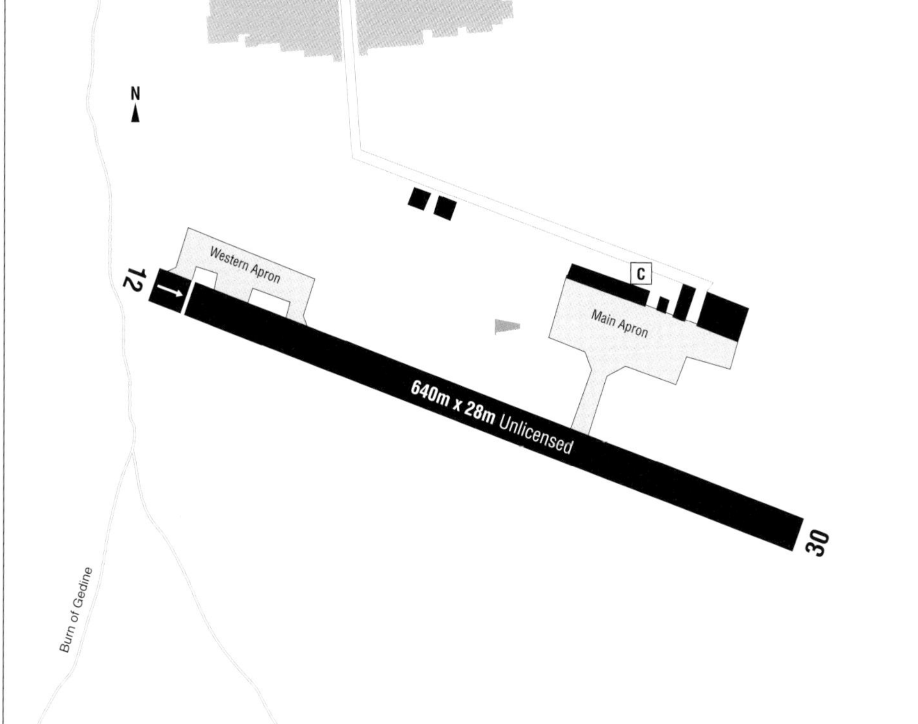

RWY	SURFACE	TORA	LDA	U/L	LIGHTING
12	Asphalt			640x28	Thr Rwy PAPI 4.5° LHS
30	Asphalt			610x28	Ap Thr Rwy PAPI 4.5° LHS

Displaced Thr Rwy12

RNAV

Remarks
ACFT operators are reminded to check with ATC availability of services before nominating this AD as a Diversion AD.
Visual aid to location: IbnGreen UT.

Warnings
Rising GND exists in take-off path Rwy30. Frequent helicopter activity outside AD Hrs. No GND signals except light signals.

Operating Hrs Emergency use or ambulance flights UFN
Circuits 30 RH, 12 LH, 1000ft QFE
Landing Fee On application
Maintenance Nil
Fuel Nil
Disabled Facilities Nil
Restaurants Nil
Taxis
PT Coaches **Tel:** 01957 711666
Car Hire Nil
Weather Info M T9 Fax 442 GWC

Operator Shetland Islands Council
Unst Aerodrome
Baltasound, Shetland, ZE2 9DT
Tel: 01957 711877 (AD)
Tel/Fax: 01957 711541

575ft 19mb	8nm NNW of Boscombe Down N5117.17 W00146.92	PPR MIL	Alternative AD **Farnborough** Thruxton **Non-standard join**

Upavon	LARS Boscombe 126.700	OPS Salisbury 122.750

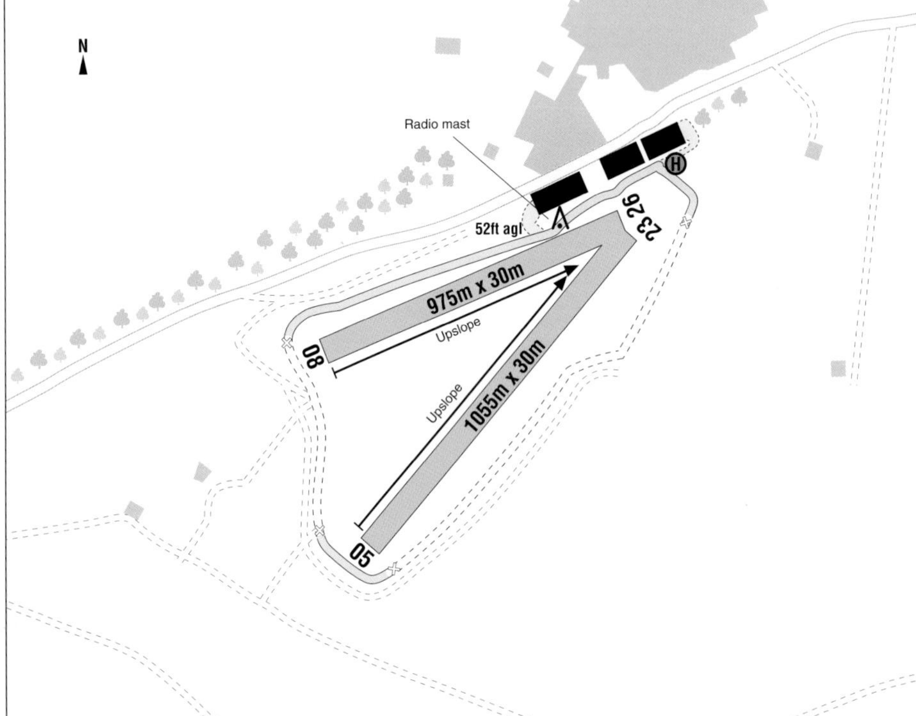

RWY	SURFACE	TORA	LDA	U/L	LIGHTING
05/23	Grass	1055	1055		Nil
08/26	Grass	975	975		Nil

Rwy26 surface suitable for ACFT equipped with low pressure tyres
Rwys upslope W-E 1.77%

RNAV			
CPT	114.35	244	24.5

Remarks
Strict PPR by telephone, 24Hrs notice. Army AD. ATC manned for certain pre-notified operations. Non-ATC qualified personnel give advisory information on UHF freq. During daylight hours call Salisbury Ops, 5 minutes before ETA passing ACFT type, ETA & intentions.

Warnings
AD situated within EG D126/128 range information available from 'Salisbury Ops'. S Twy closed to Helicopter and fixed wing operations. Glider flying takes place during daylight hrs.
Caution: Radio mast 52ft agl just to W of TWR. Netheravon AD is 2.5nm S, Larkhill Range 3nm W. Everleigh drop zone 3.5nm to the SE.
Noise: Arr/Dept will be at pilots own discretion. All APP to be from N sector (290-040°).

Operating Hrs SR-SS
Circuits Info available with PPR
Landing Fee Charges in accordance with MOD policy
Contact Station Ops for details
Maintenance Nil
Fuel Nil
Disabled Facilities Nil
Restaurant Nil
Taxi/Car Hire Nil

Weather Info Air SW MOEx
Operator MOD (Army)
Upavon Airfield
Salisbury Plain, Wilts
Tel: 01980 615381 (PPR)
Tel: 01980 615068
Tel: 01980 674710/674730
(Salisbury Ops)

U-V

UPFIELD

10ft 0mb	4nm SE of Newport N5133.50 W00253.00	PPR	**Alternative AD** **Bristol Filton** Bristol

Upfield	**LARS** **Filton 122.725**	**LARS** **Cardiff 126.625**	**A/G** **119.500**

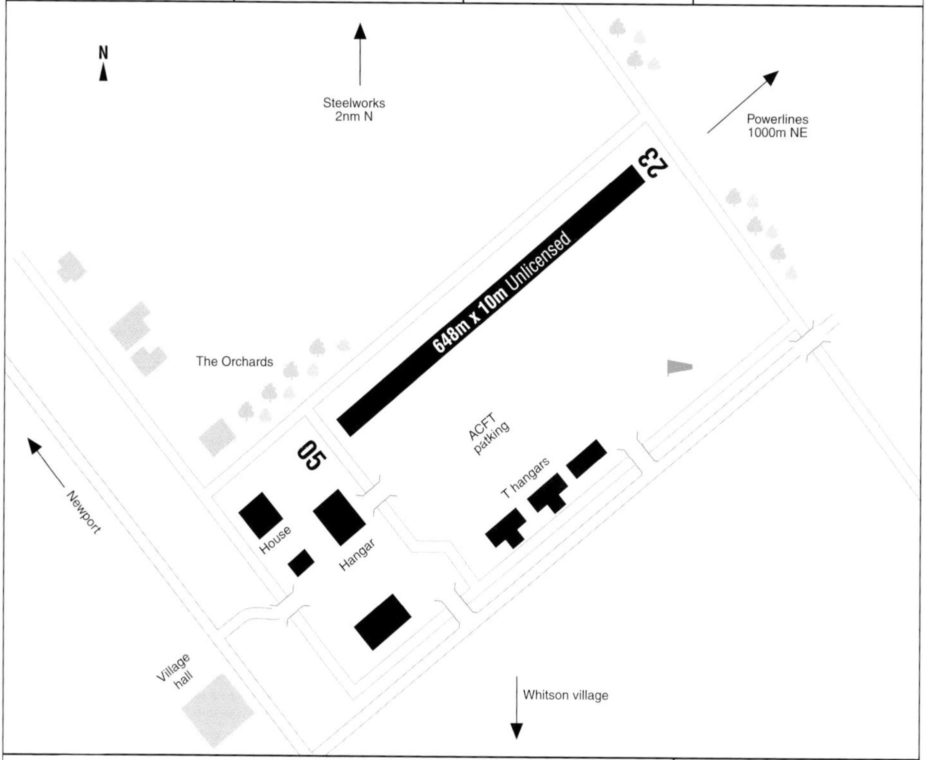

RWY	SURFACE	TORA	LDA	U/L	LIGHTING
05/23	Concrete			648x10	Nil

Concrete Rwy raised 4ins agl, flood avoidance

RNAV			
BCN	**117.45**	**129**	**17.3**

Remarks
PPR. Visiting ACFT welcome at own risk.

Warnings
All ACFT movements must be confined to Rwy only. Other areas are very soft all year round. Use full length of Rwy for take-off. Low flying military ACFT may be encountered in vicinity, particularly during the week.
Noise: Operate considerately. Do not over fly The Orchards. Avoid over flying Redwick village to NE, Goldcliffe village and houses on Whiston Road to SE.
Ensure downwind leg is over the coast. Climb out on Rwy centre line to 1000ft before turning onto course.
Dept Rwy 23: clear road and farm opposite, turn right over steelworks.
Dept Rwy05: Climb straight ahead.

Operating Hrs	SR-SS
Circuits	To N 1000ft QFE
Landing Fee	Single £5, Twin £10, Microlight £3
Maintenance	Emergency repairs, PFA inspector on site Long term parking available
Fuel	MOGAS available on request
Disabled Facilities	Nil
Restaurants	Local Pub B & B Celtic Manor (Ryder Cup Venue) 6 miles from AD
Taxis	Operator can advise
Car Hire	Nil
Weather Info	Air S MOEx

Operator
K M Bowen
Upfield Farm
Whitson, Newport
Gwent, NP18 2PG
Tel: 01633 279222
Fax: 01633 279922
milesbowen@aol.com

UPPER HARFORD

750ft 25mb	2.5nm W of Bourton on the Water N5153.32 W00149.28	PPR	Alternative AD	Gloucestershire Kemble

Non-Radio	LARS Brize 124.275	Safetycom 135.475

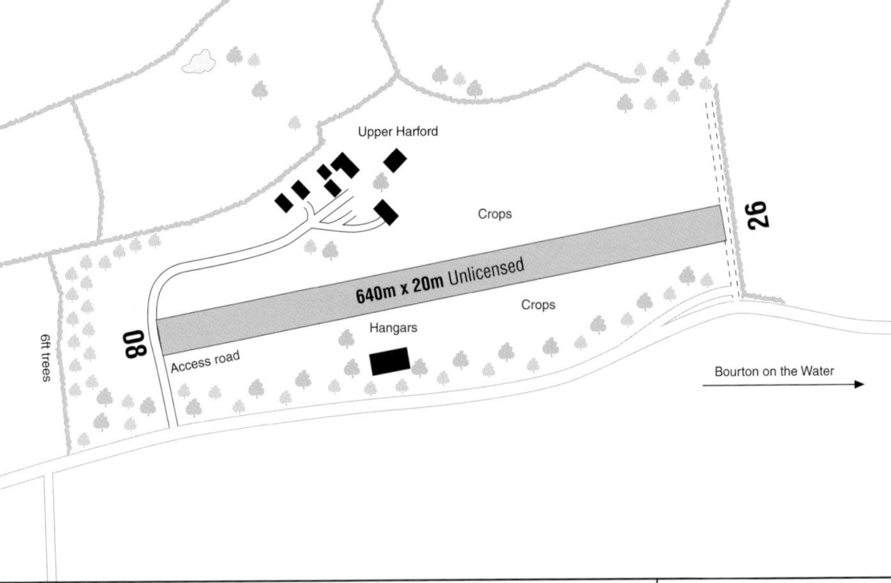

RWY	SURFACE	TORA	LDA	U/L	LIGHTING
08/26	Grass			640x20	Nil

RNAV			
HON	113.65	195	28.7

Remarks
Strictly PPR by telephone. AD operated by flying community, which has strict planning constraints on visiting ACFT. PPR for visitors will normally only be granted for pilots visiting residents or local villages. Casual visitors will not be accepted. Strip is well maintained and is located between a disused railway line and Bourton on the Water.

Warnings
Hedge at Rwy08 Thr and disused electrical supply poles, (no wires), adjacent to Rwy26 APP.
Noise: Avoid over flight of all local habitation.

Operating Hrs	SR-SS daily
Circuits	N 1000ft QFE
Landing Fee	Nil
Maintenance	Nil
Fuel	Nil
Disabled Facilities	Nil
Restaurants	Nil
Taxis/Car Hire	Nil
Weather Info	Air Cen MOEx

Operator
Mr M Jones
Upper Harford House
Upper Harford
Bourton on the Water
Glos GL54 3BY
Tel/Fax: 01451 821455

36ft 1mb	1nm NW of Rhosneigr N5314.89 W00432.12	PPR MIL	Alternative AD Diversion AD	Hawarden Caernarfon **Non-standard join**

Valley	ATIS 120.725	LARS/APP 125.225	DIR 123.300	TWR/GND 122.100

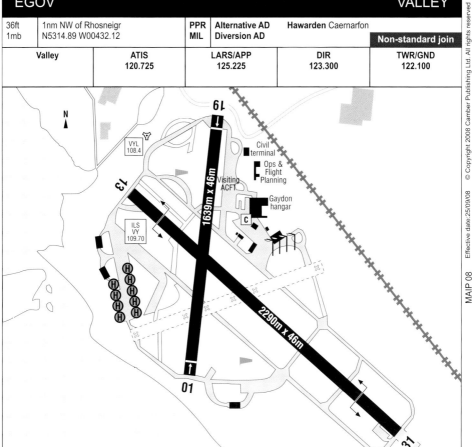

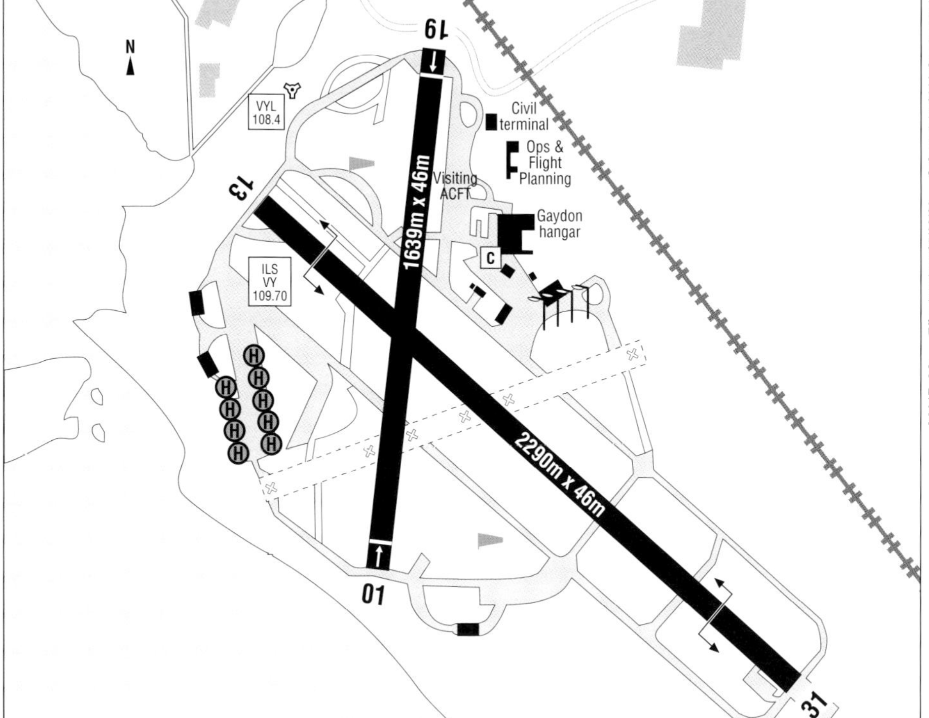

RWY	SURFACE	TORA	LDA	U/L	LIGHTING
13/31	Asphalt	2290	2290		Ap Thr Rwy PAPI 3°
01	Asphalt	1572	1572		Thr Rwy PAPI 3°
19	Asphalt	1571	1571		Ap Thr Rwy PAPI 3°

RNAV

Remarks
PPR to all ACFT other than emergency. Inbound civil ACFT make contact with ATC at min range 30nm. Flying training takes place 0800-1800. Helicopter training H24. Valley can only accept 1 visiting ACFT movement during any 30 min period. Limited radar service at a range exceeding 12nm in sector SE of AD.
Visual aid to location: Ibn VY Red.

Warnings
Intensive visual circuit flying at Mona (094°/6nm). Arrester gear 390m from Rwy13/31 Thr.
Noise: Avoid over flying Rhosneigr (SSE of AD) below 1000ft agl.

Operating Hrs Mon-Thu 0800-1800 Fri 0800-1700 (L)

Circuits 31, 19 RH
2 Rwys may be in use at once

Landing Fee Charges in accordance with MOD policy
Contact Station Ops for details

Maintenance Nil

Fuel JET A1

Disabled Facilities

T

Restaurants Nil

Taxis/Car Hire Nil

Weather Info M T Fax 444 MOEx

Operator RAF Valley
Holyhead, Ynys Mon
Isle of Anglesey LL65 3NY
Tel: 01407 762241 Ex 7582 (Ops)
Fax: 01407 767335

Effective date:25/09/08 MAIP 08

231ft 8mb	4nm S of Lincoln N5309.97 W00031.43	PPR MIL	Alternative AD Diversion AD	**East Midlands** Wickenby Non-standard join

Waddington	LARS	APP	DIR	TWR
	127.350	127.350	123.300	122.100 121.300

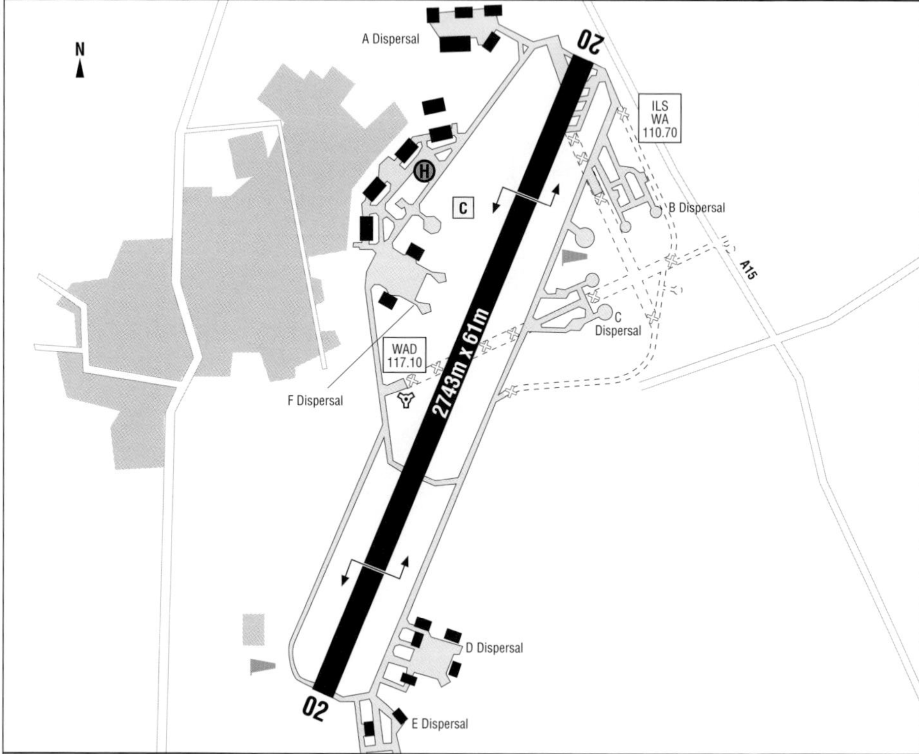

RWY	SURFACE	TORA	LDA	U/L	LIGHTING
02/20	Asphalt	2743	2742		Ap Thr Rwy PAPI 3°

Arrester gear Rwy02/20 610m from Thr

RNAV			
GAM	112.80	118	16.7

Remarks

PPR 24Hrs notice required. ATZ active H24. Inbound ACFT contact Waddington Zone 20nm before MATZ boundary. For Scampton MATZ crossings, contact Waddington Zone. Air Ambulance and flying club operate outside normal Hrs.

Warnings

Public Rd cross final APP Rwy20. Due to high usage slot times must be adhered to. Dept into sector 130-220 will not normally be approved due to Cranwell Ops, plan to avoid this sector. Strong W Winds can produce marked turbulence on final for Rwy20.
Noise: Pilots joining or flying in visual circuit are to avoid over flying Harmston & Waddington villages below 1000fty QFE. Do not over fly Boothby Graffoe, Bracebridge Heath, Branston, Washingborough, Heighington, Coleby & Navenby villages below 500ft QFE.

Operating Hrs	Mon-Thu 0800-2359 Fri 0800-1800
Circuits	02 RH, 20 LH, 1000ft QFE
Landing Fee	Charges in accordance with MOD policy Contact Station Ops for details
Maintenance	Nil
Fuel	AVTUR
Disabled Facilities	Nil
Restaurants	Nil
Taxis/Car Hire	Nil
Weather Info	M T Fax 446 MOEx ATIS **Tel:** 01522 720271 Ex 7305
Met Office	**Fax**: 01522 726525 **Tel:** 01522 727305

Operator

RAF Waddington
Lincoln
Lincs LN5 9NB
Tel: 01522 727451 (ATC)
Tel: 01522 727301 (Ops)
opswad@btconnect.com

WALLIS INTERNATIONAL

0ft 0mb	1nm NNE of Whittlesey N5234.70 W00007.15	PPR	**Alternative AD** **Cambridge** Peterborough Sibson

Non-Radio	**LARS** **Cottesmore 130.200**	**Safetycom** **135.475**

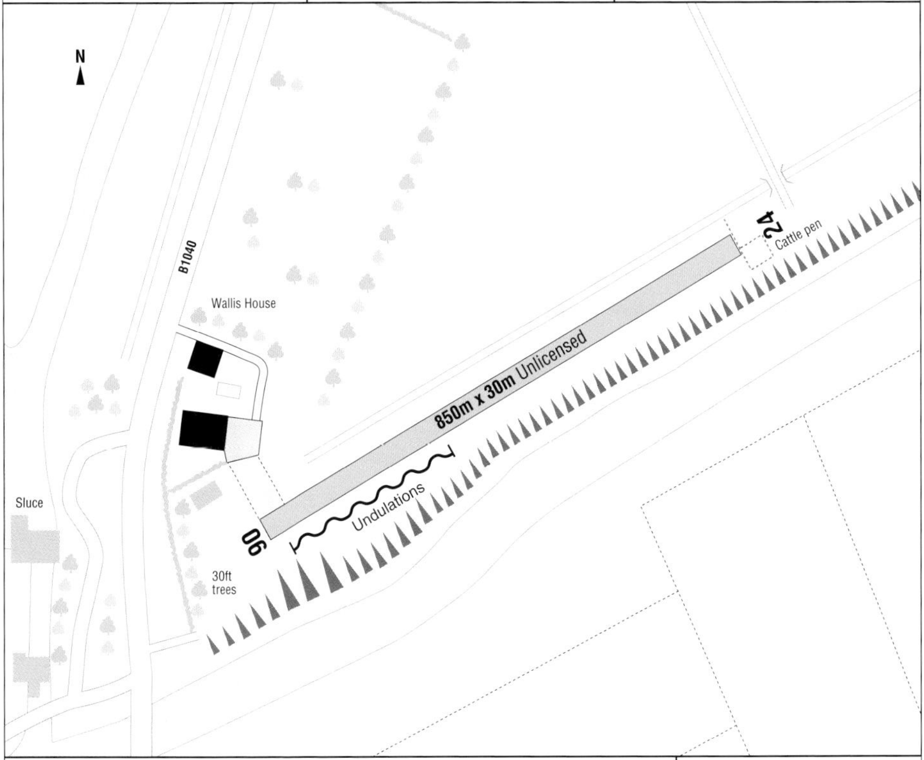

N
B1040
Wallis House
Sluce
30ft trees
06
24
Cattle pen
850m x 30m Unlicensed
Undulations

RWY	SURFACE	TORA	LDA	U/L	LIGHTING
06/24	Grass			850x30	Nil

RNAV

Remarks
PPR by telephone. Visiting ACFT welcome at pilots own risk. AD situated close to River Nene, midway between Thorney & Whittlesey. Strip is mainly flat but there are undulations for first third of Rwy06.

Warnings
30ft trees on short final Rwy06. Wire fence 4ft high and cattle pen Rwy24 Thr.
Noise: Avoid over flying all local houses.

Operating Hrs	SR-SS
Circuits	LH 1000ft QFE
Landing Fee	Nil
Maintenance	Nil
Fuel	Nil
Disabled Facilities	Nil
Restaurant	Pub adjacent strip (5 min walk)
Taxi/Car Hire	Nil
Weather Info	Air SE MOEx

Operator

Tony Wallis
Wallis House
Thorney
Peterborough
Cambridgeshire
PE6 0RL
Tel: 01733 202070
Tel: 07958 224545
jrfisher.farming@virgin.net

Effective date:25/09/08

WALTON WOOD

180ft 6mb	4.5nm S of Pontefract N5337.77 W00115.55	PPR	**Alternative AD** **Diversion AD**	**Leeds Bradford** Sherburn in Elmet

Walton Wood	**APP** **Doncaster Sheffield 126.225**	**A/G** **123.625**

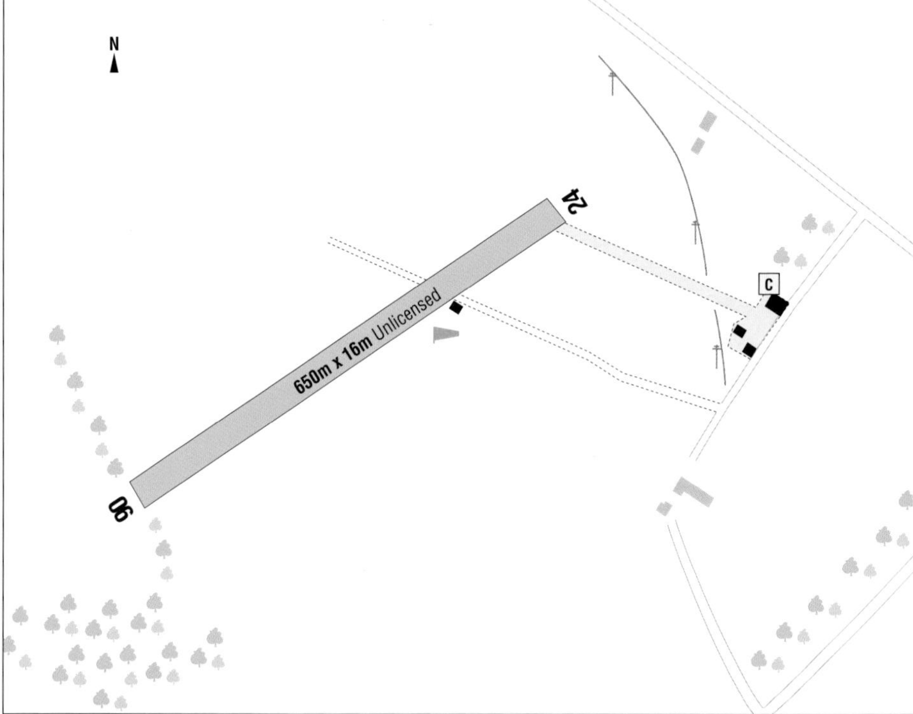

RWY	SURFACE	TORA	LDA	U/L	LIGHTING
06/24	Grass			650x16	Nil

RNAV			
GAM	**112.80**	**335**	**23.8**

Remarks
PPR by telephone. Visiting ACFT welcome at own risk. Rwy can become water logged in winter.

Warnings
Located inside Doncaster Sheffield CTA. Power lines cross Rwy24 APP 10m from Thr. Public footpath & bridle way cross Rwy.
Noise: Avoid over flying all local villages.

Operating Hrs	Available on request
Circuits	24 LH, 06 RH 1000ft
Landing Fee	Single £10 Twin £20
Maintenance	Helicopter Part 145
Fuel	AVGAS JET A1 100LL
Disabled Facilities	
Restaurants	Nil
Taxis/Car Hire	Nil
Weather Info	Air Cen MOEx

Operator
Aero Maintenance Ltd
Walton Wood Airfield
Thorpe Audlin
Pontefract, Yorkshire, WF83HQ
Tel: 01977 620631
Tel: 01977 620769
Fax: 01977 620868
info@amltd.co.uk
www.amltd.co.uk

W

EGNO WARTON

55ft 2mb	6nm W of Preston N5344.70 W00252.98	PPR	**Alternative AD** **Diversion AD**	**Blackpool** Manchester Barton **Non-standard join**

Warton	ATIS	LARS/APP	TWR	FIRE
	121.725	129.525	130.800	121.600

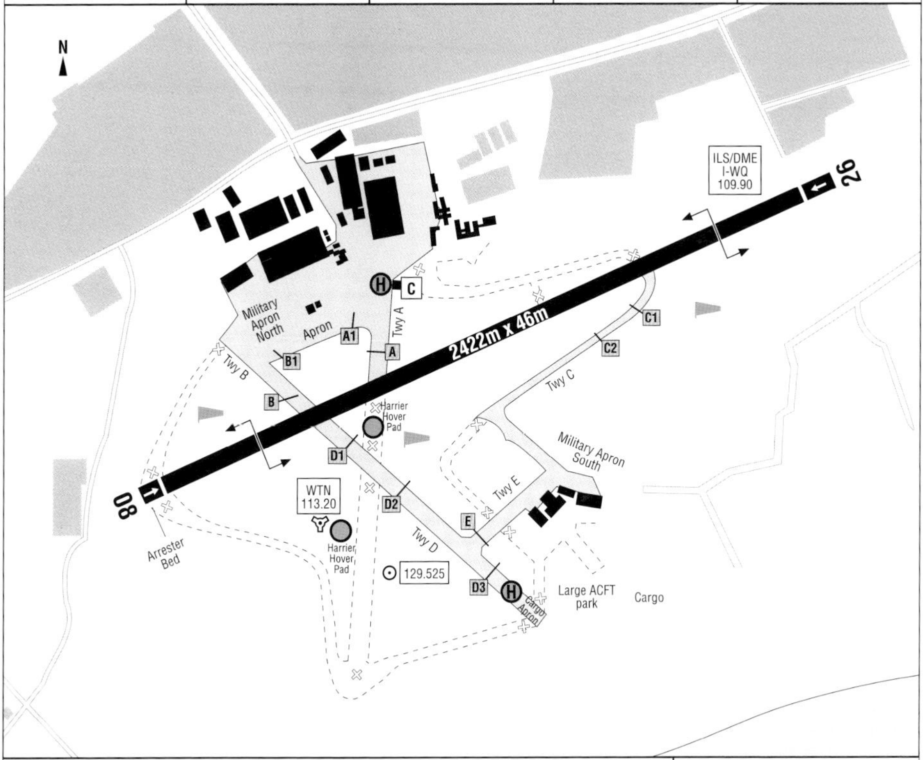

N
ILS/DME
I-WQ
109.90
26
08
2422m x 46m
Military Apron North
Apron
Twy A
Twy B
Twy C
Twy D
Twy E
A1
A
B1
B
C
C1
C2
D1
D2
D3
E
H
Harrier Hover Pad
Harrier Hover Pad
WTN
113.20
129.525
Military Apron South
Arrester Bed
Large ACFT park
Cargo
Cargo Apron

RWY	SURFACE	TORA	LDA	U/L	LIGHTING
08	Asphalt	2422	2358		Ap Thr Rwy PAPI 3°
26	Asphalt	2341	2341		Ap Thr Rwy PAPI 3°

RNAV			
WAL	**114.10**	**028**	**23.0**

Remarks

PPR non-radio ACFT not accepted. Hi-vis. Visiting ACFT on business with BAE only. Red & white marker boards positioned 35m S Rwy08/26 for its full length, 1000m apart. A marshaller must be present for engine starts. Model ACFT flying on AD when closed. Lancashire Police Helicopter operates H24.

Aids to Navigation: NDB WTN 337.00

Warnings

Arrester gear on Rwy08/26. Arrester cable housing located 395m after the start of the full width pavement flush with Rwy. Pilots of light ACFT advised to touchdown after cable housing. Beware close proximity of Springfields Restricted Area and Blackpool AD.

Noise: Avoid over flying factory buildings.

Operating Hrs 0630-1730 (Summer) +1Hr (Winter) & by arr

Circuits All circuits S

Landing Fee On application

Maintenance Ltd

Fuel JET A1

Disabled Facilities

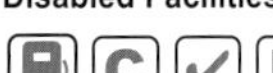

Handling **Tel:** 01772 852303

Restaurants Pub & Motel nr AD
Birley Arms **Tel:** 01772 632201

Taxis/Car Hire Can be arr on site

Weather Info M* Air Cen MOEx
ATIS **Tel:** 01772 856060

Operator BAE Systems
Warton Aerodrome, Preston
Lancshire, PR4 1AX
Tel: 01772 633333 (AD)
Tel: 01772 852303 (Civil Ops)
Tel: 01772 852374 (ATC)
Fax: 01772 634706

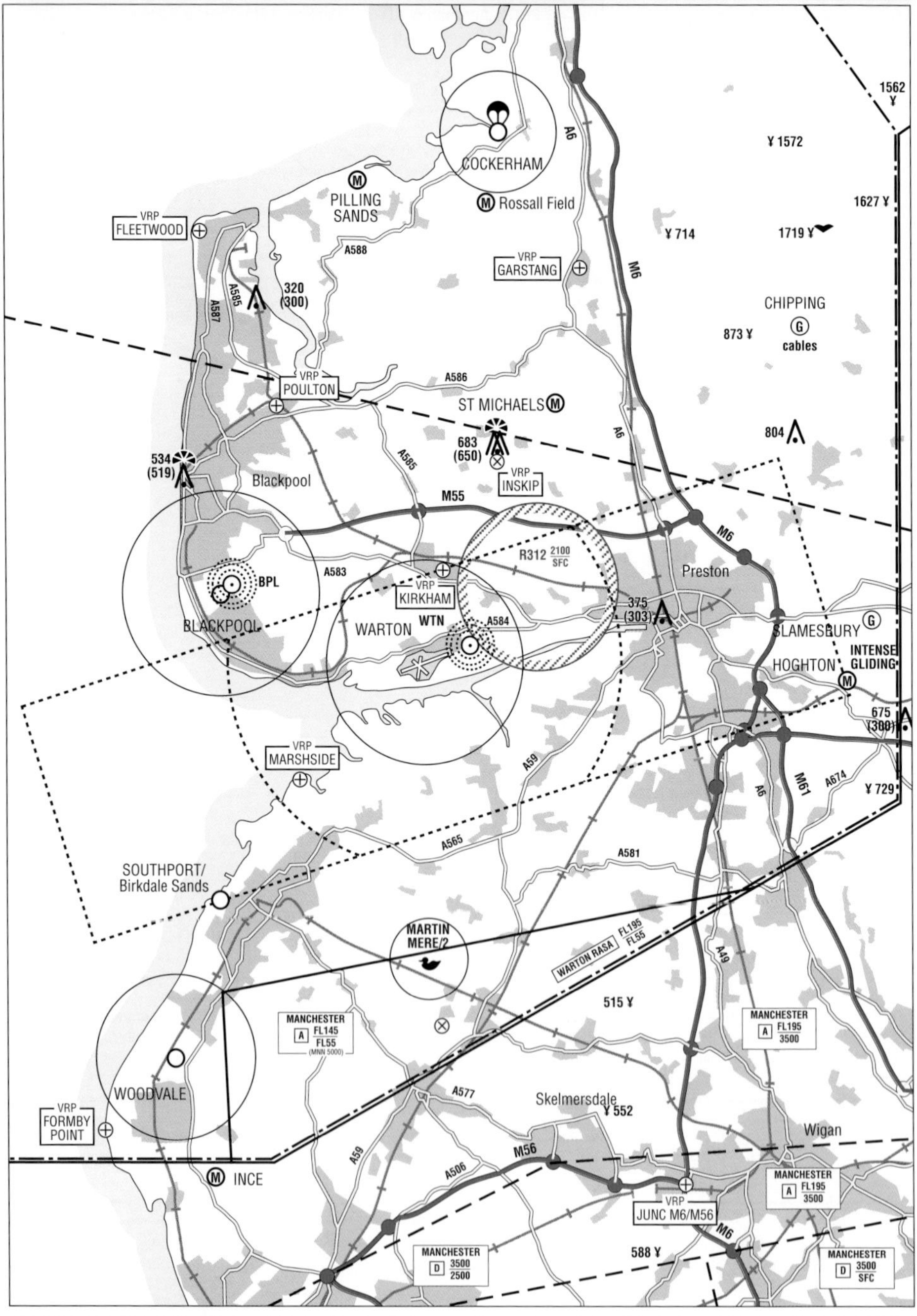

Visual Reference Points (VRP)

Blackburn	N5344.85 W00228.78
Formby Point	N5333.12 W00306.32
Garstang	N5354.38 W00246.55
M6/M58 Junction	N5332.07 W00241.87

283ft 9mb	4nm SSW of Stowmarket N5207.64 E00057.64	PPR MIL	Alternative AD **Southend** Elmsett

Non-standard join

Wattisham	APP	DIR	TWR	A/G
	125.800	123.300	122.100	125.800

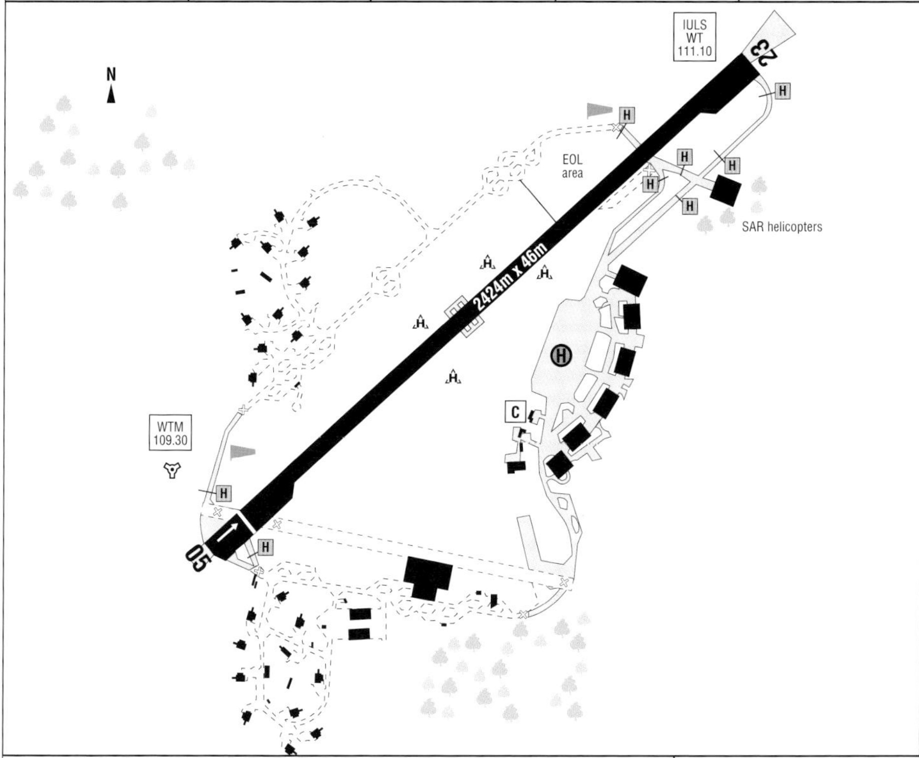

RWY	SURFACE	TORA	LDA	U/L	LIGHTING
05	Asphalt	2424	2284		Ap Thr Rwy PAPI 3°
23	Asphalt	2424	2422		Ap Thr Rwy PAPI 3°

RNAV			
CLN	114.55	340	18.2

Remarks
Strict PPR. Flight plans must be addressed to EGUWZGZX and EGUWYWYO.
Visual aid to location: Ibn WT Red.

Warnings
The first and last third of Rwy is slippy when wet. Intense helicopter flying at all times. Possible laser hazards on apron when Apache helicopters running. Glider flying weekends & PH SR-SS. Aeromodel flying takes place on AD on Friday evenings, W/E & PH. Outside normal Ops Hrs if no answer on APP/TWR freq call A/G freq and request gliders to cease launching prior to Arr & Dept. Full time bird control unit in operation on AD. Elmsett AD 3.3nm S.
Caution: SAR & Police Helicopters operate H24. 3m fence Rwy23 undershoot. TV mast 933ft aal/1210ft amsl 9nm NE of AD.
Noise: Avoid 10m from nose area.

Operating Hrs Mon-Fri 0800-1800 (L)
Circuits Variable up to 1000ft QFE
No dead side
Landing Fee Charges in accordance with MOD policy
Contact Station Ops for details
Maintenance Nil
Fuel AVTUR FS 11
Disabled Facilities Nil
Restaurants Nil
Taxis/Car Hire Nil

Weather Info M T Fax 448 MOEx
Operator Army Air Corps
Wattisham
Suffolk
IP7 7RA
Tel: 01449 728234/35
Tel: 01449 728234 Ex 8241
Fax: 01449 728232

EGBW — WELLESBOURNE MOUNTFORD

159ft 5mb	3.3nm E of Stratford upon Avon N5211.53 W00136.87	PPR	**Alternative AD** **Birmingham** Turweston **Diversion AD**

Wellesbourne	APP	AFIS
	Birmingham 118.050	124.025

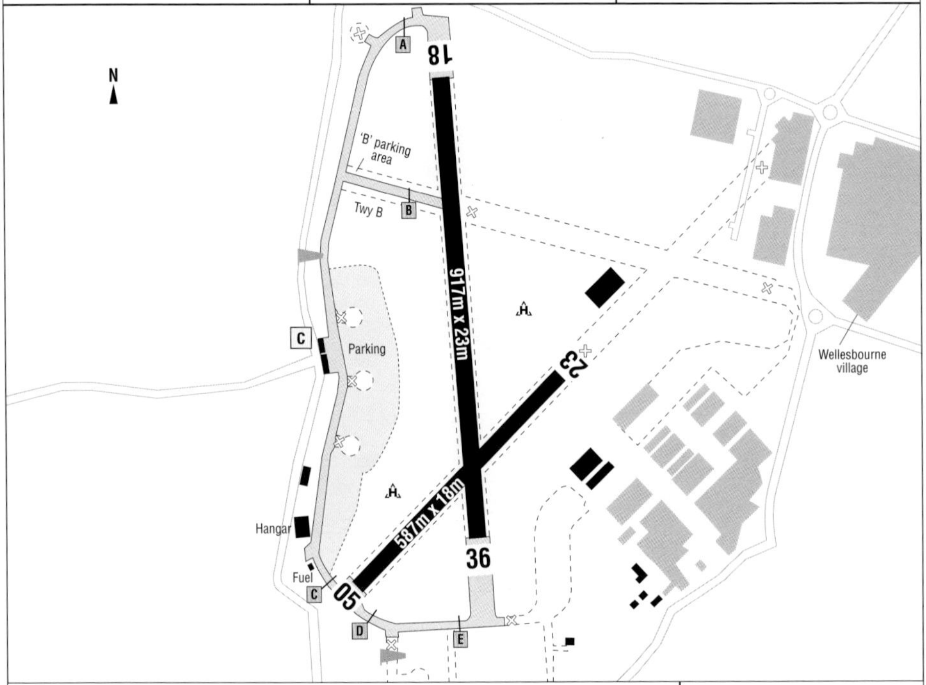

RWY	SURFACE	TORA	LDA	U/L	LIGHTING
05/23	Asphalt	587	587		Nil
18	Asphalt	917	917		Thr Rwy APAPI 3° LHS
36	Asphalt	917	917		Thr Rwy APAPI 4.25° LHS

Rwy23 not available Sat & PH due to market

RNAV			
HON	113.65	174	10.0

Remarks
PPR non-radio ACFT not accepted. Pilots requested to contact Wellesbourne at least 10 mins before ETA Wellesbourne. Certain customs facilities available.
Visual aid to location: Abn white flashing

Warnings
Rwy05/23 not available from Fri 1600–Sun 1000 (Tue after PH). AD situated 3nm S boundary of Birmingham CTA (base 1500ft) & below CTA base 3500 ft. Deviation from marked manoeuvring area hazardous. Industrial buildings E of AD may cause turbulence and/or wind shear.

Operating Hrs	0800-1630 (Summer) 0900-1730 or SS +30mins whichever earlier (Winter) & by arr
Circuits	Fixed wing variable 1000ft QFE Heli variable 600ft QFE
Landing Fee	Fixed wing Single £10, Twin £15 Heli Single £5, Twin £10
Parking	Single £5.00, Twin £10, over night
Maintenance	**Tel:** 01789 470225
Fuel	AVGAS JET A1 100LL 0900-1715 or SS (L)

Disabled Facilities

Restaurants
Touchdown Inn **Tel:** 01789 470575

Taxis	
Local	**Tel:** 01789 841729
Stratford	**Tel:** 01789 414514
Car Hire	Nil
Weather Info	Air Cen MOEx www.wellesbourneairfield.com
Operator	Radarmoor Ltd Wellesbourne Mountford Aerodrome Wellesbourne Warks, CV35 9EU **Tel:** 01789 842007 (Office) **Tel:** 01789 842000 (TWR) **Fax:** 01789 470112 (Office) **Fax:** 01789 470465 (TWR) tower@wellesbourneairfield.com www.wellesbourneairfield.com

Wellesbourne Mountford Noise Abatement Procedures

Effective date:25/09/08

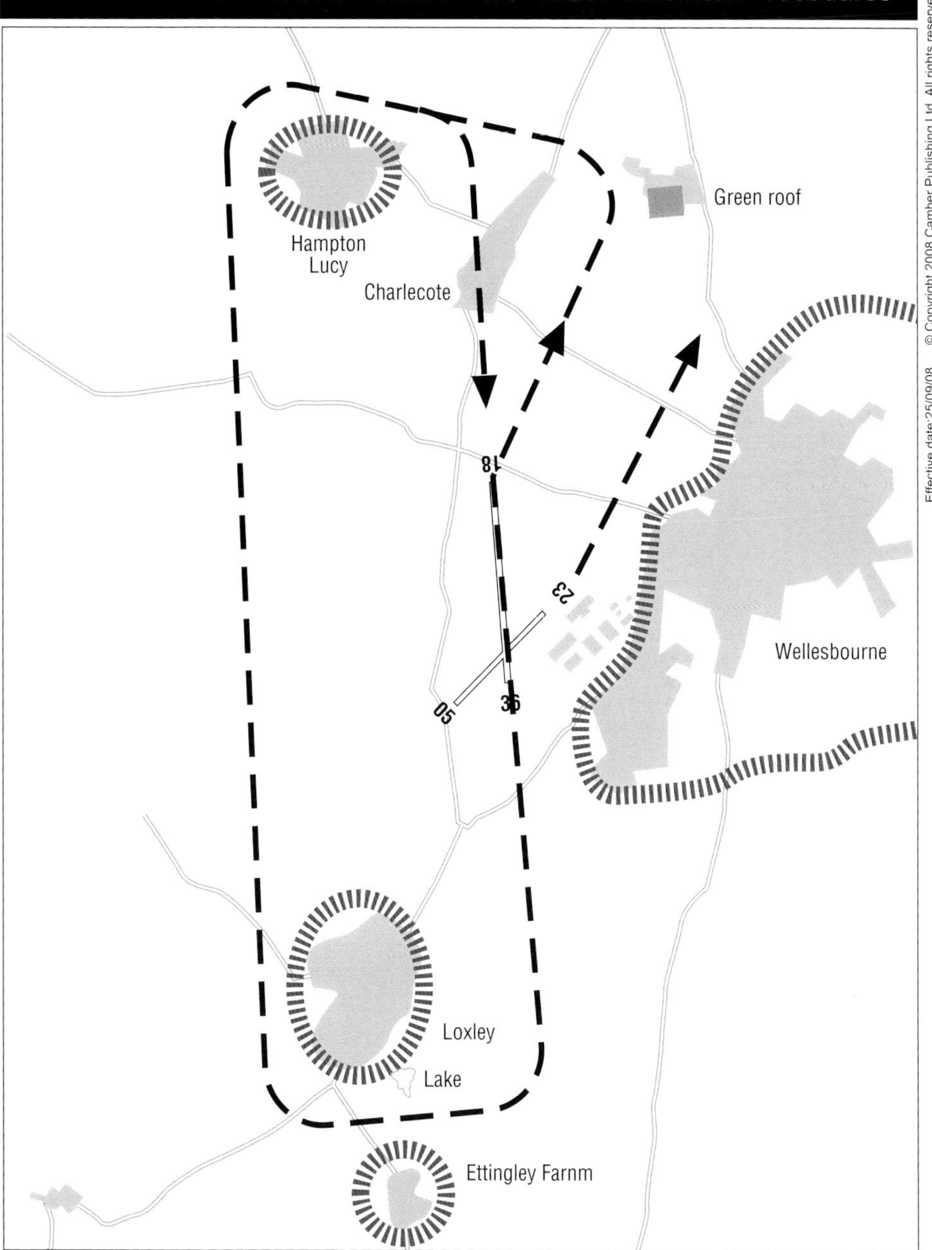

The villages of Wellesbourne, Charlecote, Hampton Lucy and Loxley are very noise sensitive, every effort must be made to avoid over flying.

Rwy36: After dept, turn right, track 030°, towards the green roofs, climb to 1000ft QFE before turning crosswind. Continue outside the villages and the lake shown in the diagram.

Rwy18: Climb straight ahead past the lake SE of Loxley, continue outside the villages as shown in the diagram.

Rwy05: After dept, turn left, track 030°, avoid the villages as far as possible.

233ft 8mb	2nm S of Welshpool N5237.72 W00309.20	PPR	Alternative AD Diversion AD	Hawarden Sleap

Non-standard join

Welshpool	A/G 128.000

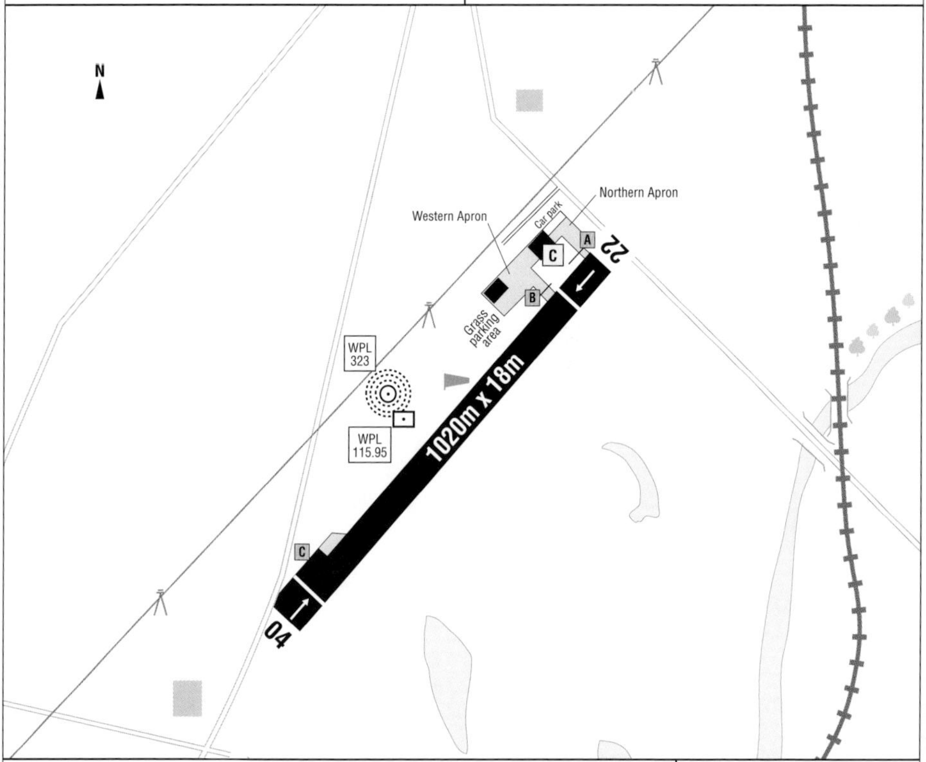

N
Western Apron
Northern Apron
Car park
Grass parking area
A
B
C
22
04
1020m x 18m
WPL 323
WPL 115.95

RWY	SURFACE	TORA	LDA	U/L	LIGHTING
04	Asphalt	880	902		APAPI 3° LHS
22	Asphalt	880	879		APAPI 3° LHS

Displaced Thr Rwy04 100m, Displaced Thr Rwy22 123m

RNAV			
SWB	116.80	245	20.6

Remarks
PPR non-radio ACFT not accepted.

Warnings
AD situated in the Severn Valley with high GND on both sides. Pilots should not descend below safety height until the Rwy has been positively identified. The fins of parked ACFT on the W apron may infringe AD transitional area. Trees infringe the transitional surface by 2nm ESE AD.

Operating Hrs 0900-1700 (L)
Circuits LH 1500ft QFE
Landing Fee Single £10, Twin £20
Maintenance Nil
Fuel AVGAS JET A1 100LL
Hrs as AD

Disabled Facilities

Restaurants Cafe at AD

Taxis
Amber Cabs **Tel:** 01938 556611
Yellow Cabs **Tel:** 01938 555533
Car Hire Nil

Weather Info Air N MOEx

Operator Mid Wales Airport Ltd
Welshpool Aerodrome
Welshpool, Powys, SY21 8SG
Tel: 01938 555560
Fax: 01938 555062
www.welshpoolairport.co.uk

428ft 15mb	4nm E of Cardigan N5206.92 W00433.42	PPR	**Alternative AD** **Pembrey** Haverfordwest

West Wales	A/G 122.150	AFIS 122.150	Range Control 119.650

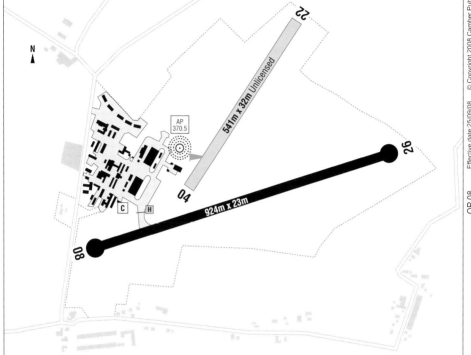

N
22
541m x 32m Unlicensed
AP
370.5
04
26
924m x 23m
08
C
H

RWY	SURFACE	TORA	LDA	U/L	LIGHTING
08	Asphalt	883	845		Nil
26	Asphalt	886	845		Nil
04/22	Grass			541x32	Nil

RNAV			
STU	113.10	073	19.2

Remarks

Strict PPR by telephone. Non-Radio ACFT not accepted. Hi vis. AD U/L weekends & PH, licensed operations by arr. While airside pilots are responsible for safety of passengers and other crew members. Carriage of dangerous goods as specified in ANO is prohibited without written approval of AD manager.

Warnings

Part of ATZ located within Danger Area EGD201. ACFT must NOT penetrate range without permission during notified hours of range ops. PPR & Radio contact with West Wales Radio is sufficient for ACFT Arr/Dept AD. Subject to Rwy in use circuit entry must be made via downwind or base leg aircraft are to specify where the circuit will be joined. Road close to Rwy08 APP. Road traffic is controlled by traffic lights. A/G station will advise if any vehicles are observed not complying with signals. Helicopters must fly fixed wing circuit procedures unless otherwise approved. All wheel equipped Helicopters must use the Rwy. **Caution:** Turbulence Rwy08 Try with strong N winds

Noise: ACFT should operate in such a manner as to create minimum noise impact.

Operating Hrs	0800-1600 (Summer) 0900-SS (Winter) & by arr
Circuits	26 LH, 08 RH, 1000ft QFE. No O/H joins
Landing Fee	Single £12 Twin £25, Other £10 per tonne
Maintenance	Nil
Fuel	AVGAS JET A1 100LL

Disabled Facilities

Restaurants	Light refreshments available

Taxis	Information available with PPR
Car Hire	Hourly bus service passes AD
Weather Info	Air S MOEx
Operator	West Wales Airport Ltd Blaenanarch Ceredigion SA43 2DW **Tel:** 01239 811100 **Fax:** 01239 811555

Effective date:25/09/08

282ft 9mb	8nm N of Oxford N5152.71 W00112.82	**PPR** **Mil**	Alternative AD **Oxford** Turweston **Non-standard join**

Weston on the Green	**Brize Zone** **124.275**	**TWR** **133.65**

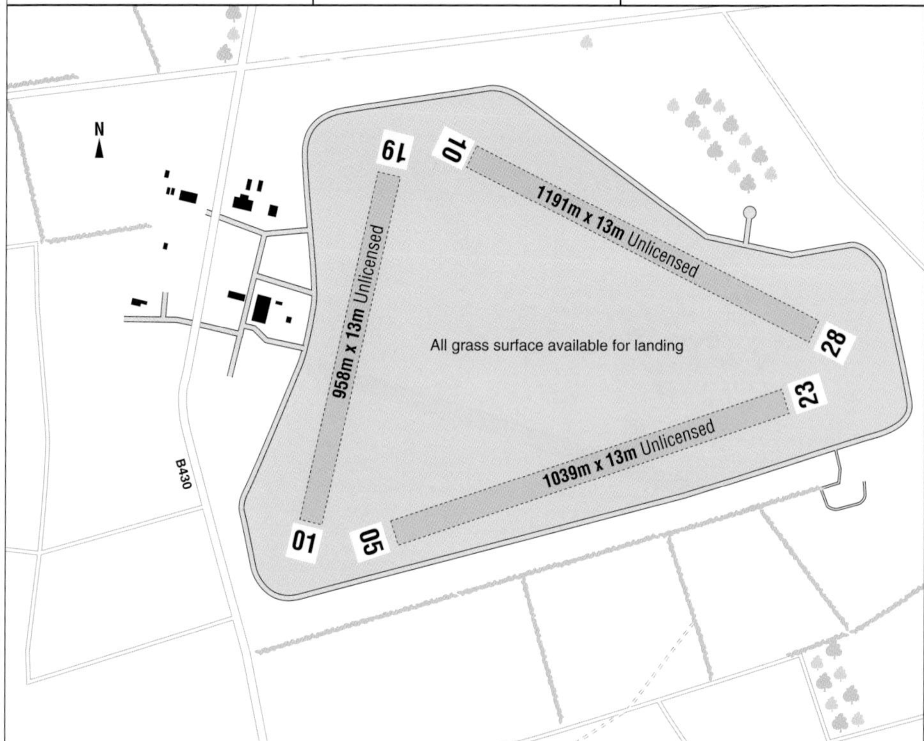

RWY	SURFACE	TORA	LDA	U/L	LIGHTING
01/19	Grass			958x13	Nil
05/23	Grass			1039x13	Nil
10/28	Grass			1191x13	Nil

RNAV			
DTY	116.40	196	18.4

Remarks

PPR essential, 24hrs notice required. AD is established as a Drop Zone for No1 Parachute Training School at Brize Norton and is not configured as a normal AD. After landing head for Twy on W edge of the drop zone, next to Operations Building. ACFT must call TWR before entering Zone, ACFT may be asked to hold if parachuting in progress.

Warnings

AD located in D129. Intensive parachuting operations and winch launched and motor gliders on AD.
Noise: Avoid over flying Middleton Stoney, Weston on the Green and in particular Kirtlington and Bletingdon villages.

Operating Hrs	Operational Hrs vary due to weather & parachuting commitments.
Circuits	Nil
Landing Fee	Charges in accordance with MOD policy. Contact Station Ops for details
Maintenance	Nil
Fuel	Nil
Disabled Facilities	Nil
Restaurants	Nil
Taxi/Car Hire	Nil
Weather Info	Air SW MOEx

Operator

RAF Weston on the Green
Bicester
Oxfordshire
OX25 8TQ
Tel: 01869 343246 (Ops)

W

WESTONZOYLAND

30ft 1mb	4nm SE of Bridgewater N5106.60 W00255.58	PPR	Alternative AD	Exeter Dunkeswell

Zoyland Microbase	LARS Yeovil Radar 127.350	A/G 129.825

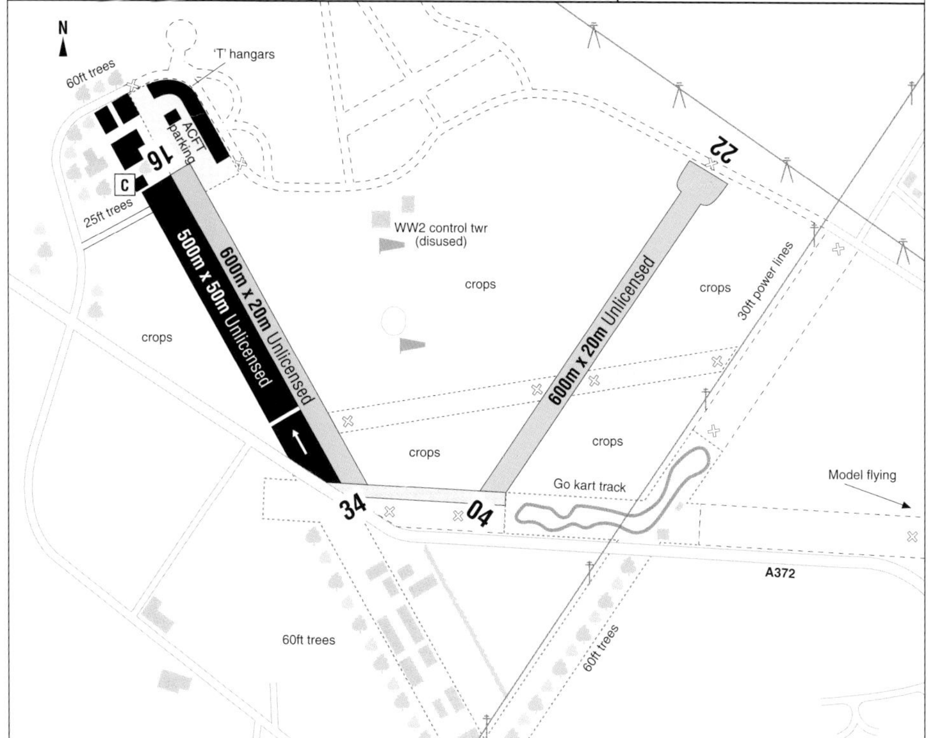

RWY	SURFACE	TORA	LDA	U/L	LIGHTING
16/34	Asphalt			500x50	Nil
16/34	Grass			600x20	Nil
04/22	Grass			600x20	Nil

RNAV

Remarks

PPR by telephone. Visiting ACFT welcome at pilots own risk. Ab Initio Microlight training takes place. AD uses part of WW2 site, marked areas are useable. AD has other uses. Twy between Rwy16/34 and Rwy04/22 not open to visiting ACFT on Sunday.

Warnings

Rwy16/34 Asphalt in good condition there are substantial trees final APP Rwy16 which may cause turbulence/windshear. Garden Centre on Rwy34 final.

Caution: Power lines Rwy22 APP 100m from Rwy22 Thr. AD has no deadside due to the close proximity of Westonzoyland village.

Noise: ACFT to join overhead the windsock or control TWR at 1500ft, descending to join downwind, remaining clear of Westonzoyland village. See circuit diagram.

Operating Hrs	0900-SS or 2100 whichever earlier
Circuits	See Circuit diagram 800ft QFE
Landing Fee	£3 for non members
Maintenance	Nil
Fuel	Nil
Disabled Facilities	Nil
Restaurant	Nil
Taxi/Car Hire	Nil
Weather Info	Air SW MOEx

Operator

Tim Bawden
Manor Farm
Westonzoyland
Bridgewater
Somerset
Tel: 07881 447782 (Tim Bawden)
Tel: 07811 194640 (Jeff Thomas)
info@westonzoylandflyingclub.co.uk
www.westonzoylandflyingclub.co.uk

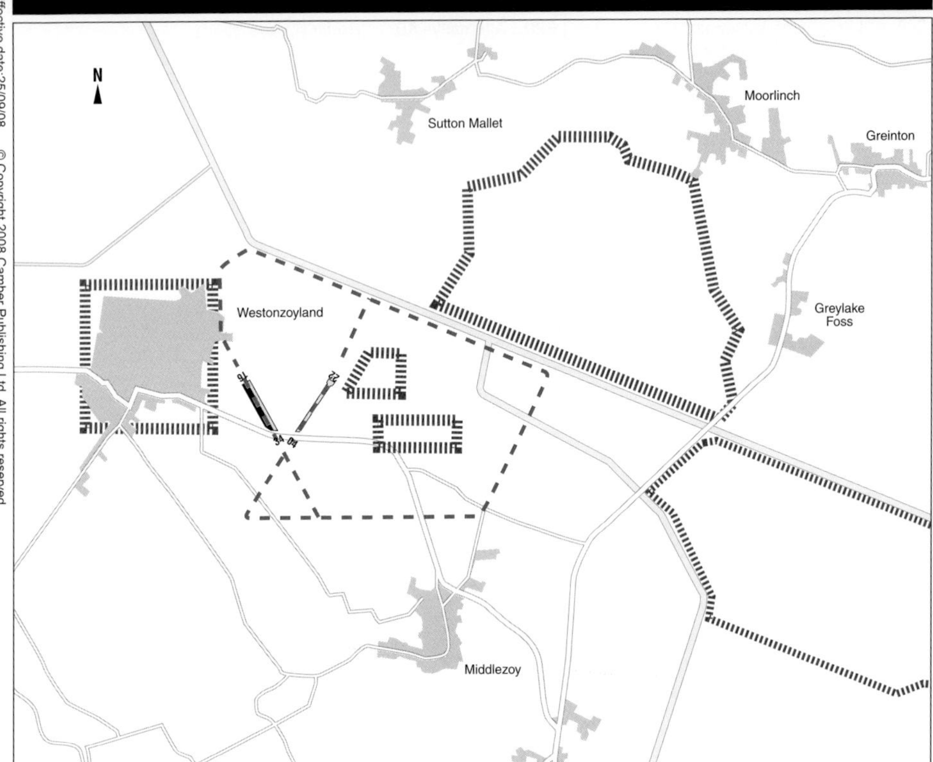
N
Sutton Mallet
Moorlinch
Greinton
Westonzoyland
Greylake
Foss
Middlezoy

EGEW WESTRAY

29ft 1mb	22nm N of Kirkwall Airport N5921.02 W00257.00	PPR	**Alternative AD** **Diversion AD**	**Kirkwall** Sanday

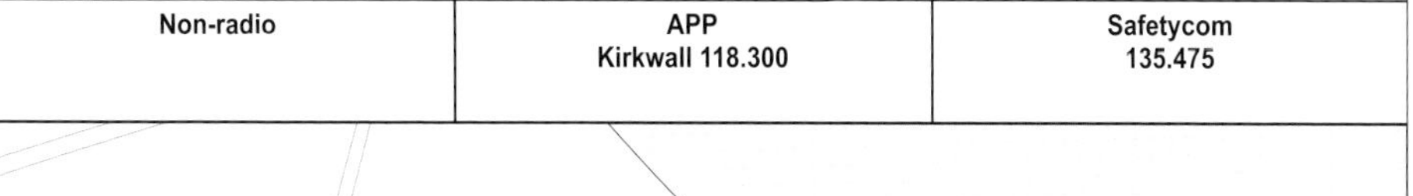

Non-radio	APP Kirkwall 118.300	Safetycom 135.475

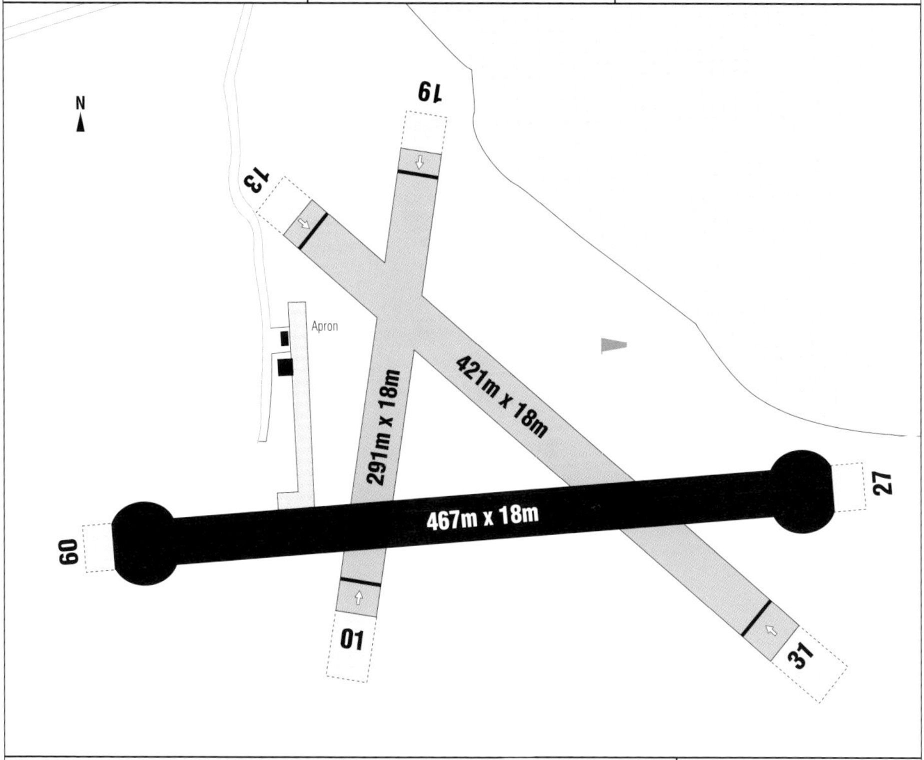

RWY	SURFACE	TORA	LDA	U/L	LIGHTING
09/27	Hard Core	467	467		Nil
13	Grass	394	359		Nil
31	Grass	421	359		Nil
01	Grass	261	235		Nil
19	Grass	291	218		Nil

RNAV			
KWL	**108.60**	**002**	**23.5**

Remarks
PPR essential. Scheduled service operates Mon-Sat. Contact AD Manager before landing.

Warnings
Grass Rwys flooded/soft after heavy rain.

Operating Hrs SR-SS
Circuits Nil
Landing Fee Nil
£36.95 if fire cover required
Maintenance Nil
Fuel Nil
Disabled Facilities

Restaurants
Cleaton House **Tel:** 01857 677508
cleaton@orkney.com57
Pierowall Hotel **Tel:** 01857 677208

Taxis/Car Hire
Westrak **Tel:** 01857 677528
Harcus **Tel:** 01857 677450
Mrs Groat **Tel:** 01857 677374 (Sand O'Gill)
Bike Hire
Mrs Bain **Tel:** 01857 677319 (Rapness)
Mrs Groat **Tel:** 01857 677374 (Sand O'Gill)
Weather Info Air Sc GWC
Operator Orkney Islands Council
Kirkwall, Orkney
Tel: 01856 873535
Fax: 01856 876094
Tel: 01857 677226 (AD Manager)
stephenhagan@onetel.net.uk

WEYBOURNE

30ft 1mb	3nm W of Sheringham N5256.81 E00107.32	PPR	Alternative AD	Norwich Old Buckenham

Non-radio	LARS Norwich 119.350	Safetycom 135.475

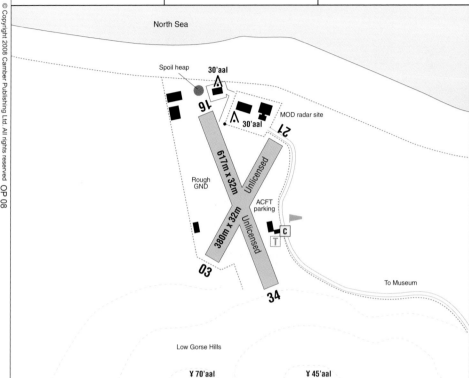

North Sea

Spoil heap

30'aal

16

MOD radar site

30'aal

21

617m x 32m

Unlicensed

Rough GND

ACFT parking

380m x 32m

Unlicensed

C

T

03

34

To Museum

Low Gorse Hills

¥ 70'aal

¥ 45'aal

RWY	SURFACE	TORA	LDA	U/L	LIGHTING
16/34	Grass			617x32	Nil
03/21	Grass			380x32	Nil

Rwy21 slight upslope, Rwy16 slight upslope first half

RNAV

Remarks
Smallest WW2 RAF AD. Housing Muckleburgh collection of military vehicles (open Feb-Nov). Strips very well prepared & cut. Book-in at caravan key at side. Museum is short walk. Fly-ins welcome, special facilities can be arr (ie tank demonstrations). For personal tours or party arr at restaurant contact Collection manager.

Warnings
Rwy suface may suffer from rabbit scrapes, please exercise caution. Low gorse hills S of strip. White post at corner of MOD perimeter fence, encroaches edge Rwy16 Thr. Model ACFT may operate, one circuit before landing will GND aero-modellers. **Noise:** Avoid over flying Weybourne & Kelling villages & MOD RAD site close Rwy21Thr. RAD site also has a number of other antennae (see AD chart).

Operating Hrs SR-SS

Circuits 1000ft QFE

Landing Fee £5 (Donation if not going to museum)
£5.50 (Museum admission)

Maintenance Nil

Fuel Nil

Disabled Facilities

Restaurants Restaurant in museum complex

Taxis **Tel:** 01263 822228

Car Hire Nil

Weather Info Air S MOEx

Operator Muckleburgh Estates
Weybourne
Norfolk, NR25 7EG
Tel: 01263 588210/588608
(Museum Office)
Fax: 01263 588425

W

EGEH WHALSAY

100ft 3mb	Shetland Islands N6022.62 W00055.33	**PPR**	**Alternative AD** **Scatsta** Lerwick

Non-radio	**APP** **Sumburgh 131.300**	**Safetycom** **135.475**

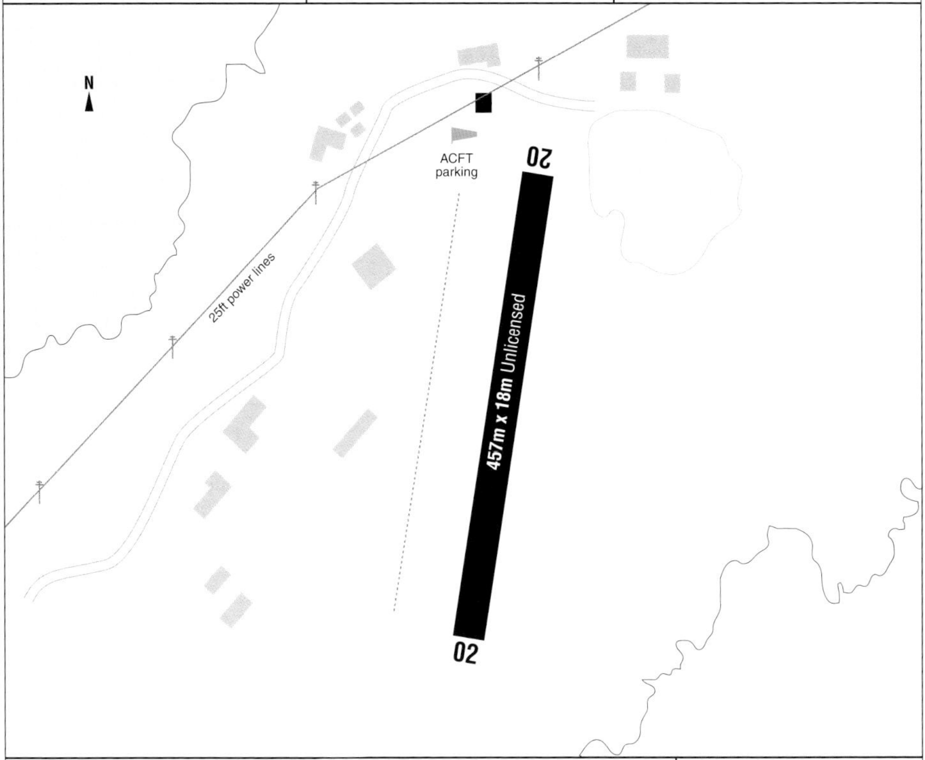

RWY	SURFACE	TORA	LDA	U/L	LIGHTING
02/20	Asphalt			457x18	Nil

Heavily weathered surface with many loose stones

RNAV

Remarks
PPR by telephone. Main function is Air Ambulance Ops.

Warnings
Rwy surface poor with loose stones. Hill 390ft amsl 222° 3.4nm. AD used during daylight Hrs only. Sheep may be present on Rwy. Fence W of Rwy has been known to blow across the strip after high winds.

Operating Hrs	SR-SS
Circuits	Suggest standard overhead join LH 1000ft QFE
Landing Fee	£4
Maintenance	Nil
Fuel	Nil
Disabled Facilities	Nil
Restaurants	Nil
Taxis Angus Irvine	Transport can be provided by **Tel:** 01806 566208
Car Hire	Nil
Weather Info	Air Sc GWC

Operator Whalsay Development Committee
Whalsay Aerodrome, Skaw
Whalsay, Shetland Islands
Tel: 01806 566449
(PPR via agent Mr Williamson)

Effective date:25/09/08 OP 08

WHARF FARM

295ft 9mb	0.25nm W of Market Bosworth N5237.40 W00124.59	PPR	Alternative AD	East Midlands Leicester

Non Radio	ATIS East Mids 128.225	APP East Mids 134.175	Safetycom 135.475

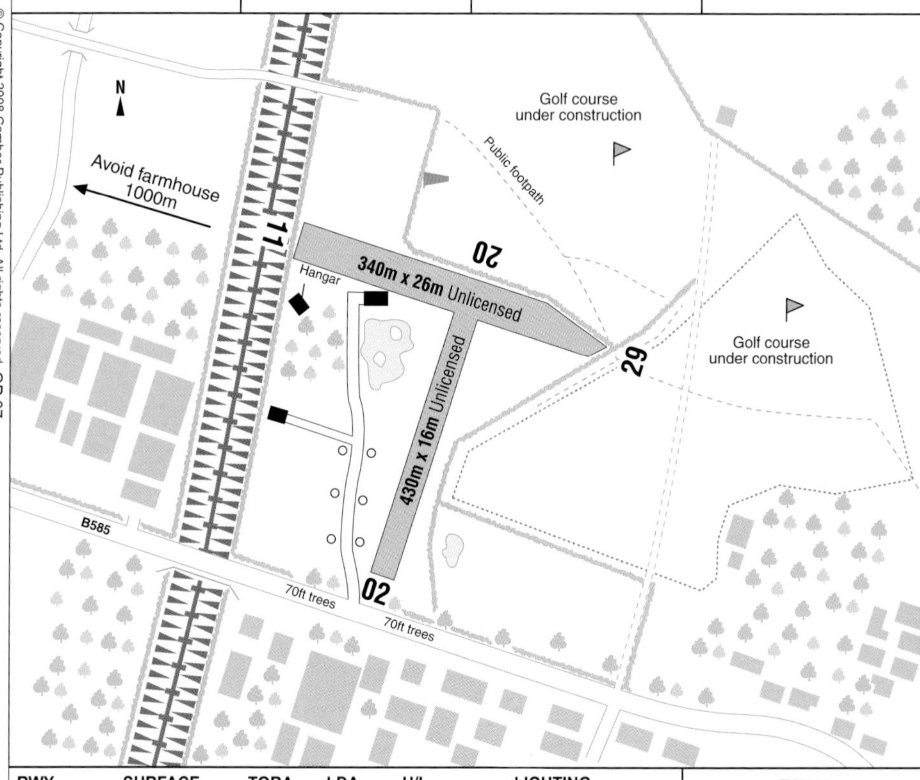

RWY	SURFACE	TORA	LDA	U/L	LIGHTING
02/20	Grass			430x16	Nil
11/29	Grass			340x26	Nil

RNAV			
HON	113.65	034	18.0

Remarks
PPR by telephone. Suitable STOL ACFT welcome at pilots own risk.

Warnings
Mature trees either side of short final Rwy02. Industrial buildings on opposite side of B585 from Rwy. Public footpath crosses short final Rwy29.Railway cutting crosses short final Rwy11, operated by Battlefield line preserved steam railway, operates daily.
Caution: Position of low hedges adjacent to Rwy Thr. Electric fences at the side of Rwy. Construction traffic Crosses Rwy29 Thr,
Noise: Avoid over flying Market Bosworth E of AD and farmhouse 1000m out on Rwy29 climb out.

Operating Hrs	SR-SS
Circuits	02, 20 W, 11, 29 N, 800ft QFE
Landing Fee	Nil
Maintenance	Nil
Fuel	Nil
Disabled Facilities	
Restaurants	Nil
Taxis/Car Hire	Nil
Weather Info	Air Cen MOEx

Operator
Mr L James
Wharf Farm
Station Road, Market Bosworth
Leicestershire, CV13 0PG
Tel: 01455 290258
wharf.farm@tiscali.co.uk

WHITERASHES

360ft 12mb	7nm N of Aberdeen Airport N5719.40 W00214.30	PPR	Alternative AD Aberdeen Insch

Non-standard join

Non-Radio	APP Aberdeen 119.050	Safetycom 135.475

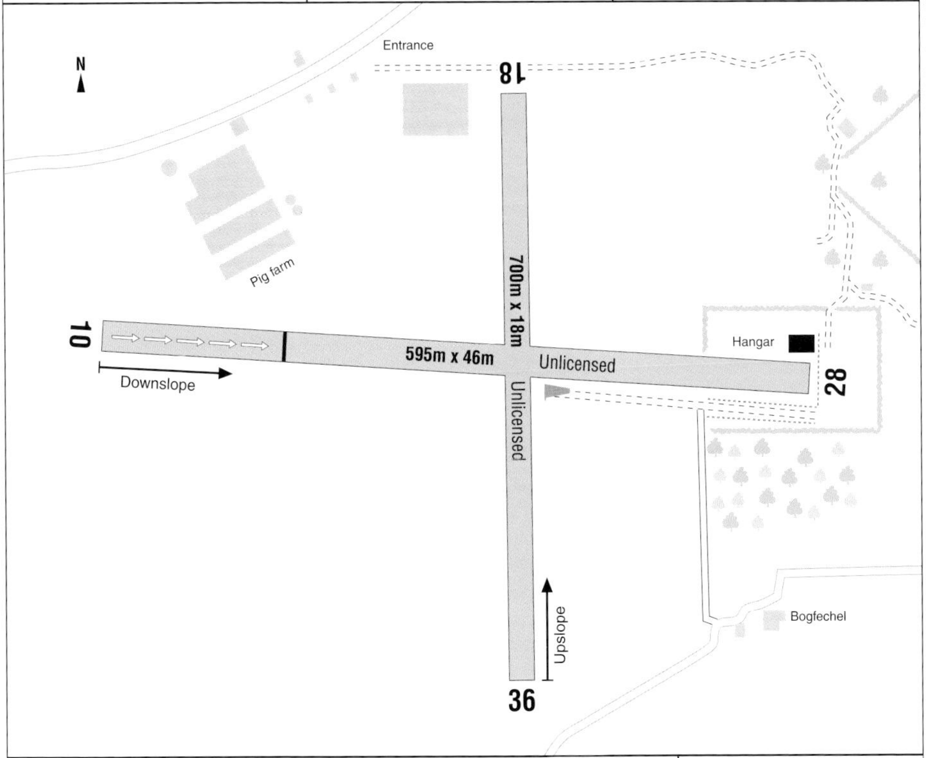

N
Entrance
18
700m x 18m
Pig farm
10
Downslope
595m x 46m
Unlicensed
Unlicensed
Hangar
28
Bogfechel
Upslope
36

RWY	SURFACE	TORA	LDA	U/L	LIGHTING
10/28	Grass			595x46	Nil
18/36	Grass			700x18	Nil

Starter extension Rwy10 275m, Rwy10 downslope over first 300m
Rwy36 upslope on initial portion

RNAV			
AND	114.30	052	1.2

Remarks
PPR by telephone essential. AD situated within Aberdeen Airspace. Hangarage available by arr. Pilots must read & comply with booking out procedure posted on hanger door.

Warnings
Exercise caution taxiing to hangar due to close proximity of parked ACFT at Rwy edge. Agricultural work takes place on grass up to Rwy edges.
Caution: 30ft trees Rwy28 Thr and along S egde of Rwy for first 150m. Grass cutting may be in progress periodically. Hills 678ft amsl 1.5nm SE. Windmill generator 0.8nm S. TV masts (Meldrum VRP) 1245ft amsl 5.5nm WNW. There are specific restrictions applied to Inbound and Dept ACFT by Aberdeen ATC please see specific VFR/SVFR routings.

Operating Hrs Mon-Fri 0630-SS Sat-Sun 0730-SS

Circuits Circuit patterns must be strictly followed to avoid conflict with Aberdeen APP traffic. Circuits should be kept within 1nm laterally from AD & maximum of 1.5nm final. 10 LH 28 RH 800ft but not above 600ft on base leg 36 LH 18 RH 800ft. All altitudes QNH

Landing Fee £5

Maintenance Nil
Fuel Nil

Disabled Facilities Nil

Restaurant Nil

Taxi
Swift Taxi **Tel:** 01651 862862
Car Hire Nil

Weather Info Air Sc GWC

Operator John Thorogood
Gadie House
Leslie
Insch
Aberdeenshire
AB52 6NT
Tel: 01464 820492

Effective date:25/09/08

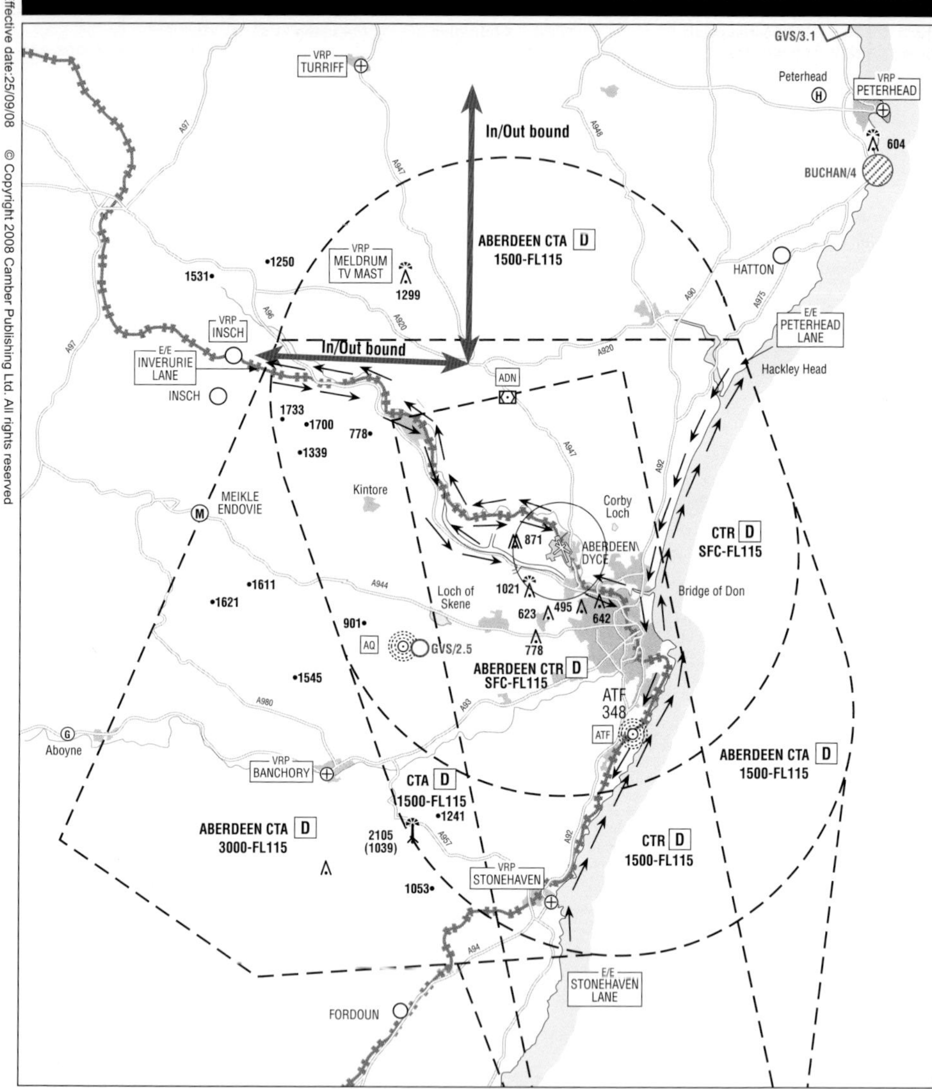

Mandatory Actions
PPR essential and contact with Aberdeen ATC for flights to/from AD.

Pre-Take Off Actions:
Contact Aberdeen APP by Telephone to book out Tel: 01224 727159
A dept slot must be adheres to ± 5mins, or re-negotiated.
Attempt to establish contact with Aberdeen APP on GND, or at very latest 500ft, if unsuccessful, you **must** return to field and phone Aberdeen ATC.

Approach & Departure Routes:
Standard APP – from the N at less than 1000ft QNH. APP Old Meldrum Mast from N, (golf course with country house is entry point). Track 138°M to AD. DO NOT CONTINUE FURTHER S INTO THE ZONE IF AD NOT IN SIGHT.
Standard Dept – Track 312°M from AD to Old Meldrum Mast.
Alternative arr may be made with ATC, but remember you are in Controlled Airspace, close to ILS APP Rwy16.

EGLM WHITE WALTHAM

133ft 5mb	2nm SW of Maidenhead N5130.05 W00046.47	**Alternative AD** **Farnborough** Wycombe **Diversion AD**

Waltham	LARS Farnborough West 125.250	A/G 122.600

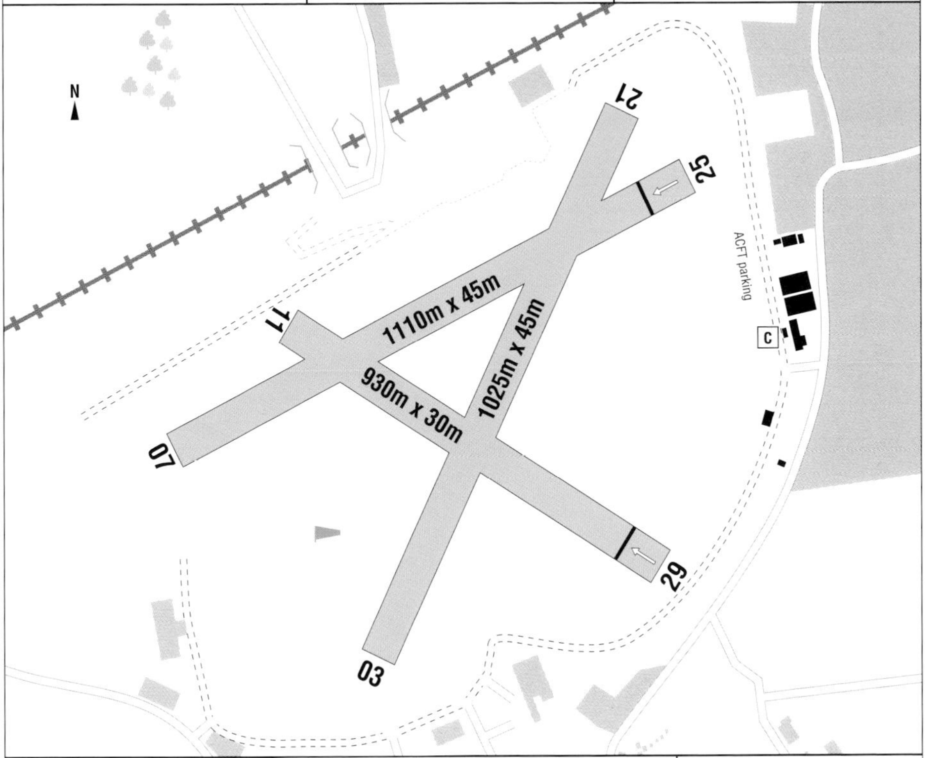

N

21

25

ACFT parking

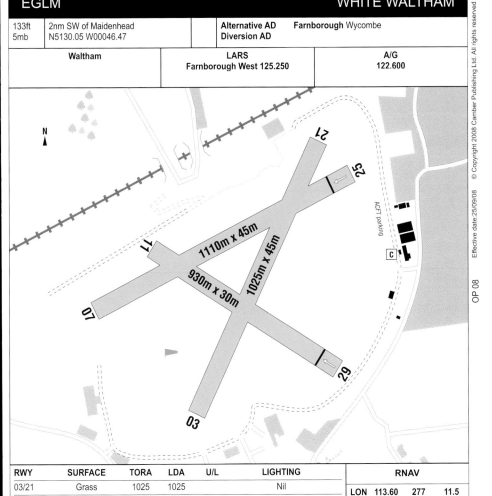

C

1110m x 45m

1025m x 45m

930m x 30m

11

07

29

03

RWY	SURFACE	TORA	LDA	U/L	LIGHTING
03/21	Grass	1025	1025		Nil
07	Grass	1110	1110		Nil
25	Grass	1110	1045		Nil
11	Grass	930	930		Nil
29	Grass	930	867		Nil

Displaced Thr Rwy25 65m, Displaced Thr Rwy29 63m

RNAV			
LON	**113.60**	**277**	**11.5**

Remarks
Aerobatic practice takes place on AD. No night operations on AD. No overhead depts. Run and break manoeuvres prohibited.

Warnings
Vehicular traffic not under control of AD uses the perimeter track which bounds the manoeuvring area to N & E of AD Pilots are to exercise extreme vigilance when taxiing.
Noise: Pilots of Dept ACFT are requested to conform with local noise abatement procedures. Available in the briefing room.

Operating Hrs 0700-SS +30mins or 1900 if earlier (Summer) 0800-SS +30mins (Winter) & by arr

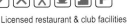

Circuits 07, 29 RH, 03, 11, 21, 25 LH, 800ft QFE Join overhead 1300ft QFE

Landing Fee Single £12, Twin £18. Free with fuel uplift, single 50ltr, twin 100ltr

Maintenance
WLAC **Tel:** 01628 823276

Fuel AVGAS JET A1 100LL
0700 – 1hr before SS (Summer)
0800 – 1hr before SS (Winter)

Disabled Facilities

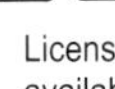

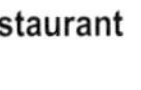

Restaurant Licensed restaurant & club facilities available

Taxis
Ace Cabs **Tel:** 01628 773855
U-want **Tel:** 01628 622110

Car Hire
National **Tel:** 0118 9352088

Weather Info Air SE MOEx

Operator	West London Aero Club White Waltham Aerodrome, Maidenhead, Berks, SL6 3NJ **Tel:** 01628 823272 **Fax:** 01628 826070 www.wlac.co.uk

White Waltham Joining Procedures

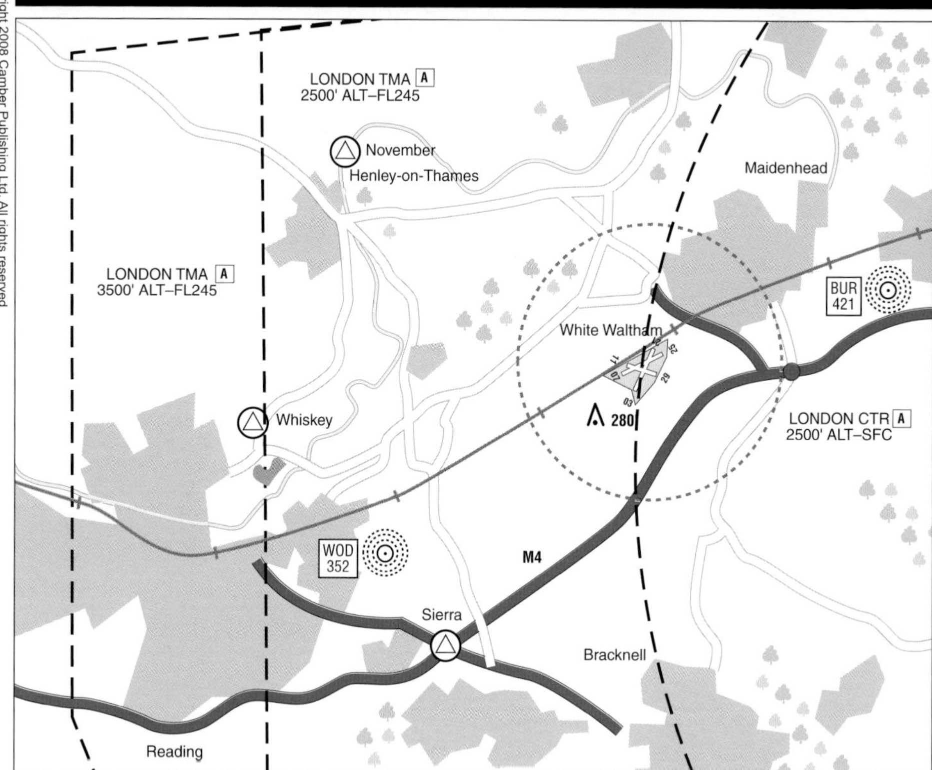

Although E portion of ATZ is within London CTZ, flights within ATZ may take place without compliance with IFR requirements provided that:

1 ACFT must remain clear of cloud & in sight of surface.

2 ACFT must fly **not above 1500ft QNH** provided that ACFT can remain at least **500ft below cloud otherwise 1000ft QNH.**

3 Minimum flight visibility **3km.**

Pilots operating in local flying area are responsible for their own separation from other air traffic.

Departures

Rwy03 LH turn at end of Rwy, track 010°M until turning onto crosswind.

Rwy07 RH turn at end of Rwy, track 100°M until turning onto crosswind.

Rwy29 RH turn at end of Rwy, track 300°M until turning onto crosswind.

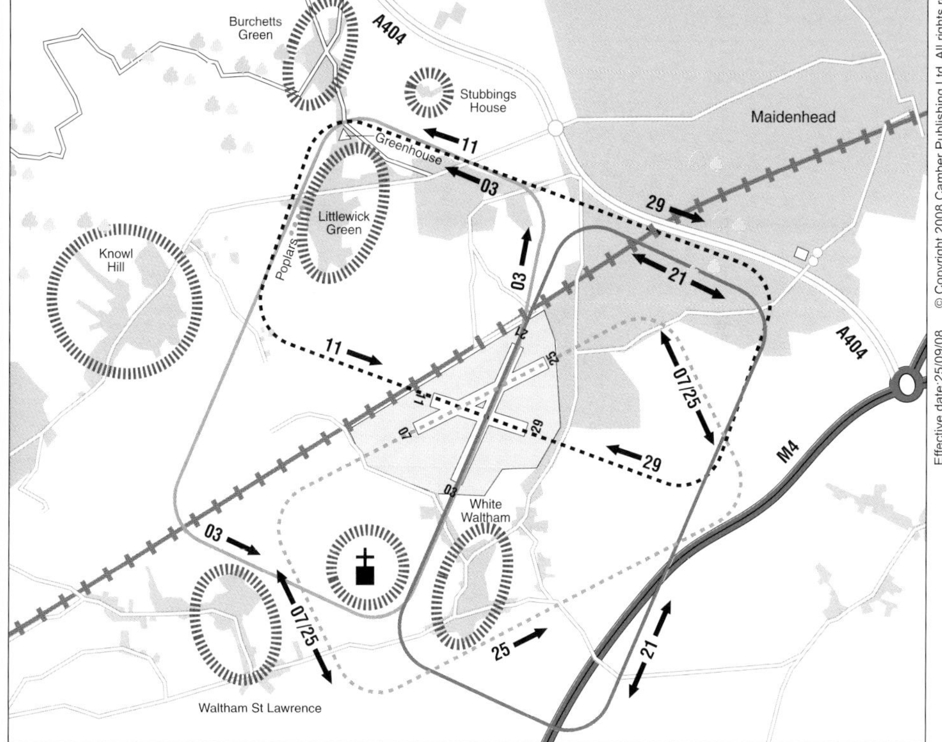

Effective date:25/09/08

Fixed Wing – join overhead at 1300ft QFE.
Helicopters – Arr and Dept low level from the centre of the AD avoiding fixed wing circuit traffic and noise sensitive areas.

Visual Reporting Point (**VRP**)

From N:	**November**	Bend in the Thames N of Henley-on-Thames
From W:	**Whiskey**	N of gravel pits by Reading gasometers
From S:	**Sierra**	M4/A329M Jct N of Wokingham (M4 Jct 10)

126ft 4mb	1nm N of Wick N5827.53 W00305.58	PPR	Alternative AD Diversion AD	Kirkwall Sanday

Wick	ATIS	APP	AFIS	TWR	FIRE	Handling
	113.600	119.700	119.700	119.700	121.600	Farnor 130.375

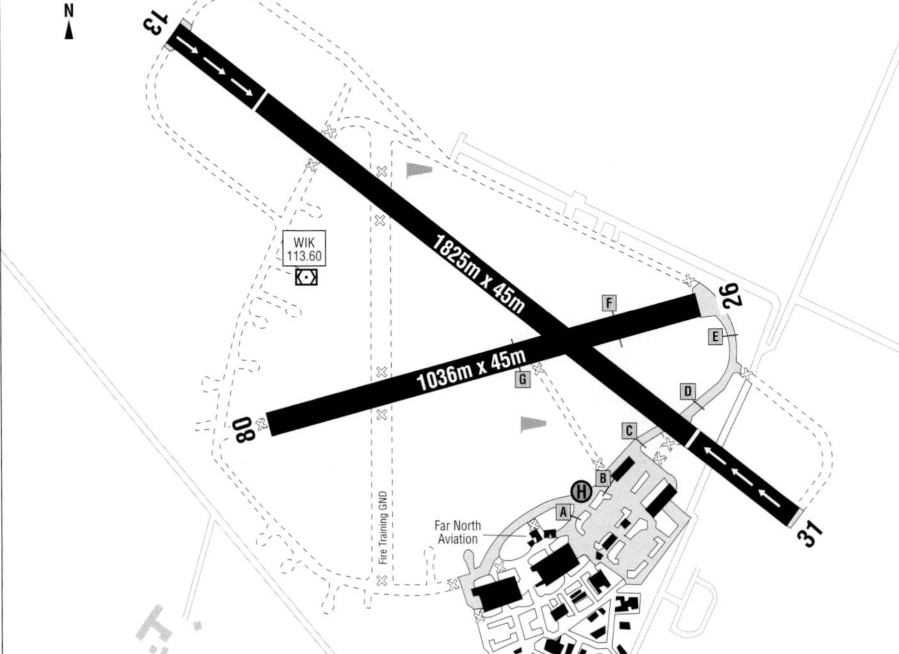

RWY	SURFACE	TORA	LDA	U/L	LIGHTING
08/26	Asphalt	1036	1036		Thr Rwy APAPI 4° LHS
13	Asphalt	1740	1400		Ap Thr Rwy PAPI 3° LHS
31	Asphalt	1708	1398		Ap Thr Rwy PAPI 3° LHS

RNAV
WCK 113.60 On AD

Remarks
Grass areas soft sand unsafe, only marked Twys to be used.
Aids to Navigation: NDB WCK 344.00

Warnings
No GND signals except light signals. Loop Twy (N of disused Control TWR, linking apron with Hangar 2) is available for ACFT with outer main gear span <6m. Rwy08/26 not available to jet ACFT, helicopters of ACFR with MTWA >2730kg.AD has deer hazard, particularly during dawn/dusk. Pilots are requested to report any animals on AD to ATC.

Operating Hrs Mon-Fri 0600-1730 1800-1945
Sat 0800-0924 1000-1345 (Summer)
+1Hr (Winter) & by arr

Circuits Nil

Landing Fee £12 ACFT under 3MT
VFR cash/cheque on day

Maintenance By arr with Far North Aviation

Fuel AVGAS JET A1 100LL
Refuelling Hrs during AD Hrs with Far North outside AD Hrs by arr
Tel: 01955 602201 (H24)

Disabled Facilities

Handling **Tel:** 01955 602201 (Far North Aviation)
Fax: 01955 602203 (Far North Aviation)
www.farnorthaviation.co.uk

Restaurant Buffet facilities available at AD

Taxis Via Far North

Car Hire Via Far North or
Practical Car Hire **Tel:** 01955 604125

Weather Info M T9 Fax 452 GWC
ATIS **Tel:** 01955 607596

Visual Reference Points (VRP)

Castletown Aerodrome	N5835.12 W00321.02
Duncansby Head Lighthouse	N5838.63 W00301.52
Keiss Village	N5832.00 W00307.40
Loch Watten	N5829.00 W00320.10
Lybster Village	N5818.00 W00317.10
Thrumster Masts	N5823.58 W00307.43

Operator HIAL, Wick Aerodrome
Wick, Highland KW1 4QP
Tel: 01955 602215 (HIAL)
Fax: 01955 604750 (ATC)
wickatc@hial.co.uk
www.hial.co.uk/wick-airport.html

84ft 3mb	8nm NE of Lincoln N5319.02 W00020.93	PPR	Alternative AD	**Humberside** Retford Gamston

Wickenby	LARS Waddington 127.350	A/G 122.450

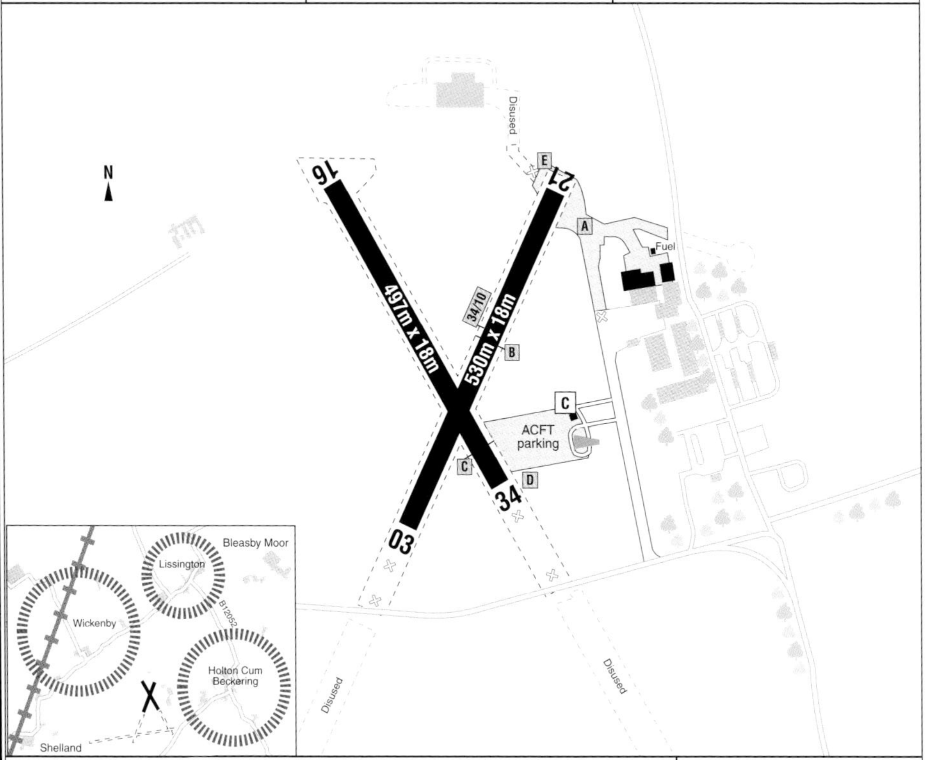

RWY	SURFACE	TORA	LDA	U/L	LIGHTING
03/21	Concrete	530	530		Nil
16/34	Concrete	497	497		Nil

RNAV			
GAM	112.80	088	21.5

Remarks

PPR by telephone. AD U/L on Monday. Inbound ACFT requested to contact RAF Waddington.

Visual aid to location: Ibn WN Green.

Warnings

Aerobatic training takes place SE corner of ATZ 800-3000ft, times notified by radio. No overhead joins during active periods. AD is divided by public road and only Rwys N of road can be used. A third Rwy09/27 is closed. HGVs cross Rwy21 Thr. All ACFT flying in ATZ must contact Waddington before climbing above 1500ft QFE.

Noise: Avoid over flying the villages of Wickenby, Holton Cum Becking and Lissington.

Operating Hrs	0900-1800 (Summer) 0900-SS (Winter)
Circuits	LH Light ACFT 1000ft QFE LH Microlights & Helicopters 700ft QFE
Landing Fee	Single £7, Twin £14, Microlights £3.50
Maintenance	JAR 145, FAA & LAA **Tel:** 01673 885966
Fuel	AVGAS JET A1 100LL

Disabled Facilities

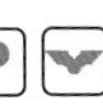

Restaurant	Club facilities & restaurant
Accomodation	
Redhurst B&B	**Tel:** 01673 857927

Taxis/Car Hire

Marriot Taxis	**Tel:** 01673 858541 **Tel:** 07813 932282
County Cars	**Tel:** 01522 567878
Weather Info	Air N MOEx
Operator	Wickeny Aerodrome LLP The Old Control Tower Wickenby Aerodrome Langworth, Lincoln, LN3 5AX **Tel/Fax:** 01673 885000 cas.projects@talk21.com **Tel:** 01673 885111 (Fly365 Ltd Microlight School) info@fly365.co.uk www.fly365.co.uk

WING FARM

420ft 14mb	2nm SSW of Warminster N5109.80 W00212.51	PPR	Alternative AD	Bristol Compton Abbas

Non-Radio	LARS Boscombe 126.700	LARS Yeovil Radar 127.350	Safetycom 135.475

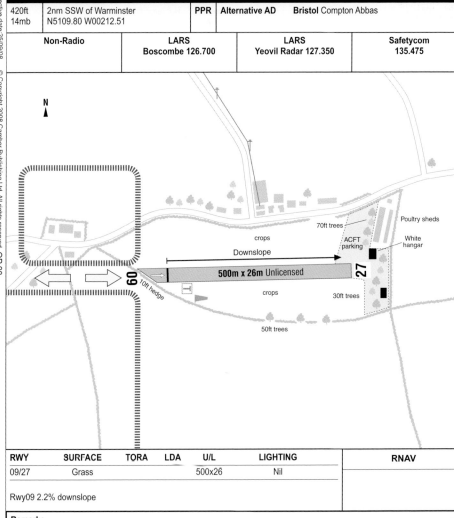

RWY	SURFACE	TORA	LDA	U/L	LIGHTING
09/27	Grass			500x26	Nil

Rwy09 2.2% downslope

RNAV

Remarks
PPR. Visiting ACFT welcome at pilot's own risk. Pilots MUST be capable of STOL operations. Take off run ltd to 350m, leaving 150m stopping distance. Rwy is well prepared cut strip. White 'T' markers mark Rwy. Long-term parking available.

Warnings
Surface may be soft especially Jan-Apr. Movements confined to strip and parking area. Electric power cables 500m out on Rwy09 APP. Glider site, 'The Park' 3nm SSW of AD. Beware cables up to 2000ft agl. D123 3nm NNE of AD activity info available from Boscombe APP.
Noise: Avoid low flying over the local habitation, particularly the houses marked either side of Rwy09 APP. Make straight in APP/climb-out until well clear of the houses.

Operating Hrs SR-SS

Circuits 600ft QFE

Landing Fee Private ACFT £5, Microlights £3
Have correct money, no change available
Overnight parking: Private ACFT £3, Microlights £2

Maintenance Galaxy Mircrolights
Tel: 07841 614577
mark@galaxymicrolights.co.uk

Fuel Nil, Petrol station 0.75 of mile

Disabled Facilities By arrangement

Restaurants/Accommodation
The George Inn **Tel:** 01985 840396 Longbridge Deverill

Taxis
DJ's Taxis **Tel:** 01985 215151

Car Hire

Weather Info Air SW MOEx

Operator Mr Earl W B Trollope
Wing Farm
Longbridge Deverill
Warminster
Wilts BA12 7DD
Tel/Fax: 01985 840401
earl.t@virgin.net

W

10ft 0mb	3nm NE of Holbeach N5248.00 E00006.00	PPR	Alternative AD	Fenland

Wingland	LARS Marham 124.150	A/G 129.825

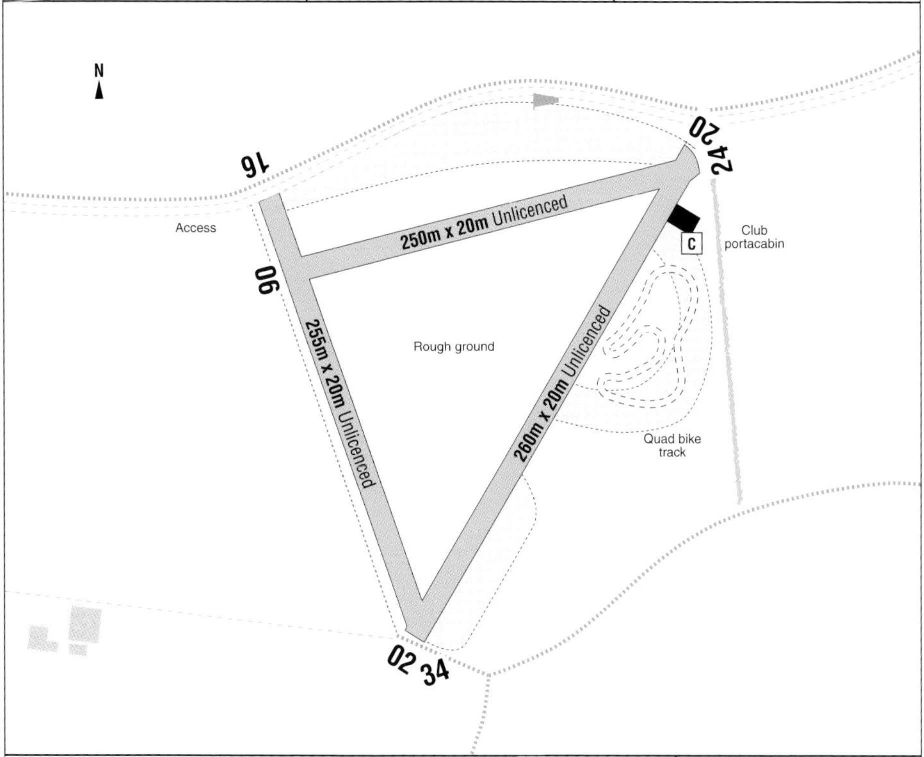

RWY	SURFACE	TORA	LDA	U/L	LIGHTING
02/20	Grass			260x20m	Nil
06/24	Grass			250x20m	Nil
16/34	Grass			255x20m	Nil

RNAV

Remarks

PPR by telephone. Microlights welcome. Visitors welcome at pilots own risk

Warnings

Model aircraft flying takes place at the AD.

Noise: Avoid over flying Gedney Dyke to the W and Lutton to the SE of the AD.

Operating Hrs	SR-SS
Circuits	Nil
Landing Fee	Discretionary – pilots choice
Maintenance	Nil
Fuel	Nil
Disabled Facilities	Nil
Restaurant	Nil
Taxi/Car Hire	Nil
Weather Info	Air S MOEx

Operator Peter Higgins
Lincs
Tel: 01406 362488
winglandairfield@aol.com

Effective date:25/09/08

273ft 9mb	10nm NW of Peterborough N5236.75 W00028.60	PPR MIL	**Alternative AD** **East Midlands** Peterborough Conington **Diversion AD** **Non-standard join**

Wittering	LARS/APP	DIR	Talkdown	TWR
	Cottesmore 130.200	130.200	123.300	125.525

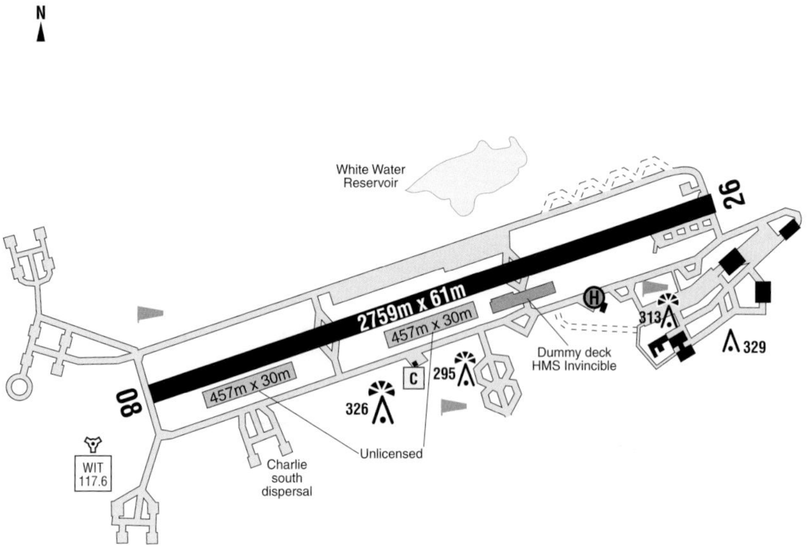

N
White Water Reservoir
26
2759m x 61m
457m x 30m
457m x 30m
08
Dummy deck HMS Invincible
313
329
295
326
C
WIT 117.6
Unlicensed
Charlie south dispersal

RWY	SURFACE	TORA	LDA	U/L	LIGHTING
08	Asphalt	2759	2744		Ap Thr Rwy PAPI 3° RHS
26	Asphalt	2759	2759		Ap Thr Rwy PAPI 3°

RNAV

Remarks
PPR by telephone essential. RAF AD with based high performance ACFT. AD Situated within CMATZ with Cottesmore who are the controlling authority.
Visual aid to location: Ibn Red

Warnings
AD has various areas of Twy & dispersals carrying non-standard markings associated with Harrier STOL strips. Also numerous cut grass strips within AD boundary. These areas are for use of based AD ONLY. Hovering and variable circuits in operation at all times. Gliding winch launch to 3000ft Mon-Fri 0800-1515 Sat 0900-1030 1600-SS Sun 1200-1300 1600-SS (Summer) + 1Hr (Winter) & by arr
Noise: Over flight of domestic site to SE and fenced compounds to SW is forbidden to fixed wing ACFT below 1000ft QFE.

Operational Hrs Mon-Thu 0730-1630 Fri 0730-1600 (Summer) + 1Hr (Winter)

Circuits Light ACFT 26 LH, 08 RH, 1200ft QFE
Jet ACFT 1500ft
No deadside

Landing Fee Charges in accordance with MOD policy
Contact Station Ops for details

Maintenance Not available to visiting ACFT
Fuel JET A1 strictly by prior arr only

Disabled Facilities Nil

Taxi/Car Hire Nil

Weather Info M T Fax454 MOEx

Operator RAF Wittering
Peterborough
PE8 6HB
Tel: 01780 783838 Ex 7052
Fax: 01780 783838
witops-airoperations@wittering.raf.mod.uk

EGBO WOLVERHAMPTON HALFPENNY GREEN

283ft 10mb	5nm E by S of Bridgnorth N5231.05 W00215.57	**PPR**	**Alternative AD** **Birmingham** Tatenhill

Halfpenny Green	**AFIS** **123.000**

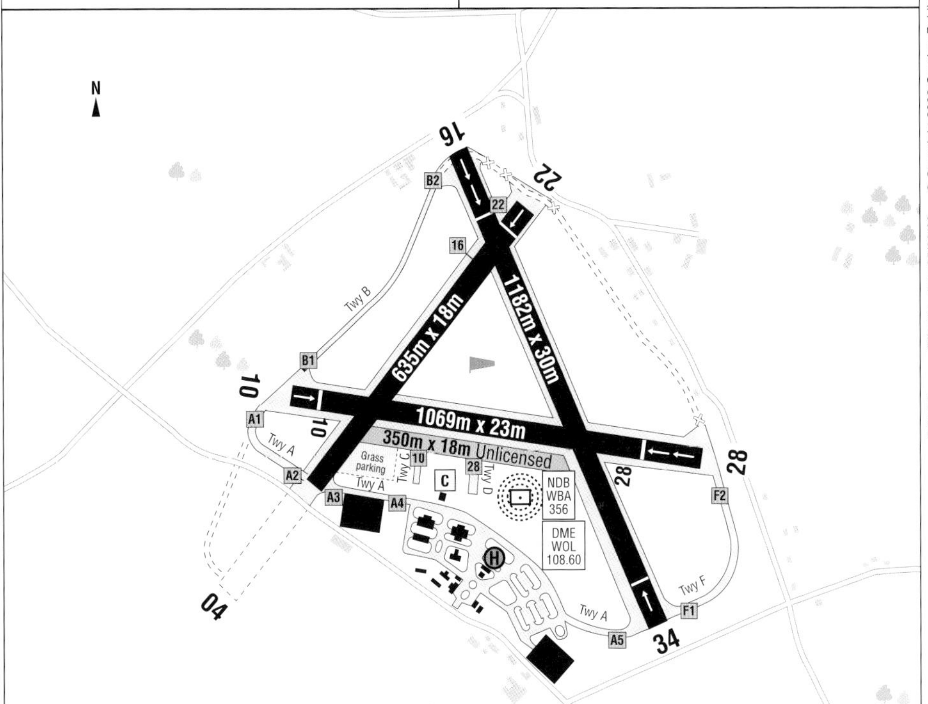

RWY	SURFACE	TORA	LDA	U/L	LIGHTING
04	Asphalt	604	574		Nil
22	Asphalt	604	515		Nil
10/28	Asphalt	771	771		Thr Rwy APAPI 4° LHS
16	Asphalt	1025	858		Nil
34	Asphalt	1096	910		Nil
10/28	Grass			350x18	Nil

Starter extension Rwy10 49m
Starter extension Rwy28 45m
Displaced Thr Rwy22 90m
Displaced Thr Rwy10 158m
Displaced Thr Rwy28 140m
Displaced Thr Rwy16 219m
Displaced Thr Rwy34 187m

RNAV			
SWB	**116.80**	**143**	**22.3**

Remarks
PPR. Hi Vis only. Rwy10/28 licensed for night use. Pilots are responsible for their passengers whilst airside. Helicopters not to be flown within 50m of DME mast NE of apron.
Visual aid to location: IBn flashing green WBA.

Warnings
Rwy10/28 lighting outside Hrs for police ops only. Police helicopters may operate outside normal Hrs.
Noise: Dept Rwy16 to maintain track for 600m before turning, avoid Highgate Farm. No fan stop Rwy34 until beyond 1000m past Thr.

Operating Hrs	0900-1800 (Summer) 0900-1700 (Winter)	**Landing Fee**	Singles £10, Twin <3Tonne £25 Twin >3 Tonne £45 + £15 per tonne, Microlights £7
Circuits	Helicopters RH 800ft QFE. Joining ACFT keep >1300ft QFE dead side		

Maintenance	
Aircraft Maintenance Halfpenny Green	**Tel:** 01384 221302
Fuel	AVGAS JET A1 100LL Oil W80 W100.80 100 by arr

Disabled Facilities

Restaurants	Café open daily
Taxis	**Tel:** 01384 404040 **Tel:** 01902 892888
Car Hire	**Tel:** 01384 424666
Weather Info	Air Cen MOEx

Operator

Wolverhampton Airport Ltd
Wolverhampton Airport
Stourbridge
West Midlands, DY7 5DY
Tel: 01384 221350 (Admin)
Tel: 01384 221378 (ATC)
Tel: 0808 1003362
Fax: 01384 221514 (ATC)
info@wolverhamptonairport.co.uk
atc@wolverhamptonairport.co.uk
www.wolverhamptonairport.co.uk

W

XWOM WOMBLETON

120ft 4mb	8nm W of Pickering N5414.02 W00058.13	PPR	**Alternative AD** **Diversion AD**	**Humberside** Sherburn in Elmet

Non-radio	LARS Leeming 127.750	Safetycom 135.475

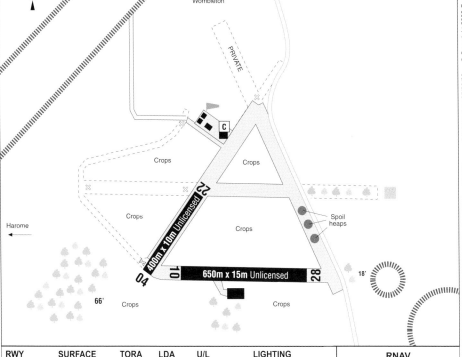

N
Wombleton
PRIVATE
C
Crops
Crops
22
Crops
Crops
Spoil heaps
Harome
400m x 10m Unlicensed
04
10
650m x 15m Unlicensed
28
18'
66'
Crops
Crops

RWY	SURFACE	TORA	LDA	U/L	LIGHTING
10/28	Concrete			650x15	Nil
04/22	Asphalt			400x10	Nil

Rwy10/28 prefered

RNAV

Remarks
PPR by telephone. Visitors welcome at own risk. Park ACFT near old TWR & enter flight details in AD log. Microlight activity. Former Twy and Rwy to W of Rwy04/22 are unusable by ACFT.

Warnings
Farm vehicles, pedestrians, animals & model ACFT may be encountered on AD, please be alert to Rwy incursion at any time. AD surfaces rough with loose stones & grass growth at joints. 70ft trees 200m Rwy10 Thr. Public road bounded by25ft trees 150m Rwy28 Thr. 2 private strips in N portion of AD not to be used by visitors. Kirkbymoorside AD 1.5nm NE of Wombleton.
Noise: Avoid over flying Wombleton & Harome to W & N of AD. Modify APP to avoid local houses & obstructions.

Operating Hrs Available on request

Circuits Light ACFT 04, 10 RH, 22, 28 LH, 1000ft QFE. Microlights 04, 28 RH, 10, 22 LH, 500ft QFE

Landing Fee Private Nil
Commercial may be charged a small fee

Maintenance Nil

Fuel Nil

Disabled Facilities

Restaurant Tea & coffee available

Taxis/Car Hire Can be arr on Arr

Weather Info Air N MOEx

Operator Windsports Centre Ltd
Wombleton Airfield
North Yorkshire
Tel/Fax: 01751 432356

EGOW WOODVALE

37ft 1mb	1.5nm NE of Formby N5334.89 W00303.33	PPR MIL	Alternative AD Diversion AD	Liverpool Blackpool Non-standard join

Woodvale	LARS	APP	A/G	TWR
	Warton 125.925	Liverpool 119.850	121.000	119.750

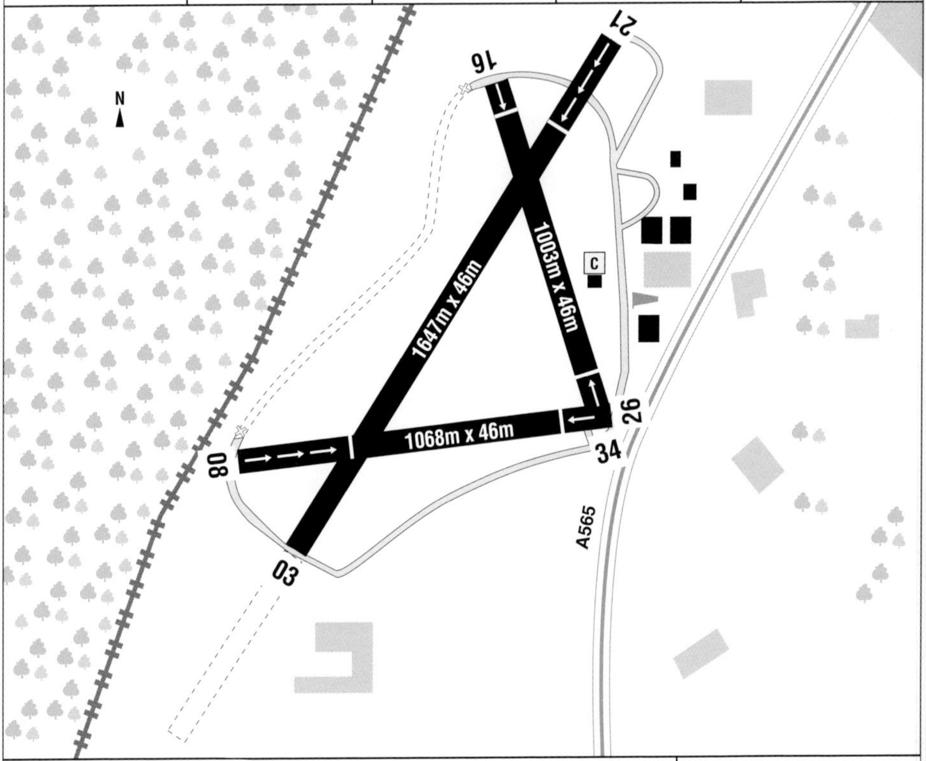

N
16
21
1647m x 46m
1003m x 46m
1068m x 46m
08
26
34
03
C
A565

RWY	SURFACE	TORA	LDA	U/L	LIGHTING
03/21	Asphalt	1647	1642		Nil
08	Asphalt	1068	710		Nil
26	Asphalt	1068	914		Nil
16	Asphalt	1003	644		Nil
34	Asphalt	1003	865		Nil

RNAV			
WAL	114.10	019	11.7

Remarks
PPR to private and charter ACFT. Light ACFT activity SR-SS +30min outside AD Hrs. Circuit can be very busy with University Air Squadron ACFT. Police helicopter activity H24

Warnings
Full obstacle clearance criteria not met on APP to all Rwys. Considerable risk of bird strike. Taxi routes as per ATC.

Operating Hrs: Tue-Sun 0700-1700 or SS if earlier
Available in summer any 6 days out of 7
Sometimes 7 days a week notified by NOTAM

Circuits: 03 08 LH, 21 26 RH 800ft QFE

Landing Fee: Charges in accordance with MOD policy
Contact Station Ops for details

Maintenance: Nil

Fuel: AVGAS 100LL (Ltd)
Military Account holders only

Disabled Facilities

Restaurants: Numerous in Formby

Taxis
White **Tel:** 01704 527777
Yellow **Tel:** 01704 531000

Car Hire
Dewerdens **Tel:** 01704 533066

Weather Info: Air Cen MOEx

Operator: RAF Woodvale
Formby
Liverpool
Merseyside L37 7AD
Tel: 01704 872287 Ex 7243
Fax: 01704 834805 (Flight Plans)

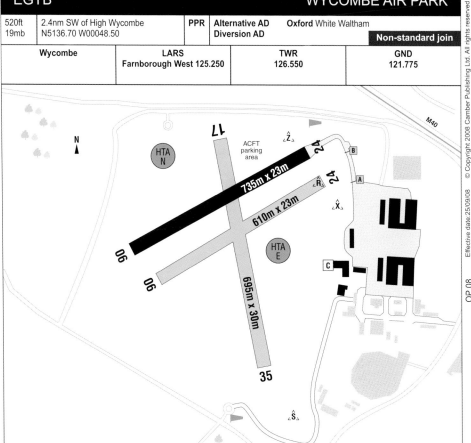

520ft 19mb	2.4nm SW of High Wycombe N5136.70 W00048.50	PPR	**Alternative AD** **Diversion AD**	**Oxford** White Waltham **Non-standard join**

Wycombe	LARS	TWR	GND
	Farnborough West 125.250	126.550	121.775

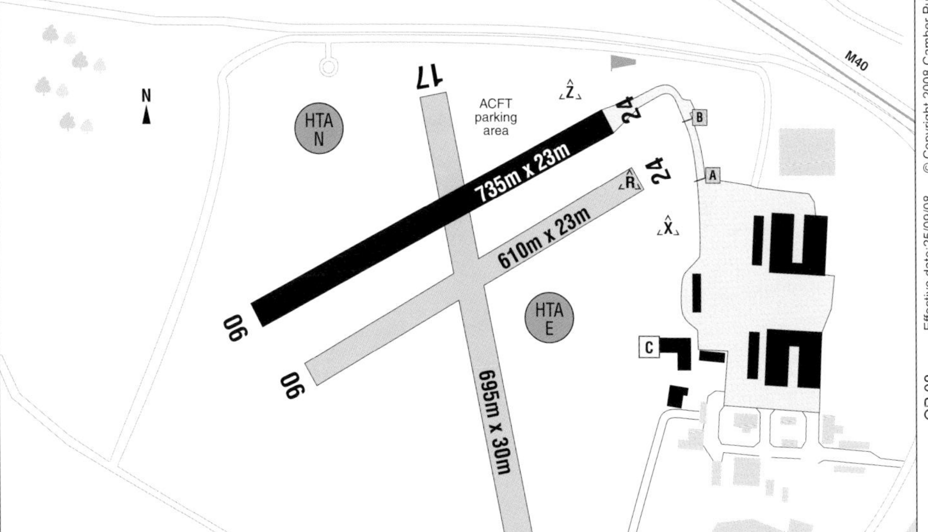

RWY	SURFACE	TORA	LDA	U/L	LIGHTING
06/24	Asphalt	735	735		Thr Rwy APAPI 4°
06/24	Grass	610	610		Nil
17/35	Grass	695	695		Nil

RNAV			
BNN	113.75	238	11.8

Remarks

PPR. When Rwy17/35 in use, Rwy06/24 is PPR Mon-Fri Sat-Sun 2Hrs. Gliders fly a circuit opposite direction to powered ACFT. Joining ACFT must position to over fly Rwy in use at 1200ft QFE on Rwy QDM. When overhead the midpoint of Rwy turn left or right (depending on circuit direction) to level at circuit height 1000ft QFE on cross wind leg prior to turning downwind.
Visual aid to location: Ibn WP Green.

Warnings

AD is situated below London Terminal Control Area. AD is liable to water logging. Intense gliding takes place on & around AD. Helicopters operate inside fixed-wing circuits. Helicopters must remain well clear of housing area E of Rwy17/35.
Noise: Procedures are enforced – pilots must obtain a briefing before dept Visiting ACFT will not be accepted without PPR including a briefing

Operating Hrs 0800-1630 (Summer)
0900-1600 (Winter) & by arr

Circuits Fixed wing variable 1000ft QFE
Helicopter 750ft QFE

Landing Fee £14 up to 1.5MT

Maintenance Available

Fuel AVGAS JET A1 100LL

Disabled Facilities

Restaurants Restaurant & refreshments available

Taxis
Neales **Tel:** 01494 463399

Car Hire
National **Tel:** 01494 527853

Weather Info Air SE MOEx

Operator Airways Aero Associations Ltd
Wycombe Air Park, Booker, Marlow
Buckinghamshire, SL7 3DP
Tel: 01494 529261 (Admin/ATC)
Tel: 01494 529262 (BA Flying Club)
Fax: 01494 438657 (ATC)
Fax: 01494 461237 (Admin)
www.bafc.co.uk

Effective date:25/09/08 OP 08

N
High wycombe
High Wycombe
M40
Lane End
Ditchfield
Frieth
Ragmans Castle
17
24
06
35

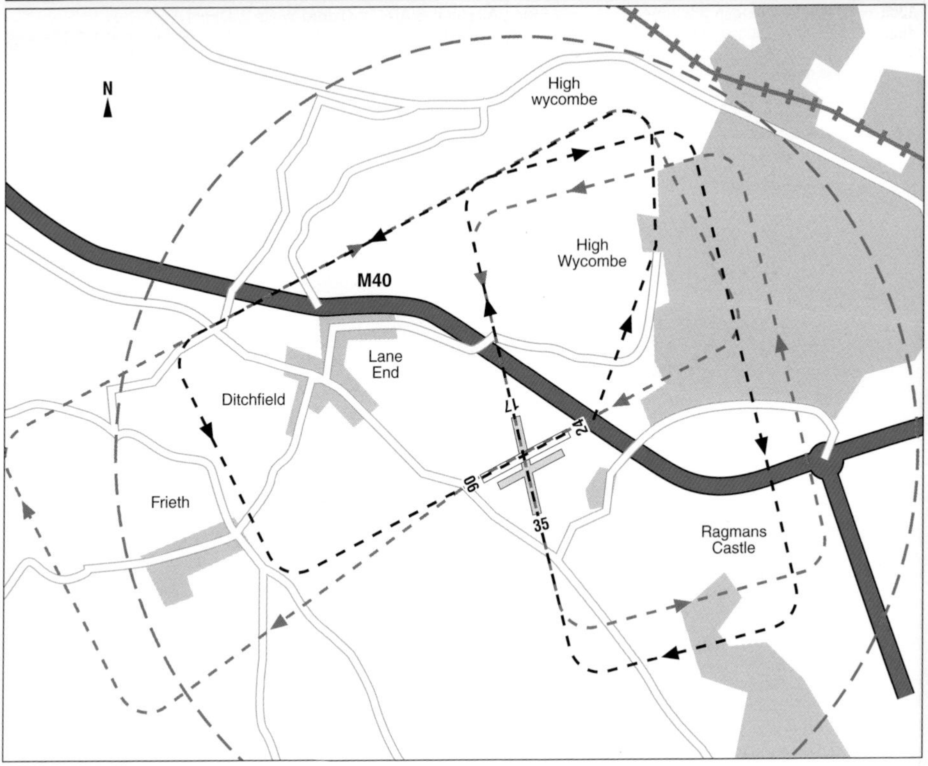

All pilots MUST obtain a briefing on Noise Abatement Procedures before Dept.

EGUY WYTON

135ft 4mb	3nm NE of Huntingdon N5221.43 W00006.47	PPR MIL	Alternative AD Diversion AD	Cambridge Peterborough Conington **Non-standard join**

Wyton	APP	TWR	A/G
	134.050	119.975	134.050

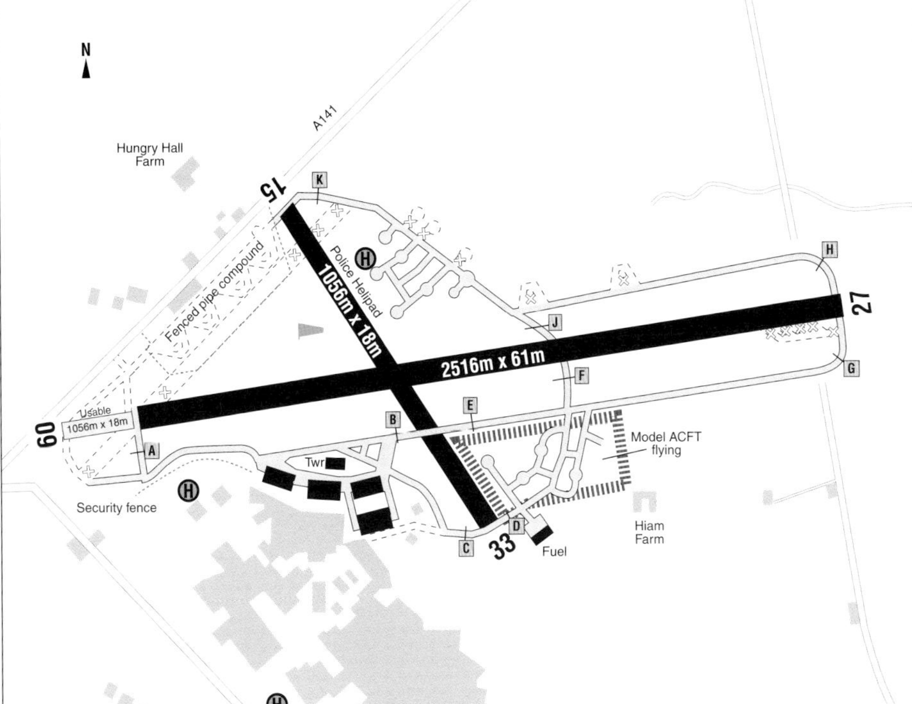

RWY	SURFACE	TORA	LDA	U/L	LIGHTING
09/27	Asph/Conc	2516	2516		Nil
15	Asph/Conc	1056	1056		Nil
33	Asph/Conc	1056	770		Nil

RNAV			
BKY	116.25	347	22.9

Remarks

PPR. Strictly by telephone. RAF AD, intensive ab-initio flying training by UAS ACFT.

Warnings

Turbulence may be encountered over Rwy when wind from S and greater than 15kts. Twy clearance reduced to 17.5 m from centreline to fence S of Rwy09 holding point, Twy available to light ACFT only. Locally based ACFT and Microlights operate outside normal AD Hrs. Model ACFT operate outside AD Hrs within designated area. Rwy27 non standard markings.

Noise: Avoid Huntingdon town, the village of Woodhurst 1.5nm N of Rwy27 Thr and Raptor foundation 2.75nm Rwy27 final APP.

Operating Hrs	Mon-Sun 0830-1700 & by arr
Circuits	09 LH, 27 RH, 800ft QFE
Landing Fee	Charges in accordance with MOD policy Contact Station Ops for details
Maintenance	Nil
Fuel	AVGAS 100LL by prior arr
Disabled Facilities	Nil
Restaurant	Nil
Taxi/Car Hire	Nil
Weather Info	Air Cen MOEx

Operator RAF Brampton &Wyton
Huntingdon, Cambs, PE17 2EA
Tel: 01480 52451 Ex 6412
Fax: 01480 446783 (ATC)

Effective date:25/09/08 OP 08

30ft 1mb	2nm S of Redcar N5435.01 W00103.93	PPR	**Alternative AD**	**Durham Tees Valley** Fishburn

Non-radio	**LARS** **Durham 118.850**	**Safetycom** **135.475**

ICI industrial complex
A174
N
Crops
25
Low hedge
635m x 12m Unlicensed
Farm track
125ft power lines
C
07
Pond
B1269
Yearby village

RWY	SURFACE	TORA	LDA	U/L	LIGHTING
07/25	Grass			635x12	Nil

RNAV

Remarks
PPR by telephone essential. Windsock displayed with PPR. AD located close to boundary of Durham Tees Valley CTR/CTA. Contact Durham APP on Arr/Dept. Full AD details and aerial photographs on website.

Warnings
Power lines 125ft agl cross Rwy25 final APP approx 600m from Thr with a pylon on the centreline.
Noise: Avoid over flying the village of Yearby and the ICI chemical plant NW & Redcar.

Operating Hrs SR-SS

Circuits Any convenient height
Over head joins essential

Landing Fee Private Nil
Commercial rates with PPR

Maintenance Nil

Fuel Nil

Disabled Facilities

Restaurants Nil

Taxis **Tel:** 01642 474849

Car Hire Nil

Weather Info Air N MOEx

Operator Yearby Airstrip Trust
Turners Arms Farm
Yearby
Redcar
North Yorkshire
TS11 8HH
Tel: 01642 470322 (Barry Smith)
acro@btinternet.com
www.acro.co.uk

202ft 7mb	1nm W by S of Yeovil N5056.40 W00239.52	PPR	**Alternative AD** **Diversion AD**	**Bristol** Compton Abbas

Westland	LARS	APP	TWR	A/G
	Yeovil Radar 127.350	130.800	125.400	125.400

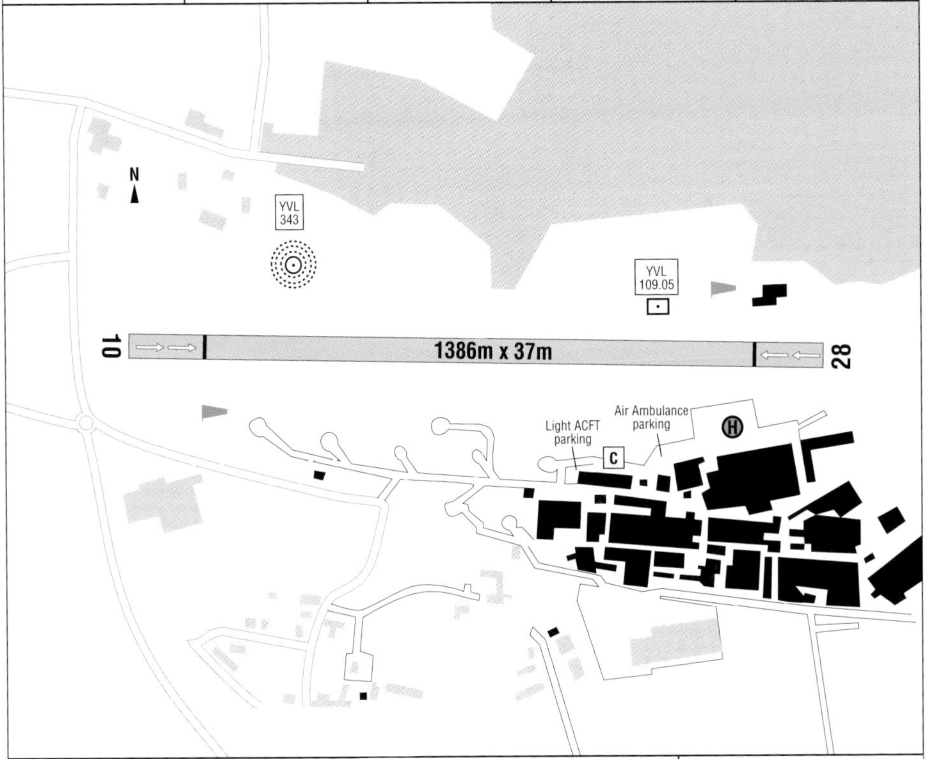

N
YVL 343
YVL 109.05
10
1386m x 37m
28
Light ACFT parking
Air Ambulance parking
C
H

RWY	SURFACE	TORA	LDA	U/L	LIGHTING
10	Grass	1319	1224		Nil
28	Grass	1319	1124		Nil

RNAV

Remarks
PPR 24Hrs Licensed for night Ops by helicopters only. Circuits S of Rwy due to proximity of Yeovilton. Visiting ACFT may be delayed due to helicopter test flying.

Warnings
Windshear on Rwy28 APP. Displaced landing Thr. AD surface is convex with a pronounced gradient to S at Rwy10 Thr. Caution required after heavy rain. Model ACFT, light ACFT & helicopter flying takes place outside normal Hrs. High GND rising to 442ft amsl 2.5nm to SW with radio mast 528ft amsl. Trees on high GND rising to 400ft amsl 1nm to E. Aerial mast 471ft amsl 0.8nm NW. Beware of bird concentrations.
Noise: Avoid over flying houses adjacent to NW, N & E boundaries.

Operating Hrs Mon-Thu 0800-1530 Fri 0800-1430 except PH (Summer) +1Hr (Winter)

Circuits S 1000ft
See Remarks

Landing Fee Available with PPR

Maintenance Nil

Fuel JET A1 by arr with PPR

Disabled Facilities

Restaurant Light refreshments available

Taxis/Car Hire On request to ATC before or after landing (Booked via ATC to comply with security restrictions)

Weather Info M* T9 MOEx

Operator Westland Helicopters Ltd
Yeovil Aerodrome, Yeovil
Somerset, BA20 2YB
Tel: 01935 475222 ask for ATC
Fax: 01935 703055

Effective date:25/09/08 OP 08

EGDY — YEOVILTON

75ft 3mb	4nm N of Yeovil N5100.56 W00238.33	PPR MIL	Alternative AD Diversion AD	Bristol Compton Abbas Non-standard join

Yeovil	LARS	APP	RAD	DIR	TWR	GND
	127.350	127.350	127.350	123.300	122.100	122.100

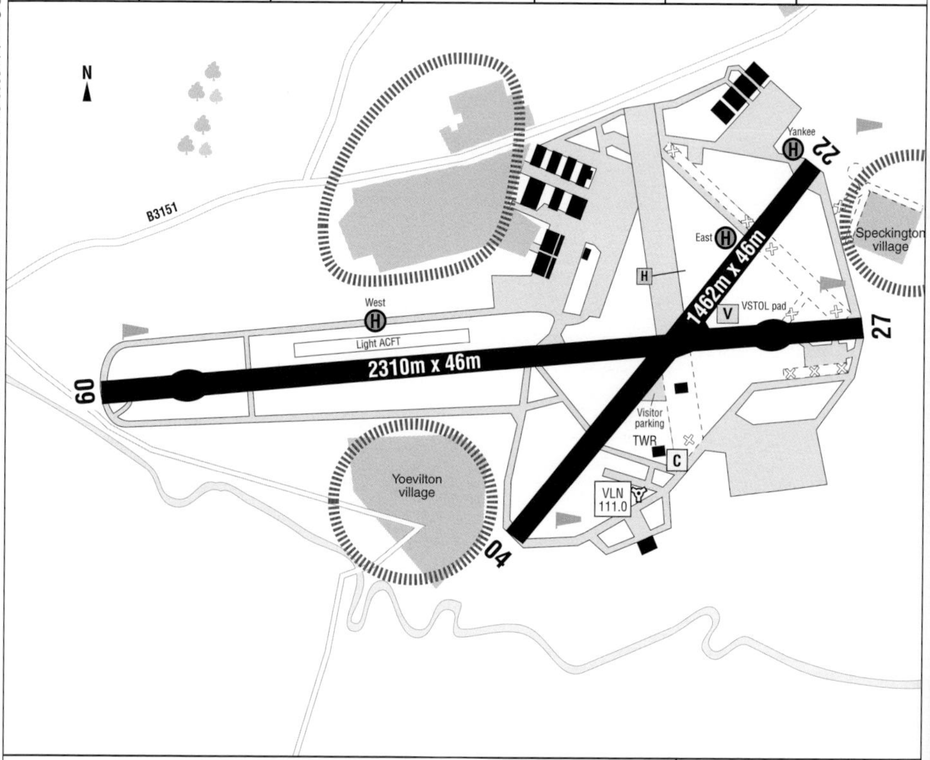

RWY	SURFACE	TORA	LDA	U/L	LIGHTING
09/27	Concrete	2310	2310		Ap Thr Rwy PAPI 3°
04	Concrete	1463	1463		Ap Thr Rwy PAPI 3°
22	Concrete	1463	1463		Ap Thr Rwy PAPI 3.25°

RNAV

Remarks
Strict PPR. Visiting ACFT call APP at 20nm range. Outside published Ops Hrs AD is not available to civil ACFT.

Warnings
Glider flying takes place outside normal Ops Hrs. High intensity mixed jet and helicopter activity. 2 Rwys may be in use at the same time. Special rules for helicopters. Constant helicopter transit traffic between Yeovilton and Merryfield 11nm WSW. Turbulence and windshear may be experienced on short final Rwy27. For all Rwys there is a limited deadside which is restricted to the area between the Rwy in use and a line drawn parallel to Rwy in use which passes through the spherical radar dome to the N of AD.

Operating Hrs Mon-Thur 0830-1700 Fri 0800-1400 (L)
Circuits 04, 09 RH, 22, 27 LH, 1000ft QFE
Landing Fee Charges in accordance with MOD policy Contact Station Ops for details
Maintenance Nil
Fuel AVGAS JET A1 100LL
Disabled Facilities
Restaurants Nil
Taxis/Car Hire Nil

Weather Info M T Fax 456 MOEx
Tel: 01935 455426

Operator RNAS Yeovilton
Yeovilton, Somerset, BA22 8HT
Tel: 01935 455497 (PPR)
Tel: 01935 455262 (ATC)

XRUF YORK

65ft 2mb	3nm W of York N5356.83 W00110.24	PPR	**Alternative AD** **Leeds Bradford** Sherburn in Elmet **Diversion AD** **Non-standard join**

Rufforth	**LARS** **Linton 118.550**	**LARS** **Fenton 126.500**	**A/G** **129.975**

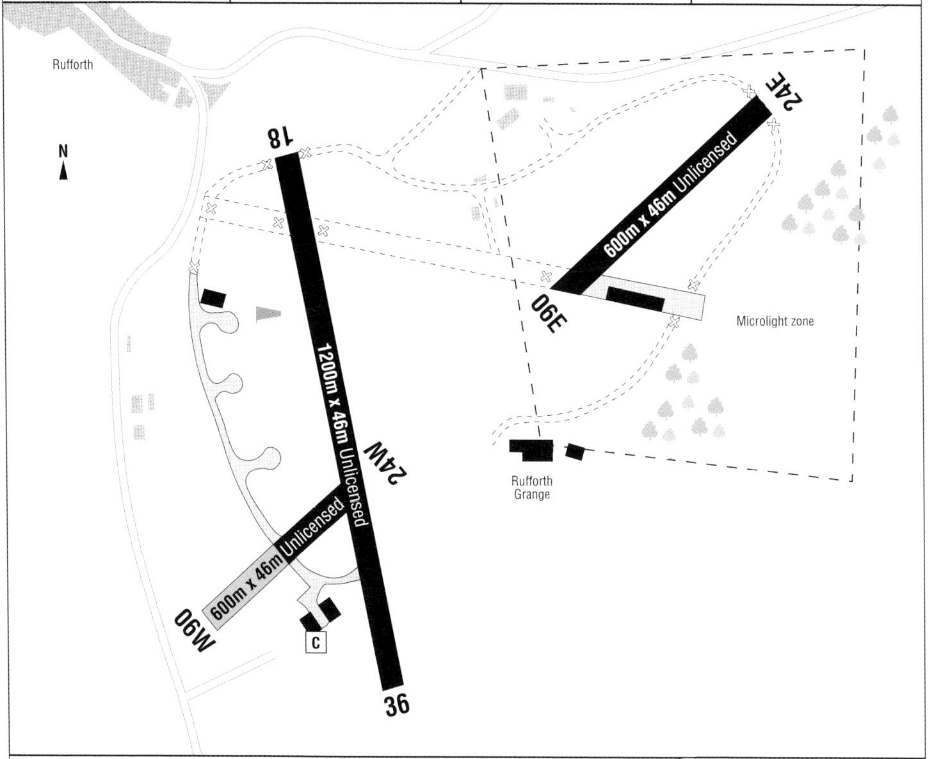

Rufforth
N
18
24E
600m x 46m Unlicensed
06E
Microlight zone
1200m x 46m Unlicensed
24W
Rufforth Grange
600m x 46m Unlicensed
06W
C
36

RWY	SURFACE	TORA	LDA	U/L	LIGHTING
18/36	Asphalt			1200x46	Nil
06/24W	Asph/Grass			600x46	Nil
06/24E	Asphalt			600x46	Nil

Rwy36 ignore Displaced Thr markings, Rwy24W 300m grass & 300m tarmac
Rwy24E microlight acft only

RNAV

Remarks
ACFT landing Rwy24W avoid microlight circuits on Rwy24E/06E. Beware gliders and powered ACFT on same circuit. Tug ACFT operate variable circuits.

Warnings
AD located on part of disused AD. Disused parts of AD are obstructed by farm buildings & equipment. AD is between Church Fenton and Linton-on-Ouse MATZs. Intense gliding activity. Rwys18/36 have displaced Thr marks which should be ignored. Microlights operating from disused Rwy at NE side of AD which is now re-activated as Rwy06E/24E. No overhead joins due to cables up to 2000ft agl. No dead side, join downwind.
Noise: Avoid over flying local farms and villages

Operating Hrs	SR-SS
Circuits	18 RH, 36 LH 24W RH, 06W LH, 800ft QFE Microlights 24E LH, 06E RH, 500ft QFE
Landing Fee	Rufforth E Nil Rufforth W £6-£50 depending on size
Maintenance	Nil
Fuel	AVGAS 100LL (Rufforth W)

Disabled Facilities

Restaurants	Vending machine in clubhouse Pub lunches The Tankard Rufforth 1m
Taxis	**Tel:** 01423 359000
Car Hire National	**Tel:** 01904 612141
Weather Info	Air N MOEx
Operator	York Gliding Centre Rufforth Aerodrome York, YO23 3NA **Tel:** 01904 738694 (W) **Fax:** 01904 738109 (W) **Tel:** 01904 738877 (Microlights E)

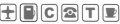

12ft 0mb	3.5nm ENE of Calais N5057.65 E00157.80	PPR	Alternative AD	Le Touquet

Non-standard join

Calais	ATIS Lille 119.320	ATIS Calis 135.450	APP Lille 120.275	TWR 128.920

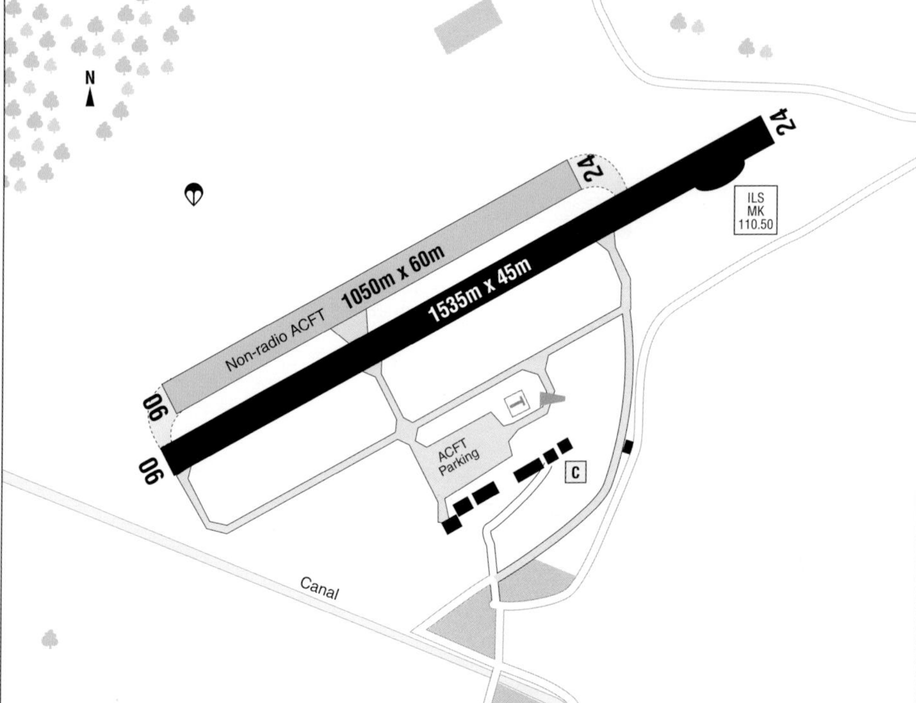

RWY	SURFACE	TORA	LDA	U/L	LIGHTING
06	Asphalt	1535	1535		Thr Rwy
24	Asphalt	1535	1535		Ap Thr Rwy
06/24	Grass	1050	1050		Nil

RNAV			
BNE	113.80	007	20.3

Remarks

PPR for Ops at certain times see Ops Hrs. Situated within Calais TMA (Class E airspace). SVFR flights requested to contact Lille APP if above 2000ft QNH, if operating below this alt, call Calais direct. Non-radio ACFT MUST use grass Rwy. DZ is to NW Rwy06/24 grass. Customs available 0800-1900 (L).

Aids to Navigation: NDB MK 418.00

Warnings

AD surface unusable outside marked or asphalt areas. Danger area 1.5nm NNW AD 0.5nm radius, up to 1650ft agl/ Coastal location gives high risk of sea fog. Heli & parachute activity on AD.

Operating Hrs	0800-1900 (1900-2300 PPR for IFR or training flights only). PPR requests must be made before 1700 same day. PPR for flights wishing to operate 0600-0800 must be obtained previous day
Circuits	Asphalt 06 RH, 24 LH, 1000ft QFE Grass 06 LH, 24 RH, 1000ft QFE
Landing Fee	On application
Maintenance	Nil
Fuel	AVGAS JET A1 100LL
Hangarage	By arrangement
Disabled Facilities	Nil

Restaurants	On Airfield
Taxis/Car Hire	Arranged locally
Weather Info	MT **Fax:** 552
Operator	**Tel:** 00 33 321 00 1100 (ATC) **Tel:** 00 33 32182 7066 (AD) **Tel:** 321 97 90 66 (Customs) **Fax:** 00 33 328 613 327 (AD)

LFRD DINARD

219ft 7mb	3nm S of Dinard N4835.26 W00204.80	PPR	Alternative AD	Avranches Dinard

Non-standard join

Dinard	ATIS 124.575	APP Rennes 124.900	TWR 120.150	Lighting 120.150

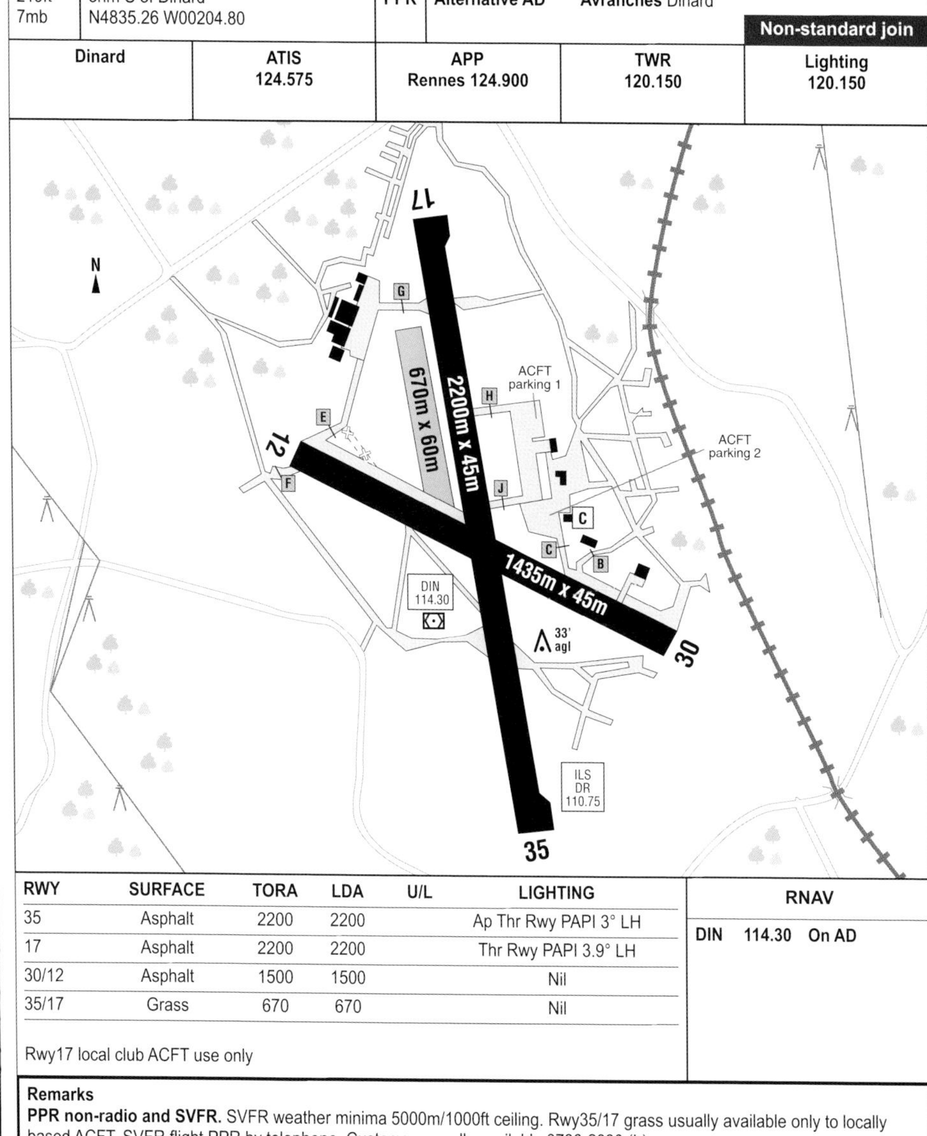

RWY	SURFACE	TORA	LDA	U/L	LIGHTING
35	Asphalt	2200	2200		Ap Thr Rwy PAPI 3° LH
17	Asphalt	2200	2200		Thr Rwy PAPI 3.9° LH
30/12	Asphalt	1500	1500		Nil
35/17	Grass	670	670		Nil

Rwy17 local club ACFT use only

RNAV

DIN 114.30 On AD

Remarks

PPR non-radio and SVFR. SVFR weather minima 5000m/1000ft ceiling. Rwy35/17 grass usually available only to locally based ACFT. SVFR flight PPR by telephone. Customs normally available 0730-2030 (L)

Warnings

Birds on AD. Mandatory SVFR routing, please check with SVFR request. Rwy unuseable outside ATC Hrs.

Operating Hrs Mon-Fri 0515-1845, Sat 0615-2015, Sun 0615-1845 (L)

Circuits Asphalt 17, 30 RH, 12, 35 LH, 1000ft QFE
Grass 17 RH, 35 LH, 1000ft QFE

Landing Fee On application

Maintenance Available

Fuel AVGAS JET A1 100LL

Disabled Facilities Nil

Restaurants In the terminal

Taxis At the terminal

Car Hire Available in Dinard

Weather Info M T Fax 544 A
ATIS **Tel:** 00 33 299 163 158

Visual Reference Points (VRP)

Echo/Pont du Port St Hubert	DIN 131°/5nm
November/Ile de Cezembre	DIN 010°/5nm
November Bravo/Barrage de la Rance	DIN 054°/3nm
November Echo/Pointe du Grouin	DIN 057°/12nm
November Whisky/Cap Frehel	DIN 307°/11nm
Sierra Whisky/Ploancoet	DIN 241°/7nm
Whisky Juliet/LeGuildo	DIN 264°/5nm

Operator **Tel:** 00 33 299 16 3803 (AD)
Tel: 00 33 299 16 3805 (Operator)

Effective date:25/09/08 JEP 08

EIDW DUBLIN

242ft 8mb	5nm N of Dublin City N5325.52 W00615.12	PPR	Alternative AD Belfast City Trim Non-standard join

Dublin	ATIS 124.525	APP 121.100 119.550 119.925	DEL 121.875
GND 121.800	FIS 118.500	RAD 129.175	TWR 118.600

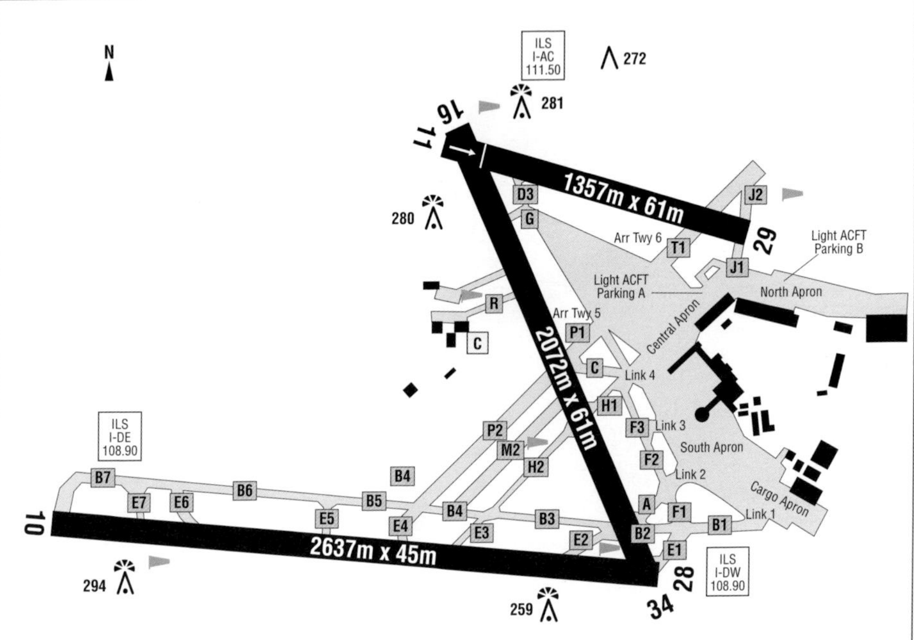

RWY	SURFACE	TORA	LDA	U/L	LIGHTING
10/28	Concrete	2637	2637		Ap Thr Rwy PAPI 3°
16/34	Asphalt	2072	2072		Ap Thr Rwy PAPI 3°
11	Asph/Conc	1339	1254		Ap Thr Rwy PAPI 3.5°
29	Asph/Conc	1339	1339		Ap Thr Rwy PAPI 3°

RNAV			
DUB	114.90	164	4.9

Remarks

PPR. Flight plans are mandatory for all ACFT wishing to use Dublin AD and CTA. Contact DEL at least 15 minutes prior to start up. ACFT prohibited from entering stands without marshalling guidance. ACFT are prohibited to hold on Twy B2. Twy E4 for daylight use only, ACFT with wingspan <30m taxiing from Rwy28. Twy E5 for use by ACFT with wingspan <36m. Twy T1 for daylight use only. Mandatory GND handling for all ACFT. AD closed on Christmas day.

Visual aid to location: Abn White Green

Warnings

Obstacle 700ft amsl 5nm SE of Rwy34 Thr.

Noise: ACFT operators must ensure at all times that the ACFT is operated in a manner that will cause the least disturbance practicable to areas surrounding the AD. Dept ACFT from all Rwys must maintain heading straight after take-off to 5nm before commencing turn unless otherwise instructed by ATC.

Operating Hrs	H24
Circuits	Not available on Rwy10/28 & Rwy16/34 11 LH 29 RH 800ft aal
Landing Fee	Available with PPR
Maintenance	Available
Fuel	AVGAS 100LL (0700-2230 (L) AVTUR JET A1 (H24)
Disabled Facilities	Available
Handling	Tel: 00 353 18145232 (Signature)

Restaurants	Available inside terminal
Taxi/Car Hire	Available outside terminal
Weather Info	**Tel:** 00 353 570 123123 **Fax:** 00 353 570 131838
Operator	Aer Rianta Cpt Dublin airport Co Dublin **Tel:** 00 353 18141111 **Fax:** 00 353 18144643 www.dublin-airport.com

For

Dublin Circuit Procedures

Rwy10/28 & Rwy16/34 are not available for circuit traning.

Rwy11

LH 800ft

After take-off/passing end of Rwy turn onto 100°M. Turn onto crosswind leg before crossing N1 main road.
Downwind leg - to be flown to S of Rathingle House and Rivervalley Estate.
Base leg – turn to be E of Rivermeade Estate.
Finals – ACFT must not position S of Rwy centreline.

Rwy29

RH 800ft

Dept on Rwy heading, climb to 500ft by 0.75nm upwind. Climb and turn through crosswind at 800ft aal remaining E of Rivermeade (Toberburr) Estate.
Downwind – Must be S of rathingle House and Rivervalley Estate.
Base leg – to be over the N! road.
Finals – ACFT must not position So of Rwy29 extended centreline.

Dublin Visual Approach Chart

Flight plans are mandatory for flights within Dublin CTR/CTA. When the flight destination is not an AD licensed for public use the address, telephone number and name of property owner of the place of intended landing must be included in field 18.
Special VFR is available within Dublin CTR.
Flight information Service is H24. 118.50 is allocated for ACFT in class G airspace.
Landing lights should be shown at all times during flights within Dublin CTR.
Take-off without 2 way communications with Dublin ATC either by RTF or telephone is not permitted.

Dublin CTA/CTR Clearance Procedures

Prior to penetration of Dublin CTA/CTR contact must be made at least 10 minutes before ETA at airspace boundary to the relevant ATSU as follows:
Dublin TWR 118.60 for entry into Dublin CTR
Dublin ACC North Sector 129.17 for entry to Dublin CTA North Sector
Dublin ACC South Sector 124.65 for entry to Dublin CTA South Sector
Dublin ACC North Sector is divided from Dublin ACC South Sector by:
Rwy10/28 active – boundary line along extended centreline of Rwy10/28
Rwy16/34 active – boundary line along extended APP line of Rwry16/34

Dublin VFR Arrival & Departure Routes

Flights arr/dept at Dublin AD are cleared as follows:
N arr/dept: via Skerries VFR route
W arr/dept: via Skerries VFR route or Dunshaughlin VFR route
S arr/dept: as instructed by TWR.
SW arr: fixed wing via Dunboyne or Dunshaughlin. Helis via Redcow Roundabout or The Square, Tallaght.
S dept: as instructed by ATC or flights intending to transit EIR15 are cleared to either Palmerston Roundabout Hold or Marley Park to await onwards clearance from Baldonnel TWR.

Flights with arr/dept destinations other than Dunlin AD are normally cleared as follows:
N arr/dept: As instructed by Dublin TWR or Skerries VFR route
W arr/dept: As instructed by Dublin TWR or Dunshaughlin VFR route
SW arr: as Instructed by Dublin TWR or Heli – via Red Cow roundabout or The square, Tallaght. Fixed wing – via Dunboyne or Dunshaughlin
S arr: as instructed by Dublin TWR
S dept: as instructed by Dublin TWR or flights intending to transit EIR15 route either the Palmerstown Roundabout Hold or the Marley Park Hold to await onwards clearance from Baldonnel TWR.

Dublin Holding Patterns

Broad Meadows Bridge

N532756.45 W00611.25

LH pattern based on the M1 motorway bridge, which crosses Broad Meadow estuary. Outbound leg is 1 minute at 90 kts on track 190°M. Minimum holding alt 100ft QNH.
Arr overhead, turn L onto outbound leg before southern shore of the Broad Meadow estuary.
Turn L onto inbound leg E of N1 road, remaining E of N1 road at all times.

Finglas Church Spire

N5323.17 W00618.41

LH pattern based on the W Finglas Church Spire. Outbound leg is 1minute at 90 kts on track 010°M. Minimum holding alt 1700ft QNH.
Arr overhead, turn onto outbound leg before M50 motorway remaining S of the motorway at all times.
Turn L onto inbound leg remaining W of N2 road at all times.

Palmerston Roundabout

N5321.25 W00623.00

LH pattern based on Palmerston roundabout which intersects the M50 motorway and N4 road.
Outbound leg is 1 minute at 90 kts on track 281°M.
Minimum alt is 1700ft QNH.

Marley Park House

N5316.36 W00616.00

RH pattern based on Marley Park House (large manor house in Marley Public Park)
Outbound leg is 1 minutes at 90 kts on track 291°M.
Minimum Alt is 1700ft QNH.

Effective date:25/09/08

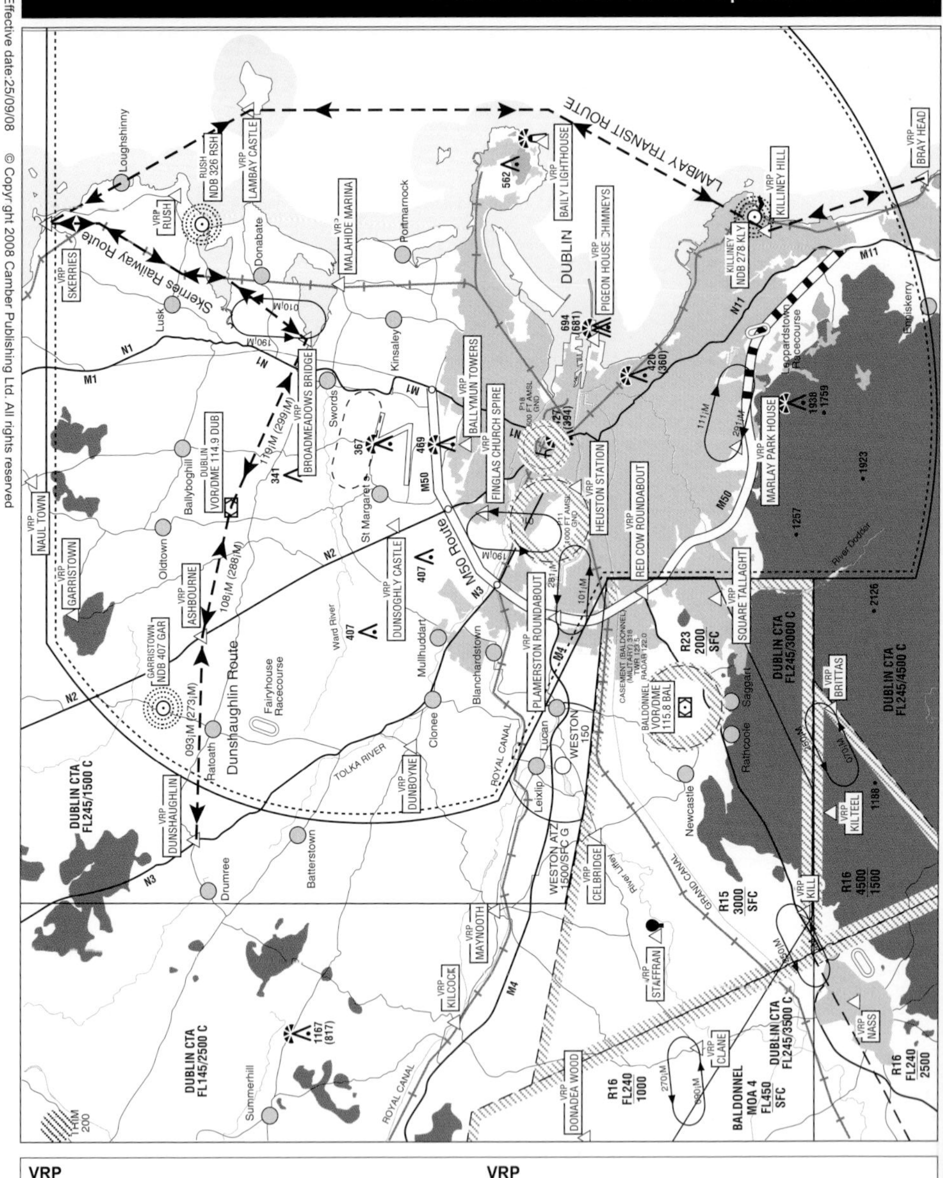

VRP		VRP	
Ashbourne	N5330.70 W00623.90	Kill	N5314.80 W00635.50
Baily Lighthouse	N5321.80 W00603.30	Killiney Hill	N5315.80 W00606.90
Ballymun Towers	N5323.80 W00615.80	Kilteel	N5314.10 W00631.30
Bray Head	N5311.70 W00604.80	Lambay Castle	N5329.40 W00601.80
Brittas	N5314.20 W00627.20	Malahide Marina	N5327.10 W00609.10
Broadmeadows Bridge	N5327.90 W00611.40	Marley Park House	N5316.60 W00616.00
Cellbridge	N5320.30 W00632.20	Maynooth	N5322.90 W00635.40
Clane	N5317.60 W00641.20	Naas	N5313.50 W00639.20
Donadea Wood	N5320.60 W00645.00	Naul Town	N5335.20 W00617.30
Dunboyne	N5325.10 W00628.50	Palmerston Roundabout	N5321.40 W00623.00
Dunshauglin	N5330.80 W00632.50	Pigeon House Chimneys	N5320.40 W00611.40
Dunsoghly Castle	N5325.60 W00619.30	Red Crow Roundabout	N5319.10 W00622.10
Finglas church Spire	N5323.30 W00618.70	Rush	N5331.40 W00605.40
Garristown	N5334.00 W00623.00	Skerries	N5334.70 W00606.50
Heuston Station	N5320.80 W00617.70	Square Tallaght	N5317.20 W00622.30
Kilcock	N5324.00 W00640.00	Straffan	N5318.70 W00636.40

LFBH LA ROCHELLE

74ft 3mb	1.4nm NW of La Rochelle N4610.75 W00111.71	**Alternative AD** **Le Thou**

Non-standard join

La Rochelle	ATIS	FIS	TWR
	126.870	Bordeaux Info 125.300	118.000

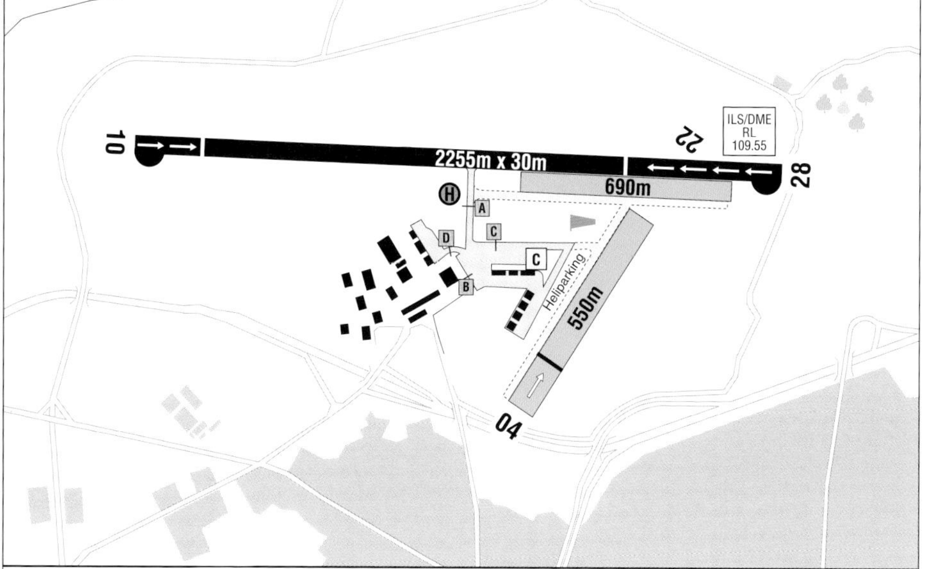

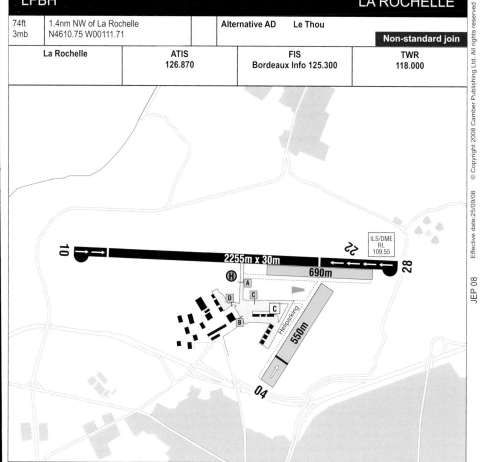

RWY	SURFACE	TORA	LDA	U/L	LIGHTING
28	Asphalt	2140	1605		Thr Rwy PAPI 3.1° LHS
10	Asphalt	2140	1940		Thr Rwy PAPI 3° LHS
28/10	Grass	690	–		Nil
22/04	Grass	550	–		Nil

Rwy28/10 Grass available only to local ACFT

RNAV

Remarks
Microlights not accepted. SVFR minima 1500m, ceiling 700ft. Rwy28 preferred in winds of less than 4 kts.
Aids to Navigation: NDB RL 322.00

Warnings
Only Rwys and marked Twys available for the movement of ACFT.
Noise: In the visual circuit avoid over flying built-up areas.

Operating Hrs Mon-Fri 0400-2100 Sat/Sun & PH 0600-2000 (Summer) Mon-Fri 0500-2200 Sat/Sun & PH 0800-1800 (Winter) & by arr
Circuits 28, 22 RH, 700ft QFE
Landing Fee On application
Maintenance Available plus hangerage
Fuel AVTUR JET A1 100LL
Disabled Facilities Nil
Restaurants In the terminal
Taxis/Car Hire Available in the terminal

Weather Info M T
Visual Reporting Points (VRP)
Charron Usseau Nieul-s-Mer & St Vivien
Operator CCI La Rochelle
14 Rue du Palais, 17000 La Rochelle
Tel: 00 33 46 42 3026 (AD)
Fax: 00 33 46 43 1254 (AD)

Effective date:25/09/08 JEP 08

LFAT LE TOUQUET

20ft 1mb	1nm E of Le Touquet N5030.90 88137.65	PPR	Alternative AD Calais Non-standard join

Le Touquet	ATIS 123.125	FIS Paris N 125.700	APP 125.30 118.450

APP Lille 120.275	TWR 118.450	GND 125.300

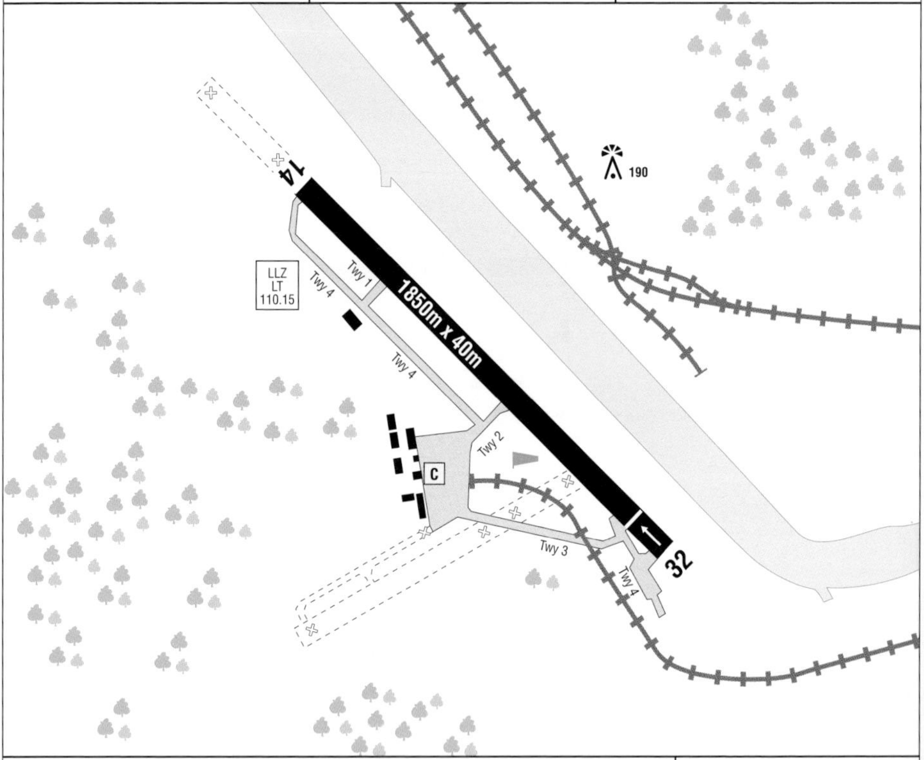

RWY	SURFACE	TORA	LDA	U/L	LIGHTING
14	Asphalt	1850	1554		Ap Thr Rwy
32	Asphalt	1850	1700		Thr Rwy PAPI 3° LHS

RNAV			
BNE	113.80	240	12.5

Remarks

PPR non-radio ACFT. Call TWR before starting engine for Dept. SVFR weather minima 3000m/820ft ceiling (Arr); 1500m / 660ft ceiling (Dept) fixed wing. In winds of less than 4kts use of Rwy14 is preferred.

Aids to Navigation: NDB LT 358.00

Warnings

Due to AD location is it susceptible to sea fog which can arrive without warning, have an in-land diversion planned. Mandatory SVFR routing, please check with SVFR request. When Rwy32 in use, ACFT may be cleared to Rwy14, straight in. With a break right of the LT locator onto a track of 181°(M) for 2.1nm before turning left into circuit.

Operating Hrs	Mon-Fri 0800-1700, Sat 0700-1700 (Summer) Mon-Sat 0900-1700 (Winter)
Circuits	32 RH, 14 LH, 1000ft QFE
Landing Fee	On application
Maintenance	Available
Fuel	AVGAS JET A1 100LL
Disabled Facilities	Nil
Restaurants	In the terminal
Taxis	At the terminal
Car Hire	Available in Le Touquet

Weather Info M T Fax 552 A
ATIS **Tel:** 00 33 2105 5126

Visual ReferencePoints (VRP)

Echo/Neuville	N5028 50 E00146.70
November/Hardelot Plage	N5038 00 E00168.00
November Echo/Samer	N5038 10 E00144.80
November Mike/Wimereux	N5045 90 E00138.00
Sierra/Rang duFliers	N5025.00 E00138.60

Operator **Tel:** 00 33 321 05 0066 (ATC)
Tel: 00 33 321 050 399 (AD)
Fax: 00 33 321 055 934 (AD)

For

EBOS OSTEND

13ft 1mb	3nm S of Ostend N5111.93 E00251.73	PPR	Alternative AD Kokjoide **Non-standard join**

Ostend	ATIS	FIS	APP	TWR	GND
	136.100	Brussels 126.900	120.600	118.175	121.975

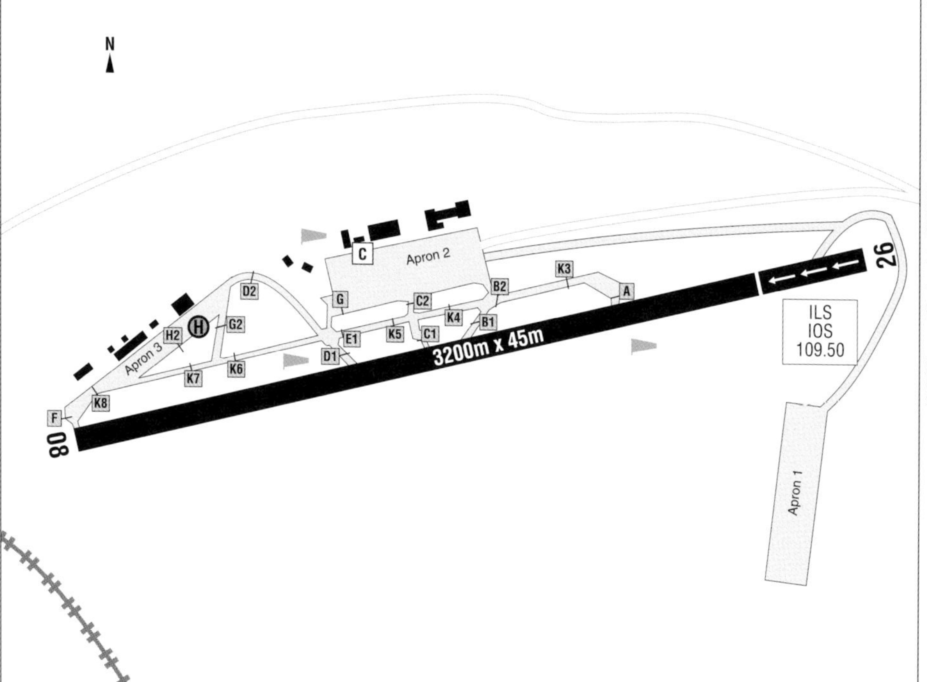

RWY	SURFACE	TORA	LDA	U/L	LIGHTING
26	Asphalt	3200	2785		Ap Thr Rwy PAPI 3° LH
08	Asphalt	2400	2900		Ap Thr Rwy PAPI 3° LH

RNAV			
KOK	114.50	054	10.0

Remarks

PPR non-radio ACFT (may be subject to prohibition). AD situated within Class C Airspace.

Aids to Navigation: NDB ONO 399.50. NDB DD 352.50. NDB OO 375.262.

Warnings

ACFT APP visually should not descend below 1500ftamsl before intercepting the PAPI glide slope, or fly below this slope once established.

Operating Hrs	H24
Circuits	Nil
Landing Fee	On application
Maintenance	Available
Fuel	AVGAS Jet A1 100LL
Disabled Facilities	Nil
Restaurants	In the terminal
Taxis/Car Hire	At the terminal
Weather Info	M T **Fax:** 562 A **Tel:** 00 32 59 551452

Visual Reference Points (VRP)

Aalter	N5105.12 E00327.00
Breskens	N5125.00 E00333.00
Dunkerque	N5102.00 E00222.30
Torhout	N5104.10 E00306.11

Operator

Tel: 00 32 59 551411 (AD)
Tel: 00 32 59 551464 (Self briefing)
Tel: 00 32 59 551452 (Met)
Fax: 00 32 59 512951 (AD)

Effective date:25/09/08 JEP 08

UK VFR Flight Guide
Private Airfields

Private Airfields DELETED this year

The airfield below has been deleted from this guide for various reasons. Often because of inconsiderate visitor use that has caused annoyance to neighbours and put the strip at risk. The owners therefore have requested that we no longer publish details. The fact that an airfield is listed below **does not necessarily mean that the airfield no longer exists.**

Donemana
Nesscliffe Camp
Sennybridge

Private Airfields ADDED for 2009

The airfields below have agreed to let us publish details for the first time this year. **Please remember that should you use them – and they are all strictly PPR – consideration and good airman ship will ensure they are still available in future years.**

Alcester
Bowerswaine Farm
Forwood Farm
Glendoe
Hook Norton
Octon
Willow Farm

Private Airfields New map pages 2009

The airfields below have agreed to become full page map pages this year. Please see the map section listed alphabetical.

Breidden
Coll
Kimbolton
Main Hall Farm
Portmoak
Shifnal
Sollas
Strathaven
Weston on the Green
Ballykelly
Fairford

ABOYNE

N5704.52 W00250.08, 1.1nm W of Aboyne (N of River Dee), 460ft amsl

Rwy09L/27R Tarmac 520x5.5m Rwy09R/27L Tarmac 540x7m. **Remarks:** Gliding or maintenance related ACFT only. Gliders launch by Aerotow, keep good look out at all times. Windsock N of Rwy. **Radio:** A/G 130.100. **Circuits:** Nil.. **Maintenance:** Light ACFT & Glider available Alan Middleton, Aboyne ACFT Maintenance **Tel:** 01339 885236. **Fuel:** Nil. **Landing Fee:** Gliding Club business or Maintenance £6. Non Gliding Club business £17 Motor Gliders £4 Light ACFT £7.50. **Operator:** Deeside Gliding Club, Waterside, Dinnet. **Tel:** 01339 885339 (Club Office) office@deesideglidingclub.co.uk www.deesideglidingclub.co.uk

Disabled Facilities:

ALCESTER

N5213.84 W00152.67, 4nm S of Redditch, 250ft amsl

Rwy18/36 Grass 430x19m. **Remarks:** Good level strip. Windsock displayed. Located between A435 and River Arrow. **Warnings:** Road crosses Rwy at mid point. Gliding activity at Snitterfield AD to N of AD. Located on the edge of Birmingham CTA. **Caution:** Cables run along both ends of Rwy. **Landing:** From N – land short under cables or long over flying road. From S – Land short over S boundary hedge and stop before field or long over fly over road. **Noise:** Avoid over flying Alcester village. **Operating Hrs:** SR-SS. **Circuits:** Nil. **Landing Fee:** Nil. **Maintenance:** Nil. **Fuel:** Nil. **Operator:** Mr Turner, Mill House, Kings Coughton, Alcester, Warks. **Tel:** 01789 72180 **Tel:** 07785 954988

ALLENSMORE

N5200.02 W00250.07, 4nm SW of Hereford, 300ft amsl

N/S Grass 550x50m. **Remarks:** Animals grazing. Large letter A on white back ground on hangar roof at N end of strip. **Circuits:** Nil **Landing Fee:** Subscription to Mission Aviation Fellowship. **Maintenace**: Nil. **Fuel:** Nil. **Operator:** Mr Powell, Locks Garage, Allensmore, Hereford HR2 9HS. **Tel:** 07879 883406

BINSTEAD

N5043.00 W00112.00, 2nm W of Ryde, 150ft amsl

Rwy18/36 Grass 400x16m. **Remarks:** PPR. Microlights not accepted. Well maintained strip. Power lines APP Thr Rwy36 but go underground APP. **Visual Aid to Location:** 0.5nm S of Abbey on N coast of Isle of Wight. Southampton CTR close by. **Noise:** Do not over fly the abbey and villages. **Operating Hrs:** SR-SS. **Circuits:** Please fly straight in APP. **Maintenance:** Nil. **Fuel:** Nil. **Operator:** John Cleaver, Newnham Farm, Binstead, Isle of Wight, PO33 4ED. **Tel:** 01983 882423

BOWERSWAINE FARM

N5053.00 W00159.00, 5nm W of Wimbourne Minster, 150ft amsl.

Rwy09/27 Grass 500x12m. **Remarks:** PPR essential. Grass high on both sides of Rwy. Rwy09 APP and first section runs across cricket pitch. Windsock displayed. **Warnings:** Located inside Bournemouth CTR/Solent CTA. AD boggy during winter months. Animals graze AD, removed with PPR. **Caution:** Cables on short finals Rwy09 APP. Stream and hedge on short finals Rwy27. Trees to N of Rwy09 Thr may cause turbulence with N/NE winds. **Noise:** Avoid over flying Village NW of AD. **Operating Hrs:** SR-SS. **Circuits:** Variable. **Landing Fee:** Nil. **Maintenance:** Nil. **Fuel:** Nil. **Operator:** Mr J C Haycock, Bowerswaine Farmhouse, Gussage All Saints, Wimborne, Dorset, BH21 5ES. **Tel:** 01258 840577 **Tel:** 07831 626820

BROADMEADOW

N5202.00 W00246.00. 3nm SW Hereford. 325ft amsl

Rwy09/27 Grass 400x18m. **Remarks:** PPR by telephone. Microlight ACFT only. Windsock at both ends of Rwy. Good clear APP to both Rwy. **Warnings:** Slight Rwy upslope. Madley AD close to S of strip. **Noise:** Avoid over flying all local houses and villages, especially to E of AD. Over fly the field to identify not below 1500ft agl. Decend to circuit height over open farmland 1nm W of AD for ling final Rwy10R and tight circuit for Rwy28L. **Radio:** 129.825. **Operating Hrs:** 0900-2000. **Circuits:** All to N. 500ft agl **Landing Fee:** Nil. **Fuel:** MOGAS by arrangement. **Maintenance:** Nil. **Operator:** Mr Powell, Broadmeadow Farm, Haywood, Hereford, HR2 9RU. **Tel:** 01432 278421 **Tel:** 07749 702699 (PPR) **Tel:** 07787 564170 (PPR).

Disabled Facilities:

For

BROMSGROVE (Stoney Lane)

N5220 W00159, 2nm NW of Redditch. 425ft amsl

Rwy075/255 Grass 375x15m. **Remarks:** PPR is essential. Strip is only suitable for experienced STOL pilots due to windshear and turbulence. Rwy slope to SW. A windsock may be shown in S of AD. Join overhead at 1500ft QFE. **Noise:** Avoid over flying Blakenhurst Prison 0.5m to S and all local habitation. **Circuits:** SE at 800ft QFE. **Landing Fee:** £5 for business use, £2.50 for recreational flyers. **Maintenance:** Nil. **Fuel:** Available (MOGAS) 3nm away 24 Hrs. **Accommodation:** Immediately to S of AD. **Operator:** P Whittaker, 'Longlands', Stoney Lane, Bromsgrove, Worcs, B60 1LZ. **Tel:** 01527 875228 **Tel:** 07966 275154 (Mobile)

CAMPHILL

N5318.28 W0143.88, 12nm WSW of Sheffield. 1300ft amsl

Rwy18/36 Grass. **Remarks:** Gliding Site, Strictly PPR. No Rwy markings, landing area along centreline of AD. No powered ACFT except motor gliders permitted. Surface is undulating, APP can be hazardous in poor weather. **Warnings:** Area of intense gliding activity with winch launches up to 2000ft agl (3300ft asml). **Noise:** Avoid over flying adjacent villages. **Radio:** Camphill GND 129.975. **Maintenance:** Nil. **Fuel:** Nil. **Accommodation:** Available in club house inc food. **Operator:** Derbyshire & Lancashire Gliding Club, Camphill, Great Hucklow, Tideswell, Buxton, SK17 8RQ. **Tel:** 01298 871270/871207 dlgc@gliding.u-net.com www.dlgc.org.uk

CAUNTON

N5307.05 W00053.50, 4.5NM NW of Newark, 160ft amsl

Rwy03/21 Grass 400m, Rwy11/29 Grass 400m. **Radio:** Caunton Radio 129.825. **Remarks:** PPR essential. Microlights only enter and leave AD from E or W. Arrive 1000ftagl, descend in circuit. High performance 3-axis microlights may use alternative circuit pattern – call for briefing if flying said machine. **Warnings:** Rwy21 has displaced Thr– keep finals short and land 1/3 along Rwy. Rwy03/11 down slope. High power cables to E. Keep a good look out for hang gliders on aerotow and foot launched powered hang gliders. **Circuits:** 03/11 RH, 21/29 LH 500ft agl. No deadside **Landing Fee:** Nil. **Maintenance:** Nil. **Hangarage:** Ltd available. **Fuel:** Available on request. **Accommodation:** B & B available on site. **Operator:** Andy Buchan, Pebbles, Southwell Road, Farnsfield, Notts, NG22 8EB. **Tel:** 01623 883802 **Tel:** 07850 942096 (Mobile) andy@lightflight.co.uk.

Disabled Facilities:

CHALLOCK (EGKE)

N5112.50 E00049.75, 4nm NNW of Ashford, 600ft amsl

NE/SW Grass 800m, N/S Grass 800m. **Remarks:** PPR by telephone essential. Glider towing by winch and aerotow takes place here. **Warnings:** There are unmarked electric lines along NE side of AD. All APP are over tall trees. Rwy surface is undulating and SW corner is not useable. **Noise:** Do not join over head. **Operating Hrs:** By arrangement. **Maintenance:** Nil **Fuel:** Nil. **Landing Fee:** Nil. **Operator:** Kent Gliding Club, Challock Aerodrome, Squids Gate, Challock, Ashford, Kent, TN25 4DR. **Tel:** 01233 740274 **Tel:** 01233 740307 **Fax:** 01233 740811. **Disabled Facilities:**

CRAYSMARSH FARM

N5121.80 W00205.30, 4nm N of Keevil AD, 180ft amsl

Rwy18/36 Grass 500x15m approx. **Remarks:** PPR. Rwy waterlogged during winter months. **Warnings:** Power cables 800m from Rwy18 APP. **Noise:** Avoid over flying all local villages. **Radio:** Safetycom 135.475. **Operating Hrs:** SR-SS. **Maintenance:** Nil. **Fuel:** Nil. **Landing Fee:** Available with PPR. **Circuits:** Operator will advise with PPR. **Fuel:** MOGAS available with PPR. **Operator:** Mr Cottle, Craysmarsh Farm, Melksham, Wiltshire, SN12 6RG. **Tel:** 01380 828258

DOWLAND

N5053.00 W00402.00, 3.5nm W Winkleigh Disused AD. 450ft amsl

Rwy09/27 Grass 461x8m. **Remarks:** Strict PPR. Rwy in excellent condition. Windsock displayed at W end of Rwy. **Warnings:** Slight upslope Rwy09. Trees on APP Rwy27. High GND to NE of AD. Eaglescott ATZ close to NNE. **Noise:** Avoid over flying Dowland village. **Operating Hrs:** SR-SS. **Circuits:** LH at 800ft QFE. **Landing Fee:** Nil. **Maintenance:** Nil. **Fuel:** Nil. **Operator:** Mr W.G. Dunn, Croft, Dowland, Winkleigh, Devon, EX19 8PD. **Tel:** 01805 804627 wgdunn100@tiscali.co.uk.

Disabled Facilities:

DUNSTABLE DOWNS

N5151.98 W00032.90, 1nm SW of Dunstable, 500ft amsl

Rwy04/22 Grass 900x50m, Rwy15/33 Grass 750x50m, Rwy18/36 Grass 500x50m. **Radio:** A/G 119.900. **Remarks:** PPR essential. Permission for use normally restricted to pilots with at least a Silver Gliding Badge and on gliding business. Inbound ACFT contact Luton APP. AD located within the Luton CTR. ACFT to taxi behind glider launch points. Intensive gliding activity including winch launching takes place. There are no AD markings. The Downs up to 817ft amsl are located to E & S of AD. Rwys have undulating surfaces. For landing information please telephone. Intensive hang gliding takes place along the ridge. **Operating Hrs:** by arr. **Circuits:** variable to NW of Downs, powered ACFT circuit is outside glider circuit. **Maintenance:** London light ACFT **Tel:** 01582 663419. **Fuel:** AVGAS 100LL available by arr. **Operator:** London Gliding Club, Dunstable Downs, Dunstable, Bedfordshire, **Tel:** 01582 663419 (PPR) **Fax:** 01582 665744 andy@londonglidingclub.com www.londonglidingclub.com.

EAST LOCHLANE FARM

N5622.00 W00352.30, 1.5nm W of Crieff, 800ft amsl

Rwy06/24 Grass 440x15m. **Remarks:** PPR essential for brief on AD conditions. Animals graze on field. Windsock displayed N Rwy06 Thr. **Warnings:** Upslope Rwy24 Thr. Trees border S edge of strip, may cause turbulence. **Noise:** Avoid over flying all houses and farms, especially the stud farm next door. **Operating Hrs:** SR-SS. **Circuits:** Nil. **Landing Fee:** Nil. **Maintenance:** Nil. **Fuel:** Nil. **Operator:** Gordon Halley, East Lochlane Farm, Crieff, **Tel:** 01764 652686 **Tel:** 07710 488640 **Fax:** 01764 753042 gordon@lochlane.co.uk

EAST WINCH

N5243.33 E00031.90, 4nm SE of Kings Lynn, 49ft amsl
Rwy10/28 Grass 850x16m. **Remarks:** Situated on edge of Marham MATZ. Pilots Arr & Dept should contact Marham APP Visiting ACFT not normally accepted unless a customer of Scanrho Aviation. Crop spraying ACFT operate from AD. **Noise:** Avoid overflying East Winch village **Circuits:** 10 LH, 28 RH, 800ft QFE. **Maintenance:** Scanrho Aviation. **Operator:** Three Ways, East Winch, Kings Lynn, Norfolk. **Tel:** 01553 840396 **Tel:** 01553 840262 (Mr Burman) **Fax:** 01485 600413

ERROL

N5624.30 W00310.92, 6nm SW of Dundee Airport, 31ft amsl
Rwy05/23 Asphalt 630x46m (E of disused AD). **Radio:** A/G 123.45 **Remarks:** Contact Leuchars APP & Dundee APP. Before entering circuit call DZ Control Errol. Free-fall parachuting up to FL150. Visiting pilots should report to Fife Parachuting Centre, Muirhouses Farm or Harbour Sawmills Ltd (on disused Rwy11). **Noise:** On APP/climb-out maintain Rwy heading for at least 1nm to avoid houses. **Operating Hrs:** SR-SS closed Mon & Thur. **Maintenance:** Nil. **Fuel:** Nil. **Landing Fee:** Single £5, Twin £10. **Operator:** Mr L Doe, Muirhouses Farm, Errol. **Tel:** 01821 642555 (Operator work) **Tel:** 01821 642333 (Operator home) **Tel:** 01821 642355 (Harbour Sawmills AD) **Tel:** 01821 642454 (Parachute Club) **Fax:** 01821 642825 (Mr Doe)

FANNERS FARM

N5147.00 E00026.00. 4nm N Chelmsford. 210ft amsl
Rwy06/24 Grass 415x14m. **Remarks:** Strict PPR by telephone. **Warnings:** 8ft hedges at both Thrs. Rwy 06 APP is between two large poplars. Also electricity poles on Rwy24 APP. AD is on SE edge of Stansted CTA, (base 2000ft). **Noise:** Avoid over flying Great Waltham and Chignall Smealy villages. **Operating Hrs:** SR-SS. **Circuits:** 800ft QFE to NW. **Landing Fee:** Nil. **Maintenance:** Nil. **Fuel:** Nil. **Operator:** Peter Lee, Fanners Farm, Great Waltham, Essex, CH3 1EA. **Tel:** 01245 360470

FEARN

N5745.48 W00356.58, 1nm S of Fearn, 25ft amsl
Rwy11/29 Asphalt 1097x46m (other Rwys are obstructed by fences). Rwy surface – Asphalt over concrete, W 2/3rds very broken, Loose surface on all Rwy. **Remarks:** AD situated in D703. An entry/exit sector is established from GND level to1000ft agl in the segment S of a line joining N5745.00 W00400.42 & N5745.00 W00353.25. Maximum height S of this line is 1000ft agl. DAAIS Tain Range 122.750. Wind monitoring mast adjacent Rwy11/29 to N side on west cross Rwy. **Fuel:** Nil. **Operator:** Mrs D Sutherland, Tullich Farm, Fearn, Ross-Shire, Highland Region, IV18 0PE **Tel:** 01862 832278

FLOTTA

N5849.58 W00308.53, 9.5nm SE of Stromness, Orkney, 70ft amsl
Rwy16/34 Asphalt 759x18m. **Remarks:** Heliport operated by Talisman Energy (UK) Ltd. Fixed wing ACFT accepted when operating Ambulance flights or in emergency only. There is a significant longitudinal slope on Rwy. No facilities. **Visual aid to Location:** A flare stack 1.4nm from AD. **Fuel:** Nil. **Operator:** **Tel:** 01856 884359. **Disabled Facilities:**

FOLKESTONE (Lyminge)

N5109 E00104, 7nm S of Canterbury, 600ft amsl
Rwy06/24 Grass 440x10m. **Remarks:** Strip is surrounded to W, E and N by Lyminge Forest – a large wooded area. **Caution:** trees to 50ft are a hazard at N end of strip. PPR is essential as there may be farm machinery or people working in soft fruit fields in close proximity. **Noise:** Visiting ACFT are requested to avoid all houses. **Circuits:** 24 LH, 06 RH, 800ft QFE. **Fuel**: Nil. **Operator:** Mr G G Boot **Tel:** 01624 801027 geoffreyboot@supanet.com

FORWOOD FARM

N5318.20 W00051.00, 5nm E of Retford, 200ft amsl.
Rwy02/20 Grass 500x27m. **Remarks:** PPR essential. Windsock displayed. Large wood to W of AD. Intense military activity in area. **Warnings:** Located inside Doncaster CTA. Darlton Gliding site to W of AD. AD located close to Scampton/Waddington MATZ. AD boggy after heavy rain and during winter months. Power cables (20ft), 100m from Rwy02 Thr. **Noise:** Avoid over flying Rampton Hospital and Treswell village. **Operating Hrs:** SR-SS. **Circuits:** To E. **Landing Fee:** Nil. **Maintenance:** Nil. **Fuel:** Nil. **Operator:** David Bell, Forwood Farm, Treswell, Notts, DN22 0EE. **Tel:** 01777 248719 **Tel:** 07970 883448. Steph.bell@tiscali.co.uk

GLENDOE

N5775.70 W00044.03, 1nm SE of Fort Augustus, 300ft amsl.
Rwy04/22 Grass 650x20m. **Remarks:** Located on shores of Loch Ness. Windsock displayed. **Warnings:** Rwy slopes to W. AD boggy when wet and during winter months. Windshear on APP with S winds. Trees and hills to E. Windfarm to NW of AD. **Operating Hrs:** SR-SS. **Circuits:** 22 RH, 04 LH. **Landing Fee:** Nil. **Maintenance:** Nil. **Fuel:** Nil. **Operator:** Greville Vernon, Bowldown Farms Ltd, Bowldown, Weston Birt, Tetbury, Glos. **Tel:** 01666 890224 **Fax:** 01666 890433 gv@bowldown.com

GREEN FARM

N5209.00 W00133.30, 3nm SE of Wellesbourne Mountford AD, 375ft amsl
Rwy04/22 Grass 613x30. **Remarks:** Displaced Thr Rwy04 marked by red cones to avoid hedge close to Rwy04 Thr and rough GND which reduces take off run on Rwy04 also. Rough area is suitable as over run Rwy22. Call Wellsbourne Radio due to close proximity of ATZ. Ettington strip is 1.5nm to WSW. Strip is regularly over flown by low level fast jets. Windsocks displayed. AD regularly crossed by horse riders. **Warnings:** Rwy04 undershoot slopes steeply upwards, suitable for Rwy22 over run. **Noise:** Do not over fly Kineton and Butlers Marston village E of AD. **Circuits:** 22 LH, 04 RH. **Fuel:** Nil. **Landing Fee:** Nil. **Operator:** Terry Cooper, Green Farm, Combrook, Warwickshire. CV35 9HP. **Tel:** 01926 640162. **Disabled Facilities:**

GUNTON PARK (Hanworth)

N5250.30 E000119.16, 2nm N of Suffield and 3nm W of Antingham, 100ft amsl
N/S Grass 800x30m. **Remarks:** PPR imperative due to location of Rwy in middle of a deer park. Rwy has 2m deer fence at each end, some high trees on S APP, also undulating with mown dry grass. Electric power line goes under GND in centre of Rwy. There is a line of trees S of Rwy and also trees at N end. Windsock is displayed on E side. **Noise:** Visiting ACFT are requested not to over fly Observatory TWR 1nm N and Hall 1nm W of AD. **Fuel:** Nil. **Operator:** Sally Martin, Park Farm, Gunton Park, Hanworth, Norwich, Norfolk NR11 7HL. **Tel:** 01263 761202 **Tel:** 01263 768667 (Office) **Fax:** 01263 768642

HALWELL

N5021.55 W00342.35, 5nm WNW of Dartmouth, 625ft amsl
Rwy09/27 Grass 480x12m. **Remarks:** PPR. Rwy09 has up slope. Well prepared/mowed Rwy. Mainly used by Microlights but light ACFT are welcome at pilots own risk. **Noise:** All ACFT APP AD from NW. Do not over fly houses to the W of the AD. **Operating Hrs:** SR-SS. **Circuits:** should be to N and kept very tight. **Landing Fee:** Nil. **Fuel:** MOGAS available by prior arr. **Restaurant/Accomodation:** The Old Inn, Halwell (shortwalk from AD) **Tel:** 01803 712329. **Operator:** Keith Wingate, South Hams Flying Group, Chakdina, 16 Buckwell Road, Kingsbridge, South Devon, TQ7 1NQ. **Tel:** 01548 857513 **Fax:** 01548 853556 **Tel:** 07971 480078 keithwinga@aol.com www.btinernet.com/~south.hams/shfc/index.html

HATTON

N5724.40 W00154.71, 1nm S of Hatton, 265ft amsl
Rwy08/26 Grass 650x18m. **Remarks:** Visiting ACFT welcome with PPR at pilots own risk. 2% up slope on Rwy08. 30ft agl domestic power line crosses Rwy26 APP on short final. Strip may be waterlogged during winter months. Strip is close to boundary of Aberdeen CTA/CTR Aberdeen APP, and is beneath HMR Whiskey, a published helicopter route for off shore traffic. Heavy commercial helicopters can be expected entering/leaving Aberdeen zone. Useful weather information can be obtained from Aberdeen ATIS. **Noise:** Avoid over flight of local habitation. **Landing Fee:** Donations to upkeep welcomed. **Circuits:** 26 LH, 08 RH, 800ft QFE. **Fuel:** Nil. **Operator:** James Anderson, Ardiffery Mains, Hatton, Peterhead, Aberdeenshire AB42 0SD. **Tel:** 01779 841207 **Tel:** 07947 127560.
Disabled Facilities:

HOME FARM

N5206.50 W00143.00, 5nm S Stratford upon Avon, 250ft amsl
Rwy02/20 Grass 650x20m. **Remarks:** Strict PPR. **Warnings:** Rwy has up slope at S end. Power lines cross APP Rwy20. Large oak tree 2/3 along Rwy on W side. Low flying military ACFT operate in AD vicinity. **Caution:** Microlight activity from Long Marston 2nm NW. **Noise:** Avoid over flying local villages to NW and NE. **Operating Hrs:** SR-SS. **Circuits:** To W 500ft QFE. **Fuel:** Nil. **Maintenance:** Nil. **Operator:** Paul Collicutt, Lower Farm, Admington, Shipton on Stour, Warks, CV36 4JW. **Tel:** 01789 450329 **Tel:** 07801 466990 paul@ebonystar.demon.co.uk

HOOK

N5116.50 W00056.53, 5nm E of Basingstoke, 225ft amsl
Rwy08/26 Grass 609x20m. **Remarks:** Slight up slope on Rwy08, grass can become water logged in winter. Power lines and trees on both APP. Preferred landing Rwy26, take off Rwy08. Windsock by Rwy08 Thr. **Noise:** Do not over fly Hook village. **Fuel:** Nil. **Operator:** Chris Hill, Scotland Farm, Holt Lane, Hook, Hampshire, RG27 9ES **Tel:** 01256 762423.
Disabled Facilities:

HOOK NORTON

N5200.58 W00129.53, 7nm SW of Banbury, 580ft amsl
Rwy06/24 Grass 340x15m. **Remarks:** PPR essential. Windsock displayed. **Warnings:** Dowslope Rwy06. Hedges on Rwy06/24 APP. Cables to E of AD in valley. Gliding at Shennington AD to N of AD. **Noise:** Avoid over flying all local houses and farms. **Operating Hrs:** SR-SS. **Circuits:** to N 800ft. **Landing Fee:** £10 to Katherine House Hospice. **Maintenance:** Nil. **Fuel:** MOGAS from garage opposite. **Operator:** Dean Wood, Scotts Hedge, Hook Norton, Oxon, OX15 5DD. **Tel:** 01608 737349. **Tel:** 07860 580944 enquiries@firsgarage.co.uk

KINGFISHER BRIDGE

N5219.50 E00016.50. 5nm S of Ely. 16ft asml
Rwy09/27 Grass 570x38m. **Remarks**: PPR by telephone. Rwy in excellent condition. Windsock displayed N of Rwy. **Visual aid to location:** Cement works to N of AD. River cam to W of AD. **Warnings**: Power lines 400m W of Rwy27 Thr. AD situated within Lakenheath/Mildenhall MATZ, call for info. **Operating Hrs:** SR-SS. **Circuits**: LH 1000ft QFE. **Landing Fee:** Nil. **Maintenance**: Nil. **Fuel**: Nil. **Operator**: Andrew Green, Kingfishers Bridge, High Fen Farm, Wicken, Ely, Cambs, CB7 5XJ. **Tel:** 01353 72112. agreen@plr.net

KING'S LYNN (Tilney St. Lawrence)

N5243 E00019. 4.5nm SW of Kings Lynn,2nm W of River Great Ouse, 10ft amsl
Rwy16/34 Grass 400x32m. **Remarks:** Operated for private use, Strict PPR, visiting ACFT welcome at pilot's own risk. Pylons 200ft high 0.5nm to N. Orange Windsock displayed. **Landing Fee:** Nil. **Fuel:** Nil. **Operator:** J. Goodley & Sons, Hirdling House, Tilney St. Lawrence **Tel:** 01945 880237
Disabled Facilities:

KNOCKBAIN FARM

N5735.75 W00428.00, 1nm SW Dingwall, 600ft amsl

Rwy08/26 Grass 650x15m. **Remarks:** PPR. AD well marked, located on top of hill between Dingwall and Loch Ussie, may not suitable for use during winter months. PFA types welcome. 2 windsocks displayed on AD. Power lines present E of AD. Beware low flying jets. Rwys slope up to centre, Rwy08 6%, Rwy26 4%. **Noise:** Dept: Rwy26 turn right as soon as practicable possible. **Operating Hrs:** SR-SS. **Circuits:** To N at 800ft. Make standard calls on 135.475. **Landing Fee:** Nil. **Maintenance:** Nil. **Fuel:** Nil. **Operator:** David Lockett, Knockbain Farm, Dingwall, Ross-shire, IV15 9TJ. **Tel:** 01349 862476 **Tel:** 07736 629838 davidlockett@avnet.co.uk.

Disabled Facilities:

LAINDON

N5135.67 E00026.76, 1.25nm NNW of Basildon, 90ft amsl

Rwy08/26 Grass 475x18m. **Remarks:** Up slope on Rwy26. Crops may be grown right up to strip edge. There is a public road at Rwy26 Thr, keep a good lookout for vehicles and pedestrians. Power lines 80ft agl parallel the strip to S. AD located within Southend LARS. Preferred landing Rwy in light winds Rwy26. **Noise:** Do not over fly built up area to S of AD. **Circuits:** 1000ft to N. **Fuel:** Nil. **Operator:** George French, High View, 16 Wash Road, Basildon, Essex, SS15 4ER. **Tel:** 01268 411464 **Tel:** 07802 887338

LANE FARM

N5207 W00312, 4nm NW of Hay-on-Wye, 830ft amsl

Rwy06/24 Grass 730x50m (strip width narrows to min of 30m). **Remarks:** Strip situated in a valley with high GND all around up to 1671ft amsl to W and 1361ft amsl to SW. 50ft trees on N side of AD and close to both Thrs. Cables run close down NW side of AD and cross Rwy06 APP on very short final (30ft agl). Windsock displayed when AD active. Lane farm is on the NW side of AD. This strip is ONLY available to pilots visiting the locality or using Lane farm holiday properties. No casual visitors or strip training. Farmed deer graze AD. **Noise/Circuits:** To be flown to avoid local villages, the area is very rural. **Landing Fee:** £5. **Fuel:** Nil. **Operator:** John Bally, Lane Farm, Paincastle, Hay-on-Wye, Radnorshire LD2 3JS. **Tel:** 01497 851605

LANGHAM

N5256.30 E00057.38,9nm W of Sheringham, 120ft amsl

Rwy10/28 Concrete 700x15m (former Twy), Rwy02/20 Grass 550x18m. (SW end of disused AD). **Warnings:** Mast 98ft aal, 250m N of Rwy25 Thr. Trees and huts on Rwy28 APP. Due to obstructions exercise extreme caution. **Circuits:** Nil. **Landing Fee:** £20. **Maintenance:** M3 available. **Fuel:** AVGAS 100LL by arr. **Operator:** H Labouchere Esq **Tel:** 01328 830003 **Fax:** 01328 830232. **Disabled Facilities:**

LARK ENGINE FARMHOUSE

N5224.96 E00022.18, 4.5nm ENE of Ely, 0ft amsl

Rwy06/24 Grass 600xm. **Remarks:** Flat strip situated within the Mildenhall/Lakenheath CMATZ. Call Lakenheath APP 128.900. **Warnings:** Trees very close to Rwy24 APP on very short final which, as well as constituting an obstruction may also generate rotor in S winds. Farm equipment may be parked close to Rwy edge. Windsock displayed. **Noise:** Do not over fly the village of Prickwillow 1nm NW of AD. **Operating Hrs:** SR-SS. **Circuits:** Join directly downwind LH for both Rwys 1000ft QFE. **Landing Fee:** Nil. **Fuel:** Nil. **Operator:** Mr Clinton Judd, Lark Engine Farmhouse, Lark Bank, Prickwillow, Ely, Cambs. CB7 4SW, **Tel/Fax:** 01353 688428

LITTLE CHASE FARM

N5221.00 W00137.00, 1.5nm WNE of Kenilworth, 325ft amsl

Rwy08/26 Grass 500x30m. **Remarks:** PPR essential. Experienced STOL pilots welcome at own risk. Rwy in good condition. **Warnings:** Live stock graze AD, removed with PPR. AD within Birmingham CTR. **Caution:** High level power lines cross Rwy26 Thr and electric fence half way along Rwy. **Noise:** Avoid over flying all local houses and farms. **Operating Hrs:** SR-SS. **Circuits:** To S of AD, avoiding Birmingham CTR. **Landing Fee:** Nil. **Maintenance:** Nil. **Fuel:** Nil. **Operator:** David Sansome, Little Chase Farm, Chase Lane, Kenilworth, Warks, CV8 1PR. **Tel:** 01926 853029

LOWER BOTREA

N5007.00 W00538.00, 1.5nm SE of St Just, 400ft amsl

Rwy07/25 Grass 600x50m. Rwy17/35 Grass 500x50m. **Remarks:** PPR essential. Strip may be water logged and unusable during winter months. Windsock displayed at Rwy intersection. Trees surround AD. **Noise:** Avoid over flying all local habitation. **Operating Hrs:** SR-SS. **Circuits:** Any direction - See noise. **Fuel:** Nil. **Operator:** Mr Hunt, Lower Botrea Farm, Newbridge, Penzance, Cornwall. **Tel:** 01736 787768

MANBY

N5321.30 E0005.06 3nm SE Louth. 60ft amsl.

Rwy08/26 Grass 500x20m. **Remarks:** PPR essential. Visitors welcome at pilots own risk. AD located in NW corner of ex RAF Manby AD. **Warnings:** Do not use the straight length of perimeter track on N side of AD. Helicopters arrive from W or South of AD onto S Apron only. **Caution:** Motor rallying activities and grazing animals on AD. Keep good look out for obstacles and defects in/on the perimeter track. **Noise:** Avoid over flying all houses and local villages. **Operating Hrs:** SR-SS. **Circuits:** To S of AD. **Landing Fee:** £6. **Fuel:** Nil. **Maintenance:** Nil. **Operator:** Manby Motorplex, Manby, Louth, Lincs, LN11 8UZ **Tel:** 01507 668119. **Tel:** 07831 585211 **Fax:** 01507 327955 **Fax:** 01507 328111 sales@manbymotorplex.com www.manbymotorplex.com

MELBOURNE (Melrose Farm)

N5352.03 W00050.27, 6nm SSW of Pocklington, 25ft amsl

Rwy06/24 Tarmac 1000x46m. **Remarks:** Only active Rwy on disused AD. Power line 120ft, crosses Rwy06 APP, farm tractors maybe on AD. Drag racers, microlights and autogyros all operate here. Windsock displayed to N of Rwy24 Thr. **Noise:** Avoid over flying local habitation. **Fuel:** Nil. **Operator:** J Rowbottom, Melrose Farm, Melbourne, York, YO42 4SS, **Tel:** 01759318392 **Fax:** 01759 318948

NETHER HUNTLYWOOD

N5540.60 W00236.42, 8nm NW of Kelso, 550ft amsl

Rwy07/25 Grass 400x25m. **Remarks:** PPR essential. Sheep graze AD. Always fly low past Rwy to check status. Windsock displayed N edge of AD. Rwy has small undulations. **Warnings:** Power lines 1nm W of AD. **Operating Hrs:** SR-SS. **Circuits:** To S of Rwy. **Landing Fee:** Nil. **Maintenance:** Nil. **Fuel:** MOGAS by arrangement. **Restaurants:** Toilets on site. **Operator:** Richard Lawrence, Nether Huntlywood, Earlston, Berwickshire, TD4 6BB. **Tel:** 01573 410502 **Tel:** 07968 862518 www.huntlywood.co.uk

NEWARK (Beeches Farm)

N5309 W00044. 2nm W of Swinderby AD and 5nm NE of Newark. 50ft amsl

Rwy10/28 Grass 517x18m. **Remarks:** Visiting ACFT welcome PPR. Rwy is level with good surface. Windsock displayed on hangar roof. Newark – Lincoln railway runs at 90° close to Rwy28 Thr. N side of AD there is a ditch running from hangar to railway. Contact Waddington MATZ when in the area. **Noise:** Avoid over flying local villages. **Circuits:** 800ft aal. **Fuel:** Nil. **Operator:** P L Clements, Beeches Farm, South Scarle, Newark, Notts NG23 7JH. **Tel:** 01636 892273 **Fax:** 01636 893556

NYMPSFIELD (Stroud)

N5142.51 W00217.01, 4nm SW of Stroud,700ft amsl

E/W Grass 1120m. **Remarks:** PPR by telephone essential for gliding business only. Visiting ACFT welcome at pilots own risk. Field is undulating, areas N & S side of AD very boggy. Gliding site, caution cables!. Trees close to AD boundary and hilly situation of site generates turbulence and wind gradients in cross winds. NW wind is to be avoided. **Landing Fee:** £5. **Maintenance:** Roger Targett Sailplanes **Tel:** 01453 860861. **Fuel:** Nil. **Operator:** Bristol & Gloucestershire Gliding Club **Tel:** 01453 860342/860060. office@bggc.co.uk.

Disabled Facilities:

OCTON

N5407.00 W00025.00, 9nm N of Driffield, 350ft amsl

Rwy18/36 Grass 900x30m. **Remarks:** PPR essential for briefing. Experienced STOL pilots welcome at own risk. **Warnings:** Rwy18 steep upslope. Intense military activity in area. Eddsfield AD 2.5nm SW of AD. Octon and Eddsfield circuit pattern overlap. **Noise:** Avoid over flying all local villages and farms. **Operating Hrs:** SR-SS. **Circuits:** LH 1000ft QFE. **Landing Fee:** Nil. **Maintenance:** Nil. **Fuel:** Nil. **Operator:** Mr Howitt, Low Octon Grange, Foxholes, Driffield, Yorks, YO25 3HJ. **Tel:** 01377 267661

PAYDEN STREET

N5115.12 E00044.50, 7nm NE of Ashford. 630ft amsl

Rwy02/20 Grass 1000x12m. **Remarks:** Strict PPR by telephone. Rwy in good condition. Windsock displayed to W of Rwy midpoint. **Visual aid to location:** 2 Dutch barns on Rwy02 APP. AD located in the middle of arable land. **Noise:** Avoid over flying all local houses especially house adjacent Rwy02 Thr. **Operating Hrs:** SR-SS. **Circuits:** Join over head, descend on dead side. **Landing Fee:** £20. **Maintenance:** Nil. **Fuel:** Nil. **Operator:** John Boyd, Court Lodge Farm, Lenham, Maidstone, Kent, ME17 2QD. **Tel:** 01622 858403 **Tel:** 07791 040578 **Fax:** 01622 850624 jarthurboyd@aol.com

PENT FARM

N5106.32 E00104.30, 2.5nm NNW Hythe, 240ft amsl

Rwy05/23 Grass 950x20m. **Remarks:** Strict PPR by telephone. AD not suitable for inexperience pilots due to proximity of hills. Windsock displayed on S side approx mid point. Model ACFT active at weekends. **Warnings:** Rwy05 slight up slope. Hills rising to 550ft amsl at NE end of AD. Masts 221ft agl 1nm NE of AD. **Noise:** Avoid over flying the villages of Stanford and Postling. **Operating Hrs:** SR-SS. **Circuits:** N at 1000ft. **Landing Fee:** £5. **Maintenance:** M3 & M5 available **Fuel:** Nil. **Operator:** Mr C R Reynolds, Pent Farm, Postling, Hythe, Kent, CT21 4EY. **Tel:** 01303 862436. **Tel:** 07850 628981

RHIGOS

N5144.34 W00335.05, 8nm W of Merthyr Tydfil, 780ft amsl

Rwy09/27 Grass 550m. **Remarks:** Hill top site, primarily for gliding. Surface is rough. Field slopes down from E to W. After rain due to soft surface. Not suitable for light ACFT in strong S & N winds. Beware of launch cables. **Noise:** Avoid over flying Rhigos village. **Circuits:** 09 RH, 27 LH. **Fuel:** Nil. **Operator:** Vale of Neath Gliding Club, Rhigos Airfield, Aberdare, Glamorgan, South Wales. **Tel:** 01685 811023

ROSEMARKET

N5144.32 W00458.59, 4nm S of Haverford W, 160ft amsl

Rwy08/26 Grass 600x15m. **Remarks:** Up slope on Rwy08. Can be unusable after heavy rain. Public road close to Rwy08 Thr, look out for vehicles and pedestrians. Car park close to Rwy08 Thr. Windsock displayed at E end of strip. Strip is part of a leisure complex and is situated within a 9 hole Golf course. Because of the Rwy site prior telephone contact would be appreciated. Golfers are particularly welcomed. **Noise:** Avoid over flying riding school on N edge of woods to NE of strip **Circuits:** 800ft QFE. **Fuel:** MOGAS at Haverfordwest. **Operator:** Bill & Bridie Young, Dawn till Dusk Golf course, Rosemarket, Milford Haven, Pembrokeshire SA73 1JY **Tel:** 01437 890281 www.dawntilldusk.co.uk.

Disabled Facilities:

SHACKLEWELL

N5239.00 W00034.00, 3nm W Stamford, 535ft amsl

Rwy06/24 Grass 600x15m. **Remarks:** PPR by telephone. Well prepared strip, with clear APP. Windsock displayed at E end. Contact Cottesmore MATZ inbound and before Dept. **Noise:** Avoid over flying Empingham village 1nm S of AD. **Operating Hrs:** SR-SS. **Circuits:** Nil. **Landing Fee:** Nil. **Maintenance:** Nil. **Fuel:** Nil. **Operator:** Richard Watt, Shacklewell Lodge, Empingham, Oakham, Rutland, LE15 8QQ. **Tel:** 01780 460646 **Tel:** 07801 585480 **Fax:** 01780 460306 wattrichard@hotmail.com

STOODLEIGH BARTON

N5057.50 W00332.00, 4nm NW of Tiverton, 830ft amsl

Rwy09/27 Grass 800x75m. **Remarks:** Rwy27 has up slope and lateral slope down to S. A building on short final Rwy09. **Noise:** Avoid Stoodleigh village. **Radio:** A/G 129.825. **Operating Hrs:** SR-SS. **Circuits:** S 1000ft QFE. **Landing Fee:** donation to the RNLI would be most welcome. **Fuel:** MOGAS available by prior arr. **Restaurant:** Red Lion, Oakford **Tel:** 01398 351219. **Operator:** Mr W Knowles, Stoodleigh Barton, Tiverton, Devon **Tel:** 01398 351568 **Tel:** 0753 0071157.

Disabled Facilities:

STRETTON

N5320.70 W00231.50, 3nm SE of Warrington, 270ft amsl

Rwy09/27 parallel Concrete/Grass 400x20m. **Remarks:** Rwy N of disused Rwy09/27 Rwy on Stretton disused AD. 6ft high hedge and public road close to Rwy27Thr. APP from S directly to base leg. When landing Rwy09 make offset APP to avoid M56. This will also provide clearance from a cellular telephone mast 130ft agl, 700m out and to N Rwy09 APP. Located within the Manchester Low Level Route – intensive light ACFT traffic up to 1250ft amsl, also VRP for Liverpool/Manchester VFR traffic. PFA or Vintage type ACFT only accepted. **Noise:** Do not over fly house E of AD. **Fuel:** Nil. **Operator:** J Sykes, Invergordon Nurseries, Swineyard Lane, High Leigh, Knutsford, Cheshire **Tel:** 01925 754027

SUTTON BANK (Thirsk)

N5413.72 W00112.58, 5nm E of Thirsk,18nm N of York, 920ft amsl

E/W Grass 549m NE/SW Grass 732m. **Radio:** A/G 129.975. **Remarks:** PPR Surface may be soft in places. There are trees to N & E. Do not APP over steep S & W cliffs with insufficient speed to overcome local down draughts. Windsock displayed. **Landing Fee:** £5. **Fuel:** Nil. **Operator:** Yorkshire Gliding Club (PTY) Ltd, Sutton Bank, Thirsk, North Yorkshire YO7 2EY. **Tel:** 01845 597237. enquiry@ygc.co.uk. www.ygc.co.uk.

Disabled Facilities:

THORNBOROUGH GROUNDS

N5201.00 W00058.30, 2nm ENE of Buckingham, 260ft amsl

Rwy06/24 Grass 500m. **Remarks:** Visiting ACFT welcome with PPR and at pilots own risk. Field wet in winter. AD not suitable for low wing, long spat ACFT. **Warnings:** Pylons and power lines on both Rwy APP. **Noise:** Avoid over flying local farm houses, village and stud farm N of Rwy. **Landing Fee:** Voluntary. **Fuel:** Nil. **Maintenance:** Nil. **Operator:** C M Moore, Thornborough Grounds, Buckingham MK18 2AB. **Tel:** 01280 814675 cmm@morecorporation.com.

TOWER FARM

N5215.44 W00039.55, 2nm SSE of Wellingborough, 370ft amsl

Rwy10/28 Grass 640x24m. **Remarks:** Briefing essential for first time visitors. Rwy28 has up slope which increases in severity at midpoint then becomes less severe from midpoint on. This aids landing but could constitute a significant hazard on Dept. Owner recommends that visitors call or listen out with Sywell A/G for local traffic information. Beware microlights operating from field to w of AD. AD is situated 2nm NW of Podington disused AD, (Santa Pod Raceway) where large numbers of spectators congregate for drag racing events spring to autumn mainly PH & weekends. **Visual aid to location:** White concrete water TWR at W end of strip. **Noise:** Avoid Wollaston, to W of AD. **Operating Hrs:** SR-SS **Circuits:** To N. **Fuel:** Nil. **Landing Fee:** Nil. **Operator:** Mrs S Sumner and Chris Sumner, Tower Farm, Wollaston, Wellingborough, Northants, NN29 7PJ **Tel:** 01933 664225 **Tel:** 07803 715736. pgs@clara.co.uk

TRULEIGH FARM

N5053.85 W00015.30, 3nm SSE of Henfield VRP (Shoreham), 132ft amsl

Rwy10/28 Grass 500x15m. **Remarks:** Sheep may be grazing so PPR essential. Strip slopes upward from E until midpoint. Rwy is situated between two groups of trees which may cause rotor/windshear. AD can be very wet after prolonged precipitation. Power lines to E of AD crossing the Rwy28 APP 900m from Thr. Radio masts on hill 1nm S of AD. There are numerous Hang gliding and Paracending sites in the area around AD. Shoreham ATZ is close to S. Arr/Dept ACFT are advised to contact Shoreham APP. Useful weather information can be obtained from Shoreham ATIS. Windsock displayed to NW of Rwy. **Noise:** Avoid all local habitation, especially the houses 0.5nm NE of AD. **Operating Hrs:** SR-SS. **Circuits:** LH 1000ft QFE. **Landing Fee:** Nil. **Fuel:** Nil. **Operator:** Robin Windus, Truleigh Manor, Edburton, Henfield, Sussex. BN5 9LL **Tel:** 01903 813186.

Disabled Facilities:

VALLANCE BY-WAYS GATWICK

N5109.17 W00011.40, Adjacent to NW corner of Gatwick AD, 202ft amsl

Rwy08/26 Grass 553x9m. **Remarks:** PPR strictly required. Helicopter welcome handled by Interflight **Tel:** 01293 509000 **Fax:** 01293 567010. Permission from Gatwick must be obtained. 60ft trees Rwy26 APP and deer may encroach the strip. Windsock displayed. **Circuits:** To N away from Gatwick but avoiding Charlwood NW of AD. **Landing Fee:** Donation to Gatwick Aviation Museum on AD. **Fuel:** Nil. Handling: Interflight **Tel:** 01293 509000 **Fax:** 01293 567010. **Operator:** P G Vallance Ltd, Lowfield, Heath Road, Charlwood, Surrey. RH6 0BT **Tel:** 01293 862915 or **Tel:** 07836 666817 gpvgat@aol.com www.gatwick-aviation-museum.co.uk.

Disabled Facilities:

WADSWICK STRIP

N5124 W00212, 2.2nm SE of Colerne AD, 400ft amsl

Rwy10/28 Grass 700x25m. **Remarks:** PPR. Café on AD. **Caution:** Access road crosses the strip at W end. Traffic is controlled by traffic lights, which are activated on Freq 123.100. Ensure you use this facility before landing and take off. Wires at E end of strip are buried. The pole is still in position close to Thr on S side of Rwy. Windsock displayed. AD within Lynham CTR always contact APP. **Noise:** Avoid over flying he village to N of strip on initial APP particularly avoiding Hazelbury Manor which is close to W of strip. **Circuits:** to S. **Fuel:** Nil. **Operator:** Tim Barton, Manor Farm, Wadswick, Corsham, Wiltshire. SN13 8JB. **Tel:** 01225 810706 **Fax:** 01225 810307. tim@wadswick.co.uk www.wadswick.co.uk

WEST HORNDON

N5133.72 E00021.30, 3nm S of Brentwood. 80ft amsl

Rwy06/24 Grass 500x20m. **Remarks:** PPR by telephone. Rwy in good condition. Windsock displayed S of Rwy24. Gardens opens Thursday April-July, £5 donation to National Garden Scheme. Lunch available during this period. **Warnings:** Power lines run close to N AD boundary parallel with Rwy. **Caution:** Farm machinery on AD. **Noise:** Avoid over flying all local houses and farms. **Operating Hrs:** SR-SS. **Circuits:** To S 1000ft QFE. **Landing Fee:** Nil. **Maintenance:** Nil. **Fuel:** Nil. **Operator:** Bernard Holmes, Barnards Farm, Brentwood Road, West Hordon, Essex, CM13 3LX. **Tel:** 01277 811262 www.barnardsfarm.eu.

Disabled Facilities:

WHITBY (Egton)

N5427.00 W00045.00 4nm W of Whitby, 3nm NE of Grosmont, 650ft amsl

E/W Grass 450x100m. **Remarks:** Level, but surface may be bumpy and strip is surrounded by trees. During summer sheep graze on Rwy. Situated beside the main Whitby to Guisborough road. Windsock S side at midpoint. **Fuel:** Nil. **Operator:** P A Jackson, Finkle Bottoms, Great Fryup, Whitby, North Yorkshire. **Tel:** 01947 897367 (Home).

Disabled Facilities:

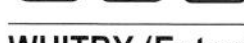

WIGTOWN

N5450.93 W00426.95, 1nm S of Wigtown, 20ft amsl

Rwy06/24 Concrete 446x18m, (30m starter extensions available at both ends of Rwy). **Remarks:** Rwy surface rough. Baldoon Hill – 129ft amsl/109ft aal – located 300m NW Rwy06 Thr, care should be taken when APP/Dept from this direction. **Operating Hrs:** PPR by arr. **Circuits:** 06/24 LH 800ft. **Landing Fee:** Nil. **Fuel:** Nil. **Operator:** Mr A H Sproat **Tel:** 01988 402215

WILLOW FARM

N5325.25 W00054.50, 1nm NW of Gringley on the Hill, 12ft amsl

Rwy06/24 Grass 405x30m. **Remarks:** PPR essential. Windsock displayed. **Warnings:** AD located inside Doncaster Sheffield CTA and close by Scampton/Waddington MATZ. Trees on APP Rwy24. Displaced Thr Rwy06 due to public road – vehicles and pedestrians crossing. **Operating Hrs:** SR-SS. **Circuits:** To N 800ft QFE. **Landing Fee:** Nil. **Maintenance:** Nil. **Fuel:** Nil. **Restaurants:** Nil. **Taxi/Car Hire:** Nil. **Operator:** Stuart Beresford, Willow Farm, Gringley on the Hill, Doncaster, DN10 4SL. **Tel:** 01777 816967 **Tel:** 07836 737935 jetfresh@hotmail.com

WOODLANDS (Roche)

N5025.31 W00448.80, 5nm SW of Bodmin, 531ft amsl

Rwy16/34 Grass 320x15, Rwy01/19 Grass 320x15m, Rwy13/31 Grass 320x15m, Rwy07/25 175x15m. **Remarks:** Strict PPR. AD situated very close to St Mawgan MATZ. No facilities on AD. Rwy34/31 APP trees and power lines present. Rwy07 APP large hedge on short finals. Windsock displayed 200m on E side Rwy31. **Noise:** Avoid over flying all local habitation, especially the farm to S of AD and N of main Rd. **Operating Hrs:** SR-SS. **Circuits:** No local circuits. **Fuel:** Nil **Operator:** Woodlands Flying Group, Woodlands Aerodrome, Camelford, Cornwall, PL32 9YF. **Tel:** 01872 560771 (Mr Hanley) **Tel:** 01872 510495 (Mr Gibbs)

WOONTON

N5209.72 W0256.74, 5nm SSW of Shobdon AD, 400ft amsl

Rwy16/34 Grass 500x15m. **Remarks:** Rwy34 has a marked up slope. Land Rwy34, Dept Rwy16 only. Surface can be soft after prolonged precipitation. Sheep graze the strip so PPR essential. Public footpath crosses Rwy34 touchdown point. Windsock displayed. Low flying military ACFT transit area during weekdays. Operator can sometimes provide transport if arranged in advance. **Noise:** Avoid local habitation, particularly the village of Woonton to N of AD. **Operating Hrs:** SR-SS. **Landing Fee:** Nil. **Fuel:** Available by arr. **Operator:** Mike Hayes, Chapel Stile Cottage, Woonton Almeley, Herefordshire. HR3 6QN. **Tel:** 01432 377371 (Office Hrs) **Tel:** 01544 340635 (Evenings) **Fax:** 01432 355988 mike.hayes@denco.co.uk

YATESBURY

N5126.00 W00154.00 4nm E of Calne. 525ft amsl

Rwy10/28 Grass 410x19m. **Remarks:** PPR essential by telephone. Airfield located within Lyneham MATZ, contact Lyneham APP for traffic information. See website for details. **Warnings:** East end of strip lower then west end, Set altimeters at the holding point. **Noise:** Please avoid over flying all local habitation. **Operating Hrs:** SR-SS. **Landing Fee**: Available with PPR. **Circuits:** See website for details 600ft QFE. **Fuel:** Nil. **Maintenance**: Nil. **Operator:** Tony Hughes, Wiltshire Microlight Centre, 1 White Horse View, Cherhill, Calne, Wiltshire, SN11 5UR. **Tel:** 07836 554554. tonyhughes@wiltsmicrolights.com www.wiltsmicrolights.com